1991
Novel & Short Story Writer's Market

Editor: Robin Gee

Assistant Editor: Roseann Shaughnessy

Writer's Digest Books

Cincinnati, Ohio

Distributed in Canada by McGraw-Hill,
330 Progress Ave.,
Scarborough, Ontario M1P 2Z5.
Also distributed in Australia by Kirby Books, Private Bag No. 19, P.O. Alexandria NSW2015.

Managing Editor, Market Books Department:
Constance J. Achabal; Assistant Managing Editor: Glenda Tennant Neff

1991 Novel & Short Story Writer's Market.

International Standard Serial Number
ISSN 0897-9812
International Standard Book Number
0-89879-427-7

Cover art by Nicholas Wilton

Contents

From the Editors

Many people, especially those who do not write, would describe a writer's life as isolated or even lonely. The generally accepted image is that of a writer scribbling away alone in a tiny room, usually in the wee hours before dawn. Yet people who do write know, while writing can indeed be lonely at times, writers do not stay isolated very long. Life has a way of intruding upon art and for most writers it's a necessary and welcome intrusion.

This year, as every year, we visited writers at conferences to find out what kind of information they need and what questions concern them. While the subject of writing was almost always the starting point for our conversations, we noticed this year in particular, the subject turned quickly to national and world events—to the "life" that intrudes upon the writing. Editors and publishers we spoke with also mentioned several of the same "non-writing" topics as having an impact on the writing and publishing community.

The subject of intellectual freedom, for example, came up again and again. Part of the discussion involved the restrictions placed on funds for the National Endowment for the Arts. Many small magazines and publishers rely on NEA funds. A few magazines, including the *Boston Review* and the *Kenyon Review* rejected grants from the NEA this year rather than accept the funds with restrictions. In addition to the obvious effects NEA restrictions have on a few writers, more writers will be affected if magazines have less money to buy stories—and it could mean the demise of some very important markets. We've heard a whole spectrum of terms connected with this issue—censorship, pornography, free expression, free speech—but whatever term is used, writers and editors agree intellectual freedom is one of the most important issues we face in this decade.

The environment was another popular topic. Less controversial than the freedom of expression issue, writers and editors wanted to work together to find ways to conserve energy and resources. Perhaps because writers and editors rely so much on paper, they seemed particularly concerned with saving and protecting the world's forests.

In fact very few world events escaped discussion—from the fall of the Berlin Wall to the situation in the Middle East, writers everywhere we visited were concerned, involved and open to life. In our interview with writer Allan Gurganus he says the old adage is true: you must live life before you can write about it. And if there is any lesson to be learned here it's that life makes our writing richer, and hopefully, all the better.

It's your interest in life around you as well as your professional concerns that make doing this book so challenging and rewarding. You'll notice we've gone from a mix of original and reprint articles to all original material this year as we strive to bring you a fresh variety of articles. We've included words of encouragement and wisdom from fellow writers including Gurganus, Sue Miller, Rachel Simon and Melissa Pritchard. Other articles deal with the mechanics of writing such as John Tibbetts' piece on characterization, Monica Wood's article on dialogue and Stephen Minot's piece on creating tension.

We've also included articles on form from short story writer Tom Chiarella and the associate editor of *Story* magazine, Jack Heffron. Michael Banks gives tips on meeting editors at science fiction conventions and three agents answer your most frequently asked questions in the "Agents' Roundtable." Finally, we round out our articles section with a description of a few markets you may not have considered before.

Check the "Business of Writing Fiction" section and the introductions to each section for the "hard facts" of the writing business. The listings, of course, are the nitty-gritty of the book, but we've scattered 14 Close-up interviews with writers, editors and publishers throughout the listing sections to entertain as well as inform. This year we're happy to include even more interviews with writers including western writer Cameron Judd, mystery writer Barbara Mertz and romance writer Laura Resnick. And no matter where your writing interests lie, we've included interviews with editors at a variety of publications and publishers. This year's interviews feature editors at *Byline*, a magazine devoted to new writers; *Potato Eyes*, for writers interested in a pro-rural journal and *Thema*, a magazine built around different themes. We spoke with the editors of the *Boston Review* and *New Mystery* about their special needs and the editors from David Godine, Four Walls Eight Windows and Zoland Books discuss how they got started as well as what makes their books special. Finally, we spoke with the director of a state arts agency to find out how and why you should apply for grants and fellowships, important sources of financial support for writers.

While *Novel & Short Story Writer's Market* includes listings for just about every type of fiction writing, writers with special interests may want to take a look at one of our "sister" publications. Markets for poetry may be found in *Poet's Market* and markets for both writing and illustration for children are featured in *Children's Writer's and Illustrator's Market*. If your writing leans toward the lighter side, check out the newest member of our family, *Humor and Cartoon Markets*, now in its second year.

We invite you to write us about new markets or trends you may come across or just drop us a line to let us know how you are doing, how the book has helped you or what you'd like to see included in our next edition. We hope you'll enjoy this edition and make our book a regular part of your writing life.

Roseann Shaughnessy

Robin Gee

Writing Techniques

An Interview with Allan Gurganus

by Anne Bowling

Improbable may best describe the pairing of an irascible 99-year-old widow with a fifth grade education and a 43-year-old male writer of contemporary fiction. At first blush, novelist Allan Gurganus and his heroine Lucy Marsden share nothing but their birthplace, the South.

But fortunately for the some 250,000 people who have read and loved Gurganus' best-seller, *The Oldest Living Confederate Widow Tells All*, they also share a love for the telling of a good story. By the end of the novel, the two are quite inseparable.

The character of Lucy Marsden surfaced for Gurganus while he was a writer in residence at the Yaddo artist's colony in Saratoga, New York. Transcending gender and time, Gurganus crafted the story of the child-bride of a 50-year-old veteran of the Civil War, told from her bed·in a nursing home.

Seven years and 718 pages later, Alfred A. Knopf Co. published *The Oldest Living Confederate Widow Tells All*, which critics have hailed as "exuberant" and "unforgettable reading." The novel has been featured as a Book-of-the-Month main selection and reviewed for screen possibilities by such notables as Stanley Kubrick, David Lynch and Steven Spielberg.

© Marion Ettlinger

Gurganus studied under author Grace Paley while earning his B.A. at Sarah Lawrence College. From there he went on to the Iowa Writer's Workshop where he studied with Stanley Elkin, John Irving and John Cheever, who became mentor, friend and professional advocate for the young writer.

Gurganus teaches fiction writing at Sarah Lawrence College and has taught at Stanford University, Duke University and the Iowa Writer's Workshop. His short fiction has been published in *The New Yorker*, *The Atlantic* and *The Paris*

Anne Bowling *is a Cincinnati-based freelance writer.*

Review. A collection of short stories and novellas, *White People*, was released by Alfred A. Knopf in January, 1991.

AB: I read that you began serious and voracious reading during a stint in the Navy. Were there books that you read then that affected you most and writers whose styles you tried to emulate?

AG: The first book that really happened to me was Henry James' *Portrait of a Lady*. I was then living on an aircraft carrier in a room with 65 other guys, bunks stacked five high and a bathroom that didn't have doors on the toilet booths, no shower curtains, no privacy, with the war in Vietnam going on. So for me the sense of privacy that happened to me when I began to read gave me an enormous consolation and helped me through that period, and also reinforced the concept that character is really enormously important both in life and in fiction. The thing that thrilled me most in *Portrait of a Lady* was the first 30 pages in which James analyzes the character of Isabel Archer, and finds her—in his words—a young lady who had an unquenchable desire to think well of herself. And that described me under those circumstances. I was trying to get the best out of a bad experience, and tell myself that four years was not a lifetime and there was a life after this life. James was a great comfort.

AB: So the reading and the writing were therapeutic?

AG: Well, I think they were me creating company for myself. I think that's one of the underestimated qualities of fiction. When children make up their imaginary pals they are in some ways doing what writers do, and for me *The Oldest Living Confederate Widow* became an ideal traveling companion. She was someone you would want on your life raft with you, a person who has seen and done it all. One who has suffered but is not completely embittered by her suffering and has a kind of life that keeps her going in the moment.

AB: Her humor?

AG: Yes. I think it's really essential. It's mandatory equipment for the trail.

AB: So you began writing when you were in the Navy?

AG: Yes. What I did was imitate the writers I had read. I would write a story in the mode of Henry James or Conrad or Balzac, and my first masters were 19th Century writers. The writer I read most often is Chekhov. Young writers should read not only what's happening now but also read the great writers of the past. The past has a way of editing out the writers who aren't important. There's a kind of service that history has paid you by saying that of all of the people writing, these 12 or 14 were the greatest.

AB: They endured?

AG: That's right. They're the ones the readers have voted for. I think what every writer wants is to be listed not just on the bestseller list but in that list of great writers who are read forever. That's certainly my ambition.

AB: Was there a transition point, a point at which you realized the writing wasn't recreational but you were a writer?

AG: I had started out to be a painter. I went to art school at the Pennsylvania Academy of Fine Arts at the University of Pennsylvania. I've always thought of myself as an artist, even when I was a little kid, because I had a lot of ability as a draftsman. I still illustrate my work and do a lot of drawing in relation to my writing. I sometimes do sketches of scenes from my fiction. It adds an extra dimension that readers can feel without quite knowing they've been sketched out for them in advance.

AB: That says something about the creative process.

AG: It's all connected. That's part of the beauty of being a novelist, that everything is admissable. In some fields, only things that are directly pertinent to your particular area are valid. I'm one of those people who's always talking to the guy who's fixing my car at the service station and I want to know everybody's occupation and everybody's ambitions and skills and it all goes somewhere. I think a real novelist is a fabulous interviewer and knows how to talk to everybody, not just people from the same educational level or the same class or race or social background. A novelist must have the ability to transcend gender and time and everything to find out what we all have in common.

AB: When did you first begin to write professionally?

AG: I published my first story in *The New Yorker* in 1974 when I was 26 years old. I had been writing since I was 18, and had studied writing at Sarah Lawrence. I had studied with Grace Paley and then at the writer's workshop with Stanley Elkin and John Cheever.

AB: It seems you developed quickly as a writer. You were published in *The New Yorker* a year after you were graduated from Sarah Lawrence. To what do you attribute that early success?

AG: Part of it is that I was slightly older than that sounds, because I had been in the Navy for three and a half years. I was grown up when I started publishing even though I was very young. Vietnam made us all ancient spirits. All of us who survived came back 150 years old, because we had seen more than three lifetimes worth of sadness and grief. I think that old line about whatever doesn't kill you makes you stronger is right. So I had a sense of urgency by the time I went back and got my B.A. at Sarah Lawrence. I was really ready to get on with it.

AB: Did you ever have a crisis of confidence, or get to the point where you said, "There's no way I'll be able to survive on a writer's income. I should think about getting an M.B.A. and forget about writing."?

AG: I thought about going to medical school. I think doctors and writers have a lot in common. They see the world symptomatically and they believe in a cure, they listen to people's complaints. But teaching was really how I supported myself. I hadn't made a living as a writer until the novel came out, and even now I don't know how long that will continue. But teaching has always seemed to be a beautiful career independent of writing. There's something about being around young believers in literature, people who are new to the world and new to language, that inspires me and keeps me honest. I've received an enormous amount of wonderful mail about the novel, but one of the best letters was from a former student of mine, who said, "This is the kind of book you told us it was possible to write and this book meets your own high standard." It's a cliché, but teaching really teaches the teacher more than it teaches the student.

AB: What did the Iowa Writer's Workshop do for your writing as a craft, and your career as a writer?

AG: As a craft, it was very important, because it meant that I could spend as many hours a week on my writing as I wanted without apologizing. As an undergraduate you have to study physics and French and all this. Part of the genius of the Iowa program is that they really just let you write. They don't require you to take too many other kinds of classes, so the writing is the center of your life. The greatest bonus was the friendships with some very wonderful and serious writers. I had a sense of being one of many people in the vineyard, and that the occupation was worthy and exciting. It was all right to spend as much time as possible trying to learn your craft. What the workshop did for my career was it introduced me to John Cheever who sold my first substantial story to *The New Yorker*. The editor, William Maxwell, called up and said, "Congratulations, we've just bought your story." And I said, "Yeah, and I'm Mae West." I had no idea that it was an actual person from New York on the phone, and it took a lot of convincing before I believed it. Having somebody sponsor me was a great benefit. It's something I try to do for my students.

AB: How do you rate the value of mentors for writers?

AG: I think they're essential. We all need role models, in life and in art. One reason you have mentors is so you can learn from how they fail as well as succeed. I think there's a kind of negative benefit from having a mentor, in that nobody can be everything to you. Part of my pleasure in suddenly having a little money came from being able to set up a scholarship at Sarah Lawrence in honor of Grace Paley, my first fiction writing teacher. I'm trying very hard in my life to go from being a pauper to a philanthropist and skip being a Republican. That's always been my dream, and I'm actually managing to implement it. I want to give back some of what was given to me, which was a very great deal.

AB: You strike me as a person who appreciates community in all that you do. I noticed it in the beginning of *Oldest Living Confederate Widow* in which you credit a number of different people for their input while you were putting the book together.

AG: I used to think the ideal editor was somebody with a Ph.D. in comparative literature. But I've changed my opinion, and I even listen to my parents, if you can believe that. I don't think that writing works only on a symbolic level. I think it has to work on the level of story, and the level of narrative detail, so I listen carefully to everything everyone tells me about the work. Then, of course, I do exactly what I would do anyway. But I think it's very important to have a test readership before you send something out into the world and to pay attention to them. One of the secrets of telling is that telling is only 50% of it. Listening is the other 50%. I don't think any writer can afford not to be a good listener. That's part of the reason writers are such good conversationalists. They tell their own tales uninterrupted and then they sit and listen to another's tales with exactly the same attention. Beginning writers get cranked up. Sometimes they hear only the sound of their own voices. The longer you stay a writer, the more voices you find in your own voice and the more voices you find in the world. So I think literature provides community, it gives people who never had anything to talk about something to hold dear and in common.

AB: With regard to formal writing instruction, do you believe that writing talent can develop on its own or is it a combination of talent and instruction?

AG: I think there are certain shortcuts that a teacher can help you with. Finally, we're all alone in the struggle, and the fact that you're enrolled in a program doesn't mean that you're actually learning. You have to learn how to learn. I once met the actress Ruth Gordon, who said something wonderful. She said there are people who are talented and there are people who are talented at being talented. I think that finally the real writers are the people in the latter category. They will find a way to write if they have 12 children and work 80 hours a week. They will still wake up at 4 a.m. and work until 6 every morning. People who write have to write. They don't do it as an option or a hobby, they do it as a way of seeing the world. I think a lot of people benefit enormously from having this imposed discipline. And I think everybody can also benefit from having a teacher who's spent six days a week for 20 years writing, and can say, "You're better in first person than you are in third," or "there's too much dialogue and you're making the conversation literal." But they can't tell you what to write about, and they can't make a writer out of a sow's ear.

AB: Did you sell your early work through an agent?

AG: I sold some of the early stories myself, two to *The Atlantic* and one to the *American Review*. Then I had an agent for 15 years or so. When the novel was about to appear, I changed agents to Amanda Urban at ICM (International Creative Management). She's extraordinarily wonderful.

AB: Do you think an agent is essential for success?

AG: No, I don't. I think the tendency is to feel that an agent is everything and I think what young writers don't always realize is that every literary magazine is read by New York publishers. It's the business of editors in New York and at university presses to find future writers. All editors are professional talent scouts, and they want to find new talent. It's very hard to convince people of this sometimes.

AB: So you would advise new writers to submit their work to small presses?

AG: Absolutely. To think that you have to get into *The New Yorker* your first time out is complete and utter folly. It's much more convincing to an editor to get a letter from somebody who says, "I've been published in *Prairie Schooner,* the *Iowa Review* and the *Carolina Review* and here's my story for *The New Yorker.*" You establish your credentials by publishing where you can publish and by finding your own audience. I think there's also a danger in wanting to publish everything you write as soon as you write it, whether you've been writing for a long time or not. Some young writers spend more time at the post office than they do at their desks. I think it's very dangerous to give authority for your work to an editor too soon. You have to assume sovereignty over your own work before you try to sell it.

AB: Get your own house in order first?

AG: Yes. You don't invite a potential buyer into a house whose back wall is missing. Furnish the house, get it in working order, put some food on the table and then invite people in. I think there's a lot of rushing to judgment, looking to the publishing world for your confirmation when in fact you can only get that from yourself and your three closest readers. That's the rule of thumb. When three people urge you to send your work to a magazine, do it. But not before.

AB: What's your work routine?

AG: Well, I tend to get up around 6:30 a.m. and work until one in the afternoon, six days a week. It sounds like a lot, but it means that every day doesn't have to be a genius day. There are days when what I'm doing is just implementing the changes I made yesterday, but it keeps me in contact with the material, and it allows me to sort of dream continuously. It gives me a kind of patience with other people when I see how hard writing is. It does not get any easier. If anything, it gets harder because you let yourself get away with less. You know what the tricks are and they don't satisfy you. So there's this continual upping of the ante.

AB: How do you generate ideas for your stories?

AG: It seems to me that ideas are growing under every bush. Any copy of any newspaper contains enough stories to keep a career alive for a lifetime. It's a question of what angle and what tales you choose to emphasize and how you can make those tales personal to you and your readers. But I think a lot of what attracts readers is a pure adoration for language, and I think one of the things that's missing from a lot of contemporary fiction is an abiding interest in language as an end in itself. There are certain chapters of my novel which I know by heart and I can recite them like a kind of liturgy. Language can be musical, and that's the quality I miss in a lot of contemporary fiction. My teachers were all incredible musicians. You can read any passage of their work aloud and hear an amazing kind of sonorous love of language and connection to language. They let ideas grow out of language, rather than use the language to kind of wallpaper up the ideas.

AB: I've read that you don't get writer's block often. What is your advice to those who do?

AG: My theory is you don't get it if you don't believe in it. I've never heard of anyone getting plumber's block, or traffic cop's block. To make writing an exalted occupation above and beyond other occupations seems to me to invite trouble. I think of myself as a serious craftsperson. I think it's a mistake to sit down and say, "Now I will write a great masterpiece." I think that's where the trouble comes in. But if you just tell the truth in the most effective way you can, chances are you will come closer to doing what you want to do. I heard a wonderful phrase from a psychoanalyst: Perfect is the enemy of good. So if you think you're going to write perfectly chances are you'll write nothing, but if you hope to write well chances are you'll write perfectly.

AB: Do you propel a story or does the story propel you? A lot of writers use outlines, and they know pretty much where the story's going when they start out. I wondered if you work that way?

AG: I think that would be very dull indeed. Imagine if you were giving a dinner party and had a list of everything that would be discussed and what each person would say. There would be no point in throwing the dinner party. The whole element of inviting people into your life is that they surprise you, and please you, and stir things that you had not intended to be stirred. I think the same is true of writing. I don't want to write to blueprint specifications. I want to be surprised by the material. Grace Paley says everybody deserves the open destiny of life and I think every character deserves that, too.

AB: I read that Lucy Marsden hit you like a flash at Yaddo, and that you sat down then and wrote about 30 pages.

AG: That's right. I got her voice immediately, and I had to do some magic later in the book to keep the voice various enough to cover almost 720 pages. I thought at first the book would have several voices, but Lucy's turned out to be such a torrent of voice that I had faith that she could tell everything she needed to tell, which meant telling all, as the title suggests.

AB: Is this kind of flash of creativity something a young writer can prepare for?

AG: You have to put this in context. I had been writing for 13 years when this flash of creativity struck. I had been preparing the tools and honing my skills, so when this happened it did not happen to someone who had never written before. I had all the technique available to me that allowed me to follow the inspiration to its logical conclusion after seven years of working in the voice. But I think we are given gifts, and I think the great place for young writers to look for these gifts is in their own neighborhoods. Frequently what you find in your writing is that you're not just a person with an autobiography that begins the year you were born. You're part of a continuum of history. And if you can line yourself up with the history of tradition, you see how that history can influence you in the present to write stories about people who are long dead. You wind up being a much bigger writer than just the first-person narrow "I." You wind up putting yourself into a kind of oracle position, and allowing history to speak through you. I would encourage people to look at the stories of their grandparents and great-grandparents and their neighborhood, to see how they can become the sage of their own neighborhood.

AB: Would you say that's a common mistake on the part of young writers, that they try to flee their upbringing and go to something that's more interesting or not as well known, and they miss some really good material?

AG: Well, I think that's maybe a first step. I think people fall in love with the sound of their own voice and then they find other people's voices in that, and I think it's inevitable that you're suspicious of your own material in the beginning. But I think that the cliché that writing novels only begins when you're 40 is true. I know very few great books that were written by people in their 20s. I think you have to be alive in the world a certain number of years before you understand that you're going to die, which is the first equipment a young writer needs. To understand that you're mortal puts you in touch with the real subject matter, people and time. All novels are about people and time, and how time changes them or doesn't change them.

AB: You were very perceptive as your main character, Lucy. There were some cracks you made about men that made me chuckle, and then I sat back and realized this was a male writer writing through the voice of a woman about men.

AG: I think the differences between men and women cannot be exaggerated. It's as if the Lord put a cocker spaniel and a giraffe in the same house and said, "Go forth and multiply and spend 50 years together and let's see how it turns out." It's miraculous that marriages work as often and well as they do. I think men, in particular, are lazy about imagining women, and I think to me part of the joy and education of the book was saying "I" and meaning "her" and saying "I" and meaning "she." There's nothing more instructive than literally becoming someone else. The world's justice and injustice is completely re-aligned.

AB: Do you like writing short stories or novels better?

AG: I really love both forms. I think in some ways the story is more difficult than the novel, because each individual unit of the novel need not be completely perfect, whereas every story has to be utterly concise, utterly consistent and extraordinarily fast and felt. But I'm just feeling my way. In some ways I feel I'm very much in my apprenticeship as a novelist and a story writer. That's part of the beauty of writing is that the apprenticeship goes on forever. I don't think I'll ever be as good as Chekhov, although I'd like to be. And so it keeps me honest, it keeps me sympathetic to beginning writers because I think of myself in some ways as a beginner, although I've been doing it for 20 years.

AB: What's the most frustrating aspect of writing fiction?

AG: I'm a very slow writer. I wish I could write a novel in a year and a half instead of seven years, but I think the novel accumulates for me like geological strata and it takes time to pile up enough experience and connections in the context of the work to make it real, to give it the sense of lived history. I think I'm just going to have to live with this as a writer. My most recent book, *White People*, accumulated over more years than the novel. It's my whole history of short stories. And now I'm working on the next slow novel, for Knopf as well, *The Erotic History of a Southern Baptist Church*.

AB: What about commercial success?

AG: I don't know anyone who became a serious writer in hopes of becoming a commercial success. You don't do it for that purpose. Sometimes some kind of commercial good luck overtakes you, but I don't know anybody who I respect as a writer who started out in hopes of being a commercial success. What they set out to do was investigate the world in their own voice, with their own cultural history and their own subject matter, and in the process people become interested. That's the right sequence. It's not looking around and seeing what will sell and writing that, but looking around and deciding, "What do I want to leave as my note in the bottle? What's crucial to me, and what needs investigating? What needs saving from my life and what needs telling?" When that's rendered on the page, people come forward to read it and therefore buy it. But it's the wrong sequence to start looking around for sales. Honest writing always finds that a secondary and tertiary consideration.

AB: How do you feel about your own success?

AG: It never occurred to me that I would have any kind of commercial success. I had hoped for good reviews and serious literary attention, so for me the business of having a novel on the bestseller list is a kind of incredible bonus. It's like the grace of God: You can't ask for it, it's sort of visited upon you. It thrills me to have had so many people read my book. I get letters every day from book groups and librarians and young people, and the whole experience has confirmed my belief that there are many serious and intelligent readers in this country. It flies in the face of the statistics we've been force-fed. I think readers in America don't know how to find important and serious books because they are subjected to a commercial barrage of publicity. But when they find a book that moves them, seems important to them, and entertains them, they do buy it. Storytelling has the imperative that you shall not bore your reader. You do everything you can to engage and excite and stimulate and move and amuse your reader and, when those needs are met, you stand a good chance of communicating to a lot of people.

AB: How does it feel to be on a big book tour after living on or under the poverty line most of your adult life?

AG: That's a good question. I learned a lot very quickly. One thing I learned is just how many readers there are in this country, serious and passionate readers. Everywhere I went I met people who were avid to read good stuff. The tour is exhausting and exhilarating at the same time. I thought I was going to be a stranger but really felt that I was talking to my cousins in every city. I felt I had found that community we talked about earlier. Not only am I a writer, but a reader. In some ways, I'm a reader first. I think that every writer is a reader trying to pay back a debt, who's trying to leave a book that is as good as the book he has loved most.

66 People who write have to write. They don't do it as an option or a hobby, they do it as a way of seeing the world. 99

—Allan Gurganus

An Interview with Sue Miller

by Carol Lloyd

Sue Miller has encouraging words for beginning writers. The author of two hugely successful novels, *The Good Mother* and *Family Pictures*, and one collection of stories, *Inventing the Abbotts*, Miller says, "I'm not as despairing as some others about people with talent moving ahead solely on the basis of their talent. The idea that the world of publishing is closed to you unless you know someone, have a network, or have someone who can get you in at *The New Yorker*—that's just not true. People out there are eager to publish good stuff and are, in fact, looking for it."

Jerry Bauer

She should know. After selling her first two stories to *Ploughshares* and *North American Review*, Miller received several letters from agents and editors. One agent, Maxine Groffsky, wrote repeatedly, stating that she wasn't sure, but she might be able to help with short fiction. "Several other agents, it seemed to me," says Miller, "were hoping I could turn one of the stories into a novel. They seemed like they were just trying to score with a novel. Maxine presented herself differently."

Groffsky went on to represent Miller's *The Good Mother* and *Family Pictures*. Miller dedicated her 1987 collection of stories, *Inventing the Abbotts*, to the agent, whom Miller says has become a dear friend as well as trusted advisor.

Another reader of her stories in literary magazines was James Atlas, formerly of the *New York Times Book Review*. Atlas wrote a very encouraging letter to Miller, to which she responded. Several years later when he moved to *The Atlantic*, he wrote again, asking whether she had any fiction he might see. In this way Miller began selling to *The Atlantic*.

"I remember thinking that it would be very nice if I could actually make some money on the early stories," she says, "so I sent them off to *The New Yorker* and *The Atlantic* and *Redbook*. When they were rejected, I just checked them off my list and kept sending the stories off. I had a very curious sense of real confidence about the stories. I remember thinking that it was too bad they weren't going to make money, but I thought they would get taken *somewhere*."

She had enrolled in a writer's workshop in Cambridge taught by writer Anne Bernays, during a period she describes as a real "turn" in her life. Having written on and off since undergraduate days but seldom finishing her pieces, Miller looked to a workshop for the deadlines she had been unable to impose on herself. "I was always working on a novel. In fact, I finished one after college which was very bad.

"People (in the workshop) were very positive about my work, but it was more just an internal confidence that I'd managed to do this thing. I'd suddenly written a story which I felt stood on its own."

Carol Lloyd *is a Cincinnati-based freelance writer.*

Up to that point, an eight-year stint as a day care worker and the stresses of single parenthood with a young child left her little time to write, but plenty of opportunity to read. "I read everything I could get my hands on by certain writers, always with a great deal of attention to technique. Not that I could've articulated it, but by some sort of nearly osmotic-type process I took in a sense of what a complete story might be like."

Enrolled in the Boston University writing program in 1979 on a full fellowship, she completed the program and obtained another small fellowship before she began to teach at Boston University in 1981. She still teaches there one semester a year, this term leading a graduate writing workshop and a literature course on the short story.

Family Pictures grew from her desire to write a "family" novel. "*The Good Mother* was so much in one character's mind, so tight. I wanted to write a more expansive novel with a lot of characters." *Family Pictures* traces more than 20 years in the life of a Chicago family.

An admirer of such "family" novels as *The Man Who Loved Children* by Christina Stead and *Beyond the Bedroom Wall* by Larry Woiwode, she saw such an enterprise as the "next step in doing more complicated" writing.

Miller asked herself what the bad thing was that would happen to the whole family, "something that would change and reverberate for a long time among all the members." There is, she says, a "curious sort of cold bloodedness to imagine the worst thing possible and live through it imaginatively. The scenes which are painful in fiction are wonderful fictional opportunities. There's a kind of glee about them that is unavoidable if you're looking at your work as your work as well as thinking of the impact it will have."

The result in *Family Pictures* was the autism, long undiagnosed, of Randall, the second oldest boy in the Eberhardt family. "I've always been interested in that kind of endless impact on a family's life. It seemed to be an extraordinary fictional opportunity," says Miller, who adds that she has always been angered by the Freudian understanding of that kind of illness that blames the parents for the child's condition.

In the initial period of writing *Family Pictures*, Miller read many accounts of raising a child with autism, schizophrenia, severe retardation or other significant problem. "I felt I understood an awful lot after reading some of these testimonies."

All told, she spent nearly a year researching and making notes about the characters, events, and what she wanted to show through those events.

The period of laying the groundwork is characteristic of Miller's approach. "I tend to know very clearly what I want to do and why, what I would like the feeling of the book to be. I'm not clear in everything that's going to happen. Certainly in *Family Pictures*, which is not plot driven — it holds a series of events that explore the dynamics of the family — there was always a lot of choice about which character to turn to next.

"There was a lot I didn't know before I started each chapter but I certainly knew what I wanted the book to be and do."

Yet *Family Pictures* proceeded anything but smoothly. Having begun in the first person, Miller produced 200 pages which her agent, husband, and finally she herself thought were not working. They told her, and she eventually concurred, that it was time to stop and try again. "Then I began to work in the third person. I decided the story really had to be in the third person, but I always had these first-person chapters sitting around. It just wouldn't pull together. I had notes to myself that I wrote in moments of real perplexity. I just kept going at it, thinking somehow I would pull it together.

"Only near the end did I see how I could integrate the two parts of the book and make it work. My husband (novelist Douglas Bauers) helped me edit, cutting about 100 pages throughout."

Miller's solution was to intersperse first-person accounts by Nina, the second oldest girl, with third-person narrative about the Eberhardt family.

Currently in the preliminary stages of her third novel, she is writing short scenes, making notes, "trying to figure out, again, how to tell it." The "how" seems to be a central question in her writing.

Her advice to new and mid-career writers? "Mostly don't think of writing as a career. I think that's death. Think of writing as a process, one of growth, as a gift, which it surely is if you're good. The question is really what use to make of it, not to be strategic. It always makes me nervous to talk to people who are thinking of how to position themselves in the market in terms of what seems to be selling well.

"I think it's a real disaster not to keep in mind that you have to enjoy the process. I know that's easy for me to say, since I've had such financial success, but I honestly don't feel any differently about the process of writing from the way I felt when I had no financial success at all. It's sometimes been a struggle to keep the notion of whether or not this will be as commercial as the last, but it seems to me that's what you have to do.

"I've had a very lucky writing career," she continues. "But to publish in a little literary magazine is a real achievement. There are people—agents and editors—reading those journals. To try to write a story because someone will buy it is a mistake.

"There's too much focus on career and what comes next, with young writers particularly. The question is much more internal about what to do next. It seems to me the question is what would enlarge your gift.

"If you're writing good work people will notice it. Somehow it will happen. That may be naive, and I know there certainly arc a lot of people who struggle and struggle. My work may in some sense be more mainstream than other people writing truly eccentric kinds of fiction who may have more difficulty than I did, so I don't mean to gloss over the whole issue."

She urges writers to remember that among the readers of literary magazines with circulations of 1,500 or 3,000 are people eagerly looking for someone with talent to represent or publish.

As to her writing habits, Miller laughs and says, "They are not to be recommended. I work very irregularly and sporadically, with periods of working frantically for short shots and then feeling there's nothing more to say about it."

She and her husband have markedly different styles, she says. "He is more diurnal. He wakes in the morning and goes to work. But in the end he and I work at about the same pace." They have recently purchased a country house near their Cambridge home where she plans to do much of her writing. "I'll go away for a day or two. When I'm working I like not to talk to anyone, be sort of grumpy, then spend a longer stretch of time being sociable."

Miller acknowledges that her good fortune has extended to her choice of agents, as well. "People need an agent at the point when they are trying to sell a book. It's their business to know who would be interested in a book, not even just which house, but which editors in the house would embrace it.

"Increasingly, publishers read through agents. Most agents are willing to do much more reading than publishers are. They're willing to look at what comes in. They welcome new talent."

She suggests that writers with a finished work "write a letter out of the blue with a small sample of your work, something that represents your prose and the movement of whatever it is you're writing. I think it's a mistake to send in 500 pages, but most agents are willing to look at a few pages, even if it comes in very cold."

Aside from choosing an agent with appropriate credentials, she suggests finding some-one with genuine enthusiasm for your work, someone who's not trying to push to change things you don't feel confident changing. "Once you've published, you're likely to hear about other agents, if you want to change. One asks everyone one knows."

She sold the film rights to *The Good Mother*, she admits, "because I wanted to make the money. It bought us both a lot of writing time." She acknowledges that *Family Pictures* may also be sold for film treatment. Yet, just as she didn't see the movie *Good Mother*, neither would she watch *Family Pictures*. "I didn't want to have to think of my characters as someone else portrayed them. I wanted to have my own images. Seeing the movie would make my images always have this kind of filter."

66 **Think of writing as a process, one of growth, as a gift, which it surely is if you're good. The question is really what use to make of it . . .** 99

—Sue Miller

___ *Adding Life with Dialogue*

by Monica Wood

Have you ever read a transcript of a presidential press conference? Even the most lively and intelligent-sounding presidential answers can look like idiocy on the page. How about the conversation you overheard in a cafeteria? You wrote it down verbatim on a napkin:

"So her mother says to me, not the mother but the one that I thought was her except for that one green tooth? She says to me, you know your friend Danny, that's the guy I went out with just before I dumped Kevin . . . "

"That one green tooth" is kind of interesting, and the convolutions of mothers and boyfriends might be a promising place to start from or go toward, but to make this "found" conversation fiction-worthy you'll have to run it through a dialogue filter a few times.

As a writer, you must choose your characters' words wisely: dialogue sets pace, controls tone, reveals character, and moves the story forward. Good dialogue isn't a representation of how people really talk; it only *reads* that way. To get dialogue to read well, you have to practice writing a lot of it; and it helps to follow a few guidelines.

Using dialogue to reveal story

It is common knowledge that in order to keep up with the storyline on a "daytime drama," all you have to do is tune in for 20 minutes every month or so. In this case common knowledge is actually true, because of dialogue like this:

Aging Ingenue: Well, if it isn't my little brother Max.
Lead Male Hunk: I guess we haven't seen each other since Mother left her modeling job in Los Angeles to search for Justin.
Aging Ingenue: A lot's happened since then. The fire at Cross Enterprises that left Paige and Whitney dead—
Lead Male Hunk: And who would have guessed that our own father would turn out to the Port City Stalker.

This is not story revelation; this is shameless plot review. Rather than push the story forward, as good dialogue should do, this kind of information-giving dialogue stops the story altogether in order to identify characters and convey plot information. Useful in daytime drama, death in fiction. To write good dialogue, you must not think of dialogue as a *device*. If you have certain pieces of information that your reader must discover, don't depend on dialogue to do the whole job for you unless you want something akin to a soap opera exchange. Dialogue *can* do some of the job for you, however, in a way that straight prose cannot.

Let's look at an example. Your main character, Roddy, is a little boy with the face of Gabriel and the soul of Lucifer. In your story Roddy wreaks havoc on his unsuspecting

Monica Wood's fiction has appeared in numerous magazines, including Redbook, Yankee, North American Review *and* Fiction Network. *She is one of 16 American writers whose work was selected for the anthology,* Sudden Fiction International. *She also edits an anthology of work for high school readers,* 20 for the 90s.

parents and spins their lives out of focus, illuminating nuances of parenthood that reverberate with rare and important truths about the human condition. That's your hope, anyway.

So far you have seven pages of clear prose, packed with telling detail. It reads flat.
Roddy's manipulation of his parents lacks tension somehow. If this is like most first drafts,
chances are the story suffers from an overdose of exposition and an underdose of revelation. The reader probably envisions the author at the end of each paragraph holding up a
cue card that says DO YOU GET IT YET?

Try giving Roddy a shot of dialogue. Four lines of good dialogue can save you four pages
of exposition. Forget your six-paragraph description of diabolical little Roddy. Forget the
two-page passage you wrote about Catherine, Roddy's mother, that included the phrase
"her heart quivered every time Roddy opened his mouth to speak." Try the old "show,
don't tell" routine:

Catherine set the last of the groceries on the checkout counter. An enormous woman
with a "We Please" button clipped to her bosom smiled down at Roddy as she blipped
each item through the scanner. She had to lean halfway over the counter to really see him.
Carrots, soup cans, boxes of cereal beeped as Roddy, unsmiling, returned her gaze.

"Aren't you a cute little buzzard," she said, running a block of cheese over the scanner.

Catherine saw the purse of his lips, the stony set of his shoulders. She clasped her hands
together. "He's not very talkative," she said, hopefully.

The woman laughed. "He's just shy, aren't you, little fellow?"

Roddy raised his tiny eyes. "I hope you die."

Within a few lines of dialogue, fortified by gestural pauses and a well-placed dialogue
tag (more on that later) you have conveyed plenty of information about Roddy: He is a
child ("cute little buzzard"); he is short (the woman has to lean over to see him; he has
tiny eyes; his mother is afraid of him ("she said, hopefully"). You have revealed the two
crucial elements of the story: Roddy is an unpredictable, and possibly evil, little brat; and
Catherine is an ineffective and somewhat fearful mother. Not bad for a few inches of type.

Dialogue tags and gestural pauses

In the Roddy-Catherine scene you probably noticed that the dialogue does not exist
alone. The actual words of dialogue are no more crucial than the dialogue tags and gestural
pauses that set the tone and pace of the dialogue sequence. *Dialogue tags* are the "he said/
she said" 's of a dialogue sequence; *descriptive dialogue tags* are tags with a gesture attached
(" ' . . . buzzard,' she said, running a block of cheese over the scanner"); and *gestural pauses*
are the full-sentence interruptions ("Roddy raised his tiny eyes") that you sprinkle through
a dialogue sequence to fatten up the scene and avoid endless dialogue tags. Look how the
impact of Roddy's scene is diminished by eliminating gestural pauses:

Catherine set the last of the groceries on the checkout counter. An enormous woman
with a "We Please" button clipped to her bosom smiled down at Roddy as she blipped
each item through the scanner. She had to lean halfway over the counter to really see him.
Carrots, soup cans, boxes of cereal beeped as Roddy, unsmiling, returned her gaze.

"Aren't you a cute little buzzard," she said.

"He's not very talkative," Catherine said.

"He's just shy, aren't you, little fellow?"

"I hope you die," Roddy said.

Not only is the "he said/she said" overbearing, but the pace of the scene, the sense of a life (in this case the bustle of a grocery store) going on around this little beast and his mother, is completely lost. Gone are the block of cheese being swept over the scanner, the woman's laugh and Roddy's tiny eyes. Gone are Catherine's nervousness and the checkout woman's heartiness, both of which combine to infuse tension into this small exchange. By eliminating gestural pauses you are left with too swift a pace, a sliver of a scene and too many dialogue tags in order to identify the speakers.

It is best to dispense with dialogue tags altogether whenever you can, but sometimes a well-placed tag can inform the scene in a way a gestural pause cannot. Consider the "she said, hopefully" after Catherine's one line: This is a woman afraid of her own child. While the best writing advice I ever received (from George Garrett, 11 years ago at a writers' conference) was "Circle all your adverbs, dear, and then kill 'em," a well-chosen adverb in a dialogue tag can be most effective. Use them sparingly, however, and watch for redundancy: If the description is in the dialogue already (and in most cases it should be), leave it out of the tag. (For example: "I hate your guts!" she said angrily. Or: "I can't go on," he murmured sadly.)

Another mistake some writers make when creating dialogue tags is trying too hard to jazz them up. He said/she said is just fine. Spare the reader from she hissed/I laughed/he groaned. The aforementioned functions cannot actually be performed simultaneously with speaking, anyway. He shouted/ she whispered/ I screamed are probably all right, since they can at least be performed with words, but your best bet is to avoid tags in favor of gestures. Consider this scene from a story you have just written:

Frank presented the daisies. "I picked these."
"So?" She gave them a brief glance. "What do you want, a medal?"
"You said you liked romantic men."
"I said I liked romance." She put up one finger. "There's a big difference, Frank. Huge."
He stared into the flowers for a moment. "Are you real mad, or only a little bit mad?"
"Real mad."
Frank turned the flowers around a few times in his hands, considering. "I guess this would be a lousy time to ask for that 60 bucks you owe me."
She snatched the flowers and tore off their yellow tops one by one. "That's right," she said, handing him the bunch of stems. "It would."

In this scene it is easy to keep track of who is speaking, with minimal use of dialogue tags. In the girlfriend's final line you have used a descriptive dialogue tag for a certain effect—her line is slowed down, by virtue of the tag ("she said, handing him the bunch of stems"), and as a result she is rendered imperious rather than impetuous. This is how the last line would look minus the descriptive dialogue tag:

Frank turned the flowers around a few times in his hands, considering. "I guess this would be a lousy time to ask for that 60 bucks you owe me."
She snatched the flowers and tore off their yellow tops one by one.
"That's right, it would."

The girlfriend's action is less controlled in this second version, for she does not hand the stems back; and her line, uninterrupted, reads snappish and petulant. In the original version the girlfriend is much more self-possessed. Small decisions about how to present dialogue have large consequences for your characters.

One caution about using any of these presentation devices: One device used exclusively will make the dialogue sequence monotonous:

"Over here," she said, waving her program in the air.

"I thought I'd never find you," he told her, picking his way over the row to the seat beside her.

"I've been waiting for hours," she said, pushing the sticky strands of hair from her face.

In other words, vary your construction. (This goes for all aspects of a story, of course, not just dialogue.) Your best bet for presenting realistic, snappy dialogue is to use a combination of presentation devices: tagless dialogue, gestural pauses, descriptive tags, and simple tags. This is especially true when long tags serve as a connector for an already long line of dialogue:

"I can't see you again, Marilyn," Neville said, extracting his pocket handkerchief with a magician's flourish and presenting it to her with a trembling hand, "because Mother's wheelchair broke and she's asked me to fly to Japan with her to have it fixed."

Two mistakes here: The obvious one is the endless dialogue tag, and the other is the long line of dialogue with the connector "because." You might salvage a line like this as follows:

"I can't see you again, Marilyn," Neville said. He presented his pocket handkerchief with a magician's flourish. "Mother's wheelchair broke and she's asked me to fly to Japan with her to have it fixed."

Once you begin to write dialogue with a better sense of the importance of presentation, you will notice that character and story revelation depend as much on the surrounding details as they do on the dialogue itself.

Revealing character

Now that you know something about the function of dialogue and its nuts and bolts, you're stuck with a blank page and a character aching to say something. But what?

It depends on the character. Children don't talk like teenagers; teenagers don't talk like adults; southerners don't talk like northerners. Ethnic and cultural diversities also make for dialogue challenges: a Hopi Indian doesn't talk like a Boston Catholic; a steel worker doesn't talk like a lifeguard.

This is not a simple matter of vocabulary, either. Your character's words reflect so much about him—his background, motivation, inner and outer life—that the words he speaks are barely as important as how he speaks them. The cadence of dialogue, its syntax and grammar, and even the number of words it contains help show the reader who your character is.

You might have a character whose world view is maddeningly simple: things are either good or bad. His dialogue is a series of platitudes that drives the other characters nuts. Another character might be painfully shy, or burdened by a terrible secret: she can't seem to eke out more than a few words at a time.

In the Roddy-Catherine scene, Roddy's line is not "I hope you get sick," or "I hope you get sick and die," or "I bet you're going to die someday." He says, in the stripped, direct, bottom-line vocabulary *of a child*: "I hope you die."

Similarly, in the scene between Frank and his girlfriend, the verbal exchange has a certain cultural color. How differently would the reader perceive them if you were to change their words:

Frank presented the daisies. "These are for you."
She gave them a brief glance. "I suppose you thought they would thrill me?"
"You said you liked romantic men."
"I said I liked romance. There's a difference, isn't there?"
He stared into the flowers for a moment. "Are you horribly angry, or only a little?"
"Horribly."
Frank turned the flowers around a few times in his hands, considering. "I suppose it would be unwise to ask for the money you owe me?"
She snatched the flowers and tore off their yellow tops one by one. "Indeed."

The changes are small but the ramifications are great. The difference between "horribly angry" and "real mad," or "that's right" and "indeed," is entrenched in the education, class, goals, and expectations of your characters.

Interesting dialogue, in fiction and in life, depends as much on what you leave out as what you put in. In the following scene you are trying to reveal some aspect of the relationship between a mother and daughter, from the daughter's point of view.

"I'd just like to see you settled, that's all," my mother says.
"What do you mean?" I know exactly what she means.
"Settled," she says, glaring. "I mean *settled*."
"I'm settled, for heaven's sake. I have a job, a house, a dog. I send out for pizza every Friday night." She's still looking at me. "Mom, I'm *settled*."
She purses her lips, drums her spotted fingers on the tabletop. "There's more to this life, young lady, than the company of a dog."

In this scene, what the mother and daughter *do not* say is what makes the scene work. The daughter knows what the mother is getting at, the mother knows the daughter knows, and yet each is refusing to acknowledge the other's meaning. This unspoken argument provides the scene with emotional tension and reveals the characters as two strong wills locked in struggle. If you rewrite the scene using the dialogue the first version left out, you get something like this:

"I wish you'd get married," my mother says.
"I don't want to get married, Mom. I have everything I need right now."
She is glaring at me. "A husband would make your life a lot fuller."

The scene loses its punch when you write the "real" dialogue. Remember, people seldom say exactly what they mean. That's what makes stories, and real life, so interesting.

In the mother-daughter scene the language itself is not readily identifiable as belonging to any particular social stratum, but the words and cadences are carefully chosen nonetheless, for they illuminate a universal mother-daughter struggle. The mother's use of "young lady" illuminates her desire to establish position. The daughter's deliberate misinterpretation of the word "settled" as meaning, among other things, "I send out for pizza every

Friday night" is understandably infuriating to the mother. The word "settled," repeatedly and deliberately misunderstood, is the ping-pong ball in this back-and-forth game the mother and daughter are playing.

Varying the length of the sentences also reinforces the push-pull of this scene. By keeping the words but slightly altering their order and cadence, you get a scene robbed of some of its tension and most of its rhythm:

> "I'd just like to see you settled, that's all," my mother says.
> "What do you mean?" I ask, though I know exactly what she means.
> "Settled, I mean settled."
> "I'm settled, for heaven's sake, Mom." She's still looking at me. "I have a job, a house, a dog, and I send out for pizza every Friday night, so I'm settled."
> She purses her lips and drums her spotted fingers on the tabletop. "Young lady, there's more to this life than a dog's company."

The alterations are slight but the rhythm is much changed. Treat each line of dialogue like a line of poetry. If you make every word count and pay attention to line breaks, your character will stay alive.

One more observation about the original version of this scene: Notice the one line of internal monologue: "I know exactly what she means." This line sets up the ensuing tension and lets the reader in on the daughter's part of the push-pull. Combining dialogue with internal monologue—making the reader privy to the difference between a character's thoughts and words—is a fascinating way for the reader to get to know a character.

The pitfalls of writing dialect

Let's say you have done everything right—labored over word choice, meticulously laid out cadences, chosen a syntactical pattern peculiar to and compatible with your character—and still the dialogue looks stiff and unconvincing. Your character is Patsy, an old, angry, southern lady, but you wouldn't know it by reading what she has to say. To solve this problem, you decide to literally spell it out for the reader:

> "Buddy's been playin' bluegrass all naht long," Patsy said. "An mah haid's 'bout to explode."

This technique is not only out of vogue, it can be vexing to a reader who must slow down in order to figure out what the character is saying. Besides, if the line doesn't sound southern in the first place, spelling it out won't make much difference. The translation for the above line is: "Buddy's been playing bluegrass all night long," Patsy said. "And my head's about to explode." With the possible exception of the word "bluegrass," this line could be attributed to anybody from Boston to Seattle. It has no particular regional slant. (This is not necessarily bad, except that you want to identify Patsy as southern through her speech.)

If you can't get Patsy to sound southern, it's probably because you're northern—or western, or Canadian, or Bulgarian. If you insist on using Patsy, you have two choices: Move to Memphis or find some southerners to make friends with. Otherwise, you will probably resort to feeding Patsy lines like "shut my mouth and pass the grits," which will not endear her to many readers, particularly your new southern friends.

Creating true speech is a noble goal. To make your character as real as possible, though, you don't have to write full-blown, phonetically spelled dialect. Some well-chosen phrases and a general rhythm in the language will suffice, allowing readers from outside the particular region to appreciate the linguistic differences while still being able to read the words.

Let's say you're from northern New England. Why not move the story to Maine, where you're more familiar with the local dialect? This way you can give Patsy a believable voice without resorting to dropped letters and suspicious spellings.

"Howard's been wailing on that guitar all night long," Patsy might say from her new location. "You better believe I got one wicked headache."

A beautiful example of dialect that comes from the language itself, with no spelling variations, comes from the great Irish playwright, J.M. Synge (pronounced, appropriately, "sing"). Here is a line delivered by Pegeen, the barkeep's daughter from *The Playboy of the Western World*, after she meets Christy Mahon, a stranger who wanders into her father's tavern:

Pegeen: "Well, you'll have peace in this place, Christy Mahon, and none to trouble you, and it's near time a fine lad like you should have your good share of the earth."

It's difficult to read that line in anything other than an Irish brogue.

Knowing when to stop

Finally, you've got your characters talking to your satisfaction. Now it's time to learn how to shut them up. Real people have a habit of repeating themselves and drifting off in conversation, but fictional characters can afford no such luxury.

As a general (and arbitrary) rule, don't let your characters say more than three sentences at once unless they have a compelling reason. You'll be surprised how well this works. Let's look at Spike and Arnold, two high school boys hanging around outside a school gymnasium.

Arnold leaned against the scarred brick, his jacket slung over one shoulder. It was cold but his black shirt looked good. "You were the one who was dying to come to this stupid dance," he said to Spike. "Just because Sherrie might show up within the next century is no reason to stand out here freezing. We've been waiting over an hour and she still isn't here. I wouldn't be surprised if she didn't even show up at all. It wouldn't surprise me one bit, considering her past history."

"What makes you think I care if Sherrie shows up? I didn't say anything about Sherrie," Spike said. He huddled inside his leather jacket, sucking on a cigarette. "We're through, anyway. I wouldn't give her the time of day at this point, if you want the truth. Six months was enough of her, let me tell you. I would've given her the shirt off my back in those days, but now I wouldn't lend her my extra jacket if she was freezing to death in Siberia. Sherrie's nothing to me. I don't care if she lives or dies."

"I think I see her."

"Where?" Spike's head whirled around like the light on top of a squad car.

This scene has possibilities, but the characters are too long-winded to move the scene forward. There's plenty of story revelation here—Spike and Sherrie dated for six months and Spike is still smitten; Arnold and Spike have been waiting outside the gym for over an hour; Sherrie has a history of not showing up when she's supposed to—but how important are these facts to the real story? Doesn't it read a little like a daytime drama? Try putting a muzzle on this pair and see what you get:

Arnold leaned against the scarred brick, his jacket slung over one shoulder. It was cold but his black shirt looked good. "You were the one who was dying to come to this stupid dance," he said to Spike. "How much longer are we supposed to wait for her? Another century or what?"

"Did I say I was waiting for Sherrie?"

"It's pretty obvious."

"A lot you know," Spike said. He huddled inside his leather jacket, sucking on a cigarette. "I wouldn't give her the time of day at this point, if you want the truth. I don't care if she lives or dies."

"I think I see her."

"Where?" Spike's head whirled around like the light on top of a squad car.

In this second version, not as much information is conveyed, but the essence of the scene—the difference between Spike's words and actions—is distilled from the cluttered original.

We don't need to know how long Spike and Sherrie dated; the interesting part is that he's still carrying a torch for her. We don't need to know they've been waiting over an hour. Arnold's impatience and the cold air already imply a long wait. This revised version is cleaner and more effective. Where the original scene hovered, the revision moves.

Dialogue is not always a solution; in the wrong place, dialogue can burden a story. Even in the right place, good dialogue can drag a story if it is too long.

All of these suggestions for writing good dialogue are, of course, simply guidelines that you are welcome to sidestep. Fiction isn't much fun to write if you go strictly by the rules. In John Irving's novel, *A Prayer for Owen Meany*, Owen's entertaining dialogue sometimes goes on for paragraphs (in capital letters!). Alice Walker's luminous novel, *The Color Purple*, is full of spelling variations. However, when you're stuck, when you get to the inevitable point in a story where *something* stops working, the "rules" are a handy refuge for getting your story moving again.

Jump-Start Your Fiction Through Your Characters

by John Tibbetts

All fiction writers—young and old, the novice and the experienced—are intimidated by a blank page. Many writers have blocks that can last for days, months or years. Consider some of the brilliant writers who have been fallow for long periods: Herman Melville, Katherine Ann Porter, Tillie Olsen, to name just a few. So how do you get started when your mind is empty, when you're staring at that blank page, stumped?

When I can't get started writing, it's because I am concentrating on the wrong thing; that is, I am focusing on the plot of the story. Instead, I've learned that I should concentrate on my character or characters. If can understand my characters, then the plot will take care of itself. To break through a block, I must find out where and how my characters have lived, how they make their living, who are their mothers and fathers.

To learn about your characters, do some research. I don't mean research in a library. No, this is the research of your own life and imagination. You need to explore the people you have known and within them you'll find your story.

Plot is character, said Henry James. About Russian writer Ivan Turgenev, James wrote: "The germ of the story . . . was never an affair of plot—that was the last thing he thought of. The first form in which a tale appeared to him was the figure of an individual, or a combination of individuals, whom he wished to see in action, being sure that such people must do something very special and interesting."

So, in effect, James advised you should think of someone interesting, someone you find intriguing—and write about him. Put your character into a situation that would make him uncomfortable and then watch what he does.

I have six exercises that will help you get a story rolling. If one of these exercises doesn't work for you, try another. These strategies are all ways of keeping your story alive. At the same time these exercises can help you discover and develop your characters, because when you make a character live and breathe, your reader will follow that person for page after page. After all, we all remember Huck Finn, Anna Karenina and Pip better than we remember the plot details of the novels written by Mark Twain, Tolstoy and Dickens.

1. Name your character

Elmore Leonard, that wonderful writer of crime thrillers, once said that he can't get a story straight in his mind until he gets the names of his characters right.

Same with me. I can't start a short story until I choose an appropriate name for my protagonist. How a writer chooses a name for his characters will tell you a lot about that writer's methods—and philosophy—of storytelling.

For instance, the novelist and filmmaker John Sayles has said that he chooses the shortest name possible for his main character. He doesn't want to type a long name over and over again. I agree. It sounds superficial, but I don't want to type Christopher, Jonathon

John Tibbett's stories have appeared in Mss, Kansas Quarterly, Cimarron Review, Confrontation *and other publications. His work has been nominated for a Pushcart Prize and he is the recipient of a General Electric Award for Younger Writers. He writes for the South Carolina Sea Grant Consortium.*

or Elizabeth dozens of times if I can type Chris, Jon or Liz. So when I look over the stories I've written, I see the following names of my characters: Jeff, Ned, Ann, Tim, Bert.

These names fit my characters. The people I write about would go by a short name rather than a long one. Informal people, they would likely have nicknames. They are usually Midwestern and they dislike pretension. Their tastes tend toward the simple rather than the complex, the unornamented rather than the rococo. These characters are common people—they're not rich or particularly successful or remarkable in any superficial way. But generally they're intelligent, politically aware, well-read and perceptive about the people and the world around them. They are an unhearalded group: schoolteachers, small-time musicians, students and small-town or alternative journalists.

No matter how hard I try to change the kinds of people I write about, I can't do it. Frank O'Connor, the Irish storyteller, wrote that the short story is usually about a member of a "submerged population." My characters are indeed members of a submerged group—a group submerged under the stream of attention given to the more successful, the more flamboyant.

But perhaps the flamboyant is what interests you, as it did F. Scott Fitzgerald. Think of "Amory Blaine" in *This Side of Paradise*. It's a name that fits the romanticism of Fitzgerald's protagonist.

2. Writing from the point of view of some alien

I often start a story by basing the main character on myself. Most writers probably do the same thing; we know ourselves better than we know anyone else. But the character based on myself becomes boring very quickly. Soon I want to write about someone else—without losing that freshness that comes from confessional writing. But it's tough to write about strange people—people with different backgrounds from ourselves. The trick here is to find a common element between yourself and another person.

Begin by writing an account of something that has happened to you. It can be something ordinary. Let's take, for example, this common experience: your close friend has just married someone whom you find unsuitable.

Include details about how everything looked to you: the groom, the bride, the cake, the families, the music. Tell us about the smells, the sounds of the wedding. After all, the experience was different for you than for anyone else.

Now pick someone you know—a friend or an acquaintance from a different social or economic or ethnic background. Make this person the main character of your story; he will have some of your qualities and some of his own.

Put your character into your unhappy situation: his friend is marrying badly. See this scene from your character's eyes.

How will your character's experience differ from your own? How will it be the same?

You might learn that all people have similar basic emotions: for instance, we want our friends to be happy. But we express those basic emotions in different ways. You might smile and congratulate the bride and groom while someone else might brood, drink too much, and say hostile, inappropriate things.

If you can identify with the emotions of people who are different from you, then you can understand their actions. By concentrating on emotions that each of us have, you can write from the point of view of a truckdriver or a debutante, a sailor or a senator. After all, each of us at some time feels envy, disappointment and pride. And sooner or later, each of us probably copes with a friend marrying someone we dislike.

The filmmaker Stephen Spielberg is a master of creating characters from varying backgrounds—and a master of showing how these characters would respond to the world and to conflict. (You can learn a lot about storytelling from the best movie-makers, after all.) In the movie, *E.T.*, for instance, the opening sequence is a lesson in an unusual character's point-of-view—a creature from another planet. Remember, the movie's first sequence shows us the creature's first night on Earth. Spielberg's camera is fixed at waist level for much of the first five minutes of the movie, because the creature's eyes are at that level. What E.T. sees, the audience sees, too.

The camera shows cars approaching. The camera is positioned low to the ground, from E.T.'s point of view. Then men emerge from the cars, and the audience, along with the creature, hears keys jingling—these keys are attached to a man's belt, at waist level.

As the creature tries to escape, running to his space ship, which will soon fly away without him, the camera *becomes* E.T. The camera pushes through the undergrowth of the forest, striking bushes and you hear the panicked breathing of terror. So the audience experiences the mad dash along with the creature.

In this sequence, Spielberg masterfully illuminates how to get inside someone different from yourself. Spielberg identifies with an emotion that is common to everyone: fear. It is the fear of the unknown, of being left behind, of being hurt by someone bigger and stronger.

Spielberg does not concentrate on the differences between ourselves and the creature—but the similarities. Of course, as Spielberg continues to tell his story, he sentimentalizes his creature and neglects to give him any ugly attributes—meanness or selfishness. But his strategy of getting inside a character is consistent with Tolstoy's approach: Tolstoy noted that once he got inside a character's skin, once he saw the world through that person's eyes, he took pity on him.

It's Spielberg's empathy for the creature that makes that first sequence work so effectively.

3. Create composite characters

After a time, you may come to a dead end with your character. He's not complicated enough or interesting to you anymore. Now you might think of grafting another person onto your character. Many storytellers have noted how their characters are composites—bits of many people they've known over the years. A writer takes attributes of qualities from one person and then grafts those onto someone else—generally someone similar in a certain respect. I always have at least two—sometimes three or four—different models for each major character in my stories, though one model generally is predominant.

But first you need to learn to ignore the boundaries of time and space. Start this exercise by picking a friend from childhood, someone you haven't seen in years. Imagine what he would be like today. Describe his marriage, his work, his education.

The idea here is to avoid the literal truth; you need to find another, more playful truth, an artist's truth. Fiction writers and poets create their art by mixing people and situations, by disregarding temporal boundaries. Robert Frost wrote, "The artist . . . snatches a thing from some previous order in time and space into a new order with not so much as a ligature clinging to it of the old place where it was organic."

One of the pleasure of storytelling is finding the similarities among disparate people.

I began a story once about an old girlfriend. I wrote about her humor, gentleness, resourcefulness, toughness and her fierce independence. But what I remembered most was her mulish stubbornness that made her difficult to be with. As I wrote about her, she suddenly reminded me of my grandfather. I saw similarities between a woman I cared for when I was 24 and a man who died when I was 16. I saw the connections between a redhead with long legs and a fierce old country doctor. I saw the connection between the qualities that I intermittently found attractive in a woman and the spoken and unspoken values of my family.

My old girlfriend and my grandfather both came from hardscrabble families; they both had alcoholic fathers; they both pushed away those they loved; they were both tender, sarcastic and harsh. So in my story, I gave my girlfriend a little bit of my grandfather's background. By blending their histories, I made sense of something that never made sense before—my attraction to this difficult person. And I created a richer, more complicated story.

4. Make your readers use at least two senses

I can't get rolling on a story unless I know the setting. If I am going to live imaginatively in a place for the duration of a story, then I'd better find it stimulating in some way. Also, my character must have some emotional reaction to the place where he lives or where he's visiting—he must be in conflict with it somehow.

One way to learn about your character is to put him into a place, then have him respond to that environment. It's important for your character to sense things around him—to smell, to touch, to hear, etc. Flannery O'Connor, the short-story writer and novelist, wrote that she always tried to get at least two senses into the first paragraph of a story, preferably three. That is, she wanted her protagonist to respond physically to his setting. After all, human beings are not of another world; we are grounded to the earth; we sweat, we lust, and we fight.

Consider the first few sentences of Ralph Ellison's "King of the Bingo Game." "The woman in front of him was eating roasted peanuts that smelled so good that he could barely contain his hunger. He could not even sleep and wished they'd hurry up and begin the bingo game. There, on his right, two fellows were drinking wine out of a bottle wrapped in a paper bag, and he could hear the soft gurgling in the dark. His stomach gave a low, gnawing growl."

In these few sentences, we learn about the setting: a dark, crowded theater with a potentially rowdy audience (the wine). And we learn about the protagonist. He probably doesn't have a home; if he had a place to live, he probably wouldn't be trying to sleep in a theater. He's poor, tired and hungry. And we, the readers, become absorbed in this character because we perceive the environment along with him. Ellison has provoked our senses with the smell of peanuts, the sound of the wine gurgling and the sound of protagonist's stomach growling. Two senses are evoked; one sense evoked twice.

And essence of storytelling is absorbing the reader in the world of your character. Making your reader smell, touch, feel, hear and see (along with your character) will get that reader hooked on your story.

5. Create smart characters

Most of us enjoy stories about intelligent, savvy people. A fictional character may not realize that he is intelligent (Huck Finn) or he may think he is more astute than he really is (Pip and Anna Karenina), but in one way or another we continue reading about, and believing in, a fictional creation because we admire his alertness to the world. Even Vladimir Nabokov's child-molesting Humbert Humbert is admirable to the extent that he is resourceful and perceptive, if only on the basest level.

Consider how Anton Chekhov in his great story, "The Lady with the Pet Dog," shows us the perceptiveness of his protagonist, Gurov: "One evening while (Gurov) was dining in the public garden, the lady in the beret walked up without haste to take the next table.

Her expression, her gait, her dress, and the way she did her hair told him that she belonged to the upper class, that she was married, that she was in Yalta for the first time and alone, and that she was bored there."

We know a variety of things about both Gurov and the woman. We know that Gurov is attracted to her, that he is a lady's man, and that he can read character—both good and bad. We also know that he is cynical. About the woman, we know her class, her marital status and her willingness to have an affair. Would Gurov be capable of making so many judgments about a woman he's never met? Of course. Most of us make swift judgments like this every day about people we don't know, and frequently we are correct.

What makes this strategy so effective, however, is the fact that Chekhov does not allow his narrator to make these observations. In most cases, the ominiscient narrator—one that sees the truth about characters and tells us the meaning of a scene or a story—is a monotonous and outdated strategy. Instead Chekhov filters these perceptions through the mind of his protagonist, Gurov. Notice that all the information comes to the reader by way of Gurov's perceptions. Thus, the story has a greater richness and complexity.

Allow your characters their full intelligence and perceptiveness. Allow them to know as much about human nature as you do on your best, most enlightened days.

6. Show character through action

Sometimes the simplest thing in storytelling is the toughest—and the most important—that is, showing characters moving through the world without the crutch of getting inside their heads. As thousands of creative writing teachers have pointed out, it is more difficult to show than to tell. When you find yourself getting too fancy, or when you are stuck, return to this simple principle: what a person does tells us about his character.

Try writing a page showing a person involved in action. Don't enter your character's mind. Just concentrate on what your character does. Gesture, said the 18th century French novelist and philosopher Denis Dierot, is more illuminating than explanation.

A suggested start: "After lunch he went to the porch to get the mail and found a large brown package."

Dramatize how your character responds, step-by-step, as if you were writing a play. Does your character throw out the package without opening it? Does he open it? What does he find? How does he react? If a story is going badly, or if I can't get a story started, I usually try this exercise. It forces me to concentrate on action.

This strategy reduces a story to "something happens and my character must react."

And isn't life like that? Something happens and we must react. We react badly or well. Then we judge and measure our reaction.

Think of the plot of Shakespeare's *Othello*. Without realizing it, Othello has made an enemy of the evil Iago, who is determined to destroy him. The story is about how Othello reacts clumsily and foolishly to the challenges of this evil plotter.

The plot of *Hamlet* is similar in this respect. Something has happened to Hamlet's family—and how the hero reacts to this event and subsequent events is the story.

Again, we are reminded of what Henry James wrote about Turgenev: plot is character. Action defines character.

But grand heroics are rare for most of us. You could go through a lifetime without an opportunity for obvious heroism. Most of us, in fact, live quietly. However, underneath the quiet a drama is going on, and the best writers are attuned to this everyday drama. They are attuned because each of our responses to the small stuff is the genuine barometer of character, good or bad, and is the heart of storytelling.

Creating Tension In Your Fiction

by Stephen Minot

"Well, it's a pleasant story." When you hear that comment about a work you have just written, don't smile. It may sound like a compliment, but it isn't.

Editors are flooded with "pleasant little stories," and they reject most of them. Often, the rejection slip is without comment. If there is a note it may say, "Pleasant reading, but a bit mild for us." Or, more bluntly, "Needs more impact."

What's puzzling for the author is the fact that these are often stories that receive very little adverse criticism from friends and fellow writers. Readers nod, smile, mutter phrases like "very nice" or "I enjoyed it." And there the comments stop. It's not that "bland" is a hard word to pronounce, it's that the solution seems elusive.

A dull story is like a dull meal at a restaurant. Patrons don't complain, but they don't come back. The sad aspect is that the chef, hearing no specific complaints, never improves.

No, it's not true that only sex and violence sell. In fact, for most magazines, excessive use of sex and violence is the sign of an immature writer. The solution is far more subtle.

What those pleasant little stories lack is *tension*. While tension can be created in a number of different ways, it always consists of pitting one element against another.

The most obvious type of tension, the type we are most familiar with, is *conflict*. A more subtle form of tension is created by arousing *curiosity*. When curiosity is intensified and made dramatic, the result is *suspense*. And surprisingly, a different but effective type of tension can be achieved by the use of *irony* and *satire*.

Any story that seems bland, limp, lifeless, flat or just plain dull is lacking in tension. Tension provides the energy and the vitality that hold a reader's attention and interest. Although these five forms of tension can overlap and be used simultaneously with others, it helps to examine each separately.

Conflict: Add essential vitality

The first of these, dramatic conflict, is found in all types of narrative including plays, films, and some types of poetry. We call it "dramatic" partly because it is associated with plays, but mainly in the sense of being vivid or striking.

When handled blatantly, dramatic conflict is the mainspring of relatively simple fiction and drama. Adventure stories and television thrillers pit characters against each other with great regularity. Occasionally an individual faces a group or, less often, some aspect of nature. The conflict in such works tends to be simple, straightforward, and not complicated with inner debate. In the case of television scripts, the plots are often rather similar.

With associations like these, it is no wonder that some beginning writers unconsciously avoid all forms of conflict and keep their characters passive or isolated. But there is no

Stephen Minot *has been a professor of English at Trinity College in Oxford and recently took over as Chair of Creative Writing at the University of California at Riverside. He has published short stories and three novels, including his most recent,* Surviving the Flood, *published by Atheneum in the U.S. and Granada in England. He is currently preparing the fifth edition of his creative writing textbook,* Three Genres.

need to avoid conflict in even the most sensitive fiction. It will serve you well and will add essential vitality to your fiction as long as you make sure that it is reasonably subtle, insightful and appropriate to the length of your story.

Suppose, for example, your story deals with a recently widowed mother and the ways in which she and her teenaged daughter adjust to life without a man in the house. It may be that they will go through similar stages and have somewhat similar reactions, but unless we see some form of conflict between mother and daughter, the story may well seem bland and somewhat unrealistic. If they are totally harmonious, the tone may even become sentimental. Conflict between mother and daughter does not have to be harsh, and it can always be resolved in the end, but it should be clear and unmistakable if it is to provide the kind of vitality that every story needs.

When one bases fictional characters on personal friends, there is a natural tendency to mute or even suppress signs of conflict. Who wants to antagonize a spouse, a parent or close friends who might recognize themselves in the fiction? It's a bad sign when you catch yourself saying, "I can't write it that way, it would be just too embarrassing." It means you have not yet divorced the story from your life. Psychologically, you are writing an autobiographical fragment, not fiction.

Whenever you shy away from conflict for fear of hurting the feelings of someone you know, radically alter the story even before you write the first draft. Change the ages, alter the setting, shift the season. In some cases you can even reverse the sex—particularly of children. This is called *metamorphosing* a personal experience—shifting it so fundamentally that you are psychologically free to develop the fiction as fiction.

Try a subtle approach

We often associate conflict between a character and an aspect of nature with high adventure. Mountain climbing, survival at sea, floods and fires all come to mind. Such situations can all make good fiction—particularly when the writer knows the subject and is not merely imitating someone else's work.

But don't forget that nature has its subtle challenges as well. Four days of rain may not make an epic film, but it can have a significant effect on a couple on vacation who are doing their best to hold a marriage together. One-hundred-degree temperature may not make headlines in August, but it could be a central factor in a story about a father who agrees to go jogging with his son and is determined not to show his age.

The same applies to conflict with aspects of society. We have all seen gripping accounts in films of men and women threatened by mob violence, but that may be too big a scope for a short story. Prejudice, for example, can take very subtle forms—a child excluded from a party, a veteran who finds old friendships dissolve when back in civilian life. Society can also be the enemy for an immigrant in a new country. Even a benign community may seem like an opponent to be conquered. And every time we battle a bureaucracy—be it a hospital, a large corporation or a governmental agency, we are St. George facing the dragon.

One way to make conflict of any type more insightful and subtle is to combine it with an inner conflict. Returning to our example of the mother and daughter making a new life together in the absence of the father, outer conflict may be made clear by verbal disputes and perhaps the slamming of a door. But if the daughter, say, goes back to her own room, only to return to her mother's door again, we have a picture of her inner conflict over whether to sustain the rift or make up. Details like these add depth to our view of a relationship.

One word of warning: When working with internal conflict, be careful not to rely too heavily on your protagonist's thoughts. Long passages in which characters "debate" with themselves begin to sound like explanatory essays. It is far more subtle and effective to imply an inner conflict through some kind of action or revealing dialogue.

Curiosity: Hook the reader

Arousing curiosity is an equally important way to create tension in your fiction. It usually takes time to develop conflict, but you can arouse the reader's curiosity in the very first paragraph. Commercial writers often refer to this as *the hook* — the creation of a situation that seizes the reader's attention from the start. No, you don't have to have bodies slump to the floor or bridges collapse into raging water; what draws the reader may be as mild as the appearance of a perfect stranger standing there at the front door with his suitcase, the six-year-old child who gets off the bus in a small town with no parents and no knowledge of English, the loving wife and mother of three who quietly announces that the family can get its own supper because she is taking the next bus to El Paso. Situations like that are openings waiting for a story; and once written the opening paragraph is a baited hook for any reader.

Important as the opening hook often is, don't forget that arousing curiosity is an important form of tension straight through to the end of a story. That stranger at the door isn't going to hold the reader very long if he turns out to be dull Uncle Harry who would like to stay over one night on his way to Omaha. As soon as that opening situation has been established, there have to be more questions to hold the reader's interest.

Think of these *dramatic questions*. As soon as the stranger's identity is clarified (a not-so-dull Uncle Harry from Australia, for example), we could raise another: Is he *really* an uncle; or, Can we trust him? or, Will he ask for money? And overlapping with that, How long will he stay? When you read a short story, notice how often the plot keeps generating new questions that hold your interest.

Dramatic questions are a natural form of tension because readers at any age want to know, "What happens next?" And every story teller knows that you can't tell too much too soon. The detective story is a highly stylized sequence of dramatic questions with the ultimate dramatic question, "Who done it?" But even subtle stories that deal with the unfolding of character use the technique of playing the reader's desire to know against the withholding of that information.

Depending on a single dramatic question has its risks. If the reader has the feeling that there are only two possible outcomes, the result will seem to be predictable. We see this occasionally in the sports story that poses the too-simple question, "Will they win or lose?" Or the mountain-climbing story that asks, "Will they make it to the top or not?" One solution is to find a conclusion that is not quite one or the other. They lose the game but preserve their sense of honor. The climbers make it to the top but for complex reasons the victory brings no sense of satisfaction.

Suspense: Increase the voltage

Suspense, our third form of tension, is a heightened form of curiosity. It too uses a dramatic question, but the voltage has been increased. Since it takes time to build suspense convincingly, it is not often found in short short stories — those under 2,000 words. Even in longer stories and novels, suspense is frequently limited to specific scenes rather than becoming the primary energizing force. So-called suspense thrillers will, of course, continue to be popular just as will television dramas of the same sort. Entertaining as highly suspenseful fiction can be, it has a certain limitation. Suspense tends to overpower subtle characterization and theme. Dick Tracy, like Batman before him, is a cardboard character designed to sustain suspense.

If you have a compelling plot, however, don't shy away from suspense. Just make sure that it doesn't cause you to settle for stereotyped characters and win-or-lose plots. If you feel the story sliding in that direction, remember that because suspense is merely an intensified form of curiosity, it can always be muted a bit to give other literary elements a chance.

Conflict, arousing curiosity and creating suspense are three closely related approaches to creating tension in fiction. How much should you use? To a large degree, this is simply a matter of choice. It depends on the degree to which subtle insights into character and theme are important and conversely the degree to which you want to stress dramatic impact. But consider the degree of tension in terms of the length of the story. In some ways, tension is like electricity—a heavy wire can take high voltage. In the same way, a novel can absorb life-and-death conflicts and gripping suspense, but a short short story packed with that much drama may seem like an outline of an unsuccessful television plot. It becomes *melodrama*—drama that is so overdone that the reader no longer takes it seriously. In such cases, it is fairly easy to convert murder to insult and suicide to an act reflecting deep despair.

Irony: Surprise with contrast

Irony and satire provide two more methods of creating tension in fiction. Although they seem at first to be completely unrelated to conflict, curiosity and suspense, they also place two elements in opposition. Both irony and satire create tension by playing the author's apparent intent against the actual meaning. Both can be used to add spice to an otherwise bland story.

Before one can use irony effectively, it helps to be able to identify examples and understand how it works. Basically, there are two ways we use the word *ironic*. One refers to the way we speak or write and the other to events.

Verbal irony, that having to do with words, occurs when characters make statements that are knowingly different or even the opposite of what they really mean. In casual conversation we sometimes call it *sarcasm*, though sarcasm is generally hostile and critical. Irony can take the form of simple understatement, as when someone describes a hurricane as "quite a blow." Stronger irony can be a full reversal of meaning as if the same character, while watching his house being washed away in the storm, says "Great day for a sail."

Verbal irony in fiction occurs most often in dialogue. It suggests a character who is wry and given to understatement. There is a significant difference between a character who, having just learned that he has just lost his life savings, says, "I'm ruined, totally ruined," and one who says, "Well, that kind of spoils a nice day." The use of this kind of irony can help to define character.

It is also possible, however, to use verbal irony in passages of exposition. Author's intrusion is not widely used in contemporary writing, but it is always possible to adopt a wry tone when one does step into a story. There is a difference between describing a character directly as "a pathological liar" and employing ironic understatement such as, "He never felt at ease speaking the truth." The difference is simply a matter of style.

When irony refers to events rather than the use of words, it is sometimes called irony of fate. In actual use, it may take the form of a very minor event. It refers to any outcome that is the opposite of normal expectations. One often hears it used in a careless way to describe anything that is unexpected—"Ironically, the weaker team won." True irony, however, is a real reversal. It is ironic for a composer like Beethoven to lose his hearing or for an Olympic swimmer to drown in his own bathtub. Life occasionally provides ironic twists that are too blatant for fiction. Bad enough that America's first major toxic waste disaster should actually occur in something known as the Love Canal, but what story writer would have dared call the culprit the Hooker Chemical Corporation?

Ironic reversals in fiction tend to be muted so that they don't become obtrusive. A elderly bachelor who constantly complains about the children in the neighborhood turns out to be the only one who makes contact with a deeply withdrawn teenager; the loss of a job that a man and his wife had been dreading turns out to redirect their lives and strengthen the bond between them.

Irony provides tension in fiction because there is a surprising contrast between what is said and what is meant or between expectations and what actually occurs. The reader is caught off balance, jolted.

Satire: Sustain the attack

Satire is almost always rooted in irony. Essentially it is exaggeration for the purpose of ridicule. Through the use of irony, the author is able to ridicule a person or institution with a "straight face." Many young people are introduced to satire through magazines such as *Mad* and/or *National Lampoon* long before they read more subtle versions in fiction. And the skits on *Saturday Night Live* have entertained an entire generation. Satire on that level is good fun but rather obvious. It is designed for quick entertainment.

Satire in fiction, however, can be developed into a complex and sustained attack. Many have become enduring aspects of our literary heritage. The butt or target of satiric fiction is often a group or institution that takes itself too seriously. George Orwell's *Animal Farm*, for example, sharply attacks the old leadership of the Soviet Union by presenting them as barnyard animals. Joseph Heller ridicules war through arch and sometimes bitter irony in *Catch-22*. Mary McCarthy lashes the academic world in *The Groves of Academe*. J.P. Marquand gently satirizes Bostonians in *The Late George Apley*.

If this approach interests you, watch out for three dangers in the writing of satire. The first is lack of focus. Decide in advance just what kind of person, institution or tradition you wish to ridicule. Keep your satiric attack precise and detailed.

The second danger is a matter of excess. If your exaggeration becomes extreme, you will find the piece turning into slapstick. Such work may, like cartoons and TV scripts, be very funny, but they may also be rather superficial and quickly forgotten.

The third and most serious danger is the risk of cruelty. Remember that satire is an attack. As with telling jokes, everyone has the right to poke fun or even sharply criticize his or her own race or religious group, but when you turn satire against someone else's group, it can become nasty.

Charge it with tension

These, then, are ways of establishing tension in fiction, ways you can keep your work lively and "charged." Although I have presented them separately for analysis, I should make it clear that this does not describe how one goes about writing a story. One doesn't sit down and try to think of ways to arouse curiosity or develop irony, hoping that story will appear like a genie from a bottle. It is far more fruitful to begin with a character in a particular situation—perhaps someone you have known or heard about. From that point, a fictional plot unfolds—part experience, perhaps, and part invention.

It is usually after completing the first draft that you can afford to make a careful assessment of how it went. Is it lively enough to hold a reader that is not your best friend? Would you yourself go on reading if you came across this story in a magazine? In short, does it have the vitality needed to hold a reader who might have other things to do?

If not, see if it might be possible to show or at least imply some kind of conflict between two characters or between one character and a group. Or might it be possible to develop an inner conflict—a character who both loves and dislikes another, one who both wants and doesn't want to take a particular course of action?

Then ask yourself if the opening paragraph will hold a reader. If so, are there other questions that will enliven the story as it develops?

In some cases, the use of suspense can be created simply by raising the stakes, making those dramatic questions more dramatic. Remember that no story should be limited by the events as they happened in life. A story is an artistic creation; it has a life of its own.

Finally, if you find one or more characters just a bit stuffy or pompous, consider the possibility of exaggerating their foibles, creating a bit of satire. The same applies to those highly autobiographical stories in which you begin to take yourself just a bit too seriously. Can you get outside of that character and gently poke fun at him or her? Satire is often a good remedy for sentimentality and self-pity.

When starting a new story, tension will not be your first concern. The characters and what they face at a particular moment in their lives form the core of most stories. But once your story takes shape, remember that you must give it life if you are to hold your readers. That vitality, that sense of energy, depends on how skillfully you have developed fictional tension.

Stephen Minot, *Three Genres: The Writing of Poetry, Fiction, and Drama*, 4e, 1988, pp. 201-210. Adapted by permission of Prentice Hall, Englewood Cliffs NJ.

❝A dull story is like a dull meal at a restaurant. Patrons don't complain, but they don't come back.❞

— **Stephen Minot**

Allow Me a Metaphor: Putting Together a Short Story Collection

by Tom Chiarella

Allow me this metaphor. The act of collecting short stories into a book is a lot like making soup. The cook/writer takes the best ingredient/story (the roast! the title story!) and lays it in the pot to create broth. Strong, spicy ingredients/stories then follow, each one affecting the taste and texture of those already in the pot as well as those that will follow. With cooking soup, as with pulling together a collection of short stories, the trick is to know when enough is enough, to avoid over-cooking the ingredients and to serve at the proper temperature.

I won't continue long with this metaphor, but I will say that, for me, the act of bringing stories together is very much like cooking. It involves improvising, compromising and constant taste-testing. Like the good cook, the writer constantly compares his work to other meals he has eaten. So I spent a good deal of time looking at the order and assemblage of other books—other soups—before I settled on my own. I decided that I was cooking a "soup" rather than a casserole or a layered cake because the good collection is like *pot-au-feu*. The illustration in one's cookbook is of no help. There is no ideal. The short story collection is created anew at the hand of each and every chef, simmering with its own conglomeration of individual nuances and scents.

The task of bringing together disparate stories into a collection can be as soul-taxing as tying up a novel, perhaps more so. In a novel the mechanisms are geared towards a resolution, or at the very least an ending of some sort. Whether the novel adheres to a sequential narrative structure or to a more experimental, less linear pattern, the text binds it together. To the frustrated short story writer—tinkering with his stories at all hours, stacking and restacking manuscripts in different orders—this is grounds for envy. His book is a series of different wholes—separate worlds, lives, characters, obsessions.

It is a daunting task and the easy solutions constantly beckon: wait another year; just bind it up and send it; forget the whole thing. But the writer who works past these solutions is forced to find something that binds her stories together.

Is it enough to say the stories were penned by the same person? Perhaps, but even so, for the writer trying to break through with a first collection, name carries little weight.

The problems of collecting an even, cohesive group of stories are many. The stories may have been written over many years; over that time the writer's aesthetic has surely grown, if not changed completely. The strength of one story now reminds the writer of another story's major weakness. Time may allow the writer to see the stylistic excess of early work. Rewriting begins—each story is sent through the mill yet again, and soon they begin to feel stale.

Other, more procedural, questions abound: How many of these stories need to be published? How do I convince a publisher to take a chance on a collection of stories? Do I

Tom Chiarella is a professor of English at DePauw University. His short fiction has appeared in The New Yorker *and* Story *magazine. He's currently busy in the kitchen cooking up his latest story collection.*

need an agent? Soon the greater whole—the collection—seems further from completion than ever before.

My friend the novelist once said he couldn't understand why I wrote short stories. "They're too taxing," he said. "You sink yourself in a story for a month and then, when it's finished, it's gone. You have to start all over." At this point he glanced at his manuscript. It was a neat stack at the edge of his desk; he'd been adding page upon page, every day for more than a year. "There's no time to get in a groove with short stories."

When he said this, I agreed. That is why two years ago—when the sum total of all my stories seemed to be zero, when their collection seemed as distant and fractured a dream as there ever was—I decided to bind my stories together by centering them around a single character. I vowed that I wouldn't shape the book into a novel, that each story would be just that—a story. I chose a single character—this focus—because it was a trick. I created it to make myself focus, to get on with it, to bring everything together.

It worked. After two years of struggling to see the collection of stories as something finished, it happened that one afternoon I was sitting in my office stacking and restacking manuscripts when I suddenly realized that it was a whole, that I had finished something.

Getting started on getting finished

It's trite to say more new writers are "breaking into" the publishing world with short story collections now than ever before, but it's true. The "novel first" attitude among publishers seems to be fading. Writers like Robert Olmstead, Rick Bass and Lorrie Moore published their collections first, with no small measure of success. The "whys?" of this slight shift in the publishing playbook have been pondered at great length. Some claim a resurgence of the short story, that its very form suddenly became palatable to the reading public. The source of this new interest? Everything—from MTV to Raymond Carver, from short attention spans to Anton Chekov. Trend-tracking is a cottage industry for the liberal arts graduate. I'll leave it to one of them. Suffice it to say that the short story is here to stay.

Another old ax is the question: What makes a good short story? We see text after text upon this very subject in all manner of places. This is an important, ongoing discussion. But few turn their attention to the short story collection. It exists as a form without much specification. Length, number of stories, even the presence of a common thread through the stories in a collection, all seem to be a matter of choice. I surveyed four local bookstores and found collections ranging from 62 pages in length to more than 500, from three stories to 27. Some collections appeared to be tightly centered on a person or a place; others were as beautifully diverse and mottled as an infra-red photograph.

So what makes a good collection then? The writer's aesthetic, for one thing. No matter what the writer's vision of the world is—fractious or frenetic, gothic or minimal, cyberpunk or neo-romantic—the bottom line is: Does that vision dwell in the work? The good writer knows the world—in one way or many ways—and the writer's aesthetic gives that knowledge to others. A good story does that and more. Good stories, drawn together with purpose, work to shape this vision even further.

Other than that, the diversity of the market may suggest that anything goes. First, read. Be familiar with what's out there. Some good collections are like glancing in several directions from the same spot. At first the stories seem disconnected and yet as you finished the collection you see that this disconnectedness may be at the heart of the character's lives. Other collections are firmly tied up in the life of a single character, or a family, or a city, or a region. With these books, reading the stories is more like looking inward. At their heart is a more singular knowledge of character, no smaller than the first, merely angled differently.

Some collections are rock-solid steady in their tone; a firm realism or a self-reflexive sweep may infect an entire work. Other collections involve wild variations in tone: quick shifts from fantastic to sarcastic to satiric.

All writers know the watch words. Knowing the market is the most important part of assessing the marketability of your own work. If you don't know the jungle it's harder to cut a swath. You can't write if you don't read. Use whatever handy saying you want, just keep reading.

Use the knowledge you gain from reading to see where your group of stories fits. There may seem to be natural models—that's good. If you find one or two books that echo the heart of your work somehow, then chances are you're hitting the same nerves. On the other hand, if you find 20 books that feel about the same as yours, you're likely to find the fear rising in your throat. With good reason, too. No one wants his work to be perceived of as formulated or heavily patterned. Yet it's obviously better to know if your book is riding the coattails of some stylistic trend than to send off the same book naively thinking that you may be redefining the whole question of style. So, read.

Perhaps your collection doesn't seem to fit. That could be the best news of them all. It's cliché to say that editors are always looking for something new, yet there's some truth in the statement. Don't talk yourself out of the collection merely because no one's doing anything quite like you. Celebrate that fact. Just be even more certain that the work is tight—the prose, the shape of the stories, the shape of the book—before considering yourself finished.

The trick is to find your own path. To do so you must know your own abilities. Assess your work as thoroughly as you assess the work of others. A good collection needs quality and connection. When you are satisfied with your work turn the question of quality over to the reader. As for connection, you decide. The connections may be as overt as a single character, a family history or a gritty neighborhood running throughout your stories, as subtle as an attitude in the narration, as obtuse as your own world view or as fractured as the visions of a chronic channel flipper. Whatever the connection, it must exist. As the writer, you must be sure it's there.

Pulling it together

Let me use another metaphor. The short story writer is like an old tomato gardener. He diddles. It's in his very nature. Just as the tomato gardener stoops to slip a twist-tie over his newest vine, just as he prunes back the flowers and lays in the manure around the base of his beloved plants at the just-right moments, so too does the short story writer fuss. Stories demand this sort of attention—tilling, pruning, trimming and fertilizing. But the old tomato gardener visits his garden every day and soon he grows nostalgic for the smell of the place as he lies in bed at night. So when his tomatoes begin to hang ripe and heavy on the vine, he sees this as a symbol for the impending death of his garden, for the coming of winter, the passing of another year. He lets the tomatoes hang there and for a while they ripen further. But ultimately the tomatoes fall into the late summer dust. The rabbits come out at night and take their bites; the bugs start in soon after.

In this way the short story writer may not be able to judge when his collection is finished. After years of diddling, stories become so familiar that they are hard to assess—individually or as whole. But the process of assessment, as discussed above, is the first step towards finishing. Do it.

After that only the mechanics remain. Don't let them stumble you. As for length of the manuscript, set yourself a goal — one that seems reasonable to the shape of your own work. Ten stories is a good middle ground (but by no means is it a minimum). Remember that editors prefer to cut stories to suit their needs, rather than ask for another (as this can often take months). So, to a certain extent, more is better. Yet don't weaken the chances of a collection by including obviously flawed or incomplete stories.

When you have finished the body of your collection — that is to say the tomatoes are on the vine, the stories are in place — you may wish to have a procedure to follow to tie up the loose ends. I'll suggest one:

1. Do a quick, but thorough, read-through and revision of each and every story. This can only help. It will allow you to snag any typos and/or grammatical errors (the finished manuscript should be error free) and will afford you a new familiarity with the group of stories.

2. Rearrange the stories. Unless your book has some natural sequence, the order of the stories may seem to be pretty much up for grabs. Think about the collections you admire. Perhaps they started with the strongest story and ended with another strong one (most do). Be conscious of the variation of tone from one story to the next. You may not want that gory story about the demons in the barbecue pit right next to that story about lost innocence in the Berkshires. Or perhaps you do. Make the decision; just be sure it's informed by the content. Don't allow lulls. Don't string two weaker stories back-to-back.

Give the collection to different readers in different orders and ask them to read it from start to finish. Their differing responses (and suggestions) should help you gauge the effect of one particular order over another. Change and shift things until it feels right. The order of your stories creates the effect of the book. You owe it to yourself to see your collection wearing all of its masks.

3. Look at the table of contents. Many readers of short story collections don't read them in order, but pick and choose, using the table of contents as a sort of menu. Titles matter. A table of contents should be provocative, inviting.

If the collection takes its title from one of the stories, you may wish to give this story prominent placement — typically, first or last. Again, models come into play.

4. Look for the weak link. You probably already know the strong point, but be sure you know the weak point of the book too. You are looking for the one point that may make the collection itself unmarketable. It could be a particular story, or the way two or three are strung together. Perhaps the whole manuscript is too short. It's sad but true that editors knock first books and collections out of the circuit for reasons like this. At least try to gauge the weakest link, so that you can know why you're standing by it. Again, this goes back to making informed decisions.

5. Submit any unpublished stories to magazines. Track record. That's what an editor looks for. If stories in the collection have been published in high quality journals, then the flag of credibility goes up for the writer. If every story in the collection is unpublished, the editor will most likely take that as a sign of some underlying weakness in the group. Prior publication is not an absolute, but it matters. If you haven't been trying to get the stories published individually, get started. If you've been at it for years, try one more time.

6. When it's finished, send it. Don't wait around forever. When you decide it's finished, it most likely is. Send it out. Start something new. Plant a new garden.

Where do you send it? There are options:

a) To an agent. This can be a good bet for any number of reasons. Agents are obviously as in tune with the market as anybody. They generally respond quickly and with some sort of critique, even in the event of a brush-off. If two or three of the stories have been previously published your chances improve significantly. Agents want proven material, even in their riskier ventures.

Still, submitting to an agent puts more time between getting your manuscript to an editor. Some agents won't consider collections. Many agents aren't willing to look at collections alone (they may ask for novel chapters too) and most agents won't market individual stories for you. Be sure to check each individual agent's submission guidelines carefully.

b) To a publishing house. It's possible to send directly to the publishers, but be prepared for a long wait. Don't let that hinder you though; editors really do like to "discover" new writers. The least you may come away with is a decent, thoughtful response to your book or good suggestions for change. The problem is that publishers get hundreds of manuscripts, so yours really has to grab them. Make the manuscript orderly, free of grammatical errors, user friendly. Don't include statements of purpose or theme. Don't send one or two stories as a teaser (they'll only think you're biding for time as you crank out a few quick ones). Be thorough and professional.

c) To publishing contests. The advantage here is that many contests require blind submission, so the identity of the writer, including her past publication record is of no consequence. But, while I think of these contests as important, the odds are a lot like Lotto. Again, be prepared for a long wait.

What I did

When I put my book of stories together this past year I followed the procedure I outlined above. I got a lot of advice, asked a lot of questions, and finally, did a lot of work. I can't say I'd follow that same procedure every time, but I change all my habits as a matter of course. One summer I'll write exclusively in the front room, next summer only in a diner. One autumn I'll insist on reading the box scores before writing anything, next autumn I won't touch the sports section until I've written three pages. For me the procedure itself was like a shopping list, which I checked off as I went down it. When I found myself at the bottom, I felt that I was pleasantly floating. I went right to the top and began checking before I knew it I was at the bottom all over again. I had finished. Using the list forced me to confront that.

Finishing a project of any scale is often difficult. For a writer, there's a built-in emotional attachment to the material. For me the attachment was like a narcotic. I had built a book of stories around a character whom I knew better than myself. After 14 stories, I instinctively sensed his reaction to every situation.

I knew my character's entire life. I wrote the last three stories to bridge gaps in the collection, gaps in my character's life. While I was single-minded about finishing, it taxed me. I began to sense myself falling into a pattern and worse still I saw the collection looking more and more like a novel.

I love novels, but I wanted to work with the short story and within the collection as a whole, to create a life for this character full of both variation and pattern. I had worked consciously to shift style and voice and tense from story to story. I had thought of each story as a separate unit, a part of a larger whole. My character's mindset changed in each story as he got older. I began to see his life as a collection of moments. I wanted that. What I didn't want was to see an easy pattern, to have to pull one thread clumsily through the whole thing in order to make it sing.

That was when I began to look at other collections very carefully. I was looking at their assemblage as much as their content. I wanted to see what held them together. The collections I admired, and there were many, seemed connected—by a sensibility, by a place, or by a person. That steeled me. I loved those books and wanted mine to be as good. It was a matter of taste I know, for other sorts of collections—ones I liked not as much or not at all—sold and sold well. But for me that final process of consideration gave me a sense that completion was near.

Either way, the final step involved jumping over all the built-in doubts about a collection, allowing me to build my own sort of collection and ultimately pushing forward. I decided I couldn't wait around forever for someone to publish a book like the one I had written. Mine had to be strong enough to create the model. That's the challenge of all short story collections.

One final thing

I opened this piece with the metaphor which equated bringing together a collection of short stories with making soup. Not accurate really. Let me explain.

For a long time I put off finishing my collection. ("Another year," I'd say.) Still, I felt I was up against it. My trick for finishing had been to focus on one character. But I'd been at it too long and soon I faced a new set of problems. Each story worked against the last one. They seemed to wash together. I couldn't see them as separate. I had begun to think I might never escape my character or the collection.

One afternoon my mother called. She teaches in a city elementary school in Rochester, New York. When I asked about her class, she said, "We made stone soup today."

I hadn't remembered stone soup until that moment. It comes from a folktale—the starving man starts soup with water and a stone, then offers to share it with the townfolk if they each put a different ingredient into the pot. The soup is delicious. The moral is sharing, cooperation.

"You do that in school?" I asked.

"Certainly," she said. "Each child brings one ingredient. It makes very good soup."

"How many ingredients?" I said. "How much of each one?" I know I sounded tense because my mother laughed.

"Whatever we get," she said. "Every soup is different."

"How do you know when it's done?"

My mother laughed again."When it's time to eat."

Every writer procrastinates. The short story writer can give himself a hundred reasons to work another day or add another story before pulling his book together. Eventually, though, it's time to eat.

Allow me just one more metaphor. Here's the true simile I was searching for in the first paragraph here: Collecting stories is like making *stone* soup. Each ingredient, each story, comes from its own garden, in its own variety, in its own amount. They all work together. The trick is to know yourself and your stories, to know your soup and when to serve it.

More Than Form: The Novel and the Short Story

by Jack Heffron

I doubt there is a fiction writer anywhere who would need more than a moment to define the difference between a novel and a short story. The primary difference, of course, is *length*. And yet, that simple, easily discerned difference creates a good many other differences in the writer's approach to the work, her relationship to it, the strategies she uses to complete successfully a piece of fiction, long or short.

Still, we discuss the forms as if they were very much the same, though we make clear distinctions between, say, the short story and the poem. Early in our literary careers, most of us define ourselves as either a fiction writer or a poet. For the majority of fiction writers, those early years are served writing short stories. We began writing 'seriously' (that is, for others, strangers, to read and criticize our work) in an undergraduate creative writing course. And though the syllabus may not have called for a short story instead of a novel chapter, we all banged away at the smaller form. A short story, to the novice, seems a good bit easier and, well, less presumptuous.

We planned to learn the finer points of plot, characterization and point of view in the shorter form, then to graduate to the longer one, the assumption being that the novel was simply a much longer short story. Such thinking denies some very real differences in the forms. In fact, the short story's demands for economy, compression and unity may be more difficult to satisfy for the novice than the novel's need for endurance and stamina. As William Faulkner once said, "All the trash must be eliminated in the short story, whereas one can get away with some of it in a novel."

The story demands that every detail, every word, serve a specific and clearly focused end in order to achieve an overall unity of effect, the goal of this form. In many ways the short story is closer to the poem. Rick DeMarinis, who has published a number of story collections and novels, (most recently *The Year of the Zinc Penny*, a novel, and *The Voice of America*, stories), believes the notion of writing stories in order to graduate into novels is wrong-headed.

"I did serve such an 'apprenticeship' in the misguided belief that a short story was easier [than the novel] because it was shorter," he explains. He perceives the difference as largely a matter of discipline and attitude. "The novel requires the discipline of the endurance runner; the short story requires the discipline of the tight-rope walker."

In a novel, problems in character development, plot, tone and others, can be solved by adding whatever seems necessary, just as a painter will brush in a new image. In a story, any addition requires achieving a new balance, a realignment of all the other parts. The process of revision often involves a good bit more taking out than putting in. The task is getting the piece to read as though it were written in a single sitting, as though the writer simply took dictation from the muse—an occurrence not nearly as common as story writers

Jack Heffron is associate editor of Story magazine. His short fiction has appeared in several literary journals, most recently in the North American Review and the Chariton Review.

would have their readers believe. More often, the story writer revises over and over, tinkering with sentences, scenes, dialogue. He lives by inference, by suggesting a world outside the story to create the illusion that we are examining a detail from a very large canvas.

Word by word

Thus, the short story, because of its demands, seems an unlikely place for the apprentice writer to begin, unless the writer's goal is to work for a good long while within that form. "In terms of creativity, a week of a short story is far more exhausting than a month of a novel," says Robert Olmstead, who has enjoyed success with stories (*River Dogs*) and with novels (*Soft Water* and *A Trail of Heart's Blood Wherever You Go*). "I take great pleasure in working on novels. There's a generous pace to them. It's leisurely. You can take time to get up and walk around, refill the coffee cup, light a cigarette."

Olmstead, a graduate of Syracuse University's M.F.A. program (where he worked under Raymond Carver and Tobias Wolff) and who now is writer-in-residence at Dickenson College, believes that the apprenticeship is served with short stories because the workshop setting handles the shorter form more easily. He also believes, however, that apprentice writers should concentrate more on sentences and paragraphs than on the larger structures. "The best apprenticeships are word by word, line by line, two people sitting next to each other discussing a paragraph for an hour."

His belief is echoed by Kate Braverman, a novelist (*Lithium for Medea* and *Palm Latitudes*) and story writer (*Squandering the Blue*) who teaches creative writing at U.C.L.A. She believes that young writers should not be so concerned with form. "Structure gives people a superficial concept of what writing is. I'm interested in people writing good lines and being aware of the fact that good lines are built on a choice of words, how they sound, how they resonate, what they suggest."

Like Olmstead, she feels the emphasis, in the early years, should be on writing for its own sake, divested of a defining form. "The best apprenticeship that people can put in is to go and sit in front of a building and do five pages on what that building looks like. Go around and learn your world, what the architecture is, and what the trees are and what the history of your street is, and the names of the Indians who used to live there, the gods they believed in."

If the apprentice writer feels he must choose one form over the other to work in, there are, admittedly, advantages to the shorter one. It does allow the young writer to finish work, an important aspect of the learning stage, since a finished product offers a sense of accomplishment, a feeling that one has met his goals. The shorter form also allows for a greater range of experimentation. The writer can vary points of view from story to story and can play with different narrative structures.

Developing characters

The strategies a writer uses in developing characters for a novel are different from those used in a short story. A short story, first of all, allows the writer to develop only a few characters, seldom more than two, into complex, rounded fictional people. Since the story must be focused on the character's crisis of the moment — the story's central impulse — little room is left for supplying background and exposition. The character's history as well as his life beyond the current crisis must be implied by a few well-chosen details — a pocketwatch passed down from a great-grandfather, a ribbon won at the seventh-grade track meet. Through these details the reader senses lives being lived, so that the characters seem more real. Without them, the characters will appear flat, mere props to carry out the story's conflict, or worse, to serve some agenda beyond the story—a message the author wants to convey or an issue the author wants to explore through fiction.

A telling gesture or detail can help character development—a scar, a beard that is constantly stroked, fingernails manicured to perfection that the character flashes at odd moments. These details summon forth the character, make him or her clear in the eyes of the reader by inferring behavioral traits and patterns that the story does not have room to show at greater length: a 'tip of the iceberg' approach.

Finally, the old truism is true—action is character—and a short story simply offers fewer opportunities to show your character in action. Thus, a character can be complicated by a single act—a harsh man tenderly pulling a blanket over a child, a kindly, soft-spoken woman demanding her due from an impudent store clerk.

"You don't really have the leisure to develop character in a short story," says DeMarinis. "You present character, and with a few telling gestures, you give the reader enough clues for him to understand who he's dealing with."

A short story that, for me, offers textbook strategies in characterization is Richard Giles's "The Whole World," which appeared in the Winter 1990 issue of *Story*. In it, Giles quickly establishes his main character, Pope, a hard-bitten, tough old farmer whose daughter returns home, pregnant, having been driven off years before by her father's inability to accept her adult sexuality. Pope's primary physical detail, his *tag*, is a missing finger, a stump which "he stroked as another man might pick his teeth." The detail suggests Pope's past, his life before the story, giving him a history. It also suggests how tough his life has been, full of harsh physical labor, and perhaps it hints at his stunted emotional development.

But rather than settle for a one-dimensional, American-Gothic image of the stoic farmer, Giles also offers a few of what DeMarinis calls "telling gestures." We glimpse behind Pope's mask and find that while lying in bed waiting for sleep he fantasizes about being a night bird, free in the dark sky to fly and to screech. Later, in a vain attempt to keep his daughter entertained (and thus away from the men in town) he retells the story of losing his finger, relishing her laughter. He becomes suddenly vulnerable in the reader's eyes, and a complex individual.

The best stories, those whose characters linger in our memories long after the story is over, employ characters, that, like real people, are full of contradictions, of fantasy lives that are not even suggested on the surface. Since the story writer does not have room enough and time to show a character in a variety of fully developed and revealing scenes, he or she must find other ways to move quickly past the character's masks (and past the *type* with which the character is most easily identified). The surest means to this end is asserting a great deal of pressure on the character. He must want something very badly, must need desperately to escape whatever torment dogs him so that the reader can see the character without disguises or defenses, a naked self that is weak or strong, passionate or indifferent, brave or cowardly (or both, depending on the situation).

Asserting that pressure by constantly raising the stakes, constantly creating new road-blocks for the character, can also lead to some nice surprises for the writer. A character we thought of in one way—shy or arrogant or friendly, suddenly bursts off in a new direction. In such cases, the cozy confines of the story help the writer assert this dramatic pressure, since both the writer and the reader can live with a heightened narrative tension over the short haul. If the character is under tremendous pressure from the start in a novel, the reader and the writer will be exhausted after the first hundred pages (if that long). The novel demands that the tension be modulated, rising and falling like waves or, depending on the story, like a roller coaster.

Showing change

The writer of the short story also is limited in his ability to convincingly show a character's change. Of course, many stories lead to an epiphany, to a change in perspective about the subject of the story, but length prohibits showing more fundamental changes in character. Therefore, when we show a character working her way through a bad time, say the months following a divorce, we can suggest at the end, given the events of the narrative, she will be able to cope better in the future. But if her selfishness and basic dishonesty caused the divorce, it is difficult, in five thousand words, to convince the reader that the action of the story has ignited a significant reversal in behavior and that the character will now be a considerably more generous, giving person.

"In the novel, not only one, but other characters can and do change," explains James B. Hall, who has published novels (*Mayo Sergeant, Racers to the Sun*, and *Not By the Door*) and story collections (*The Short Haul*). " 'Life' changes them and we see it happen and believe. The novel involves process, and given enough process, a change in character becomes acceptable. Whereas short fiction's commitment to unity of effect, to only a very few full scenes, legislates for revelation within a character, but precludes the melodrama of a character's fundamental change, let us say, from a bad man to a good man."

One way the story writer might attempt to circumvent this limitation is by opening the story with a catastrophic event that changes the character's life view, then developing this change throughout the story. In "The Country Husband," John Cheever's protagonist, Francis Weed, survives a plane crash and returns to his repressive suburban world a 'changed' man. The story documents his rebellion in comic detail, but even here, the 'change' is only temporary and Francis returns to his 'normal' self.

In developing characters into complex, rounded literary folk, the novelist has many more options. She can sketch entire scenes for the sole purpose of developing an aspect of a main character. In a novel I'm working on I've written a five-page scene to show my protagonist—who the reader knew to be a desperate, reckless individual—as a caring, empathic person, so caring, in fact, that he is easily manipulated.

"The novel allows tremendous latitude in the introduction and treatment of characters," says DeMarinis. "You can give ten pages, if you want, to the description of a cab driver or of a psychiatric nurse just for the joy of exercising your powers of description or to indulge your insights into the varieties of human behavior."

The novel's latitude not only allows, it *forces* the writer beyond the short story's limits of inference and gesture. For a classic example, consider F. Scott Fitzgerald's *The Great Gatsby*. We first see Gatsby bathed in moonlight, his arms spread wide to the green light at the end of Daisy's dock. He is the distant, enigmatic, romantic hero. Before seeing him, we learned a bit about his legend, heard the rumors about him. Then we watch as he presides over one of his grand parties. Then we meet him, along with Nick, and our early perception of him as mysterious hero is complicated by his laughably bogus 'life story.' Later still we see him as gangster, as shy boy-man made vulnerable by love, and finally as a desperate dreamer. And Gatsby, despite all the scenes in which he is developed, remains somewhat vague. Think of the complexity of Nick Carraway, even Daisy. All are shown in a number of contradictory ways.

The larger canvas allows for such contradictions without suggesting that the character's development is somehow *wrong*, inconsistent. In the story, a number of contradictions would make us wonder who the character *really* is. Thus, we tell the writer that we don't believe the sweet, vulnerable protagonist we've come to know in the story's first fifteen pages would *do* such a thing on page sixteen. We insist that the writer foreshadow such a contradiction earlier, give us some clue as to the character's complexity before foisting such a change upon us.

Plot, pace and structure

One reason I took the time to write that five-page scene which developed another side of my character was to slow the pace of the novel. It had opened very quickly, and neither reader nor writer could have continued at such a fast pace for the course of several hundred pages. A novel demands greater modulation of pace, a rising and falling action rather than a bee-line for the exit. While short stories do not *require* a fast, linear, forward movement, they must be focused on one or two very specific goals. Even daring, fragmented structures such as those used by Donald Barthelme, Robert Coover and William Gass have a clear direction.

"It's the very rare short story that can accommodate a subplot," says DeMarinis, "but a true novel almost requires such excursions. The pace of a story is obviously faster than that of a novel. Like a poem, a short story has a detectable rhythm. Some novels do, but most do not. Or if they do, it is not as crucial an element to their esthetic success."

In a story, I would not enjoy the luxury of that five-page scene since such a drastic change in intensity—such a shift in the established rhythm—would have registered on the reader as a "soft spot," and an alert editor would trim or cut the scene, or perhaps combine it with another one so that at least it would be working on a number of levels, accomplishing several necessary chores for the story.

Likewise, the length of scenes, by necessity, must be shorter in the story. A scene's success is judged by its precision, its control, its tightness. When writing a scene in a short story, I write everything that transpires between the characters. I record all the dialogue, the gestures, the asides, all the starts and stops and hems and haws to make sure that I have done well by the scene in my head—given it plenty of time to develop on its own, to take over and become something different, such as when a character suddenly says something I had not foreseen. Once completed, I go back to trim fastidiously, reviewing the scene dozens of times until I'm sure all the fat is gone, that the scene is tight.

In a scene from a novel, my agenda is different and so, therefore, are my strategies. I am still concerned about pace, about tightness, but these are lower priorities than the rhythm of the scene. Here I've got room to modulate the tone a bit more, to play with rising and falling action, to explore the emotional undercurrents informing the scene. The short story rarely allows such freedom unless the writer uses only a few characters and very few fully developed scenes.

A master at creating and sustaining long dramatic scenes within the short story is J.D. Salinger. In his classic story "Uncle Wiggily in Connecticut," he uses, primarily, only two characters who remain, for the most part, in a single room, talking and drinking during a long afternoon. But such stories require wonderful dialogue in order to sustain the reader's interest, and their *apparent* aimlessness must be controlled with a deft hand.

Several years ago Madison Smartt Bell told us that "Less Is Less" and the past few years have seen a slight shift away from minimalism to more fully developed narratives. Still, the story writer (and to a lesser extent, the novelist) in order to compete in the marketplace, must make more of less. Robert Olmstead, defending his former teacher Raymond Carver from the (now pejorative) tag of "minimalist," noted, "I read a Carver story and the word that comes to my mind always is generosity. He's an immensely giving writer."

Point of view

Today's novelists and short story writers enjoy great freedom when choosing a work's point of view, but each form offers slightly different freedoms and limitations. In both cases, the caveat remains—it must seem natural—an organic part of the work. The writer fails if the chosen point of view is too limited, too self-conscious or too distracting.

For this reason, unusual points of view—second person, for instance—tend to be easier to execute in a short story simply because the writer is not forced to sustain that device over many pages. Thus, Bob Shacochis uses second person with wonderful results in his story "Lord ShortShoe Wants the Monkey." The use of "you" rather than "I," "he" or "she" does not become a bothersome convention of the story. Sustaining that very idiosyncratic approach over the course of a novel is extremely difficult, since it calls such attention to itself, drawing the spotlight away from the characters and plot. (Of course, it can be employed occasionally with great effect, the most famous recent example being Jay Mac-Inerny's *Bright Lights, Big City*.)

The same reasoning holds true for first-person narratives in which the voice is very idiosyncratic, a dialect perhaps. The novelty of such a voice can engage a reader for a short while and can add a delightfully fresh perspective to one's material, but the writer must ask herself: Can the reader tolerate such a voice through hundreds of pages? Can this voice communicate my entire story, even the more subtle aspects or those that require keen observation? Or will the limitations and eccentricities which seem so charming and which allow me to sustain a strong element of mystery for twenty pages become annoying or overly confining in a much longer work?

Of course, examples in which an unreliable, idiosyncratic first-person voice tells a long story are legion: Twain's *Huckleberry Finn*, for one; Allan Gurganus's *The Oldest Living Confederate Widow Tells All* is a more recent example. But a writer making such a strategic choice here must be aware of the challenge he has set for himself. For all the novelty and freshness this voice gives the work, it creates a great many demands.

The most common point of view technique currently in use is, of course, the limited third person, which focuses on the thoughts of a single character but allows the writer to move in and out of that character's mind and to make more general observations. The writer also can sustain tension through what his main character does not know. This point of view seems to be the easiest one to employ in a short story. Over the course of a novel, however, it may become too confining. Locked into the mind of just one character without the benefit of a rich voice, the reader can feel claustrophobic. He may want to jump into the consciousness of another character—or two, or three or more.

Novelists, therefore, often choose an omniscient point of view, though not in the 19th-century mode of jumping from one character to the next even within a single scene. They use a more limited omniscient but with a number of characters changing, say, with each new chapter. This technique gives the novel an openness, allowing the reader a fresh look at the events of the narrative. In fact, the switching perspectives can become the central focus of the novel as a number of characters investigate the same events. The master of this approach was Faulkner, particularly in *The Sound and the Fury* and in *As I Lay Dying* (in which first-person narrators are mixed). A more recent example is Tobias Wolff's *The Barrack's Thief* in which first person and third person are mixed to great effect.

Such shifts within a story are more difficult to execute since the goals here are economy and unity. The reader does not take kindly to shifts in perspective unless the writer establishes this openness early in the story—within the first several pages. Certainly writers can use an omniscient point of view, and can even use more than one first-person or limited third-person narrator. A recent (and excellent) example of the latter is T. Coraghessan Boyle's story "If the River Was Whiskey" in which the very tight third-person perspective switches between father and son. But Boyle marks the shifts by inserting a space break each time. The reader may be jarred if the switches simply occur without apparent pattern. A writer also risks jarring the reader (and violating that reader's trust) when, after the first ten or twelve pages of a single point of view, he changes to a new one.

Of course, such 'rules' have never limited the creative mind and should, instead, be used as guideposts that can save the writer time spent on trial and error. Even better, they might be used as challenges the writer creates for herself—barriers to be broken through.

"If you can write in a voice I want to hear I don't care how long, in fact I don't care what form or even what subject matter. I will read, read, read," says Olmstead. "For everything we can say about the nature of the endeavor, there's a writer out there running roughshod over our tenets."

The switch-hitter

Most of us do not consider ourselves short story writers or novelists so much as simply, fiction writers. Of course, many of us prefer one form over the other, but even these opinions are subject to change. In fact, it's a safe bet that we prefer the form in which we're *not* working at the moment.

Truth is, one's talent for storytelling is best served by a willingness to work in both forms. A good friend of mine who is an excellent and well-published short story writer made great strides in his stories after undertaking what turned out to be a failed novel. He was unhappy, naturally, about having "wasted" eight months on the project. But suddenly there was a new elasticity in his writing style, which had previously suffered, at times, from a stiffness, a rigidity. Now his short fiction is airier and, frankly, better. Of course, the same lesson can be learned by the writer more given to verbosity and who for that reason works more easily within the novel. Through short stories, that writer can gain a stronger sense of economy and precision.

"One way to stay inventive and alert is to go back and forth between forms," Kate Braverman says. "You learn different moves. In order to survive as a writer you really need a lot in your arsenal. You need different kinds of punches and feints and combinations."

For those writers who can and do move back and forth between forms, the question can arise, What have I got here—a novel or a short story? The first novel I ever wrote began as a short story and just kept growing. I tried to finish it in twenty pages but couldn't, then headed for one hundred pages, thinking I had hooked a novel. Having reached one hundred pages, I stopped, used the piece for my M.F.A. thesis, and went back to stories. But the characters continued to pry their way through my subconscious, begging for further attention, which I gave them, finally shutting them up after another two hundred pages.

Hall feels that the forms are so inherently different one cannot be easily confused with the other. "That a short story would 'grow' into a novel, or the reverse, is not in my vocabulary," he explains, adding that such confusion could arise from mishandling the material at the point of conception. "There are always uneasy minutes about which form literary material may possibly take, and on some occasions I have taken an 'idea' for a novel and have said everything germane about it in the short story form. Never the reverse."

Olmstead agrees that the forms are easy to distinguish. "Some people wait to see what it's going to be," he says. "I always know which is which. Short stories come to me, novels don't. There's a wholeness there, something complete. I feel it, I sense it, I experience it."

Other writers recognize the beast less easily. Braverman says, "I am always looking for something big. I never go out looking for something small." Nevertheless, she is quick to accept a short story. "I'm not a sport fisherman. Some people can go out and say, 'Just the two-hundred-pound marlin for me.' I fish to survive. Whatever goes into the net, that's dinner."

A common mistake writers make, she adds, is labeling the impulse too quickly. The temptation for most of us is to gain control of the material quickly—the easiest way to kill it. A student once complained to me that her story was going badly because it was out of control. "I don't know where it's going," she said, "or even what it is." She was writing frantically to keep us with the torrent of words. My advice: Be thankful for the torrent; drink from it until it stops, then go back and figure out what it is.

Naming the thing is the first step toward controlling it. By naming it "my short story" or "my novel," we have stabbed the flag of ownership into the virgin soil and can stand smiling for the snapshot: Mine! Unfortunately, like good parents, we must resist the temptation to control our children. The writer must, in the early stages, risk a leap of faith and allow the story impulse to tromp around on the page or the screen for a while—giving it room to grow and develop naturally while trying to keep it in some way contained.

"If you move too fast, you can lose it," Braverman warns. "Moving too fast, before it's coalesced in the subconscious, can just abort the entire thing. The concept of form defeats a lot of people, and I think it's unnecessary. It doesn't have to. Writing is about good lines, whether you're writing a poem or a short story or a novel."

Olmstead feels the 'I might lose this' anxiety more in stories than in longer works. "Short stories are like trying to remember your dreams," he says. "They drift in and out of consciousness. You have to get hold of them, try to coax them onto the page. You hold too tight, they go smash. You don't hold tight enough, they fade away."

As with so many aspects of writing, experience is the best teacher. The more the fiction writer works at his craft, the more easily he can distinguish between these two forms. As Hall notes, "The experienced husbandman, even past dusk, will seldom mistake a rooster for a peahen."

A different dynamic

In discussing how a writer decides between novel and short story, Braverman says, "Finally, it's not enough that you choose it, it must choose you. It's a dynamic." It seems to me the notion of a dynamic between writer and work cuts to the heart of the difference between novels and short stories. The primary difference is one of our relationship to the form in which we are working. Since fiction writers are very different from each other so, too, are their relationships with their work.

Though I truly love the short story form and would never want to choose between forms, I find myself more at ease when working on a novel. As Olmstead noted, there is a leisurely quality to the relationship, an awareness as I write that tomorrow I will return to this world and the next day, and the day after that. In fact, while writing in this longer form, the writer lives, at least part of the time, within that world. And so much of what happens in the 'real' world seems somehow to fit that other one, so that I find myself writing notes constantly— in supermarkets, theaters, restaurants, everywhere.

Some writers can avoid the keyboard for days, maybe weeks, while allowing ideas to incubate. When ready, they attack—whipping out short stories in a single sitting or a section of a novel in a week. Unfortunately, I am not one of those writers. I must face the keyboard nearly every day, and novels ease that chore by prolonging the process of creation: tomorrow I will write what comes next. With short stories, I write as the pieces come to me, in whatever order, and the process of creation is a good bit shorter than the process of revision. And though the short story offers that sense of completion more often—undeniably, a wonderful feeling—the writer is then faced with the task of beginning again, of starting over from scratch.

DeMarinis agrees. "Beginning a short story is almost as hard as ending one, which always takes some miracle of insight. This involves some agony. I think a writer of short stories needs to depend on the inspired moment. The novelist is more of a plow horse than a gazelle."

So each writer must ask himself or herself which am I—plow horse or gazelle? And it is unlikely that any of us are one as opposed to the other: we're both. The question then becomes, which am I most often? James B. Hall considers himself more a story writer.

"Over the years, I am drawn more steadily to short fiction," he explains. "I've been told I am quick tempered, reactive, and my hand-eye reactions once were said to be notably quick. In a long, sustained exercise, such as writing a book-length fiction, I want results quicker than is quite rational. It never seems as good as it should be at that moment, and I can't keep thinking about it. So I sometimes think if I were only more like a German-trained engineer, a bridge specialist, then I would write more and better novels. Too late, I think, to take that up with mother."

Braverman sums it up this way: "A story is like a love affair, and a novel is like a marriage." A story offers initial exhuberance and, since the end is never far from sight, plenty of romance. The novel offers more certainty, a stronger sense—for better or for worse—of permanence.

Though she enjoys both forms, Braverman feels the novel grants a greater sense of achievement. "For a writer, I think the novel is the ultimate performance," she says. "It's the ultimate test of intelligence and stamina and the ruthless will to succeed. The ability to embrace ghastly solitude. And you cannot conceal who you are across the dimensions of a novel. A novel ultimately reveals the quality of the soul."

The important point here is to remember that the forms, indeed, are different, and that the young writer who charges into the sunset armed for battle must remember that his strategies must change to fit the opponent.

Off the Beaten Path: Publishing Alternatives

by Robin Gee and Anne Thompson

We divide *Novel & Short Story Writer's Market* neatly into five market categories: two for magazines, two for book publishers and one for contests and awards. Yet from time to time we come across markets that don't quite fit into these categories. We agonize a bit and finally put them into the section that seems most appropriate.

Yet these "different" markets offer writers unique alternatives to the usual publishing route. Some publish traditional fiction but take a nontraditional approach to the method of publication. They look for the same material as that published by regular markets. Others are completely new endeavors—experiments in both form and presentation. As with traditional markets, these new markets are often the most open to new writers. And since the form is new, they may be more willing to look at fiction that is experimental or at least atypical.

The markets in this article also appear as listings in the book, but since they do not represent typical markets, we would not feature them as Close-ups. They do deserve special attention, however, so we decided to highlight them here.

One type of alternative market is a direct result of the revolution in computer technology. As the number of people who have access to a personal computer continues to grow, so will the computerized magazine field. At this time there are only a handful of magazines on disk and even fewer available as on-line systems, but the number is growing rapidly. *The Black Hole Literary Review* is an on-line literary magazine—accessible by computer modem.

Eclipse Books and Fantagraphics are two publishers of graphic novels and comic books. While material included in graphic novels follows the same structure as any other type of novel or long short story, the difference is the way the story is presented. Graphic novels are highly illustrated. Often the illustrations are similar to those included in comic books, but the subject matter is more serious. The story accompanies the visuals scene by scene, not unlike a movie or play.

Books that invite readers to participate either by creating their own endings or by finding a solution to a problem have become trendy sellers in recent years. People still remember *Masquerade*, a book that included clues to the discovery of a buried golden rabbit. The first reader to discover the location of the rabbit would win prize money. More recently, Martin Handford's Waldo books ask readers to find a character, Waldo, or an item of his clothing in illustrations included in the book. Although this started as a children's book, the book has attracted an enthusiastic adult audience. Capitalizing on "reader participation," Lombard Marketing, Inc., has taken a unique approach. The company has created bePuzzled, a line of puzzles based on mystery stories. Each puzzle includes a jigsaw picture and a written mystery story. The picture puzzle offers at least six visual clues and the booklet offers at least six written clues. Together they help readers solve the mystery.

There are several well-known newspaper syndicates and these offer a lucrative market for columnists, essayists, feature writers and cartoonists. The PEN Syndicated Fiction project is a syndicate created exclusively for fiction. As with newspaper syndicates, the PEN

Anne Thompson *is a freelance writer from Tiffin, Ohio.*

project sells to a number of outlets. The project was initially created to sell short fiction to newspapers, but clients also include a literary magazine and a radio program, as well as a number of Sunday newspaper magazines.

For the new writer the following markets offer additional opportunities for publication. For the experienced writer, they offer a chance to publish something a little different. Together they offer writers variety and a chance to follow the "road less traveled."

Computer magazines:
The Black Hole Literary Review

The Black Hole Literary Review is like any other literary journal in that it accepts fiction and poetry submissions. Everything else about this magazine, however, is vastly different. Of course the main difference is its computer format. The review is available only on computer, accessible by a modem. But, more importantly, it is an *interactive* publication. As with other electronic bulletin boards, users can leave messages to each other through E-mail. For writers, this is an attractive benefit — immediate reader feedback.

"There are no rejections," says Editor Bill Allendorf, who simply proofreads before approving a file. And there's no page limit, either. Allendorf will accept everything from poetry, short fiction and essays to full-length novels.

The best way to submit material, he says, is as an ASCII text file via the modem. ASCII is a universal computer language for IBM compatible computers. If you do not have an IBM compatible, you may still be able to access the magazine — check with your computer dealer for the appropriate telecommunications software.

The computer magazine operates on a system of small fees, credits and royalties. Subscribers pay an initial $5 fee. The fee buys a limited bank of time credits. As stories are read, credits are deducted according to the length of the story. Writers are charged from 50 cents to $2 to submit material, but each time a piece is read, the writer also receives a royalty. Assuming writers will want to be subscribers, they can have their charges deducted from the $5 initial fee. Royalties may be paid out in cash or in time credits added to your "bank."

"In the first year, I would have paid out hundreds of dollars in royalties," says Allendorf, "but the writers took them all in free credits."

Allendorf admits writers won't get rich on the system, but in addition to the cash or credit royalties, they receive free and immediate feedback from readers, many of whom are also writers. Criticism, advice and messages may be left through E-mail. As a subscriber you receive an identification name that enables you to access your mail, leave messages for others, read material and participate in a number of the review's services.

In addition to stories, *The Black Hole* includes polls and questionnaires, classified ads, teleconferencing, an information center and SIG files. SIG files are files belonging to Special Interest Groups. Participants interested in certain subjects use the files to exchange information. Also included in the SIG files are a number of interactive stories. Readers are invited to add a paragraph and help build a group story.

Since 1989 the magazine has obtained more than 250 entries. "Within the first month," says Allendorf, "we had 100 subscribers." Based on *The Black Hole*'s current success, he sees a bright future. He hopes to attract other publications to buy material from the magazine. "They could simply call into *The Hole*, enter a keyword and find a collection of pieces pertaining to that subject," he says. He is also exploring tying into a national data network. This would make access easier and cheaper for long-distance subscribers to access *The*

Black Hole. Allendorf says he knows computer magazines are just beginning to catch on, but the possibilities, he says, are staggering.

Graphic novels:
Eclipse and Fantagraphics

Graphic novels are not new, but they do require a unique blend of fiction and artwork. Like comic books, each scene is illustrated and accompanied by narrative in the form of captions or balloons. Yet, unlike comics, graphic novels follow a longer story line and often the subject matter is more serious. Few, if any, feature traditional super heroes.

Publishers of graphic novels look for action-oriented fiction, material that lends itself well to heavy illustration. Yet the subject matter can vary widely. "Any subject suitable for a prose novel can be presented as a graphic novel," says Catherine Yronwode of Eclipse Books. These can include "action-adventure, gothic horror, science fiction, fantasy, western, detective/crime fiction, etc. 'Slice of Life,' romances, 'coming of age' stories also can work easily in a graphic novel format. It's the *medium*, not the message."

Robert Boyd, assistant editor at Fantagraphics Books, says he is also open to a wide variety of material. "We look for subject matter that is more or less the same as that you would find in 'mainstream' fiction. Graphic novels we've published either in book or serial form have been about life in a Los Angeles barrio, the life of a Parisian jazz musician . . . a story about a middle-aged radio talk show host. The common factor is their artfulness and quality."

Both Eclipse and Fantagraphics publish reprints as well as original material. Many of these reprints are collections of material that originally appeared as serialized comics. These might be either classic comics or collections of comics originally published by the company. Foreign translations are also very popular sellers.

As with other small or independent presses, publishers of graphic novels survive and flourish by carving their own niche in the market. Eclipse has become known for its colorful adaptations of classic stories such as *The Hobbit* and *The Magic Flute*.

Fantagraphics, on the other hand, has gone in another direction. Although the publisher reprints collections of classic comics such as *Popeye* and *Little Nemo*, it has become best known for its graphic novel series, including the popular *Love and Rockets* books.

Writers interested in graphic novels must be able to think visually, but often do not need to be artists themselves. If you are a good artist, it can help, but most graphic novels are collaborations. Fantagraphics prefers to work with a writer/artist or a writer who has already paired up with an artist. Eclipse will work with a writer who is also an artist, but will help in finding a suitable artist collaborator.

Trends on the graphic novel scene include more translations and foreign publications, especially by European, South American and Japanese publishers. Both publishers agreed that while action-adventure remains a big seller, subtle, sophisticated graphic novels aimed at a more discerning audience are becoming increasingly popular.

Actually, the term graphic novel can be misleading. Since most comic books are 32 to 48 pages, says Yronwode, the longer graphic form is called a novel. Yet it is considerably shorter than a mainstream book. Most graphic novels are closer to the length of a novella or long short story. Graphic novels generally range from 48 to 80 pages.

Payment for graphic novels is similar to arrangements with mainstream book publishers. Writers are paid an advance against royalties. Artists also usually receive a separate advance. In most cases artist and writer must split the royalties, with the artist receiving slightly more.

Submission policies are also very similar to that of a book publishers. Samples of artwork are required if the writer is the artist or is submitting with the collaborator. If you have art samples, send photocopies of finished art. If you do not have art, but you do have ideas about illustrations, send along your ideas. For stories, send a plot summary or synopsis and a chapter or a sample of dialogue. The ability to write strong dialogue is essential. And it goes without saying, lush, detailed scenes will attract attention.

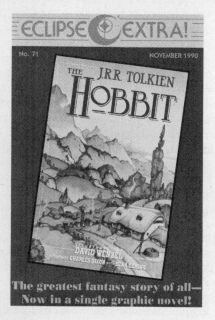

Charles Dixon and Sean Deming adapted this version of The Hobbit by J.R.R. Tolkien for Eclipse Comics. Dixon is better known, says Editor Catherine Yronwode, for his original action adventure stories, also presented in graphic novel form. The illustrator was David Wenzel.

Interactive fiction: bePuzzled

Part of the joy of reading a good mystery is trying to solve the puzzle—who done it—before the final chapters. Jigsaw puzzles work much the same way. Only by assembling the pieces does the picture become clear. With this in mind, Mary Ann and Robert Lombard came up with an idea to combine both verbal and visual puzzles. They formed Lombard Marketing in 1987 to oversee sales of a unique line of jigsaw puzzles, aptly called bePuzzled.

What makes these puzzles different is the combination of verbal and visual clues. Each bePuzzled package contains a 125-, 500-, or 1,000-piece jigsaw puzzle and a 4-5,000-word short story. The puzzle contains a minimum of six visual clues to the mystery posed in the story. The story sets up the scenario and characters and contains six additional clues. The mysteries are not meant to be easy, but all have been tested to make sure they are solvable given the clues. Yet the solution is made available in mirror type on the back of the story booklet.

The bePuzzled line is divided into categories that include bePuzzled (traditional mystery thrillers), bePuzzled Romance, bePuzzled Interactive, bePuzzled Bestseller and bePuzzled Jr.—each sharing the same concept, but different in story themes.

Unlike traditional mysteries, of course, Editor Lucy Seccareccia is looking for "thoughtful, challenging mysteries that can be concluded with a visual element of a puzzle."

A story must contain at least six verbal and six visual clues. The trick is to make no single clue solve the mystery, says Seccareccia. The clues must work together to reveal the solution. She advises writers to try to divide their clues into thirds—one-third should be vague, one-third obvious and one-third bluffs. "Our most successful mystery stories are those in which the writer has a visual for the puzzle already in mind and then directs the story to include clues that support the solution."

Writers interested in submitting should send an SASE for free guidelines. You are not expected to include artwork, but a sketch or description of the visual element is appreciated. Send a list of both visual and literal clues, a list and description of characters, a story synopsis and a writing sample. Writing samples should reflect the genre you are interested in writing for bePuzzled. Also include a brief biography.

Subjects for mysteries include thrillers, suspense and classic whodunits. For the other lines, the company is interested in a variety of topics including romance, horror, humor and mainstream fiction. Some of the current line include *Sweet Revenge*, the mystery of the death of Armande Decoca, noted gourmand and hopeless chocoholic; *Mysteries at the Magic Bazaar*, a collection of three crimes at the Magic Bazaar; and *A Ghost of a Chance*, a suspenseful romance between a beautiful ghost and a handsome heir to a mysterious New England estate.

This cover for "Sweet Revenge," one of the bePuzzled mystery series packages, illustrates the company's unique contribution to the mystery genre. BePuzzled publishes 15 puzzles per year, and each contains an accompanying story with clues.

Fiction syndicates: The PEN Project

Before World War II newspapers frequently featured stories and serialized fiction. In fact, such well-known and loved writers as Twain and Hemingway gained much of their early popularity through newspaper exposure. In 1982 the international writers' organization, PEN, decided to revive this practice and created the PEN Syndicated Fiction Project. The project was created specifically to market fiction to newspapers, especially Sunday supplements. Since that time the project has sold fiction to some 28 papers including the *Chicago Tribune* and the *Kansas City Star*.

Since other media also use syndicates it was not long before the group added radio to its list of clients. National Public Radio now features a half-hour show, "The Sound of Writing," with some stories selected from the PEN program.

Writers whose stories are selected for the project receive an initial $500 for serial and audio rights and $100 per publication by participating newspapers. If a story is selected for the radio program, the writer receives an additional $100. Caroline Marshall, director of the project, says the group just signed an agreement with the new literary magazine, *American Short Fiction*. Stories selected for syndication will be made available to the literary journal as well.

Each year PEN also selects three authors from the program to receive the "Annual Best" citation. The authors are invited to read their work and attend a reception in Washington, D.C.

Writers interested in submitting should note there is only one reading period. Work must be submitted during the month of January only. Although writers can submit up to 10 stories at a time, explains Marshall, no individual story should exceed 2,500 words. Previously published material is accepted as long as it was published in a periodical with less than 2,000 circulation.

Keep in mind the audience, says Marshall. Newspapers are looking for quality stories of general, topical or family interest, and shorter stories have the best chance of radio air play.

Attending Science Fiction Conventions for Fun and Profit

by Michael A. Banks

With the exception of those who live in or near cities where publishers are located, professional freelance writers lead solitary lives. We communicate with editors almost exclusively by mail and telephone, and only on rare occasions meet them or our peers. While solitude is conducive to writing, too much solitude can make writing tough. You can only go so far with everything happening in your head, as it were, and no direct, in-person feedback. Besides, humans are social creatures and need at least occasional contact with their peers and co-workers.

In virtually any other occupation, one meets with his or her co-workers and clients on a regular basis. The same should be true for writers, but usually isn't—except for science fiction and fantasy writers.

SF and fantasy writers have access to a unique network of support, contacts and resources in the form of science fiction and fantasy conventions (called "cons" for short). These events offer writers the opportunity to meet with other writers, SF fans and often with editors and publishers.

Typically organized and hosted by SF fan clubs, cons center around guests of honor and/or specific themes. They feature programming of interest to writers, as well as panel discussions of SF and fantasy, readings by well-known authors, costume competitions and a wide variety of other events.

SF cons originated in the late 1930s as informal meetings of a dozen or fewer SF fans, writers and would-be writers. They've since evolved into much larger events, held quite frequently on a regional, national and international basis. The venue is usually a hotel, and attendance at a regional con ranges from under 100 to over 2,000. Attendance depends on the location (major cities draw more people than smaller towns), the con's writer and artist guests and other factors.

The majority of regional SF cons are held on weekends. During the summer months, there are several cons over any given weekend, and there's at least one con somewhere in the U.S. or Canada on almost any weekend of the year.

The annual World Science Fiction Convention, or "Worldcon," is held over the Labor Day holiday. The location is usually in the U.S., but not always (last year it was in the Netherlands), and draws anywhere from 5,000 to 10,000 people. The Worldcon is a five- or six-day event. (Related cons of special interest include the annual World Fantasy Convention and the World Horror Convention, along with the National Science Fiction Convention—held when the Worldcon is not in the U.S.)

In case you're wondering, the professionals who attend SF cons are not limited to the guests of honor. Most cons invite writers other than the main guest of honor (typically one

A frequent con attendee, **Michael Banks** *is the author of 22 books, both fiction and nonfiction, 41 short stories and more than 1,000 articles. He is the author of* Word Processing Secrets for Writers *(with Ansen Dibell) and the novel* The Odysseus Solution *(with Dean Lambe).*

of the best-selling "name" writers such as Isaac Asimov, C.J. Cherryh or Larry Niven at the larger conventions). Some are special guests, while others attend on their own and participate in convention programming. The same is true of editors and publishers. The reason writers, editors and publishers attend cons on their own (as opposed to being a guest of convention) is simple: They want to meet editors and other writers. Which, not incidentally, is why you should be attending SF conventions if you are writing SF, fantasy or related genre fiction. (You'll find that writers and editors make up anywhere from 5% to 30% of a convention's membership.)

So, what exactly goes on at these conventions? Quite a bit, as you might imagine. Having been to more than 120 SF cons since 1973, I can give you a good idea of what to expect. (Too, I'm writing this a few days after returning from a medium-sized convention where I was guest of honor.) I'll give you an overview of an average regional convention (300 to 600 attendees).

Most conventions begin on Friday and run through Sunday. The con committee (the people running the con) often host a party the Thursday before the con and a "dead dog" party the Monday after, but at either of these points very few fans and fewer professionals are present. (It is nice to go in a day early or stay a day after, if you can, to acclimate yourself to the environment or recover from the whirl of events, as the case may be.)

Most con-goers arrive Friday afternoon or evening, check into the hotel and register with the convention. There's always a registration fee, payable in advance or at the door. Rates for regional cons average $25, with Worldcon memberships sometimes more than $100. (Larger cons—the Worldcon included—offer lower membership rates for those who register in advance. The earlier you register, the less it costs.)

When you register, you're given a program book and an identifying badge. Con staff members make sure nobody is admitted to program items or open events without a badge.

Since most con-goers arrive on Friday, that's the busiest time at the registration table. It's also the best time to meet or at least identify writers and editors. Standing in line waiting to check in is a fairly boring business, and thus presents an opportunity to strike up conversations.

With the exception of a few conventions that have little or no formal programming, an opening ceremony is held early in the evening of the first day. At this time, the guests of honor are introduced, and each may give a small speech. (In addition to a writer or editor guest of honor, there's usually a fan guest of honor and an artist guest of honor.) Special guests are also introduced, along with other writers and editors attending the con.

Following the opening ceremonies, there is usually a reception, party, dance or some other event to allow the guests to mingle. Panel discussions or other program items may also be scheduled.

Concurrent with first day registration and throughout the con, you will usually find a bourse, or "huckster room," where books, magazines and other SF and fantasy-related merchandise are available. Most cons feature an art show, and many have special exhibit rooms. Huckster rooms, arts shows and exhibits are normally open during daytime and early evening hours. There are usually video or film programs, too.

Panels and other program items continue through the daytime and evening hours on succeeding days of the convention. Programming is normally held in hotel function space (meeting rooms and auditoriums). At large cons, especially worldcons where two or more hotels are used, programming may be held in more than one hotel. (Large events, like presentations of science fiction's annual "Hugo" awards, may make use of a civic or convention center.)

Program items can include any of the following:

- two or more writers or editors discussing specific aspects of writing SF and fantasy
- one writer discussing his or her work
- readings by guest writers
- fans and/or writers discussing the SF and fantasy fields
- writers' workshops, conducted by one or more published writers (these often require advance registration, but usually are free of extra charge)
- art or benefit auctions
- a banquet, at which the guests of honor give speeches and awards are presented
- author autograph sessions
- "meet the author" parties and parties hosted by publishers or clubs

Cons also provide a hospitality suite, which serves as a meeting-place for fans and professionals alike. This "con suite" is often open 24 hours a day. Individuls or groups may also give room patyties. Less formal gatherings of this type usually provide thebest opportunities to meet editors and other writers.

Speaking of meeting editors and writers, you'll find it worthwhile to spend time with both. Writers, published or unpublished, are easy to meet and talk with, and are a good source of information, inspiration and contact. Be sure to attend all the panels or events having to do with writing and participate if you can (audience interaction is expected during panels). You'll also learn quite a bit just listening to the pros "talk shop," something they do quite a bit. So once you've made some acquaintances and know you're welcome, sit in on informal hallway, lobby or party chats whenever you can.

Don't be afraid to strike up a conversation with pro writers or editors if they seem affable. There are few writers and editors who aren't approachable, as long as you don't make a pest of yourself or approach them at the wrong time.

In case you're wondering, one of the best ways to make a pest of yourself is to bring a manuscript to a con with you and ask an editor or writer to read it. Most pro writers don't read other writers' work, except in professional situations, or for friends. No matter how much you want or need some professional feedback, the fastest way to turn off a writer is to ask him or her to read your work. (Unless, of course, having your work read and critiqued is a part of the writers' conference program.) Every published author, from Stephen King to Ray Bradbury to me, is frequently asked to read beginning writers' work, and we normally decline the honor.

Editors have no time for reading manuscripts at cons; most are there for business and a little fun (and their business at cons doesn't include reading unsolicited manuscripts. Despite the demand, they aren't on duty 24 hours a day.) Don't expect an editor to take your work back to the office, either. As Betsy Mitchell, associate publisher of Bantam/Spectra Books, says: "Editors don't plan on taking a lot of extra luggage back with them from a convention or conference. If an editor's interested in your manuscript, you'll be asked to mail it in."

An additional point of editorial etiquette: When meeting editors informally, you shouldn't try to press business matters on the editor. You can conduct little, if any, business at a reception or party, since other writers are seeking editors for the same reasons as you. The best you can hope for is to be able to meet the editor or agent, make a good impression, and be remembered by that person when your work crosses his or her desk.

If there is one cardinal rule for making a good impression with an editor, it is "Don't force your writing into the conversation." Doing so gives the editor the idea that the only reason you're interested in talking with him or her is to push your work—just like 9,000 other writers. If the editor asks you about your writing, fine. Otherwise, concentrate on making a good impression. Most editors feel it's somewhat tasteless and rude to press business on someone in such an informal situation.

But, if you can't bring up your writing during an informal meeting, when can you do so? Easy: Set up a private meeting. You can do this by inviting the editor to meet the next day, or by writing or phoning the editor a month or more in advance of the conference or convention. Explain who you are and ask if it would be possible to meet for lunch (or dinner, breakfast or whatever) during the conference. You'll find many editors open to such a suggestion (especially if you offer to buy). Either is more tasteful than trying to discuss your writing in a crowded room.

Set a definite day and time, have a definite project (or projects) to present, and don't be pushy or oversell yourself.

Incidentally, you'll often find agents at cons. The "rules of etiquette" for agents are slightly different. While you shouldn't expect an agent to read your work at a con, agents are usually more open to direct questions about representation and discussion of your work.

Beyond professional considerations, you should go to a SF con with the attitude that you are going to have a fun and interesting weekend, whether or not you meet editors or make contacts with writers who might help you advance your career. And relax—don't push yourself to spend time with every writer and editor present. Take some time to browse the huckster room, chat with fans and enjoy some of the activities not related to writing. Cons always feature unique events you won't find anywhere else—showings of rare films, special space or scientific displays, costume balls and more.

By sitting in on the right programming and getting in on the right conversations, you will learn more about writing and marketing your work in a weekend at a con than you would in a month otherwise.

And there's an additional benefit: After several days' exposure to writers and editors, you will return home recharged, inspired and ready to work!

Sources of information about science fiction and fantasy conventions:

Watch for announcements in science fiction magazines (*Aboriginal SF*, *Analog* and *Isaac Asimov's Science Fiction Magazine* are the best sources). You'll also find detailed listings in magazines that cover the science fiction field, such as *Locus* (P.O. Box 13305, Oakland, CA 94661).

In addition to the aforementioned sources, genre fiction writers will find organizations such as the Science Fiction Writers of America (SFWA, Box 4236, West Columbia SC 29171) publish fan and reader publications that are good sources of convention listings.

Each year we visit writers' conferences across the country to find out what writers want and need to know. Invariably they ask about agents—how to find one, how to work with one and how to know if an agent is doing a good job. This year we decided to go straight to the source and asked three well-respected agents to answer these and other frequently asked questions about their roles.

To find out more about working with agents see the introduction to the Literary Agents section in this book. To find out more about the agents we questioned, check their listings, also in the Literary Agents section. We've included responses from the following agents:

Eileen Fallon was an agent with Lowenstein Associates for eight years before establishing her own agency, The Fallon Literary Agency, in the summer of 1990. The agency handles mainstream fiction, mysteries and romances, as well as a range of nonfiction.

Jeff Herman founded The Jeff Herman Literary Agency, Inc., in 1985. The agency handles general nonfiction, business reference, commercial self-help, computer books and is becoming increasingly active in general fiction. Prior to opening his own agency, Herman worked in a New York public relations firm and as a publicity associate for Schocken Books. He is the author of *The Insider's Guide to Book Editors & Publishers: Who They Are! What They Want! And How to Win Them Over!*

Evan Marshall is president of The Evan Marshall Agency, which specializes in books of adult fiction and nonfiction, as well as original screenplays. He was previously an agent for Sterling Lord Literistic, Inc., and before that held editorial positions with Dodd, Mead, Everest House and New American Library. He is also a contributor to *Writer's Digest*.

It seems to be getting harder for a first-time author to find an agent; at the same time fewer publishers are accepting unsolicited material. How can new authors increase their chances of attracting an agent's attention?

Eileen Fallon: One attracts an agent's attention through professionalism, pure and simple. Professionalism encompasses everything from putting your name, return address and a daytime phone number on correspondence to spelling the agent's name correctly (and sending mail to the right address) to just about the most important aspect—researching the market *before* you write, through haunting local bookstores and using *Writer's Market* or *Novel & Short Story Writer's Market* and then contacting an agent who definitely handles the kind of material you are writing. For instance, do not send a science fiction novel to someone who does not represent books in that genre.

Jeff Herman: The first thing to do to attract an agent is to remember the agent is probably being flooded with submissions and that the vast majority of them will be rejected for a variety of reasons. At the same time, most agents are seeking the next jewel. To be that jewel, the writer should avoid the most common disqualifiers. Briefly, here are some basic do's and don'ts:

Establish contact with a query letter describing the project. Don't send anything that can't fit into a #10 envelope unless requested to do so. Include an SASE to facilitate a response. Make sure the letter provides a good "sales pitch," is personalized and professionally written. You want the agent to think she may need you more than you need her. You want to turn the tables so you have some leverage in the equation.

Get good, personalized stationery. Have your name turned into an impressive logo. This will make you look sharp and business-like.

If the agent doesn't know you, don't assume he will want to talk to you. Most projects, especially fiction, have to be read for proper assessment. Hearing about it on the phone is a poor use of the agent's time and won't be appreciated.

Evan Marshall: I look first for evidence that the writer knows the market for which he or she is writing, the conventions of the genre. Then I look for writing that is technically well crafted and a story that embodies fresh ideas and plot concepts as well as characters that are interesting and somehow unique. If all these are present, and the writer exhibits a professional manner in the way he or she corresponds with me and presents material, chances are I'll be interested.

How important are referrals? Any suggestions on how to obtain some?

Eileen Fallon: If a writer is referred by someone I know, usually another writer or an editor, I will most likely consider that material sooner than I would that of someone who hasn't been referred personally to me. But it has no bearing on whether or not I take the material on for representation. Similar to other agents, I take on projects I can sell and don't take on those I can't.

Jeff Herman: Referrals are invaluable as door-openers. Anytime someone calls or writes and states that they've been referred by someone I respect, they get serious attention. It doesn't mean I'll represent them, but I will notice them. It also means that the person didn't just get my name from one of the many public directories of agents.

To get referrals, the writer should talk to or gain access to anyone that has been published and is using an agent. The writer should join local and national writers' groups to network and gather information about agents and the industry as a whole.

Evan Marshall: A referral is helpful but not vital. Many editors refer writers to me, and I do take special notice of these writers because the editors feel their material is of good quality and right for me. My clients also will refer writers to me and I look carefully at their work too, because obviously I respect the literary judgment of the people I represent.

Please explain agent contracts. What should an author look for in a contract and how long should such a contract be binding?

Eileen Fallon: In such a contract, authors should look for a clear spelling out of terms — what the commissions are on both domestic and foreign sales, what fees or deductions (if any) there are in addition to the commission, a clause telling you how to end the relationship. Contracts call for a variety of lengths of time that they are in effect. I prefer a book by book contract; I don't think that you can represent someone who no longer wants to be represented by you, since this is a very personal relationship.

Jeff Herman: In my opinion, the contract should be brief and easy to read. Some of the basic points that should be addressed include:

What will the agent represent? Will it only be the work in question? All future works, too? Anything and everything the writer ever writes, including non-books? My personal belief is it should only apply to the work(s) at hand and not be binding regarding anything else.

What is the agency commission? (10-15 percent is normal) What expenses will the writer be responsible for? (Photocopying, postage and long-distance calls are often charged back to the author.)

How and when will the contract terminate? In my opinion, there should be no time limit here. Either party should be able to terminate the agreement at any time upon written notice. However, the agent should be entitled to remain as agent-of-record regarding any deals that were made or any that may result from efforts that were made prior to the termination. In other words, if I submit your work to 10 publishers on Monday and on Tuesday you fire me, but on Wednesday we receive an offer from one of those 10, I shall be entitled to be the agent of record if you enter into an agreement with that publisher or any of the other nine.

Evan Marshall: A representation agreement should state the types of material the agent will handle for the writer (books? short stories? screenplays? plays?); the commissions the agent will receive on sales made domestically as well as overseas for the various types of material he or she will represent; whether the agreement covers a specified period (I have heard of periods of up to five years) or simply continues in effect until either party terminates by letter; how much time the agent has, after notice of termination, to complete deals he or she has begun; and whether the agent may deduct from the author's monies expenses such as photocopying, messengers and overseas postage.

How can an author judge how an agent is doing (apart from sales)? What can authors expect from an agent?

Eileen Fallon: Authors should expect to be updated about the status of projects; if they are not happy with how frequently their agent gives them status reports, they should let the agent know right away (any problem should be aired as soon as possible).

Jeff Herman: The way to judge your agent is to request frequent reports about who the work is being submitted to and what the status of those submissions is. You should request to receive copies of all publisher correspondence in response to your work. Even if no sales are resulting, your agent may be making aggressive and appropriate efforts to sell the work. What you need to know is that he or she is indeed making ongoing efforts to get a deal and hasn't forgotten about you. Don't be a pest, but you are entitled to call at least twice a month for status reports and strategy discussions.

Evan Marshall: Apart from sales, an agent should be submitting a client's material both aggressively and judiciously. Beyond this, an author should expect career guidance, which includes editorial feedback based on the agent's knowledge of the markets and advice as to which projects the author would be wisest to pursue. Finally, the author should expect reasonable communication regarding the status of active projects and prompt remittance of monies the agent receives on the author's behalf.

With all the mergers, etc., causing an unstable environment for the editor/writer relationship, many agents say they're taking over some of the role previously played by editors—they have become the stable factor in the writer's career. Do you agree? Why or why not?

Eileen Fallon: Yes, most definitely—agents are now often the sole stable factor in a writer's career, due to the fact that editors often change companies or sometimes leave the field. The markets are also more competitive, so agents must do a great deal of editing work on material before it is submitted; editors do not have the time to rethink a writer's proposal.

Jeff Herman: I partially agree with this statement. Editor turnover is rampant. Therefore, most writers today will have many editors in their careers. Some may even end up having many editors for just one title—I've seen it happen. So the agent will be the only constant player. Still, the editor acts as the book's "director" throughout the editorial process and the agent cannot usurp this role.

Because the editors will quickly come and go, the agent will be primarily responsible today for managing the writer's long-term goals. The editor's role is short-lived and probably only pertains to the project at hand.

Evan Marshall: With editors changing jobs more frequently than ever, agents have indeed become the stable factor in a writer's career. Additionally, editors are, for the most part, unable to work with authors' material as they once could and so the agent often serves as a preliminary editor, helping to conceive and shape material.

What are some of the things writers ask for that they should not expect from an agent?

Eileen Fallon: In my experience two things writers should not expect: 1) publicity advice and 2) their agent to take on unsaleable material (once a relationship has been established). Frequently, a good, competent nonfiction writer, someone who does practical books, wants to work on something more literary—unfortunately, just because one writes good nonfiction, one doesn't necessarily have the artistic skill to pull off fiction.

Jeff Herman: Many agents can and do help authors write and revise their manuscripts. But this is a luxury. The writer should not automatically expect this service. After all, they are the writers.

Writers should not assume the agent has a lot of time for unproductive chit chat, especially during business hours.

Writers should not assume the agent is responsible when the publisher screws up and the book is unavailable in most bookstores. In such cases, the agent is also the victim, as may be the editor.

Evan Marshall: A writer should not expect constant (for example, daily) communication with his or her agent, who, after all, must serve a number of clients. A writer should not expect an agent to lend money, make travel arrangements or publicize a writer's book.

Perhaps, most importantly, a writer should not expect an agent to market material the agent does not feel is marketable or to make demands of publishers that the agent believes are unreasonable.

What are some of the basic steps you take to market a writer's work? What happens from the time a writer signs on to the time a contract is negotiated?

Eileen Fallon: I keep abreast of the fields I handle and keep my ears open for opportunities. I keep constantly in touch with editors. I look for two things first when examining manuscripts: 1) I must feel excited about the writing and 2) I must feel I am knowledgeable about the market for the material. Next, based on my knowledge of the market, I work with the writer to shape the material. I must have the very best material to submit. Editors really are overworked, so I must prepare a good package. Just as with a job interview, put your best foot forward and submit a well-prepared package — both in content and mechanical presentation. That is why I spend a lot of my time helping authors reshape the material before presenting it to an editor.

Jeff Herman: In general, the steps are: 1) Make the proposal or manuscript as perfect as possible. Develop a sales concept and strategy. 2) Discuss the project with several appropriate editors, and submit it to those who showed significant interest. 3) Make follow-up calls to further massage their interest. 4) If and when an offer is received, call all the others who are still considering it and see if they would like to make an offer. If yes, set a deadline and create a bidding situation, whereby the project will be sold to the highest bidder.

Evan Marshall: Once a writer and I have agreed to work together, I go right into the market with his or her material. Often this means calling or meeting with editors who I believe would like this material. Submission methods vary widely, from the single submission to the auction-with-rounds and I try to market a book in the most effective way possible for that book. During the marketing process, I try to keep my client informed about where the project has been and how the editors have responded. When an editor (or editors) makes an offer, it is of course my job to negotiate as effectively as possible on behalf of the client, explaining terms and policies as necessary and always offering my advice. Once a book is sold, it is up to me not only to monitor its progress up to and through publication, but to pursue subsidiary rights such as television and film rights, serial rights and rights overseas. Later, when royalty statements arrive, I must scrutinize them for accuracy and be ready to explain them to the author.

What about fees in addition to a commission? What should a writer expect from a reading or critique fee? (Answer only if you charge fees or if you feel strongly about the subject.)

Eileen Fallon: I do not charge a fee, but I feel strongly about the subject because it always comes up at writers' conferences. Yes, a number of very reputable agents charge reading fees. But I think it is important for a writer to learn exactly what he or she will receive for that fee — will they get a written critique, for example.

Evan Marshall: The fee I charge to consider the work of unpublished writers is what I use to pay my readers. This is the only way I can consider the work of unpublished writers. I feel it's most important that a writer know up front exactly what he or she will get for the fee—a critique, or simply a yes or no. I am not a critiquing service; however, since my readers do give me an assessment of a manuscript, I pass this assessment along to the writer if I cannot take on the manuscript. If I do take on a writer, the reading fee is refunded from the commission on his or her first sale.

When should an author and agent part company?

Eileen Fallon: When one or the other feels that they are no longer the best partnership in terms of furthering the writer's career.

Jeff Herman: The author should leave if he or she believes the agent is no longer providing reasonable or honest service.

Evan Marshall: When an agent has lost enthusiasm for a writer's work, when a writer has lost faith in an agent's ability to handle his or her work or when any sort of tension has crept into the relationship—these are times when it is probably best for the agent and the author to part.

Should an author also hire a publishing lawyer to go over the final contract, or are most agents well-versed in the nitty-gritty legalities of such contracts?

Eileen Fallon: A publishing lawyer is not necessary—a good agent knows contracts.

Jeff Herman: It's usually not necessary to bring in a lawyer. But if the writer does, he should make sure the lawyer actually understands book contracts.

Evan Marshall: No; this would be a waste of the author's money. Agents know—or should know—book contracts well enough to negotiate the most favorable contract possible for the author.

Explain your role as business manager. How does an agent keep track of royalties, etc.?

Eileen Fallon: This sort of business duty is handled the same way as in any other business—through a workable system set up by the firm.

Jeff Herman: Essentially, the agent is the conduit for the author's due income from the publisher. This money should be turned around within 10 business days. In most cases, there's nothing extraordinary about this role. Sometimes an agent can spot errors and be effective in having them promptly corrected.

Evan Marshall: As a writer's business manager, I handle all the details of the publishing process so that the writer can attend to what he or she does best—write. It is my job to see that a client's book is published well and to intercede when it is not. Perhaps, most importantly, having an agent allows the writer to keep his or her relationship with the publisher "pure," preventing the awkwardness that can arise when a writer represents him or herself.

Important Listing Information

● *Listings are* not *advertisements. Although the information herein is as accurate as possible, the listings are not endorsed or guaranteed by the editor of* Novel & Short Story Writer's Market.
● Novel & Short Story Writer's Market *reserves the right to exclude any listing that does not meet its requirements.*

Key to Symbols and Abbreviations

‡ New listing in all sections
* Subsidy publisher in Small Press and Commercial Book publishers sections
■ Book packager or producer
ms — manuscript; mss-manuscripts
b&w — black and white (photo)
SASE — self-addressed, stamped envelope
SAE — self-addressed envelope
IRC — International Reply Coupon, for use on reply mail in Canada and foreign markets.
FAX — a communications system used to transmit documents over the telephone lines.

(See Glossary for definitions of words and expressions used in writing/publishing.)

The Markets

How to Get the Most Out of This Book

Once you've completed your novel or short story, your next step will be to begin your search for a publisher. Finding the right market for your work requires careful research and planning. This book is designed to help you with that search by providing listings of magazine and book publishers looking for fiction submissions. To make your search easier, the listings are divided into six sections: literary and small circulation magazines, commercial periodicals, small presses, commercial book publishers, contests and awards, and literary agents. Following each main section is a list of similar foreign markets (for more information on approaching foreign publishers, see the "Business of Fiction Writing").

If you are not sure what category your work fits into or if you just want to explore the possibilities, start by browsing through the sections to find a market that interests you. The browsing method will also help you get an idea of what types of fiction are most needed, payment ranges and other general information about the magazine or book publishing industry. Read the section introductions to learn more about current trends and information specific to the type of listing featured in each section.

To help narrow your search, we've also included a Category Index located immediately preceding the Markets Index at the back of the book. The Category Index is divided into sections (e.g. literary and small circulation magazines, commercial magazines, etc.) and each section is divided by specific fiction categories or genres. For example, if you are looking for a small press publisher that accepts science fiction, look under "Small Press" in the category index and find the "Science Fiction" heading. There you will find an alphabetical list of all the small press publishers of science fiction listed in the book.

Once you've selected a listing, it is important to read it carefully. A dagger (‡) before a listing indicates a listing new to the 1991 edition. In the book publisher sections, a listing may also have an asterisk, indicating it is a subsidy publisher or a square indicating a book packager. For quick reference see the "Key to Symbols and Abbreviations." Further explanation of these and other symbols and terms can be found in the section introductions and in the glossary.

We've also ranked the magazine and book publishers with the following codes to help you select those markets most appropriate for your work.

I **Open to beginners. Especially encourages new writers to submit fiction;**
II **Accepts work both from beginning and established writers, depending on quality;**
III **Prestige market, generally hard to break into, usually accepting work only by established or agented writers and a very few outstanding new writers;**
IV **Specialized publication or press, limited to contributors from certain regions**

or within a specific age group or to those writing on specialized subjects or themes.

We occasionally receive letters asking why a certain magazine, book publisher, contest or agent is not in the book. Sometimes when we contact a listing, the editor or agent does not want to be listed because they: do not use very much fiction; are overwhelmed or backlogged with submissions; are having financial difficulty or have been recently sold; use only solicited material; accept work from a select group of writers; do not have the staff or time for the many unsolicited manuscripts a listing may bring.

Some listings do not appear because we have chosen not to list them. We investigate complaints about misrepresentation by editors or agents in the information they provide us or about unethical or unprofessional activities in a publisher's dealings with writers. If we find these reports to be true, after thorough investigation, we will delete a listing. See "Important Listing Information" for more about our listing policies.

If you feel you have not been treated fairly by a market listed in our book we advise you take the following steps:
● First, try to contact the listing. Sometimes one phone call or letter can quickly clear up the matter.
● Be sure to document all your correspondence with the listing. When you write to us with a complaint, we will ask for the name of your manuscript, the date of your submission and the dates and nature of your subsequent correspondence.
● We will write to the publisher, editor or agent and ask them to resolve the problem. We will then enter your letter into our files.
● The number, frequency and severity of unresolved complaints will be considered in our decision whether or not to delete the listing from the book.

To find out what happened to listings that appeared in the 1990 edition, but not in the 1991 edition, check the list of "Other Markets" at the end of each section. This list also includes a few well-known markets that have declined a listing.

Listings appearing in *Novel & Short Story Writer's Market* are compiled from detailed questionnaires, phone interviews and information provided by editors, publishers, awards directors and agents. The publishing industry is volatile and changes of address, editor, policies and needs happen frequently. To keep up with the changes we suggest you check the monthly Markets column in *Writer's Digest* magazine.

We also rely on our readers for information on new markets and changes in the markets listed in the book. Write us if you have any new information or if you have suggestions on how to improve our listings to better suit your writing needs.

Sample listing

The following is a sample listing. Each element of the listing is numbered and numbers correspond to the explanations following the listing. For more information on specific terms, see the glossary and the introductions to each section.

(1)‡BOTTOMFISH MAGAZINE (II), Language Arts Division, De Anza College, 21250 Steven Creek Blvd., Cupertina CA 95014. (409)996-4545. (2) Editor-in-Chief: Robert E. Brock. (3) Magazine: 7×8½; 80-100 pages; White Bristol vellum cover; b&w high contrast illustrations and photos; (4) "Contemporary poetry, fiction, excerpts of novels, b&w graphics and photos for literary and writing community." (5)Annually. (6) Estab. 1976. (7) Circ. 500.
(8) **Needs:** Experimental, literary and prose poem. "Literary excellence is our only criteria. We will consider all subjects except pornography." (9) Receives 10-20 unsolicited mss/month. (10)Accepts 2-3 mss/issue. (11) Publishes ms "about 6 months-1 year after acceptance. (12)

Recently published work by Janet Sisk. **(13)** Length: 500 words minimum; 5,000 words maximum; 2,500 words average.
(14) How to Contact: Send complete ms with cover letter, brief bio and SASE. **(15)** Reports in 8-10 weeks. **(16)** SASE. **(17)** Photocopied submissions OK. No multiple submissions or reprints. Accepts computer printout submissions, prefers letter quality. **(18)** Sample copy $3.50; back issue $2.50.
(19) Payment: Payment: 2 free contributor's copies. Charges $3.50 for extra copy.
(20) Terms: Acquires one-time rights.
(21) Advice: "Strive for originality and high level of craft; avoid cliched or stereotyped characters and plots. We don't print slick, commercial fiction, regardless of quality."

(1) Symbols, names, addresses and phone numbers. One or more symbols may precede the name of the market. A dagger symbol (‡) indicates the listing is new. Other symbols include subsidy (*) or book packager (■).

(2) Contact name. Whenever possible send your query or submission to a specific person. Use the fiction editor's name, if available. If you are not sure of the gender, it is best to use the full name (e.g. Robin Jones). If no name is given in the listing, check other sources (the masthead, if it is a magazine or, for the book publishing industry, check the directory, *Literary Market Place*).

(3) Physical description. Listings for publications often include physical description—the number of pages, type of paper, binding, number of illustrations or photos. This information is provided to give you some idea of the quality and type of publication. Magazines with inexpensive paper and binding may be more open to the work of new writers.

(4) Descriptive quote. This is a quote from the publisher describing the magazine or book publisher. The statement sometimes focuses on the publisher's philosophy and often contains a description of the audience. In book publishers' listings this is followed by a description of the types of books published (e.g., hardbound originals, paperback reprints).

(5) Frequency of publication. Some literary magazines published by universities are not published in the summer; the listing will then include a line beginning with "Does not read manuscripts from . . ."

(6) Date established. New magazines are often receptive to new writers.

(7) Circulation. For many of the literary and all of the small circulation magazines, circulation is under 10,000. In book publisher listings information is included on the number of titles and percentage of fiction titles published each year.

(8) Needs. This section lists the types of fiction needed. Sometimes a quote about what is most needed and what material should not be submitted.

(9) Number of manuscripts received. This can give you an idea of the competition. If a publisher receives several hundred manuscripts each week, but only publishes two or three, response time will be slow and competition high.

(10) Number of manuscripts published. See number 9.

(11) Time between publication and acceptance. This is especially important if you will not be paid until publication. Some small journals may take up to one year to publish.

(12) Recently published. Names of authors and, if the listing is an agent or book publisher, book titles will appear in this section.

(13) Length requirements. Minimum and maximum word lengths are often given. Short shorts are short pieces under 700 words, unless otherwise indicated.

(14) How to contact. This section gives details on how to contact the listing including whether it is necessary to query first or to send a complete manuscript. If sample chapters are required, send *consecutive* chapters, preferably starting with the first chapter. Cover letter and other submission requirements are listed here.

(15) Reporting time. This is a rough estimate of the time it will take for the publisher to respond to your query or submission. New publishers sometimes miscalculate the time needed to respond to the submissions generated by this book. Add three weeks to the time given, but if you have waited much longer, feel free to check the status of your submission with a letter, return postcard or a phone call.

(16) SASE. A self-addressed, stamped envelope in a size to fit your manuscript or letter is usually required.

(17) Acceptable submissions. If reprints, simultaneous or photocopied submissions are accepted, it will say so here. If not mentioned, they probably are not acceptable. When in doubt, call or write to obtain fiction guidelines. Computer printout submissions should be double-spaced, dark and legible — at least near-letter quality. If computer disk submissions are accepted, contact the publisher to find out specifics.

(18) Sample copy and guidelines. To find out more about a publisher, it is best to obtain a sample copy, catalog or fiction guidelines.

(19) Payment. Some small and literary magazines only pay in copies, others pay excellent rates. Note whether payment is made on acceptance or on publication. For book publishers, advances are upfront payments, made in one or more installments against royalties. You will not receive royalties until the advance has been covered.

(20) Terms. This is an important section. Note what type of rights you are selling. If the publication is not copyrighted, all rights belong to the author. Often the rights will revert to the author upon publication. Both of these agreements are the same as one-time rights — the publisher acquires or buys the right to publish your piece one time only. For more information on rights, see the "Business of Fiction Writing."

(21) Advice. Read the information in this section carefully. It is here where publishers and editors have the opportunity to pass on inside information on how to approach their magazine or publishing firm.

We include in the listings as much specific information as possible, but there are some items we do not mention because they are basically the same for all listings. See "The Business of Fiction Writing" for more on the basic requirements of all fiction markets.

Remember your market research should begin with a careful study of the listing but it should not end there. Whenever possible try to obtain a sample copy or catalog. For book publishers, check *Books in Print* at the library to find a publisher's titles and take a look a some of their books. The library also has publishing industry magazines such as *Publishers Weekly* as well as magazines for writers. These can help you keep informed of new publishers and changes in the field.

The Business of Fiction Writing

The listings in *Novel & Short Story Writer's Market* contain most of the essential information necessary for submission to the markets. Yet over the years we've made them as concise as possible in order to make room for more listings. We've left out some of the very basic information common to all the listings. These we call the "givens," the unwritten rules of which writers, especially beginners, should be aware. We've included much of this information in this section—a compilation of information on submission, approaching markets and manuscript mechanics.

Approaching magazine markets. While it is essential for nonfiction markets, a query letter by itself is usually not needed by most magazine fiction editors. If you are approaching a magazine to find out if fiction is accepted, a query is fine, but editors looking for short fiction want to see *how* you write. Many editors don't even read queries—they want to go right to the story. A cover letter, however, can be useful as a letter of introduction, but it must be accompanied by the actual piece. Include basic information in your cover letter—name, address, a brief list of previous publications—if you have any—and two or three sentences about the piece (why you are sending it to *this* magazine or how your experience influenced your story). Keep it to one page and remember to include a self-addressed, stamped envelope for reply.

Approaching book publishers. Some book publishers do ask for queries first, but most want a query plus sample chapters or an outline or, occasionally, the complete manuscript. Again, make your letter brief. Include the essentials about yourself—name, address, phone number and publishing experience. Include only the personal information related to your story. For example, if your story takes place in a hospital and you are a nurse, mention it—it adds credibility. Show that you have researched the market with a few sentences about why you chose this publisher. For example, if you chose the publisher because you feel your book would fit nicely into their action adventure line, let them know.

Book proposals. A book proposal is a package sent to a publisher that includes a cover letter and one or more of the following: sample chapters, outline, synopsis, author bio, publications list. When asked to send sample chapters, send up to three *consecutive* chapters. An outline covers the highlights of your book chapter by chapter. Be sure to include details on main characters, the plot and subplots. Outlines can run up to 30 pages, depending on the length of your novel. The object is to tell what happens in a concise, but clear, manner. A synopsis is a very brief description of what happens in the story. Keep it to two or three pages. The terms synopsis and outline are sometimes used interchangeably, so be sure to find out exactly what each publisher wants.

Agents. Agents are not usually needed for short fiction and most do not handle it unless they already have a working relationship with you. For novels, you may want to consider working with an agent, especially if you are interested in marketing to publishers who do not look at unsolicited submissions. For more on approaching agents see the introduction to the Literary Agents section and "Agents' Roundtable," starting on page 59.

Approaching foreign markets. When sending return postage to another country, do not send stamps. You must purchase International Reply Coupons (IRCs). The foreign publisher can use the IRCs to buy stamps from his/her own country. IRCs cost 95 cents each and can be purchased at the main branch of your local post office. This rule applies between countries in North America—U.S. writers sending return postage to Canadian publishers (and vice versa) must use IRCs.

Main branches of local banks will cash foreign checks, but keep in mind payment quoted in our listings by foreign publishers is usually payment in their currency. Also note reporting time is longer in most overseas markets. To save time and money, you may want to include a return postcard (with IRC) with your submission and forego asking for a manuscript to be returned.

Some mailing tips. Manuscripts under five pages long can be folded into thirds and sent in a business-sized (#10) envelope. For submissions of five pages or more, however, mail it flat in a 9×12 or 10×13 envelope. Your manuscript will look best if it is mailed in an envelope only slightly larger. For the return envelope, fold it in half, address it to yourself and add a stamp (or clip IRCs to it with a paper clip).

Mark both of your envelopes in all caps, FIRST CLASS MAIL or SPECIAL FOURTH CLASS MANUSCRIPT RATE. The second method is cheaper, but it is handled the same as Parcel Post (Third Class) and is only for manuscripts weighing more than one pound and mailed within the U.S. First Class mailing assures fastest delivery and better handling.

Book manuscripts should be mailed in a sturdy box (a ream-size typing paper box works well). Tape the box shut and tape corners to reinforce them. To ensure your manuscript's safe return, enclose a self-addressed and stamped insulated bag mailer. You may want to check with the United Parcel Service (UPS) or other mailing services for rates when mailing large manuscript packages.

If you use an office or personal postage meter, do not date the return envelope—it could cause problems if the manuscript is held too long before being returned. First Class mail is forwarded or returned automatically. Mark Third or Fourth Class return envelopes with "Return Postage Guaranteed" to have them returned.

If you send a cover letter with a Fourth Class manuscript, you must indicate this on the envelope (FIRST CLASS LETTER ENCLOSED) and include First Class postage.

It is not necessary to insure or certify your submission. In fact, many publishers do not appreciate receiving unsolicited manuscripts in this manner. Your best insurance is to always keep a copy of all submissions and letters.

Manuscript mechanics. A professionally presented manuscript will not guarantee publication. Yet on the other hand, a handwritten story in pencil on the back of your shopping list will almost always be rejected no matter how well written it is. A sloppy, hard-to-read manuscript will not be read—publishers simply do not have the time. Here's a list of suggested submission techniques for polished manuscript presentation:

● Use white, $8\frac{1}{2} \times 11$ bond paper, preferably 16 or 20 lb. weight. The paper should be heavy enough so that it will not show pages underneath it and strong enough to take handling by several people. Do not use onion skin or erasable paper.

● Type your manuscript on a typewriter with a dark ribbon. Make sure the letters are clean and crisp. You can also use a computer printer, but avoid hard-to-read dot matrix. Near-letter or letter quality is acceptable.

● Proofread carefully. Most editors will not mind an occasional white-out, but do not send a marked up manuscript or one with many typos. Also keep a dictionary, thesaurus and stylebook handy.

● Always double space and leave a 1¼ inch margin on all sides of the page. For a short story manuscript, your first page should include your name, address and phone number (single-spaced) in the upper left corner. In the upper right, indicate an approximate word count. Center the name of your story about one-third of the way down, skip two or three lines and center your byline (byline is optional). Skip three lines and begin your story.

- For subsequent pages, include your last name and page number in the upper right hand corner.
- For book manuscripts, use a separate cover sheet. Put your name, address and phone number in the upper left corner and word count in the upper right. Some writers list their agent's name and address in the upper right (word count is then placed at the bottom of the page). Center your title and byline about halfway down the page. Start your first chapter on the next page. Begin by centering the chapter number and chapter title (if there is one) about one-third of the way down the page. Be sure to include your last name and page number in the upper right of this page and each page to follow. Start each chapter with a new page.
- There are a number of ways to count the number of words in your piece. One way is to count the number of words in five lines and divide that number by five to find an average. Then count the number of lines and multiply to find the total words. For long pieces, you may want to count exactly how many words in the first three pages, divide by three and multiply by the number of pages you have.
- Always keep a copy. Manuscripts do get lost. To avoid expensive mailing costs, send only what is required. If a publisher asks for two sample chapters, only send two. If you are including artwork or photos, but you are not positive they will be used, send photocopies. Artwork is hard to replace.
- Most publishers do not expect you to provide artwork and some insist on selecting their own illustrators, but if you have suggestions, please let them know. Magazine publishers work in a very visual field and are usually open to ideas.
- If you want a reply or if you want your manuscript returned, enclose a self-addressed, stamped envelope (SASE). For most letters, a business-size (#10) envelope will do. Avoid using any envelope too small for an 8½×11 sheet of paper. For manuscripts, be sure to include enough postage and an envelope large enough to contain it. If you are requesting a magazine, send an envelope big enough to fit. When in doubt, you can send a label with your address and stamps.
- When sending electronic (disk or modem) submissions, contact the publisher first for specific information and follow the directions carefully.
- Keep accurate records. This can be done in a number of ways, but be sure to keep track of where your stories are and how long they have been "out." Write down submission dates. If you do not hear about your submission for a long time—about three weeks to one month longer than the reporting time stated in the listing—you may want to contact the publisher. When you do, you will need an accurate record for reference.

Rights. Know what rights you are selling. The Copyright Law states that writers are selling one-time rights (in almost all cases) unless they and the publisher have agreed otherwise. Below is a list of various rights. Be sure you know exactly what rights you are selling before you agree to the sale.

- All Rights allow a publisher to use the manuscript anywhere and in any form, including movie and book club sales, without further payment to the writer.
- Copyright is the legal right to exclusive publication, sale or distribution of a literary work. This right is that of the writer or creator of the piece and you need simply to include your name, date and the copyright symbol on your piece in order to copyright it. You can also register your copyright with the Copyright Office, although it is not necessary. Request information and forms from the Register of Copyrights, Library of Congress, Washington DC 20559.
- First Serial Rights mean that the publisher has the right to publish your work for the first time in any periodical.

- First North American Serial Rights are the same as First Serial, but they are only for publication on the North American Continent.
- One-time Rights allow a publisher to publish a story one time.
- Reprint Rights are permission to print a piece that was first published somewhere else.
- Second Serial Rights allow a publisher to print a piece in another periodical after it appeared for the first time in book form or in a magazine.
- Subsidiary Rights are all rights other than book publishing rights included in a book contract such as book club rights, movie rights and paperback rights.
- Work-for-hire is work that does not belong to the creator. If you do work-for-hire, you do not own the copyright and cannot sell any rights. For example, if you write a pamphlet for your company as an employee, generally the rights to that material do not belong to you. Writers doing work-for-hire are usually paid a flat fee for the work and do not collect royalties or other payments.

Samples

The samples on pages 74, 75 and 76 were selected to give you an idea of how to set up a short story cover letter, book proposal letter and a table of contents for a book proposal. Professionalism is the key here. Copy should be free of typos, paper should be clean bond (preferably white) and the type must be dark and clear. Keep your correspondence concise and always include an SASE or a return postcard.

We borrowed these samples from another Writer's Digest book, but we'd like to include samples from our readers. If you have a successful cover letter, outline, summary or other proposal piece we might use for an example in our next edition, please send us a copy. We'd also like to hear from you about what samples you would like to see in the future.

Following the letter samples are our postage-by-the-page charts. We've included them to help you determine mailing costs, but figures are subject to change in early 1991, so check with your post office for exact amounts. Be sure to mail manuscripts in a sturdy box mailer. Since postal rates are going up, many writers are finding it more economical to send photocopies that they do not expect to be returned. Some include a simple reply postcard with responses to be checked off by the publisher and returned.

I. WRIGHT
222 Tudor Street
Toonerville TX 01100
Telephone: 111-555-1234

June 20, 1988

Mr. Rod Rambeau, Editor
Courage Magazine
999½ Beacon Way
Boston, MA 02222

Dear Mr. Rambeau:

I am enclosing my short story *The Secret of 'Gator Grandy: America's Unknown Hero*. I feel certain your readers will enjoy reading this story, which, although fiction, is based on a legendary character who supposedly lived in the Louisiana swamps and, with his mysterious concoctions, helped save the lives of hundreds of people stricken with yellow fever.

My story runs approximately 7,500 words.

I am a published writer. My mystery novel will soon be brought out by Jones Publishing. I have also published stories in *Valor Times* and *Glory Review*.

I have enclosed a stamped, self-addressed mailer.

I look forward to hearing from you.

Sincerely,

I. Wright

Encls.

This is a cover letter for a short story sent to a magazine. Notice it is brief. Information about the story is mentioned early—within the first paragraph. Publishing credits are mentioned in the third paragraph and the author points out an SASE is enclosed. This and the following two samples were taken from the book, **The Writer's Digest Guide to Manuscript Formats,** *copyright © 1987, by Dian Dincin Buchman & Seli Groves, (Writer's Digest Books).*

I. WRIGHT
222 Tudor Street
Toonerville TX 01100
111-555-1234

January 5, 1987

Ms. Wilma B. White, Editor
Jones Publishing Co.
888 E. 57th Street
New York, NY 10166

Dear Ms. White:

What if a series of brutal murders were being committed in Paris, Texas, and everyone thought a maniac was responsible, but the real culprit wasn't even human? My
book, *The Rueful Murders in the Morgue*, shows how several women were torn apart
by the creature until brilliant detective work ended the rampage.

Today's readers have shown they want to read books that combine the classic elements of mystery with the modern techniques available for solving them. My book
provides the experience of horror that comes with the realization that terrible murders are being committed. The book also shows how a detective's observations and
his scientific expertise solve the mystery.

Readers also appreciate carefully introduced subplots that add different textures to
the story. I have included a love story that grows out of the experiences of two of
the characters, and I have also shown how the sailor came into possession of the
ape that plays a major role in the way the murders are committed and in the way
they are solved.

Enclosed is my proposal, along with three chapters of the book, and synopses of
these chapters. I have thoroughly researched the material on which my book is
based, including the actual case, which occurred in Paris, France, in 1832. I have
studied both the psychology of humans facing the terrors of the unknown and the
behavior of primates in a frightening environment.

The book will run 250 pages and can be ready for submission one year from contract.

Also enclosed: A post card on which I would appreciate your noting that you received
this material, as well as a stamped, addressed envelope in which this material can
be returned to me if necessary.

I look forward to hearing from you.

Sincerely,

I. Wright

Encl.

*This is a cover letter accompanying a book proposal. The first paragraph is like a
story lead. It pulls the reader (the editor) into the story immediately. Paragraph four
includes details on research. This is where qualifications and experience might be
mentioned. Notice the letter includes much information about the story, but is confined to one page.*

Morgue/Wright

Table of Contents

Introduction

Chapter-by-Chapter Outline

Sample Chapters

Writing samples

Enclosed in folder.

This is a table of contents for a book proposal. Material to be included in a proposal will vary according to publishers' guidelines. This proposal includes bio information, an overview, a chapter-by-chapter outline and list of sample chapters. The writer also included other writing samples.

U.S. Postage by the Page

by Carolyn Hardesty

Mailing costs can be an appreciable part of writing expenditures. The chart below can help save money as well as time by allowing you to figure the fees for sending your manuscripts to prospective publishers.

Postage rates are listed by numbers of pages (using 20 lb. paper) according to the most commonly used envelopes and their self-addressed, stamped envelopes (SASEs). While most writers prefer to send their work First Class, Third Class is becoming a choice for some. Third Class moves more slowly, but it costs less than First Class after the first 4 ounces. Also, it is permissible in Third Class to include a letter pertaining to the material inside.

First Class mail weighing more than 11 ounces is assessed according to weight plus geographical zone so it needs to be priced at the Post Office.

Postcards can be a bargain for writers. If the postage costs are higher than another computer printout or photocopied version of a manuscript, a postcard can be used for the editor's reply. The cost is 20¢.

For short manuscripts or long queries, use a #10 (business-size) envelope with a 30¢ stamp. Four pages is the limit if you are including a SASE. Another option is the 6×9 envelope. For 1-3 pages, postage is 30¢ in the U.S. For 1-7 pages with SASE, cost is 54¢ in the U.S.

Ounces	9×12 9×12 SASE number of pages	9×12 SASE (for return trips) number of pages	First Class Postage	Third Class Postage **	Postage from U.S. to Canada **
under 2	. . .	1 to 2	$ .40*	$ .45	$ .40*
2	1 to 4	3 to 8	.54	.45	.52
3	5 to 10	9 to 12	.78	.65	.74
4	11 to 16	13 to 19	1.02	.85	.96
5	17 to 21	20 to 25	1.26	1.00	1.18
6	22 to 27	26 to 30	1.50	1.00	1.40
7	28 to 32	31 to 35	1.74	1.10	1.62
8	33 to 38	36 to 41	1.98	1.10	1.84
9	39 to 44	42 to 46	2.22	1.20	2.06
10	45 to 49	47 to 52	2.46	1.20	2.28
11	50 to 55	53 to 57	2.70	1.30	2.50

*This cost includes an assessment for oversized mail that is light in weight.
**Postage to other countries and increments for Third Class had not been determined at the time we went to press. Check with your post office for increases.

Prices listed above were correct as of press time (may change due to recent budget negotiations).

Carolyn Hardesty's *short fiction has appeared in* Four Minute Fictions, The North American Review *and the* Montana Review. *She is the editor of* Goldfinch, *a prize winning history magazine for children.*

Canadian Postage by the Page

by Barbara Murrin

The following chart is for the convenience of Canadian writers sending domestic mail and American writers sending an envelope with International Reply Coupons (IRCs) or Canadian stamps for return of a manuscript from a Canadian publisher. Unfortunately these figures are approximate, because the Canadian Postal Service meets to determine new fees in January each year, after we go to press. Check with your local post office for changes.

Manuscripts returning from the U.S. to Canada will take a U.S. stamped envelope although the original manuscript was sent with Canadian postage. This applies to return envelopes sent by American writers to Canada, too, which must be accompanied with IRCs or Canadian postage.

In a #10 envelope, you can have up to five pages for 39¢ (on manuscripts within Canada) or 45¢ (on manuscripts going to the U.S.). If you enclose a SASE, four pages is the limit. If you use 10×13 envelopes, send one page less than indicated on the chart.

IRC's are worth 45¢ Canadian postage but cost 95¢ to buy in the U.S.

Canada Post has made major changes in designation of types of mail, as follows:

Standard Letter Mail   Minimum size: 9cm × 14cm (3⅝″ × 5½″); Maximum size: 14cm × 24.5cm (5½″ × 9⅝″); Maximum thickness: 5mm (³⁄₁₆″)

Oversize Letter Mail   Minimum size: 14cm × 24.5cm (5½″ × 9⅝″); Maximum size: 27cm × 38cm (10⅞″ × 15″); Maximum thickness: 2cm (¹³⁄₁₆″)

International Letter Mail   Minimum size: 9cm × 14cm (3⅝″ × 5½″); Maximum size: Length + width + depth 90cm (36″) Greatest dimension must not exceed 60cm (24″)

Insurance: To U.S. and within Canada—45¢ for each $100 coverage to a maximum coverage of $1000. International—65¢ for each $100 coverage to a maximum coverage of $1000. **Registered Mail:** $3 plus postage (air or surface—any destination). Legal proof of mailing provided.

Weight up to	9×12 envelope, 9×12 SASE number of pages*	9×12 SASE (for return trips) number of pages	Canada		First Class to U.S.	
			Standard	Oversize	Standard	Oversize
30 g/1.07 oz.	...	1 to 3	$ .39	$ .49	$ .45	$ .55
50 g/1.78 oz.	1 to 4	4 to 7	.61	.78	.65	1.00
100 g/3.5 oz.	5 to 14	8 to 18	.78	.78	...	1.00
200 g/7.1 oz.	15 to 46	19 to 49	(1.17)	1.17		1.90
300 g/10.7 oz.	47 to 57	50 to 61	(1.56)	1.56		2.35
400 g/14.2 oz.	58 to 79	62 to 82	(1.95)	1.95		3.25
500 g/17.8 oz.	80 to 101	83 to 104	(2.34)	2.34		4.15
1.0 kg/2.2 lbs.	102 to 208	105 to 212	**	**	(air pkt.)	7.30

*Based on 20 lb. paper and 2 adhesive labels per envelope.
**For Canadian residents mailing parcels 1 kg. and over within Canada (domestic mail), rates vary according to destination. Ask your Post Master for the chart for your area.

Barbara Murrin *owns and operates a desk-top publishing business in Williams Lake, British Columbia. She teaches music and business subjects at a nearby community college and, when there is time, writes romance. One of her short stories has been included in* Insight's Most Unforgettable Stories, *a compilation of stories from 20 years of publication.*

Literary and Small Circulation Magazines

Little/literary magazines provide perhaps the greatest opportunity for publication to new and unpublished writers. This is due to the vast number and variety of these magazines now in publication, 723 of which are listed in the 1991 edition.

While some listings have been lost from last year's edition, many new ones have been included. Most publications listed in this section can be located in the Category Index, with the exception of those with no categorical specifications (i.e., those accepting "all types of fiction.") A list of those magazines not included in this year's edition is provided at the end of this section with reasons for exclusion.

The diversity of the market

Whether you are a published veteran or a new writer submitting a story for the first time, you'll find it easy to locate a publication that is receptive to the type of work you are submitting. In the course of your search for a suitable market, it is helpful to realize that a magazine's name reveals much about the type of fiction it publishes. For example, magazines that are very open to submissions from new writers will frequently contain the word "writer" in their title (with the exception of *Writer's Forum*, a university-published literary magazine.) Fanzines, small circulation magazines with eccentric titles (i.e., *Baby Sue, Blonde on Blonde*) are a viable market for writers of highly experimental works that may be unpublishable elsewhere. It should be noted that fanzines rarely, if ever, pay writers. Journals affiliated with universities or colleges often use state names and generally accept only literary fiction.

Information such as paper quality, binding, type and number of pages, is helpful in determining the level of prestige that a publication carries. While magazines printed on high quality acid-free paper will frequently carry more prestige than those printed on 20 lb. photocopied paper, the latter will be more inclined to publish the work of a new writer.

Experience and exposure

Although a large number of magazines listed in this section do not pay writers, publication in them can lead to important long-term rewards. Among the most significant of these is publishing experience. As the new writer begins to develop a portfolio of publication credits, he gains the crucial exposure needed to gain the attention of commercial magazine editors and book publishers. This exposure is obviously important for the writer who hopes to have a collection of short stories published. Publication in prestige journals such as *The North American Review*, *The Antioch Review* and *Ploughshares* leads to recognition in the literary community. In fact, many book publishers and agents regularly peruse these journals in search of promising new writers.

Many prestige journals are subsidized by universities and state arts councils, enjoying a foundation of stability and financial support, whereas most new, small and independent literary magazines "stand on their own." Unfortunately, this lack of stability forces many small literary magazines to suspend publication after only one year. However, the fact remains that these less-renowned, often non-paying publications are the most accessible means of publication for the new writer.

How to submit

Before submitting your work to a potential market, be it a fanzine or a literary journal, it is essential that you read the listing first and obtain a sample copy of the publication. When you have studied the magazine carefully and decided that it is appropriate for your work, you can prepare to send it out. Your manuscript should exhibit a professionalism that shows an editor you are serious about your writing endeavor. It should be typed, double spaced, on clean, typo-free regular typing paper (no erasable or onion-skin). The complete manuscript should be accompanied by a cover letter and an SASE with sufficient postage for a reply. If you are sending material to Canada or overseas, include International Reply Coupons (IRC's) instead of stamps. These are available at most main post offices. When composing your cover letter, remember that its purpose is to pique the editor's interest in your story without *explaining* or *justifying* the story. Let the story speak for itself. It is not necessary to give a detailed biography unless this relates directly to your story.

When your manuscript is ready for submission, avoid sending it out arbitrarily. Don't waste your time with alphabetic submission, i.e., sending your manuscript to all of the "A's," then the "B's,"etc. This method causes magazines at the beginning of the section to become flooded with manuscripts. In addition, it can prevent you from discovering important markets at the end of the section.

As mentioned before, it is best to obtain sample copies of the publications seeking your type of work, after you have carefully read the listings in this secton. Some writers choose to read through the section first, while others check the category index at the back of the book before the markets index. The category index is divided into sections identical to those in the book. Find the Literary and Small Circulation category index and look for headings that best describe your work—such as literary, horror, mystery, experimental, etc. Once you have sent your manuscript on its way, try to be patient. Don't assume that it has been rejected if the editor fails to respond within the time frame designated in the listing. It is possible that the editor is simply deluged with manuscripts and has not yet come across yours. It is also possible that your manuscript is under consideration. Wait an additional three or four weeks before querying a magazine about the status of your piece.

If you are interested in learning more about fanzines, see the quarterly magazine, *Factsheet Five* (6 Arizona Ave., Rensselaer NY 12144-4502). For more literary magazines that feature poetry, see *Poet's Market* (Writer's Digest Books, 1507 Dana Ave., Cincinnati OH 45207) and *The International Directory of Little Magazines and Small Presses* (Dustbooks, Box 100, Paradise CA 95967). The following is the ranking system we have used to categorize the listings in this section:

I   **Publication encourages beginning writers or unpublished writers to submit work for consideration and publishes new writers regularly;**

II **Publication accepts work by established writers and by new writers of exceptional talent;**

III **Publication does not encourage beginning writers; prints mostly writers with previous publication credits and very few new writers;**

IV **Special-interest or regional publication, open only to writers in certain genres or on certain subjects or from certain geographical areas.**

‡**ABYSS MAGAZINE (II, IV), "Games and the Imagination,"** Ragnarok Enterprises, 3716 Robinson, Austin TX 78722. (512)472-6534. Editor: David F. Nalle. Fiction Editor: Patricia Fitch. Magazine: 8½x11; 28 pages; bond paper; glossy cover; illustrations; photos. "Heroic fantasy fiction: some fantasy, horror, SF and adventure fiction, for college-age game players." Bimonthly. Plans special fiction issue. Estab. 1979. Circ. 1,500.

Needs: Adventure, fantasy, horror, psychic/supernatural/occult, cyberpunk, science fiction, heroic fantasy, sword and sorcery. "Game-based stories are not specifically desired." Receives 20-30 unsolicited mss/month. Buys 1 ms/issue; 7 mss/year. Publishes ms 1-12 months after acceptance. Recently published work by Antoine Sadel, Kevin Anderson, Alan Blount; published new writers within the last year. Length: 2,000 words average; 1,000 words minimum; 4,000 words maximum. Publishes short shorts occasionally. Sometimes critiques rejected mss or recommends other markets.

How to Contact: Send for sample copy first. Reports in 1 month on queries; 2 months on mss. "Do send a cover letter, preferably entertaining. Include some biogaphical info and a precis of lengthy stories." SASE. Photocopied submissions OK. Accepts computer printout submissions. "Call IIBBS at (512)472-6905 for modem ASCII info." Sample copy and fiction guidelines $3.

Payment: Pays 1-3/word or by arrangement, plus contributor's copies.

Terms: Pays on publication for first North American serial rights.

Advice: "We are particularly interested in new writers with mature and original style. Don't send us fiction which everyone else has sent back to you unless you think it has qualities which make it too strange for everyone else but which don't ruin the significance of the story. Make sure what you submit is appropriate to the magazine you send it to. More than half of what we get is completely inappropriate. We plan to include more and longer stories."

ACM, (ANOTHER CHICAGO MAGAZINE) (II), Another Chicago Press, 3709 N. Kenmore, Chicago IL 60613. (312)524-1289. Editor: Barry Silesky. Fiction Editor: Sharon Solwitz. Magazine: 5½ × 8½; 150-200 pages; "art folio each issue." Estab. 1977.

Needs: Contemporary, literary, experimental, feminist, gay/lesbian, ethnic, humor/satire, prose poem, translations and political/socio-historical. Receives 75-100 unsolicited fiction mss each month. Recently published work by David Michael Kaplan, Diane Wakoski, Gary Soto; published new writers in the last year. Sometimes recommends other markets.

How to Contact: Unsolicited mss acceptable with SASE. Accepts computer printout submissions. Publishes ms 6 months to 1 year after acceptance. Sample copies are available for $8 ppd. Reports in 2 months.

Payment: Small honorarium plus contributor's copy.

Terms: Acquires first North American serial rights.

Advice: "Get used to rejection slips, and don't get discouraged. Keep query and introductory letters short. Make sure ms has name and address on every page, and that it is clean, neat and proofread. We are looking for stories with freshness and originality in subject angle and style, and work that encounters the world and is not stuck in its own navel."

‡**THE ACORN (I,II),** 1530 7th St., Rock Island IL 61201. (309)788-3980. Editor: Betty Mowery. Newsletter: 8½ × 11; 8-10 pages; illustrations. "Manuscripts of interest to K-12th grade audience or K-12th grade librarians and teachers." Bimonthly. Estab. 1989. Circ. 100.

Needs: Ethnic, juvenile, mainstream, preschool/picture book, prose poem, regional, religious/inspirational, romance (contemporary, historical, young adult), science fiction, suspense/mystery, young adult. "We use one adult manuscript per issue, if it is of interest to young people. No erotica or anything degrading to race or religion or background." Receives 50 unsolicited fiction mss/month. Accepts 10-12 mss/issue; 60-70 mss/year. Publishes ms within two months after acceptance. Length: 500 words preferred; 200 words minimum; 500 words maximum. Accepts short shorts. Length: 200 words. Sometimes critiques or comments on rejected mss and recommends other markets.

How to Contact: Send complete ms with cover letter. Reports in 1 week. SASE. Simultaneous, photocopied and reprints OK. Sample copy for $1. Fiction guidelines are contained in publication.

Payment: Pays in contributor's copies.

Terms: Acquires first rights.

Advice: Looks for "tight writing and a manuscript that has something to say and isn't prcachy, but still gets the point across. I am open to all manuscripts from both published and unpublished writers. I'm eager to help a beginning author get into print. "

ACTA VICTORIANA (I, II), 150 Charles St. West, Toronto, Ontario M5S 1K9 Canada. Editor: Emma Thom. Magazine: 9½×13; 40 pages; glossy paper; cornwall cover; illustrations and photos. "We publish the poetry, prose, drawings and photographs of university students as well as of other writers. The magazine reaches the University of Toronto community as well as students of other universities. Semiannually. Estab. 1875. Circ. 1,500+.
Needs: Contemporary, ethnic, experimental, humor/satire, literary, mainstream, prose poem. Accepts 4-5 mss/issue; 8-10 mss/year. Publishes ms 2 months after acceptance. Recently published work by Craig Stephenson, Peter McCallum and Douglas Brown; published new writers within the last year. Length: 1,500 words maximum.
How to Contact: Send complete manuscript with cover letter, which should include information about the writer's previous publishing credits and biography. Reports in 2 months on mss. International Reply Coupons if in U.S. Simultaneous and photocopied submissions OK. Accepts computer printout submissions. Sample copy and fiction guidelines for $3 and 9×12 SAE.
Payment: Pays contributor's copies.
Advice: "University publications such as ours offer beginning fiction writers good opportunities to get published. If your piece is innovative and exciting, yet at the same time well-crafted, you will have a good chance of getting published. Editors change yearly in this student journal, yet our editorial policy remains roughly the same."

ADRIFT(II), Writing: Irish, Irish American and . . ., #4D, 239 E. 5th St., New York NY 10003. Editor: Thomas McGonigle. Magazine: 8×11; 32 pages; 60 lb paper stock; 65 lb cover stock; illustrations; photos. "Irish-Irish American as a basis—though we are interested in advanced writing from anywhere." Semiannually. Estab. 1983. Circ. 1,000+.
Needs: Contemporary, erotica, ethnic, experimental, feminist, gay, lesbian, literary, translations. Receives 40 unsolicited mss/month. Buys 3 mss/issue. Recent issues have included work by Francis Stuart. Published new writers within the last year. Length: open. Sometimes critiques rejected mss and recommends other markets.
How to Contact: Send complete ms. Reports as soon as possible. SASE for ms. Photocopied submissions OK. Accepts computer printout submissions. Sample copy $5.
Payment: Pays $7.50-300.
Terms: Pays on publication for first rights.
Advice: "The writing should argue with, among others, James Joyce, Flann O'Brien, Juan Goytisolo, Ingeborg Bachmann, E.M. Cioran, Max Stirner, Patrick Kavanagh."

AERIAL (II), Box 25642, Washington DC 20007. (202)333-1544. Editor: Rod Smith. Magazine: 6x9; 64 pages; 75 lb paper; 10 pt. CIS cover stock; photos on cover only. Semiannually. Estab. 1984. Circ. 750.
Needs: Experimental, literary, translations. Receives 10 mss/month. Accepts 1-2 mss/issue; 3-4 mss/year. Publishes ms within 3-12 months of acceptance (average). Length: ½ page-10 pages. Sometimes critiques rejected mss.
How to Contact: Send ms—short fiction or excerpts—with or without cover letter. Reports in 1 week to 1 month. SASE. Photocopied and reprint submissions OK. Accepts computer printout submissions. Sample copy for $6.
Payment: Pays in contributor's copies.
Terms: Acquires one-time rights.
Advice: "We consider ourselves politically and aesthetically 'dissident.' Believe that it is important and necessary to explore alternative modes of conceptualization given the current dangerous global situation."

AFTER HOURS (II), When Fantasy Meets the Darkness, P.O. Box 538, Sunset Beach CA 90742-0538. Editor: William G. Raley. Magazine: 8½×11; 48-56 pages; #3 grade offset paper; #3 grade uncoated cover; about 3 illustrations per issue; photographs sometimes with interviews. "*After Hours* features stories too weird or off-the-wall to happen during the day. Therefore, all stories *must* take place after dark! For adults and young adults." Quarterly. Estab. 1989. Circ. 500.

 The double dagger before a listing indicates that the listing is new in this edition. New markets are often the most receptive to freelance contributions.

Needs: Condensed/excerpted novel, fantasy, horror, humor/satire, psychic/supernatural/occult, suspense/mystery. "No science fiction, 'typical' crime stories (where the only motive is murder, rape, or robbery), religious, political or military." Receives 200 unsolicited mss/month. Buys 12 mss/issue; 50 mss/year. Publishes ms "about 9 months" after acceptance. Recently published work by J.N. Williamson, Steve Rasnic Tem, Tanith Lee and Mort Castle. Length: 2,500 words preferred; 6,000 words maximum. Publishes short shorts.
How to Contact: Send complete ms with cover letter. Include "where you heard about *After Hours*, *brief* list of credits. Cover letter is optional." Reports in 4 months on mss. SASE for ms or query. Photocopied submissions OK. Accepts computer printout submissions. Accepts electronic submissions via disk. Sample copy for $4. Fiction guidelines for #10 SAE and 1 first class stamp.
Payment: Pays $60 maximum (1¢/word) and one contributor's copy.
Terms: Pays on acceptance for first North American serial rights. Sends galleys to author.
Advice: "Readers don't want to wait around for something to happen. I need action (or at least an atmosphere of dread) on page one. Good characterization is a must. As far as plots go, don't be afraid to be original. I avoid overdone plots. There are so many stories where people come back from the dead, or turn into a monster, that it's no longer entertaining. Characters should be believable, with women portrayed as equals. No excessive blood or violence. If your story has a fresh plot (or a new twist on an old one) or is just plain strange, you've probably got a sale."

AGNI (II), Creative Writing Program, Boston University, 236 Bay State Rd., Boston MA 02215. (617)354-8522. Editor-in-Chief: Askold Melnyczuk. Magazine: 5½ × 8½; 212-300 pages; 55 lb booktext paper; glossy cover stock; occasional illustrations and photos. "Eclectic literary magazine publishing first-rate poems and stories." Semiannually. Estab. 1972.
Needs: Stories, excerpted novels, prose poems and translations. Receives 200 unsolicited fiction mss/month. Accepts 4-7 mss/issue, 8-12 mss/year. Recently published work by Stephen Minot, Heidi Jon Schmidt, Volodymyr Dibrova and Marco Papa. Rarely critiques rejected mss or recommends other markets.
How to Contact: Send complete ms with SASE and cover letter listing previous publications. Simultaneous and photocopied submissions OK. Accepts computer printout submissions. Reports in 1 month. Sample copy $6, $12 for double issue.
Payment: Pays $8/page; 2 contributor's copies; extra copies 40% of retail price.
Terms: Pays on publication for first North American serial rights. Sends galleys to author. Copyright reverts to author upon publication.
Advice: "Read *Agni* carefully to understand the kinds of stories we publish. Read—everything, classics, literary journals, bestsellers."

‡AGORA (IV), The Magazine for Gifted Students, AG Publications, P.O. Box 10975, Raleigh NC 27605. (919)787-6832. Editor: Thomas E. Humble. Magazine: 8½ × 11; 32 pages; illustrations and photographs. "We publish winners of our writing competitions for students in grades 7-12." Bimonthly (4 issues per school year). Estab. 1986. Circ. 3,200.
Needs: Ethnic, historical (general), humor/satire, literary, regional, religious, science fiction. Receives 2-4 unsolicited mss/month. Length: 450-1,500 words average. Publishes short shorts.
How to Contact: "Subscribe to magazine or attend a school that subscribes to a class set." Accepts electronic submissions via disk. Sample copy $4. Free fiction guidelines.

ALABAMA LITERARY REVIEW (II), Smith 264, Troy State University, Troy AL 36082. (205)566-8112, ext. 330. Editor: Theron Montgomery. Fiction Editor: Jim Davis. Magazine: 6 × 11½; 100+ pages; top paper quality; some illustrations; photos. "National magazine for a broad range of the best contemporary fiction, poetry, essays and drama that we can find." Semiannually. Estab. 1987.
Needs: Condensed novel, contemporary, erotica, ethnic, experimental, fantasy, feminist, historical (general), humor/satire, literary, prose poem, regional, science fiction, serialized/excerpted novel, suspense/mystery, translations. "Serious writing." Receives 50 unsolicited fiction mss/month. Buys 2 fiction mss/issue. Publishes ms 5-6 months after acceptance. Published work by Manette Ansay, Ed Peaco, Peter Fromm and Rick Shelton; published new writers within the last year. Length: 2,000-3,000 words average. Publishes short shorts of 1,000 words. Sometimes comments on rejected mss and recommends other markets.
How to Contact: Send complete ms with cover letter or submit through agent. Reports on queries in 2 weeks; on mss in 2-4 weeks (except in summer). SASE. Simultaneous submissions OK. Accepts computer printouts, no dot-matrix "unless Xeroxed." Sample copy $4 plus 50¢ postage.

Payment: Pays in contributor's copies. Hope to pay honorarium by January.
Terms: First rights returned to author.
Advice: "Read our publication first. Avoid negative qualities pertaining to gimmickry and a self-centered point of view. We are interested in any kind of writing if it is *serious* and *honest* in the sense of 'the human heart in conflict with itself.' "

ALASKA QUARTERLY REVIEW (II), University of Alaska, Anchorage, 3211 Providence Dr., Anchorage AK 99508. (907)786-1327. Fiction Editor: Ronald Spatz. Magazine: 6x9; 146 pages; 60 lb Glatfelter paper; 10 pt. C15 black ink varnish cover stock; photos on cover only. Magazine of "contemporary literary art and criticism for a general literary audience." Semiannually. Estab. 1982.
Needs: Contemporary, experimental, literary, prose poem and translations. Receives 100 unsolicited fiction mss/month. Accepts 5-11 mss/issue, 15-22 mss/year. Does not read mss May 15-August 15. Published new writers within the last year. Publishes short shorts. Occasionally critiques rejected mss.
How to Contact: Send complete ms with SASE. Photocopied submissions OK. Reports in 2 months. Publishes ms 6 months to 1 year after acceptance. Sample copy $4.
Payment: 1 free contributor's copy and a year's subscription.
Terms: Acquires first rights.
Advice: "We have made a significant investment in fiction. The reason is quality; serious fiction *needs* a market. Try to have everything build to a singleness of effect."

THE ALCHEMIST (II), Box 123, Lasalle, Quebec H8R 3T7 Canada. Editor: Marco Fraticelli. Magazine: 5½ × 8½; b&w illustrations and photographs. "We publish prose in most issues with no prejudices in regard to style, but we tend to favor the experimental rather than the traditional." Published irregularly. Estab. 1974. Circ. 500.
Needs: Literary, feminist, gay, lesbian and psychic/supernatural/occult. Buys 1 ms/issue.
How to Contact: Send complete ms with SASE or IRC. Accepts computer printout submissions. Accepts disk submissions compatible with Apple. Prefers hard copy with disk submission. Reports in 1 month. Publishes ms an average of 6 months after acceptance. Sample copy $2.
Payment: Pays in contributor's copies.
Terms: Rights remain with author.
Advice: "Please—no American stamps on the SASE."

ALDEBARAN (II), Roger Williams College, Ferry Rd., Bristol RI 02809. (401)253-1040. Editor: Alfred Levitt. Magazine: 5½ × 8½; 60-80 pages; illustrations; photos. Literary publication of prose and poetry for a general audience. Published annually or twice a year. Estab. 1970.
Needs: Will consider all fiction. Receives approximately 10 unsolicited fiction mss each month. Does not read mss in summer. Preferred length: 3,000 words or shorter. Critiques rejected mss when there is time.
How to Contact: Send complete ms with SASE and cover letter, which should include "information for possible contributor's notes—but cover letters will not influence decision on publication." Accepts computer printout submissions. Reports in 1 month. Sample copy $3 with SASE.
Payment: 2 free author's copies.
Terms: Copyright reverts to author on publication.
Advice: Mss are rejected because of "incomplete stories, no live character, basic grammatical errors; usually returned with suggestions for revision and character change."

ALPHA BEAT SOUP (IV), 68 Winter Ave., Scarborough, Ont. M1K 4M3 Canada. Editor: Dave Christy. Magazine: 7½ × 9; 95-125 pages; illustrations. "Beat and modern literature—prose, reviews and poetry." Semiannually. Plans special fiction issue. Estab. 1987. Circ. 250.
Needs: Erotica, experimental, literary and prose poem. Published work by Charles Bukowski, Joy Walsh and Richard Nason; published new writers within the last year. Length: 600 words minimum; 1,000 words maximum. Sometimes recommends other markets.

Market categories: (I) Beginning; (II) General; (III) Prestige; (IV) Specialized.

How to Contact: Query first. Reports on queries ASAP. SASE. Simultaneous, photocopied and reprint submissions OK. Sample copy for $4.
Payment: Pays in contributor's copies.
Terms: Rights remain with author.
Advice: "*ABS* is the finest journal of its kind available today, having, with 7 issues, published the widest range of published and unpublished writers you'll find in the small press scene."

AMARANTH (II), Tales of the Supernatural, MKASHEF Enterprises, P.O. Box 368, Poway CA 92074-0368. Editor: Ms. Alayne Gelfand. Magazine: 8½ × 11; 150 pages; 60 lb paper; full-color cover; illustrations. "Any supernatural, paranormal, inexplicable situation *EXCEPT* vampires, 'devil worship horror' *or* 'sword and sorcery' for adult, sophisticated, educated, literary audience." Annually. Estab. 1990.
Needs: Adventure, contemporary, erotica, ethnic, experimental, feminist, gay, historical (general), lesbian literary, prose poem, romance (contemporary), science fiction, suspense/mystery. "We are *not* looking for 'gore horror' but the emotional/spiritual/psychic side of the supernatural. Bizarre or inexplicable situations; the odd, fantastic, peculiar, curious are only a few examples of acceptable subjects. Ghosts, werewolves, witches, wraiths are also acceptable subjects *if* depicted as never done before. Your werewolf should be the most unique beast ever written about." No victimization of women. No 'singles bar' settings." Receives 5-50 unsolicited mss/month. Buys 5-15 mss/issue. Does not read mss September-March. Publishes ms 1 month to 1 year after acceptance. Agented fiction 1%. Length: 2,000 words preferred; 10,000 maximum. Publishes short shorts. Sometimes critiques rejected mss and recommends other markets.
How to Contact: Query first. Very important that you send for detailed guidelines. Include a *brief* biography of writing experience. Reports in 3 weeks on queries; 4 months on mss. SASE. Accepts photocopies, computer printouts or disk submissions (IBM WordPerfect). Sample copy $15 available March '91. Fiction guidelines for #10 SAE and one 1st class stamp.
Payment: Pays 1¢/word and contributor's copies.
Terms: Pays on publication for first North American serial rights.
Advice: "I am looking for unique ideas told in unique, beautiful, interesting ways. A story must grab me from word one and keep me moving through it and with it to the end. A manuscript that is handled professionally, that tells an unusual story with detailed characterization, that has lyrical writing and avoids clichéd situations and word usage will stand out of the pack. *Please* do not waste your time or mine by submitting without having seen the guidelines. The needs of *AMARANTH* are highly specified."

THE AMARANTH REVIEW (I, II), Window Publications, P.O. Box 56235, Phoenix AZ 85079. Editor: Dana L. Yost. Magazine: 8½ × 11; 60-80 pages; 60 lb offset paper; 90 lb cover stock; illustrations and occasional photos. "Our theme is eclectic—we are interested in poetry and short fiction which deals with the human condition in its broadest possible expression. For an educated, thinking audience of those who enjoy quality poetry and fiction." Estab. 1989. Circ. 1,500.
Needs: Literary and contemporary. Plan to publish special fiction issue or an anthology in the future. Receives 100+ unsolicited mss/month. Accepts 8-10 mss/issue; 20 mss/year. Publishes ms 2-6 months after acceptance. Published work by Genni Gunn and Richard Ploetz. Length: 2,500 words average; 3,500 words maximum. Publishes short shorts. Sometimes critiques rejected mss and recommends other markets.
How to Contact: Send complete ms with cover letter. Include how the writer heard about us—brief bio is also welcome. Reports in 2 weeks on queries; 1 month on ms. SASE. Simultaneous and photocopied submissions OK. Accepts computer printout submissions. Accepts electronic submissions (IBM Word Perfect 5.0 only). Sample copy $5.50. Writer's guidelines for #10 SAE and 1 first class stamp.
Payment: Free subscription to magazine; pays in contributor's copies; charges for extras (40% discount.)
Terms: Acquires first North American serial rights.
Advice: "The one basic requirement is that the piece be good, quality fiction. But more specifically, we look for the piece to deal with some basic condition of the human existence, and we look for the piece to hit hard and knock us into thinking—really thinking—about the issue or circumstances of the story. I also think that today's fiction writers need to take some chances—a lot of the stories we receive could have been written by a dozen other writers, and that almost always means that they will end up being rejected. Fiction is about voice, and it's about tone—quite simply, it's about the unique perspective of the author. Tell the story in the way that only you can tell it and forget about the rubber-stamp

approach to writing fiction—it just doesn't cut it in today's highly competitive market."

AMBERGRIS (I, II), P.O. Box 29919, Cincinnati OH 45229. Editor: Mark Kissling. Magazine: 5 × 8; 80-90 pages; 40 lb offset paper; 60 lb offset cover; illustrations; photographs. "*Ambergris* is a non-profit magazine dedicated to the discovery and publication of quality art and literature." Annual. Estab. 1987. Circ. 500.
Needs: "Excellent short fiction showing stylistic distinction. Contemporary themes, any subject." *No simultaneous submissions accepted.* No strictly preschool, juvenile, romance, serialized/excerpted novel or young adult. Receives 30-40 mss/month. Accepts 6 mss/issue. Publishes ms "up to one year" after acceptance. Word length open, prefers under 5,000 words.
How to Contact: Send complete ms with cover letter which should include a three-line biographical sketch. One work of fiction per submission. Reports on mss in 2 months. Enclose SASE for return of mss. Sample copy $4; back issue $3. Fiction guidelines free with #10 SASE.
Payment: Pays 2 contributor's copies, extras available at half cover price.
Terms: Acquires first North American serial rights.
Advice: "We give special consideration to works by Ohio writers and about the Midwest in general. We attempt to foster the emerging writer, but encourage beginning writers and others unfamiliar with our format to look at a sample copy before submitting work." Sponsors annual contest with $100 cash prize for best short story. Send SASE for information.

AMELIA (II), 329 E St., Bakersfield CA 93304. (805)323-4064. Editor-in-Chief: Frederick A. Raborg, Jr. Magazine: 5½ × 8½; 124-136 pages; perfect bound; 60 lb high quality moistrite matte paper; kromekote cover; four-color covers; original illustrations; b&w photos. "A general review using fine fiction, poetry, criticism, belles lettres, one-act plays, fine pen-and-ink sketches and line drawings, sophisticated cartoons, book reviews and translations of both fiction and poetry for general readers with catholic tastes for quality writing." Quarterly. Plans special fiction issue each July. Estab. 1984. Circ. 1,250.
Needs: Adventure, contemporary, erotica, ethnic, experimental, fantasy, feminist, gay, historical (general), humor/satire, lesbian, literary, mainstream, prose poem, regional, science fiction, senior citizen/retirement, sports, suspense/mystery, translations, western. Nothing "obviously pornographic or patently religious." Receives 160-180 unsolicited mss/month. Buys up to 9 mss/issue; 25-36 mss/year. Published 4 new writers within the last year. Published Judson Jerome, Jack Curtis, Maxine Kumin, Eugene Dubnov and Merrill Joan Gerber. Length: 3,000 words average; 1,000 words minimum; 5,000 words maximum. Usually critiques rejected ms. Sometimes recommends other markets.
How to Contact: Send complete manuscript. Cover letter with previous credits if applicable to *Amelia* and perhaps a brief personal comment to show personality and experience. Reports in 1 week on queries; 2 weeks-3 months on mss. SASE. Photocopied submissions OK. Accepts computer printout submissions; prefers letter-quality. Sample copy for $7.95. Fiction guidelines free for #10 SAE and 1 first class stamp.
Payment: Pays $35-50 plus 2 contributor's copies; extras with 20% discount.
Terms: Pays on acceptance. Buys first North American serial rights. Sends galleys to author "when deadline permits."
Advice: "Write carefully and well, but have a strong story to relate. I look for depth of plot and uniqueness, and strong characterization. Study manuscript mechanics and submission procedures. Neatness does count. There is a sameness—a cloning process—among most magazines today that tends to dull the senses. Magazines like *Amelia* will awaken those senses while offering stories and poems of lasting value."

AMERICAN DANE (II,IV), The Danish Brotherhood in America, 3717 Harney, Box 31748, Omaha NE 68131. (402)341-5049. Editor: Pamela K. Dorau. Magazine: 8¼ × 11; 20-28 pages; 40 lb paper; slick cover; illustrations and photos. "The *American Dane* is the official publication of the Danish Brotherhood. Corporate purpose of the Danish Brotherhood is to promote and perpetuate Danish culture and traditions and to provide Fraternal benefits and family protection." Estab. 1916. Circ. 8,900.

**Read the Business of Fiction section to learn the correct way
to prepare and submit a manuscript.**

Needs: Ethnic. "Danish!" Receives 4 unsolicited fiction mss/month. Accepts 1 ms/issue; 12 mss/year. Reads mss during August and September only. Publishes ms up to one year after acceptance. Length: 1,000 words average; 3,000 words maximum. Publishes short shorts.
How to Contact: Query first. SASE. Simultaneous submissions OK. Accepts computer printout submissions. Sample copy for $1 and 9×12 SAE with 54¢ postage. Fiction guidelines free for 4×9½ SAE and 1 first class stamp.
Payment: Pays $15-$50.
Terms: Pays on publication for first rights. Publication not copyrighted.
Advice: "Think Danish!"

‡**AMERICAN FICTION (II)**, English Dept., Springfield College, Springfield MA 01095. Editor: Michael C. White. Magazine: 5¾x8¼; 200-300 pages; Annually. For "serious readers of fiction." Circ. 5,000 paper.
Needs: Contemporary, experimental, traditional literary. Receives 700-800 mss/year. Buys or accepts 20-25 mss/year. Does not read mss June-December. "Send *only* after our *AWP* and *Poets & Writers* ads appear." Publishes ms within 12 months of acceptance. Charges $7.50 reading fee. Recently published work by Ursula Hegi, Florri McMillan, Clint McCown, Perry Glasser, Antonya Nelson. Length: 5,000 words average 10,000 words maximum. Publishes short shorts. Sometimes critiques rejected mss.
How to Contact: "Send ms, cover/bio, *after* reading our ads in *AWP* and *Poets & Writers* each spring" SASE for query. "We don't return mss." Simultaneous and photocopied submissions OK. Accepts computer printout submissions, including dot-matrix. Fiction guidelines for #10 SAE and 1 first class stamp. For sample copy (strongly encouraged) write Birch Lane Press, 600 Madison Ave., New York, NY 10022.
Payment: Pays $50 maximum and contributor's copies. "$1,000, 500, 250 awards to top 3 stories based on guest judge's decision."
Terms: Pays on publication for first North American serial rights. "The *American Fiction* series is a contest. Top 20-25 stories published, with awards given to judge's top 3 stories. 1988 judge was Raymond Carver; 1989 Anne Tyler; 1990 Louise Erdrich."
Advice: Looks for "moving, interesting, engaging characters, action, language."

‡**AMERICAN LITERARY REVIEW (II), A National Journal of Poems and Stories**, University of North Texas, P.O. Box 13615, Denton TX 76203. (817)565-4670, 565-2124. Editor: Scott Cairns. Fiction Editor: Clay Reynolds. Magazine: 7x10; 128 pages; 60 lb. Glatfelter paper; 60 lb. Springhill Vellum cover. "Publishes poems and stories for a general audience." Semiannually. Estab. 1990. Circ. 200.
Needs: Mainstream and literary only. No genre works. Receives 25 unsolicited fiction mss/month. Accepts 7-10 mss/issue; 14-20 mss/year. Publishes ms within 2 years after acceptance. Recently published work by Gordon Weaver, Gerald Haslam and William Miller. Length: 3,500 words preferred; 5,000 words maximum. Critiques or comments on rejected mss and recommends other markets.
How to Contact: Send complete ms with cover letter. Reports in 6-8 weeks. SASE. Simultaneous and photocopied submissions OK. Sample copy for $5. Fiction guidelines free.
Payment: Pays in contributor's copies.
Terms: Acquires one-time rights. Sends pre-publication galleys to author.
Advice: "We want to publish poems and stories that reflect the kinds of writing being done in various regions of America. We are not looking for a 'style' or an aesthetic to make us distinctive." Looks for "literary quality and careful preparation."

THE AMERICAS REVIEW (II,IV) A Review of Hispanic Literature and Art of the USA, Arte Publico Press, 4800 Calhoun, University of Houston, Houston, TX 77204-2090. (713)749-4768. Editors: Dr. Julian Olivares and Evangelina Vigil-Pinon. Magazine: 5½×8½; 128 pages; illustrations and photographs. "*The Americas Review* publishes contemporary fiction written by U.S. Hispanics—Mexican Americans, Puerto Ricans, Cuban Americans, etc." Quarterly. Estab. 1972.
Needs: Contemporary, ethnic, literary, women's, hispanic literature. No novels. Receives 12-15 fiction mss/month. Accepts 2-3 mss/issue; 8-12 mss/year. Publishes mss "6 months to 1 year" after acceptance. Length: 3,000-4,500 average number of words; 1,500 words minimum; 6,000 words maximum. Publishes short shorts. Sometimes critiques rejected mss and recommends other markets.
How to Contact: Send complete manuscript. Reports in 3 months. SASE. Photocopied submission OK. Accepts computer printout submissions, no dot-matrix. Accepts electronic submissions via IBM compatible disk. Sample copy $5; $10 double issue.

Payment: $50-200; 5 contributor's copies.
Terms: Pays on acceptance for first rights, and rights to 40% of fees if story is reprinted. Sponsors award for fiction writers.
Advice: "There has been a noticeable increase in quality in U.S. Hispanic literature."

THE AMHERST REVIEW (II), Box 1811, Amherst College, Amherst MA 01002. (413)542-2250. Editor: Josh Jacobs. Fiction Editor: Lisa Stanton. Magazine: 7½×8½; 60-70 pages; illustrations and photographs. "We are a college literary magazine publishing work by students, faculty and professionals. We seek submissions of poetry, fiction, and essay for the college community." Annually.
Needs: Adventure, confession, contemporary, ethnic, experimental, fantasy, feminist, gay, historical (general), horror, humor/satire, lesbian, mainstream, prose poem, psychic/supernatural/occult, regional, romance, science fiction, suspense/mystery, translations, western. "No sentimentality." Receives 10-20 unsolicited mss/month. Does not read mss March-August. Length: 4,500 words; 7,200 words maximum.
How to Contact: Send complete ms with cover letter. Reports in 4 months on mss. Accepts computer printout submissions. Sample copy for $5, SAE and $1 postage.
Payment: 2 free contributor's copies; $5 charge for extras.
Terms: Acquires first rights.

‡ANIMAL TALES (II, IV) Stories About Animals and the People Who Love Them, Pet Publications, 2113 W. Bethany Home Rd., Phoenix AZ 85015. (602)246-7144. Editor: Berta I. Cellers. Magazine: 8½×11; 32-40 pages; 20 lb. bond paper; 20 lb. bond cover; sketches; 8½×11 photographs. "Realistic animal stories that would be enjoyed by adults and can be read to children for all age groups." Bimonthly. Estab. 1989. Circ. 1,000.
Needs: Adventure, humor/satire, animal stories. "Does not accept material where animals are given human characteristics—such as talking." Receives 200 unsolicited mss/month. Buys 8-12 mss/issue; 48-60 mss/year. Publishes ms 4-12 months after acceptance. Recently published work by Chris Carter, William K. Church and Joe Whetstone. Length: 2,500-3,500 words average; 2,000 words minimum; 6,000 words maximum. "Occasionally publishes short shorts as fillers." Length: 500 words. Sometimes critiques rejected mss.
How to Contact: Send complete manuscript with cover letter including Social Security number and author information. Reports in 2 months on mss. SASE. Sample copy for $4.95. Fiction guidelines for legal size SAE and 1 first class stamp.
Payment: Pays $5-50.
Terms: Buys first rights. "Request writer's contest entry."
Advice: "Appearance makes a manuscript stand out. When a writer has taken some time and care in preparing a manuscript they usually have done the same in writing the material. I look for a unique story line, with an easy-to-read format."

ANTAEUS (III), The Ecco Press, 26 W. 17th St., New York NY 10011. (212)645-2214. Editor-in-Chief: Daniel Halpern. Managing Editor: Cathy Jewell. Magazine: 6½×9; 275 pages; Warren old style paper; illustrations and photographs sometimes. "Literary magazine of fiction and poetry, literary documents, and occasional essays for those seriously interested in contemporary writing." Quarterly. Estab. 1970. Circ. 5,000.
Needs: Contemporary, literary, prose poem, excerpted novel, and translations. No romance, science fiction. Receives 600 unsolicited fiction mss/month. Recently published fiction by Richard Ford, Donald Hall, Joyce Carol Oates; published new writers within the last year. Rarely critiques rejected mss.
How to Contact: Send complete ms with SASE. Photocopied submissions OK; no multiple submissions. Accepts computer printout submissions; prefers letter-quality. Reports in 6-8 weeks. Sample copy $5. Fiction guidelines free with SASE.
Payment: Pays $10/page and 2 free contributor's copies. 40% discount for extras.
Terms: Pays on publication for first North American serial rights and right to reprint in any anthology consisting of 75% or more material from *Antaeus*.
Advice: "Read the magazine before submitting. Most mss are solicited, but we do actively search the unsolicited mss for suitable material. Unless stories are extremely short (2-3 pages), send only one. Do not be angry if you get only a printed rejection note; we *have* read the manuscript. Always include an SASE. Keep cover letters short, cordial and to the point."

ANTIETAM REVIEW (II,IV), Washington County Arts Council, 82 W. Washington St., Hagerstown MD 21740. (301)791-3132. Editor: Susanne Kass. Magazine: 8½×11; 42 pages; photos. A literary journal of short fiction, poetry and black-and-white photographs. Annually. Estab. 1982. Circ. 1,000.
Needs: Contemporary, ethnic, experimental, feminist, literary and prose poem. "We read manuscripts from our region—Delaware, Maryland, Pennsylvania, Virginia, West Virginia and Washington D.C. only. We read from October 1 to March 1." Receives about 100 unsolicited mss/month; accepts 7-9 stories/year. Published work by Rachel Simon, Elisavietta Ritchie, Philip Bufithis; published new writers within the last year. Length: 3,000 words average.
How to Contact: "Send ms and SASE with a cover letter. Let us know if you have published before and where." Photocopies OK. Accepts computer printouts; prefers letter-quality. Reports in 1 to 2 months. "If we hold a story, we let the writer know. Occasionally we critique returned ms or ask for rewrites." Sample copy $5. Back issue $2.50.
Payment: "We believe it is a matter of dignity that writers and poets be paid. We have been able to give $100 a story and $25 a poem, but this depends on funding. Also 2 copies." Prizes: "We offer a $100 annual literary award in addition to the $100, for the best story."
Terms: Acquires first North American serial rights. Sends pre-publication galleys to author if requested.
Advice: "We look for well crafted work that shows attention to clarity and precision of language. We like relevant detail but want to see significant emotional movement within the course of the story—something happening to the central character. This journal was started in response to the absence of fiction markets for emerging writers. Its purpose is to give exposure to fiction writers, poets and photographers of high artistic quality who might otherwise have difficulty placing their work."

THE ANTIGONISH REVIEW, St. Francis Xavier University, Antigonish, Nova Scotia B2G 1C0 Canada. (902)867-3962. Editor: George Sanderson. Literary magazine for educated and creative readers. Quarterly. Estab. 1970. Circ. 800.
Needs: Literary, contemporary, prose poem and translations. No erotic or political material. Accepts 6 mss/issue. Receives 25 unsolicited fiction mss each month. Published work by Arnold Bloch, Richard Butts and Helen Barolini; published new writers within the last year. Length: 3,000-5,000 words. Sometimes comments briefly on rejected mss.
How to Contact: Send complete ms with cover letter. SASE or IRC. Accepts disk submissions compatible with Apple and Macintosh. Prefers hard copy with disk submission. Reports in 3 months. Publishes ms 3 months to 1 year after acceptance.
Payment: 2 free author's copies.
Terms: Acquires first rights.
Advice: "Learn the fundamentals and do not deluge an editor."

ANTIOCH REVIEW (II), Box 148, Yellow Springs OH 45387. (513)767-6389. Editor: Robert S. Fogarty. Associate Editor: Nolan Miller. Magazine: 6×9; 128 pages; 60 lb book offset paper; coated cover stock; illustrations "seldom." "Literary and cultural review of contemporary issues in politics, American and international studies, and literature for general readership." Quarterly. Published special fiction issue last year; plans another. Estab. 1941. Circ. 4,000.
Needs: Literary, contemporary, translations and experimental. No children's, science fiction or popular market. Buys 3-4 mss/issue, 10-12 mss/year. Receives approximately 175 unsolicited fiction mss each month. Approximately 1-2% of fiction agented. Length: any length the story justifies.
How to Contact: Send complete ms with SASE, preferably mailed flat. Accepts computer printout submissions, prefers letter-quality. Reports in 2 months. Publishes ms 6-9 months after acceptance. Sample copy $5; free guidelines with SASE.
Payment: $10/page; 2 free author's copies. $2.70 for extras.
Terms: Pays on publication for first and one-time rights (rights returned to author on request).
Advice: "Our best advice, always, is to *read* the *Antioch Review* to see what type of material we publish. Quality fiction requires an engagement of the reader's intellectual interest supported by mature emotional relevance, written in a style that is rich and rewarding without being freaky. The great number of stories submitted to us indicates that fiction apparently still has great appeal. We assume that if so many are writing fiction, many must be reading it."

APAEROS (I), 960 S.W. Jefferson Ave., Corvallis OR 97333. Clerks: Kathe and John Burt. Newsletter: 8½×5½; 24-32 pages; photos if photocopyable. "Sex, erotica, relationships (het, lesbian, gay), turn-ons, nudism, VD and rape prevention, etc. For sharing feelings, knowledge, questions, problems, stories, drawings and fantasies. Ready-to-photocopy pages published unedited." Bimonthly. Estab. 1985. Circ. 100.

Needs: Confession, erotica, feminist, gay, lesbian, romance (contemporary, historical, young adult), comic strips, prose poem, science fiction, serialized/excerpted novel, spiritual. Published new writers within the last year. Publishes short shorts. Sometimes comments on rejected mss or recommends other markets.

How to Contact: Send $2 and SASE for sample and guidelines. SASE for mss. Simultaneous, photocopied and reprint submissions OK. Accepts computer printouts. "State that you are over 18."

Payment: "Increased pages; maybe free subscription extensions."

Terms: Publication copyrighted via "common law."

Advice: "*Apaeros* is *un*edited, reader-written. The amateur press is good for learning the trade."

APPALACHIAN HERITAGE (I, II), Berea College, Hutchins Library, Berea KY 40404. (606)986-9341. Editor: Sidney Farr. Magazine: 7 × 9½; 80 pages; 60 lb stock; 10 pt Warrenflo cover; drawings and clip art; b&w photos. "*Appalachian Heritage* is a southern Appalachian literary magazine. We try to keep a balance of fiction, poetry, essays, scholarly works, etc., for a general audience and/or those interested in the Appalachian mountains." Quarterly. Estab. 1973. Circ. 1,100.

Needs: Regional, literary, historical. Receives 20-25 unsolicited mss/month. Accepts 2 or 3 mss/issue; 10 or more mss/year. Published work by Robert Morgan, Richard Hague and James Still; published new writers within the last year. No reading fee, but "would prefer a subscription first." Length: 2,000-2,500 word average; 3,000 words maximum. Publishes short shorts. Length: 500 words. Occasionally critiques rejected mss and recommends other markets.

How to Contact: Send complete ms with cover letter. Reports in 1-2 weeks on queries; 3-4 weeks on mss. SASE for ms. Simultaneous, photocopied submissions OK "if clear and readable." Accepts computer printout submissions, no dot-matrix. Sample copy for $4.

Payment: 3 free contributor's copies; $4 charge for extras.

Terms: Acquires one-time rights.

Advice: "Trends in fiction change frequently. Right now the trend is toward slick, modern pieces with very little regional or ethnic material appearing in print. The pendulum will swing the other way again, and there will be a space for that kind of fiction. It seems to me there is always a chance to have really good writing published, somewhere. Keep writing and keep trying the markets. Diligent writing and rewriting can perfect your art. Be sure to study the market. Do not send me a slick piece of writing set in New York City, for example, with no idea on your part of the kinds of things I am interested in seeing. It is a waste of your time and money. Get a sample copy, or subscribe to the publication, study it carefully, then send your material."

‡ARARAT QUARTERLY (IV), Ararat Press, AGBU., 585 Saddle River Rd., Saddle Brook NJ 07662. (201)797-7600. Editor: Dr. Leo Hamalian. Magazine: 8½ × 11; 72 pages; illustrations and b&w photographs. "*Ararat* is a forum for the literary and historical works of Armenian intellectuals or non-Armenian writers writing about Armenian subjects."

Needs: Condensed/excerpted novel, contemporary, historical (general), humor/satire, literary, religious/inspirational, translations. Publishes special fiction issue. Receives 25 unsolicited mss/month. Buys 5 mss/issue; 20 mss/year. Length: 1,000 words average. Publishes short shorts. Length: 250 words. Sometimes critiques rejected mss and recommends other markets.

How to Contact: Send complete manuscript with cover letter. Reports in 1 month on queries; 3 weeks on mss. SASE. Simultaneous, photocopied and reprint submissions OK. Accepts computer printout submissions. Sample copy $4 and $1 postage. Free fiction guidelines.

Payment: Pays $10-75 plus 2 contributor's copies.

Terms: Pays on publication for one-time rights. Sometimes sends galleys to author.

‡ARCHAE (II), A Paleo-literary Review, Cloud Mountain Press, 10 Troilus, Old Bridge NJ 08857-2724. (908)679-8373. Editor: Alan Davis Drake. Magazine: 7x8½; 50-70 pages; illustrations. "For a literary, anthropological, general audience." Semiannually. Estab. 1990. Circ. 150.

Needs: Contemporary, experimental, historical, humor/satire, literary, mainstream, prose poem, translations. "No confessional material." Plans special fiction issue. Receives 3-5 unsolicited fiction mss/month. Accepts 2-3 mss/issue; 4-6 mss/year. Publishes mss 2-3 months after acceptance. Length: 3,000-6,000 words preferred; 8,000 words maximum. Publishes short shorts. Length: 500 words. Critiques or comments on rejected mss and recommends other markets.

How to Contact: Query first. Reports in 2 weeks on queries; in 6 weeks on mss. SASE. Simultaneous, photocopied and computer printout submissions OK. Accepts electronic submissions. Sample copy for $6, 8x9 SAE and 4 first-class stamps. Fiction guidelines for #10 SAE and 1 first-class stamp.
Payment: Pays in contributor's copies.
Terms: Aquires first North American serial rights. Sends pre-publication galleys to author. Sponsors fiction contest — send for details.

ARGONAUT (II), Box 4201, Austin TX 78765-4201. Editor: Michael Ambrose. Magazine: 5¼ × 8¼; 60 or more pages; 60 lb paper; varied cover stock; illustrations; "*Argonaut* is a weird fantasy/science fiction magazine. Our readers want original, literate, unusual stories with a strong science fiction or weird element." Annually. Estab. 1972. Circ. 500.
Needs: Science fiction and weird fantasy. Buys 5-8 mss/issue. Receives 40-50 unsolicited fiction mss each month. Published work by Charles R. Saunders, Albert J. Manachino, John Alfred Taylor, Ardath Mayhar and Dale Hammell. Length: 2,500-10,000 words. Sometimes recommends other markets.
How to Contact: Send complete ms with SASE. "It is nice to know a little something about the author." Reports in 1-2 months. Sample copy $3.
Payment: 2 or more copies. Extras at 50% discount.
Terms: Acquires first North American serial rights.
Advice: "We are not interested in heroic or 'high' fantasy, horror, or media-derived stories. Our main focus is upon science fiction, particularly of the 'hard' variety, although we also publish weird fantasy of a highly original, unusual nature. If unsure about a story, try us."

ARNAZELLA (II), Arnazella's Reading List, English Department, Bellevue Community College, Bellevue WA 98007. (206)641-2021. Advisor: Roger George. Magazine: 5 × 6; 104 pages, 70 lb paper; heavy coated cover; illustrations and photos. "For those interested in quality fiction." Annually. Estab. 1976. Circ. 500.
Needs: Adventure, contemporary, erotica, ethnic, experimental, fantasy, feminist, gay, historical, humor/satire, lesbian, literary, mainstream, prose poem, regional, religious/inspirational, science fiction, suspense/mystery, translations. Submit in fall and winter for issue to be published in spring. Published new writers within the last year. Publishes short shorts. *Preference may be given to local contributors.*
How to Contact: Send complete ms with cover letter. Reports on mss in spring. "The months of June through October are very hard for us to read mss because we have no staff at that time. The best times to submit are October through January." SASE. Photocopied submissions OK. Accepts computer printout submissions. Sample copy for $5. Fiction guidelines for #10 SAE and 1 first class stamp.
Payment: Pays in contributor's copies.
Terms: Acquires first rights. "Best student story earns $25."
Advice: "Read this and similar magazines, reading critically and analytically."

ART BRIGADE, 2400 Braxton Cove, Austin TX 78741. Editor: Ben Davis. Fiction Editors: Ben Davis and Mark Capps. Tabloid: 11 × 14; 24-32 pages; newsprint paper; book stock cover; illustrations and photographs. "*Art Brigade* exists for the purpose of publishing bold new fiction and poetry, covering personalities in the arts, and helping people link up with other alternative media outlets. For other writers, musicians, independent publishers and artists. Also distributed to college students and others in Texas." Annually. Also publishes *Surface Tension,* quarterly art/fiction supplement with experimental/political focus. Estab. 1987. Circ. 5,000.
Needs: Contemporary, erotica, experimental, fantasy, feminist, gay, horror, humor/satire, lesbian, literary, science fiction, serialized/excerpted novel, translations, political. "No pointless pornographic nonsense, insipid or two-dimensional genre fiction, hate literature, pieces with a specialized perspective, aimless or amateurish ranting, anything incoherent, new age/pseudoscientific gobbledygook." Receives 25 unsolicited fiction mss/month. Accepts approx. 10 mss/issue; 40-50 mss/year. Publishes fiction an average of 1 month after acceptance. Length: 3,500 words averge; 4,500-5,000 words maximum. Publishes short shorts. Sometimes comments on rejected mss and recommends other markets.
How to Contact: Send complete manuscript with cover letter. Reports in 6-8 weeks on mss. Simultaneous, photocopied and reprint submissions OK. Computer printout submissions OK. Sample copy $1; fiction guidelines free.
Payment: Pays in contributor's copies.
Terms: Acquires one-time rights. Sends pre-publication galleys to author.
Advice: "*Art Brigade* strives to be more than a forum for challenging art and fiction. We seek to be an active part of a larger artistic community, boosting regional music and arts, linking illustrators and comic artists with writers, working with writers on special projects and in general providing a place

where our contributors can grow and explore, as well. Be confident and be sure what you are doing is good and worthwhile, and be persistent and aggressive. Any good writer can find an enthusiastic readership if he tries hard enough, and works on his craft. Be original, innovative, and don't rely on the obvious, but seek to teach and reveal as well as teach or shock. Whatever else, be true to your own personal literary instincts, and persevere."

ARTEMIS (IV), An art/literary publication from the Blue Ridge and Virginia, Box 8147, Roanoke VA 24014. (703)365-4326. Contact: Fiction Editors. Magazine: 8×8; 85 pages; heavy/slick paper; colored cover stock; illustrations; photos. "We publish poetry, art and fiction of the highest quality and will consider any artist/writer who lives or has lived in the Blue Ridge or Virginia. General adult audience with literary interest." Annually. Estab. 1976. Circ. 2,000.
Needs: Literary. Wants to see "the best contemporary style." Receives 40 unsolicited fiction mss/year. Accepts 3-4 mss/issue. Does not read mss Jan.-Aug. Publishes ms 4-5 months after acceptance. Published works by Rosanne Coggeshall, Jeanne Larsen, Kurt Rheinheimer; published work by new writers within the last year. Length: 1,500 words average; 2,500 words maximum.
How to Contact: Submit 2 copies of unpublished ms between Sept. 15-Nov. 15, name, address and phone on title page only. Reports in 2 months. SASE for ms. Photocopied submissions OK. Accepts computer printout. No dot-matrix unless high quality. Sample copy $6.50. "Ms not adhering to guidelines will be rejected."
Payment: 1 complimentary copy.
Terms: Acquires first rights.
Advice: "We look for polished quality work that holds interest, has imagination, energy, voice."

ARTFUL DODGE (II), Department of English, College of Wooster, Wooster OH 44691. Editor-in-Chief: Daniel Bourne. Magazine: 100-130 pages; illustrations; photos. "There is no theme in this magazine, except literary power. We also have an ongoing interest in translations from Eastern Europe and elsewhere." Semiannually. Estab. 1979. Circ. 1,000.
Needs: Experimental, literary, prose poem, translations. "We judge by literary quality, not by genre. We are especially interested in fine English translations of significant contemporary prose writers." Receives 40 unsolicited fiction mss/month. Accepts 2-3 mss/issue, 5 mss/year. Recently published fiction by Edward Kleinschmidt, William S. Burroughs and Elizabeth Bartlett; published 2 new writers within the last year. Length: 10,000 words maximum; 2,500 words average. Occasionally critiques rejected mss.
How to Contact: Send complete ms with SASE. Do not send more than 30 pages at a time. Photocopied submissions OK. Reports in 2-3 months. Sample copies of older, single issues are $2.75 or five issues for $5; recent issues are double issues, available for $5.75. Free fiction guidelines for #10 SAE and 1 first class stamp.
Payment: 2 free contributor's copies and small honorarium.
Terms: Acquires first North American serial rights.
Advice: "If we take time to offer criticism, do not subsequently flood us with other stories no better than the first. If starting out, get as many readers, good ones, as possible. Above all, read contemporary fiction and the magazine you are trying to publish in."

‡ASYLUM (II), P.O. Box 6203, Santa Maria CA 93456. Editor: Greg Boyd. Magazine: 5½×8½; 48-112 pages; 10 pt C1S cover. "For a literary audience." Estab. 1985.
Needs: Contemporary, erotica, experimental, literary, prose poem, translations. Publish special fiction issue. Receives 20 unsolicited mss/month. Accepts 5 mss/issue; 25 mss/year. Publishes ms 3-9 months after acceptance. Agented fiction 1%. Publishes short shorts. Rarely critiques rejected mss or recommends other markets. Circ. 500.
How to Contact: Send complete manuscript with cover letter. Reports in 1-4 weeks on queries; 1-4 months on mss. SASE. Sample copy $2.50.
Payment: Pays contributor's copies.
Terms: Acquires first rights. Sends galleys to author.
Advice: "Short, tightly written prose fiction and prose poems stand the best chance of gaining acceptance in *Asylum*. Writers should read the magazine before submitting work."

‡ASYMPTOTE (II), Fiction by Musicians, Essays on Popular Culture, P.O. Box 11627. Memphis TN 38111-0627. Editor: Robert Gordon. Magazine: 8½×11; 40 pages; hi-brite paper; b&w illustrations and photographs. "No theme or guidelines per se. Lengths vary, looking for the thought-provoking pieces and stories not comfortable elsewhere. For a youngish audience—under 45; many are

music listeners." Published 2/3 times/year, or so. Estab. 1988. Circ. 5,000.
Needs: "Will accept all; need not be a musician to contribute. Typed double-spaced preferred. MacIntosh Microsoft word disc preferred." Plans special fiction issue. Accepts 4-8 mss/issue. Recently published work by Ann Magnuson, John Doe, Jim Dickinson, Tav Falco, Mojo Nixon. Publishes short shorts. Sometimes critiques rejected mss and recommends other markets.
How to Contact: Query with clips of published work or send complete manuscript with cover letter and brief bio. Reports on queries in as quickly as 1 week up to 8 months. SASE. Photocopied submissions OK. Accepts computer printout submissions. Accepts electronic submissions. Sample copy $2.
Payment: Pays in free subscription to magazine and contributor's copies.
Terms: Acquires one-time rights. "Sometimes" sends galleys to author.
Advice: "If a piece seems like a rehashed idea or is too common, we're not interested. The cutting edge is just as effective and alive in traditional formats as experimental techniques. We look for things that push boundaries, but do not necessarily need to be experimental."

THE ASYMPTOTICAL WORLD (II), Box 1372, Williamsport PA 17703. Editor: Michael H. Gerardi. Magazine: 8½×11; 54 pages; glossy paper; illustrated cover; b&w illustrations. *"The Asymptotical World* is a *unique* collection of psychodramas, fantasies, poems and illustrations which elucidates the moods and sensations of the world created in the mind of men, for 18 year olds and older; those who enjoy work completed in style and mood similar to Poe." Annually. Estab. 1984. Circ. 1,300.
Needs: Experimental, fantasy, horror, psychic/supernatural/occult. Receives 30 unsolicited fiction mss/month; accepts 10 fiction mss/issue. Publishes ms 6 months to 1 year after acceptance. Length: 1,000 words minimum; 2,000 words maximum.
How to Contact: Query first. SASE. Reports in 1-2 months on queries; 1-2 months on mss. Simultaneous and photocopied submissions OK. Accepts computer printouts. Sample copy $6.95 with SAE and 8 first class stamps. Fiction guidelines for 4x9 SAE and 1 first class stamp.
Payment: Pays $20-50.
Terms: Pays on publication. Acquires first rights.
Advice: *"The Asymptotical World* is definitely unique. It is strongly suggested that a writer review a copy of the magazine to study the format of a psychodrama and the manner in which the plot is left 'open-ended.' The writer will need to study the atmosphere, mood and plot of published psychodramas before preparing a feature work."

ATALANTIK (II, IV), 7630 Deer Creek Drive, Worthington OH 43085. (614)885-0550. Editor: Prabhat K. Dutta. Magazine: 8½×11; approx. 80 pages; paper quality and cover stock vary; illustrations and photos. "The publication is bilingual: Indian (Bengali) and English language. This was started to keep the Indian language alive to the Indian immigrants. This contains short stories, poems, essays, sketches, book reviews, cultural news, children's pages, etc." Quarterly. Plans special fiction issue. Estab. 1980. Circ. 400.
Needs: Adventure, condensed novel, contemporary, ethnic, experimental, historical (general), humor/satire, juvenile (5-9 years), literary, mainstream, psychic/supernatural/occult, romance, science fiction, suspense/mystery, translations, travelogue, especially to India. No politics and religion. Receives 15 unsolicited fiction mss/month. Publishes about 2-4 fiction mss/issue; about 20-50 mss/year. Publishes ms an average of at least 6 months after acceptance. Length: 2,000-5,000 words average. Publishes short short stories. Length: 1-2 pages. Sometimes comments on rejected mss and recommends other markets.
How to Contact: Query with clips of published work or send complete ms with cover letter; "author's bio data and a synopsis of the literary piece(s)." Reports on queries in 1 month; on mss in 4 months. SASE. Photocopied submissions OK. Computer laser printout submissions OK. Sample copy $6; fiction guidelines for #10 SASE.
Payment: Pays in contributor's copies; charge for extras.
Terms: Acquires all rights. Sponsors contests for fiction writers.
Advice: "A short story has to be short and should have a story too. A completely imaginative short story without any real life linkage is almost impossible. The language should be lucid and characters kept to a small number. A short story is not simply the description of an incident. It goes far beyond, far deeper. It should present the crisis of a single problem. Usually a successful short story contains a singular idea which is developed to its most probable conclusion in a uniquely charted path."

ATLANTIS (II), A Women's Studies Journal, Institute for the Study of Women, Mt. St. Vincent University, Halifax, Nova Scotia B3M 2J6 Canada. (902)443-4450. Editors: Susan Clark, Deborah Poff. Magazine: 7½×9½; 170-200 pages; matte quality paper; glossy cover stock; b&w illustrations and photos. "Interdisciplinary women's studies journal, accepts original research and some fiction in French and English for academics and researchers interested in feminism." Semiannually. Estab. 1975. Circ. 800.

Needs: Feminist research and creative work (short stories, poetry, etc.). Receives 20 unsolicited fiction mss/month. Accepts 1-2 mss/issue; 2-4 mss/year. Publishes ms 6-12 months after acceptance. Publishes short shorts. Critiques rejected mss.

How to Contact: Send complete ms with cover letter. Photocopied submissions OK. Accepts computer printouts. Current issue for $10; back issue for $7.50 (Canadian).

Payment: Pays 1 contributor's copy.

Advice: "We welcome and have published work by previously unpublished writers."

ATROCITY (I), Publication of the Absurd Sig of Mensa, 2419 Greensburg Pike, Pittsburgh PA 15221. Editor: Hank Roll. Newsletter: 8½×11; 8 pages; offset 20 lb paper and cover; illustrations; photographs occasionally. Humor and satire for "high IQ-Mensa" members. Monthly. Estab. 1976. Circ. 250.

Needs: Humor/satire. Liar's Club, parody, jokes, funny stories, comments on the absurdity of today's world. Receives 20 unsolicited mss/month. Accepts 5 mss/issue. Publishes ms 3-6 months after acceptance. Published 10 new writers within the last year. Length: 150 words preferred; 650 words maximum.

How to Contact: Send complete ms. "No cover letter necessary if ms states what rights (e.g. first North American serial/reprint, etc.) are offered."Reports in 1 month. SASE. Simultaneous, photocopied and reprint submissions OK. Accepts computer printout submissions; no dot-matrix. Sample copy for 50¢, #10 SAE and 2 stamps.

Payment: Pays with contributor's copies.

Terms: Acquires one-time rights.

Advice: Manuscript should be single spaced, copy ready. Horizontal format to fit on one 8½×11 sheet. "Be funny."

AURA Literary/Arts Review (II), University of Alabama at Birmingham, Box 76, University Center, Birmingham AL 35294. (205)934-3216. Editor: Stefanie Truelove and Adam Pierce. Magazine: 6×9; 150 pages; b&w illustrations and photos. "We publish various types of fiction with an emphasis on short stories. Our audience is college students, the university community and literary-minded adults, the arts community." Semiannually. Estab. 1974. Circ. 1,000.

Needs: Literary, contemporary, science fiction, regional, romance, men's, women's, feminist and ethnic. No mss longer than 7,000-8,000 words. Accepts 3-4 mss/issue. Receives 15-20 unsolicited fiction mss each month. Published works by Nickell Romjue, Josephine Marshall, Rodolfo Tomes; published new writers within the last year. Length: 2,000-8,000 words. Publishes short shorts; length according to editor's decision. Critiques rejected mss when there is time.

How to Contact: Send complete ms with SASE. No simultaneous submissions; please include biographical information. Reports in 2 months. Sample copy $2.50

Payment: 2 free author's copies.

Terms: Acquires first North American serial rights.

Advice: "We welcome experimental or traditional literature on any subject."

AXE FACTORY REVIEW (III), The Axe Factory, Box 11186, Philadelphia PA 19136. (215)331-7389. Editor: Louis McKee. Fiction Editor: Joseph Farley. Magazine: 8×10; 56 pages. Published irregularly. Estab. 1986. Circ. 500.

Needs: Contemporary, erotica, humor/satire, literary. Receives 2-4 unsolicited mss each month. Does not read during the summer. Publishes short shorts. Sometimes critiques rejected mss.

How to Contact: Send complete ms with cover letter. Reports in 2 weeks on queries; 2-6 weeks on mss. SASE. Simultaneous submissions OK. Accepts computer printout submissions; no dot-matrix. Sample copy $5.

Payment: Pays 2 contributor's copies.

Terms: Acquires first rights.

THE AZOREAN EXPRESS (I, IV), Seven Buffaloes Press, Box 249, Big Timber MT 59011. Editor: Art Cuelho. Magazine: 6¾×8¼; 32 pages; 60 lb book paper; 3-6 illustrations/issue; photos rarely. "My overall theme is rural; I also focus on working people (the sweating professions); the American Indian and Hobo; the Dustbowl era; and I am also trying to expand with non-rural material. For rural and library and professor/student, blue collar workers, etc." Semiannually. Estab. 1985. Circ. 600.

Needs: Contemporary, ethnic, experimental, humor/satire, literary, regional, western, rural, working people. Receives 10-20 unsolicited mss/month. Accepts 2-3 mss/issue; 4-6 mss/year. Publishes ms 1-6 months after acceptance. Length: 1,000-3,000 words. Also publishes short shorts 500-1,000 words. "I take what I like; length sometimes does not matter, even when longer than usual. I'm flexible." Sometimes recommends other markets.

How to Contact: "Send cover letter with ms; general information, but it can be personal, more in line with the submitted story. Not long rambling letters." Reports in 1-4 weeks on queries; 1-4 weeks on mss. SASE. Photocopied submissions OK. Accepts computer printouts. Sample copy $3. Fiction guidelines for SASE.

Payment: Pays in contributor's copies. "Depends on the amount of support author gives my press."

Terms: Acquires first North American serial rights. "If I decide to use material in anthology form later, I have that right." Sends pre-publication galleys to the author upon request.

Advice: "There would not be magazines like mine if I was not optimistic. But literary optimism is a two-way street. Without young fiction writers supporting fiction magazines the future is bleak, because the commercial magazines allow only formula or name writers within their pages. My own publications receive no grants. Sole support is from writers, libraries and individuals."

BABY SUE (I), Box 1111, Decatur GA 30031-1111. (404)875-8951. Editor: Don W. Seven. Magazine: 8½ × 11; 20 pages; illustrations and photos. "*Baby Sue* is a collection of music reviews, poetry, short fiction and cartoons," for "anyone who can think and is not easily offended." Bi-annual. Plans special fiction issue. Estab. 1983. Circ. 1,500.

Needs: Erotica, experimental and humor/satire. Receives 5-10 mss/month. Accepts 3-4 mss/year. Publishes ms within 3 months of acceptance. Publishes short shorts. Length: 1-2 single-spaced pages.

How to Contact: Query with clips of published work. Reports in 1 month. SASE. Accepts computer printout submissions. Send one first class stamp for a sample copy.

Payment: Pays 1 contributor's copy.

Advice: "If no one will print your work, start your own publication—it's easy and cheap. It's also a great way to make contact with other people all over the world who are doing the same."

BAD HAIRCUT (II), 3115 S.W. Roxbury, Seattle WA 98126. Editors: Ray Goforth, Kim Goforth. Magazine: 5½ × 8½; 30 pages; illustrations. Published irregularly. Estab. 1987. Circ. 1,000.

Needs: Experimental, humor/satire, prose poem, translations, political, world-conscious. Receives 20 fiction ms/month. Accepts 1-3 mss/issue; 4-12 mss/year. Publishes short shorts. Almost always critiques rejected mss and recommends other markets.

How to Contact: Query with or without clips of published work; send complete ms with cover letter; or "send by special messenger." Reports in 1 week on queries; 2 months on mss. SASE. Simultaneous, photocopied and reprint submissions OK. Accepts computer printout submissions. Sample copy $4. Fiction guidelines for #10 SAE and 1 first class stamp.

Payment: Free subscription to magazine or contributor's copies; charge for extras. Payment "depends on our financial state."

Terms: Acquires first North American serial rights. Rights revert to author.

Advice: "Keep on trying. You reap what you sow. Love is love. Enjoy your life. Always include a nice cover letter describing who you are and why you're sending your stuff to us."

‡BAHLASTI PAPERS (I), The Newsletter of the Kali Lodge, O.T.O., P.O. Box 15038, New Orleans LA 70115. (504)899-7439. Editor: Chén. Newsletter: 8½ × 11; 12 pages; 20 lb. paper; 20 lb. cover; 2 illustrations; occasional photographs. "Mythological, artistic, alternative and political material for the lunatic fringe." Monthly. Estab. 1986. Circ. 200.

Needs: Condensed/excerpted novel, erotica, ethnic, experimental, fantasy, feminist, gay, horror, humor/satire, lesbian, literary, psychic/supernatural/occult, science fiction, serialized novel, suspense/mystery. "We do not publish poetry." Receives 5 unsolicited mss/month. Accepts 2 mss/issue; 24/year. Publishes mss approx. 1 month after acceptance. Recently published work by Steve Canon and Darius James. Publishes short shorts.

How to Contact: Send complete manuscript with cover letter telling "why author is interested in being published in *Bahlasti Papers*." Reports in 2 weeks on queries and 1 month on mss. SASE. Simultaneous, photocopied and reprint submissions OK. Accepts computer printout submissions. Sample copy for $2.25 with 5½ × 8½ and 2 first class stamps.

Payment: Pays free subscription to magazine.
Terms: Publication not copyrighted.
Advice: "We look for the odd point-of-view; the individual; independence of thought; work which breaks down established archetypes and so liberates us from social programming."

‡**BARDIC RUNES,** 424 Cambridge St, Ottawa, Ontario K1S 4H5 Canada. (613)231-4311. Editor: Michael McKenny. Magazine. Estab. 1990.
Needs: Fantasy. "Traditional or high fantasy." Length: 3,500 words or less.
Payment: ½¢/word on acceptance.

‡**BEING (I,IV), A Celebration of Spirit, Mind & Body,** M. Talarico Publications, P.O. Box 417, Oceanside CA 92049-0417. (619)722-8829. Editor: Marjorie E. Talarico. Magazine: Digest size; 40-50 pages; copy paper; vellum cover; black-and-white, pen-and-ink illustrations. "General and New Age short stories, poems and articles for those interested in the correlation of spirit, mind and body to the culmination of being." Quarterly. Estab. 1989. Circ. 300.
Needs: New Age, reincarnation, pagan. Also adventure, ethnic, experimental, fantasy, horror, literary, prose poem, psychic/supernatural/occult, religious/inspirational, science fiction. "Looking for New Age and science fiction stories for children. Length: 500 to 2,500 words. Also need articles on crystals, astrology, magick for a better life, herbs, past and future lives, psychic/metaphysical experiences. No AIDS, drugs or porno stories." Has published special fiction issue and plans one in the future. Receives 50 unsolicited fiction mss/month. Accepts 6-8 mss/issue; 36 mss/year. Does not read mss from October 1 to December 31. Publishes mss 2-4 months after acceptance. Recently published work by Paul Meyers, Sylvia Anders, Ruth Innes. Length: 2,500 words preferred; 300 words minimum; 7,500 words maximum. Publishes short shorts. Length: 650 words. Critiques or comments on rejected mss and recommends other markets.
How to Contact: Send complete mss with cover letter. "I like to know a little bit about the author, credits (if any) and what prompted author to write this particular story." Reports in 8-10 weeks. SASE. Simultaneous, photocopied, reprint and computer printout submissions OK. Sample copy for $3, 7½ × 10¼ SAE and 3 first-class stamps. Fiction guidelines for #10 SAE and 1 first-class stamp.
Payment: Pays in contributor's copies; charges for extras.
Terms: Acquires one-time rights.
Advice: Looks for "Originality! I like to see an author really bend their imagination and keep me wanting to turn the pages. (if there is artwork to go along, I would like to see it.)"

LA BELLA FIGURA (I,II,IV), Box 411223, San Francisco CA 94141-1223. Editor: Rose Romano. Magazine: 8½ × 11; 10 pages. Publishes "work by Italian-American women, mostly about us. We now publish men also." Quarterly. Estab. 1988. Circ. 150.
Needs: Ethnic, feminist, lesbian, literary, prose poem, translations and Italian-American culture and heritage. "It is the purpose of *LBF* to provide a space for a much-neglected group of people. It is our space to share ourselves with each other and to help others understand us." Receives 10-15 mss/ month. Accepts 1-2 mss/issue; 4-8 mss/year. Publishes ms within 3-6 months of acceptance. Recently published work by Maria Mazziotti Gillan, Rina Ferrarelli, Jennifer Lagier and Anna Bart. Length: about 5 double-spaced pages preferred. Publishes short shorts. Sometimes critiques rejected mss and recommends other markets.
How to Contact: Send complete manuscript with cover letter, which should include previous publications and any other credits. Reports within 4 months. No longer use themes. SASE. Photocopied and reprint submissions OK. Accepts computer printout submissions. Sample copy $2.
Payment: Pays 2 contributor's copies; charge for extras.
Terms: Acquires one-time rights.
Advice: "There's not enough work by and about Italian-Americans published yet. The writer must find that space between stereotyped and assimilated. Although any good writing is considered, I'm most interested in work about Italian-American culture."

THE BELLINGHAM REVIEW (II), 1007 Queen St., Bellingham WA 98226. Editor: Susan Hilton. Magazine: 5½ × 8; 64 pages; 60 lb white paper; varied cover stock; photos. "A literary magazine featuring original short stories, novel excerpts, short plays and poetry of palpable quality." Semiannually. Estab. 1977. Circ. 700.

Needs: All genres/subjects considered. Acquires 1-2 mss/issue. Publishes short shorts. Published new writers within the last year. Length: 5,000 words or less. Critiques rejected mss when there is time.
How to Contact: Send complete ms. Reports in 2 weeks to 3 months. Publishes ms an average of 1 year after acceptance. Sample copy $2.
Payment: 1 free author's copy plus 2-issue subscription. Charges $1.50 for extras.
Terms: Acquires first North American serial and one-time rights.
Advice: Mss are rejected for various reasons, "but the most common problem is too much *telling* and not enough *showing* of crucial details and situations. We also look for something that is different or looks at life in a different way."

BELLOWING ARK (II), A Literary Tabloid, Box 45637, Seattle WA 98145. (206)545-8302. Editor: R.R. Ward. Tabloid: 11½×16; 20 pages; electro-brite paper and cover stock; illustrations; photos. "We publish material which we feel addresses the human situation in an affirmative way. We do not publish academic fiction." Bimonthly. Plans special fiction issue. Estab. 1984. Circ. 500.
Needs: Contemporary, literary, mainstream, serialized/excerpted novel. "Anything we publish will be true." Receives 100-150 unsolicited fiction mss/year. Accepts 1-2 mss/issue; 7-12 mss/year. Time varies, but publishes ms not longer than 6 months after acceptance. Recently published work by Kim Silvera Wolterbeek, Grace Cash and Catherine Marley; published new writers within the last year. Length: 3,000-5,000 words average. Publishes short shorts. Sometimes critiques rejected mss and recommends other markets.
How to Contact: No queries. Send complete ms with cover letter and short bio. "I always cringe when I see letters listing 'credits' and stating the 'rights' offered! Such delights indicate the impossible amateur. Many beginners address me by first name—few of my close friends do." Reports in 6 weeks on mss. SASE. Sample copy for $2, 9x12 SAE and 85¢ postage.
Payment: Pays in contributor's copies.
Terms: Acquires first rights.
Advice: "*Bellowing Ark* began as (and remains) an alternative to the despair and negativity of the Workshop/Academic poetry scene; we believe that life has meaning and is worth living—the work we publish reflects that belief. Learn how to tell a story before submitting. Avoid 'trick' endings—they have all been done before and better."

BELOIT FICTION JOURNAL (II), Box 11, Beloit College WI 53511. (608)363-2308. Editor: Clint McCown. Magazine: 6×9; 130 pages; 60 lb paper; 10 pt. CIS cover stock; illustrations and photos on cover. "We are interested in publishing the best contemporary fiction and are open to all themes except those involving pornographic, religiously dogmatic or politically propagandistic representations. Our magazine is for general readership, though most of our readers will probably have a specific interest in literary magazines." Semiannually. Estab. 1985.
Needs: Contemporary, literary, mainstream, prose poem, spiritual and sports. No pornography, religious dogma, political propaganda. Receives 75 unsolicited fiction mss/month. Accepts 8-10 mss/issue; 16-20 mss/year. Replies take longer in summer. Publishes ms within 9 months after acceptance. Length: 5,000 words average; 250 words minimum; 10,000 words maximum. Sometimes critiques rejected mss and recommends other markets.
How to Contact: Send complete ms with cover letter. Reports in 1 week on queries; 1-6 weeks on mss. SASE for ms. Simultaneous and photocopied submissions OK, if identified as such. Accepts computer printouts. Sample copy $5. Fiction guidelines free for #10 envelope and 1 first class stamp.
Advice: "Many of our contributors are writers whose work we have previously rejected. Don't let one rejection slip turn you away from our—or any—magazine."

‡BERKELEY FICTION REVIEW (II), 700 Eshelman Hall, University of California, Berkeley CA 94720. Editors: Jennifer Englander and Bruno Fazzolari. Magazine: journal size; 200 pages; some illustrations and photographs. "We publish fresh, inventive fiction and poetry, as well as non-academic essays." Published annually. Estab. 1981. Circ. 500.
Needs: No "self-consciously trendy fiction." Receives up to 50 unsolicited mss/month. Accepts 8-20 mss/issue. Published work by new writers in the last year. Occasionally critiques rejected mss.
How to Contact: Send complete ms with short author's note. SASE. Photocopied submissions OK. Sample copy $5.
Payment: 1 free contributor's copy.
Advice: "As time in our society becomes a more and more precious commodity it seems to me that short fiction collections and anthologies are gaining ground. However, I am not sure that the fiction itself has responded to this change. I have yet to see short fiction which attempts to be as encompassing

and unifying as the novel. Our goal is to publish innovating new writing which, if it doesn't exemplify perfection, explores possibilities."

BEYOND . . . SCIENCE FICTION & FANTASY (I,II,IV), Other Worlds Books, Box 1124, Fair Lawn NJ 07410. (201)791-6721. Editor: Shirley Winston; Fiction Editor: Roberta Rogow. Magazine: 8½ × 11; 56 pages; illustrations. Science fiction and fantasy fiction, art and poetry. Audience is "mostly adults, some younger." Quarterly. Estab. 1985. Circ. 300.
Needs: Fantasy and science fiction. No pornography. Receives 100 unsolicited mss/month. Accepts 11 mss/issue; 44 mss/year. Publishes ms "up to 2 years after acceptance." Length: 5,000 words average; 500 words minimum; 12,000 words maximum. Publishes short shorts. Sometimes critiques rejected mss and recommends other markets.
How to Contact: Send complete ms with cover letter. Reports in 2 months. SASE. Photocopied submissions OK. Accepts computer printout submissions. Sample copy $4.50; fiction guidelines free for SASE.
Payment: ⅓¢ per word and contributor's copies.
Terms: Pays on publication for first North American serial rights.

BIG TWO-HEARTED (II,IV), Mid-Peninsula Library Cooperative, 424 Stephenson Ave., Iron Mountain MI 49801. (906)774-3005. Editor: Gary Silver. Magazine: 5½ × 8¼; 60 pages; 20 lb bond; 60 lb stock. "Creative, wholesome and understandable stories and poems about nature and the independent human spirit." Published every 4 months. Estab. 1985. Circ. 110.
Needs: Humor/satire, literary, prose poem and regional. No profanity, morbidity or erotica. Receives 3 mss/month. Accepts 3 mss/issue. Publishes ms within 3-6 months of acceptance. Recently published work by John O'Connor and Gene Washington; published new writers within the last year. Length: 2,000 words preferred; 500 words minimum; 3,000 words maximum. Sometimes critiques rejected mss.
How to Contact: Send complete ms with cover letter, which should include a short bio. Reports in 3 months. SASE. Photocopied submissions OK. Accepts computer printout submissions. Sample copy for $1 and 6 × 9 SAE.
Payment: Pays in contributor's copies.
Terms: Acquires all rights (returned to author).
Advice: "Tell a good story. Send us a clean manuscript with double-checked spelling and punctuation. Use of the traditional taboo words is an automatic rejection. Our readers like upbeat stories set in the out-of-doors."

BILINGUAL REVIEW (II, IV), Hispanic Research Center, Arizona State University, Tempe AZ 85287. (602)965-3867. Editor-in-Chief: Gary D. Keller. Scholarly/literary journal of US Hispanic life: poetry, short stories, other prose and theater. Magazine: 7 × 10; 96 pages; 55 lb acid-free paper; coated cover stock. Published 3 times/year. Estab. 1974. Circ. 2,000.
Needs: US Hispanic creative literature. "We accept material in English or Spanish. We publish original work only—no translations." US/Hispanic themes only. Receives 50 unsolicited fiction mss/month. Accepts 3 mss/issue, 9 mss/year. Often critiques rejected mss. Recently published work by Demetria Martínez, Alicia Gaspar de Alba, Tomás Rivera; published work of new writers within the last year.
How to Contact: Send 2 copies of complete ms with SAE and loose stamps. Simultaneous and high-quality photocopied submissions OK. Reports in 1 month on mss. Publishes ms an average of 1 year after acceptance. Sample copy $9.
Payment: 2 contributor's copies. 30% discount for extras.
Terms: Acquires all rights (50% of reprint permission fee given to author as matter of policy).
Advice: "We do not publish literature about tourists in Latin America and their perceptions of the 'native culture.'"

THE BLACK HOLE LITERARY REVIEW (I), 1312 Stonemill Court, Cincinnati OH 45215. (513)821-6670. Editor: Wm. E. Allendorf. Electronic Bulletin Board. "This is an attempt to revolutionize publishing—no paper, no rejection slips, no deadlines. For any person with access to a home computer and a modem." Estab. 1989. Circ. 150.
Needs: "Any or all fiction and nonfiction categories are acceptable. Any size, topic, or inherent bias is acceptable. The only limitation is that the writer will not mind having his piece read, and an honest critique given directly by his readership." Plans future hardcopy anthology. Publishes ms 1-2 days after acceptance. Length: 2,000-10,000 words. Publishes short shorts, poetry, essays. "Critique given if not by editor, then by reader through Email."

How to Contact: Upload as EMAIL to the editor. Cover letter should include "titles, description (abstract), copyright notice." Reports in 1-2 days. Simultaneous submissions OK. Fiction guidelines free.
Payment: Pays in royalties, but charges fee for initial inputting (see below).
Terms: Charges $5 minimum subscription. Submissions cost $.50+ (deducted from subscription). Royalties are accrued each time the piece is read. Contact editor for details. Buys one-time rights.
Advice: "If the concept of the electronic magazine goes over with the public, then the market for fiction is limitless. Any piece that an author has taken the trouble to set to print is worth publishing. However, The Hole is looking for writers that want to be read—not ones that just want to write. The electronic magazine is an interactive medium, and pieces are judged on their ability to inspire a person to read them." Writers interested in submitting should: "Do it. You would be the first to be rejected by The Hole, if we did not use your piece; to make matters easier for all concerned, submit your piece as a ASCII text file via the modem. If you do not have access to a home computer with a modem, buy one, borrow one, steal one. This is the wave of the future for writers."

‡**BLACK ICE (IV)**, Campus Box 494, Boulder CO 80306. (303)492-8947. Editor: Ron Sukenick. Fiction Editor: Mark Amerika. Magazine: 5½ × 8½; 100 pages; glossy cover; photography on cover. "Publishes the most experimental innovative writing being written today for writers, critics, sophisticated readers." Published 3 times/year. Estab. 1984. Circ. 700.
Needs: Experimental, literary, translations. Does not want to see "anything that's not ground-breaking." Plans special fiction issue. Receives 35-50 unsolicited mss/month. Accepts approx. 12 mss/issue; approx. 36 mss/year. Publishes ms 2-4 months after acceptance. Agented fiction 5-10%. Recently published work by Hal Jaffe, Stacey Levine, Phil Henderson, Kathryn Thompson. Sometime critiques rejected mss and recommends other markets.
How to Contact: Send complete manuscript with cover letter. Reports in 1-2 months on queries; 2-3 months on mss. SASE. Simultaneous and photocopied submissions OK. Accepts computer printout submissions. Sample copy $7. Fiction guidelines for #10 SAE and 1 first class stamp.
Payment: "Small payment when grant money permits."
Terms: Buys first rights.
Advice: "Expand your 'institutionalized' sense of what a story should be so that you include (open yourself up to) language play, innovative spatial composition, plots that die trying, de-characterizations whipped up in the food processor, themes barely capable of maintaining equilibrium in the midst of end-of-the-century energy crisis/chaos, etc."

BLACK JACK (I), Seven Buffaloes Press, Box 249, Big Timber MT 59011. Editor: Art Cuelho. "Main theme: Rural. Publishes material on the American Indian, farm and ranch, American hobo, the common working man, folklore, the Southwest, Okies, Montana, humor, Central California, etc. for people who make their living off the land. The writers write about their roots, experiences and values they receive from the American soil." Annually. Estab. 1973. Circ. 750.
Needs: Literary, contemporary, western, adventure, humor, American Indian, American hobo, and parts of novels and long short stories. "Anything that strikes me as being amateurish, without depth, without craft, I refuse. Actually, I'm not opposed to any kind of writing if the author is genuine and has spent his lifetime dedicated to the written word." Buys 5-10 mss/year. Receives approximately 10-15 unsolicited fiction mss/month. Length: 3,500-5,000 words (there can be exceptions).
How to Contact: Query for current theme with SASE. Reports in 1 week on queries, 2 weeks on mss. Sample copy $4.75.
Payment: Pays 1-2 author's copies.
Terms: Acquires first North American serial rights and reserves the right to reprint material in an anthology or future *Black Jack* publications. Rights revert to author after publication.
Advice: "Enthusiasm should be matched with skill as a craftsman. That's not saying that we don't continue to learn, but every writer must have enough command of the language to compete with other proven writers. Save postage by writing first to the editor to find out his needs. A small press magazine always has specific needs at any given time. I sometimes accept material from country writers that aren't all that good at punctuation and grammar but make up for it with life's experience. This is not a highbrow publication; it belongs to the salt-of-the-earth people."

BLACK RIVER REVIEW (II), 855 Mildred Ave., Lorain OH 44052. (216)244-9654. Editor: Kaye Coller. Fiction Editor: Jack Smith. Magazine: 8½ × 11; 60 pages, "quality stock" paper; mat card cover stock; b&w drawings. "Contemporary writing and contemporary American culture; poetry, book reviews, essays on contemporary literature, short stories." Annually. Estab. 1985. Circ. 400.

Needs: Contemporary, experimental, humor/satire and literary. No "erotica for its own sake, stories directed toward a juvenile audience." Accepts up to 5 ms/year. Does not read mss May 1-Dec. 31. Publishes ms no later than July of current year. Recently published work by Willie Smith and Stephen Dunning. Length: up to 3,500 words but will consider up to 4,000 maximum. Publishes short shorts. Sometimes critiques rejected mss and recommends other markets.

How to Contact: Reports on mss no later than July. SASE. Photocopied submissions OK. Sample copy $3 back issue; $3.50 current. Fiction guidelines for #10 SAE and 1 first class stamp.

Terms: Acquires one-time rights.

Payment: Pays in contributor's copies.

Advice: "Since it is so difficult to break in, much of the new writer's creative effort is spent trying to match trends in popular fiction, in the case of the slicks, or adapting to narrow themes ('Gay and Lesbian,' 'Vietnam War,' 'Women's Issues,' etc.) of little and literary journals. An unfortunate result, from the reader's standpoint, is that each story within a given category comes out sounding like all the rest. Among positive developments of the proliferation of small presses is the opportunity for writers to decide what to write and how to write it. My advice is support a little magazine that is both open to new writers and prints fiction you like. 'Support' doesn't necessarily mean 'buy all the back issues,' but, rather, direct involvement between contributor, magazine and reader needed to rebuild the sort of audience that was there for writers like Fitzgerald and Hemingway."

THE BLACK SCHOLAR (II, IV), The Black World Foundation, Box 2869, Oakland CA 94609. (415)547-6633. Editor: Robert Chrisman. Magazine: 7×10; 56+ pages; newsprint paper; glossy, 24 lb cover; illustrations; b&w photos. Magazine on black culture, research and black studies for Afro-Americans, college graduates and students. "We are also widely read by teachers, professionals and intellectuals, and are required reading for many black and Third World Studies courses." Bimonthly. Estab. 1969. Circ. 10,000.

Needs: Literary, contemporary, juvenile, young adult and ethnic. No religious/inspirational, psychic, etc. Receives approximately 75 unsolicited fiction mss each month. Published new writers within the last year. Length: 2,000-5,000 words.

How to Contact: Query with clips of published work and SASE. Reports in 2 months on queries, 1 month on mss.

Payment: 10 author's copies and 1 year's subscription.

Terms: Acquires all rights.

Advice: "Poetry and fiction appear almost exclusively in our annual culture issue (generally, Sept./ Oct. of given year)."

BLACK WARRIOR REVIEW (II), Box 2936, Tuscaloosa AL 35487. (205)348-4518. Editor-in-Chief: Jim Jones. Fiction Editor: Alicia Griswold. Magazine: 6×9; approx. 144 pages; illustrations and photos sometimes. "We publish contemporary fiction, poetry, reviews, essays and interviews for a literary audience." Semiannually. Estab. 1974. Circ. 1,300-2,000.

Needs: Contemporary, literary, mainstream and prose poem. No types that are clearly "types." Receives 100 unsolicited fiction mss/month. Accepts 5 mss/issue, 10 mss/year. Approximately 25% of fiction is agented. Recently published work by Scott Gould, Max Phillips and Lynda Sexson; published new writers within the last year. Length: 7,500 words maximum; 3,000-5,000 words average. Occasionally critiques rejected mss.

How to Contact: Send complete ms with SASE. Photocopied submissions OK. Reports in 2-3 months. Publishes ms 2-5 months after acceptance. Sample copy $4. Free fiction guidelines for SAE and 1 first class stamp.

Payment: $5-10/page and 2 contributor's copies.

Terms: Pays on publication.

Advice: "Become familiar with the magazine(s) being submitted to; learn the editorial biases; accept rejection slips as part of the business; keep trying. We are not a good bet for 'commercial' fiction. Each year the *Black Warrior Review* will award $500 to a fiction writer whose work has been published in either the fall or spring issue, to be announced in the fall issue. Regular submission deadlines are August 1 for fall issue, January 1 for spring issue."

BLACK WRITER MAGAZINE (II), Terrell Associates, Box 1030, Chicago IL 60690. (312)995-5195. Editor: Mable Terrell. Fiction Editor: Herman Gilbert. Magazine: 8½×11; 40 pages; glossy paper; glossy cover; illustrations. "To assist writers in publishing their work." For "all audiences, with a special emphasis on black writers." Quarterly. Estab. 1972.

Needs: Ethnic, historical, literary, religious/inspirational, prose poem. Receives 20 unsolicited mss/month. Accepts 15 mss/issue. Publishes ms on average of 6 months after acceptance. Length: 3,000 words preferred; 2,500 words average; 1,500 words minimum. Sometimes critiques rejected mss and recommends other markets.

How to Contact: Send complete ms with cover letter, which should include "writer's opinion of the work, and rights offered." Reports in 3 weeks. SASE. Simultaneous submissions OK. Does not accept dot-matrix computer submissions. Sample copy for 8½×11 SAE and 70¢ postage. Fiction guidelines for SASE.

Payment: Free subscription to magazine.

Terms: Acquires one-time rights. Sponsors awards for fiction writers. Contest deadline May 30.

Advice: "Write the organization and ask for assistance."

BLATANT ARTIFICE (IV), Hallwalls Annual Anthology of Short Fiction, Hallwalls Contemporary Arts Center, 700 Main St., Buffalo NY 14202. (716)854-5828. Editor: Edmund Cardoni. Magazine: 7×9; 150 pages; high quality paper; glossy 2-color cover; illustrations; photos. "Innovative contemporary short fiction by visitors to our reading series. Fiction writers may submit work to be considered for inclusion in the reading series, but all contributors to the publication must first have been readers in the series." Audience is readers of contemporary fiction, writers, artists. Annually. Estab. 1986. Circ. 1,000.

Needs: Contemporary, erotica, ethnic, feminist, gay, humor/satire, lesbian, literary, excerpted novel, translations only if submitted by the original author, not by the translator, political fiction. No "genre fiction, so-called 'minimalist' fiction, Iowa-style fiction, realistic fiction, yuppie fiction." Receives 2-4 unsolicited mss/month. Buys 30 mss/year. Length: 1,500 words preferred; 1,250 words minimum; 2,500 words maximum. Publishes short shorts. Sometimes critiques rejected mss and recommends other markets.

How to Contact: Submit a résumé, list of publications, readings, awards, etc., and samples of writing to be considered for inclusion in the reading series. All writers invited to do readings will subsequently be invited to submit work to the annual anthology. Reports in 3 months on mss. SASE. Simultaneous and photocopied submissions OK. Published work may be submitted for consideration for inclusion in the reading series. Accepts computer printout submissions. Sample copy for SAE and $10.

Payment: Pays $35. "This is the payment for publication only, but publication ensues from first doing a reading, for which there is a separate, negotiable payment."

Terms: Pays on publication for first or one-time rights. One 3-month writer's residency *for fiction writers only* is occasionally offered, depending on availability of funding in any given year.

Advice: "Be daring or forget it, which means write as only you can write, and not as you perceive others around you (or *out there*) writing; take my word for it, most of them are wrong. Submit work and a résumé to be considered for inclusion in our reading series; if invited to give reading, subsequent publication in *Blatant Artifice* is automatic. Women writers as well as black, hispanic, and other minority writers are particularly encouraged to apply for readings and residencies at Hallwalls."

‡THE BLIZZARD RAMBLER (I), World's Most Unique Magazine, Box 54, Weiser ID 83672. Editor: Ron Blizzard. Fiction Editor: Dale Blizzard. Magazine: 7x8½; 80-120 pages; 20 lb paper; 60 lb cover; no art. Publishes "humor/satire and adventure (SF, fantasy, western), for those who don't take themselves too seriously." Publishes 3-4 issues/yr. Plans special fiction issue. Estab. 1983. Circ. 400.

Needs: Adventure, fantasy, humor/satire, prose poem, suspense/mystery, western. "We also like fictional 'news' stories." No erotica. Receives 35-50 unsolicited mss/month. Buys 70-90 mss/issue; 220-280 mss/year. Publishes ms 6-12 months after acceptance. Recently published work by Kenneth Wisman, Jess Wilbanks, Celeste Paul. Length: 3,000 words preferred; 2,500 words average; 50 words minimum; 8,000 words maximum. Sometimes critiques rejected mss and recommends other markets.

How to Contact: Send complete ms with cover letter. "Cover letter optional." Reports in 4-6 weeks on queries; 1-3 months on mss. Photocopied submissions OK. Accepts computer printout submissions, including dot-matrix. Sample copy for $4 with writer's guidelines. Fiction guidelines for #10 SAE and 1 first class stamp.

Payment: Pays ¼¢/word. Free contributor's copy.

Terms: Pays on acceptance. Acquires first rights. Sends galleys to author if requested.

Advice: "Is it entertaining? Is it a story, or just part of one? Is it clear what's happening? We would like to see old style westerns submitted. Send for a sample copy or writer's guidelines. Aim to entertain and send in the stories."

‡**BLUE LIGHT RED LIGHT (III), A Periodical of Speculative Fiction & the Arts,** Suite F-42, 496A Hudson St., New York NY 10014. (201)432-3245. Publisher: Alma Rodriguez. Magazine: 6×9; 170 pages. Semiannually. Estab. 1989.
Needs: Ethnic, experimental, fantasy, literary, prose poem. No horror, cyber punk. Agented fiction 20%. Publishes short stories. Length 6-8 pages. Recommends other markets.
How to Contact: Send complete manuscript with cover letter. Reports in 3 weeks on queries; 2 months on mss. SASE. Simultaneous and photocopied submissions OK. Accepts computer printout submissions. Sample copy $5.50.
Payment: Pays contributor's copies.
Terms: Acquires first rights.
Advice: "*Blue Light Red Light* is open to any nationality or ethnicity. We accept the finest works of new and established writers, fusing mainstream writing, magic realism and surrealism together with speculative fiction. As an interdiciplinary periodical, we seek not to isolate these genres but to discover the points of contact between them and mainstream writing itself. As contemporary life becomes fragmented, the search for meaning, for personal myths becomes all the more intense. We want to participate in this search for meaning. Everyone interested in *BLRL* should read a copy before submitting their work."

THE BLUE WATER REVIEW (II), 6226 S.W. 10th St., West Miami FL 33144. (305)266-0050. Editor/ Publisher: Dennis M. Ross. Magazine. 5½×7; 45 pages; 60 lb paper; standard cover stock; illustrations and photos. "No theme. We want quality writing: fiction, interviews with well known writers and critics, poetry, and photos." Semiannually. Estab. 1989. Circ. 5,000.
Needs: Adventure, contemporary, ethnic, experimental, humor/satire, literary, mainstream, regional, sports, suspense/mystery. "No pornography, no handwritten or single spaced submissions, no manuscripts without SASE." Receives 15 unsolicited mss/month. Accepts 3-4 mss/issue; 10 mss/year. Publishes ms 1-3 months after acceptance. Agented fiction 10%. Length: 3,000 words maximum. Publishes short shorts. Sometimes critiques rejected mss.
How to Contact: Send complete manuscript with cover letter. Reports in 1 month on queries; 3 months on mss. SASE. Photocopied submissions OK. Fiction guidelines for #10 SAE and 1 first class stamp.
Payment: 1 free contributor's copy; charge for extras.
Terms: Acquires one-time rights.
Advice: "Manuscripts should have classic elements of short story, such as meaningful character change. Submit your best work no matter the publication. We want quality. Use standard form as illustrated in *Writer's Digest* (short stories)."

BLUELINE (II, IV), English Dept., SUNY, Potsdam NY 13676. Editor-in-Chief: Anthony Tyler. Magazine: 6×9; 112 pages; 70 lb white stock paper; 65 lb smooth cover stock; illustrations; photos. "*Blueline* is interested in quality writing about the Adirondacks or other places similar in geography and spirit. We publish fiction, poetry, personal essays, book reviews and oral history for those interested in the Adirondacks, nature in general, and well-crafted writing." Annually. Estab. 1979. Circ. 700.
Needs: Adventure, contemporary, humor/satire, literary, prose poem, regional, reminiscences, oral history and nature/outdoors. Receives 8-10 unsolicited fiction mss/month. Accepts 6-8 mss/issue. Does not read January-August. Recently published fiction by Jeffrey Clapp. Published new writers within the last year. Length: 500 words minimum; 3,000 words maximum; 2,500 words average. Occasionally critiques rejected mss. Sometimes recommends other markets.
How to Contact: Send complete ms with SASE and brief bio. Photocopied submissions OK. Submit mss Aug. 1-Nov. 30. Accepts computer printout submissions, prefers letter-quality. Reports in 2-10 weeks. Publishes ms 3-6 months after acceptance. Sample copy $5.75. Free fiction guidelines for 5×10 SASE with 1 first class stamp.
Payment: 1 contributor's copy. Charges $3 each for 3 or more extra copies; $4 each for less than 3.
Terms: Acquires first rights.
Advice: "We look for concise, clear, concrete prose that tells a story and touches upon a universal theme or situation. We prefer realism to romanticism but will consider nostalgia if well done. Pay attention to grammar and syntax. Avoid murky language, sentimentality, cuteness or folksiness. We would like to see more good fiction related to the Adirondacks. Please include short biography and word count. If manuscript has potential, we work with author to improve and reconsider for publication. Our readers prefer fiction to poetry (in general) or reviews. Write from your own experience, be specific and factual (within the bounds of your story) and if you write about universal features such

as love, death, change, etc., write about them in a fresh way. Triteness and mediocracy are the hallmarks of the majority of stories seen today."

‡BLUR (II), Boston Literary Review, Box 357, W. Somerville MA 02144. (617)625-6087. Editor: Gloria Mindock. Magazine: 5¼×13; 24 pages; 70 lb. offset paper; 80 lb. cover. Contemporary poetry and fiction. Semiannually. Estab. 1985. Circ. 500.
Needs: Contemporary, experimental. "Non-mainstream work that has a strong and unique voice and that takes risks with form or content." Receives 50 unsolicited mss/month. Accepts 1-2 mss/issue; 2-4 mss/year. Publishes ms 6 months-1 year after acceptance. Length: 2,500 words maximum. Publishes short shorts. Sometimes critiques rejected mss.
How to Contact: Send complete manuscript with cover letter. Reports in 2-4 weeks on queries. SASE. Photocopied submissions OK. Sample copy $4.
Payment: Pays 2 contributor's copies.
Terms: Acquires first North American serial rights. Sends galleys to author.

BOGG (II), A Magazine of British & North American Writing, Bogg Publications, 422 N. Cleveland St., Arlington VA 22201. (703)243-6019. U.S. Editor: John Elsberg. Magazine: 9×16; 64-68 pages; 50 lb white paper; 50 lb cover stock; line illustrations. "American and British poetry, prose poems and other experimental short 'fictions,' reviews, and essays on small press." Published 3 times a year. Estab. 1968. Circ. 1,750.
Needs: Very short experimental and prose poem. Nothing over 1 typewritten page. Receives 25 unsolicited fiction mss/month. Accepts 1-2 mss/issue; 3-6 mss/year. Published 50% new writers within the last year. Occasionally critiques rejected mss.
How to Contact: Query first or send ms (2-6 pieces) with SASE. Photocopied submissions OK. Accepts computer printout submissions. Prefers letter-quality. Reports in 1 week on queries; 2 weeks on mss. Publishes ms 3-12 months after acceptance. Length: 300 words maximum. Sample copy $3 or $4 (current issue).
Payment: 2 contributor's copies. Reduced charge for extras.
Terms: Acquires one-time rights.
Advice: "Read magazine first. We are most interested in work of experimental or wry nature to supplement poetry. No longer (with issue #60) accepts traditional narrative short stories."

BOTTOMFISH MAGAZINE (II), Bottomfish Press, Language Arts Division, De Anza College, 21250 Steven Creek Blvd., Cupertino CA 95014. (408)996-4545. Editor-in-Chief: Robert E. Brock. Magazine: 7×8½; 80-100 pages; White Bristol vellum cover; b&w high contrast illustrations and photos. "Contemporary poetry, fiction, excerpts of novels, b&w graphics and photos for literary and writing community." Annually. Estab. 1976. Circ. 500.
Needs: Experimental, literary and prose poem. "Literary excellence is our only criteria. We will consider all subjects except pornography." Receives 10-20 unsolicited fiction mss/month. Accepts 2-3 mss/issue. Does not read mss in summer. Recently published work by Janet Sisk. Length: 500 words minimum; 5,000 words maximum; 2,500 words average.
How to Contact: Send complete ms with cover letter, brief bio and SASE. Photocopied submissions OK. No multiple submissions or reprints. Accepts computer printout submissions, prefers letter-quality. Reports in 8-10 weeks. Publishes ms an average of 6 months-1 year after acceptance. Current issue: $3.50; back issue: $2.50.
Payment: 2 free contributor's copies. Charges $3.50 for extra copies.
Terms: Acquires one-time rights.
Advice: "Strive for orginality and high level of craft; avoid clichéd or stereotyped characters and plots. We don't print slick, commercial fiction, regardless of quality."

BOULEVARD (III), Opojaz Inc., 2400 Chestnut St., Philadelphia PA 19103. (215)561-1723. Editor: Richard Burgin. Magazine: 5½×8½; 150-220 pages; excellent paper; high-quality cover stock; illustrations; photos. "*Boulevard* aspires to publish the best contemporary fiction, poetry and essays we can print." Published 3 times/year. Estab. 1986. Circ. about 2,500.
Needs: Contemporary, experimental, literary, prose poem. Does not want to see "anything whose first purpose is not literary." Receives over 400 mss/month. Buys about 6 mss/issue. Publishes ms less than a year after acceptance. Agented fiction ⅓-¼. Length: 5,000 words average; 10,000 words maximum. Publishes short shorts. Published work by Madison Smartt Bell, Francine Prose, Alice Adams. Sometimes critiques rejected mss and recommends other markets.

How to Contact: Send complete ms with cover letter. Reports in 2 weeks on queries; 2 months or less on mss. SASE. Simultaneous and photocopied submissions OK. Accepts computer printout submissions. Accepts electronic submissions. Sample copy for $5 and SAE with 5 first class stamps.
Payment: Pays $50-150; contributor's copies; charges for extras.
Terms: Pays on publication for first North American serial rights. Does not send galleys to author unless requested.
Advice: "Master your own piece of emotional real estate. Be patient and persistent."

MARION ZIMMER BRADLEY'S FANTASY MAGAZINE, Box 245-A, Berkeley CA 94701. Business Address; P.O. Box 11095, Oakland CA 94611-9991. (415)601-9000. Editors and Publishers: Marion Zimmer Bradley and Jan Burke. Magazine: 8½×11; 64 pages; 60 lb text paper; 10 lb cover stock; b&w interior and 4 color cover illustrations. "Fantasy only; strictly family oriented." Quarterly.
Needs: Adventure, contemporary, fantasy, humor/satire, psychic/supernatural/occult, suspense/mystery and young adult/teen (10-18) (all with fantasy elements). "No avant garde or romantic fantasy. No computer games!" Receives 50-60 unsolicited mss/month. Buys 8-10 mss/issue; 36-40 mss/year. Publishes 3-12 months after acceptance. Agented fiction 5%. Length: 3,000-4,000 words average; 5,000 words maximum. Publishes short shorts. Critiques rejected mss and recommends other markets.
How to Contact: Send complete ms with cover letter "including Social Security number, telephone number and previous credits in the field (only) and personal info. Maximum length 500 words." 1 month on mss. SASE. Photocopied submissions OK. Accepts computer printout submissions; no dot matrix that is hard to read. Sample copy $3.50. Fiction guidelines for 9×12 SAE and 1 first class stamp.
Payment: Pays 3-10¢/word; contributor's copies.
Terms: Pays on acceptance. $25 kill fee "if held 12 months or more." Buys first North American serial rights. Sometimes sends galleys to author.
Advice: "If I want to finish reading it—I figure other people will too. A manuscript stands out if I care whether the characters do well, if it has a rythm. Make sure it has characters I will know *you* care about. If you don't care about them, how do you expect me to?"

‡BRAIN DEAD (II), 4503 Washington St., Kansas City MO 64111. (816)561-3320. Editor: John Bergin. Magazine: 7×8½; 48 pages; 60 lb. bond paper; 60 lb. cover stock; illustrations and photographs. "All kinds of people read *Brain Dead*."
Needs: Experimental, science fiction, horror, weird stuff, poetry, essays, politics. Receives 2-3 unsolicited mss/month. Accepts 1-2 mss/issue; 4-5 mss/year. Publishes ms 3-7 months after acceptance. Length: 500 words average; up to 500 words maximum. Publishes short shorts. Critiques rejected mss and recommends other markets.
How to Contact: Query with clips of published work. Reports in 2 weeks on queries; 3 weeks on mss. SASE. Photocopied and reprint submissions OK. Accepts computer printout submissions. Sample copy for $2. Fiction guidelines for #10 SAE and 1 first class stamp.
Payment: Pays contributor's copies.
Terms: Acquires one-time rights.
Advice: "I don't really have a set of criteria. I'll print it if it moves me . . . if it's a good work, honest, revealing, well-written, different . . . or just interesting. The manuscripts that seem to stand out are the vicious ones. Pieces that bite. And the experimental work. . . ."

BREAKTHROUGH! (II), Aardvark Enterprises, 204 Millbank Dr. S.W., Calgary, Alberta T2Y 2H9 Canada. (403)256-4639. Editor: J. Alvin Speers. Magazine: 5½×8½; 52 pages; bond paper; color paper cover; illustrations. "Up-beat, informative and entertaining reading for general audience—articles, short stories, poetry, fillers and cartoons. General interest—popular with writers and readers for information and entertainment." Quarterly. Estab. 1982. Circ. 200+.
Needs: Adventure, historical (general), humor/satire, literary, regional, religious/inspirational, romance (contemporary, historical, young adult), suspense/mystery. "No pornography, uncouth language, crudely suggestive, gay or lesbian." Receives 25 mss/month. Accepts 8-10 mss/issue; 30-40 mss/year. "Publication time varies with available space, held for season, etc." Length: 1,500 words; 500 words minimum; 2,500 words maximum. Publishes short shorts. Sometimes critiques rejected mss.
How to Contact: Subscribe, or buy sample and submit ms. Include brief bio. Reports in 1 week on queries. SASE. Simultaneous, photocopied and reprint submissions OK. Accepts computer printouts. Sample copy $4. Fiction guidelines for #10 SAE, IRC, Canadian 45¢ stamp, or $1 U.S. quite acceptable.

Payment: By readers' vote small cash honorarium for best 3 items each issue, plus 4th place Honorable Mention Certificate.
Terms: Acquires one-time rights.
Advice: "We look for quality in line with editorial guidelines, clarity of presentation of story or information message. Be familiar with our style and theme—do not submit inappropriate material. We treat submittors with respect and courtesy."

‡**THE BRIDGE (II), A Journal of Fiction & Poetry,** The Bridge, 14050 Vernon St., Oak Park MI 48237. Editor: Jack Zucker. Fiction Editor: Helen Zucker. Magazine: 5½×8½; 120 pages; 60 lb. paper; heavy cover. "Fiction and poetry for a literary audience." Semiannually. Estab. 1990.
Needs: Ethnic, feminist, humor/satire, mainstream, regional. Receives 40 unsolicited mss/month. Buys 5-7 mss/issue; 10-14 mss/year. Publishes ms within one year of acceptance. Length: 3,000 words average; 7,500 words maximum. Publishes short shorts. Length: 1,000 words.
How to Contact: Send complete manuscript with cover letter. Reports in 1 week on queries; 2 months on mss. SASE. Photocopied submissions OK. Accepts computer printout submissions. Sample copy $4 ($5 for 2).
Payment: Pays $5 maximum and contributor's copies.
Terms: Buys first North American serial rights. Will be copyrighted soon.
Advice: "Don't give us fiction intended for a popular/commercial market—we'd like to get 'real literature.' "

‡**BROOMSTICK (II, IV), A National, Feminist Periodical by, for, and About Women Over Forty,** 3543 18th St. #3, San Francisco CA 94110. (415)552-7460. Editors: Mickey Spencer and Polly Taylor. Magazine: 8½x11; 40 pages; line drawings. "Our first priority in selecting and editing material is that it convey clear images of women over 40 that are positive, that it show the author's commitment against the denigration of midlife and long-living women which pervades our culture, and that it offer us alternatives which will make our lives better." For "women over 40 interested in being part of a network which will help us all develop understanding of our life situations and acquire the skills to improve them." Quarterly. Estab. 1978. Circ. 3,000.
Needs: Feminist experience in political context, old women, age, and ageism, humor, ethnic. No mss of "romantic love, nostalgic, saccharine acceptance, by or about men or young women." Receives 10 unsolicited fiction mss/month. Accepts 2-3 mss/issue; 20 mss/year. Recently published work by Astro, Wilma Elizabeth McDaniel, Ruth Harriet Jacobs; published new writers within the last year. Recommends magazine subscription before sending ms. Critiques rejected mss.
How to Contact: Send complete mss with 2 SASEs. Simultaneous, photocopied and previously published submissions OK. Accepts computer printout submissions. Prefers letter-quality. Reports in 3 months on queries and mss. Sample copy for $5. Writer's guidelines for 50¢ or SASE.
Payment: 2 free contributor's copies; $3.50 charge for extras.
Advice: "Don't use stereotypes to establish character. Give protagonists names, not just roles (e.g. 'mother'). Avoid using "you," which sounds preachy. Read our editorials."

BVI-PACIFICA NEWSLETTER (I), Tahuti/Quetzlcoatl Press, Box 45792, Seattle WA 98145-0792. (206)547-2364 or 547-2202. Editor: Yael Dragwyla. Magazine: 5½×8½; 32-36 pages; 20 lb paper; 60 lb cover; illustrations; some photographs. "Theme: Breaking new trails in the Inner Planes (world of the mind)." Quarterly. Plans special fiction issue. Estab. 1985. Circ. 200+.
Needs: Erotica, experimental, fantasy, horror, humor/satire, psychic/supernatural/occult, science fiction, serialized/excerpted novel, suspense/mystery, SubGenius. "We want fiction, humor, poetry or graphics that make the mind turn unusual or new corners—like juxtaposition of dissonant material such that it almost makes sense—like good satire, with Punkeon, SubGenius or end-of-the-world overtones. No romance, children's, New Ager or Norman Vincent Peale-type inspirational, anything saccharine." Receives 1-2 unsolicited mss/month. Accepts 6-12 mss/issue; 6-24 mss/year. Publishes ms 3 months-1 year after acceptance. Length: 450 words preferred; 100 words minimum; 1,000 words maximum. Sometimes critiques rejected mss and recommends other markets.
How to Contact: Send complete ms with cover letter. Reports in 1-4 weeks. SASE. Simultaneous, photocopied and reprint submissions OK. Accepts computer printout submissions. Sample copy for $2.50.

Payment: Pays in contributor's copies.

Terms: Acquires first North American serial rights.

Advice: "Write with your heart as well as your head. As the state of the world today is both horrifying and disgusting in many places and respects, often the most honest and gripping fiction and the best humor deals with the terror and anger this provokes, head-on. We want fiction, humor, poetry and graphics that free up and change the mind, so that the actions underlaid by mind will change, and in the changing, maybe open up new cracks in the Cosmic Egg."

BYLINE (II), Box 130596, Edmond OK 73013. (405)348-5591. Editor-in-Chief: Marcia Preston. Managing Editor: Kathryn Fanning. Monthly magazine "aimed at encouraging and motivating all writers toward success, with special information to help new writers." Estab. 1981.

Needs: Literary, suspense/mystery and general fiction. Especially like stories with a literary or writing twist. Receives 50-75 unsolicited fiction mss/month. Accepts 1 ms/issue, 12 mss/year. Recently published work by C.C. Howerton and Jennifer Gostin. Published many new writers within the last year. Length: 4,000 words maximum; 1,000 words minimum.

How to Contact: Send complete ms with SASE. Photocopied submissions OK. "For us, no cover letter is needed." Reports in 2-6 weeks. Publishes ms an average of 3 months after acceptance. Sample copy, guidelines and contest list for $3.

Payment: $50 and 2 free contributor's copies.

Terms: Pays on acceptance for first North American rights.

Advice: "We're very open to new writers. Submit a well-written, professionally prepared ms with SASE. No erotica or senseles violence; otherwise, we'll consider most any theme. Writing connection is a plus. We also sponsor short story and poetry contests."

‡CACANADADADA REVIEW (II), P.O. Box 1283, Port Angeles WA 98362. (206)457-8001. Editor: Jack Estes. Magazine: 5½×8½; 50 pages; 55 lb paper; good cover stock; illustrations; photographs. "Irreverent and satiric works for a college-age, educated audience with a sense of humor." Semiannual. Estab. 1990. Circ. 300.

Needs: Confession, contemporary, erotica, experimental, fantasy, humor/satire, literary, prose poem, science fiction and translations. "No heavy, boring stories. Nothing 'anarchist,' violently sexual or handwritten." Receives 6-8 unsolicited mss/month. Buys 4 mss/issue; 8 mss/year. Publishes ms 6 months after acceptance. Recently published work by Ken Nattinger, Shari McNabb, Celia Lustgarten. Length: 1,000 words average; 100 words minimum; 3,000 words maximum. Publishes short shorts. Length: 200-300 words. Sometimes critiques rejected mss.

How to Contact: Send complete manuscript with cover letter. Reports in 2 months. SASE. Accepts simultaneous and photocopied submissions, reprints and computer printouts. Accepts electronic submissions via disk. Sample copy $4. Fiction guidelines for SASE.

Payment: Pays $2-20 and 2 contributor's copies.

Terms: Pays on publication for one-time rights.

Advice: "A piece must be unusual in form or content, i.e., biting or humorous or both. Read an issue first—ours is unusual."

CACHE REVIEW (II), Cache Press, Box 19794, Seattle WA 98109-6794. (206)789-2073. Editor: Steven Brady. Magazine: 8½×11; 50 pages; 20 lb bond paper; classic laid cover; cover photos and illustrations. Magazine which publishes "quality writing in all styles." Published irregularly. Estab. 1982. Circ. 200-500.

Needs: Experimental, fantasy, historical (general), horror, humor/satire, mainstream, prose poem, regional, science fiction, serialized/excerpted novel, sports, suspense/mystery and translations. Receives 10-20 unsolicited fiction mss/month. Accepts 3-6 mss/issue, 6-12 mss/year. Does not read June-August. Recently published work by Jacques Servin, David Mouat, Jim Finley. Length: 10,000 words maximum. Publishes short shorts.

How to Contact: Send complete ms with SASE. Photocopied submissions OK, "but we prefer the original." Accepts computer printout submissions; prefers letter-quality. Reports in 1 month on mss. Publishes ms 6-12 months after acceptance. Sample copy $3.50.

Payment: 2 free contributor's copies; $3.00 charge for extras.

Terms: All rights revert to the author. "Cash awards may be presented for the best pieces of fiction and/or poetry in each issue."

Advice: "Send your best. Don't be afraid to experiment, but remember that editors have seen all the tricks."

Close-up

Marcia Preston
Editor-in-Chief
Byline

The process by which *Byline* magazine evolved is an inspiring one. Introduced in 1981 as a newsletter for new writers, it immediately filled a void in the Oklahoma writing community. *Byline* gradually developed into a slick-cover magazine subsidized primarily by subscriptions, with little advertising. Eventually, a decrease in subscription numbers threatened the existence of the magazine.

At that critical juncture in 1985, Marcia Preston, who had been a supporter of *Byline* since its introduction, stepped in and purchased the magazine. Preston, a graduate of Central Oklahoma State University with a degrees in creative writing and English, was teaching high school English and was eager to become more involved in a writing career. She recalls, "I had always been a supporter of *Byline* and saw its great potential, even though it (the magazine) was slipping. I decided to purchase it because I saw it as an opportunity to pursue a career that involved writing. It was a way to further my own interest in writing, as well as a way to help other writers."

Immediately, she and Managing Editor Katherine Fanning tackled the circulation problem. They instituted a program of state representatives to promote *Byline* in other states across the country. With these improvements underway, Preston began to focus on improving the editorial content, as well as the physical quality, of the magazine.

Today *Byline* is published monthly and regularly features works of fiction, nonfiction and poetry, as well as motivational and "how-to" articles. Preston receives approximately 50-75 fiction manuscripts per month, but publishes only one per issue. While she accepts all types of general, short fiction (with the exception of any that include gratuitous sex or violence), she prefers literary, genre, women's and popular fiction. Preston looks specifically for pieces that are well-crafted and convincing, with "believable characters— characters that I can really care about in the first paragraph." Preston advises new writers to actively peruse current literary magazines to familiarize themselves with the types of fiction being published. "If a writer is widely-read in fiction, he or she is aware of the things that have become clichés," she says.

Although her duty as editor-in-chief of *Byline* is a full-time endeavor, Preston diligently pursues a freelance writing career in her spare moments. Her fiction has been published in magazines such as *'Teen* and *Woman's World*. Aware of the struggles inherent in being a writer, Preston applies this fundamental empathy to *Byline's* philosophy: "We really believe that almost anyone with a good grasp of craft can succeed as a writer at his or her own particular level. It isn't always major talent that makes a writer succeed, it is the drive and the willingness to work towards succcss."

—Roseann Shaughnessy

CAESURA (I), English Dept., 9030 Haley Center, Auburn University, Auburn AL 36849. (205)844-4620. Editor: Lex Williford. Fiction Editor: Tess Scogan. Magazine: 6×9; 60-80 pages. Literary journal of fiction, creative non-fiction and poetry, for a college-educated audience. Annually. Estab. 1984. Circ. 600.

Needs: Contemporary, literary, mainstream. Does not want to see work by any whose goal is to fit a genre formula. Receives 10 unsolicited mss/month. Accepts 3-6 mss/issue; 12-15/year. Does not read mss in summer. Deadline for each year's issue: January 15. Publishes ms 3-9 months after acceptance. Length: 3,000 words average; 2,000 words minimum; 7,500 words maximum. Publishes short shorts. Occasionally critiques rejected ms.

How to Contact: Send mss, SASE. Reports in 1-2 months. Accepts computer printout submissions. Sample copy $3.

Payment: Free subscription to magazine and contributor's copies. Payment varies, based upon funding.

Terms: Acquires one-time rights. Holds annual contest for short stories.

Advice: "We're looking for stories with a strong sense of scene and dramatic structure—rising action, complications, and reversals—and a subtle lyricism. Surprise us."

IL CAFFÉ (II, IV), The Italian Experience, 900 Bush, #418, San Francisco CA 94109. (415)928-4886. Editor: R.T. LoVerso. Magazine: 8×12; 36 pages; illustrations and photos. Publishes serialized novels, short stories, interviews, politics, economy and art for American and Italian-American professional people. Bimonthly. Estab. 1981. Circ. 20,000.

Needs: Adventure, comics, condensed novel, confession, contemporary, ethnic, humor/satire, literary, mainstream, prose poem, romance (contemporary, historical, young adult), serialized/excerpted novel and translations. Receives 5 unsolicited mss/month. Accepts 1-2 mss/issue; 6-12 mss/year. Recently published work by Masini; published new writers within the last year. Length: 3,000 words average. Also publishes short shorts. Occasionally critiques rejected mss.

How to Contact: Send complete ms with SASE. Reports in 1 month. Publishes ms 2-6 months after acceptance. Simultaneous, photocopied and previously published submissions OK. Accepts computer printout submissions, prefers letter-quality. Sample copy $2.25.

Payment: Pays in contributor's copies; $1.25 charge for extras.

Terms: Acquires first rights. Buys reprints.

Advice: Fiction should reflect "international views."

‡CALAPOOYA COLLAGE, Box 309, Monmouth OR 97361. Fiction Editor: John Hart. Tabloid: 12x16; 40 pages; b&w photographs. Annually. Estab. 1975. Circ. 1,500.

Needs: Mainstream, Native American. Receives 20-30 unsolicited mss/year. Accepts 1 or 2 mss/issue. Does not read mss in summer. Length: 1,600 words preferred; 1,200 words minimum; 2,000 maximum. Publishes short shorts. Sometimes recommends other markets. "We receive over 3,000 submissions a year—mostly poetry."

How to Contact: Send complete ms with cover letter. Reports in 2 months on mss. SASE. Does not accept dot-matrix computer printouts. Sample copy $4.

Payment: Pays in contributor's copies.

‡CALIFORNIA QUARTERLY (I), 100 Sproul Hall, U.C. Davis, Davis CA 95616. Senior Editor: Elliot L. Gilbert. Managing Editor: Debbie Perreaux Collins. Magazine: 6×10; 80 pages; "book quality" paper; glossy cover; drawings and glossy photos. Magazine for fiction, poetry and graphics. Estab. 1971.

Needs: Contemporary, experimental and literary. Receives approximately 300 mss/month. Does not read mss from June to the end of September. Published new writers within the last year. Length: 8,000 words average.

How to Contact: Send complete manuscript. Reports in 4-6 weeks on mss. SASE. Photocopied submissions OK. Accepts computer printout submissions. Sample copy $4.

Payment: 1 contributor's copy plus $3/page for prose.

Terms: Pays on publication for first North American serial rights.

Advice: "We suggest that you read our publication to familiarize yourself with the range and quality of acceptable work. We do not publish genre work (e.g., science fiction, romance). Professional-quality graphics, poetry, and short fiction with substance, texture, heart, wit and craft stand a good chance of being published."

CALLALOO (II, IV), A Journal of Afro-American and African Arts and Letters, Dept. of English, University of Virginia, Charlottesville VA 22903. (804)924-6637. Editor: Charles H. Rowell. Magazine: 7×10; 200 pages. Scholarly magazine. Quarterly. Plans special fiction issue in future. Estab. 1976. Circ. 1,000.
Needs: Contemporary, ethnic (black culture), feminist, historical (general), humor/satire, literary, prose poem, regional, science fiction, serialized/excerpted novel, translations. Accepts 3-5 mss/issue; 10-20 mss/year. Length: no restrictions. average.
How to Contact: Submit complete ms and cover letter with name and address. Reports on queries in 2 weeks; 2-3 months on mss. Simultaneous and photocopied submissions OK. Previously published work "occasionally" OK. Accepts computer printout submissions. Sample copy $5.
Payment: Pays in contributor's copies.
Terms: Acquires all rights. Sends galleys to author.

CALLIOPE (II, IV), Creative Writing Program, Roger Williams College, Bristol RI 02809. (401)253-1040, ext 2217. Co-ordinating Editor: Martha Christina. Magazine: 5½×8½; 40-56 pages; 50 lb offset paper; vellum or 60 lb cover stock; occasional illustrations and photos. "We are an eclectic little magazine publishing contemporary poetry, fiction, and occasionally interviews." Semiannually. Estab. 1977. Circ. 300.
Needs: Literary, contemporary, experimental/innovative. "We try to include 2 pieces of fiction in each issue." Receives approximately 10-20 unsolicited fiction mss each month. Does not read mss mid-March to mid-August. Published new writers within the last year. Length: 3,750 words. Publishes short shorts under 15 pages. Critiques rejected mss when there is time.
How to Contact: Send complete ms with SASE. Reports immediately or up to 3 months on mss. Sample copy $1.
Payment: 2 free author's copies and one year's subscription beginning with following issue.
Terms: Rights revert to author on publication.
Advice: "We are not interested in reading anyone's very first story. If the piece is good, it will be given careful consideration. Reading a sample copy of *Calliope* is recommended. Let the characters of the story tell their own story; we're very often (painfully) aware of the writer's presence. Episodic is fine; story need not (for our publication) have traditional beginning, middle and end."

‡CALYPSO (II), Journal of Narrative Poetry and Poetic Fiction, 175 E. Washington #C, El Cajon CA 92020. Editor: Susan Richardson. Magazine: 6×9; 60-100 pages; 70# French linen paper; 65# French linen cover. "Theme: How the characteristics of poetry can strengthen fiction and vice versa. Types: narrative and lyric poetry, poetic and other types of fictions, essays, book reviews for readers of contemporary literature; scholars." Annually. Estab. 1989. Circ. 200.
Needs: Contemporary, experimental, literary, mainstream, prose poem, poetic fiction. No religious/inspirational. Receives 40 unsolicited mss/month. Accepts 7-10 mss/issue; 7-10 mss/year. Does not read July through December. Publishes ms 1 month-1 year after acceptance. Recently published work by William R. Johnson, Paul Milenski, Ilán Stavans, David Hopes, Lu Vickers. Publishes short shorts. Sometimes critiques rejected mss and recommends other markets.
How to Contact: Send manuscript; no cover letter required. "We request biographical notes on acceptance." Reports in 1 week on queries and 1-2 months on mss. SASE. Photocopied submissions OK. Accepts computer printout submissions "only if readable." Sample copy for $6. Fiction guidelines for SAE and 1 first class stamp.
Payment: Pays in contributor's copies.
Terms: "Rights revert to author after publication as long as appearance in *Calypso* is acknowledged in subsequent anthologization."
Advice: "Poetic fiction uses the characteristics of poetry: rhythm, imagery, figurative language, etc. and other characteristics such as described in *Calypso 2*'s upcoming essay, 'Toward a Definition of Poetic Fiction,' by Angus Woodward."

CANADIAN AUTHOR & BOOKMAN (II), Canadian Authors Association, Suite 104, 121 Avenue Rd., Toronto, Ontario M5R 2G3 Canada. (416)926-8084. Editor: Gordon Symons. Magazine: 8½×11; 32 pages; illustrations; photos. "Craft magazine for Canadian writers, publishing articles that tell how to write and where to sell. We publish half a dozen poems and one short story per issue as well as the craft articles. We aim at the beginning or newly emerging writer." Quarterly. Estab. 1921. Circ. 3,000.
Needs: Contemporary, humor/satire, literary. "Will not accept writing for children or 'young' adult market." Receives 100-200 unsolicited mss/year. Buys 8-10 mss/issue, 30-40 mss/year. Publishes ms 3-6 months after acceptance. Published new writers within the last year. Length: 2,500 words average;

2,000 words minimum; 3,000 words maximum. Occasionally recommends other markets.
How to Contact: Send complete ms with cover letter, which should include introduction and brief bio. Reports in 1-2 weeks on queries; 1-2 months on mss. SASE. Photocopied submissions OK. Accepts computer printout submissions. Sample copy $4.50, 9 × 12 SAE and IRC. Fiction guidelines #10 SAE and IRC.
Payment: "Our magazine publishes one short-fiction piece per issue, which receives the Okanagan Short Fiction Award of $125 Canadian funds." Contributor's copy to the author.
Terms: Pays on publication for first North American serial rights.
Advice: "We are looking for originality, flair and imaginative work. The writer's strategy is examined from the overall structure, to the rise and fall of the sentences to the placement of the punctuation. For more specific information, send $2.50 Canadian funds to the Canadian Authors Association with your request for a reprint of *The Green Glad Bag Review*, by Geoff Hancock."

CANADIAN FICTION MAGAZINE (II,IV), Box 946, Station F, Toronto, Ontario M4Y 2N9 Canada. Editor: Geoffrey Hancock. Magazine: 6×9; 148-300 pages; book paper; overweight cover stock; 16-32 page portfolio. "This magazine is a quarterly anthology devoted exclusively to the contemporary creative writing of writers and artists in Canada and Canadians living abroad. Fiction only, no poetry. The ideal reader of *CFM* is a writer or somebody interested in all the modes, manners, voices, and conventions of contemporary fiction." Quarterly. Estab. 1971. Circ. 1,800.
Needs: Literary. "Theme, style, length and subject matter are at the discretion of the author. The only requirement is that the work be of the highest possible literary standard." Buys 10 mss/issue, 35 mss/year. Publishes short shorts. Published new writers within the last year.
How to Contact: Send complete ms with SASE or IRC. Reports in 6 weeks on mss. Publishes ms up to 18 months after acceptance. "It is absolutely crucial that three or four issues be read. We sell back issues up to 1976 for $3; current issue $9.95 (postage included). Some double issues are $15. CFM Writers Kit: Guidelines, reading list and selected back issues available ($60 resource) for only $30." (Canadian funds.)
Payment: $10/page (Canadian) plus one-year subscription.
Terms: Pays on publication for first North American serial rights. Sends galleys to author.
Advice: "*CFM* publishes Canada's leading writers as well as those in early stages of their careers. A wide knowledge of contemporary literature (in English and in translation) plus expertise in creative writing, modern fiction theories, current Canadian literature, and the innovative short story would be of great help to a potential contributor. *CFM* is an independent journal not associated with any academic institution. Each issue includes French-Canadian fiction in translation, interviews with well-known Canadian writers on the techniques of their fiction, forums and manifestoes on the future of fiction, as well as art work and reviews. $500 annual prize for the best story submitted in either French or English. Contributors might study anthology spin-offs, such as *Magic Realism; Illusion: Fables, Fantasies* and *Metafictions; Shoes and Shit: Stories for Pedestrians; Canadian Writers at Work: Interviews* or *Singularities: Physics and Fiction.*"

‡CAN(N)ON MAGAZINE (II), P.O. Box 3132, Winnipeg, Manitoba R3C 4E6 Canada. Magazine: 5½×8½; 50 pages; illustrations 4-5 full pages; photographs. "Innovative, experimental, challenging." Quarterly. Estab. 1990.
Needs: Confession, contemporary, erotica, experimental, fantasy, feminist, gay, humor/satire, lesbian, prose poem, psychic/supernatural/occult, science fiction, suspense/mystery. "Our mandate: To publish, promote and create a forum for works which are innovative in form and/or content; work which challenges existing boundaries or 'types'; (also) work which is exemplary in an established medium." No fiction more than (approx.) 2,000 words. Receives 15 unsolicited mss/month. Buys 12-36 mss/year. Reports within 3 months. Length: 2,000 words maximum. Publishes short shorts.
How to Contact: Send complete manuscript with cover letter. Publishable bio of author if work is accepted. Reports on mss in 3 months. SASE. Photocopied submissions OK. Accepts computer printout submissions via disk. Sample copy for $5 (Canadian). Fiction guidelines for #10 SAE; International Reply Coupon or appropriate stamp rate.
Payment: Pays in contributor's copies.
Terms: Rights reverted to author.

THE CARIBBEAN WRITER (IV), The Caribbean Research Institute, RR 02, Box 10,000—Kingshill, St. Croix, Virgin Islands 00850. (809)778-0246. Magazine: 6×9; 110 pages; 60 lb paper; glossy cover stock; illustrations and photos. "*The Caribbean Writer* is an international magazine with a Caribbean focus.

The Caribbean should be central to the work, or the work should reflect a Caribbean heritage, experience or perspective." Annually. Estab. 1987. Circ. 1,500.

Needs: Contemporary, historical (general), humor/satire, literary, mainstream and prose poem. Receives 300 unsolicited mss/year. Accepts 10 mss/issue. Length: 300 words minimum; 3,750 words maximum.

How to Contact: Send complete ms with cover letter. "Blind submissions only. Send name, address and title of ms on separate sheet. Title only on ms. Mss will not be considered unless this procedure is followed." Reports "once a year." SASE. Simultaneous and photocopied submissions OK. Accepts computer printout submissions. Sample copy for $7 and $2 postage. Fiction guidelines for SASE.

Payment: 1 contributor's copy.

Terms: Acquires one-time rights.

A CAROLINA LITERARY COMPANION (II), Community Council for the Arts, Box 3554, Kinston NC 28501. (919)527-2517. Editors: Nellvena Duncan Eutsler, Mike Parker. Magazine: 5½×8½; 65-75 pages; 80 lb matte paper; 80 lb card matte cover. "The original focus of the magazine was on providing a forum for NC writers, but that emphasis has been expanded to include both established and emerging writers from any geographic area. Priority is given to manuscripts submitted by writers living in or natives of the following states: Alabama, Florida, Georgia, Kentucky, Maryland, North Carolina, South Carolina, Tennessee, Virginia, West Virginia. Subscriptions are held by individuals, academic and public libraries." Annually. Estab. 1985. Circ. 500.

Needs: Adventure, contemporary, ethnic, historical, humor/satire, literary, mainstream, regional, senior citizen/retirement, suspense/mystery. No horror stories, religious material, children's/teenager's stories, erotic or specifically sexually oriented fiction. Receives 10-15 unsolicited mss/month. Accepts 5-6 mss/issue; 10-12 mss/year. "Recently published work by Ron Rash, who won a General Electric Foundation 1987 Award for Younger Writers, sponsored by The Coordinating Council of Literary Magazines." Published new writers within the last year. Publishes short-shorts.

How to Contact: Send complete ms with cover letter including brief bio. statement and SASE for return of ms. Reports in 1-2 weeks on queries; 2-4 months on mss. Photocopied submissions OK. Accepts computer printout submissions. Sample copy for $4.25, 6×9 SAE and 3 first class stamps.

Payment: Pays in contributor's copies.

Advice: "Submit! Just be sure your manuscript is legible, correctly spelled and correctly punctuated (the number of illegible and/or misspelled/mispunctuated submissions we receive is appalling). Fiction published in *A Carolina Literary Companion* is limited by space requirements to short and short-short stories. We are committed to providing a forum for emerging Southern writers in particular."

CAROLINA QUARTERLY (II), Greenlaw Hall CB #3520, University of North Carolina, Chapel Hill NC 27599-3520. (919)962-0244. Editor-in-Chief: David Kellogg. Fiction Editor: William Keith Hall. Literary journal: 90-100 pages; illustrations; photos. "Fiction, poetry, graphics and some reviews, for that audience—whether academic or not—with an interest in the best in poetry and short fiction." Triquarterly. Estab. 1948. Circ. 1,000.

Needs: No pornography. Receives 150-200 unsolicited fiction mss/month. Buys 5-7 mss/issue, 15-20 mss/year. Publishes ms an average of 10 weeks after acceptance. Recently published work by Ian MacMillan, Jessica Weber, Rick Bass. Published new writers within the last year. Length: 7,000 words maximum; no minimum; no preferred length. Also publishes short shorts. Occasionally critiques rejected mss.

How to Contact: Send complete ms with cover letter (no synopsis of story) and SASE to fiction editor. Photocopied submissions OK. Reports in 2-4 months. Sample copy $4; Writer's guidelines for SASE and $1 postage.

Payment: $3/printed page; 2 free contributor's copies. Regular copy price for extras.

Terms: Pays on publication for first North American serial rights.

Advice: "We publish a good many unsolicited stories and yes, I love publishing a new writer for the first time; *CQ* is a market for newcomer and professional alike. Write 'Fiction Editor' on envelope of submitted manuscript. Keep story to decent length—it's hard to publish very long stories. Also—read what gets published in the journal/magazine you're interested in. Write the kind of story you would like to read. Make your packet look professional yet modest."

CAROUSEL LITERARY ARTS MAGAZINE (II), Room 217, University of Guelph, Guelph, Ontario N1G 2S1 Canada. Editor: Michael Carbert. Magazine: 5½×8½; 80 pages; illustrations and photographs. Annually. Estab. 1985. Circ. 500.

Needs: Adventure, contemporary, ethnic, experimental, fantasy, feminist, gay, horror, humor/satire, lesbian, literary, prose poem, religious/inspirational, romance, science fiction, sports, suspense/mystery and western. Receives 5 unsolicited mss each month; accepts 5-6 mss per issue. Publishes ms 1-2 months after acceptance. Recently published work by Leon Rooke and J.J. Steinfield. Length: 3,000 words maximum. Publishes short shorts of 1,500-2,000 words.
How to Contact: Include bio with manuscript. Reports in 2 weeks on queries; 2 months on mss. SASE. Simultaneous and photocopied submission OK. Accepts computer printout submissions. Sample copy $3.50 (Canadian) and 2 first class stamps. Fiction guidelines for SAE.
Payment: Pays in contributor's copies.
Terms: Acquires one-time rights.
Advice: "We want work which takes chances in style, point of view, characterization. We are open to new writers."

CATHEDRAL OF INSANITY (II), 1216 W. Ivesbrook, Lancaster CA 93534. Editor: Julie Luce. Magazine: 5½ × 8½; 120 pages; illustrations. "The theme is mainly humor with a bit of seriousness. Publishes short stories and poetry for underground intellectuals." Irregular. Estab. 1988. Circ. 50.
Needs: Contemporary, experimental, humor/satire, psychic/supernatural/occult, serialized/excerpted novel and strange personal experiences. "I would like something with an underground or avant-garde feel. Nothing mainstream." Accepts 1 ms/issue; 2 mss/year. Publishes ms within 1-2 months of acceptance. Publishes short shorts. Sometimes critiques rejected mss.
How to Contact: Query with clips of published work. Reports in 2 weeks. Simultaneous and reprint submissions OK. Accepts computer printout submissions. Sample copy for $2 — cash or check payable to Julie Luce. Fiction guidelines free.
Payment: No payment.
Advice: "Send some work. My magazine is eager for material. Short-shorts are best, nothing over 3 pages. Something humorous/satirical (I am fond of word play) or unnatural (drug experiences) is a good thing to send."

CEILIDH (II), An Informal Gathering for Story & Song, Box 6367, San Mateo CA 94403. (415)591-9902. Editors: Patrick S. Sullivan and Perry Oei. Associate Editor: Denise E. Sullivan. Magazine: 5½ × 8½; 32-64 pages; illustrations. "We are a growing literary magazine looking for literary fiction, drama and poetry." Quarterly. Two issues annually devoted to fiction. Estab. 1981. Circ. 500.
Needs: Experimental, literary, prose poem, science fiction, serialized/excerpted novel and translations. No romance, juvenile, erotica, preschool or young adult. Receives 25 unsolicited mss/month. Accepts 5 mss/issue; 10-12 mss/year. Published work by Karlton Kelm and Anne Brashler. Published new writers within the last year. Length: 3,000 words average; 6,000 words maximum. Also publishes short shorts. Sometimes recommends other markets.
How to Contact: Send complete ms with SASE. Reports in 6-8 weeks. Photocopied submissions OK. Accepts computer printout submissions. Publishes ms 2-3 months after acceptance. Sample copy $3.50. Fiction guidelines for #10 SAE and 1 first class stamp.
Payment: 2 contributor's copies; $3 charge for extras.
Terms: "At this point we cannot pay for every piece, but we occasionally sponsor a contest." Acquires one-time rights.
Advice: "We lean toward experimental, more serious fiction, with a strong sense of voice. Send a neat manuscript with a descriptive cover letter, SASE. Fiction is a good voice for our times. Poetry is also, but people seem to enjoy a short story over a long poem."

CENTRAL PARK (II), A Journal of the Arts and Social Theory, Neword Productions, Inc. Box 1446, New York NY 10023. (212)362-9151. Editor: Stephen-Paul Martin. Magazine: 7½ × 10, 100 pages; glossy cover stock; illustrations; photos. Magazine of theoretical essays, poetry, fiction, photos and graphics for intellectual audience. Semiannually. Estab. 1981. Circ. 1,000.
Needs: Contemporary, erotica, ethnic, experimental, feminist, gay, historical (general), lesbian, literary, prose poem, serialized/excerpted novel and translations. Approximately 10% of fiction is agented. Receives 50 unsolicited mss/month. Publishes short shorts of 5-10 pages. Accepts 5 mss/issue; 10 mss/year. Published works by Ron Sukenick, Clarence Major, Dick Higgins. Published new writers within the last year. Usually critiques rejected mss. Sometimes recommends other markets.
How to Contact: Send complete ms and cover letter with "publication credits, relevant personal data, reasons for sending to us. We prefer submissions from people who are familiar with the magazine. We suggest that prospective contributors order a sample copy before submitting." Reports in 2 months.

SASE. Simultaneous and photocopied submissions OK. Accepts computer printout submissions. Publishes ms an average of 3 months after acceptance. Sample copy $5.
Payment: 2 contributor's copies; $5 for extras.
Terms: Acquires first rights.
Advice: "We would like to publish more short fiction, especially if it is experimental, aggressively sexual and political in nature. Write what seems to be an authentic representation of how *your* feelings interact with the social world. Let your imagination have free reign in evolving the form your work takes. Be aware of, *but not harnessed by,* conventions. We like to know who our writers are: what they do, their literary background and activities. Writers should include a cover letter and expect a personal letter in response."

CHAKRA (I, II), Box 8551, FDR Station, New York NY 10022. Editor: Liz Camps. Magazine; 8½×11; 16-28 pages; illustrations. "A journal of the speculative arts and sciences: magick, mysticism, philosophy, erotica, discordia, cybershamanism for artists and others with keen curiosity."Published irregularly—2 or 3 times/year. Estab. 1988. Circ. "several hundred."
Needs: Condensed/excerpted novel, erotica, experimental, fantasy, feminist, gay, horror, lesbian, literary, prose poem, psychic/supernatural/occult, religious, science fiction, philosophy and socio politics. Receives 10 unsolicited mss/month. Accepts 2-6 mss/issue; 5-15 mss/year. Time between acceptance and publication varies. Recently published work by George Smyth, Richard Behrens, Lorraine Schein. Length: 4,000 words maximum. Publishes short shorts. Occasionally critiques rejected mss.
How to Contact: Send complete ms with cover letter. Reports in 1 month. SASE. Simultaneous, photocopied and reprint submissions OK. Accepts computer printout submissions. Sample copy $2, 9×12 SAE and 65¢ postage. Fiction guidelines for #10 SAE and 1 first class stamp.
Payment: Pays in contributor's copies. Publication not copyrighted.
Advice: "Please submit all queries, manuscripts, etc. on *used paper* to encourage amateur recycling. If two manuscripts would fit *Chakra*'s theme, but one was obviously 'written to be published' whereas the other seems primarily to fulfill the emotional needs of the writer, the latter will be chosen over the former. Sincerity of feeling is more important than genre, but it must be expressed well to be accepted in *Chakra*."

‡CHALK TALK (IV), 1550 Mills Road, RR2, Sidney, British Columbia V8L 3S1 Canada. (604)656-1858. Editor: Virginia Lee. Magazine: Pony tabloid size; 24 pages; recycled newsprint paper. "Writing by children only for children, ages 5-14." Monthly. Estab. 1988. Circ. 3,600.
Needs: Children writers only. Juvenile, young adult. "No war or violence." Publishes mss 1-4 months after acceptance. Length: 200 words preferred. Publishes short short. Critiques or comments on rejected mss and recommends other markets.
How to Contact: Send complete ms with cover letter. Reports in 3 months. SASE. (IRCs) Sample copy and fiction guidelines free.
Payment: Pays in contributor's copies.
Terms: Acquires one-time rights. Sponsors occasional contests for children only.

CHAMINADE LITERARY REVIEW (II), Chaminade Press, 3140 Waialae Ave., Honolulu HI 96816. (808)735-4826. Editor: Loretta Petrie; Fiction Editor: James Robinson. Magazine: 6×9; 175 pages; 50# white paper; 10 pt cis cover; photographs. "Multicultural, particularly Hawaii—poetry, fiction, artwork, criticism, photos, translations for all English-speaking internationals, but primarily Hawaii." Semiannually. Estab. 1987. Circ. 350.
Needs: Excerpted novel, ethnic, experimental, humor/satire, literary, religious/inspirational, translations. "We have published a variety including translations of Japanese writers, a fishing story set in Hawaii, fantasy set along the Amazon, but the major point is they are all 'literary.' No erotica, horror, children's or young adult, confession, lesbian, gay." Receives 8 unsolicited mss/month. Accepts 5-8 mss/issue. Publishes ms 3-6 months after acceptance. "We haven't published short shorts yet, but would depending on quality." Sometimes critiques rejected ms.
How to Contact: Send complete ms with cover letter. Include short contributor's note. Reporting time depends on how long before deadlines of May 15 and December 15. SASE. Photocopied and reprint submissions OK. If clear, near letter quality computer printout submissions are accepted. Sample copy for $3.50.

Payment: Free subscription to magazine.

Terms: Acquires one-time rights.

Advice: "We look for good writing; appeal for Hawaii audience and writers everywhere. *CLR* was founded to give added exposure to Hawaii's writers, both here and on the mainland, and to juxtapose Hawaii writing, with mainland and international work."

‡**CHAMPAGNE HORROR,** Champagne Productions, 2419 Klein Place, Regina, Saskatchewan S4V 1M4 Canada. (306)789-2419. Art Editor: Randy Nakoneshny. Fiction Editor: Cathy Buburuz. Magazine: 8½×11; 60 pages; semi-gloss cover stock; illustrations; photographs. "Psychological, thought-provoking horror fiction, poetry, artwork and photographs for horror fans." Annually. Estab. 1990. Circ. 500+.

Needs: Horror. Receives 50 unsolicited mss/month. Buys approximately 20 mss/issue. Does not read mss January-June. Publishes ms within 6 months after acceptance. Recently published work by Cliff Burns, Alan Catlin, John-Ivan Palmer, Diana Kemp-Jones. Length: 1,000 average; 300 words minimum; 2,000 words maximum. Publishes short shorts. Length: 500 words. Sometimes critiques rejected mss and recommends other markets.

How to Contact: Send complete manuscript with cover letter and biography. Reports in 3 weeks. SASE. "Send loose (unaffixed) postage or International Reply Coupons as US postage cannot be used in Canada." Photocopied submissions OK. Accepts computer printout submissions. Sample copy $5.95. Fiction guidelines for SAE and 50¢ (unaffixed postage stamps).

Payment: Pays $5-40 (Canadian) and contributor's copies.

Terms: Pays on publication for first rights.

Advice: "If your work contains one or more of the following elements, we want to see it: psychological or thought provoking horror, chilling mystery, a touch of morbid humor, unique situations or locations. Especially interested in the work of established and upcoming artists, writers and poets."

CHAPTER ONE (I), For the Unpublished Writer in All of Us, JAB Publishing, Box 4086, Cary NC 27519-4086. (919)460-6668. Editor: Belinda J. Puchajda. Magazine: 5¼×8. "For short stories and poems." Bimonthly. Estab. 1989.

Needs: Adventure, confession, contemporary, erotica, ethnic, experimental, fantasy, feminst, historical (general), horror, humor/satire, juvenile (5-9 years), literary, mainstream, preschool (1-4 years), prose poem, psychic/supernatural/occult, regional, religious/inspirational, romance (contemporary, historical, young adult), science fiction, senior citizen/retirement, sports, suspense/mystery, western, young adult/teen (10-18 years). "No pornography." Publishes annual special fiction issue. Receives 50-100 unsolicited mss/month. Buys 10-20 mss/issue; 60-100 mss/year. Publishes ms 3 months after acceptance. Length: 4,500 words; 100 words minimum; 6,000 maximum. Publishes annual children's special issue. Publishes short shorts. Length: 100 words. Sometimes critiques rejected mss and recommends other markets.

How to Contact: Send complete ms with cover letter. Include biographical information. Reports in 1 month on queries; 2 months on ms. Simultaneous, photocopied and reprint submissions OK. Accepts computer printout submissions. Sample copy $1. Fiction guidelines for #10 SAE and 1 first class stamp.

Payment: Pays $30 maximum; free contributor's copies.

Terms: Publication not copyrighted.

Advice: "We feel that there is a lot of talent out there, and we want to see it. Whether it be a story from a housewife who never wrote anything before, or a writer who has been writing for years and has never got published. We want to get you in print."

THE CHARITON REVIEW (II), Northeast Missouri State University, Kirksville MO 63501. (816)785-4499. Editor: Jim Barnes. Magazine: 6×9; 100+ pages; 60 lb paper; 65 lb cover stock; photographs on cover. "We demand only excellence in fiction and fiction translation for a general and college readership." Semiannually. Estab. 1975. Circ. 700+.

Needs: Literary, contemporary and translations. Buys 3-5 mss/issue, 6-10 mss/year. Published work by Steve Heller, John Deming, Judy Ray. Published new writers within the last year. Length: 3,000-6,000 words. Critiques rejected mss when there is time. Sometimes recommends other markets.

How to Contact: Send complete ms with SASE. No book-length mss. Reports in less than 1 month on mss. Publishes ms an average of 6 months after acceptance. Sample copy $3 with SASE.
Payment: $5/page up to $50 maximum. Free author's copy. $2.50 for extras.
Terms: Pays on publication for first North American serial rights; rights returned on request.
Advice: "Do not ask us for guidelines: the only guidelines are excellence in all matters. Write well and study the publication you are submitting to. We are interested only in the very best fiction and fiction translation. We are not interested in slick material. We do not read photocopies or carbon copies. Know the simple mechanics of submission—SASE, no paper clips, no odd-sized SASE, etc. Know the genre (short story, novella, etc.). Know the unwritten laws."

THE CHATTAHOOCHEE REVIEW (II), DeKalb College, 2101 Womack Rd., Dunwoody GA 30338. (404)551-3166. Editor: Lamar York. Magazine: 6×9; 150 pages; 70 lb paper; 80 lb cover stock; illustrations; photographs. Quarterly. Estab. 1980. Circ. 1,250.
Needs: Contemporary, erotica, experimental, feminist, gay, humor/satire, literary, mainstream, regional and translation. No juvenile, romance, sci-fi. Receives 500 unsolicited mss/month. Accepts 5 mss/issue. Recently published work by Leon Rooke, R.T. Smith; published new writers within the last year. Length: 2,500 words average. Sometimes critiques rejected mss and recommends other markets.
How to Contact: Send complete ms with cover letter, which should include sufficient bio for notes on contributors' page. Reports in 6 months. SASE. Photocopied submissions OK. Accepts computer printout submissions. Sample copy $3.50. Fiction guidelines printed in magazine.
Payment: Pays in contributor's copies.
Terms: Acquires first rights. "We sponsor a prize awarded to the best story printed in *The Review* throughout the year. Judged by a professional writer, not the editor."
Advice: "Arrange to read magazine before you submit to it."

‡CHICAGO REVIEW, 5801 S. Kenwood Ave., Chicago IL 60637. (312)702-0887. Fiction Editor: Andy Winston. Magazine for a highly literate general audience: 6½x9; 96 pages; offset white 60 lb paper; illustrations; photos. Quarterly. Estab. 1946. Circ. 2,000.
Needs: Literary, contemporary, and especially experimental. Accepts up to 5 mss/issue, 20 mss/year. Receives 80-100 unsolicited fiction mss each month. No preferred length, except will not accept book-length mss. Critiques rejected mss "upon request." Sometimes recommends other markets.
How to Contact: Send complete ms with cover letter. SASE. Simultaneous submissions OK. Accepts computer printout submissions. Reports in 4-5 months on mss. Sample copy $4.50. Free guidelines with SASE.
Payment: 3 free author's copies and subscription.
Advice: "We look with interest at fiction that addresses subjects inventively, work that steers clear of clichéd treatments of themes. We're always eager to read writing that experiments with language, whether it be with characters' viewpoints, tone or style."

CHIPS OFF THE WRITER'S BLOCK (I), Box 83371, Los Angeles CA 90083. Editor: Wanda Windham. Newsletter. "Freelancer's forum, the beginner's chance to be published." Bimonthly.
Needs: "We will consider all categories of fiction, as our publication gives writers a chance to be 'critiqued' by fellow writers." No pornographic or offensive material. Published new writers within the last year. "Always" critiques rejected mss.
How to Contact: Submit complete ms. "Cover letters are not necessary. Please note the word count on the first page of the story." Reports in 3 weeks on queries; 1 month on mss. SASE. Considers simultaneous submissions; "prefers" photocopies. Accepts computer printout submissions. Sample copy $2. Fiction guidelines for #10 SAE and 1 first class stamp.
Payment: Pays in contributor's copies.
Advice: "The editor works directly with the author if editing is necessary or if the story needs to be reworked. The writer's peer group also sends in comments, suggestions, etc., once the story is in print. The comments are discussed in later issues."

CHIRON REVIEW (I), Rt. 2, Box 111, St. John KS 67576. (316)549-3933. Editor: Michael Hathaway. Tabloid: 10×13; 24+ pages; newsprint; illustrations; photos. Publishes "all types of material, no particular theme; traditional and off-beat, no taboos." Estab. 1982. Circ. 1,200.
Needs: Contemporary, experimental, humor/satire, literary. Receives 6 mss/month. Accepts 1 ms/issue; 4 mss/year. Publishes ms within 6-18 months of acceptance. Length: 3,500 words preferred. Publishes short shorts. Sometimes recommends other markets to writers of rejected mss.

How to Contact: Send complete ms with cover letter. Reports in 4-8 weeks. SASE. Photocopied submissions OK. Accepts computer printout submissions. Sample copy $2 ($4 overseas). Fiction guidelines for #10 SAE and 1 first class stamp.
Payment: Pays 1 contributor's copy. Charge for extra copies, 50% discount.
Terms: Acquires first rights.

CHRISTIAN OUTLOOK (I,IV), Hutton Publications, Box 1870, Hayden ID 83835. (208)772-6184. Editor: Linda Hutton. Newsletter: 8½×11; 3 pages; b&w illustrations. "Magazine nondenominational, inspirational for middle-of-the-road Christian (*not* evangelical)." Quarterly. Estab. 1988. Circ. 300.
Needs: Religious/inspirational. "Do not use present tense." Receives 50 unsolicited mss/month. Buys 2-3 mss/issue; 8-12 mss/year. Publishes ms up to one year after acceptance. Recently published work by May Wareberg and Margaret Shauer. Length: 300-1,500 words; 1,000 average. Publishes short shorts. Length: 300 words. Sometimes critiques rejected mss and recommends other markets.
How to Contact: Submit complete manuscript. Reports in 3 weeks on mss. SASE. Accepts simultaneous, photocopied and reprint submissions. Accepts computer printout submissions. Sample copy free for #10 SAE and 2 first class stamps. Fiction guidelines for #10 SAE and 1 first class stamp.
Payment: ¼¢/word and contributor's copies.
Terms: Pays on acceptance for one-time rights.
Advice: "A dash of humor is always welcome; religious writers tend to take themselves too seriously and be too intense. The arrogant attitude of some religious publications, demanding that freelancers be members of their denominations, infuriated me and led me to start publishing an open, nondenominational newsletter to encourage beginning religious writers."

CHRYSALIS (II), Journal of the Swedenborg Foundation, The Swedenborg Foundation, 139 E. 23rd St., New York NY 10010. (212)673-7310. Send mss to: Rt. 1, Box 184, Dillwyn VA 23936. (804)983-3021. Editor-in-Chief: Carol S. Lawson. Fiction Editor: Phoebe Loughrey. Magazine: 7½×10; 80 pages; archival paper; coated cover stock; illustrations; photos. "A literary magazine centered around one theme per issue (e.g., 'Wise Woman: A Human Process' and 'Aspects of African Spirit' and 'Tree of Knowledge'). Publishes fiction, articles, poetry, book and film reviews for intellectually curious readers interested in spiritual topics." Triannually. "Would like to publish special fiction issues, but we need more writers!" Estab. 1985. Circ. 2,000.
Needs: Adventure (leading to insight), contemporary, experimental, historical (general), literary, mainstream, science fiction, spiritual, sports, suspense/mystery. No religious, juvenile, preschool. Receives 40 mss/month. Buys 2-3 mss/issue; 6-9 mss/year. Publishes ms within 9 months of acceptance. Recently published work by Stephen Larsen, Robert Beum, Julia Randall; published new writers within the last year. Length: 1,500 words minimum; 2,500 words maximum. Publishes short shorts. Sometimes critiques rejected mss and recommends other markets. Does not accept reprinted or in-press material.
How to Contact: Query first and send SASE for guidelines. Reports in 1 month on queries; in 2 months on mss. SASE. Photocopied submissions OK. Accepts computer printout submissions, "prefers letter quality." Sample copy for $5. Fiction guidelines for #10 SAE and 1 first class stamp.
Payment: Pays $75-250, free subscription to magazine and 5 contributor's copies.
Terms: Pays on publication for one-time rights. Sends galleys to author.
Advice: Looking for "1. *Quality*; 2. appeal for our audience; 3. relevance to/illumination of an aspect of issue's theme."

CICADA (II, IV), 329 "E" St., Bakersfield CA 93304. (805)323-4064. Editor: Frederick A. Raborg, Jr. Magazine: 5½×8¼; 24 pages; Matte cover stock; illustrations and photos. "Oriental poetry and fiction related to the Orient for general readership and haiku enthusiasts." Quarterly. Estab. 1985. Circ. 600.
Needs: Adventure, contemporary, erotica, ethnic, experimental, fantasy, feminist, historical (general), horror, humor/satire, lesbian, literary, mainstream, psychic/supernatural/occult, regional, contemporary romance, historical romance, young adult romance, science fiction, senior citizen/retirement, suspense/mystery and translations *all with Oriental slant.* "We look for strong fiction with Oriental (especially Japanese) content or flavor. Stories need not have 'happy' endings, and we are open to the experimental and/or avant-garde. Erotica is fine (the Japanese love their erotica); pornography, no." Receives 30+ unsolicited mss/month. Buys 1 ms/issue; 4 mss/year. Publishes ms 6 months-1 year after acceptance. Agented fiction 5%. Recently published work by Gilbert Garand and Jim Mastro. Length: 2,000 words average; 500 words minimum; 3,000 words maximum. Critiques rejected ms when appropriate. Always recommends other markets.

How to Contact: Send complete ms with cover letter. Include Social Security number and appropriate information about the writer in relationship to the Orient. Reports in 2 weeks on queries; 3 months on mss (if seriously considered). SASE. Photocopied submissions OK. Accepts computer printout submissions. Sample copy $4.50. Fiction guidelines for #10 SAE and 1 first class stamp.
Payment: Pays $10-25 plus contributor's copies; charge for extras.
Terms: Pays on publication for first North American serial rights. $5 kill fee.
Advice: Looks for "excellence and appropriate storyline. Strong characterization and knowledge of the Orient are musts. Neatness counts high on my list for first impressions. A writer should demonstrate a high degree of professionalism."

CIMARRON REVIEW (II), Oklahoma State University, 205 Morrill, Stillwater OK 74078-0135. (405)744-9476. Editor: Gordon Weaver. Managing Editor: Deborah Bransford. Magazine: 6×9; 100 pages; illustrations on cover. "Poetry and fiction on contemporary themes; personal essay on contemporary issues that cope with life in the 20th century, for educated literary readers. We work hard to reflect quality." Quarterly. Estab. 1967. Circ. 500.
Needs: Literary and contemporary. No collegiate reminiscences or juvenilia. Accepts 6-7 mss/issue, 24-28 mss/year. Recently published works by Peter Makuck, Mary Lee Settle, W. D. Wetherell, John Timmerman; published new writers within the last year. Sometimes recommends other markets.
How to Contact: Send complete ms with SASE. "Short cover letters are appropriate but not essential, except for providing *CR* with the most recent mailing address available." Accepts computer printout submissions, prefers letter-quality. Reports in 4-6 weeks on mss. Publishes ms 6-9 months after acceptance. Free sample copy with SASE.
Payment: 3 free author's copies.
Terms: Acquires all rights on publication.
Advice: "Short fiction is a genre uniquely suited to the modern world. *CR* seeks an individual, innovative style that focuses on contemporary themes."

‡CIPHER (II), 5415 Connecticut Ave., NW, #819, Washington DC 20015. (202)966-3583. Editor: James Heynderickx. Magazine: 5½×8½; 62 pages; 24 lb. paper; vellum cover, 5 illustrations/issue. "We present contemporary art, fiction, poetry and critical essays to an open-minded, educated audience." Quarterly. Estab. 1990.
Needs: Contemporary, experimental, literary, mainstream, prose poem, translations. "We also have a 'Works in Progress' section in each issue. In this section, excerpts from developing and yet-to-be-published novels, books of poetry and major works of criticism will be presented." Does not want to see "anything that is imitative. We can also pass on adventure, fantasy, science fiction and romance." Plans special fiction issue. Receives 30-40 unsolicited fiction mss/month. Accepts 3-4 mss/issue; 12-16 mss/year. Publishes mss 4-6 months after acceptance. Recently published work by Sarah Freligh. Length: 2,000 words preferred; 300 words minimum; 4,000 words maximum. Publishes short shorts. Length: 300-500 words. Critiques or comments on rejected mss and recommends other markets.
How to Contact: Send complete ms with cover letter. "Include name, address, phone number, but no publishing history or background on the specific piece." Reports in 2 months. SASE. Photocopied submissions are OK. Sample copy for $4. Fiction guidelines for #10 SAE and 1 first-class stamp.
Payment: Pays in contributor's copies.
Terms: Acquires first North American serial rights.
Advice: "More than anything else, we are looking for a clarity of voice in the fiction we publish. This clarity is usually achieved by writers who are conscious of their purpose and use of language. We admire stories in which both content and form attempt to offer insight...Our editors believe that 'a lack of revision' is the number one reason that fiction from beginning writers is often passed over...Our main recommendation is that writers should investigate and revise a piece of fiction as much as possible if they are interested in discovering its true potential."

‡CITY SCRIPTUM (I, II), City College of San Francisco, 50 Phelan Ave., San Francisco CA 94112. (415)239-3000. Editor: H. Brown Miller. Magazine: 8½×11; 50-60 pages. "Our publication is a college literary magazine that publishes short fiction, essays and poetry for a college/general audience." Semiannually. Revived 1989. Circ. 1,000.
Needs: Adventure, condensed/excerpted novel, confession, contemporary, ethnic, experimental, fantasy, feminist, gay, historical (general), horror, humor/satire, lesbian, literary, mainstream, prose poem, psychic/supernatural/occult, science fiction, suspense/mystery, western. We accept manuscript *only* two times per year: 1) 9/1-10/31 and 2) 2/1-3/31. Manuscript will be published during semester it

was accepted. Length: 2,100 words average for prose/75 lines max for poetry. Publishes short shorts. Length: No preference.

How to Contact: Send complete manuscript with cover letter. Request writers guidelines including author's name, address and phone number. SASE. Simultaneous and photocopied submissions OK. Accepts computer printouts. Sample copy $2. Fiction guidelines for #10 SAE and 1 first class stamp.
Payment: Pays in contributor's copies.
Terms: Acquires one-time rights.

‡CLIFTON MAGAZINE (II), University of Cincinnati Communications Board, 204 Tangeman University Center, Cincinnati OH 45221. Editor: Rich Roell. Fiction Editor: Solomon Davidoff. Magazine: 8x11; 64 pages; 70 lb enamel coated paper; illustrations; photos. "*Clifton* is the magazine of the University of Cincinnati, presenting fiction, poetry and feature articles of interest to the University community. It is read by a highly literate audience of students, academics and professionals looking for original and exciting ideas presented in our award-winning format." Quarterly. Estab. 1972. Circ. 30,000.
Needs: Literary, contemporary, science fiction, fantasy, feminist, erotica, humor, prose poem, spiritual, regional and ethnic. "Will consider anything we haven't read a thousand times before. We try to have no preconceptions when approaching fiction." Accepts 1-2 mss/issue, 5 mss/year. Recently published work by Karen Heuler, Evelyn Livingston and Adrienne Gosselin. Length: 6,000 words maximum. Publishes short shorts. Receives approximately 30 unsolicited fiction mss each month.
How to Contact: Send complete ms with SASE. Reports in 1 month on mss. Sample copy $1.75. Free guidelines with #10 SASE.
Payment: 3 free author's copies.
Terms: Acquires first rights.
Advice: "*Clifton* often publishes work by unpublished authors and is quite open to any fiction. We look forward to continuing the publication with both young and established writers. *Clifton* tries to find mechanically sound, intricate, original work for publication. The unusual is popular. Be unique. Don't give up. Send at least one follow-up letter. All stories will receive comments if rejected."

‡THE CLIMBING ART (IV), The FreeSolo Press, P.O. Box 816, Alamosa CO 81101. (719)589-5579. Editor: David Mazel. Magazine: 8½ × 11; 32 pages; 50 lb. book paper; 10 pt. cover; 10/issue illustrations; 10/issue photographs. "Themes of mountaineering, rock climbing, mountains, outdoors and environmental for mountaineers and mountain enthusiasts." Quarterly. Estab. 1986. Circ. 1,000.
Needs: Adventure, condensed/excerpted novel, confession, contemporary, experimental, feminist, historical (general), humor/satire, literary, mainstream, prose poem, science fiction, translations. Receives 5-10 unsolicited mss/month. Buys 1-3 mss/issue; 4-10 mss/year. Publishes ms 3-12 months after acceptance. Recently published work by Barry Greer. Length: 3,000 words average; 12,000 words maximum. Publishes short shorts. All lengths will be considered. Sometimes critiques rejected mss and recommends other markets.
How to Contact: Send complete manuscript with cover letter. Reports in 2 months. SASE. Simultaneous, photocopied and reprint submissions OK. Accepts computer printout submissions. Accepts electronic submissions. Sample copy $2.75.
Payment: $100 maximum and free subscription to magazine for all rights. Sends galleys to author.

CLOCKWATCH REVIEW (II), A Journal of the Arts, Dept. of English, Illinois Wesleyan University, Bloomington IL 61702. (309)556-3352. Editor: James Plath. Magazine: 5½ × 8½; 64-80 pages; coated stock paper; glossy cover stock; illustrations; photos. "We publish stories which are *literary* as well as alive, colorful, enjoyable—stories which linger like shadows," for a general audience. Semiannually. Estab. 1983. Circ. 1,500.
Needs: Contemporary, experimental, humor/satire, literary, mainstream, prose poem and regional. Receives 50-60 unsolicited mss/month. Accepts 2 mss/issue; 4 mss/year. Recently published work by Ellen Hunnicutt, V.K. Gibson, J.W. Major; published new writers within the last year. Length: 2,500 words average; 1,200 words minimum; 4,000 words maximum. Occasionally critiques rejected mss if requested.
How to Contact: Send complete ms. Reports in 2 months. SASE. Photocopied submissions OK. Accepts computer printout submissions. Prefers letter-quality. Publishes ms 3-12 months after acceptance. Sample copy $4.

Payment: 3 contributor's copies and small cash stipend. (Currently $50, but may vary).
Terms: Acquires first serial rights.
Advice: "*Clockwatch* has always tried to expand the audience for quality contemporary poetry and fiction by publishing a highly visual magazine that is thin enough to invite reading. We've included interviews with popular musicians and artists in order to further interest a general, as well as academic, public and show the interrelationship of the arts. Give us characters with meat on their bones, colorful but not clichéd; give us natural plots, not contrived or melodramatic. Above all, give us your *best* work."

COCHRAN'S CORNER (I), Box 2036, Waldorf, MD 20601. (301)843-0485. Editor: Debra G. Tompkins. Magazine: 5½×8; 52 pages. "We publish both fiction and nonfiction and poetry. Our only requirement is no strong language." For a "family" audience. Plans a special fiction issue. Quarterly. Estab. 1986. Circ. 500.
Needs: Adventure, historical (general), horror, humor/satire, juvenile (5-9 years), preschool (1-4 years), prose poem, religious/inspirational, romance, science fiction, suspense/mystery and young adult/teen (10-18 years). "Mss must be free from language you wouldn't want your/our children to read." Receives 50 mss/month. Accepts 4 mss/issue; 8 mss/year. Publishes ms by the next issue after acceptance. Published work by Juni Dunkin, Ruth Cox Anderson, Becky Knight. Length: 500 words preferred; 300 words minimum; 1,000 words maximum. Sometimes critiques unsolicited mss and recommends other markets.
How to Contact: Send complete ms with cover letter. Reports in 3 weeks on queries; 3 months on mss. SASE for manuscript. Simultaneous, photocopied and reprint submissions OK. Accepts computer printout submissions. Sample copy for $3, 5×9 SAE and 90¢ postage. Fiction guidelines for #10 SAE and 1 first class stamp.
Payment: Pays in contributor's copies.
Terms: Acquires one-time rights.
Advice: "I feel the quality of fiction is getting better. The public is demanding a good read, instead of having sex or violence carry the story. I predict that fiction has a good future. We like to print the story as the writer submits it if possible. This way writers can compare their work with their peers and take the necessary steps to improve and go on to sell to bigger magazines. Stories from the heart desire a place to be published. We try to fill that need."

THE COE REVIEW (II), Student Senate of Coe College, 1220 1st St., Cedar Rapids IA 52402. Contact: Cyrus Cramer. Magazine: 8½×5½; 100-150 pages; illustrations; photos. Annual anthology of "quality experimental writing in both poetry and fiction. Especially directed to an academic or experimental literary audience that is concerned with current literature." Annually. Estab. 1972. Circ. 500.
Needs: Literary, contemporary, psychic/supernatural, science fiction, fantasy, feminist, gay/lesbian, erotica, quality ethnic, regional, serialized and condensed novels, translations. "We publish students, unsolicited professional and solicited professional mss. *The Coe Review* is growing and it is our goal to become nationally acknowledged in literary circles as a forerunner in the publication of experimental writing. We support writing workshops and invite both writing professors and student writers to submit." No "religious propaganda, gothic, romance, western, mystery or adventure." Length: 500-4,000 words.
How to Contact: Send complete ms with SASE. "Mss sent in summer will possibly not be returned until fall depending on availability of a fiction editor in summer." Accepts computer printout submissions. Sample copy $4.
Payment: $25-100 for solicitations. 1 free author's copy. $4 charge for extras.
Terms: Pays on publication for all rights "but possibly sooner with solicited mss. Upon request we will reassign rights to the author."
Advice: "We desire material that seeks to explore the vast imaginative landscape and expand the boundaries thereof. Study experimental writers such as Borges, Vonnegut, Brautigan, J. Baumbach and Manual Puig. Avoid sentimentalism. Do not be afraid to experiment or to write intelligent fiction."

COLD-DRILL MAGAZINE (IV), English Dept., Boise State University, 1910 University Dr., Boise ID 83725. (208)385-1999. Editor: Tom Trusky. Magazine: 6×9; 150 pages; Beckett text paper; illustrations; photos. Material submitted *must be by Idaho authors or deal with Idaho.* For adult audiences. Annually. Estab. 1970. Circ. 500.
Needs: Adventure, contemporary, erotica, ethnic, experimental, fantasy, feminist, gay, horror, humor/satire, lesbian, literary, mainstream, science fiction, serialized/excerpted novel, suspense/mystery, translations, western, Idaho topics. "Manuscripts are selected in December for the annual issue in

March. Authors may submit any time, but they will not be notified unless they are selected; if they are, notification will be in late December, early January." No children's literature, romance, gothic, true confession, psychic, religious or inspirational. Receives 10 fiction mss/month. Accepts 5-7 mss/year. Publishes short shorts.

How to Contact: Query first. Reports in 2 weeks. SASE. Simultaneous and photocopied submissions OK. Accepts computer printouts. Sample copy $5. Fiction guidelines for #10 SAE and 1 first class stamp.

Payment: Pays in contributor's copies.

Terms: Acquires first rights.

Advice: "We publish the best in Idaho literature, regardless of the genre. Know the publication."

COLLAGES AND BRICOLAGES (II), The Journal of International Writing, Office of International Programs, 212 Founders Hall, Clarion University of Pennsylvania, Clarion PA 16214. (814)226-2340. Editor: Marie-José Fortis. Magazine: 8 × 11; 100-150 pages; illustrations. "The theme, if there is any, is international post-modern/avant-gardist culture. The magazine may include essays, short stories, short plays, poems that show innovative promise." Annually. Estab. 1987. Plans special fiction issue.

Needs: Contemporary, ethnic, experimental, feminist, humor/satire, literary, mainstream, philosophical, prose poem and science fiction. "Also post-modern, surrealist designs/illustrations are welcome." Receives about 10 unsolicited fiction mss/month. Publishes ms 6-9 months after acceptance. Recently published work by Margaret Del Guercio, Marcia Yudkin and Daniel Quinn; published new writers within the last year. Publishes short shorts. Sometimes critiques rejected ms; recommends other markets when there is time.

How to Contact: Send complete ms with cover letter. Reports in 2-3 months. SASE. Simultaneous submissions OK. Accepts computer printout submissions. Sample copy $5.

Payment: Pays two contributor's copies.

Terms: Acquires first rights.

Advice: "As far as fiction is concerned, it seems that everything has been said before. Hence, the writer's despair. This literary despair should be an asset to today's young writer. It should be his motif. The only innovation that can still be done is language innovation, playfulness, humor (with a sense of doom). We are now living in a neo-dada age, in a 'post-modern aura.' Hence, the writer's input should concentrate on these premises. Writing about the decadence of inspiration can bring us to a new age in literature. (The Dadaist despair was, after all, answered with surrealism.)We encourage experimental and literary writers that do not shy away from reading the classics."

COLORADO REVIEW (II), English Department, Colorado State University, Fort Collins CO 80523. (303)491-6428. Managing Editor: Bill Tremblay. Fiction Editor: David Milofsky. Translation Editor: Mary Crow. Literary magazine: 128 pages; 70 lb book weight paper; glossy cover stock. Semiannually. Estab. 1977. Circ. 1,000.

Needs: Contemporary, ethnic, experimental, literary, mainstream, translations. Receives 100 unsolicited fiction mss/month. Accepts 2-3 mss/issue. Recently published work by David Huddle, Francois Camoin, Patricia Eakins. Published new writers within the last year. Length: under 6,000 words. Does not read mss May-August. Occasionally critiques rejected mss and recommends other markets.

How to Contact: Send complete ms with SASE and brief bio and previous publications. Accepts computer printout submissions; prefers letter-quality. Reports in 3 months. Publishes ms 3-6 months after acceptance. Sample copy $5.

Payment: $10/printed page; 1 subscription to magazine; 2 free contributor's copies; $5 charge for extras.

Terms: Pays on publication for first North American serial rights. "We assign copyright to author on request." Sends galleys to author.

Advice: "We are interested in manuscripts which show craft, imagination and a convincing voice. Character development, strong story lines and thematic insight are always desired. If a story has reached a level of technical competence, we are receptive to the fiction working on its own terms. The oldest advice is still the best: persistence. Approach every aspect of the writing process with pride, conscientiousness—from word choice to manuscript appearance."

COLORADO-NORTH REVIEW (I, II), University of Northern Colorado, Greeley CO 80639. (303)351-1350. Editor: Joel Long. Magazine: 5½ × 8½; 64 pages; 70 lb paper; 80 lb cover stock; illustrations; photos. Magazine of poetry, short fiction, translations, photography, interviews and graphic arts for writers or those interested in contemporary creativity. Published in winter and spring. Estab. 1968. Circ. 2,500.

Needs: Contemporary, literary and prose poem. Receives 100 unsolicited fiction mss/month. Accepts 70 mss/issue (including poetry), 140 mss/year. Published work by James Lentestey and Dennis Vannatta. Length: 1,000 words maximum. Critiques rejected mss by request.
How to Contact: Send complete ms with SASE and brief biographical info for contributor's section. Photocopied submissions OK. Reports in 3 months. Publishes ms 2-3 months after acceptance. Sample copy $3.50; free guidelines with SASE.
Terms: Pays in contributor's copies.
Advice: "We print poetry, art, and short fiction, so space is limited for short fiction, averaging three to four stories an issue. Obviously we must be very selective so send your best work. We are looking for stories whose form is dictated by its content. Innovative work is welcome as long as the innovation meets its own standards for quality. Work with insight is always appreciated. Please do not send simultaneous submissions."

COLUMBIA: A MAGAZINE OF POETRY & PROSE (II), 404 Dodge Hall, Columbia University, New York NY 10027. (212)854-4391. Editors: Rotating. Magazine: 5¼×8¼; approximately 200 pages; coated cover stock; illustrations, photos. "We accept short stories, novel excerpts, translations, interviews, nonfiction and poetry." Annually.
Needs: Literary, prose poem and translations. Accepts 3-10 mss/issue. Receives approximately 125 unsolicited fiction mss each month. Does not read mss April 1 to August 31. Recently published work by Philip Lopate, Amy Hempel, Madison Smartt Bell; published 5-8 unpublished writers within the year. Length: 25 pages maximum. Publishes short shorts.
How to Contact: Send complete ms with SASE. Accepts computer printout submissions. Reports in 1-2 months. Sample copy $5.
Payment: Pays in author's copies. $3 charge for extras. Offers annual fiction awards.
Advice: "Don't overwhelm editors. Send work that's not longer than 20 pages."

COLUMBUS SINGLE SCENE (II,IV), Box 30856, Gahanna OH 43230. (614)476-8802. Editor: Jeanne Marlowe. Magazine: 8×11; 24 pages; illustrations; photos. Single living, male-female relationship topics covered for single adults. Monthly. Estab. 1985. Circ. 5,000.
Needs: Confession, contemporary, experimental, fantasy, humor/satire, mainstream, suspense/mystery. Buys 12 mss/year. Publication time varies "now that I have a backlog." Published work by Lori Ness, Robert Weinstein, John Birchler; published new writers within the last year. Length: 5,000 words maximum; "shorter ms more likely to be accepted." Publishes short shorts. Occasionally critiques rejected mss.
How to Contact: Send complete ms with a statement granting one time rights in exchange for copies. Reports in 1 week on queries; 2-4 weeks on mss. SASE for ms, "unless you don't want ms returned." Simultaneous, photocopied and reprint submissions OK, "if not from local publications." Accepts computer printout submissions. Sample copy $1.
Payment: Contributor's copies and advertising trade for most; $25 plus advertising trade maximum.
Terms: Pays on acceptance for one-time rights.
Advice: "My readers are primarily interested in meeting people, dating/relating to the other sex. I like to include a biographical note about my contributors' relation to singles. Although I have little space, I like to tackle tough problems and integrate fiction with editorial and personal experience. I don't shy away from the controversial, but reject the superficial."

COMMON LIVES/LESBIAN LIVES (IV), A Lesbian Quarterly, Box 1553, Iowa City IA 52244. Contact: Tess Catalano and Tracy Moore. "*CL/LL* seeks to document the experiences and thoughts of lesbians for lesbian audience." Magazine: 5×8½; 112-128 pages; illustrations; photos. Quarterly.
Needs: Adventure, comics, contemporary, erotica, ethnic, experimental, fantasy, feminist, historical (general), humor/satire, juvenile, lesbian, prose poem, psychic/supernatural/occult, regional, romance, science fiction, senior citizen/retirement, suspense/mystery, western and young adult/teen. "*All pertaining to lesbian culture.*" Length: 4-10 pages. Occasionally critiques rejected mss.
How to Contact: Send complete ms with cover letter; a short bio sketch is required. Reports in 4 months. SASE. Photocopied submissions OK. Accepts computer printout submissions. Publishes ms up to 4 months after acceptance. Published "many" new writers within the last year. Sample copy $5.
Payment: 2 contributor's copies.
Advice: "Readers relate stories to their lives; fiction is an interesting and accessible way for lesbians to document their experience and express their opinions."

A COMPANION IN ZEOR (I,II,IV), 17 Ashland Ave., RR 5, R Box 82, Cardiff NJ 08232. Editor: Karen Litman. Fanzine: 8½x11; 60 pages; "letter" paper; heavy blue cover; b&w line illustrations; occasional b&w photographs. Publishes science fiction based on the various Universe creations of Jacqueline Lichtenberg. Occasional features on Star Trek, and other interests, convention reports, reviews of movies and books, recordings, etc. Published irregularly. Estab. 1978. Circ. 300.

Needs: Fantasy, humor/satire, prose poem, science fiction. "No vicious satire. Nothing X rated. Homosexuality prohibited unless *essential* in story. We run a clean publication that anyone should be able to read without fear." Occasionally receives one manuscript a month. Accepts "as much as can afford to print." Publication of an accepted ms "can take years, due to limit of finances available for publication." Occasionally critiques rejected mss and recommends other markets.

How to Contact: Query first or send complete ms with cover letter. "Prefer cover letters about any writing experience prior, or related interests toward writing aims." Reports in 1 month. SASE. Simultaneous and photocopied submissions OK. Accepts computer printout submissions. Sample copy price depends on individual circumstances. Fiction guidelines for #10 SAE and 1 first class stamp. "I write individual letters to all queries. No form letter at present." SASE preferred for guidelines, but not required (our present contact with writers is small). If volume of inquiries becomes larger, a SASE will be required.

Payment: Pays in contributor's copies.

Terms: Acquires first rights.

Advice: "We take fiction based on any and all of Jacqueline Lichtenberg's published novels. The contributor should be familiar with these works before contributing material to my fanzine. Also accepts manuscripts on cassette from visually handicapped if submitted. 'Zines also on tape for those individuals."

COMPOST NEWSLETTER (IV), Compost Coven, 729 Fifth Ave., San Francisco CA 94118. (415)751-9466. Editor: Valerie Walker. Newsletter: 7×8½; 20 pages; bond paper; illustrations and scanned photographs. Publishes "humor/satire from a pagan/punk perspective." Published 8 times/year. Estab. 1981. Circ. under 100.

Needs: Experimental, fantasy, feminist, gay, humor/satire, lesbian, psychic/supernatural/occult, science fiction, serialized novel, pagan. No Christian. Publishes ms within 1 or 2 issues after acceptance. Length: 500 words minimum; 2,000 words maximum.

How to Contact: Query with clips of published work. Reports in 2 months. SASE. Simultaneous, photocopied and reprint submissions OK. Accepts dot-matrix computer printouts; accepts electronic submissions via Macintosh disk. Sample copy $2. (Make checks/MO's out to Valerie Walker; mark "for CNL".)

Payment: Pays in contributor's copies.

Terms: Acquires one-time rights. Publication not copyrighted.

Advice: "If you don't like the magazine market, go out and make one of your own. Type single space on white paper, or send a Macintosh disk in MacWrite or Microsoft Word. Don't bother to format unless it's essential for the feel of the piece. Entertain us, even if you're serious. Get strange." Publishes ms "if it is funny, bizarre, or we agree with its politics."

CONCHO RIVER REVIEW (I, II, IV), Fort Concho Museum Press, 213 East Avenue D, San Angelo TX 76903. (915)657-4441. Editor: Terence A. Dalrymple. Magazine: 6½×9; 100-125 pages; 60 lb Ardor offset paper; Classic Laid Color cover stock; b&w drawings. "We publish any fiction of high quality—no thematic specialties—contributors must be residents of Texas or the Southwest generally." Semiannually. Estab. 1987. Circ. 300.

Needs: Contemporary, ethnic, historical (general), humor/satire, literary, regional and western. No erotica; no science fiction. Receives 10-15 unsolicited mss/month. Accepts 3-6 mss/issue; 8-10 mss/year. Publishes ms 4 months after acceptance. Published work by Robert Flynn, Clay Reynolds, Roland Sodowsky. Length: 3,500 words average; 1,500 words minimum; 5,000 words maximum. Sometimes critiques rejected mss and recommends other markets.

How to Contact: Send complege ms with SASE; cover letter optional. Reports in 3 weeks on queries; 3-8 weeks on mss. SASE for ms. Simultaneous and photocopied submissions OK. Accepts computer printout submissions. Sample copy $4. Fiction guidelines for #10 SAE and 1 first class stamp.

Payment: Pays in contributor's copies; $4 charge for extras.

Terms: Acquires first rights.

Advice: "We prefer a clear sense of conflict, strong characterization and effective dialogue."

CONFRONTATION (II), English Dept., C.W. Post of Long Island University, Greenvale NY 11548. (516)299-2391. Editor: Martin Tucker. Magazine: 6×9; 190-250 pages; 70 lb paper; 80 lb cover; illustrations; photos. "We like to have a 'range' of subjects, form and style in each issue and are open to all forms. Quality is our major concern. Our audience is literate, thinking people; formally or self-educated." Semiannually. Published special fiction issue last year; plans another. Estab. 1968. Circ. 2,000.
Needs: Literary, contemporary, prose poem, regional and translations. No "proseletyzing" literature. Buys 30 mss/issue, 60 mss/year. Receives 400 unsolicited fiction mss each month. Does not read June-September. Approximately 10-15% of fiction is agented. Recently published work by Jerzy Kosinski, Irvin Faust, Lore Segal; published new writers within the last year. Length: 500-4,000 words. Publishes short shorts. Critiques rejected mss when there is time. Sometimes recommends other markets.
How to Contact: Send complete ms with SASE. "Cover letters acceptable, not necessary. We accept simultaneous submissions but do not like it." Accepts computer printout submissions, letter-quality only. Reports in 6-8 weeks on mss. Publishes ms 6-12 months after acceptance. Sample copy $3.
Payment: $10-$100. 1 free author's copy. Half price for extras.
Terms: Pays on publication for all rights "with transfer on request to author."
Advice: "Keep trying."

‡**CONJUNCTIONS (II)**, 33 W. 9th St., New York NY 10011. Editor: Bradford Morrow. Magazine: 6x9; 294 pages; 55 lb woven paper; heavy cream laid paper cover stock; illustrations; photos. "*Conjunctions*: a conjoining of texts by many diverse writers: a forum of work-in-progress by both well-known and new writers. We represent no clique but are concerned solely with publishing works of high artistic and technical calibre." Semiannually. Estab. 1981. Circ. 5,500.
Needs: Experimental, literary and translations. Receives 200 unsolicited fiction mss/month. Accepts 65 mss/year. "Recent issues have included new work by John Hawkes, William T. Vollman and Mary Caponegro."Published new writers within the last year. No preferred length.
How to Contact: Send complete ms with SASE. Reports in 8-12 weeks on mss.
Payment: 3 free contributor's copies; extra copies available at 40% discount to contributors.
Terms: Acquires one-time rights. Sends galleys to author.
Advice: "Gain a far wider personal experience than that which is possible in writing schools. A broader reading base than is evident in most of the unsolicited work we receive would be useful. So much has already been accomplished, and it seems to us the literacy rate among writers is only barely higher than any other community or profession."

‡**CONVERGING PATHS (IV)**, Three Sisters, Ltd., P.O. Box 63, Mt. Horeb WI 53572. Editor: Kyril Oakwind. Newsletter: 8½×11; 36 pages; 20 lb. paper; 67 lb. cover; black-and-white illustrations. "Pagan/Wiccan/religio-occult for a pagan/Wiccan audience." Quarterly. Estab. 1986.
Needs: Traditional Wiccan, psychic/supernatural/occult, pagan. Publishes mss 3-6 months after acceptance. Length: open. Publishes short shorts. Recommends other markets.
How to Contact: Query first. Reports in 2-4 weeks. SASE. Photocopied and computer printout submissions OK. Accepts electronic submissions. Sample copy for $4, #10 SAE and 1 first-class stamp. Fiction guidelines for #10 SAE and 1 first-class stamp.
Payment: Pays in contributor's copies.
Terms: Acquires one-time rights.
Advice: "It must be pagan or Wiccan oriented, preferably inspirational, a good story or humorous. It should be reasonably well-written, but can be from a first-time writer."

CORONA (II), Marking the Edges of Many Circles, Department of History and Philosophy, Montana State University, Bozeman MT 59717. (406)994-5200. Magazine: 7×10; 130 pages; 60 lb "mountre matte" paper; 65 lb hammermill cover stock; illustrations; photos. "Interdisciplinary magazine—essays, poetry, fiction, imagery, science, history, recipes, humor, etc., for those educated, curious, with a profound interest in the arts and contemporary thought." Annually. Estab. 1980. Circ. 2,000.
Needs: Comics, contemporary, experimental, fantasy, feminist, gay, lesbian, humor/satire, literary, preschool, prose poem, psychic/supernatural/occult, regional, romance and senior citizen/retirement. "Our fiction ranges from the traditional Talmudic tale to fiction engendered by speculative science, from the extended joke to regional reflection—if it isn't accessible and original, please don't send it." Receives varying number of unsolicited fiction mss/month. Accepts 6 mss/issue. Publishes short shorts. Published work by Rhoda Lerman and Stephen Dixon; published new writers within the last year. Occasionally critiques rejected mss. Sometimes recommends other markets.

How to Contact: Send complete ms with SASE. Accepts computer printout submissions. Reports in 6 months on mss. Sample copy $7.
Payment: Minimal honorarium; 2 free contributor's copies; discounted charge for extras.
Terms: Acquires first rights. Sends galleys to author upon request.
Advice: "Be knowledgeable of contents other than fiction in *Corona*; one must know the journal."

COSMIC LANDSCAPES (I), An Alternative Science Fiction Magazine, % Dan Petitpas, 6 Edson St., Hyde Park MA 02136. (617)361-0622. Editor: Dan Petitpas. Magazine: 7×8½; 32-56 pages; white bond paper and cover stock; illustrations; photos occasionally. "A magazine which publishes science fiction for science-fiction readers; also articles and news of interest to writers and SF fans. Occasionally prints works of horror and fantasy." Annually. Estab. 1983. Circ. 100.
Needs: Science fiction. Receives 10-15 unsolicited mss/month. Accepts 8 mss/issue. Published new writers in the last year. Length: 2,500 words average; 25 words minimum. Will consider all lengths. "Every manuscript receives a personal evaluation by the editor." Sometimes recommends other markets.
How to Contact: Send complete ms with info about the author. Reports usually in 1 week-3 months. SASE. Photocopied submissions preferred. Accepts readable computer printout submissions. Sample copy $3. Fiction guidelines free with SASE.
Payment: 2 contributor's copies; charges $1.50 for extras.
Terms: Acquires one-time rights.
Advice: "Writers should send a cover letter; include SASE and a return address. I like to know a little about them. Please give some background, and how the story pertains to their experience. Learn manuscript formats. Get E. B. White's *Elements of Style*. Don't get all your ideas from TV shows or movies. Try to know the basics."

CRAB CREEK REVIEW (II), 4462 Whitman Ave. N., Seattle WA 98103. (206)633-1090. Editor: Linda Clifton. Fiction Editor: Carol Orlock. Magazine: 6×10 minitab; 32 pages; ultrabright newsprint paper; self cover; line drawings. "Magazine publishing poetry, short stories, art and essays for adult, college-educated audience interested in literary, visual and dramatic arts and in politics." Triquarterly. Estab. 1983. Circ. 350.
Needs: Contemporary, humor/satire, literary and translations. No confession, erotica, horror, juvenile, preschool, religious/inspirational, romance or young adult. Receives 20-30 unsolicited mss/month. Accepts 2 mss/issue; 6 mss/year. Recently published work by Rebecca Wells, Jack Cady, Paloma Diaz-Mas; published new writers within the last year. Length: 3,000 words average; 1,200 words minimum; 4,000 words maximum. Publishes short shorts. Occasionally critiques rejected mss.
How to Contact: Send complete ms with short list of credits. Reports in 3 months. SASE. Photocopied submissions OK "but no simultaneous submissions." Accepts computer printout submissions; prefers letter-quality. Sample copy $3.
Payment: 2 free contributor's copies; $2 charge for extras.
Terms: Acquires first rights. Rarely buys reprints.
Advice: "We appreciate 'sudden fictions.' Type name and address on each piece. Enclose SASE. Send no more than one story in a packet (except for short shorts—no more than 3, 10 pages total)."

CRAZYHORSE (III), Dept. of English, Univ. of Arkansas, Little Rock, AR 72204. (501)569-3160. Managing Editor: Zabelle Stodola. Fiction Editor: David Jauss. Magazine: 6×9; 140 pages; cover and front page illustrations only. "Publishes original, quality literary fiction." Biannually. Estab. 1960. Circ. 1,000.
Needs: Literary. No formula (science-fiction, gothic, detective, etc.) fiction. Receives 100-150 unsolicited mss/month. Buys 4-5 mss/issue; 8-10 mss/year. Does not read mss in summer. Publishes short shorts. Past contributors include Lee K. Abbott, Frederick Busch, Andre Dubus, Pam Durban, H.E. Francis, James Hannah, Gordon Lish, Bobbie Ann Mason and Maura Stanton. Published new writers within the last year. "Rarely" critiques rejected mss.
How to Contact: Send complete ms with cover letter. Reports in 1 week on queries; 1-4 weeks on mss. SASE. Photocopied submissions OK. Accepts computer printout submissions. Sample copy $4.
Payment: Pays $10/page and contributor's copies.
Terms: Pays on publicaton for first North American serial rights. *Crazyhorse* awards $500 to the author of the best work of fiction published in a given year.
Advice: "Read a sample issue and submit work that you believe is as good as or better than the fiction we've published."

CRAZYQUILT (II), 3341 Adams Ave., San Diego CA 92116. (619)688-1029. Editor: Marsh Cassady. Magazine: 5½ × 8½; 92 pages; illustrations and photos. "We publish short fiction, poems, nonfiction about writing and writers, one-act plays and b&w illustrations and photos." Quarterly. Estab. 1986. Circ. 175.
Needs: Contemporary, ethnic, fantasy, gay, historical, humor/satire, literary, mainstream, science fiction, excerpted novel, suspense/mystery. "Shorter pieces are preferred." Receives 85-100 unsolicited mss/quarter. Accepts 1-3 mss/issue; 4-12 mss/year. Publishes 1 year after acceptance. Recently published work by Louis Phillips, Geraldine Little, David Mouat; published new writers within the last year. Length: 1,500 words minimum; 5,000 words maximum. Occasionally critiques rejected mss.
How to Contact: Send complete ms with cover letter. Reports in 3 weeks on mss. Simultaneous and photocopied submissions OK. Accepts computer printout submissions. Sample copy $4.50 ($2.50 for back issue). Fiction guidelines for SAE and 1 first class stamp.
Payment: 2 free contributor's copies.
Terms: Acquires first North American serial rights or one-time rights. Holds annual poetry and fiction contest ($100, $50 and $25 prizes) and annual chapbook contest.
Advice: "Write a story that is well constructed, develops characters and maintains interest."

‡THE CREAM CITY REVIEW (II), University of Wisconsin-Milwaukee, Box 413, Milwaukee WI 53201. (414)229-5041.Editor: Kit Pancoast. Fiction Editor: Joe Gahagan. Magazine: 8½x5½; 120-200 pages; 70 lb offset/perfect bound paper; 80 lb cover stock; illustrations; photos. "General literary publication—an electric selection of the best we receive." Semiannually. Plans to publish special fiction issue Semiannually. Estab. 1975. Circ. 1,000-1,500.
Needs: Ethnic, experimental, humor/satire, literary, prose poem, regional and translations. Receives approximately 100-200 unsolicited fiction mss each month. Accepts 6-10 mss/issue. Published work by Eve Shelnutt, Ellen Hunnicut and F.D. Reeve; published new writers within the last year. Length: 1,000-10,000 words. Publishes short shorts. Critiques rejected mss when there is time. Recommends other markets "when we have time."
How to Contact: Send complete ms with SASE. Photocopied submissions OK. Reports in 2 months. Sample copy $4.50.
Payment: 2 free author's copies.
Terms: Acquires first rights. Sends galleys to author. Rights revert to author after publication.
Advice: "Read as much as you write so that you can examine your own work in relation to where fiction has been and where fiction is going."

CREATIVE KIDS (I, IV), GCT, Inc., Box 6448, Mobile AL 36660. (205)478-4700. Editor: Fay L. Gold. Magazine: 8½ × 11; 32 pages; illustrations; photos. Material by children for children. Published 8 times/year. Estab. 1980. Circ: 10,000.
Needs: "We publish work by children ages 5-18." Juvenile (5-9 years); young adult/teen (10-18 years). No sexist, racist or violent fiction. Accepts 8-10 mss/issue; 60-80 mss/year. Publishes ms up to one year after acceptance. Published new writers within the last year. Publishes short shorts.
How to Contact: Send complete ms with cover letter, which should include name, age, home address, school name and address. Reports in 2 weeks on queries; 1 month on mss. SASE. Accepts computer printout submissions, no dot-matrix. Sample copy $3.
Payment: Pays contributor's copy only.
Terms: Acquires all rights.
Advice: "Ours is a magazine to encourage young creative writers to use their imaginations, talent and writing skills. Type the manuscript—double space. Include all vital information about author. Send to one magazine at a time."

THE CREATIVE WOMAN (I,IV), Governors State University, University Park IL 60466. (708)534-5000, ext. 2524. Editor: Dr. Helen Hughes. Magazine: 8½ × 11; 48 pages; illustrations; photos. "Focus on a special topic each issue, presented from a feminist viewpoint." Estab. 1977. Circ. 800.
Needs: Feminist, humor/satire, prose poem, spiritual and sports. Receives 30-40 unsolicited fiction mss/month. Accepts 1 ms/issue; 3 mss/year. Publishes ms 3-12 months after acceptance. Recently published work by Susan Griffin. Also publishes short shorts. Occasionally critiques rejected mss and recommends other markets.
How to Contact: Send complete ms with cover letter. Reporting time varies. "Sometimes very backlogged." SASE for ms. Photocopied submissions and reprints OK. Accepts computer printouts. Sample copy $3.

Payment: Pays in contributor's copies.
Advice: "Read our magazine before submitting. Don't give up."

THE CRESCENT REVIEW (II), The Crescent Review, Inc., Box 15065, Winston-Salem NC 27113. (919)924-1851. Editor: Guy Nancekeville. Magazine: 6×9; 128 pages. "A fiction writer's magazine." Estab. 1983. Circ. 286.
Needs: All kinds of stories. Receives 1,000 unsolicited mss/year. Accepts 30 mss/year. Published new writers within the last year. Length: 3,500 words average.
How to Contact: Reports in 6 weeks to 6 months. SASE. Next issue, $5. Back issue $6.
Payment: 2 free contributor's copies; discount for contributors.
Terms: First North American serial rights.
Advice: "Keep trying."

CROSS TIMBERS REVIEW (II), Cisco Junior College, Cisco TX 76437. (817)442-2567. Editor: Monte Lewis. Fiction Editor: Sue Doak. Magazine: 6×9½; 64 pages average; 65 lb paper; 80 lb cover stock; pen and ink illustrations. "To serve as a medium through which regional ideas and works may be presented to a broader readership, while at the same time not excluding the works of international writers, for academic and general audience." Semiannually. Estab. 1983. Circ. 250.
Needs: Adventure, ethnic, historical (general), humor/satire, literary, regional, western, southwestern material. Receives 5-10 unsolicited fiction mss/month. Accepts 2-3 mss/issue; 4-6 mss/year. Does not read mss June/July. Publishes ms 3-6 months after acceptance. Length: 3,000-4,000 words average; 1,000 words minimum; 4,000 words maximum. Sometimes critiques rejected mss.
How to Contact: Send complete ms and cover letter with name, address. Reports in 6 weeks on queries; 6 months on mss. SASE for ms. Photocopied submissions OK. Accepts computer printouts. Sample copy $3.
Payment: Pays in 3 contributor's copies, $3 charge for extras.
Terms: Acquires one-time rights. Sends galleys to author.
Advice: "We like stories with *impact*. The story must say something with preciseness and punch. The Southwest has a rich tradition of fiction; we want to encourage writers to keep the tradition alive. We attempt to showcase Texas writers."

CROSSCURRENTS (III), 2200 Glastonbury Rd., Westlake Village CA 91361. Editor: Linda Brown Michelson. Magazine: 6×9; 176 pages; 60 lb paper stock; laminated cover; line drawings and halftone photos. "*Crosscurrents* is a literary magazine offering another corner for today's artistry. We publish short fiction, poetry, graphic arts and nonfiction. We direct our publication toward an educated audience who appreciate good writing and good art and who enjoy a periodic sampling of current trends in these fields." Quarterly. Estab. 1980. Circ. 3,000.
Needs: Most categories except heavy erotica, juvenile, science fiction and young adult. "Good writing is what we look for and consider first. We want high quality literary fiction." Buys 7-12 mss/issue, 45 mss/year. Approximately 10% of fiction is agented. Recently published fiction by Alvin Greenberg, Joyce Carol Oates and Alice Adams; published new writers in the last year. Length: 6,000 words maximum. Critiques rejected mss when there is time.
How to Contact: Send complete ms with SASE. Reviews material June 1-Nov 30 each year. No simultaneous submissions. Accepts computer printout submissions. Prefers letter-quality. Reports in 6 weeks on mss. Publishes ms 2-12 months after acceptance. Sample copy $6.
Payment: $35 minimum. Offers 50% kill fee for assigned ms not published.
Terms: Pays on publication for first North American serial rights.
Advice: "Look at a sample issue to see what we publish. Include a short letter with your manuscript to let us know who you are. If given encouragement, submit three or four times each year, not every week. Study the awards collections and make sure your work measures up. Even small publications receive submissions from Nobel winners, and so self-monitoring will, in the long run, save postage."

CUTBANK (II), English Department, University of Montana, Missoula MT 59812. (406)243-5231. Editor-in-Chief: David Curran. Magazine: 5½×8½; 115-130 pages. "Publishes highest quality fiction, poetry, artwork, for a general, literary audience." Two issues or one double issue/year. Estab. 1972. Circ. 450.
Needs: "No overt stylistic limitations. Only work of high quality will be considered." Receives 200 unsolicited mss/month. Accepts 6-12 mss/year. Does not read mss from February 2-August 15. Publishes ms up to 6 months after acceptance. Published new writers within the last year. Length: 3,750

words average; 1,000 words minimum; 12,500 words maximum. Occasionally critiques rejected mss and recommends other markets.

How to Contact: Send complete ms with cover letter, which should include "name, address, publications." Reports in 1 month on queries; 1-6 months on mss. SASE. Accepts computer printout submissions; no dot-matrix. Sample copy $4 (current issue $9) and 6½×9 SAE. Fiction guidelines 50¢, #10 SAE and 1 first class stamp.

Payment: Free contributor's copies, charges for extras, 10% discount for over 15 copies.

Terms: Acquires all rights. Rights returned upon writtern request.

Advice: "Tight market, improving. Strongly suggest contributors read an issue. Send 3 line bio and note whether mss is available on disk. Every submission is read several times, by several editors. We have published both numerous new and established fiction writers, including William Pitt Root, Ralph Beer, Neil McMahon, Gordon Lish, Madeline Defrees, James Welch, Rick DeMarinis, Fred Haefele, William Yellow Robe, Leonard William Robinson, etc. Send only your best work. Note: We do not return phone calls."

‡CWM (II, III, IV), 4801 Cypress Creek #1004, Tuscaloosa AL 35405. (205)553-2284. Editor: David C. Kopaska-Merkel. Co-editor: Geof Huth, 225 State St., Apt. 451, Schenectady NY 12305. (518)374-7143. Magazine: variable size; pages variable; paper quality variable; cover variable; ink drawings or others possible. "Each issue has a theme; that of the 1st issue is: 'Water in all its forms.' We publish fiction, art and poetry for anyone interested in something a little bit different." Estab. 1990.

Needs: "Any submission fitting the theme." Receives 5-10 mss/months. Accepts 1-5 mss/issue; 2-10 mss/year. Publishes ms 1-11 months after acceptance. Length: 10,000 words maximum. Publishes short shorts; any length is acceptable. Sometimes comments on rejected mss and recommends other markets.

How to Contact: Query first or send complete manuscript with cover letter. Reports in 1-4 weeks on queries; 1-8 weeks on mss. SASE. Photocopied submissions OK. Accepts computer printout submissions. Accepts electronic submissions via disk. Fiction guidelines for #10 SAE and 1 first class stamp.

Payment: Pays contributor's copies.

Terms: Acquires one-time rights.

Advice: "A manuscript must meet our theme for the issue in question. It stands out if it begins well and is neatly and clearly prepared. Given a good beginning, the story must hold the reader's interest all the way to the end and not let go. It helps if a story haunts the reader even after it is put aside."

‡D.C. (I), K3, 18 Taylor Ave., Earlville NY 13332. (315)691-9431. Editor: Katrina Kelly. Newsletter: 8½×11; 6-10 pages; illustrations. "*D.C.* is interested in funny and/or interesting materials, sick humor is good, too. Our audience is people of the punk genre and the sarcastically morbid." Monthly. Estab. 1988. Circ. 150.

Needs: Confession, ethnic, experimental, horror, humor/satire, prose poem, psychic/supernatural/occult. Receives 2-6 unsolicited mss/month. Acquires 3 (depending on length) mss/issue. Publishes ms in the next issue after acceptance. Recently published work by Katrina Kelly, Jenn Nixon, Ben White. Publishes short shorts. Length: less than one page typed.

How to Contact: Query first. Reports in 1 week. Simultaneous and photocopied submissions OK. Accepts computer printout submissions. Sample copy for $1. Fiction guidelines for SAE and 1 first class stamp.

Payment: Pays free subscription to magazine.

Advice: "I like submissions that are well written, are *somewhat* logical and interest or amuse."

‡DAGGER OF THE MIND (II), Beyond The Realms Of Imagination, K'yi-Lih Productions (a division of Breach Enterprises), 1317 Hookridge Dr., El Paso TX 79925. (915)591-0541. Editor: Arthur William Lloyd Breach. Magazine. 8½×11; 62-86 pages; hibright paper; high glossy cover; from 5-12 illustrations. Quarterly. Estab. 1990. Circ. 5,000.

Needs: Lovecraftian. Adventure, experimental, fantasy, horror, prose poem, science fiction, suspense/mystery. Nothing sick and blasphemous, vulgar, obscene, racist, sexist, profane, humorous, weak, exploited women stories and those with idiotic puns. Plans special paperback anthologies. Receives 120 unsolicited mss/month. Publishes 8-15 mss/issue depending on length; 90-100 mss/year depending upon length. Publishes ms 1 year after acceptance. Agented fiction 30%. Recently published work by Sidney Williams, Jessica Amanda Salmonson, Donald R. Burleson. Length: 4,500 words average; 5,000 minimum; 10,000 words maximum. Publishes short shorts. Length: Under 1,000 words. Sometimes comments on rejected mss.

How to Contact: Send complete manuscript with cover letter. "Include a bio and list of previously published credits with tearsheets. I also expect a brief synopsis of the story." Reports in 2 weeks on queries; 2 months on mss. SASE. Photocopied submissions OK. Accepts computer printout submissions. Accepts electronic submissions. Sample copy for $3.50, 9×12 SAE and 5 first class stamps. Fiction guidelines for #10 SAE and 1 first class stamp.

Payment: Pays ½-1¢/word plus one contributor's copy.

Terms: Pays on publication for first rights (possibly anthology rights as well).

Advice: "I'm a big fan of the late H.P. Lovecraft. I love reading through Dunsanian and Cthulhu Mythus tales. I'm constantly on the lookout for this special brand of fiction. If you want to grab my attention immediately, write on the outside of the envelope. 'Lovecratian submission enclosed.' There are a number of things which make submissions stand out for me. Is there any sensitivity to the tale? I like sensitive material, so long as it doesn't become mushy. Another thing that grabs my attention is characters which leap out of the pages and grab you. Then there are those old standards for accepting a manuscript: good imagery, story plot and originality. Move me, bring a tear to my eye; make me stop and think about the world and people around me. Frighten me with little spoken of truths about the human condition. In short, bring out all my emotions (except humor, I detest humor) and show me that you can move me in such a way as I have never been moved before."

THE DALHOUSIE REVIEW (II), Room 314, Dunn Building, Dalhousie University, Halifax, Nova Scotia B3H 3J5 Canada. Editor: Dr. Alan Andrews. Magazine: 14cm×23cm; approximately 165 pages; photographs sometimes. Publishes articles, short stories and poetry. Quarterly. Circ. 1,000.

Needs: Literary. Length: 5,000 words maximum.

How to Contact: Send complete ms with cover letter. SASE (Canadian stamps). Sample copy $5.50 (Canadian dollars) plus postage.

DAN RIVER ANTHOLOGY (I), Box 123, South Thomaston ME 04858. (207)354-6550. Editor: R. S. Danbury III. Book: 5½x8½; 156 pages; 60 lb. paper; gloss 65 lb. full-color cover; b&w illustrations. For general/adult audience. Annually. Estab. 1984. Circ. 1,200.

Needs: Adventure, contemporary, ethnic, experimental, fantasy, historical (general), horror, humor/satire, literary, mainstream, prose poem, psychic/supernatural/occult, regional, romance (contemporary and historical), science fiction, senior citizen/retirement, suspense/mystery and western. No "evangelical Christian, pornography or sentimentality." Receives 20-30 unsolicited mss/month. Accepts about 8-10 mss/year. Reads "mostly in March." Length: 2,000-2,400 words average; 800 words minumum; 4,000 words maximum.

How to Contact: *Charges reading fee: $1 for poetry; $3 for prose.* Send complete ms with SASE. Reports in April each year. Accepts computer printout submissions. Sample copy $9.95 paperback, $19.95 cloth, plus $2.50 shipping. Fiction guidelines for #10 SASE.

Payment: 10% of all sales attributable to writer's influence: readings, mailings, autograph parties, etc., plus up to 50% discount on copies, plus other discounts to make total as high as 73%.

Terms: Acquires first rights.

Advice: "Also: The CAL Anthology—Same Guidelines. Acceptance/Rejection—November."

‡DANCE CONNECTION (II, IV), A Canadian Dance Journal, 603, 815 1st St. SW, Calgary, Alberta, T2P 1N3 Canada. (403)237-4327. Editor: Heather Elton. Magazine: 8½×11; 52 pages; recycled bond paper; illustrations and b&w photographs. "Dance: Interview, essay, commentary, reviews for dance lovers, academics, educators, professionals, artists." Published 5 times per year. Estab. 1983. Circ. 5,000.

Needs: Dance. "Do not send anything not related to dance or poems about ballet." Plans special fiction issue. Receives 10 unsolicited mss/month. Accepts 1 mss/issue; 3 mss/year. Publishes ms 3 months after acceptance. Length: 1,100 words average; 400 words minimum; 2,500 words maximum. Publishes short shorts. Length: 800 words.

How to Contact: Query with clips of published work or send complete manuscript with cover letter. Reports in 6 weeks. SASE. Simultaneous, photocopied and reprint submissions OK. Accepts computer printout submissions. Accepts electronic submissions. Sample copy for 9×12 SAE. Fiction guidelines for #10 SAE.

Payment: Pays $25-250 (Canadian), free subscription to magazine and contributor's copies.

Terms: Pays on publication. Buys first rights or one-time rights.

‡**THE DANGEROUS TIMES,** 32 Chestnut Hill, Greenfield MA 01301. (413)772-6441. Editor: Josh. Magazine: 5½×8½; 28-40 pages; 20 lb. bond paper; 20 lb. cover; b&w illustrations and photographs. "Anarchist-oriented music and literary zine. Reviews, fiction, comics, political/social analysis and commentary, art and a very small dose of poetry for a small but dedicated readership with a wide range of interests. Very few anarchist readers, mostly a "leftist" crowd. Two large portions of the readership are fans of alternative music and members of the academic community." Quarterly. Estab. 1985. Circ. 200.

Needs: Adventure, condensed/excerpted novel, contemporary, erotica, ethnic, experimental, fantasy, feminist, gay, historical (general), horror, humor/satire, juvenile (5-9 years), lesbian, literary, preschool (1-4 years), psychic/supernatural/occult, regional, religious/inspirational, science fiction, senior citizen/retirement, serialized novel, suspense/mystery, translations, western, young adult/teen (10-18 years), anarchist. Receives 1-2 unsolicited mss/month. Accepts 0-1 ms/issue; 1-6 mss/year. Publishes ms 4 months after acceptance. Recently published work by Christopher Willingham, O.S. Publishes short shorts. Sometimes critiques rejected mss and recommends other markets.

How to Contact: Send complete manuscript with cover letter. SASE if return desired. Simultaneous and photocopied submissions OK. Accepts computer printout submissions. Accepts electronic submissions (Apple IIe only). Sample copy for $1.50.

Payment: Pays one contributor's copy.

Terms: Author retains all rights. Publication is not copyrighted.

‡**DARK SIDE (I,IV), The Modern Magazine of Horror,** Rt. 3, Box 272-D, Ripley Magazine MS 38663. (601)837-8670. Editor: S.C. Riley. Magazine: "A quarterly magazine featuring horror fiction, poetry, art, interviews, reviews, commentary, market news." Quarterly. Estab. 1990.

Needs: Horror. Length: 5,000 words maximum. Publishes short shorts.

How to Contact: Send complete manuscript with cover letter. SASE. Photocopied and reprint submissions OK. Accepts computer printout submissions. Sample copy for $4.50 in US, $5 (US) in Canada. Fiction guidelines free.

Payment: Pays $4 and up and one contributor copy.

Terms: Pays on acceptance for first or one-time rights.

Advice: "I welcome but do not limit subjects to Gothic or occult material. Prefer stories with modern setting. The emphasis is on well-written material with strong openings, well-developed plots and endings that are not too predictable nor seem contrived. I would like to see new stories with fresh ideas or fresh twists to known themes. Dare to extend your creativity."

‡**DARK TOME (I, IV),** P.O. Box 705, Salem OR 97308. Editor: Michelle Marr. Magazine: 5½×8½; 30-80 pages; 20 lb. paper; 60 lb. cover; illustrations. "We publish horror fiction for mature readers who are not easily offended." Bimonthly. Estab. 1990. Circ. 75.

Needs: Horror, psychic/supernatural/occult. "I want original stories, not classic ghost stories. I also tend to stay away from purely gothic material. No science fiction, gay and lesbian material or juvenile." Receives 60 unsolicited mss/month. Acquires 6-10 mss/issue; 30-60 mss/year. Publishes manuscript 2 months after acceptance. Recently published work by John Bien, Roger Dale Trexler. Length: 1,500 words average; 3,000 words maximum. Always comments on rejected mss.

How to Contact: Send complete manuscript with cover letter. Include something about the author. Reports in 1 week on queries; 3 weeks on mss. SASE. Photocopied submissions OK. Accepts computer printout submissions. Sample copy for $2 payable to Michelle Marr. Fiction guidelines for #10 SAE and 1 first class stamp.

Payment: Pays in contributor's copies.

Terms: Acquires first North American serial rights.

Advice: "I am looking for *horror* fiction *only*. What makes a manuscript stand out is originality, a believable plot, stories that leave a lasting image in the mind of the reader. Check for inconsistencies in plot; do something original; if an editor suggests a change that you strongly disagree with, *don't* do it (even if it means not selling the story). AND DON'T GIVE UP!"

DAUGHTERS OF SARAH (II, IV), 3801 N. Keeler, Box 416790, Chicago IL 60618. (312)736-3399. Editor: Reta Finger. Magazine: 5½×8½; 32 pages; illustrations and photos. "Christian feminist publication dealing with Christian theology, history, women and social issues from a feminist point of view." Bimonthly. Estab. 1974. Circ. 6,000.

Needs: Historical, religious/inspirational, feminist and spiritual (Christian feminist). "No subjects unrelated to feminism from Christian viewpoint." Receives 6-8 unsolicited fiction mss/month. Buys 4-6 mss/year. Recently published work by Mary Cartledge-Hayes. Length: 1,800 words maximum. Publishes short shorts. Occasionally critiques rejected mss "if related and close to acceptance."

How to Contact: Cover letter stating why ms was written; biography of author. Query first with description of ms and SASE. Simultaneous, photocopied and previously published submissions OK "but won't pay." Accepts computer printout submissions. Reports in 2 weeks on queries. Publishes "most" ms 3 months to 1 year after acceptance. Sample copy for $2.50.

Payment: Pays $15/printed page; 3 free contributor's copies. Offers kill fee of one-half stated fee.

Terms: Pays upon publication for first North American serial or one-time rights.

Advice: "Make sure topic of story fits with publication. We get many stories that are either Christian stories, women's stories, Christian women's stories, but not necessarily feminist. We believe that the Christian gospel was meant to be radically egalitarian and we try to integrate it with the feminist insights and analysis available today."

DEATHREALM (II), 3223-F Regents Park, Greensboro NC 27405. (919)288-9138. Editor: Mark Rainey. Magazine: 5½x8½; 50-60 pages; 20 lb bond paper; 8 pt glossy coated cover stock; pen & ink, screened illustrations; b&w photos. Publishes "fantasy/horror," for a "mature" audience. Quarterly. Estab. 1987. Circ. 1,200.

Needs: Experimental, fantasy, horror, psychic/supernatural/occult and science fiction. "Sci-fi tales should have a horror slant. *Do not* send tales that are not in the realm of dark fantasy. *Strongly* recommend contributor buy a sample copy of *Deathrealm* before submitting." Receives 200-300 mss/month. Buys 6-8 mss/issue; 30 mss/year. Publishes ms within 1 year of acceptance. Published work by Joe R. Lansdale, Fred Chappell, Thomas Ligotti. Length: 5,000 words average; 10,000 words maximum. Publishes short shorts. Sometimes critiques rejected mss and recommends other markets.

How to Contact: Send complete manuscript with cover letter, which should include "publishing credits, some bio info, where they heard about *Deathrealm*. Never reveal plot in cover letter." Reports in 1 week on queries; 2-6 weeks on ms. SASE. Photocopied submissions OK. Accepts computer printout submissions, *only* if high-quality. Sample copy for $4 and 65¢ postage. Fiction guidelines for #10 SAE and 1 first class stamp.

Payment: Pays $5 minimum; $8 maximum; contributor's copies.

Advice: "Concentrate on characterization; development of ideas; strong atmosphere, with an important setting. I frown on gratuitous sex and violence unless it is a mere side effect of a more sophisticated story line. Stay away from overdone themes—foreboding dreams come true; being a frustrated writer; using lots of profanity and having a main character so detestable you don't care what happens to him."

This cover of Deathrealm *by Jeffrey Osier was drawn to accompany his story, "Little Skull Girl." Editor Mark Rainey says "Osier's illustration captures the eerie, grotesque mood that prevails throughout most of this magazine that leans toward supernatural, atmospheric fiction." Osier is an art director at* Encyclopedia Britannica *in Chicago. Copyright © 1990 by Jeffrey Ossier.*

DELIRIUM (II), Route One, Box 7X, Harrison ID 83833. Editor: Judith Shannon Paine. Magazine: 6½×9; 60 pages; 50 lb. paper; 65 lb. cover; illustrations; photos occasionally. "Themes will vary. The material must be lively, well-developed. For adult audience interested in contemporary, literary, avant garde." Quarterly. Estab. 1989. Circ. 200.
Needs: Contemporary, experimental, horror, humor/satire, prose poem, romance (contemporary), western, young adult/teen (10-18). "No religious, political rant, juvenile, pornography, occult." Plans special fiction issue in the future. Acquires 5-10 mss/issue; 30-40 mss/year. Publishes ms 3 months after acceptance. Length: 500 words preferred; 250 words minimum; 1,000 words maximum. Publishes short shorts. Length: 350 words. Sometimes critiques rejected mss and recommends other markets.
How to Contact: Send complete ms with cover letter and SASE sufficient for its return. Reports in 2 weeks-3 months on mss. SASE. Accepts photocopied submissions. Sample copy for $4. (Make checks payable to publisher: Frank L. Nicholson, Muggwart Press, POB 7814, Riverside CA 92503). Fiction guidelines for #10 SAE and 1 first class stamp.
Payment: Pays one contributor's copy.
Terms: Acquires one-time rights. Rights revert to author.
Advice: "Seek pride and pleasure by doing your very very best. A manuscript must be finely crafted, lively, original, from start to finish, neat, well-spelled and syntaxically acceptable. A fresh, funny, warm, bold or gripping manuscript will get my attention. Like fine wine, it should have its very own bouquet and have time to breathe. Be your own meanest editor. Don't be afraid. I don't bite. Have fun when you write. Structure is important. Get naked. I want to see the bare bones in your work, please."

DENVER QUARTERLY (II, III), University of Denver, Denver CO 80208. (303)871-2892. Editor: Donald Revell. Magazine: 6×9; 144-160 pages; occasional illustrations. "We publish fiction, articles and poetry for a generally well-educated audience, primarily interested in literature and the literary experience. They read *DQ* to find something a little different from a strictly academic quarterly or a creative writing outlet." Quarterly. Estab. 1966. Circ. 1,200.
Needs: "We are now interested in experimental fiction (minimalism, magic realism, etc.) as well as in realistic fiction."
How to Contact: Send complete ms with SASE. Does not read mss May-September 15. Do not query. Reports in 1-2 months on mss. Publishes ms within a year after acceptance. Published work by Joyce Carol Oates, Jay Clayton, Charles Baxter; published new writers within the last year. No simultaneous submissions. Sample copy $5 with SASE.
Payment: Pays $5/page for fiction and poetry, 2 free author's copies plus 3 tear sheets.
Terms: Buys first North American serial rights.
Advice: "We'll be looking for serious, realistic and experimental fiction. Nothing so quickly disqualifies a manuscript as sloppy proofreading and mechanics. Read the magazine before submitting to it. Send clean copy and a *brief* cover letter. We try to remain eclectic and I think we do, but the odds for beginners are bound to be long considering the fact that we receive nearly 8,000 mss per year and publish only about 16 short stories."

DESCANT (II), Box 314, Station P, Toronto, Ontario M5S 2S8 Canada. (416)927-7059. Editor: Karen Mulhallen. Magazine: 5¾×8¾; 100-300 pages; heavy paper; good cover stock; illustrations and photos. "High quality poetry and prose for an intelligent audience who wants to see a broad range of literature." Published 4 times/year. Published special fiction issue last year; plans another. Estab. 1970. Circ. 1,000.
Needs: Literary, contemporary, translations. "Although most themes are acceptable, all works must have literary merit." Receives 100-200 unsolicited mss/month. Recently published work by Tim Lilburn, Douglas Glover, George Bowering. Publishes short shorts. Critiques rejected mss when there is time.
How to Contact: Send complete ms with cover letter. SAE, IRC. Reports in 4 months on mss. Sample copy $7.50 plus $2 for postage to U.S.
Payment: Pays a modest honorarium and 1 year subscription. Extra author's copies at discount.
Advice: "*Descant* has plans for several special issues in the next two years. Unsolicited work is less likely to be accepted in the coming months, and will be kept on file for longer before it appears."

DESCANT (II), Department of English, Texas Christian University, Fort Worth TX 76129. (817)921-7240. Editors: Betsy Colquitt, Stanley Trachtenberg. "*Descant* uses fiction and poetry. No restriction on style, content or theme. *Descant* is a 'little' literary magazine, and its readers are those who have interest in such publications." Semiannually. Estab. 1955. Circ. 500.

Needs: Literary, contemporary and regional. No genre or category fiction. Receives approximately 50 unsolicited fiction mss each month. Does not read mss in summer. Published new writers within the last year. Length: 1,500-5,000 words. Publishes short shorts. Sometimes recommends other markets. **How to Contact:** Send complete ms with SASE. Accepts computer printout submissions. Reports usually within 6 weeks on ms. Sample copy $4.50 (old copy).
Payment: Pays 2 free author's copies. (Pays $4.50 charge/extra copy.)
Advice: "Submit good material. Even though a small publication, *Descant* receives many submissions, and acceptances are few compared to the total number of mss received." Mss are rejected because they "are badly written, careless in style and development, shallow in characterization, trite in handling and in conception. We offer a $300 annual prize for fiction—the Frank O'Connor Prize. Award is made to the story considered (by a judge not connected to the magazine) to be the best published in a given volume of the journal."

DESERT SUN, 840 Ortiz SE #1, Albuquerque NM 87108. (505)266-8905. Editor: Craig W. Chrissinger. Magazine: 7 × 8½; 24-40 pages; 20 lb bond paper and cover; illustrations and photographs. Theme: science fiction, fantasy and horror. Publishes fiction, articles, essays, book reviews, movie reviews, interviews. Semiannually. Estab. 1986. Circ. 120.
Needs: Science fiction, fantasy, horror, humor/satire, erotica. "Almost any element is allowed as long as it ties in with science fiction, fantasy or horror." Receives 10-15 fiction mss/month. Accepts 10-20 mss/issue. Does not read mss March-May or August-December. Publishes ms 2-4 months after acceptance. Recently published work by William Rasmussen, D.M. Vosk, Anke Kriske; published new writers within the last year. Length: 1,000-2,000 words average; 3,200 words maximum. Sometimes critiques rejected ms and recommends other markets.
How to Contact: Send complete ms with cover letter and name, source of information about magazine. Reports on queries in 1 month; 2 months on mss. SASE. Photocopied submissions OK. Accepts computer printout submissions, including dot-matrix. Sample copy $2. Make all payments to Craig Chrissinger. Fiction guidelines for #10 SASE.
Payment: Pays in contributor's copies; charge for extras.
Terms: Acquires one-time rights. Publication copyrighted.
Advice: "First off, be as original as possible and have fun with your manuscripts. Work at your writing every day. When you're ready to submit, know about the magazine's focus and send only appropriate material. Watch out for typographical errors, and spelling and punctuation mistakes."

DEVIANCE, Opus II Writing Services, Box 1706, Pawtucket RI 02862. (401)722-8187 (evenings, weekends only). Editor: Lin Collette. Magazine. 8½ × 11; 36-48 pages; 20 lb. bond paper; heavier bond cover; b&w drawings; b&w photographs on occasion. "*Deviance* is a magazine dedicated to publishing work by persons espousing views that may not be in favor of the 'majority.' This includes feminists, lesbian/gay, non-religious or religious (i.e. discussions of religious issues that are not Judeo-Christian or which may be an unorthodox view of Christianity or Judaism), political (non-republican or democrat) and so on." Published three times yearly. Plans special fiction issue. Estab. 1987. Circ. 500.
Needs: Condensed novel, contemporary, ethnic, experimental, fantasy, feminist, gay, historical (general), horror, humor/satire, lesbian, literary, prose poems, psychic/supernatural/occult, science fiction, serialized/excerpted novel, spiritual, suspense/mystery, translations. "Nothing homophobic, racist, sexist, violent for violence's sake." Receives 5 fiction mss/month. Accepts 1-2 mss/issue. May publish ms up to 2 years after acceptance. Published work by Rombakis; published new writers within the last year. Length: 2,500 words average; 25 words minimum; 2,500 words maximum. Sometimes critiques rejected ms and recommends other markets.
How to Contact: Send complete ms with cover letter, a biography including other places published, a whimsical description of author, no longer than 10 lines. Reports on queries in 2 weeks; 1 month on mss. SASE. Simultaneous, photocopied and reprint submissions OK. Accepts computer printout submissions. Sample copy $4.50, SAE with 85¢ postage. Fiction guidelines for #10 SAE with 1 first class stamp. *Make checks out to Lin Collette please!*
Payment: Pays in contributor's copies; $4 charge for extras.
Terms: Acquires first rights.
Advice: "Read the magazine! We have people sending in material that is so 'mainstream' (as in inspirational, children's, Harlequin-type love stories) that we know nobody's bothering to check us out. If you can't afford a back issue, at least send for guidelines. We are looking for offbeat ways of looking at the world—we publish gay, lesbian, feminist, horror, slice-of-life, *New Yorker*-style pieces, so if you've been rejected by *The New Yorker*, give us a try."

‡**DOOR COUNTY ALMANAK (IV)**, The Dragonsbreath Press, 10905 Bay Shore Dr., Sister Bay WI 54234. (414)854-2742. Editor: Fred Johnson. Magazine: 6x9; 200-300 pages; good uncoated paper; antique vellum cover stock; illustrations; photos. "The major focus is Door County WI and its surrounding areas. Covering the history, recent and distant, of the area and its people, including contemporary profiles of people and businesses. Each issue has a major theme. Also uses poetry and fiction for general audience, mainly aimed at people familiar with the area." No set publication schedule. Estab. 1982.

Needs: Adventure, contemporary, fantasy, historical (general), humor/satire, literary, regional, suspense/mystery. "Prefer to have the fiction in some way related to the area, at least to the issue's theme." No romance. Receives 10-20 unsolicited fiction mss/month. Buys 1-2 mss/issue. Does not read mss April-September. Published new writers within the last year. Length: 4,000 words average; 500 words minimum; 6,000 words maximum.

How to Contact: Query first. Reports in 3-4 weeks on queries; 2-3 months on mss. SASE for query and ms. Simultaneous, photocopied submissions and reprints OK. Accepts computer printouts. Sample copy: $5.95 for issue #2; $7.95 for issue #3 with 7x10 SAE and $1 postage. Fiction guidelines free for #10 SAE and 1 first class stamp.

Payment: Pays $10-$35 plus contributor's copies.

Terms: Pays on publication for first North American serial rights and other rights.

Advice: "Query first to find out what coming issue's theme is and what the needs are. We're always looking for nonfiction articles also. Keep in mind this is definitely a regional magazine."

DREAM INTERNATIONAL/QUARTERLY (II, IV), U.S. Address: Charles I. Jones, 121 N. Ramona St. #27, Ramona CA 92065. Australia address: Dr. Les Jones, 256 Berserker St., No. Rockhampton, Queensland 4701, Australia. Editors: Les and Chuck Jones. Magazine: 5 × 7; 60-80 pages; Xerox paper; parchment cover stock; some illustrations and photos. Publishes fiction and nonfiction that is dream-related or clearly inspired by a dream. Quarterly. Estab. 1981. Circ. 200.

Needs: Adventure, confession, contemporary, erotica, ethnic, experimental, fantasy, historical (general), horror, humor/satire, juvenile (5-9 years), literary, mainstream, prose poem, psychic/supernatural/occult, romance, science fiction, senior citizen/retirement, serialized/excerpted novel, spiritual, suspense/mystery, translations, western, young adult/teen (10-18). Receives 20-40 unsolicited mss/month. Publishes ms 6-8 months after acceptance. Length: 1,500 words minimum; 2,000 words maximum. Published new writers within the last year. Publishes short shorts. Length: 1,000 words. Occasionally critiques rejected mss. Sometimes recommends other markets.

How to Contact: Reports in 6 weeks on queries; 3 months on mss. SASE. Photocopied and reprint submissions OK. Accepts computer printout submissions. Sample copy for $4 (add $1 to single copy purchases and $3 to subscriptions to cover postage and handling), SAE and 2 first class stamps. Guidelines for $1, SAE and 1 first class stamp. "Accepted mss will not be returned unless requested at time of submission."

Payment: Pays in contributor's copies; sometimes offers free magazine subscription.

Terms: Acquires one-time rights.

Advice: "Use your nightly dreams to inspire you to literary flights. Avoid stereotypes and clichés. Avoid Twilight Zone type stories. When contacting editor, make all checks, money orders, and overseas drafts payable to *Charles Jones.*"

‡**DREAMS & NIGHTMARES (IV)**, **The Magazine of Fantastic Poetry**, 4801 Cypress Creek #1004, Tuscaloosa AL 35405. (205)553-2284. Editor: David C. Kopaska-Merkel. Magazine: 5½×8½; 20 pages; ink drawing illustrations. "*DN* is mainly a poetry magazine, but I *am* looking for short-short stories. They should be either fantasy, science fiction, or horror." Estab. 1986. Circ. 200.

Needs: Experimental, fantasy, horror, humor/satire, science fiction. "Try me with anything *except*: senseless violence, misogyny or hatred (unreasoning) of any kind of people, sappiness." Receives 4-8 unsolicited mss/month. Buys 0-1 ms/issue; 0-2 mss/year. Publishes ms 1-9 months after acceptance. Recently published work by Ron McDowell. Length: 500 words average; 1,000 words maximum. Publishes short shorts. Length: 500 or fewer words. Sometimes critiques rejected mss and recommends other markets.

How to Contact: Query first, then send complete manuscript. Reports in 1-3 weeks on queries; 1-6 weeks on mss. SASE. Photocopied submissions OK. Accepts computer printout submissions. Accepts electronic submissions. Sample copy for $1. Fiction guidelines for #10 SAE and 1 first class stamp.

Payment: Pays $2 and one contributor's copy.

Terms: Pays on acceptance for one-time rights.

Advice: "A story must grab the reader and hold on to the end. I want to be *involved*. Start with a good first line, lead the reader where you want him/her to go and end with something that causes a reaction or provokes thought."

DREAMS & VISIONS (II), New Frontiers in Christian Fiction, Skysong Press, RR1, Washago, Ontario L0K 2B0 Canada. Editor: Steve Stanton. Fiction Editor: Wendy Stanton. Magazine: 5½ × 8½; 48 pages; 20 lb. bond paper; Cornwall coated cover; illustrations on cover. "Contemporary Christian fiction in a variety of styles for adult Christians." Quarterly. Estab. 1989. Circ. 1,000.

Needs: Contemporary, experimental, fantasy, humor/satire, literary, religious/inspirational. "All stories should portray a Christian world view or expand upon Biblical themes or ethics in an entertaining or enlightening manner." Receives 10 unsolicited mss/month. Accepts 7 mss/issue; 30 mss/year. Publishes ms 2-6 months after acceptance. Length: 2,500 words; 1,200 words minimum; 8,000 words maximum. Sometimes critiques rejected mss and recommends other markets.

How to Contact: Send complete ms with cover letter. "Bio is optional: degrees held and in what specialties, publishing credits, service in the church, etc." Reports in 2 weeks on queries; 6-8 weeks on mss. SASE. Photocopied submissions OK. Accepts computer printout submissions. Sample copy for $3. Fiction guidelines for SAE and 1 IRC.

Payment: Pays in contributor's copies; charge for extra at ⅓ discount.

Terms: Acquires first North American serial rights and one-time, non-exclusive reprint rights.

Advice: "In general we look for work that has some literary value, that is in some way unique and relevant to Christian readers today. Our first priority is technical adequacy, though we will occasionally work with a beginning writer to polish a manuscript. Ultimately, we look for stories that glorify the Lord Jesus Christ, stories that build up rather than tear down, that exalt the sanctity of life, the holiness of God, and the value of the family."

EAGLE'S FLIGHT (I), A Literary Magazine, 203 N. Weigle, Watonga OK 73772. (405)623-7333. Editor: Shyamkant Kulkarni. Fiction Editor: Rekha Kulkarni. Tabloid: 8½ × 11; 2-4 pages; bond paper; broad sheet cover. Publication prints "fiction and poetry for a general audience." Quarterly.

Needs: Literary, mainstream, romance, suspense/mystery. Plans to publish special fiction issue in future. Accepts 1-2 mss/year. Does not read mss June-December. Length: 1,500 words preferred; 1,000 words minimum; 2,000 maximum. Publishes short shorts.

How to Contact: Query first. Reports in 6 weeks on queries; 3 months on mss. Combine SASE. Photocopied submissions OK. Accepts computer printout submissions. Sample copy or fiction guidelines for $1 and 4 × 9½ SAE and 1 first class stamp.

Payment: Pays $5-20 or free subscription to magazine, contributor's copies; charge for extras.

Terms: Pays on publication for first North American serial rights or one-time rights.

Advice: "We look for form, substance and quality. Read and study what one wants to write and work at."

EARTH'S DAUGHTERS (II), A Feminist Arts Periodical, Box 41, Central Park Station, Buffalo NY 14215. (716)835-8719. Collective editorship. Business Manager: Bonnie Johnson. Magazine: usually 5½ × 8½; 50 pages; 60 lb paper; coated cover; 2-4 illustrations; 2-4 photos. "We publish poetry and short fiction; also graphics, art work and photos; our focus is the experience and creative expression of women." For a general/women/feminist audience. Quarterly. Published special topical issues last year; plans more this year. Estab. 1971. Circ. 1,000.

Needs: Contemporary, erotica, ethnic, experimental, fantasy, feminist, humor/satire, literary, prose poem. "Keep the fiction short." Receives 25-50 unsolicited fiction mss/month. Accepts 2-4 mss/issue; 8-12 mss/year. Recently published work by Gabrielle Burton, Mary Jane Markell, Meredith Sue Willis and Julia Alvarez; published several new writers within the last year. Length: 400 words minimum; 1,000 words maximum; 800 words average. Occasionally critiques rejected mss and recommends other markets.

How to Contact: Send complete ms. SASE. Simultaneous and photocopied submissions OK. Accepts computer printout submissions, "must be clearly legible." Reports in 3 weeks on queries; 3 weeks to 3 months on mss. Publishes ms an average of 1 year after acceptance. Sample copy for $4.

Payment: 2 free contributor's copies, additional copies half price.
Terms: Acquires first rights. Copyright reverts to author upon publication.
Advice: "We require work of technical skill and artistic intensity; we welcome submissions from unknown writers. Send SASE in April of each year for themes of upcoming issues. Please do not inquire as to the status of your work too soon or too often—the US Mail is dependable, and we have yet to lose a manuscript."

ECHOES (I,II), The Hudson Valley Writers Association, Box 365, Wappingers Falls NY 12590. (914)298-8556. Editor: Marcia Grant. Fiction Editors: Casey Clark Grant, Don Monaco. Magazine: 5½×8½; 44 pages; illustrations. Quarterly. Estab. 1985. Circ. 300.
Needs: "We do not categorize material—we consider material of *all* types." Receives 15-30 unsolicited mss/month. Buys or accepts 2-5 mss/issue; 8-20 mss/year. Publishes ms 8-12 weeks after acceptance. Recently published work by Arnold Lipkind, C.C. Doucette. Length: 1,500 words preferred; 750 words minimum; 3,000 words maximum. Publishes short shorts. Sometimes critiques rejected mss and recommends other markets.
How to Contact: Send complete manuscript with cover letter. Reports in 6-8 weeks on queries/mss. SASE. Simultaneous, photocopied and reprint submissions OK if author owns rights. Accepts computer printout submissions. Sample copy for $4.50. Back issues $3. Fiction guidelines for SAE.
Payment: Pays 1 contributor's copy.
Terms: Acquires one-time rights.
Advice: "Suggest reading a sample copy. We look for quality writing, engaging ideas and writing that we can get excited about."

‡THE ECPHORIZER (II), A Mensa Magazine of Literature and Ideas, American Mensa Ltd., Region 8, 481 Century Dr., Campbell CA 95008. (408)378-8820. Editor: Michael J. Eager. Magazine: 7×8½; 36 pages; 60 lb. offset paper; Astrobrite cover; 5-8 line art illustrations and limited photographs. "Eclectic magazine for Mensa members and friends." Bimonthly. Estab. 1981.
Needs: Adventure, contemporary, erotica, experimental, fantasy, historical (general), humor/satire, literary, mainstream, prose poem, psychic/supernatural/occult, regional, science fiction, serialized novel, suspense/mystery, translations. Receives 4-5 unsolicited mss/month. Accepts 2-3 mss/issue; 18-25 mss/year. Publishes ms 2-4 months after acceptance. Recently published work by Redge Mahaffey, Albert Russo. Length: 3,000 words average; 500 words minimum; 6,000 words maximum. Publishes short shorts. Sometimes critiques rejected mss.
How to Contact: Send complete manuscript with cover letter. Reports in 2-4 weeks. SASE. Simultaneous, photocopied and reprint submissions OK. Accepts computer printout submissions. Accepts electronic submissions (preferred method). Sample copy $2.
Payment: Pays contributor's copies.
Terms: Acquires first North American serial or one-time rights.
Advice: Looks for "interesting presentation, well-thought-out, unique approach to situation. Have clear idea of what you are trying to say and who you are saying it to. Too many articles received which are technically well written but appear to have no point or purpose. One gets to the end and says 'So? What next?' "

EIDOS: (IV), Erotic Entertainment for Women, Men & Couples, Box 96, Boston MA 02137-0096. (617)262-0096. Editor: Brenda L. Tatelbaum. Tabloid: 10×14; 48 pages; web offset printing; illustrations; photos. Magazine of erotica for women, men and couples of all sexual orientations, preferences and lifestyles. "Explicit material regarding language and behavior formed in relationships, intimacy, moment of satisfaction—sensual, sexy, honest. For an energetic, well informed, international erotica readership." Quarterly. Estab. 1984. Circ. 7,000.
Needs: Erotica. Humorous or tongue-in-cheek erotic fiction is especially wanted. Publishes at least 4 pieces of fiction/year. Published new writers within the last year. Length: 1,000 words average; 500 words minimum; 2,000 words maximum. Occasionally critiques rejected mss and recommends other markets.
How to Contact: Send complete ms with SASE. "Cover letter with history of publication or short bio is welcome." Reports in 1 month on queries; 2 months on mss. Simultaneous and photocopied submissions OK. Accepts computer printout submissions. Sample copy $10. Fiction guidelines for #10 envelope with 1 first class stamp.

Payment: Pays in contributor's copies.
Terms: Acquires first North American serial rights.
Advice: "We receive more erotic fiction manuscripts now than in the past. Most likely because both men and women are more comfortable with the notion of submitting these manuscripts for publication as well as the desire to see alternative sexually explicit fiction in print. Therefore we can publish more erotic fiction because we have more material to choose from. There is still a lot of debate as to what erotic fiction consists of. This is a tough market to break into. Manuscripts must fit our editorial needs and it is best to order a sample issue prior to writing or submitting material. Honest, explicitly pro-sex, mutually consensual erotica is void of power, control and degradation—no rape or coercion of any kind."

ELDRITCH SCIENCE (II,IV), Greater Medford Science Fiction Society, 87-6 Park, Worcester MA 01605. Editor: George Phillies. Magazine: 8½×11; 30 pages; 20 lb paper; 60 lb cover; illustrations. Science fiction and fantasy for adults. Semiannually. Estab. 1988.
Needs: Adventure, fantasy, literary, science fiction. "No horror, contemporary, erotica." Receives 5-10 unsolicited mss/month. Accepts 4 mss/issue; 8 mss/year. Publishes mss 4-6 months after acceptance. Published work by Cabot, Moxley, Reedman. Length: 8,000 words; 5,000 words minimum; 15,000 words maximum. Sometimes critiques rejected mss and recommends other markets.
How to Contact: Send complete ms with cover letter. Reports in 2 weeks on queries; 6-8 weeks on mss. SASE for mss. Photocopied submissions OK. Accepts computer printout submissions. Accepts electronic submissions via disk. Sample copy for 8½×11 SAE and 4 first class stamps. Free fiction guidelines.
Payment: Pays in contributor's copies.
Terms: Acquires one-time rights. Publication not copyrighted.
Advice: "Clear plots, heroes who think and solve their problems, and sparkling, literary prose. Make a manuscript stand out. Read the guidelines!"

ELDRITCH TALES (II, IV), Yith Press, 1051 Wellington Rd., Lawrence KS 66044. (913)843-4341. Editor-in-Chief: Crispin Burnham. Magazine: 5½×8; 120 pages (average); glossy cover; illustrations; "very few" photos. "The magazine concerns horror fiction in the tradition of the old *Weird Tales* magazine. We publish fiction in the tradition of H.P. Lovecraft, Robert Bloch and Stephen King, among others, for fans of this particular genre." Semiannually. Estab. 1975. Circ. 1,000.
Needs: Horror and psychic/supernatural/occult. "No mad slasher stories or similar nonsupernatural horror stories." Receives about 8 unsolicited fiction mss/month. Accepts 12 mss/issue, 24 mss/year. Published work by J.N. Williamson, William F. Wu and Charles Grant. Published new writers within the last year. Length: 50-100 words minimum; 20,000 words maximum; 10,000 words average. Occasionally critiques rejected mss. Sometimes recommends other markets.
How to Contact: Send complete ms with SASE and cover letter stating past sales. Photocopied and previously published submissions OK. Accepts computer printout submissions, prefers letter-quality. Reports in 4 months. Publication could take up to 5 years after acceptance. Sample copy $6 and $1 for postage and handling.
Payment: ¼¢/word; 1 contributor's copy. $1 minimum payment.
Terms: Pays in royalties on publication for first rights.
Advice: "Buy a sample copy and read it thoroughly. Most rejects with my magazine are because people have not checked out what an issue is like or what type of stories I accept. Most rejected stories fall into one of two categories: non-horror fantasy (sword & sorcery, high fantasy) or non-supernatural horror (mad slasher stories, 'Halloween' clones, I call them). When I say that they should read my publication, I'm not whistling Dixie. We hope to up the magazine's frequency to a quarterly. We also plan to be putting out one or two books a year, mostly novels, but short story collections will be considered as well."

THE ELEPHANT-EAR (II, IV), Irvine Valley College, 550 Irvine Center Dr., Irvine CA 92720. (714)559-3327 ext. 299. Editor: Linda Thomas. Magazine: 6×9; 150+ pages; matte paper and cover stock; illustrations and photos. "The journal prints the work of Orange County writers only." Annually. Estab. 1983. Circ. 2,000.
Needs: Contemporary, ethnic, experimental, feminist, humor/satire, literary, regional. Receives 100 mss/year. Accepts 5 mss/issue. "Reads only between Feb. 14 and June 1; reports thereafter." Publishes ms within 3 months of acceptance. Length: 25 pages maximum. Publishes short shorts. Sometimes critiques rejected mss.

How to Contact: Send completed ms with cover letter, which should include "the name, address and phone number of author, the title(s) of work submitted. Author's name must not appear on manuscript." SASE. Photocopied submissions OK. Accepts computer printout submissions. Sample copy for 6x9 SAE. Free fiction guidelines.
Payment: Pays in contributor's copies.
Terms: Acquires one-time rights.

‡11TH STREET RUSE (II), 322 E. 11th St., #23, New York NY 10003. Editor: Violet Snow. Newsletter: 8½ × 11; 4 pages; bond paper. "Mythical travel; goddess religion; the homeless; for young intellectuals with poor spelling." Bimonthly. Estab. 1988. Circ. 150.
Needs: "We need humorous writers, who can *hear* what they write—preferably have studied poetry. Accepts all types of fiction." No "Romance or genre that's dumb and obvious." Receives 5 unsolicited mss/month. Accepts 1 ms/year. Publishes ms 2 months after acceptance. Recently published work by RLS, Violet Snow and Lucid. Length: 500 words average; 6 words minimum; 1,000 words maximum. Publishes short shorts. Length: 300 words. Sometimes comments on rejected mss.
How to Contact: Send complete manuscript with cover letter. Include "bio, hatsize." Reports in 3 months. SASE. Simultaneous and photocopied submissions OK. Accepts computer printout submissions. Sample copy for $1, #10 SAE and 1 first class stamp. Fiction guidelines for #10 SAE and 1 first class stamp.
Payment: Pays contributor's copies.
Terms: Acquires one-time rights. Publication not copyrighted.

‡ELLIPSIS . . . (II), 105A N. Santa Cruz Ave., Los Gatos CA 95030. Editor: Joy Oestreicher. Journal: 96 pages; illustrations. "*Ellipsis* . . . represents those writings which have been mistakenly omitted from academic literature. We publish unique literary poetry, short fiction and essays of epistemological comment." Biannual. Estab. 1988.
Needs: Literary, humor/satire, prose poem, experimental, essay, traditional poetry and b&w art. "We're interested in serious fiction and poetry which has a humorous twist and vice versa. In particular, we are looking for work which contains a strong, philosophical, psychological or social theme." Receives 50 mss/month. Accepts 15-20 mss/issue. Publishes ms within 6-12 months of acceptance. Length: 5,000 words maximum. Publishes short shorts. Sometimes critiques rejected mss and recommends other markets.
How to Contact: Send SASE for writer's guidelines! Reports on mss in 1-6 months. SASE. Simultaneous and photocopied submissions OK. Accepts computer printout submissions, including dot-matrix (please use a dark ribbon). Accepts electronic submissions (Macintosh). No more than 2 short stories or 6 poems per submission. Sample copy $6.
Advice: "In order to be published in *Ellipsis* . . ., a poem or short story must show the passionate writer's command of language, either through a unique use of the written word, or through the creative use of imagery and metaphor. We don't want to see stories that simply meander for 10 pages and then stop. We seek writing which leaves the reader with a sense that something important and wonderful has been said. (Not to make the whole thing sound too forbidding, we also happen to like puns, and enjoy odd stories that strike our fancy.) It is strongly suggested that you purchase a sample copy."

‡EMERALD CITY COMIX & STORIES, Wonder Comix, P.O. Box 95402, Seattle WA 98145-2402. (206)784-0162. Editor: Nils Osmar. Newsletter (Tabloid): 35″ tab (folds to 8½ × 11½); 8-12 pages; newsprint paper; illustrations and photographs. "Eclectic material for an eclectic audience (mostly adults, somewhat sophisticated)." Quarterly. Estab. 1987. Circ. 10,000.
Needs: Adventure, erotica, experimental, fantasy, humor/satire, literary, mainstream, prose poem, science fiction, suspense/mystery. No "misogynist." Receives 30 unsolicited mss/month. Accepts 1-2 mss/issue; 4-6 mss/year. Publishes ms 1-6 months after acceptance. Recently published work by Jerome Gold. Length: 2,500 words average. Publishes short shorts. "Sometimes" recommends other markets.
How to Contact: Send complete manuscript with cover letter. Reports in 2-4 weeks. SASE. Simultaneous, photocopied and reprint submissions OK. Accepts computer printout submissions. Sample copy for $2. Fiction guidelines for 1 first class stamp.
Payment: Pays 2 contributor's copies.
Terms: Writer retains all rights.
Advice: "Don't be discouraged if your work isn't immediately published. Commercial potential isn't necessarily related to artistic merit. In fact, there may be an inverse equation in today's marketplace."

EMRYS JOURNAL (II), The Emrys Foundation, Box 8813, Greenville SC 29604. (803)288-5154. Editor: Linda Julian. Magazine: 6×9; 96 pages; 60 lb. paper and cover stock; calligraphy illustrations. "We publish short fiction, poetry, essays and book reviews. We are particularly interested in hearing from women and other minorities. We are mindful of the southeast but not limited to it." Annually. Estab. 1984. Circ. 300.
Needs: Contemporary, feminist, literary, mainstream and regional. "We read only during September 1-February 15. During reading periods we receive around 800 manuscripts." Accepts 3-7 stories per issue. Publishes ms 2 months after acceptance. Length: 3,500 words average; 2,500 word minimum; 6,000 word maximum. Publishes short shorts. Length: 1,600 words. Sometimes recommends other markets.
How To Contact: Send complete ms with cover letter. Put no identification on manuscript; include separate sheet with title, name, address and phone. "No queries." Reports in 2 months. SASE. Photocopied submissions OK. Accepts computer printout submissions. Sample copy $4 and 7×10 SAE with 4 first class stamps. Fiction guidelines for #10 SAE and 1 first class stamp.
Payment: Pays in contributor's copies.
Terms: Acquires first rights. "Send to managing editor for guidelines."

EOTU (I, II), Magazine of Experimental Fiction, 1810 W. State, #115, Boise ID 83702. Editor: Larry D. Dennis. Magazine 5½×8½; 70-80 pages; 20 lb paper; illustrations. "We publish short stories that try to say or do something new in literature, in prose. New style, new story structures, new voice, whatever." Bimonthly. Estab. 1988. Circ. 500.
Needs: Experimental, prose poem. No stories whose express purpose is to advance a religious or political belief. No pornography. Receives 150-200 unsolicited fiction mss/month; accepts 10-12 mss/issue; 60-70 mss/year. Publishes ms 4-6 months after acceptance. Recently published work by Don Webb, Bruce Boston, H. Andrew Lynch; published new writers within the last year. Length: 2,500 words average; 2 words minimum; 5,000 words maximum. Sometimes comments on rejected mss or recommends other markets.
How to Contact: Send complete ms. "Cover letter isn't really necessary, but it's nice to know where they heard of us." Reports on queries in 1 week; on mss in 6-8 weeks. SASE. Photocopied submissions OK. Accepts computer printouts. Sample copy for $4; fiction guidelines for #10 SAE and 1 first class stamp.
Payment: Pays $5 minimum; $25 maximum and contributor's copies.
Terms: Pays on acceptance for first North American serial rights. Sends pre-publication galleys to author "only when a story has been edited and a writer's approval of the changes is needed."
Advice: "I've got this time and money and want to invest it in something. So, do I buy a Jiffy Lube or start a new Wendy Burger place? Or do I choose to create a business that caters to my strengths, my loves and desires? Well, that's what I'm doing. I always wanted to publish a magazine, and I've always loved short stories. I urge beginning writers to keep sending stories out. You'll never sell the one in your drawer. If a story comes back with a handwritten note, if it looks like someone really read it, send that editor another. When an editor takes time to critique, it means he's interested and he's trying to help."

EPOCH MAGAZINE (II), 251 Goldwin Smith Hall, Cornell University, Ithaca NY 14853. (607)256-3385. Editor: Michael Koch. Magazine: 6×9; 80-100 pages; good quality paper; good cover stock. "Top level fiction and poetry for people who are interested in and capable of being entertained by good literature." Published 3 times a year. Estab. 1947. Circ. 1,000.
Needs: Literary, contemporary and ethnic. Buys 4-5 mss/issue. Receives approximately 100 unsolicited fiction mss each month. Does not read in summer. Recently published work by Dallas Wiebe, Harriet Doerr, Darrell Spencer; published new writers in the last year. Length: 10-30 typed, double-spaced pages. Critiques rejected mss when there is time. Sometimes recommends other markets.
How to Contact: Send complete ms with SASE. Accepts computer printout submissions. "No dot-matrix please." Reports in 2-8 weeks on mss. Publishes ms an average of 3 months after acceptance. Sample copy $4.
Terms: Pays on publication for first North American serial rights.
Advice: "Read and be interested in the journals you're sending work to."

ERGO! (II), The Bumbershoot Literary Magazine, Bumbershoot, Box 9750, Seattle WA 98109-0750. (206)622-5123. Editor: Judith Roche. Magazine: 6×9; 100 pages; 60 lb offset stock; gloss cover; illustrations; photos. "Magazine publishes articles of interest to the literary community, book reviews,

and poems and prose by competition winners and invited writers who read at the Bumbershoot Festival." Annually. Circ. 1,500.
Needs: Literary. Accepts approximately 4 mss/issue. Agented fiction 4%. Publishes short shorts.
How to Contact: Query first. Reports in 2 weeks on queries; 2 months on mss. SASE for ms. Simultaneous, photocopied and reprint submissions OK. Accepts computer printout submissions. Sample copy for $5 and 9 × 12 SAE.
Payment: $25-75 for articles and reviews. $150 award honoraria for Bumbershoot writers; contributor's copies.
Terms: Pays on acceptance for one-time rights.
Advice: Request application for annual contest.

EROTIC FICTION QUARTERLY (I, II, IV), EFQ Publications, Box 4958, San Francisco CA 94101. Editor: Richard Hiller. Magazine: 5 × 8; 186 pages; perfect bound; 50 lb offset paper; 65 lb cover stock. "Small literary magazine for thoughtful people interested in a variety of highly original and creative short fiction with sexual themes. Irregularly published."
Needs: Any style heartfelt, intelligent erotica. Also, stories not necessarily erotic whose subject is some aspect of authentic sexual experience. No standard pornography; no "men's magazine" stories; no contrived plots or gimmicks; no broad satire, parody or obscure "literary" writing. Length: 500 words minimum; 5,000 words maximum; 1,500 words average. Occasionally critiques rejected ms.
How to Contact: Send complete ms only. Photocopied submissions, non-returnable copy OK with SASE for reply. Fiction guidelines free with SASE.
Payment: $50.
Terms: Pays on acceptance for first rights.
Advice: "I specifically encourage unpublished as well as published writers who have something to say regarding sexual attitudes, emotions, roles, etc. Story ideas should come from real life, not media; characters should be real people. There are essentially no restrictions regarding content, style, explicitness, etc.; *originality*, *clarity* and *integrity* are most important. The philosophy is this: *EFQ* publishes stories *about* sex by persons who have something, grand vision or small insight, to say. We try not to publish anything that could easily be printed somewhere else, and what we need is original viewpoints not really describable in advance."

‡THE ESCAPIST (I), A Biannual Literary Journal for Fans of C.S. Lewis, 6861 Catlett Rd., St. Augustine FL 32095. Editor: T.M. Spell. Magazine: 5½ × 8½; 4-16 pages; 20-50 lb. paper; 20-50 lb. cover. "Escapism is viewed in a very positive light here, and stories in some way related to this theme are welcome. Looking for stories in the Lewisian tradition, or work that evokes what Lewis defined as 'Joy.' For teens to seniors who enjoy Christian fiction without the didactics, and who aren't afraid to ask themselves the tough questions about 'reality.' " Estab. 1990. Circ. 100 + .
Needs: Adventure, ethnic, experimental, fantasy, humor/satire, literary, prose poem, religious/inspirational, science fiction, suspense/mystery, translations. Receives 15-25 unsolicited mss/month. Accepts 4-10 mss/issue; 8-20 mss/year. Publishes ms 6 months to 1 year after acceptance. Recently published work by Roxanne Royer Smolen, Ron Blizzard, B.Z. Niditch. Length: 2,500 words average; 25 words minimum; 3,000 words maximum. Publishes short shorts. Sometimes critiques rejected mss and recommends other markets.
How to Contact: "Tell me a little about what you're submitting (is it a story, poem(s), or essay?), and where you saw *The Escapist* listed. If you would like me to comment on or critique your submission, just ask." Reports in 1-3 weeks on queries; 2-8 weeks on mss. SASE. Simultaneous, photocopied and reprint submissions OK. Accepts computer printout submissions. Sample copy for $1. Fiction guidelines for #10 SAE and 1 first class stamp.
Payment: Pays 2 contributor's copies.
Terms: Acquires first North American serial rights or one-time rights (if a reprint).
Advice: "Whether your story deals with global warming, space travel, or an alternate world adventure, strive through the use of imagery and the development of ideas to make the reader feel that sudden stab of Joy or unnameable longing that characterizes the effect that C.S. Lewis's work has had on you in the past. One story might be the feature piece of an entire issue, so I'm looking for especially excellent, vividly rendered, thought provoking writing."

EVENT (II), Douglas College, Box 2503, New Westminster, British Columbia V3L 5B2 Canada. Editor: Dale Zieroth. Fiction Editor: Maurice Hodgson. Managing Editor: Bonnie Bauder. Magazine: 6x9; 120 pages; good quality paper; good cover stock; illustrations; photos. "Primarily a literary magazine, publishing poetry, fiction, reviews, occasionally plays and graphics; for creative writers, artists, anyone interested in contemporary literature." Published 3 times/year. Estab. 1970. Circ. 1,000.

Needs: Literary, contemporary, feminist, adventure, humor, regional. No technically poor or unoriginal pieces. Buys 6-8 mss/issue. Receives approximately 50+unsolicited fiction mss/month. Recently published work by Jane Rule, H.E. Francis, Ally McKay; published new writers within the last year. Length: 5,000 words maximum. Critiques rejected mss "when there is time."

How to Contact: Send complete ms with SASE and bio (*must* be Canadian postage or IRC). Accepts computer printout submissions. Prefers letter-quality. Reports in 4 months on mss. Publishes ms an average of 6-12 months after acceptance. Sample copy $5.

Payment: Pays $10-$15 and 2 author's copies.

Terms: Pays on publication for first North American serial rights.

Advice: "A good narrative arc is hard to find."

‡**EXIT 13 MAGAZINE (II)**, 22 Oakwood Ct., Fanwood NJ 07023. (908)889-5298. Editor: Tom Plante. Magazine: 5½×8½; 52 pages. "Mostly poetry; 10-20% prose per issue." Annually. Estab. 1988. Circ. 400.

Needs: Adventure, contemporary, literary, regional. "Needs short fiction of four pages or less." No religious, juvenile, sci-fi. Receives 1 unsolicited ms/month. Accepts 1-2 mss/year. Publishes ms "within six months" of acceptance. Recently published work by Ruth Moon Kempher. Publishes short shorts 4 pages or less.

How to Contact: Send complete manuscript with cover letter. Reports in 2 weeks on queries; 2 months on mss. SASE. Simultaneous and photocopied submissions OK. Accepts computer printout submissions. Sample copy $5. Fiction guidelines for #10 SAE and 1 first class stamp.

Payment: Pays contributor's copy. Charges for extras.

Terms: Acquires one-time rights.

‡**EXPERIMENT IN WORDS (II), The Magazine of the 1990's**, Homemade Ice Cream Publications, P.O. Box 470186, Fort Worth TX 76147. Editor: Robert W. Howington. Magazine: 8½×11; 20-30 pages; 20-60 lb. paper; 20-60 lb. bond cover; b&w illustrations. "The theme is experimental. I publish stories that create unique thoughts, images, dialogue and narrative for those who appreciate originality and are open to new ideas and thoughts, and are not easily offended by someone else's point of view." To be published 3 times in 1991.

Needs: Experimental. "Use a different structure, content, style or voice. Don't get your ideas from the newspaper or TV or movies. Since this is an experimental magazine, I don't want any stories that fall into a so-called category. I want original pieces that create *new* categories." Receives 50-60 mss/month. Accepts 3-5 mss/issue; 9-15 mss/year. Publishes ms 3-6 months after acceptance. Recently published work by Charles Bukowski, Julie R Ragan, Dennis Beck. Length: 1,500 words average; 6 words minimum; 3,500 words maximum. Publishes short shorts. Length: 6-500 words. Sometimes critiques rejected mss and recommends other markets.

How to Contact: Send complete manuscript with cover letter. "Tell me who you are and what you do. Give me your literary background and/or activities. List your most cherished credits or awards. In one sentence give me your philosophy on writing (it can be a long sentence)." Reports in 1-2 months on mss. SASE. Simultaneous, photocopied and reprint submissions OK. Accepts computer printout submissions. Sample copy for $2 in cash or stamps, or both. Fiction guidelines for #10 SAE and 1 first class stamp.

Payment: Pays 2 contributor's copies.

Terms: Acquires one-time rights. "Each story, poem and drawing published is eligible for our Writer, Poet and Artist of the Year awards. The story, poem and drawing judged best (by me) for that calendar year (3 issues in 1991) will garner a monetary prize for its creator. The award winners and monetary amounts will be announced in the year's final issue."

Advice: "I like writing that extracts from me an emotional response or an intellectual pondering. My taste is in writing that is way off the beaten path. I want stuff that is so far out there they don't even have a map to tell you where it is. I don't require or encourage writers to purchase a sample copy. You will not figure out what I want by reading an issue. What it simply comes down to is this: I'll accept what I like, period. 'It's ALIVE! It's ALIVE!' describes my magazine. I want the words to walk off the page and jump onto my readers and show them something they've never seen before in the written word. Since I've become bored with the commercial fiction published today, I felt I could contribute to a new wave of fiction by offering pages to writers who hold my same beliefs—to be able to create fiction that has never before been offered to the reading public."

EXPLORATIONS '91, University of Alaska Southeast, 11120 Glacier Highway, Juneau AK 99801. (907)789-4418. Editors: Art Petersen and Ron Silva. Magazine: 5½ × 8¼; 44 pages; heavy cover stock; illustrations and photographs. "Poetry, prose and art—we strive for artistic excellence." Annually. Estab. 1980. Circ. 250.
Needs: Experimental, humor/satire. Receives 1,700 mss/year.
How to Contact: Send complete ms with cover letter, which should include bio. Reports in 2-3 months. SASE. Simultaneous, photocopied and reprint submissions OK. Accepts computer printout submissions. Sample copy $4 ($3 for back issues).
Payment: Pays 2 contributor's copies. *Charges $4 reading fee for non-UAS fiction contributors.* Also awards two annual prizes of $100 each: one for poetry, one for fiction. Write for information.
Terms: Acquires one-time rights (rights remain with the author).

EXPLORER MAGAZINE (I), Flory Publishing Co., Box 210, Notre Dame IN 46556. (219)277-3465. Editor: Ray Flory. Magazine: 5½ × 8½; 20-32 pages; 20 lb. paper; 60 lb. or stock cover; illustrations. Magazine with "basically an inspirational theme including love stories in good taste." Christian writing audience. Semiannually. Estab. 1960. Circ. 200 +.
Needs: Literary, mainstream, prose poem, religious/inspirational, romance (contemporary, historical, young adult) and science fiction. No pornography. Buys 2-3 mss/issue; 5 mss/year. Length: 600 words average; 300 words minimum; 900 words maximum. Occasionally critiques rejected mss.
How to Contact: Send complete ms with SASE. Reports in 1 week. Publishes ms up to 3 years after acceptance. Photocopied submissions OK. Sample copy $3. Fiction guidelines for SAE and 1 first class stamp.
Payment: Up to $25; $3 charge for extras.
Terms: Cash prizes of $25, $20, $15 and $10 based on subscribers' votes. A plaque is also awarded to first place winner.
Advice: "See a copy of magazine first; have a good story to tell—in *good* taste! Most fiction sent in is too *long*! Be yourself! Be honest and sincere in your style. Write what you know about. Our philosophy is to reach the world with Christian literature, drawing others closer to God and nature."

F.O.C. REVIEW (I,II), Box 101, Worth IL 60482. Editor: Michael Ogorzaly. Managing Editor: William L. Roach. Magazine: 5½ × 8½; more than 60 pages. "We publish original stories, poems, essays, one-act plays, drawings and sketches. In addition, we seek book and film reviews." Quarterly. Plans special fiction issue. Estab. 1988. Circ. 500.
Needs: Adventure, condensed/excerpted novel, contemporary, experimental, fantasy, feminist, humor/satire, literary, prose poem, science fiction, serialized novel, sports and suspense/mystery. No romance, erotica. Receives more than 30 mss/month. Accepts 10-12 mss/issue; 36 mss/year. Publishes ms in next or following issue after acceptance. Published work by James Linn, Rama Rao, John Nerone and Gregory Burnham. Published new writers within the last year. Length: 4,000 words maximum; publishes short shorts. Sometimes critiques rejected mss.
How to Contact: Send 2 copies of complete ms with cover letter. Reports in 2 months. SASE. Simultaneous, photocopied and reprint submissions OK. Accepts computer printout submissions. Sample copy $5. Fiction guidelines for #10 SAE and 1 first class stamp.
Payment: Pays in contributor's copies.
Terms: Acquires one-time rights.

FAG RAG, Box 331, Kenmore Station, Boston MA 02215. (617)661-7534. Editor: Collective. Magazine of gay male liberation. Annually. Estab. 1970. Circ. 5,000.
Needs: Gay male material only: adventure, comics, confession, erotica, fantasy, historical, men's, prose poem. Receives 5 unsolicited fiction mss/month. Accepts 5 mss/issue. Length: 1-10,000 words average.
How to Contact: Query first. Reports in 2 months on queries; 9 months on mss. SASE for query. Photocopied submissions OK. Accepts computer printout submissions. Accepts disk submissions compatible with IBM-PC/Macintosh. Sample copy $5.
Payment: Pays in 2 contributor's copies.
Terms: Acquires first North American serial rights.

THE FARMER'S MARKET (II), Midwestern Farmer's Market, Inc., Box 1272, Galesburg IL 61402. Editor: Jean C. Lee. Magazine: 5½ × 8½; 100-140 pages; 60 lb. offset paper; 65 lb. cover; b&w illustrations and photos. Magazine publishing "quality fiction, poetry, nonfiction, plays, etc., with a Midwestern theme and/or sensibility for an adult, literate audience." Semiannually. Estab. 1982. Circ. 500.

Needs: Contemporary, feminist, humor/satire, literary, regional and excerpted novel. "We prefer material of clarity, depth and strength; strong plots, good character development." No "romance, avant-garde, juvenile, teen." Accepts 6-12 mss/year. Published work by Donn Irving, Mary Maddox, David Williams; published new writers within the last year. Occasionally critiques rejected mss or recommends other markets.

How to Contact: Send complete ms with SASE. Reports in 1-2 months. Photocopied submissions OK. Accepts computer printout submissions. Publishes ms 4-8 months after acceptance. Sample copy for $4.50 and $1 postage and handling.

Payment: Pays 1 free contributor's copy. (Other payment dependent upon grants).

Terms: Authors retain rights.

Advice: "We're always interested in regional fiction. We are trying to publish more fiction and we are looking for exceptional manuscripts. Read the magazines before submitting. If you don't want to buy it, ask your library. We receive numerous mss that are clearly unsuitable."

FAT TUESDAY (II), 8125 Jonestown Road, Harrisburg PA 17112. Editor-in-Chief: F.M. Cotolo. Editors: B. Lyle Tabor and Thom Savion. Associate Editors: Lionel Stevroid and Kristen vonOehrke. Journal: 8½ × 11 or 5 × 8; 27-36 pages; good to excellent paper; heavy cover stock; b&w illustrations; photos. "Generally, we are an eclectic journal of fiction, poetry and visual treats. Our issues to date have featured artists like B. Lyle Tabor, Dom Cimei, Mary Lee Gowland, Patrick Kelly, Cheryl Townsend, Joi Cook, Chuck Taylor and many more who have focused on an individualistic nature with fiery elements. We are a literary mardi gras—as the title indicates—and irreverancy is as acceptable to us as profundity as long as there is fire! Our audience is anyone who can praise literature and condemn it at the same time. Anyone too serious about it on either level will not like *Fat Tuesday*." Annually. Estab. 1981. Circ. 700.

Needs: Comics, erotica, experimental, humor/satire, literary, prose poem, psychic/supernatural/occult, serialized/excerpted novel and dada. "Although we list categories, we are open to feeling out various fields if they are delivered with the mark of an individual and not just in the format of the particular field." Receives 10 unsolicited fiction mss/month. Accepts 4-5 mss/issue. Published new writers within the last year. Length: 1,000 words maximum. Publishes short shorts. Occasionally critiques rejected mss.

How to Contact: Send complete ms with SASE. Photocopied submissions OK. Accepts computer printout submissions. "No previously published material considered." Reports in 1 month. Publishes ms 3-10 months after acceptance. Sample copy $5.

Payment: Pays 1 free contributor's copy.

Terms: Acquires one-time rights.

Advice: "Retain your enthusiasm. Never write and submit anything without it. Buy an issue and eat it up, page by page. Then, go into your guts and write something. If you're not on fire, we'll tell you so and encourage you to try again. Don't be self-critical when you have something to say that reflects how you feel. Most of all, be aware of life outside of literature, and then let life influence your writing. It is essential that a potential submitter buy a sample issue and experience the 'zine to understand what would work and get a better idea of what we're talking about and help support all free forms of expression."

‡FELICITY (I), Weems Concepts, Star Route, Box 21AA, Artemas PA 17211. (814)458-3102. Editor: Kay Weems-Winter. Newsletter: 8½ × 11; 20 lb. bond paper; illustrations. "Publishes articles, poetry and short stories. Poetry has different theme each month. No theme for stories." Monthly. Estab. 1988. Circ. 200.

Needs: Adventure, confession, ethnic, fantasy, historical (general), horror, humor/satire, juvenile (5-9 years), prose poem, psychic/supernatural/occult, religious/inspirational, romance (contemporary, historical, young adult), science fiction, senior citizen/retirement, suspense/mystery, western and young adult/teen (10-18 years). No erotica, translations. Receives 6-10 unsolicited mss/month. Accepts 1 ms/issue (for *Felicity* contest); 12 mss/year (for *Felicity* contest—sometimes more). Publishes ms 3-4 months after acceptance. $5 entry fee for contest entries. Length: 2,000 words preferred; 800 words minimum; 2,500 words maximum. Sometimes critiques rejected mss and recommends other markets.

How to Contact: Send complete ms with cover letter or enter our monthly contests. "Send SASE for return of ms or tell me to destroy it if not accepted." Reports in 3-4 months. SASE. Simultaneous, photocopied and reprint submissions OK as long as author still retains rights. Accepts computer printout submissions. Sample copy for $2, #10 SAE and 65¢ postage. Fiction guidelines for #10 SAE and 1 first class stamp.

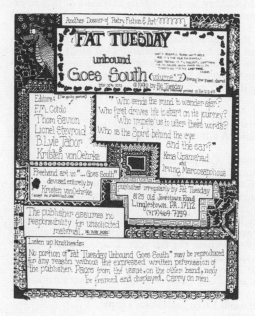

According to Editor-in-Chief Frank Cotolo, Fat Tuesday "has always strived to 'make words live,' and have 'color and depth.' The concept of a 'visual, hand-drawn' issue seemed in tune," he says. "Fat Tuesday is a celebration of voices, and therefore of the senses—which lends itself to expand upon the common, linear format in which writing is presented." Illustrator Kristen vonOehrke-Cotolo says she didn't choose this cover, "it just came out that way." Copyright © 1990 Kristen vonOehrke-Cotolo.

Payment: Pays in contributor's copies and ½ of entry fee collected for Short Story Contest.
Terms: Acquires one-time rights. "We will be" copyrighted. "We sponsor monthly contests. Winner receives half of entry fees collected for the short story contest. Submit ms along with entry fee and you will be entered in the contest. Deadline is the 30th of each month. Read both of our publications— *Felicity* and *The Bottom Line Publications*. Our contests are listed there."
Advice: Looks for "good opening sentence, realistic characters, nice descriptions, strong plot with believable ending. Use natural conversations. Let me *feel* your story. Keep me interested until the end. Keep trying. A lot of mss I read are from new writers. Personally I enjoy stories and articles which will create a particular emotion, build suspense, or offer excitement or entertainment. Don't spell out everything in detail—keep me guessing."

FICTION (II), % Dept. of English, City College, 138th St. & Convent Ave., New York NY 10031. (212)690-8170/690-8120. Editor: Mark Jay Mirsky. Managing Editor: Allan Aycock. Magazine: 6×9; 150-250 pages; illustrations and occasionally photos. "As the name implies, we publish *only* fiction; we are looking for the best new writing available, leaning toward the unconventional and off-beat. *Fiction* has traditionally attempted to make accessible the unaccessible, to bring the experimental to a broader audience." Biannually. Estab. 1972. Circ. 3,000.
Needs: Contemporary, experimental, feminist, humor/satire, literary and translations. No romance, science-fiction, etc. Plan to publish special fiction issue or an anthology in the future. Receives 30-50 unsolicited mss/month. Accepts 12-20 mss/issue; 24-40 mss/year. Does not read mss May-October. Publishes ms 1-6 months after acceptance. Agented fiction 10-20%. Recently published work by Joyce Carol Oates, Peter Handke, Max Frisch and Adolfo Bioy-Casares. Length: Open. Publishes short shorts. Sometimes critiques rejected mss and recommends other markets.
How to Contact: Send complete ms with cover letter. Reports in 5 weeks on mss. SASE. Simultaneous submissions OK, but please advise. Photocopied submissions OK. Accepts computer printout submissions. Sample copy $6.95. Fiction guidelines free.
Payment: Pays in contributor's copies.
Terms: Acquires first rights.
Advice: Submit "something different, off-the-wall—we would favor a less-polished but stylistically adventurous piece over a more-polished formulaic piece."

FICTION INTERNATIONAL (II), English Dept., San Diego State University, San Diego CA 92182. (619)594-6220. Editors: Harold Jaffe and Larry McCaffery. Serious literary magazine of fiction, extended reviews, essays. 200 pages; illustrations; photos. "Our twin biases are progressive politics and post-modernism." Biannually. Estab. 1973. Circ. 2,500.
Needs: Literary, political and innovative forms. Receives approximately 300 unsolicited fiction mss each month. Published new writers within the last year. No length limitations but rarely use manuscripts over 25 pages. Portions of novels acceptable if self-contained enough for independent publication. Unsolicited mss will be considered only from September 1 through December 15 of each year.
How to Contact: Send complete ms with SASE. Reports in 1-3 months on mss. Sample copy for $9: query Ed Gordon, managing editor.
Payment: Varies.
Terms: Pays on publication for first rights and first North American serial rights.
Advice: "Study the magazine. We're highly selective. A difficult market for unsophisticated writers."

THE FIDDLEHEAD (II), University of New Brunswick, Campus House, Box 4400 Fredericton, New Brunswick E3B 5A3 Canada. (506)453-3501. Editor: K.T. Thompson. Fiction Editors: Anthony Boxill, Diana Austin and K.T. Thompson. Magazine: 6×9; 104-128 pages; ink illustrations; photos. "No criteria for publication except quality. For a general audience, including many poets and writers." Quarterly. Estab. 1945. Circ. 1,000.
Needs: Literary. No non-literary fiction. Receives 100-150 unsolicited mss/month. Buys 4-5 mss/issue; 20-40 mss/year. Publishes ms up to 4 months after acceptance. Small percent agented fiction. Published work by Arych Leo Stollman; published new writers within the last year. Length: 50-3,000 words average. Publishes short shorts. Occasionally critiques rejected mss.
How to Contact: Send complete ms with cover letter. SASE. "Canadian stamps or international coupons!" for mss. Photocopied and reprint submissions OK. Accepts computer printout submissions. Sample copy for $5.50 (Canadian).
Payment: Pays $10-12 (Canadian)/published page and 1 free contributor's copy.
Terms: Pays on publication for first or one-time rights.
Advice: "Less than 5% of the material received is published."

FIGMENT MAGAZINE (I, II, IV), Tales from the Imagination, P.O. Box 3566, Moscow ID 83843-0477. Editors: Barb & J.C. Hendee. Magazine: 5½×8½; 48-56 pages; slick stock cover; illustrations. "Poetry/stories/vignettes/novelettes in genres of sf, fantasy, and sf/f related horror, for adults." Quarterly. Estab. 1989.
Needs: Fantasy, science fiction and horror based on sf/f themes and plots. "We're open to standard plotting through slightly experimental, as long as the story is interesting, comprehensible and always entertaining." Receives 200+ mss/month. Buys 8-12 mss/issue; 32-48 mss/year. Publishes ms within 6 months after acceptance. Recently published work by Dean Wesley Smith, Kristine Kathryn Rusch, Kevin J. Anderson, Don Webb. Length: 500-7,500 words; 3,000 words preferred. Sometimes critiques rejected manuscripts and recommends other markets.
How to Contact: Send complete ms with cover letter; include Social Security number, bio, SASE and listing of publishing credits (year to date only) including where and when. Reports in 2 weeks on queries; 1 month average on mss. Photocopied submissions OK. Accepts computer printout submissions. Does not accept electronic or simultaneous submissions. Sample copy $4. Fiction guidelines for #10 SASE.
Payment: Vignettes and short shorts (1,000 words): $5. Stories (3-5,000 words): $17. Novelettes (7,500 words): $35. Poems: $2-4.
Terms: Pays within 30 days of acceptance for first North American serial rights only. Sends galleys to author.
Advice: "Looks for original ideas or original methods used with old ideas. Cutting edge material that is entertaining, fantastical, and far-reaching. Don't tell us what your story is about in your cover letter; if we can't figure it out from the manuscript, then some more work needs to be done before your submit. We expect professional submissions in the proper format."

FINE MADNESS (II), Box 15176, Seattle WA 98115-0176. Magazine: 5×8; 80 pages; 65 lb. paper; 60 lb. cover stock. Estab. 1981. Circ. 800.
Needs: Contemporary, experimental, literary, prose poem and translations. Receives 10 unsolicited mss/month. Accepts 1-2 mss/issue; 2-4 mss/year. Publishes ms no more than 1 year after acceptance. Recently published work by Naomi Nye, David Downing, Hillel Schwarz and Michael Novak. Length: "approx. 12 pages max." Publishes short shorts.

How to Contact: Query first or send complete ms with cover letter. Reports in 3 weeks on queries; 3 months on mss. Sample copy $4. Fiction guidelines free.
Payment: Free subscription to magazine and contributor's copies.
Terms: Acquires first North American serial rights.

FIREWEED, A Feminist Quarterly, Box 279, Station B, Toronto, Ontario M5T 2W2 Canada. Editors: The Fireweed Collective. Women's literary and cultural journal, with an emphasis on race, class and sexuality. Quarterly. Estab. 1978. Circ. 2,000.
Needs: Fiction, poetry, nonfiction, articles, book reviews, lesbian, working class, and women of color content No "women's formula style." Receives 60 unsolicited fiction mss/month. Accepts 30 mss/issue; 120 mss/year. Length: 1,200 words minimum; 18,000 words maximum; 6,000 words average. Occasionally critiques rejected ms.
How to Contact: Query first with SASE. Photocopied submissions OK. Reports in 6 months on queries. Sample copy $4 in Canada, $5 in U.S.
Payment: $20 and 2 free contributor's copies.
Terms: Author retains copyright.

‡FISH DRUM MAGAZINE (II), Santa Fe Council for the Arts, % 626 Kathryn Ave., Santa Fe NM 87501. Editor: Robert Winson. Magazine: 5½×8½; 40-odd pages; glossy cover; illustrations and photographs. "Lively, emotional vernacular modern fiction, art and poetry." Published 2-4 times a year. Estab. 1988. Circ. 500.
Needs: Contemporary, erotica, ethnic, experimental, fantasy, feminist, gay, lesbian, literary, mainstream, prose poem, psychic/supernatural/occult, regional, religious/inspirational, science fiction. "We're interested in material by New Mexican writers; also on the practice of Zen. Most of the fiction we've published is in the form of short, heightened prose-pieces." Receives 2-4 unsolicited mss/month. Accepts 1-2 mss/issue; 2-8 mss/year. Publishes ms 6 months-1 year after acceptance. Recommends other markets.
How to Contact: Send complete manuscript with cover letter. Reports on mss in 1-3 months. SASE. Sample copy for $3.
Payment: Pays in contributor's copies. Charges for extras.
Terms: Acquires first North American serial rights. Sends galleys to author.

FIVE FINGERS REVIEW (II), Box 15426, San Francisco CA 94115. (415)661-8052. Editor: "rotating." Magazine: 6×9; 125-150 pages; photographs on cover. "*Five Fingers* is dedicated to publishing well wrought poetry and prose from various aesthetic viewpoints. The magazine provides a forum from which talented writers (new and known, traditional and experimental) act as conscientious objectors, as creative witnesses to the passions and possibilities of our time." Semiannually. Estab. 1984. Circ. 1,000.
Needs: Ethnic, experimental, feminist, gay, humor/satire, lesbian, literary, regional, prose poems, prose vignettes and works that move between the genres. Receives 15-20 unsolicited mss/month. Accepts 2-5 mss/issue. Published work by Molly Giles, W.A. Smith and Peter Johnson; published new writers in the last year. Publishes short shorts.
How to Contact: Query with clips of published work. SASE. Simultaneous, photocopied and reprint submissions OK. Sample copy for $6.
Payment: Pays in contributor's copies.
Advice: "We are particularly looking for short-short stories, prose poems, prose vignettes and works of translations."

THE FLORIDA REVIEW (II), Dept. of English, University of Central Florida, Orlando FL 32816. (407)275-2038. Contact: Russell Kesler. Magazine: 5½×8½; 128 pages. Semiannually. Plans special fiction issue. Estab. 1972. Circ. 1,000.
Needs: Contemporary, experimental and literary. "We welcome experimental fiction, so long as it doesn't make us feel lost or stupid. We aren't especially interested in genre fiction (science fiction, romance, adventure, etc.), though a good story can transcend any genre." Receives 80 mss/month. Buys 8-10 mss/issue; 16-20 mss/year. Publishes ms within 3-6 months of acceptance. Published work by Stephen Dixon, Richard Grayson and Liz Rosenberg. Publishes short shorts.
How to Contact: Send complete ms with cover letter. Reports in 2-4 months. SASE. Simultaneous and photocopied submissions OK. Accepts computer printout submissions. Sample copy $4.50; free fiction guidelines.

Payment: Pays $5/printed page and contributor's copies. Charges for extra copies.
Terms: Pays on publication. "Copyright held by U.C.F.; reverts to author after publication. (In cases of reprints, we ask that a credit line indicate that the work first appeared in the *F.R.*)"
Advice: "We publish fiction of high 'literary' quality—stories that delight, instruct, and aren't afraid to take risks."

FOLIO: A LITERARY JOURNAL (II), Literature Department, American University, Washington DC 20016. (202)885-2971. Editor changes yearly. Magazine: 6×9; 64 pages. "Fiction is published if it is well written. We look specifically for language control and skilled plot and character development." For a scholarly audience. Semiannually. Estab. 1984. Circ. 400.
Needs: Contemporary, literary, mainstream, prose poem, sports, suspense/mystery, translations, essay, b&w art or photography. No pornography. Receives 50 unsolicited mss/month. Accepts 25 mss/issue; 50 mss/year. Does not read mss during May-August or December-January. Published work by Henry Taylor, Kermit Moyer, Linda Pastan; publishes new writers. Length: 2,500 words average; 4,500 words maximum. Publishes short shorts. Length: 3 pages. Occasionally critiques rejected mss. Occasional theme-based issues. See guidelines for info.
How to Contact: Send complete ms with cover letter, which should include a brief biography. Reports in 1-2 weeks on queries; 1-2 months on mss. SASE. Simultaneous, photocopied and reprint submissions OK. Accepts computer printout submissions. Sample copy for $4.50. Guidelines for #10 SAE and 1 first class stamp.
Payment: Pays in contributor's copies.
Terms: Acquires all rights. "$75 award for best fiction or poetry. Spring issue only. Query for guidelines."

FOOTWORK (I,II), The Paterson Literary Review, Passaic County Community College, College Blvd., Paterson NJ 07509. (201)684-6555. Editor: Maria Gillan. Magazine: 8×11; 120 pages; 60 lb. paper; 70 lb. cover; illustrations; photos. Plans fiction issue in future.
Needs: Contemporary, ethnic, experimental, translations. "We are interested in quality short stories, with no taboos on subject matter." Receives about 60 unsolicited mss/month. Accepts 4 mss/issue. Publishes ms about 6 months to a year after acceptance. Published new writers within the last year. Length: 2,500-3,000 words.
How to Contact: Reports in 3 months on mss. SASE. No simultaneous submissions or reprints. Accepts computer printouts. Sample copy $5.
Payment: Pays in contributor's copies.
Terms: Acquires first North American rights.
Advice: "We look for original, vital, powerful work. The short story is—when successful—a major achievement. Because we publish relatively little work, we cannot consider stories which are slight, however charming."

‡FOUR QUARTERS (III), LaSalle University, 20th and Olney Ave., Philadelphia PA 19141-1199. (215)951-1610, 1700. Editor: John C. Keenan. Magazine: 7x9; 64 pages; 70 lb. paper; 65 lb. cover. Magazine of poetry, ficiton and nonfiction for college educated audience. Semiannual in Fall and Spring. Estab. 1951. Circ. 750.
Needs: Literary and contemporary. "Fiction strong on characterization leading to a revelation for character or reader. Receives about 50 unsolicited mss per month. Buys 5 mss/issue, 20 mss/year. Prefer published writers who have received recognition in one of the "Best" collections. Recently published work by Douglas Angus, Mary Clearman Blew, Peter LaSalle, and T. Alan Broughton. Length: 2,000-5,000 word, 10-20 pages.
How to Contact: Send complete ms with SASE. Reports in 2 months on mss. Sample copy $5. Free guidelines with SASE.
Payment: Pays up to $200 and 3 free author's copies. $4 charge for extras.
Terms: Pays on acceptance for first North American rights.
Advice: "Read the magazine before submitting. We are open to all fiction, experimental or traditional, but our tastes lean toward stories strong on characterization, leading to a significant revelation. Polished craftsmanship will always get a sympathetic reading."

FRONTIERS (II), A Journal of Women Studies, Mesa Vista Hall 2142, University of New Mexico, Albuquerque NM 87131. Editor: Nancy D. Mann. Magazine: 8½×11; 92 pages; photos. "Women studies; academic articles in all disciplines; criticism, book and film reviews; exceptional creative work (art, short fiction, photography, poetry)."

Close-up

Rachel Simon
Writer

Jerry Bauer

Rachel Simon's work has appeared in several literary magazines, including *North American Review*, *Story* and *Quarterly West*. Her newly published collection of short stories is titled *Little Nightmares, Little Dreams*. While the book is named for one of the 16 stories in the collection, the title aptly describes the way Simon works as well.

"The writing process for me is an experience like dreaming. I become submerged in my subconscious," she says. Initial stories come to her quickly like dreams and she will often write the first draft in one sitting. "The first draft is the scariest part to many people, but to me it's the most fun."

This is not to say the writing comes easy. "I've learned to have a lot of patience. I go over the draft, combing it through dozens of times, changing a word here and there. I may work on a piece for two or three hours and change only 10 words."

Simon's day usually starts around 6 a.m.. She begins writing very early and writes through until late afternoon, takes a walk, has dinner, and returns to her writing until bedtime. Sometimes it's hard to maintain this vigorous writing schedule, she admits, "but I try to write at least eight hours every day."

Before her book was accepted, Simon taught classes in writing and did some temporary work. Two generous grants and the advance from the book have made it possible for her to quit teaching for awhile and devote herself to writing full-time. "Still, I've learned to live frugally—I don't go shopping, don't buy a lot of things. Actually the process has been liberating. I've learned to simplify my life."

She began sending out work seriously while in graduate school at Sarah Lawrence. She sent to several "slick" publications without success. "One magazine that had my story since June, contacted me in October to say they were considering the piece. I heard nothing so I finally called in February. They didn't remember it and couldn't find it. After a search, they said it had fallen down behind a desk and they would like more time to look at it again. So I waited. A week later I got a rejection letter. I was furious."

Yet Simon turned the anger to use and sent out a flurry of submissions. Soon after, she won third place in the *Playboy* College Fiction Contest and her stories began to sell. About this time a friend suggested she attend the Writers at Work conference in Utah. The only way she could afford the trip was to try to win the contest sponsored by the conference. So Simon entered the contest and won. She met an editor from Houghton Mifflin at the conference and subsequently sold her manuscript.

Her advice to writers is simple: "Send only your best. Read magazines, of course, and also the annual collections such as *Best American Short Stories*, the O. Henry Award winners and Pushcart Prize winners." Keep trying, she says. Yet, if you've tried several times with no success, put the work aside and start something new.

Her experience is a lesson. "Fight bitterness," she says. "Don't let your anger work against you. Use it to increase your action. Above all, writers must learn to be very patient."

—Robin Gee

Needs: Feminist, lesbian. Receives 15 unsolicited mss/month. Accepts 1 ms/issue. Publishes ms 6 months to 1 year after acceptance. Sometimes critiques rejected mss and recommends other markets.
How to Contact: Send complete ms with cover letter. Reports in 1 week on queries; 3 months on mss. SASE. Accepts computer printout submissions. Sample copy for $8.
Payment: Pays 2 contributor's copies.
Terms: Buys first North American serial rights.
Advice: "We are a *feminist* journal. *FRONTIERS* aims to make scholarship in women studies, and *exceptional* creative work, accessible to a cross-disciplinary audience inside and outside the university."

‡**THE G.W. REVIEW (II),** The George Washington University, Box 20, The Marvin Center, 800 21st St., N.W., Washington DC 20052. (202)994-7288. Editor: Adam H. Freedman. Fiction Editor: Joe Dodson. Magazine: 6×9; 64 pages; 60 lb. white offset paper; 65 lb. Patina cover; cover photo and inside photos. "The G.W. Review is a literary magazine that publishes poetry, short fiction, essays and graphic arts for the university community, the Washington, DC metropolitan area and an increasing number of national subscribers." Semiannually. Estab. 1980. Circ. 4,000 (annually).
Needs: Condensed/excerpted novel, contemporary, experimental, humor/satire, literary, mainstream, prose poem, translations. "The G.W. Review does not accept previously published material. No pornography or proselytizing religious manuscripts." Does not read mss May 15-August 15. Publishes ms up to 6 months after acceptance. Recently published work by Blanche Boyd and Richard McCann. Length: 2,500 words average; 3,500 words maximum. Publishes short shorts. Sometimes critiques rejected mss.
How to Contact: Send complete manuscript with cover letter. Include biographical information, places previously published, previous books, etc. Reports in 3-6 weeks on queries; 4-10 weeks on mss. SASE. Simultaneous and photocopied submissions OK. Accepts computer printout submissions. Sample copy for $3. Fiction guidelines for 9×12 SASE.
Payment: Pays in contributor's copies.
Terms: Acquires one-time rights.
Advice: "The G.W. Review seeks to publish the best contemporary writing from outside the University community as well as the best from within. Initially intended for distribution to university students and the surrounding Washington D.C. metropolitan area, *The G.W. Review* has since begun to attain a more widespread national distribution and readership."

THE GAMUT (II), A Journal of Ideas and Information, Cleveland State University, 1218 Fenn Tower, Cleveland OH 44115. (216)687-4679. Editor: Louis T. Milic. Managing Editor: Susan Dumbrys. Magazine: 7×10; 96 pages; 70 lb Patina Matte paper; Patina Matte cover stock; illustrations; photos. "*The Gamut* is a general-interest magazine that *mainly* publishes well-researched, interesting articles; however, we like to publish one or two pieces of fiction per issue, if we find something suitable." For the college-educated audience. Triannually. Estab. 1980. Circ. 1,200.
Needs: Contemporary, experimental, feminist, humor/satire, literary, mainstream, prose poem, regional, translations. "Our only requirement is high quality fiction." No genre fiction, no fiction for specific age groups. Receives 100 unsolicited mss/month. Accepts 1-2 mss/issue; 4-6 mss/year. Publishes mss usually 3 months, certainly 1 year after acceptance. Reading fee "only when we have contest, then $5." Published work by Margot Livesey, Nancy Potter, John Gerlach; published new writers within the last year. Length: 3,000 words average; 1,000 words minimum; 6,000 words maximum.
How to Contact: Send complete ms with cover letter. Reports in 1 month on queries; 3 months on mss. SASE for ms. Simultaneous and photocopied submissions OK. Accepts computer printouts. Sample copy $2.50. Fiction guidelines for #10 SAE and 1 first class stamp.
Payment: Pays $25-150, depending on length; contributor's copies; charges reduced rate for extras.
Terms: Pays on publication for first North American serial rights.
Advice: "The best advice we have for writers who wish to be published in our magazine is that they should care about the quality of their writing. Further, we are interested neither in stale approaches to fictional situations nor in avant-garde experiments that have lost touch with the purpose of literature."

GARM LU (II, IV), A Canadian Celtic Arts Journal, St. Michael's College, University of Toronto, 81 St. Mary St., Toronto, Ontario M5S 1J4 Canada. (416)926-1300 (Celtic Studies Dept.). Magazine: 140mm×215mm; 60 pages; bond paper; almost cardboard cover; illustrations. "A register of the concerns and interests of those involved in Celtic studies." Semiannually. Estab. 1986. Circ. 400.
Needs: Adventure, condensed novel, confession, contemporary, erotica, ethnic, feminist, gay, historical, humor/satire, lesbian, literary, regional, religious/inspirational, serialized/excerpted novel, translations, Celtic. Receives 4 unsolicited mss/month. Buys 1 or 2 mss/issue; 3 or 4 mss/year. Length: 1,000

words preferred; 250 words minimum; 2,500 words maximum. Sometimes critiques rejected mss.
How to Contact: Query with clips of published work or send complete ms with cover letter. Reports in 1 month on queries; 5 weeks on mss. SASE. Simultaneous, photocopied and reprint submissions OK. Accepts computer printouts. Sample copy for $3 (US).
Payment: Free contributor's copy; charge for extras.
Terms: Acquires all rights. "In future, we will be having contests that will be worth about $20 (Canadian)."
Advice: "Read it over 100 times and edit it 100 times."

GAS (I, II, IV), Journal of The Gross Americans' Society, Box 397, Marina CA 93933. (408)384-2768. Editor: Jeannette M. Hopper. Magazine: digest size; 20-50 pages; 20 lb paper; non-gloss heavy cover; pen-and-ink illustrations; photos if screened. "*Gas* is dedicated to the fine art of the gross-out; accepts humorous horror, horrible humor and blends of those genres, with an emphasis on short-short horror fiction." For "people mature enough to see that this is all strictly for fun and entertainment, and not an attempt to make any real social statement." Quarterly. Estab. 1986. Circ. 250.
Needs: Adventure, confession, contemporary, erotica, experimental, fantasy, horror, humor/satire, mainstream, prose poem, psychic/supernatural/occult, science fiction, suspense/mystery, gross humor/horror. "All fiction must have some aspect of grossness, but story is of utmost importance. Characters must be someone the reader can identify with (no utterly detestable creeps as protagonists). No scatalogical or cannibal-related stories. No hard pornography. No children placed in sexual situations. No politics, racism, religion or heavy dogma." Receives 50 unsolicited mss/month. Buys 5-10 mss/issue; 40 mss/year at most. Publishes ms 3 months to 1 year after acceptance. Published work by J.N. Williamson, Bruce Boston, Cheryl Sayre; published new writers within the last year. Length: 1,500 words maximum. Publishes short shorts of 100-1,000 words. Sometimes critiques rejected mss and recommends other markets.
How to Contact: Send complete ms with cover letter, which should include brief introduction of author and previous publications. Reports in 1 week on queries; 1-2 weeks on mss. SASE. No simultaneous submissions. Photocopied and reprint (5 years after publication) submissions OK. Accepts computer printout submissions. Sample copy for $3.50. Fiction guidelines for #10 SASE.
Payment: Pays ¼¢/word with a $2 minimum; contributor's copies; charge for extras.
Terms: Pays on publication for one-time rights. Occasional contests announced in magazine.
Advice: "Now concentrating more on humorous *horror*, whereas we were open to almost anything sick and funny in the past. Now the emphasis will be upon the frightening and bizarre, rather than just 'funny stuff.' I receive too many submissions from people who never should have passed English proficiency exams; spelling is terrible, punctuation is a mystery, grammar is pathetic. Master your basic tools, and that means master English. Also, read, read, read to get the feel of how the pros do it. Finally: GAS is unlike any other magazine; please read a copy before submitting."

‡THE GASLIGHT REVIEW (II), Foreword Publishing, 2476 Glenwood Ave., Toledo OH 43620. Editor: Barbara Mann. Newspaper/Tabloid: 10⅛×15; 16 pages; newsprint paper; pen & ink illustrations. "Literary review—reviews, commentary, autobiography, short stories and essays for a college-educated audience." Bimonthly. Estab. 1989. Circ. 1,000.
Needs: Feminist, social commentary, humor/satire, lesbian, literary. Considers experimental, gay/lesbian and sci-fi. No "romance or christian evangelical reviews." Receives 10+ mss/month. Accepts 1 or 2 mss/issue; 8+ mss/year. Publishes ms 3-4 months after acceptance. Recently published work by Barbara Mater, John O'Connor and Sam Wright. Length: 3,500 words average; 6,000 words maximum. Publishes short shorts. Sometimes critiques rejected ms and recommends other markets.
How to Contact: Send complete manuscript with cover letter with "short bio plus any comment author thinks is necessary to fair consideration." Reports in 3 weeks to 1 month on queries. SASE. Photocopied submissions OK. Accepts computer printout submissions. Sample copy for $2.50 with 9×12 SAE and 65¢ postage. Fiction guidelines for #10 SAE and 1 first class stamp.
Payment: Pays contributor's copies.
Terms: Acquires first North American serial rights. Usually sends galleys to author.

‡GAUNTLET (II), Exploring the Limits of Free Expression, 309 Powell Rd., Dept. WD, Springfield PA 19064. (215)328-5476. Editor/Publisher: Barry Hoffman. Magazine: 6x9; 150-200 pages; 50 lb. bond; 10 pt. CIS cover; illustrations and photographs. "Censorship and free expression for a general audience (music, art, records, film, fiction, etc.) Fiction wanted on any of these themes." Annually. Estab. 1990. Circ. 4,000.

Needs: Censorship, erotica, ethnic, fantasy, feminist, gay, horror, humor/satire, mainstream, suspense/mystery. "No hard science fiction, romance or stories not on censorship theme." Receives 20 unsolicited fiction mss/month. Buys 8-12 mss/issue. Does not read mss October 1-May 1. Publishes ms before March of next year after acceptance. Recently published work by Ray Bradbury, Graham Masterton, Bill Relling. Length: 1,000-2,500 words preferred. Publishes short shorts. Critiques or comments on rejected mss and recommends other markets.
How to Contact: Send complete ms with cover letter. Include general background, where your heard about *Gauntlet*. Reports in 1 week on queries; 3-4 weeks on mss. SASE. Simultaneous, photocopied and computer printout submissions OK. Accepts electronic submissions on disk (5¼ floppy, IBM compatible, ASCII format). Sample copy for $8.95. Fiction guidelines for #10 SAE and 1 first-class stamp.
Payment: Pays ¼-1 cent/word and contributor's copies; charges $5 for extras.
Terms: Pays on publication for first or one-time rights. Offers kill fee—½ of acceptance fee. Sends pre-publication galleys to author.
Advice: "Take issues out of the headlines of any paper, give them a twist and you might have something special...Show the impact on the censored individual or society. A story on the ultimate censorship (other than the destruction of the world) is fodder for a good tale. *You* determine what the ultimate censorship is. Hints: Don't be predictable (come up with an original ending) and strong characterization is more important than setting.. I want horror, fantasy, even mainstream and would *kill for a good mystery or suspense story*."

GAY CHICAGO MAGAZINE (II), Ultra Ink, Inc. 3121 N. Broadway, Chicago IL 60657-4522. (312)327-7271. Editor: Jerry Williams. Magazine: 8½x11; 80-144 pages; newsprint paper and cover stock; illustrations; photos. Entertainment guide, information for the gay community.
Needs: Erotica (but no explicit hard core), lesbian, gay and romance. Receives "a few" unsolicited mss/month. Accepts 10-15 mss/year. Published new writers within the last year. Length: 1,000-3,000 words.
How to Contact: Send complete ms with SASE. Photocopied submissions OK. Accepts computer printout submissions. Accepts disk submissions compatible with Merganthaler Crtronic 200. Must have hard copy with disk submissions. Reports in 4-6 weeks on mss. Free sample copy for 9×12 SAE and $1.45 postage.
Payment: Minimal. 5-10 free contributor's copies; no charge for extras "if within reason."
Terms: Acquires one-time rights.
Advice: "I use fiction on a space-available basis, but plan to use more because we have doubled our format size to 8½×11."

THE GEORGIA REVIEW (II,III), The University of Georgia, Athens GA 30602. (404)542-3481. Editor-in-Chief: Stanley W. Lindberg. Associate Editor: Stephen Corey. Journal: 7×10; 216 pages (average); 50 lb. woven old style paper; 80 lb. cover stock; illustrations; photos. "*The Georgia Review*, winner of the 1986 National Magazine Award in Fiction, is a journal of arts and letters, featuring a blend of the best in contemporary thought and literature—essays, fiction, poetry, graphics and book reviews—for the intelligent nonspecialist as well as the specialist reader. We seek material that appeals across disciplinary lines by drawing from a wide range of interests." Quarterly. Estab. 1947. Circ. 5,300.
Needs: Experimental and literary. "We're looking for the highest quality fiction—work that is capable of sustaining subsequent readings, not throw-away pulp magazine entertainment. Nothing that fits too easily into a 'category.'" Receives about 300 unsolicited fiction mss/month. Buys 3-4 mss/issue; 12-15 mss/year. Does not accept unsolicited mss in June, July or August. Would prefer *not* to see novel excerpts. Recently published work by Lee K. Abbott, Marjorie Sandor, John Edgar Wideman; published new writers within the last year. Length: open. Occasionally critiques rejected mss.
How to Contact: Send complete ms with SASE. Photocopied submissions OK; no multiple submissions. Accepts computer printout submissions. Reports in 2-3 months. Sample copy $4; free guidelines for #10 SAE with 1 first class stamp.
Payment: Minimum: $25/printed page; 1 year complimentary subscription; 1 contributor's copy, reduced charge for extra.
Terms: Pays on publication for first North American serial rights. Sends galleys to author.

GESTALT (I,II), Anti-matter Publishing, 516 W. Wooster, Bowling Green OH 43402. Editor: Jeff Fearnside. Magazine: 8½×11; 48 pages; glossy paper and stock; illustrations; photographs. "The theme of our magazine is on newer, less traditional literature. Our audience is anyone interested in art, ideas and literature. They are *generally* college-aged to young professional (18-35 years old)." Quarterly. Estab. 1988. Circ. 2,000.

Needs: Adventure, condensed/excerpted novel, contemporary, ethnic, experimental, fantasy, feminist, historical (general), horror, humor/satire, literary, prose poem, regional, science fiction, serialized novel, suspense/mystery, translations and western. "We would like to see a wide range of subjects." Has published a special fiction issue or an anthology (with fiction). Receives 40-60 unsolicited mss/ month. Accepts 1-5 mss/month, depending on length; 4-20/year depending on length. Publishes ms 2 weeks-3 months after acceptance. "Length varies. The number of words is unique to each ms." Publishes short shorts. Sometimes critiques rejected mss.

How to Contact: Send complete ms with cover letter. "Include a return address, possibly a phone number, and, if desired, a personal autobiography—but I do *not* want to see any list of publishing credits." Reports in 1 week on queries; 2-3 months on mss. SASE. Accepts simultaneous, photocopied, reprinted and computer printed submissions. Sample copy $4.75. Fiction guidelines free for SASE.

Payment: Pays in contributor's copies.

Terms: Acquires first serial rights only; "all other rights remain with the author."

Advice: "The single most important criteria I have in choosing fiction is this: If I like it, I'll print it. I don't think there is any higher praise for a work than to have someone say, 'I like it.' First and foremost, it must be realized that the short story is a written form of what originally was a verbal art: storytelling. Thus, it is the voice of the story, the movement of the words, that make the good ones stand apart from the poor. Beginning writers, my advice to you is to destroy one of the oldest conventions of a writer: know your audience. Forget the audience; write for yourself. You don't necessarily have to write from experience, but you should write from a familiar and deep-felt emotion. Put fear aside. Don't be afraid to run up to the edge where convention and insanity meet, and to take a long look over that edge. Embrace convention when it suits your needs, and defy convention when that suits your needs."

THE GETTYSBURG REVIEW (II), Gettysburg College, Gettysburg PA 17325. (717)337-6770. Editor: Peter Stitt. Assistant Editor: Elizabeth Tornes. Magazine: 6¾ × 10; approx. 200 pages; acid free paper; full color illustrations and photos. "Quality of writing is our only criterion; we publish fiction, poetry and essays." Quarterly. Estab. 1988. Circ. 1,500.

Needs: Contemporary, experimental, historical(general), humor/satire, literary, mainstream, regional and serialized novel. "We require that fiction be intelligent, and intelligently and aesthetically written." Receives approx. 60 mss/month. Buys approx. 4-6 mss/issue; 16-24 mss/year. Publishes ms within 3-6 months of acceptance. Published work by Frederick Busch, Ed Minus and Gloria Whelan. Length: 3,000 words average; 1,000 words minimum; 20,000 words maximum. Publishes short shorts. Sometimes critiques rejected mss.

How to Contact: Send complete mss with cover letter, which should include "education, credits." Reports in 3 months. SASE. Photocopied submissions OK. Accepts computer printout submissions.

Payment: Pays $25/printed page plus free subscription to magazine, contributor's copy. Charge for extra copies.

Terms: Pays on publication for first North American serial rights.

Advice: Reporting time can take three months. It is helpful to look at a sample copy of *The Gettysburg Review* to see what kinds of fiction we publish before submitting.

GOLDEN ISIS MAGAZINE (I, IV), Box 726, Salem MA 01970. Editor: Gerina Dunwich. Magazine: digest size; approx. 30-40 pages; 20 lb stock; paper cover; illustrations. "*Golden Isis* is a mystical New Age literary magazine of occult fiction, Goddess-inspired poetry, artwork, Wiccan news, letters, occasional book reviews and classified ads." Quarterly. Estab. 1980. Circ. 4,000.

Needs: Psychic/supernatural/occult, bizarre fantasy and mystical Egyptian themes. "Please do not send us pornographic, religious, racist or sexist material. We will not consider stories written in present tense." Receives 100+ mss/month. Buys 2 mss/issue; 8 mss/year. Published fiction by Rod R. Vick, Cary G. Osborne and Gypsy Electra; published many new writers within the last year. Maximum length for manuscripts (including artwork, diagrams, etc.): 100 pages. Publishes short shorts. Occasionally critiques rejected mss and often recommends other markets.

How to Contact: *"A reading fee of $5 plus return postage is required with each ms. submission."* Send complete ms with cover letter. Reports in 1 month. SASE. Simultaneous, photocopied and reprint submissions OK. Accepts computer printout submissions. Sample copy $5. Fiction guidelines for #10 SAE and 1 first class stamp.

Payment: Payment varies from 1 free contributor's copy to $5.
Terms: Pays on publication for first North American serial rights.
Advice: "Submit short fiction that is well-written, atmospheric and equipped with a good surprise ending. Originality is important. Quality writing is a must. Avoid clichés, poor grammar, predictable endings, unnecessary obscenity and run-on sentences, for these things will only bring you a fast rejection slip."

GOTTA WRITE NETWORK LITMAG (I), Maren Publications, 612 Cobblestone Circle, Glenview IL 60025. Editor: Denise Fleischer. Magazine: 8½×11; 48 pages; saddle-stapled ordinary paper; matte card or lighter weight cover stock; illustrations. Magazine "serves as an open forum to discuss new markets, victories and difficulties. Gives beginning writers their first break into print." Quarterly. Estab. 1988. Circ. 200.
Needs: Adventure, contemporary, fantasy, historical, humor/satire, literary, mainstream, prose poem, romance, science fiction and young adult/teen. Receives 10-20 unsolicited ms per month; accepts 3-5 mss per issue; up to 20 mss a year. Publishes mss 1-2 months after acceptance. Recently published work by Don Stockard, Chuck Howland, Carol Vinci and Jeff Vander Meer. Length: 8 pages maximum for short stories; publishes short shorts of 1-2 pages. Critiques rejected mss and recommends other markets.
How to Contact: Send complete ms with cover letter and query letter. Include "who the writer is, type of work submitted, previous publications and the writer's focused area of writing." Reports in 2 weeks. SASE. Photocopied submissions OK; reprints considered "at times." Accepts computer printouts and electronic submissions via Macintosh disks. Sample copy $2.50. Fiction guidelines free with SASE.
Payment: Pays in contributor's copies; charge for extras.
Terms: Acquires first North American serial rights.
Advice: "If I still think about the direction of the story after I've read it, I know it's good. Organize your thoughts on the plot and character development (qualities, emotions) before enduring 10 drafts. Make your characters come alive by giving them a personality and a background and then give them a little freedom. Let them take you through the story."

GRAIN (I, II), Saskatchewan Writers' Guild, Box 1154, Regina, Saskatchewan S4P 3B4 Canada. Editor: Geoffrey Ursell. Fiction Editor: Edna Alford. Literary magazine: 6×9; 96-112 pages; Chinook offset printing; chrome-coated stock; illustrations; photos sometimes. "Fiction and poetry for people who enjoy high quality writing." Quarterly. Estab. 1973. Circ. 600-1,000.
Needs: Contemporary, experimental, literary, mainstream and prose poem. "No propaganda—only artistic/literary writing." No mss "that stay *within* the limits of conventions such as women's magazine type stories, science fiction; none that push a message." Receives 60-80 unsolicited fiction mss/month. Buys 4-7 mss/issue; 16-28 mss/year. Approximately 1% of fiction agented. Recently published two short stories by emerging writers selected for the first *Journey Prize Anthology*. Length: "No more than 30 pages." Occasionally critiques rejected mss.
How to Contact: Send complete ms with SAE, IRC and brief of one-two sentences. "Let us know if you're just beginning to send out." Reports within 6 months on ms. Publishes ms an average of 4 months after acceptance. Sample copy $5.
Payment: $30-100; 2 free contributor's copies.
Terms: Pays on publication for one-time rights. "We expect acknowledgment if the piece is republished elsewhere."
Advice: "Submit a story to us that will deepen the imaginative experience of our readers. *Grain* has established itself as a first-class magazine of serious fiction. We receive submissions from around the world. Canada is a foreign country, so we ask that you *do not* enclose US postage stamps on your return envelope. If you live outside Canada and neglect the International Reply Coupons, we *will not* read nor reply to your submission."

GRASSLANDS REVIEW (I), Mini-Course—University of North Texas, N.T. Box 13706, Denton TX 76203. Editor: Laura B. Kennelly. Magazine: 6×9; 55 pages. *Grasslands Review* prints creative writing of all types; poetry; fiction,essays for a general audience. Semiannually. Estab. 1989. Circ. 100.
Needs: Adventure, contemporary, ethnic, experimental, fantasy, horror, humor/satire, literary, prose poem, regional, science fiction, suspense/mystery and western. Nothing pornographic or overtly political or religious. Accepts 4-5 mss/issue. Reads only in October and March. Publishes ms 6 months after acceptance. Recently published work by Ivars Balkits, Edward Mycue, Kathleen Fitzpatrick and Mike

Newland. Length: 1,500 words average; 100-3,500 words. Publishes short shorts (100-150 words). Sometimes critiques rejected mss and recommends other markets.
How to Contact: Send complete ms in October or March *only* with cover letter. Reports on mss in 2 months. SASE. Sample copy $1.
Payment: Pays in contributor's copies.
Terms: Acquires one-time rights. Publication not copyrighted.
Advice: "We are looking for fiction which leaves the reader with a strong feeling or impression—or a new perspective on life. The Review began as an in-class exercise to allow experienced creative writing students to learn how a little magazine is produced. We now wish to open it up to outside submissions so that our students can gain an understanding of how large the writing community is in the United States and so that they may have experience in working with other writers."

‡GREAT STREAM REVIEW (II), Lycoming College, Box 66, Williamsport PA 17701. Editor: Penelope Wilkerson Austin. Fiction Editor: G.W. Hawkes. Magazine: 6×9; 100+ pages. "The best fiction, nonfiction and poetry we can find for an educated adult audience." Estab. 1989.
Needs: Contemporary, literary, mainstream, regional. Buys 2-4 mss/issue; 4-8 mss/year. Publishes ms within year of acceptance. Recently published work by Moses, Gridley, Barber, Paul. Length: 6,000-9,000 words average. Publishes short shorts. Length open. Sometimes critiques rejected mss and recommends other markets.
How to Contact: Send complete manuscript with cover letter including "name, address, phone number, brief bio." Reports in 1 week on queries; 2 months on mss. SASE. Simultaneous and photocopied submissions OK. Accepts computer printout submissions. Sample copy $4.
Payment: Pays $10/published page maximum $100 and contributor's copies.
Terms: Buys first North American serial rights. "Contests are announced."

GREEN MOUNTAINS REVIEW (II), Johnson State College, Box A-58, Johnson VT 05656. (802)635-2356, ext. 339. Editor: Neil Shepard. Editor: Tony Whedon. Magazine: digest size; 90-100 pages. Semiannually. Estab. 1987. Circ. 1,000.
Needs: Adventure, contemporary, experimental, humor/satire, literary, mainstream, regional (New England), serialized/excerpted novel, translations. Receives 20 unsolicited mss/month. Accepts 5 mss/issue; 10 mss/year. Publishes ms 1-2 months after acceptance. Length: 25 pages maximum. Publishes short shorts. Sometimes critiques rejected mss.
How to Contact: Send complete ms with cover letter. Reports in 1 month on queries; 2 months on mss. SASE. Simultaneous and photocopied submissions OK. Accepts computer printout submissions; no dot-matrix. Sample copy for $4.
Payment: Pays in contributor's copies.
Terms: Acquires first North American serial rights. Sends galleys to author upon request.

GREEN'S MAGAZINE (II), Fiction for the Family, Green's Educational Publications, Box 3236, Regina, Saskatchewan S4P 3H1 Canada. Editor: David Green. Magazine: 5¼×8; 100 pages; 20 lb. bond paper; matte cover stock; line illustrations. Publishes "solid short fiction suitable for family reading." Quarterly. Estab. 1972.
Needs: Adventure, fantasy, humor/satire, literary, mainstream, science fiction and suspense/mystery. No erotic or sexually explicit fiction. Receives 20-30 mss/month. Accepts 10-12 mss/issue; 40-50 mss/year. Publishes ms within 3-6 months of acceptance. Agented fiction 2%. Recently published work by Solomon Pogarsky, Ann Beacham, Hélène Scheffler-Mason. Length: 2,500 words preferred; 1,500 words minimum; 4,000 words maximum. Sometimes critiques rejected mss and recommends other markets.
How to Contact: Send complete ms. "Cover letters welcome but not necessary." Reports in 2 months. SASE. "Must include international reply coupons." Photocopied submissions OK. Accepts computer printout submissions. No simultaneous submissions. Sample copy $4 (Canadian). Fiction guidelines for #10 SAE and international reply coupon.
Payment: Pays in contributor's copies.
Terms: Acquires first North American serial rights.

GREENSBORO REVIEW (II), University of North Carolina at Greensboro, Dept. of English, Greensboro NC 27412. (919)334-5459. Editor: Jim Clark. Fiction Editor: Sarah Nawrocki. Magazine: 6×9; approximately 136 pages; 60 lb. paper; 65 lb. cover. Literary magazine featuring fiction and poetry for readers interested in contemporary literature. Semiannually. Circ. 500.

Needs: Contemporary and experimental. Accepts 6-8 mss/issue, 12-16 mss/year. Published work by Julia Alvarez, Larry Brown and Madison Smartt Bell; published new writers within the last year. Length: 7,500 words maximum.

How to Contact: Send complete ms with SASE. Unsolicited manuscripts must arrive by September 15 to be considered for the winter issue and by February 15 to be considered for the summer issue. Manuscripts arriving after those dates may be held for the next consideration. Photocopied submissions OK. Sample copy $2.50.

Payment: Pays in contributor's copies.

Terms: Acquires first North American serial rights.

Advice: "We want to see the best being written regardless of theme, subject or style. Recent stories from *The Greensboro Review* have been included in *The Best American Short Stories*, *Prize Stories: The O. Henry Awards*, *New Stories from the South* and *Best of the West*, anthologies recognizing the finest short stories being published."

GROUNDSWELL, A Literary Review (II), P.O. Box 13013, Albany NY 12212-2093. (518)449-8069. Editor: Kristen Murray. Fiction Editor: F.R. Lewis. Magazine. 5½×8½; 150 pages; 70 lb paper; occasional line drawings/graphics. "Variable themes; fiction, poetry reviews of small press publications, critical essays, focus on prominent writer with work (new) by focused-on writer. Annually. Estab. 1984.

Needs: Contemporary, ethnic, experimental, fantasy, feminist, gay, humor/satire, lesbian, literary, mainstream, regional, excerpted novel, suspense/mystery, translations. "We are open to any high quality, significant, honest fictions." No formula stories; stories that are racist, sexist; stories that ignore craft and clarity. Accepts up to 5 mss/issue; 4-10 mss/year. Recently published work by Elizabeth Adams, Kirpal Gordon, Beth Weatherby, Lisa Kroger; published new writers within the last year. Length: 7,500 words maximum. Publishes short shorts. Length 1-6 pages. Sometimes critiques rejected ms.

How to Contact: Send complete ms with brief bio note. "We want something that can be used as a contributor's note if the story is accepted." Reports in 3 months (varies). SASE. Photocopied submissions OK. Accepts computer printout submissions, no dot-matrix. Sample copy $6 and 6×9 SAE with 6 first class stamps.

Payment: 2 contributor's copies; other payment depends on funding.

Terms: Pays for first North American serial rights. Copyright reverts to author.

Advice: "Read the magazine in which you want to publish. Polish your work. Please, please—no onion skin, no dot matrix. Send work that looks like you are proud to be sending it. Before being concerned about *where* you're going to publish it, pay attention to writing well and courageously."

GRUE MAGAZINE (II, IV), Hell's Kitchen Productions, Box 370, New York NY 10108. Editor: Peggy Nadramia. Magazine: 5½×8½; 96 pages; 60 lb. paper; 10 pt. CIS film laminate cover; illustrations; photos. "Quality short fiction centered on horror and dark fantasy—new traditions in the realms of the gothic and the macabre for horror fans well read in the genre, looking for something new and different, as well as horror novices looking for a good scare." Published 3 times/year. Estab. 1985.

Needs: Horror, psychic/supernatural/occult. Receives 250 unsolicited fiction mss/month. Accepts 10 mss/issue; 25-30 mss/year. Publishes 1-2 years after acceptance. Published work by Thomas Ligotti, Joe R. Lansdale, Don Webb; published new writers within the last year. Length: 4,000 words average; 6,500 words maximum. Sometimes critiques rejected ms and recommends other markets.

How to Contact: Send complete ms with cover letter. "I like to hear where the writer heard about *Grue*, his most recent or prestigious sales, and maybe a word or two about himself." Reports in 3 weeks on queries; 4 months on mss. SASE for ms. Photocopied submissions OK. Accepts computer printouts. Sample copy $4.50. Fiction guidelines for #10 SAE and 1 first class stamp.

Payment: Pays in 2 contributor's copies plus ½¢ per word.

Terms: Pays on publication for first North American serial rights.

Advice: "Editors actually vie for the work of the better writers, and if your work is good, you will sell it—you just have to keep sending it out. But out of the 250 mss I read in September, maybe three of them will be by writers who cared enough to make their plots as interesting as possible, their characterizations believable, their settings unique, and who took the time to do the rewrites and polish their prose. Remember that readers of *Grue* are mainly seasoned horror fans, and *not* interested or excited by a straight vampire, werewolf or ghost story—they'll see all the signs, and guess where you're going long before you get there. Throw a new angle on what you're doing; put it in a new light. How? Well, what scares *you*? What's *your* personal phobia or anxiety? When the writer is genuinely, emotionally involved with his subject matter, and is totally honest with himself and his reader, then we can't help being involved, too, and that's where good writing begins and ends."

‡**GULF COAST (II), A Journal of Literature & Art,** Dept. of English, University of Houston, 4800 Calhoun Rd., Houston TX 77204-5641. (713)749-3431. Editors: Stewart James and Randall Watson. Fiction Editors: Mark O'Connor and Randy Brieger. Magazine: 6×9; 108 pages; stock paper, gloss cover; illustrations and photographs. "Fiction on the cusp for the literary-minded." Estab. 1984. Circ. 1,000.
Needs: Condensed/excerpted novel, contemporary, ethnic, experimental, humor/satire, literary, regional, translations, special interest: *translations* from emerging literatures, South America, Africa, China, etc. No children's, religious/inspirational. Plans special fiction issue. Receives 40 unsolicited mss/month. Accepts 3-4 mss/issue; 6-8 mss/year. Publishes ms 6 months to 1 year after acceptance. Agented fiction 5%. Recently published work by Larry Woiwode, John Hawkes and Oscar Hijuelos. Length: No limit. Publishes short shorts. Sometimes critiques rejected mss.
How to Contact: Send complete manuscript with cover letter. "As few words as possible; please notify us if the submission is being considered elsewhere." Reports in 3 weeks to 6 months. Simultaneous and photocopied submissions OK. Sample copy for $4, 9×12 SAE and 4 first class stamps. Fiction guidelines for #10 SAE and 1 first class stamp.
Payment: Pays contributor's copies.
Terms: Acquires one-time rights. Also sponsors fiction contest. "Write for guidelines."
Advice: "We are most intrigued by those who take risks, experiment with language."

‡**GULF STREAM MAGAZINE (II),** Florida International University, English Dept., North Miami Campus, N. Miami FL 33181. (305)940-5599. Editor: Lynne Barrett. Associate Editors: Pamela Gross, Virginia Oesterle. Magazine: 5½×8½; 96 pages; bond paper; laminate (1 color, b&w) cover; cover illustrations only; cover photographs only. "We publish all *good quality*—fiction nonfiction and poetry for a predominately literary market." Semiannually. Estab. 1989. Circ. 350.
Needs: Contemporary, humor/satire, literary, mainstream, regional, suspense/mystery. Nothing "radically experimental." Plans special issues. Receives 80 unsolicited mss/month. Acquires 5 mss/issue; 10 mss/year. Does not read mss during the summer. Publishes ms 6 weeks to 3 months after acceptance. Recently published work by Alan Cheuse, Ann Hood. Length: 5,000 words average; 7,500 words maximum. Publishes short shorts. Sometimes critiques rejected mss.
How to Contact: Send complete manuscript with cover letter including "previous publications/short bio." Reports in 2 months. SASE. Photocopied submissions OK. Sample copy $4. Free fiction guidelines.
Payment: Pays 2 free subscriptions and contributor's copies.
Terms: Acquires first North American serial rights.
Advice: "Looks for good concise writing—well plotted; interesting and quixotic characters."

‡**GYPSY (II),** Die Sympathische Alternative, Vergin Press, 10708 Gay Brewer, El Paso TX 79935. (915)592-3701. Editors: Belinda Subraman and S. Ramnath. Magazine: 8½×11; 84 pages; 20-60 lb. offset paper; 60 lb. card cover; drawings; sometimes photographs. "Quality writing, not limited to theme, for the literary and artistic community." Semiannually. Estab. 1990. Circ. 1,000.
Needs: Experimental, feminist, literary, serialized novel, translations. Receives 100 unsolicited fiction mss/month. Accepts 2-4 mss/issue; 6-10 mss/year. Publishes ms 1-8 months after acceptance. Length: "open, but short is better—perhaps 500-2,500 words." Publishes short shorts. Critiques or comments on rejected mss. Sometimes recommends other markets.
How to Contact: Query first or send complete ms with cover letter. Reports in 2 weeks. SASE. Photocopied submissions OK. Reprint submissions sometimes OK. Sample copies for $5, #10 SAE and 1 first-class stamp. Fiction guidelines for #10 SAE and 1 first-class stamp.
Payment: Pays in contributor's copies.
Terms: Acquires one-time rights.

HAIGHT ASHBURY LITERARY JOURNAL (II), 558 Joost Ave., San Francisco CA 94127. (415) 221-2017. Editors: Alice Rogoff, William Walker and Joanne Hotchkiss. Tabloid: 11×17; 16 pages; newsprint paper; illustrations and photographs. Annually. Estab. 1979. Circ. 2,000.
Needs: Confession, contemporary, erotica, ethnic, experimental, feminist, gay, humor/satire, lesbian, literary, mainstream and prose poem. Plans special fiction issue in the future. Receives 2 unsolicited mss/month; accepts 2-4 mss/issue; 4-8 mss/year. Publishes ms 4-6 months after acceptance. Length: 2,000 words preferred; 3,500 words maximum. Publishes short shorts of 250-300 words.

How to Contact: Send complete ms with cover letter; reports in 2 months. SASE. Photocopied submissions OK. Sample copy $1.50 with 9×12 SAE and 4 first class stamps.
Payment: Pays in contributor's copies.

‡**HALF TONES TO JUBILEE (II)**, English Dept. Pensacola Junior College, 1000 College Blvd., Pensacola FL 32504. (904)484-1416. Editors: Allan Peterson and Walter Spara. Magazine: 6×9; approx. 100 pages; 70 lb. laid stock; 80 lb. cover. "No theme, all types published." Annually. Estab. 1985. Circ. 500.
Needs: Open. Receives approx. 2 unsolicited mss/month. Accepts approx. 6 mss/issue. Publication of ms "depends when submitted. We publish in September." Recently published work by Rachel Cann, Dusty Sklar, Johnathan Gillman. Length: 1,500 words average. Publishes short shorts. Sometimes critiques rejected mss and recommends other markets.
How to Contact: Send complete manuscript with cover letter. SASE. Photocopied submissions OK. Accepts computer printout submissions. Sample copy $4. Free fiction guidelines.
Payment: Pays 2 contributor's copies.
Terms: Acquires one-time rights.

HARDBOILED, (I,II,IV), (formerly *Detective Story Magazine*), Gryphon Publications, Box 209, Brooklyn NY 11228. Editor: Gary Lovisi. Magazine: digest size; more than 50 pages; offset paper; card stock cover; illustrations. Publishes "stories 2,000-4,000 words where detective (in whatever guise) is central character—stories should be *fun* and enjoyable to read. We are now publishing harder, more cutting-edge fiction, mostly in the hardboiled or noir area." Quarterly. Estab. 1988.
Needs: Some mystery, but mostly detective. No "blood for blood's sake." Receives 20 mss/month. Accepts 9-12 mss/year. Publishes ms within 6 months to 2 years of acceptance. Published work by Will Murray, Robert Sampson and C.J. Henderson; published new writers within the last year. Length: 2,000 words minimum; 4,000 words maximum. Sometimes critiques rejected mss and recommends other markets.
How to Contact: Query first or send complete ms with cover letter. Reports in 2 weeks on queries; 1 month on mss. SASE. Photocopied submissions OK. Accepts computer printout submissions. Sample copy $4.
Payment: Pays in contributor's copies.
Terms: Acquires first North American serial rights. Copyright reverts to author.

This cover of Detective Story Magazine *(recently renamed* Hardboiled*), showcases the cover story "Tangled Web," by Jeffrey Denhart. Editor Gary Lovisi says "it also shows off the hardboiled aspect of the magazine" which publishes "fiction about all manners of detectives, all types of stories." Ron Wilber, the cover artist, is a regular artist for the magazine. Artwork copyright © 1990 by Ron Wilber.* Detective Story Magazine *copyright © 1990 by Gryphon Publications.*

HAUNTS (II,IV), Tales of Unexpected Horror and the Supernatural, Nightshade Publications, Box 3342, Providence RI 02906. (401)781-9438. Editor: Joseph K. Cherkes. Magazine: 6×9 digest; 80-100 pages; 50 lb. offset paper; perfect bound; pen and ink illustrations. "We are committed to publishing only the finest fiction in the genres of horror, fantasy and the supernatural from both semi-pro and established writers. We are targeted towards the 18-35 age bracket interested in tales of horror and the unknown." Quarterly. Plans special fiction issue. Estab. 1984. Circ. 1,200.

Needs: Fantasy, horror, psychic/supernatural/occult. No pure adventure, explicit sex, or blow-by-blow dismemberment. Receives 400-450 unsolicited fiction mss/month. Accepts 10-12 mss/issue; 50-75 mss/year. Publishes ms 6-9 months after acceptance. Published work by Mike Hurley, Kevin J. Anderson, Frank Ward; published new writers within the last year. Length: 3,500 words average; 1,000 words minimum; 8,500 words maximum. Publishes short shorts of not less than 500 words. Critiques rejected mss. Recommends other markets.

How to Contact: Query first. "Cover letters are a nice way to introduce oneself to a new editor." Open to submissions June 1 to December 1, inclusive. Reports in 2-3 weeks on queries; 2-3 months on mss. SASE for query. Photocopied submissions OK. Accepts computer printouts. Accepts magnetic media (IBM PC-MS/DOS Ver 2.0 or higher). Sample copy $3.50 postpaid. Fiction guidelines for #10 SASE.

Payment: Pays $5-50 (subject to change), contributor's copies, charge for extras.

Terms: Pays on publication for first North American serial rights.

Advice: "Follow writers' guidelines closely. They are a good outline of what your publisher looks for in fiction. If you think you've got the 'perfect' manuscript, go over it again—carefully. Check to make sure you've left no loose ends before sending it out. Keep your writing concise. If your story is rejected, don't give up. Try to see where the story failed. This way you can learn from your mistakes. Remember, success comes to those who persist. We plan to open to advertising on a limited basis, also plan a media campaign to increase subscriptions and distributed sales."

HAWAII PACIFIC REVIEW (II), Hawaii Pacific University, 1060 Bishop St., Honolulu HI 96813. (808)544-0259. Editor: Frederick Hohing. Magazine: 6×9; 100-150 pages; quality paper; glossy cover; illustrations and photos. "As a literary magazine located in Hawaii, we are interested in material that concerns or is set in the Pacific Rim and Asia. Categories: fiction, poetry, essays and scholarly writing." Annually. Estab. "nationwide in 1988."

Needs: Adventure, contemporary, ethnic, experimental, fantasy, humor/satire, literary, mainstream, regional, science fiction, suspense/mystery, translations. No romance, confessions, religious or juvenile. Receives approx. 50 unsolicited fiction mss/month. Accepts 4-8 mss/issue. Deadline for the Spring annual issue is January 1. Does not read in summer. Publishes ms 3-12 months after acceptance. Published work by Ruth Shigezawa, Marilyn Shoemaker, Susan B. Weston; published new writers within the last year. Length: 5,000 words maximum. Publishes short shorts. Sometimes critiques rejected mss or recommends other markets.

How to Contact: Send complete manuscript with cover letter, which should include a brief bio. Reports in 3 months. SASE. Simultaneous and photocopied submissions OK. Accepts computer printouts. Fiction guidelines for #10 SAE and 1 first class stamp.

Payment: Pays in contributor's copies.

Terms: Acquires first North American serial rights. Rights revert to author upon publication. "A fiction contest is in the planning stages."

Advice: "A beginning writer should take pride in his work. Professional appearance of the manuscript, therefore, is a must."

HAWAII REVIEW, (II), University of Hawaii English Dept., 1733 Donaghho Rd., Honolulu HI 96822. (808)956-8548. Editor: Teya Maman. Fiction Editor: Jeanne Tsutsui. Magazine: 6½×9½; 150-170 pages; illustrations; photos. "We publish short stories as well as poetry and reviews by new and experienced writers. As an international literary journal, we hope to reflect the idea that cultural diversity is of universal interest." For residents of Hawaii and non-residents from the continental US and abroad. Triannually. Plans special fiction issue on environmental concerns. Estab. 1972. Circ. 5,000.

Needs: Contemporary, ethnic, experimental, humor/satire, literary, prose poem, regional and translations. Receives 40-50 mss/month. Accepts no more than 40 mss/issue; 130 mss/year. Published work by William Pitt Root, Ursule Molinaro and Ian Macmillan; published new writers within the last year. Length: 4,000 words average; no minimum; 8,000 words maximum. Occasionally critiques mss. Recommends other markets.

How to Contact: Send complete manuscript with SASE. Reports in 3-4 months on mss. Photocopied submissions OK. Accepts computer printout submissions. Sample copy for $5. Fiction guidelines free.
Payment: "Varies depending upon funds budgeted. Last year, we paid $35-70 per story." 2 contributor's copies.
Terms: Pays on publication for all rights. Sends galleys to author upon request. After publication, copyright reverts to author upon request.

‡**HAYDEN'S FERRY REVIEW (II)**, Arizona State University, Matthews Center A.S.U., Tempe AZ 85287-1502. (602)965-1243. Managing Editor: Salima Keegan. Magazine: 6 × 9; 128 pages; fine paper; illustrations and photographs. "Contemporary material by new and established writers for a varied audience." Semiannually. Estab. 1986. Circ. 600.
Needs: Contemporary, ethnic, experimental, fantasy, feminist, gay, historical (general), humor/satire, literary, mainstream, prose poem, psychic/supernatural/occult, regional, romance (contemporary), science fiction, senior citizen/retirement. Possible special fiction issue. Receives 60 unsolicited mss/ month. Accepts 5 mss/issue; 10 per year. Does not read mss in the summer. Publishes mss 3-4 months after acceptance. Recently published work by Chuck Rosenthal and Rick Bass. Length: No preference. Publishes short shorts.
How to Contact: Send complete manuscript with cover letter that includes bio. Reports in 8-10 weeks from deadline on mss. SASE. Photocopied submissions OK. Accepts computer printout submissions. Sample copy for $6. Fiction guidelines for SAE.
Payment: Pays contributor's copies.
Terms: Acquires first North American serial rights. Sends galleys to author.

HEARTLAND JOURNAL, (IV), Box 55115, Madison WI 53705. Affiliated with the Wisconsin Academy of Sciences, Arts & Letters. (800)263-3020. Editor: Jeri McCormick, Senior Editor: Lenore M. Coberly. Quarterly. "Writers and artists must be over 60 years old."
Needs: "Uses short stories, poems, essays and articles that are carefully told." Length should suit the material. "See the magazine for guidance about what we publish." Sample copy is $5.
How to Contact: Send complete mss and SASE. Will accept carefully written handwriting. Published work by Doris Kerns Quinn, Judson Jerome and Leroy Shoemaker.
Payment: Pays in contributors' copies and awards annual cash prizes.

‡**HEATHENzine (I, II)**, Split Personality Press, P.O. Box 587, Olean NY 14760. Editor: Ken Wagner. Magazine: standard size; 18 pages; regular paper; paper cover; illustrations and photographs. "Underground material for an adult, educated audience that is not easy to offend." Bimonthly. Estab. 1990. Circ. 150.
Needs: Erotica, ethnic, experimental, fantasy, feminist, gay, humor/satire, lesbian, literary, prose poem. "Work should be off-beat." Receives 1-10 unsolicited mss/month. Accepts 2-5 mss/issue; 12- 60 mss/year. Publishes ms 2-6 months after acceptance. Recently published work by Richard Paul Schmonses. Length: 1,000 words average; 2,500 words maximum. Publishes short shorts. Sometimes critiques rejected mss.
How to Contact: Send complete manuscript with cover letter that includes "credits, info. about writer." SASE. Simultaneous, photocopied and reprint submissions OK. Accepts computer printout submissions. Sample copy for $2. Fiction guidelines for #10 SAE and 1 first class stamp.
Payment: Pays in contributor's copies. Charges for extras.
Terms: Acquires one-time rights.
Advice: "*HEATHEN* is intense. Write with intensity, not just swearing either—really bite into that heat."

HEAVEN BONE (IV), New Age Literary Arts, Heaven Bone Press, Box 486, Chester NY 10918. (914)469-9018. Editors: Steven Hirsch, Kirpal Gordon. Magazine: 8½ × 11; 49-78 pages; 60 lb. recycled offset paper; recycled CIS cover; computer clip art, graphics, line art, cartoons, halftones and photos scanned in tiff format. "New age, new consciousness, expansive, fine literary, earth and nature, spiritual path. We use current reviews, essays on new age topics, creative stories and fantasy. Also: reviews of current poetry releases and expansive literature." Readers are "spiritual seekers, healers, poets, artists, musicians, students." Semiannually. Estab. 1987. Circ. 500.
Needs: Experimental, fantasy, psychic/supernatural/occult, esoteric/scholarly, regional, religious/inspirational, spiritual, new age. "No violent, thoughtless or exploitive fiction." Receives 45-110 unsolicited mss/month. Accepts 5-15 mss/issue; 12-30 mss/year. Publishes ms 2 weeks to 6 months after acceptance. Published work by Richard Paul Schmonses, Joe Richey, Jeanine Pommy-Vega; published

new writers within the last year. Length: 3,500 words average; 1,200 words minimum; 6,000 words maximum. Publishes short shorts. Sometimes critiques rejected mss and may recommend other markets.

How to Contact: Send complete ms with cover letter, which should include short bio of recent activities. Reports in 2 weeks on queries; 2 weeks-6 months on mss. SASE. Reprint submissions OK. Accepts computer printout submissions. Accepts electronic submissions via "Apple Mac SE/30 versions of Macwrite, Microsoft Word v. 4.0 or Writenow v. 2.0." Sample copy $4.50. Fiction guidelines free.

Payment: Pays in contributor's copies; charges for extras.

Terms: Acquires first North American serial rights. Sends galleys to author, if requested.

Advice: "Our fiction needs are tempermental, so please query first before submitting. We prefer shorter fiction. Do not send first drafts to test them on us. Please refine and polish your work before sending. Always include SASE. We are looking for the unique, unusual and excellent."

‡HEMISPHERES (I, II), Paisano Press, Route 1, Box 28, Eden WI 53019. Editor: Gary A. Scheinoha. Magazine: 5½ × 8½; 16-24 pages; plain white paper; colored paper cover; b&w illustrations and photographs. "Theme is open, we don't do special issues or themes. Leave it pretty much to the individual writer. For a general audience." Semiannually. Estab. 1989. Circ. 40-50.

Needs: Adventure, contemporary, ethnic, horror, humor/satire, literary, mainstream, prose poem, romance (contemporary), suspense/mystery, western. Does not want to see "anything pornographic, promoting prejudice; definitely no occult, excessive violence, gore or bad language." Acquires 1-2 mss/issue (when available); 3-4 mss/year. Publishes ms usually next issue after acceptance. Recently published work by Tom Pyle, Roger Meyer, Donna J. Dodson. Length: 500-700 words average; 300 words minimum; 1,000 words maximum. Publishes short shorts (occasionally). Length: 300-400 words. Sometimes critiques rejected mss and recommends other markets.

How to Contact: Send complete manuscript with cover letter. Include "what rights are offered, something about writer, very brief summary of material." Reports in 1 month. SASE. Simultaneous, photocopied and reprint submissions OK. Sample copy $2. Fiction guidelines for #9 SAE and 1 first class stamp.

Payment: Pays in contributor's copies.

Terms: Acquires one-time rights.

Advice: "The best way to know what I want is to buy a sample and read it cover to cover. While I have no preconceptions of what I'm looking for in fiction, it shows what we have done in the past and what might be open to future exploration. Above all, don't be afraid/intimidated to send a story to us. Let us see what you're capable of. As a freelance writer myself, I know the pitfalls, perils of the profession. As such, I am always willing/eager to work with new writers. This magazine was founded with the specific intent of giving writers a break into print."

HERESIES (IV): A Feminist Publication on Art & Politics, Box 1306, Canal St. Station, New York NY 10013. Magazine: 8½ × 11; 96 pages; non-coated paper; b&w illustrations and photos. "We believe that what is commonly called art can have a political impact and that in the making of art and all cultural artifacts our identities as women play a distinct role . . . A place where diversity can be articulated." International and North American-wide readership; carried by many libraries, alternative bookshops, and art schools. Published two times a year. Estab. 1977. Circ. 8,000.

Needs: Feminist and lesbian. Published new writers within the last year. Publishes stories up to 25 typed pages maximum.

How to Contact: Query. Free guidelines with SASE.

Payment: Small payment post publication and several free author's copies.

Advice: "Try not to imitate what you think is a successful, saleable style. Try to stick to concrete stuff you've experienced yourself so as to sharpen your narrative/dialogue skills on a foundation of familiarity."

HIBISCUS MAGAZINE (II), Short Stories, Poetry and Art, Hibiscus Press, Box 22248, Sacramento CA 95822. Editor: Margaret Wensrich. Magazine: 8½ × 11; 24-28 pages; 50 lb. paper; 1 ply vellum cover stock; pen-and-ink illustrations. Magazine of short stories, poetry and drawings. Estab. 1985. Published three times/year. Circ. 1,000-2,000.

Needs: Adventure, contemporary, fantasy, humor/satire, literary, mainstream, science fiction, suspense/mystery and western. Receives 500 unsolicited mss/month. Buys 3 mss/issue; 9 mss/year. Does not read mss in August or December. Published new writers within the last year. Length: 1,500-2,500 words average; 1,500 words minimum; 3,000 words maximum.

How to Contact: Send complete ms with SASE. Reports in 6-8 weeks on mss. Photocopied submissions OK. Accepts computer printout submissions. Sample copy $5. Fiction guidelines with #10 SAE and 1 first class stamp.
Payment: One year subscription, 2 free copies.
Terms: Acquires first rights.
Advice: "We do not return manuscripts if writers and/or poets do *not* include enough postage on SASE. We do not attempt to return mail without enough postage. International mail, especially from Canada, often does not have sufficient postage for return of ms. Writers and poets need to go to the post office and have mail weighed and then put on correct postage. We do not answer queries without an SASE."

HIGH PLAINS LITERARY REVIEW (II), 180 Adams Street, Suite 250, Denver CO 80206. (303)320-6828. Editor-in-Chief: Robert O. Greer, Jr. Magazine: 6×9; 135 pages; 70 lb. paper; heavy cover stock. "The *High Plains Literary Review* publishes poetry, fiction, essays, book reviews and interviews. The publication is designed to bridge the gap between high-caliber academic quarterlies and successful commercial reviews." Three times per year. Estab. 1986. Circ. 650.
Needs: Most pressing need: outstanding essays. Serious fiction, contemporary, humor/satire, literary, mainstream, regional. No true confessions, romance, pornographic, excessive violence. Receives approximately 200 unsolicited mss/month. Buys 4-6 mss/issue; 12-18 mss/year. Publishes ms usually 6 months after acceptance. Published work by Richard Currey, Joyce Carol Oates, Nancy Lord and Rita Dove; published new writers within the last year. Length: 4,200 words average; 1,500 words minimum; 8,000 words maximum; prefers 3,000-6,000 words. Occasionally critiques rejected mss. Sometimes recommends other markets.
How to Contact: Send complete ms with cover letter, which should include brief publishing history. Reports in 6 weeks. SASE. Simultaneous and photocopied submissions OK. Accepts computer printout submissions. Sample copy for $4.
Payment: Pays $5/page for prose and 2 contributor's copies.
Terms: Pays on publication for first North American serial rights. "Copyright reverts to author upon publication." Sends copy-edited proofs to the author.
Advice: "*HPLR* publishes *quality* writing. Send us your very best material. We will read it carefully and either accept it promptly, recommend changes or return it promptly. Do not start submitting your work until you learn the basic tenants of the game including some general knowledge about how to develop characters and plot and how to submit a manuscript. I think the most important thing for any new writer interested in the short story form is to have a voracious appetite for short fiction, to see who and what is being published, and to develop a personal style."

HILL AND HOLLER: Southern Appalachian Mountains, Seven Buffaloes Press, Box 249, Big Timber MT 59011. Editor: Art Cuelho. Magazine: 5½×8½; 80 pages; 70 lb offset paper; 80 lb cover stock; illustrations; photos rarely. "I use mostly rural Appalachian material: poems and stories. Some folklore and humor. I am interested in heritage, especially in connection with the farm." Annually. Published special fiction issue. Estab. 1983. Circ. 750.
Needs: Contemporary, ethnic, humor/satire, literary, regional, rural America farm. "I don't have any prejudices in style, but I don't like sentimental slant. Deep feelings in literature are fine, but they should be portrayed with tact and skill." Receives 10 unsolicited mss/month. Accepts 4-6 mss/issue. Publishes ms 6 months to a year after acceptance. Length: 2,000-3,000 words average. Also publishes short shorts of 500-1,000 words.
How to Contact: Query first. Reports in 2 weeks on queries. SASE. Accepts computer printouts. Sample copy $4.75.
Payment: Pays in contributor's copies; charge for extras.
Terms: Acquires first North American serial rights "and permission to reprint if my press publishes a special anthology." Sometimes sends galleys to author.
Advice: "In this Southern Appalachian rural series I can be optimistic about fiction. Appalachians are very responsive to their region's literature. I have taken work by beginners that had not been previously published. Be sure to send a double-spaced clean manuscript and SASE. I have the only rural press in North America; maybe even in the world. So perhaps we have a bond in common if your roots are rural."

HIPPO (II), Chautauqua Press, 28834 Boniface Dr., Malibu CA 90265. (213)457-7871. Editor: Karl Heiss. Magazine: 5½×8½; 42-48 pages; #20 lb. bond paper; card cover; hi-contrast b&w illustrations. "Surreal and Hyper-real writing—writing that is honest and unpretentious—has a good chance of being considered. For open-minded, artistic, optimistic, cynical, paradoxical and all encompassing minds of all ages etc." Semiannually. Estab. 1988. Circ. 150.

Needs: Adventure, confessions, contemporary, erotica, experimental, fantasy, horror, humor/satire, literary, mainstream, prose poem, psychic/supernatural/occult, regional, science fiction, western and surreality. "No pure genre fiction, but love the inclusion of genre style and content elements. No pretentious stuff that could only possibly live within the confines of academia." Receives 12 unsolicited mss/month. Accepts 5-9 mss/issue; 10-18 mss/year. Publishes ms "no more than 3 months" after acceptance. Published work by Stephen-Paul Martin, B.Z. Niditch, Greg Boyd and Gerald Locklin. Length: 500-3,000 words average; 4,000 words maximum. Publishes short shorts. Sometimes critiques rejected mss and recommends other markets.

How to Contact: Send complete ms with cover letter. Reporting time varies. SASE. Photocopied and reprint submissions OK. Accepts computer printout submissions. Sample copy $2.50. "The magazine itself is the best guide for the submitter."

Payment: Pays in contributor's copies.

Terms: Acquires first or first North American serial rights.

Advice: "Be real, be unafraid, be spontaneous, tell me whatever you want about why you like your story—or even why you don't (and that's just the cover letter). The worst I'll do is tell you I don't need the manuscript for *Hippo*—but I may be able to steer you to someone who would want it."

‡HOBO JUNGLE (II), A Quarterly Journal of New Writing, 33 Rucum Rd., Roxbury CT 06783. (203)354-4359. Editors: Marc Erdrich and Ruth Boerger. Magazine: 8x10½; 64 pages; newsprint paper; Groove cover; illustrations. "Magazine of new writing, considering poetry, fiction, essays, artwork and musical scores–works of high quality by serious writers for a general audience." Quarterly. Estab. 1987. Circ. 11,000.

Needs: Adventure, condensed/excerpted novel, contemporary, erotica, ethnic, experimental, fantasy, feminist, historical, humor/satire, literary, mainstream, prose poem, regional, science fiction, serialized novel, suspense/mystery, translations. "Young Hobos' section publishes work of young people through high school. No special requirements." Receives 25 unsolicited fiction mss/month. Buys 2-3 mss/issue; 10-12 mss/year. Publishes ms 1 month after acceptance. Agented fiction 5%. Length: Open. Publishes short shorts. Always comments on or critiques rejected mss.

How to Contact: Send complete ms with cover letter. If pseudonym is being used, please include real name. Reports in 3-6 months. SASE. Simultaneous, photocopied and computer printout submissions OK. Accepts electronic submissions. Sample copy and fiction guidelines free.

Payment: Pays $10 plus 2 contributor's copies.

Terms: Pays on publication for one-time rights.

Advice: "We seek tightly written prose, displaying a command of the language. The beginning writer should read work aloud; read it to others who can offer constructive criticism; make sure the piece is accurate in terms of sentence construction, punctuation and spelling. Avoid cliché's (unless relevant to work)."

HOBO STEW REVIEW (I, II), 2 Eliot St.#1, Somerville MA 02143. Editor: Hobo Stew. Magazine: 8½×11; photocopy paper; 65 lb. card stock cover; illustrations (use black ink on white 8½x11 paper). "*H.S.R.* encourages fiction, essays, letters to editor, poetry and journalism." Quarterly. Estab. 1984. Circ. 40.

Needs: Contemporary, feminist, humor/satire, senior citizen/retirement, translations, young adult/teen (10-18). No ageist or sexist fiction, or "slices of life that are 2 dimensional." Receives 40-50 unsolicited mss/month. Accepts 5-7 mss/issue; 20-30 mss/year. Publishes short shorts. Sometimes critiques rejected mss and recommends other markets.

How to Contact: Send complete ms with cover letter. Reports in 3-4 weeks. SASE. Photocopied submissions OK. Sample copy $2. Fiction guidelines for #10 SAE with 1 first class stamp.

Payment: Pays 1 contributor's copy.

Terms: Publication not copyrighted.

Advice: "Hobo does *HSR* for the fun of it; and sometimes he does not appreciate a particular approach to funning. He will tell you so. Do not burst a blood vessel. Do you want to be seen as a crybaby? No, Hobo thought not. Merely look toward the thousands of other places that you might share your thoughts with. Keep those tempers cool; rejection is an honorable place. *OR* you can write Hobo back, try again, and see what happens. It all is a game of chance—in your writing take those chances. Hobo does. Sometimes he loses . . . sometimes he gets by."

HOBSON'S CHOICE (I), (formerly *Starwind*), Starwind Press, Box 98, Ripley OH 45167. (513)392-4549. Editor: Susanne West. Magazine: 8½×11; 16 pages; 60 lb offset paper and cover; b&w illustrations; line shot photos. "Science fiction and fantasy for young adults (teen to 25 or so) with interest in science, technology, science fiction and fantasy." Monthly. Estab. 1974. Circ. 2,000.

Needs: Fantasy, humor/satire, science fiction. "We like SF that shows hope for the future and protagonists who interact with their environment rather than let themselves be manipulated by it." No horror, pastiches of other authors, stories featuring characters created by others (i.e. Captain Kirk and crew, Dr. Who, etc.). Receives 50+ unsolicited mss/month. Buys 4-6 mss/issue; 16-24 mss/year. Publishes ms between 4 months-2 years after acceptance. Published work by Barbara Myers, Allen Byerle, Kurt Hyatt; published new writers within the last year. Length: 3,000-8,000 words average; 1,000 words minimum; 8,000 words maximum. Occasionally critiques rejected mss.

How to Contact: Send complete ms. Reports in 6-8 weeks. SASE for ms. Photocopied submissions OK. Accepts computer printouts. Accepts electronic submissions via disk for the IBM PC or PC compatible; MacIntosh; word processors: Multimate, WordStar, MacWrite, or ASCII. Sample copy $3.50; issue #2-4 $2.50. Fiction guidelines free for #10 SAE and 1 first class stamp.

Payment: Pays 1-4¢/word and contributor's copies.

Terms: Pays 25% on acceptance; 75% on publication. "25% payment is kill fee if we decide not to publish story." Rights negotiable. Sends galleys to the author.

Advice: "I certainly think a beginning writer can be successful if he/she studies the publication *before* submitting, and matches the submission with the magazine's needs. Get our guidelines and study them *before* submitting. Don't submit something *way over* or *way under* our word length requirements. Be understanding of editors; they can get swamped very easily, *especially* if there's only one editor handling all submissions. You don't need to write a synopsis of your story in your cover letter—the story should be able to stand on its own."

‡HOOFSTRIKES NEWSLETTER (II, IV), Gweetna Press, Box 106, Mt. Pleasant MI 48858. (517)772-0139. Editor: Cathy Ford. Newsletter: 8½×11; 10-12 pages; offset stock; illustrations. Publishes fiction, nonfiction, poetry, art, puzzles, games. etc. "Published every other month. Distributed free as a service to animal welfare. Subject matter: Animal-related with emphasis on horses. Fantasy animal material is desired also." Estab. 1983. Circ. 400.

Needs: Adventure, contemporary, ethnic, experimental, fantasy, historical (general), horror, humor/satire, juvenile (5-9 years), literary, mainstream, psychic/supernatural/occult, regional, religious/inspirational, romance, science fiction, suspense/mystery, western, young adult/teen (10-18 years). "Must be animal-related material, but can use any of above themes." Receives 10-12 unsolicited mss/month. Accepts 1-2 mss/issue; 6-12 mss/year. Length: 1,500 words maximum. Publishes short shorts. Length: 1,500 words. Occasionally critiques rejected mss.

How to Contact: Send complete ms with cover letter, which should list "previously published material." Reports in 6-10 weeks. SASE. Photocopied submissions OK. Accepts computer printout submissions. Sample copy $2. Fiction guidelines for #10 SAE and 1 first class stamp.

Payment: Pays in 1-5 copies "per editor's discretion."

Terms: Acquires one-time rights.

HOR-TASY (II, IV), Ansuda Publications, Box 158-J, Harris IA 51345. Editor/Publisher: Daniel R. Betz. Magazine: 5½×8½; 72 pages; mimeo paper; index stock cover; illustrations on cover. "*Hor-Tasy* is bringing back actual *horror* to horror lovers tired of seeing so much science fiction and SF passed off as horror. We're also very much interested in true, poetic, pure fantasy."

Needs: Fantasy and horror. "Pure fantasy: Examples are trolls, fairies and mythology. The horror we're looking for comes from the human mind—the ultimate form of horror. It must sound real—so real that in fact it could very possibly happen at any time and place. We must be able to feel the diseased mind behind the personality. No science fiction in any way, shape or form. We don't want stories in which the main character spends half his time talking to a shrink. We don't want stories that start out with: 'You're crazy,' said so and so." Accepts 6 mss/issue. Receives 15-20 unsolicited fiction mss each month. Published work by Charmaine Parsons, M. C. Salemme, Jude Howell; published new writers within the last year. Critiques rejected mss "unless it's way off from what we're looking for." Sometimes recommends other markets.

How to Contact: Query or send complete ms with SASE. Accepts computer printout submissions. Reports in 1 day on queries. "If not interested (in ms), we return immediately. If interested, we may keep it as long as 6 months." Publishes ms an average of 1 year after acceptance. Sample copy $2.95. Guidelines for #10 SASE.

Payment: Pays 2 free author's copies. Charge for extras: Cover price less special discount rates.
Terms: Acquires first North American serial rights.
Advice: "Most stories rejected are about spooks, monsters, haunted houses, spacemen, etc. Because *Hor-Tasy* is a unique publication, I suggest the potential writer get a sample copy. Only unpublished work will be considered."

HOUSEWIFE-WRITER'S FORUM (I), P.O. Box 780, Lyman WY 82937. Editor: Diane Devine Wolverton. Magazine: 5½ × 8½; 32-40 pages and 20 lb bond paper and cover stock; illustrations. "Support for the woman who juggles writing with family life. We publish short fiction, poetry, essays, nonfiction, line drawings, humor and hints. For women of all ages; house husbands who write." Quarterly. Estab. 1988. Circ. over 1,200.
Needs: Confession, contemporary, experimental, historical (general), humor/satire, literary, mainstream, romance (contemporary, historical), suspense/mystery—with writing theme, preferably. No pornographic material. Receives 50-100 mss/month. Buys 1-2 mss/issue; 4-8 mss/year. Publishes ms within 6 months to 1 year after acceptance. Published work by Elaine McCormick, Carol Shenold and Sherry Zanzinger. Length: 1,500 words preferred; 500 words minimum; 2,000 words maximum. Publishes short shorts. Sometimes critiques rejected mss and if possible recommends other markets.
How to Contact: Send complete ms with cover letter. Cover letter should include "the basics." Reports in 1 month on queries; 3 months on mss. SASE. Simultaneous, photocopied and reprint submissions OK. Accepts computer printout submissions. Sample copy for $4. Fiction guidelines for #10 SAE and 1 first class stamp.
Payment: Pays $1-10, plus one contributor's copy. Half price for extra copies.
Terms: Pays on acceptance for one-time rights. Sponsors awards for fiction writers. "We sponsor occasional contests geared to the interests of housewife-writers. First place winners are published in the magazine. Entry fees: $4. Prize: $25. Send #10 SAE with 1 first class stamp for guidelines and further information."
Advice: "Just write it the best you can and submit it. If time allows, I'll share whatever thoughts come to mind as I read it. Play with your basic idea, try to imagine the plot unfolding in different ways. And this is something few other editors will say, but share with me any worries you have about your story as presently submitted. I read every submission as a friend would. I look for the good parts and encourage you to develop your strengths. At the same time, I try to help minimize your weaknesses (we all have them!). I think two heads are better than one, and as long as you realize that my opinion isn't perfect, we can learn from each other; and we'll both be better writers as a result. In 1990, I launched a humor-only publication, *Housewives' Humor*. It will include humorous fiction as well as Jean Kerr/ Peg Bracken/Kathleen Quinlan/Erma Bombeck-like accounts of modern womanhood—but with a dash of the sardonic."

HOWLING DOG (II), 8419 Rhode, Utica MI 48317. Magazine: 6 × 9; 64 pages; 65 lb paper; some illustrations; some photographs. "A wild and crazy literary magazine for a diverse audience." Estab. 1985. Circ. 500.
Needs: Contemporary, experimental, humor/satire, literary and mainstream. Receives 40 unsolicited mss/month. Accepts 2 mss/issue. Publishes ms 6 months after acceptance. Recently published work by M.L. Liebler and Gregory Burnham. Length: 1,000 words average; 300 words minimum; 1,500 words maximum. Publishes short shorts. Sometimes critiques rejected mss and recommends other markets.
How to Contact: Send complete ms with cover letter. Reports in 1 year. Sample copy $4.
Payment: Pays in contributor copies; discount charge for extras.
Terms: Acquires one-time rights.
Advice: "We look for crazy, *provocative*, quick, detailed, memorable, smooth reading, emotional or otherwise interesting. Keep it *less than* 1,500 words."

‡HURRICANE ALICE (II), A Feminist Quarterly, Hurricane Alice Fn., Inc., 207 Church St. SE, Minneapolis MN 55455. Executive Editors: Martha Roth, Janet Tripp. Fiction is collectively edited. Tabloid: 11 × 17; 12-16 pages; newsprint stock; illustrations and photos. "We look for feminist fictions with a certain analytic snap, for serious readers, seriously interested in emerging forms of feminist art/artists." Quarterly. Estab. 1983. Circ. 600-700.
Needs: Erotica, experimental, feminist, gay, humor/satire, lesbian, science fiction, translations. No coming-out stories, defloration stories, abortion stories. Receives 20 unsolicited mss/month. Publishes 4-6 stories annually. Publishes ms up to 1 year after acceptance. Published work by Jodi Stutz, Martha Clark Cummings, Pearl Cleage; published new writers within the last year. Length: up to 3,000 words maximum. Publishes short shorts. Occasionally critiques rejected mss.

How to Contact: Send complete ms with cover letter. "A brief biographical statement is never amiss. Writers should be sure to tell us if a piece was commissioned by one of the editors." Reports in 3 months. SASE for ms. Simultaneous and photocopied submissions OK. Accepts computer printout submissions. Sample copy for $2.50, 11x14 SAE and 2 first class stamps.
Payment: Pays 5-10 contributor's copies.
Terms: Acquires one-time rights.
Advice: "Fiction is a craft. Just because something happened, it isn't a story; it becomes a story when you transform it through your art, your craft."

‡**IMAGINATION (I),** LMH Media, P.O,. Box 781, Dolton IL 60419. Editor: Lisa Hake. Magazine. Monthly. Estab. 1990. Circ. 150.
Needs: Adventure, confession, contemporary, experimental, fantasy, humor/satire, literary, mainstream, prose poem, psychic/supernatural/occult, romance (contemporary), science fiction, senior citizen/retirement, serialized novel, suspense/mystery. No erotica or ethnic. Plan special fiction issue. Receives 100 unsolicited mss/month. Accepts 1 ms/issue; 12 mss/year. Publishes ms 1-12 months after acceptance to change to 1-6 months after Jan. 1, 1991. Recently published work by Kelly Davis, H. Ray Nail and Sigmund Weiss. Length: 300-1,200 words average; 200 words minimum; 1,500 words maximum. Publishes short shorts. Length: 300 words. Sometimes critiques rejected mss and recommends other markets.
How to Contact: Send complete manuscript with cover letter including "name, address, phone, if it was published previously, if so, by whom, when, where, etc. Brief intro." Reports in 2-11 weeks. SASE. Simultaneous, photocopied and reprint submissions OK. Accepts computer printout submissions. Sample copy $2. Fiction guidelines for #10 SAE and 1 first class stamp.
Payment: Pays 2 copies. "May change in 1991 to free subscription."
Terms: Acquires one-time rights. "Watch for special bulletins. Also have monthly fiction contest. 'Finish Me.' We supply the 1st sentence—you supply the rest, 300-700 words. Prizes. Send SASE for current sentence and guidelines."

‡**INDIAN YOUTH OF AMERICA NEWSLETTER (II, IV),** Indian Youth of America, Inc., P.O. Box 2786, Sioux City IA 51106. (712)252-3230. Newsletter: 8½×11; 12 or more pages; 100 lb. lustre paper; illustrations and photographs. "We are looking for Native American authors who write on a variety of themes for a broad audience, from children (former campers and others) through adults; nationwide, international." Quarterly. Estab. 1987.
Needs: Adventure, condensed/excerpted novel, contemporary, historical, literary, western, Native American. "Unsolicited manuscripts are welcome, and should be about 5-6 pages typed, double-spaced. Author should include biographical information and a photo (returnable) of himself/herself. Illustrations for the story can also be used, provided space is available. The author should also include tribal affiliation. All authors should be of Native American descent." "Does not want to see extremely abstract themes; extreme violence; sexual situations." Unsolicited mss received each month "varies greatly." Acquires one ms/issue; 4 mss/year. Publishes ms usually within a year after acceptance. Agented fiction 50%. Published work by Joseph Bruchac, Mary Tall Mountain, Louis Littlecoon Oliver, Virginia Driving Hawk Sneve. Length: 800 words average; 650-700 words minimum; 1,200 words maximum. Recommends other markets.
How to Contact: Send complete manuscript with cover letter that includes information about the author, tribal affiliation, other published works and awards, if applicable. Reports in 2-4 weeks on queries; 4-6 weeks on mss. Simultaneous, photocopied and reprint submissions OK. Accepts computer printout submissions. Sample copy and fiction guidelines free.
Payment: Pays free subscription to magazine and contributor's copies.

INDIANA REVIEW (II), 316 N. Jordan Ave., Indiana University, Bloomington IN 47405. (812)855-3439. Editor: Reneé Manfredi. Associate Editor: Allison Joseph. Magazine: 6×9; 128 pages; 60 lb paper; Glatfelter cover stock. "Magazine of contemporary fiction and poetry in which there is a zest for language, some relationship between form and content, and some awareness of the world. For fiction writers/readers, followers of lively contemporary poetry." Triannually. Estab. 1976. Circ. 500.
Needs: Literary, contemporary, experimental, mainstream. "We are interested in innovation, logic, unity, a social context, a sense of humanity. All genres that meet some of these criteria are welcome." Accepts 3-4 mss/issue. Recently published work by Charles Baxter, Wright Morris, H.E. Francis, Francine Prose, Amy Herrick; published new writers within the last year. Length: 1-35 magazine pages.

How to Contact: Send complete ms with cover letter. "Don't describe or summarize the story." SASE. Accepts computer printout submissions, prefers letter-quality. Reports in 3 weeks-3 months. Publishes ms an average of 2-10 months after acceptance. Sample copy $5.
Payment: $5/page.
Terms: Buys North American serial rights.
Advice: "Refrain from the chatty cover letter. Send one story at a time (unless they're really short), and no simultaneous submissions."

INDIGO (II), 5704 McMurray, Cote St. Luc, Montreal Quebec H4W 262 Canada. Editors: Brian A. Burke and Gretta Henderson. Magazine: 8×11; 45-60 pages; 45 lb premium paper quality; glossy cover stock; illustrations and photographs. Semiannually. Estab. 1989. Circ. 1,500-2,500.
Needs: Contemporary, experimental, horror, humor/satire, literary, mainstream, psychic/supernatural/occult and serious science fiction. No juvenile, preschool, religious or silly science fiction. Plans special fiction issue. Receives 20 unsolicited mss per month; accepts 6-10 mss per issue; 12-20 mss per year. Agented fiction less than 5%. Length: 2,800-3,500 words average; 1,200 words minimum; 7,000 words maximum. Comments on rejected mss and recommends other markets.
How to Contact: Send complete ms with cover letter; bio if possible. Reports within 2 months. SASE. Photocopied, reprint and computer printout submissions OK. Sample copy $2 (Canadian) and SAE with IRCs. Fiction guidelines free with SASE.
Payment: Pays contributor's copies.
Terms: Pays for first North American serial rights.
Advice: "Rewrite your manuscript until you know it's the best you can write. Why stop with a rough precious stone if you could produce a polished gem?"

INLET (II), Virginia Wesleyan College, Norfolk VA 23502. Editor: Joseph Harkey. Magazine: 7×8½; 32-38 pages. "Poetry and short fiction for people of all ages." Annually. Estab. 1970. Circ. 700.
Needs: Literary, contemporary, mainstream, fantasy and humor. "Our main interest is well written fiction." Accepts 2-5 mss/issue. Receives 10-20 unsolicited fiction mss each month. Does not read in summer. Recently published work by Myron Taube and John H. Timmerman. Length: 750-2,000 words but "will consider up to 3,500." Sometimes recommends other markets.
How to Contact: "Manuscripts are read September through March only." Send complete ms to fiction editor with SASE. Reports in 2 months. Sample copy for 75¢ postage (Do not send personal checks.)
Payment: Free author's copies.
Advice: "Write carefully and present a neatly typed manuscript with SASE. Send an example of your best work; short shorts preferred. Some rejected manuscripts are poorly written. Some lack imaginative treatments of the problems they raise."

INNISFREE (I, II), Box 277, Manhattan Beach CA 90266. (213)545-2607. FAX (213)546-5862. Editor: Rex Winn. Magazine: 8½×11; 44 pages; 90 lb cover stock; illustrations and photos. Publishes "fiction, poetry, essays—open forum." Bimonthly. Estab. 1981. Circ. 300.
Needs: Adventure, contemporary, ethnic, fantasy, literary, mainstream, regional, science fiction and suspense/mystery. "No political or religious sensationalism." Accepts 10-12 mss/issue; approx. 80 mss/year. Publishes ms within 6 months of acceptance. Recently published work by Ron Fleshman, Peter McGinn, Clem Portman and John Birchler. Length: 3,000 words average. Publishes short shorts. Sometimes critiques rejected mss.
How to Contact: Send complete mss with cover letter. Reports in 1 month. SASE. Accepts electronic submissions via IBM disk. Sample copy $2. Free fiction guidelines.
Payment: No payment. Prizes offered.
Terms: Acquires one-time rights.
Advice: "Fiction market is on the decline. This is an attempt to publish new writers who take pride in their work and have some talent."

INTERIM (II), Dept. of English, University of Nevada, Las Vegas NV 89154. (702)739-3172. Editor and Founder: A. Wilber Stevens. Magazine: 6×9; 48-64 pages; heavy paper; glossy cover; cover illustrations. Publishes "poetry and short fiction for a serious, sophisticated, educated audience." Semiannually. Estab. 1944; revived 1986. Circ. 600-800.
Needs: Contemporary, experimental, literary and prose poem. Accepts 2-3 mss/issue. Publishes ms within 6 months to 1 year of acceptance. Recently published work by Peter Parsons. Length: 4,000 words preferred; 7,500 words maximum.

How to Contact: Send complete ms with cover letter. Reports on mss in 2 months. SASE. Photocopied submissions OK. Accepts computer printout submissions. Sample copy $3.
Payment: Pays in contributor's copies and free subscription to magazine.

‡THE IOWA REVIEW (II), University of Iowa, 308 EPB, Iowa City IA 52242. (319)335-0462. Editor: David Hamilton. Magazine: 6×9; 200 pages; first grade offset paper; Carolina CIS-10 pt. cover stock. "Stories, essays, poems for a general readership interested in contemporary literature." Published triannually. Estab. 1970. Circ. 1,200.
Needs: Receives 150-200 unsolicited fiction mss/month. Less than 10% of fiction is agented. Buys 4-5 mss/issue, 12-16 mss/year. Does not read mss May-August. Recently published work by Mary Swander, Charles Baxter and Donald Hall. Published new writers within the last year.
How to Contact: Send complete ms with SASE. "Don't bother with queries." Simultaneous and photocopied submissions OK. Accepts computer printout submissions. Reports in 4 months on mss. Publishes ms an average of 4-12 months after acceptance. Sample copy $5.
Payment: $10/page; 2 free contributor's copies; charge for extras: 30% off cover price.
Terms: Pays on publication for first North American serial rights. Hardly ever buys reprints.
Advice: In cover letters, "be moderate. Be decent. Be brief."

IOWA WOMAN, P.O. Box 680, Iowa City IA 52244. Contact: Editor. Nonprofit magazine "dedicated to encouraging and publishing women writers and artists internationally." Quarterly. Estab. 1979. Circ. 2,500.
Needs: Historical, literary, women's. Receives 10-15 unsolicited mss/month. Accepts 2 mss/issue; 8 mss/year. Length: 5,000 words maximum.
How to Contact: Send complete ms. Reports in 3 months. SASE. Sample copy for $4 and SAE with $1.25 postage. Fiction guidelines for SAE with 1 first class stamp.
Payment: 2 free contributor's copies; $3 charge for extras.
Terms: Acquires all rights. Publication copyrighted.
Advice: "Our editorial collective often responds critically with rejections. Our guidelines are clear, but we still get stories without women or women's experience as the center. New writers have a better chance with regular submissions than with our annual writing contest which is quite competitive. We rarely publish work written by men, and only as insightful essays about relationships with women."

Associate Editor Marianne Abel says that at Iowa Woman "we are committed to using art only by Iowa women on our cover." Ames, Iowa resident Linda Emmerson's papercut "State Fair" reflects the traditional, multigenerational celebration of Iowa's state fair. "Many readers of our magazine might well recognize themselves and their friends and families in the silhouettes," commented Abel. Copyright © 1989 Linda Emmerson.

‡**IT'S A MAD, MAD, MAD, MAD, MAD WORLD (I,II), The Open Forum Magazine for Open Minds,** Flybreeder Publications, 8830 Nesbit Ave. N., Seattle WA 98103. Editor: Steve Anger. Magazine: 8½ × 11; approx. 20 pages; photocopy paper and cover; illustrations and photographs. "An open forum, leftist, weird, warped and otherwise elsewhere unpublishable for weird, warped, sci-fi, drug-addicts and ultra intellectuals (who can't spell)." Bimonthly. Estab. 1989. Circ. 200.

Needs: "The weirder, the better." Erotic, ethnic, experimental, fantasy, feminist, gay, lesbian, prose poem, psychic/supernatural/occult, science fiction, serialized novel, suspense/mystery. "No western, romance, children's, sports, normal or work from authors without a sense of humor." Receives 3-4 unsolicited fiction mss/month. Accepts 1-2 mss/issue. Publishes ms 1-2 months after acceptance. Recently published work by Frank Lee Disko, Debz Roraback. Length: 2-3 pages. Publishes short shorts. Length: 10 words or more.

How to Contact: Send complete ms with cover letter. Include name, address, how you heard of the magazine. Reports in 1 month. SASE. Simultaneous, photocopied, reprint, computer printout submissions OK. Sample copy free. Fiction guidelines for #10 SAE and 1 first-class stamp.

Payment: Pays in contributor's copies.

Terms: Publication not copyrighted.

Advice: "The more abnormal and weird it is the better. Also must have a sense of humor and intelligence to it. Do whatever you feel in your heart."

JACARANDA REVIEW (II), Dept. of English, UCLA, Los Angeles CA 90024. (213) 825-4173. Editor: Bruce Kijewski. Fiction Editor: Katherine Swiggart. Magazine: 5½ × 8; 200 pages; high quality paper; Archer cover stock; cover illustrations. "We publish anything that we think is high quality, for serious readers of fiction and poetry." Semiannually. Estab. 1984. Circ. 1,000.

Needs: Condensed/excerpted novel, contemporary, experimental, literary, mainstream, prose poem and translations. "We're not particularly interested in what people call 'genre' fiction. We're interested in fiction that reflects contemporary sensibilities about contemporary life." Receives 25 mss/month. Accepts 3 mss/issue; 6 mss/year. Publishes ms within 1-2 months of acceptance. Recently published work by Jorge Luis Borges, Ed Minus and Charles Bukowski; published new writers within the last year. Length: 2,500-5,000 words preferred; 500 words minimum; 10,000 words maximum. Sometimes critiques rejected mss and recommends other markets.

How to Contact: Send complete mss with cover letter. Cover letter should include "contributor's note." Reports on queries in 2 weeks; on mss in 2 months. SASE. Simultaneous and photocopied submissions OK. Accepts computer printout submissions. Sample copy for $3.50, 6x9 SAE and 3 first class stamps.

Payment: Pays in contributor's copies. Discount for extra copies.

Terms: Acquires one-time rights.

Advice: Sees "too much *unexamined* minimalist fiction; that is, fiction that dwells in passivity and is almost ashamed of passion. Not enough fiction inspired by Garcià Marquez or Kundera. Lately we tend to like fiction that avoids minimalist mannerisms (though we do publish work in the Robison-F. Barthelme mode), that has an energetic sense of humor, and which aspires to be psychologically fearless. We're interested in good experimental fiction, too, if we can find some, and fiction about and by women. A lot of the fiction we receive seems inspired in conception but underdeveloped and unrealized in execution. Care—deeply—about the reader, and care deeply about your work."

JAPANOPHILE (II, IV), Box 223, Okemos MI 48864. (517)349-1795. Editor-in-Chief: Earl Snodgrass. Magazine: 5¼ × 8½; 50 pages; illustrations; photos. Magazine of "articles, photos, poetry, humor, short stories about Japanese culture, not necessarily set in Japan, for an adult audience, most with college background; travelers." Quarterly. Published special fiction issue last year; plans another. Estab. 1974. Circ. 600.

Needs: Adventure, historical (general), humor/satire, literary, mainstream, and suspense/mystery. Receives 40-100 unsolicited fiction mss/month. Buys 1 ms/issue, 4-10 mss/year. Recently published work by Gerald Dorset, Bobbi Crudup, Joan Van De Moortel; published new writers within the last year. Length: 2,000 words minimum; 9,000 words maximum; 4,000 words average. Sometimes recommends other markets.

How to Contact: Send complete ms with SASE and cover letter with author bio and information about story. Photocopied and previously published submissions OK. Accepts computer printout submissions. Reports in 2 months on mss. Sample copy $4; guidelines for #10 SAE and 1 first class stamp.

Payment: Pays $20 on publication.

Terms: Pays on publication for all rights, first North American serial rights or one-time rights (depends on situation).

Advice: "Short stories usually involve Japanese and 'foreign' (non-Japanese) characters in a way that contributes to understanding of Japanese culture and the Japanese people. However, a *good* story dealing with Japan or Japanese cultural aspects anywhere in the world will be considered, even if it does not involve this encounter or meeting of Japanese and foreign characters. Some stories may also be published in an anthology." Annual contest pays $100 plus publication for the best short story. Deadline December 31. Entry fee is $5.

JAZZIMINDS MAGAZINE, Box 237, Cold Spring Harbor NY 11724. Editor: Joan H. Callahan. Fiction Editor: Jiliann Coran. Magazine: 8½×11; 20-30 pages; bond paper; heavy cover stock. "We like to emphasize the 'dark' and wild sides of life for an adult audience." Annually with quarterly supplemental issues. Estab. 1987.

Needs: Condensed/excerpted novel, contemporary, experimental, literary, prose poem and translations. Plan to publish special fiction issue or anthology in the future. Accepts 6 mss/issue; 24-30 mss/ year. Publishes ms 3 months-1 year after acceptance. Recently published work by Albert Rosso and L. Taesczch. Length: 1,000-2,000 words; 1,000-1,500 average. Publishes short shorts. Sometimes critiques rejected mss and recommends other markets.

How to Contact: Query first. Query with clips of published work or send complete ms with cover letter. Include brief auto-bio data. (Please send work vertically, not folded preferred.) Reports in 3 weeks on queries; 2 months on mss. SASE. Photocopied and reprint submissions OK. Accepts computer printout submissions. Sample copy $6 (make checks and mo's payable to: J. Callahan.) Fiction guidelines for SASE.

Payment: Acquires first or first North American serial rights.

Advice: "If someone has written about the 'dark' smokey wild side of life on the fringes, classic jazz, speakeasy, Billy Holliday or the bohemic life from which jazz was born, we are very interested. We suggest you get a sample copy, and take in your market. Aim high!"

JEOPARDY (II), Literary Arts Magazine, CH 132, Western Washington University, Bellingham WA 98225. (206)676-3118. Contact: Editors. Magazine: 6×9; 108 pages; 70 lb paper; Springhill 215 cover stock; illustrations and photographs. Material published: fiction, nonfiction, poetry, photographed artwork (slide form) for "all inclusive" audience. Annually. Estab. 1965. Circ. 3,000-4,000.

Needs: Adventure, contemporary, ethnic, experimental, fantasy, feminist, humor/satire, literary, mainstream, prose poem, regional, contemporary romance, science fiction and translations. No long stories. Accepts 7-10 mss/year. Length: 4 pages (average 800-1,000 words).

How to Contact: Submissions accepted between September and February. Mss sent during summer months may not be read immediately. Send complete ms. SASE. Simultaneous and previously published submissions OK. Accepts computer printout submissions. Sample copy $2.

Payment: Two contributor's copies. "Sometimes *Jeopardy* awards cash prizes or special recognition to winners in various categories."

Advice: "We are a student-run university literary publication. We are happy to look at any fiction. Sometimes, if staff is large enough, at writer's request we will comment on the work."

THE JOURNAL (II), Creative Writing Program, Ohio State University, 164 W. 17th St., Columbus OH 43210. (614)292-4076. Editors: Kathy Fagan (poetry); Michelle Herman (fiction). Magazine: 6×9; 80 pages. "We are open to all forms of quality fiction." For an educated, general adult audience. Semiannually. Estab. 1973. Circ. 1,300.

Needs: Contemporary, erotica, ethnic, experimental, feminist, gay, literary, prose poem and regional. No romance or religious/devotional. Accepts 2-12 mss/issue. Receives approximately 100 unsolicited fiction mss each month. Publishes ms within 8 months of acceptance. Agented fiction 10%. Recently published work by Anne Brashler and Kent Meyers; published new writers within the last year. Length: 4,000 words maximum. Critiques rejected mss when there is time. Sometimes recommends other markets.

How to Contact: Send complete ms with cover letter, which should list previous publications. Reports in 2 weeks on queries; 3 months on mss. SASE. Photocopied submissions OK. "No simultaneous submissions please." Accepts computer printout submissions. Prefers letter-quality. Publishes ms 1-12 months after acceptance. Sample copy $4.50; fiction guidelines for SASE.

Payment: Pays $25 stipend when funds are available. Free author's copies. $4.50 charge for extras.
Terms: Acquires First North American serial rights. Sends galleys to author.
Advice: Mss are rejected because of "lack of understanding of the short story form, shallow plots, undeveloped characters. Cure: read as much well-written fiction as possible. Our readers prefer 'psychological' fiction rather than stories with intricate plots. Take care to present a clean, well-typed submission."

JOURNAL OF POLYMORPHOUS PERVERSITY (II), Wry-Bred Press, Inc., 10 Waterside Plaza, Suite 20-B, New York NY 10010. (212)689-5473. Editor: Glenn Ellenbogen. Magazine: 6¾×10; 24 pages; 60 lb paper; antique india cover stock; illustrations with some articles. "*JPP* is a humorous and satirical journal of psychology, psychiatry, and the closely allied mental health disciplines." For "psychologists, psychiatrists, social workers, psychiatric nurses, *and* the psychologically sophisticated layman." Semiannually. Plans special fiction issue. Estab. January, 1984.
Needs: Humor/satire. "We only consider materials that are 1) funny, 2) relate to psychology *or* behavior." Receives 10 unsolicited mss/month. Accepts 8 mss/issue; 16 mss/year. Published work by Kathleen Donald, Ph.D. Most writers published last year were previously unpublished writers. Length: 1,500 words average; 4,000 words maximum. Comments on rejected ms.
How to Contact: Send complete ms *in triplicate.* Reports in 1-3 months on mss. SASE. Simultaneous and photocopied submissions OK. Accepts computer printout submissions; prefers letter-quality. Accepts disk submissions compatible with Morrow MD-11. Prefers hard copy with a disk submission. Sample copy $5. Fiction guidelines free for #10 SAE and 1 first class stamp.
Payment: 2 contributor's copies; charge for extras: $5.
Advice: "We will *not* look at poetry or short stories. We only want to see intelligent spoofs of scholarly psychology and psychiatry articles written in scholarly scientific languages. Take a look at *real* journals of psychology and try to lampoon their *style* as much as their content. Avoid writing in first person; rather use more quasi-scientific style. There are few places to showcase satire of the social sciences, thus we provide one vehicle for injecting a dose of humor into this often too serious area."

JOURNAL OF REGIONAL CRITICISM (II), Arjuna Library Press, 1025 Garner St. D, Space 18, Colorado Springs CO 80905. Editor: Joseph A. Uphoff, Jr. Pamphlet: size variable; number of pages variable; Xerox paper; Bristol cover stock; b&w illustrations and photos. "Surrealist and dreamlike prose poetry and very short surrealist stories to illustrate accompanying mathematical, theoretical material in the fine arts for a wide ranging audience interested in philosophical sophistication and erudite language." Variable frequency. Estab. 1979.
Needs: Adventure, contemporary, ethnic, experimental, fantasy, historical (general), horror, humor/satire, literary, mainstream, prose poem, psychic/supernatural/occult, regional, religious/inspirational, contemporary romance, science fiction. Receives 1 or fewer unsolicited fiction ms/month. Accepts 1-5 mss/issue. Recently published work by Gayle Teller, Ron Ellis and Randall Brock. Short short stories preferred. Sometimes critiques rejected mss and recommends other markets.
How to Contact: Send complete ms with cover letter. Manuscript will *not* be returned. Cover letter should include goals, behind-the-scenes explanation, and biographical material or résumé, date of birth, degrees, awards, offices and publications. SASE for query. Simultaneous, photocopied and reprint submissions OK. Accepts computer printouts. Sample copy, if and when available, for $1 postage.
Payment: By contract after profit; contributor's copies.
Terms: Acquires "prototype presentation rights." Publication copyrighted—limited edition procedure copyrights.
Advice: "Reality is, itself, a kind of fiction, but we seldom have personal control over our lives like we can have over our writings. Language can convey beautiful stories, crisis, tragedy, or merely form. That which does not exist can be made to exist in fiction. In writings, we can, through image, violate the natural laws of the universe to make fantasy. This technique is often applied to cartoons and comedy. Writings can also be made to influence the course of events rather than relating unreal situations. The news is often the basis of a good, fictional adventure. Those who do not know what surrealism is are urged to read *Nadja* by Andre Breton and the literature of Amos Tutuola."

K (II), 351 Dalhousie St., Brantford, Ontario N3S 3V9 Canada. Editor: G.J. McFarlane. Magazine: 8½×11; 50 pages. Has an "open theme that provides a forum for writers whose contemporary ideas establish a voice for turbulent times." Published as funds permit. Estab. 1985.

Needs: Condensed novel, confession, contemporary, erotica, experimental, feminist, humor/satire, literary, mainstream, science fiction, serialized/excerpted novel. Accepts mss "as quality and space permit." Mss published an undetermined time after acceptance. Publishes short shorts. Occasionally critiques rejected mss and recommends other markets.

How to Contact: Send complete ms with cover letter. Reports in 1 month on queries. SASE. Simultaneous, photocopied and reprint submissions OK. Accepts computer printout submissions. Sample copy $4.

Payment: Pays in contributor's copies.

KALEIDOSCOPE (II, IV), International Magazine of Literature, Fine Arts, and Disability, 326 Locust St., Akron OH 44302. (216)762-9755, ext. 27. Editor-in-Chief: Darshan Perusek, Ph.D. Magazine: 8½×11; 56-64 pages; non-coated paper; coated cover stock; illustrations (all media); photos. Semiannually. Estab. 1979. Circ. 1,500.

Needs: Personal experience, drama, fiction, essay, humor/satire, prose poem. Receives 20-25 unsolicited fiction mss/month. Accepts 10 mss/year. Approximately 1% of fiction is agented. Recently published work by Oliver Sacks, M.D., Constance Kunin, Dallas Denny and Mary Holmes. Published new writers within the last year. Length: 3,000 words minimum; 5,000 words maximum.

How to Contact: Query first or send complete ms and cover letter, which should include author's educational and writing background; if author has a disablty, how the disability has influenced the writing. SASE. Accepts computer printout submissions. Reports in 1 month on queries; 6 months on mss. Sample copy $2. Guidelines for #10 SAE and 1 first class stamp.

Payment: Cash payment ranging from $25-75. 2 free contributor's copies; charge for extras: $4.50.

Terms: Pays on publication for first rights. Reprints are permitted with credit given to original publication.

Advice: "Read the magazine and get fiction guidelines. Writers with disablties may write on any topic; non-disabled writers must limit themselves to the theme of disability. Avoid the trite and sentimental. Fiction should be fresh, original and imaginative. We seek thought-provoking subject matter with fresh language and imagery and effective handling of technique. Expect minor editing."

KALLIOPE (II), A Journal of Women's Art, Florida Community College at Jacksonville, 3939 Roosevelt Blvd., Jacksonville FL 32205. (904)387-8211. Editor: Mary Sue Koeppel. Magazine: 7¼×8¼; 76-88 pages; 70 lb coated matte paper; Bristol cover; 16-18 halftones per issue. "A literary and visual arts journal for women, *Kalliope* celebrates women in the arts by publishing their work and by providing a forum for their ideas and opinions." Short stories, poems, plays, essays, reviews and visual art. Published 3 times/year. Estab. 1978. Circ. 1,000.

Needs: "Quality short fiction by women writers." Accepts 2-4 mss/issue. Receives approximately 100 unsolicited fiction mss each month. Recently published work by Layle Silbert, Robin Merle, Claudia Brinson Smith, Colette; published new writers within the last year. Preferred length: 750-3,000 words, but occasionally publishes longer (and shorter) pieces. Critiques rejected mss "when there is time and if requested."

How to Contact: Send complete ms with SASE and short contributor's note. Reports in 2-3 months on ms. Publishes ms an average of 1-6 months after acceptance. Sample copy $7 for current issue; $4 for issues from '78-'88.

Payment: 3 free author's copies or year's subscription. $7 charge for extras, discount for large orders.

Terms: Acquires first rights. "We accept only unpublished work. Copyright returned to author upon request."

Advice: "Read our magazine. The work we consider for publication will be well written and the characters and dialogue will be convincing and have strength and movement. We like a fresh approach and are interested in new or unusual forms. Make us believe your characters; give readers an insight which they might not have had if they had not read you. We would like to publish more work by minority writers." Manuscripts are rejected because "1) nothing *happens!*, 2) it is thinly disguised autobiography (richly disguised autobiography is OK), and 3) ending is either too pat or else just trails off."

KANA (II), Box 36091, Towson MD 21286. (301)828-6123. Editor: Laurie Precht. Magazine: 5½×8½; 40 pages; 60 lb paper; 70 lb cover; illustrations. "Any material as long as it makes sense," for a "college educated and above" audience. Semiannually. Estab. 1988. Circ. 200.

Needs: Adventure, confession, contemporary, ethnic, experimental, fantasy, feminist, gay, historical (general), humor/satire, lesbian, literary, mainstream, regional, senior citizen/retirement, translations. Does not want to see "the type of fiction that drags on without saying anything; confusing material."

Receives 5-10 unsolicited mss/month. Accepts 1-2 mss/issue; 2-4 mss/year. Publishes ms 1-6 months after acceptance. Length: 500-750 words preferred; 2,000 words maximum. Publishes short shorts. Sometimes critiques rejected mss.

How to Contact: Send complete ms with cover letter. Cover letter should include "a bio, return address (on work, too)." Reports in 2-3 months. SASE. Simultaneous and photocopied submissions OK "when noted as such." Accepts computer printout submissions. No previously published material. Sample copy for 5½×8½ SAE and 2 first class stamps. Fiction guidelines for #10 SAE and 1 first class stamp.

Payment: Pays in contributor's copies.

Terms: All rights remain with author.

Advice: "I gear my magazine towards the public instead of the literary private sectors. I believe that the hairdresser down the street enjoys reading just as much as the professor at the university, but the material in literary magazines is often too deep for non-literature majors (or otherwise), so I keep *Kana* simple, understandable, and free to whomever wants to read it or submit to it. I believe that Steinbeck and William Carlos Williams grasped best the contemporary short story (American, anyway)."

KANSAS QUARTERLY (I, II), Kansas Quarterly Association, 122 Denison Hall, English Dept., Kansas State University, Manhattan KS 66506-0703. (913)532-6716. Editors: Harold Schneider (emeritus), Ben Nyberg, Jonathen Holden and John Rees. Magazine: 6×9; 104-356 pages; 70 lb offset paper; Frankcote 8 pt. coated cover stock; illustrations occasionally; unsolicited photos rarely. "A literary and cultural arts magazine publishing fiction and poetry. Special material on selected, announced topics in literary criticism, art history, folklore and regional history. For well-read, general and academic audiences." Quarterly. Published double and single fiction issues last year; plans repeat. Estab. 1968. Circ. 1,300.

Needs: "We consider most categories as long as the fiction is of sufficient literary quality to merit inclusion, though we have no interest in children's literature. We resist translations and parts of novels, but do not absolutely refuse them." Accepts 30-50 mss/year. Limited reading done in summer. Approximately 1% of fiction is agented. Recently published work by Rick Bass, Stephen Dixon, Kathleen Spivak and George Blake. Published new writers within the last year. Length: 350-12,000 words. Sometimes recommends other markets.

How to Contact: Send complete ms with SASE. Reports in 3 months+ on mss. Publishes ms an average of 18-24 months after acceptance. Sample copy $6.

Payment: 2 free author's copies and annual awards to the best of the stories published.

Terms: Acquires all rights. Sends galleys to author. "We reassign rights on request at time of republication." Sponsors awards: *KQ*/KAC (national); Seaton awards (for Kansas natives or residents). Each offers 6-10 awards from $25-$250.

Advice: "Always check a sample copy of the magazine to which you send your stories—note its editors' likes and interests. Send your story with SASE—do not appear to devalue them by asking they be discarded rather than returned."

KARAMU (II), English Dept., Eastern Illinois University, Charleston IL 61920. (217)581-5614. Editor: Peggy L. Brayfield. Magazine: 5×8; 60 pages; cover illustrations. "We like fiction that builds around real experiences, real images and real characters, that shows an awareness of current fiction and the types of experiments that are going on in it, and that avoids abstraction, sentimentality, over-philosophizing and fuzzy pontifications. For a literate, college-educated audience." Annually. Estab. 1967. Circ. 500.

Needs: Literary, contemporary. Receives approximately 20-30 unsolicited fiction mss/month. Recently published work by J. Carol Goodman, F.R. Lewis and Sheila Goldburgh Johnson. Accepts 4-5 mss/issue. Published new writers within the last year. Length: 2,000-7,000 words. Critiques rejected mss when time permits.

How to Contact: Send complete ms with SASE. Accepts computer printout submissions, prefers letter-quality. Reports in 2-3 months on mss. Publishes ms an average of 1 year after acceptance. Sample copy $2.

Payment: 1 free author's copy. Half price charge for extras.

Advice: "Send for a sample copy, read it, and send a complete ms if your stories seem to match our taste. Please be patient—we sometimes get behind in our reading, especially between May and September. Mss submitted between January and June have the best chance. We feel that much of the best writing today is being done in short fiction."

KENNEBEC (II, IV), A Portfolio of Maine Writing, University of Maine at Augusta, University Heights, Augusta ME 04330. (207)622-7131. Editors: Carol Kontos, Terry Plunkett. Tabloid: 11x14; 36-40 pages; newsprint; illustrations and photos. We publish mostly Maine-related stories and poetry for a Maine and New England audience." Annually. Estab. 1975. Circ. 5,000.
Needs: Condensed novel, contemporary, experimental, fantasy, humor/satire, literary, regional, serialized/excerpted novel. Reads mss Sept. 15-Dec. 15. Published new writers within the last year. Length: 1,500-3,000 words. Publishes short shorts. "Rarely" critiques rejected mss.
How to Contact: Send complete ms with cover letter; which should include information about writer's connection with Maine. SASE. Simultaneous submissions OK. Accepts computer printout submissions. Sample copy free.
Payment: Pays in contributor's copies.
Advice: "We have limited paper available, so long manuscripts are generally not suitable."

‡KENNESAW REVIEW (II), Kennesaw State College, English Dept., P.O. Box 444, Marietta GA 30061. (404)423-6297. Editor: Dr. Robert W. Hill. Fiction Editors: Drs. Greg Johnson and Paula Yow. Magazine. "Just good fiction, all themes, for a general audience." Quarterly. Estab. 1987.
Needs: Condensed/excerpted novel, contemporary, ethnic, experimental, fantasy, feminist, gay, horror, humor/satire, literary, mainstream, psychic/supernatural/occult, regional. No romance. Plans special fiction issue. Receives 25-60 mss/month. Accepts 2-4 mss/issue. Publishes ms 6 months after acceptance. Recently published work by Lisa Koger, Michael Lee West, Eve Shelnutt, David Bottom. Length: 9-30 pages. Publishes short shorts. Length: 500 words. Often comments on or critiques rejected mss.
How to Contact: Send complete ms with cover letter. Include previous publications. Reports in 3 weeks on queries; in 2 months on mss. SASE. Simultaneous, photocopied and computer printout submissions OK. Sample copy and fiction quidelines free.
Payment: Pays in contributor's copies.
Terms: Acquires all rights.
Advice: "Use the language well and tell an interesting story. Send it on. Be open to suggestions."

THE KENYON REVIEW (II), Kenyon College, Gambier OH 43022. (614)427-3339. Editor: Marilyn Hacker. "Fiction, poetry, essays, book reviews for primarily academic audience." Quarterly. Estab. 1939. Circ. 4,000.
Needs: Condensed/excerpted novel, contemporary, ethnic, experimental, fantasy, feminist, gay, historical, humor/satire, lesbian, literary, mainstream, prose poem, senior citizen/retirement, translations. Receives 300 unsolicited fiction mss/month. Accepts up to 3 mss/issue; up to 12 mss/year. Does not read mss June-August. Publishes ms 12-18 months after acceptance. 50% of fiction is agented. Length: 3-15 (typeset) pages preferred. Rarely publishes short shorts. Sometimes comments on rejected ms.
How to Contact: Send complete ms with cover letters. Reports on mss in 1 month. SASE. Simultaneous and photocopied submissions OK. Does not accept dot-matrix computer printouts. Sample copy $7.
Payment: $10/page for fiction.
Terms: Pays on publication for one-time rights and option on anthology rights. Sends copy-edited version to author for approval.
Advice: "Read several issues of our publication."

‡KEY WEST REVIEW (II), P.O. Box 2082, Key West FL 33045. (305)296-1365. Editor: William J. Schlicht. Magazine: 6x9; 100 pages; classic laid cover, some illustrations and photographs. "Fiction, poetry, graphics—like to use some Key West-related material. For an audience interested in good literature." Quarterly. Estab. 1988. Circ. 500.
Needs: Excerpted novel, contemporary, experimental, feminist, gay, humor/satire, lesbian, literary, mainstream, regional. No romance, confessional, sentimental, violence. Receives 20 unsolicited fiction mss/month. Accepts 20 mss/issue; 60 mss/year. Does not read mss June-September. Publishes ms 1 month after acceptance. Recently published work by Alice Adams, Hal Bennett, Joan Williams. Length: varies. Comments on or critiques rejected mss. Might recommend other markets.
How to Contact: Send a complete ms with cover letter. Reports in 2 months. SASE. Photocopied and computer printout submissions OK. Sample copy $3. Fiction guidelines for #10 SAE and 1 first-class stamp.
Payment: Pays in contributor's copies; charges for extras.
Terms: Acquires one-time rights.

KINGFISHER (II), Box 9783, N. Berkeley CA 94709. Editors: Ruthie Singer, Barbara Schultz, Lorraine Gray, Andrea Beach. Magazine: 6×9; 120 pages; 60 lb paper; 80 lb cover. "*Kingfisher* sports no particular political or intellectual doctrine. We are interested in innovative short fiction primarily, but we will also consider poetry and translations." Biannually. Estab. 1987.
Needs: Contemporary, experimental, literary, serialized/excerpted novel and translations. No science fiction. Receives 100 unsolicited fiction mss/month. Accepts up to 20 mss/issue; up to 40 mss/year. Recently published work by Campbell McGrath, Ruth Barzel and Brian Boyd. Published new writers within the last year. Length: 3,000 words average; 12,000 words maximum. Publishes short shorts. Sometimes comments on rejected mss and recommends other markets.
How to Contact: Send complete ms with cover letter, which should include short bio and list of publication credits. Reports on queries in 1 month; on mss in 3 months. SASE. Simultaneous and photocopied submissions OK. Accepts computer printout submissions. Sample copy $5.
Payment: Pays in contributor's copies.
Terms: Acquires one-time rights.
Advice: "We will continue to publish short works of fiction as long as we can find ones of the quality we require. The writer should please mention if he or she would like to receive specific reaction to his/her work. We are more than happy to help in that way."

‡KINGS REVIEW, P.O. Box 1933, S. San Francisco CA 94083-1933. Editor: Larry Sparks. Magazine; illustrations. "We publish mostly poetry. However, we are open to prose; usually for an academic audience." Estab. 1988.
Needs: Experimental, literary, prose poem. "All work should come with SASE." Receives "several" unsolicited mss/month. Accepts "few" mss/issue. Publishes ms "various periods" after acceptance. Recommends other markets.
How to Contact: Send complete manuscript with cover letter and "some biographical information." Reports in 6 weeks on queries; 3 months on mss. SASE. Simultaneous, photocopied and reprint submissions OK. Accepts computer printout submissions. Accepts electronic submissions. Sample copy $3.50. Fiction guidelines for SAE and standard postage.
Payment: Usually.
Terms: Payment may be either on acceptance or publication for one-time rights.

KIOSK (II), English Department, S.U.N.Y. at Buffalo, 302 Clemens Hall, Buffalo NY 14260. (716)636-2570. Editor: N. Gallespie. Magazine: 5½×8½; 100 pages; card stock cover. "We seek innovative, non-formula fiction and poetry." Plans special fiction issue. Annually (may soon be Biannual). Estab. 1986. Circ. 750.
Needs: Excerpted novel, erotica, experimental, feminist, gay, humor/satire, lesbian, prose poem and translations. "No genre or formula fiction; we seek fiction that defies categorization—lush, quirky, flippant, subversive, etc." Receives 15 mss/month. Accepts 6 mss/issue. Publishes ms within 6 months of acceptance. Published work by Ray Federman, Carol Berge, Tom Whalen. Length: 3,000 words preferred; 7,500 words maximum. Publishes short shorts "the shorter the better." Sometimes critiques rejected mss; rarely recommends other markets.
How to Contact: Send complete mss with cover letter. Does not read from May to September. Reports in 2-3 weeks on queries; 2-3 months on mss. "Most sooner; if we keep it longer, we're considering it seriously." SASE. Simultaneous, photocopied and reprint submissions OK. Accepts computer printout submissions. Sample copy for 9x6 or larger SAE and 2 first class stamps.
Payment: Pays in contributor's copies.
Terms: Acquires one-time rights.
Advice: "*Kiosk* was started because it seemed to us that most little mags were publishing the same type of stuff—slick, literary, polished fluff that writing programs churn out like hot dogs. If you've got a different vision of writing than others seem to be buying, then maybe this mag is for you. Literary magazine writing is exciting when editors take chances and offer a place for writers who find other avenues closed." Looks for "a writer's unique vision and care for the language. Striking, unexpected images. New forms, new thinking. A certain level of technical accomplishment."

KOLA (IV), A Black Literary Magazine, Box 1602, Place Bonaventure, Montreal Quebec H5A 1H6 Canada. Editor: Dr. Horace I. Goddard. Magazine: 6×9; 40 pages; black and white illustrations. "Manuscripts that focus on the black experience in Africa and the African diaspora for a general audience." Estab. 1987. Circ. 300.

Needs: Contemporary, ethnic, feminist, literary, black. Accepts 3 mss/issue. Publishs ms 2 months after acceptance. Recently published work by Dr. Nigel Thomas, Randolph Homer and Yvonne Anderson. Length: 3,000-5,000 words; 2,000 words minimum; 6,000 words maximum. Sometimes critiques rejected mss.
How to Contact: Send complete manuscript with cover letter. Include bio-vita, previous publications. Reports in 3 months on mss. SASE for ms, not needed for query. Photocopied submissions OK. Accepts computer printout submissions. Sample copy for $4 and 6×9 SAE.
Payment: Two free contributor's copies.
Terms: Acquires first rights.
Advice: "The fiction must relate to the black experience. It must be of a high standard in structure: theme, plot, characterization, etc. Make sure you can follow grammar rules, use a dictionary, accept criticism, and keep on writing even though the rejection slips get you down."

LACTUCA (II), Box 621, Suffern NY 10901. Editor: Mike Selender. Magazine: folded 8½×14; 60-70 pages; 24 lb bond; soft cover; illustrations. Publishes "poetry, short fiction and b&w art, for a general literary audience." Published 2-3 times/year. Estab. 1986. Circ. 400.
Needs: Adventure, condensed/excerpted novel, confession, contemporary, erotica, literary, mainstream, prose poem and regional. No "self-indulgent writing or fiction about writing fiction." Receives 30 or more mss/month. Accepts 3-4 mss/issue; 10-12 mss/year. Publishes ms within 3-12 months of acceptance. Published work by Douglas Mendini, Tom Gidwitz, Ruthann Robson; published new writers within the last year. Length: around 12-14 typewritten double-spaced pages. Publishes short shorts. Often critiques rejected mss and recommends other markets.
How to Contact: Query first or send complete ms with cover letter. Cover letter should include "just a few brief notes about yourself. Please no long 'literary' résumés or bios. The work will speak for itself." Reports in 2 weeks on queries; 6-8 weeks on mss. SASE. Photocopied submissions OK. No simultaneous or previously published work. Accepts computer printouts. Accepts electronic submissions via "MS DOS or Macintosh formatted disk. We can convert most word-processing formats." Sample copy for $3.50. Fiction guidelines for #10 SAE and 1 first class stamp.
Payment: Pays 2-5 contributor's copies, depending on the length of the work published.
Terms: Acquires first North American serial rights. Sends galleys to author if requested. Copyrights revert to authors.
Advice: "Too much of the poetry and fiction I have been reading over the past two years has been obsessed with the act of writing or life as a writer. We're not interested in this kind of writing. I place a strong emphasis on the readability of fiction. The dialogue should be clear, and the characters speaking readily discernible. It is worth making the extra revisions necessary to obtain this level of quality. We strongly suggest that writers send a SASE for our guidelines before submitting any fiction."

LAKE EFFECT (II), Lake County Writers Group, Box 59, Oswego NY 13126. (315)635-5714. Editor: Jean O'Connor Fuller, M.E. Tabloid: 11½×17; 32 pages; newsprint paper and cover; illustrations; photos. "We publish short fiction, poetry, humor, reviews, b&w art and photographs and one nonfiction piece of interest to the area each issue. Our circulation is principally upstate NY." Quarterly. Estab. 1986. Circ. 10,000.
Needs: Contemporary, fantasy, historical (general), humor/satire, literary, mainstream, regional. "We want previously unpublished, honest stories." Accepts 2-3 mss/issue. Does not read mss in August. Publishes ms within 6 months after acceptance. Recently published work by David Shields, Zina Collier; published new writers within the last year. Length: 5,000 words maximum. Publishes short shorts. Occasionally critiques rejected mss and recommends other markets.
How to Contact: Send complete ms with cover letter, which should include biographical information on author. Reports in 2 months. SASE for ms. Photocopied submissions OK. No simultaneous submissions. Accepts computer printout submissions; "dot-matrix must be readable." Sample copy for $2. Fiction guidelines for #10 SAE and 1 first class stamp.

The double dagger before a listing indicates that the listing is new in this edition. New markets are often the most receptive to freelance contributions.

Payment: $25 and 1 free contributor's copy; charge $2 for extras.

Terms: Acquires first North American serial rights.

Advice: "We exist primarily to give outlet to the writers of this region, but also will use good work from outside if we like it. Send us stories about human beings we can believe in, in neat, professional style. We prefer upbeat to downbeat work, but deplore sentimentality. Do not send us your death stories."

LANGUAGE BRIDGES QUARTERLY (II,IV), Polish-English Literary Magazine, Box 850792, Richardson TX 75085-0792. (214)530-2782. Editor: Eva Ziem. Fiction Editor: Zofia Przebindowska-Tousty. Magazine: 8½×11; 20+ pages; 60 lb paper; 65 lb cover; illustrations. "Today's Poland and Polish spirit are the main subject; a picture of life in Poland, with emphasis on the recent Polish emigration wave problems, however topics of general nature are being accepted. For both English and Polish speaking readers." Quarterly. Estab. 1989. Circ. 300.

Needs: Condensed/excerpted novel, fantasy, historical (general), humor/satire, literary, prose poem, religious/inspirational, translations, young adult/teen (10-18 years). "No horror, no vulgar language." Receives 1 unsolicited ms/month. Accepts one fiction ms every second issue. Publishes ms 3-6 months after acceptance. "Length does not matter. The longer works are broken into parts." Publishes short shorts. Sometimes critiques rejected mss and recommends other markets.

How to Contact: Send complete ms with cover letter. Reports in 2-3 months on mss. Simultaneous, photocopied and reprint submissions OK. Accepts computer printouts. Accepts electronic submissions via disk. Free sample copy and fiction guidelines.

Payment: Pays contributor's copies.

Terms: Pays for one-time rights. Sends galleys to author.

Advice: "Fiction has to be original and meaningful for us. We wish to introduce English speaking readers to Polish culture and to the current problems of Poles in Poland and abroad."

‡LATE KNOCKING (II), Harford Poetry Society, Inc., Box 336, Forest Hill MD 21050. Editors: Vonnie Crist and Jean E. Keenan. Magazine: 5½×8½; 50-100 pages; 80 lb stock; illustrations. "Good quality prose, poetry and artwork for a literate, adult audience." Semiannually. Estab. 1985. Circ. 500.

Needs: Adventure, confession, contemporary, ethnic, experimental, fantasy, feminist, historical, horror, humor/satire, literary, mainstream, science fiction, suspense/mystery, translations. Receives 60-100 unsolicited mss/month. Accepts 3-6 mss/issue. Publishes ms 3-9 months after acceptance. Length: 3,200 words average; 150 words minimum; 4,000 words maximum. Publishes short shorts. Occasionally critiques rejected mss or recommends other markets.

How to Contact: Send complete ms with cover letter. Reports in 8 weeks on mss. Photocopied and reprint submissions OK. Accepts computer printout submissions, including dot-matrix. Sample copy $3. Fiction guidelines free with SAE and 1 first class stamp.

Payment: Pays in contributor's copies.

Terms: Acquires first North American serial rights or one-time rights. Publication copyrighted.

Advice: "Read everything—from ancient classics to modern pop, and listen, and apprentice yourself—learn, study, practice, talk with other people, nature, yourself, your coffee pot, your onion patch. Learn the difference between 'nauseous' and 'nauseated.' Know words before you make up your own."

LAUREL REVIEW (II), Northwest Missouri State University, Dept. of English, Maryville MO 64468. (816)562-1265. Editors: Craig Goad, David Slater and William Trowbridge. Fiction Readers: Jim Simmerman, Randy Freisinger, Parker Johnson. Magazine: 6×9; 124-128 pages; good quality paper. "We publish poetry and fiction of high quality, from the traditional to the avant-garde. We are eclectic, open and flexible. Good writing is all we seek." Biannually. Estab. 1960. Circ. 700.

Needs: Literary and contemporary. Accepts 3-5 mss/issue, 6-10 mss/year. Receives approximately 60 unsolicited fiction mss each month. Approximately 1% of fiction is agented. Length: 2,000-10,000 words. Critiques rejected mss "when there is time." Reads September to May.

How to Contact: Send complete ms with SASE. Accepts computer printout submissions. Reports in 1 week to 4 months on mss. Publishes ms an average of 1-12 months after acceptance. Sample copy $3.50.

Payment: 2 free author's copies, 1 year free subscription.

Terms: Acquires first rights. Copyright reverts to author upon request.

Advice: Send $3.50 for a back copy of the magazine.

THE LEADING EDGE (II,IV), Magazine of Science Fiction and Fantasy, 3163 JKHB, Provo UT 84604. Editor: Scott R. Parkin. Fiction Editor: Carl Rossi. Magazine: 5×8; 100-120 pages; 20 lb bond paper; 40 lb card stock; 15-20 illustrations. "We are a magazine dedicated to the new and upcoming author, poet, and artist involved in the field of science fiction and fantasy. We are for the upcoming professional." Published 3 times/year. Circ. 400.
Needs: Adventure, experimental, fantasy, humor/satire, prose poem, science fiction. "We are very interested in experimental sf and humorous stories, but all pieces should fall within the category of sf and fantasy. No graphic sex, violence, dismemberment, etc. No outrageous religious commentary. No fannish/media stories; i.e., no Star Wars, Star Trek, Dr. Who, etc." Receives 40 unsolicited mss/month. Buys 6-8 mss/issue; 20-30 mss/year. Publishes ms 1-4 months after acceptance. Recently published work by Michael R. Collings, Thomas Easton and L.E. Carroll. Length: 5,000 words; 500 words minimum; 17,000 words maximum. Publishes short shorts. Sometimes critiques rejected mss.
How to Contact: Send complete ms with cover letter. Include name and address, phone number, title of story and classification of story (leave name off manuscript—put it on cover letter only). Reports in 2-3 months on mss. SASE. Simultaneous and photocopied submissions OK. Accepts computer printout submissions. Sample copy for $2.50. Fiction guidelines #10 SAE and 1 first class stamp.
Payment: Pays $5-75 plus contributor's copies.
Terms: Pays on publication for first North American serial rights. Sends galleys to author.
Advice: "All fiction must be original, innovative and interesting. We are very familiar with the body of sf and fantasy work, and look for new stories. Too many writers of sf and fantasy rely on existing cliché and convention. Humor, hard science, and experimental fantasy have the best chance for publication. Accurate science, vivid imagery, and strong characterization will impress the editors. We want stories about people with problems; the setting is there to illustrate the problem, not vice versa. Proofread!!! Please send clean, proofread copy. Just because we're small doesn't mean we're sloppy. Research! Be accurate. Our readers are *very* aware of science and history. We do not publish graphic violence or sex. Violence is okay if it is necessary to the story."

‡**THE LEDGE POETRY AND PROSE MAGAZINE (II),** 64-65 Copper Ave., Glendale NY 11385. (718)366-5169. Editor: Timothy Monaghan. Magazine: 5½×7; 72 pages; offset paper; gloss cover; cover art. "Our only criteria is material of high literary merit." Tri-annually. Estab. 1988. Circ. 450.
Needs: Condensed/excerpted novels, confession, contemporary, erotica, humor/satire, literary, mainstream, prose poem, romance. Receives approx. 12 unsolicited fiction mss/month. Accepts 1-2 mss/issue; 3-6 mss/year. Publishes mss 2 weeks-3 months after acceptance. Recently published work by Tim Sheehan, Chris Woods. Length: "up to 4 pages, double-spaced." Publishes short shorts. Comments on or critiques rejected mss occasionally, if warranted. Recommends other markets.
How to Contact: Send complete ms with cover letter. Reports in 2-3 weeks on queries; 1-2 months on mss. SASE. Photocopied, reprint and computer printour submissions OK. Accepts electronic submissions. Sample copy for $3.50. Fiction guidelines for #10 SAE and 1 first-class stamp.
Payment: Pays in contributor's copies.
Terms: Acquires one-time rights.
Advice: A manuscript stands out when "it overwhelms me every time I read it--in other words, stamina is the key to a successful piece. Fiction is not meant to be a one-time thrill."

LEFT CURVE (II), Box 472, Oakland CA 94604. (415)763-7193. Editor: Csaba Polony. Magazine: 8½×11; 96 pages; 60 lb paper; 100 pt. CIS Durosheen cover; illustrations; photos. "*Left Curve* is an artist-produced journal addressing the problem(s) of cultural forms emerging from the crises of modernity that strive to be independent from the control of dominant institutions, based on the recognition of the destructiveness of commodity (capitalist) systems to all life." Published irregularly. Estab. 1974. Circ. 1,000.
Needs: Contemporary, ethnic, experimental, historical, humor/satire, literary, prose poem, regional, science fiction, translations, political. Receives approx. 1 unsolicited fiction ms/month. Accepts approx. 1 ms/issue. Publishes ms a maximum of 6 months after acceptance. Length: 1,200 words average; 500 words minimum; 2,500 words maximum. Publishes short shorts. Sometimes comments on rejected mss or recommends other markets.

Market categories: (I) Beginning; (II) General; (III) Prestige; (IV) Specialized.

How to Contact: Send complete ms with cover letter, which should include "statement on writer's intent, brief bio., why submitting to *Left Curve*." Reports on queries in 1 month; on mss in 3 months. SASE. Accepts computer printouts. Sample copy for $5, 9×12 SAE and 90¢ postage. Fiction guidelines for 2 first class stamps.
Payment: Pays in contributor's copies.
Terms: Acquires first rights.
Advice: "Be honest, realistic and gorge out the truth you wish to say. Understand yourself and the world. Have writing be a means to achieve or realize what is real."

LEFT-FOOTED WOMBAT (II), Literary Eccentricity, Vishnu-Ala Dav Press, 615 Ratone Ln., Manhattan KS 66502. (913)539-9273. Editor: David McGhee. Magazine: 5½×8½; 20-24 pages; bond paper; illustrations and photographs. "Unusual theme and/or writing style for an eccentric audience." Published 2 times a year. Estab. 1988.
Needs: Adventure, contemporary, erotica, ethnic, experimental, fantasy, feminist, gay, horror, humor/satire, lesbian, prose poem, psychic/supernatural/occult, regional, religious/inspirational, science fiction, senior citizen/retirement, suspense/mystery, translations. "No sap, bad science fiction, fantasies or same old stories." Receives 8 unsolicited mss/month. Accepts 1 ms/issue; 2 mss/year. Publishes ms 2-3 weeks after acceptance. Length: 2,000 words; 1,000 words minimum; 3,000 words maximum. Sometimes critiques rejected mss.
How to Contact: Send complete ms. Reports in 1 week on queries; 3-4 months on mss. SASE. Simultaneous, photocopied and reprint submissions OK. Sample copy for $1. Fiction guidelines for #10 SAE and 1 first class stamp.
Payment: Pays in contributor's copies; charges for extras.
Terms: "Author retains rights."
Advice: Looking for "writing that evokes an emotional response in a clever, subtle manner; original thoughts, plots, characters, and/or writing style; eccentric topics, themes, plots, characters; but especially written well, flowing, graceful. Keep writing as long as you enjoy. If you're writing for money, forget it. The Big Bucks are rare to find. It is about the love of the word, communicating a personal emotion, not cash. Practice and wading through dry spells are important, which is why enjoying it is a necessity."

LEGEND (I, II, IV), A "Robin of Sherwood" Fanzine, 1036 Hampshire Rd., Victoria, British Columbia V8S 4S9 Canada. (604)598-2197. Editor: Janet P. Reedman. Magazine: size varies; 120+ pages; bond paper; cover varies; illustrations. "Fantasy: Based on TV series 'Robin of Sherwood.' Retold myths/legends; Celtic preferred. Some historical, if set in pre-1600 Europe." Semiannually. Estab. 1989. Circ. 200+.
Needs: Adventure, fantasy, historical, retold myths/legends. "Mostly need material based on 'Robin of Sherwood' in these genres. Original fantasy accepted only rarely. Nothing excessively violent/sexual. Nothing sticky-sweet and saccharine, either!" Receives 2-3 unsolicited mss/month. Accepts 9-15 mss/issue; 9-15 mss/year. Publishes ms 4-18 months after acceptance. Length: 3,000 words preferred; 150 words minimum; 20,000 words maximum. Sometimes critiques rejected mss and recommends other markets.
How to Contact: Query first. (I'll accept mss without queries, but it might be wise to write and ask if we're still open, overstocked, etc.). Reports in 2-3 weeks on queries; 5-6 weeks on mss. SASE. "Will accept loose stamps or IRCs, as I can use stamps from other countries." Photocopied and reprint submissions OK. Accepts computer printout submissions. Sample copy $12. Fiction guidelines for #10 SAE and 1 loose first class stamp.
Payment: Pays in contributor's copies for material over 3 pages long.
Terms: Acquires first North American serial rights.
Advice: "Please support small publications, so they can *survive* to publish your work! *Read* a sample copy, so you don't waste postage and the editor's time! We have had handwritten mss, juveniles, no SASE, satires, experimental fiction, 5 stories crammed in one envelope . . . *despite explicit* guidelines!"

Read the Business of Fiction section to learn the correct way to prepare and submit a manuscript.

‡LIBIDO (II, IV), The Journal of Sex and Sensibility, Libido, Inc. P.O. Box 146721, Chicago IL 60614. (312)728-5979. Editors: Jack Hafferkamp and Marianna Beck. Magazine 5½×8½; 72 pages; 70 lb. non-coated; b&w illustrations and photographs. "Erotica is the focus. Fiction, poetry, essays, reviews for literate adults." Quarterly. Estab. 1988. Circ. 7,000.
Needs: Condensed/excerpted novel, confession, erotica, gay, lesbian. No "Dirty words for their own sake, violence, sexual exploitation." Plans special fiction issue. Receives 25-50 unsolicited mss/month. Buys about 5/issue; about 20 per year. Publishes ms up to 1 year after acceptance. Recently published work by Marco Vassi, Anne Rampling (Ann Rice), Larry Tritten. Length: 1,000-5,000 words; 300 words minimum; 3,000 words maximum. Sometimes critiques rejected ms and recommends other markets.
How to Contact: Send complete manuscript with cover letter including Social Security number and brief bio for contributor's page. Reports in 1-3 months on mss. SASE. Photocopied and reprint submissions OK. Accepts computer printout submissions. Accepts electronic submissions via disk. Sample copy $6. Free fiction guidelines.
Payment: Pays $15-50 and 2 contributor's copies.
Terms: Pays on publication for one-time or anthology rights.
Advice: "Humor is a strong plus. There must be a strong erotic element, and it should celebrate the joy of sex."

LIGHTHOUSE (II), Box 1377, Auburn WA 98071-1377. Editor: Tim Clinton. Magazine: 5½×8½; 56 pages; illustrations. "Timeless stories and poems for family reading—G rated." Bimonthly. Estab. 1986. Circ. 500.
Needs: Adventure, contemporary, historical, humor/satire, juvenile (5-9 years), mainstream, preschool (1-4 years), prose poem, regional, romance (contemporary, historical and young adult), senior citizen/retirement, sports, suspense/mystery, western, young adult/teen (10-18 years). Receives 300 mss/month. Accepts 15 mss/issue; 90 mss/year. Publishes ms within 2 years of acceptance. Recently published work by Birdie L. Etchison, Louise Hannah Kohr, Robert E. Kelly; published new writers within the last year. Length: 5,000 words maximum. Publishes short shorts.
How to Contact: Send complete mss, include Social Security number. No queries, please. Reports in 2 months on mss. SASE. Photocopied submissions OK. Accepts computer printout submissions. Sample copy $2 (includes guidelines). Fiction guidelines for #10 SAE and 1 first class stamp.
Payment: Pays up to $50 for stories; up to $5 for poetry.
Terms: Author copies discounted at $1.50 each. Payment on publication for first rights and first North American serial rights.
Advice: "If there is a message in the story, we prefer it to be subtly hidden in the action. We feel there is a market for quality fiction stories that are entertaining and have standards of decency as well."

LIMESTONE: A LITERARY JOURNAL (II), University of Kentucky, Dept. of English, 1215 Patterson Office Tower, Lexington KY 40506-0027. Editor: Matthew J. Bond. Magazine: 6×9; 50-75 pages; standard text paper and cover; illustrations; photos. "We publish a variety of styles and attitudes, and we're looking to expand our offering." Annually. Estab. 1981. Circ. 1,000.
Needs: Contemporary, experimental, humor/satire, literary, mainstream, prose poem, regional. "Avoids stories and poetry that 'say something.'" Receives 200 mss/year. Accepts 15 mss/issue. Does not read mss May-Sept. Publishes ms an average of 6 months after acceptance. Recently published work by Guy Davenport, Wendell Berry, James Baker Hall; publishes new writers every year. Length: 3,000-5,000 words preferred; 5,000 words maximum. Publishes short shorts. Sometimes critiques rejected mss.
How to Contact: Send complete ms with cover letter, which should include "publishing record and brief bio." Reports in 1 month on queries; 7 months on mss. SASE. Simultaneous and photocopied submissions OK. Accepts computer printout submissions. Sample copy $3.
Payment: Pays 2 contributor's copies.
Terms: Rights revert to author.
Advice: "We encourage all writers to send their most exacting, thought-filled writing. Send us writing where every word tells."

LININGTON LINEUP (IV), Elizabeth Linington Society, 1223 Glen Terrace, Glassboro NJ 08028-1315. Editor: Rinehart S. Potts. Newsletter: 8½×11; 16 pages; bond paper and cover stock; illustrations and photographs. "For those interested in the publications of Elizabeth Linington (a/k/a Lesley Egan, Egan O'Neill, Anne Blaisdell, Dell Shannon)—historical fiction and detective mysteries—therefore material must relate in some way thereto." Bimonthly. Plans special fiction issue. Estab. 1984. Circ. 400.

Needs: *Charges reading fee of $1. Requires magazine subscription of $12 before reading.* Historical (general), literary, suspense/mystery. Receives 3-4 fiction mss/month. Accepts 1 ms/issue; 4 mss/year. Publishes ms 3 months after acceptance. Publishes short shorts. Sometimes comments on rejected mss.

How to Contact: Query first. Reports in 1 month. SASE. Photocopied and reprint submission's OK. Accepts computer printout submissions. Sample copy $3.

Payment: Free subscription to magazine.

Terms: Acquires first rights.

Advice: "Become familiar with Miss Linington's books and continuing characters. We have been receiving material which completely disregards the information cited above."

‡LITERARY CREATIONS (II), Imagery Publications, P.O. Box 1339, Albany OR 97321. (503)451-1372. Editor/Publisher: M. L. Ingram. Newsletter: 17-22; 4 pages; bond paper; illustrations. "A showcase for unpublished writers of poetry, fiction and nonfiction." Monthly. Estab. 1990. Circ. 300.

Needs: Genealogy, life story, adventure, historical, humor/satire, literary, prose poem. "No pornography." Plans special fiction issue. Receives 1-3 unsolicited fiction mss/month. Accepts 1 ms/issue; 12 mss/year. Publishes ms within 30 days after acceptance. Recently published work by T.R. Healy. Length: 1,000 words preferred; 250 words minimum; 1,200 words maximum. Publishes short shorts. Critiques or comments on rejected mss. Recommends other markets.

How to Contact: Send complete ms with cover letter. Reports in 2 weeks. SASE. Simultaneous, photocopied and computer printout submissions OK. Sample copy for $2, #10 SAE and 1 first-class stamp. Fiction guidelines for #10 SAE and 1 first-class stamp.

Payment: Pays in contributor's copies.

Terms: Acquires one-time rights. Sponsors fiction contests—send SASE for guidelines.

Advice: "If the story line interests the editor, it is assumed there are others sharing that interest. The story line should be within the comprehension of a person of average intelligence."

THE LITERARY REVIEW, An International Journal of Contemporary Writing, Fairleigh Dickinson University, 285 Madison Ave., Madison NJ 07940. (201)593-8564. Editor-in-Chief: Walter Cummins. Magazine: 6×9; 128-152 pages; illustrations; photos. "Literary magazine specializing in fiction, poetry, and essays with an international focus." Quarterly. Estab. 1957. Circ. 1,800.

Needs: Works of high literary quality only. Receives 30-40 unsolicited fiction mss/month. Approximately 1-2% of fiction is agented. Published Anne Brashler, Thomas E. Kennedy, Steve Yarbrough; published new writers within the last year. Accepts 10-12 mss/year. Occasionally critiques rejected mss. Sometimes recommends other markets.

How to Contact: Send complete ms with SASE. "Cover letter should include publication credits." Photocopied submissions OK. Accepts computer printout submissions. Reports in 10 weeks on mss. Publishes ms an average of 1-1½ years after acceptance. Sample copy $5; free guidelines with SASE.

Payment: 2 free contributor's copies; 25% discount for extras.

Terms: Acquires first rights.

Advice: "Too much of what we are seeing today is openly derivative in subject, plot and prose style. We pride ourselves on spotting new writers with fresh insight and the ability to express it."

‡THE LITTLE MAGAZINE (II), State University of New York at Albany, English Department, Albany NY 12222. Editor: Jan Ramjerdi. Magazine: 5½×8½; 300 pages; 70 lb. Nikusa paper; 10 pt. high gloss cover; cover illustrations. "Fiction and poetry for a literary audience." Annually. Estab. 1965.

Needs: Ethnic, experimental, feminist, gay, humor/satire, lesbian, literary, prose poem. No romance. Receives "roughly" 600 mss/issue over a 3-month reading period. Accepts 10 mss/issue. Reads only from September 15 to December 15. Publishes ms 6 months after acceptance. Recently published work by Edward Kleinschmidt, William Roorback and Patricia Kain. Length: 4,500 words preferred; 6,000 words maximum. Publishes short shorts. Critiques or comments on rejected mss.

How to Contact: Send complete ms with SASE, but only send between September 15 and December 15. Reports in 1 month on queries; in 2 months on mss. Simultaneous, photocopied, reprint and computer printout submissions OK. Sample copy for $6.

Payment: Pays 2 contributor's copies.

Terms: Acquires first North American serial rights.

Advice: "We like a wide variety of work from traditional to experimental."

‡LIVING AMONG NATURE DARINGLY MAGAZINE (II), A guide for folks who dare to live life their way, Bill Anderson—Living Among Nature Daringly, 4466 Ike Mooney Rd., Silverton OR 97381. (503)873-8829. Editor: Bill Anderson. Magazine: 8½ × 10; 40 pages; newsprint paper; newsprint cover; illustrations and photographs. "Environmentally concerned, 'back to the land' material for a senior citizen audience with a mid to low income." Published 5 times a year. Estab. 1986. Circ. 500 paid.
Needs: Adventure, historical (general), senior citizen/retirement, suspense/mystery, western. "Should place reader in a farming and/or trapping situation." No erotica, gay, lesbian, romance, fantasy. Plans special fiction issue. Buys 2-4 mss/year. Publishes ms 2-3 months after acceptance. Length: Open. Publishes shorts shorts. Length: 400 words. Sometimes critiques rejected mss and recommends other markets.
How to Contact: Query with clips of pubished work or send complete manuscript with cover letter. Reports in 5 weeks on queries; 2 months on mss. Accepts computer printout submissions. Accepts electronic submissions via (MacIntosh format only). Sample copy $2 with 9 × 12 SAE and 8 first class stamps. Fiction guidelines for $2 with 9 × 12 SAE and 8 first class stamps.
Payment: Pays $10-100. Charges for extras.
Terms: Buys first North American serial rights, one-time rights. Sends galleys to author.

‡LIVING STREAMS (II, IV), The Christian Writers' Journal, P.O. Box 1321, Vincennes IN 47591. Editor: Kevin Hrebik. Fiction Editor: Marilyn Phemister. Magazine: 5½ × 8½; 80 pages; glossy color cover, illustrations, some photographs. "Christian—evangelical. Uses allegories of Christian themes or straight fiction with at least a good strong moral point. Audience is mature adults—mostly Christian, including many writers." Quarterly. Estab. 1988. Circ. 1,000.
Needs: Christian, contemporary, humor/satire, mainstream, religious/inspirational, science fiction, Christian allegory. No immorality, profanity, etc. Accepts 3-4 mss/issue; 9-12 mss/year. Publishes ms 6 months after acceptance. Length: 1,000 words average; 500 words minimum; 1,500 words maximum. Occasionally critiques rejected mss.
How to Contact: Write for info sheet. *Must subscribe—nonsubscribers' work not accepted.* Reports in 3-4 days on queries; in 3-4 weeks on mss. SASE. Simultaneous, photocopied, reprint and computer printout submissions OK. Sample copy for $3.75. Fiction guidelines for #10 SAE and 1 first-class stamp.
Payment: Pays in contributor's copies and free subscription. Five free tear sheets also for SASE.
Terms: Acquires one-time rights.
Advice: "Buy a sample issue. Get the feel of the publication. There are many columns and features that should appeal to virtually any type of writer. Look for regularly printed tips on things we specifically need. Learn to self-edit your material—and be open to further editing by our staff. We do try to work with those pieces and writers who show potential and are flexible."

LLAMAS MAGAZINE (IV), The International Camelid Journal, Clay Press Inc., Box 100, Herald CA 95638. (916)448-1668. Editor: Cheryl Dal Porto. Magazine: 8½ × 11; 112+ pages; glossy paper; 80 lb glossy cover stock; illustrations and pictures. For llama owners and lovers. 8 issues/year. Estab. 1979. Circ. 5,500.
Needs: Adventure, historical, humor/satire. Receives 15-25 unsolicited fiction mss/month. Accepts 1-6 mss/issue; 12-24 mss/year. Publishes ms usually 3-4 months after acceptance. 15% of fiction is agented. Length: 2,000-3,000 words average. Publishes short shorts 300-1,000 words in length. Sometimes critiques rejected mss.
How to Contact: Send query to: Susan Ley, *Llamas* Asst. Editor, Box 1038, Dublin OH 43017. Reports in 1 month. Reprint submissions OK. Accepts computer printout submissions. Accepts electronic submissions via Apple 2 disk. Fiction guidelines free.
Payment: $25-500, free subscription to magazine and contributor's copies.
Terms: Pays on publication for first rights, first North American serial rights and one-time rights. Sends pre-publication galleys to author if requested.

LONG SHOT, Box 6231, Hoboken NJ 07030. Editors: Danny Shot, Caren Lee Michaelson, Jack Wiler. Magazine: 5½ × 8½; 128 pages; 60 lb paper; 10 pt. CIS cover; illustrations; photos. Estab. 1982. Circ. 1,500.
Needs: Adventure, confession, contemporary, erotica, ethnic, experimental, fantasy, feminist, gay, horror, humor/satire, lesbian, political, prose poem, psychic/supernatural/occult, science fiction, suspense/mystery, western. Receives 100 unsolicited mss/month. Accepts 4-5 mss/issue. Does not read mss in August. Publishes ms 6 months at longest after acceptance. Published work by Sean Penn,

Charles Bukowski, Robert Press; published new writers within the last year. Publishes short shorts. Sometimes recommends other markets.

How to Contact: Send complete ms. Reports in 4-6 weeks. SASE. Simultaneous and photocopied submissions OK. Sample copy $5 plus $1 postage.

Payment: Pays in contributor's copies.

Terms: Acquires one-time rights.

THE LONG STORY (II), 11 Kingston St., North Andover MA 01845. (508)686-7638. Editor: R.P. Burnham. Magazine: 5½ × 8½; 150-200 pages; 60 lb paper; 65 lb cover stock; illustrations (b&w graphics). For serious, educated, literary people. No science fiction, adventure, romance, etc. "We publish high literary quality of any kind, but especially look for committed fiction; working class settings, left-wing themes, etc." Annually. Estab. 1983. Circ. 500.

Needs: Contemporary, ethnic, feminist and literary. Receives 30-40 unsolicited mss/month. Buys 6-7 mss/issue. Length: 8,000 words minimum; 20,000 words maximum. ("To accept 20,000 word story it would have to be right down our alley—about poor, oppressed people, i.e., committed fiction.") Sometimes recommends other markets.

How to Contact: Send complete ms with a brief cover letter. Reports in 2+ months. Publishes ms an average of 3 months to 1 year after acceptance. SASE. Photocopied submissions OK. Accepts computer printout submissions, prefers letter-quality. Sample copy $5.

Payment: Pays in 2 free contributor's copies; $4 charge for extras.

Terms: Acquires first rights.

Advice: "Read us first and make sure submitted material is the kind we're interested in. Send clear, legible manuscripts. We're not interested in commercial success; rather we want to provide a place for long stories, the most difficult literary form to publish in our country."

LOONFEATHER (II), Bemidji Arts Center, 426 Bemidji Ave., Bemidji MN 56601. (218)751-4869. Editors: Betty Rossi and Jeane Sliney. Magazine: 6 × 9; 48 pages; 60 lb Hammermill Cream woven paper; 65 lb vellum cover stock; illustrations; occasional photos. A literary journal of short prose, poetry and graphics. Mostly a market for Northern Minnesota, Minnesota and Midwest writers. Semiannually. Estab. 1979. Circ. 300.

Needs: Literary, contemporary, prose poem and regional. Accepts 2-3 mss/issue, 4-6 mss/year. Published work by Richard Jewell, Gary Erickson, James C. Manolis. Published new writers within the last year. Length: 600-1,500 words (prefers 1,500).

How to Contact: Send complete ms with SASE, and short autobiographical sketch. Reports in 3 months. Sample copy $2 back issue; $4.95 current issue.

Payment: Free author's copies.

Terms: Acquires one-time rights.

Advice: "Send carefully crafted and literary fiction. Because of increase in size of magazine, we can include more, slightly longer fiction. The writer should familiarize himself/herself with the type of fiction published in literary magazines as opposed to family magazines, religious magazines, etc."

‡LOST (II), A Magazine of Horror and Dark Humor, Lupus Publishing, 67 Seyler St., New Hamburg, Ontario N0B 2G0 Canada. (519)662-2725. Editor: Adam Thornton. Magazine: 5¾ × 8½; approx. 40 pages; stiff bond cover; illustrations and photographs. "Horrific or black comedy in both stories and artwork. Graphic or quiet poems accepted as well." Estab. 1990.

Needs: Experimental, horror, prose poem, psychic/supernatural/occult. "Must be morbid or horrific." No "fantasy or science." Receives 10 or 11 unsolicited mss/month. Accepts 5 mss/issue. Publishes ms 1 or 2 months after acceptance. Recently published work by Detlef Burghardt. Length: 500 words average; 100 words minimum; 2,000 words maximum. Publishes short shorts. Length: 400 words. Always comments on rejected mss and recommends other markets.

How to Contact: Send complete manuscript with cover letter that includes some biographical info. Reports in 1 week. Simultaneous, photocopied and reprint submissions OK. Accepts computer printout submissions. Accepts electronic submissions. Free sample copy and fiction guidelines.

Payment: Pays in contributor's copies. Publication is not copyrighted.

Advice: "Read popular horror stories, then send us something unlike the stuff you read. We are looking for fiction along the lines of Steve Rasnic Tem, Charles L. Grant, Douglas E. Winter, Richard Christian Matheson."

LOST AND FOUND TIMES (II), Luna Bisonte Prods, 137 Leland Ave., Columbus OH 43214. (614)846-4126. Editor: John M. Bennett. Magazine: 5½×8½; 40 pages; good quality paper; good cover stock; illustrations; photos. Theme: experimental, avant-garde and folk literature, art. Published irregularly. Estab. 1975. Circ. 300.
Needs: Literary, contemporary, experimental, prose poem. Prefers short pieces. Accepts approximately 2 mss/issue. Published work by Joachim Frank, Al Ackerman, Jack Saunders. Published new writers within the last year. Sometimes recommends other markets.
How to Contact: Query with clips of published work. SASE. Accepts computer printout submissions. Reports in 1 week on queries, 2 weeks on mss. Sample copy $4.
Payment: 1 free author's copy.
Terms: Rights revert to authors.

‡LOST CREEK LETTERS (I, II), Lost Creek Publications, Box 373A, Rushville MO 64484. (816)688-7834. Editor: Pamela Montgomery. Magazine: 5½×8½; 40-44 pages; copy bond paper; line cover art illustrations. "The only theme we have is *quality*. Completely open, with some taboos on genre for a college and post-college audience." Quarterly. Estab. 1990. Circ. 200.
Needs: Adventure, condensed/excerpted novel, contemporary, ethnic, experimental, fantasy, feminist, humor/satire, literary, mainstream, regional, science fiction, surrealism. No romance, western, religious, juvenile. Plans special fiction issue. Receives 25+ unsolicited mss/month. Buys 3-5 mss/issue; 12-20 mss/year. Publishes ms 1-6 months after acceptance. Recently published work by John Weston and J.L. Lauinger. Length: 3,000 words average; 200 words minimum; 5,000 words maximum. Publishes short shorts. Sometimes critiques rejected ms and recommends other markets.
How to Contact: Send complete manuscript with cover letter. "Please *never* query." SASE. Simultaneous and photocopied submissions OK. Accepts computer printout submissions. Accepts electronic submissions via disk (must be IBM 5¼). Sample copy $4.50. Fiction guidelines for #10 SAE and 1 first class stamp.
Payment: Pays $2-5 or contributor's copies.
Terms: Pays on publication for one-time rights. "We are read for *Best American Short Stories*. I nominate stories for the Pushcart Prize."
Advice: "A ms stands out if it is *rich* in detail and its characters are fully developed. A fine story is meaningful on more than an obvious superficial level. Polish is absolutely essential and can only be achieved by dedicated revising."

LOUISIANA LITERATURE (II), A Review of Literature and Humanities, Southeastern Louisiana University, Box 792, Hammond LA 70402. (504)549-5022. Editor: Tim Gautreaux. Magazine: 6¾×9¾; 84 pages; 70 lb paper; card cover; illustrations; photos. "We publish literary quality fiction and essays by anyone. Essays should be about Louisiana material, but creative work can be set anywhere." Semiannually. Estab. 1984. Circ. 400 paid; 1,000 printed.
Needs: Literary, mainstream, regional. No sloppy ungrammatical manuscripts. Receives 25 unsolicited mss/month. Accepts 3 mss/issue; 6 mss/year. Does not read mss June-July. Publishes ms 6 months maximum after acceptance. Published work by William Caverlee and Ingrid Smith; published new writers within the last year. Length: 2,500 words preferred; 1,000 words minimum; 6,000 words maximum. Publishes short shorts. Sometimes comments on rejected mss.
How to Contact: Send complete ms. Reports in 1-2 months on mss. SASE. Photocopied submissions OK. Accepts computer printout submissions. Sample copy $4.
Payment: Pays up to $25 and contributor's copies.
Terms: Pays on publication for one-time rights.
Advice: "Cut out everything that is not a functioning part of the story. Make sure everything is spelled correctly. Use relevant specific detail in every scene."

THE LOUISVILLE REVIEW (II), Department of English, University of Louisville, Louisville KY 40292. (502)588-6801. Editor: Sena Naslund. Magazine: 6×8¾; 100 pages; Warren's Old Style paper; cover photographs. Semiannually. Estab. 1976. Circ. 750.
Needs: Contemporary, experimental, literary, prose poem. Receives 30-40 unsolicited mss/month. Accepts 6-10 mss/issue; 12-20 mss/year. Publishes ms 2-3 months after acceptance. Recently published work by Maura Stanton, Patricia Goedicke, Michael Cadnum; Length: 50 pages maximum. Publishes short shorts.
How to Contact: Send complete ms with cover letter. Reports on queries in 2-3 weeks; 2-3 months on mss. SASE. Photocopied submissions OK. Accepts computer printout submissions, including dot-matrix, "if readable." Sample copy for $3. Fiction guidelines for #10 SAE and 1 first class stamp.

Payment: Pays in contributor's copies.
Terms: Acquires first North American serial rights.
Advice: Looks for "original concepts, fresh ideas, good storyline, engaging characters, a story that works."

THE MACGUFFIN (II), Schoolcraft College, Department of English, 18600 Haggerty Rd., Livonia MI 48152. (313)591-6400, ext. 449. Editor: Arthur J. Lindenberg. Fiction Editor: Elizabeth Hebron. Magazine: 5½ × 8½; 128 pages; 60 lb paper; 110 lb cover; b&w illustrations and photos. *"The MacGuffin* is a literary magazine which publishes a range of material including poetry, nonfiction and fiction. Material ranges from traditional to experimental. We hope our periodical attracts a variety of people with many different interests." Published 3 times per year. Quality fiction a special need. Estab. 1984. Circ. 500.
Needs: Adventure, contemporary, ethnic, experimental, fantasy, historical (general), humor/satire, literary, mainstream, prose poem, psychic/supernatural/occult, science fiction, translations. No religious, inspirational, confession, romance, horror, pornography. Receives 25-40 unsolicited mss/month. Accepts 5-10 mss/issue; 10-30 mss/year. Does not read mss between July 1 and August 15. Publishes 6 months to 2 years after acceptance. Agented fiction: 10-15%. Published work by Richard Kostelantz, Gayle Boss, Ann Knox; published new writers within the last year. Length: 2,000-2,500 words average; 400 words minimum; 4,000 words maximum. Publishes short shorts. Length: 400 words. Occasionally critiques rejected mss and recommends other markets.
How to Contact: Send complete ms with cover letter, which should include: "1. *Brief* biographical information; 2. Note that this *is not* a simultaneous submission." Reports in 6-8 weeks. SASE. Photocopied and reprint submissions OK. Accepts computer printout submissions. Sample copy $3. Fiction guidelines free.
Payment: Pays in 2 contributor's copies.
Terms: Acquires one-time rights.
Advice: "Be persistent. If a story is rejected, try to send it somewhere else. When we reject a story, we may accept the next one you send us. When we make suggestions for a rewrite, we may accept the revision. There seems to be a great number of good authors of fiction, but there are far too few places for publication. However, I think this is changing. Make your characters come to life. Even the most ordinary people become fascinating if they live for your readers."

THE MAD ENGINEER, c/o Mosier, 4550 Flake Rd., Martinsville IN 46151. (317)342-0554. Editor: Mary Hagan. Magazine: digest size; 24 pages; illustrations; photos. Publishes "science fiction with a technical slant; short fiction (7,000 words or less); technical information or essays (innovative or unusual)." Quarterly. Plans special fiction issue. Estab. 1986. Circ. 150.
Needs: Science fiction and stories with technical slant. "No stories based on TV or movies (Star Trek, Dr. Who, etc.). Parody or satire on the above is acceptable." Receives less than 1 ms/month. Accepts 1-2 mss/issue; 4-6 mss/year. Publishes ms generally within 6 months of acceptance. Published work by Lee Strong, Andrew Looney. Length: 500 words minimum; 7,000 words maximum. Publishes short shorts. Sometimes critiques rejected mss.
How to Contact: Send complete mss with cover letter. Cover letter should include "short biographic information." Reports in 4 weeks on queries; in 6 weeks on mss. SASE. Photocopied and reprint submissions OK. Accepts computer printout submissions. Sample copy 75¢.
Payment: Pays in contributor's copies.
Terms: Acquires one-time rights.
Advice: "Just send me something. I'll never say 'no' without telling you why."

THE MADISON REVIEW (II), Department of English, Helen C. White Hall, 600 N. Park St., University of Wisconsin, Madison WI 53706. Contact: Fiction Editor. Magazine: 6 × 9; 180 pages. "Magazine of fiction and poetry with special emphasis on literary stories and some emphasis on midwestern writers." Published semiannually. Estab. 1978. Circ. 500.
Needs: Experimental and literary stories, prose poems and excerpts from novels. Receives 50 unsolicited fiction mss/month. Accepts 7-12 mss/issue. Published work by Richard Cohen, Fred Chappell and Janet Shaw. Published new writers within the last year. Length: no preference.
How to Contact: Send complete ms with cover letter and SASE. "The letters should give one or two sentences of relevant information about the writer—just enough to provide a context for the work." Reports in 2 months on mss. Publishes ms an average of 4 months after acceptance. "We often do not report on mss during the summer." Sample copy $4.

Payment: 2 free contributor's copies; $2.50 charge for extras.
Terms: Pays for first North American serial rights.
Advice: "We are now willing to accept chapters of novels in progress and short short fiction. Write with surgical precision—then revise. Often the label 'experimental' is used to avoid reworking a piece. If anything, the more adventurous a piece of fiction is, the more it needs to undergo revision."

THE MAGE (II, IV), A Journal of Fantasy and Science Fiction, Colgate University Student Association, Hamilton NY 13346. Contact: Editor. Magazine: 8½×11; about 64 pages; good-quality paper stock and cover; b&w illustrations. "Fiction, essays, poetry, artwork and commentary within the genre of science fiction and fantasy. Emphasis is on a balance of poetry, fiction and nonfiction. We do serialize longer works of exceptional quality." Semiannually. Estab. 1984. Circ. 900.
Needs: Experimental, fantasy, horror, science fiction. No sword-and-sorcery adventure or stories based on Dungeons and Dragons and its ilk; no erotica. Receives 15-25 unsolicited fiction mss/month. Accepts 6-10 mss/issue; 12-20 mss/year. Does not read mss June through August. Generally publishes ms within 3 months of acceptance. Recently published work by Patricia Anthony, Eric Davin and David Lunde. Published new writers within the last year. Length: 3,500-4,500 words average; 1,000 words minimum. Usually critiques rejected mss.
How to Contact: Query first or send complete ms and cover letter with list of previous works published. Reports in 2 weeks on queries; 3-5 weeks on mss (report time is longer if submitted just before or during the summer). SASE for ms. Simultaneous and photocopied submissions OK. Accepts computer printouts. Sample copy $3.
Payment: Pays in contributor's copies.
Terms: Acquires first North American serial rights or one-time rights. Sometimes sends galleys to author.
Advice: "We are interested in writers who have practiced enough (even if nothing has been published) to develop a refined writing style. We are interested in presenting good writing first, but we do publish capsule reviews of new fiction. Submitting several of these to us will help a new writer develop some recognition of *The Mage*'s standards, which might help him/her when submitting a first manuscript to us."

MAGIC CHANGES (II), Celestial Otter Press, P.O. Box 658, Warrenville IL 60555. (708)416-3111. Editor: John Sennett. Magazine: 8½×11; 110 pages; 60 lb paper; construction paper cover; illustrations; photos. "Theme: transformation by art. Material: poetry, songs, fiction, stories, reviews, art, essays, etc. For the entertainment and enlightenment of all ages." Annually. Estab. 1979. Circ. 500.
Needs: Literary, prose poem, science fiction, sports fiction, fantasy and erotica. "Fiction should have a magical slant." Accepts 8-12 mss/year. Receives approximately 15 unsolicited fiction mss each month. Published work by J. Weintraub, David Goodrum, Anne F. Robertson; published new writers within the last year. Length: 3,000 words maximum.
How to Contact: Send complete ms with SASE. Accepts computer printout submissions, prefers letter-quality. Accepts disk submissions compatible with IBM or Macintosh. Prefers hard copy with disk submissions. Reports in 1 month. Publishes ms an average of 5 months after acceptance. Sample copy $5. Make check payable to John Sennett.
Payment: 1-2 free author's copies. $5 charge for extras.
Terms: Acquires first North American serial rights.
Advice: "Write about something fantastic in a natural way, or something natural in a fantastic way. We need good stories—like epic Greek poems translated into prose."

THE MALAHAT REVIEW (II), University of Victoria, Box 3045, Victoria, British Columbia V8W 3P4 Canada. (604)721-8524. Editor: Constance Rooke. Magazine: 6×9; 132 pages; photographs occasionally. Publishes fiction, poetry and reviews. Quarterly. Estab. 1967. Circ. 1,800.
Needs: Receives 100 unsolicited mss/month. Buys approximately 6 mss/issue; 25 mss/year. Publishes short shorts. Occasionally critiques rejected mss.
How to Contact: Send complete ms with cover letter. SASE (Canadian postage or IRCs). Photocopied submissions OK. Accepts computer printout submissions. Sample copy $6. Fiction guidelines free.
Payment: Pays $40 per 1,000 words; and contributor's copies.
Terms: Acquires first rights.
Advice: "If it's good, we publish it. *The Malahat Review* is a "generalist" literary magazine, which is to say that it is open to all schools of writing and does not espouse any particular ideology or aesthetic. We believe that new writers should have the opportunity of appearing with celebrated writers, and

we find that a mix of unknown and famous names results very naturally from our choice of the best work we receive."

MANOA (III), A Pacific Journal of International Writing, English Dept., University of Hawaii Press, Honolulu HI 96822. (808)948-8833. Editor: Robert Shapard. Fiction Editors: Roger Whitlock and Jeff Carroll. Magazine: 7×10; 200 pages. "An American literary magazine, emphasis on top US fiction and poetry, but each issue has a major guest-edited translated feature of recent writings from an Asian/Pacific country." Semiannually. Estab. 1989.

Needs: Excerpted novel, contemporary, literary, mainstream and translation (from nations in or bordering on the Pacific). "Part of our purpose is to present top U.S. fiction from throughout the US, not only to US readers, but to readers in Asian and Pacific countries. Thus we are not limited to stories related to or set in the Pacific—in fact, we do not want exotic or adventure stories set in the Pacific, but good US literary fiction of any locale." Plans to publish special fiction issue or an anthology in the future. Accepts 10-12 mss/issue; 20-24/year. Publishes ms 6 months-1 year after acceptance. Agented fiction 50%. Published work by Anne Beattie, Ron Carlson and Francois Camoin. Publishes short shorts.

How to Contact: Send complete ms with cover letter or through agent. Reports in 1-6 weeks. SASE. Simultaneous and photocopied submissions OK. Sample copy $7.

Payment: "Highly competitive rates paid so far." Pays in contributor copies.

Terms: Pays for first North American serial, plus one-time reprint rights. Sends galleys to author.

Advice: "Hawaii has come of age literarily and wants to contribute to the best of US mainstream. It's readership is (and is intended to be) mostly national, not local. It also wants to represent top US writing to a new international market, in Asia and the Pacific. Altogether we hope our view is a fresh one; that is, not facing East toward Europe but west toward 'the other half of the world.' We mostly run short stories."

MARK (II), A Journal of Scholarship, Opinion, and Literature, University of Toledo, 2801 W. Bancroft SU2514, Toledo OH 43606. (419)537-4463. Editor: Brenda Wyatt. Magazine: 6×9; 72 pages; acid-free paper; some illustrations; photographs. "General theme is exploration of humanity and man's effort to understand the world around him." Annually. Estab. 1967. Circ. 3,500.

Needs: Contemporary, ethnic, humor/satire, literary, regional and science fiction. "We do not have the staff to do rewrites or heavy copyediting—send clean, legible mss only." No "typical MFA first-person narrative—we like stories, not reportage." Receives 20-25 unsolicited fiction mss/month. Accepts 7-10 mss/year. Does not read June to September. Publishes ms 6 months after acceptance. Publishes short shorts.

How to Contact: Send complete ms with cover letter, name, address and phone. Reports in January each year. Photocopied submissions OK. Accepts computer printouts. Sample copy $3 plus 7x10 SAE with 72¢ postage.

Payment: Pays two contributor's copies.

Terms: Acquires one-time rights.

Advice: "Beginning fiction writers should write in a style that is natural, not taught to them by others. More importantly, they should write about subjects they are familiar with. Be prepared for rejection, but good writing will always find a home."

THE MARYLAND REVIEW, Department of English, University of Maryland Eastern Shore, Princess Anne MD 21853. (301)651-2200, ext. 262. Editor: Chester M Hedgepeth. Magazine: 6×9; 100-150 pages; good quality paper stock; heavy cover; illustrations; photos "possibly." "We have a special interest in black literature, but we welcome all sorts of submissions. Our audience is literary, educated, well-read." Annually. Estab. 1986. Circ. 500.

Needs: Contemporary, humor/satire, literary, mainstream, black. No genre stories; no religious, political or juvenile material. Accepts approx. 12-15 mss/issue. Publishes ms "within 1 year" after acceptance. Published work by John K. Crane, David Jauss. Published new writers within the last year. Publishes short shorts. "Length is open, but we do like to include some pieces 1,500 words and under."

How to Contact: Send complete ms with cover letter, which should include a brief autobiography. Reports "as soon as possible." SASE, *but do not return mss.* Photocopied submissions acceptable. No simultaneous submissions. Accepts computer printout submissions. Sample copy for $6.

Payment: Pays in contributor's copies.
Terms: Acquires all rights.
Advice: "Think primarily about your *characters* in fiction, about their beliefs and how they may change. Create characters and situations that are utterly new. We will give your material a careful and considerate reading. Any fiction that is flawed by grammatical errors, misspellings, etc. will not have a chance. We're seeing a lot of fine fiction these days, and we approach each story with fresh and eager eyes. Ezra Pound's battle-cry about poetry refers to fiction as well: 'Make it New!' "

‡**THE MASSACHUSETTS REVIEW (II)**, Memorial Hall, University of Massachusetts, Amherst MA 01002. (413)545-2689. Editors: Mary Heath, Fred Robinson, Paul Jenkins. Magazine: 6x9; 172 pages; 52 lb paper; 65 lb vellum cover; illustrations and photos. Quarterly.
Needs: Short stories. Published new writers within the last year. Approximately 5% of fiction is agented. Critiques rejected mss when time permits. Guidelines available by SASE.
How to Contact: Send complete ms. No ms returned without SASE. Reports in 2 months. Publishes ms an average of 9-12 months after acceptance. Sample copy $5.50.
Payment: Pays $50 maximum.
Terms: Pays on publication for first North American serial rights. Publication copyrighted.
Advice: "Shorter rather than longer stories preferred (up to 28 pages). There are too many stories about 'relationships,' domestic breakups, etc. Fiction not read June 1 through Oct. 1."

MATI, Ommation Press, 5548 N. Sawyer, Chicago IL 60625. Editor: Effie Mihopoulos. "Primarily a poetry magazine, but we do occasional special fiction and science fiction issues." Quarterly. Estab. 1975. Circ. 1,000.
Needs: Literary, contemporary, science fiction, feminist, translations. No mystery, gothic, western, religious. Receives approximately 20 unsolicited fiction ms each month. Length: 1-2 pages. Occasionally sends ms on to editors of other publications. Sometimes recommends other markets.
How to Contact: Send complete ms with SASE. Reports in 1 week-2 months. Sample copy $1.50 with 9 × 12 SASE (preferred) plus 90¢ postage.
Payment: 1 free author's copy. Special contributor's rates available for extras.
Terms: Acquires first North American serial rights. "Rights revert to authors but *Mati* retains reprint rights."
Advice: "We want to see good quality writing and a neat ms with sufficient return postage; same size return as outside envelope and intelligent cover letter. Editor to be addressed as 'Dear Sir/Ms' instead of 'Dear Sir' when it's a woman editor."

MERLYN'S PEN, The National Magazine of Student Writing, Grades 7-10, (IV), Box 1058, East Greenwich RI 02818. (401)885-5175. Editor: R. Jim Stahl. Magazine 8⅛ × 10⅞; 36 pages; 50 lb paper; 70 lb gloss cover stock; illustrations; photos. Student writing only—grades 7 through 10, for libraries, homes and English classrooms. Bimonthly (September-April). Estab. 1985. Circ. 22,000.
Needs: Adventure, experimental, fantasy, historical (general), horror, humor/satire, literary, mainstream, regional, romance, science fiction, suspense/mystery, western, young adult/teen, editorial reviews, puzzles, word games, poetry. Must be written by students in grades 7-10. Receives 300 unsolicited fiction mss/month. Accepts 25 mss/issue; 100 mss/year. Publishes ms 3 months to 1 year after acceptance. Length: 1,500 words average; 25 words minimum; 4,000 words maximum. Publishes short shorts. Responds to rejected mss.
How to Contact: Send complete ms and cover letter with name, grade, age, home and school address, home and school telephone number, supervising teacher's name and principal's name. Reports in 10-12 weeks. SASE for ms. Accepts computer printouts. Sample copy $3.
Payment: Three contributor's copies, charge for extras. Each author published receives a free copy of *The Elements of Style*.
Terms: Author retains own copyright.
Advice: "Write what you *know*; write where you are."

MICHIGAN QUARTERLY REVIEW, University of Michigan, 3032 Rackham, Ann Arbor MI 48109-1070. (313)764-9265. Editor: Laurence Goldstein. "An interdisciplinary journal which publishes mainly essays and reviews, with some high-quality fiction and poetry, for an intellectual, widely read audience." Quarterly. Estab. 1962. Circ. 1,800.

Needs: Literary. No "genre" fiction written for a "market." Receives 200 unsolicited fiction mss/ month. Buys 2 mss/issue; 8 mss/year. Published work by Charles Baxter, Bell Gale Chevigny and Jay Neugebored; published new writers within the last year. Length: 1,500 words minimum; 7,000 words maximum; 5,000 words average.

How to Contact: Send complete ms with cover letter. "I like to know if a writer is at the beginning, or further along, in his or her career. Don't offer plot summaries of the enclosed story, though a background comment is welcome." SASE. Photocopied submissions OK. Accepts computer printout submissions (margins *not* justified). Sample copy for $2 and 2 first class stamps.

Payment: Pays $8-10/printed page.

Terms: Pays on publication for first rights. Awards the Lawrence Foundation Prize of $500 for best story in *MQR* previous year.

Advice: "Read back issues to get a sense of tone; level of writing. *MQR* is very selective; only send the very finest, best-plotted, most-revised fiction."

MID-AMERICAN REVIEW (II), Department of English, Bowling Green State University, Bowling Green OH 43403. (419)372-2725. Contact: Ken Letko, editor-in-chief. Magazine: 5½ × 8½; 200 pages; 60 lb bond paper; coated cover stock. "We publish serious fiction and poetry, as well as critical studies in modern literature, translations and book reviews." Published biannually. Estab. 1981.

Needs: Experimental, traditional, literary, prose poem, excerpted novel and translations. Receives about 50 unsolicited fiction mss/month. Buys 5-6 mss/issue. Does not read June-August. Approximately 5% of fiction is agented. Recently published work by Steven Schwartz, Eve Shelnut, Dan O'Brien; published new writers within the last year. Occasionally critiques rejected mss. Sometimes recommends other markets.

How to Contact: Send complete ms with SASE. Reports in about 2 months. Publishes ms an average of 3-6 months after acceptance. Sample copy $3.

Payment: $5/page up to $50; 2 free contributor's copies; $2 charge for extras.

Terms: Pays on publication for one-time rights.

Advice: "We just want *quality* work of whatever vision and/or style. We are now looking for more translated fiction."

Editor Ken Letko says this cover was chosen for Mid-American Review *because "its contemporary treatment of an image expresses both control and strength, characteristics that we hope invite the viewer to explore the literary work within—similarly strong, controlled and contemporary." This print was created by Cat Crotchett who currently teaches painting at Bowling Green State University. Reprinted with the permission of Cat Crotchett.*

‡THE MIDCOASTER (II), 2750 N. 45th St., Milwaukee WI 53210. Editor: Peter Blewett. Magazine: 8½×11; 48 pages. Literary magazine for a general audience. Annually. Estab. 1988. Circ. 300.
Needs: Condensed/excerpted novel, confession, contemporary, erotica, ethnic, experimental, feminist, gay, horror, humor/satire, lesbian, literary, mainstream, prose poem, regional, sports, suspense/ mystery, translations. Receives 6-10 unsolicited mss/month. Accepts 4-8 mss/issue. Publishes ms up to one year after acceptance. Recently published work by Dona Hickey, Jana Harris, José Dalísay. Length: 1,000 words average. Publishes short shorts. Sometimes critiques rejected mss.
How to Contact: Query first, or send complete manuscript (with cover letter). Reports in 2 weeks on queries; 8-10 weeks on mss. SASE. Simultaneous and photocopied submissions OK. Accepts computer printout submissions. Sample copy $4.50. Free fiction guidelines.
Payment: Pays contributor's copies.
Terms: Acquires first rights. Sends galleys to author.

MIDDLE EASTERN DANCER (II), The International Monthly Magazine of Middle Eastern Dance & Culture, Box 181572, Casselberry FL 32718-1572. (407)831-3402. Editor: Karen Kuzsel. Fiction Editor: Tracie Harris. Magazine: 8½×11; 36 pages; 60 lb stock; enamel cover; illustrations; photos. "Our theme is Middle Eastern dance and culture. We run seminar listings, professional directory, astrology geared to dancers, history, interviews, poetry, recipes, reviews of movies, clubs, shows, records, video, costuming, personal beauty care, exercise and dance choreography." Monthly. Estab. 1979. Circ. 2,500.
Needs: No fiction that does not relate to Middle-Eastern dance or culture. Receives 5 unsolicited ms/ month. Publishes ms within 4 months after acceptance. Published work by Alan Fisher, Jeanette Larson and Sid Hoskins; published new writers within the last year. *Charges $10 if comments are desired.* Occasionally critiques rejected mss. Recommends other markets.
How to Contact: Send complete ms with cover letter, which should include "background in Middle Eastern dance or culture, why they came to write this story and how they know of the magazine." Reports in 1 month on queries. SASE. Photocopied and reprint submissions OK "if not to other Middle Eastern Dance and culture publication." Accepts computer printout submissions. Sample copy $1 or send 9x12 SAE and 75¢ postage.
Payment: Pays $10-25 and 2 contributor's copies.
Terms: Pays on acceptance for one-time rights.
Advice: "Stick strictly to Middle Eastern dance/culture."

MINAS TIRITH EVENING-STAR (IV), W.W. Publications, Box 373, Highland MI 48357-0373. (313)887-4703. Editor: Philip Helms. Magazine: 8½×11; 40+ pages; typewriter paper; black ink illustrations; photos. Magazine of J.R.R. Tolkien and fantasy—fiction, poetry, reviews, etc. for general audience. Quarterly. Published special fiction issue; plans another. Estab. 1967. Circ. 500.
Needs: "Fantasy and Tolkien." Receives 5 unsolicited mss/month. Accepts 1 ms/issue; 5 mss/year. Published new writers within the last year. Length: 1,000-1,200 words preferred; 5,000 words maximum. Also publishes short shorts. Occasionally critiques rejected ms.
How to Contact: Send complete ms and bio. Reports in 1 week on queries; 2 weeks on mss. SASE. Photocopied and previously published submissions OK. Accepts computer printout submissions, prefers letter-quality. Sample copy $1.
Terms: Acquires first rights.
Advice: Goal is "to expand knowledge and enjoyment of J.R.R. Tolkien's and his son Christopher Tolkien's works and their worlds."

MIND IN MOTION (II), A Magazine of Poetry and Short Prose, Box 1118, Apple Valley CA 92307. (619)248-6512. Editor: Céleste Goyer. Magazine: 5½×8½; 54 pages; 20 lb paper; 50 lb cover. "We prefer to publish works of substantial brilliance that engage and encourage the readers' mind." Quarterly. Estab. 1985. Circ. 350.
Needs: Experimental, fantasy, humor/satire, literary, prose poem, science fiction. No "mainstream, romance, nostalgia, un-poetic prose; anything with a slow pace or that won't stand up to re-reading." Receives 50 unsolicited mss/month. Buys 5 mss/issue; 40 mss/year. Publishes ms 2 weeks to 3 months after acceptance. Published work by Robert E. Brimhall, Warren C. Miller, Michael K. White. Length: 2,000 words preferred; 250 words minimum; 3,500 words maximum. Sometimes critiques rejected mss and occasionally recommends other markets.
How to Contact: Send complete ms. "Cover letter or bio not necessary." SASE. Simultaneous (if notified) and photocopied submissions OK. Accepts computer printout submissions. Sample copy for $3.50. Fiction guidelines for #10 SAE and 1 first class stamp.

Payment: One contributor's copy when financially possible; charge for extras.
Terms: Acquires first North American serial rights.
Advice: "We look for fiction with no wasted words that demands re-reading, and startles us continually with the knowledge that such genius exists. Send works of cosmic pressure written poetically."

MINNESOTA INK (II), Box 9148, N. St. Paul MN 55109. (612)433-3626. Managing Editor: Valerie Hockert. Variable number of pages; 40 lb paper; illustrations and photographs. "A bimonthly publication designed to provide guidance and advice as well as inspiration for writers and other people interested in writing (e.g., the college student, the business person)." Monthly. Estab. 1987.
Needs: Adventure, contemporary, experimental, fantasy, humor/satire, mainstream, regional, romance (contemporary, historical), science fiction, senior citizen/retirement, suspense/mystery, western, young adult/teen (12-18 years). Receives about 100 unsolicited mss/month. Publishes mss "usually a couple months" after acceptance. Length: 500 words minimum; 1,500 words maximum. Sometimes critiques rejected mss.
How to Contact: Send complete ms with cover letter and biographical sketch. Reports in 1-2 months. SASE. Photocopied submissions OK. Sample copy $4. Fiction guidelines for SASE.
Payment: Pays in contributor's copies or subscription.
Terms: Acquires first rights. Sponsors contests and awards for fiction writers. "Contest announcements are published in publication."

THE MINNESOTA REVIEW (II), A Journal of Committed Writing, English Dept., SUNY-Stony Brook, Stony Brook NY 11794. (516)632-7400. Editors: Helen Cooper, William J. Harris, Michael Sprinker, Susan Squier. Fiction Editor: Fred Pfeil. Magazine: 5¼ × 8; approximately 160 pages; some illustrations; occasional photos. "We emphasize political writing, favoring especially socialist and feminist work." Semiannually. Estab. 1960. Circ. 1,000.
Needs: Experimental, fantasy, feminist, gay, historical (general), lesbian, literary, science fiction. Receives 20 mss/month. Accepts 3-4 mss/issue; 6-8 mss/year. Publishes ms within 6 months to 1 year after acceptance. Published work by Enid Dame, Ellen Gruber Garvey, John Berger. Length: 5,000-6,000 words preferred. Publishes short shorts. Sometimes critiques rejected mss and recommends other markets.
How to Contact: Send complete ms with cover letter (cover letter optional). Reports in 2-3 weeks on queries; 2-3 months on mss. SASE. Accepts computer printout submissions. Sample copy $4. Fiction guidelines are free.
Payment: Pays in contributor's copies. Charge for extra copies.
Terms: Acquires first rights.
Advice: "Write good stories with explicit political themes. Read back issues of *MR* for a sense of our collective taste."

MIORITA, A JOURNAL OF ROMANIAN STUDIES (IV), The Dept. FLLL, Dewey 482, University of Rochester, Rochester NY 14627. (716)275-4258 or (716)275-4251. Co-Editors: Charles Carlton and Norman Simms. Magazine: 5½ × 8½; Xerox paper; occasional illustrations. Magazine of "essays, reviews, notes and translations on all aspects of Romanian history, culture, language and so on," for academic audience. Annually. Estab. 1973. Circ. 200.
Needs: Ethnic, historical, literary, regional and translations. "All categories contingent upon relationship to Romania." Receives "handful of mss per year." Accepts "no more than one per issue." Length: 2,000 words maximum. Occasionally critiques rejected mss.
How to Contact: Send complete ms. SASE preferred. Previously published work OK (depending on quality). Accepts computer printout submissions.
Payment: "We do not pay."

THE MIRACULOUS MEDAL, The Central Association of the Miraculous Medal, 475 E. Chelten Ave., Philadelphia PA 19144. (215)848-1010. Editor: Rev. Robert P. Cawley, C.M. Magazine. Quarterly.
Needs: Religious/inspirational. Receives 25 unsolicited fiction mss/month; accepts 2 mss/issue; 8 mss/year. Publishes ms up to two years or more after acceptance.
How to Contact: Query first with SASE. Sample copy and fiction guidelines free.
Payment: Pays 2¢/word minimum.
Terms: Pays on acceptance for first rights.

THE MISS LUCY WESTENRA SOCIETY OF THE UNDEAD, 125 Taylor Street, Jackson TN 38301. (901)427-7714. Editor: Lewis Sanders. Newsletter: "Vampires/Dracula, modern/classic, very, very short fiction." Estab. 1989.
Needs: Vampires. "Very, very short fiction on vampires, Gothic, modern, erotic, but no porno or sleaze. Must be sent camera ready with a proper SASE." Length: 500 words average. Publishes short shorts of 500 words or less.
How to Contact: Send complete ms with cover letter. Reports on queries "as soon as possible." SASE. Simultaneous and reprint submissions OK. Sample copy $2.50, #10 SAE and 2 first class stamps. Fiction guidelines for #10 SAE and 2 first class stamps.
Payment: Pays 1 contributor's copy.
Terms: Acquires one-time rights. Publication not copyrighted.

MISSISSIPPI REVIEW (I, II), University of Southern Mississippi, Southern Station, Box 5144, Hattiesburg MS 39406. (601)266-4321. Editor: Rick Barthelme. "Literary publication for those interested in contemporary literature—writers, editors who read to be in touch with current modes." Semiannually. Estab. 1972. Circ. 1,500.
Needs: Literary, contemporary, fantasy, humor, translations, experimental, avant-garde and "art" fiction. No juvenile. Buys varied amount of mss/issue. Does not read mss in summer. Length: 100 pages maximum.
How to Contact: Send complete ms with SASE including a short cover letter. Accepts computer printout submissions. Sample copy $5.50.
Payment: Pays in author's copies. Charges cover price for extras.
Terms: Acquires first North American serial rights.

MISSISSIPPI VALLEY REVIEW (III), Western Illinois University, Dept. of English, Simpkins Hall, Macomb IL 61455. Editors: Carl Bean, Loren Logsdon, John Mann and Forrest Robinson. Magazine: 128 pages; original art on cover. "A small magazine, *MVR* has won 16 Illinois Arts Council awards in poetry and fiction. We publish stories, poems and reviews." Biannually. Estab. 1971. Circ. 2,000.
Needs: Literary, contemporary. Does not read mss in summer. Published work by Ray Bradbury, Gwendolyn Brooks, Louise Erdrich, Al Hirschfeld, Doris Lessing, Jack Matthews.
How to Contact: Send complete ms with SASE. Reports in 3 months. Sample copy $5.
Payment: 2 free author's copies.
Terms: Individual author retains rights.
Advice: "Persistence."

THE MISSOURI REVIEW (II), 1507 Hillcrest Hall, University of Missouri, Columbia MO 65211. (314)882-4474. Editor: Greg Michalson. Magazine: 6×9; 256 pages. Theme: fiction, poetry, essays, reviews, interviews, cartoons. "All with a distinctly contemporary orientation. For writers, and the general reader with broad literary interests. We present non-established as well as established writers of excellence. The *Review* frequently runs feature sections or special issues dedicated to particular topics frequently related to fiction." Published 3 times/academic year. Estab. 1977. Circ. 2,400.
Needs: Literary, contemporary; open to all categories except juvenile, young adult. Buys 6-8 mss/issue, 18-25 mss/year. Receives approximately 300 unsolicited fiction mss each month. Published new writers within the last year. No preferred length. Critiques rejected mss "when there is time."
How to Contact: Send complete ms with SASE. Reports in 10 weeks. Sample copy $5.
Payment: $20/page minimum.
Terms: Pays on signed contract for all rights.
Advice: Awards William Peden Prize in fiction; $1,000 to best story published in *Missouri Review* in a given year.

MODERN LITURGY (IV), Resource Publications, Inc., Suite 290, 160 E. Virginia St., San Jose CA 95112. Fiction Editor: John Gallen. Magazine: 8½×11; 48 pages; 60 lb glossy paper and cover stock; illustrations and photographs. "*Modern Liturgy* is focused on the liturgical arts—music, visual art, architecture, drama, dance and storytelling. We use short pieces that lend themselves to religious education or preaching. Readers are professionals and volunteers who plan and organize worship for Roman Catholic churches." 10 issues/year. Estab. 1973.
Needs: Liturgical. "Storytelling should be creative. Short pieces that tell you you how so-and-so came to a personal relationship with Jesus don't make it here." Receives 10 unsolicited fiction mss/month. Accepts 1 ms/issue; 9 mss/year. Length: 1,500 words average; 600 words minimum; 2,500 words maximum. Publishes short shorts.

How to Contact: Send complete ms with cover letter. Reports in 6 weeks. Sample copy $4 with 9x12 SAE and 3 first class stamps. Fiction guidelines for #10 SAE and 1 first class stamp.

Payment: Free subscription and 5 contributor's copies; charge for extras.

Terms: Acquires first rights plus right to grant non-commercial reprint permission to customers.

Advice: "We don't publish 'short stories' in the classic literary sense, but we do publish much fictional material (stories, plays, skits, humor) that is of use to worship leaders and planners."

‡**THE MONOCACY VALLEY REVIEW (II),** Mt. St. Mary's College, Emmitsburg MD 21701. (301)447-6122. Editor: William Heath. Fiction Editor: Roser Camiacals-Heath. Magazine: 8½x11; 20 pages; high-quality paper; illustrations and photographs. For readers in the "Mid-Atlantic region; all persons interested in literature." Semiannually. Estab. 1986. Circ. 250.

Needs: Adventure, contemporary, experimental, historical, humor/satire, literary, mainstream, prose poem. "We would not exclude any categories of fiction, save pornographic or obscene. Our preference is for realistic fiction that dramatizes things that matter." Receives 10-15 unsolicited mss/month. Buys 3 mss/issue; 6 mss/year. Does not read mss Decemer-March; June-October. Publishes ms 6 weeks after acceptance. Recently published work by Ann Knox; Maxine Combs; Doris Selinsky. Length: 3,000-4,000 words preferred; no minimum; 10,000 words maximum. Sometimes critiques rejected mss.

How to Contact: Query first or ask for submission guidelines. Cover letter unnecessary. Reports in 4 weeks on queries; 1-4 months on mss. SASE. Simultaneous and photocopied submissions OK. Accepts computer printout submissions. Sample copy $5. Fiction guidelines for #10 SAE and 1 first class stamp.

Payment: Pays $10-25. Free contributor's copies.

Terms: Pays on publication.

Advice: "Be patient in receiving a response. Manuscript readings take place about eight weeks before the two publication dates (June 15 and December 15). If you submit in July, your work will likely not be read until October. I would not advise submitting in November and December."

THE MOUNTAIN LAUREL, Monthly Journal of Mountain Life, Foundation Inc., P.O. Box 562, Wytheville VA 24382. (703)228-7282. Editor: Susan M. Thigpen. Tabloid: 28 pages; newsprint, illustrations and photographs. "Everyday details about life in the Blue Ridge Mountains of yesterday, for people of all ages interested in folk history." Monthly. Estab. 1983. Circ. 20,000.

Needs: Historical, humor, regional. "Stories must fit our format—we accept seasonal stories. There is always a shortage of good Christmas stories. A copy of our publication will be your best guidelines as to what we want. We will not even consider stories containing bad language, sex, gore, horror." Receives approximately 40 unsolicited fiction mss/month. Accepts up to 5 mss/issue; 60 mss/year. Publishes ms 2 to 6 months after acceptance. Length: 500-600 words average; no minimum; 1,000 words maximum. Publishes short shorts. Length 300 words. Sometimes critiques rejected mss. Recommends other markets.

How to Contact: Send complete ms with cover letter, which should include "an introduction to the writer as though he/she were meeting us in person." Reports in 1 month. SASE. Simultaneous and photocopied submissions OK. Accepts computer printout submissions. Sample copy for 9x12 SAE and 5 first class stamps. Fiction guidelines for #10 SAE and 1 first class stamp.

Payment: Pays in contributor's copies.

Terms: Pays for one-time rights.

Advice: "Tell a good story. Everything else is secondary. A tightly written story is much better than one that rambles. Short stories have no room to take off on tangents. *The Mountain Laurel* has published the work of many first-time writers as well as works by James Still and John Parris. First publication ever awarded the Blue Ridge Heritage Award."

‡**MOVING OUT (IV), Feminist Literary & Arts Journal,** Box 21249, Detroit MI 48221. Contact: Margaret Kaminski, co-editor. Magazine: 8½x11; 75 pages; medium paper; heavy cover; illustrations; photos. Magazine of "material which captures the experience of women, for feminists and other humane human beings." Published annually. Estab. 1970. Circ. 1,000.

Needs: Feminist, lesbian and senior citizen/retirement. No androcentric creations. Accepts about 10-20 mss/issue. Recently published poetry by Jan Worth and Denise Bergman. Occasionally critiques rejected mss.

How to Contact: Send complete ms with SASE. Accepts computer printout submissions. Reports in 6-12 months. Sample copy $9 (old issue $3.50); free guidelines with SASE.
Payment: 1 free contributor's copy.
Terms: Acquires first rights. Publication copyrighted.
Advice: "We like to see work that explores women's aesthetics, as well as that which represents varied experiences of the poor, the handicapped, the minorities, the lonely. Be fearless. Do not add to the mountains of sappy poetry and prose out there. Show us the reality of what you know, not what you think might sound 'poetic'."

‡**MUD CREEK (II),** The Loess Press, P.O. Box 19417, Portland OR 97219. (503)238-6329. Editor: Marty Brown (Ms.). Magazine: 5x7¼; 96-120 pages; illustrations and photographs. "We publish short fiction, poetry and non-academic essays on all themes for a college-educated, literary, artistic audience." Semiannually. Estab. 1989. Circ. 1,000.
Needs: Contemporary, literary, mainstream, serialized novel, translations. "We consider all types of fiction except 'formula' fiction. We are not adverse to publishing science fiction, romance, feminist, gay, lesbian, fantasy, etc., but it should test the limits of the genre. We do not publish material that is genre specific." Receives approx. 20 unsolicited fiction mss/month. Accepts 2-5 mss/issue; 4-10 mss/year. Publishes ms 1-9 months after acceptance. Recently published work by Stanley Poss, Charles Varani, M.K. Smith. Length: Open. Publishes short shorts. Critiques or comments on rejected mss, "if it shows promise and if time allows." Recommends other markets.
How to Contact: Send complete ms with cover letter. Include brief biographical statement (50 words or less). SASE. Photocopied and computer printout submissions OK. Sample copy for $5. Fiction guidelines for #10 SAE and 1 first-class stamp.
Payment: Pays 2 contributor's copies; charges for extras.
Terms: Acquires first North American serial rights.
Advice: "If you don't enjoy reading it, you probably won't enjoy writing for it. Our allegiance is to the audience, not to the writer who wants to have an outlet. We often accept stories by beginners, but never stories that are amateurish. Mistakes beginners make are: unnecessary descriptive passages; inconsistant narrative voice; unbelievable plots; hommages to elders; poor pacing; tense problems; grammatical errors. Pay attention to details."

MYSTERY NOTEBOOK (II, IV), Box 1341, F.D.R. Station, New York NY 10150. Editor: Stephen Wright. Journal and Newsletter: 8½×11; 10-16 pages and occasional double issues; photocopied; self cover; illustrations and photos sometimes. "Mystery books, news, information; reviews and essays. Separate section covers books of merit that are not mysteries." For mystery readers and writers. Quarterly. Estab. 1984. Circ. (approx.) 1,000.
Needs: Excerpted novel (suspense/mystery). Receives few unsolicited mss. Length: brief. Short shorts considered. Occasionally comments on rejected ms.
How to Contact: Query first or query with clips of published work (preferably on mystery). Reports in 3 weeks on queries; 4 weeks on mss. SASE for ms. Photocopied and previously published submissions OK (if query first). All submissions must be letter-quality. Sample copies or back issues $10.
Payment: None. "If author is a regular contributor, he or she will receive complimentary subscription. Usually contributor receives copies of the issue in which contribution appears."
Advice: "Mystery magazines use all kinds of stories in various settings. This is also true of mystery books except that no matter what kind of detective is the protagonist (private eye, amateur, police and all the rest) the novel must be the best of its kind—even for consideration. Mystery fiction books have increased in demand—*but* the competetion is more keen than ever. So only those with real talent *and* a superb knowledge of mystery-writing craft have any chance for publication. It also helps if you know and understand the market."

MYSTERY TIME (I), An Anthology of Short Stories, Box 1870, Hayden ID 83835. (208)772-6184. Editor: Linda Hutton. Booklet: 5½×8½; 44 pages; bond paper; illustrations. "Annual collection of short stories with a suspense or mystery theme for mystery buffs." Estab. 1983.
Needs: Suspense/mystery only. Receives 10-15 unsolicited fiction mss/month. Accepts 10-12 mss/year. Published work by Elizabeth Lucknell, Loretta Sallman Jackson, Vickie Britton. Published new writers within the last year. Length: 1,500 words maximum. Occasionally critiques rejected mss and recommends other markets.

How to Contact: Send complete ms with SASE. "No cover letters."Simultaneous, photocopied and previously published submissions OK. Accepts computer printout submissions. Prefers letter-quality. Reports in 1 month on mss. Publishes ms an average of 6-8 months after acceptance. Sample copy $3.50. Fiction guidelines for #10 SAE and 22¢ postage.
Payment: ¼¢/word minimum; 1¢/word maximum. 1 free contributor's copy; $2.50 charge for extras
Terms: Acquires one-time rights. Buys reprints. Sponsors annual short story contest.
Advice: "Study a sample copy and the guidelines. Too many amateurs mark themselves as amateurs by submitting blind."

THE MYTHIC CIRCLE (I), The Mythopoeic Society, Box 6707, Altadena CA 91001. Co-Editors: Tina Cooper and Christine Lowentrout. Magazine: 8½ × 11; 50 pages; high quality photocopy paper; illustrations. "A tri-quarterly fantasy-fiction magazine. We function as a 'writer's forum,' depending heavily on letters of comment from readers. We have an occasional section called 'Mythopoeic Youth' in which we publish stories written by writers still in high school/junior high school. We have several 'theme' issues (poetry, American fantasy) and plan more of these in the future." Tri-quarterly. Estab. 1987. Circ. 150.
Needs: Short fantasy. "No erotica, no graphic horror, no 'hard' science fiction." Receives 25 + unsolicited ms/month. Accepts 19-20 mss/issue. Publishes ms 2-8 months after acceptance. Published work by Charles de Lint, Gwyneth Hood, Angelee Sailer Anderson; published new writers within the last year. Length: 3,000 words average. Publishes short shorts. Length: 8,000 words maximum. Always critiques rejected mss; may recommend other markets."
How to Contact: Send complete ms with cover letter. "We like to know if the person is very young— we give each ms a personal response. We get many letters that try to impress us with other places they've appeared in print—that doesn't matter much to us." Reports in 2-8 weeks. SASE. Photocopied submissions OK; no simultaneous submissions. Accepts computer printout submissions and IBM or MAC floppies. Sample copy $5; fiction guidelines for #10 SASE.
Payment: Contributor's copies; charges for extras.
Terms: Acquires one-time rights.
Advice: "There are very few places a fantasy writer can send to these days. *Mythic Circle* was started up because of this; also, the writers were not getting any kind of feedback when (after nine or ten months) their mss were rejected. We give the writers personalized attention—critiques, suggestions— and we rely on our readers to send us letters of comment on the stories we publish, so that the writers can see a response. Don't be discouraged by rejections, especially if personal comments/suggestions are offered."

‡NCASA NEWS (II), Newsletter of the National Coalition Against Sexual Assault, Suite 500, 123 S. 7th St., Springfield IL 62701. (217)753-4117. Editor: Becky Bradway. Newsletter: 8½ × 11; 30 pages; illustrations and photographs. "*NCASA News* is a forum for commentary, information and creative work concerning sexual assault and the anti-sexual assault movement." Quarterly. Estab. 1985. Circ. 850.
Needs: Condensed/excerpted novel, contemporary, ethnic, experimental, feminist, gay, humor/satire, literary, prose poem, regional, serialized novel, translations. Fiction and poetry are included in a special section, "Voices of Survivors." Work should be written by survivors of rape or incest. "All fiction must be grounded in a feminist perspective. We will not accept work that is racist, classist, or heterosexist." Accepts 1-2 mss/issue; 4-6 mss/year. Publishes ms up to 1 year after acceptance. Length: 3,000 words average; 500 words minimum; 10,000 words maximum. Publishes short shorts. Sometimes critiques rejected mss and recommends other markets.
How to Contact: Send complete manuscript with cover letter. Include publication and professional background, if any. Reports in 6 weeks on mss. SASE. Simultaneous and reprint submissions OK. Accepts computer printout submissions. Accepts electronic submissions (MS/DOS). Sample copy $3. Fiction guidelines for SASE and 1 first class stamp.
Payment: Pays 3 contributor's copies.
Terms: Acquires first rights.
Advice: "*NCASA News* is looking for well-written, thoughtful fiction and poetry from survivors of rape and incest. Fiction may be based upon personal experience, but should utilize the mechanics of the story form: plot, characterization, dialogue, etc. Think through your story. Spend time with it. Revise it, many times. A strong scene showing an experience is almost always more powerful than a personal monologue."

NEBO (I), A Literary Journal, Arkansas Tech University, Dept. of English, Russellville AR 72801. (501)968-0256. Contact: Editor. Literary, fiction and poetry magazine: 5×8; 50-60 pages. For a general, academic audience. Annually. Estab. 1983. Circ. 500.
Needs: Literary, mainstream, reviews. Receives 20-30 unsolicited fiction mss/month. Accepts 2 mss/issue; 6-10 mss/year. Does not read mss May 1-Sept. 1. Published new writers within the last year. Length: 3,000 words maximum. Occasionally critiques rejected mss.
How to Contact: Send complete ms with SASE and cover letter with bio. Accepts computer printout submissions, prefers letter-quality. Reports in 3 months on mss. Publishes ms an average of 6 months after acceptance. Sample copy $1. "Submission deadline for all work is April 5th."
Payment: 1 free contributor's copy.
Terms: Acquires one-time rights.
Advice: "A writer should carefully edit his short story before submitting it. Write from the heart and put everything on the line. Don't write from a phony or fake perspective. Frankly, many of the manuscripts we receive should be publishable with a little polishing. Manuscripts should *never* be submitted with misspelled words or on 'onion skin' or colored paper."

THE NEBRASKA REVIEW (II), University of Nebraska at Omaha, ASH 212, Omaha NE 68182. (402)554-2771. Fiction Editor: Richard Duggin. Magazine: 5½×8½; 72 pages; 60 lb text paper; chrome coat cover stock. "*TNR* attempts to publish the finest available contemporary fiction and poetry for college and literary types." Publishes 2 issues/year. Estab. 1973. Circ. 500.
Needs: Contemporary, humor/satire, literary and mainstream. Receives 20 unsolicited fiction mss/month. Accepts 3-5 mss/issue, 8 mss/year. Does not read April 1-September 1. Published work by Elizabeth Evans, Stephen Dixon and Peter Leach; published new writers within the last year. Length: 5,000-6,000 words average.
How to Contact: Send complete ms with SASE. Photocopied submissions OK. Reports in 1-2 months. Publishes ms an average of 4-6 months after acceptance. Sample copy $2.50.
Payment: 2 free contributor's copies plus 1 year subscription; $2 charge for extras.
Terms: Acquires first North American serial rights.
Advice: "Don't consider us as the last place to submit your mss. Write 'honest' stories in which the lives of your characters are the primary reason for writing and techniques of craft serve to illuminate, not overshadow, the textures of those lives. Sponsors a $300 award/year — write for rules."

NEGATIVE CAPABILITY (II), A Literary Quarterly, 62 Ridgelawn Dr. E., Mobile AL 36608. (205)661-9114. Editor-in-Chief: Sue Walker. Managing Editor: Richard G. Beyer. Magazine: 5½×8½; 160 pages; 70 lb offset paper; 4 color/varnish cover stock; illustrations; photos. Magazine of short fiction, prose poems, poetry, criticism, commentaries, journals and translations for those interested in contemporary trends, innovations in literature. Published tri-quarterly. Estab. 1981. Circ. 1,000.
Needs: Adventure, contemporary, ethnic, experimental, fantasy, feminist, gothic/historical romance, historical (general), literary, prose poem, psychic/supernatural/occult, regional, romance (contemporary), science fiction, senior citizen/retirement, suspense/mystery, translations. Accepts 2-3 mss/issue, 6-10 mss/year. Does not read July-Sept. Publishes short shorts. Published work by A.W. Landwehr, Gerald Flaherty and Richard Moore; published new writers within the last year. Length: 1,000 words minimum. Sometimes recommends other markets.
How to Contact: Query or send complete ms. SASE. Reports in 2 weeks on queries; 6 weeks on mss. Publishes ms an average of 6 months after acceptance. Sample copy $5.
Payment: 2 free contributor's copies.
Terms: Acquires first rights, first North American serial rights and one-time rights. Sends galleys to author.
Advice: "We consider all manuscripts and often work with new authors to encourage and support. We believe fiction answers a certain need that is not filled by poetry or nonfiction." Annual fiction competition. Deadline Dec. 1.

NEW BLOOD MAGAZINE (I,II), Suite 3730, 540 W. Foothill Blvd., Glendora CA 91740. Editor: Chris B. Lacher. Magazine: 8½×11; 64-96 pages; slick paper; gloss cover; b&w and color illustrations and photos. "Of course, story counts, but *New Blood* publishes fiction considered too strong or gory to appear in today's periodicals; note, emphasis does not have to be on gore or grue — I just want a story that knocks me out! Fans of Clive Barker and *Fangoria* magazine, for example, will appreciate *New Blood*." Quarterly. Estab. 1986. Circ. 15,000.

Needs: Horror, occult, dark fantasy, splatter punk, erotica, suspense/mystery, slice-of-life. "Any genre or theme is acceptable, actually, as long as it portrays a different slant or outlook. I am not looking for generic overviews of generic themes. *Do not* submit stories of elves, faeries, vampires— especially concerning AIDS—werewolves (were-bats, were-rats, were-babies, or were-anything), ghosts, or psycho-killers disposing of their victims in a 'unique' manner—these types of stories are too routine for my tastes. I do not consider 'bar' stories, 'road' stories, or nautical tales (I don't want to see *anything* about the sea or boats or mermaids), nor do I want 'appliances/household/office items from Hell' stories (i.e., monsters in the toilet; killer washing machines), or stories told from the point-of-view of an animal/insect/plant."Receives 200 unsolicited mss/month. Accepts 10-20 mss/issue; 45-90 mss/ year. Publishes ms 3-9 months after acceptance. Agented fiction 1%. Recently published work by Clive Barker, Joe R. Lansdale, Robert R. McCammon; published new writers within the last year. Length: 2,500 words average; 5,000 words maximum. Always comments on rejected mss. Sometimes recommends other markets.
How to Contact: Send complete ms with cover letter, which should include a brief bio. Query only for fiction more than 5,000 words. Reports on queries and mss "within 3 weeks." SASE. Photocopied and reprint submissions OK. Sample copy $4.
Payment: Pays 3¢/word minimum.
Terms: Rights revert to author on publication.
Advice: "Becoming familiar with the unique type of fiction I publish by purchasing a subscription is your key to a quick sale. Discover why you enjoy it as a fan, and you will, in turn discover what we seek from a prospective contributor."

THE NEW CRUCIBLE (I), A Magazine About Man and His Environment, Box 7252, Spencer IA 51301. Editor: Garry De Young. Magazine: 8½×11; variable number of pages; 20 lb paper; soft cover; illustrations and photographs. Publishes "environmental material—includes the total human environment." Monthly. Plans special fiction issue. Estab. 1964.
Needs: Atheist. "Keep material concise, use clear line drawings. Environmentalists must be Materialists because the environment deals with matter. Thus also evolutionists. Keep this in mind. Manuscripts not returned. Will not accept religious or other racist or sexist material." *Charges $1/page reading fee.* Length: concise preferred. Publishes short shorts. Sometimes critiques rejected mss. Publishes original cartoons.
How to Contact: Send complete ms with cover letter. Cover letter should include "biographical sketch of author." SASE. Simultaneous, photocopied and reprint submissions OK. Accepts computer printout submissions. Sample copy for $2, 8½x11 SAE and 4 first class stamps.
Payment: Pays in contributor's copies.
Terms: "Will discuss rights with author."
Advice: "Be gutsy! Don't be afraid to attack superstitionists. Attack those good people who remain so silent—people such as newspaper editors, so-called scientists who embrace superstition such as the Jesus myth or the Virgin Mary nonsense."

NEW DELTA REVIEW (II), English Dept./Louisiana State University, Baton Rouge LA 70803. (504)388-4079. Editor: Kathleen Fitzpatrick. Fiction Editor: David Racine. Magazine: 6×9; 75-125 pages; high quality paper; glossy card cover; illustrations; photographs possible. "No theme or style biases. Poetry, fiction primarily; also creative essays and reviews." Semi-annually. Estab. 1984.
Needs: Contemporary, erotica, experimental, humor/satire, literary, mainstream, prose poem, translations. Receives 120 unsolicited mss/ month. Accepts 4-8 mss/issue. Recently published work by Susan Sonde, John McNally, Thomas E. Kennedy; published new writers within the last year. Length: 2,500 words average; 250 words minimum; 5,000 words maximum. Publishes short shorts. Sometimes critiques rejected mss.
How to Contact: Send complete ms with cover letter. Cover letter should include "credits, if any; no synopses, please." Reports on mss in 6-8 weeks. SASE. Mss deadlines October 15 for fall; April 15 for spring. Prefers photocopied submissions. No dot-matrix. Sample copy $4.
Payment: Pays in contributor's copies. Charge for extras.
Terms: Acquires first North American serial rights. Sponsors award for fiction writers in each issue. Eyster Prize-$50 plus notice in magazine. Mss selected for publication are automatically considered.
Advice: "The question we are asked most is still what *kind* of fiction we like. All we can say is this: The good kind. The second most asked question is what we mean when we ask for 'breakthrough' fiction. Here we shrug and smile coyly and say 'try us.' Be brave. Explore your voice. Make sparks fly off your typewriter. And don't forget the SASE if you want a response."

NEW ENGLAND REVIEW (III), (formerly *New England Review and Bread Loaf Quarterly*), Middlebury College, Middlebury VT 05753. (802)388-3711, ext. 5075. Editors: T.R. Hummer, Devon Jersild. Magazine: 6 × 9; 140 pages; 70 lb paper; coated cover stock; illustrations; photos. A literary quarterly publishing fiction, poetry and essays on life and the craft of writing. For general readers and professional writers. Quarterly. Estab. 1977. Circ. 2,000.

Needs: Literary. Receives 250 unsolicited fiction mss/month. Accepts 5 mss/issue; 20 mss/year. Does not read ms June-August. Recently published work by Jeanne Schinto, Robert Minkoff, Kathryn Davis; published new writers within the last year. Publishes ms 3-9 months after acceptance. Agented fiction: less than 5%. Publishes short shorts. Sometimes critiques rejected mss.

How to Contact: Send complete ms with cover letter. "Cover letters that demonstrate that the writer knows the magazine are the ones we want to read. We don't want hype, or hard-sell, or summaries of the author's intentions. Will consider simultaneous submissions, but must be stated as such, and author must know we may not read a submission that is also being considered elsewhere if we receive too many submissions sent only to us." Reports in 6-8 weeks on mss. SASE. Photocopied submissions OK. Accepts computer printouts.

Payment: Pays $5 per page; $10 minimum; free subscription to magazine, offprints; contributor's copies; charge for extras.

Terms: Pays on publication. Acquires first rights and reprint rights on *NER/BLQ* and Middlebury College. Sends galleys to author.

Advice: "We look for work that combines intelligence with craft and visceral appeal. To break into the prestige or literary market, writers should avoid formulae and clichés and assume that the reader is at least as intelligent and well informed as they are."

NEW FRONTIER (IV), 46 North Front, Philadelphia PA 19106. (215)627-5683. Editor: Sw. Virato. Magazine: 8 × 10; 48-60 pages; pulp paper stock; illustrations and photos. "We seek new age writers who have imagination yet authenticity." Monthly. Estab. 1981. Circ. 60,000.

Needs: New age. "A new style of writing is needed with a transformation theme." Receives 10-20 unsolicited mss/month. Accepts 1-2 mss/issue. Publishes ms 3 months after acceptance. Agented fiction "less than 5%." Published work by John White, Laura Anderson. Published work by new writers within the last year. Length: 1,000 words average; 750 words minimum; 2,000 words maximum. Publishes short shorts. Length: 150-500 words. Occasionally critiques rejected mss and recommends other markets.

How to Contact: Send complete ms with cover letter, which should include author's bio and credits. Reports in 2 months on mss. SASE for ms. Simultaneous, photocopied and reprint submissions OK. Accepts computer printout submissions. Sample copy for $2. Fiction guidelines for #10 SAE and 1 first class stamp.

Terms: Acquires first North American serial rights and one-time rights.

Advice: "The new age market is ready for a special kind of fiction and we are here to serve it. Don't try to get an A on your term paper. Be sincere, aware and experimental. Old ideas that are senile don't work for us. Be fully alive and aware—tune in to our new age audience/readership."

NEW LAUREL REVIEW (II), 828 Lesseps St., New Orleans LA 70117. Editor: Martha Farrin. Magazine: 6 × 9; 120 pages; 60 lb book paper; Sun Felt cover; illustrations; photo essays. Journal of poetry, fiction, critical articles and reviews. "We have published such internationally known writers as Martha McFerren, Tomris Uyar and Yevgeny Yevtushenko." Readership: "Literate, adult audiences as well as anyone interested in writing with significance, human interest, vitality, subtlety, etc." Annually. Estab. 1970. Circ. 500.

Needs: Literary, contemporary, fantasy and translations. No "dogmatic, excessively inspirational or political" material. Accepts 1-2 fiction mss/issue. Receives approximately 50 unsolicited fiction mss each month. Length: about 10 printed pages. Critiques rejected mss when there is time.

How to Contact: Send complete ms with SASE. Reports in 3 months. Sample copy $6.

Payment: 2 free author's copies.

Terms: Acquires first rights.

Advice: "We are interested in international issues pointing to libraries around the world. Write fresh, alive 'moving' work. Not interested in egocentric work without any importance to others. Be sure to watch simple details such as putting one's name and address on ms and clipping all pages together. Caution: Don't use overfancy or trite language." (Note: At press time this magazine was about to move; mail will be forwarded to new address.)

NEW LETTERS MAGAZINE (I, II), University of Missouri-Kansas City, 5100 Rockhill Rd., Kansas City MO 64110. (816)276-1168. Editor: James McKinley. Magazine: 14 lb cream paper; illustrations. Quarterly. Estab. 1971 (continuation of *University Review*, founded 1935). Circ. 2,500.
Needs: Contemporary, ethnic, experimental, humor/satire, literary, mainstream, translations. No "bad fiction in any genre." Published work by Richard Rhodes, Jascha Kessler, Josephine Jacobsen; published work by new writers within the last year. Agented fiction: 10%. Also publishes short shorts. Occasionally critiques rejected mss.
How to Contact: Send complete ms with cover letter. Does not read mss May 15-October 15. Reports in 3 weeks on queries; 6 weeks on mss. SASE for ms. Photocopied submissions OK. No multiple submissions. Accepts computer printouts. Sample copy: $8.50 for issues older than 5 years; $5.50 for 5 years or less.
Payment: Honorarium—depends on grant/award money; 2 contributor's copies. Sends galleys to author.
Advice: "Seek publication of representative chapters in high-quality magazines as a way to the book contract. Try literary magazines first."

NEW METHODS (IV), The Journal of Animal Health Technology, Box 22605, San Francisco CA 94122-0605. (415)664-3469. Editor: Ronald S. Lippert, AHT. Newsletter ("could become magazine again"): 8½×11; 4-6 pages; 20 lb paper; illustrations; photos "rarely." Network service in the animal field educating services for mostly professionals in the animal field; e.g. animal health technicians. Monthly. Estab. 1976. Circ. 5,608.
Needs: Animals: adventure, condensed novel, contemporary, experimental, historical, mainstream, regional. No stories unrelated to animals. Receives 12 unsolicited fiction mss/month. Buys one ms/ issue; 12 mss/year. Length: open. "Rarely" publishes short shorts. Occasionally critiques rejected mss. Recommends other markets.
How to Contact: Query first with theme, length, expected time of completion, photos/illustrations, if any, biographical sketch of author, all necessary credits or send complete ms. Report time varies. SASE for query and ms. Simultaneous and photocopied submissions OK. Accepts computer printouts. Sample copy $2 for *NSSWM* readers. Fiction guidelines free for #10 SAE and 1 first class stamp.
Payment: Varies.
Terms: Pays on publication for one-time rights.
Advice: Contests: theme changes but is generally the biggest topics of the year in the animal field. "Emotion, personal experience—make the person feel it. We are growing."

NEW MEXICO HUMANITIES REVIEW (II), Humanities Dept., New Mexico Tech, Box A, Socorro NM 87801. (505)835-5445. Editors: John Rothfork and Jerry Bradley. Magazine: 5½×9½; 150 pages; 60 lb lakewood paper; 482 ppi cover stock; illustrations; photos. Review of poetry, essays and prose of Southwest. Readership: academic but not specialized. Published 3 times/year. Estab. 1978. Circ. 650.
Needs: Literary and regional. "No formula." Accepts 40-50 mss/year. Receives approximately 50 unsolicited fiction mss/month. Published work by John Deming, Fred Chappell; published new writers within the last year. Length: 6,000 words maximum. Publishes short shorts. Critiques rejected mss "when there is time." Sometimes recommends other markets.
How to Contact: Send complete ms with SASE. Accepts computer printout submissions. Reports in 2 months. Publishes ms an average of 6 months after acceptance. Sample copy $5.
Payment: 1 year subscription.
Terms: Sends galleys to author.
Advice: Mss are rejected because they are "unimaginative, predictable and technically flawed. Don't be afraid to take literary chances—be daring, experiment."

NEW MOON, A Journal of Science Fiction and Critical Feminism, Box 2056, Madison WI 53701. (608)251-3854. Editor: Janice Bogstad. "Speculative fiction, fantastic feminist fiction, reviews and criticism of such works. Copies found in university libraries, feminist and literary collections, women's studies programs." Semiannually. Estab. 1981. Circ. 600.
Needs: Experimental, fantasy, feminist, literary, prose poem, science fiction, translations. Receives 3-5 unsolicited fiction mss/month. Accepts 2-4 mss/issue; 15 mss/year. Published new writers within the last year. Length: 1,000-1,500 words average; 1,000 words minimum; 3,000 words maximum. Occasionally critiques rejected mss.
How to Contact: Query first. Cover letter should include "other interests, other publications of your work." Reports in 2 months on queries; 4 months on mss. SASE. Simultaneous, photocopied submissions and previously published work OK. "No originals." Accepts computer printout submis-

sions. Sample copy $4. Fiction guidelines free for #10 SAE and 1 first class stamp.
Payment: Pays 1 contributor's copy; 60% of cover price charge for extras.
Terms: Acquires one-time rights.
Advice: "Send photocopies only. Send clean, clear copy and advise as to turnaround time expected."

NEW ORLEANS REVIEW (II), Box 195, Loyola University, New Orleans LA 70118. (504)865-2294.
Editor: John Mosier. Magazine: 8½×11; 100 pages; 60 lb Scott offset paper; 12+ King James C15
cover stock; photos. "Publishes poetry, fiction, translations, photographs, nonfiction on literature and
film. Readership: those interested in current culture, literature." Published 4 times/year. Estab. 1968.
Circ. 1,000.
Needs: Literary, contemporary, translations. Buys 9-12 mss/year. Length: under 40 pages.
How to Contact: Send complete ms with SASE. Does not accept simultaneous submissions. Accepts
computer printout submissions. Accepts disk submissions; inquire about system compatibility. Prefers
hard copy with disk submission. Reports in 3 months. Sample copy $9.
Payment: "Inquire."
Terms: Pays on publication for first North American serial rights. Sends galleys to author.

THE NEW PRESS (II), 87-40 Francis Lewis Blvd. A44, Queens Village NY 11427. (718)217-1464.
Publisher: Bob Abramson. Magazine: 8½×11; 32 pages; medium bond paper and glossy cover stock;
illustrations and photographs. "Poems, short stories, commentary, personal journalism. Original and
entertaining." Quarterly. Estab. 1984.
Needs: Adventure, confession, ethnic, experimental, fantasy, humor/satire, literary, mainstream,
prose poem, serialized/excerpted novel, spiritual, sports, translations. No gratuitous violence. Receives
10 unsolicited mss/month. Accepts 2 mss/issue; 8 mss/year. Publishes ms 6 months after acceptance.
Published new writers within the last year. Length: 3,000 words maximum; 100 words minimum.
Sometimes critiques rejected mss and recommends other markets.
How to Contact: Send complete ms with cover letter. Reports in 2 months. SASE. Simultaneous,
photocopied and reprint submissions OK. Accepts computer printout submissions. Sample copy $2;
fiction guidelines free. $8 for one-year (4 issues) subscription.
Payment: Pays in contributor's copies and awards $50 for most significant prose in each issue.
Terms: Pays for one-time rights.

THE NEW QUARTERLY (II, IV), New Directions in Canadian Writing, ELPP, University of Waterloo, Waterloo, Ontario N2L 3G1 Canada. (519)885-1212, ext. 2837. Managing Editor: Mary Merikle.
Fiction Editors: Peter Hinchcliffe, Kim Jernigan. Magazine: 6×9; 80-120 pages; perfect bound cover,
b&w cover photograph; photos with special issues. "We publish poetry, short fiction, excerpts from
novels, interviews. We are particularly interested in writing which stretches the bounds of realism.
Our audience includes those interested in Canadian literature." Quarterly. Published recent special
issues on magic realism in Canadian writing and family fiction. Upcoming issue on Canadian Mennonite writing.
Needs: "I suppose we could be described as a 'literary' magazine. We look for writing which is fresh,
innovative, well crafted. We promote beginning writers alongside more established ones. Ours is a
humanist magazine – no gratuitous violence, though we are not afraid of material which is irreverent
or unconventional. Our interest is more in the quality than the content of the fiction we see." Receives
approx. 50 unsolicited mss/month. Buys 5-6 mss/issue; 20-24 mss/year. Publishes ms usually within 6
months after acceptance. Recently published work by Diane Schoemperlen, Patrick Roscoe and Steven Heighton; published new writers within the last year. Length: up to 20 pages. Publishes short
shorts. Sometimes recommends other markets.
How to Contact: Send complete ms with cover letter, which should include a short biographical note.
Reports in 1-2 weeks on queries; approx. 3 months on mss. SASE for ms. Photocopied submissions
OK. Accepts computer printout submissions. Sample copy for $3.50.
Payment: Pays $100 and contributor's copies.
Terms: Pays on publication for first North American serial rights.
Advice: "Send only one well polished manuscript at a time. Persevere. Find your own voice. The
primary purpose of little literary magazines like ours is to introduce new writers to the reading public.
However, because we want them to appear at their best, we apply the same standards when judging
novice work as when judging that of more established writers."

‡**the new renaissance (II)**, 9 Heath Rd., Arlington MA 02174. Fiction Editors: Louise T. Reynolds, Harry Jackel and Patricia Mechoud. Magazine: 6×9; 144-152 pages; 70 lb paper; laminated cover stock; artwork; photos. "An international magazine of ideas and opinions, emphasizing literature and the arts, *tnr* takes a classicist position in literature and the arts. Publishes a variety of quality fiction, always well crafted, sometimes experimental. *tnr* is unique among literary magazines for its marriage of the literary and visual arts with political/sociological articles and essays. We publish the beginning as well as the established writer." Biannually. Estab. 1968. Circ. 1,500.
Needs: Literary, humor, prose poem, translations, off-beat, quality fiction and, occasionally, experimental fiction. "We don't want to see heavily plotted stories with one-dimensional characters or heavily academic or obviously 'poetic' writing, or fiction that is self-indulgent." Buys 5-6 mss/issue, 8-13 mss/year. Receives approximately 50-70 unsolicited fiction mss each month. Requires $5.60 for 2 sample back issues or $6.25 for recent issue before reading mss. Overstocked. Reads only from Jan. 2 thru June 30 of any year. Approximately 8-12% of fiction is agented. Recently published work by M.E. McMullen, Vitaliano Brancati and Stewart O'Nan; published new writers within the last year. Length of fiction: 3-36 pages. Comments on rejected mss "when there is time and when we want to encourage the writer or believe we can be helpful."
How to Contact: Send complete ms with SASE or IRCs of sufficient size for return. "Inform us if multiple submission." Reluctantly accepts computer printout submissions but prefers letter-quality. Reports in 4-6 months. Publishes ms an average of 18-24 months after acceptance. Sample copy $5.60 for 2 back issues, or $6.25 for recent issue. Current issue is $7.30.
Payment: $30-$75 after publication. 1 free author's copy. Query for additional copies.
Terms: Acquires all rights in case of a later *tnr* book collection; otherwise, rights return to the writer. Publication copyrighted.
Advice: "We represent one of the best markets for writers, because we publish a greater variety (of styles, statements, tones) than most magazines, small or large. Study *tnr* and then send your best manuscript; we will read 2 manuscripts if they are 5 pages or less; for mss 6 pages or more, send only one ms. Manuscripts are rejected because writers do not study their markets and send out indiscriminately. Fully one-quarter of our rejected manuscripts fall into this category; others are from tyro writers who haven't yet mastered their craft, or writers who are not honest, or who haven't fully thought their story through, or from writers who are careless about language. Also, many writers feel compelled to 'explain' their stories to the reader instead of letting the story speak for itself."

NEW VIRGINIA REVIEW (II), An anthology of literary work by and important to Virginians, 1306 East Cary St., 2A, Richmond VA 23219. (804)782-1043. Rotating guest editors. Contact: Mary Flynn. Magazine: 6½×10; 300+ pages; high quality paper; coated, color cover stock. "Approximately one half of the contributors have Virginia connections; the other authors are serious writers of contemporary fiction. Occasionally guest editors set a specific theme for an issue, e.g. 1986 Young Southern Writers." Annually. Estab. 1978. Circ. 2,000.
Needs: Contemporary, experimental, literary, mainstream, serialized/excerpted novel. No blue, sci-fi, romance, children's. Receives 50-100 unsolcited fiction mss/month. Accepts an average of 15 mss/issue. Does not read from April 1 to September 1. Publishes ms an average of 6-9 months after acceptance. Length: 5,000-6,500 words average; no minimum; 8,000 words maximum. Sometimes critiques rejected mss.
How to Contact: Send complete ms with cover letter, name, address, telephone number, brief biographical comment. Reports in 6 weeks on queries; up to 6 months on mss. "Will answer questions on status of ms." SASE. Photocopied submissions OK. Accepts computer printout submissions. Sample copy $13.50 and 9x12 SAE with 5 first-class stamps.
Payment: $10/printed page; contributor's copies; charge for extras, ½ cover price.
Terms: Pays on publication for first North American serial rights. Sponsors contests and awards for Virginia writers only.
Advice: "Since we publish a wide range of styles of writing depending on the tastes of our guest editors, all we can say is—try to write good strong fiction, stick to it, and try again with another editor."

NeWEST REVIEW (II, IV), Box 394, Sub P.O. 6 Saskatoon, Saskatchewan S7N 0W0 Canada. Editor: Naomi Frankel. Fiction Editor: Lewis Horne. Magazine: 48 pages; book stock; illustrations; photos. Magazine devoted to western Canada regional issues; "fiction, reviews, poetry for middle- to high-brow audience." Bimonthly (6 issues per year). Estab. 1975. Circ. 1,000.
Needs: "We want fiction of high literary quality, whatever its form and content. But we do have a heavy regional emphasis." Receives 15-20 unsolicited mss/month. Buys 1 ms/issue; 10 mss/year. Length: 2,500 words average; 1,500 words minimum; 5,000 words maximum. Sometimes recommends other markets.

How to Contact: "We like *brief* cover letters. Reports very promptly in a short letter. SAE, IRCs or Canadian postage. Photocopied submissions OK. No multiple submissions. Accepts computer printout submissions. Sample copy $3.50.
Payment: Pays $100 maximum.
Terms: Pays on publication for one-time rights.
Advice: "Polish your writing. Develop your story line. Give your characters presence. If we, the readers, are to care about the people you create, you too must take them seriously."

‡NEXT PHASE (I, II), Phantom Press, 325 Humphrey St., New Haven CT 06511. (203)777-1762. Editor: Michael White. Fiction Editor: Kim Means. 8½×11; 12 pages. "Science fiction fantasy with humane twist for experimental comic/graphic novel/sci fi fantasy fans." Quarterly. Estab. 1989. Circ. 500.
Needs: Experimental, fantasy, horror, science fiction. Publishes annual special fiction issue. Receives 4-10 unsolicited mss/month. Accepts 2 mss/issue; 8 mss/year. Publishes short shorts. Sometimes critiques rejected mss and recommends other markets.
How to Contact: Send complete manuscript with cover letter. SASE. Simultaneous, photocopied and reprint submissions OK. Accepts computer printout submissions. Sample copy for $1 per issue includes postage.
Payment: Pays contributor's copies.
Terms: Acquires one-time rights.

‡NEXUS (II), Wright State University, 006 University Center, Dayton OH 45435. (513)873-2031. Editor: Chris Rue. Magazine: 8½x11; 90-140 pages; good coated paper; heavy perfect-bound cover; b&w illustrations and photography. "International arts and literature for those interested." 3 times per year. Circ. 2,000.
Needs: Contemporary, experimental, literary, regional, translations. No sci-fi, western, romance. Receives 25-30 unsolicited mss/month. Accepts 2-3 mss/issue; 6-10 mss/year. Does not read mss June-Sept. Publishes ms 2-6 months after acceptance. Recently reprinted Alain Robbe Grillet and Stuart Dybek (audial reading). Length: 4,000 words average; 500 words minimum; 7,500 words maximum. Publishes short shorts of any length. Sometimes critiques rejected mss and recommends other markets.
How to Contact: Send complete manuscript with cover letter including "any previous publishers of your work. *Do Not* explain anything about the story." Reports in 2 weeks on queries; 1-2 months on mss. SASE. Simultaneous, photocopied and reprint submissions OK. Sample copy for $4, 10×13 SAE and 5 first class stamps. Fiction guidelines for #10 SAE and 1 first class stamp.
Payment: Pays contributor's copies.
Terms: Acquires first North American serial rights.
Advice: "Simplicity and a perfection of style (description, simile, dialogue) always make a lasting impression. Good, careful translations receive favored readings."

‡NIGHT OWL'S NEWSLETTER (II, IV), Julian Associates, 6831 Spencer Hwy., #203, Pasadena TX 77505. (713)930-1481. Editor: Debbie Jordan. Newsletter: 8½×11; 16 pages; 20 lb. copy paper; cartoons. A newsletter for "night owls—people who can't sleep through much of the hours between midnight and 6 a.m. and usually want to sleep late in the morning." Quarterly. Estab. 1990.
Needs: Excerpted novel, experimental, fantasy, humor/satire, literary. "All variations must relate to the subject of night owls. No erotica." Accepts 1-2 mss/issue; 4-10 mss/year. Publishes ms 3-9 months after acceptance. Recently published work by Michael Thibodeaux. Length: 500-700 words preferred; 250 words minimum; 1,000 words maximum. Publishes short shorts. Critiques or comments on rejected mss. Recommends other markets.
How to Contact: Send complete ms with cover letter. Include short bio and credits. Reports in 1 month. SASE. Simultaneous, photocopied, reprint and computer printout submissions OK. Accepts electronic submissions. Sample copy for $3.50. Fiction guidelines for #10 SAE and 1 first-class stamp.
Payment: Pays $1 minimum plus 2 contributor's copies; charges for extras.
Terms: Buys first North American serial rights.
Advice: "We are most interested in a humorous and intelligent approach to the problem of people not being able to get to sleep or stay asleep at night and/or unable to wake up in the morning. This means the writer must understand the problem and have information to help others (besides suggesting drugs, alcohol or sex) or offer humorous support."

NIGHT SLIVERS (I,IV), A Journal of Nocturnal Pain, P.O. Box 389, Mt. Prospect IL 60056. Editor: Patricia Kocis. Publisher: Kevin Kocis. Magazine: 5½ × 8½; 60-80 pages; 20 lb paper; 60 lb cover; some illustrations. Publishes "short-short stories of horror and pain, like a sliver evokes pain—thus, the title." Semiannually. Estab. 1988. Circ. 200.
Needs: Experimental, horror, literary, psychic/supernatural/occult. "Our main interest is horror; therefore, any other fiction category must centralize around a horrific theme. We are also in literary and experimental horror, though these are difficult to write. No revenge, monsters, slasher, cannibalism, child situations, blatant religious (including satanism) and racism." Receives 30-60 unsolicited mss/month. Buys 15-20 mss/issue; 45-60 mss/year. Publishes ms 6 months-1 year after acceptance. Length: 800 words preferred; 100 words minimum; 1,000 words maximum. Publishes short shorts. Sometimes critiques rejected mss and recommends other markets.
How to Contact: Send complete ms with cover letter. Cover letter should include "informal bio, credits, interests (personal and literary)." Reports in 2 weeks on queries; 1 month on mss. SASE. Photocopied submissions OK. Sample copy for $4.50 postpaid. Fiction guidelines for #10 SAE and 1 first class stamp.
Payment: Pays $5. Two free contributor's copies; charge for extras.
Terms: Pays on publication for first North American serial rights.
Advice: "Read all the literary greats—Hemingway, Updike, Steinbeck, along with the great writers of short horror—Bradbury, Etchison, Matheson, Barker. Since there isn't a lot of time or space to produce strong characterization in a short-short, mood and feeling are important. Think about that before you write. Be brief, neat and professional."

‡NIGHTSUN, Department of English, Frostburg State University, Frostburg MD 21532. Co-Editors: Doug DeMars and Barbara Wilson. Magazine: 5½ × 8½; 120 pages; acid free paper; varied cover stock; illustrations; photos sometimes. "Although *Nightsun* is now primarily a poetry journal, we are still looking for excellent short-short fiction (5-6 pgs. maximum)." Annually. Estab. 1981. Circ. 500-1,000 (varying).
How to Contact: Send inquiry with SASE. Accepts computer printout submissions. Reports in 3 months. Sample copy $6.95.
Payment: Pays 1 free contributor's copy.
Terms: Acquires one-time rights (rights revert to author after publication).

NIMROD (II), International Literary Journal, Arts & Humanities Council of Tulsa, 2210 S. Main, Tulsa OK 74114. Editor-in-Chief: Francine Ringold. Magazine: 6 × 9; 160 pages; 60 lb white paper; illustrations; photos. "We publish one thematic issue and one awards issue each year. A recent theme was *From the Soviets,* a compilation of poetry, prose and fiction from and about many of the diverse cultures in the Soviet Union." We seek vigorous, imaginative, quality writing." Published semiannually. Estab. 1956. Circ. 2,000+.
Needs: "We accept contemporary poetry and/or prose. May submit adventure, ethnic, experimental, prose poem, science fiction or translations." Receives 120 unsolicited fiction mss/month. Published work by Sharon Sakson and Anita Noble; published new writers within the last year. Length: 7,500 words maximum.
How to Contact: Reports in 3 weeks-3 months. Sample copy: "to see what *Nimrod* is all about, send $5.90. Be sure to request an awards issue."
Payment: 3 free contributor's copies.
Terms: Acquires one-time rights.
Advice: "Read the magazine. Write well. Be courageous. No superfluous words. No clichés. Keep it tight but let your imagination flow. Read the magazine. Strongly encourage writers to send #10 SASE for brochure. Rules are fairly explicit. Disqualification a possiblility if procedures not followed." Annual literary contest. Send #10 (business-size) SASE for full contest details.

NO IDEA MAGAZINE (I), P.O. Box 14636, Gainesville FL 32604-4636. Editors: Var Thëlin and Sarah Dyer. Magazine: 8½ × 11; 64 pages, 16 four-color pages; 37 lb newsprint; illustrations and photographs. Each issue comes with a hard-vinyl 7-inch record. "Mostly underground/punk/hardcore music and interviews, but we like delving into other art forms as well. We publish what we feel is good—be it silly or moving." Sporadically. Estab. 1985.
Needs: Adventure, contemporary, experimental, fantasy, horror, humor/satire, science fiction, suspense/mystery. "Humor of a strange, odd manner is nice. We're very open." Receives 5-10 mss/month. Publishes ms up to 6 months after acceptance. Publishes mostly short shorts. Length: 1-6 pages typed.

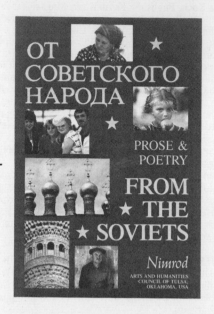

According to Nimrod editor Francine Ringold, these photographs were featured on the "From the Soviets" issue because "they all represent different republics or areas of the Soviet Union, and convey an immediate visual representation on the cover of what is contained inside." Copyright © 1990 Nimrod.

How to Contact: Send complete manuscript with cover letter. Photocopied submissions OK. Accepts computer printout submissions. Sample copy $3. Checks to Var Thëlin.
Payment: Pays in contributor's copies.
Terms: Acquires one-time rights.
Advice: "A query with $3 will get you a sample of our latest issue and answers to any questions asked. Just because we haven't included a writer's style of work before doesn't mean we won't print their work. Perhaps we've never been exposed to their style before."

THE NOCTURNAL LYRIC (I), Box 2602, Pasadena CA 91102-2602. (818)796-4801. Editor: Susan Ackerman. Digest: 5½×8½; 22 pages; illustrations. "We are a non-profit literary journal, dedicated to printing fiction by new writers for the sole purpose of getting read by people who otherwise might have never seen their work." Bimonthly. Estab. 1987. Circ. 150.
Needs: Experimental, fantasy, horror, humor/satire, psychic/supernatural/occult, science fiction, poetry, suspense/mystery. "We will give priority to unusual, creative pieces." Receives approx. 50 unsolicited mss/month. Publishes ms 4-8 months after acceptance. Publishes short shorts. Length: no more than 8 double-spaced typed pages.
How to Contact: Send complete ms with cover letter. Cover letter should include "something about the author, what areas of fiction he/she is interested in." Reports in 1 week on queries; 4-6 weeks on mss. SASE. Simultaneous, photocopied and reprint submissions OK. Accepts computer printout submissions. Sample copy $1.25 (checks made out to Susan Ackerman, editor). Fiction guidelines for #10 SAE and 1 first class stamp.
Terms: Publication not copyrighted. Pays neither in cash nor contributor's copies.
Advice: "We are not really impressed by the stories found in current fiction magazines. They seem to be too mainstream—too ordinary. We are saddened that writers who write from their soul are frequently rejected because their material is too controversial—or not too 'commercial.' Be as original and creative as you can be—search the depths of your being for an unusual way of expressing a story that has meaning for you. This will truly impress us."

‡NOMOS (II, IV), Studies in Spontaneous Order, Nomos Press, Inc., 257 Chesterfield, Glen Ellyn IL 60137. (708)858-7184. Editor: Carol B. Low. 8½×11; 32 pages; original illustrations. "Essays, poems, fiction, letters relating to Libertarian concepts and culture for a Libertarian audience." Quarterly. Estab. 1982. Circ. 450 paid; 1,000 total.

Needs: Historical (general), humor/satire, science fiction, suspense/mystery. "We are a strictly hard-core Libertarian magazine and only consider relevant fiction. Reviews of novels also accepted." Receives 1 unsolicited ms/month. Accepts 1 ms/issue; 4 mss/year. Publishes ms 4-8 months after acceptance. Length: 500-2,000 words average; 2,000 words maximum. Publishes short shorts. Occasionally critiques rejected mss.
How to Contact: Send complete manuscript with cover letter. Reports in 5-6 months on mss. SASE. Photocopied submissions OK. Accepts computer printout submissions. Accepts electronic submissions. Sample copy $3. Fiction guidelines for #10 SAE.
Payment: Choice of free subscription to magazine or contributor's copies.
Terms: Acquires one-time rights. Sends galleys or letter detailing edits or desired corrections to author.

THE NORTH AMERICAN REVIEW, University of Northern Iowa, Cedar Falls IA 50614. Editor: Robley Wilson. Publishes quality fiction. Quarterly. Estab. 1815. Circ. 4,500.
Needs: "We print quality fiction of any length and/or subject matter. Excellence is the only criterion." Reads fiction *only* from Jan. 1 to March 31. Published new writers (about 25%) within the last year. No preferred length.
How to Contact: Send complete ms with SASE. Reports in 2-3 months. Sample copy $3.50.
Payment: Approximately $10/printed page. 2 free author's copies. $3.50 charge for extras.
Terms: Pays on acceptance for first North American serial rights.
Advice: "We stress literary excellence and read 3,000 manuscripts a year to find an average of 35 stories that we publish. Please *read* the magazine first."

THE NORTH AMERICAN VOICE OF FATIMA (II), Barnabite Fathers, 1023 Swan Rd., Youngstown NY 14174-0167. (716)754-7489. Editor: Rev. Paul M. Keeling, C.R.S.P. Marian Magazine fostering devotion to Mary, the Mother of God. Bimonthly. Estab. 1961. Circ. 3,000.
Needs: Religious/inspirational. Recently published work by Starlette L. Howard. Length: 1,000 words average.
How to Contact: Send complete ms with SASE. Reports in 1 month on ms. Sample copy free.
Payment: 2¢/word.
Terms: Pays on publication.

‡**NORTH ATLANTIC REVIEW (II),** North Eagle Corp. of NY, 15 Arbutus Ln., Stony Brook NY 11790. (516)751-7886. Editor: John Gill. Fiction Editor: Carolyn McGrath. Magazine: 7 × 9; 200 pages; glossy cover. "Sixties and general interest." Estab. 1989. Circ. 500.
Needs: "General fiction and fiction about the sixties—1960-1975—JFK, Vietnam, RFK, King, Kent State, etc." Has published special fiction issue. Accepts 12 mss/issue; 25 mss/year. Publishes ms 6-10 months after acceptance. Length: 3,000-7,000 words average. Publishes short shorts. Sometimes critiques rejected ms and recommends other markets.
How to Contact: Send complete manuscript with cover letter. Reports in 4-6 months on queries. SASE. Simultaneous and photocopied submissions OK. Accepts computer printout submissions. Sample copy for $7 and SAE. Fiction guidelines $7.

NORTH DAKOTA QUARTERLY (II), University of North Dakota, Box 8237, University Station, Grand Forks ND 58202. (701)777-3321. Editor: Robert W. Lewis. Fiction Editor: William Borden. Magazine: 6 × 9; 200 pages; bond paper; illustrations; photos. Magazine publishing "essays in humanities; some short stories; some poetry." University audience. Quarterly. Estab. 1910. Circ. 600.
Needs: Contemporary, ethnic, experimental, feminist, historical (general), humor/satire and literary. Receives 15-20 unsolicited mss/month. Accepts 2 mss/issue; 8 mss/year. Recently published work by Jerry Bumpus, Dusty Sklar, Daniel Curley; published new writers within the last year. Length: 3,000-4,000 words average. Sometimes critiques rejected mss.
How to Contact: Send complete ms with cover letter. "But they need not be much more than hello; please read this story; I've published (if so, best examples) . . ." SASE. Reports in 3 months. Publishes ms an average of 6-8 months after acceptance. Sample copy $5.
Payment: 5 contributor's copies; 20% discount for extras; year's subscription.
Terms: Acquires one-time rights.
Advice: "We may publish a higher average number of stories in the future—3 rather than 2. Read widely. Write, write; revise, revise."

THE NORTHERN REVIEW (II, IV), University of Wisconsin-Stevens Point, 018 LRC, Stevens Point WI 54481. (715)346-3568. Editor: Richard Behm. Fiction Editor: Lawrence Watson. Magazine: 7×8½; 48 pages; b&w photos. Semiannually. Estab. 1987. Circ. 1,000.
Needs: Essays, literary, regional. Receives 25 unsolicited fiction mss/month. Accepts 4 mss/issue; 2 mss/year. Publishes ms 6-18 months after acceptance. Recently published work by Jack Driscoll, Nancy Lord, Dinty Moore. Length: 2,000 words average. Publishes short shorts. Sometimes critiques rejected mss.
How to Contact: Send complete ms with cover letter. Reports in 1 month. SASE. Accepts computer printouts. Sample copy $4.
Payment: Pays in contributor's copies.

NORTHLAND QUARTERLY (II,IV), Salt River Publishing Services, 1522 E. Southern Ave. Box 2161, Tempe AZ 85282. Editor: Jody Wallace. Magazine: 5×8; approx. 100-125 pages; 60 lb offset paper; 10 pt cover stock; b&w illustrations; line drawings; cover photos. "Contemporary writing for discriminating reader. Short fiction, poetry, commentary and reviews. International publication, with emphasis on writers in upper-tier states and Canada. *Quarterly* features politically oriented writings, as well as regional writers and contemporary fiction from throughout US." Quarterly. Estab. 1987.
Needs: Condensed/excerpted novel, contemporary, feminist, literary, mainstream, regional, romance, serialized novel, progressive issues, political fiction. No religious, young romance. Receives 20-40 mss/month. Accepts 3-5 mss/issue. Publishes ms within 3-6 months of acceptance. Published work by Robert Flaum, Marcella Taylor, Robert Funge. Length: 1,500 words minimum; 4,000 words maximum. Publishes short shorts. Length: 300 words minimum. Sometimes critiques rejected mss and recommends other markets.
How to Contact: Query first, query with clips of published work or send complete ms with cover letter, which should include "general description of work, genre. Other places submitted, if any." Reports on queries in 2-3 weeks; in 3-4 weeks on mss. SASE. Simultaneous, photocopied and some reprint submissions OK. Accepts computer printout submissions. Accepts electronic submissions via disk. Sample copy for $4, 5×8 SAE and 4 first class stamps. Fiction guidelines for #10 SAE and 1 first class stamp.
Payment: Pays in contributor's copies.
Terms: Sends galleys to author if requested. Sponsors awards for fiction and poetry writers. "Write for information."
Advice: Looks for "contemporary, adult fiction of high quality. We adopt an unprejudiced, open attitude for all manuscripts submitted, and have published world-class writers as well as beginners."

‡THE NORTHWEST GAY & LESBIAN READER (I, IV), Art, Opinion and Literature, Beyond the Closet Bookstore, 1501 Belmont Ave., Seattle WA 98122. (206)322-4609. Editor: Ron Whiteaker. Tabloid: 11x17; 16 pages; newsprint paper, illustrations, photographs. "A wide range of formats reflecting the gay/lesbian/bisexual experience." Bimonthly. Estab. 1989. Circ. 4,000.
Needs: Gay, lesbian, bisexual. "Light erotica OK. No hard-core erotica, or 'abusive attitude' fiction." Receives 2 unsolicited mss/month. Accepts 1 ms/issue. Publishes ms 2 months after acceptance. Recently published work by William Freeberg, Aubrey Hart Sparks, Jill Sunde. Length: 2,000 words preferred; 1,000 words minimum; 3,000 words maximum. Publishes short shorts.
How to Contact: Send complete ms with cover letter. Include "a bit about the story and its author." Reports in 2 weeks on queries; 2 months on mss. SASE. Photocopied submissions OK. Accepts electronic submissions—IBM compatible disk in generic (ASCII) word processing format. Sample copy for 75 cents, 9x12 SAE and 3 first-class stamps. Fiction guidelines for #10 SAE and 1 first class stamp.
Payment: Pays in contributor's copies and free subscription.
Terms: Acquires one-time rights.
Advice: "A story that is clever and well-written and contains original ideas is considered first, rather than the hackneyed, over-done story lines containing redundant dogma and irritating buzzwords. Reflect the gay/lesbian/bisexual experience."

NORTHWEST REVIEW (II), 369 PLC, University of Oregon, Eugene OR 97403. (503)346-3957. Editor: John Witte. Fiction Editor: Cecelia Hagen. Magazine: 6×9; 140-160 pages; coated paper; high quality cover stock; illustrations; photos. "A general literary review featuring poems, stories, essays and reviews, circulated nationally and internationally. For a literate audience in avant-garde as well as traditional literary forms; interested in the important younger writers who have not yet achieved their readership." Published 3 times/year. Estab. 1957. Circ. 1,200.

Needs: Literary, contemporary, feminist, translations and experimental. Accepts 4-5 mss/issue, 12-15 mss/year. Receives approximately 100 unsolicited fiction mss each month. Recently published work by Susan Stark, Madison Smartt Bell, Maria Flook, Charles Marvin. Published new writers within the last year. Length: "Mss longer than 40 pages are at a disadvantage." Critiques rejected mss when there is time. Sometimes recommends other markets.

How to Contact: Send complete ms with SASE. "No simultaneous submissions are considered." Accepts computer printout submissions; prefers letter-quality. Reports in 3-4 months. Sample copy $3.

Payment: 3 free author's copies. 40% discount.

Terms: Acquires first rights.

Advice: "Persist. Copy should be clean, double-spaced, with generous margins. Careful proofing for spelling and grammar errors will reduce slowing of editorial process." Mss are rejected because of "unconvincing characters, overblown language, melodramatic plot, poor execution."

‡NORTHWEST WRITERS, PHOTOGRAPHERS AND DESIGN ARTISTS (II), Northwest Publishers, #801, 1011 Boren Ave., Seattle WA 98104. Editor: William L. Brown, Jr.. Fiction Editor: Kay Kinghammer. Magazine: 8½ × 11; 28-36 pages; Topkot paper; Topkit cover; illustrations and photographs. "Fiction, poetry, photographic layouts, illustrations, articles on the creative process for the reading public, photographers and artists." Quarterly.

Needs: Adventure, condensed/excerpted novel, contemporary, ethnic, experimental, fantasy, horror, humor/satire, literary, prose poem, psychic/supernatural/occult, romance (contemporary), science fiction, serialized novel, suspense/mystery, translations. Nothing religious, children stories, heavy political. Receives 10-15 unsolicited mss/month. Buys 3-6 mss/issue. Publishes ms 1 year after acceptance. Recently published work by Diane Mapps, Kay Kinghammer. Length: 3,500 words average. Publishes short shorts. Rarely (for a fee) critiques rejected mss.

How to Contact: Send complete manuscript with cover letter. Reports in 3 months on mss. SASE. Photocopied and reprint submissions OK. Accepts computer printout submissions. Sample copy $3 each with 9 × 12 SAE and $1 postage. Fiction guidelines for #10 SAE and 1 first class stamp.

Payment: Pays $150 maximum plus contributor's copies. Charge for extras.

Terms: Pays on publication for one-time rights.

‡NOSTOC MAGAZINE (II), Arts End Books, Box 162, Newton MA 02168. Editor: Marshall Brooks. Magazine: size varies; 60 lb book paper; illustrations; photos. Biannually. Estab. 1973. Circ. 300.

Needs: "We are open-minded." Receives approximately 15 unsolicited fiction mss each month. Published new writers within the last year. Publishes short shorts. Prefers brief word length. Frequently critiques rejected mss and recommends other markets.

How to Contact: Query. SASE for ms. Reports in 1 week on queries, 2-3 weeks on mss, ideally. Sample copy $2.50. Send SASE for catalog.

Payment: Modest payment.

Terms: Sends galleys to author. Rights revert to author.

Advice: "We tend to publish *short* short stories that are precise and lyrical. Recently, we have been publishing *short* short story collections by one author, which are issued as a separate number of the magazine. We are always on the outlook for new material for these small collections. We publish fiction because of the high quality; quite simply, we believe that good writing deserves publication."

NOTEBOOK/CNADERNO: A LITERARY JOURNAL (II, IV), Esoterica Press, Box 170, Barstow CA 92312-0170. Editor: Ms. Yoly Zentella. Magazine: 5½ × 8½; 100 pages; bond paper; 90 lb cover stock; illustrations. "Accepting fiction and nonfiction. *Notebook*'s emphasis is on history, culture, art and literary critique and travel pieces. For ages 25-50, writers, artists, educators, some academia." Semiannually. Publishes special ethnic issues, e.g. Native American, Pacific, Asian. Estab. 1985. Circ. 100, "including many libraries."

Needs: Ethnic, (focusing especially on Chicano and Latino American pieces in English and Spanish), historical (Latino American, European and Muslim), humor/satire, literary, regional. "One yearly issue featured exclusively Chicano and Latino American writers, and we need black-American writers." Absolutely no explicit sex or obscenities accepted, but tasteful eroticism considered. Receives approximately 20-25 unsolicited fiction mss/month. Published work by Jan Beastrom, R. Ivanov Rehez, Tom Lane; published new writers within the last year. Length: 2,000 words average; 2,500 words maximum. Sometimes critiques rejected mss.

How to Contact: Send complete ms with cover letter and short biography. Reports in 2 weeks on queries; 1-2 months on mss. Always SASE for ms and correspondence. Accepts computer printouts. Sample copy $6 plus $1 p/h. Expects contributor to subcribe, or buy subscription for a Library of their choice. Make checks payable to Yoly Zentella. Fiction guidelines for #10 SAE and 1 first class stamp.
Payment: 1 free contributor's copy, charges for extras.
Terms: Acquires first North American serial rights. "Rights revert to author upon publication."
Advice: "We are now planning more fiction in our issues and less poetry. We are also considering novellas for publication, appearing exclusively in one issue." Planning an issue dealing exclusively with the African influence on the American (North and South) continents.

NOW & THEN (IV), Center for Appalachian Studies and Services, East Tennessee State University, Box 19180A, Johnson City TN 37614-0002. (615)929-5348. Editor: Pat Arnow. Magazine: 8½ × 11; 36-52 pages; coated paper and cover stock; illustrations; photographs. Publication focuses on Appalachian culture, present and past. Readers are mostly people in the region involved with Appalachian issues, literature, education." 3 issues/year. Estab. 1984. Circ. 880.
Needs: Ethnic, literary, regional, serialized/excerpted novel, prose poem, spiritual and sports. "Absolutely has to relate to Appalachian theme. Can be about adjustment to new environment, themes of leaving and returning, for instance. Nothing unrelated to region." Accepts 2-3 mss/issue. Publishes ms 3-4 months after acceptance. Published work by Gurney Norman, Lance Olsen, George Ella Lyon; published new writers within the last year. Length: 3,000 words maximum. Publishes short shorts.
How to Contact: Send complete ms with cover letter. Reports in 3 months. Include "information we can use for contributer's note." SASE. Simultaneous and photocopied submissions OK. Accepts computer printout submissions. Sample copy $3.50.
Payment: Pays up to $50 per story, contributor's copies, one year subscription.
Terms: Buys first-time rights.
Advice: "We're emphasizing Appalachian culture, which is not often appreciated because analysts are so busy looking at the trouble of the region. We're doing theme issues. Beware of stereotypes. In a regional publication like this one we get lots of them, both good guys and bad guys: salt of the earth to poor white trash. Sometimes we get letters that offer to let us polish up the story. We prefer the author does that him/herself." Send for list of upcoming themes.

NRG (II), Skydog Press, 6735 SE 78th, Portland OR 97206. Editor: Dan Raphael. Magazine/tabloid: 11 × 17; 20 pages; electrobrite paper; illustrations; photos. For the "creative and curious." Theme is "open-ended, energized, non-linear emphasis on language and sounds"; material is "spacial, abstract, experimental." Semiannually. Estab. 1976. Circ. 1,000.
Needs: Contemporary, experimental, literary and prose poem. Receives 8 unsolicited mss/month. Accepts 6 mss/issue; 11 mss/year. Recently published work by S.P. Stressman, Willie Smith, Don Webb. Length: 1,000 words average; 3,000 words maximum. Occasionally critiques rejected mss.
How to Contact: Send complete ms with SASE and cover letter stating where you learned of magazine; list of 3-5 previous publications. See copy of magazine. Reports in 1 month on mss. Simultaneous and photocopied submissions OK. Accepts computer printout submissions. Publishes ms an average of 1 year after acceptance. Sample copy $1.50. "Best guideline is sample copy."
Payment: Pays in free contributor's copies only, ½ cover price charge for extras.
Terms: Acquires one-time rights.
Advice: "I'm trying to get more fiction, but am strict in my editorial bias. I don't want it to add up or be purely representational. Energy must abound in the language, or the spaces conjured. Forget what you were taught. Let the story tell you."

NUCLEAR FICTION (II,V), 2518 Leon St., #107, Austin TX 78705. (512)478-7262. Editor: Brian Martin. Magazine. "A bi-monthly magazine of sci-fi, fantasy and horror. Includes film and book reviews." Estab. 1988.
Needs: Horror, fantasy and science fiction. Film and book reviews. Length: Open.
How to Contact: Send complete ms with cover letter. Reports in 2-4 weeks on average. Sample copy $3.
Payment: Pays ¼¢/word. (Minimum payment $5.)
Terms: Pays on acceptance; buys first North American serial rights for fiction, all rights for reviews.
Advice: "*Nuclear Fiction* strives to present a wide range of studies in a variety of styles. The traditionalist and the experimentalist will each find a home in *Nuclear Fiction*. Film and book reviews are an excellent way to break into *Nuclear Fiction*."

‡**LA NUEZ (II, IV)**, P.O. Box 1655, New York NY 10276. (212)260-3130. Editor: Rafael Bordao. Magazine: 8½×11; 32 pages; 60 lb. offset paper; glossy cover; illustrations and photographs. *"Spanish language* literary magazine (poetry, short fiction, criticism, reviews) for anyone who reads Spanish and loves poetry and literature. Many of our readers are professors, writers, critics and artists. Quarterly. Estab. 1988. Circ. 1,000.
Needs: Spanish only. Literary. "Nothing more than 6 pages. No political or religious themes." Publishes "very few" mss/issue, "because of space limitations." Publishes ms 3-6 months after acceptance. Length: 6 pages or less. Publishes short shorts.
How to Contact: Send complete ms with cover letter and short bio, SASE. Reports in 6-8 weeks. Sample copy for $3.50. Fiction guidelines for #10 SAE and 1 first-class stamp.
Payment: Pays 2 contributor's copies.
Advice: Publication's philosophy is "to publish the high quality poetry and literature in Spanish of writers from the rich diversity of cultures, communities and countries in the Spanish-speaking world."

OBSIDIAN II: BLACK LITERATURE IN REVIEW (II, IV), Dept. of English, North Carolina State University, Raleigh NC 27695-8105. (919)737-3870. Editor: Gerald Barrax. Fiction Editor: Linda Beatrice Brown. Magazine: 6×9; approx. 130 pages. "Creative works in English by Black writers, scholarly critical studies by all writers on Black literature in English." Published 3 times/year (spring, summer and winter). Estab. 1975. Circ. 500.
Needs: Ethnic (pan-African), feminist. No poetry, fiction or drama mss not written by Black writers. Accepts 7-9 mss/year. Published new writers within the last year. Length: 1,500-10,000 words.
How to Contact: Send complete ms in duplicate with SASE. Reports in 3 months. Publishes ms an average of 4-6 months after acceptance. Sample copy $5.
Payment: Pays in contributor's copies.
Terms: Acquires one-time rights. Sponsors contests occasionally; guidelines published in magazine.

THE OHIO REVIEW (II), 209C Ellis Hall, Ohio University, Athens OH 45701-2979. (614)593-1900. Editor: Wayne Dodd. Assistant Editor: Robert Kinsley. Magazine: 6×9; 144 pages; illustrations on cover. "We attempt to publish the best poetry and fiction written today. For a mainly literary audience." Triannually. Estab. 1971. Circ. 2,000.
Needs: Contemporary, experimental, literary. "We lean toward contemporary on all subjects." Receives 150-200 unsolicited fiction mss/month. Accepts 3 mss/issue. Does not read mss June 1-August 31. Publishes ms 6 months after acceptance. Agented fiction: 1%. Sometimes critiques rejected mss and/or recommends other markets.
How to Contact: Query first or send complete ms with cover letter. Reports in 6 weeks. SASE. Photocopied submissions OK. Accepts computer printouts. Sample copy $4.25. Fiction guidelines free for #10 SASE.
Payment: Pays $5/page, free subscription to magazine, 2 contributor's copies.
Terms: Pays on publication for first North American serial rights. Sends galleys to author.
Advice: "We feel the short story is an important part of the contemporary writing field and value it highly. Read a copy of our publication to see if your fiction is of the same quality. So often people send us work that simply doesn't fit our needs."

OLD HICKORY REVIEW (II), Jackson Writers Group, Box 1178, Jackson TN 38302. (901)424-3277 or (901)664-5959. Editor: Edna Lackie. Fiction Editors: Dorothy Stanfill and Donald Phillips. Magazine: 8½×11; approx. 90 pages. "Usually two short stories and 75-80 poems—nothing obscene or in poor taste. For a family audience." Semiannually. Plans special fiction issue. Estab. 1969. Circ. 300.
Needs: Contemporary, experimental, fantasy, literary, mainstream. Receives 4-5 unsolicited fiction mss/month. Accepts 2 mss/issue; 4 mss/year. Publishes ms no more than 3-4 months after acceptance. Length: 2,500-3,000 words. Publishes short shorts. Sometimes critiques rejected mss and recommends other markets.
How to Contact: Send complete ms with cover letter, which should include "credits." Reports on queries in 2-3 weeks; on mss in 1-2 months. SASE. Photocopied submissions OK. Accepts computer printouts. Sample copy available. Fiction guidelines free for SAE.
Payment: Pays in contributor's copies; charge for extras. Sponsors contests for fiction writers, "advertised in literary magazine and with flyers."
Advice: "We are tired of war, nursing homes, abused children, etc. We are looking for things which are more entertaining. No pornographic fiction, no vile language. Our publication goes into schools, libraries, etc."

Editor Jo Anne Starnes says this cover "reflects our unusual title, but does not necessarily reflect the work inside — which includes poetry, fiction and art of all types and subjects." Genna Carstarphen, former art editor of The Old Red Kimono created this cover. Copyright © Genna Carstarphen.

THE OLD RED KIMONO (II), Box 1864, Rome GA 30162. (404)295-6312. Editors: Jo Anne Starnes and Jonathan Hershey. Magazine: 8×11; 65-70 pages; white offset paper; 10 pt. board cover stock. Annually. Estab. 1974. Circ. 1,000.
Needs: Literary. "We will consider good fiction regardless of category." Receives 20-30 mss/month. Buys 2-4 mss/issue. Does not read mss April-September. "Issue out in May every year." Recently published work by John Morrison, Hubert Whitlow, Jeanne Cunningham. Length: 2,000-3,000 words preferred; 5,000 words maximum. Publishes short shorts. "We prefer short fiction."
How to Contact: Send complete ms with cover letter. Reports in 2 weeks on queries; 4-5 weeks on mss. SASE. Photocopied submissions OK. Accepts computer printout submissions. Sample copy for $2, 8×11 SAE and 4 first class stamps. Fiction guidelines for #10 SAE and 1 first class stamp.
Payment: Pays in contributor's copies.
Terms: Acquires first rights.

‡ONCE UPON A WORLD (II), Route 1, Box 110A, Nineveh IN 46164. Editor: Emily Alward. Magazine: 8½×11; 80-100 pages; standard white paper; colored card stock cover; pen & ink illustrations. "A science fiction and fantasy magazine with emphasis on alternate-world cultures and stories of idea, character and interaction. Also publishes book reviews and a few poems for an adult audience, primarily readers of science fiction and fantasy." Annually. Estab. 1988. Circ. 100.
Needs: Fantasy, science fiction. "No realistic" stories in contemporary settings; horror; stories using Star Trek or other media characters; stories with completely negative endings." Receives 20 unsolicited mss/month. Accepts 8-12 mss/issue; per year "varies, depending on backlog." Publishes ms from 2 months to 1½ years after acceptance. Recently published work by Janet Reedman and Mark Andrew Garland. Length: 3,000 words average; 400 words minimum; 10,000 words maximum. Publishes short shorts. Sometimes critiques rejected mss and recommends other markets.
How to Contact: Send complete manuscript with $1 reading fee. Reports in 2-4 weeks on queries; 2-16 weeks on mss. SASE. Photocopied submissions OK. Accepts computer printout submissions. Sample copy $8. Fiction guidelines for #10 SAE and 1 first class stamp.
Payment: Pays contributor's copies.
Terms: Acquires first rights. "Stories copyrighted in author's name; copyrights not registered."
Advice: "Besides a grasp of basic fiction technique, you'll need some familiarity with the science fiction and fantasy genres. We suggest reading some of the following authors whose work is similar to what we're looking for: Isaac Asimov, Poul Anderson, Norman Spinrad, David Brin, Anne McCaffrey, Marion Zimmer Bradley, Mercedes Lackey, Katharine Kimbriel."

‡ONIONHEAD (II), Literary Quarterly, Arts on the Park, Inc., 115 N. Kentucky Ave., Lakeland FL 33801. (813)680-2787. Editors: Charles Kersey, Dennis Nesheim, Dudley Uphoff. Editorial Assistant: Lavonne Nesheim. Magazine: digest-size; 48 pages; 20 lb. bond; glossy card cover. "Provocative political, social and cultural observations and hypotheses for a literary audience – an open-minded audience." Estab. 1989. Circ. 250.

Needs: Contemporary, ethnic, experimental, feminist, gay, humor/satire, lesbian, literary, prose poem, regional. "Must have a universal point (International)." Publishes short fiction in each issue. Receives 100-150 unsolicited titles/month. Acquires approximately 28 mss/issue; 100 titles (these numbers include: poetry, short prose and essays)/year. Publishes ms within 18 months of acceptance. Recently published work by Marilyn Trail, Mary Jane Ryals, Harriet Calkins, Jack Matthews, Ann Miller Fadley, Tim Coats. Length: 3,000 words average; 4,000 words maximum. Publishes short shorts. Recommends other markets.

How to Contact: Send complete manuscript with cover letter that includes brief bio and SASE. Reports in 2 weeks on queries; 2 months on mss. Photocopied submissions OK. Accepts computer printout submissions (prefer letter quality). Sample copy $3 postpaid. Fiction guidelines for #10 SAE and 1 first class stamp.

Payment: Pays in contributor's copy. Charge for extras.

Terms: Acquires first North American serial rights. "A short story competition is planned for 1991. Awards will be announced in October 1991. Guidelines available for SASE beginning January 1991."

Advice: "Review a sample copy of *Onionhead* and remember *literary quality* is the prime criterion. Avoid heavy-handed approaches to social commentary – be subtle, not didactic."

OREGON EAST (II, IV), Hoke College Center, EOSC, La Grande OR 97850. (503)963-1787. Editor: Angela Dierdorff. Magazine: 6×9; 80 pages; illustrations and photographs. "*Oregon East* prefers fiction about the Northwest. The majority of our issues go to the students of Eastern Oregon State College; staff, faculty and community members receive them also, and numerous high school and college libraries." Annually. Estab. 1950. Circ. 900.

Needs: Humor/satire, literary, prose poem, regional, translations. No juvenile/children's fiction. Receives 20 unsolicited mss/month. Accepts 3-6 mss/issue. Does not read April to August. Publishes ms an average of 5 months after acceptance. Published work by Ursula LeGuin, Madeline de Trees and George Venn. Published new writers within the last year. Length: 2,000 words average; 3,000 words maximum. Publishes short shorts. Sometimes critiques rejected mss.

How to Contact: Send complete mss with cover letter which should include name, address, brief bio. Reports in 1 week on queries; 3 months on mss. SASE. Photocopied submissions OK. Accepts computer printout submissions, no dot-matrix. Sample copy $5; fiction guidelines for #10 SASE.

Payment: 2 contributor's copies.

Terms: Rights revert to author.

Advice: "Follow our guidelines, please! Keep trying: we have limited space because we must publish 50% on-campus material. *Oregon East* has been around for almost 40 years, and it has always strived to represent the Northwest's great writers and artists, as well as several from around the world."

OTHER VOICES (II), 820 Ridge Rd., Highland Park IL 60035. (708)831-4684. Editors: Sharon Fiffer and Lois Hauselman. Magazine: 5⅞×9; 168-205 pages; 60 lb paper; coated cover stock; occasional photos. "Original, fresh, diverse stories and novel excerpts" for literate adults. Semiannually. Estab. 1985. Circ. 1,500.

Needs: Contemporary, experimental, humor/satire, literary, excerpted novel. No taboos, except ineptitude and murkiness. No fantasy, horror, juvenile, psychic/occult. Receives 45 unsolicited fiction mss/ month. Accepts 20-23 mss/issue. Publishes ms approx. 3-6 months after acceptance. Agented fiction: 40%. Published work by Barbara Lefcowitz, Susan B. Weston; published new writers within the last year. Length: 4,000 words average; 5,000 words maximum. Also publishes short shorts "if paired together" of 1,000 words. Only occasionally critiques rejected mss or recommends other markets.

How to Contact: Send mss with SASE or submit through agent. Cover letters "should be brief and list previous publications. Also, list title of submission. Most beginners' letters try to 'explain' the story – a big mistake." Reports in 10-12 weeks on mss. SASE. Photocopied submissions OK; no simultaneous submissions or reprints. Accepts computer printouts. Sample copy $5.90 (includes postage). Fiction guidelines for #10 SAE and 1 first class stamp.

Payment: Pays in contributor's copies and modest cash gratuity.

Terms: Acquires one-time rights.

Advice: "There are so *few* markets for *quality* fiction! We—by publishing 40-45 stories a year—provide new and established writers a forum for their work. Send us your best voice, your best work, your best best. Don't expect to earn a living at it—no matter how talented."

OTHER WORLDS (II), Science Fiction-Science Fantasy, Gryphon Publications, Box 209, Brooklyn NY 11228. Editor: Gary Lovisi. Magazine: 5×8; 40-60 pages; offset paper; card/color cover; illustrations and photographs. "Adventure—or action-oriented SF—stories that are fun to read." Annually. Estab. 1988. Circ. 300.

Needs: Science fiction. No high fantasy, sword and sorcery. Receives 6 unsolicited mss/month. Buys 2-4 mss/issue. Publishes ms 1-2 years (usually) after acceptance. Length: 3,000 words preferred; 2,000 words minimum; 4,000 words maximum. Publishes short shorts. Length: 500-1,000 words. Sometimes critiques rejected mss and recommends other markets.

How to Contact: Send complete ms with cover letter. Reports in 2 weeks on queries; 1 month on mss. SASE. Photocopied submissions OK. Accepts computer printout submissions. Sample copy $4. Free fiction guidelines.

Payment: Pays in contributor's copies.

Terms: Acquires first North American serial rights. Copyright reverts to author.

OUROBOROS (II), 3912 24th St., Rock Island IL 61201-6223. Editor and Publisher: Erskine Carter. Magazine: 6×9; 76 pages; 60 lb offset paper; 80 lb cover; b&w illustrations. "We publish fiction (short stories), poetry and art for thoughtful readers." Semiannually. Estab. 1985. Circ. 400.

Needs: Adventure, contemporary, experimental, fantasy, historical (general), horror, humor/satire, literary, mainstream, psychic/supernatural/occult, science fiction, suspense/mystery. "We are mainly interested in stories about people, in situations of conflict or struggle. We want to see *real* characters at odds with others, themselves, their universe. No racist/right-wing/anti-minority material." Receives 40-50 unsolicited mss/month. Accepts 8-10 mss/issue; 32-40 mss/year. Publishes ms 3 months to 1 year after acceptance. Published work by T.B. Ward, W. Sheidley, T. Angle; published new writers within the last year. Length: 2,500 words average; 3,500 words maximum. Publishes short shorts. Length: 500 words. Sometimes critiques rejected mss and recommends other markets.

How to Contact: Request guidelines and a sample copy. Reports in 2 weeks. SASE. Photocopied and reprint submissions OK. Accepts computer printout submissions. Sample copy of current issue $4.50. Back issues available.

Payment: Pays in contributor's copies.

Terms: Rights revert to author. Sends galleys to author.

Advice: "The beginning writer *can* break in here and learn valuable lessons about writing and publishing. Obtain a sample copy, write something you think will grab us, then submit. Get to know the markets. Don't waste time, energy and postage without researching."

‡OUT MAGAZINE (II, IV), YOU the Publications, Box 5, 359 Davenport Rd., Toronto, Ontario M5R 1K5 Canada. Editor: Shawn Venasse. Tabloid: 11×17; 16 pages; newsprint; illustrations and photographs. "*By* and *for gay men*—short fiction, essays, poetry, interviews, photos, illustrations for gay men, age 18-54." Bimonthly. Estab. 1986. Circ, 4,000+.

Needs: Gay, adventure, condensed/excerpted novel, erotica, ethnic, experimental, fantasy, historical (general), humor/satire, literary, prose poem, suspense/mystery, translations. "We are looking for 'original' bold, innovative, distinctive writing that both explores and celebrates the *gay male* spirit. We are not particularly interested in cliched work, i.e. 70's porn, 'coming out' stories (unless they are really good) nor AIDS stories (again, not unless they are exceptional)." Nothing homophobic, sexist, racist nor *porn* written in a cliched manner. Plans special fiction issue. Receives 10 unsolicited mss/month. Accepts 2 mss/issue; 12 mss/year. Publishes ms up to 2 months after acceptance. Agented fiction 10%. Recently published work by Peter Crossley, Jim Nason. Length: 1,500 words average; 1,000 words minimum; 2,000 words maximum. Publishes short shorts. Length: 400-500 words. Sometimes critiques rejected mss and recommends other markets.

How to Contact: Send complete manuscript with cover letter. Include bio material, intent of story, why writer chose *Out!* Reports in 2 weeks on queries; 4-6 weeks on mss. SASE. Photocopied submissions OK. Accepts computer printout submissions. Accepts electronic submissions via disk (Word Perfect 5.0 preferred). Sample copy $2.

Payment: Pays free subscription and contributor's copies.

Terms: Acquires one-time rights.

Advice: "We look for bold, innovative words coupled with a strong voice. A writer who is not afraid to challenge his readers. A strong visual/descriptive sense. 'Passionate, honest, thoughtful' — key words."

‡**OUTERBRIDGE (II)**, English A-323, The College of Staten Island (CUNY), 715 Ocean Terr., Staten Island NY 10301. (212)390-7654. Editor: Charlotte Alexander. Magazine: 5½ × 8½; approx. 110 pages; 60 lb white offset paper; 65 lb cover stock. "We are a national literary magazine publishing mostly fiction and poetry. To date, we have had three special focus issues (the 'urban' and the 'rural' experience, 'Southern'), 2 special 10th anniversary issues and a double issue for 1986-88 with 200 pages and 73 contributors ($8). For anyone with enough interest in literature to look for writing of quality and writers on the contemporary scene who deserve attention. There probably is a growing circuit of writers, some academics, reading us by recommendations." Annually. Estab. 1975. Circ. 500-700.

Needs: Literary. "No *Reader's Digest* style; that is, very popularly oriented. We like to do interdisciplinary features, e.g., literature and music, literature and science and literature and the natural world." Accepts 8-10 mss/year. Does not read in July or August. Recently published work by William Davey, Ron Berube, Patricia Ver Ellen; published new writers within the last year. Length: 10-25 pages. Sometimes recommends other markets.

How to Contact: Query. Send complete ms with cover letter. "Don't talk too much, 'explain' the work, or act apologetic or arrogant. If published, tell where, with a brief bio." SASE. Reports in 2 weeks on queries, 2 months on mss. Sample copy $5 for annual issue.

Payment: 2 free author's copies. Charges ½ price of current issue for extras to its authors.

Terms: Acquires one-time rights. Requests credits for further publication of material used by *OB*.

Advice: "Read our publication first. Don't send out blindly; get some idea of what the magazine might want. A *short* personal note with biography is appreciated. Competition is keen. Read an eclectic mix of classic and contemporary. Beware of untransformed autobiography, but *everything* in one's experience contributes."

OWLFLIGHT (I, IV), Magazine of Science Fiction and Fantasy, Unique Graphics, 1025 55th St., Oakland CA 94608. (415)655-3024. Editor: Millea Kenin. Magazine: 8½ × 11; 64-80 pages; 60 lb stock; b&w, line and half tone illustrations, and b&w photos. Magazine publishes "the full range of the science fiction/fantasy genre, for readers familiar with sf/fantasy." Irregularly published. Estab. 1980. Circ. 1,500.

Needs: Fantasy, science fiction. No horror. "We do not want to see anything *not* sf or fantasy, or anything racist, sexist or pro-war." Receives 100-200 unsolicited mss/month. Buys at least 10 mss/issue. Publishes ms up to 2 years after acceptance. Published work by Janet Fox, Ardath Mayhar, Eric M. Heidemann; published new writers in the last issue. Length: 6,000 words average; 2,500 words minimum; 8,000 words maximum (10 to 32 double-spaced pages — nothing that falls outside these limits will be considered, as different word-counting methods produce different copy-fitting results). Usually briefly critiques rejected mss. Sometimes recommends other markets.

How to Contact: "Never submit mss without querying (with SASE) for guidelines, *which tell what categories are open or overstocked.* Cover letter may include a brief background of the writer, but should never contain a long credit list nor a description of an enclosed story." Reports in 1 week on requested guidelines; 2-6 weeks on mss. SASE. Simultaneous, photocopied and reprint submissions OK. State whether ms is simultaneous submission. Accepts computer printout submissions, dot-matrix only if truly near letter quality. Sample copy $2.50; check must be payable to Unique Graphics. Fiction guidelines free with sample order; otherwise for #10 SASE.

Payment: Pays 1¢/word plus 3 free contributor's copies, charge for extras — ½ cover price.

Terms: Pays on acceptance for first North American serial rights or one-time rights. If total at 1¢/word is under $10, it is paid on acceptance; if over $10, a $10 deposit is paid on acceptance with the balance paid on publication.

Advice: "I recommend the top-down method: Send a story first to the biggest circulation, highest paying publication that is a relevant market. If it doesn't get picked out of the slush pile, send it to the relevant newsstand magazines, or original anthologies stated for commercial publicaton. If it still hasn't been accepted, send it to the small press. That's better than sticking it in a drawer. We'd love to see experimental work that stretches the limits of the genre, but not work that is outside it or work to which the sf elements are irrelevant."

OXFORD MAGAZINE (II), Bachelor Hall, Miami University, Oxford OH 45056. (513)529-5221. Magazine: 6×9; 85-100 pages; illustrations. Biannually. Estab. 1985. Circ. 500-1,000.
Needs: Ethnic, experimental, feminist, gay, humor/satire, lesbian, literary, translations. Receives 50-60 unsolicited mss/month. Does not read mss May through August. Published new writers within the last year. Length: 2,000-3,000 words average; 4,000 words maximum. Publishes short shorts.
How to Contact: Send complete ms with cover letter, which should include a short bio or interesting information. Reports in 3-4 months on mss. SASE. Photocopied submissions OK. Accepts computer printout submissions. Sample copy for $4, 10×12 SAE and 4 first class stamps.
Payment: Pays a small honorarium and 1 year subscription.
Terms: Acquires one-time rights.
Advice: "We look for writing that makes sense: fiction that makes you put down your spoon and reread the page until your soup goes cold."

OYEZ REVIEW (I, II), 430 S. Michigan Ave., Chicago IL 60605. (312)341-2017. Editor: Angela Lewis. Magazine: 5½×8½; 91 pages; b&w camera ready illustrations and photos. Looking for "what is fresh and good" for Chicago audience. Annually. Estab. 1967. Circ. 500.
Needs: Contemporary, experimental, feminist, literary, poetry and regional. Accepts 2-5 mss/issue. Length: "about 10 pages, double-spaced."
How to Contact: Send complete ms with SASE. Reports in 3 months on ms. Photocopied submissions OK. Sample copy $4.
Payment: 5 contributor's copies.
Terms: Acquires one-time rights.
Advice: "*Oyez* encourages imaginative fiction, good dialogue, good characterization. Because our magazine is small and we have more poetry than fiction, we need/want *good*, but short fiction. We are interested in seeing what all writers can do—not just previously published writers. Since our staff changes from year to year, so does the philosophy of the publication—this year we are trying to delve into the collective American unconscious!"

P.I. MAGAZINE (II), Fact and Fiction about the World of Private Investigators, 755 Bronx, Toledo OH 43609. (419)382-0967. Editor: Bob Mackowiak. Magazine: 8½×11; about 50 pages; coated white paper and cover; illustrations and photographs. "All about private eyes: personality profiles and stories about professional investigators; original fiction; books, movie, video, games, etc. Audience includes private eye and mystery fans." Quarterly. Estab. 1988. Circ. 750
Needs: Adventure, humor/satire, suspense/mystery. "Principal character must be a private detective—not a police detective, spy or school teacher who solves murders on the side. No explicit sex." Buys 4-6 mss/issue. Publishes ms 2-3 months after acceptance. Recently published work by Curtis Fischer; column by Bill Palmer. Length: 2,500 words preferred; 500 words minimum; 5,000 words maximum. Publishes short shorts. Sometimes critiques rejected ms and recommends other markets if possible.
How to Contact: Send complete ms with cover letter. Reports in 4 months. SASE. Simultaneous and photocopied submissions OK. Accepts computer printout submissions. Single copy for $3.75."
Payment: Pays $15 minimum; $25 for fiction; contributor's copies; charge for extras.
Terms: Pays on publication. Acquires one-time rights.
Advice: "Private eye stories do not need to be murder mysteries, and they do not need to start with a client walking into the detective's run-down office. How about two successful private investigators making good money—most of the real P.I.s run profitable businesses."

THE P.U.N. (PLAY ON WORDS) (II), The Silly Club and Michael Rayner, Box 536-583, Orlando FL 32853. (407)898-0463. Editor: Danno Sullivan. Newsletter: 8 pages; cartoons. "All polite humor. Polite, meaning no foul language, sex, etc. As a joke, something like 'Child Abuse with Dr. Seuss' is OK. We have an intelligent readership. They don't mind puzzling a bit to get the joke, but they also enjoy plain silliness." Published bimonthly. Estab. 1982. Circ. 400.
Needs: Humor/satire. Receives 20 unsolicited fiction mss/month. Accepts 1-3 mss/issue; 10-20 mss/ year. Publishes ms "usually next issue" after acceptance. Length: short shorts, 1 page or less. Sometimes critiques rejected mss.
How to Contact: Send complete ms with cover letter. Reports in 2-3 weeks. SASE. Simultaneous, photocopied and reprint submissions OK. Accepts computer printouts. Sample copy for #10 SASE and $1.

Payment: Pays $1 minimum, $15 maximum; contributor's copies.
Terms: Pays on acceptance for one-time rights.
Advice: "Keep it short. Keep it obviously (even if it's subtle) funny. Above all, don't write like Erma Bombeck. We get a lot of 'cute' material—*Readers Digest*-style, which is not for us. We like short *articles*, as opposed to stories. Fiction presented as fact."

PABLO LENNIS (I, IV), The Magazine of Science Fiction, Fantasy and Fact, Halcyon Press, Fandom House, 30 North 19th St., Lafayette IN 47904. Editor: John Thiel. Magazine: 8½×11; 22 pages; standard stock; illustrations and "occasional" photos. "Science fiction, fantasy, science, research and mystic for scientists and science fiction and fantasy appreciators." Published 4-5 times/year.
Needs: Fantasy, psychic/supernatural/occult, science fiction, spiritual. Receives 25 unsolicited mss/ year. Accepts 3 mss/issue; 15 mss/year. Publishes ms 6 months after acceptance. Published work by Eugene Flinn, Archie Taylor, Martha Collins; published new writers within the last year. Length: 1,500 words average; 3,000 words maximum. Occasionally critiques rejected mss and recommends other markets.
How to Contact: "Method of submission is author's choice but he might prefer to query. No self-statement is necessary." Reports in 2 weeks. Does not accept computer printouts.
Payment: Pays in contributor's copies.
Terms: Publication not copyrighted.
Advice: "*Novel and Short Story Writer's Market* has brought in many new manuscripts, so my rate of publication has slowed down, but I don't reject frequently and then with good reasons. If you want to write a really good story, stick to materially perceived reality in setting scenes and saying something the reader would like to hear. Always have an understandable framework from which to depart imaginatively. I like an optimistic approach and one which is elevating to readers, and do have editorial taboos against unpleasant and abusive language."

PACIFIC REVIEW (II), Dept. of English and Comparative Lit., San Diego State University, San Diego CA 92182-0295. Contact: Editor. Magazine: 6×9; 100-150 pages; book stock paper; paper back, extra heavy cover stock; illustrations, photos. "There is no designated theme. We publish high-quality fiction, poetry, and familiar essays: academic work meant for, but not restricted to, an academic audience." Biannually. Estab. 1973. Circ. 1,000.
Needs: "We do not restrict or limit our fiction in any way other than quality. We are interested in all fiction, from the very traditional to the highly experimental. Acceptance is determined by the quality of submissions." Does not read June-August. Published new writers within the last year. Publishes short shorts. Length: 4,000 words max.
How to Contact: Send original ms with SASE. Reports in 2-4 months on mss. Sample copy $6.
Payment: 1 author's copy.
Terms: "First serial rights are *Pacific Review's*. All other rights revert to author."

PAINTED BRIDE QUARTERLY (II), Painted Bride Art Center, 230 Vine St., Philadelphia PA 19106. (215)925-9914. Co-editors: Louis Camp and Joanna DiPaulo. Literary magazine: 6×9; 96-100 pages; illustrations; photos. Quarterly. Estab. 1975. Circ. 1,000.
Needs: Contemporary, ethnic, experimental, feminist, gay, lesbian, literary, prose poem and translations. Receives 10 unsolicited mss/week. Accepts 2 mss/issue; 8 mss/year. Published new writers within the last year. Length: 3,000 words average; 5,000 words maximum. Publishes short shorts. Occasionally critiques rejected mss.
How to Contact: Send complete ms. Reports in 3 weeks-3 months. SASE. Accepts computer printout submissions. Prefers letter-quality. Sample copy $5.
Payment: 2 contributor's copies, 1 year free subscription, 50% off additional copies.
Terms: Acquires first North American serial rights.
Advice: "We want quality in whatever—we hold experimental work to as strict standards as anything else. Many of our readers write fiction; most of them enjoy a good reading. We hope to be an outlet for quality. A good story gives, first, enjoyment to the reader. We've seen a good many of them lately, and we've published the best of them."

THE PANHANDLER (II), A Magazine of Poetry and Fiction, The University of West Florida, English Dept, Pensacola FL 32514. (904)474-2923. Editors: Michael Yots and Stanton Millet. Magazine: 6×9; 64 pages; 40 lb paper; 70 lb cover stock. Semiannually. Estab. 1976. Circ. 500.

Needs: Contemporary, ethnic, experimental, humor/satire, literary and mainstream. No Sci Fi, horror, erotica. Plans to publish special fiction or anthology issue in the future. Receives 10 unsolicited mss/month. Accepts 2-4 mss/issue; 8-10 mss/year.Publishes ms 3-8 months after acceptance. Length: 1,500-3,000 words; 2,500 average. Sometimes critiques rejected mss and recommends other markets.

How to Contact: Send complete ms with cover letter. Including writing experience, publications. Reports in 1-4 months. SASE. Simultaneous submissions OK. Sample copy $2. Fiction guidelines for #10 SAE and 1 first class stamp.

Payment: Pays in contributor's copies.

Terms: Acquires first rights.

Advice: "We look for engaging narrative voice. Characters whose concerns are of interest to readers. Real, everyday problems, dilemmas. Clear, efficient narrative style. Manuscript must lead the reader through the story and make him feel on completion that it was worth the trip."

THE PAPER BAG (I, II), Box 268805, Chicago IL 60626-8805. (312)285-7972. Editor: Michael H. Brownstein. Magazine: 5½ × 8½; 25-40 pages; cardboard cover stock; illustrations. Quarterly. Estab. 1988. Circ. 300.

Needs: Adventure contemporary, erotica, ethnic, experimental, fantasy, feminist, horror, literary, mainstream, prose poem, suspense/mystery and western. Plans to publish special fiction or anthology issue in the future. Receives 10 unsolicited mss/month. Accepts 2-4 mss/issue; 36-60 mss/year. Publishes mss 3 months to 1 year after acceptance. Under 500 words preferred; 500 words maximum. "Has to be under 500 words." Sometimes critiques rejected mss and recommends other markets.

How to Contact: Send complete ms with cover letter. "Include brief bio for our contributor's page." Reports in 1 week on queries; 1 week to 3 months on mss. SASE. Photocopied submission OK. Sample copy $2.50. Fiction guidelines for SAE and 1 first class stamp.

Payment: Pays in contributor's copies.

Terms: Acquires first rights. Sometimes sends pre-publication galleys to the author.

PAPER RADIO (I,II), Loose Milk Review, Box 85302, Seattle WA 98145. Editors: N.S. Kvern and Dagmar Howard. Magazine: 8½ × 11; 28-36 pages; photocopied paper and cover; illustrations; high contrast b&w photographs. "We're open to anything, but it has to be short—usually less than 2,500 words, and only one or two per issue." Readers are "mostly people who are interested in avant garde, mail art, Xerox art, political, bizarre, surrealism, punk, literary/experimental writing and computers." Published 3 times/year. Estab. 1986. Circ. 500.

Needs: Erotica, experimental, fantasy, literary, prose poem, science fiction. Receives 10 unsolicited fiction mss/month. Accepts 4-5 mss/issue; 12-15 mss/year. Publishes ms an average of 2-3 months after acceptance. Length: 2,000 words average; 3,500 words maximum. Publishes short shorts. Sometimes critiques rejected mss.

How to Contact: Send complete ms with cover letter. "some autobiographical information is helpful—one or two paragraphs—and I like to know where they hear about our magazine." Reports in 3 weeks. SASE. Simultaneous or photocopied submissions OK. Accepts computer printout submissions. Sample copy $3.

Payment: Contributor's copies.

Terms: Acquires first rights, "artist can publish material elsewhere simultaneously."

Advice: "We are devoted to the cause of experimentation and literature and we like a wide variety of fiction. Best to see a sample copy. Our publication is orderly in its chaos, wild and untameable in its order."

‡PARAGRAPH (II), A Magazine of Paragraphs, Oat City Press, Inc., 1423 Northampton St., Holyoke MA 01040. (413)533-8767. Co-Editors: Walker Rumble and Karen Donovan. Magazine: 4¼ × 5½; 38 pages. "No particular theme—we publish single collection of paragraphs for a general audience." Published 3 times/year. Estab. 1985. Circ. 700.

Needs: "Any topic is welcome, including experimental writing. Our only requirement is that paragraphs must be 200 words or less." Receives 30-40 unsolicited mss/month. Accepts 30-33 mss/issue; 90 mss/year. Publishes ms 2-3 months after acceptance. Recently published work by Lisa Shea, Laurel Speer, Conger Beasley Jr., Jennifer Lodde, Gary Fincke. Length: 200 words average; 200 words maximum. Publishes short shorts. Length: 200 words. Sometimes critiques rejected mss.

How to Contact: Send complete manuscript with cover letter. Reports in 1 week on queries; 2 months on mss. SASE. Simultaneous and photocopied submissions OK. Accepts computer printout submissions. Sample copy $3. Fiction guidelines for SAE and 1 first class stamp.

Payment: Pays contributor's copies and charges for extras.
Terms: Acquires first rights. Sends galleys to author.

‡PARA*phrase (II), Newsletter of Cosmic Trend, Cosmic Trend, Box 322 Clarkson Rd., Mississauga, Ontario L5J 3Y2 Canada. Editor: George LeGrand. Fiction Editor: Tedy Asponsen. Newsletter: 7 × 8½; 24 pages; photocopy paper; color paper cover; b&w illustrations. "Mature audience with a New Age slant." Published approx. 2-3 times a year. Estab. 1990. Circ. 200.
Needs: Confession, contemporary, erotica, experimental, fantasy, humor/satire, prose poem, psychic/supernatural/occult, science fiction, New Age. Does not want to see "Rhymed, structured poetry, run-of-the-mill romance, politically focused material." Receives 1-2 unsolicited mss/month. Accepts 2-3 mss/issue; 6-9 mss/year. Publishes ms 6 months to one year after acceptance. Recently published work by Victor C. Klein, Aida M. Jirasek. Length: 500-1,000 words average; 3,000 words maximum. Publishes short shorts. Length: 100-200 words. Sometimes critiques rejected mss and recommends other markets.
How to Contact: Send complete manuscript with cover letter including previous credits of publishing. Reports in 2 weeks on queries; 1 month on mss. SASE or International Reply Coupon. Simultaneous, photocopied and reprint submissions OK. Accepts computer printout submissions. Sample copy for $2. Fiction guidelines for $1 and 4 × 9½ SAE and 1 first class stamp.
Payment: Pays in contributor's copies. Charge for extras.
Terms: Acquires one-time rights.
Advice: "Looks for authenticity of inner human experience, beyond the obvious, effectively communicated and presented."

THE PARIS REVIEW (II), 45-39 171 St. Pl., Flushing NY 11358. Editor: George A. Plimpton. Managing Editor: James Linville. Magazine: 5¼ × 8½; about 240 pages; 50 lb paper; 10 pt Cls cover stock; illustrations and photographs. "Fiction and poetry of superlative quality, whatever the genre, style or mode. Our contributors include prominent, as well as little-known and previously unpublished writers. Recent issues have included the work of Raymond Carver, Elizabeth Tallent, Rick Bass, John Koethe, Sharon Olds, Derek Walcott, Carolyn Kizer, Tess Gallagher, Peter Handke, Denis Johnson, Bobbie Ann Mason, Harold Brodkey, Joseph Brodsky, John Updike, Andre Dubus, Galway Kinnell, E.L. Doctorow and Philip Levine. 'The Art of Fiction' interview series includes important contemporary writers discussing their own work and the craft of writing." Quarterly.
Needs: Committed work of boldness and originality, combining excellence of form and voice. Receives several hundred unsolicited fiction mss each month. Published new writers within the last year. No preferred length. Also publishes short shorts.
How to Contact: *Send complete ms with SASE to 541 E. 72nd St., New York NY 10021.* Reports in 6-8 weeks on mss. Sample copy $6.90.
Payment: $100-$500. 2 free author's copies. Regular charge for extras.
Terms: Pays on publication for first North American serial rights. Sends galleys to author.
Advice: *"The Paris Review* has the widest circulation of any literary journal. We are devoted to helping talented, original writers find larger audiences."

PARTING GIFTS (II), 3006 Stonecutter Terrace, Greensboro NC 27405. Editor: Robert Bixby. Magazine: 5 × 8; 40 pages. "High quality insightful fiction, very brief and on any theme." Semiannual. Plans special fiction issue. Estab. 1988.
Needs: "Brevity is the second most important criterion behind literary quality." Publishes ms within one year of acceptance. Length: 250 words minimum; 1,000 words maximum. Sometimes critiques rejected mss.
How to Contact: Send complete ms with cover letter. Reports in 1 day on queries; in 1-7 days on mss. SASE. Accepts computer printout submissions.
Payment: Pays in contributor's copies.
Terms: Acquires one-time rights.
Advice: Magazine fiction today "seems to celebrate drabness and disconnection. Read the works of Amy Hempel, Jim Harrison, C.K. Williams and Janet Kauffman, all excellent writers who epitomize the writing *Parting Gifts* strives to promote."

PARTISAN REVIEW (II), 236 Bay State Rd., Boston MA 02215. (617)353-4260. Editor: William Phillips. Executive Editor: Edith Kurzweil. Magazine: 6 × 9; 160 pages; 40 lb paper; 60 lb cover stock. Theme is of world literature and contemporary culture: fiction, essays and poetry with emphasis on the arts and political and social commentary, for the general intellectual public; scholars. Quarterly. Estab. 1934. Circ. 8,000.

Needs: Contemporary, experimental, literary, prose poem, regional and translations. Receives 100 unsolicited fiction mss/month. Buys 2 mss/issue; 8 mss/year. Recently published work by José Donoso, Isaac Bashevis Singer, Doris Lessing; published new writers within the last year. Length: open. Publishes short shorts.

How to Contact: Send complete ms with SASE and cover letter listing past credits. Photocopied submissions OK. Accepts computer printout submissions; prefers letter-quality. Reports in 4 months on mss. Sample copy for $5 and $1 postage.

Payment: Pays $25-200; 1 free contributor's copy.

Terms: Pays on publication for first rights.

Advice: "Please, research the type of fiction we publish. Often we receive manuscripts which are entirely inappropriate for our journal. Sample copies are available and this is a good way to determine audience."

‡PASSAGER (II, IV), A Journal of Remembrance and Discovery, University of Baltimore, 1420 N. Charles, Baltimore MD 21201-5779. Editor: Kendra Kopelke. Fiction Editor: Sally Darnowsky. Magazine: 8¼ square; 32-36 pages; 70 lb. paper; 80 lb. cover; photographs. "We publish stories and novel excerpts to 5,000 words, poems to 50 lines, interviews." Quarterly. Estab. 1990. Circ. 750.

Needs: "Publishes personal voices that speak about the strangeness and wonder of the passage of time; age as a time of more rather than less. Special interest in older writers, but publishes all ages." Receives 200 unsolicited mss/month. Accepts 2-3 mss/issue; 8-12 mss/year. Publishes ms up to 1 year after acceptance. Recently published work by Elisavietta Ritchie, Lucille Clifton, Mary Carter Smith. Length: 250 words minimum; 5,000 words maximum. Publishes short shorts. Length: 250 words. Often critiques rejected mss.

How to Contact: Send complete manuscript with cover letter. Reports in 1 week-3 months on mss. SASE. Photocopied submissions OK. Accepts computer printout submissions. Sample copy for $2.50 and 9 × 12 SAE. Fiction guidelines for #10 SAE and 1 first class stamp.

Payment: Pays free subscription to magazine and contributor's copies.

Terms: Acquires first North American serial rights. Sometimes sends galleys to author.

Advice: "*Get a copy* so you can see the quality of the work we use. We often reject beautifully written work that is bland in favor of rougher work that has the spark we're looking for. In those cases, we try to work with the author to bring the work to a publishable condition — if possible."

‡PASSAGES NORTH (II), Kalamazoo College, 1200 Academy St., Kalamazoo MI 49007. Editors: Ben Mitchell; Mark Cox, Poetry; Mary La Chapelle, Fiction. Tabloid: 11¼ × 14; 32 pages; white uncoated paper; original art and photography. Readership: general and literary. Semiannual. Estab. 1979. Circ. 2,500.

Needs: Short fiction. Excellence is our only criteria. Subjects and genre are open. Accepts 5-10 mss/ year. Recently published works by Susan Straight, Gary Gildner; published new writers within the last year. Length: 500-10,000 words. Critiques returned mss when there is time.

How to Contact: Send complete mss with SSE and brief letter of previous publication, awards. Reports in 3 weeks to 2 months. Publishes an average of 3-6 months after acceptance. Sample copy $3.

Payment: Three free author's copies. Frequent honoraria.

Terms: Rights revert to author on publication. No reprints.

Advice: "*Passages North* seeks excellent writing in a variety of genres including short fiction, memoirs, natural history and criticism."

PAVOR NOCTURNUS (I, IV), Starbuck Publishing, Suite N, 412 Maverick Dr., Palestine TX 75801. Editor: S.K. King. Magazine: 8½ × 11; 24-30 pages; 20 lb. paper; "heavy" cover stock; b&w illustrations. "Publishes dark fantasy, horror and psychic/supernatural/occult." Semiannually. Estab. 1989. Circ. about 250.

Needs: Experimental, fantasy, horror, psychic/supernatural/occult and science fiction. No *Star Trek* or *Star Wars* clones. Plans to publish a special fiction issue or an anthology in the future. Receives 12-15 unsolicited mss/month. Accepts 6 mss/issue; 12 mss/year. Publishes ms up to 6 months after acceptance. Published work by John Yarbrough, Denise Xavier. Length: 2,000 words average; 100 words minimum; 3,500 words maximum. Publishes short shorts. Length: 100-150 words. Sometimes critiques rejected mss and sometimes recommends other markets.

How to Contact: Send complete ms. Include brief bio. Reports in 2 months on mss. SASE. Simultaneous, photocopied, and reprint submissions OK. Accepts computer printout submissions. Accepts electronic submissions via disk or modem. Sample copy $3.95 and 2 first class stamps. Fiction guidelines

for SAE and 1 first class stamp. "Make check/money order payable to Starbuck Publishing."
Payment: Pays in contributor's copies.
Terms: Acquires first rights or one-time rights. Sends galleys to author. Publication not copyrighted.
Advice: Looks for "something that really sticks in my mind and haunts me for a few days. Characterization is important. I look for something that borders on insanity, yet maintains an anchor in the real world—something to tie it with everyday people in everyday situations. Even a retelling of old tales can fit this category. I am a beginning writer myself and I know what you're going through. I also know that there was a first time for folks such as King and Straub."

‡PEARL (II, IV), A Literary Magazine, Pearl, 3030 E. Second St., Long Beach CA 90803. (213)434-4523. Editors: Joan Jobe Smith, Marilyn Johnson and Barbara Hauk. Magazine: 5½×9½; 64 pages; 60 lb. bond paper; 80 lb. gloss cover; b&w drawings and graphics. "We are primarily a poetry magazine, but we do publish some *very short* fiction and nonfiction. We are interested in lively, readable prose that speaks to *real* people in direct, living language; for a general literary audience." Semiannually. Estab. 1974 ("folded" after 3 issues but began publishing again in 1987). Circ. 500.
Needs: Contemporary, humor/satire, literary, mainstream, prose poem. "We will only consider short-short stories up to 1,200 words. For longer stories, we suggest entering our annual short story contest. Although we have no taboos stylistically or subject-wise, obscure, predictable, sentimental, or cliché-ridden stories are a turn-off." Plan special fiction issue. Receives 4-5 unsolicited mss/month. Accepts 1-2 mss/issue; 2-4 mss/year. Publishes ms 6 months to 1 year after acceptance. Recently published work by MacDonald Harris, Josephine Marshall, Mark Weber, Annerose Schneider. Length: 1,000 words average; 500 words minimum; 1,200 words maximum. Publishes short shorts. Length: 1,000 words.
How to Contact: Send complete manuscript with cover letter including publishing credits and brief biographical information. Reports in 6-8 weeks on mss. SASE. Photocopied submissions OK. Accepts computer printout submissions. Sample copy $5 (postpaid). Fiction guidelines for 4½×9½ legal SAE and 1 first class stamp.
Payment: Pays 2 contributor's copies.
Terms: Acquires first North American serial rights. Sends galleys to author. "*Pearl* holds an annual short story contest. Submission period: January 1-March 1. Award: $50, publication in *Pearl*, 10 copies. $5 entry fee. Maximum length: 2,000 words. Send SASE for complete guidelines."
Advice: "We look for vivid, *dramatized* situations and characters, stories written in an original 'voice,' that make sense and follow a clear narrative line. What makes a manuscript stand out is more elusive, though—more to do with feeling and imagination than anything else . . ."

THE PEGASUS REVIEW (I, IV), Box 134, Flanders NJ 07836. (201)927-0749. Editor: Art Bounds. Magazine: 5½×8½; 6-8 pages; illustrations. "Our magazine is a bimonthly, done entirely in calligraphy, illustrated. Each issue is based on a specific theme for those who appreciate quality in both writing and presentation. Plans new features, more pages in 1991." Estab. 1980. Circ. 200.
Needs: Humor/satire, literary, prose poem and religious/inspirational. Themes for 1990: January/February-Beginnings; March/April-Language; May/June-Parents; July/August-Children; September/October-God; November/December-Memories. "Themes may be approached by humor, satire, inspirational, autobiographical, prose. Try to avoid the obvious." Receives 50 unsolicited mss/month. Accepts 60 mss/year. Recently published work by William Call, Leslie D. Foster, Valerie Rossetti; published new writers within the last year. Publishes short shorts 3 pages; 500 words. Themes are subject to change, so query if in doubt. Critiques rejected mss and sometimes recommends other markets.
How to Contact: Send complete ms. SASE "a must." Cover letter with author's background and full name—no initials. Photocopied submissions OK. Accepts computer printout submissions. Simultaneous submissions acceptable, if so advised. Sample copy $1.50. Fiction guidelines for SAE.
Payment: 2 contributor's copies. Occasional book awards.
Terms: Acquires one-time rights.
Advice: "Write, write, write. And read, read, read. The classics and good contemporary writers. Pap is common. Study your markets as well as marketing your work. Say the usual in an unusual manner. Keep with the magazine's slant. Persevere."

PEMBROKE MAGAZINE (I, II), Box 60, Pembroke State University, Pembroke NC 28372. (919)521-4214, ext. 433. Editor: Shelby Stephenson. Fiction Editor: Stephen Smith. Magazine: 9×10; 225 pages; illustrations; photos. Magazine of poems and stories plus literary essays. Annually. Estab. 1969. Circ. 500.

Needs: Open. Receives 40 unsolicited mss/month. Publishes short shorts. Published work by Fred Chappell, Robert Morgan; published new writers within the last year. Length: open. Occasionally critiques rejected mss and recommends other markets.
How to Contact: Send complete ms. Reports immediately to 3 months. SASE. Accepts computer printout submissions. Sample copy $3 and 9 × 10 SAE.
Payment: 1 contributor's copy.
Advice: "Write with an end for *writing*, not publication."

PENNSYLVANIA ENGLISH (II), English Department, Penn State University—Erie, Humanities Division, Erie PA 16563. Editor: Dean Baldwin. Fiction Editor: Chris Dubbs. Magazine: 7 × 8½; 100 pages; 20 lb bond paper; 65 lb matte cover. For "teachers of English in Pennsylvania at the high school and college level." Semiannually. Estab. 1985. Circ. 300.
Needs: Literary, contemporary mainstream. Does not read mss from May to August. Publishes ms an average of 6 months after acceptance. Length: 5,000 words maximum. Publishes short shorts. Sometimes critiques rejected mss.
How to Contact: Send complete ms with cover letter. Reports in 2 months. SASE. Simultaneous and photocopied submissions OK. Accepts dot-matrix computer printouts.
Payment: Pays in contributor's copies.
Terms: Acquires first North American serial rights.

PENNSYLVANIA REVIEW, University of Pittsburgh, 526 C.L./English Dept., Pittsburgh PA 15260. (412)624-0026. Managing Editor: Lori Jakiela. Magazine: 7 × 10; 70-100 pages. Magazine of fiction, poetry, nonfiction, interviews, reviews, novel excerpts, long poems for literate audience. Semiannually. Estab. 1985. Circ. 1,000.
Needs: Ethnic, experimental, feminist, gay, humor/satire, lesbian, literary, prose poem, regional, translations. "High quality!" Receives 75 unsolicited fiction mss/month. Accepts 3-5 mss/issue; 6-10 mss/year. Deadlines: Dec. 1 and March 1. Mss not read in summer months. Recently published work by Sharon Doubiago and Maggie Anderson; published new writers within the last year. Length: 5,000 maximum words for prose. Comments on rejected mss "rarely and only if we've had some interest."
How to Contact: Send complete ms. Reports in 1 week on queries; 6-8 weeks on ms. SASE for ms. Photocopied submissions OK. Accepts computer printout submissions. Prefers letter-quality. Sample copy $5. Fiction guidelines for #10 SAE and 1 first class stamp.
Payment: $5/page for prose; 1 contributor's copy.
Terms: Pays on publication for first North American serial rights.
Advice: "Don't be discouraged when your work is returned to you. Returns are not necessarily a comment on the quality of the writing. Keep trying."

PEOPLENET (IV), "Where People Meet People", Box 897, Levittown NY 11756. (516)579-4043. Editor: Robert Mauro. Newsletter: 8½ × 11; 12 pages; 20 lb paper; 20 lb cover stock. "Romance stories featuring disabled characters." Quarterly. Estab. 1987. Circ. 200.
Needs: Romance, contemporary and disabled. Main character must be disabled. Accepts 1-2 mss/issue; 4-8 mss/year. Publishes ms up to 2 years after acceptance. Length: 500-1,000 words; 800-1,000 average. Publishes short shorts.
How to Contact: Send complete ms and SASE. Reports in 1 week "*only* if SASE there." Accepts computer printout submissions. Fiction guidelines for #10 SAE and 1 first class stamp.
Payment: Pays 1¢/word on acceptance.
Terms: Acquires first rights.
Advice: "We are looking for stories under 1,000 words on romance with a disabled man or woman as the main character. No sob stories or 'super crip' stories. Just realistic romance. No porn. Love, respect, trust, understanding and acceptance are what I want."

PERCEPTIONS (I), 1945 S. 4th W., Missoula MT 59801. (406)543-5875. Editor: Temi Rose. Magazine: 4 × 5; 20 pages. Publishes "primarily women's perceptions," for readers of "all ages, both sexes." Published 3 times/year. Plans special fiction issue. Estab. 1983. Circ. 100.
Needs: Adventure, condensed/excerpted novel, confession contemporary, experimental, fantasy, feminist, prose poem, psychic/supernatural/occult, religions/inspirational, science fiction, suspense/mystery. Accepts 1 ms/issue. Length: four pages tops. Publishes short shorts. Collected by University of Wisconsin, Madison Serials Library; produces poetry videos with permission of writers. Critiques rejected mss "only if requested."

How to Contact: Query first. Reports in 2-3 weeks on queries; in 1 month on mss. SASE. Simultaneous, photocopied and reprint submissions OK. Accepts computer printout submissions. Accepts electronic submissions via disk or modem. Sample copy $3. Fiction guidelines free for SASE and 1 first class stamp.
Payment: Pays in contributor's copies. Sponsors awards for fiction writers "occasionally."

PHOEBE (II), The George Mason Review, George Mason University, 4400 University Dr., Fairfax VA 22030. (703)323-3730. Editor: Patricia Bertheaud. Fiction Editors: Patricia Stacey and Patricia Snell. Magazine: 6×9; 72 pages; 80 lb quality paper; 0-5 illustrations per issue; 0-10 photographs per issue. "We publish fiction, poetry, photographs, illustrations and some reviews." Quarterly. Estab. 1972. Circ. 3,500.
Needs: Experimental, literary, mainstream, prose poem, regional, serialized/excerpted novel, translations. No romance, western, juvenile, erotica. Receives 20 mss/month. Accepts 5-7 mss/issue; 20-28 mss/year. Does not read mss June-July. Publishes ms 3-6 months after acceptance. Published work by Alan Cheuse, Richard Bausch, Paul Milensky. Length: 4,500 words average; 8,000 words maximum. Publishes short shorts. Sometimes comments on rejected mss.
How to Contact: Send complete ms with cover letter. Include "name, address, phone; if and where you've published previously. Brief bio." Reports in 1 week on queries; 6 weeks on mss. SASE. Photocopied submissions OK. Sample copy $3.25. Fiction guidelines for #10 SAE with 1 first class stamp.
Payment: Pays in 4 contributor's copies.
Terms: Acquires one-time rights.
Advice: "*Phoebe* is committed to furthering the arts and particularly to helping new writers of poetry and fiction. Many of our staff are associated with the M.F.A. program in writing at George Mason University. While we are receptive to all kinds of good writing, we particularly appreciate stories that tell stories: clean, honest prose. Studying a recent issue would be helpful."

PIG IRON (II), Box 237, Youngstown OH 44501. (216)783-1269. Editor: Jim Villani. Fiction Editor: Nate Leslie. Magazine. 8½×11; 96 pages; 60 lb offset paper; 85 pt coated cover stock; b&w illustrations; b&w 120 line photographs. "Contemporary literature by new and experimental writers." Annually. Estab. 1975. Circ. 1,000.
Needs: Literary and thematic. No mainstream. Buys 10-20 mss/issue. Receives approximately 75-100 unsolicited fiction mss each month. Recently published work by Jerry Bumpus, Angela Woodward, Catherine Reid and Mark S. Franko. Length: 8,000 words maximum.
How to Contact: Send complete ms with SASE. No simultaneous submissions. Accepts computer printout submissions. Reports in 3 months. Sample copy $3.
Payment: $5/printed page. 2 free author's copies. $3 charge for extras.
Terms: Pays on publication for first North American serial rights.
Advice: "Looking for works that do not ignore psychological development in character and plot/action." Mss are rejected because of "lack of new ideas and approaches. Writers need to work out interesting plot/action and setting/set. Read a lot; read for stylistic innovation. Send SASE for current theme list. Also publishes thematic anthologies. Query for theme."

THE PIKESTAFF FORUM (II), Box 127, Normal IL 61761. (309)452-4831. Editors: Robert D. Sutherland, James Scrimgeour, James McGowan and Curtis White. Tabloid: 11½×17½; 40 pages; newsprint paper; illustrations; photos. "*The Pikestaff Forum* is a general literary magazine publishing poetry, prose fiction, drama." Readership: "General literary with a wide circulation in the small press world. Readers are educated (but not academic) and have a taste for excellent serious fiction." Published irregularly—"whenever we have sufficient quality material to warrant an issue." Estab. 1977. Circ. 1,000.
Needs: Literary and contemporary with a continuing need for good short stories or novel excerpts. "We welcome traditional and experimental works from established and non-established writers. We look for writing that is clear, concise and to the point; contains vivid imagery and sufficient concrete detail; is grounded in lived human experience; contains memorable characters and situations. No confessional self-pity or puffery; self-indulgent first or second drafts; sterile intellectual word games or five-finger exercises or slick formula writing, genre-pieces that do not go beyond their form (westerns, mysteries, gothic, horror, science fiction, swords-and-sorcery fantasy), commercially oriented mass-market stuff, violence for its own sake, racist or sexist material or pornography (sexploitation)." Accepts 1-4 mss/issue. Receives approximately 15-20 unsolicited fiction mss each month. Recently published work by Constance Pierce, Linnea Johnson; published new writers within the last year. Length: from 1 paragraph to 4,000 or 5,000 words. Critiques rejected mss when there is time.

How to Contact: Query. Send complete ms. SASE. Accepts computer printout submissions. Prefers letter-quality. Reports in 3 weeks on queries, 3 months on mss. Publishes ms up to 1 year after acceptance. Sample copy $2.
Payment: 3 free author's copies. Cover price less 50% discount for extras.
Terms: Acquires first rights. Copyright remains with author.
Advice: "We are highly selective, publishing only 3% of the stories that are submitted for consideration. Read other authors with an appreciative and critical eye; don't send out work prematurely; develop keen powers of observation and a good visual memory; get to know your characters thoroughly; don't let others (editors, friends, etc.) define or 'determine' your sense of self-worth; be willing to learn; outgrow self-indulgence. Develop discipline. Show, don't tell; and leave some work for the reader to do. Write for the fun of it (that way there's a sure return for the investment of time and effort). Always write to achieve the best quality you can; be honest with yourself, your potential readers, and your story. Learn to become your own best editor: know when you've done well, and when you haven't done as well as you can. Remember: there's a lot of competition for the available publication slots, and editorial bias is always a factor in what gets accepted for publication. Develop a sense of humor about the enterprise."

‡**PIKEVILLE REVIEW (II)**, Pikeville College, Pikeville KY 41501. (606)432-9341. Editor: James Alan Riley. Magazine: 5 × 8; 80-100 pages; 60 lb. paper. "Fiction, poetry, interviews, essays and book reviews for literate audience." Annually. Estab. 1988. Circ. 500.
Needs: Contemporary, experimental, literary, prose poem, translations. Receives 20 unsolicited mss/month. Accepts 1 mss/issue. Recently published work by Malcolm Glass and Jim Wayne Miller. Publishes short shorts. Sometimes critiques rejected mss and recommends other markets.
How to Contact: Send complete manuscript with cover letter. Reports in 6 weeks to 5 months on mss. SASE. Photocopied submission OK. Accepts computer printout submissions. Sample copy $3. Fiction guidelines for SAE.
Payment: Pays contributor's copies.
Terms: Acquires one-time rights. "$50 for best story and $50 for best essay each issue."

‡**THE PINEHURST JOURNAL**, Pinehurst Press, P.O. Box 360747, Milpitas CA 95036. (408)945-0986. Editor: Michael K. McNamara. Magazine: 8½ × 11; 32 pages; 24 lb. paper; 60 lb. cover; occasional illustrations. "Fiction, nonfiction and poetry for an educated audience appreciative of polished, thought-provoking work." Quarterly. Estab. 1990. Circ. 150.
Needs: Contemporary, erotica, experimental, feminist, gay, historical (general), horror, humor/satire, lesbian, literary, mainstream, prose poem, suspense/mystery, translations. "No hard sci-fi, fantasy, occult, swords and sorcery, slasher or porn: no travel or religious. No formula western or romance." Receives 30-35 mss/month. Accepts 9-11 mss/issues; 35-45 mss/year. Publishes ms 1-4 months after acceptance. Length: 2,000 words average; 750 words minimum; 4,000 words maximum. Publishes short shorts. Length: 200-400 words. Sometimes critiques mss and recommends other markets.
How to Contact: Send complete manuscript with cover letter and short bio which includes publishing successes, if any. Indicate whether piece is a simultaneous submittal. Reports in 1 month or less on queries; 2 months or less on mss. SASE. Simultaneous, photocopied and reprint submissions OK. Accepts computer printout submissions. Sample copy for $4.50 and SAE. Guidelines for #10 SAE and 1 first class stamp.
Payment: $5 maximum, free 1 year subscription and contributor's copies. Charge for extras.
Terms: Offers $5 + subscription. Buys one-time rights.
Advice: "Try to make each word pull its own weight and polish, polish, polish. Failing that, punctuate, punctuate, punctuate."

THE PIPE SMOKER'S EPHEMERIS (I, II, IV), The Universal Coterie of Pipe Smokers, 20-37 120 St., College Point NY 11356. Editor: Tom Dunn. Magazine: 8½ × 11; 54-66 pages; offset paper and cover; illustrations; photos. Pipe smoking and tobacco theme for general and professional audience. Irregular quarterly. Estab. 1964.
Needs: Historical (general), humor/satire, literary, pipe smoking related. Publishes ms up to 1 year after acceptance. Length: 2,500 words average; 5,000 words maximum. Also publishes short shorts. Occasionally critiques rejected mss.
How to Contact: Send complete ms with cover letter. Reports in 2 weeks on mss. Simultaneous, photocopied submissions and reprints OK. Accepts computer printouts. Sample copy for 8½x11 SAE and 6 first class stamps.
Terms: Acquires one-time rights.

PLÉIADES MAGAZINE/PHILAE MAGAZINE (I), Box 357, Suite D, 6677 W. Colfax, Lakewood CO 80214. (303)237-3398. John Moravec, Editor of Pléiades Magazine; Cyril Osmond, editor of Philae Magazine. Magazine: 8½×11; 30-50 pages; 30 lb paper; illustrations; b&w photographs. "We want well thought out material; no sex stories, and good poetry and prose. We want articles about national issues." Pléiades published twice a year; Philae is published quarterly. Estab. 1984. Circ. 10,000.
Needs: Fantasy, historical (general), horror, literary, senior citizen/retirement, serialized/excerpted novel, suspense/mystery, western. "No sex or hippie material." Receives 50-70 unsolicited mss/month. Accepts 3 mss/issue. Publishes ms three months or less after acceptance. Length: 1,200-1,500 words average; 500-800 words minimum. Occasionally critiques rejected mss and recommends other markets.
How to Contact: Send complete ms with cover letter. Reports in 1 week on queries; 2 weeks on mss. SASE. Simultaneous submissions OK. Sample copy $1.75. Fiction guidelines for #10 SAE and 1 first class stamp.
Payment: Pays in contributor's copies.
Terms: Rights remain with author. Offers awards and trophies for best work.
Advice: "Today's magazine fiction stinks. We want authors who can write non-stereotype material, and who are not brainwashed by a bureaucratic society. Learn to write, and take lessons on punctuation. We want shorter good fiction and articles."

PLOUGHSHARES (II), Emerson College, 100 Beacon St., Boston MA 02116. (617)926-9875. Executive Director: DeWitt Henry. "Our theme is new writing (poetry, fiction, criticism) that addresses contemporary adult readers who look to fiction and poetry for help in making sense of themselves and of each other." Quarterly. Estab. 1971. Circ. 3,800.
Needs: Literary, prose poem. "No genre (science fiction, detective, gothic, adventure, etc.), popular formula or commercial fiction whose purpose is to entertain rather than to illuminate." Buys 20+ mss/year. Receives approximately 400-600 unsolicited fiction mss each month. Published work by Rick Bass, Alice Hoffman, Theodore Weesner; published new writers within the last year. Length: 300-6,000 words.
How to Contact: "Query for guidelines and examine a sample issue. Reading periods and needs vary." Cover letter should include "previous pubs." SASE. Reports in 5 months on mss. Sample copy $5. (Please specify fiction issue sample.)
Payment: $10/page to $50 maximum, plus copies. Offers 50% kill fee for assigned ms not published.
Terms: Pays on publication for first North American serial rights.
Advice: "Be familiar with our fiction issues, fiction by our writers and by our various editors (e.g., Rosellen Brown, Tim O'Brien, Jay Neugeboren, Jayne Anne Phillips, James Alan McPherson) and more generally acquaint yourself with the best short fiction currently appearing in the literary quarterlies, and the annual prize anthologies (*Pushcart Prize, O. Henry Awards, Best American Short Stories*). Also realistically consider whether the work you are submitting is as good as or better than—in your own opinion—the work appearing in the magazine you're sending to. What is the level of competition? And what is its volume? (In our case, we accept about 1 ms in 200.) Never send 'blindly' to a magazine, or without carefully weighing your prospect there against those elsewhere. Always keep a copy of work you submit."

THE PLOWMAN (II), Box 414, Whitby Ontario L1N 5S4 Canada. Editor: Tony Scavetta. Tabloid: 112 pages; illustrations and photos. "We are the largest chapbook publisher in the world, over 300 books to our name." Monthly. Estab. 1988. Circ. 10,000.
Needs: Adventure, confession contemporary, ethnic, historical (general), juvenile (5-9 years), literary, mainstream, preschool (1-4 years), prose poem, regional, religious/inspirational, romance, senior citizen/retirement, translations, western and young adult/teen (10-18). Plans to publish special fiction issue or an anthology in the future. Publishes ms 3 months after acceptance. Length: 1 typewritten page. Sometimes critiques rejected mss and recommends other markets.
How to Contact: Send complete ms with cover letter. Reports in 1 week. Enclose IRCs. Simultaneous, photocopied and reprint submissions OK. Accepts computer printout submissions.Sample copy and fiction guidelines for $2 and large SAE.
Payment: Pays in contributor's copies; charges for extras.
Terms: Acquires one-time rights. Sends galleys to author.

‡**POETIC SPACE (I, II), Poetry & Fiction,** P.O. Box 11157, Eugene OR 97440. Editor: Don Hildenbrand. Fiction Editor: Thomas Strand. Magazine: 8 × 11; 12 pages; light paper; medium cover; b&w art. "Social, political, avant-garde, erotic, environmental material for a literary audience." 3 times a year. Estab. 1983. Circ. 600.

Needs: Contemporary, erotica, ethnic, experimental, fantasy, feminist, gay, humor/satire, lesbian, literary, prose poem, regional, serialized novel, translations. No sentimental, romance, mainstream. Plans special fiction issue. Receives 10-12 unsolicited mss/month. Accepts 1-2 mss/issue; 6-8 mss/year. Publishes ms 3-4 months after acceptance. Recently published work by Nathan Versace and Maia Penfold. Length: 1,500-2,000 words average. Publishes short shorts. Sometimes critiques rejected mss and recommends other markets.

How to Contact: Send complete manuscript with cover letter that includes basic info/credits. Reports in 1-2 weeks on queries; 1-2 months on mss. SASE. Photocopied submissions OK. Accepts computer printout submissions. Sample copy for $2, 4 × 9 SAE and 45¢ postage. Fiction guidelines for #10 SAE and 1 first class stamp.

Payment: Pays contributor's copies.

Terms: Acquires one-time rights or "reserves anthology rights."

‡**POETRY FORUM SHORT STORIES (I, II),** Poetry Forum, 5713 Larchmont Dr., Erie PA 16509. (814)866-2543. Editor: Gunver Skogsholm. Newspaper: 7 × 8½; 34 pages; card cover; illustrations. "Human interest themes-(no sexually explicit or racially biased or blasphemous material) for the general public—from the grassroot to the intellectual." Quarterly. Estab. 1989. Circ. 200-400.

Needs: Confession, contemporary, ethnic, experimental, fantasy, feminist, historical, literary, mainstream, prose poem, religious/inspirational, romance, science fiction, senior citizen/retirement, suspense/mystery, young adult/teen. "No blasphemous, sexually explicit material." Publishes annual special fiction issue. Receives 50 unsolicited mss/month. Accepts 12 mss/issue; 40 mss/year. Publishes ms 6 months after acceptance. Agented fiction less than 1%. Recently published work by Bernard Hewitt, Don Peyer, Jess Wilbanks. Length: 2,000 words average; 500 words minimum; 5,000 words maximum.

How to Contact: Send complete manuscript with cover letter. Reports in 6 weeks to 2 months on mss. SASE. Simultaneous, photocopied and reprint submissions OK. Accepts computer printout submissions. "Accepts electronic submissions via disk gladly." Sample copy $3. Fiction guidelines for SAE and 1 first class stamp.

Terms: Acquires one-time rights.

POETRY HALIFAX DARTMOUTH (I, II), BS Poetry Society, Box 7074 North, Halifax Nova Scotia B3K 5J4 Canada. Editor: Mark Hamilton. Magazine: 7 × 8½; 24 pages; bond paper; card stock cover. Bimonthly. Estab. 1986. Circ. 300.

Needs: Experimental, humor/satire, literary and prose poem. Receives 1 or 2 unsolicited mss/month; accepts 3-4 mss/year. Publishes ms 3-6 months after acceptance. Puslishes short shorts. Sometimes critiques rejected mss.

How to Contact: Send complete ms with cover letter and short bio. Reports in 3 months on queries. SASE. Photocopied submissions OK. Accepts computer printout submissions. Sample copy $2. Fiction guidelines for #10 SAE and 1 first class stamp (IRC).

Payment: $5 (Canadian) and 2 contributor's copies.

Terms: Pays on publication for first North American serial rights.

POETRY MAGIC PUBLICATIONS (I), 1630 Lake Dr., Haslett, MI 48840. (517)339-8754. Editor: Lisa Roose-Church. Magazine: 8½ × 11; b&w illustrations. "Publishes poetry and articles relating to writing. Have used other themes. We will consider just about anything of high quality." Quarterly. Estab. 1988.

Needs: Contemporary, humor, prose poem. No pornography, science fiction, horror, fantasy. Receives over 100 mss/month. Accepts 2 mss/issue. Publishes ms within 6 months of acceptance. Published work by Scott Sonders. Length: 50-500 words preferred; 50 words minimum; 1,000 words sometimes. Sometimes critiques rejected mss and recommends other markets.

How to Contact: Query first, query with clips of published work or send complete ms with cover letter. Reports in 2-4 weeks. SASE. Simultaneous (if stated), photocopied and reprint submissions OK. Accepts computer printout submissions. Sample copy for $4.50. Fiction guidelines for #10 SAE and 30¢ postage.

Payment: Pays in contributor's copies (minimum) to $100 (maximum).
Terms: Acquires first rights or one-time rights.
Advice: "Correct usage of grammar, punctuation, etc. is important. We prefer fiction that is quality reading, which entices the reader for more from that author. Because we get less fiction than poetry, we are selective because our readers want to be enticed, enthralled and overwhelmed with a story. If it doesn't do this for the editor she will not accept it. Experiment and create your own style."

‡POETRY MOTEL (II), Suburban Wilderness Press, 1619 Jefferson, Duluth MN 55812. (218)728-3728. Editor: Pat McKinnon. Fiction Editor: Bud Bracken. Magazine: 7×8½; 50-80 pages; 20 lb. paper; various cover; various amount of illustrations and photographs. "We're wide open though we lean toward wry satire and hilarity." 1-2 times annually. Estab. 1984. Circ. 500.
Needs: Condensed/excerpted novel, contemporary, erotica, ethnic, fantasy, feminist, gay, humor/satire, lesbian, literary, prose poem, science fiction. "Nothing along the popular/genre lines." Receives 2-5 unsolicited mss/month. Accepts 2-5 mss/issue; 2-10 mss/year. Publishes ms 1 month to 2 years after acceptance. Recently published work by Willie Smith, Gregory Burnham, Hugh Knox. Length: 300 words average; 25 words minimum; 1,500 words maximum. Publishes short shorts. Length: 300-500 words. Sometimes critiques rejected mss.
How to Contact: Send complete manuscript with cover letter. Reports in 1 week on queries; 1 week to 1 month on mss. SASE. Simultaneous, photocopied and reprint submissions OK. Accepts computer printout submissions. Sample copy $5. Fiction guidelines for #10 SAE and 1 first class stamp.
Payment: Pays contributor's copies. Charge for extras.
Terms: Acquires one-time rights.
Advic: "Read what we print first since it is beyond description and never what you might imagine."

‡THE POINTED CIRCLE (II), Portland Community College-Cascade, 705 N. Killingsworth St., Portland OR 97217. (503)244-6111 ext. 5405. Editor: Student Editorial Staff. Magazine: 7×8½; approx. 80 pages; b&w illustrations and photographs. "Anything of interest to educationally/culturally mixed audience." Annually. Estab. 1980.
Needs: Contemporary, ethnic, literary, prose poem, regional. "We will read whatever is sent, but encourage writers to remember we are a quality literary/arts magazine intended to promote the arts in the community." Accepts 3-7 mss/year. We accept submissions only December 1-March 1, for October 1 issue. Length: 3,500 words average; 500 words minimum; 5,000 words maximum. Publishes short shorts. Length: 100 words. Rarely critiques rejected mss and sometimes recommends other markets.
How to Contact: Send complete manuscript with cover letter and brif bio. SASE. Simultaneous and photocopied submissions OK. Accepts good quality computer printouts. Sample copy for $3.50. Fiction guidelines for #10 SAE and 1 first class stamp.
Payment: Pays in contributor's copies.
Terms: Acquires one-time rights.
Advice: "Looks for quality—topicality—nothing trite. The author cares about language and acts responsibly toward the reader, honors the reader's investment of time and piques the reader's interest."

‡POOR ROBERT'S ALMANAC (II), Poor Robert's Publications, 80 South 900 East, Apt. 1, Provo UT 84606. (801)377-4147. Editor: Robert Raleigh. Magazine: 8½×11; 20 pages; 60 lb. white paper; 60 lb. white cover; illustrations vary (art, cartoons). " A publication for writers and artists who produce, and readers who enjoy, short stories, poetry, essays and art. Contemporary, literary fiction (no particular theme) for college-educated adults." Quarterly. Estab. 1989. Circ. 400.
Needs: Contemporary, ethnic, experimental, feminist, literary, mainstream, serialized novel, translations. No mystery, sci fi. Plans special fiction issue. Receives 1-2 unsolicited mss/month. Accepts 2-3 mss (depending on length)/issue; 8-12 mss/year. Publishes ms 3 months after acceptance. Recently published work by Derek Gullino, J.R. Rodriguez. Length: 3,000 words average; 5,000 words maximum. Publishes short shorts. Sometimes critiques rejected mss and recommends other markets.
How to Contact: Send complete manuscript with cover letter. Include "Name and address *only*. No information about having published elsewhere, books published, etc." Reports in 4 weeks on queries; 6 weeks on mss. SASE. Simultaneous submissions OK. Accepts electronic submissions via disk or modem. Sample copy $2. Fiction guidelines for #10 SAE and 1 first class stamp.

Payment: Pays in contributor's copies.
Terms: Acquires one-time rights.
Advice: "I am particularly interested in fiction that is not formulaic, and that denies the reader ideological or literary closure. I like to read fiction that undermines authority and hierarchy, whether literary, political, social, religious or personal, although this is less important than how the fiction operates as fiction."

THE PORTABLE WALL (II), Basement Press, 215 Burlington, Billings MT 59101. (406)256-3588. Editor: Daniel Struckman. Fiction Editor: Gray Harris. Magazine: 6¼×9¼; 40 pages; cotton rag paper; best quality cover; line engravings; illustrations. "We consider all kinds of material. Bias toward humor." Twice annually. Estab. 1977. Circ. 400.
Needs: Adventure, contemporary, ethnic, experimental, feminist, historical, humor/satire, literary, mainstream, prose poem, regional, science fiction, senior citizen, sports, translations. "We hand set all type; therefore, we favor short pieces and poetry." Receives less than 1 unsolicited ms/month. Accepts one or two mss/issue; one or two mss/year. Publishes ms 6 months to a year after acceptance. Published works by Gray Harris, Wilbur Wood. Length: 2,000 words preferred. Publishes short shorts. Sometimes critiques rejected mss.
How to Contact: Send complete ms with cover letter. Reports in 2 weeks on mss. SASE. Accepts computer printout submissions. Sample copy $5.
Payment: Free subscription to magazine.
Terms: Acquires one-time rights.
Advice: "We like language that evokes believable pictures in our minds and that tells news."

PORTLAND REVIEW (I, II), Portland State University, Box 751, Portland OR 97207. (503)725-4533. Editor: Greg Needham. "The *Review* is looking for fiction, poetry and essays that linger in the mind's eye with frightful clarity after the magazine has been put aside and the business of life resumed." Publishes three times yearly. Estab. 1955. Circ. 1,500.
Needs: "More good fiction and essays and less bad poetry." Length: 6,000 words maximum.
How to Contact: Submit complete ms with personal biographical note, SASE. Photocopied submissions OK. Reports in 6 weeks. Sample copy for $5.
Payment: 1 free contributor's copy.
Terms: Acquires one-time rights.
Advice: "We want to increase the ratio of fiction to poetry. Stick with a few magazines and let them really get to know your work."

‡POSKISNOLT PRESS (I, II, IV), Yesterday's Press, Yesterday's Press, 224 82nd St., Brooklyn NY 11209. (718)680-3899. Editor: Patricia D. Coscia. Fiction Editor: Richard B. Murray. Magazine: 7×8½; 20 pages; regular typing paper. Estab. 1989. Circ. 100.
Needs: Contemporary, erotica, ethnic, experimental, fantasy, feminist, gay, humor/satire, lesbian, literary, mainstream, prose poem, psychic/supernatural/occult, romance, young adult, senior citizen/ retirement, western, young adult/teen (10-18 years). "X-rated material is not accepted!" Plans to publish a special fiction issue or anthology in the future. Receives 50 unsolicited mss/month. Accepts 30 mss/issue; 100+ mss/year. Publishes ms 6 months after acceptance. Length: 200 words average; 100 words minimum; 500 words maximum. Publishes short shorts. Length: 100-500 words. Sometimes critiques rejected mss and recommends other markets.
How to Contact: Query first with clips of published work or send complete manuscript with cover letter. Reports in 1 week on queries; 6 months on mss. SASE. Accepts simultaneous, photocopied and computer printout submissions. Sample copy for $2 with #10 SASE and $2 postage. Fiction guidelines for #10 SASE and $2 postage.
Payment: Pays with free subscription to magazine or contributor's copies; charges for extras.
Terms: Pays on acceptance for all rights, first rights or one-time rights. Sends galleys to author.

THE POST (II), Publishers Syndication International, Suite 856, 1377 K St., Washington DC 20005. Editor: A.P. Samuels. Newspaper: 8½×11; 32 pages. Monthly. Estab. 1988.
Needs: Adventure, romance and suspense/mystery. "No explicit sex, gore, extreme violence or bad language." Receives 75 unsolicited mss/month. Buys 1 ms/issue; 12 mss/year. Time between acceptance and publication varies. Agented fiction 10%. Length: 10,000 words average.

How to Contact: Send complete manuscript with cover letter. Reports on mss in 5 weeks. Accepts computer printout submissions. Fiction guidelines for #10 SAE and 1 first class stamp.
Payment: ½¢ to 4¢/word.
Terms: Pays on acceptance for all rights.

POTATO EYES (II), Appalachian Voices, Nightshade, Box 76, Troy ME 04987. (207)948-3427. Editors: Carolyn Page and Roy Zarucchi. Magazine: 6×9; 80 pages; 60 lb text paper; 80 lb Curtis flannel cover. "We tend to showcase Appalachian talent from Alabama to Quebec, and in doing so, we hope to dispel hackneyed stereotypes and political borders. Our subscribers have included: boat builder, teacher, dairy farmer, college prof, doctor, lawyer, world traveler, lumberman . . . and that was just in last week's batch."
Estab. 1988. Circ. 800.
Needs: Contemporary, humor/satire, literary, mainstream, regional, and rural themes. Receives 20 unsolicited mss/month. Accepts 3-4 mss/issue; 6-8 mss/year. Publishes ms 6 months-1 year after acceptance. Recently published work by Simone Poirier-Bures, Lynn Taesch and Gary Barker. Length: 3,000 words maximum; 2,000 average. Publishes short shorts. Length: 450 words. Sometimes critiques rejected mss and recommends other markets.
How to Contact: Send complete ms with cover letter. Reports in 2 weeks-2 months on mss. SASE. Accepts computer printouts, no dot matrix. Sample copy $4.75, including postage. Fiction guidelines with #10 SAE.
Payment: Contributor's copies.
Terms: Acquires first North American serial rights.
Advice: "We care about the larger issues, including pollution, ecology, bio-regionalism, uncontrolled progress and 'condominia,' as well as the rights of the individual, particularly the elderly. We care about television, the great sewer pipe of America, and what it is doing to America's youth. We are exploring these issues with writers who have originality, a reordered perspective, and submit to us generous sprinklings of humor and satire. Although we do occasionally comment on valid fiction, we have walked away unscathed from the world of academia and refuse to correct manuscripts. We respect our contributors and treat them as professionals, however, and write personal responses to every submission if given an SASE. We expect the same treatment—clean copy without multi folds or corrections. We like brief non-Narcissistic cover letters containing the straight scoop. We suggest that beginning fiction writers spend the money they have set aside for creative writing courses or conferences and spend it instead on subscriptions to good little literary magazines."

THE POTTERSFIELD PORTFOLIO (II,IV), New Writing From Atlantic Canada, Crazy Quilt Press, 19 Oakhill Dr., Halifax Nova Scotia B3M 2V3 Canada. (902)443-9600. Editors: Donalee Moulton-Barrett, Barb Cottrell, Peggy Amirault. Magazine: 8½×11; 52 pages; good quality paper; coated cover stock; illustrations. "All material in *The Portfolio* is written by Atlantic Canadians or those with a connection—significant—to the region." Semi-annually. Estab. 1979.
Needs: Contemporary, ethnic, experimental, fantasy, feminist, gay, humor/satire, lesbian, literary, mainstream, prose poem, regional, science fiction. Receives 30-50 fiction mss/month. Buys 8-10 mss/issue. Published work by Lesley Choyce, Spider Robinson, Silver Donald Cameron; published new writers within the last year. Publishes short shorts. Sometimes comments on rejected mss and recommends other markets.
How to Contact: Send complete ms with cover letter and enough information for short bio in journal. Reports in 2 months. SASE. Simultaneous and photocopied submissions OK. Accepts computer printout submissions. Sample copy $5 (US).
Payment: Fiction $30, poetry $10, and contributor's copies.
Terms: Pays on publication for first Canadian English-language serial rights.
Advice: "Still believe the marketplace is open to beginning writers. Tailor your fiction to a particular market—it helps to break in more quickly and avoids unnecessary rejections from publications that are not buying the type of work you're producing."

PRAIRIE FIRE (II), Prairie Fire Press Inc., Room 423, 100 Arthur St., Winnipeg, Manitoba R3B 1H3 Canada. (204)943-9066. Managing Editor: Andris Taskans. Fiction Editor: Ellen Smythe. Magazine: 6×9; 96 pages; offset bond paper; sturdy cover stock; illustrations; photos. "Essays, critical reviews, short fiction and poetry. For writers and readers interested in Canadian literature." Published 4 times/year. Estab. 1978. Circ. 1,200.

Close-up

Carolyn Page and Roy Zarucchi
Co-editors
Potato Eyes

"We know of no other literary magazine that focuses specifically on the entirety of the Appalachian chain, from Alabama to the Laurentians in Quebec," say *Potato Eyes* co-editors, Carolyn Page and Roy Zarucchi. "We set out to showcase talent from this geographical sphere of influence that transcends international borders."

Page and Zarucchi established *Potato Eyes* in 1989 because they wanted a means of maintaining contact with the network of writers they had met years before in North Carolina. Page attended Western Carolina University on a writing fellowship. She and Zarucchi met when they became involved with a community college literary magazine in the early 1980s.

"When we quit the classroom, we broke the red pencil," they say. "We refuse to spend our time correcting nitpick items such as punctuation and spelling. We have seen the frustration of academicians who refuse to play by the institutional rules," they say. "Try being a rogue narrative poet in a Neo-formalist environment." Their 1991 *Novel and Short Story Writer's Market* listing says "We have walked away unscathed from the world of academia."

As a result, Page and Zarucchi founded *Potato Eyes*, a publication subtitled Appalachian Voices. "There's a danger to being called Appalachian," the editors admit. "To some that means dialect, which is very difficult to write well." Therefore, they ask, as many editors do, that potential contributors send for a sample copy before submitting. The 6x9, 90-page magazine has a flannel cover and quality natural paper: a handsome product even for those with no desire to have their work appear between the covers.

"We publish for a general audience, educated but not expert, in literature," Page and Zarucchi say. "We stress accessibility of the written word." They publish pieces with a strong sense of place and immediacy. Their preferences run to rural rebelliousness, attention to environment and natural setting, and "wicked good" satire. "We don't get enough of this."

Science fiction and romance will not find a home in *Potato Eyes*. The editors have also been called anti-urban. "That doesn't entirely displease us," they say. "We'd rather be considered pro-rural, though." The average time for handling a submission is about four weeks. "This allows us to consider work in batches and thus make some comparative decisions." Both editors read every submission.

"Send us your short stories flat, neat and with a cover letter that is written by a human being," Page and Zarucchi say. "Don't tell us how famous you are, or how many MFA degrees you've collected, or whose coat tails you're riding. Be internal and real with us." They return the favor with a hand-written note for every acceptance or rejection.

The editorial diligence of Page and Zarucchi has not gone unnoticed in the magazine's brief history. *Potato Eyes* is perhaps one of the last three literary magazines to earn a seed

grant from the Coordinating Council of Literary Magazines. The grant had been awarded to magazines that had published fewer than three issues. Now known as the Council of Literary Magazines and Presses, the Council's grant money has regrettably dried up.

Page and Zarucchi also operate Nightshade Press, which publishes and promotes 10 poetry chapbooks per year. "We are constantly amazed by the number of good manuscripts that we and other small press editors have to turn away," the editors say. "Because we are such a small house, we are currently reading only poetry chaps." They hope to publish short story collections in 1992, and will begin accepting queries at that time. "We would like to stress *queries* only, please." Preference will be given to writers whose work has appeared in *Potato Eyes*.

"We like to think that universality of meaning and regionality of setting are not mutually exclusive. The small press movement promotes diversity and individuality and runs contrary to current notions that homogeneity is desirable," Page and Zarucchi say. "Large publishing houses tend not to publish what they can't mass market and sell in the mall. The small press has an important role to play and audience to serve in offering an alternative. One of the keys to success is to treat writers and subscribers as if they were human beings and not marketing units." The editors of *Potato Eyes* do indeed take a very human approach, and their magazine reflects this dedication.

— Mark Kissling

Needs: Literary, contemporary, experimental, prose poem, reviews. "We will consider work on any topic of artistic merit, including short chapters from novels-in-progress. We wish to avoid gothic, confession, religious, romance and pornography." Buys 4-5 mss/issue, 8-10 mss/year. Does not read mss in summer. Recently published work by Sandra Birdsell, George Bowering, Robert Kroetsch; published new writers within the last year. Receives 18-20 unsolicited fiction mss each month. Publishes short shorts. Length: 8,000 maximum; no minimum; 3,000 words average. Critiques rejected mss "if requested and when there is time." Sometimes recommmends other markets.
How to Contact: Send complete ms with IRC w/envelope and short bio. Reports in 2-3 months. Sample copy for $7 (Canadian).
Payment: $60 for the first page, $30 for each additional page. 1 free author's copy. 60% of cover price for extras.
Terms: Pays on publication for first North American serial rights. Rights revert to author on publication.
Advice: "We are publishing more fiction, and we are commissioning illustrations. Read our publication before submitting. We prefer Canadian material. Most mss are not ready for publication. Be neat, double space. Be the best writer you can be."

THE PRAIRIE JOURNAL OF CANADIAN LITERATURE (I, II, IV), Prairie Journal Press, Box 997, Station G, Calgary, Alberta T3A 3G2 Canada. Editor: A.E. Burke. Journal: 7 × 8½; 50-60 pages; white bond paper; Cadillac cover stock; cover illustrations. Journal of creative writing and scholarly essays, reviews for literary audience. Semiannually. Published special fiction issue last year. Estab. 1983.
Needs: Contemporary, literary, prose poem, regional, excerpted novel, novella, typed single space on camera-ready copy. Canadian authors given preference. No romance, erotica, pulp. Receives 20-40 unsolicited mss each month. Accepts 10-15 ms/issue; 20-30 mss/year. *Charges reading fee of up to $1/page "if help requested."* Suggests sample issue before submitting ms. Recently published work by Nancy Ellen Russell, Carla Mobley, Patrick Quinn; published new writers within the last year. Length: 2,500 words average; 100 words minimum; 3,000 words maximum. Sometimes critiques rejected mss and recommends other markets.
How to Contact: Send complete ms. Reports in 1 month. SASE or SAE and IRC. Photocopied submissions OK. Accepts computer printout if letter quality, no dot-matrix. Sample copy $3 (Canadian) and SAE with $1.10 for postage or IRC. Include cover letter of past credits—a friendly introduction to a new acquaintance. Reply to queries for SAE with 48¢ for postage or IRC. No American stamps.
Payment: Contributor's copies.
Terms: Acquires first North American serial rights. In Canada author retains copyright.
Advice: Interested in "innovational work of quality. Beginning writers welcome. I have chosen to publish fiction simply because many magazines do not. Those who do in Canada are, for the most part, seeking formulaic writing. There is no point in simply republishing known authors or conventional, predictable plots. Of the genres we receive fiction is most often of the highest calibre. It is a very competitive field. Be proud of what you send. You're worth it."

PRAIRIE SCHOONER (II), University of Nebraska, English Department, 201 Andrews Hall, Lincoln NE 68588-0334. (402)472-3191. Magazine: 6 × 9; 144 pages; good stock paper; heavy cover stock. "A general literary quarterly of stories, poems, essays and reviews for a general, educated audience that reads for pleasure." Quarterly. Estab. 1927. Circ. 2,000.
Needs: Good fiction. Accepts 4-5 mss/issue. Receives approximately 150 unsolicited fiction mss each month. Recently published work by Antonya Nelson, Stephen Pett, Josephine Jacobsen; published new writers within the last year. Length: varies.
How to Contact: Send complete ms with SASE and cover letter listing previous publications—where, when. Reports in 3 months. Sample copy $2.
Payment: 3 free author's copies.
Terms: Acquires all rights. Will reassign rights upon request after publication. Annual prize of $500 for best fiction, $500 for best new writer (poetry or fiction), $500 for best poetry; additional prizes, $250-1,000.
Advice: "*Prairie Schooner* is eager to see fiction from beginning and established writers. Be tenacious. Accept rejection as a temporary setback and send out rejected stories to other magazines."

THE PRESIDENT JOURNAL (II), President Productions, General Delivery, Tofield, Alberta T0B 4J0 Canada. Editor: Chris Laursen. Magazine: 5½ × 8½; 36-64 pages; recycled paper; recycled paper cover; illustrations and photographs. "Promotes multiculturalism, anti-fascism, anti-racism, anti-sexism, freedom of speech, human rights. Publishes fiction, mail art, reviews and articles for a wide audience. Some audience members are 16; some are in their 60s. Open-minded, exploring audience." Estab. 1990. Circ. 125+.

Needs: Ethnic, experimental, horror, humor/satire, literary, psychic/supernatural/occult, suspense/mystery, translations, surreal. "No pornography or racist literature. We only wish to see what is quoted to our interest." Publishes annual special fiction issue. Receives 50+ mss/month. Accepts 10-20 mss/issue; 40-100 mss/year. Publishes ms 3 months after acceptance. Recently published work by B.Z. Niditch, Torben Rolfsen, Randy MacKenzie. Length: 1,000 words average; 2,000 words maximum. Publishes short shorts. Length: 50-500 words. Always comments on rejected mss and recommends other markets.

How to Contact: Query first or send complete manuscript with cover letter including "where previously published; any literary, art, musical activites involved in." Reports in 1-4 weeks. SASE. Simultaneous, photocopied and reprint submissions OK. Accepts computer printout submissions (in special cases only!) Sample copy for $3 Canadian, (or currency equivalent) or 3 IRCs. Fiction guidelines for #10 SAE and 1 IRC.

Payment: Pays contributor's copies.

Terms: All rights reverted to author upon publication.

Advice: "Escape endings are *never* acceptable and the story must be memorable. I notice enthusiastic writers who need an alternative outlet for their work, and there are many of them; many of them who also write for the mainstream. Enthusiasm plus uniqueness stand out. Your story should make a comment of some sort, individual or major. Write about what concerns you."

PRIMAVERA (II, IV), University of Chicago, 1448 E. 52nd St. #274, Chicago IL 60615. (312)324-5920. Editorial Board. Magazine: 5½ × 8½; 100 pages; 60 lb paper; glossy cover; illustrations; photos. Literature and graphics reflecting the experiences of women: poetry, short stories, photos, drawings. Readership: "an audience interested in women's ideas and experiences." Annually. Estab. 1975. Circ. 1,000.

Needs: Literary, contemporary, science fiction, fantasy, feminist, gay/lesbian and humor. "We dislike slick stories packaged for more traditional women's magazines. We publish only work reflecting the experiences of women, but also publish mss by men." Accepts 6-10 mss/issue. Receives approximately 40 unsolicited fiction mss each month. Recently published work by Ann Harleman, Janet Sisk; published new writers within the last year. Length: 25 pages maximum. Critiques rejected mss when there is time. Often gives suggestions for revisions and invites re-submission of revised ms. Occasionally recommends other markets

How to Contact: Send complete ms with SASE. Cover letter not necessary. Accepts computer printout submissions, "if assured it is not a multiple submission." Prefers letter-quality. Reports in 1 week – 5 months on mss. Publishes ms up to 1 year after acceptance. Sample copy $5; $6 for recent issues. Guidelines for #10 SASE.

Payment: 2 free author's copies.

Terms: Acquires first rights.

PRISM INTERNATIONAL (II), E462-1866 Main Mall, University of British Columbia, Vancouver, British Columbia V6T 1W5 Canada. (604)228-2514. Executive Editor: Heidi Neufeld Raine. Editor: Blair Rosser. Magazine: 6 × 9; 72-80 pages; Zephyr book paper; Cornwall, coated one side cover; photos on cover. "A journal of contemporary writing – fiction, poetry, drama, creative non-fiction and translation. *Prism*'s audience is world-wide, as are our contributors." Readership: "Public and university libraries, individual subscriptions, bookstores – an audience concerned with the contemporary in literature." Published 4 times/year. Estab. 1959. Circ. 1,200.

Needs: Literary, contemporary, prose poem or translations. "Most any category as long as it is *fresh*. No overtly religious, overtly theme-heavy material or anything more message- or category-oriented than self-contained." Buys approximately 70 mss/year. Receives 50 unsolicited fiction mss each month. Published new writers within the last year. Length: 5,000 words maximum "though flexible for outstanding work." Publishes short shorts. Critiques rejected mss when there is time. Occasionally recommends other markets.

How to Contact: Send complete ms with SASE or SAE, IRC and cover letter with bio, information and publications list. "Keep it simple. US contributors take note: US stamps are not valid in Canada and your ms will not likely be returned if it contains US stamps. Send International Reply Coupons instead." Accepts computer printout submissions. Prefers letter-quality. Reports in 3 months. Sample copy $4 (Canadian).

Payment: $20/printed page, 1 free year's subscription.
Terms: Pays on publication for first North American serial rights.
Advice: "Too many derivative, self-indulgent pieces; sloppy construction and imprecise word usage. There's not enough attention to voice and not enough invention. We are committed to publishing outstanding literary work in all genres."

PRISONERS OF THE NIGHT (II), An Adult Anthology of Erotica, Fright, Allure and . . . Vampirism, MKASHEF Enterprises, Box 368, Poway CA 92074-0368. Editor: Alayne Gelfand. Magazine: 8½×11; 100-150 pages; 20 lb paper; slick cover; illustrations. "An adult, erotic vampire anthology of original character stories and poetry. Heterosexual and homosexual situations included." Annually. Estab. 1987. Circ. approx. 5,000.
Needs: Adventure, contemporary, erotica, experimental, fantasy, feminist, gay, horror, lesbian, literary, prose poem, psychic/supernatural/occult, science fiction, suspense/mystery, western. "All stories must be vampire stories, with unique characters, unusual situations." No fiction that deals with anyone else's creations, i.e. no "Dracula" stories. Receives 30-50 unsolicited fiction mss/month. Accepts 10-20 mss/issue. Publishes ms 1-11 months after acceptance. Recently published work by Elaine C. Crombie, Sonia and Naomi Hughes, Wendy Rathbone, Della Van Hise; published new writers within the last year. Length: under 10,000 words. Publishes short shorts. Sometimes critiques rejected mss. Recommends other markets.
How to Contact: Send complete ms with short cover letter. "A brief introduction of author to the editor; name, address, *some* past credits if available." Reports in 1 week on queries; 2-4 months on mss. Reads *only* September-March. SASE. Photocopied submissions OK. Accepts computer printout submissions. Accepts electronic submissions via IBM Word Perfect (4.2), disk—files no longer than 18 pages each. Sample copy $15. Fiction guidelines for #10 SAE and 1 first class stamp.
Payment: Pays 1¢/word for fiction.
Terms: Pays on publication for first North American serial rights.
Advice: "The unique *type* of vampire will catch my eye quickest. Don't be trite, don't do the expected with your plot. Erotic, sensual elements are preferred to the cerebral. Detailed characterization is required. No pornography; I do not want cheap or tawdry sex for shock value. Graphic erotica *is* acceptable. Be original, stretch your imagination."

PROCESSED WORLD (II), #1829, 41 Sutter St., San Francisco CA 94104. (415)626-2160. Editor: Chris Carlson. Magazine: 8½×11; 44-48 pages; 20 lb bond paper; glossy cover stock; illustrations; photos. Magazine about work, office work, computers and hi-tech (satire). Triannually. May publish special fiction issue. Estab. 1981. Circ. 4,000.
Needs: Comics, confession, contemporary, fantasy, humor/satire, literary, science fiction. Accepts 1-2 mss/issue; 3-6 mss/year. Recently published work by James Pollack. Published new writers within the last year. Length: 1,250 words average; 100 words minimum; 1,500 words maximum. Occasionally critiques rejected ms.
How to Contact: Send complete ms. Reports in 4 months. SASE. Simultaneous and photocopied submissions OK. Accepts computer printout submissions. Prefers letter-quality. Sample copy $4.
Payment: Subscription to magazine.
Terms: Acquires one-time rights.
Advice: "Make it real. Make it critical of the status quo. Read the magazine before you send us a story."

‡PROPHETIC VOICES (II), An International Literary Journal, Heritage Trails Press, 94 Santa Maria Dr., Novato CA 94947. (415)897-5679. Editor: Goldie L. Morales. Fiction Editors: Ruth Wildes Schuler and Jeanne Leigh Schuler. Magazine: 6¾×8¼; 100-144 pages; bond paper; textured cover; illustrations and photographs. "Material with a social awareness/ecology slant for an adult audience. Interested in material from other countries." Semiannually.
Needs: Historical (general) and prose poem. "We want gripping material that is also educational." No religious, sexual, juvenile, sports, young adult. Receives 10 unsolicited mss/month. Accepts 1 or 2 mss/issue; 3 or 4 mss/year. Publishes ms 1-3 years after acceptance. Recently published work by P. Raja, Denver Stull and Kirpal Gordon. Publishes short shorts. Recommends other markets.

How to Contact: Send complete manuscript. Reports in 5 weeks on queries; 3 months on mss. SASE. Simultaneous, photocopied and reprint submissions OK. Sample copy $6.
Payment: Pays contributor's copy.
Terms: Acquires one-time rights.
Advice: "A story should be different, educational—one that a reader is not likely to forget. Material must have universal and timeless appeal. We are not interested in trendy stories or those appealing only to a limited region or geographical locale."

‡**PROVINCETOWN ARTS (II)**, Provincetown Arts, Inc., 650 Commercial St., P.O. Box 35, Provincetown MA 02657. (508)487-3167. Editor: Christopher Busa. Magazine: 9×12; 184 pages; 60 lb. uncoated paper; 12 pcs cover; illustrations and photographs. "*PA* focuses broadly on the artists, writers and theater of America's oldest continuous art colony." Annually. Estab. 1985. Circ. 5,000.
Needs: Plans special fiction issue. Receives 90 unsolicited mss/year. Buys 3 mss/issue. Publishes ms 3 months after acceptance. Recently published work by Carole Maso and Hilary Masters. Length: 3,000 words average; 1,500 words minimum; 5,000 words maximum. Publishes short shorts. Length: 1,500-5,000 words. Sometimes critiques rejected mss and recommends other markets.
How to Contact: Send complete manuscript with cover letter including previous publications. Reports in 2 weeks on queries; 3 months on mss. SASE. Photocopied submissions OK. Sample copy $7.50.
Payment: Pays $75-300.
Terms: Pays on publication for first rights. Sends galleys to author.

PSI (II), Suite 856, 1377 K Street NW, Washington DC 20005. Editor: A.P. Samuels. Magazine: 8½×11; 32 pages; bond paper; self cover. "Mystery and romance for an adult audience." Bimonthly. Estab. 1987.
Needs: Romance (contemporary, historical, young adult), suspense/mystery. Receives 35 unsolicited mss/month. Buys 1-2 mss/issue. Published work by Sharon K. Garner, Michael Riedel; published new writers within the last year. Length: 10,000 words average. Publishes short shorts. Critiques rejected mss "only on a rare occasion."
How to Contact: Send complete ms with cover letter. Reports in 2 weeks on queries; 4 weeks on mss. SASE. Accepts computer printout submissions. Accepts electronic submissions via disk.
Payment: Pays 1-4¢/word plus royalty.
Terms: Pays on acceptance for first North American serial rights.
Advice: "Manuscripts must be for a general audience. Just good plain story telling (make it compelling). No explicit sex or ghoulish violence."

THE PUB (I, II), Ansuda Publications, Box 158J, Harris IA 51345. Editor/Publisher: Daniel R. Betz. Magazine: 5½×8½; 72 pages; mimeo paper; heavy stock cover; illustrations on cover. "We prefer stories to have some sort of social impact within them, no matter how slight, so our fiction is different from what's published in most magazines. We aren't afraid to be different or publish something that might be objectionable to current thought. *Pub* is directed toward those people, from all walks of life, who are themselves 'different' and unique, who are interested in new ideas and forms of reasoning. Our readers enjoy *Pub* and believe in what we are doing." Published 2 times/year. Estab. 1979. Circ. 350.
Needs: Literary, psychic/supernatural/occult, fantasy, horror, mystery, adventure, serialized and condensed novels. "We are looking for honest, straightforward stories. No love stories or stories that ramble on for pages about nothing in particular." Buys reprints. Accepts 4-6 mss/issue. Receives approximately 35-40 unsolicited fiction mss each month. Published new writers within the last year. Length: 8,000 words maximum. Sometimes recommends other markets.
How to Contact: Send complete ms with SASE. Accepts computer printout submissions. Prefers letter-quality. Reports in 1 month. Publishes ms an average of 6 months after acceptance. Sample copy $3. Guidelines for #10 SASE.
Payment: 2 free author's copies. Cover price less special bulk discount for extras.
Terms: Acquires first North American serial rights and second serial rights on reprints.
Advice: "Read the magazine—that is *very* important. If you send a story close to what we're looking for, we'll try to help guide you to exactly what we want. We appreciate neat copy, and if photocopies are sent, we like to be able to read all of the story. Fiction seems to work for us—we are a literary magazine and have better luck with fiction than articles or poems."

‡**PUCKERBRUSH REVIEW (I, II)**, Puckerbrush Press, 76 Main St., Okono ME 04473. (207)866-4868/ 581-3832. Editor: Constance Hunting. Magazine: 9×12; 80-100 pages; illustrations. "We publish mostly new Maine writers; interviews, fiction, reviews, poetry for a literary audience." Semiannually. Estab. 1979. Circ. approx. 500.
Needs: Experimental, gay (occasionally), literary, belles letters. "Nothing cliché." Receives 30 unsolicited mss/month. Accepts 6 mss/issue; 12 mss/year. Publishes ms 1 year after acceptance. Recently published work by Dwight Cathcart, Tema Nason. Sometimes publishes short shorts. Sometimes critiques rejected mss and recommends other markets.
How to Contact: Send complete manuscript with cover letter. Reports in 2 months. SASE. Simultaneous submissions OK. Sample copy $2. Fiction guidelines free.
Payment: Pays in contributor's copies.
Advice: "Fiction is getting energetic again. Just write the story as it would like you to do."

PUERTO DEL SOL (I), New Mexico State University, Box 3E, Las Cruces NM 88003. (505)646-3931. Editor-in-Chief: Kevin McIlvoy. Poetry Editor: Joe Somoza. Magazine: 6×9; 200 pages; 60 lb paper; 70 lb cover stock; photos sometimes. "We publish quality material from anyone. Poetry, fiction, art, photos, interviews, reviews, parts-of-novels, long poems." Semiannually. Estab. 1961. Circ. 1,000.
Needs: Contemporary, ethnic, experimental, literary, mainstream, prose poem, excerpted novel and translations. Receives varied number of unsolicited fiction mss/month. Accepts 8-10 mss/issue; 12-15 mss/year. Does not read mss May-August. Published work by Ken Kuhlken, Susan Thornton; published new writers within the last year. Occasionally critiques rejected mss.
How to Contact: Send complete ms with SASE. Simultaneous and photocopied submissions OK. Accepts computer printout submissions. Reports in 2 months. Sample copy $4.
Payment: 3 contributor's copies.
Terms: Acquires one-time rights (rights revert to author).
Advice: "We are open to all forms of fiction, from the conventional to the wildly experimental, as long as they have integrity and are well written. Too often we receive very impressively 'polished' mss that will dazzle readers with their sheen but offer no character/reader experience of lasting value."

PULPHOUSE (II), The Hardback Magazine of Dangerous Fiction, Box 1227, Eugene OR 97440. Editor: Kristine Kathryn Rusch. Magazine: 200-250 pages; 70 lb paper; hard cover. Quarterly. Estab. 1988. Circ. 1,250 (1,000 cloth-bound trade editions; 250 leather-bound editions).
Needs: Fantasy, horror, science fiction, speculative fiction. Recently published work by Harlan Ellison, Kate Wilhelm, Michael Bishop, Charles de Line, George Alec Effinger; published new writers within the last year. Length: 7,500 words maximum.
How to Contact: Send complete ms with cover letter "that gives publication history, work history, or any other information relevant to the magazine. Don't tell us about the story. The story will tell us about the story." SASE. Sample copy for $20 (cloth); $60 (leather). Fiction guidelines for #10 SAE and 1 first class stamp.
Payment: Pays 3-6¢/word.
Terms: Pays on acceptance for one-time anthology rights.
Advice: "*Pulphouse* is subtitled The Hardback Magazine of Dangerous Fiction. By 'dangerous,' we mean fiction that takes risks, that presents viewpoints not commonly held in the field. Although such fiction can include experimental writing, it is usually best served by clean, clear prose. We are looking for strong characterization, fast-moving plot, and intriguing settings."

‡**PULSAR (II), Science Fiction and Fantasy**, Tony Ubelhor, P.O. Box 886, Evansville IN 47706. (812)479-7022. Editor: Tony Ubelhor. Magazine: 8×11; 72 pages; 20 lb. paper; glossy cover; b&w illustrations and photographs. "Science fiction and fantasy stories, articles, interviews for an adult audience." Semiannually. Estab. 1986. Circ. 400.
Needs: Experimental, fantasy, science fiction. "Always looking for articles and retrospectives on the science fiction field, as well as interviews with writers and notable fans." No horror. Publishes annual special fiction issue. Receives 10 unsolicited mss/month. Accepts 5-10 mss/issue; 10-20 mss/year. Publishes ms 1-6 months after acceptance. Recently published work by Mike Resnick, Arlan Andrews, Yvonne Navarro, C.S. Williams. Length: 6,000 words average; 1,500 words minimum; 12,000 words maximum. Publishes short shorts. Length: about 6,000-10,000 words. Sometimes critiques rejected mss.
How to Contact: Send complete manuscript with cover letter. Reports in 4-6 weeks on queries; 3-4 months on mss. SASE. Photocopied and reprint submissions OK. Accepts computer printout submissions. Sample copy $3.50. Fiction guidelines free for SAE and 1 first class stamp.

Payment: Pays contributor's copies. Charge for extras.
Terms: Acquires first North American serial rights.
Advice: "We encourage beginning writers. A rejection from us is always an invitation to submit again."

QUARRY (II), Quarry Press, Box 1061, Kingston, Ontario K7L 4Y5 Canada. (613)548-8429. Editor: Steven Heighton. Magazine: 5½×8½; 120 pages; #1 book 120 paper; 160 lb Curtis Tweed cover stock; illustrations; photos. "Quarterly anthology of new Canadian poetry, prose. Also includes graphics, photographs and book reviews. We seek readers interested in vigorous, disciplined, new Canadian writing." Published special fiction issue; plans another. Estab. 1952. Circ. 1,100.
Needs: Experimental, fantasy, literary, science fiction, serialized/excerpted novel and translations. "We do not want highly derivative or clichéd style." Receives 60-80 unsolicited fiction mss/month. Buys 4-5 mss/issue; 20 mss/year. Does not read in July. Less than 5% of fiction is agented. Published work by Diane Schoemperlen, David Helwig, Joan Fern Shaw. Published new writers within the last year. Length: 3,000 words average. Publishes short shorts. Usually critiques rejected mss and recommends other markets.
How to Contact: Send complete ms with SAE, IRC and brief bio. Photocopied submissions OK. Accepts computer printout submissions; prefers letter-quality. Publishes ms an average of 3-6 months after acceptance. Sample copy $5 with 4×7 SAE and 50¢ Canadian postage or IRC.
Payment: $10/page; 1 year subscription to magazine and 1 contributor's copy.
Terms: Pays on publication for first North American serial rights.
Advice: "Read previous *Quarry* to see standard we seek. Read Canadian fiction to see Canadian trends. We seek aggressive experimentation which is coupled with competence (form, style) and stimulating subject matter. We also like traditional forms. Our annual prose issue (spring) is always a sellout. Many of our selections have been anthologized. Don't send US stamps or SASE. Use IRC. Submit with brief bio."

QUARTERLY WEST (II), University of Utah, 317 Olpin Union, Salt Lake City UT 84112. (801)581-3938. Editors: C.F. Pinkerton, Regina Oost. Fiction Editor: Tom Hazuka. Magazine: 6×9; 150+ pages; 60 lb paper; 5-color cover stock; illustrations and photographs rarely. "We try to publish a variety of fiction by writers from all over the country. Our publication is aimed primarily at an educated audience which is interested in contemporary literature and criticism." Semiannually. "We sponsor biennual novella competition." Estab. 1976. Circ. 1,000.
Needs: Literary, contemporary, translations. Buys 4-6 mss/issue, 10-12 mss/year. Receives approximately 100 unsolicited fiction mss each month. Recently published work by Andre Dubus and Chuck Rosenthal; published new writers within the last year. No preferred length. Critiques rejected mss when there is time. Sometimes recommends other markets.
How to Contact: Send complete ms. Cover letters welcome. SASE. Accepts computer printout submissions; prefers letter-quality. Reports in 2 months; "sooner, if possible." Sample copy for $4.50.
Payment: $15-$300.
Terms: Pays on publication for first North American serial rights.
Advice: "Write a clear and unified story which does not rely on tricks or gimmicks for its effects." Mss are rejected because of "poor style, formula writing, clichés, weak characterization. We solicit quite frequently, but tend more toward the surprises—unsolicited. Don't send more than one story per submission, but submit as often as you like."

QUEEN OF ALL HEARTS (II), Queen Magazine, Montfort Missionaries, 26 S. Saxon Ave., Bay Shore NY 11706. (516)665-0726. Managing Editor: Roger M. Charest, S.M.M. Magazine: 7¾×10¾; 48 pages; self cover stock; illustrations; photos. Magazine of "stories, articles and features on the Mother of God by explaining the Scriptural basis and traditional teaching of the Catholic Church concerning the Mother of Jesus, her influence in fields of history, literature, art, music, poetry, etc." Bimonthly. Estab. 1950. Circ. 5,000.
Needs: Religious/inspirational. "No mss not about Our Lady, the Mother of God, the Mother of Jesus." Receives 3 unsolicited fiction mss/month. Buys 3-4 mss/issue; 24 mss/year. Length: 1,500-2,000 words. Sometimes recommends other markets.
How to Contact: Send complete ms with SASE. Photocopied submissions OK. Reports in 1 month on mss. Publishes ms 6 months to one year after acceptance. Sample copy $1.75 with 9×12 SAE.
Payment: Varies. 6 free contributor's copies.
Advice: "We are publishing stories with a Marian theme."

QUEEN'S QUARTERLY: A Canadian Review (II, IV), John Watson Hall, Queen's University, Kingston, Ontario K7L 3N6 Canada. (613)545-2667. Editors: Ms. Martha Bailey. Magazine: 6 × 9; 800 pages/year; 50 lb Zephyr antique paper; 65 lb Mayfair antique britewhite cover stock; illustrations. "A general interest intellectual review, featuring articles on science, politics, humanities, arts and letters. Book reviews, poetry and fiction." Published quarterly. Estab. 1893. Circ. 1,700.
Needs: Adventure, contemporary, experimental, fantasy, historical (general), humor/satire, literary, mainstream, science fiction and women's. *"Special emphasis on work by Canadian writers."* Buys 2 mss/issue; 8 mss/year. Published work by Janette Turner Hospital; published new writers within the last year. Length: 5,000 words maximum.
How to Contact: "Send complete ms and a copy on disk in Wordperfect—only one at a time—with SASE." Photocopied submissions OK if not part of multiple submission. Accepts computer printout submissions. Prefers letter-quality. Reports within 3 months. Sample copy $5.
Payment: $100-300 for fiction, 2 contributor's copies and 1-year subscription. $5 charge for extras.
Terms: Pays on publication for first North American serial rights. Sends galleys to author.

QUINTESSENTIAL SPACE DEBRIS (I, IV), Box 42, Worthington OH 43085. Editor: Kathleen Gallagher. Newsletter: 8½ × 11; illustrations and photographs. "Humorous articles, anecdotes, parodies of book reviews or movie reviews, serious articles about the use of humor in science-fiction books and movies. For fans and readers of science fiction and fantasy, comic books and media." Semiannually. Plans special fiction issue. Estab. 1987. Circ. 500.
Needs: Fantasy, humor/satire, science fiction. No "Star Trek, Star Trek: The Next Generation or Dr. Who pastiches using established television and movie characters." Receives "not many" unsolicited mss/month. Publishes ms 6 months-1 year after acceptance. Publishes short shorts. Sometimes critiques rejected mss.
How to Contact: Query first or send complete ms with cover letter. Reports in 2 months on queries; 3 months on mss. SASE for query, not needed for ms. Simultaneous, photocopied and reprint submissions OK. Accepts computer printout submissions. Sample copy for 9 × 12 SAE and 4 first class stamps. Fiction guidelines for #10 SAE and 1 first class stamp.
Payment: Free subscription to magazine and contributor's copies.
Terms: All rights revert on publication.

‡RADIO VOID (II), Radio Zero, P.O. Box 5983, Providence RI 02903. Editor: Brian T. Gallagher. Fiction Editor: Christopher Pierson. Magazine: 8½ × 11; 48 pages; newsprint paper; illustrations and photographs (varies). "Conflicting, themeless writers...an eclectic blend in which, when sifted, can be found a common literary thread. We publish anything. Originally for a college audience, we are in the throes of audience change." Quarterly. Estab. 1986. Circ. 3,000.
Needs: Open to all types of fiction. Receives approx. 20 unsolicited fiction mss/month. Accepts 10-12 mss/issue; 20-60 mss/year ("it truly varies"). Publishes ms 3-4 months after acceptance. Recently published work by JLS Schneider, Marthayn Pelegrimas. Length: Open. Publishes short shorts. Critiques or comments on rejected mss. Recommends other markets.
How to Contact: Send complete ms with cover letter. Include name, address, biographical paragraph. Reports in 1 month on queries; in 2 months on mss. SASE. Simultaneous and photocopied submissions OK. Sample copy for $2. Fiction guidelines for #10 SAE and 1 first-class stamp.
Payment: Pays in contributor's copies and free business card-size ad.
Terms: "We do not purchase rights--author offers us a loan."

‡RAFALE (II), Supplement Littéraire, Franco-American Research Organization Group, University of Maine, Franco American Center, Orono ME 04469. (207)581-3704. Editor: Richard Belair. Tabloid insert: 4 pages; newsprint; illustrations and photos. Publication was founded to stimulate and recognize creative expression among Franco-Americans, all types of readers, including literary and working class." Monthly except July and August. Estab. 1986. Circ. 5,000.
Needs: "We will consider any type of short fiction, poetry and critical essays of good quality, in French as well as English." Receives about 10 unsolicited mss/month. Accepts 2-4 mss/issue. Recently published work by Robert Cormier; published new writers within the last year. Length: 1,000 words average; 750 words minimum; 2,500 words maximum. Occasionally critiques rejected mss.
How to Contact: Send complete ms with cover letter, which should include a short bio and list of previous publications. Reports in 3 weeks on queries; 4 weeks on mss. SASE. Simultaneous, photocopied and reprint submissions OK.

Payment: Pays $10 and 3 copies.
Terms: Buys one-time rights. Publication copyrighted.
Advice: "Write honestly. Start with a strongly felt personal experience and develop it with a beginning, middle and end. If you make us feel what you have felt, we will publish it."

RAG MAG (II), Box 12, Goodhue MN 55027. (612)923-4590. Publisher and editor: Beverly Voldseth. Magazine: 5½×8½; 60 pages; varied paper quality; illustrations; photos. "We are eager to print poetry, prose and art work. We are open to all styles." Semiannually. Estab. 1982. Circ. 200.
Needs: Adventure, comics, contemporary, erotica, ethnic, experimental, fantasy, feminist, literary, mainstream, prose poem, regional. "Anything well written is a possibility. No extremely violent or pornographic writing." Receives 20 unsolicited mss each month. Accepts 1-2 mss/issue. Published work by Sigi Leonhard, Lynne Burgess and Pat McKinnon; published new writers within the last year. Length: 1,000 words average; 2,200 words maximum. Occasionally critiques rejected mss. Sometimes recommends other markets.
How to Contact: Send complete ms. Reports in 2 months. SASE. Simultaneous, photocopied and previously published submissions OK. Accepts computer printout submissions. Prefers letter-quality. Single copy $4.50.
Payment: 1 contributor's copy; $4.50 charge for extras.
Terms: Acquires one-time rights.
Advice: "Submit clean copy on regular typing paper (no tissue-thin stuff). We want fresh images, sparse language, words that will lift us out of our chairs. I like the short story form. I think it's powerful and has a definite place in the literary magazine."

RAINBOW CITY EXPRESS (I,II,IV), Box 8447, Berkeley CA 94707-8447. Editor: Helen B. Harvey. Magazine: 8½×11; 60-80 pages; 20 lb bond paper; illustrations. "We are only interested in topics pertaining to spiritual awakening and evolution of consciousness. For highly educated, well-read, psychologically sophisticated, spiritually evolving and ecologically conscious free-thinkers." Feminist orientation. Quarterly. Estab. 1988. Circ. 1,000.
Needs: Feminist, literary, prose poem, religious/inspirational and spirituality. "We only accept *short fiction* and absolutely no novels or long fiction. No immature, romantic, violent, sexist material." Receives 60-90 unsolicited mss/month. Buys 4-10 mss/issue; 20-40 mss/year. Publishes ms 3-6 months after acceptance. Will publish in the coming year work by David Warner, Helen B. Harvey and Daniel Panger. Length: 200-1,000 words; 500-800 average. Almost always critiques rejected mss and sometimes recommends other markets.
How to Contact: "Order a sample copy and *read it first!* Then send a complete manuscript with SASE." Reports on queries in 2-4 weeks; 3-6 months on mss. All submissions *must* contain SASE! Sample copy $6 postpaid. Writer's guidelines for #10 SASE and 2 first class stamps.
Payment: "Payment is arranged on individual basis. Some cash 'honorariums' and every contributor always receives a copy of issue containing her or his work." Pays $5-50.
Terms: Pays on publication. Buys one-time rights.
Advice: Looks for "intelligent, lively, well-written material, with a substantial and plausible plot and characters. Topics must be related to our Spirituality/Consciousness slant. *Read* 1-2 copies of *RCE* first! We prefer *true* (nonfiction) stories related to spiritual awakening."

‡RAJAH (I, II), The Rackham Journal of the Arts and Humanities, 411 Mason Hall, University of Michigan, Ann Arbor MI 48109. Fiction Editors: Catharine Krieps, Thomas Mussio and Mary Lacey. Staff: Raymond Lee, Julie Burch, Giha Hausknecht and John Cantu. Magazine: 6×9; approx. 100 pages; 60 lb off-white stock; 10 pt, perfect bound cover; illustrations and photos. "Our interest is in quality poetry, short fiction, essays, criticism and translations by new and established authors who are mostly graduate students at the University of Michigan, for an educated reading public." Annually. Estab. 1971. Circ. 500.
Needs: Adventure, confession, contemporary, ethnic, experimental, fantasy, feminist, historical (general), horror, humor/satire, lesbian, literary, mainstream, regional, serialized/excerpted novel, translations. No children's, pornographic or obscene fiction. Receives 2 unsolicited mss/month. Accepts approximately 1 ms/issue from author outside University of Michigan. Publishes ms no more than 2 years after acceptance. Published work by Gail Gilliland; published new writers within the last year. Length: 2,500 words average; 5,000 words maximum. Critiques rejected mss. Occasionally recommends other markets.

How to Contact: Send complete ms with cover letter, which should include date, brief bio, publications record (if any). Reports on mss in 6-10 months. SASE. Photocopied submissions OK. Accepts computer printout submissions. Accepts electronic submissions compatible with Apple Macintosh (preferred), or IBM compatible floppy disk using Microsoft Word. Sample copy for $1.50, 6½×9½ SAE and 95¢ postage.
Advice: "We are especially interested in material focusing on social issues and current culture, and we are always on the lookout for manuscripts by unpublished authors. We believe that both fiction and scholarly articles reflect that kind of work being produced by talented young people around the world. *RaJAH* is primarily a graduate student publication but accepts a limited number of manuscripts from unsolicited authors."

RAMBUNCTIOUS REVIEW (II), Rambunctious Press, Inc., 1221 W. Pratt Blvd., Chicago IL 60626. Editors: Mary Dellutri, Richard Goldman, Beth Hausler and Nancy Lennon. Magazine: 7½×10; 48 pages; b&w illustrations and photos. "Quality literary magazine publishing short dramatic works, poetry and short stories for general audience." Annually. Estab. 1984. Circ. 500.
Needs: Adventure, contemporary, erotica, ethnic, experimental, feminist, historical, humor/satire, literary, mainstream, prose poem and contemporary romance. No murder mysteries. Receives 10-20 unsolicited mss/month. Accepts 6 mss/year. Does not read June 1-August 31. Recently published work by Neal Lulofs, Rod Kessler, Ronald Levitsky; published new writers within the last year. Length: 12 page maximum. Publishes short shorts. Occasionally comments on rejected mss.
How to Contact: Send complete ms. Reports in 2 months on mss. SASE. Simultaneous and photocopied submissions OK. Accepts computer printout submissions. Prefers letter-quality. Sample copy $4.
Payment: 2 contributor's copies.
Terms: Acquires first rights.
Advice: "We sponsor a yearly fiction contest in the fall. Send SASE for details. Fiction lives—if you can grasp the essentials of fiction, you can recreate a bit of life."

THE RAMPANT GUINEA PIG (II), A Magazine of Fantasy & Subcreative Fiction, 20500 Enadia Way, Canoga Park CA 91306. Editor-in-Chief: Mary Ann Hodge. Magazine: 8½×11; 30 pages; 20 lb stock; illustrations. "Though we emphasize fantasy fiction, we also publish some poetry and material relating to the life and works of Donald K. Grundy. Our readers are literate and well read in fantasy. Many have an interest in children's literature." Published biannually. Estab. 1978. Circ. 100.
Needs: Fantasy, science fantasy and religious fantasy (Christian or otherwise). "Humorous, satire, parody and pastiche okay. All stories should be rated G or PG. No sword and sorcery/barbarian fiction, no *Star Trek* or *Star Wars* stories. No thinly disguised sermons or religious bigotry. I'm particularly looking for mythopoeic and subcreative fantasy, high fantasy, and stories that convey a sense of wonder and the proximity of faerie." Receives 4-8 unsolicited fiction mss/month. Accepts 5-7 mss/issue; 10-14 mss/year. Published work by Lawrence D. Myers, Barbara Rosen; published new writers within the last year. Length: 8,000 words maximum; 5,000 words average (serials may be longer); also publishes short shorts. Occasionally critiques rejected mss. Sometimes recommends other markets.
How to Contact: Send complete ms with SASE. Photocopied submissions OK. Accepts computer printout submissions. Accepts disk submissions compatible with Macintosh Plus. Reports in 6 weeks on mss. Sample copy $3, checks payable to Mary Ann Hodge. Fiction guidelines with #10 SAE and 1 first class stamp.
Payment: 2 contributor's copies. $3 charge for extras.
Terms: Pays for first North American serial rights.
Advice: "I'm publishing more fiction per issue. Read as much fantasy as you can. But don't try to clone Tolkien. Remember that tight plotting and believable characterization and dialogue are essential in fantasy. And read one or more issues of *The Rampant Guinea Pig* before submitting so you'll know the niche we occupy in the genre. At least send for the fiction guidelines. I'm always looking for humorous stories to balance the more serious ones."

Market conditions are constantly changing! If you're still using this book and it is 1992 or later, buy the newest edition of Novel & Short Story Writer's Market at your favorite bookstore or order directly from Writer's Digest Books.

RE ARTS & LETTERS [REAL] (II), "A Liberal Arts Forum," Stephen F. Austin State University, P.O. Box 13007, Nacogdoches TX 75962. (409)568-2101. Editor: Lee Schultz. Academic Journal, 6×10 perfect bound, 120-150 pages; "top" stock. "65-75% of pages composed of fiction (2-4 stories per issue), poetry (20-60 per issue), an occasional play, book reviews (assigned after query), and interviews. Other 25-35% comprised of articles in scholarly format. Work is reviewed based on the intrinsic merit of the scholarship and creative work and its appeal to a sophisticated international readership (U.S., Canada, Great Britain, Ireland, Brazil, Puerto Rico, Italy)." Semiannual. Estab. 1968. Circ. 400+.
Needs: Adventure, contemporary, genre, feminist, science fiction, historical, experimental, regional. No beginners. Receives 35-70 unsolicited mss per month. Accepts 2-5 fiction mss/issue. Publishes 1-6 months after acceptance; one year for special issues. Recently published work by Joe R. Lansdale, Lewis Shiner, Walter McDonald, Peter Mattheisson. Length 1,000-7,000 words. Occasionally critiques rejected mss and conditionally accepts on basis of critiques and changes. Recommends other markets.
How to Contact: Send complete ms with cover letter. No simultaneous submissions. Reports in 2 weeks on queries; 3-4 weeks on mss. SASE. Accepts "letter quality" computer submissions. Sample copy and writer's guidelines $4. Guidelines for SASE.
Payment: Pays one contributor's copy; charges for extras.
Terms: Rights then revert to author.
Advice: "Please study an issue. Have your work checked by a well published writer—who is not a good friend."

‡REALMS (II), Black Matrix Press, P.O. Box 5737, Grants Pass OR 97527. (503)476-7039. Editor: Guy Kenyon. Magazine: 5½×8½; 52 pages; 20 lb. bond paper; slick cover; b&w illustrations. "*REALMS* is dedicated to printing only stories within the genre of Sword & Sorcery, heroic fantasy, etc. for a general audience that likes traditional fantasy fiction." Bimonthly. Estab. 1989. Circ. 150.
Needs: Fantasy fiction, serialized novel. "No experimental or erotic fiction." Receives 30-40 mss/month. Accepts 4-6 mss/issue; 35-40 mss/year. Publishes ms 3-6 months after acceptance. Recently published work by Gerard Houarner, Janet Peedman and Amy Wolf. Length: 10,000 words average; 2,000 words minimum; 15,000 words maximum. Sometimes critiques rejected mss and recommends other markets.
How to Contact: Send complete manuscript with cover letter. "Also include a brief bio of the author. Just a few lines so that we can get some idea of who we are dealing with." Reports in 2 weeks on queries; 4-6 weeks on mss. Photocopied submissions OK. Accepts computer printout submissions. Sample copy $2. Fiction guidelines for #10 SAE and 1 first class stamp.
Payment: Pays in contributor's copies.
Terms: Pays on publication for first North American serial rights.
Advice: "We look for strong characters. The emphasis in a story should be on human behavior, no matter how exotic the setting or complex the plot. Stories are about people and if the reader cannot identify with the characters in the story, it is not likely they will stick around long enough to witness the outcome. The old saying that a sloppy manuscript usually means sloppy writing is not always true, but a professional looking submission will make it to the top of the readers pile before one that looks amateurish."

RECONSTRUCTIONIST (II), Federation of Reconstructionist Congregations & Havurot, Church Rd. and Greenwood Ave., Wyncote PA 19095. (215)887-1988. Editor: Joy Levitt. Magazine: 8½×11; 32 pages; illustrations; photos. Review of Jewish culture—essays, fiction, poetry of Jewish interest for American Jews. Published 6 times/year. Estab. 1935. Circ. 9,000.
Needs: Send mss only to Joy Levitt, Box 1336, Roslyn Heights NY 11577. All other material should be sent to the Pennsylvania address. Ethnic. Receives 10 unsolicited mss/month; buys 15 mss/year. Publishes ms 1-2 years after acceptance. Recently published work by Myron Taube, Lev Raphael. Published new writers within the last year. Length: 2,500 words average; 3,000 words maximum. Publishes short shorts. Recommends other markets.
How to Contact: Send complete ms with cover letter. Reports in 6-8 weeks. SASE for mss. Photocopied submissions OK. Accepts computer printouts. Sample copy free.
Payment: Pays $25-36 and contributor's copies.
Terms: Pays on publication for first rights.

 The double dagger before a listing indicates that the listing is new in this edition. New markets are often the most receptive to freelance contributions.

RED BASS (I, II), Red Bass Productions, 216 Chartres St., New Orleans LA 70130. Editor: Julia Hodges. Magazine: 8½×11; 136-256 pages; 60 lb offset paper; illustrations and photos. *"Red Bass* features interviews, fiction, poetry, reviews and essays in different thematic context, strongly emphasizing experimental work and a forceful, progressive political orientation. Irregularly. Estab. 1981. Circ. 3,000.

Needs: "We publish a variety of short fiction, and excerpts from novels; writers need to check with editors about upcoming themes; since each issue is restricted to one topic, no unsolicited fiction is being accepted until 1992. Receives 20 or more unsolicited fiction mss/month. Accepts 2-3 ms/issue; 4-5 mss/year. Publishes ms in variable time after acceptance. Recently published work by Luisa Valenzuela, Kathy Acker, Lynn Tillman; published new writers within the last year. Length: 1,500 words average; 500 words minimum; 3,000 words maximum. Also publishes short shorts. Sometimes critiques rejected mss and recommends other markets.

How to Contact: Send complete manuscript with cover letter. Reports in 1 month or more on queries; 2 months on mss. SASE for ms. Simultaneous submissions OK. Accepts computer printouts. Sample copy $7.50.

Payment: Free contributor's copies; sometimes cash as funds allow.

Terms: Acquires first North American serial rights.

Advice: "It is best to look at a few issues before submitting material. We do plan to publish more fiction and experimental writing when the themes of the book/magazine allow. Special issues have included 'Conspiracy Charges' and 'Gerard Malanga: A Thirty Year Survey in the Arts' as well as planned issues 'From Haiti; and 'What's Hot in Havana: A Look at the New Cuban art.' "

Red Bass has been referred to as "one of the few true political journals left," and "the kind of intellectual jolt one needs." Gary Panter created this cover, calling it "a stained glass panel of chaos," with the art and articles of the issue in mind. Panter is a painter and graphic artist living in Brooklyn, New York. Reprinted with the permission of Red Bass.

RED CEDAR REVIEW (II), Dept. of English, Morrill Hall, Michigan State University, East Lansing MI 48825. (517)355-7570. Contact: Fiction Editor. Magazine: 5½×8½; 60-80 pages; quality b&w illustrations; good b&w photos. Theme: "literary—poetry, fiction, book reviews, one-act plays, interviews, graphics." Biannually. Estab. 1963. Circ. 400+.
Needs: Literary, feminist, regional and humorous. Accepts 3-4 mss/issue, 6-10 mss/year. Published new writers within the last year. Length: 500-7,000 words.
How to Contact: Send complete ms with SASE. Reports in 2-3 months on mss. Publishes ms up to 4 months after acceptance. Sample copy $2.
Payment: 2 free author's copies. $2.50 charge for extras.
Terms: Acquires first rights.
Advice: "Read the magazine and good literary fiction. There are many good writers out there who need a place to publish, and we try to provide them with that chance for publication. We prefer short stories that are experimental and take risks. Make your style unique—don't get lost in the mainstream work of the genre."

THE REDNECK REVIEW OF LITERATURE (II, IV), Box 730, Twin Falls ID 83301. (208)734-6653. Editor: Penelope Reedy. Magazine: 8½×11; 80 pages; offset paper; cover varies from semi-glossy to felt illustrations; photos. "I consider *Redneck* to be one of the few—perhaps the only—magazines in the West seeking to bridge the gap between literate divisions. My aim is to provide literature from and to the diverse people in the western region. *Redneck* is not a political publication and takes no sides on such issues. Readership is extremely eclectic including ranchers, farmers, university professors, writers, poets, activists, civil engineers, BLM conservation officers, farm wives, attorneys, judges, truck drivers." Semiannually. Estab. 1975. Circ. 500.
Needs: "Publishes poetry, fiction, plays, essays, book reviews and folk pieces. *Redneck* deals strictly with a contemporary viewpoint/perspective, though the past can be evoked to show the reader how we got here. Nothing too academic or sentimental reminiscences. I am not interested in old-time wild west gunfighter stories." Receives 10 "or so" unsolicited mss/month. Receives 4-5 mss/issue. Recently published work by Rafael Zepeda, Clay Reynolds and Gerald Haslam; published new writers within the last year. Length: 1,500 words minimum; 2,500 words maximum.
How to Contact: Send complete ms. SASE. No simultaneous submissions. Reprint submissions from established writers OK. Sample copy for $6 with $1 postage.
Payment: Contributor's copies.
Terms: Rights returned to author on publication.
Advice: "Use strong sense of place. Give characters action, voices. Tell the truth rather than sentimentalize."

‡REFLECT (II, IV), 3306 Argonne Ave., Norfolk VA 23509. (804)857-1097). Editor: W.S. Kennedy. Magazine: 5½×8½; 48 pages; pen & ink illustrations. "Spiral Mode fiction and poetry for writers and poets—professional and amateur." Quarterly. Estab. 1979.
Needs: Spiral fiction. "The four rules to the Spiral Mode fiction form are : (1) The story a situation or condition. (2) The outlining of the situation in the opening paragraphs. The story being told at once, the author is not overly-involved with dialogue and plot development, may concentrate on *sound*, *style*, *color*—the superior elements in art. (3) The use of a concise style with euphonic wording. Good poets may have the advantage here. (4) The involvement of Spiral Fiction themes—as opposed to Spiral Poetry themes—with love, and presented with the mystical overtones of the Mode." No "smut, bad taste, anarchist . . ." Accepts 2-6 mss/issue; 8-24 mss/year. Publishes ms 3 months after acceptance. Recently published work by Ruth Wildes Schuler, B.Z. Niditch, Patricia Anne Treat. Length: 1,500 words average; 2,500 words maximum. Publishes short shorts. Sometimes critiques rejected mss and recommends other markets.
How to Contact: Send complete manuscript with cover letter. Reports in 2 months on mss. SASE. Accepts computer printout submissions. Sample copy $2. Free fiction guidelines.
Payment: Pays contributor's copies.
Terms: Acquires one-time rights. Publication not copyrighted.
Advice: "Subject matter usually is not relevant to the successful writing of Spiral Fiction, as long as there is some element or type of *love* in the story, and provided that there are mystical references. (Though a dream-like style may qualify as 'mystical.')"

‡**REFLECTIONS (II, IV)**, Journalism Class, Box 368, Duncan Falls OH 43734. (614)674-5209. Editor: Dean Harper. Magazine: 8½x11; 32 pages; "very good" paper; "excellent" cover stock; illustrations; photos. Publishes "good wholesome stories primarily for 10-18 year olds." Estab. 1980. Circ. 1,000.
Needs: Adventure, juvenile, religious/inspirational, science fiction, senior citizen/retirement, prose poem, spiritual, sports, suspense/mystery, western, young adult/teen (10-18 years). Receives 10-20 mss/ month. Accepts 1-5 mss/issue; 2-10 mss/year. Publishes ms within 1-5 months of acceptance. Published work by Celia and Melissa Pinson, Michelle Hurst, Natasha Snitkovsky; pulblished new writers within the last year. Length: 500 words minimum; 5,000 words maximum. Publishes short shorts. Sometimes critiques rejected mss and recommends other markets.
How to Contact: Send complete mss with cover letter. Reports in 2 weeks. SASE. Simultaneous, photocopied and reprint submissions OK. Accepts computer printout submissions, including dot-matrix. Sample copy for $2, #10 SAE and 1 first class stamp. Fiction guidelines for #10 SAE and 1 first class stamp.
Payment: Pays in contributor's copies.
Terms: Acquires one-time rights. Publication copyrighted.
Advice: "We always welcome good writing. Please avoid overuse of 'got.' Keep sending your writing. Read it first to others for opinions. Ask for suggestions from editors."

RENAISSANCE FAN (I, II, IV), 2214 SE 53rd, Portland OR 97215. (503)235-0668. Editor: Rosalind Molin. Magazine: 8½×11; 15-30 pages; illustrations and photos. "This is an amateur fanzine (fan magazine) related to science fiction and fantasy. Each issue has a theme." Readers are "science fiction and fantasy fans." Quarterly. Estab. 1988. Circ. 150.
Needs: Fantasy, science fiction. "We do not promote abuse and violence." Receives 3 unsolicited mss/month. Accepts up to 4 mss/issue. Publishes ms in next issue that relates to theme. Published work by Eleanor Malin, Dennis Hoggatt; published new writers within the last year. Length: 5,000 words preferred; 600 words minimum; 15,000 words maximum. Publishes short shorts. Sometimes critiques rejected mss and recommends other markets.
How to Contact: "It is best to query, but if not, find out what the themes are—a phone call is OK— no calls after 8:00 PST." SASE for ms. Simultaneous and photocopied submissions OK "must know where and when." Accepts computer printout submissions and electronic submission in ASCII, Kaypro CP/M or IBM PC. Sample copy for 9×12 SAE and 85¢. Fiction guidelines free.
Payment: Free subscription to magazine.
Terms: Acquires one-time rights.
Advice: "Readers are not mind readers. A tree is not just a tree. It is a birch or an elm or a maple. A car is an Olds, a Ford, a Chevy, a Mustang, a Pinto, etc. Be visual—use colors, sounds, smells, tastes. Appeal to the senses. Write an active story, not just a passive one. Practice. Rewrite. Submit. Listen to what you have written. Read it aloud. Know your subject. Look at what is happening around you. An everyday activity can be turned into a fantasy or science fiction story. Do not use two words where one will do—edit, edit, edit. Become a storyteller."

RENEGADE (II), Box 314, Bloomfield MI 48303. (313)972-5580. Editor: Michael E. Nowicki. Magazine: 5½×8½; 32 pages; 4-5 illustrations. "We are open to all forms except erotica and we publish whatever we find good." Estab. 1988. Circ. 100.
Needs: Adventure, condensed/excerpted novel, contemporary, experimental, fantasy, feminist, historical (general), horror, humor/satire, literary, mainstream, prose poem, psychic/supernatural/occult, religious/inspirational, romance, science fiction, suspense/mystery, translations and western. Receives 40-50 unsolicited mss/month. Accepts 2 mss/issue; 4 mss/year. Publishes ms 6 months after acceptance. Published work by Sam Astrachan. Length: 400-4,000 words; 3,000 average. Publishes short shorts. Length: 400 words. Sometimes critiques rejected mss and recommends other markets.
How to Contact: Send complete ms with cover letter. Reports in 2 weeks to 1 month on queries; 3 weeks to 2 months on mss. SASE. Sample copy $2. Fiction guidelines for #10 SAE and 1 first class stamp.
Payment: Pays in contributor's copies.
Terms: All rights revert to author. Publication not copyrighted.
Advice: "We look for characters which appear to be real and deal with life in a real way, as well as the use of plot to forefront the clash of personalities and the theme of the work. Take advice cautiously and apply what works. Then submit it. We are always happy to critique work we read."

‡RENOVATED LIGHTHOUSE PUBLICATIONS (II), Box 21130, Columbus OH 43221. Editor: R. Allen Dodson. Chapbooks and magazines; 5½×8½; 40 pages; standard paper; card cover; illustrations and photographs. "Mostly poetry-related, but will consider all literary and artistic mediums and subjects for freelancers and general audiences with literary interest." Bimonthly in 1991. Estab. 1986. Circ. 100.
Needs: Adventure, experimental, fantasy, historical (general), literary, mainstream, prose poem, regional, science fiction, New Age. Publishes annual special fiction issue. Receives 1 unsolicited ms/ month. Buys 1 ms/year. Publishes ms 1 year after acceptance. Always critiques rejected mss and sometimes recommends other markets.
How to Contact: Send complete manuscript with cover letter. "Personal information and comments about the story—I like to get to know my writers." Reports in 1 week on queries; 1 months on mss. SASE. Photocopied and reprint submissions OK. Accepts computer printout submissions. Sample copy $2. Fiction guidelines in each issue.
Payment: Pays 25% royalties for 1 year. For chaps,$1 plus copy for appearance in magazine.
Terms: Royalty payments made quarterly. Sends galleys to author. Publication not copyrighted.

RESPONSE (II, IV), A Contemporary Jewish Review, 27 W. 20th St., 9th Floor, New York NY 10011. (212)675-1168. Editor: Bennett Graff. Magazine: 6×9; 96 pages; 70 lb paper; 10 pt. CIS cover; illustrations; photos. Fiction, poetry and essays with a Jewish theme, for Jewish students and young adults. Quarterly. Estab. 1967. Circ. 1,500.
Needs: Contemporary, ethnic, experimental, feminist, historical (general), humor/satire, literary, prose poem, regional, religious, spirituals, translations. "Stories in which the Holocaust plays a major role must be exceptional in quality. The shrill and the morbid will not be accepted." Receives 5-10 unsolicited mss/month. Accepts 5-10 mss/issue; 10-15 mss/year. Publishes ms 2-4 months after acceptance. Length: 15-20 pages (double spaced). Publishes short shorts. Sometimes recommends other markets.
How to Contact: Send complete ms with cover letter; include brief biography of author. "Do not summarize story in cover letter." Reports in 2 months on mss. SASE. Photocopied submissions are OK. Accepts computer prinout submissions. Sample copy $6; free guidelines.
Payment: Pays in contributor's copics.
Terms: Acquires all rights.
Advice: "In the best pieces, every word will show the author's conscious attention to the craft. Subtle ambiguities, quiet ironies and other such carefully handled tropes are not lost on *Response*'s readers. Pieces that also show passion that is not marred by either shrillness or pathos are respected and often welcomed. Writers who write from the gut or the muse are few in number. *Response* personally prefers the writer who thinks about what he or she is doing, rather than the writer who intuits his or her stories."

‡RESURGENS (I, II), Resurgens, P.O. Box 725006, Atlanta GA 30339-9006. Editors: David Blanchard and Paul Beard. Magazine: 5½×8½; 64 pages. Quarterly. Estab. 1990. Circ. 500.
Needs: Literary, mainstream, serialized novel, poetry and literary criticism. "We prefer stories that emphasize plot and character development." No "horror/gothic; modern minimalist stuff." Plans special fiction issue. Receives 10+ unsolicited mss/month. Accepts 2-3 mss/issue; 8-12 mss/year. Publishes ms 1-3 months after acceptance. Critiques rejected mss.
How to Contact: Send complete manuscript with cover letter and bio. Reports in 1 week on queries; 2 months on mss. SASE. Photocopied submissions OK. disk or modem. Sample copy for $3.
Payment: Pays contributor's copies.

‡REVIEW LA BOOCHE (II), Columbia Daily Tribune and Waters Publication, 110 S. 9th, Columbia MO 65201. (314)874-8772. Editors: Michel Jabbour and Gerald Dethrow. 6×9; 100 pages; 60 lb. paper; 80 lb. Irish linen cover. "No theme. Tightly constructed stories with strong use of poetics for everyone." Annually. Estab. 1976. Circ. 500.
Needs: Adventure, contemporary, experimental, historical (general), juvenile (5-9 years), literary, mainstream, young adult/teen (10-18 years). "Needs short stories under 5,000 words." Recently published work by Nancy Lord, Nolan Briterfield and Dennis Danvers. Length: 5,000 words. Publishes short shorts. Sometimes critiques rejected mss and recommends other markets.
How to Contact: Send complete manuscript with cover letter. Reports in 2 wccks-1 month. SASE. Accepts photocopied and computer printout submissions. Sample copy for #10 SAE. Fiction guidelines free.

Payment: Contributor's copies.
Terms: Acquires first rights.
Advice: "Charge up the language with active verbs and use adjectives sparingly unless they contribute to expanding the boundaries of the nouns they border."

RIVER CITY, Memphis State Review, Dept. of English, Memphis State University, Memphis TN 38152. (901)678-8888. Editor: Sharon Bryan. Magazine: 6×9; 100 pages. National review of poetry, fiction and nonfiction. Semiannually. Estab. 1980. Circ. 1,200. Published work by Fred Busch. Published new writers within the last year.
Needs: Novel excerpts, short stories.
How to Contact: Send complete ms with SASE. Sample copy $4.
Payment: Annual $100 prize for best poem or best short story and 2 free contributor's copies. "We pay if grant monies are available."
Terms: Acquires first North American serial rights.
Advice: "We're soliciting work from writers with a national reputation, and are occasionally able to pay, depending on grants received. I would prefer no cover letter. *River City* Writing Awards in Fiction: $2,000 1st prize, $500 2nd page, $300 3rd prize. See magazine for details."

RIVER STYX (II), Big River Association, 14 S. Euclid, St. Louis MO 63108. (314)361-0043. Editor: Lee Schreiner. Magazine: 6×8; 90 pages; visual art (b&w). "No theme restrictions, high quality, intelligent work." Triannual. Estab. 1975.
Needs: Excerpted novel chapter, contemporary, ethnic, experimental, feminist, gay, satire, lesbian, literary, mainstream, prose poem, translations. "Avoid 'and then I woke up' stories." Receives 15 unsolicited mss/month. Buys 1-3 mss/issue; 3-8 mss/year. Reads only in September and October. Published work by Bonita Friedman, Leslie Becker, Fred Viebahn. Length: no more than 20-30 manuscript pages. Publishes short shorts. Sometimes critiques rejected mss and recommends other markets. Send complete manuscript with name and address on every page. Reports in 2 months on mss. Photocopied and reprint submissions OK. Accepts computer printout submissions. Sample copy $7. Fiction guidelines for #10 SAE and 1 first class stamp.
Payment: Pays $8/page maximum, free subscription to magazine and contributor's copies.
Terms: Pays on publication for first North American serial rights.
Advice: Looks for "writer's attention to the language and the sentence; responsible, controlled narrative."

RIVERSIDE QUARTERLY (II,IV), 807 Walters #107, Lake Charles LA 70605. (817)756-4749. Editor: Leland Sapiro. Fiction Editor: Redd Boggs. Magazine: 5½×8½; 64 pages; illustrations. Quarterly. Estab. 1964. Circ. 1,100.
Needs: Fantasy and science fiction. Accepts 1 mss/issue; 4 mss/year. Publishes ms 6 months after acceptance. Length: 3,500 words maximum; 3,000 words average. Publishes short shorts. Critiques rejected mss.
How to Contact: *Send directly to fiction editor, Redd Bogg, Box 1111, Berkeley, CA 94701.* Send complete ms with cover letter. Reports in 2 weeks. SASE. Simultaneous submissions OK. Accepts electronic submissions. Sample copy $2.
Payment: Pays in contributor's copies.
Terms: Acquires one-time rights. Sends galleys to author.
Advice: "Would-be contributors are urged to first inspect a copy or two of the magazine (available at any major college or public library) to see the *kind* of story we print."

RIVERWIND (II,IV), General Studies/Hocking Technical College, Nelsonville OH 45764. (614)753-3591 (ext. 2375). Editor: Audrey Naffziger. Associate Editor: Cindy Dubielak. Magazine: 6×9; 60 lb paper; cover illustrations. "College press, small literary magazine." Annually. Estab. 1975.
Needs: Adventure, contemporary, erotica, ethnic, feminist, historical (general), horror, humor/satire, literary, mainstream, prose poem, spiritual, sports, regional, translations, western. No juvenile/teen fiction. Receives 30 mss/month. Published work by Lee Martin, Roy Bentley, Kate Hancock; published new writers within the last year. Sometimes critiques rejected mss.
How to Contact: Send complete mss with cover letter. Reports on mss in 1-4 months. SASE. Photocopied submissions OK.
Payment: Pays in contributor's copies.
Advice: "Your work must be strong, entertaining. It helps if you are an Ohio/West Virginia writer. We hope to print more fiction."

ROANOKE REVIEW (II), Roanoke College, English Department, Salem VA 24153. (703)375-2500. Editor: Robert R. Walter. Magazine: 6×9; 40-60 pages. Semiannually. Estab. 1967. Circ. 300.
Needs: Receives 30-40 unsolicited mss/month. Accepts 2-3 mss/issue; 4-6 mss/year. Publishes ms 6 months after acceptance. Length: 2,500 words minimum; 7,500 words maximum. Publishes short shorts. Occasionally critiques rejected mss.
How to Contact: Send complete ms with cover letter. Reports in 1-2 weeks on queries; 8-10 weeks on mss. SASE for query. Photocopied submissions OK. Accepts computer printout submissions. Sample copy $2.
Payment: Pays in contributor's copies.

THE ROCKFORD REVIEW (II), The Rockford Writers Guild, Box 858, Rockford IL 61103. (815)962-2552. Fiction Editor: Olivia Diamond. Magazine: 5⅜×8½; 96 pages; b&w illustrations; b&w photos. "Eclectic in approach, we look for poetry with control of poetic line and devices with a fresh approach to old themes or new insights into the human condition whether in prose or poetry." Annually. Estab. 1971. Circ. 500.
Needs: Ethnic, experimental, fantasy, feminist, historical (general), humor/satire, literary and regional. No erotica, gay/lesbian. Accepts 5-6 mss/issue. Publishes ms 6-9 months after acceptance. Recently published work by Eugene C. Flinn, John Pesta, George Keithly, Stacy Tuthill, Peter Blunett and Robert Klein Engler. Length: 2,000-4,000 words; 2,500 average. Sometimes critiques rejected mss and recommends other markets.
How to Contact: Send complete ms. "Include a short biographical note—no more than four sentences." Reports in 4-6 weeks on mss. SASE. Accepts simultaneous and photocopied submissions, reprints (as long as acknowledgement included) and computer printouts. Sample copy $5. Fiction guidelines for SAE.
Payment: Pays contributor's copies. "One editor's choice cash prize per issue."
Terms: Acquires first North American serial rights. *Charges reading fee of $5 for poems and $5 for prose works.*
Advice: "Any subject or theme goes as long as it enhances our understanding of our humanity. We want strongly plotted stories where the action takes place in other settings besides the character's head. Experiment with point-of-view. Make sure you've got it right for your story. We would like to see a lot more short stories than we receive."

ROHWEDDER (II, IV), International Journal of Literature & Art, Rough Weather Press, Box 29490, Los Angeles CA 90029. Editor: Hans-Jurgen Schacht. Fiction Editors: Robert Dassanowsky-Harris and Nancy Antell. Magazine: 8½×11; 50+ pages; 20 lb paper; 90 lb cover; illustrations; photos. "Multilingual/cultural poetry and short stories. Graphic art and photography." Published semi-annually. Estab. 1986.
Needs: Contemporary, ethnic, experimental, feminist, literary, regional, translations (with rights). No fillers. Receives 20-50 unsolicited mss/month. Accepts 1-3 mss/issue; 6 mss/year. Publishes ms 1-3 months after acceptance. Length: 1,500-2,500 words average; 200 words minimum; 2,500 words maximum. Publishes short shorts. Sometimes critiques rejected mss and recommends other markets.
How to Contact: Include bio with submission. Reports in 2 weeks on queries; 2 months on mss. SASE. Photocopied submissions OK. Accepts computer printout submissions. Sample copy $5.50.
Payment: Pays in contributor's copies, charges for extras.
Terms: Acquires one-time right.
Advice: "Go out as far as you have to but remember the basics: clear, concise style and form."

ROOM OF ONE'S OWN (II), Growing Room Collective, Box 46160, Station G, Vancouver, British Columbia V6R 4G5 Canada. Editors: Editorial Collective. Magazine: 5×6; 100 pages; bond paper; bond cover stock; illustrations; photos. Feminist literary: fiction, poetry, criticism, reviews. Readership: general, nonscholarly. Quarterly. Estab. 1975. Circ. 1,200.
Needs: Literary, feminist and lesbian. No "sexist or macho material." Buys 6 mss/issue. Receives approximately 40 unsolicited fiction mss each month. Approximately 2% of fiction is agented. Recently published work by Janette Turner Hospital, Anne E. Norman, Judith Monroe; published new writers within the last year. Length: 3,000 words preferred. "No critiques except under unusual circumstances."
How to Contact: Send complete ms with SASE or SAE and IRC. "Please include cover letter. State whether multiple submission or not (we don't consider multiple submissions) and whether previously published." Reports in 3-6 months. Publishes ms within a year after acceptance. Sample copy $5 with SASE or SAE and IRC.

Payment: Varies, plus 2 free author's copies.
Terms: Pays on publication for first rights.
Advice: "Write well and unpretentiously." Mss are rejected because they are "unimaginative."

‡**ST. ANDREWS REVIEW (II)**, St. Andrews Presbyterian College, Laurinburg NC 28352. (919)276-3652. Director: Ron Bayes. Fiction Editor: Jackson Morton. General literary magazine for literary and fine arts audience. Semiannually. Estab. 1970. Circ. 1,000.
Needs: Condensed novel, contemporary, experimental, fantasy, historical (general), humor/satire, literary, mainstream and prose poem. Receives 75 unsolicited mss/month. Accepts 2-6 mss/issue; 5-12 mss/year. Recently published work by Fred Chappell, Michael McFee, Edward Falco. Published new writers within the last year.
How to Contact: Send complete ms. Reports in 2 months. SASE. Simultaneous and photocopied submissions OK. Accepts computer printout submissions. Prefers letter-quality. Sample copy $5 with legal-size SAE and 3 first class stamps.
Payment: 2 contributor's copies.
Terms: Rights to individual works revert to author after publication. Publication copyrighted.
Advice: "Please write about what really concerns you and tell the truth, no matter how unseasonal or unsalable your kind of fiction appears to be. Please don't copy anyone else; and please attend workshops, formal and informal, in which you share your work with those who will offer constructive criticism."

SALOME: A JOURNAL OF THE PERFORMING ARTS (I, II, IV), Ommation Press, 5548 N. Sawyer, Chicago IL 60625. Editor: Effie Mihopoulos. "*Salome* seeks to cover the performing arts in a thoughtful and incisive way." Quarterly. Estab. 1976. Circ. 1,000.
Needs: Literary, contemporary, science fiction, fantasy, women's, feminist, gothic, romance, mystery, adventure, humor, serialized novels, prose poems, translations. "We seek good quality mss that relate to the performing arts or fiction with strong characters that somehow move the reader." Receives approximately 25 unsolicited fiction mss each month; accepts 40 mss/year. No preferred length. Sometimes sends mss on to editors of other publications and recommends other markets.
How to Contact: Send complete ms with SASE. Reports in 1 month. Sample copy $4, 9×12 SASE with 90¢ (book-rate) postage preferred.
Payment: 1 free author's copy. Contributor's rates for extras upon request.
Terms: Acquires first North American serial rights. "Rights revert to author, but we retain reprint rights."
Advice: "Write a well-written story or prose poem." Rejected mss are "usually badly written—improve style, grammar, etc.—too often writers send out mss before they're ready. See a sample copy. Specify fiction interest."

SALT LICK PRESS (II), Salt Lick Foundation, 1804 E. 38½ St., Austin TX 78722. Editor: James Haining. Magazine: 8½×11; 64 pages; 60 lb offset stock; 80 lb text cover; illustrations and photos. Irregular. Estab. 1969.
Needs: Contemporary, erotica, ethnic, experimental, feminist, gay, lesbian, literary. Receives 15 unsolicited mss each month. Accepts 2 mss/issue. Length: open. Occasionally critiques rejected mss.
How to Contact: Send complete ms with cover letter. Reports in 2 weeks on queries; 4 weeks on mss. SASE. Simultaneous, photocopied and reprint submissions OK. Accepts computer printout submissions. Sample copy $5, 9×12 SAE and 3 first class stamps.
Payment: Free contributor's copies.
Terms: Acquires first North American serial rights. Sends galleys to author.

SAMISDAT (II), 456 Monroe Turnpike, Monroe CT 06468. Editor: Merritt Clifton. Magazine: 5½×8½; 60-80 pages; offset bond paper; vellum bristol cover stock; illustrations; photos. Publication is "environmentalist, anti-war, anti-nuke, emphatically non-leftist—basically anarchist." Publishes essays, reviews, poetry and original artwork in approximately equal proportions. Audience consists of "people constructively and conscientiously engaged in changing the world." Subscribers include many secretaries, journalists, blue-collar workers and housewives "but very few bureaucrats." Annually. Estab. 1973. Circ. 400+.
Needs: Adventure, contemporary, erotica, ethnic, experimental, fantasy, feminist, gay, historical (general), humor/satire, lesbian, literary, mainstream, prose poem, regional, science fiction, serialized/excerpted novel, sports, suspense/mystery, translations, western. "We're pretty damned eclectic if something is done well. Formula hackwork and basic ineptitude, though, won't ever hack it here. No

whimsy; no self-indulgent whines about the difficulty of being a sensitive writer/artist." Receives approximately 10-100 unsolicited mss/month. Accepts 2-5 mss/issue. Publishes ms 2-5 months after acceptance. Recently published work by Miriam Sagan, Thomas Michael McDade, Robert Swisher; published new writers within the last year. Length: 1,500-5,000 words. Publishes short shorts. Length: up to 1,000 words. Sometimes recommends other markets or critiques rejected mss.

How to Contact: Send complete ms with cover letter. "I like to know how old the author is, what he/she does for a living, and get a ballpark idea of writing experiences, but I do not want to see mere lists of credits. I also like to know why a writer is submitting here in particular." Reports in 1 week on queries and mss. SASE. Reprint submissions OK. "Does not read photocopies or multiple submissions of any kind." Accepts computer printout submissions. Sample copy $2.50.

Payment: Pays in contributor's copies.

Terms: Acquires one-time rights.

Advice: "I'm editor, publisher, printer, distributor, and therefore I do as I damned well please. Over the past 18 years I've found enough other people who agree with me that short stories are worthwhile that my magazine manages to support itself, more or less in the tradition of the old-time radical magazines that published the now-classical short story writers. Know the factual background to your material, e.g., if writing a historical piece, get the details right."

SAN GABRIEL VALLEY MAGAZINE (IV), Miller Books, 2908 W. Valley Blvd., Alhambra CA 91803. (213)284-7607. Editor: Joseph Miller. Magazine: 5¼×7¼; 48 pages; 60 lb book paper; vellum bristol cover stock; illustrations; photos. "Regional magazine for the Valley featuring local entertainment, dining, sports and events. We also carry articles about successful people from the area. For upper-middle class people who enjoy going out a lot." Bimonthly. Published special fiction issue last year; plans another. Estab. 1976. Circ. 3,000.

Needs: Contemporary, inspirational, psychic/supernatural/occult, western, adventure and humor. No articles on sex or ERA. Receives approximately 10 unsolicited fiction mss/month. Buys 2 mss/issue; 20 mss/year. Length: 500-2,500 words. Also publishes short shorts. Recommends other markets.

How to Contact: Send complete ms with SASE. Accepts computer printout submissions. Reports in 2 weeks on mss. Sample copy $1 with 9×12 SASE.

Payment: 5¢/word; 2 free author's copies.

Terms: Payment on acceptance for one-time rights.

SAN JOSE STUDIES (II), San Jose State University, One Washington Square, San Jose CA 95152. Editor: Fauneil J. Rinn. Magazine: digest size; 112-144 pages; good paper and cover; occasional illustrations and photos. "A journal for the general, educated reader. Covers a wide variety of materials: fiction, poetry, interviews, interdisciplinary essays. Aimed toward the college-educated common reader with an interest in the broad scope of materials." Triannually. Estab. 1975. Circ. 500.

Needs: Social and political, literary, humor, ethnic and regional. Accepts 1-2 mss/issue, 3-6 mss/year. Receives approximately 12 unsolicited fiction mss each month. Published work by Molly Giles, Richard Flánagán. Length: 2,500-5,000+ words. Critiques rejected mss when there is time. Sometimes recommends other markets.

How to Contact: Send complete ms with SASE. Accepts computer printout submissions. Prefers letter-quality. Reports in 2 months. Publishes ms an average of 6 months to 1 year after acceptance. Sample copy $4.

Payment: 2 free author's copies. Annual $100 award for best story, essay or poem.

Terms: Acquires first rights. Sends galleys to author.

Advice: "Name should appear *only* on cover sheet. We seldom print beginning writers of fiction or poetry."

‡SANSKRIT (II), Literary Arts Publication of UNC Charlotte, University of North Carolina at Charlotte, Highway 49, Charlotte NC 28223. (704)547-2326. Editor: Tina McEntire. Fiction Editor: Steven Sherrill. Magazine: 9×15, 60-90 pages. "We are a general lit/art mag open to all genres if well written for college students, alumni, writers and artists across the country." Annually. Estab. 1968.

Needs: Contemporary, erotica, ethnic, experimental, feminist, gay, humor/satire, lesbian, literary, mainstream, prose poem, regional, science fiction, translations. No formula, western, romance. Receives 2-4 unsolicited mss/month. Accepts 3-6 mss/issue. Does not read mss in summer. Publishes in late March. Recently published work by Nann Budd, Rob Walker, Bronwyn Mauldin. Length: 250 words minimum; 5,000 words maximum. Publishes short shorts. Sometimes critiques rejected mss.

How to Contact: Send complete manuscript with cover letter. SASE. Simultaneous and photocopied submissions OK. Accepts computer printout submissions. Sample copy $6. Fiction guidelines for #10 SAE.
Payment: Pays contributor's copies.
Terms: Acquires one-time rights. Publication not copyrighted.
Advice: "A tight cohesive story, in an often shattered world, wins my heart. I like quirkiness just to the point of self indulgence. There is a fine line . . . there are many fine lines . . . walk as many as you can."

SANTA MONICA REVIEW (III), Santa Monica College, 1900 Pico Blvd., Santa Monica CA 90405. (213)450-5150. Editor: James Krusoe. Magazine: 5½×8; 140 pages, rag paper. Semiannually. Estab. 1988. Circ. 1,000.
Needs: Contemporary, literary. Accepts 5 mss/issue; 10 mss/year. Publishes mss varying amount of time after publication. Published work by Ann Beattie, Arturo Vivante and Guy Davenport.
How to Contact: Send complete ms with cover letter. Reports in 3 months on mss. SASE. Simultaneous and photocopied submissions OK. Sample copy $6.
Payment: Free subscription to magazine, contributor's copies.
Terms: Acquires one-time rights.
Advice: "We are *not* actively soliciting beginning work. We want to combine high quality West Coast, especially Los Angeles, writing with that from the rest of the country."

‡SATORI (II), Fact & Fiction, Hands Off The Press, Inc., P.O. Box 318, Tivoli NY 12583. (914)757-4443. Editor: Gary Green and Pat Sims. Magazine: 8½×11; 20 pages. "Regional (Hudson Valley, NY) but not exclusively. New and unique writing—short (1,500 to 2,000 words) and very short (from a paragraph on)." Quarterly. Estab. 1988. Circ. 500.
Needs: Condensed/excerpted novel, contemporary, experimental, humor/satire, regional, translations. Receives 5 unsolicited mss/month. Accepts 1-2 mss/issue; 4-8 mss/year. Recently published work by Dick Higgins and Cynde Gregory. Length: 1,500 words average; 500 words minimum; 2,500 words maximum. Publishes short shorts. Length: Paragraph (50 words) to 250 words. Sometimes critiques rejected mss.
How to Contact: Send complete manuscript with cover letter. "Sample copy recommended. Cover letter should include general background, other publications work has been included in, how our publication came to their attention." SASE. Simultaneous and photocopied submissions OK. Accepts computer printout submissions. Accepts electronic submissions via disk (Macintosh 3.5" disk only). Sample copy $3. Fiction guidelines for #10 SAE and 1 first class stamp.
Payment: Pays 3 contributor's copies. Charges for extras.
Terms: Acquires one-time rights.
Advice: "Unique voice, precision of language and originality."

SCREAM MAGAZINE (II), Fiction in a Fantastic Vein, Alternating Crimes (AC) Publishing, Box 10363, Raleigh NC 27605. (919)834-7542. Consulting Editor: Russell Boone. Managing Editor: Katie Boone. 8¼×10½; 64 pages; 24 lb bond/60 lb offset paper; 80 lb uncoated cover; illustrations and photographs. "We publish fiction with a darker theme, as well as poetry and nonfiction. Readers enjoy serious literature *and* formula fiction. They are open-minded enough to explore the unfamiliar." Biennial. Estab. 1985. Circ. 1,500.
Needs: Contemporary, erotica, experimental, fantasy, feminist, gay, historical (general), horror, crime, lesbian, literary, psychic/supernatural/occult, regional, science fiction, serialized/excerpted novel, suspense/mystery. No religious fiction. Receives 15-25 unsolicited mss/month. Accepts 5-8 mss/issue; 12-20 mss/year. Publishes ms 3-12 months after acceptance. Length: 2,500 words preferred; 900 words minimum; 3,500 words maximum. Frequently critiques rejected mss and recommends other markets.
How to Contact: Send complete ms with cover letter. Reports in 16 weeks on mss. SASE. Photocopied submissions OK. Accepts computer printout submissions. Sample copy for $5. Free fiction guidelines. No simultaneous submissions.
Payment: Pays in contributor's copes.
Terms: Acquires first North American serial rights.
Advice: "I believe there is a 'fiction revival' on the way via the underground/small press express. The audience, the readers are out there but they can't get their fix at the general public newsstands. For the last decade (1976-1988) these discerning readers of American fiction have had to go to 'alternative bookstores' or make their discovery by word of mouth. But all this is changing. The news agencies and booksellers have already begun picking up on this and new titles are beginning to appear at newsstands

around the country. In turn, I think the mainstream publications wil begin picking up on this new mood and in the next few years open up their fiction markets. Get a recent issue of *Scream*, study it and submit your work."

SCRIVENER (II), 853 Sherbrooke St. W., Montreal, Quebec H3A 2T6 Canada. Editors: Thea Boyanowsky, Sam Anson and Peter Samson. Magazine: 8½×11; 40 pages; glossy paper; illustrations; b&w photos. "*Scrivener* is a creative journal publishing fiction, poetry, graphics, photography, reviews, interviews and scholarly articles. We publish the best of new and established writers. We examine how current trends in North American writing are rooted in a pervasive creative dynamic; our audience is mostly scholarly and in the writing field." Annually. Estab. 1980. Circ. 800.
Needs: Good writing. Receives 40 unsolicited mss/month. Accepts 20 mss/year. Does not read mss May 1-Sept 1. Publishes ms up to 6 months after acceptance. Recently published work by James Conway, Colin Wright, Louis Phillips; published new writers within the last year. Length: 25 pages maximum. Occasionally publishes short shorts. Often critiques rejected mss. Sometimes recommends other markets.
How to Contact: Query first. Order sample copy ($5); send complete ms with cover letter with "critical statements; where we can reach you; biographical data; education; previous publications." Reports in 4 months on queries and mss. SASE/IRC preferred but not required. Simultaneous, photocopied submissions and reprints OK. Accepts computer printouts. Sample copy $5 (US in USA; Canadian in Canada). Fiction guidelines for SAE/IRC.
Payment: Sometimes pays $3-25; provides contributor's copies; charges for extras.
Terms: Pays on publication.
Advice: "Send us your best stuff. Don't be deterred by rejections. Sometimes a magazine just isn't looking for your *kind* of writing. Don't neglect the neatness of your presentation."

THE SEATTLE REVIEW (II), Padelford Hall GN-30, University of Washington, Seattle WA 98195. (206)543-9865. Editor: Donna Gerstenberger. Fiction Editor: Charles Johnson. Magazine: 6×9. "Includes general fiction, poetry, craft essays on writing, and one interview per issue with a Northwest writer." Semiannually. Published special fiction issue. Estab. 1978. Circ. 1,000.
Needs: Contemporary, ethnic, experimental, fantasy, feminist, gay, historical, horror, humor/satire, lesbian, literary, mainstream, prose poem, psychic/supernatural/occult, regional, science fiction, excerpted novel, suspense/mystery, translations, western. "We also publish a series called Writers and their Craft, which deals with aspects of writing fiction (also poetry)—point of view, characterization, etc., rather than literary criticism, each issue." Does not want to see "anything in bad taste (porn, racist, etc.)." Receives about 50 unsolicited mss/month. Accepts about 3-6 mss/issue; about 4-10 mss/year. Reads mss all year but "slow to respond in summer." 25% of fiction is agented. Recently published work by David Milofsky, Lawson Fusao Inada and Liz Rosenberg; published new writers within the last year. Length: 3,500 words average; 500 words minimum; 10,000 words maximum. Publishes short shorts. Sometimes critiques rejected mss. Occasionally recommends other markets.
How to Contact: Send complete ms. "If included, cover letter should list recent publications or mss we'd seen and liked, but been unable to publish." Reports in 3 months. SASE. Accepts computer printout submissions. Sample copy "half-price if older than one year." Current issue $4.50; some special issues $5.50—6.50.
Payment: Pays 0-$100, free subscription to magazine, 2 contributor's copies; charge for extras.
Terms: Pays on publication for first North American serial rights. Copyright reverts to writer on publication; "please request release of rights and cite *SR* in reprint publications." Sends galleys to author.
Advice: "Beginners do well in our magazine if they send clean, well-written manuscripts. We've published a lot of 'first stories' from all over the country and take pleasure in discovery."

SEEMS (II), Lakeland College, Sheboygan WI 53081. (414)565-3871. Editor: Karl Elder. Magazine: 7×8½; 40 pages. "We publish fiction and poetry for an audience which tends to be highly literate. People read the publication, I suspect, for the sake of reading it." Published irregularly. Estab. 1971. Circ. 300.
Needs: Literary. Accepts 4 mss/issue. Receives approximately 12 unsolicited fiction mss each month. Published work by John Birchler; published new writers within the last year. Length: 5,000 words maximum. Also publishes short shorts. Critiques rejected mss when there is time.
How to Contact: Send complete ms with SASE. Accepts computer printout submissions. Prefers letter-quality. Reports in 2 months on mss. Publishes ms an average of 1-2 years after acceptance. Sample copy $3.

Payment: 1 free author's copy; $3 charge for extras.

Terms: Rights revert to author.

Advice: "Send clear, clean copies. Read the magazine in order to help determine the taste of the editor." Mss are rejected because of "lack of economical expression, or saying with many words what could be said in only a few. Good fiction contains all of the essential elements of poetry; study poetry and apply those elements to fiction. Our interest is shifting to story poems, the grey area between genres."

SENSATIONS (I,II), 2 Radio Ave., A5, Secaucus NJ 07094. Founder: David Messineo. Magazine: 8½×11; 48 pages; 20 lb inside paper, 67 lb cover paper; vellum cover; black ink line illustrations. "We publish short stories and poetry, no specific theme, for a liberal, worldly audience who reads for pleasure." Annually. Estab. 1987. Circ. 250. "Releasing five issues between 1990 and 1992."

Needs: Adventure, contemporary, fantasy, gay, historical, horror, humor/satire, lesbian, literary, mainstream, prose poem, regional, romance (historical), science fiction, suspense/mystery. "We're not into gratuitous profanity, pornography, or violence. Sometimes these are needed to properly tell the tale. We'll read anything unusual, providing it is submitted in accordance with our submission policies. No abstract works only the writer can understand." Receives approx. 30 unsolicited mss/issue. Accepts 4 mss/issue. Publishes ms 2 months after acceptance. Published work by Patricia Flinn, Karl Luntta and Ed Condon. "No more than 14 pages double-spaced." Publishes short shorts. Always critiques rejected mss; sometimes recommends other markets.

How to Contact: "Send name, address, a paragraph of background information about yourself, a paragraph about what inspired the story. We'll send submission guidelines when we are ready to judge material." Reports in 1-2 weeks on queries; 4-6 weeks on mss. SASE for brochure. Simultaneous and photocopied submissions OK. Accepts computer printout submissions. Accepts electronic submissions (Macintosh only). *Must first purchase* sample copy $6. Check payable to "David Messineo." "Do not submit material before reading brochure and following its guidelines."

Payment: No payment.

Terms: Acquired one-time rights.

Advice: "Each story must have a strong beginning that grabs the reader's attention in the first two sentences. Characters have to be realistic and well-described. Readers must like, hate, or have some emotional response to the characters other than boredom. Setting, plot, construction, attention to detail—all are important. We work with writers to help them improve in these areas, but the better stories are written before they come to us, the greater the chance for publication. Purchase sample copy first and read the stories. Our fourth issue includes part one of a five part research project detailing poetry written in and about America in the 1500s and 1600s, which may be of interest to you."

THE SEWANEE REVIEW (III), University of the South, Sewanee TN 37375. (615)598-1245. Editor: George Core. Magazine: 6x9; 192 pages. "A literary quarterly, publishing original fiction, poetry, essays on literary and related subjects, book reviews and book notices for well-educated readers who appreciate good American and English literature." Quarterly. Estab. 1892. Circ. 3,500.

Needs: Literary, contemporary. No translations, juvenile, gay/lesbian, erotica. Buys 10-15 mss/year. Receives approximately 100 unsolicited fiction mss each month. Does not read mss June 1-August 31. Published work by Andre Dubus, Helen Bell, Merrill Joan Gerber. Published new writers within the last year. Length: 6,000-7,500 words. Critiques rejected mss "when there is time." Sometimes recommends other markets.

How to Contact: Send complete ms with SASE and cover letter stating previous publications, if any. Accepts computer printout submissions. Reports in 1 month on mss. Sample copy $6 plus 50¢ postage.

Payment: $10-12/printed page. 2 free author's copies. $3.50 charge for extras.

Terms: Pays on publication for first North American serial rights and second serial rights by agreement.

Advice: "Send only one story at a time, with a serious and sensible cover letter. We think fiction is of greater general interest than any other literary mode."

SHATTERED WIG REVIEW (I, II), Shattered Wig Productions, 523 E. 38th St., Baltimore MD 21218-1930. (301)467-4344. Editor: Collective. Magazine: 40-50 pages; "average" paper; cardstock cover; illustrations and photos. "Open forum for the discussion of the political aspects of everyday life. Fiction, poetry, graphics, essays, photos." Semiannually. Estab. 1988. Circ. 300.

Needs: Confession, contemporary, erotica, ethnic, experimental, feminist, gay, humor/satire, juvenile (5-9 years), lesbian, literary, preschool (1-4 years), prose poem, psychic/supernatural/occult, regional, senior citizen/retirement, serialized/excerpted novel, translations, young adult/teen (10-18), meat, music, film, art, pickles, revolutionary practice." Does not want "anything by Ann Beattie or John Irving." Receives 15-20 unsolicited mss/month. Publishes ms 2-4 months after acceptance. Published work by Al Ackerman, Jake Berry, Bella Donna; published new writers within the last year. Publishes short shorts. Sometimes critiques rejected mss and recommends other markets.
How to Contact: Send complete ms with cover letter or "visit us in Baltimore." Reports in 1 month. SASE for ms. Simultaneous, photocopied and reprint submissions OK. Accepts computer printout submissions. Sample copy for $3 and SAE.
Payment: Pays in contributor's copies.
Terms: Acquires one-time rights.
Advice: "The arts have been reduced to imploding pus with the only material rewards reserved for vapid stylists and collegiate pod suckers. The only writing that counts has no barriers between imagination and reality, thought and action. We publish any writing that addresses vital issues. Send us at least 3 pieces so we have a choice."

SHAWNEE SILHOUETTE (II), Shawnee State University, 940 Second St., Portsmouth OH 45662. (614)354-3205. Fiction Editor: Tamela Carmichael. Magazine: 5 × 7; 40 pages; illustrations and photos. Quarterly.
Needs: Adventure, contemporary, historical, humor/satire, literary, mainstream, regional, romance, science fiction, suspense/mystery. Receives 3 unsolicted mss/month. Accepts 3 mss/issue. Does not read mss in summer. Publishes ms an average of 3-6 months after acceptance. Published new writers within the last year. Length: 800 words average; 400 words minimum; 1,000 words maximum. Publishes short shorts. Occasionally critiques rejected mss.
How to Contact: Send complete ms with cover letter. Reports in 3 weeks on queries. SASE. Photocopied submissions OK. Accepts computer printout submissions. Sample copy $2, 5 × 7 SAE and 6¢ postage.
Payment: Free contributor's copies.
Terms: Acquires one-time rights.

SHOE TREE (I), The Literary Magazine by and for Young Writers, National Association for Young Writers, Inc., 215 Valle del Sol Dr., Sante Fe NM 87501. (505)982-8596. Editor: Sheila Cowing. Magazine: 6 × 9; 64 pages; 70 lb vellum/white stock; 10 pt. cover; illustrations (photos occasionally). "*Shoe Tree* is a nationwide publication dedicated to nurturing young talent. All stories, poems and artwork are done by children between the ages of 6 and 14." Published 3 times a year. Estab. 1985. Circ. 1,000.
Needs: Adventure, contemporary, fantasy, historical, horror, humor/satire, literary, mainstream, science fiction, suspense/mystery. "No formulas or classroom assignments." Receives 100-150 unsolicited mss/month. Accepts 6 fiction mss/issue; 18 mss/year. Publishes ms 3-6 months after acceptance. Published new writers within the last year. Length: 2,000 words average; 150 words minimum; 5,000 words maximum. Occasionally critiques rejected mss. Recommends other markets sometimes.
How to Contact: Send complete ms with cover letter, which should include name, address, age, school and name of teacher. Reports in 2-4 weeks on queries; 10-12 weeks on mss. SASE. Photocopied submissions OK. Accepts computer printout submissions. Sample copy $5. Fiction guidelines for #10 SAE.
Payment: 2 free contributer's copies.
Terms: Acquires all rights. "The National Association for Young Writers sponsors three annual *Shoe Tree* contests. The contests are open to all children between the ages of 6 and 14. Categories: fiction, nonfiction and poetry. First prize in each category: $25. Deadlines: Dec. 1 (fiction); April 1 (poetry); June 1 (nonfiction). When writing for contest rules, please provide SASE."
Advice: "Because the purpose of our magazine is to nurture talented young writers, to encourage them to explore their world in words, and to help them improve their writing skills, we are very 'optimistic' toward beginning fiction writers. We look for freshness and originality. Draw on your own experiences whenever possible. Avoid formulas and stories assigned in the classroom."

SHOOTING STAR REVIEW (II, IV), 7123 Race St., Pittsburgh PA 15208. (412)731-7039. Editor: Sandra Gould Ford. Magazine: 8½ × 11; 32 pages; 60 lb white paper; 80 lb enamel glossy cover; generously-illustrated; photos. "Dedicated to the Black African-American experience." Quarterly. Estab. 1987. Circ. 1,500.

Needs: Contemporary, experimental, literary, regional, young adult, translations. Each issue has a different theme: "Behind Bars" (deadline March 1); "Marching to a Different Beat" (deadline June 1); "A Salute to African-American Male Writers" (deadline September 1); "Mothers and Daughters" (deadline November 15). Writers should send a SASE for guidelines. No juvenile, preschool. Receives 30-40 unsolicited mss/month. Publishes 5-8 mss/issue. Publishes ms 4-12 months after acceptance. Length: 1,800 words preferred; 3,500 words maximum. Publishes short shorts. Length: 1,000 words or less. Sometimes critiques rejected mss and recommends other markets.

How to Contact: Send complete ms with cover letter. "We like to promote the writer as well as their work and would appreciate understanding who the writer is and why they write." Reports within 1 month on queries; 10-12 weeks on mss. SASE. Simultaneous, photocopied and reprint submissions OK. Accepts computer printout submissions. Accepts electronic submissions via "IBM compatible, 5¼" double sided/double density disk, ASCII non-formated." Sample copy for $3. Fiction guidelines for #10 SAE and 1 first class stamp.

Payment: Pays $15-50 maximum and 2 contributor's copies; charge for extras.

Terms: Pays on publication for first North American serial rights. Sends galleys to author upon request, if time permits.

Advice: "*Shooting Star Review* was started specifically to provide a forum for short fiction that explores the Black experience. We are committed to this art form and will make space for work that satisfies our guidelines. Upcoming themes — "Home & Community" — exploring the worlds that make us (deadline April 21, 1991); "Star Child" — fanciful studies of the zodiac (deadline July 14, 1991); "The Heritage" — thoughts about what growing old can mean (deadline Oct. 24, 1991); "Juneteenth" — the celebration of emancipation (deadline Jan. 15, 1992).

‡SHORT STUFF MAGAZINE FOR GROWN-UPS (II), Bowman Publications, P.O. Box 7057, Loveland CO 80537. (303)669-9139. Editor: Donna Bowman. Magazine: 8½ × 11; 40 pages; bond paper; enamel cover; b&w illustrations and photographs. "Nonfiction is regional — Colorado and adjacent states. Fiction and humor must be tasteful, but can be any genre, any subject. We are designed to be a 'Reader's Digest' of fiction. We are found in professional waiting rooms, etc." Monthly.

Needs: Adventure, contemporary, fantasy, historical (general), humor/satire, mainstream, regional, romance (contemporary/historical), science fiction, senior citizen/retirement, suspense/mystery, western. No erotica. Plans special fiction issue. Receives 100 unsolicited mss/month. Buys 8 mss/issue; 76 mss/year. Publishes ms 3 months after acceptance. Recently published work by Dean Ballenger and Dorothy Roberts. Length: 1,500 words average; 2,000 words maximum.

How to Contact: Send complete manuscript with cover letter. Include SASE. Reports in 3 months. Photocopied and reprint submissions OK. Accepts computer printout submissions. Sample copies with SAE and 65¢ postage. Fiction guidelines for SAE.

Payment: Pays $10-50 and free subscription to magazine.

Terms: Pays on publication for first North American serial rights.

Advice: "We seek a potpourri of subjects each issue. A new slant, a different approach, fresh viewpoints — all of these excite us. We don't like gore, salacious humor or perverted tales. Prefer third person. Be sure it is a story with a beginning, middle and end. It must have dialogue. Many beginners do not know an essay from a short story."

‡SIDETREKKED (I, IV), Science Fiction London, 172 William St., London, Ontario N6B 3B7 Canada. (419)433-7001. Editor: Bill Stephens. Newspaper: 7x8½; 36-40 pages; bond paper, black-and-white drawings, halftone photographs. "Science fiction for science fiction readers, mostly adults." Quarterly. Estab. 1980. Circ. 200.

Needs: Fantasy, science fiction. "We will consider any story with a science fictional slant. Because sf tends to be all-embracing, that could include horror, humor/satire, romance, suspense, feminist, gay, ethnic, etc. — yes, even western — but the science fiction classification must be met, usually by setting the story in a plausible, futuristic universe." Receives 3-5 unsolicited fiction mss/month. Accepts 3-8 mss/issue. Time between acceptance and publication varies. Recently published work by Joe Beliveau, Dave Seburn. Length: 1,000-5,000 words preferred. "No hard-and-fast rules, but we can't accommodate novelettes or novellas." Publishes short shorts. Critiques or comments on rejected mss, if requested by the author. Recommends other markets on occasion.

How to Contact: Send complete ms with cover letter. Reports in 3 weeks on queries; in 1 month on mss. SASE. Photocopied and computer printout submissions OK. Sample copy for $2 (Canadian) and 9x10 SAE.

Payment: Pays in contributor's copies.
Terms: Acquires first North American serial rights. "We are presently running a short fiction contest in celebration of our sponsoring club's 10th anniversary. If sponsorship can be arranged, we would consider making it an annual event."
Advice: "We are more forgiving than most fiction markets and we try to work with new writers. What makes us want to work with a writer is some suggestion that he or she understands what makes a good story. What makes a manuscript stand out? Tell a good story. The secondary things are fixable if the story is there, but if it is not, no amount of tinkering can fix it."

SIGN OF THE TIMES (II), A Chronicle of Decadence in the Atomic Age, 3819 NE 15th, Portland OR 97212. (206)323-6779. Editor: Mark Souder. Tabloid: 8×10; 32 pages; book paper; 120 lb cover stock; illustrations; photos. "Decadence in all forms for those seeking literary amusement." Semiannually. Published special fiction issue last year; plans another. Estab. 1980. Circ. 750.
Needs: Comics, erotica, experimental, gay, lesbian. No religious or western manuscripts. Receives 6 unsolicited mss/month. Buys 10 mss/issue; 20 mss/year. Published work by Gary Smith, Willie Smith, Ben Satterfield. Length: 3,000 words average; 500 words minimum, 5,000 words maximum. Publishes short shorts. Sometimes comments on rejected mss and recommends other markets.
How to Contact: Send complete ms with cover letter and bio. Reports in 6 weeks on mss. SASE. Photocopied submissions OK. Accepts computer printout submissions. Prefers letter-quality. Sample copy $3.50. Fiction guidelines for #10 SASE.
Payment: Up to $20, subscription to magazine, 2 contributor's copies; 1 time cover price charge for extras.
Terms: Pays on publication for first rights plus anthology in the future.

THE SIGNAL (II), Network International, Box 67, Emmett ID 83617. Editors: Joan Silva and David Chorlton. Magazine: 8½×11; 68 pages; good paper; some art; photos. "Wide open. Not restricted to 'literature.' Poetry, essays, reviews, comment, interviews, speculative thought." Semiannually. Estab. 1987.
Needs: Literary, translations. No "religious dogma, journeys of self-discovery in a '57 Chevrolet, catalogues of family members." Receives few unsolicited mss/month. Accepts "perhaps 1" ms/issue. Publishes ms 6 months to 1 year after acceptance. Length: 3,000 words maximum. Publishes short shorts.
How to Contact: "Just send us the story. Cover letter optional." Reports in 10 weeks on mss. SASE. Photocopied submissions OK. Accepts computer printout submissions. Sample copy $4. Fiction guidelines for #10 SAE and 1 first class stamp.
Payment: Pays in contributor's copies.
Terms: Acquires first rights.
Advice: "We want to remain open to all writing. Although unable to publish very much fiction, we do look for ideas expressed in any form."

SILVERFISH REVIEW (IV), Silverfish Press, Box 3541, Eugene OR 97403. (503)344-5060. Editor: Rodger Moody. High quality literary material for a general audience. Published irregularly. Estab. 1979. Circ. 750.
Needs: Literary. Accepts 1-2 mss/issue.
How to Contact: Send complete ms with SASE. Reports in 1 month on mss. Sample copy $3 and $1 for postage.
Payment: 5 free author's copies. $5/page when funding permits.
Terms: Rights revert to author.
Advice: "We publish primarily poetry; we will, however, publish good quality fiction."

SING HEAVENLY MUSE! (II), Box 13299, Minneapolis MN 55414. Editor: Sue Ann Martinson. Magazine: 6x9; 125 pages; 55 lb acid-free paper; 10 pt. glossy cover stock; illustrations; photos. Women's poetry, prose and artwork. Semiannually. Estab. 1977.
Needs: Literary, contemporary, fantasy, feminist, mystery, humor, prose poem and ethnic/minority. Receives approximately 30 unsolicited fiction mss each month. "Accepts mss for consideration only in April and September." Published work by Helene Cappuccio, Erika Duncan, Martha Roth. Publishes short shorts. Sometimes recommends other markets.

How to Contact: Query for information on theme issues or variations in schedule. Include cover letter with "brief writing background and publications." Accepts computer printout submissions. Reports in 1-3 months on queries and mss. Publishes ms an average of 1 year after acceptance. Sample copy $3.50.
Payment: Honorarium; 2 free copies.
Terms: Pays on publication for first rights.
Advice: "Try to avoid preaching. Look for friends also interested in writing and form a mutual support-and-criticism group."

SINISTER WISDOM (IV), Box 3252, Berkeley CA 94703. Editor: Elana Dykewomon. Magazine: 5½×8½; 128-144 pages; 55 lb stock; 10 pt CIS cover; illustrations; photos. Lesbian-feminist journal, providing fiction, poetry, drama, essays, journals and artwork. Quarterly. 1990 issues were on disability, Italian-American women, lesbian voices. Estab. 1976. Circ. 3,000.
Needs: Lesbian, adventure, contemporary, erotica, ethnic, experimental, fantasy, feminist, historical, humor/satire, literary, prose poem, psychic, regional, science fiction, sports, translations. No heterosexual or male-oriented fiction; nothing that stereotypes or degrades women. Receives 50 unsolicited mss/month. Accepts 25 mss/issue; 75-100 mss/year. Publishes ms 1 month to 1 year after acceptance. Published work by Melanie Kaye/Kantrowitz, Adrienne Rich, Terri L. Jewell and Gloria Anzaldúa; published new writers within the last year. Length: 2,000 words average; 500 words minimum; 4,000 words maximum. Publishes short shorts. Occasionally critiques rejected mss. Sometimes recommends other markets.
How to Contact: Send 2 copies of complete ms with cover letter, which should include a brief author's bio to be published when the work is published. Reports in 2 months on queries; 6 months on mss. SASE. Photocopied submissions OK. Accepts computer printout submissions. Sample copy $6.25; subscription $17.
Payment: Pays in contributor's copies.
Terms: Rights retained by author.
Advice: The philosophy behind *Sinister Wisdom* is "to reflect and encourage the lesbian movements for social change, especially change in the ways we use language."

SIX LAKES ARTS (I), Art & Entertainment Between the Lakes, (formerly *In-Between*), Six Lakes Arts Communication, Inc., 43 Chapel St., Seneca Falls NY 13148. (315)568-4265. Publisher: Stephen Beals. Associate Editor: Jim Porto. Magazine: 8½×11; 32 pages minimum; 60 lb offset paper; glossy cover; illustrations; photos. "Art and entertainment. Music, theatre, short stories, poetry. Exclusive to Finger Lakes region of New York State, for upscale arts enthusiasts." Bimonthly. Estab. 1987. 1,500 copies distributed to members, arts groups and media.
Needs: Historical (general), humor/satire, prose poem, senior citizen/retirement, suspense/mystery, music, theatre. Finger Lakes writers given preference. "We are a new magazine for the Finger Lakes. We are interested in art and entertainment with a very broad view of what constitutes art. We have a rural flavor and a 'family' audience. Work must be reflective of Finger Lakes region." No erotica, sci fi, psychic, religious, romance, gay/lesbian. Accepts 1-2 mss/issue. Publishes ms 1-3 months after acceptance. Published work by Richard Cicarelli, Barbara Mater and David Downey. Length: 800 words average; 500 words minimum; 2,000 words maximum. Will consider longer pieces in serial form. Publishes short shorts.
How to Contact: Send complete ms with cover letter. Reports in 2-4 weeks on queries; 4-6 weeks on mss. SASE. Simultaneous, photocopied and reprint submissions OK. Accepts computer printout submissions. Accepts electronic submissions via Apple Macintosh. Sample copy and fiction guidelines free.
Payment: $25 articles and short stories; $10 poetry.
Advice: Most of our writers are first-timers. Keep in mind our audience is rural by choice and shouldn't be talked down to. We have published a book of mystery short stories."

SKYLARK (I), Purdue University, 2233 171st St., Hammond IN 46323. (219)844-0520. Editor: Marcia F. Jaron. Magazine: 8½×11; 100 pages; illustrations; photos. Fine arts magazine—short stories, poems and graphics for adults. Annually. Estab. 1971. Circ. 500-1,000.
Needs: Contemporary, ethnic, experimental, fantasy, feminist, humor/satire, literary, mainstream, prose poem, regional, science fiction, serialized/excerpted novel, spiritual, sports, suspense/mystery and western. Receives 20 mss/month. Accepts 6-7 mss/issue. Published work by Michael Beres, Anthony Schneider, O.A. Fraser, Amy Garza. Published new writers within the last year. Length: 1-15 double-spaced pages.

How to Contact: Send complete ms. SASE for ms. Photocopied submissions OK. Accepts computer printout submissions. Prefers letter-quality. Sample copy $5; back issue $3.
Payment: 1 contributor's copy.
Terms: Acquires first rights. Copyright reverts to author.
Advice: "The goal of *Skylark* is to encourage *creativity* and give beginning and published authors showcase for their work. Check for spelling errors or typos."

‡SLATE AND STYLE (IV) Magazine of the National Federation of the Blind Writers Division, NFB Writer's Division, 2704 Beach Drive, Merrick NY 11566. Editor: Loraine E. Stayer. Fiction Editor: Tom Stevens. Newsletter: 8 × 10; 25 print/Braille pages; cassette and large print. "Articles of interest to writers, and resources for blind writers. Quarterly. Estab. 1982. Circ. 200.
Needs: Adventure, contemporary, fantasy, humor/satire, blindness. No erotica. Does not read June, July. Length: 2,000 words average; 1,000 words minimum; 6,000 words maximum. Publishes short shorts. Critiques rejected mss only if requested. Sometimes recommends other markets.
How to Contact: Query first. Reports on queries in 2 weeks; 4 weeks on mss. Photocopied submissions OK. Sample copy $2.50 and cassette mailer if tape requested. Large print copies also available. "Sent Free Matter For The Blind. If not blind, send 2 stamps."
Payment: Pays in contributor's copies.
Terms: Acquires one-time rights. Publication not copyrighted. Sponsors contests for fiction writers.
Advice: "Planning 'showcase' publication of poetry, articles, stories by blind writers or members of writers' division. Request that writer take responsibility of copyright permission if piece previously published. Aiming for 6,000 word length per piece. Write *Slate & Style* for details. We aren't interested in demeaning attitudes toward blindness!" Members/subscribers only. Payment for showcase (now termed Far Horizon) $10-25 depending on length.

SLIPSTREAM (II, IV), Box 2071, New Market Station, Niagara Falls NY 14301. (716)282-2616. Editor: Dan Sicoli. Fiction Editors: R. Borgatti, D. Sicoli and Livio Farallo. Magazine: 7 × 8½; 80-120 pages; high quality paper and cover; illustrations; photos. "We use poetry and short fiction with a contemporary urban feel." Estab. 1981. Circ. 300.
Needs: "We are currently backlogged with fiction. Submit after July 1, 1991." Contemporary, erotica, ethnic, experimental, fantasy, feminist, gay, humor/satire, lesbian, literary, mainstream, prose poem and science fiction. No religious, juvenile, young adult or romance. Receives over 75 unsolicited mss/ month. Accepts 2-8 mss/issue; 6-12 mss/year. Publishes short shorts under 15 pages. Recently published work by Gregory Burnham, Nan D. Hayes and Kurt Nimmo. Rarely critiques rejected mss. Sometimes recommends other markets.
How to Contact: Send complete ms. Reports within 2 months. SASE. Accepts computer printout submissions. Sample copy $4. Fiction guidelines for #10 SASE.
Payment: 2 contributor's copies.
Terms: Acquires one-time rights on publication.
Advice: "Writing should be honest, fresh; develop your own style. Check out a sample issue first. Don't write for the sake of writing, write from the gut as if it were a biological need. Write from experience and mean what you say, but say it in the fewest number of words."

THE SMALL POND MAGAZINE (II), Box 664, Stratford CT 06497. (203)378-4066. Editor: Napoleon St. Cyr. Magazine: 5½ × 8½; 42 pages; 60 lb offset paper; 65 lb cover stock; illustrations (art). "Features contemporary poetry, the salt of the earth, peppered with short prose pieces of various kinds. The college educated and erudite read it for good poetry, prose and pleasure." Triannually. Estab. 1964. Circ. 300.
Needs: "Rarely use science fiction or formula stories you'd find in *Cosmo, Redbook, Ladies Home Journal*, etc." Buys 10-12 mss/year. Longer response time in July and August. Receives approximately 50 unsolicited fiction mss each month. Length: 200-2,500 words. Critiques rejected mss when there is time. Sometimes recommends other markets.
How to Contact: Send complete ms with SASE and short vita with publishing credits. Accepts good copy computer printout submissions. Prefers letter-quality. Reports in 2 weeks-1 month. Publishes ms an average of 2 months to 1 year after acceptance. Sample copy $2.50.

Payment: 2 free author's copies. $2/copy charge for extras.
Terms: Pays for all rights.
Advice: "Send for a sample copy first. All mss must be typed. Name and address and story title on front page, name of story on succeeding pages and paginated." Mss are rejected because of "tired plots and poor grammar; also over-long—2,500 words maximum. Don't send any writing conference ms unless it got an A or better."

SMILE (IV), Box 3502, Madison WI 53704. (608)258-1305. Editor: Fred Wagwroth. Magazine: 8½×11; 28 pages; colored cover; illustrations; photos. Publishes material on "non-mainstream politics; political theory and practice." Semiannually. Plans special fiction issue. Estab. 1987. Circ. 1,500.
Needs: "Anarchist or communist topics that deal with the psychosocial liberation from the oppressive society." Receives 2 unsolicited fiction mss/month. Length: 200 words minimum; 800 words maximum. Sometimes critiques rejected mss.
How to Contact: Query with clips of published work or send complete mss with cover letter. Simultaneous, photocopied and reprint submissions OK. Accepts computer printout submissions. Accepts electronic submissions via disk or modem. Sample copy for SAE and 6 first class stamps.
Payment: Pays in 2 contributor's copies.
Terms: "Everything printed is free to be copied by anyone." Publication is not copyrighted.

‡SNAKE NATION REVIEW (II), Snake Nation Press, Inc. 2920 North Oak, Valdosta GA 31602. (912)242-1503. Editor: Roberta George. Fiction Editor: Janice Daugharty. Newspaper: 6×9; 110 pages; acid free 70 lb. paper; 90 lb. cover; illustrations and photographs. "We are interested in all types of stories for an educated, discerning, sophisticated audience." Semiannually. Estab. 1989. Circ. 500.
Needs: "Short stories of 5,000 words or less, poems (any length), art work that will be returned after use." Condensed/excerpted novel, contemporary, erotica, ethnic, experimental, fantasy, feminist, gay, horror, sumor/satire, lesbian, literary, mainstream, prose poem, psychic/supernatural/occult, regional, science fiction, senior citizen/retirement, suspense/mystery. "We want our writers to have a voice, a story to tell, not a flat rendition of a slice of life." Receives 50 unsolicited mss/month. Buys 8-10 mss/issue; 20 mss/year. Publishes ms 3-6 months after acceptance. Agented fiction 1%. Recently published work by Starky Flythe and Peter Meinke. Length: 3,500 words average; 300 words minimum; 5,500 words maximum. Publishes short shorts. Length: 500 words. Sometimes critiques rejected mss and recommends other markets.
How to Contact: Send complete manuscript with cover letter. Reports on queries in 3 months. SASE. Photocopied submissions OK. Accepts computer printout submissions. Sample copy for $5, 8×10 SAE and 90¢ postage. Fiction guidelines for SAE and 1 first class stamp.
Payment: Pays $100 maximum and contributor's copies.
Terms: Buys first rights. Sends galleys to author. "Spring contest: short stories (5,000 words); $300 first prize, $200 second prize, $100 third prize; entry fee $5 for stories $1 for poems."
Advice: "Looks for clean, legible copy and an interesting, unique voice that pulls the reader into the work."

SNAKE RIVER REFLECTIONS (I), (formerly *Writing Pursuits*), 1863 Bitterroot Dr., Twin Falls ID 83301. (208)734-0746 (evenings). Editor: Bill White. Newsletter: 8×11; 3-5 pages; illustrations. Newsletter for writers. 10 issues per year. Estab. 1990. Circ. approximately 200.
Needs: Literary, regional, suspense/mystery, humor/satire and western. No erotica, gay, lesbian, religious or occult fiction. Accepts 1 ms/issue; 10 mss/year. Publishes ms within 1-2 months of acceptance. Length: 500 words maximum. Sometimes critiques rejected mss and recommends other markets.
How to Contact: Query first. Reports in 1-2 weeks. SASE. Photocopied submissions OK. Accepts computer printout submissions; also electronic submissions via disk or modem. Sample copy 55¢. Fiction guidelines for #10 SASE.
Payment: Pays in contributor's copies.
Terms: Acquires first rights.
Advice: "Be persistent. Study a sample of our publication. Make your story exciting."

THE SNEAK PREVIEW (I), Box 639, Grants Pass OR 97526. (503)474-3044. Editor: Curtis Hayden. Fiction Editor: Claire Pennington. Tabloid: 9¾×14; 24-32 pages; newsprint paper; newsprint cover; illustrations; photos. "News and arts biweekly of local events, with one page reserved for writers and poets to submit stories and poems." Biweekly. Estab. 1986. Circ. 12,500.

Needs: Humor/satire (especially), prose poem, regional. "Nothing that would offend the scruples of a small town in southern Oregon." Receives 2 unsolicited mss/month. Buys 1 ms/issue; 26 mss/year. Publishes ms within 2 weeks-6 months of acceptance. Published work by Leo Curzen, Cher Manuel, Garfield Price. Length: 250 words average; 200 words minimum; 300 words maximum.

How to Contact: Query first. Reports in 2 weeks. SASE (65¢ postage is a must). Simultaneous, photocopied and reprint submissions OK. Accepts computer printout submissions. Guidelines for SASE.

Payment: Contributor's copies.

Terms: Publication not copyrighted.

Advice: "We need more people like Hunter Thompson. Everybody thinks the New-York-City-let's-get-serious-about-life-and-our-'art' is where it's at."

SOJOURNER, A Women's Forum (II,IV), 42 Seaveins, Jamaica Plain MA 02130. (617)524-0415. Editor: Karen Kahn. Magazine: 11×17; 48 pages; newsprint paper; illustrations; photos. "Faminist journal publishing interviews, nonfiction features, news, viewpoints, poetry, reviews (music, cinema, books) and fiction for women." Published monthly. Estab. 1975. Circ. 33,000.

Needs: Contemporary, ethnic, experimental, fantasy, feminist, lesbian, humor/satire, literary, prose poem and women's. Receives 20 unsolicited fiction mss/month. Accepts 10 mss/year. Approximately 10% of fiction is agented. Published new writers within the last year. Length: 1,000 words minimum; 4,000 words maximum; 2,500 words average. Recommends other markets.

How to Contact: Send complete ms with SASE and cover letter with description of previous publications; current works. Photocopied submissions OK. Publishes ms an average of 6 months after acceptance. Sample copy $2 with 10×13 SASE and 86¢ postage. Free fiction guidelines with SASE.

Payment: Subscription to magazine and 2 contributor's copies, $15. No extra charge up to 5; $1 charge each thereafter.

Terms: First rights only.

Advice: "Pay attention to appearance of manuscript! Very difficult to wade through sloppily presented fiction, however good. Do write a cover letter. If not cute, it can't hurt and may help. Mention previous publication(s)."

‡THE (something) (II, IV), The M Press, 1520 Bryn Mawr Ave., Racine WI 53403. (414)637-1503. Editor: Mark M. Newsletter: 8½×11; 12 pages; plain paper; plain paper cover; illustrations and photographs. "Short, short oddball stuff for oddballs." Bimonthly. Estab. 1985. Circ. about 100.

Needs: Experimental, humor/satire, prose poem. Receives 1 mss/month. Accepts 1 mss/issue; 6 mss/year. Publishes ms 2 months after acceptance. Length: 500 words average 500 words maximum. Publishes short shorts. Length: "as short as possible." Sometimes critiques rejected mss.

How to Contact: Send complete manuscript with cover letter. Reports in 1 week on queries; 3 weeks on mss. SASE. Accepts photocopied submissions. Sample copy $1. Fiction guidelines for legal SAE and 1 first class stamp.

Payment: Pays contributor's copy.

Terms: Acquires first right.

Advice: "Keep it short, short, short and odd."

SONORA REVIEW (II), University of Arizona, Department of English, Tucson AZ 85721. (602)621-8077. Editors: Martha Ostheimer and Layne Schorr. Fiction Editors: Ellen Devos, Robert Schirmer. Magazine: 6×9; 150 pages; 16 lb paper; 20 lb cover stock; photos seldom. *The Sonora Review* publishes short fiction and poetry of high literary quality. Semiannually. Estab. 1980. Circ. 500.

Needs: Literary. "We are open to a wide range of stories with accessibility and vitality being important in any case. We're not interested in genre fiction, formula work." Buys 4-6 mss/issue. Approximately 10% of fiction is agented. Published work by Nancy Lord, Robyn Oughton, Ron Hansen. Length: open, though prefers work under 25 pages. Sometimes recommends other markets.

How to Contact: Send complete ms with SASE and cover letter with previous publications. Accepts computer printout submissions. Prefers letter-quality. Reports in 2 months on mss, longer for work received during summer (May-August). Publishes ms an average of 2-6 months after acceptance. Sample copy $4.

Payment: 2 free author's copies. $2 charge for extras. Annual cash prizes.
Terms: Acquires first North American serial rights. Fall issue features fiction contest winnter: 1st prize, $150; 2nd prize $75. Submit by October 1.
Advice: "We have increased the size of the magazine at 50% and are developing more special features connecting special themes and regions. Let the story sit for several months, then review it to see if you still like it. If you're unsure, keep working on it *before* sending it out. All mss are read carefully, and we try to make brief comments if time permits. Our hope is that an author will keep us interested in his or her treatment of a subject by using fresh details and writing with an authority that is absorbing." Mss are rejected because "1) we only have space for 6-8 manuscripts out of several hundred submissions annually, and 2) most of the manuscripts we receive have some merit but are not of publishable quality. It would be helpful to receive a cover letter with all manuscripts."

SOUNDINGS EAST (II), English Dept., Salem State College, Salem MA 01970. (508)741-6270. Advisory Editor: Rod Kessler. Magazine: 5½ × 8½; 64 pages; illustrations; photos. "Mainly a college audience, but we also distribute to libraries throughout the country." Biannually. Estab. 1973. Circ. 2,000.
Needs: Literary, contemporary, prose poem. No juvenile. Publishes 4-5 stories/issue. Receives 30 unsolicited fiction mss each month. Does not read April-August. Published work by James Brady, Terry Farish and Christina Shea. Published new writers within the last year. Length: 250-5,000 words. "We are open to short pieces as well as to long works."
How to Contact: Send complete ms with SASE between September and March. Accepts computer printout submissions. Prefers letter-quality. Reports in 2 months on mss. Sample copy $3.
Payment: 2 free author's copies.
Terms: All publication rights revert to authors.
Advice: "We're impressed by an excitement—coupled with craft—in the use of the language. It also helps to reach in and grab the reader by the heart."

SOUTH CAROLINA REVIEW (II), Clemson University, Clemson SC 29634-1503. (803)656-3229. Editors: R.J. Calhoun, Frank Day and Carol Johnston. Managing Editor: Mark Winchell. Magazine: 6 × 9; 200 pages; 60 lb cream white vellum paper; 65 lb cream white vellum cover stock; illustrations and photos rarely. Semiannually. Estab. 1967. Circ. 700.
Needs: Literary, contemporary, humor and ethnic. Receives approximately 50-60 unsolicited fiction mss each month. Does not read mss June-August. Recently published work by Joyce Carol Oates, Rosanne Coggeshall, Stephen Dixon; published new writers within the last year. Rarely critiques rejected mss.
How to Contact: Send complete ms with SASE. Accepts computer printout submissions. Reports in 2 months on mss. Sample copy $5.
Payment: Pays in contributor's copies.
Advice: Mss are rejected because of "poorly structured stories, or stories without vividness or intensity. The most celebrated function of a little magazine is to take a chance on writers not yet able to get into the larger magazines—the little magazine can encourage promising writers at a time when encouragement is vitally needed. (We also publish 'name' writers, like Joyce Carol Oates, Stephen Dixon, George Garrett.) Read the masters extensively. Write and write more, with a *schedule*. Listen to editorial advice when offered. Don't get discouraged with rejections. Read what writers say about writing (e.g. *The Paris Review* Interviews with George Plimpton, gen. ed.; Welty's *One Writer's Beginnings*,etc). Take courses in writing and listen to, even if you do not follow, the advice."

SOUTH DAKOTA REVIEW (II), University of South Dakota, Box 111, University Exchange, Vermillion SD 57069. (605)677-5966. Editor: John R. Milton. Magazine: 6 × 9; 150+ pages; book paper; glossy cover stock; illustrations sometimes; photos on cover. Literary magazine for university and college audiences and their equivalent. Emphasis is often on the West and its writers, but will accept mss from anywhere. Issues are generally fiction and poetry with some literary essays. Quarterly. Estab. 1963. Circ. 500.
Needs: Literary, contemporary, ethnic, experimental, excerpted novel, regional and translations. "We like very well-written stories. Contemporary western American setting appeals, but not necessary. No formula stories, sports or adolescent 'I' narrator." Receives 30 unsolicited fiction mss/month. Accepts about 10-20 mss/year, more or less. Assistant editor accepts mss in June-July, sometimes August. Approximately 5% of fiction is agented. Publishes short shorts of 5 pages double-spaced typescript. Published work by Ed Loomis, Max Evans, Dennis Lynds; published new writers the last year. Length: 1,300 words minimum; 6,000 words maximum. (Has made exceptions, up to novella length.) Sometimes recommends other markets.

How to Contact: Send complete ms with SASE. "We like cover letters that are not boastful and do not attempt to sell the stories but rather provide some personal information about the writer." Photocopied submissions OK if not multiple submission. Reports in 1 month. Publishes ms an average of 1-6 months after acceptance. Sample copy $5.
Payment: 2-4 free author's copies, depending on length of ms. $2.50 charge for extras.
Terms: Acquires first rights and second serial rights.
Advice: Rejects mss because of "careless writing; often careless typing; stories too personal ('I' confessional), adolescent; working manuscript, not polished; subject matter that editor finds trivial. We are trying to use more fiction and more variety. We would like to see more sophisticated stories. Do not try to outguess editors and give them what you think they want. Write honestly. Be yourself."

‡**THE SOUTH HILL GAZETTE (II)**, A.D. Images, P.O. Box 547, Rochester MI 48307. (313)656-9777. Editor: Leigh A. Arrathoon. Newsletter: 8½×11; 12 pages; illustrations and b&w photographs. "Upbeat fiction suitable for family reading." Weekly. Circ. 6,000/week.
Needs: Adventure, ethnic, historical (general), humor/satire, prose poem, regional, romance (contemporary and historical), science fiction, suspense/mystery, western, seasonal. "The style must be clear, the words well-chosen (but not affected); the parts of the fiction should work together at the service of the whole. We do use dialect if it is well-done." No erotica, horror, religious, political, juvenile, fantasy, gay, feminist, lesbian. "Anything written to shock, impress or horrify – anything illogical." Receives 1 or 2 unsolicited mss/month. Accepts 1 ms/issue; 6-10 4 week pieces (20 pages each). "Our publication reflects the seasons – publication date depends upon how the material fits into that scheme." Recently published work by Antonia Baquet Cyres, Steve Adolph, Lianna S.M. Wright, Leigh A. Arrathoon. Publishes short shorts.
How to Contact: Query first. "Please call and discuss – 9:00 p.m. or later (313)656-9777." SASE. Photocopied submissions OK. Accepts computer printout submissions. "Only if done on a Mac IIX." Sample copy for 9×12 SAE and 3 first class stamps.
Payment: Pays contributor's copies.
Terms: Acquires first rights.
Advice: "The story is the thing. All the devices in the fiction should work together at the service of the statement. If the fiction doesn't have a statement to make, it isn't worth writing. Stories are units of communication that are simply larger constructs than words, sentences and paragraphs. They are a way to teach, amuse or move the reader."

SOUTHERN CALIFORNIA ANTHOLOGY (II), Master of Professional Writing Program – USC, MPW-WPH 404 USC, Los Angeles CA 90089-4034. (213)743-8255. Contact: Melissa Hartman. Magazine: 5½×8½; 142 pages; semi-glossy cover stock. "The *Southern California Anthology* is a literary review that is an eclectic collection of previously unpublished quality contemporary fiction, poetry and interviews with established literary people, published for adults of all professions; of particular interest to those interested in serious contemporary literature." Annually. Estab. 1983. Circ. 1,500.
Needs: Contemporary, ethnic, experimental, feminist, historical (general), humor/satire, literary, mainstream, regional, serialized/excerpted novel. No juvenile, religious, confession, romance, science fiction. Receives 30 unsolicited fiction mss each month. Accepts 10-12 mss/issue. Does not read February-September. Publishes ms 4 months after acceptance. Length: 10-15 pages average; 2 pages minimum; 25 pages maximum. Publishes short shorts.
How to Contact: Send complete ms with cover letter or submit through agent. Cover letter should include list of previous publications. Reports on queries in 1 month; on mss in 4 months. SASE. Photocopied submissions OK. Accepts computer printout submissions, no dot-matrix. Sample copy $2.95. Fiction guidelines for #10 SAE and 1 first class stamp.
Payment: Pays in contributor's copies.
Terms: Acquires first rights.
Advice: "The *Anthology* pays particular attention to craft and style in its selection of narrative writing."

‡**SOUTHERN EXPOSURE (III, IV)**, Institute for Southern Studies, P.O. Box 531, Durham NC 27702. (919)688-8167. Editor: Eric Bates. Magazine: 8½×11; 64 pages. "Southern politics and culture – investigative reporting, oral history, fiction for an audience of Southern changemakers – scholars, journalists, activists." Quarterly. Estab. 1972. Circ. 5,000.
Needs: Contemporary, ethnic, feminist, gay, humor/satire, lesbian, literary, regional. Plans special fiction issue. Receives 50 unsolicited mss/month. Buys 1 mss/issue; 4 mss/year. Publishes ms 3-6 months after acceptance. Agented fiction 25%. Recently published work by Clyde Egerton, Jill McCorkle and Larry Brown. Length: 3,500 words preferred.

How to Contact: Send complete ms with cover letter. Reports in 4-6 weeks on mss. SASE for ms. Photocopied submissions OK. Accepts computer printout and photocopied submissions. Sample copy for $4, 8½×11 and $1.85 postage. Fiction guidelines for #10 SAE and 1 first class stamp.
Payment: Pays $100, free subscription to magazine and contributor's copies.
Terms: Pays on publication for first rights.

SOUTHERN HUMANITIES REVIEW (II, IV), Auburn University, 9088 Haley Center, Auburn University AL 36849. Co-Editors: Thomas L. Wright and Dan R. Latimer. Magazine: 6×9; 96 pages; 60 lb neutral pH, natural paper, 65 lb neutral pH med. coated cover stock; occasional illustrations and photos. "We publish essays, poetry, fiction and reviews. Our fiction has ranged from very traditional in form and content to very experimental. Literate, college-educated audience. We hope they read our journal for both enlightenment and pleasure." Quarterly. Estab. 1967. Circ. 800.
Needs: Serious fiction, fantasy, feminist, humor and regional. Receives approximately 25 unsolicited fiction mss each month. Accepts and prints 1-2 mss/issue, 4-6 mss/year. Slower reading time in summer. Published work by Anne Brashler, Heimito von Doderer and Ivo Andric; published new writers within the last year. Length: 3,500-5,000 words. Critiques rejected mss when there is time. Sometimes recommends other markets.
How to Contact: Send complete ms with SASE and cover letter with an explanation of topic chosen—special, certain book, etc., a little about author if they have never submitted. Accepts computer printout submissions. Prefers letter-quality. Reports in 90 days. Sample copy $4.
Payment: 1 copy; $4 charge for extras.
Terms: Acquires all rights. Sends galleys to author.
Advice: "Send us the ms with SASE. If we like it, we'll take it or we'll recommend changes. If we don't like it, we'll send it back as promptly as possible. Read the journal. Send a typewritten, clean copy carefully proofread. We also award annually the Hoepfner Prize of $100 for the best published essay or short story of the year. Let someone whose opinion you respect read your story and give you an honest appraisal. Rewrite, if necessary, to get the most from your story."

THE SOUTHERN REVIEW (II), Louisiana State University, 43 Allen Hall, Baton Rouge LA 70803. (504)388-5108. Editors: James Olney and Dave Smith. Magazine: 6¾×10; 240 pages; 50 lb Glatfelter paper; 65 lb #1 grade cover stock; occasional photos. A literary quarterly publishing critical essays, poetry and fiction for a highly intellectual audience. Quarterly. Published special fiction issue. Estab. 1935. Circ. 3,000.
Needs: Literary and contemporary. "We emphasize style and substantial content. No mystery, fantasy or religious mss." Buys 7-8 mss/issue. Receives approximately 100 unsolicited fiction mss each month. Approximately 5% of fiction is agented. Recently published work by William Hoffman, Rick Bass, Jill McCorkle. Published new writers within the last year. Length: 2,000-10,000 words. Sometimes recommends other markets.
How to Contact: Send complete ms with cover letter and SASE. "Prefer brief letters giving information on author concerning where he/she has been published before. Biographical info and what he/she is doing now." Accepts computer printout submissions. Prefers letter-quality. Reports in 2 months on mss. Publishes ms an average of 1-2 years after acceptance. Sample copy $5.
Payment: Pays $12/printed page. 2 free author's copies.
Terms: Pays on publication for first American serial rights. "We transfer copyright to author on request." Sends galleys to author.
Advice: "Develop a careful style with characters in depth." Sponsors annual contest for best first collection of short stories published during the calendar year.

SOUTHWEST REVIEW (II), 6410 Airline, Southern Methodist University, Dallas TX 75275. (214)373-7440. Editor: Willard Spiegelman. Magazine: 6×9; 144 pages. "The majority of our readers are college-educated adults who wish to stay abreast of the latest and best in contemporary fiction, poetry, literary criticism and books in all but the most specialized disciplines." Quarterly. Estab. 1915. Circ. 1,600.
Needs: "High literary quality; no specific requirements as to subject matter, but cannot use sentimental, religious, western, poor science fiction, pornographic, true confession, mystery, juvenile or serialized or condensed novels." Receives approximately 200 unsolicited fiction mss each month. Recently published work by Brad Conard, Ellen Akins, Rick Bass and Millicent Dillon. Length: prefers 3,000-5,000 words. Occasionally critiques rejected mss. Sometimes recommends other markets.

How to Contact: Send complete ms with SASE. Accepts computer printout submissions. Prefers letter-quality. Reports in 3 months on mss. Publishes ms 6 months to 1 year after acceptance. Sample copy $5. Free guidelines with SASE.
Payment: Payment varies; writers receive 3 free author's copies.
Terms: Pays on publication for first North American serial rights. Sends galleys to author.
Advice: "We have become less regional. A lot of time would be saved for us and for the writer if he looked at a copy of the *Southwest Review* before submitting. We like to receive a cover letter because it is some reassurance that the author has taken the time to check a current directory for the editor's name. When there isn't a cover letter, we wonder whether the same story is on 20 other desks around the country."

SOU'WESTER (II), English Dept., Southern Illinois University-Edwardsville, Edwardsville IL 62026-1438. (618)692-3190. Managing Editor: Fred W. Robbins. Magazine: 6×9; 88 pages; Warren's Olde style paper; 60 lb cover. General magazine of poetry and fiction. Published three times/year. Estab. 1960. Circ. 300.
Needs: Receives 40-50 unsolicited fiction mss/month. Accepts 3 mss/issue, 9 mss/year. Published work by Robert Wexelblatt, Robert Solomon; published new writers within the last year. Length: 5,000 words minimum; 10,000 words maximum. Occasionally critiques rejected mss.
How to Contact: Send complete ms with SASE. Simultaneous and photocopied submissions OK. Accepts computer printout submissions. Reports in 3 months. Publishes ms an average of 6 months after acceptance. Sample copy $1.50.
Payment: 2 contributor's copies. $1.50 charge for extras.
Terms: Acquires all rights.

SPACE AND TIME (II, IV), 138 W. 70th St., New York NY 10023. Editor-in-Chief: Gordon Linzner. Magazine: 5½×8½; 120 pages; 20 lb paper; index cover stock; illustrations. Magazine of "fantasy fiction of all types and sub-genres (including science fiction)—the less categorizable, the better. *S&T* tends to feature new writers and odd pieces for which there are few if any other markets. Some poetry (overstocked). *S&T* attracts readers who cannot get enough of this material or who want something new and different. Because it is small, *S&T* can take chances on stories that are either too traditional or too experimental, and prides itself on its variety of styles and story types. Also well illustrated." Published semiannually. Estab. 1966. Circ. 400.
Needs: Adventure, fantasy, horror, humor/satire, psychic/supernatural/occult and science fiction. "Actually, will consider almost any type of fiction as long as it has a fantastic slant. No media clones— no tales involving characters/situations that are not your creation (*Star Trek*, et al) except for certain types of satire. No stories based on Von Daniken, etc., type cults." Receives 75-100 unsolicited fiction mss/month. Accepts 10 mss/issue, 20 mss/year. Published work by Phyllis Ann Karr, Mickey Zucker Reichert, Doug Beason; published new writers within the last year. Length: 12,000 words maximum. Occasionally critiques rejected mss. Sometimes recommends other markets.
How to Contact: Query first. *No unsolicited mss.* Photocopied submissions OK. Accepts computer printout submissions. Reports in 2 months. Publishes ms an average of 1-2 years after acceptance. Sample copy $5.
Payment: ½¢/word and 2 contributor's copies. Charges cover price less 40% contributor discount for extras.
Terms: Pays on acceptance for first North American serial rights.
Advice: "At the moment we cannot tell when we will be an open market again—potential contributors should inquire. We remain a closed market at present."

SPECTRUM (II), Anna Maria College, Box 72-C, Sunset Lane, Paxton MA 01612. (617)757-4586. Editor: Robert H. Goepfert. Fiction Editor: Joseph Wilson. Magazine: 6×9; 64 pages; illustrations and photos. "An interdisciplinary publication publishing fiction as well as poetry, scholarly articles, reviews, art and photography. Submissions are especially encouraged from those affiliated with liberal arts colleges." Semiannually. Estab. 1985. Circ. 1,000.
Needs: Contemporary, experimental, historical, literary, mainstream. No western, mystery, erotica, science fiction. Receives an average of 15 unsolicited fiction ms/month. Accepts 4-6 mss/issue. Publishes ms approx. 6 months after acceptance. Length: 2,000-5,0000 words preferred; 3,000 words average; 10,000 words maximum. Publishes short shorts. Sometimes critiques rejected mss and recommends other markets.

How to Contact: Send complete ms with cover letter. Reports in 6 weeks. SASE for ms. Photocopied submissions OK. Accepts computer printouts, no dot-matrix. Sample copy for $3. Fiction guidelines free with SASE.
Payment: Pays $20 and 2 contributor's copies.
Terms: Pays on publication for first North American serial rights. Sends pre-publication galleys to author. Publication not copyrighted.
Advice: "Our chief aim is diversity."

SPINDRIFT (II), Shoreline Community College, 16101 Greenwood Ave. North, Seattle WA 98133. (206)546-4785. Editor: Carol Orlock, adviser. Magazine: 140 pages; excellent quality paper; photographs; b&w artwork. "We look for fresh, original work that is not forced or 'straining' to be literary." Annually. Estab. around 1967. Circ. 500.
Needs: Contemporary, ethnic, experimental, historical (general), prose poem, regional, science fiction, serialized/excerpted novel, translations. No romance, religious/inspirational. Receives up to 150 mss/year. Accepts up to 20 mss/issue. Does not read during spring/summer. Publishes ms 3-4 months after acceptance. Published work by David Halpern, Jana Harris; published new writers within the last year. Length: 250 words minimum; 3,500-4,500 words maximum. Publishes short shorts.
How to Contact: Send complete ms, and "bio, name, address, phone and list of titles submitted." Reports in 2 weeks on queries; 6 months on mss with SASE. Photocopied submissions OK. Accepts computer printout submissions. Sample copy for $6, 8×10 SAE and $1 postage.
Payment: Pays in contributor's copies; charge for extras.
Terms: Acquires first rights. Publication not copyrighted.
Advice: "The tighter the story the better. The more lyric values in the narrative the better. Read the magazine, keep working on craft. Submit several pieces by February 1."

THE SPIRIT THAT MOVES US (II), Box 820-W, Jackson Heights NY 11372-0820. (718)426-8788. Editor: Morty Sklar. Publishes fiction, poetry and artwork. "We want feeling and imagination, work coming from the human experience." Semiannually. Estab. 1975. Circ. 1,500-2,000.
Needs: "SASE first to find out what our needs are." Literary and contemporary, feminist, gay/lesbian, humor, ethnic, prose poem, spiritual, sports and translations. No sensational. Buys 5-6 mss/issue and about 15 mss for special fiction issues. Receives approximately 90 unsolicited fiction mss each month. Recently published work by Susan Fradkin, Sam Gridley, Carolyn Moore; published new writers within the last year. Length: 10,000 words maximum. Critiques rejected mss when there is time.
How to Contact: Send SASE first for theme and plans. "A cover letter sort of makes the exchange more personal." Accepts computer printout submissions. Prefers letter-quality. Reports in 1 week-1 month on mss. Publishes ms an average of 6 months after acceptance. Sample copy $5 for *The Spirit That Moves Us Reader* or current 176-page special issue.
Payment: Free cloth copy, 40% discount for paperbacks; 25% on all other publications.
Terms: Pays for first rights. Buys reprints for anthology issue.
Advice: "Query first for theme with SASE. We're small but good and well-reviewed. Send the work you love best. Write from yourself and not from what you feel is the fashion or what the editor wants. This editor wants what you want if it has heart, imagination and skill. Aside from the obvious reason for rejection, poor writing, the main reason for rejection is lack of human concerns—that is, the writer seems to be concerned with style more than content. Read a copy of the magazine you'll be submitting work to. Don't rely on your writing for money unless you're in it for the money. Have time to write, as much time as you can get (be anti-social if necessary)."

SPITBALL (I), 6224 Collegevue Pl., Cincinnati OH 45224. Editor: Mike Shannon. Magazine: 5½×8½; 52 pages; 20 lb white paper; 65-67 lb cover stock; illustrations; photos. Magazine publishing "fiction and poetry about *baseball* exclusively for an educated, literary segment of the baseball fan population." Quarterly. Estab. 1981. Circ. 1,000.
Needs: Confession, contemporary, experimental, historical, literary, mainstream and suspense. "Our only requirement concerning the type of fiction written is that the story be *primarily* about baseball." Receives "100 or so" unsolicited fiction mss/year. Accepts 7-8 mss/year. Published work by Dallas Wiebe, Michael Gilmartin, Rick Wilber. Published new writers within the last year. Length: no limit. The longer it is, the better it has to be. Will critique rejected mss if asked.
How to Contact: Send complete ms with SASE, and cover letter with brief bio about author. Photocopied and previously published submissions OK. Reporting time varies. Publishes ms an average of 3 months after acceptance. Sample copy $5.

Payment: "No monetary payment at present. We may offer nominal payment in the near future." 2 free contributor's copies per issue in which work appears.
Terms: Acquires first North American serial rights. Buys reprints "if the work is good enough and it hasn't had major exposure already."
Advice: "Our audience is mostly college educated and knowledgeable about baseball. The stories we have published so far have been very well written and displayed a firm grasp of the baseball world and its people. In short, audience response has been great because the stories are simply good as stories. Thus, mere use of baseball as subject is no guarantee of acceptance. We are always seeking submissions. Unlike many literary magazines, we have no backlog of accepted material. Consult *The Best of Spitball* (1988) by Pocket Books, Div. of Simon & Schuster. Still in print even if not in local bookstore. Fiction is a natural genre for our exclusive subject, baseball. There are great opportunities for writing in certain areas of fiction, baseball being one of them. Baseball has become the 'in' spectator sport among intellectuals, the general media and the 'yuppie' crowd. Consequently, as subject matter for adult fiction it has gained a much wider acceptance than it once enjoyed."

SPOOFING! (I, IV), Yarns and Such, Creative With Words Publications, Box 223226, Carmel CA 93922. (408)649-5627. Editor: Brigitta Geltrich. Booklet: 5½×8½; approx. 60 pages; bond paper; illustrations. Folklore. Semiannually. Estab. 1975. Circ. varies.
Needs: Ethnic, humor/satire, juvenile (5-9 years), preschool (1-4 years), regional, young adult/teen (10-18 years), folklore. "Once a year we publish an anthology of the writings of young writers, titled: *We are Writers Too!*" No erotica, religious fiction. Receives 50-100 unsolicited fiction mss/month. Does not read mss July-August. Publishes ms 2-6 months after acceptance. Published new writers within the last year. Length: 1,000 words average. Critiques rejected mss "when requested, *then we charge $20/prose, up to 1,000 words.*"
How to Contact: Query first or send complete ms with cover letter. "Reference has to be made to which project the manuscript is being submitted." Reports in 1 week on queries; 2 months on mss; longer on specific seasonal anthologies. SASE. Photocopied submissions OK. Accepts computer printout submissions, no dot-matrix. Accepts electronic submissions via Radio Shack Model 4/6 disk. Sample copy price varies. Fiction guidelines for #10 SAE with 2 first class stamps.
Payment: Charge for contributor's copies; 20% reduction on each copy ordered.
Terms: Acquires one-time rights.

SPSM&H (II, IV), *Amelia* Magazine, 329 "E" St., Bakersfield CA 93304. (805)323-4064. Editor: Frederick A. Raborg, Jr. Magazine: 5½×8¼; 24 pages; Matte cover stock; illustrations and photos. "*SPSM&H* publishes sonnets, sonnet sequences and fiction, articles and reviews related to the form (fiction may be romantic or Gothic) for a general readership and sonnet enthusiasts." Quarterly. Estab. 1985. Circ. 600.
Needs: Adventure, confession, contemporary, erotica, ethnic experimental, fantasy, feminist, gay, historical (general), horror, humor/satire, lesbian, literary, mainstream, regional, contemporary and historical romance, science fiction, senior citizen/retirement, suspense/mystery, translations and western. All should have romantic element. "We look for strong fiction with romantic or Gothic content, or both. Stories need not have 'happy' endings, and we are open to the experimental and/or avant-garde. Erotica is fine; pornography, no." Receives 30+ unsolicited mss/month. Buys 1 ms/issue; 4 mss/year. Publishes ms 6 months-1 year after acceptance. Agented fiction 5%. Recently published work by Mary Louise R. O'Hara and Clara Castelar Bjorlie. Length: 2,000 words average; 500 words minimum; 3,000 words maximum. When appropriate critiques rejected ms; Recommends other markets.
How to Contact: Send complete ms with cover letter. Should include Social Security number. Reports in 2 weeks. SASE. Photocopied submissions OK. Accepts computer printout submissions. Sample copy $4.50. Fiction guidelines for #10 SAE and 1 first class stamp.
Payment: Pays $10-25; contributor's copies; charge for extras.
Terms: Pays on publication for first North American serial rights.
Advice: "A good story line (plot) and strong characterization are vital. I want to know the writer has done his homework and is striving to become professional."

SQUARE ONE (I, II), A Magazine of Fiction, Box 11921-0921, Milwaukee WI 53211. Editor: William D. Gagliani. Magazine: 7×8½; 75-90 pages; 20 lb white bond paper; 80 lb colored linen cover; illustrations; pen and ink drawings or any black on white. "There is no specific theme at *Square One*, but we publish only fiction and illustrations. Aimed at a general literate audience—people who *enjoy* reading fiction." Annually (currently). Estab. 1984. Circ. 250.

Needs: Open to all categories including mainstream, mystery, science fiction, horror, fantasy, suspense, etc. "We like exciting stories in which things happen and characters *exist*." Receives 40-50 unsolicited fiction mss/month. Does not read mss between May and September. Accepts 6-12 mss/ issue, depending on lengths; 6-12 mss/year. Publishes ms generally 1-11 months after acceptance. Recently published work by Kent Glenzer and Cheryl Sayre; published new writers within the last year. Length: 3,000 words average; 7,500 words maximum. Publishes short shorts but not vignettes. "It is editorial policy to comment on at least 75% of submissions rejected, but please be patient—we have a very small staff."
How to Contact: Send complete ms with cover letter. "Too many letters explain or describe the story. Let the fiction stand on its own. If it doesn't, the letter won't help. We like a brief bio and a few credits, but some writers get carried away. Use restraint and plain language—don't try to impress (it usually backfires)." Reports in 1-11 months on mss. SASE for ms. Simultaneous (if so labeled), photocopied and reprint submissions OK. Accepts computer printouts. Can accept electronic submissions via disk, but "We can accept DS/DD, 3½" Atari Mega Disks (using Wordwriter St or PKS Write). Hard copy should accompany any electronic submissions." Sample copy $3.50, 9×12 SAE, and 6 first class stamps (recent issue). Fiction guidelines for #10 SAE and 1 first class stamp. Please make checks payable to William D. Gagliani.
Payment: Two contributor's copies.
Terms: Pays for one-time rights.
Advice: "*Square One* is not a journal for beginners, despite what the name may imply. Rather, the name refers to the back-to-basics approach that we take—fiction must first and foremost be compelling. We want to see stories that elicit a response from the reader. We will give slight preference to Wisconsin writers, but will gladly consider submissions from anywhere. We must stress that, since we are an irregular publication, contributors should expect long response lags. Our staff is small and *Square One* is a part-time endeavor. Patience is the best advice we can offer. Also, we oppose the absurdity of asking that writers subscribe to every magazine they would like to write for, especially given most writers' financial state. Check local public and college libraries and bookstores to see what's going on in the small press and literary markets, and—as a matter of dignity—consider carefully before submitting to magazines that routinely charge reading fees."

STAR ROUTE JOURNAL (II), Box 1451, Redway CA 95560. (707)923-3256. Editor: Mary Siler Anderson. Magazine: 10¾×14½; 24 pages usually; newsprint paper and cover; b&w illustrations and photos. "Counter-culture—still think of ourselves as hippies—interested in environment, politics, philosophy, exploring ideas and changing consciousness. For people who are dissatisfied with pop culture and looking for new meaning." Monthly. Plans special fiction issue. Estab. 1978. Circ. 700.
Needs: Erotica, ethnic, experimental, feminist, gay, humor/satire, lesbian, literary, prose poem, science fiction, translations. Special interest: fiction having to do with hippies/1960s. Nothing "supportive of right-wing politics, racist views, militarism, mainstream conformist culture, consumerism." Receives 4-5 unsolicited fiction mss/month. "Would like to publish 1 short story/month. Plan to devote December issue to fiction and poetry." Publishes ms 1-4 months after acceptance. Published work by Paul Encimer, Leslie Craig and Pat Music; published new writers within the last year. Length: 1,700 words average; 1,000 words minimum; 2,500 words maximum. Publishes short shorts. Sometimes comments on rejected mss and recommends other markets.
How to Contact: Send complete ms. Reports in 3-4 weeks. SASE. Simultaneous, photocopied and reprint submissions OK. Accepts computer printouts. Sample copy $1. Fiction guidelines for #10 SAE and 1 first class stamp.
Payment: Pays in contributor's copies, free subscription to magazine. Charge for extras.
Terms: Acquires first rights. "We publish a fiction/poetry issue every December."
Advice: "Usually everything is read by three of us and our decisions are highly subjective; either we like it or we don't. We like pieces with humor, insight, heart and imagination."

‡STARLIGHT, Star Books, Inc., 408 Pearson St., Wilson NC 27893. (919)237-1591. Editor: Irene Burk Hrrell. Magazine: digest size 5½×7½; 64 pages; 20 lb. paper; b&w illustrations and photographs. "Christian inspirational material for men and women of all ages, some children." Quarterly. Estab. 1987.
Needs: Religious/inspirational. Wants "Any genre, for any age, as long as it is exciting, God-honoring, in conformity with biblical truch." Publishes ms less than three months after acceptance. Recently published work by Ralph Filicchia. Length: "10-12 double-spaced pages but open to longer or shorter." Sometimes critiques rejected mss.

How to Contact: Send complete manuscript with cover letter. Reports in 1 month on queries. SASE. Photocopied submissions OK. Accepts computer printout submissions. Sample copy $4. Fiction guidelines for #10 SAE and 2 first class stamps.
Payment: Pays 3 contributor's copies.
Terms: Acquires first rights.

STARRY NIGHTS, Merry Men Press, 274 Roanoke Road, ElCajon CA 92020. (619) 442-5541. Editor: Robin Hood. Magazine: 8½×11; 200 pages; 20 lb paper; 90 lb cover stock. Erotic science fiction/fantasy, poetry, art "for a mature audience." Estab. 1990.
Needs: Erotica. "See guidelines for definition of erotica. There's a big difference between *E* and *pornography*." Has published special fiction issue in the past. Receives 7 unsolicited mss per month; buys up to 15 mss per issue. Publishes ms 1-11 months after acceptance. Publishes short shorts. Comments on rejected mss and recommends other markets.
How to Contact: Reports in 1 week on queries; 1 month on mss. SASE. Photocopied and computer printout submissions OK. Accepts electronic submissions, "hard copy must be included." Fiction guidelines for SAE and 1 first class stamp.
Payment: .01/word and 1 contributor's copy.
Terms: Pays on publication for first North American serial rights.

STARSONG (I, II), A Magazine of Fantasy, Science Fiction and Horror, Box 260B, St. Matthews SC 29135. Editor: Larry D. Kirby III. Magazine: 8½×11; 90 pages; Xeroxed paper; heavy cover stock; illustrations. Quarterly. Estab. 1987. Circ. 400.
Needs: Fantasy, horror, humor/satire, prose poem, psychic/supernatural/occult, science fiction. Receives 60 unsolicited fiction mss/month. Accepts 8-12 mss/issue; 32-48 mss/year. Publishes within one year of acceptance. Recently published work by Sydney Williams, William C. Rasmussen, Ardath Mayhar; published new writers within the last year. No preferred word length. Publishes short shorts. Sometimes critiques rejected mss.
How to Contact: Send complete ms with cover letter, which should include "bio." SASE. Photocopied submissions OK. Accepts computer printouts. Sample copy $5; fiction guidelines for #10 SAE and 1 first class stamp.
Payment: Pays in contributor's copies.
Terms: Acquires one-time rights.
Advice: "Larger mags won't experiment with style or subject matter. I like new ideas and particularly like new authors. Try new ideas. Experiment. Be willing to rewrite. Pay attention to your dreams. Read small press mags. By the time you change your style to match what's in the big mags, the style will change. Don't send cyberpunk. It's boring. Make me believe your characters. Make me wonder. Make me smile. Make me check the .357 before I turn the lights out."

THE STERLING WEB (II), Arachnid Publishing, Box 38383, Tallahassee FL 32315. Send submissions to Box 38190. Editors: Ann Kennedy and Amy Mann. Magazine: 8½×11; 80-100 pages; 20 lb paper; glossy cover; b&w illustrations and photographs. "Speculative fiction for those that seek to be challenged—all ages." Quarterly. Estab. 1989.
Needs: Experimental, fantasy, horror, humor/satire, psychic/supernatural/occult, science fiction. "No slash n' gore, no predictable endings." Publishes annual special fiction issue. Receives 30-40 unsolicited mss/month. Accepts 8-12 mss/issue. Publishes ms 3-9 months after acceptance. Length: 2,500 words; 5,000 words maximum. Publishes short shorts. Sometimes critiques on rejected ms and recommends other markets.
How to Contact: "Get guidelines, or better yet, a copy of our magazine, and then submit." Reports in 4-6 weeks on queries; 1 month on mss. SASE. Photocopied submissions OK. Accepts computer printout submissions. Accepts electronic submissions. Sample copy $4.75 plus 75¢ postage and handling. Fiction guidelines for #10 SAE and 1 first class stamp.
Payment: 2 contributor's copies. Discount to writers for additional copies.
Terms: Acquires first North American serial rights.
Advice: "The kind of work I look for is a piece that will stay with me long after I've finished reading it. It must paint pictures in my mind that are not easily erased. Read a copy of our magazine, at least—get our Writer's Guidelines."

STONE DRUM (II), An International Magazine of the Arts, Box 233, Valley View TX 76272. (817)665-1145. Editor: Joseph Colin Murphey. Fiction Editor: Dwight Fullingim. Magazine: 6×9; 64-108 pages; 60 lb paper; slick 80 lb cover; graphics 8-10 illustrations; photographs. "We have no stated theme: the best writing to be found in poetry, fiction, articles on the craft of the arts and book reviews for adults generally educated in the humanities." Annually. Estab. 1972. Circ. 300.

Needs: Excerpted novel, contemporary, fantasy, humor/satire, literary, mainstream, psychic/supernatural/occult. "No erotica, no pornography, no all-out, no-holds-barred adult language." Receives 3-10 unsolicited mss/month. Accepts 3-6 ms/issue,except for specials. Publishes ms 6 months after acceptance. Published work by Elizabeth/Paul Bartlett, Joseph Bruchac and Jonathan London. Length: 2,000 words; 4,000 words maximum. Publishes short shorts. Sometimes critiques rejected ms and recommends other markets.

How to Contact: Send complete ms with cover letter. Reports in 3 weeks on mss. SASE. Photocopied submissions OK. Accepts computer printout submissions. Accepts electronic submissions. Sample copy $4. Fiction guidelines for #10 SAE and 1 first class stamp. Reading period: Sept. through Nov. each year. ("We publish 1 issue per year.")

Payment: Pays in contributor's copies.

Terms: Acquires one-time rights.

Advice: "Craft and experience, seem rather simultaneous, but I look for a good story line and dialogue that is believable, fitting to the context with people talking like people talk—regional or national— the way people talk in our time. Read some good market magazine that explains what editors expect. It wouldn't hurt to know something about manuscript form and the expectation of as near a perfect presentation as possible."

STONE SOUP (I), The Magazine By Children, Children's Art Foundation, Box 83, Santa Cruz CA 95063. (408)426-5557. Editor: Gerry Mandel. Magazine: 6×8¾; 48 pages; high quality paper; Sequoia matte cover stock; illustrations; photos. Stories, poems, book reviews and art by children through age 13. Readership: children, librarians, educators. Published 5 times/year. Estab. 1973. Circ. 12,000.

Needs: Fiction by children on themes based on their own experiences, observations or special interests. No clichés, no formulas, no writing exercises; original work only. Receives approximately 500 unsolicited fiction mss each month. Accepts approx. 15 mss/issue. Published new writers within the last year. Length: 150-2,500 words. Critiques rejected mss upon request.

How to Contact: Send complete ms with cover letter. "We like to learn a little about our young writers, why they like to write, and how they came to write the story they are submitting." SASE. Accepts computer printout submissions. Prefers letter-quality. Reports in 1 month on mss. Publishes ms an average of 1-6 months after acceptance. Sample copy $4. Free guidelines with SASE.

Payment: $10 plus 2 free author's copies; $2 charge for extras.

Terms: Acquires all rights.

Advice: Mss are rejected because they are "derivatives of movies, TV, comic books; or classroom assignments or other formulas."

STORY (II), F&W Publications, 1507 Dana Ave., Cincinnati OH 45207. (513)531-2222. Editor: Lois Rosenthal. Magazine: 6¼×9½; 128 pages; uncoated, acid-free paper; uncoated index stock. "We publish finest quality short stories. Will consider unpublished novel excerpts if they are self-inclusive." Quarterly. Estab. 1931.

Needs: Condensed/excerpted novel, contemporary, experimental, humor/satire, literary, mainstream, translations. No genre fiction—science fiction, detective, young adult, confession, romance, etc. Buys approximately 10 mss/issue. Agented fiction 50-60%. Published work by Norman Mailer, Robert Olmstead and Richard Currey. Length: 1,000 words minimum; 8,000 words maximum.

How to Contact: Send complete ms with or without cover letter, or submit through agent. Reports in one month or less on mss. SASE for ms. Photocopied submissions OK. Accepts computer printout submissions. Sample copy for $5, 9×12 SAE and $2.40 postage. Fiction guidelines for #10 SAE and 1 first class stamp.

Payment: Pays $250 plus 5 contributor's copies.

Terms: Pays on acceptance for first North American serial rights. Sends galleys to author.

Advice: "We publish stories written in a variety of voices by new and established writers."

STORYQUARTERLY (II), Box 1416, Northbrook IL 60065. (312)433-0741. Co-Editors: Anne Brashler and Diane Williams. Magazine: approximately 6×9; 130 pages; good quality paper; illustrations; photos. A magazine devoted to the short story and committed to a full range of styles and forms. Published twice yearly. Estab. 1975. Circ. 3,000.

Needs: Accepts 12-15 mss/issue, 20-30 mss/year. Receives 100 unsolicited fiction mss/month. Published new writers within the last year.
How to Contact: Send complete ms with SASE. Reports in 3 months on mss. Sample copy $4.
Payment: 3 free author's copies.
Terms: Acquires one-time rights. Copyright reverts to author after publication.
Advice: "Send one manuscript at a time, subscribe to the magazine, send SASE."

‡STORYZINE (I, II), Split Personality Press, P.O. Box 587, Olean NY 14760. Editor: Ken Wagner. Magazine: illustrations and photographs. "*Storyzine* is *all* fiction, and usually all the stories in an issue are done by one writer. It's circulated to other writers for feedback. It's basically a fiction version of the poetry chaps we see abound." Bimonthly. Estab. 1990. Circ. 15-25.
Needs: Adventure, condensed/excerpted novel, confession, contemporary, erotica, ethnic, experimental, fantasy, feminist, gay, historical (general), horror, humor/satire, lesbian, literary, mainstream, prose poem, psychic/supernatural/occult, regional, religious/inspirational, science fiction, sports, suspense/mystery, translations, western. No juvenile, preschool, romance, senior citizen, serialized, novel, young adult. Publishes special fiction issue. Receives 5-25 unsolicited mss/month. Accepts 1-10 mss/issue; 6-120 mss/year. Publishes ms 1-6 months after acceptance. Recently published work by Robert Howington and Terry Havens. Length: 200-2,000 words average. Sometimes critiques rejected mss.
How to Contact: Send complete manuscript with cover letter. Include "A few credits, education (even if none it's OK), something about yourself that can be used for bio." Reports in 4-6 weeks on mss. SASE. Simultaneous, photocopied and reprint submissions OK. Accepts computer printout submissions. Sample copy $1. Fiction guidelines for legal size SAE and 1 first class stamp.
Payment: Pays contributor's copies. Charge for extras (reduced).
Terms: Acquires one-time rights. Publication not copyrighted.
Advice: "People on the whole seem to be more interested in reading stories than they were before, but it's hard to say whether that means more than that *Redbook* might begin publishing 3-5 stories rather than 1-3, so it's still the same tight market."

STRANGE PLASMA (II,IV), Science Fiction and Fantasy, Edgewood Press, Box 264, Cambridge MA 02238. Editor: Stephen Pasechnick. Magazine: 8½ × 11; 32 pages; b&w illustrations. "Literate, unusual science fiction and fantasy for an audience interested in discovering new writers." Quarterly. Estab. 1989. Circ. 500.
Needs: Experimental, fantasy, science fiction. Receives 100 unsolicited mss/month. Buys 6-8 mss/issue; 24-32 mss/year. Publishes ms 5 months after acceptance. Recently published work by Gene Wolfe, R.A. Lafferty, Terry Dowling, Carol Emshwiller and Eric Brown. Length: 3-10,000 words. Publishes short shorts. Sometimes critiques rejected mss and recommends other markets.
How to Contact: Send complete ms with cover letter. Reports in 2 weeks on queries; 2 months on mss. SASE. Photocopied submissions. Sample copy $3. Fiction guidelines for SASE.
Payment: Pays 2½¢/word.
Terms: Pays on acceptance for first North American serial rights.
Advice: "The fiction must be well written with particular emphasis on style, ideas, character."

STROKER MAGAZINE (II), 129 2nd Ave. +3, New York NY 10003. Editor: Irving Stettner. Magazine: 5½ × 8½; average 48 pages; medium paper; 80 lb good cover stock; illustrations; photos. "*An un-literary* literary review interested in sincerity, verve, anger, humor and beauty. For an intelligent audience — non-academic, non-media dazed in the US and throughout the world." Published 3-4 times/year. Estab. 1974, 46 issues to date. Circ. 600.
Needs: Literary, contemporary. No academic material. Length: "3-5 pages preferred but not essential."
How to Contact: Send complete ms with SASE. Reports in 6 weeks. Sample copy $3.50.
Payment: 2 free author's copies. $1 charge for extras.
Terms: Acquires one-time rights.
Advice: "We are interested in fiction. Be sure your name and address are on the manuscript." Published new writers within the last year.

STRUGGLE (IV), A Magazine of Proletarian Revolutionary Literature, Marxist-Leninist Party USA, Detroit Branch, Box 13261, Harper Station, Detroit MI 48213-0261. Editor: Tim Hall. Magazine: 5½ × 8½; 24-48 pages; 20 lb white bond paper; colored cover; illustrations; occasional photographs. Publishes material related to "the struggle of the working class and all progressive people against the rule of the rich—including their war policies, racism, exploitation of the workers, oppression of women, etc." Quarterly. Estab. 1985.

Needs: Contemporary, ethnic, experimental, feminist, historical (general), humor/satire, literary, prose poem, regional, science fiction, senior citizen/retirement, suspense/mystery, translations, young adult/teen (10-18). "The theme can be approached in many ways, including plenty of categories not listed here." No romance, psychic, western, erotica, religious. Receives 1-2 unsolicited fiction mss/month. Publishes ms 3 months or less after acceptance. Recently published work by Leo Paulson, Judy Fitzgerald, R.G. Wilbong; published new writers within the last year. Length: 1,000-3,000 words average; 5,000 words maximum. Publishes short shorts. Normally critiques rejected mss.

How to Contact: Send complete ms; cover letter optional but helpful. "Tries to" report in 3 months. SASE. Simultaneous, photocopied and reprint submissions OK. Accepts computer printout submissions. Sample copy for $1.50.

Payment: Pays 2 contributor's copies.

Terms: No rights acquired. Publication not copyrighted.

Advice: "Write about the oppression of the working people, the poor, the minorities, women, and if possible, their rebellion against it—we are not interested in anything which accepts the status quo. We are not too worried about plot and advanced technique (fine if we get them!)—we would probably accept things others would call sketches, provided they have life and struggle. Just describe for us a situation in which some real people confront some problem of oppression, however seemingly minor. Observe and put down the real facts. We have increased our fiction portion of our content since last year's listing. We get poetry and songs all the time. We want 1-2 stories per issue."

‡**STUDIO ONE (II, IV),** College of St. Benedict, St. Joseph MN 56374. Editors: Sarah Boettcher and Tim Pehl. Magazine: 7×10; 76-100 pages; illustrations (7-10/issue); photographs (10-15/issue). "Studio One is a regional magazine for literary and visual art. We publish photographs, drawings, paintings, poetry and short fiction for the academic community in the Midwest, particularly for the College of St. Benedict and St. John's University." Annually. Estab. 1976. Circ. 900.

Needs: Contemporary, ethnic, feminist, humor/satire, literary, mainstream, prose poem, regional. "We will consider all work submitted and we welcome submissions. The categories above reflect what we tend to publish annually." No "violent erotica, smut." Receives "maybe 1" unsolicited fiction ms/month. Accepts "5 out of 20" mss/year. Does not read mss in summer. Publishes ms 1-2 months after acceptance. Length: 500-1,000 words preferred; 5,000 words maximum. Publishes short shorts.

How to Contact: Send complete ms with cover letter. Include "return address, phone number and brief history of the work submitted (whether it has be published before)." Reports in 2-3 weeks on queries; 1-6 months on mss. SASE. Simultaneous, photocopied, reprint and computer printout submissions OK.

Payment: Pays in contributor's copies.

Terms: Acquires all rights (or reprint rights).

Advice: "If the story strikes us as interesting, we consider it. But manuscripts that arrest us with their color, word choice, form or message are the manuscripts we publish. It is so difficult to define what we look for in a work other than quality. Usually the work simply tells us that it intends to be published...Please be patient with acceptance letters. If you submitted, we will respond before publication. Our deadline is always in February, so please submit by then."

‡**STUNNINGSTORIES (II),** Coyote Publications, 3461 Hayward Pl., Denver CO 80211. Editor: E.A. Martinez. Magazine: 8½×11; 16-35 pages; 20 lb. offset paper and cover; few illustrations; purely fiction. "StunningStories publishes any genre of fiction. The main criterion is that the story captivate and entertain readers. It's for anyone willing to read it." Monthly. Estab. 1990. Circ. 1,000.

Needs: Anything but religious. Receives 200 unsolicited mss/month. Accepts 3-5 mss per issue; 36-60 per year. Publishes ms about 6 months after acceptance. Length: 300 to 8,000 words, few exceptions.

How to Contact: Send complete ms. Reports in 3 months on ms. SASE. Photocopied and reprint submissions OK. Computer printout OK. Sample copy $4.

Payment: Pays contributor's copies.

Terms: All rights revert to author after publication.

Advice: "The main criterion for any fiction we accept is that it be entertaining. Secondly, we ask that all manuscripts sent to us are as free from grammar and punctuation errors as possible. Be persistent and patient. Writing fiction is like growing a garden."

SUB-TERRAIN (I,IV), Anvil Press, Box 1575, Stn. A, Vancouver BC V6C 2P7 Canada. (604)876-8700. Editor: B. Kaufman, J.L. McCarthy and P. Petrie. Newspaper: 7×10; 16-20 pages; good-offset printed paper; 60 lb. cover stock; illustrations; photos. "We intend to function as a literary magazine with a social conscience. *SUB-TERRAIN* will provide a forum for work that pushes the boundaries in form or content." Estab. 1988.
Needs: Erotica, experimental, humor/satire and literary. Receives 6-10 unsolicited mss/month. Accepts 3-4 mss/issue. Publishes ms 1-4 months after acceptance. Length: 200-3,000 words; 400-500 average. Publishes short shorts. Length: 200 words. Sometimes critiques rejected mss and "at times" recommends other markets.
How to Contact: Send complete ms with cover letter. Reports in 3-4 weeks on queries; 6-8 weeks on mss. SASE. Sample copy $3.
Payment: Pays in contributor's copies. Acquires one-time rights.
Advice: "We look for something special in the voice or style. Not simply something that is a well-written story. A new twist, a unique sense or vision of the world. The stuff that every mag is hoping to find. Write about things that are important to you: issues that *must* be talked about; issues that frighten, anger you. The world has all the cute, well-made stories it needs. Give words power, empower yourself and make a difference."

‡SUMMERFIELD JOURNAL (II), Morning Star Design Service, Box 499, Riverdale GA 30274. (404)996-7556. Editor: Darrell Bagley. Magazine: 5½x8½; 36-48 pages; high paper quality; matte card cover. "Poetry and short fiction for a general audience." Quarterly. Plans special fiction issue. Estab. 1987. Circ. 150.
Needs: Adventure, contemporary, ethnic, experimental, fantasy, feminist, historical, horror, humor/satire, juvenile, literary, mainstream, prose poem, psychic/supernatural/occult, regional, religious/inspirational, romance (contemporary, historical, young adult), science fiction, senior citizen/retirement, sports, suspense/mystery, translations, western, young adult/teen. No graphic sex and violence. Receives 30 unsolicited fiction mss/month. Accepts 6-8 mss/issue; 24-32 mss/year. Publishes ms usually in next available issue; 1-3 months. Charges reading fee of $3 (waived for subscribers). Published work by Roberta Ross, Dan O'Neill, James R. Shott. Length: 2,000 words maximum. Publishes short shorts. Always comments on rejected mss.
How to Contact: Request guidelines or send complete ms with cover letter. Responds in 2 weeks. SASE. Simultaneous, photocopied and reprint submissions OK. Accepts dot-matrix computer printouts "if legible." Accepts electronic submissions via disk or modem; write for requirements. Sample copy $4.50 or less. Fiction guidelines for #10 SAE and 1 first class stamp.
Payment: Pays 2 contributor's copies.
Terms: Acquires first North American serial rights. Publication copyrighted. Offers $100 award quarterly for best of issue.
Advice: "Most of what we see is very poor product; either in characterization, story line, incontinuity and/or obscurity of point. We look for a solid story line with discernible beginning, middle and end, with as good characterization as can be achieved in our limits, with that certain suspension of disbelief that draws the reader fully into the tale. Show us, don't tell us. Don't be afraid to cut out your favorite passage if it does nothing to advance your story. Don't be too proud or too disheartened to accept and act on your editor's comments and recommendations."

THE SUN (II), The Sun Publishing Company, Inc., 107 N. Roberson St., Chapel Hill NC 27516. (919)942-5282. Editor: Sy Safransky. Magazine: 8½x11; 40 pages; offset paper; glossy cover stock; illustrations; photos. "*The Sun* is a magazine of ideas. We publish all kinds of writing—fiction, articles, poetry. Our only criteria are that the writing make sense and enrich our common space. We direct *The Sun* toward interests which move us, and we trust our readers will respond." Monthly. Estab. 1974. Circ. 10,000.
Needs: Open to all fiction. Accepts 3 ms/issue. Receives approximately 150 unsolicited fiction mss each month. Published work by T.L. Toma, William Penrod, Candace Perry; published new writers within the last year. Length: 10,000 words maximum.
How to Contact: Send complete ms with SASE. Reports in 3 months. Publishes ms an average of 3-6 months after acceptance. Sample copy $3.
Payment: Up to $100 on publication, plus 2 free author's copies and a complimentary subscription.
Terms: Acquires one-time rights. Publishes reprints.

SUN DOG: THE SOUTHEAST REVIEW (II), English Department, 406 Williams, Florida State University, Tallahassee FL 32306. (904)644-4230. Editor: Jamie Granger. Magazine: 6 × 9; 60-100 pages; 70 lb paper; 10 pt. Krome Kote cover; illustrations; photos. Published biannually. Estab. 1979. Circ. 2,000.
Needs: "We want stories which are well written, beautifully written, with striking images, incidents and characters. We are interested more in quality than in style or genre." Accepts 20 mss/year. Receives approximately 60 unsolicited fiction mss each month. Reads less frequently during summer. Critiques rejected mss when there is time. Occasionally recommends other markets.
How to Contact: Send complete ms with SASE. Typed, double-spaced, on good bond. Clean photocopy acceptable. "Short bio or cover letter would be appreciated." Publishes ms an average of 2-6 months after acceptance. Sample copy $4.
Payment: 2 free author's copies. $2 charge for extras.
Terms: Acquires first North American serial rights which then revert to author.
Advice: "Avoid trendy experimentation for its own sake (present-tense narration, observation that isn't also revelation). Fresh stories, moving, interesting characters and a sensitivity to language are still fiction mainstays. Also publishes winner and runners up of the World's Best Short Short Story Contest sponsored by the Florida State University English Department."

SWIFT KICK (II), 1711 Amherst St., Buffalo NY 14214. (716)837-7778. Editor: Robin Kay Willoughby. Magazine: size, number of pages, paper quality, cover stock vary; illustrations; photos, b&w line art, xerographs. Specializes in unusual formats, hard-to-classify works, visual poetry, found art, etc. for "'pataphysical, rarified audience." Published special fiction issue; plans another. Estab. 1981. Circ. 100.
Needs: Open. "If it doesn't seem to fit a regular category, it's probably what we'd like! No boring, slipshod, everyday stuff like in mass-market magazines." Receives 5 unsolicited fiction mss/month. Accepts 1-2 mss/issue. Does not read just before Christmas. Publishes ms depending on finances (6 months-1 year) after acceptance. Publishes short shorts of 1,000 words (or 1 picture). Sometimes recommends other markets.
How to Contact: Query first for longer works or send complete ms with cover letter with short work. Reports in 2 months to 1 year. SASE ("or include reply card with OK to toss enclosed work"). Simultaneous and photocopied submissions OK. Will consider reprints of astoundingly good work (out of print). Accepts computer printouts. Sample copy for $7; "sample purchase recommended to best understand magazine's needs."
Payment: Pays in contributor's copies; half price for extras.
Terms: Acquires one-time rights. Rights revert to artists/authors. Sends galleys to author if requested.
Advice: "We always get less fiction than poetry—if a story is good, it has a good chance of publication in little mags. Editorially, I'm a snob, so don't write like anyone else; be *so* literate your writing transcends literature and (almost) literacy. Don't submit over 10 pages first time. Submit a 'grabber' that makes an editor ask for more. Don't neglect the stories in your own life for someone else's castles-in-the-air."

SWORD OF SHAHRAZAD (I, II), Amazon Publications, Box 90458, Austin TX 78709-0458. Editor: Kimberli Dorris. Magazine: 5½ × 8½; 70 pages; 20 lb recycled paper; glossy color cover; illustrations. "Sword is the fiction writers' workshop-in-a-magazine. We publish fiction, feedback on published pieces, articles on writing, subscriber profiles, a markets column and many other features." Quarterly. Estab. 1988.
Needs: Adventure, condensed/excerpted novel, contemporary, erotica, ethnic, experimental, fantasy, historical, horror, humor/satire, literary, mainstream, prose poem, psychic/supernatural/occult, regional, romance, science fiction, serialized novel, sports, suspense/mystery, translations and western. No juvenile and young adult. Has published special fiction issue and plans one for the future. Receives 60 unsolicited mss per month; accepts 10-12 mss/issue; 40-50 per year. Publishes ms 2 weeks-6 months after acceptance. Length: 8,000 words maximum. Publishes short shorts. Comments on rejected mss and recommends other markets.
How to Contact: Send complete ms with cover letter. Reports on queries in 1-2 weeks; on mss in 1-4 months. SASE. Simultaneous, photocopied and reprint submissions OK. Accepts computer printout and electronic submissions. Sample copy $5. Fiction guidelines for #10 SAE and 1 first class stamp.
Payment: Pays in contributor's copies.
Terms: Acquires one-time rights; sends pre-publication galleys to author.
Advice: "We carefully read everything we receive and *always* give advice and make suggestions for improvement—even on stories that aren't right for us. That takes a lot of time, so one thing we don't tolerate is a writer who wastes our time by submitting without even reading our guidelines, much less

a copy of the magazine. It's a dead giveaway when guideline specifics are ignored or manuscripts are badly prepared. In a business this competitive, a writer who needlessly prejudices an editor against his work by submitting it unprofessionally marks himself as an amateur who intends to stay that way."

SYCAMORE REVIEW (II), Department of English, Purdue University, West Lafayette IN 47907. (317)494-3783. Editor: Henry J. Hughes. Fiction Editor: Helene Barker. Magazine: 5½×8½; 1,000 pages; heavy, textured, uncoated paper; heavy matte uncoated cover; no unsolicited art. "Journal devoted to contemporary literature. We publish both traditional and experimental fiction, personal essay and poetry." Semiannually. Estab. 1989. Circ. 1,000.
Needs: Contemporary, experimental, historical (general), humor/satire, literary, mainstream, regional, sports, translations. "We generally avoid genre literature, but maintain no formal restrictions on style or subject matter. No science fiction, romance, children's." Publishes ms 3 months-1 year after acceptance. Length: 3,750 words preferred; 250 words minimum. Sometimes critiques rejected mss and recommends other markets.
How to Contact: Send complete ms with cover letter. Cover letter should include previous publications, address changes. Reports in 3 months. SASE. Simultaneous and photocopied submissions OK. Accepts computer printout submissions. Sample copy $4. Fiction guidelines for #10 SAE and 1 first class stamp.
Payment: Pays in contributor's copies; charge for extras.
Terms: Acquires one-time rights.
Advice: "We especially recommend readers to digest work from magazines like *The Indiana Review*, *Missouri Review* and *Sewanee Review* to help shape ideas concerning the status of quality magazine fiction today. The fiction writer must read voraciously. Read stories published in *The New Yorker* and read stories appearing in your community or university magazine. When you are ready to write (you are always ready) begin writing from actual experience."

‡SYZYGY (I, II), Plaster Cramp Press, P.O. Box 1083, Wheaton IL 60189. (708)690-2577. Editor: Brad Russell. Fiction Editor: Seth Tisue. Magazine: 7×8½; 50 pages; medium paper; card stock cover; illustrations. "Humor, bizarre fiction, experimental writing, essays." Estab. 1988. Circ. 750.
Needs: Contemporary, erotica, ethnic, experimental, fantasy, feminist, gay, historical (general), horror, humor/satire, lesbian, literary, mainstream, prose poem, psychic/supernatural/occult, science fiction. Receives 10 unsolicited mss/month. Accepts 5 mss/issue; 10 mss/year. Publishes ms 1-6 months after acceptance. Recently published work by Geof Huth, John Bergin, Bob Black. Publishes short shorts. Sometimes critiques rejected mss.
How to Contact: Send complete manuscript with cover letter. "Tell us about yourself." Reports in 1 week on queries; 2 weeks on mss. Simultaneous, photocopied and reprint submissions OK. Accepts computer printout submissions. Accepts electronic submissions via disk. Sample copy for 8×9 SAE and 85¢ postage. Free fiction guidelines.
Payment: Pays free subscription to magazine and contributor's copies.
Terms: Sends galleys to author. Publication not copyrighted.
Advice: "Excellence in form and language; accessibility."

TABULA RASA (I, II), A New Page in Fiction and Poetry, Box 1920, Stn 'B', London Ontario N6A 5J4 Canada. (519)432-3488. Editor: Paul Laxon/Gord Harrison/John Kirnan. Magazine: 6×9; 70 pages; 40 lb paper; 80 lb cover stock; illustrations. "We have no specific genre of fiction in mind, though most of our submissions are contemporary—character development and plot are what we look for." Bimonthly. Estab. 1989. Circ. 500.
Needs: Contemporary, experimental, fantasy, horror, humor/satire, literary, mainstream, prose poem, science fiction, serialized novel and suspense/mystery. "We'll consider anything, though stories without a good plot or characterization won't get published in *Tabula Rasa*." Receives 15-20 unsolicited fiction mss/month. Accepts 6-10 fiction mss/issue; 40-50 mss/year. Publishes ms 1-2 months after acceptance. Length: 2,000 words average; 300 words minimum; 3,500 words maximum. Publishes short shorts of 300-500 words. Sometimes critiques rejected mss and recommends other markets.
How to Contact: Send complete ms with cover letter that includes short bio and whether the manuscript has been published elsewhere, or is being considered elsewhere. Reports in 2 weeks on queries; 1-2 months on mss. SASE. Simultaneous, photocopied and reprint submissions OK. Accepts computer printout submissions. Accepts electronic submissions via disk (IBM format) or over the CompuServe network. Sample copy $3.50. Fiction guidelines for #10 SAE and IRCs.

Payment: Pays 2 contributor's copies.

Terms: Acquires one-time rights. Sends galleys to author if there are any revisions we think are necessary.

Advice: "We're looking for stories that will entertain us and make us think at the same time. Science fiction, mystery, mainstream: genre doesn't matter, interesting characters and plots do."

THE TAMPA REVIEW (III), Humanities Division, Box 19, University of Tampa, Tampa FL 33606. (813)253-3333, ext. 424. Editor: Richard Mathews. Fiction Editor: Andy Solomon. Magazine: 7½ × 10½; approximately 100 pages; acid-free paper; illustrations; photos. "Interested in fiction of distinctive literary quality." Annually. Estab. 1988.

Needs: Contemporary, ethnic, experimental, fantasy, historical, humor/satire, literary, mainstream, prose poem, translations. "We are far more interested in quality than in genre. No sentimental as opposed to genuinely moving, nor self-conscious style at the expense of human truth." Buys 3-7 mss/issue. Publishes ms within 2 months-1 year of acceptance. Agented fiction 60%. Published work by Lee K. Abbott, Lorrie Moore, Tim O'Connor. Length: 1,000 words minimum; 6,000 words maximum. Publishes short shorts "if the story is good enough." Sometimes critiques rejected mss and recommends other markets.

How to Contact: Send complete mss with cover letter, which should include brief bio and publishing record. Include Social Security number. Reports within 3 months. SASE. Simultaneous and photocopied submissions OK. Accepts computer printout submissions. "Letter quality preferred." Sample copy for $7.50 includes postage, 9 × 12 SAE. Fiction guidelines for #10 SAE and 1 first class stamp.

Payment: Pays $10 per printed page.

Terms: Pays on publication for first North American serial rights. Sends galleys to author – upon request.

Advice: "There are more good writers publishing in magazines today than there have been in many decades. Unfortunately, there are even more bad ones. In T. Gertler's *Elbowing the Seducer*, an editor advises a young writer that he wants to hear her voice completely, to tell (he means 'show') him in a story the truest thing she knows. We concur. Rather than a trendy workshop story or a minimalism that actually stems from not having much to say, we would like to see stories that make us believe they mattered to the writer and, more importantly, will matter to a reader. Trim until only the essential is left, and don't give up belief in yourself. And it might help to attend a good writers conference, e.g. Wesleyan or Bennington."

TANDAVA (II), Box 689, East Detroit MI 48021. (313)779-9349. Editor: Tom Blessing. Magazine: 5½ × 8 or 8 × 11; 16-50 pages; illustrations. Frequency varies. Estab. 1982. Circ. 100.

Needs: Excerpted novel, contemporary, experimental, fantasy, literary, prose poem, science fiction. Plans special fiction issue. Receives 1 or less unsolicited mss/month. Accepts 2 mss/issue; 5 mss/year. Publishes ms 1½ years after acceptance. Length: 5,000 words maximum. Publishes short shorts. Length: Up to 2 pages. Sometimes critiques rejected mss and recommends other markets.

How to Contact: Send complete ms with cover letter. "Include introduction – where you heard of Tandava, goals, projects." Reports in 2 weeks. SASE. Simultaneous and photocopied submissions OK. Accepts computer printout submissions. Sample copy for $1.50.

Payment: Pays in contributor's copies.

Terms: Publication not copyrighted.

‡TEMM POETRY MAGAZINE (I, II), Split Personality Press, P.O. Box 587, Olean NY 14760. Editor: Ken Wagner. Magazine: ¼-legal; 28 pages; regular paper; heavy/good cover; illustrations and sometimes photographs. "Work that is 'accessible' without compromising truth for a general, non-literary readership." Monthly. Estab. 1990. Circ. 250.

Needs: Experimental. Accepts 1 ms/issue; 12 mss/year. Publishes ms 1-6 months after acceptance. Recently published work by Richard Kostelanetz. Length: 500 words maximum. Sometimes critiques rejected mss.

How to Contact: Query first or query with clips of published work. Include "credits, chapbooks, etc., and personal info." Reports in 2-10 weeks on queries; 2-12 weeks on mss. SASE. Simultaneous, photocopied and reprint submissions OK. Accepts computer printout submissions. Sample copy $1.25.

Payment: Pays contributor's copies. Charges for extras.

Terms: Acquires first rights. Publication is not copyrighted.

Advice: "Can you write a piece of fiction that will make new use of prose, spark stark imagery, reach in and grab me in one way or another? If so, send it – that's what I want. Remember, it must be experimental."

TERROR TIME AGAIN (II), Nocturnal Publications, 275 W. Stevens, St. Paul MN 55107. Editor: Donald L. Miller. Magazine: 5 × 8; 52-60 pages; 20 lb paper; 67 lb cover stock; illustrations. *"Terror Time Again*'s objective is to provoke a sense of fear in our readers." Annually. Estab. 1987. Circ. 200.
Needs: Only wants fear-induced stories. No science fiction or sword and sorcery. Receives up to 35 unsolicited mss/month. Accepts 15-20 mss/issue. Publishes ms in January of following year accepted. Recently published work by Steve Berman, D.A. Sale, Michael Floyd, Bob Madia and Steve Vernon; published new writers within the last year. Length: 1,000 words average; 250 words minimum; 2,000 words maximum. Publishes short shorts. Length: 250-700 words. Sometimes critiques rejected mss; recommends other markets.
How to Contact: Send complete ms with brief bio about yourself. Reports in 2-3 weeks on mss. Remember to enclose a SASE. Simultaneous, photocopied and reprint submissions OK. Accepts computer printout submissions. Sample copy $4.50; fiction guidelines free.
Payment: Pays ½¢/word plus copy.
Terms: Acquires one-time and reprint rights. Sponsors contest for writers through *The Nightmare Express*. *"Terror Time Again* has a cover contest via *The Nightmare Express* in which the cover illustration of the July/August issue of *TNE* is used by the writer to develop a story under 2,000 words. *TNE* is a newsletter for horror writers and is published bi-monthly. A one year subscription is only $10 plus *TTA* is included free."

‡TERSE TALES (II), Aurora Press, 2 Jasmine Ct., Millbrae CA 94030. (415)952-0476. Editor: Dawn Zapletal. "Story Letter." 8½ × 11; 4-8 pages; photocopy paper and cover; illustrations. "No special theme; strives for eclectic material for a general, literate audience." Quarterly. Estab. 1991.
Needs: Adventure, contemporary, fantasy, humor/satire, literary, mainstream, romance (contemporary), science fiction, senior citizen/retirement, suspense/mystery. "No racist, sexist, pornographic, religious, political or blood and guts." Receives 10-12 unsolicited mss/month. Will use 4-8 mss/issue; 15-30 mss/year. Length: 500 words average; 350 words minimum; 750 words maximum. "Exceptions will be made if story warrants it." Sometimes critiques rejected mss and recommends other markets.
How to Contact: Send complete manuscript with cover letter that includes "brief list of credits, if any. Where they heard about Terse Tales. A couple of sentences of personal info. to be included with story." Reports in 1 week to 1 month on mss. SASE. Simultaneous, photocopied and reprint submissions OK. Accepts computer printout submissions. Sample copy for #10 SAE and 4 first class stamps. Fiction guidelines for #10 SAE and 1 first class stamp.
Payment: Pays contributor's copies. Charge for extras.
Terms: Acquires one-time rights. "Sometimes" sends author galleys. "Plan special fiction issue with cash prizes. Announcement will appear in *Terse Tales* when date is set."
Advice: "Honesty and intelligence and a story that grabs me and won't let go until the last word. A tug at the heart, a laugh, a tingle up my spine are qualities I look for. I'm not hung-up on form. If I can read it and it's good, I'll use it."

THE TEXAS REVIEW (II), Sam Houston State University Press, Huntsville TX 77341. (713)294-1423. Editor: Paul Ruffin. Magazine: 6 × 9; 148-190 pages; best quality paper; 70 lb cover stock; illustrations; photos. "We publish top quality poetry, fiction, articles, interviews and reviews for a general audience." Semiannually. Estab. 1976. Circ. 700.
Needs: Literary and contemporary fiction. "We are eager enough to consider fiction of quality, no matter what its theme or subject matter. No juvenile fiction." Accepts 4 mss/issue. Receives approximately 40-60 unsolicited fiction mss each month. Published work by Richard Elman, Peter S. Scherman, Margaret Kingery; published new writers within the last year. Length: 500-10,000 words. Critiques rejected mss "when there is time." Recommends other markets.
How to Contact: Send complete ms with cover letter. SASE. Reports in 3 months on mss. Sample copy $3.
Payment: Free author's copies plus one year subscription.
Terms: Acquires all rights. Sends galleys to author.

THEMA (II,IV), Box 74109, Metairie LA 70033-4109. Editor: Virginia Howard. Magazine: 5½ × 8½; 200 pages; good paper; Grandee Strathmore cover stock; b&w illustrations. "Different specified theme for each issue—short stories, poems, b&w artwork must relate to that theme." Quarterly. Estab. 1988.
Needs: Adventure, contemporary, experimental, humor/satire, literary, mainstream, prose poem, psychic/supernatural/occult, regional, science fiction, sports, suspense/mystery, western. "Each issue is based on a specified premise—a different unique theme for each issue. Many types of fiction acceptable, but must fit the premise. No pornographic, scatologic, erotic fiction." Publishes ms within 3-4

months of acceptance. Recently published work by Ann Spiers, James W. Penha, Regina deCormier-Shekerjian. Length: 4,500 words preferred; 2,700 words minimum; 6,000 words maximum. Publishes short shorts "if very clever." Length: 300-500 words. Sometimes critiques rejected mss and recommends other markets.

How to Contact: Send complete ms with cover letter, which should include "name and address, brief introduction, specifying the intended target issue for the mss." Reports on queries in 1 week; on mss in 4-6 weeks after deadline for specified issue. SASE. Photocopied submissions OK. No dot-matrix computer printouts. Sample copy $5. Free fiction guidelines.

Payment: Pays $25.

Terms: Pays on acceptance. Purchases one-time rights.

Advice: "Do not submit a manuscript unless you have written it for a specified premise. If you don't know the upcoming themes, send for guidelines first, before sending a story. We need more stories told in the Mark Twain/O. Henry tradition in magazine fiction." Upcoming themes: 'A tattered hat, abandoned' (deadline May 1, 1991); 'It's got to be here . . . somewhere' (deadline August 1, 1991).

THIN ICE (II), 379 Lincoln Ave., Council Bluffs IA 51503. (712)322-9125. Editor/Publisher: Kathleen Jurgens. Magazine: digest size; 95-110 pages; 16-20 lb paper; enamel cover; b&w, pen and ink illustrations. "Horror and dark fantasy—short stories, poetry, interviews, art." Triannually. Estab. 1987. Circ. 250.

Needs: Experimental, fantasy (dark), horror, black humor/satire, poetry, psychic/supernatural/occult. No "racist, preachy, straight porn for shock value." Receives 80-120 unsolicited mss/month. Buys approx. 10 mss/issue; approx. 40 mss/year. Publishes ms 1-2 years after acceptance. Published work by Bentley Little, J. N. Williamson, Colleen Drippe, Jeannette Hopper. Length: 1,000-4,000 words preferred. Critiques rejected mss.

How to Contact: Send complete ms with cover letter. Cover letter should include "a personal introduction, mention a few prior 'sales' if desired (though not necessary), where the writers heard of *Thin Ice*." Reports in 1 week on queries; 1-2 months on mss. SASE. Photocopied submissions preferred. Accepts computer printout submissions, including dot-matrix (but prefer not to). Sample copy for $4.50 to Kathleen Jurgens ($6 outside of the U.S.). Fiction guidelines free with #10 SASE. Send poetry to: Marthayn Pelegrimas; 5116 S. 143 St.; Omaha NE 68137.

Payment: Pays in contributor's copies.

Terms: Acquires first North American serial rights.

Advice: "Invest in a copy of our magazine and read it from cover to cover. Get a 'feel' for the overall mood, tone, and subject matter. Don't apologize for misspellings or coffee stains on the manuscript—retype it. While we prefer informal query letters, we become quite irate when potential contributors treat us unprofessionally. We respond to all submissions personally, frequently offering editorial commentary. Always include an SASE with the correct amount of postage. Give us the full 8 weeks to repond. Absolutely no simultaneous or multiple submissions considered. Please, do not summarize the story in your cover letter."

THIRD WOMAN (II,IV), Chicano Studies Dept., Dwinelle Hall 3412, University of California, Berkeley CA 94720. (415)642-0708 or 642-0240. Editor: Norma Alarcón. Magazine: 5½ × 8½; 100-150 pages; standard good quality paper; glossy color cover; illustrations; photos. "Literature and the arts focusing on the work by/about U.S. Latinas, Hispanic World and Third World Women in general. *Third Woman* is an annual journal of art, essays and criticisms, usually with a theme. Inquire." Semiannually. Estab. 1981. Circ. 1,500.

Needs: Ethnic, feminist, translations. Receives 4 mss/month. Accepts 10 mss/year. Publishes ms within 6 months-2 years of acceptance. Length: 5,000-10,000 words preferred. Publishes short shorts.

How to Contact: Send complete ms with cover letter. Reports on queries in 6-8 weeks; on mss in 6 months. SASE. Simultaneous and photocopied submissions OK. Accepts computer printout submissions. Free sample copy.

Payment: Pays in contributor's copies.

Terms: Acquires first rights. Sends galleys to author.

‡THIRD WORLD (I, II, IV), Editora Terceiro Mundo, Rua da Gloria 122, Sala 105, Rio de Janeiro, RJ CED 20241 Brazil. (021)242-1957/222-1370. Editor: Bill Hinchlberger. Magazine: 8½ × 11; 64 pages; white, non-glossy paper; glossy/color cover; b&w illustrations; color cover, b&w inside photographs. "*Third World* is a magazine that presents world affairs from a Third World perspective for Third World professionals, university professors and students worldwide, activists and development workers interested in the Third World, intellectuals generally." Estab. 1986. Circ. 5,000.

Close-up

Virginia Howard
Editor
Thema

"Teacups in the sand." "A train wreck with a circus." "The last time I saw Jane . . ." Like lines from poems, the themes for each issue of *Thema* are vague, open for interpretation. That's the point. The magazine's purpose is to see "how various authors . . . respond to a given theme—an oddly scientific theme," says editor and publisher Virginia Howard.

The literary magazine was conceived in a Chinese restaurant when Howard and two friends had a conversation about imagination. They wondered what kind of stories and poems would be produced by different authors working with the same premise. How would they be similar? How would they differ? To find out, they agreed to all write stories based on the three fortunes in their fortune cookies and invited their writer friends to do the same.

They enjoyed the project so much they wanted to share it with others. They were also driven by curiosity, wondering how people would interpret more curious themes. "What, for example, would someone write about 'Reginald stood too close to the edge . . .'?" Howard poses. "We had to find out!" And thus, *Thema* was born.

Thema is a quarterly now in its fourth year of publication. The average issue has 11 or 12 short stories and seven to nine poems, at least one of which is usually by a new author.

Writers interested in submitting to *Thema* should be familiar with the magazine and the themes of upcoming issues (which are listed on the back page of the magazine). "Stories in which the theme is crucial to the plot seem to work best," Howard says. "Rather than trying to manipulate the theme, the author should let the premise simmer in his or her mind before writing anything down. Sometimes the 'right' plot suddenly materializes and takes shape. When that happens, you'll know it."

Writers should be creative with their interpretation of the theme without deviating or changing it. " 'The Thursday Night League' shouldn't be stretched to mean Thursday morning, or Sunday afternoon, for example."

The editors like to see plot twists and surprise endings, but these shouldn't be contrived or forced. "Try for subtlety," Howard suggests. She also asks that writers not rely on scatological clichés or obscenity. "Stories of lasting value rarely need it."

Stories should be accompanied by a cover letter stating the premise upon which the story was written. "Don't make us guess which theme you have in mind," Howard says. But avoid making the theme the title of your story.

Themes for future issues include "A tattered hat, abandoned," and "It's got to be here somewhere." "As always, we anticipate a wide variety of interpretations," says Howard.

—Kurt Scalettta

Needs: Contemporary, ethnic, feminist, translations, work by Third World authors. "While we cannot ignore poverty and disasters, we prefer work that presents the Third World in a positive light and *without stereotypes.*" "Do not want to see manuscripts that display a superficial or stereotypical understanding of the Third World—no 'erotica.' " Publishes ms 1-4 months after acceptance. Length: 500-2,000 words average; 3,000 words maximum. Publishes short shorts. Sometimes critiques rejected mss and, if possible, recommends other markets.

How to Contact: Query first with clips of published work or send complete manuscript with cover letter that includes a basic introduction of the author, indentifying him or her. Reports in 2 weeks on queries; 2-4 weeks on mss. ("Please allow for international mail.") Manuscripts will not be returned. Simultaneous, photocopied and reprint submissions OK. Accepts computer printout submissions. Accepts electronic submissions via computer network electronic mailbox: GEDNET: *TERCEIRO-MUNDO.* Free sample copy.

Payment: Pays Brazilian union scale, which varies according to exchange rages, free subscription to magazine and contributor's copies.

Terms: Buys one-time rights.

Advice: "We would be particularly receptive to work by a Third World writer writing about his or her country, culture, etc."

‡THIS MAGAZINE (II), Red Maple Foundation, 56 The Esplanade #406, Toronto, Ontario M5E 1A7 Canada. (416)364-2431. Editor: Judy MacDonald. Fiction Editor: Kevin Connolly. Magazine: 8½ × 11; 42 pages; bond paper; coated cover; illustrations and photographs. "Alternative general interest magazine." Estab. 1973. Circ. 12,000.

Needs: Ethnic, contemporary, experimental, fantasy, feminist, gay, lesbian, literary, mainstream, prose poem, regional. No "commercial/pulp fiction." Receives 15-20 unsolicited mss/month. Buys 1 mss/issue; 8 mss/year. Recently published work by Margaret Atwood and Peter McGehee. Length: 1,500 words average; 2,500 words maximum. Publishes short shorts. Length: up to 1,500 words. Sometimes critiques rejected mss.

How to Contact: Query with clips of published work. Reports in 3-5 weeks on queries; 8-10 weeks on mss. SASE. Simultaneous and photocopied submissions OK. Accepts computer printout submissions. Sample copy $2.75. Fiction guidelines for #9 SAE and 46¢ U.S., 39¢ Canadian.

Payment: Pays $100 (Canadian).

Terms: Buys one-time rights.

Advice: "Quality is foremost. We lean toward literary style. Manuscripts and queries that are clean and personalized really make a difference. Let your work speak for itself—don't try to convince us."

THUMBPRINTS (I, IV), Thumb Area Writer's Club, Box 27, Sandusky MI 48471. Editor: Janet Ihle. Newsletter: 8½ × 11; 6 pages; line drawing illustrations. Material is "primarily on writing and writers." Estab. 1983. Circ. 30.

Needs: Adventure, historical (general), humor/satire, mainstream, prose poem, regional, romance (contemporary, historical and young adult), senior citizen/retirement and sports. Accepts 1ms/issue; 10-12 mss/year. Publishes ms 3-4 months after acceptance. Length: 750 words maximum; 500 average. Publishes short shorts. Length: 250-400 words. Sometimes critiques rejected mss.

How to Contact: Send complete ms only. Reports in 1 month on queries; 2 months on mss. SASE. Photocopied submissions OK. Accepts computer printout submissions. Sample copy 50¢, #10 SASE. Guidelines for SASE.

Payment: Pays in contributor's copies; charges for extras.

Terms: Acquires first or one-time rights. Publication not copyrighted.

‡TICKLED BY THUNDER (II), A Newsletter for Writers, Tickled by Thunder Pub. Co., #4, 6280 King George Hwy., Surrey, B.C. V3X 1E9 Canada. (604)591-6095. Editor: Larry Lindner. Newsletter: 8½ × 11; 8-10 pages; bond paper; bond cover; illustrations and photographs. "Workshop-in-a-Newsletter/prefer fantasy, but totally open. For writers." Quarterly. Estab. 1990. Circ. 100.

Needs: Adventure, contemporary, fantasy, horror, humor/satire, literary, mainstream, prose poem, psychic/supernatural/occult, religious/inspirational, science fiction, suspense/mystery, western. "No pornography." Receives 40 unsolicited mss/month. Buys 1-4 mss/issue; 4-16 mss/year. Publishes ms next issue after acceptance. Length: 1,500 words average; 2,000 words maximum. Publishes short shorts. Length: No preference. Sometimes critiques rejected mss and recommends other markets.

How to Contact: Query with clips of published work including "Brief resume/history of writing experience, photo, credits, etc." Reports in 2 weeks on queries; 1 month on mss. SASE. Photocopied submissions OK. Accepts computer printout submissions. Sample copy $2.50 (Canadian Funds). Fiction guidelines for legal SAE and 1 first class stamp.
Payment: Pays $1 maximum.
Terms: Buys first rights.
Advice: "Send for guidelines."

TOAD HIWAY (II), Box 44, Universal IN 47884. (317)832-8918. Editor: Doug Martin. Fiction Editor: John Colvin. Magazine: 5½ × 8½; 24 pages; ink drawing illustrations; b&w photos. "We are especially interested in avant-garde material and quality mainstream fiction." Quarterly. Estab. 1989. Circ. 200.
Needs: Condensed/excerpted novel, contemporary, erotica, experimental, humor/satire, prose poem, science fiction and translations. Plans to publish special fiction or anthology issue in the future. Receives 25 unsolicited mss/month. Accepts 1-2 mss/issue; 4-8 mss/year. Publishes ms 3-6 months after acceptance. Length: 30,000 words maximum; 5,000 average. Publishes short shorts. Sometimes critiques rejected mss and recommends other markets.
How to Contact: Send complete ms with cover letter. "If you've been published before, be specific about magazines and dates." Reports in 6 weeks on queries; 3 months on mss. SASE. Simultaneous submissions OK. Sample copy $2. Fiction guidelines for #10 SAE.
Payment: Pays in contributor's copies.
Terms: Acquires one-time rights.

TRADESWOMEN (I,IV), A Quarterly Magazine for Women in Blue-Collar Work, Tradeswomen, Inc., P.O. Box 40664, San Francisco CA 94140. (415) 821-7334. Editors: Molly Martin and Helen Vozenilek. Magazine: 8½ × 11; 40 pages; b&w photographs. Quarterly. Estab. 1981. Circ. 1,500.
Needs: "Looking for fiction about women in blue-collar employment; on-the-job stories, 'what it's like' stories by women and men." Receives 1-2 unsolicited mss/month; accepts 1-2 mss/issue. Publishes ms 3-6 months after acceptance. Length: 2,000 words average; 3,000 words maximum. Publishes short shorts. Recommends other markets for rejected mss.
How to Contact: Send complete ms with cover letter. Reports on queries in 1 month; on ms in 2 months. SASE. Simultaneous, photocopied and reprint submissions OK. Accepts computer printout submissions. Sample copy $3. Fiction guidelines free.

TRAJECTORIES (II), The Journal of Science Fiction of the Southwest, Box 49249, Austin TX 78765. Publisher: Richard Shannon. Managing Editor: Susan Sneller. Tabloid: 11 × 14½; 32+ pages; newsprint paper and cover; b&w illustrations and photos, some color. "Speculative fiction, especially science fiction. Includes interviews, articles and news on science and culture." Quarterly. Estab. 1987. Circ. over 5,000.
Needs: Science fiction, humor/satire (of SF/nature), poetry, serialized/excerpted novel from established authors. Does not want to see "macabre 'real life' horror, slasher stories, etc. No stories involving licensed media characters. We have made a decision to not use overly violent stories, or stories where violence and/or war are glorified or otherwise shown in a positive manner." Receives 12-36 mss/month. Buys 2-3 mss/issue; 15-20 mss/year. Publishes ms within 3-9 months of acceptance. Published work by Lewis Shiner, and Steve Schlich; published new writers within the last year. Length: 2,000-5,000 words preferred; 15,000 words maximum. Publishes short shorts. Sometimes critiques rejected mss and recommends other markets.
How to Contact: Send complete ms with cover letter. Query on pieces over 15,000 words. Reports in 4-6 weeks on queries; within 2 months on mss. SASE. Photocopied submissions OK. Accepts computer printout submissions. Accepts electronic submission via disk or modem (with advance notice). "3½ inch disk, Macintosh MacWrite, MacPaint, Superpaint, Microsoft Word. 5½ inch disk—IBM word-processing programs." Sample copy for $2, 9 × 12 SAE and 4 first class stamps. Fiction guidelines for #10 SASE, also sent with sample copy if requested.
Payment: Pays $20-125 (more on longer pieces) and contributor's copies.
Terms: Pays on publication for first North American serial rights and one-time rights. Sends galleys to author on request.
Advice: "Though there seems to be more professional magazine markets in science fiction/fantasy than other genres, the number is still limited. They are, however, where most new SF/fantasy writers 'break in' the market. These cutting edge publications (such as *Asimov's*, *Analog* and *Omni*), are important vehicles for establishing new talent. Breaking these markets are tough, but can be done."

TRAMP (I, II), Box 1386, Columbia SC 29202. Editor: Alan Howard. Magazine: 5½ × 8; 32 pages; some illustrations. "contemporary poetry and prose." Quarterly. Estab. 1987. Circ. 200.
Needs: Contemporary, erotica, ethnic, experimental, fantasy, gay, humor/satire, lesbian, prose poem. "Fiction for *Tramp* must be very short, very tight, and a little off-beat. Also interested in short incidental pieces such as journal or letter excerpts." Receives 5-10 unsolicited mss/month. Buys 1-3 mss/issue; 4-12 mss/year. Publishes ms 6 months maximum after acceptance. Published work by Cliff Burns, Willie Smith, Bennie Lee Sinclair. Length: 400 words maximum. Sometimes critiques rejected mss.
How to Contact: Send complete ms with cover letter. Reports in 1-2 months. SASE. Accepts computer printout submissions. Sample copy $3. Fiction guidelines for #10 SAE and 1 first class stamp.
Payment: Pays in contributor's copies.
Terms: Acquires one-time rights.
Advice: "We prefer experimental fiction, but it should be accessible."

TRANSLATION (II), The Translation Center, Columbia University, 412 Dodge, New York NY 10027. (212)854-2305. Magazine: 6 × 9; 200-300 pages; coated cover stock; photos. Semiannually. Estab. 1972. Circ. 1,500.
Needs: Literary translations only. Accepts varying number of mss/year. Receives approximately 20-30 unsolicited fiction mss each month. Length: very short or excerpts; not in excess of 15 mss pages. Critiques rejected mss "rarely, because of time involved."
How to Contact: Send complete translation ms accompanied by original language text, 10-line autobiography, 10-line author's biography and SASE. Note required stating copyright clearance has been obtained. Reports in 3-6 months on mss. Single copy $9. Subscription $17.
Payment: 2 complimentary translator copies.
Terms: Acquires first North American serial rights for that volume publication only.
Advice: "We are particularly interested in translations from the lesser-known languages. Annual awards of $1,000 for outstanding translation of a substantial part of a book-length literary work. Translator must have letter of intent to publish from a publisher. Write for description and application for awards program."

TRIQUARTERLY (II), Northwestern University, 2020 Ridge Ave., Evanston IL 60208. (708)491-7614. Fiction Editors: Reginald Gibbons and Susan Hahn. Magazine: 6 × 9¼; 240+ pages; 60 lb paper; heavy cover stock; illustration; photos. "A general literary quarterly especially devoted to fiction. We publish short stories, novellas or excerpts from novels, by American and foreign writers. Genre or style is not a primary consideration. We aim for the general but serious and sophisticated reader. Many of our readers are also writers." Published 3 times/year. Estab. 1964. Circ. 5,000.
Needs: Literary, contemporary and translations. "No prejudices or preconceptions against anything *except* genre fiction (sci fi, romances, etc.)." Buys 10 mss/issue, 30 mss/year. Receives approximately 500 unsolicited fiction mss each month. Does not read May 1-Sept. 30. Approximately 10% of fiction is agented. Published work by Angela Jackson, Carol Bly, Leon Rooke; published new writers within the last year. Length: no requirement. Publishes short shorts.
How to Contact: Send complete ms with SASE. Reports in 3-4 months on mss. Publishes ms an average of 6 months to 1 year after acceptance. Sample copy $4.
Payment: $100-500, 2 free author's copies. Cover price less 40% discount for extras.
Terms: Pays on publication for first North American serial rights. Sends galleys to author.

TUCUMCARI LITERARY REVIEW (I), 3108 W. Bellevue Ave., Los Angeles CA 90026. Editor: Troxey Kemper. Magazine: 5½ × 8½; 32 pages; 20 lb bond paper; 110 lb cover; few illustrations; Xerox photographs. "Old-fashioned fiction that can be read and reread for pleasure; no weird, strange pipe dreams." Bimonthly. Estab. 1988. Circ. small.
Needs: Adventure, condensed/excerpted novel, contemporary, ethnic, historical (general), humor/satire, literary, mainstream, regional, (SW USA), senior citizen/retirement, suspense/mystery, western. No science fiction, sedition, blasphemy, fetishism, drugs/acid rock, pornography, horror, martial arts. Accepts 2 or 3 mss/issue; 12-18 mss/year. Publishes ms 2 to 4 months after acceptance. Length: 400-1,200 words preferred. Sometimes critiques rejected mss and recommends other markets.
How to Contact: Send complete ms with or without cover letter. Cover letter should include "anything pertinent to the submission." Reports in 2 weeks. SASE. Simultaneous, photocopied and reprint submissions OK. Accepts computer printout submissions. Sample copy $1.50 plus 50¢ postage. Fiction guidelines for #10 SAE and 1 first class stamp.

Payment: Pays in contributor's copies.
Terms: Acquires one-time rights. Publication not copyrighted.
Advice: "Does the work 'say something' or is it a hodgepodge of sentence fragments and paragraphs, not tied together into a story? No 'it was all a dream' endings."

TURNSTILE (II), Suite 2348, 175 Fifth Ave., New York NY 10010. Editor: Mitchell Nauffts. Magazine: 6×9; 128 pages; 55 lb paper; 10 pt cover; illustrations; photos. "Publishing work by new writers." Biannually. Estab. 1988. Circ. 1,500.
Needs: Contemporary, experimental, humor/satire, literary, regional. No genre fiction. Receives approx. 40 unsolicited fiction mss/month. Publishes approx. 8 short story mss/issue. Published work by Fenton Johnson, Richard Russo, Barbara Leith; published new writers within the last year. Length: 2,000 words average; 4,000 words maximum. Publishes short shorts. Sometimes comments on rejected mss or recommends other markets.
How to Contact: Query first or send complete ms with cover letter. Reports on queries in 1-2 weeks; on mss in 4-6 weeks. SASE. Simultaneous and photocopied submissions OK. Accepts computer printouts. Sample copy $6.50 and 7×10 SAE; fiction guidelines for #10 SAE and 1 first class stamp.
Payment: Pays in contributor's copies; charge for extras.
Terms: Acquires one-time rights.
Advice: "Also publishes essays and subjective nonfiction. Also interviews with writers."

TWISTED, 22071 Pineview Dr., Antioch IL 60002. (312)395-3085. Editor: Christine Hoard. Magazine: 8½×11; 152 pages; 60 lb paper; 67 lb cover; illustrations; photos. "Emphasis on contemporary horror and fantasy, anything on the dark side of reality." For readers of horror, "weird," fantasy, etc. Published irregularly. Estab. 1985. Circ. 200.
Needs: Fantasy, horror, prose poem, psychic/supernatural/occult, science fiction. "No hard science fiction, no sword and sorcery. Graphic horror or sex scenes OK if tastefully done. Sexist-racist writing turns me off." Receives approx. 12 unsolicited fiction mss/month. Accepts 10 mss/issue. Publishes ms 2 months to 2 years after acceptance. Published work by David Bruce, Joe Faust, Kathleen Jurgens; published new writers within the last year. Length: 2,000 words average; 200 words minimum; 5,000 words maximum. Sometimes critiques rejected mss and recommends other markets.
How to Contact: Reporting time varies. Cover letters not necessary but appreciated. Photocopied submissions OK. Accepts computer printouts. Sample copy $6. Fiction guidelines for #10 SAE and 1 first class stamp. No simultaneous submissions.
Payment: Pays in contributor's copies.
Terms: Acquires first rights.
Advice: "We are overstocked and not reading until after publication of *Twisted* #6—probably early '91, so writers may want to inquire before sending new work."

2 AM MAGAZINE (I, II, IV), Box 6754, Rockford IL 61125-1754. Editor: Gretta M. Anderson. Magazine: 8½×11; 60 or more pages; 60 lb offset paper; 70 lb offset cover; illustrations; photos occasionally. "Horror, science fiction, fantasy stories, poetry, articles and art for a sophisticated adult audience." Quarterly. Summer fiction issue planned. Estab. 1986. Circ. 1,000.
Needs: Experimental, fantasy, horror, humor/satire, prose poem, psychic/supernatural/occult, science fiction, suspense/mystery. No juvenile. Receives 400 unsolicited mss/month. Buys 12-14 mss/issue; 50 mss/year. Publishes ms an average of 6-9 months after acceptance. Published work by J. N. Williamson, Elizabeth Engstrom, Leonard Carpenter; published new writers within the last year. Length: 1,800 words average; 500 words minimum; 5,000 words maximum. Publishes short shorts. Sometimes critiques rejected mss and recommends other markets.
How to Contact: Send complete ms with cover letter (cover letter optional). Reports in 1 month on queries; 10-12 weeks on mss. SASE. Photocopied submissions OK. Accepts computer printout submissions, no dot-matrix. Sample copy $4.95 and $1 postage. Fiction guidelines for #10 SASE.
Payment: ½¢/word minimum, negotiable maximum; 1 contributor's copy; 40% discount on additional copies.
Terms: Pays on acceptance for one-time rights with non-exclusive anthology option. Sends prepublication galleys to author.
Advice: "Publishing more pages of fiction, more sf, and mystery, as well as horror. Put name and address on manuscript, double-space, use standard ms format. Pseudonym should appear under title on first manuscript page. True name and address should appear on upper left on first ms page."

TWO-TON SANTA (II), Box 1332, Portsmouth NH 03801. (603)427-0631. Editor: Guy Capecelatro III. Fiction Editor: Dan Leone. Magazine: 5¾ × 8¼; 4 pages. "Because of its size, only four pages, the material must be fairly short. Most tend to be stories and poems about real people dealing with somehow, ironic situations. Weekly. Estab. 1988. Circ. 200.

Needs: Condensed/excerpted novel, contemporary, erotica, experimental, feminist, gay, horror, humor/satire, juvenile (5-9 years), lesbian, preschool (1-4 years), prose poem, religious/inspirational and senior citizen/retirement. "We do not encourage writing styles that tend to alienate people. The language should not detract from or overwhelm the story itself." Publishes annual fiction issue. Receives 400 unsolicited mss/month. Accepts 2 mss/month; 112 mss/year. Publishes ms 2-4 weeks after acceptance. Recently published work by Russel Odson, Ray Halliday, Nancy Krygowski and Pagan Kennedy. Length: 3-700 words; 100-300 average. Sometimes critiques rejected mss and recommends other markets.

How to Contact: Query first. Reports in 2-3 weeks. Simultaneous, photocopied and reprint submissions OK. Accepts computer printout submissions.

Payment: Pays in contributor's copies.

Terms: Acquires one-time rights.

Advice: "The stories that stand out are ones that provide a glimpse into real life. They are imaginative in their presentation of how we exist. Stories don't necessarily follow a logical progression, but should invoke some sort of feeling within the reader. Each scene should work at being a part of the whole, if only in setting or voice. The language should not hinder an idea but be used merely as a presentation."

TYRO MAGAZINE (I), For Discriminating Readers and Developing Writers, 194 Carlbert Street, Sault Ste. Marie, Ontario P6A 5E1 Canada. (705)253-6402. Editor: Stan Gordon. Magazine: 5½ × 8½; approx. 220 pages; bond paper; firm card cover; some illustrations; photographs. Published "to provide a forum and practice medium for writers to try out almost any type of short fiction. We also publish some poetry and nonfiction, and how-to articles on writing." Special fiction issue planned. 3 times/year. Estab. 1984. Circ. 500.

Needs: Adventure, condensed novel, confession, contemporary, ethnic, experimental, fantasy, historical (general), horror, humor/satire, juvenile (5-9 years), literary, mainstream, preschool (0-4 years), prose poem, psychic/supernatural, regional, religious/inspirational, romance (contemporary, historical, young adult), science fiction, senior citizen/retirement, serialized/excerpted novel, spiritual, sports, suspense/mystery, young adult/teen (10-18 years). No "wildly experimental or legally dangerous" material. Receives about 40 unsolicited mss/month. Accepts 8-12 mss/issue; 120-160 mss/year. Publishes ms 2 months after acceptance. Published work by David Sandstad, Stephen Flocks and Robert Peterson. Published new writers within the last year. Length: 500 words minimum; 5,000 words maximum. Publishes short shorts. Usually critiques rejected mss. Sometimes recommends other markets.

How to Contact: Send complete ms with cover letter. Reports in 1 month on queries; 4-6 weeks on mss. SASE for ms. Simultaneous and photocopied submissions OK. Accepts computer printout submissions. Sample copy $10. Free fiction guidelines.

Payment: Offers awards of over 10¢/word for the best fiction in some issues.

Terms: Writers retain all rights.

Advice: "Short fiction must be trim and active; everything must advance the story."

‡THE ULTIMATE WRITER (I), Perry Terrell Publishing, 4520 Williams Blvd., Box R-328, Kenner LA 70065. (504)465-9412. Editor: Perry Terrell. Magazine: 8½ × 11; bond paper. "Poetry, fiction, essays, articles for an audience of all ages, geared toward creativity in writing and expression." Monthly. Estab. 1990. Circ. 250.

Needs: Adventure, confession, ethnic, experimental, fantasy, historical, humor/satire, juvenile, mainstream, religious/inspirational, romance, science fiction, suspense/mystery, western. No pornographic material. Plans special fiction issue. Accepts 48 mss/year. Publishes ms 4 months after acceptance. Length: 99 words minimum, no maximum, "but more than 5,000 words will be printed in 2 or 3 issues."

How to Contact: Query first or send complete ms with cover letter. Reports in 1 week on queries; 2 months on mss. SASE. Sample copy for $2. Fiction quidelines for #10 SAE and 1 first-class stamp.

Payment: Pays in contributor's copies and free three-month subscription.

Advice: Sponsors fiction contest. Write for details.

‡UNDERPASS (II), Underpass Press, #574-21, 10405 Jasper Ave., Edmonton, Alberta T5J 3S2 Canada. Editor: Barry Hammond. Magazine: 5¼ × 8¼; pages vary; 60 lb. bond paper; Mayfair cover; illustrations sometimes. "Mainly a poetry annual for an adult audience." Annually. Estab. 1987. Circ. 200-300.

Needs: Contemporary, experimental, literary, prose poem. "We have only published a few short stories. We are mainly a poetry annual. No religious or nature poetry." Receives 6 mss/month. Buys 1 or 2 mss/issue. Does not read mss Nov.-Jan. Publishes ms within 6 months after acceptance. Recently published work by Alice Major. Length: 2,000 words average; 500 words minimum; 6,000 words maximum. Publishes short shorts. Length: No preference. Sometimes critiques rejected mss.
How to Contact: Send complete manuscript with cover letter including "Brief bio. and publishing history (if any)." Reports in 6 weeks. "Our deadline is August 31st each year." SASE. Simultaneous and photocopied submissions OK. Accepts computer printout submissions. Sample copy for $6.95, 6×9 SAE and 2 first class stamps. Fiction guidelines for #10 SAE and 1 first class stamp.
Payment: Pays $10 minimum and contributor's copies.
Terms: Buys one-time rights. Sends galleys to author.
Advice: "Try poetry before submitting prose."

UNIVERSITY OF PORTLAND REVIEW (II), University of Portland, 5000 N. Willamette Blvd., Portland OR 97203. (503)283-7144. Editor-in-Chief: Thompson M. Faller. Magazine: 5×8; 40-55 pages. "Magazine for the college-educated layman of liberal arts background. Its purpose is to comment on the human condition and to present information in different fields with relevance to the contemporary scene." Published semiannually. Established 1948. Circ. 1,000.
Needs: "Only fiction that makes a significant statement about the contemporary scene will be employed." Receives 4 unsolicited mss/month. Accepts 2-3 mss/issue, 4-6 mss/year. Published new writers within the last year. Length: 1,500 words minimum; 3,500 words maximum; 2,000 words average. Sometimes recommends other markets.
How to Contact: Send complete ms with SASE. Reports in 3 weeks on queries; 6 months on mss. Publishes ms up to 1 year after acceptance. Sample copy 50¢.
Payment: 5 contributor's copies. 50¢ charge for extras.
Terms: Pays for all rights.

UNMUZZLED OX (III), Unmuzzled Ox Foundation Ltd., 105 Hudson St., New York NY 10013. Editor: Michael Andre. Tabloid. "Magazine about life for an intelligent audience." Quarterly. Estab. 1971. Circ. 20,000.
Needs: Contemporary, literary, prose poem and translations. No commercial material. Receives 10-15 unsolicited mss/month. Occasionally critiques rejected mss.
How to Contact: "Cover letter is significant." Reports in 1 month. SASE. Sample copy $7.50.
Payment: Contributor's copies.

US1 WORKSHEETS (II), US1 Poets' Cooperative, 21 Lake Dr., Roosevelt NJ 08555. (609)448-5096. Editor: Rotating board. Magazine: 11½×17; 20-25 pages; good paper. Publishes poetry and fiction. Annually. Estab. 1973.
Needs: "No restrictions on subject matter or style. Good story telling or character deliniation appreciated. Audience does not include children." Publishes ms within 3 months of acceptance. Recently published work by Alicia Ostriker, Toi Derricotte, J.A. Perkins, Cynthia Goodling, Judith McNally. Publishes short shorts.
How to Contact: Query first. Reports on queries ASAP. SASE. Photocopied submissions OK. Sample copy $4.
Payment: Pays in contributor's copies.
Terms: Acquires one-time rights. Copyright "reverts to author."

VALLEY GRAPEVINE (I, IV), Seven Buffaloes Press, Box 249, Big Timber MT 59011. Editor/Publisher: Art Cuelho. Theme: "poems, stories, history, folklore, photographs, ink drawings or anything native to the Great Central Valley of California, which includes the San Joaquin and Sacramento valleys. Focus is on land and people and the oil fields, farms, orchards, Okies, small town life, hobos." Readership: "Rural and small town audience, the common man with a rural background, salt-of-the-earth. The working man reads *Valley Grapevine* because it's his personal history recorded." Annually. Estab. 1978. Circ. 500.
Needs: Literary, contemporary, western and ethnic (Okie, Arkie). No academic, religious (unless natural to theme), gay/lesbian or supernatural material. Receives approximately 4-5 unsolicited fiction mss each month. Length: 2,500-10,000 (prefers 5,000) words.

How to Contact: Query. SASE for query, ms. Reports in 1 week. Sample copy available to writers for $4.75.
Payment: 1-2 author's copies.
Terms: Acquires first North American serial rights. Returns rights to author after publication, but reserves the right to reprint in an anthology or any future special collection of Seven Buffaloes Press.
Advice: "Buy a copy to get a feel of the professional quality of the writing. Know the theme of a particular issue. Some contributors have 30 years experience as writers; most 15 years. Age does not matter; quality does."

VALLEY WOMEN'S VOICE (II,IV), Feminist Newsjournal, 321 Student Union, University of Massachusetts, Amherst MA 01002. (413)545-2436. Newspaper: 16 pages. "Feminist analysis, feminist poetry, stories, health articles, revolution-visionary-action oriented, interviews, book reviews, music/art reviews, profiles and ideas for ongoing columns." For women readers. Monthly. Estab. 1979. Circ. 5,000.
Needs: Ethnic, feminist, lesbian, prose poem, spiritual, women's sports. Any subject "as long as it is feminist—especially news and feature articles. Photos with ms a plus." Receives 3-10 mss/month. Publishes new writers regularly. New women writers encouraged to send their best work. Length: no more than five pages. "Fiction accepted up to 20 pages, but the longer it is, the harder it is for us to print it. Please, double spaced."
How to Contact: Send complete ms with cover letter. "Cover letter should include short biographical statement which provides a context for work submitted." SASE. Simultaneous, photocopied and reprint submissions OK. Accepts computer printout submissions. Sample copy $1.
Payment: No payment. Issue in which work appears sent.

VERDICT MAGAZINE (I, IV), Journal of the Southern California Defense Counsel, 1055 Wilshire Blvd., 19th Floor, Los Angeles CA 90017. (213)580-1449. Editor: Sharon Muir. Magazine: 8½ × 11; 48 pages; slick paper; 70 lb Tahoe cover; clip art illustrations. "The magazine is geared to lawyers who specialize in insurance defense law. It is a trade publication that focuses on their work, legal cases and lifestyles." Quarterly. Estab. 1973. Circ. 5,000.
Needs: Law. Receives 10 unsolicited mss/month. Buys 2 mss/issue. Publishes ms 6 months-1 year after acceptance. Length: 2,000 words average. Publishes short shorts. Occasionally critiques rejected mss. Recommends other markets.
How to Contact: Send complete ms and cover letter with brief description of submitted ms. SASE. Simultaneous and photocopied submissions OK. Accepts computer printout submissions. Sample copy for $5 or 11 × 14 SAE and 10 first class stamps.
Payment: Pays $10.
Terms: Pays on publication for one-time rights.

‡VERVE (II), P.O. Box 3205, Simi Valley CA 93093. (805)527-8824. Editor: Ron Reichick. Fiction Editor: Marilyn Hochheiser. Magazine: Digest size, 40 pages, 70 lb. paper, 80 lb. cover, cover illustrations or photographs. "Each issue has a theme." Quarterly. Estab. 1989. Circ. 250.
Needs: Contemporary, experimental, fantasy, humor/satire, literary, mainstream, prose poem. No pornographic material. Receives 100 unsolicited fiction mss/month. Accepts 4-6 mss/issue; 16-24 mss/year. Publishes ms 2 months after acceptance. Length: 1,000 words maximum. Publishes short shorts.
How to Contact: "Request guidelines before submitting manuscript." Reports 4-6 weeks after deadline. SASE. Simultaneous, photocopied and computer printout submissions OK. Sample copy for $3.50. Fiction guidelines for #10 SAE and 1 first-class stamp.
Payment: Pays in contributor's copies.
Terms: Acquires one-time rights.

VIDEOMANIA (I,II), The Video Collectors Newspaper, LegsOfStone Publishing Co., Box 47, Princeton WI 54968. (414)295-4377. Editor: Bob Katerzynske. Tabloid; 10½ × 16; 32+ pages; newsprint paper; ground wood cover; b&w/color illustrations and photographs. "Slanted towards the home entertainment buff, individuals with a *real* interest in home video and entertainment. Publishes *anything* we feel is of interest to our readers—fiction and non-fiction. Audience is mostly male (90%), but female readership is always increasing." Bimonthly. Estab. 1982. Circ. 5-6,000.
Needs: Experimental, fantasy, feminist, horror, humor/satire, lesbian, mainstream, video/film. Receives 3-4 unsolicited mss/month. Buys 1-2 mss/issue; 6-9 mss/year. Publishes ms 2-6 months after acceptance. Length: 1,000 words maximum; 700 words minimum. Publishes short shorts. Length: 500 words. Sometimes critiques rejected mss and recommends other markets.

How to Contact: Send complete ms with cover letter. Reports in 2-4 weeks. SASE. Computer printout submissions are acceptable. Sample copy for $2.50, 9 × 12 SAE and $1 postage. Fiction guidelines for #10 SAE and 1 first class stamp.
Payment: Pays $2.50 token payment in certain cases; contributor's copies.
Terms: Pays on publication for all rights or as writer prefers.
Advice: "If the editor likes it, it's in. A good manuscript should not be too heavy; a *touch* of humor goes a long way with us. Don't expect to get rich off of us. On the other hand, we're more willing than other publications to look at the first-time, non-published writer. We've published established writers in the past that wanted to use our publication as sort of a sounding board for something experimental."

THE VILLAGE IDIOT (II), Mother of Ashes Press, Box 66, Harrison ID 83833-0066. Editor: Joe M. Singer. Magazine: Format varies; illustrations; photos.
Needs: "Beginning in 1991 *The Village Idiot* will publish 3 issues yearly and will accept letters, articles, essays and other nonfiction (as well as poems and stories). No more than 15,000 words of fiction per year will be used."
How to Contact: Send complete ms with SASE. Photocopied submissions OK. Accepts computer printouts. Sample copy $4.
Payment: Two contributor's copies.
Terms: Acquires one-time rights (copyright for author).

‡**THE VILLAGER (I,II)**, 135 Midland Ave., Bronxville NY 10707. (914)337-3252. Editor: Amy Murphy. Fiction Editor: Mrs. Anton Tedesko. Magazine: 28-40 pages. "Magazine for a family audience." Monthly, but for 9-months only—October-June. Estab. 1928. Circ. 1,000.
Needs: Adventure, historical, humor/satire, literary, prose poem, romance (historical), suspense/mystery. Length: Open. Publishes short shorts.
How to Contact: Send complete ms with cover letter. SASE. Sample copy for $1.25.
Payment: Pays 2 contributor's copies.

‡**THE VINCENT BROTHERS REVIEW (II)**, Vincent Brothers Publishing, 1459 Sanzon Dr., Fairborn OH 45324. Editor: Kimberly Willardson. Magazine: 5½ × 8½; 56-64 pages; 60 lb. white coated paper; 60 lb. Oxford (matte) cover; b&w illustrations and photographs. "There is no specific theme for *TVBR*, though we publish one theme issue per year. Writers should send SASE for information about upcoming theme issues. Each issue of *TVBR* contains poetry, b&w art, at least 1 short story and usually 1 book review. For a mainstream audience looking for an alternative to the slicks." Three issues per year. Estab. 1988. Circ. 250.
Needs: Adventure, condensed/excerpted novel, contemporary, ethnic, experimental, feminist, historical (general), humor/satire, literary, mainstream, prose poem, regional, science fiction, senior citizen/retirement, serialized novel, suspense/mystery, translations. "We don't like to exclude any category—we might very much enjoy a fantasy (or western) story if it is well crafted. We focus on the way the story is presented rather than the genre of the story. No racist, sexist, fascist, etc. work." Plans special fiction issue. Receives 3-6 unsolicited mss/month. ("We sincerely hope the number increases.") Buys 1-2 mss/issue; 3-6 mss/year. Publishes ms 1-2 months after acceptance. Recently published work by Mike Hosier, Laura E. Lehner and Rafael Alvarez. Length: 2,500 words average; 300 words minimum; 3,500 words maximum. Publishes short shorts. Length: 300-1,000 words. Sometimes critiques rejected mss and recommends other markets.
How to Contact: Send complete manuscript with cover letter. Include Social Security number. "Previous publications; if the manuscript should be returned (SASE should be included) or if the manuscript is photocopied." Reports in 3-4 weeks on queries; 3-6 months on mss. SASE. Photocopied submissions OK. Accepts electronic submissions. Sample copy $4.50. Fiction guidelines for #10 SAE and 1 first class stamp.
Payment: $10 minimum and 1 contributor's copy. Charge for extras.
Terms: Buys one-time rights.
Advice: "There are billions of great stories floating around, waiting to be told. We're looking for a writer who can wrangle one of those stories down and tame it with a compelling style and a command of lucid language. We are average readers—we want to be hooked immediately and rendered unable to put the story down until we've read the last word of it."

VINTAGE NORTHWEST (I, IV), Northshore Senior Center (Sponsor), Box 193, Bothell WA 98041. (206)487-1201. Editor: Margie Brons. Magazine: 7 × 8½; 64 pages; illustrations. "We are a senior literary magazine, published by and for seniors. All work done by volunteers except printing." For "all

ages who are interested in our seniors' experiences." Winter and summer. Estab. 1980. Circ. 500.
Needs: Adventure, comedy, condensed novel (1,000 words maximum), fantasy, historical, humor/satire, inspirational, poetry, senior citizen/retirement, suspense/mystery. No religious or political mss. Receives 2-3 unsolicited mss/month. Accepts 2 mss/issue. Published work by Bert Kowles and Marvin Harrison; published new writers within the last year. Length: 1,000 words maximum. Occasionally critiques rejected mss.
How to Contact: Send complete ms. SASE. Simultaneous, photocopied and previously published submissions OK. Accepts computer printout submissions. Sample copy $2.50. Fiction guidelines with SASE.
Payment: Pays 1 free contributor's copy.
Advice: "Our only requirement is that the author be over 50 when submission is written."

VIRGIN MEAT FANZINE (I), 2325 W.K 15, Lancaster CA 93536. (805)722-1758. Editor: Steve Blum. Digest: 5 × 8½; 26 pages. Published "about once every 3 months." Estab. 1987. Circ. 350.
Needs: "Mild erotic vampire tales. Lesbian and straight ok, no gay. Poetry should be dark and depressing." Receives 3-4 mss/day. Length: 1,000 words maximum.
How to Contact: Send complete ms with cover letter. Reports in 1 week. Simultaneous, photocopied and reprint submissions OK. Accepts computer printout submissions. Sample copy $1.
Payment: Pays in contributor's copies.
Terms: Acquires one-time rights. Publication not copyrighted.

VIRGINIA QUARTERLY REVIEW (III), 1 West Range, Charlottesville VA 22903. (804)924-3124. Editor: Staige Blackford. "A national magazine of literature and discussion. A lay, intellectual audience, people who are not out-and-out scholars but who are interested in ideas and literature." Quarterly. Estab. 1925. Circ. 4,500.
Needs: Literary, contemporary, feminist, romance, adventure, humor, ethnic, serialized novels (excerpts) and translations. "No pornography." Buys 3 mss/issue, 20 mss/year. Length: 3,000-7,000 words.
How to Contact: Query or send complete ms. SASE. Reports in 2 weeks on queries, 2 months on mss. Sample copy $5.
Payment: $10/printed page. Offers Emily Clark Balch Award for best published short story of the year.
Terms: Pays on publication for all rights. "Will transfer upon request."
Advice: "Because of the competition, it's difficult for a nonpublished writer to break in."

VISIBILITIES (IV), Box 1258, Peter Stuyvesant Station, New York NY 10009-1258. (212)473-4635. Editor: Susan T. Chasin. Magazine: 8 × 11; 32+ pages; coated paper; heavy coated cover stock; illustrations and photographs. "We are an international magazine by and for lesbians." Bimonthly. Estab. 1987. Circ. 8,000.
Needs: Lesbian. No "violence, sexist, racist, agist, etc." Accepts 1 ms/issue. Length: 2,000 words average; 1,000 words minimum; publishes short shorts. Sometimes critiques rejected mss.
How to Contact: Send complete ms with cover letter, which should include "just basics; name, address, telephone and how you heard about us." Reports in 2 weeks on queries; 3 months on mss. SASE. Accepts computer printout submissions. Sample copy $3; fiction guidelines for #10 SASE.
Payment: Contributor's copies; $5 charge for extras.
Terms: Acquires first North American serial rights.
Advice: "We are looking for life-affirming fiction—which tells us how people can live healthy, productive lives as lesbians. This does not preclude stories about painful experiences—but tell us how your characters survive and keep going."

WASCANA REVIEW (II), University of Regina, Regina, Saskatchewan S4S 0A2 Canada. Editor: Joan Givner. "Literary criticism, fiction and poetry for readers of serious fiction." Semiannually. Estab. 1966. Circ. 500.
Needs: Literary and humor. Buys 6 mss/year. Receives approximately 20 unsolicited fiction mss/month. Approximately 5% of fiction is agented. Length: no requirement. Occasionally recommends other markets.
How to Contact: Send complete ms with SASE. Accepts computer printout submissions. Prefers letter-quality. Reports in 2 months on mss. Publishes ms an average of 1 year after acceptance. Sample copy $4. Free guidelines with SAE, IRC.

Payment: $3/page for prose; $10/page for poetry. 2 free author's copies.
Terms: Pays on publication for all rights.
Advice: "Stories are often technically incompetent or deal with trite subjects. Usually stories are longer than necessary by about one-third. Be more ruthless in cutting back on unnecessary verbiage."

‡**WASHINGTON JEWISH SINGLES NEWSLETTER (II)**, Suite L, 444 N. Frederick Ave., Gaithersburg MD 20877. (301)990-0210. Editor: Ben Levitan. Magazine: 8×11; 16-50 pages; 70 lb. ivory paper; gloss cover; illustrations and photographs. "Single living for dynamic professionals, how-to, humor." Monthly. Estab. 1987. Circ. 1,000.
Needs: Singles themes. Condensed/excerpted novels, contemporary, experimental, historical, humor/satire, mainstream, psychic/supernatural/occult, romance, senior citizen/retirement, serialized novel, suspense/mystery. "Nothing depressing." Receives 8 unsolicited fictio mss/month. Buys 3 mss/year. Publishes ms 1-4 months after acceptance. Recently published work by Gowtard, Bright. Length: 500 words preferred; 100 words minimum; 700 words maximum. Publishes short shorts. Length: 500 words. Usually critiques or comments on rejected mss.
How to Contact: Send complete ms with cover letter. Include 50-word bio. Reports in 3 weeks on queries; 1 week on ms. SASE. Simultaneous, photocopied, reprint and computer printout submissions OK. Accepts electronic submissions. Sample copy for $2, large SAE and 2 first-class stamps.
Payment: Pays from byline only to $35. Pays contributor's copies.
Terms: Buys one-time rights.
Advice: Ask "1. How appropriate is it for our audience? 2. How interesting is it? 3. Humorous? (A bonus!) 4. Short and well-written? Put yourself in our audience's shoes. They are smart, busy, business-like all day. They want short, funny articles."

WASHINGTON REVIEW (II, IV), Friends of the Washington Review of the Arts, Box 50132, Washington DC 20091. (202)638-0515. Fiction Editor: Jeff Richards. "We publish fiction, poetry, articles and reviews on all areas of the arts. We have a particular interest in the interrelationships of the arts and emphasize the cultural life of the DC area." Readership: "Artists, writers and those interested in cultural life in this area." Bimonthly. Estab. 1975. Circ. 10,000.
Needs: Literary. Accepts 1-2 mss/issue. Receives approximately 50-100 unsolicited fiction mss each month. Length: Prefers 3,000 words or less. Critiques rejected mss when there is time.
How to Contact: Send complete ms with SASE. Reports in 2 months. Publishes ms an average of 6 months after acceptance. Copy for tabloid-sized SASE and $2.50.
Payment: Author's copies plus small payment whenever possible.
Terms: Pays on publication for first North American serial rights.
Advice: "Edit your writing for redundant adjectives. Make sure everything makes sense: the plot, character, motivation. Try to avoid clichés."

‡**WEBSTER REVIEW (II)**, Webster Review, Inc., Webster University, 470 E. Lockwood, Webster Groves MO 63119. (314)432-2657. Editor: Nancy Schapiro. Magazine: 5×8; 120 pages; 60 lb. white paper; 10pt. C1S; cover illustrations and photographs. "Literary magazine, international, contemporary. We publish many English translations of foreign fiction writers for academics, writers, discriminating readers." Annually. Estab. 1974.
Needs: Contemporary, literary, translations. No erotica, juvenile. Receives 100 unsolicited mss/month. Accepts 3-5 mss/issue; 6-10 mss/year. Publishes ms one year or more after acceptance. Agented fiction less than 1%. Recently published work by David Williams and Anjana Appachana. Publishes short shorts. Sometimes critiques rejected mss.
How to Contact: Send complete manuscript with cover letter. Reports in 2-4 months on mss. SASE. Simultaneous and photocopied submissions OK. Accepts computer printouts, "if legible." Free sample copy for 6×9 SAE and 2 first class stamps.
Payment: Pays contributor's copies.
Terms: Acquires first rights.

WEIRDBOOK (II), Box 149, Amherst Branch, Buffalo NY 14226. Editor: W. Paul Ganley. Magazine: 8½×11; 64 pages; self cover; illustrations. "Latter day 'pulp magazine' along the lines of the old pulp magazine *Weird Tales*. We tend to use established writers. We look for an audience of fairly literate people who like good writing and good characterization in their fantasy and horror fiction, but are tired of the clichés in the field." Annually. Estab. 1968. Circ. 1,000.

Needs: *Presently overstocked. Inquire first.* Psychic/supernatural, fantasy, horror and gothic (not modern). No psychological horror; mystery fiction; physical horror (blood); traditional ghost stories (unless original theme); science fiction; swords and sorcery without a supernatural element; or reincarnation stories that conclude with 'And the doctor patted him on ... THE END!' " Buys 8-12 mss/issue. Length: 15,000 words maximum. Sometimes recommends other markets.
How to Contact: Send complete ms with SASE. Reports in 3 months on mss. Sample copy $6.80. Guidelines for #10 SASE.
Payment: 1¢ word minimum and 1 free author's copy.
Terms: Pays on publication ("part on acceptance only for solicited mss") for first North American serial rights plus right to reprint the entire issue.
Advice: "Read a copy and then some of the best anthologies in the field (such as DAW's 'Best Horror of the Year,' Arkham House anthologies, etc.) Occasionally we keep mss longer than planned. When sending a SASE marked 'book rate' (or anything not first class) the writer should add 'Forwarding Postage Guaranteed.' "

‡**WELTER (II),** University of Baltimore, 1420 N. Charles St., Baltimore MD 21201-5779. (301)625-3270. Editor: Daniel Tessitore. Magazine: digest-size; 75 pages; matte cover; illustrations and photographs. "It is hard to nail down any trend or theme in what we publish." "For students/local writers/general audiences." Annually. Estab. 1967. Circ. 500 (approx.)
Needs: Contemporary, literary. No erotica or science fiction. Accepts 2-3 mss/issue. Does not read mss May-September. Publishes ms approx. 2 months after acceptance. Recently published work by Penny Graf, Stephen Matanle, Sarah Mayfield. Length: 3-5 typed (double-spaced) pages maximum. Publishes short shorts. Sometimes critiques rejected mss and recommends other markets.
How to Contact: Send complete manuscript with cover letter. "Bio (3 lines); SASE always." Sample copy $1. Fiction guidelines for SAE.
Payment: Pays contributor's copies (2).
Terms: Acquires one-time rights.
Advice: "No dripping sentimentality; no dream sequence unless very well done; keep it short."

WEST BRANCH (II), Bucknell Hall, Bucknell University, Lewisburg PA 17837. Editors: K. Patten and R. Taylor. Magazine: 5½×8½; 96-120 pages; good quality paper; illustrations; photos. Fiction and poetry for readers of contemporary literature. Biannually. Estab. 1977. Circ. 500.
Needs: Literary, contemporary, prose poems and translations. No science fiction. Accepts 3-6 mss/issue. Recently published work by Sharon Sheehe Stark, Gregor Hartmann, Jane McCafferty; published new writers within the last year. No preferred length.
How to Contact: Send complete ms with cover letter, "with information about writer's background, previous publications, etc." SASE. Reports in 6 weeks on mss. Sample copy $3.
Payment: 2 free author's copies and one-year subscription; cover price less 20% discount charge for extras.
Terms: Acquires first rights.
Advice: "Narrative art fulfills a basic human need—our dreams attest to this—and storytelling is therefore a high calling in any age. Find your own voice and vision. Make a story that speaks to your own mysteries. Cultivate simplicity in form, complexity in theme. Look and listen through your characters."

THE WEST TEXAS SUN (IV), NJN Inc., Box 61541, San Angelo TX 76906. (915)944-8918. Editor: Soren Nielsen. Magazine; 24-32 pages; newsprint paper and cover; b&w illustrations and photos. "Stories focusing on West Texans and the region for people interested in West Texas." Monthly. Estab. 1989. Circ. 4,000.
Needs: Contemporary, adventure, historical (general), humor/satire, literary, mainstream, regional, religious/inspirational, sports and western (ranching, horses). No erotica. Receives 4-5 unsolicited mss/month. Buys 1-2 mss/issue; 18-20 mss/year. Publishes ms 4-6 months after acceptance. Published work by Elmer Kelton, Robert Flynn and Sean Warner; published new writers within the last year. Length: 2,500 words; 500 words minimum; 4,000 words maximum. Publishes short shorts. Length: 50-200 words. Sometimes critiques rejected mss and recommends other markets.
How to Contact: Query first. Include social security number. Reports in 2-3 weeks. SASE. Simultaneous, photocopied and reprint submissions OK. Computer printout submissions are acceptable. Sample copy for 75¢ and SAE. Fiction guidelines are free with SASE.
Payment: Pays $5-200; charge for extras.
Terms: Pays on publication for first rights.

‡WESTVIEW (I, II), A Journal of Western Oklahoma, Southwestern Oklahoma State University, 100 Campus Dr., Weatherford OK 73096. (405)774-3077. Editor: Dr. Leroy Thomas. Magazine: 8½×11; up to 44 pages; 24 lb. paper; slick cover; illustrations and photographs. "Various themes for people who like nostalgia." Quarterly. Estab. 1981. Circ. 800.
Needs: Experimental, historical (general), literary, mainstream, western. "The subject must be Western Oklahoma—west of Interstate 35." Receives 2-5 unsolicited mss/month. Accepts 10 ms/issue; 40 mss/year. Publishes ms 1 month-2 years after acceptance. Recently published work by Orv Owens, Leroy Thomas and Margie Snowden North. Length: 2,000 words average; 1,000 words minimum; 3,000 words maximum. Publishes short shorts. Length: 400 words. Always critiques rejected mss and sometimes recommends other markets.
How to Contact: Query first. Reports in 3 weeks on queries. SASE. Accepts computer printout submissions. Sample copy for $4 and 9×12 SAE. Fiction guidelines for #10 SAE and 1 first class stamp.
Payment: Pays contributor's copies.
Terms: Acquires first rights.
Advice: "Write for a copy of our stylesheet and for our list of themes for future issues. Don't neglect the SASE."

WHETSTONE (II), English Dept., University of Lethbridge, Lethbridge, Alberta T1K 3M4 Canada. (403)329-2490. Contact: Editor. Magazine: approximately 6×9; 48-64 pages; superbond paper; pen or pencil sketches; photos. Magazine publishing "poetry, prose, drama, prints, photographs and occasional music compositions for a university audience." Twice yearly. Estab. 1971. Circ. 200.
Needs: Experimental, literary and mainstream. "Interested in works by native writers/artists. Interested in multi-media works by individuals or collaborators. Yearly writing contest with cash prizes." Receives 1 unsolicited fiction ms/month. Accepts 1-2 ms/issue, 3-4 mss/year. Does not read May through August. Published new writers within the last year. Length: 12 double-spaced pages maximum.
How to Contact: Send complete ms with SASE, or SAE with IRC and cover letter with author's background and experience. Simultaneous and photocopied submissions OK. Accepts computer printout submissions. Prefers letter-quality. Reports in 5 months on mss. Publishes ms an average of 3-4 months after acceptance. Sample copy $3 (Canadian) and 7½×10½ or larger SAE and 2 Canadian first class stamps or IRCs.
Payment: 1 free contributor's copy and $10 honorarium.
Terms: Acquires no rights.
Advice: "We seek most styles of quality writing. Avoid moralizing."

WHISKEY ISLAND MAGAZINE, University Center 7, Cleveland State University, Cleveland OH 44115. (216)687-2056. Editor: Matt Weiland. Magazine with no specific theme of fiction, poetry, photography. Published two times/year. Estab. 1978. Circ. 2,500.
Needs: Receives 20-30 unsolicited fiction mss/month. Acquires 3-4 mss/issue. Length: 5,000 words maximum; 2,000-3,000 words average.
How to Contact: Send complete ms with SASE. No simultaneous or previously published submissions. Reports in 2 months on mss. Sample copy $3.
Payment: 2 free contributor's copies.
Terms: Acquires one-time rights.
Advice: "Please include brief bio."

WHISPERING WIND MAGAZINE (I, II, IV), American Indian: Past & Present, Written Heritage, 8009 Wales St., New Orleans LA 70126. (504)241-5866. Editor: Jack B. Heriard. Magazine: 8½×11; 32 pages; 60 lb paper; 70 lb cover stock; color cover, b&w illustrations; b&w photos. "American Indian theme; material culture, illustrated craft articles. Articles are welcome that reflect our American Indian culture, both past and present." Audience: 52% Indian, 16+ years of age. Bimonthly. Estab. 1967. Circ. 6,000.
Needs: Special interest: American Indian. "Fiction must be American Indian related (theme) and yet historically accurate. Accuracy must also include material culture. Stories must not be stereotyped." Publishes ms up to one year after acceptance. Length: 1,500 words average. Publishes short shorts. Critiques rejected mss. Recommends other markets.
How to Contact: Send complete ms with cover letter with reasons for submission and illustration requirements. Reports in 3 months on queries. SASE for ms. Simultaneous submissions OK. Accepts computer printouts. Sample copy $4. Fiction guidelines free.

Payment: Free subscription to magazine, 6 contributor's copies, charge for extras.
Terms: Acquires first rights.
Advice: "There is a need for quality fiction about the American Indian. We publish fiction at least 4 times/year. The story must be accurate in every detail, i.e. tribal location, dress, material culture, historical perspectives, except that of the characters and basic storyline. Although fiction, it will be better received if the story is believable. Do not stereotype the characters."

‡**THE JAMES WHITE REVIEW (II, IV), A Gay Men's Literary Quarterly,** The James White Review Association, 3356 Traffic Station, Minneapolis MN 55403. (612)291-2913. Editor: Collective of 3. Tabloid: 17×26; 16 pages; illustrations; photos. "We publish work by *male* gay writers—any subject for primarily gay and/or gay sensitive audience." Quarterly. Estab. 1983. Circ. 2,500.
Needs: Contemporary, adventure, experimental, gay, humor/satire, literary, prose poem, translations. No pornography. Receives 50 unsolicited fiction mss/month. Accepts 5 mss/issue; 20 mss/year. Publishes ms 3 months or sooner after acceptance. Published work by Robert Patrick and Richard Hall. Published new writers within the last year. Length: 22 pages, double spaced. Sometimes critiques rejected mss. Recommends other markets "when we can."
How to Contact: Send complete ms with cover letter with short bio. SASE. Reports in 2-3 months. SASE for ms. Photocopied submissions OK. Sample copy $2. Fiction guidelines $1.
Payment: 3 contributor's copies.
Terms: Acquires one-time rights; returns rights to author.

WHITE WALL REVIEW, 63 Gould St., Toronto, Ontario M5B 1E9 Canada. Editor: Changes annually. Magazine: 5¾×8¾; 160 pages; Zephyr Antique paper; soft cover, glossy; two-tone illustrations; b&w photographs. Book of poetry, prose, art, plays, music and photography. Publishes both Ryerson Polytechnical Institute and professional writers. For Toronto and/or university audience. Annually. Estab. 1976. Circ. 800.
Needs: "No content 'requirements.' " Must be reasonably short. Nothing "spawning hate, prejudice or obscenity." Accepts 100+ mss/book. Recently published work by Steven Heighton, Robert Hough, Ruth Olsen Latta; published new writers within the last year.
How to Contact: Send complete ms with cover letter. "The cover letter should contain important information about why the writer is submitting to our publication, where he/she saw our information and some biographical information." Reports on mss "when accepted." SASE or SAE and IRC for ms. Simultaneous and photocopied submissions OK. Accepts computer printout submissions; prefers letter-quality. Sample copy $6 plus $1 for postage and handling.
Payment: Pays 1 contributor's copy.
Terms: Acquires first or one-time rights.
Advice: "Keep it *short*. We look for creativity but not to the point of obscurity."

THE WICAZO SA REVIEW (IV), A Journal of American Indian Studies, Eastern Washington University, Indian Studies, MS25-188, Cheney WA 99004. (509)359-2871. Editor: Elizabeth Cook-Lynn. Magazine: 8½×11; 50 pages. Publishes material relating to "Indian studies—all types, including scholarly research and reviews, for an academic audience." Plans special fiction issue. Estab. 1985. Circ. 300-500.
Needs: American Indian. "We wish to publish the creative works of American Indian writers. This is an academic journal devoted to the development of Indian studies topics. We want fiction *by* American Indians, not *about* American Indians." Recently published work by Simon Ortiz, Earle Thompson and Ralph Salisbury. Publishes short shorts.
How to Contact: Send complete ms with cover letter. Reports in 3 months. SASE. Sample copy for $4.
Payment: No payment.
Terms: Acquires first rights.
Advice: "Very little of magazine fiction today appeals to the ethnicity and the cultural diversity of America in any realistic way. Know the body of work which is now called Contemporary American Indian Fiction—the N. Scott Momaday, Simon Ortiz, Leslie Silko work, the criticism which is emerging from this development, the journals and collections which publish in this field."

WIDE OPEN MAGAZINE (II), Wide Open Press, 116 Lincoln St., Santa Rosa CA 95401. (707)545-3821. Editors: Clif and Lynn Simms. Magazine: 8½×11; 48 pages; 60 lb paper and cover. "Magazine is concerned with providing support and encouragement to writers." Quarterly. Estab. 1984. Circ. 500.

Needs: Adventure, contemporary, ethnic, experimental, fantasy, feminist, gay, historical (general), horror, humor/satire, lesbian, mainstream, psychic/supernatural/occult, science fiction, senior citizen/retirement, suspense/mystery, western. No "religious, children's, vignettes or character studies without plot." Receives 40 unsolicited mss/month. Buys 3 mss/issue; 12 mss/year. Publishes ms 1-3 months after acceptance. Published work by Ed Griffin, Robert R. Ramsey, Eric Steinman; published new writers within the last year. Length: 2,500 words maximum. Publishes short shorts. Sometimes critiques rejected mss and recommends other markets.
How to Contact: Send complete ms. "We want no clips or bios, please. Let the work stand on its own." Reports in 3 months. SASE. Photocopied and reprint submissions OK. Accepts computer printout submissions. Sample copy $7. Fiction guidelines for #10 SASE and 1 first class stamp.
Payment: Pays $5-$25; 1 contributor copy; charges $7 for extras.
Terms: Pays on publication for one-time rights.
Advice: "Send stories with logical plots in which characters solve their own problems. Study our guidelines and sample copies, if possible."

THE WIDENER REVIEW (III), Widener University, 14th and Chesnut Sts., Chester PA 19013. (215)499-4341. Fiction editor: Michael Clark. Magazine: 5¼ × 8½; 80 pages. Fiction, poetry, book reviews for general audience. Annually. Estab. 1984. Circ. 250.
Needs: Contemporary, experimental, literary, mainstream, regional, serialized/excerpted novel. Receives 15 unsolicited mss/month. Publishes 3-4 mss/issue. Does not read mss in summer. Publishes ms 3-9 months after acceptance. Length: 1,000 words minimum; 5,000 words maximum. Occasionally critiques rejected mss.
How to Contact: Send complete ms with cover letter. Reports in 3 months on mss. SASE for ms. No simultaneous or photocopied submissions or reprints. Accepts computer printouts. Sample copy $3. Fiction guidelines for #10 SAE and first class stamp.
Payment: Pays in contributor's copics; charge for extras.
Terms: Acquires first serial rights.

WILLOW SPRINGS (II, III), Box 1062, Eastern Washington University, Cheney WA 99004. (509)458-6424. Editor: Nance Van Winckel. Semiannually. Estab. 1977. Circ. 1,000.
Needs: Parts of novels, short stories, literary, prose poems, poems and translations. Receives 70 unsolicited mss/month. Accepts 3-4 mss/issue; 6-8 mss/year. Recently published work by Brett Lott, Andrea Barrett, Jay Weugeboren; published new writers within the last year. Length: 5,000 words maximum. Rarely critiques rejected mss.
How to Contact: Send complete ms with SASE. Photocopied submissions OK. No simultanious submissions. Reports in 2-3 months on mss. Publishes ms an average of 1-6 months after acceptance. Sample copy for $4.
Payment: 2 contributor's copies.
Terms: Acquires first North American rights.
Advice: "We hope to attract good fiction writers to our magazine, and we've made a commitment to publish 4 stories per issue. We like fiction that exhibits a fresh approach to language. Our most recent issues, we feel, indicate the quality and level of our commitment."

WIND MAGAZINE, Rt. 1, Box 809K, Pikeville KY 41501. (606)631-1129. Editor: Quentin R. Howard. Magazine: 5½ × 8½; 86+ pages. "Literary journal with stories, poems, book reviews from the small presses and some university presses. Readership is students, literary people, professors, housewives and others." Published irregularly. Estab. 1971. Circ. 500.
Needs: Literary and regional. "No restriction on form, content or subject." Published work by Anabel Thomas, Peter LaSalle and Mary Clearman Bleu; published new writers within the last year. Length: no minimum; 5,000 words maximum. Critiques rejected mss when there is time.
How to Contact: Send complete ms with SASE. Photocopied submissions OK. Accepts computer printout submissions; prefers letter-quality. Reports in 1 month. Publishes ms an average of 1 year after acceptance. Sample copy $2.50.
Payment: Free author's copies. $1.50 charge for extras.
Terms: Acquires first rights. Publication not copyrighted.
Advice: "We're constantly looking for beginning fiction writers. Diversity is one of our major editorial goals. No multiple submissions, please. We have no taboos, but set our own standards on reading each ms."

WISCONSIN ACADEMY REVIEW (II, IV), Wisconsin Academy of Sciences, Arts & Letters, 1922 University Ave., Madison WI 53705. (608)263-1692. Editor-in-Chief: Faith Miracle. Magazine: 8½ × 11; 64-80 pages; 75 lb coated paper; coated cover stock; illustrations; photos. "The *Review* reflects the focus of the sponsoring institution with its editorial emphasis on Wisconsin's intellectual, cultural, social and physical environment. It features short fiction, poetry, essays and Wisconsin-related book reviews for well-educated, well-traveled people interested in furthering regional arts and literature and disseminating information about sciences." Quarterly. Publishes annual fiction issue. Estab. 1954. Circ. 2,000.
Needs: Experimental, historical (general), humor/satire, literary, mainstream, prose poem. "Author must have lived or be living in Wisconsin or fiction must be set in Wisconsin." Receives 5-6 unsolicited fiction mss/month. Accepts 1-2 mss/issue; 8-10 mss/year. Published new writers within the last year. Length: 1,000 words minimum; 4,000 words maximum; 3,000 words average.
How to Contact: Send complete ms with SAE and state author's connection to Wisconsin, the prerequisite. Photocopied submissions OK. Accepts computer printout submissions. Prefers letter-quality. Publishes ms an average of 6 months after acceptance. Sample copy $2. Fiction guidelines for SAE and 1 first class stamp.
Payment: 5 contributor's copies.
Terms: Pays on publication for first rights.

THE WISCONSIN RESTAURATEUR (I, II), Wisconsin Restaurant Association, 125 W. Doty, Madison WI 53703. (608)251-3663. Editor: Jan LaRue. Magazine: 8½ × 11; 80 pages; 80 lb enamel cover stock; illustrations; photos. Published for foodservice operators in the state of Wisconsin and for suppliers of those operations. Theme is the promotion, protection and improvement of the foodservice industry for foodservice workers, students, operators and suppliers. Monthly except December/January combined. Estab. 1933. Circ. 4,200.
Needs: Literary, contemporary, feminist, science fiction, regional, western, mystery, adventure, humor, juvenile and young adult. "Only exceptional fiction material used. No stories accepted that put down persons in the foodservice business or poke fun at any group of people. No off-color material. No religious, no political." Buys 1-2 mss/issue, 12-24 mss/year. Receives 15-20 unsolicited fiction mss/month. Length: 500-2,500 words. Critiques rejected mss "when there is time."
How to Contact: Send complete ms with SASE. Accepts computer printout submissions. Reports in 1 month. Free sample copy with 8½ × 11 SASE. Free guidelines with SASE.
Payment: $2.50-$20. Free author's copy. 50¢ charge for extra copy.
Terms: Pays on acceptance for first rights and first North American serial rights.
Advice: "Make sure there is some kind of lesson to be learned, a humorous aspect, or some kind of moral to your story." Mss are rejected because they are not written for the restaurateur/reader.

WISCONSIN REVIEW (II), Box 158, Radford Hall, University of Wisconsin, Oshkosh WI 45901. (414)424-2267. Editor: Phillip John Huelsbeck. Magazine: 6 × 9; 60-100 pages; illustrations. Literary prose and poetry. Triquarterly. Estab. 1966. Circ. 2,000.
Needs: Literary and experimental. Receives 30 unsolicited fiction mss each month. Published new writers within the last year. Length: up to 5,000 words. Publishes short shorts. Critiques rejected mss when there is time. Occasionally recommends other markets.
How to Contact: Send complete ms with SASE and cover letter with bio notes. Reports in 1-2 months. Publishes ms an average of 1-2 months after acceptance. Sample copy $2.
Payment: Pays in contributor's copies.
Terms: Acquires first rights.
Advice: "We look for well-crafted work with carefully developed characters, plots and meaningful situations. The editors highly appreciate work of original and fresh thought when considering a piece of experimental fiction."

 The double dagger before a listing indicates that the listing is new in this edition. New markets are often the most receptive to freelance contributions.

WITNESS (II), Suite 200, 31000 Northwestern Hwy., Farmington Hills MI 48018. (313)626-1110. Editor: Peter Stine. Magazine: 6×9; 160 pages; 60 lb white paper; perfect bound; often illustrations and photos. "Fiction, poetry, essays that highlight the role of the modern writer as witness to the times." Tri-annually. Estab. 1987. Circ. 3,000.
Needs: Condensed/excerpted novel, contemporary, experimental, fantasy, feminist, literary and sports. "Alternate special or thematic issues: consult back issues or write for themes." Plans to publish a special fiction issue or an anthology in the future. Receives 150 unsolicited mss/month. Buys 10 mss/issue; 40 mss/year. Publishes ms 3 months-1 year after acceptance. Agented fiction 20%. Recently published work by Joyce Carol Oates, Amy Hempel and Richard Currey. Length: 3,500 words average. Publishes short shorts—500 words. Sometimes critiques rejected mss.
How to Contact: Send complete ms with cover letter. Reports in 3 months on mss. SASE. Simultaneous and photocopied submissions OK. Accepts computer printout submissions. Accepts electronic submissions. Sample copy $5. Fiction guidelines for #10 SAE and 1 first class stamp.
Payment: Pays $6/page minimum and contributor's copies.
Terms: Pays on publication for first North American serial rights.
Advice: Looks for "intelligence, compassion, lucidity, original voice. *Witness* blends features of literary and issue-oriented magazine and highlights the writer as witness. Alternate special issues (*Holocaust, Writings from Prison, Sixties*, etc.)"

WOMAN OF POWER (II, IV), A Magazine of Feminism, Spirituality, and Politics, Box 827, Cambridge MA 02238. (617)625-7885. Editor: Char McKee. Magazine: 8½×11; 88-96 pages; 60 lb offset stock; 60 lb glossy cover; illustrations and photos. "Upcoming themes include: 'Humor,' 'Women's Bodies,' 'Magic,' 'The Living Earth,' and 'Women in Community.' Our magazine is read by women." Quarterly. Estab. 1984. Circ. 15,000.
Needs: Ethnic, experimental, fantasy, feminist, humor/satire, lesbian, literary, psychic/supernatural/occult, religious/inspirational, science fiction, senior citizen/retirement, women's, young adult/teen. "We print works by women only." Receives 20 unsolicited mss/month. Accepts 1 or 2 mss/issue. Publishes ms 3-6 months after acceptance. Published new writers within the last year. Length: 1,000 words minimum; 3,500 words maximum. Publishes short shorts. Sometimes critiques rejected mss. Sometimes recommends other markets.
How to Contact: Send complete ms with cover letter, which should include "a short biography and reasons for submitting." Reports in 2 weeks on queries; 3 months on mss. SASE. Simultaneous, photocopied and reprint submissions OK. Computer printout submissions acceptable. Sample copy $7. Fiction guidelines for #10 SAE and 1 first class stamp.
Payment: Pays in 2 contributor's copies.
Terms: Acquires one-time rights. Sends galleys to author on request. Rights revert to authors.
Advice: "It is imperative that women read our magazine before submitting. We have a very *specific* focus which is related to women's spirituality and is best understood by studying past issues. And all materials must directly relate to one of our themes. We print high quality photographs and artwork by women."

THE WORCESTER REVIEW, Worcester Country Poetry Association, Inc., 6 Chatham St., Worcester MA 01609. Editor: Rodger Martin. Magazine: 6×9; 60-100 pages; 60 lb white offset paper; 10 pt C15 cover stock; illustrations and photos. "We like high quality, creative poetry, artwork and fiction. Critical articles should be connected to New England." Semiannually. Estab. 1972. Circ. 1,000.
Needs: Literary, prose poem. "We encourage New England writers in the hopes we will publish at least 30% New England but want the other 70% to show the best of writing from across the US." Receives 10-20 unsolicited fiction mss/month. Accepts 2-4 mss/issue. Publishes ms an average of 6 months to 1 year after acceptance. Less than 10% of fiction is agented. Published work by Debra Friedman, Carol Glickfeld. Length: 2,000 words average; 1,000 words minimum; 4,000 words maximum. Publishes short shorts. Sometimes critiques rejected mss and recommends other markets.
How to Contact: Send complete ms with cover letter. Reports in 2 weeks on queries; 4-5 months on mss. SASE. Simultaneous submissions OK if other markets are clearly identified. Accepts computer printout submissions. Sample copy $4; fiction guidelines free.

Market categories: (I) Beginning; (II) General; (III) Prestige; (IV) Specialized.

Payment: 2 contributor's copies and honorarium if possible.
Terms: Acquires one-time rights.
Advice: "Send only one short story—reading editors do not like to read two by the same author at the same time. We will use only one. We generally look for creative work with a blend of craftsmanship, insight and empathy. This does not exclude humor. We won't print work that is shoddy in any of these areas."

WORD & IMAGE (I), The Illustrated Journal, 3811 Priest Lake Dr., Nashville TN 37217. (615)361-4733. Editor: Joanna Long. Magazine: 7×8½; 48-64 pages; 22 lb paper; 60 lb cover; illustrations and photographs. "Strongly visual—usually up-beat material—well-crafted but not obscure or 'arty.' General interest stories and poetry, some nonfiction. No sensational or 'porn.' " Semiannually. Estab. 1986. Circ. 800.
Needs: Condensed/excerpted novel, contemporary, fantasy (occasionally), historical (general—"We feature a history topic in each issue,") humor/satire, literary prose poem, regional, religious/inspirational, romance (historical), senior citizen/retirement. *"Word & Image* is a nonprofit press committed to helping senior citizens and other worthy causes." Receives 25 unsolicited mss/month. Accepts 3-4 mss/issue; 6-8 mss/year. Length: 1,500-2,500 words preferred; 500-700 words minimum; 2,500 words maximum. Publishes short shorts. Sometimes critiques rejected mss and recommends other markets.
How to Contact: Send complete ms with cover letter. Cover letter should include "brief bio info." Reports in 2-3 weeks. SASE. Photocopied and reprint submissions OK. Accepts computer printout submissions. Sample copy $3. Fiction guidelines for #10 SAE and 1 first class stamp.
Payment: 1 contributor's copy; charge for extras: $3 each.
Terms: Acquires one-time rights. Publication copyrighted.
Advice: "Study a sample copy."

‡WORDS OF WISDOM (II), 612 Front St., Glendora NJ 08029-1133. (609)863-0610. Editor: J.M. Freiermuth. Newsletter: 5½×8½; 20-32 pages; copy paper; some illustrations and photographs. "Fiction, satire, poetry and travel for a general audience —90% of readers have B.A." Monthly. Estab. 1981. Circ. 120.
Needs: Adventure, contemporary, erotica, ethnic, feminist, historical (general), humor/satire, mainstream, regional, science fiction, suspense/mystery, western. No religion, children's, gay, romance. Plans special fiction issue. Receives 3-5 unsolicited mss/month. Accepts 1-2 mss/issue; 20 mss/year. Publishes ms 2-3 months after acceptance. Recently published work by Susan Doro, Darcy Cummings, Gloria Gary and Patrick Castellanos. Length: 2,000-3,000 words average; 1,200 words minimum; 6,000 words maximum. Publishes short shorts. Length: "Long enough to develop a good bite." Sometimes critiques rejected mss and recommends other markets.
How to Contact: Send complete manuscript copy with cover letter including "name, address, SASE." Reports in 2-3 weeks on mss. SASE. Simultaneous, photocopied and reprint submissions OK. Accepts computer printout and electronic submissions. Sample copy for $1, 6×9 SAE and 65¢ postage.
Payment: Pays free subscription to magazine and contributor's copies.
Terms: Acquires one-time rights. Publication not copyrighted.

WORKING CLASSICS (I,II,IV), Red Wheelbarrow Press, 298 Ninth Ave., San Francisco CA 94118. (415)387-3412. Editor: David Joseph. Magazine: 8½×11; 24 pages; 70 lb cover stock; illustrations; photos. Magazine of "creative work, fiction, nonfiction, poetry, interviews, reviews, comics, by and for working people—especially the organized, trade unionists (both rank and file and leadership), artists, leftists, progressives." Semiannually. Plans special fiction issue. Estab. 1982. Circ. 1,000.
Needs: Comics, contemporary, ethnic, experimental, feminist, gay, historical, humor/satire, lesbian, literary, prose poem and regional. No psychic/supernatural/occult, religious/inspirational. Receives 12 unsolicited mss/month. Accepts 2 mss/issue; 4 mss/year. Published the works of Paul Casey and Carrie Jenkins; published new writers within the past year. Length: 2,400 words average; 250 words minimum; 18,000 words maximum. Occasionally critiques rejected mss. Recommends other markets.
How to Contact: Send complete ms. "We're interested in the concrete process involved in your actual conditions. We like to know why you believe your story is for our audience of working people and working writers." Reports in 3 months. SASE. Simultaneous, photocopied and previously published submissions OK. Accepts computer printout submissions; prefers letter-quality. Accepts disk submissions for IBM or compatible. Prefers hard copy with disk submission. Sample copy $3.

Payment: 1 free contributor's copy; reduced charge for extras.
Terms: Acquires one-time rights.
Advice: "The recent expansion in the short fiction market seems to have come to a halt. I think it will remain open with room for new developments in fiction. Dirty realism is not the last word in fiction. Yet realism often may be necessary for focusing details taken from observation. The combination of imagination and observation creates the dynamics of short fiction."

‡THE WORMWOOD REVIEW (II, IV), P.O. Box 8840, Stockton CA 95208. (209)466-8231. Editor: Marvin Malone. Magazine: 5½×8½; 48 pages; 60 lb. matte paper; 80 lb. matte cover; illustrations. "Concentrated on the prose-poem specifically for literate audience." Quarterly. Estab. 1959. Circ. 700.
Needs: Prose poem. No religious or inspirational. Receives 500-600 unsolicited fiction mss/month. Buys 30-40 mss/issue; 120-160 mss/year. Publishes ms 6-18 months after acceptance. Recently published work by Charles Bukowski, Dan Lenihan. Length: 600 words preferred; 300 words minimum; 5,000 words maximum. Publishes short shorts. Critiques or comments on rejected mss. Recommends other markets.
How to Contact: Send complete ms with cover letter. Reports in 1-3 months. SASE. Photocopied submissions OK. Sample copy for $4. Fiction guidelines for #10 SAE and 1 first-class stamp.
Payment: Pays $12-140 or equivalent in contributor's copies.
Terms: Pays on publication for all rights.
Advice: A manuscript that stands out has "economical verbal style coupled with perception and human values. Have something to say--then say it in the most economical way. Do *not* avoid wit and humor."

WRIT MAGAZINE (II), 2 Sussex Ave., Toronto, Ontario M5S 1J5 Canada. (416)978-4871. Editor: Roger Greenwald. Assoc. Editor: Richard Lush. Magazine: 6×9; 96 pages; Zephyr laid paper; cover stock varies; cover illustrations. "Literary magazine for literate readers interested in the work of new writers." Annually. Publishes occasional special fiction issues. Estab. 1970. Circ. 700.
Needs: Literary, short stories, short shorts, parts of novels, translations. Accepts 10-15 mss/year. Does not read mss in summer. Recently published fiction by Leon Rooke, Nawal El Saadawi, Michael Stephens; published new writers in the last year. Length: 300-20,000 words. Critiques rejected mss "when there is time. Sometimes recommends other markets."
How to Contact: Send complete ms with SASE (Canadian stamps or IRCs) and brief biographical note on author and/or translator, and a phone number. Translators must send copy of original text. Accepts computer printout submissions if letter quality. Reports in 2-3 months. Sample copy $6.
Payment: 2 free author's copies. Negotiates charge for extras.
Terms: Acquires first North American serial rights. Copyright reverts to author.
Advice: "Look at your target magazine before submitting."

THE WRITERS' BAR-B-Q (II), Sangamon Writers, Inc., 924 Bryn Mawr, Springfield IL 62703. (217)525-6987. Fiction Editors: Tim Osburn, Becky Bradway, Gary Smith, Gael Cox Carnes, Marcia Womack. Magazine: 8½×11; 80-110 pages; slick cover stock with full-page photo; illustrations and photos. "*The Writers' Bar-B-Q* is a fiction magazine that is looking for unpretentious, fun, exciting writing. A good story with purpose and well-drawn characters is more important to us than clever phrasing. We want writing that shows the author cares, and has something to say. Every story in the magazine is accompanied by an illustration." Semiannually. Estab. 1987. Circ. 1,000.
Needs: Adventure, contemporary, erotica, ethnic, experimental, fantasy, feminist, gay, historical (general), horror, humor/satire, lesbian, literary, mainstream, psychic/supernatural/occult, regional, science fiction, serialized/excerpted novel, suspense/mystery, translations. "Display a strong personal voice, a unique view of the world, and a sense of commitment and caring toward the characters and subject. We publish novel excerpts, long stories and plays as well as shorter pieces. We are looking for inventiveness, humor and insight. No formulas—whether they be genre formulas or academic formulas. Work that is sexist, racist or homophobic should not be mailed! We do not publish poetry." Receives 50-100 unsolicited fiction mss/month. Accepts 15-20 mss/issue; 30-40 mss/year. Publishes ms 6 months to 1 year after acceptance. Recently published work by Shannon Keith Kelly, Martha Miller,

Read the Business of Fiction section to learn the correct way to prepare and submit a manuscript.

Sharon Sloan Fiffer, Myra Epping and Karen Peterson; published new writers within the last year. Length: 500-15,000 words. Sometimes critiques rejected mss.
How to Contact: Send complete ms with cover letter, which should include "a sense of who the writer is along with a list of publications." Reports in 6 weeks-4 months on mss. SASE. Simultaneous and photocopied submissions OK. Accepts computer printout submissions. Accepts electronic submissions via disk. "We have an Epson MS-DOS." Sample copy $5; subscription, $10/year, $18/2 yr.
Payment: 3 contributor's copies.
Terms: Acquires first rights. Rights revert upon publication.
Advice: "Please make sure your work is thoughtfully edited. We have returned many stories that would have been great if given more careful attention by the writer. *The Writers' Bar-B-Q* publishes fiction with spirit and energy, with an emphasis on characterization and story over style. We combine stories often put into genres and catagories (such as sci-fi, mysteries and gay/lesbian) with so-called 'literary' fiction."

WRITERS' FORUM (II), University of Colorado at Colorado Springs, Colorado Springs CO 80933-7150. Editor: Dr. Alex Blackburn. "Ten to fifteen short stories or self-contained novel excerpts published once a year along with 25-35 poems. Funded by grants from National Endowment for the Arts, Council for Literary Magazines, University of Colorado and others. Highest literary quality only: mainstream, avant-garde, with preference to western themes. For small press enthusiasts, teachers and students of creative writing, commercial agents/publishers, university libraries and departments interested in contemporary American literature." Estab. 1974.
Needs: Literary, contemporary, ethnic (Native American, Chicano, not excluding others) and regional (West). No "sentimental, over-plotted, pornographic, anecdotal, polemical, trendy, disguised autobiographical, fantasy (sexual, extra-terrestrial), pseudo-philosophical, passionless, placeless, undramatized, etc. material." Accepts 10-12 mss/issue. Receives approximately 40 unsolicited fiction mss each month and will publish new as well as experienced authors. Published fiction by Thomas E. Kennedy, Charles Baxter, Gladys Swan; published many new writers within the last year. Length: 1,500-10,000 words. Critiques rejected mss "when there is time and perceived merit."
How to Contact: Send complete ms and letter with relevant career information with SASE. Accepts computer printout submissions; prefers letter-quality. Reports in 3-5 weeks on mss. Publishes ms an average of 6 months after acceptance. Sample back copy $5.95 to *NSSWM* readers. Current copy $8.95.
Payment: 1 free author's copy. Cover price less 60% discount for extras.
Terms: Acquires one-time rights. Rights revert to author.
Advice: "Read our publication. Be prepared for constructive criticism. We especially seek submissions that show immersion in place (trans-Mississippi West) and development of credible characters. Turned off by slick 'decadent' New York-ish content. Probably the TV-influenced fiction is the most quickly rejected. Our format—a 5½ × 8½ professionally edited and printed paperback book—lends credibility to authors published in our imprint."

WRITERS NEWSLETTER (I), Writers Studio, 1530 7th St., Rock Island IL 61201. (309)788-3980. Editor: Betty Mowery. Newsletter: 8½ × 11; 8-9 pages. "Anything of help to writers." Bimonthly. Estab. 1968. Circ. 385.
Needs: Adventure, contemporary, experimental, historical (general), humor/satire, mainstream, prose poem, regional, religious/inspiration, romance, spiritual, suspense/mystery. No erotica. Receives about 12 mss/month. Buys or accepts up to 6 mss/issue. Publishes ms within 3 months of acceptance. Published work by David R. Collins, Evelyn Witter, Chris Walkowicz; published new writers within the last year. Length: 500 words maximum. Publishes short shorts. Length: 200 words.
How to Contact: Send complete ms. Reports in 1 week. SASE. Simultaneous, photocopied and reprint submissions OK. Accepts computer printout submissions. Sample copy $1. Subscription $5 for 6 issues.
Payment: Pays in contributor's copies.
Terms: Acquires first rights.
Advice: "Just send a manuscript, but first read a copy of our publication to get an idea of what type of material we take. Please send SASE. If not, manuscripts *will not* be returned. Be sure name and address is on the manuscript."

WRITERS' RENDEZVOUS (I), P.O. Box 720512, Redding CA 96099. Editor: Karen Campbell. Newsletter: 8½ × 11; approx. 24 pages; bond paper; no cover; line drawings. "Writer-oriented, publish only work relating to freelance writing and penpalling." Quarterly. Plans special fiction issue. Estab. 1986. Circ. 100.

Needs: No fiction "not related to writing/penpalling." Receives approx. 10 unsolicited fiction mss/month. Publishes approx. 2 mss/issue; approx. 10 mss/year. Publishes ms 6 weeks-1 year after acceptance. Published work by Bettye Griffin, Jan McDaniel, Linda Hutton; published new writers within the last year. Length: 750 words average; 1,500 words maximum. Publishes short shorts. Sometimes comments on rejected mss and recommends other markets. "No erotica!!"

How to Contact: Send complete ms with cover letter. Reports in 2-4 weeks. SASE. Simultaneous, photocopied and reprint submissions OK. Accepts computer printouts, including dot-matrix "with true descenders only." Sample copy for $3, #10 SAE and 3 first class stamps; fiction guidelines for #10 SAE and 1 first class stamp.

Payment: Pays in contributor's copies.

Terms: Acquires one-time rights. Publication not copyrighted. Sponsors contests for fiction writers. "SASE for guidelines; $2 entry fee. Cash prize."

Advice: "Proofread. Then proofread again. Then ask a friend or teacher to proofread. Use your dictionary—both for spelling and meaning. Read the guidelines carefully. And, if you want cash for your work, be sure you aren't submitting to markets which pay copies. (I've had several acceptances fall through when I advised the author of our non-payment policy)."

XAVIER REVIEW (I, II), Xavier University, Box 110C, New Orleans LA 70125. (504)486-7411, ext. 7481. Editor: Thomas Bonner, Jr. Magazine of "poetry/fiction/nonfiction/reviews (contemporary literature) for professional writers/libraries/colleges/universities." Published semiannually. Estab. 1980. Circ. 500.

Needs: Contemporary, ethnic, experimental, historical (general), literary, Latin-American, prose poem, Southern, religious, serialized/excerpted novel, translations. Receives 30 unsolicited fiction mss/month. Buys 2 mss/issue; 4 mss/year. Length: 10-15 pages. Occasionally critiques rejected mss.

How to Contact: Send complete ms. SASE. Sample copy $3.

Payment: 2 contributor's copies.

YELLOW SILK (II): Journal of Erotic Arts, Verygraphics, Box 6374, Albany CA 94706. Editor/Publisher: Lily Pond. Magazine: 8½ × 11; 52 pages; matte coated stock; glossy cover stock; 4-color illustrations; photos. "We are interested in nonpornographic erotic literature: joyous, mad, musical, elegant, passionate." 'All persuasions; no brutality' is our editorial policy. Literary excellence is a priority; innovative forms are welcomed, as well as traditional ones." Published quarterly. Estab. 1981. Circ. 16,000.

Needs: Comics, erotica, ethnic, experimental, fantasy, feminist/lesbian, gay, humor/satire, literary, prose poem, science fiction and translations. No "blow-by-blow" descriptions; no hackneyed writing except when used for satirical purposes. Nothing containing brutality. Buys 4-5 mss/issue; 16-20 mss/year. Published work by William Kotzwinkle, Gary Soto. Published new writers within the last year. Length: no preference. Occasionally critiques rejected ms.

How to Contact: Send complete ms with SASE and include short, *personal* bio notes. No queries. No pre-published material. No simultaneous submissions. Name, address and phone number on each page. Photocopied submissions OK. Accepts computer printout submissions; prefers letter-quality. Submissions on disk OK *with* hard copy only. Reports in 3 months on mss. Publishes ms up to 3 years after acceptance. Sample copy $6.

Payment: 3 contributor's copies plus minimum of $10 per prose item.

Terms: Pays on publication for all periodical and anthology rights for one year following publication, at which time rights revert back to author; and non-exclusive reprint and anthology rights for the duration of the copyright.

Advice: "Read, read, read! Including our magazine—plus Nabokov, Ntozake Shange, Rimbaud, Virginia Woolf, William Kotzwinkle, James Joyce. Then send in your story! Trust that the magazine/editor will not rip you off—they don't. As they say, 'find your own voice,' then trust it. Most manuscripts I reject appear to be written by people without great amounts of writing experience. It takes years (frequently) to develop your work to publishable quality; it can take many re-writes on each individual piece. I also see many approaches to sexuality (for my magazine) that are trite and not fresh. The use of language is not original, and the people do not seem real. However, the gems come too, and what a wonderful moment that is. Please don't send me anything with blue eye shadow."

‡YESTERDAY'S MAGAZETTE (I), The Magazine of Memories, Independent Publishing Co., P.O. Box 15126, Sarasota FL 34277. (813)366-9850. Editor: Ned Burke. Magazine: 8½ × 11; 24 pages, 60 lb. paper; glossy cover, illustrations. "Nostalgia themes for adults, 40 and up." Bimonthly. Estab. 1973. Circ. 1,500.

Needs: Historical, humor/satire, mainstream, religious/inspirational, senior citizen/retirement. Published special fiction issue and plans one in the future. Receives 10-30 unsolicited fiction mss/month. Buys 1-3 mss/issue; 10-15 mss/year. Publishes ms 4 months or more after acceptance. Agented fiction 10%. Length: 1,000 words preferred; 500 words minimum; 1,500 words maximum. Publishes short shorts. Length: 250-300 words. Critiques or comments on rejected mss. Recommends other markets.
How to Contact: Send complete ms with cover letter. Reports in 2 months. SASE. Computer printout submissions OK. Sample copy for $2. Fiction guidelines for #10 SAE and 1 first-class stamp.
Payment: Pays $5-25, contributor's copies and free subscription.
Terms: Pays on publication for first rights. Sponsors fiction contest—send for details.
Advice: Looks for "flow—an easy, conversational style that tells a story in much the same way you would tell it to your best friend. Keep it simple, but emotional."

YOUNG JUDAEAN (IV), Hadassah Zionist Youth Commission, 50 W. 58th St., New York NY 10019. (212)355-7900. Contact: Editor. Magazine: 8½×11; 16 pages; illustrations. *"Young Judaean* is for members of the Young Judaea Zionist youth movement, ages 9-12." Quarterly. Estab. 1910. Circ. 4,000.
Needs: Children's fiction including adventure, ethnic, fantasy, historical, humor/satire, juvenile, prose poem, religious, science fiction, suspense/mystery and translations. "All stories must have Jewish relevance." Receives 10-15 unsolicited fiction mss/month. Publishes ms up to 2 years after acceptance. Buys 1-2 mss/issue; 10-20 mss/year. Length: 500 words minimum; 1,500 words maximum; 1,000 words average.
How to Contact: Send complete ms with SASE. Photocopied submissions OK. Reports in 3 months on mss. Sample copy for 75¢. Free fiction guidelines.
Payment: Pays 5¢/word up to $50; 2 free contributor's copies; 75¢ charge for extras.
Terms: Pays on publication for first rights.
Advice: "Stories must be of Jewish interest—lively and accessible to children without being condescending."

YOUNG VOICES MAGAZINE (I, II, IV), The Magazine of Young People's Creative Work, Box 2321, Olympia WA 98507. (206)357-4863. Editor: Steve Charak. Magazine: "All materials are by elementary and middle school students for children and adults interested in children's work." Bimonthly. Estab. 1988. Circ. 1,000.
Needs: Adventure, experimental, historical (general), humor/satire, juvenile (5-14), literary, mainstream, prose poem, and science fiction. "Everything must be written by elementary or middle school students. (8th grade is the limit)" No excessive violence or sexual content. Plans a special fiction issue or an anthology in the future. Receives 50 unsolicited mss/month. Buys 30 mss/issue; 160-200 mss/year. Publishes ms 2-4 months after acceptance. Recently published work by Amanda Trause and Lani Olson. Length: 500 words average. Publishes short shorts. Always critiques rejected mss and recommends other markets.
How to Contact: Send complete ms with cover letter. Make sure age, grade and school are in the letter. Simultaneous, photocopied and reprint submissions OK. Accepts computer printout submissions. Sample copy $3. Fiction guidelines free.
Payment: Pays $3-5 and contributor's copies.
Terms: Pays on acceptance for one-time rights.

ZERO HOUR (I, II, IV), "Where Culture Meets Crime," Box 766, Seattle WA 98111. (206)621-8829. Editor: Jim Jones. Tabloid: 11×16; 36 pages; newsprint paper; illustrations and photos. "We are interested in fringe culture. We publish fiction, poetry, essays, confessions, photos, illustrations, interviews, for young, politically left audience interested in current affairs, non-mainstream music, art, culture." Semiannually. Estab. 1988. Circ. 3,000.
Needs: Confessions, erotica, ethnic, experimental, feminist, gay, humor/satire, psychic/supernatural/occult and translations. "Each issue revolves around an issue in contemporary culture: cults and fanaticism, addiction, pornography, etc." No romance, inspirational, juvenile/young, sports. Receives 5 unsolicited mss/month. Accepts 3 mss/issue; 9 mss/year. Publishes ms 2-3 months after acceptance. Recently published work by Jesse Bernstein and Mike Allmayer. Length: 1,200 words average; 400 words minimum; 1,500 words maximum. Publishes short shorts. Length: 400 words. Sometimes critiques rejected mss.
How to Contact: Query first. Reports in 2 weeks on queries; 1 month on mss. SASE. Simultaneous and photocopied submissions OK. Accepts computer printout submissions. Sample copy $3, 9×12 SAE and 5 first class stamps. Fiction guidelines free.

Payment: Pays in contributor's copies.
Terms: Acquires one-time rights. Sends galleys to author.
Advice: "Does it fit our theme? Is it well written, from an unusual point of view or on an unexplored/underexplored topic?"

ZOIKS! (I, II, IV), Curdling the Cream of the Mind, 2509 M Avent Ferry Rd., Raleigh NC 27606. (919)821-2196. Editor: Skip Elsheimer. Fiction Editor: David Jordan. Magazine: illustrations and photos. "*Zoiks!* is interested in new ideas and new ways of thinking. Or at least using old ideas in a new way. Exploring the world through cynicism." Plans special fiction issue. Estab. 1986.
Needs: Experimental, humor/satire, psychic/supernatural/occult, translations, underground literature, conspiracy-oriented fiction. "I'm interested in anything that will make you question your surroundings. No fiction that is pretentious, lacking humor." Receives 2-3 unsolicited mss/month. Accepts 1-2 mss/issue; 6-12 mss/year. Recently published work by Joe Corey, Skip Elsheimer, Karen Bartlett; published new writers within the last year. Publishes short shorts. Sometimes critiques rejected mss or recommends other markets.
How to Contact: Query first with clips of published work or send complete ms with cover letter, which should include address. Should tell something about the author. Reports in 3 weeks. Simultaneous, photocopied and reprint submissions OK. Accepts computer submissions. Accepts electronic submissions via Macintosh 800K. Sample copy $1. Make checks payable to Skip Elsheimer.
Payment: Pays in contributor's copies; charges for extras at cost plus postage.
Terms: Publication not copyrighted. Work belongs to the author.
Advice: "I feel that magazine fiction is too industry oriented. Everyone should have a shot at getting published. Express *yourself*! Not the style of another famous author."

ZYMERGY (II), (Literary Review), Box 1746, Place du Parc, Montreal, Quebec H2W 2R7 Canada. Editor: Sonja A. Skarstedt. Magazine: 6×9; 160 pages; buff paper; Cornwall/laminated cover stock; illustrations; photos. "We publish poetry, fiction and interviews, articles: all attempting to focus on and come to grips with what is happening in today's literary movements, splayed though they might happen to be." Semiannually. Estab. 1987. Circ. 500.
Needs: Short stories, feminist, literary and prose poem. Nothing gratuitous, manipulative, (pornography and violence, e.g.) or formulaic (e.g. greeting card verse). Receives 20-100 unsolicited mss/month. Accepts 1-5 mss/issue. Publishes ms 1 year after acceptance. Length: 1200 words/average. Sometimes recommends other markets.
How to Contact: Send complete ms with cover letter. Include biographical information to be used in "Contributor's Column." Reports in 3 weeks on mss. SASE. Photocopied submissions OK. Accepts computer printout submissions. (No simultaneous submissions.) Sample copy $6 (U.S.). Checks payable to S. Skarstedt, or add two dollars for banker's fee.
Payment: Pays in contributor's copies.
Terms: Acquires first rights and the right, should the story be reprinted/anthologized, to be acknowledged.
Advice: "We look for originality. The ability to 'pull' the reader inside the story's/characters' environment. Non-stylized writing. If you don't enjoy writing—don't write! Not generally seeking stories about writers or writing."

ZYZZYVA (II, IV), The Last Word: West Coast Writers and Artists, Suite 1400, 41 Sutter St., San Francisco CA 94104. (415)255-1282. Editor: Howard Junker. Magazine: 6×9; 136 pages; Starwhite Vicksburg smooth paper; graphics; photos. "Literate" magazine. Quarterly. Estab. 1985. Circ. 3,500.
Needs: Contemporary, experimental, literary, prose poem. West Coast writers only. Receives 300 unsolicited mss/month. Buys 5 fiction mss/issue; 20 mss/year. Agented fiction: 10%. Recent issues have included Marilyn Chin, Barry Lopez and Lemand Michaels; published new writers within the last year. Length: varies.
How to Contact: Send complete ms. "Cover letters are of minimal importance." Reports in 2 weeks on mss. SASE. No simultaneous submissions or reprints. Accepts computer printouts. Sample copy $8. Fiction guidelines on masthead page.

Payment: Pays $50-250.
Terms: Pays on acceptance for first North American serial rights.
Advice: "Keep the faith."

Foreign literary and small circulation magazines

The following is a list of literary and small circulation publications from countries outside the U.S. and Canada that accept or buy short fiction in English (or in the universal languages of Esperanto or Ido) by North American writers.

Before sending a manuscript to a foreign publication with which you are unfamiliar, it's a good idea to query first for information on the magazine's needs and methods of submission. Send for sample copies, or try visiting the main branch of your local library, a nearby college library or bookstore to find a copy.

All correspondence to foreign countries must include International Reply Coupons if you want a reply or material returned. You may find it less expensive to send copies of your manuscript for the publisher to keep and just enclose a return postcard with one IRC for a reply. Keep in mind response time is slow for many foreign publishers, but don't hesitate to send a reply postcard with IRC to check the status of your submission.

ACUMEN, 6, The Mount, Furzeham, Brixham, Devon TQ5 8QY England. Fiction Editor: Patricia Oxley. Circ. 500. "Literary magazine with an emphasis on poetry. I use 2-4 short stories/year (2 issues) which are around 1,500 words, have a clear statement and are written in a literary style. Writers paid in extra copies of *Acumen*. Writers receive copies of the issue containing their work. Send sufficient IRCs to cover return postage. Make sure name and address are on manuscript (not just covering letter or, worse still, on outside of envelope.)"

‡AGOG & AGOG AGO GO, 116 Eswyn Rd., Tooting, London SW17 England. Fiction Editor: E. Jewasinski. Circ. under 1,000. Humorous material. Pays 1 contributor's copy plus payment at the descretion of the fiction editor. "Make me laugh! Presentation is good from the U.S. – content is often poor. Enclose IRCs – not U.S. stamps."

AMBIT, 17 Priory Gardens, London N6 5QY England. Fiction Editor: J. G. Ballard. Circ. 2,000. Publishes 12 stories/year. "Fantasy, science fiction stories where quotidian events are seen from an extraordinary viewpoint." Pays 2 complimentary copies and £5 per page. "*Ambit* is a good place for North American writers to send work. We regularly publish U.S. writers. Writers should screen each magazine first to see whether it has an open, adventurous editorial policy. Closed parochial magazines and journals should be shunned and allowed to shrivel in their own time."

ANTIGRUPPO, Coop. Antigruppo Siciliano, via Argenteria Km4, Trapani, Sicily 91026 Italy. Editor: Nat Scammacca. Fiction Editor: Gianni Diecidue. Needs literary, contemporary, humor, translations, history (local, Sicilian, Scots, Greek, English, Yugoslavian, Israel, Hungarian and French). "Send previously published material so we can then ask for the material we want. Ask for our '21 Points of the Antigruppo', which is a pluralistic guide and encouragement to write as one speaks. Don't copy anyone but oneself and write the way the language is spoken at home in your own region, not imitating others. Material must interest the Sicilian reader."

AQUARIUS, Flat 10, Room-A, 116 Sutherland Ave., Maida-Vale, London W9 England. Fiction Editor: Sean Glackin. Circ. 5,000. Publishes five stories/issue. Interested in humor/satire, literary, prose poem and serialized/excerpted novels. "We publish prose and poetry and reviews." Payment is by agreement. "We only suggest changes. Most stories are taken on merit." Price in UK £2 50p. plus postage and packing; in US $18 plus $3 postage. Next issue devoted to women writers.

AUGURIES, 48 Anglesey Road, Alverstoke, Gosport, Hampshire P012 2EQ England. Editor: Nik Morton. Circ. 300. Averages 30-40 stories/year. "Science fiction and fantasy, maximum length 4,000 words." Pays £2 per 1,000 words plus complimentary copy. "Buy back issues, then try me!" Sample copy $5. Subscription $20 (4 issues). Member of the New SF Alliance.

CENTRAL COAST COURIER, Box 44, Oxford, Tasmania 7190 Australia. Fiction Editor: J.C. Read. Circ. 1,000. Local newspaper publishing general fiction and poetry on a bimonthly basis. Pays nominal fee; sends contributor's copy where possible. Maximum word length for short stories: 1,500 words. Also uses summaries of novels.

CREATIVE FORUM, Bahri Publications, 997A Gobindpuri Kalkaj, New Delhi 110019 India. Fiction Editor: U.S. Bahri. Circ. 1,800. Publishes 8-12 stories annually. "We accept short stories only for our journal, *Creative Forum*. Novels/novellas accepted if suitable subsidy is forthcoming from the author." Pays in copies. Manuscripts should be "neatly typed and not beyond 200 sheets."

‡EDINBURGH REVIEW, 22 George Square, Edinburgh EH8 Scotland. Circ. 2,000. Publishes 16 stories/year. "An international journal of ideas and literature. Interested in all stories, especially the experimental and unorthodox." Pays for published fiction and provides contributor's copies. "We take 10 weeks to give a decision. We are especially interested in translations and interviews of some length."

FOOLSCAP, 78 Friars Road, East Ham, London E6 1LL England. Fiction and Poetry Editor: Judi Benson. Publishes 3 items/year. "We are primarily poetry though can handle short fiction of up to 5 pages. This could include a scene from a novel. We are looking for strong quality work but will give careful consideration to all submissions. Any subject considered, also nonfiction." Pays 1 contributor's copy. "Do not send work exceeding 5 typed pages as the magazine does not have the space. Send manuscript in typed form with SASE for return (IRCs)."

FORESIGHT (IV), 44 Brockhurst Rd., Hodge Hill, Birmingham B36 8JB England. Editor: John Barklam. Fiction Editor: Judy Barklam. Magazine including "new age material, world peace, psychic phenomena, research, occultism, spiritualism, mysticism, UFOs, philosophy, etc. Shorter articles required on a specific theme related to the subject matter of *Foresight* magazine." Sample copy for 30p and 25p postage.

FORUM FABULATORUM, Cort Adelersgade 5, 2.tv., DK-1053 Copenhagen K Denmark. Fiction Editor: Morten Sorensen. Circ. 250. Publishes 60,000-80,000 words of fiction annually. "*Forum Fabulatorum* is a fiction magazine devoted to 'fantastic literature,' by which is meant fantasy, horror and science fiction, although other kinds of non-naturalist prose and poetry are welcomed. Prints both 'name' authors and beginners, and both conventional and avant-garde material. Typically, *Forum Fabulatorum* pays around Danish kroner 150 for a story with first Danish rights; all contributors receive at least two free copies of the issue where they appear. Concentrate on psychological, philosophical and perhaps supernatural content; avoid hard science fiction, pulp and formula fiction. Stylistic innovation encouraged." English language submissions welcomed.

FRANK, An International Journal of Contemporary Writing and Art (II), B.P. 29 94301 Vincennes Cedex, France. Editor: David Applefield. "Eclectic, serious fiction, favors innovative works that convey radical social, political, environmental concern — all styles, voices — and translations, novel extracts" for literary international audience. "Send your best work, consult a copy of the journal before submitting." Recently published work by Raymond Carver, Robert Coover, Rita Dove, Italo Calvino, Vaclav Havel, and Sony Labou Tansi. Sample copy $8.

GLOBAL TAPESTRY JOURNAL (II), BB Books, 1 Spring Bank, Longsight Rd., Copster Green, Blackburn, Lancashire BB1 9EU England. Editor: Dave Cunliffe. "Post-underground with avant-garde, experimental, alternative, counterculture, psychedelic, mystical, anarchist, etc. fiction for a bohemian and counterculture audience." Recently published fiction by Gregory Stephenson, Arthur Moyse and David Tipton; published work by new writers within the last year. Sample copy $4.

GOING DOWN SWINGING, Box 64, Coburg Victoria 3058 Australia. Fiction Editors: Kevin Brophy and Myron Lysenko. Circ. 800. Publishes approx. 80 pages of fiction/year. "We publish short stories, prose poetry, poetry and prose reviews. We try to encourage young or new writers as well as established writers. Interested in experimental writing. Writers not paid as we can't afford it. Writers receive a copy of the issue they are published in. Send ms, International Reply Coupons and a short biographical note." Include 2-3 stories. Deadlines: 15 December each year. "We are an annual magazine."

Editor David Applefield of Frank magazine chose this cover "to find a more original and fresh image for today." He felt "the image seemed to unify the themes of the issue—self-referential like the Dixon interview, urban and intelligent like the New York dossier and the Pakistani Foreign dossier, plus the image technically unifies the old with the contemporary." The print was done by Belgian artist Frans Masereel in 1919.

‡GRANTA, 2/3 Hanover Yard, Noel Road, Islington, London N1 8BE England. U.S. Associate Publisher: Anne Kinard. Editor: Bill Buford. U.S. office: 250 W. 57th St., New York NY 10107. "Paperback magazine (256 pages) publishing fiction and cultural and political journalism: fiction (including novellas and works-in progress), essays, political analysis, journalism, etc."

‡HATBOX, P.O. Box 336, Miller, New South Wales, Australia. Fiction Editor: David Zorate. Circ. 150. "*Hatbox* is a small press literary magazine open to all styles, content, themes, etc. The only restriction is the length: maximum 2,500 words. Fiction can be biased, sexist, gay, political, experimental, whatever--it just needs to be quality work." Pays 1 complimentary subscription.

HECATE, Box 99, St. Lucia Q4037 Australia. Fiction Editor: Carole Ferrier. Circ. 2,000. Publishes 5-8 stories annually. "Socialist feminist; we like political stories (broadly defined)." Writers receive $6/page (Australian) and 5 copies. "We only rarely publish non-Australian writers of fiction."

THE HONEST ULSTERMAN, 102 Elm Park Mansions, Park Walk, London SW10 OAP U.K. Fiction Editor: Robert Johnstone. Circ. 1,000. Publishes 3-4 stories/year. "Mainly poetry, book review, sociopolitical comment, short stories, novel extracts, etc. Main interest is Ireland/Northern Ireland." Writers receive small payment and two contributor's copies.

HRAFNHOH, 32 Strŷd Ebeneser, Pontypridd Mid Glamorgan CF37 5PB Wales. Fiction Editor: Joseph Biddulph. Circ. 200-500. "Now worldwide and universal in scope. Suitable: fictionalized history, local history, family history. Explicitly Christian approach. Well-written stories or general prose opposed to abortion and human embryo experimentation particularly welcome. No payment made, but free copies provided. Be brief, use a lot of local colour and nature description, in a controlled, resonant prose or in dialect. Suitable work accepted in Esperanto and other languages, including Creole."

INDIAN LITERATURE, Sahitya Akademi, National Academy of Letters, Rabindra Bhavan, 35 Ferozeshah Rd., New Delhi 110 001 India. Editor: Dr. D.S. Rao. Circ. 3,100. Publishes 6 issues/year; 144-240 pages/issue. "Presents creative work from 22 Indian literatures including Indian English." Sample copy $7.

‡INKSHED, 387 Beverly Road, Hull HU5 1LS England. Fiction Editor: Sue Wilsea. Circ. 400. Publishes approx. 10 stories/year. "Small press poetry/fiction magazine. Any type of fiction used up to 2,500 words." Writers receive a complimentary copy. "Just keep it neat, typed, well-spaced with name and address on front sheet." Please send International Reply Coupons for response.

IRON MAGAZINE (II), Iron Press, 5 Marden Ter., Cullercoats, North Shields, Tyne & Wear NE30 4PD England. Editor: Peter Mortimer. Circ. 800. Publishes 14 stories/year. "Literary magazine of contemporary fiction, poetry, articles and graphics." Pays approx. £10/page. No simultaneous submissions. Five poems, two stories per submission maximum. Sample copy for $5 (no bills-no checks). "Please see magazine before submitting and don't submit to it before you're ready!"

LA KANCERKLINIKO (IV), 162 rue Paradis, 13006 Marseille France. Phone: 91-3752-15. Fiction Editor: Laurent Septier. Circ. 300. Publishes 40 pages of fiction annually. "An esperanto magazine which appears 4 times annually. Each issue contains 32 pages. *La Kancerkliniko* is a political and cultural magazine. General fiction, science fiction, etc. Short stories or very short novels. The short story (or the very short novel) must be written only in esperanto, either original or translation from any other language."

LANDFALL/CAXTON PRESS, P.O. Box 25-088, Christchurch, New Zealand. Fiction Editor: Iain Sharp. Publishes 20 stories/year. "We are willing to consider any type of serious fiction, whether the style is regarded as conservative or avant-garde." Length: maximum 15,000 words. Pays NZ $30-60, depending on length of story. "In New Zealand we follow English spelling conventions. Without wishing to be unduly nationalist, we would normally give first preference to stories which contain some kind of North American-New Zealand connection."

‡LONDON MAGAZINE, 30 Thurbe Place, SW7 London England. Editor: Alan Ross. Circ. 5,000. Publishes 20-25 stories/year. Bimonthly magazine. "Quality is the only criteria." Length: 2,000-4,500 words. Pays £50-100. "Send only original and literary, rather than commercial, work."

‡MAELSTROM, 31 Chiltern, Coleman St., Southend-on-Sea SS2 5AE England. Fiction Editor: Malcolm E. Wright. Circ. 450. Publishes 36,000 words/year. "A short-story magazine publishing most types of genre fiction, including science fiction, fantasy, thriller, mystery, horror, etc." British contributors paid £35 per 100 words and one contributor copy; American contributors paid contributor copies only. "Send SAE for submission guidelines. Disposable manuscripts are probably best, but a small SAE is still necessary if a reply is required."

MEANJIN, University of Melbourne, Parkville, Victoria 3052 Australia. Fiction Editors: Jenny Lee and Gerald Murnane. Circ. 3,000. "*Meanjin*'s emphasis is on publishing a wide range of writing by new and established writers. Our primary orientation is toward Australian writers, but material from overseas sources is also published." Writer receives approx. $50 (Australian) per 1,000 words and 2 copies. "Please submit typed manuscript and enclose return addressed envelope with IRCs."

MOMENTUM, % Pamela Goodwin, Almere Farm, Rossett, Wrexham, Clwyd LL12 0BY Wales. Fiction Editor: Jeff Bell. Circ. 350. Publishes an average of 25 stories annually. "*Momentum:* A 'middle-of-the-road' general interest mag with some verse, specializing in new writers—within those parameters anything goes, but no way-out extremes of fantasy or cult stuff, etc. Fiction only. Published 3 times a year (60 page edition)." Writers receive 1 contributor's copy. "Type fairly legibly, 2,500 words maximum and a rough word count is welcome, one side of a sheet please. Address (and name) on copy. Politics *not* barred." Subscription details: £2.40 annually GB. USA add £2, elsewhere add £1. "New subscribers get 1 free back issue."

‡NEW EUROPE, P.O. Box 212, Luxemborg 2012. Fiction Editor: Nelleke Vostveen. Biannual. Publishes 20 pages of fiction/year. "*New Europe* is a pluralingual cultural magazine (arts, letters, sciences). Two double issues (128 pages each) per year, May and November." Pays in contributor's copies.

NEW HOPE INTERNATIONAL, 20 Werneth Ave., Hyde, SK14 5NL England. Fiction Editor: Gerald England. Circ. 500. Publishes 1-4 stories annually. Publishes "mainly poetry. Fiction used must be essentially literary but not pretentious. Only short fiction used (max 2,000 words). Would use more fiction but the standard submitted (in comparison to the poetry) has been rather poor." Payment: 1 complimentary copy. Guidelines available for IRC. Sample copy: $4.

‡**NEW OUTLOOK (IV), MIDDLE EAST MONTHLY,** Israel Peace Society, 9 Gordon Street, 63458 Israel. Editor: Chaim Shur. "Middle East peace issues, for a progressive audience." Monthly. Estab. 1957. Circ. 4,500. Needs: ethnic, historical (general), translations, Palestinian literature. Pays in contributor's copies. "We publish Palestinian fiction and controversial Israeli works in English in order to broaden potential audience for these works."

‡**THE NEW WELSH REVIEW,** Dept. of English, St. David's University College, Lampeter SA48 7EB UK. Fiction Editor: Belinda Humfrey. "*NWR*, a quarterly, publishes stories, poems and critical essays." Accepts 16-20 mss/year. Pays "cheque on publication and one free copy." Length: 2,000-3,000 words.

NIEUWE KOEKRAND, Box 14767, 1001 LG Amsterdam Holland. Fiction Editor: Johan Van Leeuwen. Circ. 2,000. Publishes 2-3 pages of fiction/issue. "*Nieuwe Koekrand* is basically considered a hardcore/ punk magazine but often goes beyond that. It also includes articles on writers/fiction/movies/politics/ art/comics/horror. Fiction we use is horror and political satire. Writers don't get paid. I put in 50% of the money to get the magazine published. Others put in their efforts and energy. Don't expect too much response on getting stuff published. In case you send in something, make sure it's not over 5,000 words (approximately)."

‡**NNIDNID: SURREALITY,** 3 Vale View, Ponsanooth, Truro, Cornwall England. Fiction Editor: Tony Shiels. Circ. 500-650. Publishes 5 or 6 short stories annually. "*Nnidnid: Surreality* is an irregular publication (sometimes issued in the form of an audio cassette) devoted to the current manifestations of the International Surrealist Movement. Any prose fiction submitted should be strictly surreal in content, style and intention. We have published work by Gascoyne, Roditi, Soupault, etc. Writers are unpaid, but will receive two free copies of the issue in which their work appears. Potential contributors should understand the meaning of 'surreality,' should *be* surrealists (we instantly detect fakes!). We prefer stories of rather less than 2,500 words. Unsolicited manuscripts must be accompanied by a self-addressed envelope and an IRCs."

‡**NUTSHELL QUARTERLY,** 8 George Marston Rd, Binley, Coventry CV3 2HH England. Fiction Editor: Tom Roberts. Circ. 1,000. Accepts 30-40 mss/year. "*Nutshell* is a small press (42-page) magazine featuring short stories, poetry, interviews, articles and reviews. New publisher plans to increase pages and circulation. Pleased to receive fiction of any length and of high quality." Pays in contributor's copy and choice of payment (nominal) or reduces subscription. Length: 1,000-3,000 words preferred; 7,000 words maximum. Send SAE with IRCs and a short biography. "We are also interested in hearing about the surroundings in which people work and in receiving correspondence."

PANURGE (I), P.O. Box 1QR, Newcastle-upon-Tyne, NE99 1QR, U.K. Tel: 091-232-7669. Fiction Editor: David Almond. Circ. 1,000. Published twice/year. Perfectbound, 120 pages. "Dedicated to short fiction by new and up-and-coming names. Each issue features several previously unpublished names. Several *Panurge* writers have been included in major anthologies, approached by agents, offered contracts by publishers. We seek work that shows vitality of language, command of form, an individual approach. We pay 1 month after publication and send 1 contributor's copy. Overseas subscription $15. Airmail $18. Sample copy $7."

PEACE AND FREEDOM, 17 Farrow Rd., Whaplode Drove, Spalding, Lincs. PE12 OTS England. Fiction Editor: Paul Rance. Circ. 500+. Publishes around a dozen short stories annually. "A mixture of poetry, art, short stories, music and general features. *P and F* has a general humanism slant, as the title suggests, but good literature is judged purely as literature. Anything which is inventive, compelling, compassionate and literate will stand a chance of acceptance. Any racist, sexist, American-Russian tirades will be instantly returned." Pays in copies. "A sample copy of *P and F* costs $1/50p SAE UK) and is advisable." Subscription – $6 (£3 UK) for 4 issues. "If we have a lot of work to read, of equal merit, then the work sent in by subscribers will be chosen first. No stories over 1,000 words, please. Free gift with every issue. U.S. payment should be either in bills, IRC's or cheque (but for cheques please add $5 to any overall price, due to bankcharges on overseas cheques; bills should be sent registered; 3 IRC's = $1/18 IRC's = $6). *P and F* will also be starting up a service for writers shortly. This merely involves sending details about yourself and your work, together with a story, or stories. We will then pass on to other publishers in the U.K. Writer, as we will send out 1 story for 2 IRC's (not excluding 1,000 words), and each story thereafter for 2 IRC's each. For airmail replies please double prices."

‡SCARP (II), % School of Creative Arts, University of Wollongong, Box 1144, Wollongong 2500 Australia. Editor: Ron Pretty. Circ. 1,000. Publishes 15,000-20,000 words of fiction annually. Published twice a year. "We look for fiction in a contemporary idiom, even if it uses a traditional form. Preferred length: 1,000-3,000 words. We're looking for energy, impact, quality." Payment: $20 (Australian) per 1,000 words; contributor's copies supplied. "Submit to reach us in April and/or August. Include SASE. In Australia the beginning writer faces stiff competition—the number of paying outlets is not increasing, but the number of capable writers is."

‡SEPIA (I), **Poetry & Prose Magazine**, Kawabata Press, Knill Cross House, Higher Anderton Rd., Millbrook, Nr Torpoint, Cornwall England. Editor-in-Chief: Collin David Webb. "Magazine for those interested in modern un-clichéd work." Contains 32 pages/issue; published 3 times/year. Pays one contributor's copy. Always include SAE with IRCs.

SLOW DANCER (II), Flat 4, 1 Park Valley, The Park, Nottingham NG7 1BS England. Fiction Editors: John Harvey and Jennifer Bailey. Circ. 500. Twice yearly. Reading period November 1-April 30. Averages 1-2 short stories per issue. Pays 2 contributor's copies. Back numbers from Alan Brooks, Box 3010, RFD 1, Lubec, ME 04652 for $4. Submissions must be sent to UK.

‡SMOKE (II), Windows Project, 40 Canning St., Liverpool L8 7NP England. Contact: Dave Ward. Magazine of poetry, fiction, art, long poems, collages, concrete art, photos, cartoons. "N.B. Fiction up to 2,000 words."

SOCIAL ALTERNATIVES, % Dept. of Government, University of Queensland, St. Lucia, Queensland 4067 Australia. Fiction Editor: Reba Gostand. Circ. 3,000. Publishes 2-3 stories in each quarterly issue. "The journal is socio-political, but stories of any theme or style will be considered. The criterion is excellence." Pays writers "if we have money—we usually don't." Writers receive one contributor's copy. Send "3 copies of story, immaculately presented so no sub-editing is necessary. SASE for return."

STAND MAGAZINE, 179 Wingrove Rd., Newcastle Upon Tyne, NE4 9DA England. Fiction Editor: Lorna Tracy. Circ. 4,500. Averages 16-20 stories/year. "*Stand* is an international quarterly publishing poetry, short stories, reviews, criticism and translations." Payment: £30 per 1,000 words of prose on publication; contributor's copies. "Read copies of the magazine before submitting. Enclose sufficient IRCs for return of mss/reply. No more than 6 poems or 2 short stories at any one time." Sponsors biennial short competition: First prize, $1,500. Send 2 IRCs for information.

STUDIO: A JOURNAL OF CHRISTIANS WRITING (II), 727 Peel St., Albury 2640 Australia. Fiction Editor: Paul Grover. Circ. 300. Averages 20-30 stories/year. "*Studio* publishes prose and poetry of literary merit, offers a venue for new and aspiring writers, and seeks to create a sense of community among Christians writing." Pays in copies. Sample copy $8. Subscription $37 for four issues (one year). International draft in Australian dollars.

TAK TAK TAK, P.O. Box 7, Bulwell, Nottingham NG6 OHW England. Fiction Editors: Andrew and Tim Brown. Circ. 400. "An annual anthology on a set theme containing several pieces of fiction. Also several books each year." *Tak Tak Tak* is a anthology with cassette for music and the spoken word. We use all sorts of fiction relevant to the theme, but for reasons of space it can't be too long. (2,500 words maximum)." Pays one contributor's copy. "Send a letter explaining what you want."

‡THE THIRD HALF MAGAZINE, "Amikeco," 16, Fane Close, Stamford, Lincolnshire PE9 1H9 England. Fiction Editor: Kevin Troop. "*The Third Half* literary magazine publishes mostly poetry, but editorial policy is to publish as much *short* short story writing as possible in each issue. Short stories especially for children, for use in the classroom, with 'questions' and 'work to do' are occasionally produced, along with poetry books, as separate editions. I wish to expand on this." Pays in contributor's copies.

‡TRAPANI NUOVA, Sicilian Antigruppo/Cross-Cultural Communications, Villa Schammachanat, Via Argenteria Km 4, Trapani, Sicily 91026 Italy. Editor: Nat Scammacca. "We publish materials already published elsewhere."

WESTERLY, c/o University of Western Australia, Nedlands, Western Australia 6009 Australia. A quarterly of poetry, prose and articles of a literary and cultural kind, giving special attention to Australia and Southeast Asia.

WORKS, 12 Blakestones Rd., Slaithwaite, Huddersfield HD7 5UQ England. Fiction Editor: D. Hughes. Circ. 1,000+. 70%+ of content is fiction. "52 pages speculative and imaginative fiction (SF) with poetry, illustrated." Quarterly. Price: Enclose IRC. $5 *cash only* for 1 issue, $10 *cash only* for 4 issues. Member of the New Science Fiction Alliance. Pays in copies. "All manuscripts should be accompanied by a SASE (in the UK). USA send 2 IRC's with ms, if disposable or 4 IRCs, if not. Usual maximum is 4,500 words."

‡THE WORLD OF ENGLISH, Box 1504, Beijing China. Fiction Editor: Chen Yu-lun. Circ. 300,000+. "We welcome contributions of short articles that would cater to the interest of our reading public, new and knowledgeable writings on technological finds, especially interesting stories and novels, etc. We can only pay in our currency which regrettably is inconvertible." Write for sample copy.

THE WRITERS' ROSTRUM (I), 14 Ardbeg Rd., Rothesay, Bute PA20 0NJ Scotland. Fiction Editor: Jenny Chaplin. Circ. 1,000. Publishes approx. 15 short stories annually. "My magazine, *The Writers' Rostrum*, has been described as 'cozy' and being like 'tea and cream buns on a Sunday afternoon.' From this, you will gather that I refuse to publish anything that is in any way controversial, political or obscene. Short stories are on such topics as family life, friendship, telepathy and other aspects of the supernatural. Also seasonal topics: beauties of nature, etc. Writers in Britain receive cheque (£1-£5) on publication, together with a copy of the particular issue in which their work appears. Writers abroad receive complimentary copy. Keep to the required wordage, 900 words maximum. If at all possible, study the magazine. Always send SASE and/or IRC. Where possible, I will suggest other UK markets, since my main aim is to help handicapped/beginners/retired people get started on the craft of writing and see their work published. All profits from The Writers' Rostrum are sent to a variety of medical charities, with main recipient being Parkinson's disease research funds."

‡WRITING WOMEN, 7 Cavendish Place, Newcastle Upon Tyne NE2 2NE England. Circ. 700-800. Publishes 12 stories per year. "We publish work by new and established women writers. Stories should be not more than 3,000 words. We pay £10 per 1,000 words." Contributors receive 2 copies of the issue in which they appear. "We can take 2-3 months to reach a decision."

Other literary and small circulation magazines

The following literary magazines appeared in the 1990 edition of *Novel and Short Story Writer's Market* but are not in the 1991 edition. Those publications whose editors did not respond to our request for an update of their listings may not have done so for a variety of reasons—they may be out of business, for example, or they may be overstocked with submissions. These "no responses" are listed with no additional explanation below. If an explanation was given, it appears in parenthesis next to the listing name. Note that literary magazines from outside the U.S. and Canada appear at the end of this list.

Abbey
Adara
The Adroit Expression (out of business)
Aegean Review
The Albany Review (no longer publishing)
Allegheny Review
Alternative Fiction & Poetry (out of business)
Amateur Writers Journal (asked to be left out this year)
The American Voice (asked to be deleted)
The Anglican Magazine (asked to be deleted)
Art:Mag
The Atavachron and All Our Yesterdays

Athena Incognito Magazine
Atlantis (asked to be left out this year)
Bad Newz
Ball State University Forum (no longer publishing)
Bitch
The Bloomsbury Review (asked to be deleted)
The Book of Spells
Brilliant Star
Bristlecone (out of business)
The Capilano Review
Chelsea
Choplogic (out of business)
Conditions
The Conspiracy of Silence
Cornfield Review (asked to be left out this year)
The Couch Potato Journal

Coydog Review (out of business)
The Crimson Full Moon
Cross-Canada Writer's Magazine (out of business)
Cube Literary Magazine (out of business)
Cutting Edge Irregular (out of business)
darknerve
Day Care and Early Education (no longer accepting fiction)
Dead of Night Magazine (out of business)
Dharma Combat
Encounters Magazine (no longer publishing)
The Evergreen Chronicles
(F.)lip

Feminist Baseball
Fiction Network Magazine (out of business)
Fighting Woman News
First Stories and Storyette
Formations Magazine
Galactic Discourse
Gargoyle Magazine
The Garland
Gateways (no longer publishing)
El Gato Tuerto
The Glens Falls Review (out of business)
Great River Review
Happiness Holding Tank (asked to be left out this year)
Harvest Magazine (out of business)
Hob-Nob
Ice River (out of business)
Impulse Magazine
The Independent Review
Inside Joke (out of business)
Jabberwocky (asked to be left out this year)
Jam To-Day (out of business)
Jest (out of business)
Jewish Currents Magazine (asked to be left out this year)
Journal of Quantum 'Pataphysics (asked to be left out this year)
Joyeux Erotique
Kabbalah Yichud
Kairos
Lake Street Review (no longer publishing)
Letters Magazine (asked to be left out this year)
Lilith Magazine (asked to be left out this year)
Lime Green Bulldozers (out of business)
Little Balkans Review
Lone Star
Lyra (asked to be left out this year)

m needle m (asked to be left out this year)
Meal, Ready-to-Eat
The Mickle Street Review
Microcosm
Midland Review
The Mind's Eye (no longer publishing)
The Mirror-Northern Report
Muse's Mill (moved; no forwarding address)
Musicworks (no longer publishing fiction)
Naked Man (no longer publishing)
New Pathways
Northeast Journal (out of business)
The Northern New England Review
Oak Square
On the Edge (no longer publishing)
Open Magazine
Pandora
Pencil Press Quarterly
Peregrine (asked to be left out this year)
Permafrost
The Pig Paper (no longer publishing)
Poetic Liberty (out of business)
Portents (out of business)
Poultry
Proem Canada (out of business)
Proof Rock
Ptolemy/The Browns Mills Review
Quarry West
Quimby
The Raddle Moon
The Reaper
The Reformed Journal (asked to be deleted)
Resonance
RFD
The Rose Arts Magazine (no longer publishing)
The Round Table

Science Fiction Randomly
Scifant
Sequoia
Serendipity (moved; no forwarding address)
Shenandoah (asked to be deleted)
Solid Copy (no longer publishing)
Spectrum
Stamp Axe (no longer publishing)
Starshore (out of business)
Stories
Studia Mystica
T.W.I.
Tapestry (no longer publishing)
Tentra Artnet BBS
Tidewater (moved; no forwarding address)
Timbuktu (out of business)
Treetop Panorama (ceased publication)
TV-TS Tapestry Journal (seldom takes fiction)
Union Street Review (asked to be deleted)
Unknowns
The Unspeakable Vision of the Individual
Var Tufa (asked to left out this year)
A Very Small Magazine
Wayside (asked to be left out this year)
West Coast Review (asked to be deleted)
What
Wild East (no longer publishing)
Witness PA (moved; no forwarding address)
Wyoming, the Hub of the Wheel (asked to be left out this year)
Yak (out of business)
The Yale Review (out of business)
Z Miscellaneous (not accepting fiction)

Other foreign literary and small circulation magazines

Ammonite
An Seanrvd
Brave New World
Cencrastus
Contrast
Dada Dance Magazine
Diliman Review
edge magazine (no longer publishing)
The Fred
Illuminations

Iron Magazine
The Magpie's Nest
Marang
Margin (out of business)
The Muse
Ninth Decade
Northern Perspective
Okike
Opossum
Outrider
Phlogiston

Probe
Prospice (out of business)
Rashi
Scripsi
Tears in the Fence
Think for Yourself/Flower Pot Press
Together
Verandah
Vigil
Writing (asked to be deleted)

Commercial Periodicals

It has not been a good year for commercial magazines. Faced with a slump in advertising sales, a possible recession and a planned postal rate hike, many magazines are struggling just to keep afloat. Several have changed hands, others have undergone radical redesigns, a few have attempted "repositioning" themselves with a new readership, while some have simply folded altogether. *Time* magazine recently dubbed all this twisting and turning the start of the "Big Shakeout."

Yet all is not doom and gloom. In a recent issue of *MagazineWeek*, American Express Publishing President Thomas Ryder predicted many magazines will emerge from the slump shaken, but stronger for it. Although far from the magazine boom of the early 1980s, experts still predict some growth in 1991. Despite the number of casualties, there were 584 new magazines last year. Specialized magazines, such as those focusing on a particular region, audience or subject, are actually doing quite well.

This year we have slightly more new listings than last. Most of the magazines listed in 1990 are listed again, with the notable exceptions of *Special Report: Fiction*, facing an unsure future, and *McCall's*, at their request. The list of markets added to this edition is diverse — from the environmental journal, *Buzzworm*, to the women's service magazine, *Woman's World*, to the new sports publication, *Prime Time Sports and Fitness*. Competition is keen, but there truly is something for just about everyone.

Keeping on top of it all

What does all this mean to fiction writers? It means there are still markets interested in and able to buy fiction, but the competition is getting fierce. It is more important now than ever to study the market carefully. For example, several well-known women's magazines have changed their formats and focus in an effort to boost sales. Even though you may have grown up with *McCall's* or *Woman's Day*, be sure to familiarize yourself with recent issues before submitting.

This leads to what editors have been telling us for years — READ the magazine before submitting. Marvin Gelbart, publisher of *American Accent Short Story Magazine* says, "Before sending a ms to every (or any) publisher, take time to check him out. Go to the library and look at the type of material he publishes, or pick up a copy of his publication. Ask yourself 'Do I fit into this category?' Investigate first; save time, money and anxiety."

After studying several copies, read the publication's listing and send for guidelines, if available. It is as important to keep up with policy changes as it is format, editorial or other changes. Some changes in policy have direct effects on fiction writers. *Good Housekeeping*, for example, has changed its policy on unsolicited submissions. To curb costs and reduce workload, the magazine now refuses to return unsolicited manuscripts at all (whether or not an SASE was included) and does not report or otherwise respond to inquiries. After a number of redesigns and format changes, *Ms.* magazine opted to abandon advertising altogether. The magazine is attempting to get back to its "political roots," a decision that could very well affect the type of fiction used, if any, as well as the amount of pages available for copy — fiction or nonfiction.

Do everything you can to make it easy for an editor to read your work. That is, make sure you contact the magazine in the way outlined in the listing or their guidelines. Only a few publications want queries first, but if one is required, send a brief, direct letter outlining your story idea. Cover letters can be very important to some editors, while others want to get right to the manuscript.

Be professional. There's no substitute for talent, but a manuscript that is messy, hard-to-read or full of grammatical or typing errors signals to most editors it is the work of an amateur and risks not being read at all. Make sure your name appears on each page and that pages are numbered. Again, read the submission information. Some editors ask for a brief bio and several this year asked for a word count at the top of the first page.

Of course, a professionally presented manuscript does only part of the job—it may attract an editor's attention, but more is needed to keep it. Editors look for crisp prose, realistic dialogue and interesting characters. They also seek fiction about subjects that are original, unique and appropriate to their readership.

Some visible trends

Interest in children's magazines and publications for parents continues to grow. One reason for this, of course, is the growing number of people of "childbearing" age. Another, more subtle reason, is the high interest many of the "baby boomers" seem to take in magazines and books of any sort. Whatever the reason, children's book and magazine publishing has led to new opportunities for both children's writers and for writers interested in stories about parenthood and family.

Among some of the magazines new to this edition are *The Gifted Child Today*, *Vancouver Child* and *The Baby Connection News Journal* for parents and *Ladybug* for children. The established magazines are also picking up on the strong interest. *Highlights* magazine has increased its payment for stories and has recently started a book publishing division, Boyds Mills Press.

Buzzworm, new to this edition, is looking for what the editors call "eco-fiction." This may be an early indication of an interest in fiction reflecting the growing concern for the environment. Close to eco-fiction is nature writing. For years, nature writing has combined nonfiction and fiction in a unique form. Outdoor and adventure lifestyle magazines are also interested in this type of fiction.

Regional publications also remain strong markets. As with magazines focusing on a hobby, sport or other specialized feature, these magazines are looking for fiction written specifically for them. Editors at New England magazines generally want New England settings and editors of magazines about golf are on constant alert for good fiction about the sport.

Especially in these tense times, magazines change editors, owners, location and policies quickly. In addition to reading the listings here and studying recent issues, watch the newsstand for new publications, redesigns and other changes. The markets column in *Writer's Digest*, other writers' publications and organization newsletters can also alert you to trends in the market.

To find markets in this section for particular categories of fiction, check the Commercial Periodicals section of the Category Index located just before the Markets Index at the back of the book.

Here's the ranking system used to categorize the listings in the section:

   I **Periodical encourages beginning or unpublished writers to submit work for consideration and publishes new writers frequently;**

  II **Periodical publishes work by established writers and occasionally by new writ-**

ers of exceptional talent;

III Magazine does not encourage beginning writers; prints mostly writers with substantial previous publication credits and very few new writers;

IV Special-interest or regional magazine, open only to writers on certain topics or from certain geographical areas.

ABORIGINAL SCIENCE FICTION (II, IV), Box 2449, Woburn MA 01888-0849. Editor: Charles C. Ryan. Magazine: 8½ × 11; 68 pages; 40 lb. paper; 60 lb. cover; 4-color illustrations; photos. "*Aboriginal Science Fiction* is looking for good science fiction stories. While 'hard' science fiction will get the most favorable attention, *Aboriginal Science Fiction* also wants good action-adventure stories, *good* space opera, humor and science fantasy for adult science fiction readers." Bimonthly. Estab. 1986. Circ. 31,000 + .
Needs: Science fiction. Original, previously unpublished work only. "No fantasy, sword and sorcery, horror, or Twilight-Zone type stories." Receives 120-140 unsolicited mss/week. Buys 5-7 mss/issue; 30-42 mss/year. Publishes ms 6 months to 1 year after acceptance. Agented fiction 5%. Published work by Larry Niven, David Brin and Walter Jon Williams; published new writers within the last year. Length: 6,000 words minimum; 4,500 words maximum. Publishes short shorts "no shorter than 1,500-2,000 words for fiction. Jokes may be 50-150 words." Sometimes comments on rejected mss.
How to Contact: Send complete ms. Reports on mss in 2-3 months. SASE. Good quality photocopied submissions OK. Accepts computer printout submissions. Sample copy for $3.50 plus 50¢ postage and handling. Fiction guidelines for #10 SAE and 1 first class stamp.
Payment: Pays "$250 flat" and 2 contributor's copies.
Terms: Pays on publication for first North American serial rights and non-exclusive reprint and foreign options.
Advice: "Stories with the best chance of acceptance will make unique use of science ideas, have lively, convincing characters, an ingenious plot, a powerful and well integrated theme, and use an imaginative setting. We recommend you read *Aboriginal Science Fiction* to obtain an idea of the type of stories we publish, and we also recommend you read other science fiction publications. Watching science fiction on television or at the movies will not provide adequate experience or background to write a good science fiction story."

AIM MAGAZINE (I, II), 7308 S. Eberhart Ave., Chicago IL 60619. (312)874-6184. Editor: Ruth Apilado. Fiction Editor: Mark Boone. Newspaper: 8½ × 11; 48 pages; slick paper; photos and illustrations. "Material of social significance: down-to-earth gut. Personal experience, inspirational." For "high school, college and general public." Quarterly. Published special fiction issue last year; plans another. Estab. 1973. Circ. 10,000.
Needs: Open. No "religious" mss. Receives 25 unsolicited mss/month. Buys 15 mss/issue; 60 mss/year. Recently published work by Thomas J. Cottle, Karl Damgaard, Richie Zeiler; published new writers within the last year. Length: 800-1,000 words average. Publishes short shorts. Sometimes comments on rejected mss.
How to Contact: Send complete ms. SASE with a cover letter and author's photograph. Simultaneous submissions OK. Accepts computer printout submissions. Sample copy for $3.50 with SAE (9 × 12) and $1 postage. Fiction guidelines for #10 envelope and 1 first class stamp.
Payment: Pays $15-25.
Terms: Pays on publication for first rights.
Advice: "Search for those in your community who are making unselfish contributions to their community and write about them. Write from the heart."

ALIVE NOW! (I, II), The Upper Room, Box 189, Nashville TN 37202-0189. (615)340-7218. Editor: Mary Ruth Coffman. Magazine of devotional writing and visuals for young adults. Bimonthly. Estab. 1971. Circ. 75,000.
Needs: Religious/inspirational. Buys 4 mss/issue; 12 mss/year. Length: 10 words minimum; 300 words maximum.
How to Contact: Send complete mss with SASE. Photocopied and previously published submissions OK. Accepts computer printout submissions. Prefers letter-quality. Reports in 3 months on mss. Sample copy free. Fiction guidelines free. Enclose SASE.

Payment: Pays $5-25; 12 contributor's copies.
Terms: Pays on publication for first rights, one-time rights, newspaper and periodical rights. Occasionally buys reprints.

ALOHA, The Magazine of Hawaii and the Pacific (IV), Davick Publishing Co., 49 South Hotel St., Suite 309, Honolulu HI 96813. (808)523-9871. FAX: (808)533-2055. Editor: Cheryl Tsutsumi. Magazine about the 50th state. Upscale demographics. Bimonthly. Estab. 1979. Circ. 65,000.
Needs: "Only fiction that illuminates the Hawaiian experience. No stories about tourists in Waikiki or beachboys or contrived pidgin dialogue." Receives 3-4 unsolicited mss/month. Length: 2,000 words average.
How to Contact: Send complete ms. Reports in 2 months. Publishes ms up to 1 year after acceptance. SASE. Photocopied submissions OK. Accepts computer printout submissions. Sample copy $2.95.
Payment: 10¢/word minimum.
Terms: Pays on publication for first-time rights.
Advice: "Submit only fiction that is truly local in character. Do not try to write anything about Hawaii if you have not experienced this culturally different part of America."

‡AMAZING® STORIES (II), TSR, Inc., Box 111, Lake Geneva WI 53147. (414)248-3625. Editor: Mr. Kim Mohan. Magazine: 8⅜ × 10¾; 96 (or more) pages; 80 lb. enamel; 100 lb. Northcote cover stock; perfect bound; color illustrations; rarely b&w illustrations; rarely photos. Magazine of science fiction, fantasy and horror fiction stories for adults and young adults. Monthly. Estab. 1926. Circ. 20,000.
Needs: Science fiction, fantasy, horror. "We prefer SF to dominate our content, but will not turn away a well-written story regardless of genre. Low priority to heroic, pseudo-Medieval fantasy; no hack-n'-slash or teen exploitation horror." Receives 700-1,000 unsolicited fiction mss/month. Buys 8-10 mss/issue; 100-120 mss/year. Approximately 5% of fiction is agented. Recently published work by Pamela Sargent, Paul Di Filippo, John Brunner, David Brin; published new writers within the last year. Length: 1,000 words minimum; 25,000 words maximum; will consider serialization of or excerpts from longer works. Usually critiques rejected mss.
How to Contact: Send complete ms with cover letter (list other professional credits in SF, fantasy or horror). SASE. Photocopied submissions OK. Accepts computer printout submissions. No simultaneous submissions. Reports in 2 months on mss. Publishes ms 9-18 months after acceptance. Sample copy $5. Fiction guidelines free with #10 SASE.
Payment: Pays 6-10¢/word.
Terms: Pays on acceptance for first worldwide rights in the English language. Sends prepublication galleys to author.
Advice: "*AMAZING® Stories*, formerly a digest-sized publication, has undergone a major format change, but the fiction content of the magazine is essentially the same. We are interested in all forms of science fiction, with an emphasis on strong plot lines and believable characterization. Avoid rehashes of old ideas and stereotypical story lines or characters. We encourage writers to experiment with innovative styles and approaches, but not at the expense of comprehensibility. All of that advice holds true for fantasy and horror as well. Send us a story that deserves to be called Amazing, and we'll find a place for it."

AMERICAN ACCENT SHORT STORY MAGAZINE (I), Box 80270, Las Vegas NV 89180. (702)648-2669. Publisher/Editor: Marvin Gelbart. Editor: Carol Colina. Magazine: 5⅛ × 7¼; 160 pages; newsprint paper; 70 lb. coated cover; some illustrations. "A forum for introducing new authors to the reading public—all genres." Monthly. Estab. 1988.
Needs: Adventure, contemporary, fantasy, historical, humor/satire, literary, mainstream, romance (contemporary), science fiction and suspense/mystery. Buys approx. 10 mss/issue. Length: 4,000 words preferred; 1,000 words minimum; 5,000 words maximum.
How to Contact: Send complete ms with cover letter. Reports in 4 months. SASE. Simultaneous and photocopied submissions OK. Sample copy for $2.25; fiction guidelines free with a #10 SASE.
Payment: Pays $50-250; contributor's copies.
Terms: Pays on publication for first North American serial rights or other rights.
Advice: "Before sending a ms to every publisher, take time to check him out. Go to the library and look at the type of material he publishes, or pick up a copy of his publication. Ask yourself, 'Do I fit into this category?' Investigate first; save time, money and anxieties."

AMERICAN ATHEIST (II, IV), A Journal of Atheist News and Thought, American Atheist Press, Box 140195, Austin TX 78714-0195. (512)458-1244. Editor: R. Murray-O'Hair. Magazine: 8½×11; 56 pages; 40 lb. offset paper; 80 lb. glossy cover; illustrations and photographs. "The *American Atheist* is devoted to the history and lifestyle of atheism, as well as critiques of religion. It attempts to promote an understanding of atheism, while staying aware of religious intrusions into modern life. Most of its articles are aimed at a general—but atheistic—readership. Most readers are college or self-educated." Monthly. Estab. 1958. Circ. 30,000.
Needs: Contemporary, feminist, historical (general), humor/satire, atheist, anti-religious. "All material should have something of particular interest to atheists." No religious fiction. Receives 0-6 mss/month. "We would like to publish 1 story per issue; we do *not* receive enough quality mss to do so." Publishes ms "1-3 months" after acceptance. Length: 2,000-3,000 words preferred; 800 words minimum; 5,000 words maximum. Sometimes critiques rejected mss.
How to Contact: Send complete ms with cover letter and biographical material. Reports in 10 weeks. SASE. Photocopied submissions OK. Accepts computer printout submissions. Accepts electronic submissions, "Word Perfect compatible or in ASCII. Should be accompanied by printout." Sample copy 9×12 SAE or label. Fiction guidelines for #10 SASE.
Payment: $15/1,000 words, free subscription to the magazine and contributor's copies.
Terms: Pays on acceptance for one-time rights.
Advice: "Our magazine has a preponderance of serious 'heavy' reading matter. Sometimes our readers need a break from it. There's so little atheist fiction, we would like to encourage it."

THE AMERICAN CITIZEN ITALIAN PRESS, 13681 "V" St., Omaha NE 68137. Editor: Diana C. Failla. Magazine. Quarterly (soon to be monthly).
Needs: Ethnic, historical (general), sports, celebrity, human interest, mainstream and translations. Receives 4-5 unsolicited mss/month. Buys 1-2 mss/issue. Length: 80 words minimum; 1,200 words maximum. Publishes short shorts.
How to Contact: Send complete ms with cover letter. Reports in 1 month on queries. Simultaneous and photocopied submissions OK. Accepts computer printout submissions. Sample copy and fiction guidelines for 9×12 SAE.
Payment: Pays $20-25.
Terms: Pays on publication for one-time rights.

AMERICAN DANE (II, IV), The Danish Brotherhood in America, 3717 Harney, Box 31748, Omaha NE 68131. (402)341-5049. Editor: Jennifer Denning. Magazine: 8¼×11; 20-28 pages; 40 lb paper; slick cover; illustrations and photos. "The *American Dane* is the official publication of the Danish Brotherhood. Corporate purpose of the Danish Brotherhood is to promote and perpetuate Danish culture and tradition and to provide Fraternal benefits and family protection." Monthly. Estab. 1916. Circ. 8,900.
Needs: "Danish!" Receives 4 unsolicited fiction mss/month. Accepts 1 ms up to one year after acceptance. Length: 1,000 words average; 3,000 words maximum. Publishes short shorts.
How to Contact: Query first. SASE. Simultaneous submissions OK. Accepts computer printout submissions. Sample copy for $1 and 9×12 SAE with 54¢ postage. Fiction guidelines free for 4×9½ SAE and 1 first class stamp.
Payment: Pays $15-50.
Terms: Pays on publication for first rights. Publication not copyrighted.
Advice: "Think Danish!"

THE AMERICAN NEWSPAPER CARRIER (II), Box 2225, Kernersville NC 27285. (919)788-4336. Editor: Will H. Lowry. Newsletter: 9×12; 4 pages; slick paper; b&w illustrations and photos. "A motivational newsletter publishing upbeat articles—mystery, humor, adventure and inspirational material for newspaper carriers (younger teenagers, male and female)." Monthly. Estab. 1927.
Needs: Adventure, comics, humor/satire, inspirational, suspense/mystery and young adult/teen. No erotica, fantasy, feminist, gay, juvenile, lesbian, preschool, psychic/supernatural or serialized/excerpted novel. Receives approximately 12 unsolicited mss/month. Buys 1 ms/issue; 12 mss/year. "About all" of

The double dagger before a listing indicates that the listing is new in this edition. New markets are often the most receptive to freelance contributions.

fiction is agented. Published new writers within the last year. Length: approximately 1,000 words average; 800 words minimum; 1,200 words maximum. Publishes short shorts of 1,000 words. Rarely critiques rejected mss.
How to Contact: Send complete ms. Reports in 1 month. Publishes ms 3-6 months after acceptance. SASE. Accepts computer printout submissions. Free sample copy and fiction guidelines with #10 SAE and 1 first class stamp for each.
Payment: Pays $25.
Terms: Pays on acceptance for all rights.
Advice: "We prefer that stories concern or refer to newspaper carriers. Well-written upbeat stories—happy and humorous—are rare."

AMERICAN SQUAREDANCE (IV), Burdick Enterprises, Box 488, Huron OH 44839. (419)433-2188. Editors: Stan and Cathie Burdick. Magazine: 5×8½; 100 pages; 50 lb. offset paper; glossy 60 lb. cover stock; illustrations; photos. Magazine about square dancing. Monthly. Estab. 1945. Circ. 20,000.
Needs: Adventure, fantasy, historical, humor/satire, romance, science fiction and western. Must have square dance theme. Published work by John Heisey, Marilyn Dove, David Stone. Buys 2+ mss/year. Length: 2,500 words average. Publishes short stories of 1,000 words average.
How to Contact: Send complete ms with SASE and cover letter with bio. Reports in 2 weeks on queries. Publishes ms within 6 months after acceptance. Free sample copy. Free fiction guidelines.
Payment: Pays $2/column inch minimum; free magazine subscription or free contributor's copies.
Terms: Pays on publication for all rights.

ANALOG SCIENCE FICTION/SCIENCE FACT (II), Davis Publications, Inc., 380 Lexington Ave., New York NY 10017. (212)557-9100. Editor: Stanley Schmidt. Magazine: 5³⁄₁₆×7⅜; 192 pages; illustrations (drawings); photos. "Well written science fiction based on speculative ideas and fact articles on topics on the present and future frontiers of research. Our readership includes intelligent laymen and/or those professionally active in science and technology." Thirteen times yearly. Estab. 1930. Circ. 100,000.
Needs: Science fiction and serialized novels. "No stories which are not truly science fiction in the sense of having a plausible speculative idea *integral to the story*." Buys 4-8 mss/issue. Receives 300-500 unsolicited fiction mss/month. Publishes short shorts. Approximately 30% of fiction is agented. Recently published work by Lois McMaster Bujold, Joe Haldeman, Jerry Oltion, Timothy Zahn and Charles Sheffield; published new writers within the last year. Length: 2,000-80,000 words. Critiques rejected mss "when there is time." Sometimes recommends other markets.
How to Contact: Send complete ms with SASE. Cover letter with "anything that I need to know before reading the story, e.g. that it's a rewrite I suggested or that it incorporates copyrighted material. Otherwise, no cover letter is needed." Query with SASE only on serials. Accepts computer printout submissions. Reports in 1 month on both query and ms. Free guidelines with SASE. Sample copy for $2.50.
Payment: 5¢-8¢/word.
Terms: Pays on acceptance for first North American serial rights and nonexclusive foreign rights. Sends galleys to author.
Advice: Mss are rejected because of "inaccurate science; poor plotting, characterization or writing in general. We literally only have room for 1-2% of what we get. Many stories are rejected not because of anything conspicuously *wrong*, but because they lack anything sufficiently *special*. What we buy must stand out from the crowd. Fresh, thought-provoking ideas are important. Familiarize yourself with the magazine—but don't try to imitate what we've already published."

ARIZONA COAST (II), Hale Communications, Inc., 912 Joshua, Parker AZ 85344. (602)669-6464. Editor: Jerry Hale. Magazine: 5½×8½; 40 pages; gloss 70#; illustrations; photos. Publication prints stories about tourism, old West, lifestyle for young travel oriented family audiences, snowbirds and senior citizens. Bimonthly. Estab. 1988. Circ. 15,000.
Needs: Condensed/excerpted novel, historical (general), senior citizen/retirement, serialized novel, western. Receives 1 unsolicited mss/month. Accepts 1 ms/issue; 6 mss/year. Publishes ms within 6 months after acceptance. Publishes short shorts. Sometimes critiques rejected mss and recommends other markets.
How to Contact: Send complete ms with cover letter. Reports in 2 months. Simultaneous submissions OK. Computer printout submissions are acceptable. Accepts electronic submissions. Sample copy free.

Payment: Pays free subscription to magazine.
Terms: Acquires one-time rights.

ART TIMES (II), A Cultural and Creative Journal, CSS Publications, Inc., 7484 Fite Rd., Saugerties NY 12477. (914)246-6944. Editor: Raymond J. Steiner. Magazine: 12×15; 20 pages; Jet paper and cover; illustrations; photos. "Arts magazine covering the disciplines for an over 40, affluent, arts-conscious and literate audience." Monthly. Estab. 1984. Circ. 15,000.
Needs: Adventure, contemporary, ethnic, fantasy, feminist, gay, historical, humor/satire, lesbian, literary, mainstream and science fiction. "We seek quality literary pieces. No violence, sexist, erotic, juvenile, racist, romantic, political, etc." Receives 30-50 mss/month. Buys 1 ms/issue; 11 mss/year. Publishes ms within 18-24 months of acceptance. Length: 1,500 words maximum. Publishes short shorts.
How to Contact: Send complete ms with cover letter. Reports in 6 months. SASE. Simultaneous and photocopied submissions OK. Accepts computer printout submissions; also electronic submissions via disk. Sample copy for $1.75, 9×12 SAE and 3 first class stamps. Fiction guidelines for #10 SAE and 1 first class stamp.
Payment: Pays $15, free subscription to magazine (one year); six contributor's copies.
Terms: Pays on publication for first North American serial rights.

ISAAC ASIMOV'S SCIENCE FICTION MAGAZINE (II), Davis Publications, Inc., 380 Lexington Ave., New York NY 10017. Editor: Gardner Dozois. Magazine: 5³⁄₁₆×7⅜ (trim size); 192 pages; 29 lb. newspaper; 70 lb. to 8 pt. CIS cover stock; illustrations; rarely photos. Magazine consists of science fiction and fantasy stories for adults and young adults. 13 issues a year. Estab. 1977. Circ. 120,000.
Needs: Science fiction and fantasy. No horror or psychic/supernatural. Buys 10 mss/issue. Publishes short shorts. Receives approximately 800 unsolicited fiction mss each month. Approximately 30% of fiction is agented. Recently published work by George Alec Effinger, Connie Willis, Walter Jon Williams, Gregory Benford and Judith Moffett; published new writers in the last year. Length: up to 20,000 words. Critiques rejected mss "when there is time." Sometimes recommends other markets.
How to Contact: Send complete ms with SASE. Photocopied submissions OK. Accepts letter-quality computer printout submissions only. Reports in 1-2 months on mss. Publishes ms 6-12 months after acceptance. Free fiction guidelines with #10 SASE. Sample copy $2.
Payment: Pays 6¢-8¢/word for stories up to 7,500 words; 5¢/word for stories over 12,500; $450 for stories between those limits.
Terms: Pays on acceptance for first North American serial rights plus specified foreign rights, as explained in contract. Very rarely buys reprints. Sends galleys to author.
Advice: We are "looking for character stories rather than those emphasizing technology or science. New writers will do best with a story under 10,000 words. Every new science fiction or fantasy film seems to 'inspire' writers—and this is not a desirable trend. We consider every submission. We published several first stories last year. Be sure to be familiar with our magazine and the type of story we like; workshops and lots of practice help."

THE ASSOCIATE REFORMED PRESBYTERIAN (II), The Associate Reformed Presbyterian, Inc., 1 Cleveland St., Greenville SC 29601. (803)232-8297. Editor: Ben Johnston. Magazine: 8½×11; 32-48 pages; 50 lb. offset paper; illustrations; photos. "We are the official magazine of our denomination. Articles generally relate to activities within the denomination—conferences, department work, etc., with a few special articles that would be of general interest to readers." Monthly. Estab. 1976. Circ. 7,000.
Needs: Contemporary, juvenile, religious/inspirational, spiritual and young adult/teen. "Stories should portray Christian values. No retelling of Bible stories or 'talking animal' stories. Stories for youth should deal with resolving real issues for young people." Receives 30-40 unsolicited fiction mss/month. Buys 1 ms/some months; 10-12 mss/year. Publishes ms within 1 year after acceptance. Recently published work by Connie Johnston, Jane Marlow and Harriet Spry. Length: 300-750 words (children); 1,250 words maximum (youth). Sometimes critiques rejected mss. Occasionally recommends other markets.

Market categories: (I) Beginning; (II) General; (III) Prestige; (IV) Specialized.

How to Contact: Query and cover letter preferred. Reports in 6 weeks on queries and mss. Simultaneous submissions OK. Sample copy $1.50; fiction guidelines for #10 SAE and 1 first class stamp.
Payment: Pays $20-50 and contributor's copies.
Terms: Buys first rights.

ATLANTA SINGLES MAGAZINE, Hudson Brooke Publications, P.O. Box 49286, Atlanta GA 30359. (404)636-2260. Editor: Margaret Anthony. Magazine: 8½×11; 80 pages; 50 lb. paper; 80 lb. cover; illustrations; photographs. "Magazine for singles; publishes mostly nonfiction work by local writers. Occasional fiction, but not often." Bimonthly. Estab. 1977. Circ. 15,000.
Needs: Contemporary, humor/satire, single life. No sci-fi or erotica. Receives 20-25 unsolicited mss/ month. Accepts up to 3-5 mss/year. Publishes ms 3-6 months after acceptance. Length: 1,500 words average; 1,000 words minimum; 2,500 words maximum. Sometimes critiques rejected mss and recommends other markets.
How to Contact: Query first or send complete ms with cover letter. "Include a short bio and areas of interest in cover letter." Reports in 1 month. SASE. Simultaneous, photocopied and reprint submissions OK. Accepts computer printout submissions. Sample copy for $2. Fiction guidelines free.
Payment: Pays $100-300.
Terms: Pays on publication for one-time rights.

THE ATLANTIC ADVOCATE (I, II, IV), University Press of New Brunswick Ltd., Box 3370, Fredericton, New Brunswick E3B 5A2 Canada. (506)452-6671. Editor: Marilee Little. Magazine: 8¼×10⅞; 64 pages; coated offset paper and cover; illustrations; photos. Magazine of the Atlantic Provinces of Canada—Nova Scotia, New Brunswick, Prince Edward Island and Newfoundland. For "audience 25 years and over." Monthly. Estab. 1956. Circ. 30,000.
Needs: Historical (general), humor/satire and regional. Nothing "offensive or in poor taste." Recently published work by Elda Cadogan, Eric Cameron and Muriel Miller. Receives 5 unsolicited mss/month. Buys 20 mss/year. "I plan to publish more short stories—at least one piece of fiction per issue." Length: 1,000-1,200 words average; 1,500 words maximum. Occasionally comments on rejected mss.
How to Contact: Send in mss. Reports in 3-4 weeks. Accepts computer printout submissions. Prefers letter-quality. Fiction guidelines free.
Payment: Pays 8¢-10¢/word and contributor's copies; charge for extras.
Terms: Pays on publication for first North American serial rights.

ATLANTIC MONTHLY (II), 745 Boylston St., Boston MA 02116. (617)536-9500. FAX: (617)536-3975. Editor: William Whitworth. Senior Editor: Michael Curtis. General magazine for the college educated with broad cultural interests. Monthly. Estab. 1857. Circ. 500,000.
Needs: Literary and contemporary. "Seeks fiction that is clear, tightly written with strong sense of 'story' and well-defined characters." Buys 15-18 stories/year. Receives approximately 1,000 unsolicited fiction mss each month. Published work by Alice Munro, E.S. Goldman, Charles Baxter and T.C. Boyle; published new writers within the last year. Preferred length: 2,000-6,000 words.
How to Contact: Send cover letter and complete ms with SASE. "Grudgingly" accepts dot-matrix submissions. Prefers letter-quality. Reports in 2 months on mss.
Payment: Pays $2,500/story.
Terms: Pays on acceptance for first North American serial rights.
Advice: When making first contact, "cover letters are sometimes helpful, particularly if they cite prior publications or involvement in writing programs. Common mistakes: excessive cuteness, too lengthy a list of prior publications."

ATLANTIC SALMON JOURNAL (IV), The Atlantic Salmon Federation, 1435 St. Alexandre #1030, Montreal, Quebec H3A 2G4 Canada. (514)842-8059. Editor: Terry Davis. Magazine: 8½×11; 48-56 pages; illustrations; photographs. Conservation of Atlantic salmon: History, research, angling, science and management articles for conservationists, biologists, anglers and politicians. Quarterly. Estab. 1952. Circ. 20,000.

Read the Business of Fiction section to learn the correct way to prepare and submit a manuscript.

Needs: Historical (general), humor/satire. Receives 2-3 unsolicited mss/month. Buys 2 mss/issue. Publishes ms 2-6 months after acceptance. Length: 2,000-3,000 words average; 1,500 words minimum; 3,000 words maximum. Publishes short shorts.

How to Contact: Query with clips of published work or send complete manuscript with cover letter. Reports in 4-6 weeks on queries; 6-8 weeks on mss. SASE. Simultaneous submissions OK. Accepts computer printout submissions. Accepts electronic submissions via IBM floppy diskette, Wordstar or Word-Perfect. Sample copy for 9×12 SAE and 51¢ postage. Fiction guidelines for #8 or #10 SAE and 39¢ postage.

Payment: Pays $50-350 and contributor's copies.

Terms: Pays on publication for first rights or first North American serial rights.

‡**THE BABY CONNECTION NEWS JOURNAL (IV)**, Parent Education for Infant Development, P.O. Drawer 13320, San Antonio TX 78213. (512)342-INFA [4632]. Editor: G. Morris. Newspaper: 35″ web press; 10¾×16; 16 pages; newsprint paper; newsprint cover; illustrations and photographs. "Material on pregnancy, infant sensory development, birthing and breastfeeding for new and expectant parents, midwives, nurses, ob/gyn's, tots." Bimonthly. Estab. 1986. Circ. 36.000.

Needs: Humor/satire, mainstream, preschool (1-4 years), prose poem, romance (contemporary), pregnancy. "We offer tot pages—fiction for beginner readers—we don't want, 'See Jane run.' No out-of-touch, mystical or crude, rude, demeaning fiction." Receives 6-10 unsolicited mss/month. Accepts 2-3 mss/issue; 18-20 mss/year. Publishes ms 6-8 weeks after acceptance. Recently published work by Marc Swan, George White. Length: 350 words average; 300 words minimum; 600 words maximum. Publishes short shorts.

How to Contact: Query with clips of published work. Send complete manuscript with cover letter. "Always include a personal bio—not all about works published but info. on the writer personally. Married? Children? Hobbies? Our readers like to feel they know the writers personally." SASE. "Always include a 10×13 envelope with $1.50 postage affixed. We will mail past copies of our newspaper if your manuscript is rejected so you can understand what our journal is about. If we accept your manuscript we use this 10×13 envelope to mail you 10 copies of your published work." Sample copy for 10×13 SAE with 2 first class stamps. Fiction guidelines for #10 SAE and 1 first class stamp.

Payment: Pays in contributor's copies. Charges for extras.

Terms: Acquires all rights.

Advice: "We especially encourage the male perspective. Everyone knows about kids and babies—so a fiction base should be a breeze for our selected themes of birthing, pregnancy, raising kids, finding time for self and spouse, family values."

BALLOON LIFE, The Magazine for Hot Air Ballooning (II,IV), 2145 Dale Ave., Sacramento CA 95815. (916)922-9648. Editor: Glen Moyer. Magazine: 8½×11; 48+ pages; 80 lb. Tahoe Gloss; color, b&w photos. "Sport of hot air ballooning. Readers participate in hot air ballooning as pilots, crew, official observers at events and spectators."

Needs: Humor/satire, sports and hot air ballooning. "Manuscripts should involve the sport of hot air ballooning in any aspect." Buys 4-6 mss/year. Publishes ms within 3-4 months after acceptance. Published work by Carl Kohler and Lorna Powers; published new writers within the last year. Length: 800 words minimum; 1,500 words maximum; 1,200 words average. Publishes 400-500 word shorts. Sometimes critiques rejected mss and recommends other markets.

How to Contact: Send complete ms with cover letter that includes Social Security number. Reports in 3 weeks on queries; 2 weeks on mss. SASE. Simultaneous, photocopied and reprint submissions OK. Accepts computer printout submissions. Sample copy for 9×12 SAE and $1.65 postage. Fiction guidelines for #10 SAE and 1 first class stamp.

Payment: Pays $25-75 and contributor's copies.

Terms: Pays on publication for first North American serial, one-time or other rights. 50-100% kill fee.

Advice: "Generally the magazine looks for humor pieces that can provide a light-hearted change of pace from the technical and current event articles. An example of a work we used was titled 'Balloon Astrology' and dealt with the character of a hot air balloon based on what sign it was born (made) under."

BALTIMORE JEWISH TIMES (II, IV), 2104 N. Charles St., Baltimore MD 21218. (301)752-3504. Local News Editor: Barbara Pash. Magazine: 160 pages a week, average; illustrations; photos. Magazine with subjects of interest to Jewish readers. Weekly. Estab. 1918. Circ. 19,000.

Needs: Contemporary Jewish themes only. Receives 7-10 unsolicited fiction mss/month. Buys 10-15 mss/year. Length: 3,500 words maximum (or 6-15 typed pages). Occasionally critiques rejected mss.
How to Contact: Send complete ms. Simultaneous, photocopied and previously published submissions OK "on occasion." Accepts computer printout submissions; prefers letter-quality. Reports in 2 months on mss. Sample copy $2 and legal-size envelope.
Payment: Pays $35-150.
Terms: Pays on publication.

BEAR (IV), Masculinity . . . without the trappings, COA, 2215 R Market St. #148, San Francisco CA 94114. (415)552-1506. FAX: (415)552-3244. Editor: Richard H. Bulger. Magazine: 60-120 pages; Vista paper; 70 lb. gloss cover stock; illustrations and photos. "Bear is about the average American working man—who happens to be gay. For gay men 25-55." Bimonthly. Estab. 1987. Circ. 40,000.
Needs: Confession, erotica, humor/satire and serialized novel. "Must be sex-positive. Don't make a big deal about an individual's sexual preference. Use masculine American archetypes. No youth-oriented fiction; sex-negative or self-hating pieces; leather sex." Plans to publish special fiction issue or anthology in the future. Receives 10-15 unsolicited mss/month. Buys 1-2 mss/issue. Publishes ms 3-6 months after acceptance. Published work by Jay Shaffer, Furr and C.C. Ryder. Length: 500 words minimum; 3,000 words average. Publishes short stories. Sometimes critiques rejected mss and recommends other markets.
How to Contact: Send complete ms with cover letter that includes Social Security number. Reports in 2-3 weeks on queries; 1-2 months on mss. SASE. Simultaneous, photocopied and reprint submissions OK. Accepts computer printout submissions. Prefers electronic submissions via disk or modem. Sample copy $6. Fiction guidelines for #10 SAE and 1 first class stamp.
Payment: Pays $25-150 and 1 contributors copy for first North American serial and first rights.
Terms: Pays half on acceptance, half on publication. 50% kill fee.

BECKETT BASEBALL CARD MONTHLY (IV), Statabase, 4887 Alpha Rd., Suite 200, Dallas TX 75244. (214)991-6657. Editor: Dr. James Beckett. Fiction Editor: Jay Johnson. Magazine: 8½×11; 96 pages; coated glossy paper; 8 pt. Sterling cover; 12 illustrations; 100+ photographs. "Collecting baseball cards is a leisure-time avocation. It's wholesome and something the entire family can do together. We emphasize its positive aspects. For card collectors and sports enthusiasts, 6-60." Monthly. Estab. 1984. Circ. 900,000 paid.
Needs: Humor/satire, sports, young adult/teen (10-18 years). "Sports hero worship; historical fiction involving real baseball figures; fictionalizing specific franchises of national interest such as the Yankees, Dodgers or Mets." No fiction that is "unrealistic sportswise." Publishes ms 4-6 months after acceptance. Length: 1,500 words average; 2,500 words maximum. Publishes short shorts. Sometimes comments on rejected mss or recommends other markets "if we feel we can help the reader close the gap between rejection and acceptance."
How to Contact: Send complete ms with cover letter. Include Social Security number. Reports in 6 weeks. SASE. Will consider reprints "if prior publication is in a very obscure or very prestigious publication." Accepts computer printout submissions. Sample copy $3. Fiction guidelines free.
Payment: Pays $80-400.
Terms: Pays on acceptance for first rights.
Advice: "Fiction must be baseball oriented and accessible to both pre-teenagers and adults; fiction must stress redeeming social values; fictionalization must involve the heroes of the game (past or present) or a major-league baseball franchise with significant national following. The writer must have a healthy regard for standard English usage. A prospective writer must examine several issues of our publication prior to submission. Our publication is extremely successful in our genre, and our writers must respect the sensivities of our readers. We are different from other sports publications, and a prospective writer must understand our distinctiveness to make a sale here."

‡BEPUZZLED (II,IV), Lombard Marketing, Inc., 45 Wintonbury Ave., Bloomfield CT 06002. (203)286-4222. Editor: Luci Seccareccia. "Mystery jigsaw puzzles . . . includes short mystery story with clues contained in puzzle picture to solve the mystery for preschool, 8-12 year olds, adults." Biannually. Estab. 1987.
Needs: Mystery: Adventure, juvenile, mainstream, preschool, young adult, suspense--all with mystery theme. Receives 3 unsolicited fiction mss/month. Buys 6 mss/year. Publishes ms 6-18 months after acceptance. Agented fiction 5%. Recently published work by John Lutz, Matt Christopher, Alan Robbins. Length: 4,000 words preferred; 4,000 words minimum; 5,000 words maximum. Sometimes recommends other markets.

How to Contact: Query for submission guidelines. Reports in 2 weeks. SASE. Simultaneous submissions OK. Puzzles range from $10.50 to $18.95 plus postage. Fiction guidelines free.
Payment: Pays $200 minimum.
Terms: Payment is made on delivery of final ms. Buys all rights.
Advice: "Thoughtful, challenging mysteries that can be concluded with a visual element of a puzzle. Many times we select certain subject matter and then sent out these specifics to our pool of writers ... Think out the mystery. Work backwards. Think up the solution, list clues and red herrings. Then write the story containing supporting information. Play one of our mystery thrillers so you do understand the relationship between the story and the picture."

BIKE REPORT (I, IV), Bikecentennial, Box 8308, Missoula MT 59807. (406)721-1776. Editor: Daniel D'Ambrosio. Magazine on bicycle touring: 8½×11; 24 pages; coated paper; self cover; illustrations and b&w photos. Published 9 times annually. Estab. 1974. Circ. 18,000.
Needs: Adventure, fantasy, historical (general), humor/satire, regional and senior citizen/retirement with a bicycling theme. Buys variable number mss/year. Published new writers within the last year. Length: 2,000 words average; 1,000 words minimum; 2,500 words maximum. Publishes short shorts. Occasionally comments on a rejected ms.
How to Contact: Send complete ms with SASE. Reports in 6 weeks on mss. Simultaneous, photocopied and previously published submissions OK. Accepts computer printout submissions. Prefers hard copy with disk submission. Sample copy for $1, 9×12 SAE and 60¢ postage. Fiction guidelines free for #10 SAE and 1 first class stamp.
Payment: Pays 3-5¢/word.
Terms: Pays on publication for first North American serial rights.

BLACK BELT (II), Rainbow Publications, Inc., 1813 Victory Place, Burbank CA 91504. (818)843-4444. Executive Editor: Jim Coleman. Magazine: 106 pages. Emphasizes "martial arts for both practitioner and layman." Monthly. Circ. 100,000.
Needs: Martial arts-related, historical and modern-day. Buys 1-2 fiction mss/year. Publishes ms 3 months to one year after acceptance. Published work by Glenn Yancey.
How to Contact: Query first. Reports in 1 month. Photocopied submissions OK. Accepts computer printout submissions, "prefers letter quality."
Payment: Pays $100-175.
Terms: Pays on publication for first North American serial rights, retains right to republish.

THE B'NAI B'RITH INTERNATIONAL JEWISH MONTHLY (IV), 1640 Rhode Island Ave. NW, Washington DC 20036. (202)857-6645. Editor: Jeff Rubin. Magazine: 8⅛×10⅞; 48-56 pages; coated stock; illustrations; photos. Subjects of Jewish interest—politics, culture, lifestyle, religion—for a Jewish family audience. Published 10 times annually. Estab. 1886.
Needs: Contemporary, ethnic, historical (general), humor/satire. No immigrant memoirs; holocaust memoirs. Receives 2 unsolicited mss/month. Buys 2 mss/year. Publishes ms 6 months to 1 year after acceptance. Length: 2,500 words average; 1,000 words minimum; 5,000 words maximum. Occasionally critiques rejected mss. Recommends other markets.
How to Contact: Reports in 1 month on queries; 6 weeks on mss. Include cover letter and SASE. Accepts computer printout submissions. Accepts electronic submissions via disk or modem. Sample copy $2.
Payment: Pays $100-$750.
Terms: Pays on publication for first North American serial rights. Sends galleys to author.
Advice: "A writer who submits a manuscript without a cover letter doesn't seem to have an awareness of interest in our publication. Cover letters should include a sentence or two of biographical information (publishing credits) and an introduction to the story."

‡BOMB MAGAZINE, New Art Publications, 177 Franklin St., New York NY 10013. (212)431-3943. Editor: Betsy Sussler. Magazine: 11×14; 100 pages; 70 lb. gloss cover; illustrations and photographs. "Artist-and-writer-edited magazine." Quarterly. Estab. 1981.
Needs: Contemporary, ethnic, experimental, serialized novel. Receives 40 unsolicited mss/month. Buys 6 mss/issue; 24 mss/year. Publishes ms 3-6 months after acceptance. Agented fiction 20%. Recently published work by Patrick McGrath, Lynne Tillman, Kathy Acker. Length: 10-12 pages average. Publishes short interviews.

Close-up

Margaret Roth
Editor
Boston Review

"We try to represent the kind of thinking that has embodied Boston," says Margaret Roth, editor of the *Boston Review*. The magazine celebrated its 15th year in 1990 and Roth has been with the magazine for seven years. Before joining the magazine, she worked in book publishing and later at the Boston public television station, WGBH, where she produced teachers' guides and program support materials.

"I found books and periodicals different in many ways," she says. "With magazines you have the continuity you don't have publishing books. While every article is different, the overall entity is the same issue after issue."

Boston Review has cultivated a distinctly Boston-oriented tone, although it contains material with national appeal and interest, she says.

"We try to bring a Boston sensitivity to our choice of material. People in New England tend to rarify things into an intellectual debate—we're less apt to be emotional."

Of course this outlook affects her choice in fiction, but Roth says with fiction, taste is often the deciding element. "Most people can recognize A-plus writing but at the B or B-plus level, the editor's taste is an enormous factor."

Writers looking for publication must work to catch the editor's eye, she says. "First, know your talents; know the kinds of things you do well. Secondly, in my view, neatness does count. Cover letters are important. If you can tell me very briefly why your story is good for me and *my* magazine, it can make a difference. Tell the editor how your story will strengthen the magazine."

Boston Review is very selective, says Roth. Of the nearly 300 poetry and fiction submissions she receives each week, she buys only one. Yet, the magazine is open to the work of both established and new writers. She especially tries to find talented writers who have not yet become "accomplished."

For quite awhile Roth and her staff worried about not having the time or energy to nurture new writers. They found some new writers showed promise but needed extra guidance. With the help of Walden Books and the Bydale Foundation, they came up with the New Voices project. Money was donated to pay for a special editor to work specifically with new writers—to give them feedback and encouragement. There is no formal criteria for the program, "sometimes it's just a note, sometimes a more extensive critique."

Writers must approach publication as if it were a job interview, she says. "Just as in the world of work, often the people who are good at getting jobs get them, not necessarily those best at the job. You must learn to take off your writing hat and put on a selling hat. Think shrewdly and do everything to increase your odds. Make it easy on the editor."

—*Robin Gee*

How to Contact: Send complete manuscript with cover letter. Reports in 6-8 weeks on mss. SASE. Sample copy $5 with $2.50 postage.
Payment: Pays $100 and contributor's copies.
Terms: Pays on publication for first or one-time rights. Sends galleys to author.

BOSTON REVIEW (II), Boston Critic Inc., 33 Harrison Ave., Boston MA 02111. Publisher/Editor: Margaret Ann Roth. "A bimonthly magazine of the arts and culture." Tabloid: 11×17; 24-32 pages; jet paper. Estab. 1975. Circ. 10,000.
Needs: Contemporary, ethnic, experimental, literary, prose poem, regional, and translations. Receives 100+ unsolicited fiction mss/month. Buys 4-6 mss/year. Published work by Joyce Carol Oates, Yasunari Kawabata, Stephen Dixon. Length: 3,000 words maximum; 2,000 words average. Publishes short shorts. Occasionally critiques rejected ms.
How to Contact: Send complete ms with cover letter and SASE. "You can almost always tell professional writers by the very thought-out way they present themselves in cover letters. But even a beginning writer should find some link between the work (its style, subject, etc.) and the publication — some reason why the editor should consider publishing it." Simultaneous and photocopied mss OK. Accepts computer printout submissions. Reports in 2-3 months on mss. Publishes ms an average of 4 months after acceptance. Sample copy $4.
Payment: $50-200 and 2 contributor's copies.
Terms: Pays on publication for first rights.
Advice: "We believe that original fiction is an important part of our culture — and that this should be represented by the *Boston Review*. We have embarked on a more vigorous fiction program — including a special effort to work with new writers."

BOSTONIA MAGAZINE (IV), The magazine of culture and ideas, Boston University, 10 Lenox St., Brookline MA 02146. (617)353-3081/2917. Editor: Janice Friedman. Magazine: 8½×11; 72-80 pages; 60 lb. paper; 80 lb. cover stock. "Thoughtful provocative prose for national audience." Bimonthly. Estab. 1900. Circ. 140,000.
Needs: Adventure, condensed/excerpted novel, contemporary, ethnic, experimental, horror, humor/satire, literary, mainstream, regional, serialized novel and suspense/mystery. Plans to publish fiction in each issue. Receives 30 unsolicited mss each month. Buys 1 ms/issue; 6 mss/year. Recently published work by Conall Ryan, John Auerbach and Bette Howland. Length: 3,000 words average; 1,500 words minimum; 4,000-5,000 words maximum.
How to Contact: Send complete ms with cover letter. Reporting time varies. SASE. Sample copy $2.50. Free fiction guidelines.
Payment: Pays $400-700, contributor's copies, charges for extras.
Terms: Pays on acceptance for first North American serial rights.

BOWBENDER (II, IV), Canada's Archery Magazine, Box 912, Carstairs, Alberta T0M 0N0 Canada. (403)337-3023. FAX: (403)337-3460. Editor: Kathleen Windsor. Magazine: 8¼×10⅞; 48 pages; 60 lb. gloss stock; 100 lb. gloss cover; illustrations; photos. "We publish material dealing with hunting, wildlife, conservation, equipment, nature and Olympic team coverage etc., for outdoorsmen, especially hunters and competitive archers." Published 5 times/year. Estab. 1984. Circ. 45,000.
Needs: Adventure, sports and western. "*Might* publish fiction if it concerns (bow) hunting, archery or traveling in the Canadian outdoors." Does not want to see anything veering off the topic of archery in Canada. Publishes ms within 1 year after acceptance. Length: 2,000 words average; 500 words minimum; 3,000 words maximum.
How to Contact: Query first or send complete manuscript with cover letter, which should include a brief autobiography (archery) to be included in the magazine. Reports in 1 week on queries; 2 weeks on mss. SASE for ms. Photocopied submissions OK. Accepts computer printout submissions. Sample copy for $2.95 (Canadian), 9×12 SAE and $1.12 (Canadian postage). Editorial/Photography guidelines for #10 SAE and 39¢ (Canadian), 30¢ (U.S.) postage.
Payment: Pays $300 maximum. (Roughly 10¢/word depending on regularity of submission, quality photo complement, etc.) Free contributor's copies; charge for extras.
Terms: Pays on publication for first North American serial rights, or first Canadian if requested and acceptable.
Advice: "Fiction remains a 'big' maybe. Write for guidelines and review a sample copy first."

BOWHUNTER MAGAZINE (IV), The Magazine for the Hunting Archer, Cowles Magazines, Inc., 2245 Kohn Rd., Box 8200, Harrisburg, PA 17105. (717)657-9555. FAX: (717)657-9526. Editor: M.R. James. Editorial Director: Dave Canfield. Magazine. 8¼ × 10¾; 150 pages; 75. lb glossy paper; 150 lb. glossy cover stock; illustrations and photographs. "We are a special interest publication for people who hunt with the bow and arrow. We publish hunting adventure and how-to stories. Our audience is predominantly male, 30-50, middle income." Bimonthly. Circ. 230,000.
Needs: Bowhunting, outdoor adventure. "Writers must expect a very limited market. We buy only one or two fiction pieces a year. Writers must know the market—bowhunting—and let that be the theme of their work. No 'me and my dog' types of stories; no stories by people who have obviously never held a bow in their hands." Receives 1-2 unsolicited fiction mss/month. Buys 1-2 mss/year. Publishes ms 3 months to 2 years after acceptance. Length: 2,000 words average; 500 words minimum; 3,000 words maximum. Publishes short shorts. Length: 500. Sometimes critiques rejected mss and recommends other markets.
How to Contact: Query first or send complete ms with cover letter. Reports in 2 weeks on queries; 6 weeks on mss. Accepts computer printout submissions. Sample copy for $2 and 8½ × 11 SAE with appropriate postage. Fiction guidelines for #10 SAE and 1 first class stamp.
Payment: $25-250; free subscription to the magazine, if requested; contributor's copies, if requested up to 6; charge for extras, half price over 6.
Terms: Pays on acceptance for first North American serial rights.
Advice: "We have a resident humorist who supplies us with most of the 'fiction' we need. But if a story comes through the door which captures the essence of bowhunting and we feel it will reach out to our readers, we will buy it. Despite our macho outdoor magazine status, we are a bunch of English majors who love to read. You can't bull your way around real outdoor people—they can spot a phony at 20 paces. If you've never camped out under the stars and listened to an elk bugle and try to relate that experience without really experiencing it, someone's going to know. We are very specialized; we don't want stories about shooting apples off people's heads or of Cupid's arrow finding its mark. James Dickey's *Deliverance* used bowhunting metaphorically, very effectively . . . while we don't expect that type of writing from everyone, that's the kind of feeling that characterizes a good piece of outdoor fiction."

BOYS' LIFE (III), For All Boys, Boy Scouts of America, Magazine Division, 1325 Walnut Hill Lane, Box 152079, Irving TX 75015-2079. (214)580-2000. Editor-in-Chief: William B. McMorris. Fiction Editor: William E. Butterworth IV. Magazine: 8 × 11; 68 pages; slick cover stock; illustrations; photos. "*Boys' Life* covers Boy Scout activities and general interest subjects for ages 8 to 18, Boy Scouts, Cub Scouts and others of that age group." Monthly. Estab. 1911. Circ. 1,500,000.
Needs: Adventure, humor/satire, science fiction, suspense/mystery, western and sports. "We publish short stories aimed at a young adult audience and frequently written from the viewpoint of a 10- to 16-year-old boy protagonist." Receives approximately 100 unsolicited mss/month. Buys 12-18 mss/year. Recently published work by Donald J. Sobol, Maureen Crane Wartski, Raboo Rodgers; published new writers within the last year. Length: 500 words minimum; 1,200 words maximum; 1,000 words average. "Very rarely" critiques rejected ms.
How to Contact: Send complete ms with SASE. "We'd much rather see manuscripts than queries." Simultaneous and photocopied submissions OK. Prefers letter-quality type. Reports in 2 weeks on mss. For sample copy "check your local library." Writer's guidelines available; send SASE.
Payment: Pays $500 and up, "depending on length and writer's experience with us."
Terms: Pays on acceptance for one-time rights.
Advice: "*Boys' Life* writers understand the reader. They treat them as intelligent human beings with a thirst for knowledge and entertainment. We tend to use many of the same authors repeatedly because their characters, themes, etc., develop a following among our readers."

BREAD (II), Church of the Nazarene, 6401 The Paseo, Kansas City MO 64131. (816)333-7000. FAX: (816)333-1683. Editor: Karen De Sollar. Magazine: 8½ × 11; 34 pages; illustrations; photos. Christian leisure reading magazine for junior and senior high students. Monthly.
Needs: Fiction and how-to stories on Christian living. Themes should be school and church oriented, but without sermonizing. Buys 25 mss/year. Recently published work by Alan Cliburn, Jeanette D. Gardner, Betty Everette and Mike LaCrosse; published new writers within the last year.

How to Contact: Send complete ms with SASE. Reports in 6 weeks on mss. Sample copy $1, 9 × 12 SAE and 45¢ postage. Free guidelines for SASE.
Payment: Pays 4¢/word for first rights and 3.5¢/word for second rights.
Terms: Pays on acceptance for first rights and second serial rights. Accepts simultaneous submissions. Byline given.
Advice: "Our readers clamor for fiction."

BUFFALO SPREE MAGAZINE (II, IV), Spree Publishing Co., Inc., 4511 Harlem Rd., Buffalo NY 14226. (716)839-3405. Editor: Johanna V. Shotell. Associate Editor: Gary L. Goss. "City magazine for professional, educated and above-average income people." Quarterly. Estab. 1967. Circ. 21,000.
Needs: Literary, contemporary, feminist, mystery, adventure, humor and ethnic. No pornographic or religious. Buys 10 mss/issue, 40 mss/year. Length: 1,800 words maximum.
How to Contact: Send complete ms with SASE. Reports within 3 to 6 months on ms. Sample copy for $2 with 9 × 12 SAE and $2.40 postage.
Payment: $50-125; 1 free author's copy.
Terms: Pays on publication for first rights.

‡BUZZWORM: THE ENVIRONMENTAL JOURNAL (II), Buzzworm, Inc., Suite 206, 2305 Canyon Blvd., Boulder CO 80302. (303)442-1969. Managing Editor: Elizabeth Darby Junkin. Magazine; 8½ × 11; 96 pages; glossy. "Environmental magazine with once-a-year fiction section for outdoor/environmental-interested readers, upscale and sophisticated." Bimonthly. Estab. 1988. Circ. 75,000.
Needs: Condensed/excerpted novel, fantasy, literary, "environmental fiction." "Will only look at environmental-theme fiction." Plans special fiction issue. Buys 3 ms/year. Publishes ms 6 months after acceptance. Agented fiction 100%. Recently published work by John Nichols, Edward Abbey and Doug Peacock. Length: 3,500 words preferred; 2,500 words minimum; 5,000 words maximum. Publishes short shorts. Length: 1,000 words.
How to Contact: Send complete ms with cover letter. Submit through agent. Reports on queries in 6 weeks; on mss in 2 months. SASE. Photocopied submissions OK. Sample copy for 9 × 12 SAE and $2.25 postage. Fiction guidelines for #10 SAE and 1 first class stamp.
Payment: "Varies."
Terms: Buys all rights, first North American serial rights. Sponsors award for fiction writers. Write for details.

CAMPUS LIFE MAGAZINE (II), Christianity Today, Inc., 465 Gundersen Drive, Carol Stream IL 60188. (312)260-6200. FAX: (708)260-0114. Editor: James Long. Senior Editor: Christopher Lutes. Magazine: 8¼ × 11¼; 100 pages; 4-color and b&w illustrations; 4-color and b&w photos. "General interest magazine with a religious twist. Not limited strictly to Christian content." Articles "vary from serious to humorous to current trends and issues, for high school and college age readers." Monthly except combined May-June and July-August issues. Estab. 1942. Circ. 130,000.
Needs: Condensed novel, humor/satire, prose poem, serialized/excerpted novel. All submissions must be contemporary, reflecting the teen experience in the '90s. We are a Christian magazine but are *not* interested in sappy, formulaic, sentimentally religious stories. We *are* interested in well crafted stories that portray life realistically, stories high school and college youth relate to. Nothing contradictory of Christian values. If you don't understand our market and style, don't submit." Receives 30 unsolicited fiction mss/month. Buys 5 mss/year. Reading and response time slower in summer. Published work by Barbara Durkin, Durese Cotton; published writers within the last year. Length: 1,000-3,000 words average, "possibly longer." Publishes short shorts.
How to Contact: Query with short synopsis of work, published samples and SASE. Simultaneous, photocopied and previously published submissions OK. Reports in 4-6 weeks on queries. Sample copy $2 and 9½ × 11 envelope.
Payment: Pays "generally" $250-400; 2 contributor's copies.
Terms: Pays on acceptance for one-time rights.
Advice: "We print finely crafted fiction that carries a contemporary teen (older teen) theme. First person fiction often works best. Ask us for sample copy with fiction story. Fiction communicates to our reader. We want to encourage fiction writers who have something to say to or about young people without getting propagandistic."

CANADIAN MESSENGER (IV), Apostleship of Prayer, 661 Greenwood Ave., Toronto, Ontario M4J 4B3 Canada. (416)466-1195. Editors: Rev. F.J. Power, S.J.; Alfred De Manche. Magazine: 7 × 10; 32 pages; glossy paper; self cover; illustrations; photos. Publishes material with a "religious theme or a

moral about people, adventure, heroism and humor, for Roman Catholic adults." Monthly. Estab. 1891. Circ. 17,000.
Needs: Religious/inspirational. Receives 10 mss/month. Buys 1 ms/issue. Publishes ms within 1-1½ years of acceptance. Length: 500 words minimum; 1,500 words maximum.
How to Contact: Send complete ms with cover letter. Reports on mss in "a few" weeks. SASE. Accepts computer printout submissions. Sample copy for $1. Fiction guidelines for $1 and 7½×10½ SAE.
Payment: Pays 4¢/word.
Terms: Pays on acceptance for first North American rights.

CAPPER'S (II), Stauffer Communications, Inc., 616 Jefferson, Topeka KS 66607. (913)295-1108. Editor: Nancy Peavler. Magazine: 24-48 pages; newsprint paper and cover stock; photos. A "clean, uplifting and nonsensational newspaper for families from children to grandparents." Biweekly. Estab. 1879. Circ. 400,000.
Needs: Serialized novels. "We accept only novel-length stories for serialization. No fiction containing violence or obscenity." Buys 2-3 stories/year. Receives 2-3 unsolicited fiction mss each month. Recently published work by Juanita Urbach, Colleen L. Reece, John E. Stolberg; published new writers within the last year.
How to Contact: Send complete ms with SASE. Cover letter and/or synopsis helpful. Reports in 5-6 months on ms. Sample copy 75¢.
Payment: Pays $150-200 for one-time serialization. Free author's copies (1-2 copies as needed for copyright).
Terms: Pays on acceptance for second serial (reprint) rights and one-time rights.
Advice: "Be patient. Send SASE. Copy your work before sending—mss do get lost!"

‡CAREER FOCUS, COLLEGE PREVIEW, JOURNEY, VISIONS, Communications Publishing Group, Inc., 3100 Broadway, 225 PennTower, Kansas City MO 64111. Editor: Georgia Clark. Magazines; 70 pages; 50 lb. paper; gloss enamel cover; 8×10 or 5×7 (preferred) illustrations; camera ready mat. photographs. *Career Focus*, "For Today's Professionals" includes career preparation, continuing education and upward mobility skills for advanced Black and Hispanic college students and college graduates. Published every two months. *College Preview*, "For College-Bound Students" is designed to inform and motivate Black and Hispanic high school students on college preparation and career planning. Semiannually. Circ. 600,000. *Journey*, "A Success Guide for College and Career-Bound Students" is for Asian American high school and college students who have indicated a desire to pursue higher education through college, vocational/technical or proprietary schools. Semiannually. *Visions*, "A Success Guide For Career-Bound Students" is designed for Native American students who want to pursue a higher education through college, vocational/technical or proprietary schools. Semiannually. Specialized publication limited to certain subjects or themes.
Needs: Adventure, condensed/excerpted novel, contemporary, ethnic, experimental, historical (general), humor/satire, prose poem, romance (contemporary, historical, young adult), science fiction, sports, suspense/mystery. Receives 2-3 unsolicited mss/month. Buys 2-4 mss/year. After acceptance of ms, time varies before it is published. Length: 1,000 words minimum; 4,000 words maximum. Publishes short shorts. Does not usually comment on rejected ms.
How to Contact: Query with clips of published work (include Social Security number) or send copy of resume and when available to perform. Reports in 4-6 weeks. SASE. Simultaneous, photocopied and reprint submissions OK. Sample copy and fiction guidelines for 9×10 SASE.
Payment: Pays 10¢ per word.
Terms: Pays on acceptance for first rights and second serial (reprint) rights.
Advice: "Today's fiction market is geared toward stories that are generated from real-life events because readers are more sophisticated and aware of current affairs. But because everyday life is quite stressful nowadays, even young adults want to escape into science fiction and fairytales. Fiction should be entertaining and easy to read. Be aware of reader audience. Material should be designed for status-conscious young adults searching for quality and excellence. Do not assume readers are totally unsophisticated and avoid casual mention of drug use, alcohol abuse or sex. Avoid overly ponderous, overly cute writing styles. Query describing the topic and length of proposed article. Include samples of published work if possible. Must be typed, double spaced on white bond paper (clean copy only)."

CAT FANCY (IV), Fancy Publications, Box 6050, Mission Viejo CA 92690. (714)855-8822. Editor-in-Chief: K.E. Segnar. General cat and kitten magazine, consumer oriented for cat and kitten lovers. Published monthly. Circ. 332,000.

Needs: Cat-related themes only. Receives approximately 60 unsolicited fiction mss/month. Accepts 12 mss/year. Approximately 10% of fiction agented. Recently published work by Barbara L. Diamond, Edward W. Clarke and Sandi Fisher; published new writers within the last year. Length: 3,000 words maximum. Sometimes recommends other markets.
How to Contact: Send complete ms with SASE. Simultaneous and photocopied submissions OK. Reports in 2 months. Publishes ms 2-10 months after acceptance. Sample copy $3.50. Free fiction guidelines with SASE.
Payment: Pays 5¢/word and 2 contributor's copies. $3.50 charge for extras.
Terms: Rarely buys reprints.
Advice: "Stories should focus on a cat or cats, not just be about people who happen to have a cat. No anthropomorphism. Carefully review the publication, especially the short stories we have published before, and study our writer's guidelines."

CATHOLIC FORESTER (I, II, III), Catholic Order of Foresters, 425 W. Shuman Blvd., Box 3012, Naperville IL 60566-7012. (708)983-4920. Editor: Barbara Cunningham. Magazine: 8¼ × 10¾; 40 pages; 45 lb. paper and 60 lb. cover stock; illustrations; photos. "No special theme but we want interesting, lively stories and articles. No true confessions type, no dumb romances. People who have not bothered to study the art of writing need not apply." Bimonthly. Estab. 1884. Circ. 160,000.
Needs: Adventure, contemporary, ethnic, feminist, humor/satire, mainstream, regional, senior citizen/retirement, sports and suspense/mystery. Receives 200 unsolicited fiction mss/month. Buys approximately 7-8 mss/issue; 100 mss/year. "Publication may be immediate or not for 4-5 months." Agented fiction: 5%. Recently published work by John Keefauver, William Childress and Donald Smith. Length: 2,000 words average; 3,000 words maximum. Also publishes short shorts. Occasionally critiques rejected mss. Sometimes recommends other markets.
How to Contact: Send complete ms. "Cover letters extolling the virtue of the story do not help—manuscripts stand or fall on their own merit. I do not accept queries anymore—too many problems in authors misunderstanding 'speculation.'" SASE for ms. Simultaneous, photocopied submissions and reprints OK. Sample copy for 8½ × 11 SASE and 73¢ postage. Fiction guidelines for #10 SASE.
Payment: Pays 5¢ minimum and one contributor's copy to new author. 10¢ or more for quality works and frequent contributors. Author may request more copies—no charge.
Advice: "I enjoy a short, friendly cover letter but do not appreciate a long letter telling me the author's personal history, past credits, a complicated synopsis of the story enclosed, and his/her opinion of it. The only thing that counts is the quality and suitability of the story itself. I do make short comments occasionally on rejection slips but cannot go into great detail. Before submitting a story, act out some of your scenes to see if they make sense—speak your dialogue aloud to assure that it is realistic. Ask yourself 'is this how people really talk to each other?' Also, every rejection doesn't mean that the editor thinks the story is bad. It may just simply not fit the publication's readers, or that our space is limited."

CAVALIER MAGAZINE (II), Dugent Publishing Corp., Suite 600, 2600 Douglas Rd., Coral Gables FL 33134. (305)443-2378. Editor: Douglas Allen. Fiction Editor: M. DeWalt. Magazine: 8½ × 11; 103 pages; 60 lb paper; laminated cover stock; illustrations; photos. Sexually oriented, sophisticated magazine for single men aged 18-35. Published special fiction issue last year; plans another. Monthly. Estab. 1952. Circ. 250,000.
Needs: Adventure, horror and erotica. No material on children, religious subjects or anything that might be libelous. Buys 3 mss/issue. Receives approximately 200 unsolicited fiction mss each month. Recently published work by Janris Manley, Dillon McGrath, Wayne Rogers; published new writers within the last year. Length: 1,500-3,000 words. Critiques rejected mss "when there is time." Sometimes recommends other markets.
How to Contact: Send complete ms with SASE. A cover letter is not necessary except if ms is a multiple submission or there's special information. Accepts computer printout submissions. Prefers letter-quality. Reports in 3-6 weeks on mss. Sample copy for $3. Free fiction guidelines with SASE.
Payment: $200-300. Offers 50% kill fee for assigned mss not published.
Terms: Pays on publication for first North American serial rights.
Advice: Mss are rejected because writers "either don't know our market or the manuscripts are too long or too short. Length and erotic content are crucial (erotica in *every* story). Fiction is often much sexier and more imaginative than photos. If you are a poor speller, grammarian or typist, have your work proofread. Ask for our guidelines and follow them. Occasionally sponsors contests . . . watch publication."

CHANGES, For Adult Children, U.S. Journal Inc., 3201 SW 15th St., Deerfield Beach FL 33442. (305)360-0909. Associate Editor: Andrew Meacham. Managing Editor: Jeffrey Laign. Magazine: 8½ × 11; 80 pages; slick paper; glossy cover; illustrations; photos. "Fiction often deals with recovery from dysfunctional families. Readers are children of alcoholics and other dysfunctional families." Bimonthly. Estab. 1986. Circ. 60,000.
Needs: "Quality, professional fiction, typed, double-spaced." Receives 30 mss/month. Buys 1-3 mss/ issue. Publishes ms within several months of acceptance. Agented fiction 5%. Recently published work by Lloyd Skloot, Elizabeth Benedict. Length: 2,000 words maximum. Publishes short shorts. Sometimes critiques rejected mss and recommends other markets.
How to Contact: Query with clips of published work or send complete ms with cover letter which should include Social Security number and "a short professional bio." Reports in 6 weeks. SASE. Simultaneous submissions OK. Accepts computer printout submissions. Sample copy for SAE. Fiction guidelines for #10 SAE and 1 first class stamp.
Payment: Pays 15¢/word.
Terms: Pays on publication for first North American serial rights. Publication copyrighted.
Advice: "Too much of the fiction we read is superficial and imitative. We're looking for bold new writers who have something to say. A too-subtle message is better than a predictable one."

CHESAPEAKE BAY MAGAZINE (II, IV), Chesapeake Bay Communications, Inc., 1819 Bay Ridge Ave., Annapolis MD 21403. (301)263-2662. Editor: Jean Waller. Magazine: 8½ × 11½; 88 pages; coated stock paper; coated cover stock; illustrations; photos. "*Chesapeake Bay Magazine* is a regional publication for those who enjoy reading about the Bay and its tributaries. Most of our articles are boating-related. Our readers are yachtsmen, boating families, fishermen, ecologists, anyone who is part of Chesapeake Bay life." Monthly. Estab. 1971. Circ. 32,000.
Needs: Adventure, humor and historical. "Any fiction piece *must* concern the Chesapeake Bay. Only stories done by authors who are familiar with the area are accepted. No general type stories with the Chesapeake Bay superimposed in an attempt to make a sale." Buys 4 short stories/year. Receives approximately 3 unsolicited fiction mss each month. Recently published work by Gilbert Byron and Arline Chase. Published new writers within the last year. Length: 1,250-3,000 words. Publishes short shorts.
How to Contact: Query or send ms, including cover letter with bio information to indicate familiarity with our publication. SASE always. Reports in 1 month on queries, 2 months on mss. Publishes ms an average of 12-14 months after acceptance. Sample copy $2.50. Free writer's guidelines with SASE.
Payment: Pays $85-125. 2 free author's copies.
Terms: Pays on publication for all rights or first North American serial rights.
Advice: "Make sure you have knowledge of the area. Send only material that is related to our market. All manuscripts must be typed, double-spaced, in duplicate. Our readers are interested in any and all material about the Chesapeake Bay area. Thus we use a limited amount of fiction as well as factual material. Work must be fairly short, or have clear break-points for serialization."

CHESS LIFE (IV), U.S. Chess Federation, 186 Route 9W, New Windsor NY 12553. (914)562-8350. Editor: Julie Anne Desch. Magazine: 8¼ × 10¾; 68 pages; slick paper; illustrations and photos. "Chess: news, theory, human interest, for chess players (mostly male)." Monthly. Circ. 58,000.
Needs: "Chess must be central to story." Receives 3 unsolicited mss/month. Accepts 2 mss/year. Publishes short shorts. Occasionally critiques rejected mss.
How to Contact: Query first. Sample copy and fiction guidelines free.

CHIC (II), Larry Flynt Publications, 9171 Wilshire Blvd., Suite 300, Beverly Hills CA 90210. Executive Editor: Doug Oliver. Magazine: 100 pages; illustrations; photos. "Men's magazine, for men and women." Monthly. Estab. 1976. Circ. 100,000.
Needs: Erotica. Receives 20-30 unsolicited mss/month. Buys 1 ms/issue; 12 mss/year. Publishes ms 1-6 months after acceptance. Published new writers within the last year. Length: 3,500 words average; 3,000 words minimum; 4,000 words maximum. Occasionally critiques rejected mss. Recommends other markets.
How to Contact: Send complete manuscript with cover letter, which should include "writer's name, address, telephone number and whether the manuscript has been or is being offered elsewhere." Reports in 4-6 weeks. SASE for ms. Photocopied submissions OK. Accepts computer printout submissions. Fiction guidelines free for SASE.

Payment: Pays $500.
Terms: Pays on acceptance for all rights.
Advice: "Readers have indicated a desire to read well written erotic fiction, which we classify as a good story with a sexual undercurrent. The writer should read several published short stories to see the general tone and style that we're looking for. The writer should keep in mind that the first requirement is that the story be a well written piece of fiction, and secondarily that it deal with sex; we are not interested in 'clinically descriptive' sex accounts."

CHICKADEE (II), The Magazine for Young Children from OWL, Young Naturalist Foundation, 56 The Esplanade, Suite 306, Toronto, Ontario M5E 1A7 Canada. (416)868-6001. FAX (416)868-6009. Editor: Catherine Ripley. Magazine: 8½×11¾; 32 pages; glossy paper and cover stock; illustrations and photographs. "*Chickadee* is created to give children under nine a lively, fun-filled look at the world around them. Each issue has a mix of activities, puzzles, games and read-aloud stories." Monthly except July and August. Estab. 1979. Circ. 130,000.
Needs: Juvenile. No fantasy, religious or anthropomorphic material. Buys 1 ms/issue; 10 mss/year. Recently published work by Jo Ellen Bogart, Patti Farmer and Marilyn Pond; published new writers within the last year. Length: 200 words minimum; 800 words maximum; 500 words average. Recommends other markets.
How to Contact: Send complete ms and cover letter with $1 to cover postage and handling. Reports in 2 months. Publishes ms an average of 1 year after acceptance. Sample copy for $3.25. Free fiction guidelines for SAE.
Payment: Pays $25-350 (Canadian); 1 free contributor's copy.
Terms: Pays on publication for all rights. Occasionally buys reprints.
Advice: "We are looking for shorter stories that contain a puzzle, mystery, twist or tie-in to a puzzle that follows on the next spread. Make sure the story has a beginning, middle and an end. This seems simple, but it is often a problem for new writers."

CHILD LIFE, The Benjamin Franklin Literary & Medical Society, Inc., Box 567, 1100 Waterway Blvd., Indianapolis IN 46206. (317)636-8881. Editor: Steve Charles. Juvenile magazine for youngsters ages 8-11. Looking for adventure, humor, contemporary situations, folk and fairy tales and stories that deal with an aspect of health, nutrition, exercise (sports) or safety.
Needs: Juvenile. No adult or adolescent fiction. Recently published work by Nancy Sweetland, Ben Westfried, Toby Speed and Carole Forman. Published new writers within the last year. Length: 1,200 words maximum.
How to Contact: Send complete ms with SASE. Reports in 8-10 weeks. Sample copy 75¢. Free writer's guidelines with SASE.
Payment: Approximately 10¢/word for all rights.
Terms: Pays on publication.
Advice: "Always keep in mind your audience's attention span and interests: grab their attention quickly, be imaginative, and try to make your dialogue free and as natural as possible."

CHILDREN'S DIGEST (II), Children's Better Health Institute, Box 567, 1100 Waterway Blvd., Indianapolis IN 46206. Editor: Elizabeth A. Rinck. Magazine: 6½×9; 48 pages; reflective and preseparated illustrations; color and b&w photos. Magazine with special emphasis on health, nutrition, exercise and safety for pre-teens.
Needs: "Realistic stories, short plays, adventure and mysteries. We would like to see more stories that reflect today's society: concern for the environment, single-parent families and children from diverse backgrounds. Humorous stories are highly desirable. We especially need stories that *subtly* encourage readers to develop better health or safety habits. Stories should not exceed 1,500 words." Receives 40-50 unsolicited fiction mss each month. Recently published work by Charles Ghigna, Frances Gorman Risser and Julia Lieser; published new writers within the last year.
How to Contact: Send complete ms with SASE. A cover letter isn't necessary unless an author wishes to include publishing credits and special knowledge of the subject matter. Sample copy 75¢. Queries not needed. Reports in 10 weeks. Free guidelines with SASE.
Payment: Pays approximately 10¢/word with up to 10 free author's copies.
Terms: Pays on publication for all rights.
Advice: "We try to present our health-related material in a positive—not a negative—light, and we try to incorporate humor and a light approach wherever possible without minimizing the seriousness of what we are saying. Fiction stories that deal with a health theme need not have health as the primary subject but should include it in some way in the course of events. Most rejected health-related

manuscripts are too preachy or they lack substance. Children's magazines are not training grounds where authors learn to write 'real' material for 'real' readers. Because our readers frequently have limited attention spans, it is very important that we offer them well written stories."

CHILDREN'S PLAYMATE, The Benjamin Franklin Literary & Medical Society, Inc., P.O. Box 567, 1100 Waterway Blvd., Indianapolis IN 46206. (317)636-8881. Editor: Elizabeth A. Rinck. Magazine: 6½×9; 48 pages; preseparated and reflective art; b&w and color illustrations. Juvenile magazine for children ages 6-8 years.
Needs: Juvenile with special emphasis on health, nutrition, safety and exercise. "Our present needs are for short, entertaining stories with a subtle health angle. Seasonal material is also always welcome." No adult or adolescent fiction. Receives approximately 150 unsolicited fiction mss each month. Published work by Nancy Gotter Gates, Kathleen Nekich, Jean Leedale Hobson and Marge O'Harra; published new writers within the last year. Length: 700 words or less. Indicate word count on material.
How to Contact: Send complete ms with SASE. Accepts computer printout submissions. Reports in 8-10 weeks. Sample copy for 75¢.
Payment: Approximately 10¢/word and up to 10 free author's copies.
Terms: Pays on publication for all rights.
Advice: "Stories should be kept simple and entertaining. Study past issues of the magazine—be aware of vocabulary limitations of the readers."

CHRISTIAN LIVING FOR SENIOR HIGHS (IV), David C. Cook Publishing Co., 850 N. Grove, Elgin IL 60120. (708)741-2400. Editor: Douglas Schmidt. A take-home Sunday school paper: 8½×11; 4 pages; Penegra paper and cover; full color illustrations and photos. For senior high classes. Weekly.
Needs: Christian spiritual. Writers work mostly on assignment. "Each piece must present some aspect of the Christian life without being preachy. No closing sermons and no pat answers. Any topic appropriate to senior high is acceptable." Buys 5-10 mss/year. Length: 900-1,200 words.
How to Contact: Send complete ms with SASE. No queries please. Cover letter with brief bio, religious credentials and experience with senior highs. Reports in 2 months on mss. Free guidelines with SASE.
Payment: Pays $100-125.
Terms: Pays on acceptance for all rights.
Advice: "You've got to know kids and be aware of the struggles Christian kids are facing today. Don't write about how things were when you were a teenager—kids don't want to hear it."

CHRISTMAS (IV), The Annual of Christmas Literature and Art, Augsburg Fortress, 426 S. 5th St., Box 1209, Minneapolis MN 55440. (612)330-3300. Editorial Staff: Gloria Bengtson, Jennifer Huber, Sandra Gangelhoff. Magazine: 10⅜×13¾; 64 pages; illustrations and photographs. "Christmas—its history, celebration, traditions, music, customs, literature. For anyone who observes Christmas, especially its religious significance." Annually. Estab. 1931.
Needs: Ethnic, historical, literary, mainstream, verse, religious/inspirational, Christmas. Receives 40 unsolicited mss/month. Buys 2-3 mss/issue. Publishes ms 1-3 years after acceptance. Length: Around 2,500 words preferred.
How to Contact: Send complete ms with cover letter. Reports in 2 weeks on queries; 2-10 weeks on mss. SASE. Simultaneous and reprint submissions OK. Sample copy: Call for current price (plus shipping). Writer guidelines for #10 SAE and 1 first class stamp.
Payment: Pays $150-300. Free contributor's copy; charge for extras.
Terms: Pays on acceptance. Purchases all rights, first rights and one-time rights.

THE CHURCH HERALD (II), 6157 28th St. SE, Grand Rapids MI 49546-6999. (616)957-1351. Editor: John Stapert. Managing Editor: Jeffrey Japinga. Magazine: 8½×11; 52 pages. "We deal with religious themes and other reflections of a faith in God for a general audience, most members of the Reformed Church in America." Monthly. Estab. 1944. Circ. 47,000.
Needs: Prose poem, religious/inspirational, spiritual. Length: 1,200-1,800. Sometimes critiques rejected mss and may recommend other markets. Recently published work by Louis Lotz, James Schaap.
How to Contact: Send query with story synopsis and anticipated length. Reports in 6 weeks on queries. SASE. Accepts computer printout submissions.
Payment: Pay varies according to length.
Terms: Pays on acceptance for all rights, first rights, first North American serial rights and one-time rights.

THE CHURCH MUSICIAN (IV), The Sunday School Board of the Southern Baptist Convention, 127 9th Ave. N., Nashville TN 37234. (615)251-2961. Editor: William M. Anderson Jr. *"The Church Musician* is for church music leaders in local churches—music directors, pastors, organists, pianists, choir coordinators, and members of music councils and/or other planning committees or groups. Music leaders read the magazine for spiritual enrichment, testimonials, human interest stories and other materials related to music programs in local churches." Monthly. Estab. 1950. Circ. 20,000.
Needs: Categories related to church music. Receives 1-2 unsolicited fiction mss each month. Length: 750-2,000 words.
How to Contact: Send complete ms with SAE. Reports in 2 months on ms. Free sample copy with SAE and 30¢ postage. No simultaneous submissions.
Payment: Maximum 5¢ per word.
Terms: Pays on acceptance for all rights. Publication copyrighted.
Advice: "Avoid mushy sentiment when writing. It must be believable and, of course, practical." Many mss are rejected because they are "too long, too general, too sweet and sentimental, shallow."

CLUBHOUSE (II), Your Story Hour, Box 15, Berrien Springs MI 49103. (616)471-3701. Editor-in-Chief: Elaine Trumbo. Magazine: 6×9; 32 pages; 60 lb. offset paper; self cover stock; illustrations and some photos. "A Christian magazine designed to help young people feel good about themselves. Our primary goal is to let them know there is a God and that He loves kids. Stories are non-moralistic in tone and full of adventure." Readers are "children 9-14 years old. Stories are selected for the upper end of the age range. Primary audience—kids without church affiliation." Published 6 times/year. Estab. 1951 under former name *The Good Deeder.* Circ. 12,000.
Needs: Adventure, contemporary, historical (general), religious, young adult/teen. No Christmas stories that refer to Santa, elves, reindeer, etc. No Halloween/occult stories. Receives 250+ unsolicited fiction mss/month. Buys 6 mss/issue, 40 mss/year. Reads mss in March-April only. Published new writers within the last year. Length: 1,000-1,200 words. Occasionally critiques rejected mss. Occasionally recommends other markets.
How to Contact: Send complete ms, in April. SASE always. Simultaneous and photocopied submissions and previously published work OK. Accepts computer printout submissions. Reports in 2 months. Publishes ms 6-18 months after acceptance. Free sample copy with 6×9 SAE and 3 first class stamps. Free fiction guidelines with #10 SAE and 1 first class stamp.
Payment: Pays $25-35 and contributor's copies.
Terms: Pays on acceptance for any rights offered. Buys reprints.
Advice: "Especially interested in stories in which children are responsible, heroic, kind, etc., not stories in which children are pushed into admitting that a parent, sibling, friend, etc., was right all along. I want upbeat, fun, exciting stories. Do not mention church, Sunday School, etc., just because this is a Christian magazine. General tone of the magazine is warmth, not criticism. Remember that a story should follow a plot sequence and be properly wrapped up at the end. Most stories I reject involve kids who have regrettable turns of behavior which they finally change, appeal to a too-young age group, are preachy, are the wrong length or lack sparkle. Fiction can be more exact than truths, because details can be fashioned to complete the plot which might by necessity be omitted if the account were strictly factual."

COMPUTOREDGE (IV), San Diego's MicroComputer Magazine, The Byte Buyer, Inc., Box 83086, San Diego CA 92138. (619)573-0315. FAX: (619)573-0205. Editors: Tina Berke and Wally Wang. Magazine: 8½×11; 75-100 pages; newsprint paper; 50 lb. bookwrap cover; illustrations and photos. Publishes material relating to "personal computers from a human point of view. For new users/shoppers." Weekly. Estab. 1983. Circ. 120,000.
Needs: Computers. "Fiction *really* has to speak to our audience/readership; new computer user/first-time shopper; new and enthusiastic about computing." Receives up to 3 unsolicited fiction mss/month. Buys 3 fiction mss/year. Publishes ms 1-9 months after acceptance. Length: 800 words minimum; 1,000 words maximum.
How to Contact: Send complete ms with cover letter. Include Social Security number and phone number. Reports in 1 month. SASE. Photocopied and reprint submissions OK. Accepts computer printouts. Electronic submission of *accepted* mss encouraged. Sample copy for 9x12 SAE and $1.50 postage; writer's guidelines for #10 SAE and 1 first class stamp.
Payment: Pays 10¢/word.
Terms: Pays on publication for first rights or first North American serial rights. Offers $15 kill fee.
Advice: Magazine fiction today is "too trendy. Reader should be able to come away from article moved, enlightened, edified."

CONTACT ADVERTISING, Box 3431, Ft. Pierce FL 34948. (407)464-5447. Editor: Holly Adams. Magazines and newspapers. Publications vary in size, 40-56 pages. "Group of 14 erotica, soft core publications for swingers, single males, married males." Bimonthly, quarterly and monthly. Estab. 1975. Circ. combined is 60,000.
Needs: Erotica, fantasy, feminist, gay and lesbian. Receives 8-10 unsolicited mss/month. Buys 1-2 mss/ issue; 40-50 mss/year. Publishes ms 1-3 months after acceptance. Length: 2,000 words minimum; 3,500 words maximum; 2,500-3,500 words average. Sometimes critiques rejected mss and recommends other markets.
How to Contact: Query first, query with clips of published work or send complete ms with cover letter. Reports in 1-2 weeks on queries; 3-4 weeks on mss. SASE. Simultaneous, photocopied and reprint submissions OK. Accepts computer printout submissions. Sample copy for $6. Fiction guidelines free.
Payment: 1st submission, free subscription to magazine; subsequent submissions $25-75; all receive three contributor's copies.
Terms: Pays on publication for all rights or first rights. Sends galleys to author if requested.
Advice: "Content must be of an adult nature but well within guidelines of the law. Fantasy, unusual sexual encounters, swinging stories or editorials of a sexual bend are acceptable."

COSMOPOLITAN MAGAZINE (III), The Hearst Corp., 224 W. 57th St., New York NY 10019. (212)649-2000. Editor: Helen Gurley Brown. Fiction Editor: Betty Kelly. Associate Fiction Editor: Jill Herzig. Most stories include male-female relationships, traditional plots, characterizations. Single career women (ages 18-34). Monthly. Circ. just under 3 million.
Needs: Contemporary, romance, mystery and adventure. "Stories should include a romantic relationship and usually a female protagonist. The characters should be in their 20s or 30s (i.e., same ages as our readers). No highly experimental pieces. Upbeat endings." Buys 1 short story plus a novel or book excerpt/issue. Approximately 98% of fiction is agented. Recently published excerpts by Danielle Steel, Pat Booth and Belva Plain; published new writers within the last year. Length: short shorts (1,500 words); longer (2,000-4,000 words). Occasionally recommends other markets.
How to Contact: Send complete ms with SASE. Accepts computer printout submissions. Free guidelines with legal-sized SASE. Publishes ms 6-18 months after acceptance.
Payment: Pays $750-2,000.
Terms: Pays on acceptance for first North American serial rights. Buys reprints.
Advice: "It is rare that unsolicited mss are accepted. We tend to use agented, professional writers. The majority of unsolicited short stories we receive are inappropriate for *Cosmo* in terms of characters used and situations presented, or they just are not well written."

‡COUNTRY AMERICA (IV), 1716 Locust St., Des Moines IA 50336. (515)284-3790. Editor: Danita Allen. Magazine; 8¼ × 10½; 100 pages. "*Country America* celebrates and serves the country way of life including country music for an audience who loves rural values and traditions." Monthly. Estab. 1989. Circ. 625,000.
Needs: Regional, western. Receives "very few" unsolicited mss/month. Buys 2 or 3 mss/year. Publishes ms approximately 6 months after acceptance. Recently published fiction by Charlie Daniels.
How to Contact: Query first. Reports in 1 month. SASE for mss. Sample copy $3.30.
Payment: Pays 35¢/word minimum, 75¢/word maximum.
Terms: Pays on acceptance. Kill fee negotiable. Buys all rights.

COUNTRY WOMAN (IV), Reiman Publications, Box 643, Milwaukee WI 53201. (414)423-0100. Editor: Ann Kaiser. Managing Editor: Kathleen Pohl. Magazine: 8½ × 11; 68 pages; excellent quality paper; excellent cover stock; illustrations and photographs. "Articles should have a rural theme and be of specific interest to women who live on a farm or ranch, or in a small town or country home, and/or are simply interested in country-oriented topics." Bimonthly. Estab. 1971. Circ. 650,000.
Needs: Fiction must be upbeat, heartwarming and focus on a country woman as central character. "Many of our stories and articles are written by our readers!" Recently published work by Lori Ness, Wanda Luttrell and Dixie Laslett Thompson; published new writers within last year. Publishes 1 fiction story per issue and 6-8 profiles per issue. Length: 750-1,000 words.
How to Contact: Query first. Reports in 2-3 months. Include cover letter and SASE. Simultaneous, photocopied and reprint submissions OK. "All manuscripts should be sent to Kathy Pohl, Managing Editor." Accepts computer printout submissions. Sample copy and writer's guidelines for $2 and SASE. Guidelines for #10 SASE.

Payment: Pays $90-125.
Terms: Pays on acceptance for one-time rights.
Advice: "Read the magazine to get to know our audience. Send us country-to-the-core fiction, not yuppie-country stories—our readers know the difference!"

CRICKET MAGAZINE (II), Carus Corporation, Box 300, Peru IL 61354. (815)223-1500. Publisher/Editor-in-Chief: Marianne Carus. Magazine: 7×9; 80 pages; illustrations; photos. Magazine for children, ages 6-14. Monthly. Estab. 1973. Circ. 130,000.
Needs: Juvenile, including literary, contemporary, science fiction, historic fiction, fantasy, western, mystery, adventure, humor, ethnic and translations. No adult articles. Buys 10-20 mss/year. Receives approximately 1,100 unsolicited fiction mss each month. Approximately 1-2% of fiction is agented. Length: 500-1,500 words. Recently published work by Peter Dickinson, Mary Stolz, Jane Yolen; published new writers within the last year.
How to Contact: Do not query first. Send complete ms with SASE. List previous publications. Reports in 3 months on mss. Publishes ms 6-24 months after acceptance. Sample copy $2. Free guidelines with SASE.
Payment: Up to 25¢/word; 2 free author's copies. $1 charge for extras.
Terms: Pays on publication for first North American serial rights and one-time rights. Sends edited mss for approval. Buys reprints.
Advice: "Do not write *down* to children. Write about well-researched subjects you are familiar with and interested in, or about something that concerns you deeply. Children *need* fiction and fantasy. Carefully study several issues of *Cricket* before you submit your manuscript." Published new writers within the last year. Sponsors contests for children, ages 5-14.

CRUSADER MAGAZINE (II), Calvinist Cadet Corps, Box 7259, Grand Rapids MI 49510. (616)241-5616. FAX: (616)241-5558. Editor: G. Richard Broene. Magazine: 8½×11; 24 pages; 50 lb. white paper and cover stock; illustrations; photos. Magazine to help boys ages 9-14 discover how God is at work in their lives and in the world around them. 7 issues/year. Estab. 1958. Circ. 12,000.
Needs: Adventure, comics, confession, ethnic, juvenile, religious/inspirational, science fiction, spiritual and sports. Receives 60 unsolicited fiction mss/month. Buys 3 mss/issue; 18 mss/year. Recently published work by Sigmund Brouwer, Alan Cliburn and Betty Lou Mell. Length: 800 words minimum; 1,500 words maximum; 1,200 words average. Publishes short shorts.
How to Contact: Send complete ms and SASE with cover letter including theme of story. Simultaneous, photocopied and previously published submissions OK. Accepts computer printout submissions. Reports in 3 weeks on mss. Publishes ms 4-11 months after acceptance. Free sample copy with a 9×12 SAE and 3 first class stamps. Free fiction guidelines with #10 SAE and 1 first class stamp.
Payment: Pays 2-5¢/word; 1 free contributor's copy.
Terms: Pays on acceptance for one-time rights. Buys reprints.
Advice: "On a cover sheet list the point your story is trying to make. Our magazine has a theme for each issue, and we try to fit the fiction to the theme."

DETROIT JEWISH NEWS, 27676 Franklin Rd., Southfield MI 48034. (313)354-6060. Associate Editor: Alan Hitsky. Newspaper: 120+ pages; illustrations and photos. Jewish news. Weekly. Estab. 1942. Circ. 20,000.
Needs: "For fiction, we prefer articles on any subject with a Jewish flavor." Receives 3-4 unsolicited mss/month. Buys 6 mss/year. Publishes ms 2-3 months after acceptance. Length: 1,000-2,000 words averge. Publishes short shorts. Sometimes critiques rejected mss.
How to Contact: Send complete ms with cover letter that includes Social Security number. Reports in 1 week on queries; 1 month on mss. SASE. Simultaneous, photocopied and reprint submissions OK. Accepts computer printout submissions. Sample copy for $1. Fiction guidelines for SAE.
Payment: Pays $40-100 and contributor's copies; charge for extras.
Terms: Pays on publication for one-time rights. Offers kill fee.

DIALOGUE (I, II), The Magazine for the Visually Impaired, Dialogue Publications, Inc., 3100 Oak Park Ave., Berwyn IL 60402. (708)749-1908. Editor-in-Chief: Jerry Novak. Magazine: 9×11; 235 pages; matte stock; glossy cover; illustrations. Publishes information on blind-related technology and human interest articles for blind, deaf-blind and visually impaired adults. Quarterly. Estab. 1961. Circ. 50,000.

Needs: Adventure, contemporary, humor/satire, literary, mainstream, regional, senior citizen/retirement and suspense/mystery. No erotica, religion, confessional or experimental. Receives approximately 10 unsolicited fiction mss/month. Buys 3 mss/issue, 12 mss/year. Publishes ms an average of 6 months after acceptance. Recently published work by Patrick Quinn, Marieanna Pape and John Dasney; published new writers within the last year. Length: 1,500 words average; 500 words minimum; 2,000 words maximum. Publishes short shorts. Occasionally critiques rejected mss. Sometimes recommends other markets. "We give top priority to blind or visually impaired (legally blind) authors."
How to Contact: Query first or send complete ms with SASE. Also send statement of visual handicap. Reports in 2 weeks on queries; 6 weeks on mss. Photocopied and reprint submissions OK. Accepts computer printout submissions. Sample copy for $5 and #10 SAE with 1 first class stamp; free to visually impaired. Fiction guidelines free.
Payment: Pays $5-35 and contributor's copy.
Terms: Pays on acceptance for first rights. "All fiction published in *Dialogue* automatically enters the Victorin Memorial Award Contest held annually. One winner per year.
Advice: "Study the magazine. This is a very specialized field. Remember the SASE!"

DISCOVERIES (II), Nazarene Publishing House, 6401 The Paseo, Kansas City MO 64131. Editor: Molly Mitchell. Story paper. 5½ × 8¼; 8 pages; illustrations; color photos. "Committed to reinforce the Bible concept taught in Sunday School curriculum, for ages 8 to 12 (grades 3 to 6)." Weekly.
Needs: Religious, puzzles. Buys 1-2 stories and 1-2 puzzles/issue. Publishes ms 1-2 years after acceptance. Length: 400-800 words. Publishes short shorts.
How to Contact: Send complete ms with cover letter and SASE. Send for free sample copy and fiction guidelines with SASE.
Payment: 3.5¢/word.
Terms: Pays on acceptance for first rights.
Advice: "Stories should vividly portray definite Christian emphasis or character building values, without being preachy. Stories need to be shorter because size of story paper is smaller."

DOG FANCY, Fancy Publications, Box 6050, Mission Viejo CA 92690. (714)855-8822. Editor: Kim Thornton. General dog and puppy magazine, consumer oriented, "for dog and puppy lovers." Monthly. Circ. 150,000.
Needs: Dog-centered theme. Receives approximately 40 unsolicited fiction mss/month. Buys 12 mss/year. Length: 3,000 words maximum.
How to Contact: Query first or send complete ms. SASE always. Photocopied submissions OK. Reports in 1 month on queries, 2 months on mss. Publishes ms an average of 6 months after acceptance. Sample copy $3. Free fiction guidelines with SASE.
Payment: Pays 5¢/word and 2 contributor's copies. $3 charge for extras.
Terms: Buys reprints.
Advice: "Must be about dogs (and people), candid; first person is preferable. Include *brief* cover letter. Write to style of publication so that no re-write is necessary. Please no stories written 'by the dog' or talking dogs. Dog and dog's experiences must be focus of article; dog shouldn't be incidental character in a 'people' story. We are always especially interested in Christmas fiction—something heartwarming for the season, though not necessarily specifically Christmasy in theme."

DRAGON MAGAZINE (IV), The Monthly Adventure Role-Playing Aid, Dragon Publishing, 201 Sheridan Springs Rd., Lake Geneva WI 53147. (414)248-3625. Editor: Roger E. Moore. Fiction Editor: Barbara G. Young. Magazine: 8½ × 11; 112 pages; 50 penn. plus paper; 80 lb. northcote cover stock; illustrations; rarely photos. "*Dragon* contains primarily nonfiction—articles and essays on various aspects of the hobby of fantasy and science fiction role-playing games. One short fantasy story is published per issue. Readers are mature teens and young adults; over half our readers are under 18 years of age." Monthly. Estab. 1976. Circ. 85,000.
Needs: "We are looking for all types of fantasy (not horror) stories. We are *not* interested in fictionalized accounts of actual role-playing sessions." Receives 50-60 unsolicited fiction mss/month. Buys 10-12 mss/year. Recently published work by Dean Edmonds, Peni R. Griffin, Brian A. Hopkins and Margaret Weiss; published new writers within the last year. Length: 1,500 words minimum; 8,000 words maximum; 3,000-4,000 words average. Occasionally critiques rejected mss.
How to Contact: Send complete ms, estimated word length, SASE. List only credits of professionally published materials. Photocopied submissions OK. Accepts computer printout submissions. Reports in 2-3 weeks. Publishes ms 6-12 months after acceptance. Sample copy for $4.50. Free fiction guidelines for #10 SAE and 1 first class stamp.

Payment: Pays 5-8¢/word; 2 free contributor's copies; $2 charge for extras.
Terms: Pays on acceptance for fiction only for first Worldwide English language rights.

According to Dragon Magazine editor Roger E. Moore, this cover, entitled "Dragon's Nest," was "perfect for the theme of this particular issue, which was about dragons," in addition to depicting the magazine's name. The illustrator, Gerald Brom, says he has spent most of his life drawing and painting various "monsters and evildoers." Used with permission of TSR, Inc. Copyright © 1990, TSR, Inc. All rights reserved.

DRUMMER (II, IV), Desmodus, Inc., Box 11314, San Francisco CA 94101. (415)252-1195. Editor: A.F. DeBlase. Magazine: 8½×11; 92 pages; glossy full-color cover; illustrations and photos. "Gay male erotica, fantasy and mystery with a leather, SM or other fetish twist." Monthly. Estab. 1975. Circ. 23,000.
Needs: Adventure, erotica, fantasy, gay, horror, humor/satire, science fiction, suspense/mystery and western. "Fiction must have an appeal to gay men." Receives 20-30 unsolicited fiction mss/month. Accepts 2 mss/issue. Publishes ms 3-4 months after acceptance. Agented fiction 10%. Publishes short shorts.
How to Contact: Send complete ms with cover letter. SASE. Photocopied submissions OK; reprints OK "only if previously in foreign or very local publications." Accepts computer printouts. Accepts electronic submissions compatible with IBM PC. Sample copy for $5. Fiction guidelines for #10 SASE.
Payment: Pays $50-200 and free contributor's copies.
Terms: Pays on publication for first North American serial rights. Sponsors annual fiction contest.

‡EMERGE MAGAZINE (III), Our Voice In Today's World, Emerge Communications, 599 Broadway, New York NY 10012. (212)941-8811. Editor: Mr. Wilmer C. Ames, Jr. Fiction Editor: Mr. Roberto Santiago. Magazine; 8⅛×10⅞; 84 pages; 40 lb. paper; 70 lb. cover stock; 5-6 illustrations; 45 photographs. "*Emerge* is an African American news monthly that covers politics, arts and lifestyles for the college educated, middle class African American audience." Estab. 1989.
Needs: Ethnic, fantasy, humor/satire, literary, psychic/supernatural/occult, science fiction, sports, suspense/mystery. "*Emerge* is looking for humorous, tightly written fiction about African Americans no longer than 3,000 words. We will immediately return manuscripts with sexiest themes." Plans special fiction issue. Receives 25 unsolicited mss/month. Buys 3-6 mss/year. Publishes ms within 6 months after acceptance. Length: 3,000 words preferred.
How to Contact: Send complete ms with cover letter or submit through agent. Cover letter should include "a quick summation of the story with a list of where the author has previously been published." Reports in 3 months. SASE. Simultaneous and photocopied submissions OK. Sample copy for $4 and 11×12 SAE. Fiction guidelines free.

Payment: Pays $1,000-3,000 and contributor's copies.

Terms: Pays 25% kill fee. Buys first North American serial rights.

Advice: *"Emerge* stories must accomplish with a fine economy of style what all good fiction must do: make the unusual familiar. The ability to script a compelling story is what has been missing from most of our submissions."

EVANGEL, Light & Life Press, P.O. Box 535002, Indianapolis IN 46253-5002. (317)244-3660. Editor: Vera Bethel. Sunday school take-home paper for distribution to young adults who attend church. Fiction involves young couples and singles coping with everyday crises, making decisions that show growth; for readers ages 25-35. Magazine: 5½ × 8½; 8 pages; 2-color illustrations; b&w photos. Weekly. Estab. 1896. Circ. 35,000.

Needs: Religious/inspirational. "No fiction without any semblance of Christian message or where the message clobbers the reader." Buys 1 ms/issue, 52 mss/year. Receives approximately 75 unsolicited fiction mss each month. Recently published work by C. Ellen Watts, Jeanne Zornes and Betty Steele Everett. Length: 1,000-1,200 words.

How to Contact: Send complete ms with SASE. Reports in 1 month on ms. Free sample copy and free fiction guidelines with 6 × 9 SASE.

Payment: Pays $45; 2 free author's copies; charge for extras.

Terms: Pays on publication for simultaneous, first, second serial (reprint), first North American serial or one-time rights.

Advice: "Choose a contemporary situation or conflict and create a good mix for the characters (not all-good or all-bad heroes and villains). Don't spell out everything in detail; let the reader fill in some blanks in the story. Keep him guessing." Rejects mss because of "unbelievable characters and predictable events in the story."

THE FAMILY (II, IV), Daughters of St. Paul, 50 St. Paul's Ave., Boston MA 02130. (617)522-8911. Editor: Sr. Donna William Giaimo FSP. Magazine: 8½ × 11; 40 pages; glossy paper; self-cover; illustrations and photos. Family life—themes include parenting issues, human and spiritual development, marital situations for teen-adult, popular audience predominantly Catholic. Monthly, except July-Aug. Estab. 1953. Circ. 10,000.

Needs: Religious/inspirational. "We favor upbeat stories with some sort of practical or moral message." No sex, romance, science fiction, horror, western. Receives about 100 unsolicited mss/month. Buys 3-4 mss/issue; 30-40 mss/year. Publishes ms 4-6 months after acceptance. Length: 800 words minimum; 1,500 words maximum; 1,200 words average. *$15 fee for critique.*

How to Contact: Send complete ms with cover letter that includes Social Security number and list of previously published works. Reports in 2 months on mss. SASE. Reprint submissions OK. Sample copy $1.75, 9 × 12 SAE and 5 first class stamps. Guidelines for #10 SAE and 1 first class stamp.

Payment: Pays $50-150.

Terms: Pays on publication for first North American serial or one-time rights (reprints). Sends galleys to author "only if substantive editing was required."

Advice: "We look for 1) message; 2) clarity of writing; 3) realism of plot and character development. If seasonal material, send at least 7 months in advance. We're eager to receive submissions on family topics. And we love stories that include humor."

FAMILY MAGAZINE (II), The Magazine for Military Wives, Box 4993, Walnut Creek CA 94596. (415)284-9093. Editor: Janet A. Venturino. Magazine: 80 pages; glossy paper; 80 lb glossy cover stock; illustrations; photos. Magazine with stories of interest to military wives. Audience: high school-educated, married women. Published 10 times/year. Estab. 1958. Circ. 550,000 worldwide.

Needs: Contemporary. No "singles" stories. Receives 100 unsolicited mss/month. Buys 12-20 mss/year. Published new writers within the last year. Length: 1,000-3,000 words.

How to Contact: Send complete ms. Reports in 2 months. SASE. Simultaneous and photocopied submissions OK. Accepts computer printout submissions. Prefers letter-quality. Publishes ms an average of 1 year after acceptance. Sample copy $1.25. Fiction guidelines for SASE.

Payment: Pays $75-300; 1 contributor's copy; $1.25 charge for extras.

Terms: Pays on publication for first rights.

Advice: "Good quality still jumps out as a pearl among swine."

FIRST (II), For Women, Heinrich Bauer North America Inc., 270 Sylvan Ave., Englewood Cliffs NJ 07632. (201)569-6699. Editor: Jackie High. Fiction Editor: Bibi Wein. Magazine: 150 pages; slick paper; illustrations and photos. "Women's service magazine for women age 18 up—no upper limit—middle American audience." Monthly. Estab. 1989. Circ. 4 million.
Needs: Contemporary, humor, literary, mainstream and regional. "No experimental, romance, formula fiction, fantasy, sci-fi, or stories with foreign settings." Receives 200 unsolicited mss/month. Buys 1 ms/issue; 12 mss/year. Time between acceptance and publication varies. Agented fiction 33⅓%. Recently published work by Chuck Wachtel, Tina Smith and Paulette Bates Alden. Length: 2,500 words minimum; 4,500 words maximum; 3,500-4,000 words average. "No short shorts." Sometimes critiques rejected mss.
How to Contact: Send complete ms with cover letter. "Cover letter should be brief, mention previous publications and agent if any, and tell us if material is seasonal. No queries please." Reports in 8-10 weeks on mss. SASE for ms. Photocopied and reprint submissions OK. Accepts computer printout submissions. Fiction guidelines for #10 SAE and 1 first class stamp. Send seasonal material 6 months in advance.
Payment: Pays $1,250-2,000 (less for reprinted material).
Terms: Pays on acceptance for first North American serial rights.
Advice: "We especially like a fresh sensibility and a sensitive handling of themes of interest to contemporary women. Read at least 3 issues of the magazine. Send us the story you had to write for yourself, not one you concocted 'especially for *First*.'"

FIRST HAND (II, IV), Experiences for Loving Men, First Hand Ltd., Box 1314, Teaneck NJ 07666. (201)836-9177. FAX: (201)836-5055. Editor: Bob Harris. Magazine: digest size; 130 pages; illustrations. "Half of the magazine is made up of our readers' own gay sexual experiences. Rest is fiction and columns devoted to health, travel, books, etc." Monthly. Estab. 1980. Circ. 60,000.
Needs: Erotica, gay. "Should be written in first person." No science fiction or fantasy. Erotica should detail experiences based in reality. Receives 75-100 unsolicited mss/month. Buys 6 mss/issue; 72 mss/year. Publishes ms 9-18 months after acceptance. Recently published work by John Hoff, Rick Jackson, Julian Biddle; published new writers within the last year. Length: 3,000 words preferred; 2,000 words minimum; 3,750 words maximum. Sometimes critiques rejected mss.
How to Contact: Send complete ms with cover letter. Reports in 4-6 weeks on mss. SASE. Accepts computer printout submissions. Sample copy for $5. Fiction guidelines for #10 SAE and 1 first class stamp.
Payment: Pays $100-150.
Terms: Pays on publication for all rights or first North American serial rights.
Advice: "Cover letters are a must. Should include writer's name, address, telephone and Social Security number and should advise on use of pseudonym if any. Also whether he is selling all rights or first North American serial rights. Avoid the hackneyed situations. Be original. We like strong plots."

‡FLORIDA WILDLIFE, Florida Game & Fresh Water Fish Commission, 620 South Meridian St., Tallahassee FL 32399-1600. (904)488-5563. Editor: Andrea H. Blount. Magazine: 8½×11; 52 pages. "Conservation-oriented material for an 'outdoor' audience." Bimonthly. Estab. 1947. Circ. 30,000.
Needs: Adventure, sports. "Florida-related adventure only." Buys 3-4 mss/year. Length: 1,200 words average; 500 words minimum; 1,500 words maximum.
How to Contact: Send complete manuscript with cover letter including Social Security number. "We prefer to review article. Response varies with amount of material on hand." Sample copy $1.25.
Payment: Pays $50 per published page.
Terms: Pays on publication for one-time rights. Sends galleys to author.

THE FLYFISHER (IV), Federation of Flyfishers, 1387 Cambridge Dr., Idaho Falls ID 83401. (208)523-7300. Editor: Dennis Bitton. Magazine: 8½×11; 64 pages; 70 lb. glossy stock; self cover; b&w; illustrations; color and b/w photos. Magazine for fly fishermen. "We only publish material directly related to fly fishing." Quarterly. Estab. 1967. Circ. 15,000.
Needs: Fiction related to fly fishing only. Accepts 2 ms/issue, 8 mss/year. Published new writers within the last year. Length: 750 words minimum; 2,500 words maximum; 1,500 words average (preferred).
How to Contact: Query first with SASE. Reports in 1 month on queries and mss. Sample copy $3 with 9×12 SAE and 10 first class stamps. Free fiction guidelines with #10 SAE and 1 first class stamp.
Payment: Pays $50-250.
Terms: Pays on publication for first North American serial rights or one-time rights.

FLYFISHING NEWS, VIEWS AND REVIEWS (II,IV), Bitton Inc., 1387 Cambridge, Idaho Falls, ID 83401. (208)523-7300. Editor: Dennis G. Bitton. Newspaper tabloid: 16 pages; good newsprint; b&w illustrations; b&w photos. Publishes information on flyfishing and all related subjects, flyfishermen and women. Bimonthly. Estab. 1986. Circ. 5,000.
Needs: Adventure, condensed novel, confession, historical, humor, regional. "All as flyfishing topics." Receives 20 unsolicited mss/month. Accepts 2 mss/month; 12 mss/year. Length: 1,500-2,000 words average; 250 words minimum; 4,000 words maximum. Occasionally critiques rejected mss. Recommends other markets.
How to Contact: Query first. Reports in 2 weeks. SASE.
Payment: Pays $50-250 and 5 contributor's copies. Charge for extras.
Terms: Pays 2-3 weeks after publication for one-time rights.
Advice: "I want to see all good flyfishing fiction. Write like you talk."

FREEWAY (II), Box 632, Glen Ellyn IL 60138. (708)668-6000 (ext. 216). Editor: Kyle Lennart Olund. Magazine: 8½ × 11; 4 pages; newsprint paper; illustrations; photos. Weekly Sunday school paper "specializing in first-person true stories about how God has worked in teens' lives," for Christian teens ages 15-21.
Needs: Comics, humor/satire, spiritual, allegories and parables. Length: 1,000 words average 1,200 words maximum. Occasionally critiques rejected mss.
How to Contact: Send complete ms with SASE. Reports in 2-3 months. Simultaneous and photocopied submissions OK. Accepts computer printout submissions. Sample copy or writing guidelines available with SASE. Fiction guidelines free for SASE with 1 first class stamp.
Terms: Pays on acceptance for one-time rights 6-10¢ per word.
Advice: "Send us humorous fiction (parables, allegories, etc.) with a clever twist and new insight on Christian principles. Do *not* send us typical teenage short stories. Watch out for cliché topics and approaches."

THE FRIEND MAGAZINE (II), The Church of Jesus Christ of Latter-day Saints, 50 E. North Temple, 23rd Fl., Salt Lake City UT 84150. (801)240-2210. Editor: Vivian Paulsen. Magazine: 8½ × 10½; 50 pages; 40 lb coated paper; 70 lb coated cover stock; illustrations, photos. Publishes for 3-11 year-olds. Monthly. Estab. 1971. Circ. 220,000.
Needs: Adventure, ethnic, some historical, humor, mainstream, religious/inspirational, nature. Length: 1,000 words maximum. Publishes short shorts. Length: 250 words.
How to Contact: Send complete ms. "No query letters please." Reports in 6-8 weeks. SASE. Photocopied submissions OK. Accepts computer printout submissions. Sample copy for 9½ × 11 SAE and 85¢ postage.
Payment: Pays 8-11¢ a word.
Terms: Pays on acceptance for all rights.
Advice: "The *Friend* is particularly interested in stories with substance for tiny tots. Stories should focus on character-building qualities and should be wholesome without moralizing or preaching. Boys and girls resolving conflicts is a theme of particular merit. Since the magazine is circulated worldwide, the *Friend* is interested in stories and articles with universal settings, conflicts, and character. Other suggestions include rebus, picture, holiday, sports, and photo stories, or manuscripts that portray various cultures. Very short pieces (up to 250 words) are desired for younger readers and preschool children. Appropriate humor is a constant need."

FUTURIFIC MAGAZINE (I, II, IV), Foundation for Optimism, 280 Madison Ave., New York NY 10016. (212)684-4913. Editor: B. Szent-Miklosy. News Magazine: 8½ × 11; 32 pages; glossy paper; illustrations and photos. "News indicating what the future will be for a general audience." Monthly.
Needs: The future. "Do not send material unrelated to current events." Receives 2 unsolicited mss/month. Buys 1 ms/issue. Publishes ms 1-2 months after acceptance. Length: Open. Publishes short shorts. Sometimes critiques rejected mss.
How to Contact: Send complete ms with cover letter. Reports in 1 week. SASE. Simultaneous, photocopied and reprint submissions OK. Accepts computer printout submissions. Accepts electronic submissions. Sample copy for $3; 9 × 12 SAE and 4 first class stamps. Fiction guidelines for #10 SAE and 1 first class stamp.
Payment: Negotiated.
Terms: Pays on publication for one-time rights.

GALLERY MAGAZINE, Montcalm Publishing Corporation, 401 Park Avenue South, New York NY 10016. (212)779-8900. Editor: Marc Lichter. Fiction Editor: John Bowers. Magazine. 112 pages; illustrations and photographs. Magazine for men, 18-34. Monthly. Estab. 1972. Circ. 425,000.
Needs: Adventure, erotica, humor/satire, literary, mainstream, suspense/mystery. Receives 100 unsolicited fiction mss/month. Accepts 1 mss/issue. Publishes ms 2-3 months after acceptance. Less than 10% of fiction is agented. Length: 1,500-3,000 words average; 1,000 words minimum; 3,500 words maximum. Publishes short shorts. Sometimes critiques rejected mss and recommends other markets.
How to Contact: Send complete ms. Reports in 2 months. SASE. Photocopied submissions OK. Accepts computer printout submissions. Sample copy $5. Fiction guidelines for #10 SAE and 1 first class stamp.
Payment: $400-1,000, contributor's copies.
Terms: Pays 50% on acceptance/50% on publication. Buys first North American serial rights. Publication copyrighted.

‡THE GEM (II), Churches of God, General Conference, Box 926, Findlay OH 45839. (419)424-1961. Editor: Marilyn Rayle Kern. Magazine: 6×9; 8 pages; 50 lb. uncoated paper; illustrations (clip art). "True-to-life stories of healed relationships and growing maturity in the Christian faith for senior high students through senior citizens who attend Churches of God, General Conference Sunday Schools." Weekly. Estab. 1865. Circ. 8,000.
Needs: Adventure, feminist, humor, mainstream, religious/inspirational, senior citizen/retirement. Nothing that denies or ridicules standard Christian values. Receives 30 unsolicited fiction mss/month. Buys 1 ms every 2-3 issues; 20-25 mss/year. Recently published work by Betty Steele Everett, Todd Lee and Betty Lou Mell. Publishes ms 4-12 months after submission. Length: 1,500 words average; 1,000 words minimum; 1,700 words maximum.
How to Contact: Send complete ms with cover letter ("letter not essential, unless there is information about author's background which enhances story's credibility or verifies details as being authentic"). Reports in 6 months on mss. SASE for ms. Simultaneous, photocopied submissions and reprints OK. Accepts computer printouts. Sample copy free with 4×9 SAE and 1 first class stamp. Fiction guidelines. "One 4×9 SAE will accommodate guidelines plus one sample copy for one stamp. If more than one sample copy is desired along with the guidelines, will need 2 oz. postage."
Payment: Pays $10-15 and contributor's copies. Charge for extras (postage for mailing more than one).
Terms: Pays on publication for one-time rights.
Advice: "Competition at the mediocre level is fierce. There is a dearth of well written, relevant fiction which wrestles with real problems involving Christian values applied to the crisis times and 'passages' of life. Humor which puts the daily grind into a fresh perspective which promises hope for survival is also in short supply. Write from your own experience. Avoid religious jargon and stereotypes. Conclusion must be believable in terms of the story—don't force a 'Christian' ending. Avoid simplistic solutions to complex problems. Reader should care enough about the characters and be interested enough in the plot to keep reading when story is 'continued on page 6.' Listen to the story-telling art of Garrison Keillor. Feel how very particular experiences of small town life in Minnesota become universal."

‡GENESIS MAGAZINE, Jakel Corp., 1776 Broadway, 20th Fl., New York NY 10019. (212)265-3500. Editor: Joe Kelleher. Fiction Editor: Michael Banka. Magazine: 8×10¾; 116 pages; some illustrations and photographs. "Men's magazine with frank sexual material, target audience, age 25-45." Published 13 times/year. Estab. 1972. Circ. 300,000.
Needs: Erotica. "We publish only sex fiction, and pieces must be written in a very straightforward, unembellished style with the emphasis on sexual interactions." Receives 2 unsolicited mss/month. Buys 1 ms/issue; 10 mss/year. Publishes ms 1-3 months after acceptance. Length: 2,200 words average; 2,000 words minimum; 2,500 words maximum. Sometimes critiques rejected mss.
How to Contact: Query with clips of published work. Reports in 1 month. SASE. Photocopied submissions OK. Accepts computer printout submissions. Sample copy for SAE and $1.85 postage. Fiction guidelines for SAE and $1.25 postage.
Payment: Pays $250-525 and contributor's copies.
Terms: Pays 60 days after publication. Offers kill fee of 25% of prearranged fee. Buys first North American serial rights.

GENT (II), Dugent Publishing Corp., Suite 600, 2600 Douglas Rd., Coral Gables FL 33134. (305)443-2378. Editor: Bruce Arthur. "Men's magazine designed to have erotic appeal for the reader. Our publications are directed to a male audience, but we do have a certain percentage of female readers. For the most part, our audience is interested in erotically stimulating material, but not exclusively." Monthly. Estab. 1959. Circ. 175,000.
Needs: Contemporary, science fiction, horror, erotica, mystery, adventure and humor. *Gent* specializes in "D-Cup cheesecake," and fiction should be slanted accordingly. "Most of the fiction published includes several sex scenes. No fiction that concerns children, religious subjects or anything that might be libelous." Buys 2 mss/issue, 24 mss/year. Receives approximately 30-50 unsolicited fiction mss/month. Published new writers within the last year. Approximately 10% of fiction is agented. Length: 2,000-3,500 words. Critiques rejected mss "when there is time."
How to Contact: Send complete ms with SASE. Reports in 1 month on mss. Publishes ms an average of 6 weeks after acceptance. Sample copy $5. Free fiction guidelines with legal-sized SASE.
Payment: Pays $150-300. Free author's copy.
Terms: Pays on publication for first North American serial rights.
Advice: "Since *Gent* magazine is the 'Home of the D-Cups,' stories and articles containing either characters or themes with a major emphasis on large breasts will have the best chance for consideration. Study a sample copy first." Mss are rejected because "there are not enough or ineffective erotic sequences, plot is not plausible, wrong length, or not slanted specifically for us."

GENTLEMAN'S COMPANION (I), Gentleman's Companion, Inc., Box 447, Voorhees NJ 08003. (212)564-0112. Editor: J.H. Hartley. Magazine: 8½×11; 96 pages; 50 lb coated paper; 80 lb cover stock; illustrations; photos. Men's magazine, sexually oriented material of a heavily erotic nature, geared to swinging concepts. Monthly. Published special fiction issue. Estab. 1976. Circ. 175,000.
Needs: Erotica, fantasy. No non-erotic fiction. Receives 20 unsolicited fiction mss/month; accepts 2 fiction mss/issue. Publishes ms 6 weeks to 6 months after acceptance. Length: 1,000-2,500 words.
Payment: Payment is negotiable.
How to Contact: Send complete ms with cover letter. SASE. Reports in 1 month on queries. Sample copy $4.95 and 8½×11 SAE with 2 first class stamps. Fiction guidelines for $3.95 and 8½×11 SAE with 2 first class stamps.
Terms: Pays on publication. Acquires all rights.

‡GEORGIA SPORTSMAN (II, IV), Game & Fish Publications, P.O. Box 741, Marietta GA 30061. (404)953-9222. Editor: Jimmy Jacobs. Magazine: 8×10¾; 80 pages; slick paper; slick cover; illustrations and photographs. "Adventure, humor and nostalgia dealing with hunting and fishing in Georgia for hunters and fishermen." Monthly. Estab. 1976. Circ. 48,000.
Needs: Adventure, humor/satire. "Fiction must take place in or pertain to Georgia and center on hunting and fishing. Such activities as hiking, camping, canoeing or boating are OK as long as they have a hunting or fishing connection. No strictly camping, hiking, boating or canoeing stories or pieces ascribing human characteristics to animals and fish." Receives 6-8 unsolicited mss/month. Buys 1 ms/issue; 6-12 mss/year. Publishes ms 6 months to 1 year after acceptance. Recently published work by Bob Kornegay, John E. Phillips and Bill Cherry. Length: 1,500 words average, 1,400 words minimum; 1,600 words maximum.
How to Contact: Send complete manuscript with cover letter including "who the writer is, and how to contact him/her." SASE. Simultaneous and photocopied submissions OK. Accepts computer printout submissions. Sample copy for $2.50. Fiction guidelines free.
Payment: Pays $125.
Terms: Pays 2½ months prior to publication for first North American serial rights. Offers 100% kill fee.

‡THE GIFTED CHILD TODAY (IV), GCT Inc., P.O. Box 6448, Mobile AL 36660. (205)478-4700. Editor: Marvin Gold. Magazine: 8½×11; 64 pages; coated paper; self-cover; illustrations and photographs. "Focuses on materials about gifted, creative and talented children and youth for parents and professionals." Bimonthly. Estab. 1978. Circ. 10,000.
Needs: "As long as the subject matter deals with gifted, creative, talented individuals in some way, material will be considered." Does not want to see protagonist(s) and/or antagonist(s) that are not gifted, creative and/or talented individuals." Receives 3-4 unsolicited mss each month. Accepts 1 ms/issue. Publishes ms 3-12 months after acceptance. Length: 1,800 words average; 1,000 words minimum; 5,000 words maximum. Publishes short shorts. Length: 500 words.

How to Contact: Send complete manuscript with cover letter. Reports in 1 month on queries; 2 months on mss. SASE. Photocopied submissions OK. Sample copy for $5.
Payment: Pays in contributor's copies. Charges for extras.
Terms: Acquires first rights.

GOLF JOURNAL (II), United States Golf Assoc., Golf House, Far Hills NJ 07931. (201)234-2300. Editor: Robert Sommers. Managing Editor: George Eberl. Magazine: 40-48 pages; self cover stock; illustrations and photos. "The magazine's subject is golf—its history, lore, rules, equipment and general information. The focus is on amateur golf and those things applying to the millions of American golfers. Our audience is generally professional, highly literate and knowledgeable; presumably they read *Golf Journal* because of an interest in the game, its traditions, and its noncommercial aspects." Published 8 times/year. Estab. 1949. Circ. 280,000.
Needs: Humor. "Fiction is very limited. *Golf Journal* has had an occasional humorous story, topical in nature. Generally speaking, short stories are not used. Golf jokes will not be used." Buys 10-12 mss/year. Published new writers within the last year. Length: 1,000-2,000 words. Recommends other markets. Critiques rejected mss "when there is time."
How to Contact: Send complete ms with SASE. Reports in 2 months on mss. Free sample copy with SASE.
Payment: Pays $500-1,000. 1-10 free author's copies.
Terms: Pays on acceptance.
Advice: "Know your subject (golf); familiarize yourself first with the publication." Rejects mss because "fiction usually does not serve the function of *Golf Journal*, which, as the official magazine of the United States Golf Association, deals chiefly with nonfiction subjects."

GOOD HOUSEKEEPING (II), 959 Eighth Ave., New York NY 10019. Editor: John Mack Carter. Fiction Editor: Naome Lewis. Magazine: 8 × 10; approximately 250 pages; slick paper; thick, high-gloss cover; 4-color illustrations, b&w and color photos. Homemaking magazine of informational articles, how-to's for homemakers of all ages. Monthly. Circ. 20 million.
Needs: "*Good Housekeeping* looks for stories of emotional interest to women—courtship, romance, marriage, family, friendship, personal growth, coming-of-age. The best way to know if your story is appropriate for us is to read several of our recent issues. (We are sorry but we do not furnish free sample copies of the magazine.)" Buys 2 short stories/issue. Approximately 75% of fiction is agented. Length: 1,000-3,000 words.
How to Contact: Send complete ms with cover letter. Accepts computer printout submissions. Unsolicited manuscripts *will not* be returned (see Advice). Publishes ms an average of 6 months after acceptance.
Payment: Pays standard magazine rates.
Terms: Pays on acceptance for first North American serial rights.
Advice: "It is now our policy that all submissions of unsolicited fiction received in our offices will be read and, if found to be unsuitable for us, discarded. If you wish to introduce your work to us, you will be submitting material that will not be critiqued or returned. The odds are long that we will contact you to inquire about publishing your submission or to invite you to correspond with us directly, so please be sure before you take the time and expense to submit it that it is our type of material."

THE GUIDE (II,IV): Gay Travel, Entertainment, Politics, and Sex, Box 593, Boston MA 02199. (617)266-8557. FAX: (617)266-1125. Editor: French Wall. Magazine: 8 × 10; 124-156; newsprint; 70 lb. cover stock; photos. "Gay liberation and sex positive information, articles and columns; radical political and radical religious philosophies welcome. Audience is primarily gay men, some lesbians, bar crowd and grassroots politicos." Monthly. Estab. 1981. Circ. 25,000.
Needs: Adventure, erotica, ethnic, experimental, fantasy, feminist, gay, historical (general), humor/satire, lesbian, regional, religious/inspirational romance (contemporary, historical and young adult), science fiction, senior citizen, spiritual, sports, suspense/mystery. "Focus on empowerment—avoidance of 'victim' philosophy appreciated." Receives 4 mss/month. Publishes ms within 3 months to 1 year after acceptance. Length: 1,800 words average; 500 words minimum; 5,000 words maximum. Recently published work by Lars Eighner, John Champagne and A.J. Johnson; published new writers within the last year. Publishes short shorts. Sometimes critiques rejected mss.
How to Contact: Query first. Reports in 2-4 weeks. SASE; include cover letter and phone number. Simultaneous and photocopied submissions OK. Accepts computer printout submissions. Sample copy for 9 × 13 SAE and 8 first class stamps.

Payment: Pays $40-150.

Terms: Pays on acceptance for all rights or first rights.

Advice: *"The Guide*'s format and extensive distribution in this area makes it an excellent vehicle for writers anxious to be read. *The Guide* has multiplied its press run fourfold in the past years and is committed to continued growth."

GUIDE MAGAZINE, International Northwest Edition, One in Ten Publishing, Box 23070, Seattle WA 98102. (206)323-7374. Editor: Jenny Peterson. "We publish humor pieces, fiction, poetry, feature stories and interpretive essays examining personalities, politics, science fiction, current events, the arts business and indeed the whole of culture as it relates to gay life." Monthly. Estab. 1986. Circ. 12,000.

Needs: Adventure, condensed novels, ethnic, experimental, historical, horror, humor, mainstream, romance, science fiction, mystery/suspense, western. "No erotica or porn." Publishes 6 fiction mss/ year. Length: 800 words minimum; 3,000 words maximum.

How to Contact: Send complete ms. SASE. Photocopied and reprint submissions OK. Accepts computer printout submissions. Letter quality preferred. Accepts electronic submissions via 5¼" disks formatted with MS/DOS files stored in ASCII or WordPerfect. Send hard copy with electronic submissions. Sample copy for 9 × 12 SAE and $1 postage. Writer's guidelines for #10 SAE and 1 first class stamp.

Payment: Pays subject to contributor's copies. Pay is negotiated.

Terms: Pays on publication for first North American serial rights. Publication copyrighted.

Advice: "Well researched and intellectually challenging pieces get top priority."

GUYS, First Hand Ltd., Box 1314, Teaneck NJ 07666. (201)836-9177. FAX: (201)836-5055. Editor: Bob Harris. Magazine: digest size; 160 pages; illustrations; photos. "Fiction and informative departments for today's gay man. Fiction is of an erotic nature, and we especially need short shorts and novella-length stories." Published 10 times a year. Estab. 1988.

Needs: Gay. Should be written in first person. No science fiction or fantasy. Erotica should be based on reality. Buys 6 mss/issue; 66 mss/year. Publishes ms 9-18 months after acceptance. Recently published work by Rick Jackson, Kenn Richie, Jay Shaffer; published new writers within the last year. Length: 3,000 words average; 2,000 words minimum; 3,750 words maximum. For novellas: 7,500-8,600 words. Publishes short shorts. Length: 750-1,250 words. Sometimes critiques rejected mss and recommends other markets.

How to Contact: Send complete ms with cover letter; should include writer's name, address, telephone and Social Security number and whether he is selling all rights or first North American serial rights. Reports in 6-8 weeks on mss. SASE. Accepts computer printout submissions. Sample copy for $5. Fiction guidelines for #10 SAE and 1 first class stamp.

Payment: Pays $100-150. $75 for short shorts (all rights); $250 for novellas (all rights).

Terms: Pays on publication or in 240 days, whichever comes first, for all rights or first North American serial rights.

HADASSAH MAGAZINE (IV), 50 W. 58th St., New York NY 10019. Executive Editor: Alan M. Tigay. Senior Editor: Zelda Shluker. General interest magazine: 8½ × 11; 48-70 pages; coated and uncoated paper; slick, medium weight coated cover; drawings and cartoons; photos. Primarily concerned with Israel, the American Jewish community, Jewish communities around the world and American current affairs. Monthly except combined June/July and August/September issues. Circ. 375,000.

Needs: Ethnic (Jewish). Receives 20-25 unsolicited fiction mss each month. Recently published fiction by Anita Desai and Lori Ubell; published new writers within the last year. Length: 3,000 words maximum. Also publishes short stories 1,500-2,000 words.

How to Contact: Send complete ms with SASE. Accepts computer printout submissions. Reports in 6 weeks on mss. "Not interested in multiple submissions or previously published articles."

Payment: Pays $300 minimum. Offers $100 kill fee for assigned mss not published.

Terms: Pays on publication for U.S. publication rights.

Advice: "Stories on a Jewish theme should be neither self-hating nor schmaltzy."

HARPER'S MAGAZINE (II, III), 666 Broadway, 11th Floor, New York NY 10012. (212)614-6500. Editor: Lewis H. Lapham. Magazine: 8 × 10¾; 80 pages; illustrations. Magazine for well educated, widely read and socially concerned readers, college-aged and older, those active in political and community affairs. Monthly. Circ. 190,000.

Executive Editor Alan Tigay says this issue of Hadassah, which focuses on Jewish life and tradition, "featured a story on the aesthetic resources associated with Shabbat. Lynne Feldman's painting of a woman making a Sabbath blessing was not only a perfect illustration of the subject, but itself an aesthetic resource." "The Blessing," oil on canvas by Lynne Feldman, courtesy of Oxford Gallery, Rochester, New York.

Needs: Contemporary and humor. Stories on contemporary life and its problems. Receives approximately 300 unsolicited fiction mss/month. Published new writers within the last year. Length: 1,000-5,000 words.
How to Contact: Query to managing editor, or through agent. Reports in 6 weeks on queries.
Payment: Pays $500-1,000. Negotiable kill fee.
Terms: Pays on acceptance for rights, which vary on each author and material. Sends galleys to author.
Advice: Buys very little fiction but *Harper's* has published short stories traditionally.

HARVEY FOR LOVING PEOPLE, Harvey Shapiro Inc., Box 2070, Cherry Hill NJ 08003. (212)564-0112. Editor: Harvey Shapiro. Managing Editor: Jack Hartley. Magazine dedicated to the enrichment of loving relationships between couples, offering sexually informative material in graphically erotic manner about swingers' lifestyles. "Our readership consists of people interested in highly informative sex-related information." Monthly. Estab. 1979. Circ. 200,000.
Needs: Lesbian and heterosexual erotica. No material accepted that is not sexually oriented. Buys 2-3 mss/issue. Length: 1,000-2,000 words.
How to Contact: Send mss with SASE. Reports in 1 month.
Payment: Pays $50-200.
Terms: Pays on publication for all rights.
Advice: "We reserve the right to edit. Stay within the Meese Commission guidelines."

HI-CALL (II), Gospel Publishing House, 1445 Boonville Ave., Springfield MO 65802-1894. (417)862-2781. Editor: Deanna S. Harris. Take-home Sunday school paper for teenagers (ages 12-17). Weekly. Estab. 1936. Circ. 95,000.
Needs: Religious/inspirational, mystery/suspense, adventure, humor, spiritual and young adult, with a strong but not preachy Biblical emphasis. Receives approximately 100 unsolicited fiction mss/month. Recently published work by Betty Steele Everett, Alan Cliburn and Michelle Starr. Published new writers within the last year. Length: up to 1,500 words.
How to Contact: Send complete ms with SASE. Simultaneous and previously published submissions OK. Accepts computer printout submissions. Prefers letter-quality. Reports in 1-3 months on mss. Free sample copy and guidelines.

Payment: Pays 2-3¢/word.
Terms: Pays on acceptance for one-time rights.
Advice: "Most manuscripts are rejected because of shallow characters, shallow or predictable plots, and/or a lack of spiritual emphasis. Send seasonal material approximately one year in advance."

‡**HIGH ADVENTURE (II)**, General Council Assemblies of God (Gospel Publishing Co.), 1445 Boonville, Springfield MO 65802. (417)862-2781, ext. 4178. Editor: Marshall Bruner. Magazine: 8⅚₁₆ × 11⅛; 16 pages; lancer paper; self cover; illustrations; photos. Magazine for adolescent boys. "Designed to provide boys with worthwhile, enjoyable, leisure reading; to challenge them in narrative form to higher ideals and greater spiritual dedication; and to perpetuate the spirit of the Royal Rangers program through stories, ideas and illustrations." Quarterly. Published special fiction issue; plans another. Estab. 1971. Circ. 86,000.
Needs: Adventure, historical (general), religious/inspirational, suspense/mystery and western. Published new writers within the last year. Length: 1,200 words minimum. Publishes short shorts to 1,000 words. Occasionally critiques rejected mss.
How to Contact: Send ms with SASE. Include Social Security number. Simultaneous, photocopied and previously published submissions OK. Reports in 6 weeks on mss. Free sample copy; free fiction guidelines for 9 × 12 SASE.
Payment: Pays 2-3¢/word (base) and 3 contributor's copies.
Terms: Pays on acceptance for first rights and one-time rights.
Advice: "Read the magazine; know the readership; give attention to writing style; be accurate."

HIGH TIMES (II), Trans High Corp., 211 E. 43rd St., New York NY 10017. (212)972-8484. Editor: Steven Hager. Magazine: 8½ × 11; 100 pages; glossy paper; illustrations; photos. Publishes "drug-related" material for "counter-culture" readers. Monthly. Circ. 250,000.
Needs: Psychdelic music and art, religious use of hallucinogenics, hydroponic cultivation of plants, political coverage of the counter culture. Receives 16 unsolicited mss/month. Buys 5 mss/year. Publishes ms 6-8 months after acceptance. Published new writers within the last year. Length: 2,000-4,000 preferred. Publishes short shorts.
How to Contact: Send complete ms with cover letter. Reports in 1 month on queries; 6 weeks on mss. SASE. Simultaneous, photocopied and reprint submissions OK. Accepts computer printout submissions. "Call John Holmstrom for modem information." Sample copy for $5. Fiction guidelines free.
Payment: Pays $200-600 and contributor's copies.
Terms: Pays on publication. Purchases negotiable rights.

HIGHLIGHTS FOR CHILDREN, 803 Church St., Honesdale PA 18431. (717)253-1080. Editor: Kent L. Brown Jr., Address fiction to: Beth Troop, Manuscript Coordinator. Magazine: 8½ × 11; 42 pages; uncoated paper; coated cover stock; illustrations; photos. Published 11 times/year. Circ. 2.8 million.
Needs: Juvenile (ages 2-12). Unusual stories appealing to both girls and boys; stories with good characterization, strong emotional appeal, vivid, full of action. "Begin with action rather than description, have strong plot, believable setting, suspense from start to finish." Length: 400-800 words. "We also need easy stories for very young readers (100-400 words)." No war, crime or violence. Buys 6-7 mss/issue. Receives 600-800 unsolicited fiction mss/month. Also publishes rebus (picture) stories of 125 words or under for the 3-7-year-old child. Recently published work by Nancy West, Cris Peterson and Trinka Enell; published new writers within the last year. Critiques rejected mss occasionally, "especially when editors see possibilities in story."
How to Contact: Send complete ms with SASE and include a rough word count and cover letter "with any previous acceptances by our magazine; any other published work anywhere." Accepts computer printout submissions. Reports in 1 month on mss. Free guidelines on request.
Payment: Pays 14¢ and up per word.
Terms: Pays on acceptance for all rights. Sends galleys to author.
Advice: "We accept a story on its merit whether written by an unpublished or an experienced writer. Mss are rejected because of poor writing, lack of plot, trite or worn-out plot, or poor characterization. Children *like* stories and learn about life from stories. Children learn to become lifelong fiction readers by enjoying stories." Sponsors occasional contests. Write for information.

ALFRED HITCHCOCK'S MYSTERY MAGAZINE (I, II), Davis Publications, Inc., 380 Lexington Ave., New York NY 10017. (212)557-9100. Editor: Cathleen Jordan. Mystery fiction magazine: 5¹⁄₁₆ × 7⅜; 160 pages; 28 lb newsprint paper; 60 lb machine-/coated cover stock; illustrations; photos. Published 13 times/year. Estab. 1956. Circ. 225,000.
Needs: Mystery and detection. No sensationalism. Number of mss/issue varies with length of mss. Length: up to 14,000 words. Also publishes short shorts.
How to Contact: Send complete ms and SASE. Accepts computer printout submissions. Reports in 2 months. Free guideline sheet for SASE.
Payment: 5¢/word on acceptance.

THE HOME ALTAR (II), Meditations for Families with Children, P.O. Box 590179, San Francisco, CA 94159-0179. Editor: M. Elaine Dunham. Magazine: 5¼ × 7¼; 64 pages; newsprint paper; coated 4-color cover stock; 2-color illustrations. *"The Home Altar* is a magazine of daily devotions. For each day, there is a designated Bible reading, a short story (fiction or nonfiction) which reflects the central message of the biblical passage, and a concluding prayer." Readers are "primarily Lutheran (ELCA) families—with children between 6 and 14 years of age." Quarterly. Estab. 1940. Circ. 75,000.
Needs: Juvenile (5-9 years) and religious/inspirational. "No unsolicited manuscripts are accepted for publication in *The Home Altar.* All writing is done on assignment, to reflect specific Bible readings and themes." Accepts up to 90 mss/issue; approximately 200 mss/year. Publishes ms an average of 6 months to 1 year after acceptance. Recently published work by Barbra Minar, Normajean Matzke and Jerome Koch. Length: 150 words average; 125 words minimum; 170 words maximum. Sometimes critiques rejected mss.
How to Contact: Query with clips of published or unpublished work. Reports on queries in 3 months; on mss in 2 weeks. Photocopied submissions OK. Accepts computer printout submissions. Sample copy and fiction guidelines free.
Payment: Pays $10 per "story"; contributor's copies.
Terms: Pays on acceptance for all rights.
Advice: "We're trying to serve a diverse group of readers—children of all ages as well as adults. A well written story often has several levels of meaning and will touch people of different ages and experiences in different ways. Write stories in which children are the protagonists. Keep your sentences short. Use inclusive language when referring to human beings or to God."

HOME LIFE (II), The Sunday School Board of the Southern Baptist Convention, 127 9th Ave. N., Nashville TN 37234. (615)251-2271. Editor: Charlie Warren. A Christian family magazine: 8⅛ × 11; 66 pages; coated paper; separate cover stock; illustrations; photos. "Top priorities are strengthening and enriching marriage; parenthood; family concerns and problems; and spiritual and personal growth. Most of our readers are married couples and parents between the ages of 25-50. They read it out of denominational loyalty and desire for Christian growth and discipleship." Monthly. Estab. 1947. Circ. 700,000.
Needs: Contemporary, prose poem, religious/inspirational, spiritual, humor and young adult. "We do not want distasteful, risqué or raunchy fiction. Nor should it be too fanciful or far-fetched." Buys 1-2 mss/issue, 12-24 mss/year. Receives approximately 100-200 unsolicited fiction mss/month. Recently published work by Irene J. Kutz, Mary C. Perham, Ann Beacham; published new writers within the last year. Length: 750-1,800 words. Publishes short shorts of 500+ words. Recommends other markets.
How to Contact: Query or send complete ms. SASE always. Simultaneous submissions OK. Accepts computer printout submissions. Reports in 1 month on queries, 2 months on mss. Publishes ms 1 year to 20 months after acceptance. Sample copy for $1.
Payment: Pays up to 5¢/word for unsolicited mss. 3 free author's copies.
Terms: Pays on acceptance for all rights, first rights or first North American serial rights. Rarely buys reprints.

HORROR, (II), The Illustrated Book of Fears, Northstar Publishing, Suite C-9 1004 E. Steger Rd., Crete IL 60417. Editor: Mort Castle. Magazine. 8½ × 11; 64 pages; newsprint; color, enamel cover. "Quality horror for a general audience." Quarterly. Estab. 1989. Circ. 10,000.
Needs: Horror, psychic/supernatural/occult. Receives 50 unsolicited mss/month. Buys 4-8 mss/issue; 30 mss/year. Recently published work by Graham Masterson, Mort Castle. Length is open. Publishes short stories. Sometimes critiques rejected mss and recommends other markets.
How to Contact: "Send no more than three single-page story proposals or one complete story in standard two-column comics-script format." Reports in 3 months on queries; 4 months on mss. SASE. Reprints submission OK. Sample copy for $4. Fiction guidelines for SAE and 45¢.

Payment: Pays $5 per page and contributor's copies.
Terms: Pays on publication, rights purchased vary.
Advice: "In the tradition of the classic *EC* comics and the Warren publications of the late 60s and early 70s, but geared to contemporary taste, *HORROR* stories range from classical foggy moor at midnight tales ('when the powers of evil are exalted') to new wave, chop-o-matic super-splatter. Artists and writers are today's and tomorrow's 'big names.' "

HORSE ILLUSTRATED, Fancy Publications, Box 6050, Mission Viejo CA 92690. (714)855-8822. FAX: (714)855-3045. Managing Editor: Sharon Rolls Lemon. "General all-breed horse magazine for horse lovers of all ages but mainly women riding for show and pleasure. All material is centered around horses; both English and western riding styles are profiled." Monthly. Estab. 1982. Circ. 120,000.
Needs: Adventure, humor and suspense/mystery. "Must concern horses. Liberal — nothing unsuitable to a younger audience, although we do not want mss aimed directly at young readers." Receives 3-5 unsolicited mss/month. Buys 5-6 mss/year. Recently published work by Cooky McClung, Elizabeth Vaugh; published new writers within the last year. Length: 1,500-2,000 words average; 1,000 words minimum; 2,500 words maximum. Occasionally critiques rejected mss if asked to do so.
How to Contact: Query first or send complete ms. Reports in 2 months on queries; 3 months on mss. SASE. Photocopied submissions OK. Accepts computer printout submissions. Publishes ms 4-10 months after acceptance. Sample copy $3.25. Free fiction guidelines. SASE.
Payment: Pays $50-150; 2 contributor's copies; $2 charge for extras ("free if request is for a reasonable number of copies").
Terms: Pays on publication for one-time rights.
Advice: "Write about adult women — *no* little girl, wild stallion or cowboy and Indian stories, please."

‡**HOT SHOTS (IV)**, Sunshine Publishing Company, Inc., 7366 Convoy Court, San Diego CA 92111. (619)278-9058. Editor: Ralph Cobar. Magazine; digest sized; 100 pages; Dombrite paper; 4-color cover; color centerfold and photographs. "Adult erotica, real life fantasies, and true reader experience. Explicit fiction about 18-50 year old males only. For gay males." Monthly. Plans special fiction issue. Estab. 1986. Circ. 35,000.
Needs: Confession, erotica, gay. No subjugation, rape, heavy s&m, beastiality, incest, unless characters are of consenting age. Accepts 100-150 mss/year. Publishes ms 4 months after acceptance. Length: 2,500 words average; 2,000 words minimum; 3,000 words maximum. Sometimes critiques rejected mss.
How to Contact: Send complete ms with cover letter. Reports in 1-2 month. Accepts computer printout submissions. Accepts electronic submissions via disk convertable to ASCII format. Requires hard copy when sending disk submissions. Sample copy $5. Fiction guidelines free.
Payment: Pays $75-100, contributor's copies.
Terms: Pays on publication for all rights.
Advice: "Keep all sexual activity between fictional characters within the realm of possibility. Do not overexaggerate physical characteristics. We want stimulating fiction, not comedy. The overall tone of *Hot Shots* is always exciting, up beat, compassionate."

HUMPTY DUMPTY'S MAGAZINE (II), Children's Better Health Institute, Benjamin Franklin Literary & Medical Society, Inc., 1100 Waterway Blvd., Box 567, Indianapolis IN 46206. Editor: Christine French Clark. Magazine: 6½ × 9⅛; 48 pages; 35 lb. paper; coated cover; color, 2-color, or b&w illustrations; rarely photos. Children's magazine stressing health, nutrition, hygiene, exercise and safety for children ages 4-6. Publishes 8 issues per year.
Needs: Juvenile health-related material and material of a more general nature. No inanimate talking objects. Rhyming stories should flow easily with no contrived rhymes. Buys 3-5 mss/issue. Receives 250-300 unsolicited fiction mss/month. Length: 600 words maximum.
How to Contact: Send complete ms with SASE. Reports in 8-10 weeks. Sample copy 75¢. Editorial guidelines with SASE. No queries.
Payment: Pays minimum 10¢/word for stories plus 2 author's copies (more upon request).
Terms: Pays on publication for all rights. (One-time book rights returned when requested for specific publication.)
Advice: "In contemporary stories, characters should be up-to-date, with realistic dialogue. We're looking for health-related stories with unusual twists or surprise endings. We want to avoid stories and poems that 'preach.' We try to present the health material in a positive way, utilizing a light humorous approach wherever possible." Most rejected mss "are too wordy. Cover letters should be included only if they give pertinent information — list of credits, bibliography, or mention of any special training or qualifications that make author an authority."

HUSTLER (IV), Larry Flynt Publications, Suite 300, 9171 Wilshire Blvd., Beverly Hills CA 90210. (213)858-7100. Executive Editor: Allan MacDonell. Magazine: 100 pages; illustrations; photos. "Men's magazine, for men and women." Monthly. Estab. 1976. Circ. 1 million.
Needs: Erotica. Receives 20-30 unsolicited mss/month. Buys 1 ms/issue; 12 mss/year. Publishes ms 1-6 months after acceptance. Published new writers last year. Length: 3,500 words average; 3,000 words minimum; 4,000 words maximum. Occasionally critiques rejected mss. Recommends other markets.
How to Contact: Send complete ms with cover letter which should include "writer's name, address, telephone number, and whether the manuscript has been or is being offered elsewhere." Reports in 4-6 weeks on ms. SASE for ms. Photocopied submissions OK. Accepts computer printout submissions. Fiction guidelines free.
Payment: $1,500-nonfiction; $1,000-fiction.
Terms: Pays on acceptance for all rights.
Advice: "Readers have indicated a desire to read well written erotic fiction, which we classify as a good story with sexual undercurrent. The writer should keep in mind that the first requirement is that the story be a well written piece of fiction, and secondarily that it deal with sex; we are not interested in 'clinically descriptive' sex accounts."

‡HUSTLER BUSTY BEAUTIES (II), HG Publications, Inc., Suite 300, 9171 Wilshire Blvd., Beverly Hills CA 90210. (213)858-7100. Editor: N. Morgen Hagen. Magazine: 8x11; 100 pages; 60 lb. paper; 80 lb. cover; illustrations and photographs. "Adult entertainment and reading centered around large-breasted women for an over-18 audience, mostly male." Monthly. Estab. 1988. Circ. 150,000.
Needs: Adventure, erotica, fantasy, suspense/mystery. All must have erotic theme. Receives 25 unsolicited fiction mss/month. Buys 1 ms/issue; 6-12 mss/year. Publishes mss 3-6 months after acceptance. Recently published work by Mike Dillon, H.H. Morris. Length: 1,600 words preferred; 1,000 words minimum; 2,000 words maximum.
How to Contact: Query first. Then send complete ms with cover letter. Reports in 1 week on queries; in 2-4 weeks on mss. SASE. Sample copy for $3. Fiction guidelines free.
Payment: Pays $80-500.
Terms: Pays on acceptance for all rights.
Advice: Looks for "1. Plausible plot, well-defined characters, literary ingenuity. 2. Hot sex scenes. 3. Readable, coherent, grammatically sound prose."

IDEALS MAGAZINE (II), Ideals Publishing Corp., Suite 890, 565 Mirriott Dr., Nashville TN 37210. (615)885-8270. Editor: Nancy Skarmeas. Vice President of Publishing: Patricia Pingry. Magazine: 8⁷⁄₁₆ × 10⅛; 80 pages; 60 lb Cougarpaper; 12 pt CI-S cover; illustrations; photos. "*Ideals* is a family-oriented magazine with issues corresponding to seasons and based on traditional values." Published 8 times a year. Estab. 1944.
Needs: Seasonal, inspirational, spiritual, or humorous short, short fiction or prose poem. Beginning new policy of one short story per issue. Length: 2,000 words maximum.
How to Contact: Send complete ms with SASE. Reports in 8-12 weeks on mss.
Payment: Varies.
Terms: Pays on publication for one-time rights.
Advice: "We publish fiction that is appropriate to the theme of the issue and to our audience."

IN TOUCH (II, IV), Wesley Press, Box 50434 Indianapolis IN 46250-0434. (317)576-8144. Editor: Rebecca Higgins. Magazine: 8½ × 11; 8 pages each issue; offset paper and cover stock; illustrations; photos. Publication for teens, ages 13-18. Monthly in weekly parts.
Needs: *True* experiences and Christian testimonies told in fiction style, humorous fiction, C.S. Lewis-type allegories and spiritual. Receives 100 unsolicited fiction mss/month. Length: 500-1,200 words.
How to Contact: Send complete ms with SASE. "Queries are not encouraged." Accepts computer printout submissions. Reports in 3-6 weeks on mss. Publishes ms 6-9 months after acceptance.
Payment: Pays 4¢/word, 2¢/word on reprints.
Terms: Pays on acceptance. Byline given and brief autobiographical sketch. Buys reprints.
Advice: "Send SASE for writer's guide before submitting. We are mostly using true events written in fiction style, humor and allegories. Most religious fiction is unrealistic."

IN TOUCH FOR MEN (IV), 7216 Varna St., North Hollywood CA 91605. (818)764-2288. Editor: Alec Wagner. Magazine: 8 × 10¾; 100 pages; glossy paper; coated cover; illustrations and photographs. "*In Touch* is a magazine for gay men. It features five to six nude male centerfolds in each issue, but is erotic rather than pornographic. We include fiction." Monthly. Estab. 1973. Circ. 70,000.

Needs: Confession, gay, erotica, romance (contemporary, historical, young adult). All characters must be over 18 years old. Stories must have an explicit erotic content. No heterosexual or internalized homophobic fiction. Buys 3 mss/month; 36 mss/year. Publishes ms 3 months after acceptance. Recently published work by Chuck Fallon, Christopher H. Allenson and Addison Whitney. Length: 2,500 words average; no minimum; 3,500 words maximum. Sometimes critiques rejected mss and recommends other markets.
How to Contact: Send complete ms with cover letter, name, address and Social Security number. Reports in 1 week on queries; 2 months on mss. SASE. Simultaneous, photocopied and reprint submissions, if from local publication, OK. Accepts computer printout submissions. Sample copy $4.95. Fiction guidelines free.
Payment: Pays $25-75 (except on rare occasions for a longer piece).
Terms: Pays on acceptance for one-time rights.
Advice: "Fiction is the most popular feature of our magazine. Our magazine features erotic fiction — remember *both* words. To be published, it must have some *storyline* ('fiction'), as well as sexual activity ('erotic')."

INDIA CURRENTS (II,IV), California's Guide to Indian Arts, Entertainment and Dining, Box 21285, San Jose CA 95151. (408)274-6966. FAX: (408)274-2733. Editor: Arvind Kumar. Magazine: 8½×11; 72 pages; newsprint paper; illustrations and photographs. "The arts and culture of India as seen in America for Indians and non-Indians with a common interest in India." Monthly. Estab. 1987. Circ. 27,500.
Needs: All Indian content: contemporary, ethnic, feminist, historical (general), humor/satire, literary, mainstream, prose poem, psychic/supernatural/occult, regional, religious/inspirational, romance, translations (from Indian languages). "We seek material with insight into Indian culture, American culture and the crossing from one to another." Receives 12 unsolicited mss/month. Buys 6 ms/issue; 72 mss/year. Publishes ms 2-6 months after acceptance. Recently published work by Chitra Divakaruni, C.J. Wallia, Javaid Qazi; published new writers within the last year. Length: 2,000 words average; 1,000 words minimum; 3,000 words maximum. Publishes short shorts. Length: 500 words.
How to Contact: Send complete ms with cover letter and clips of published work. Reports in 1 month on queries; 2 months on mss. SASE. Simultaneous, photocopied and reprint submissions OK. Computer printout submissions are acceptable. Accepts electronic submissions. Sample copy $2.
Payment: Pays $20/1,000 words.
Terms: Pays on publication for one-time rights.
Advice: "Story must be related to India and subcontinent in some meaningful way. The best stories are those which document some deep transformation as a result of an Indian experience, or those which show the humanity of Indians as the world's most ancient citizens."

INDIAN LIFE MAGAZINE (II, IV), Intertribal Christian Communications, Box 3765, Station B, Winnipeg, Manitoba RAW 3R6 Canada. (204)661-9333. Editor: Jim Uttley. Magazine: 8½×11; 24 pages; newsprint paper and cover stock; illustrations; photos. A nondenominational Christian magazine written and read mostly by North American Indians. Bimonthly. Estab. 1979. Circ. 63,000.
Needs: Adventure, confession, ethnic (Indian), historical (general), juvenile, men's, religious/inspirational, women's and young adult/teen. Receives 2-3 unsolicited mss/month. Buys 1 ms/issue; 4-5 mss/year. Recently published work by Margaret Primrose and Ann Dunn. Published new writers within the last year. Length: 1,000-1,200 words average. Publishes short shorts of 600-900 words. Occasionally comments on rejected mss.
How to Contact: Query first, send complete manuscript (with cover letter, bio and published clips), or query with clips of published work. Reports in 1 month on queries; in 2 months on mss. IRC or SASE ("US stamps no good up here"). Accepts computer printout submissions. Prefers letter-quality. Sample copy $1 and 8½×11 SAE. Fiction guidelines for $1 and #10 SAE.
Payment: 4¢/word and 5 contributor's copies; 50¢ charge for extras.
Terms: Pays on publication for first rights.
Advice: "Keep it simple with an Indian viewpoint at about a 5th grade reading level. Read story out loud. Have someone else read it to you. If it doesn't come across smoothly and naturally, it needs work."

INSIDE (II), The Magazine of the Jewish Exponent, Jewish Federation, 226 S. 16th St., Philadelphia PA 19102. (215)893-5700. Editor-in-Chief: Jane Biberman. Magazine: 175-225 pages; glossy paper; illustrations; photos. Aimed at middle- and upper-middle-class audience, Jewish-oriented articles and fiction. Quarterly. Estab. 1980. Circ. 80,000.

Needs: Contemporary, ethnic, humor/satire, literary and translations. No erotica. Receives approximately 10 unsolicited fiction mss/month. Buys 1-2 mss/issue, 4-8 mss/year. Published new writers within the last year. Length: 1,500 words minimum; 3,000 words maximum; 2,000 words average. Occasionally critiques rejected mss.
How to Contact: Query first with clips of published work. Reports on queries in 3 weeks. SASE. Accepts computer printouts. Simultaneous and photocopied submissions OK. Sample copy $3. Free fiction guidelines with SASE.
Payment: Pays $100-600.
Terms: Pays on acceptance for first rights. Sometimes buys reprints. Sends galleys to author.
Advice: "We're looking for original, avant-garde, stylish writing."

INSIDE TEXAS RUNNING (II, IV), The Tabloid Magazine That Runs Texas, 9514 Bristlebrook, Houston TX 77083. (713)498-3208. Publisher/Editor: Joanne Schmidt. Specialized tabloid for Texas joggers/runners—novice to marathoner, bicycling, aerobics and general fitness. Monthly. Estab. 1977. Circ. 10,000; overall readers 30,000.
Needs: Historical (general), humor/satire, literary, and serialized/excerpted books on running and general fitness. "Nothing sexually explicit—we're family-oriented." Texas-oriented mss preferred. Buys 1 ms/issue. Length: 500 words minimum; 2,000 words maximum. Occasionally critiques rejected mss.
How to Contact: *Query only.* "We're overrun with too much to read. Not accepting manuscripts at this time." Simultaneous, photocopied and previously published submissions OK. Reports in 1 month on mss. Sample copy $1.50. Free fiction guidelines with SASE.
Payment: $25-75.
Terms: Pays on acceptance for one-time rights. Publication copyrighted.
Advice: "If a writer has something useful and original to convey, editors will want to buy his work. Period. A writer should ask himself if he, as a reader, would find the story worth reading. Too many writers can't look beyond their own experiences and relate every boring detail of some personal incident, which they disguise as fiction."

INSIGHTS (II, IV), NRA News for Young Shooters, National Rifle Association of America, 1600 Rhode Island Ave. NW, Washington DC 20036. (202)828-6075. Editor: John Robbins. Magazine: 8⅛ × 10⅞; 24 pages; 60 lb. Midset paper and cover; illustrations and photos."*InSights* publishes educational yet entertaining articles, teaching young hunters and shooters ways to improve their performance. For boys and girls ages eight to 20." Monthly. Estab. 1981. Circ. 33,000.
Needs: Hunting or competition shooting. No "anti-hunting, anti-firearms." Receives 5-10 unsolicited mss/month. Accepts 1 ms/issue; 12 mss/year. Publishes ms an average of 1 month to 1 year after acceptance. Recently published work by Dan Anderson, Michael Manley and John Robbins; published new writers within the last year. Length: 1,000 words minimum; 1,500 words maximum. Publishes short shorts. Sometimes critiques rejected ms; occasionally recommends other markets.
How to Contact: Query with clips of published work and cover letter. Reports in 1 month on query; 6-8 weeks on mss. SASE. Photocopied submissions OK. Accepts computer printout submissions. Sample copy and fiction guidelines free.
Payment: Pays up to $150.
Terms: Pays on acceptance.
Advice: "Writing is an art but publishing is a business—a big business. Any writer who understands his market place has an edge over a writer who isn't familiar with the publications that want his kind of writing. We have become more discriminating in the fiction that we buy. Story has to have a strong plot and must present a lesson, whether it is gun safety, ethics or hunting knowledge."

‡INTERNATIONAL BOWHUNTER (I,II,IV), P.O. Box 67, Pillager MN 56473-0067. (218)746-3333. Editor: Johnny Boatner. Magazine; 8¼ × 10¾; 68 pages; enamel paper; illustrations and photographs. "Bowhunting articles only for bowhunters." Published 7 times/year. Estab. 1990. Circ. 50,000+.
Needs: Adventure and sports. "We want articles by people who are actually bowhunters writing about their experience." Receives 30 unsolicited mss/month. Buys 7-12 mss/issue; 49-84/year. Publishes ms 1-6 months after acceptance. Length: 1,200 words preferred; 600 words minimum; 4,000 words maximum. Publishes short shorts. Length: 500 words. Sometimes critiques rejected ms and recommends other markets.

How to Contact: Send complete ms with cover letter. Include Social Security number. Cover letter should include bio. Reports on queries in 2 weeks. SASE. Accepts computer printout submissions. Sample copy for $2, #10 SAE and 1 first class stamp. Fiction guidelines free for #10 SAE and 1 first class stamp.
Payment: Pays $25-150 and contributor's copies; charge for extras.
Terms: Buys first rights.

JACK AND JILL, The Benjamin Franklin Literary & Medical Society, Inc., 1100 Waterway Blvd., Box 567, Indianapolis IN 46206. (317)636-8881. Editor: Steve Charles. Children's magazine of articles, stories and activities many with a health, safety, exercise or nutritional-oriented theme, ages 6-8 years. Monthly except January/February, March/April, May/June, July/August. Estab. 1938.
Needs: Science fiction, mystery, sports, adventure, historical fiction and humor. Health-related stories with a subtle lesson. No religious subjects. Published work by Peter Fernandez, Adriana Devoy and Myra Schomberg; published new writers within the last year. Length: 500-1,500 words.
How to Contact: Send complete ms with SASE. Reports in 10 weeks on mss. Sample copy 75¢. Free fiction guidelines with SASE.
Payment: Pays 8¢/word.
Terms: Pays on publication for all rights.
Advice: "Try to present health material in a positive—not a negative—light. Use humor and a light approach wherever possible without minimizing the seriousness of the subject. We need more humor and adventure stories."

JIVE, BLACK CONFESSIONS, BLACK ROMANCE, BRONZE THRILLS, BLACK SECRETS (I, II), Sterling's Magazines/Lexington Library, 355 Lexington Ave., New York NY 10017. (212)949-6850. Editor: D. Boyd. Magazine: 8½×11; 72 pages; newsprint paper; glossy cover; 8×10 photographs. "We publish stories that are ultra romantic and have romantic lovemaking scenes in them. Our audience is basically young and in high school and college. However, we have a significant audience base of divorcees and housewives. The age range is from 18-49." Bimonthly (*Jive* and *Black Romance* in odd-numbered months; *Black Confessions* and *Bronze Thrills* in even-numbered months). 6 issues per year. Estab. 1962. Circ. 100,000.
Needs: Confession, romance (contemporary, young adult). No "stories that are stereotypical to black people, ones that do not follow the basic rules of writing, or ones that are too graphic in content and lack a romantic element." Receives 200 or more unsolicited fiction mss/month. Buys 6 mss/issue (2 issues/month); 144 mss/year. Publishes ms an average of 3-6 months after acceptance. Recently published work by Linda Smith; published new writers within the last year. Length: 15-19 pages. Always critiques rejected mss; recommends other markets.
How to Contact: Query with clips of published work or send complete ms with cover letter. A cover letter should include an author's bio and what he or she proposes to do. Of course, address and phone number." Reports in 3-6 months. SASE. Simultaneous and photocopied submissions OK. "Please contact me if simultaneously submitted work has been accepted elsewhere." Accepts computer printout submissions. Sample copy for 9×12 SAE and 5 first class stamps; fiction guidelines for #10 SAE and 2 first class stamps.
Payment: $75-100.
Terms: Pays on publication for first rights or one-time rights.
Advice: "Our four magazines are a great starting point for new writers. We accept work from beginners as well as established writers. Please study and research black culture and lifestyles if you are not a black writer. Stereotypical stories are not acceptable. Set the stories all over the world and all over the USA—not just down south. We are not looking for 'the runaway who gets turned out by a sweet-talking pimp' stories. We are looking for stories about all types of female characters. Any writer should not be afraid to communicate with us if he or she is having some difficulty with writing a story. We are available to help at any stage of the submission process. Also, writers should practice patience. If we do not contact the writer, that means that the story is being read or is being held on file for future publication. If we get in touch with the writer, it usually means a request for revision and resubmission. Do the best work possible and don't let rejection slips send you off 'the deep end.' Don't take everything that is said about your work so personally. We are buying all of our work from freelance writers."

JUGGLER'S WORLD (IV), International Juggler's Association, Box 443, Davidson NC 28036. (704)892-1296. Editor: Bill Giduz. Fiction Editor: Ken Letko. Magazine: 8½×11; 44 pages; 70 lb. paper and cover stock; illustrations and photos. For and about jugglers and juggling. Quarterly.

Needs: Historical (general), humor/satire, science fiction. No stories "that don't include juggling as a central theme." Receives "very few" unsolicited mss/month. Accepts 2 mss/year. Publishes ms an average of 6 months to 1 year after acceptance. Length: 1,000 words average; 500 words minimum; 2,000 words maximum. Sometimes critiques rejected mss.

How to Contact: Query first. Reports in 1 week. Simultaneous and photocopied submissions OK. Accepts computer printout submissions. Accepts electronic submissions via IBM compatible disk. Sample copy $2.

Payment: Pays $25-50, free subscription to magazine and 5 contributor's copies.

Terms: Pays on acceptance for first rights.

‡**JUNIOR TRAILS (I, II),** Gospel Publishing House, 1445 Boonville Ave., Springfield MO 65802. (417)862-2781. Elementary Editor: Sinda S. Zinn. Magazine: 8½×11; 4 pages; 36 lb. coated offset paper; coat and matte cover stock; art illustrations; photos. A Sunday school take-home paper of nature articles and fictional stories that apply Christian principles to everyday living for 9-12 year old children. Weekly. Estab. 1954. Circ. 70,000.

Needs: Contemporary, religious/inspirational, spiritual, sports and juvenile. Adventure stories are welcome. No Biblical fiction or science fiction. Buys 2 mss/issue. Publishes short shorts. Recently published work by Betty Lou Mell, Mason M. Smith, Nanette L. Dunford; published new writers within the last year. Length: 1,000-1,200 words.

How to Contact: Send complete ms with SASE. Accepts computer printout submissions. Reports 6-8 weeks on mss. Free sample copy and guidelines.

Payment: Pays 3¢/word. 3 free author's copies.

Terms: Pays on acceptance.

Advice: "Know the age level and direct stories relevant to that age group. Since junior-age children (grades 5 and 6) enjoy action, fiction provides a vehicle for communicating moral/spiritual principles in a dramatic framework. Fiction, if well done, can be a powerful tool for relating Christian principles. It must, however, be realistic and believable in its development. Make your children be children, not overly mature for their age. We would like more stories with a *city* setting."

KID CITY (II), Children's Television Workshop, 1 Lincoln Plaza, New York NY 10023. (212)595-3456. Editor: Maureen Hunter-Bone. Magazine: 8½x11; 32 pages; glossy cover; illustrations; photos. General interest for children 6-10 "devoted to sparking kids' interest in reading and writing about the world around them." Published 10 times/year. Estab. 1974. Circ. 300,000.

Needs: Adventure, mystery, juvenile (6-10 years), science fiction. Publishes ms 6 months "at least" after acceptance. Length: 600-750 words average; 1,000 words maximum.

How to Contact: Send complete ms with cover letter. Reports in 1-2 months on mss. SASE. Photocopied submissions OK. Accepts computer printout submissions. Sample copy $1.50 and 9×12 SAE with 75¢ postage. Writers' guidelines free for 9×12 SAE with 75¢ postage.

Payment: Pays $200-400 and contributor's copies.

Terms: Pays on acceptance for all rights (some negotiable).

Advice: "We look for bright and sparkling prose. Don't talk down. Don't stereotype. Don't use cutesy names, animals or plots. No heavy moralizing or pat dilemmas."

KINDERGARTEN LISTEN (IV), WordAction Publishing Company, 2923 Troost Ave., Kansas City MO 64109. (816)931-1900 or (816)333-7000 (editorial). Editor: Janet Sawyer. Fiction Editor: Lisa Ham. Tabloid: 4-page story paper; 8½×11; newsprint; newsprint cover; b&w and 4-color illustrations; 4-color photos. Stories follow a 2-year topic cycle. Readers are kindergarten 4s, 5s and early 6s. Weekly. Estab. 1981. Circ. 45,000.

Needs: Contemporary, prose poem, religious/inspirational, spiritual, Christian topic themes. Recently published work by Katharine Ruth Adams, Helen Ott, Minnie Wells. Length: 300 words minimum; 400 words maximum. Sometimes critiques rejected mss and recommends other markets.

How to Contact: Query first "if unfamiliar with 2-year topic cycle" or send complete mss. Writers must include SASE for each submission. Reports in 3 weeks on queries; in 1 month on mss. SASE. Photocopied submissions OK. Accepts computer printout submissions. Accepts electronic submissions via disk or modem in ASCII text only. Sample copy and fiction guidelines for 8½×11 SAE and 1 first class stamp.

Payment: Pays 3.5¢/word, with contributor's copies (4 each purchase). Charge for extra copies.
Terms: Pays on acceptance for all rights, first rights or reuse rights. We pay 2¢/word for reuse of same story when issues are recycled.
Advice: "A majority of submissions we've received lately are of poor quality. Dialogue and actions of main child characters are unrealistic to the young age group our magazine ministers to. Actions and dialogue of parent characters is often too unrealistic as well. They're either too good to be true or very stilted in actions and speech. Because today's children are growing up in a rough world, we seek to help them deal with a variety of situations from divorce to the simple worries of a young child, like being left with a new babysitter. We seek to portray fictional children finding real solutions in the love and guidance of Christ, assisted by parent and other adult figures. Too many submissions appear to come from writers who don't take the children's market seriously or view it as an easy area to write prose for. In fact, children's stories require research and realism, and much effort in writing and rewriting. Writers have to know the audience well, not just guess or try to recall what it was like to be a Pre-K kid. Few writers can relate well enough to produce good manuscripts without these efforts." Criteria used in choosing fiction: "(1) Does it relate to our theme titles for the 2-year cycle? (2) Is the story interesting to children? (3) Does it assist them in understanding some vital area of the Christian life, God's love, etc.? (4) Is it realistic in portrayal of all characters? (5) Does it flow naturally and make for good reading? (6) Does the story line progress logically? (7) Does it include any references to inappropriate parent behavior, or unacceptable practices, or doctrines, of the Church of the Nazarene. Ex: We've had a hair-raising number of writers portraying scenes where children are left unattended in shopping malls or some other public place—which is highly inappropriate parental behavior considering the abduction situation that has terrorized our country's parents and families. The portrayal shows little insight on the writer's part."

LADIES' HOME JOURNAL (III), (Published by Meredith Corporation), 100 Park Ave., New York NY 10017. Editor-in-Chief: Myrna Blyth. Fiction/Books Editor: Sofia Marchant. Magazine: 190 pages; 34-38 lb. coated paper; 65 lb. coated cover; illustrations and photos.
Needs: Book mss and short stories, *accepted only through an agent.* Return of unsolicited material cannot be guaranteed. Recently published work by Sue Miller, Dominick Dunne, Louise Erdrich. Length: approximately 3,500 words.
How to Contact: Cover letter with ms (credits). Publishes ms 4 months to 1 year after acceptance.
Terms: Buys First North American rights.
Advice: "Our readers like stories, especially those that have emotional impact. We are using fiction every month, whether it's an excerpt from a novel or a short story. Stories about relationships between people—husband/wife—mother/son—seem to be subjects that can be explored effectively in short stories. Our reader's mail and surveys attest to this fact: Readers enjoy our fiction, and are most keenly tuned to stories dealing with children. Fiction today is stronger than ever. Beginners can be optimistic; if they have talent, I do believe that talent will be discovered."

‡LADYBUG (II, IV), Carus Publishing, P.O. Box 300, Peru IL 61354. Editor-in-Chief: Marianne Carus. Contact: Submissions Editor. Magazine: 8x9¼; 36 pages plus 4-page pullout section; illustrations. "*Ladybug* publishes original stories and poems and reprints written by the world's best children's authors. For young children, ages 2-7." Monthly. Estab. 1990.
Needs: Juvenile, fantasy (children's), preschool, read-out-loud stories, picture stories, folk tales, fairy tales. Length: 300-750 words preferred. Publishes short shorts.
How to Contact: Send complete ms with cover letter. Include word count on ms (do not count title). Reports in 3 months. SASE. Reprints are OK. Fiction guidelines for #10 SAE and 1 first-class stamps.
Payment: Pays up to 25 cents/word (less for reprints).
Terms: Pays on publication for first North American serial rights or second North American serial rights. For recurring features, pays flat fee and copyright becomes property of Carus Corporation.

LADY'S CIRCLE (II), Lopez Publications, 111 East 35th St., New York NY 10016. (212)689-3933. Fiction Editor: Mary Bemis. Magazine. "A lot of our readers are in Midwestern states." Monthly. Estab. 1963. Circ. 300,000.
Needs: Confession, historical, humor/satire, mainstream, religious/inspirational, romance (contemporary, historical, young adult), senior citizen/retirement. Receives 100 unsolicited fiction mss/month. Buys 3-4 fiction mss/issue; about 6-7 fiction mss/year. Time between acceptance and publication "varies, usually works 2 months ahead." Length: 3,000 words preferred; 1,000 words minimum; 3,000 words maximum. Accepts short shorts "for fillers." Sometimes critiques rejected ms.

How to Contact: Query first. Reports in up to 3 months on queries. SASE. Simultaneous, photocopied and reprint submissions OK. Accepts electronic submissions via disk or modem. Sample copy for $1.95; fiction guidelines for SAE.
Payment: Pay varies, depending on ms.
Terms: Pays on publication for first North American serial rights.

LIGUORIAN (I, IV), "A Leading Catholic Magazine," Liguori Publications, 1 Liguori Dr., Liguori MO 63057. (314)464-2500. Editor-in-Chief: Allan Weinert, CSS.R. Managing Editor: Francine M. O'Connor. Magazine: 5×8½; 64 pages; b&w illustrations and photographs. "*Liguorian* is a Catholic magazine aimed at helping our readers to live a full Christian life. We publish articles for families, young people, children, religious and singles—all with the same aim." Monthly. Estab. 1913. Circ. 430,000.
Needs: Religious/inspirational, young adult and senior citizen/retirement (with moral Christian thrust), spiritual. "Stories submitted to *Liguorian* must have as their goal the lifting up of the reader to a higher Christian view of values and goals. We are not interested in contemporary works that lack purpose or are of questionable moral value." Receives approximately 25 unsolicited fiction mss/month. Buys 12 mss/year. Recently published work by Tom Dowling, Sharon Helgens, Jim Auer, Ann Urrein and Jon A. Ripslinger; published new writers within the last year. Length: 1,500-2,000 words preferred. Also publishes short shorts. Occasionally critiques rejected mss "if we feel the author is capable of giving us something we need even though this story did not suit us." Occasionally recommends other markets.
How to Contact: Send complete ms with SASE. Accepts computer printout submissions. Accepts disk submissions compatible with TRS-80 Model III. Prefers hard copy with disk submission. Reports in 6 weeks on mss. Sample copy for and free fiction guidelines. "Please enclose 6×9 SASE."
Payment: Pays 10-12¢/word and 6 contributor's copies. Offers 50% kill fee for assigned mss not published.
Terms: Pays on acceptance for all rights.
Advice: "First read several issues containing short stories. We look for originality and creative input in each story we read. Since most editors must wade through mounds of manuscripts each month, consideration for the editor requires that the market be studied, the manuscript be carefully presented and polished before submitting. Our publication uses only one story a month. Compare this with the 25 or more we receive over the transom each month. Also, many fiction mss are written without a specific goal or thrust, i.e., an interesting incident that goes nowhere is *not a story*. We believe fiction is a highly effective mode for transmitting the Christian message and also provides a good balance in an unusually heavy issue."

LIVE, Assemblies of God, 1445 Boonville, Springfield MO 65802. (417)862-2781. Editor: Lorraine Mastrorio. "A take-home story paper distributed weekly in young adult/adult Sunday school classes. *Live* is a fictional story paper primarily. True stories and articles are acceptable. Poems and first-person anecdotes, and humor are used as fillers. The purpose of *Live* is to present in short story form realistic characters who utilize biblical principles. We hope to challenge readers to take risks for God and to resolve their problems scripturally." Weekly. Circ. 180,000.
Needs: Religious/inspirational, prose poem and spiritual. No controversial stories about such subjects as feminism, war or capital punishment. Buys 2 mss/issue. Recently published work by Maxine F. Dennis, E. Ruth Glover and Larry Clark; published new writers within the last year. Length: 500-2,000 words.
How to Contact: Send complete ms. Social Security number and word count must be included. Free sample copy and fiction guidelines only with SASE.
Payment: Pays 3¢/word (first rights); 2¢/word (second rights).
Terms: Pays on acceptance.
Advice: "Stories should go somewhere! Action, not just thought-life; interaction not just insights. Heroes and heroines, suspense and conflict. Avoid simplistic, pietistic conclusions, preachy, critical or moralizing."

LIVING WITH TEENAGERS (II), Baptist Sunday School Board, 127 9th Ave. North, Nashville TN 37234. (615)251-2273. Editor: Jimmy Hester. Magazine: 10⅜×8⅛; 50 pages; illustrations; photos. Magazine especially designed "to enrich the parent-teen relationship, with reading material from a Christian perspective" for parents of teenagers. Quarterly. Estab. 1978. Circ. 50,000.

Needs: Religious/inspirational, spiritual and parent-teen relationships. Nothing not related to parent-teen relationships or not from a Christian perspective. Buys 2-5 mss/issue. Receives approximately 50 unsolicited fiction mss/month. Length: 600-1,200 words (short shorts).
How to Contact: Cover letter with reason for writing article; credentials for writing. Query with clips of published work or send complete ms. SASE always. Reports in 2 months on both queries and mss. Free sample copy with 9 × 12 SAE and proper postage.
Payment: Pays 5½¢ per published word (all rights) and 3 free author's copies for all rights.
Terms: Pays on acceptance for all and first rights.
Advice: "Sometimes a fictitious story can communicate a principle in the parent-youth relationship quite well."

LOLLIPOPS MAGAZINE (II), Good Apple, Inc., Box 299, Carthage IL 62321. (217)357-3981. Editor: Jerry Aten. Magazine: 8½ × 11; 64 pages; illustrations. "Preschool-2nd grade publication for teachers and their students. All educational material. Short stories, poems, activities, math, gameboards." Published 5 times/year. Circ. 18,000.
Needs: Preschool-grade 2. Submissions cover all areas of the curriculum. Seasonal materials considered. Receives 40-50 unsolicited mss/month. Number of fiction mss bought varies per issue. Occasionally accepts short stories (500-750 words). Published new writers within the last year.
How to Contact: Query first or write for guidelines and a free sample copy. Reports in 1 week on queries. SASE for ms. Accepts computer printouts. Send for free sample copies and guidelines.
Payment: Payment varies; depends on story.
Terms: Pays on publication for all rights.

THE LOOKOUT (II), Standard Publishing, 8121 Hamilton Ave., Cincinnati OH 45231. (513)931-4050. FAX: (513)931-0904. Editor: Simon J. Dahlman. Magazine: 8½ × 11; 16 pages; newsprint paper; newsprint cover stock; illustrations; photos. "Conservative Christian magazine for adults and young adults." Weekly. Estab. 1894. Circ. 125,000.
Needs: Religious/inspirational. No predictable, preachy material. Taboos are blatant sex, swear words and drinking alcohol. Receives 50 unsolicited mss/month. Buys 1 ms/issue; buys 45-50 mss/year. Recently published work by Bob Hartman, June Rae Wood, Wanda Trawick and Daniel Schantz; published new writers within the last year. Length: 1,200-2,000 words.
How to Contact: Send complete ms with SASE. Accepts computer printout submissions. Reports in 2 months on ms. Simultaneous, photocopied and reprint submissions OK. Publishes ms 2 months to 1 year after acceptance. Sample copy 50¢. Free guidelines with #10 SASE.
Payment: Pays 5-7¢/word for first rights; 4-5¢/word for other rights. Free author's copies.
Terms: Pays on acceptance for one-time rights. Buys reprints.
Advice: "No queries please. Send us a believable story which is inspirational and helpful but down to earth."

THE LUTHERAN JOURNAL, Outlook Publications, Inc., 7317 Cahill Rd., Minneapolis MN 55435. (612)941-6830. Editor: Rev. A.U. Deye. "A family magazine providing wholesome and inspirational reading material for the enjoyment and enrichment of Lutherans." Quarterly. Estab. 1936. Circ. 136,000.
Needs: Literary, contemporary, religious/inspirational, romance (historical), senior citizen/retirement and young adult. Must be appropriate for distribution in the churches. Buys 2-4 mss/issue. Length: 1,000-1,500 words.
How to Contact: Send complete ms with SASE. Accepts computer printout submissions. Free sample copy with SASE (59¢ postage).
Payment: Pays $10-25 and 6 free author's copies.
Terms: Pays on publication for all and first rights.

‡LUTHERAN WOMAN TODAY (IV), Published by: Augsburg Fortress, Box 1209, Minneapolis, MN 55440. LWT editorial offices: 8765 West Higgins Rd., Chicago IL 60631. (380)312-2743. Editor: Nancy Stelling. Fiction Editor: Sue Edison-Swift. Magazine: 5⅜ × 8⅜; 48 pages; 40 lb paper; illustrations; photos. Publishes solicited and freelance theological articles, fiction, good devotional pieces, articles of interest to women. "A magazine for women of the Evangelical Lutheran Church in America 'for growth in faith and mission.' " Monthly. Estab. 1988. Circ. 300,000.
Needs: Faith-related-to-life, religious/inspirational, advocacy/peace and justice, feminist. "We look for short (700-1,000 words), well written work of special interest to Christian women." Receives 100-150 mss/month. Buys 5-10 mss/year. Publishes ms within 1 year of acceptance. Recently published

work by Carol Bly, Joyce Ditmanson. Length: 700 words average; 1,200 words maximum. Publishes short shorts. Length: 350 words.
How to Contact: Send complete ms with cover letter which should include name, address, phone, word count *rights offered*. Reports on queries in 3 months; on mss in 2 months. SASE. Accepts computer printout submissions. Sample copy for $1 and 5×7 SAE. Fiction guidelines for #10 SAE and 1 first class stamp.
Payment: Pays per printed page.
Terms: Pays on acceptance for first rights and one-time rights. Sometimes offers kill fee. Publication copyrighted.

MADEMOISELLE MAGAZINE, Condé Nast Publications, Inc., 350 Madison Ave., New York NY 10017. (212)880-8690. Fiction Editor: Eileen Schnurr. Fashion magazine for women from ages 18-34 with articles of interest to women; beauty and health tips, features, home and food, fiction. Audience interested in self-improvement, curious about trends, interested in updating lifestyle and pursuing a career. Monthly. Estab. 1935. Circ. 1.1 million.
Needs: Literary and contemporary short stories. Publishes 1-2 ms/issue, 12-20 mss/year. Length: 7-25 pages.
How to Contact: Send complete ms with SASE. Reports in 6 months. Free fiction guidelines with SASE.
Payment: $1,000 minimum for short shorts; $1,500 for short stories.
Terms: Pays on acceptance for first North American serial rights.
Advice: "We are particularly interested in stories of relevance to young single women, and we continue in the *Mademoiselle* tradition of publishing fiction of literary quality. Be sure to see the listing in Contest and Awards section for guidelines for *Mademoiselle's* Fiction Writers Contest."

THE MAGAZINE FOR CHRISTIAN YOUTH! (II), The United Methodist Publishing House, 201 8th Avenue S., Nashville TN 37202. (615)749-6463. Editor: Christopher B. Hughes. Magazine: 8½×11; 52 pages; slick, matte finish paper. "*The Magazine for Christian Youth!* tries to help teenagers develop Christian identity and live their faith in contemporary culture. Fiction and nonfiction which contributes to this purpose are welcome." Monthly. Estab. 1985. Circ. 45,000.
Needs: Adventure, contemporary, ethnic, fantasy, humor/satire, prose poem, religious/inspirational, science fiction, spiritual, suspense/mystery, translations, young adult/teen (10-18 years). "Don't preach; but story should have a message to help teenagers in some way or to make them think more deeply about an issue. No Sunday school lessons, like those found in curriculum." Receives 50-75 unsolicited mss/month. Buys 1-2 mss/issue; 12-24 mss/year. Publishes ms 9-12 months after acceptance. Length: 700-2,000 words. Publishes short shorts.
How to Contact: Send complete ms with cover letter. Reports in 3-6 months. SASE. Simultaneous and reprint submissions OK. Accepts computer printouts. Sample copy and fiction guidelines free for #10 SASE.
Payment: Pays $1.50 minimum, 4¢/word.
Terms: Pays on acceptance for first North American serial rights or one-time rights.
Advice: "Get a feel for our magazine first. Don't send in the types of fiction that would appear in Sunday school curriculum just because it's a Christian publication. Reflect the real world of teens in contemporary fiction."

MAGAZINE OF FANTASY AND SCIENCE FICTION (II), Box 56, Cornwall CT 06753. (203)672-6376. Publisher/Editor: Edward L. Ferman. Magazine: illustrations on cover only. Publishes "science fiction and fantasy. Our readers are age 13 and up who are interested in science fiction and fantasy." Monthly. Estab. 1949.
Needs: Fantasy and science fiction. Receives "hundreds" of unsolicited fiction submissions/month. Buys 8 fiction mss/issue ("on average"). Time between acceptance and publication varies. Length: 10,000 words maximum. Publishes short shorts. Critiques rejected ms, "if quality warrants it." Sometimes recommends other markets.
How to Contact: Send complete ms with cover letter. Reports in 6-8 weeks. SASE. Simultaneous, photocopied and reprint submissions OK. Accepts computer printout submissions. Sample copy for $3 or $5 for 2. Fiction guidelines for SAE.
Payment: Pays 5-7¢/word.
Terms: Pays on acceptance for first North American serial rights; foreign, option on anthology if requested.

‡MAINSTREET USA, Peak Media, Box 925, Hailey ID 83333. Editor: Brad Pearson. Magazine: "Lots" of photographs. "General interest magazine for blue collar men, ages 18-55. Topics include sports, hunting, fishing, how-to, environmental." Estab. 1991. Circ. 750,000.
Needs: "We want stories about everyday American heroes and towns, humorous or upbeat preferred." Length: 900 words minimum; 1,000 words maximum.
How to Contact: Query with clips of published work. Include Social Security number. Reports in 4-6 weeks on queries. SASE. Simultaneous, photocopied and reprint submissions OK. Accepts computer printout submissions. Accepts electronic submissions. Sample copy $3. Fiction guidelines for #10 SAE and 1 first class stamp.
Payment: Pays 25¢-$1/word.
Terms: Pays on publication for first North American serial rights.
Advice: "We look for interesting or unique aspects about life in America or individual Americans pursuing the 'American Dream.'"

MANSCAPE (II, IV), First Hand Ltd., Box 1314, Teaneck NJ 07666. (201)836-9177. Editor: Bill Bottiggi. Magazine: digest sized; 130 pages; illustrations. "Magazine is devoted to gay male sexual fetishes; publishes fiction and readers' letters devoted to this theme." Monthly. Estab. 1985. Circ. 60,000.
Needs: Erotica, gay. Should be written in first person. No science fiction or fantasy. Erotica must be based on real life. Receives 25 unsolicited fiction mss/month. Accepts 5 mss/issue; 60 mss/year. Publishes ms an average of 12-18 months after acceptance. Published new writers within the last year. Length: 3,000 words average; 2,000 words minimum; 3,750 words maximum. Sometimes critiques rejected ms.
How to Contact: Send complete ms with cover letter. SASE. Accepts computer printout submissions. Sample copy $5; fiction guidelines for #10 SASE.
Payment: Pays $100-150.
Terms: Pays on publication or in 240 days, whichever comes first, for all rights or first North American serial rights.

MATURE LIVING (II), Sunday School Board of the Southern Baptist Conv., MSN 140, 127 Ninth Ave. N., Nashville TN 37234. (615)251-2191. Editor: Randy Apon. Magazine: 8½×11; 48 pages; non-glare paper; slick cover stock; illustrations; photos. "Our magazine is Christian in content and the material required is what would appeal to 60+ age group: inspirational, informational, nostalgic, humorous. Our magazine is distributed mainly through churches (especially Southern Baptist churches) that buy the magazine in bulk and distribute it to members in this age group." Monthly. Estab. 1977. Circ. 360,000.
Needs: Contemporary, religious/inspirational, humor, prose poem, spiritual and senior citizen/retirement. Avoid all types of pornography, drugs, liquor, horror, science fiction and stories demeaning to the elderly. Buys 1 ms/issue. Published work by Burndean N. Sheffy, Pearl E. Trigg, Joyce M. Sixberry; published new writers within the last year. Length: 425-900 words (prefers 900). "Also, please use 42-characters per line."
How to Contact: Send complete ms with SASE. Reports in 2 months. Publishes ms an average of 1 year after acceptance. Sample copy $1. Free guidelines with SASE.
Payment: Pays $21-73; 3 free author's copies. 85¢ charge for extras.
Terms: Pays on acceptance. First rights 15% less than all rights, reprint rights 25% less. Rarely buys reprints.
Advice: Mss are rejected because they are too long or subject matter unsuitable. "Our readers seem to enjoy an occasional short piece of fiction. It must be believable, however, and present senior adults in a favorable light."

MATURE YEARS (II), United Methodist Publishing House, 201 Eighth Ave. S., Nashville TN 37202. (615)749-6468. Editor: Donn C. Downall. Magazine: 8½×11; 112 pages; illustrations and photos. Magazine "helps persons in and nearing retirement to appropriate the resources of the Christian faith as they seek to face the problems and opportunities related to aging." Quarterly. Estab. 1953.
Needs: Religious/inspirational, nostalgia, prose poem, spiritual (for older adults). "We don't want anything poking fun at old age, saccharine stories or anything not for older adults." Buys 3-4 mss/issue, 12-16 mss/year. Needs at least one unsolicited fiction ms each month. Published new writers within the last year. Length: 1,000-1,800 words.
How to Contact: Send complete ms with SASE and Social Security number. Reports in 2 months on mss. Usually publishes ms 1 year to 18 months after acceptance. Free sample copy with 10½×11 SAE and $2.50 postage.

Payment: Pays 4¢/word.
Terms: Pays on acceptance for all and first rights.
Advice: "Practice writing dialogue! Listen to people talk; take notes; master dialogue writing! Not easy, but well worth it! Most inquiry letters are far too long. If you can't sell me an idea in a brief paragraph, you're not going to sell the reader on reading your finished article or story."

MESSENGER OF THE SACRED HEART (II), Apostleship of Prayer, 661 Greenwood Ave., Toronto, Ontario M4J 4B3 Canada. (416)466-1195. Editors: Rev. F.J. Power, S.J., and Alfred DeMauche. Magazine: 7×10; 32 pages; coated paper; selfcover; illustrations; photos. Magazine for "Canadian and U.S. Catholics interested in developing a life of prayer and spirituality; stresses the great value of our ordinary actions and lives." Monthly. Estab. 1891. Circ. 17,000.
Needs: Religious/inspirational. Stories about people, adventure, heroism, humor, drama. No poetry. Buys 1 ms/issue. Published work by Wilhelmena Raisbeck, Ida Mae Kempel and Helen Weldon Anderson; published new writers within the last year. Length: 750-1,500 words. Recommends other markets.
How to Contact: Send complete ms with SAE or IRC. Rarely buys reprints. Reports in 1 month on mss. Sample copy $1.50.
Payment: Pays 4¢/word, 3 free author's copies.
Terms: Pays on acceptance for first North American serial rights.
Advice: "Develop a story that sustains interest to the end. Do not preach, but use plot and characters to convey the message or theme. Aim to move the heart as well as the mind. If you can, add a light touch or a sense of humor to the story. Your ending should have impact, leaving a moral or faith message for the reader."

METRO SINGLES LIFESTYLES (II), Metro Publications, Box 28203, Kansas City MO 64118. (816)436-8424. Editor: Robert L. Huffstutter. Fiction Editor: Earl R. Stonebridge. Tabloid: 36 pages; 30 lb newspaper stock; 30 lb cover; illustrations; photos. "Positive, uplifting, original, semi-literary material for all singles: widowed, divorced, never-married, of all ages 18 and over." Bimonthly. Estab. 1984. Circ. 25,000.
Needs: Humor/satire, literary, prose poem, religious/inspirational, romance (contemporary), special interest, spiritual, single parents. No erotic, political, moralistic fiction. Receives 2-3 unsolicited mss/month. Buys 1-2 mss/issue; 12-18 mss/year. Publishes ms 2 months after acceptance. Length: 1,500 words average; 1,200 words minimum; 4,000 words maximum. Publishes short shorts. Recently published work by Patricia Castle, Libby Floyd, Donald G. Smith; published new writers within the last year. Length: 1,200. Occasionally critiques rejected mss. Recommends other markets.
How to Contact: Send complete ms with cover letter. Include short paragraph/bio listing credits (if any), current profession or job. Reports in 3 weeks on queries. SASE. Accepts computer printout submissions. Sample copy $2.
Payment: Pays $25-50, free subscription to magazine and contributor's copies.
Terms: Payment on publication.
Advice: "A question I ask myself about my own writing is: will the reader feel the time spent reading the story or article was worth the effort? Personally, I enjoy stories and articles which will create a particular emotion, build suspense, or offer excitement or entertainment. Features accompanied by photos receive special attention."

MIDSTREAM (II,IV), A Monthly Jewish Review, Theodor Herzl Foundation, 110 E. 59th St., New York NY 10022. (212)752-0600. Editor: Joel Carmichael. Magazine: 8½×11; 64 pages; 50 lb paper; 65 lb white smooth cover stock. "We are a Zionist journal; we publish material with Jewish themes or that would appeal to a Jewish readership." Monthly. Estab. 1955. Circ. 10,000.
Needs: Historical (general), humor/satire, literary, mainstream, translations. Receives 15-20 unsolicited mss/month. Accepts 1 mss/issue; 10 mss/year. Publishes ms 6-18 months after acceptance. 10% of fiction is agented. Recently published work by I. B. Singer, Anita Jackson, Enid Shomer. Length: 2,500 words average; 1,500 words minimum; 3,000 words maximum. Sometimes critiques rejected mss.
How to Contact: Send complete ms with cover letter, which should include "address, telephone, identification or affiliation of author; state that the ms is fiction." Reports in 1-2 weeks. SASE. Photocopied submissions OK. Accepts computer printout submissions; no dot-matrix. Sample copy for 9×12 SAE. Fiction guidelines for #10 SASE.
Payment: Pays 5¢/word and contributor's copies.
Terms: Pays on publication for first rights. Sends prepublication galleys to author.
Advice: "Always include a cover letter and double space."

MILITARY LIFESTYLE (II), Downey Communications, Inc., 1732 Wisconsin Ave. NW, Washington DC 20007. (202)944-4000. Editor: Hope M. Daniels. Magazine: 8½×11; 80-100 pages; coated paper; illustrations and photos. Monthly magazine for military families worldwide. Publishes 10 issues per year. Estab. 1969. Circ. 520,000.

Needs: Contemporary. "Fiction must deal with lifestyle or issues of particular concern to our specific military families audience." Receives 50 unsolicited mss/month. Buys 1-2 mss/issue; 10-15 mss/year. Publishes ms 2-6 months after acceptance. Published new writers within the last year. Length: 1,800 words average. Generally critiques rejected mss. Recommends other markets if applicable. ·

How to Contact: Send complete ms with cover letter, which should include info on writer and writing credits and history. Reports in 6-8 weeks on mss. SASE. Photocopied submissions OK. Accepts computer printout submissions. Sample copy for $1.50, 9×12 SAE and 4 first class stamps. Fiction guidelines for #10 SASE and 1 first class stamp.

Payment: Pays $400 minimum and 2 free copies.

Terms: Pays generally on publication unless held more than 6 months; then on acceptance for first North American serial rights.

Advice: "Fiction is slice-of-life reading for our audience. Primarily written by military wives or military members themselves, the stories deal with subjects very close to our readers: prolonged absences by spouses, the necessity of handling child-raising alone, the fear of accidents while spouses are on maneuvers or in dangerous situations, etc. The important point: Target the material to our audience — military families — and make the characters real, empathetic and believable. Read your copy over as an objective reader rather than as its author before submission. Better yet, read it aloud!"

‡MODERN GOLD MINER AND TREASURE HUNTER (II), P.O. Box 47, Happy Camp CA 96039. (916)493-2029. Editor: Dave McCracken. Fiction Editor: Linda Montgomery. Magazine: 8x10⅞; 48 pages; 50 lb. coated #5 paper; 80 lb. Sterling Web cover; pen-and-ink illustrations; photographs. "Recreational and small-scale gold mining, treasure and relic hunting. All stories must be related to these topics. For recreational, hobbyists, adventure loving, outdoor people." Bimonthly. Estab. 1988. Circ. 50,000.

Needs: Adventure, experimental, historical, humor, senior citizen/retirement, suspense/mystery. "Futuristic stories OK, but not sci-fi. No erotica, gay, lesbian--absolutely no 'cussing!' " Buys 1-2 mss/issue; 6-16 mss/year. Publishes ms 4-6 months after acceptance. Recently published work by Ken Hodgson and Michael Clark. Length: 2,000 words preferred; 900 words minimum; 2,700 words maximum. Publishes short shorts. Length: 400-500 words. Sometimes critiques or comments on rejected mss.

How to Contact: Send complete ms with cover letter. Include social security number, "brief outline of the story and something about the author." Reports in 2 weeks on queries; 4-6 weeks on mss. SASE for mss. Photocopied submissions OK. Accepts electronic submissions. Sample copy for $2.95 (U.S.), $3.50 (Canada). Fiction guidelines free.

Payment: Pays 3¢/word minimum and contributor's copies.

Terms: Pays on publication for all rights. Sponsors fiction contest — look for rules in upcoming issues.

Advice: Looks for "as always, quality writing. We can edit small changes but the story has to grab us. Our readers love 'real life' fiction. They love exploring the 'that could happen' realm of a good fiction story. Keep your story geared to gold mining or treasure hunting. Know something about your subject so the story doesn't appear ridiculous. Don't try to dazzle readers with outlandish adjectives and keep slang to a minimum."

MODERN SHORT STORIES (I), Entertaining Stories for Fiction Lovers, Claggk Inc., Building A, Suite 101, 4820 Alpine Place, Las Vegas NV 89107. FAX: (702)878-1501. Editor: Glenn Steckler. Magazine: Digest-sized; supercalendered paper; 60 lb. cover stock; illustrations; photographs. Publishes "a variety of fiction for audiences of all ages." Bimonthly. Estab. 1988.

Needs: Adventure, confession, contemporary, experimental, fantasy, historical, horror, humor/satire, mainstream, psychic/supernatural/occult, regional, religious/inspirational, romance (contemporary, historical, young adult), science fiction, sports, suspense/mystery, western. Receives 500-1,000 unsolicited fiction mss/month. Buys 12-15 fiction mss/issue. Publishes mss 4 months to 1 year after acceptance. Recently published work by Richard Brown, James Plath and Annette Bostrom; published new writers with the last year. Length: 1,000-5,000 words preferred. Publishes short shorts. Sometimes critiques rejected ms.

How to Contact: Send complete mss with cover letter. Reports in 1-4 weeks. SASE required. Photocopied submissions OK. Accepts computer printouts. Sample copy $2.50; fiction guidelines free.
Payment: Pays $50-100.
Terms: Pays on acceptance for first rights and first anthology rights.
Advice: "There is not enough space devoted to fiction today—TV has tended to replace it. However, we feel the demand is there and that is our reason for publishing *Modern Short Stories*."

THE MODERN WOODMEN (II), Modern Woodmen of America, Mississippi River at 17th St., Rock Island IL 61201. (309)786-6481. Editor: Gloria Bergh. Fiction Editor: Jodi Spurling. Magazine: 8½×11; 24 pages; 50 lb paper; self cover; illustrations and photos. "We want articles that appeal to families, emphasize family interaction, for the family audience including all age groups from children to the elderly." Quarterly. Circ. 350,000.
Needs: Adventure, contemporary, historical (general), juvenile (5-9 years), mainstream, senior citizen/retirement, young adult/teen (10-18 years). Receives approx. 35 unsolicited fiction mss/month. Accepts 1-2 mss/month; 12-24 mss/year. Length: 1,200 words preferred. Sometimes critiques rejected mss, "but very seldom."
How to Contact: Send complete ms with cover letter. Reports in up to 2 months. SASE. Simultaneous, photocopied and reprint submissions OK. Accepts computer printout submissions. Sample copy for 8½×11 SAE with 2 first class stamps. Fiction guidelines for #10 SASE.
Payment: Pays $50 and up.
Terms: Pays on acceptance for one-time rights.
Advice: "A well written short story is a drawing card to interest our readers."

MOMENT MAGAZINE (II, IV), 3000 Connecticut Ave. NW, Suite 300, Washington DC 20008. (202)387-8888. Publisher/Editor: Hershel Shanks. Managing Editor: Suzanne F. Singer. Magazine: 8½×11; 64 pages; 60 lb. coated paper; 80 lb. cover stock; illustrations and photos. Modern, historical magazine publishing material on intellectual, cultural and political issues of interest to the Jewish community. Audience is college-educated, liberal, concerned with Jewish affairs. Bimonthly. Estab. 1975. Circ. 30,000.
Needs: Contemporary, ethnic, historical, religious, excerpted novel and translations. "All fiction should have Jewish content. No sentimental stories about 'Grandma' etc. Do not encourage Holocaust themes." Receives 60-80 unsolicited fiction mss/month. Buys 2-3 mss/year. Published new writers in the past year. Length: 2,000 words minimum; 4,000 words maximum; 3,000 words average. Publishes short shorts. Occasionally recommends other markets.
How to Contact: Cover letter with bio. Query first or send complete ms. SASE always. Photocopied submissions OK. No multiple submissions. Accepts computer printout submissions; prefers letter-quality. Reports in 1 month on queries; 1-2 months on mss. Publishes ms 1-12 months after acceptance. Sample copy $2.95. Free fiction guidelines for #10 SAE and 1 first class stamp.
Payment: Varies.
Terms: Pays on publication for first rights.
Advice: "We caution against over-sentimentalized writing which we get way too much of all the time. Query first is helpful; reading stories we've published a must."

MONTANA SENIOR CITIZENS NEWS (II,IV), Barrett-Whitman Co., Box 3363, Great Falls MT 59403. (406)761-0305. Editor: Jack Love. Tabloid: 11×17; 40-50 pages; newsprint paper and cover; illustrations; photos. Publishes "everything of interest to seniors, except most day-to-day political items like social security and topics covered in the daily news. Personal profiles of seniors, their lives, times and reminiscences." Bimonthly. Estab. 1984. Circ. 19,000.
Needs: Historical, senior citizen/retirement, western (historical or contemporary). No fiction "unrelated to experiences to which seniors can relate." Buys 1 or fewer mss/issue; 4-5 mss/year. Publishes ms within 6 months of acceptance. Published work by Anne Norris, Helen Clark, Juni Dunklin. Length: 500-700 words preferred. Publishes short shorts. Length: under 500 words.
How to Contact: Send complete ms with cover letter and phone number. Reports on mss in 4 months. SASE. Simultaneous, photocopied and reprint submissions OK. Accepts computer printout submissions. Accepts electronic submission via disk or modem. Sample copy for 9×12 SAE and $2 postage and handling.
Payment: Pays $10 minimum; 4¢/word maximum.
Terms: Pays on publication for first rights or one-time rights.

MOTHER JONES MAGAZINE (II,IV), Foundation for National Progress, 1663 Mission St., San Francisco CA 94103. (415)558-8881. Editor: Douglas Foster. Fiction Editor: Peggy Orenstein. Magazine: 64 pages; illustrations and photographs. "Political—left of center." Monthly. Estab. 1976. Circ. 200,000.
Needs: Feminist, gay, lesbian and political. Receives 20 unsolicited mss/month. Accepts 1-2 mss/year. Agented fiction 95%. Recently published work by Michael Dorris, Amy Hempel and Alice Walker. Length: 2,500 words average; 700 words minimum; 3,000 words maximum. Publishes short shorts. Sometimes critiques rejected mss.
How to Contact: Send complete ms with cover letter. Reports in 6-8 weeks on mss. SASE "only if they want manuscript returned." Simultaneous submissions OK. Computer printout submissions are acceptable. Sample copy for $3.
Payment: Negotiated.
Terms: Pays on acceptance for first North American serial rights.

MY FRIEND (II), The Catholic Magazine for Kids, Daughters of St. Paul, 50 St. Paul's Ave., Boston MA 02130. (617)522-8911. Editor: Sister Anne Joan. Magazine: 8½×11; 32 pages; smooth, glossy paper and cover stock; illustrations; photos. Magazine of "religious truths and positive values for children in a format which is enjoyable and attractive. Each issue contains Bible stories, lives of saints and famous people, short stories, science corner, contests, projects, etc." Monthly during school year (September-June). Estab. 1979. Circ. 10,000.
Needs: Juvenile, prose poem, religious/inspirational, spiritual (children), sports (children). Receives 30 unsolicited fiction mss/month. Accepts 3-4 mss/issue; 30-40 mss/year. Recently published work by Eileen Spinelli, Virginia Kroll and Jean Ciavonne; published new writers within the past year. Length: 200 words minimum; 900 words maximum; 600 words average.
How to Contact: Send complete ms with SASE. Accepts computer printout submissions. Reports in 1-2 months on mss. Publishes ms an average of 1 year after acceptance. Free sample copy for 10×14 SAE and 60¢ postage.
Payment: Pays 3-7¢ per word.
Advice: "We prefer child-centered stories in a real-world setting. Children enjoy fiction. They can relate to the characters and learn lessons that they might not derive from a more 'preachy' article. We accept only stories that teach wholesome, positive values. We are particularly interested in material for boys aged 8-10."

NA'AMAT WOMAN, Magazine of Na'amat USA, The Women's Labor Zionist Organization of America, 200 Madison Ave., New York NY 10016. (212)725-8010. Editor: Judith A. Sokoloff. Magazine covering a wide variety of subjects of interest to the Jewish community—including political and social issues, arts, profiles; many articles about Israel; and women's issues. Fiction must have a Jewish theme. Readers are the American Jewish community. Published 5 times/year. Estab. 1926. Circ. 30,000.
Needs: Contemporary, literary. Receives 10 unsolicited fiction mss/month. Buys 3-5 fiction mss/year. Length: 1,500 words minimum; 3,000 words maximum. Also buys nonfiction.
How to Contact: Query first or send complete ms with SASE. Photocopied submissions OK. Accepts computer printout submissions. Prefers letter-quality. Reports in 3 months on mss. Free sample copy for 9×11½ SAE and 71¢ postage.
Payment: Pays 8¢/word; 2 free contributor's copies. Offers kill fee of 25%.
Terms: Pays on publication for first North American serial rights; assignments on work-for-hire basis.
Advice: "No maudlin nostalgia or romance; no hackneyed Jewish humor and *no poetry.*"

NATIONAL LAMPOON (II), 155 Avenue of the Americas, New York NY 10013. (212)645-5040. Executive Editor: Larry Sloman. Magazine. "We publish humor and satire." Monthly. Estab. 1970. Circ. 250,000.
Needs: Receives 200 unsolicited fiction mss/month. Buys 2 mss/issue. Publishes ms 2-3 months after acceptance. Length: 1,000 words preferred; 500 words minimum; 2,000 words maximum. Publishes short shorts.
How to Contact: Query first. Reports in 1-2 months. SASE preferred. Simultaneous and photocopied submissions OK. Accepts electronic submissions via disk or modem. Fiction guidelines free.
Payment: Payment is negotiated.
Terms: Pays on publication for first North American serial rights and anthology rights. Offers varying kill fee.

‡NEW ERA MAGAZINE (II, IV), The Church of Jesus Christ of Latter-day Saints, 50 E. North Temple St., Salt Lake City UT 84150. (801)532-2951. Editor: Richard M. Romney. Magazine: 8 × 10½; 51 pages; 40 lb. coated paper; illustrations and photos. "We will publish fiction on any theme that strengthens and builds the standards and convictions of teenage Latter-day Saints ('Mormons')." Monthly. Estab. 1971. Circ. 200,000.
Needs: Stories on family relationships, self-esteem, dealing with loneliness, resisting peer pressure and all aspects of maintaining Christian values in the modern world. "All material must be written from a Latter-day Saint ('Mormon') point of view—or at least from a generally Christian point of view, reflecting LDS life and values." Receives 30-35 unsolicited mss/month. Accepts 1 ms/issue; 12 mss/year. Publishes ms 3 months to 5 years after acceptance. 1-2% of fiction is agented. Length: 1,500 words average; 250 words minimum; 2,000 words maximum.
How to Contact: Query letter preferred; send complete ms. Reports in 6-8 weeks. SASE. Photocopied submissions OK. Accepts computer printout submissions. Sample copy for $1 and 9 × 12 SAE with 2 first class stamps. Fiction guidelines for #10 SASE.
Payment: Pays $50-375, contributor's copies.
Terms: Pays on acceptance for all rights (reassign to author on request). Sponsors contests and awards for LDS fiction writers. "We have an annual contest, entry forms are in each September issue. Deadline is January, winners published in August."
Advice: "Each magazine has its own personality—you wouldn't write the same style of fiction for *Seventeen* that you would write for *Omni*. Very few writers who are not of our faith have been able to write for us successfully, and the reason usually is that they don't know what it's like to be a member of our church. You must study and research and know those you are writing about. We love to work with beginning authors, and we're a great place to break in if you can understand us."

NEW HAMPSHIRE LIFE (II,IV), (formerly *Seacoast Life*), Masthead Communications, Inc., Box 1200, North Hampton NH 03862. (603)964-2121. Fiction Editor: John A. Meng. Magazine: 8½ × 11; 126 pages; coated freesheet paper; 65 lb. coated cover stock; 4-color illustrations, 50/issue; 4-color photographs, 75/issue. "Lifestyle magazine for New Hampshire. We publish fiction each issue plus regional events, investigative journalism, recipes, business, health, fashion and people articles for an upscale, well-educated audience 25-50." Bi-monthly. Estab. (as *Seacoast Life*) 1985. Circ. 20,000.
Needs: Adventure, contemporary, fantasy, humor/satire, literary, mainstream, regional, science fiction, senior citizen/retirement, serialized/excerpted novel, suspense/mystery and translations. No radical fiction, i.e. homosexual, pornographic, etc. We promote literature that elicits an emotional response—not the type with a purpose to horrify or impress. Receives 20-30 unsolicited fiction mss/month. Accepts 1 mss/issue; 6 mss/year (including a holiday issue). Publishes ms 3-6 months after acceptance. Published work by Jules Archer, Sharon Helgens, Lawrence Millman and Robert Baldwin; published new writers within the last year. Length: 1,500-3,000 words average. Sometimes critiques rejected ms.
How to Contact: "Subject must be regional in order to submit—New Hampshire." Send complete ms with cover letter, writer's bio. Reports in 1 month. SASE. Simultaneous and photocopied submissions OK. Accepts computer printout submissions. Sample copy $2.50 and 9 × 12 SAE with $2.40 postage. Fiction guidelines for #10 SAE and 40¢ postage.
Payment: Pays $100 minimum; varies according to individual circumstances.
Terms: Pays 30 days after publication. Rights purchased negotiated with each individual writer.
Advice: "Our readership is highly educated, critical of shabby work and loves good fiction. Our readers love to read. Writers should be patient. We will read and reply to all submissions."

‡NEW MYSTERY (III), The Best New Mystery Stories, 175 Fifth Ave., #2001, New York NY 10010. (212)353-1582. Editor: Charles Raisch. Magazine; 5 × 8; 96 pages; illustrations and photographs. "Mystery, suspense and crime." Bimonthly. Estab. 1990. Circ. 50,000.
Needs: Suspense/mystery. Plans special annual anthology. Receives 150+ unsolicited mss/month. Buys 6-10 ms/issue. Agented fiction 50%. Recently published work by Lawrence Block, Herb Resnicow, Michael Avallone, Stu Kaminsky. Length: 3-5,000 words preferred. Sometimes critiques rejected ms and recommends other markets.
How to Contact: Send complete ms with cover letter. Reports on ms in 1 month. SASE. Accepts electronic submissions. Sample copy for $5. Fiction guidelines for SAE and 2 first class stamps.
Payment: Pays $25-500.
Terms: Pays on publication for all rights. Sponsors "Annual First Story Contest."
Advice: Stories should have "believable characters in trouble; sympathetic lead; visual language."

Close-up

Charles Raisch
Editor
New Mystery

Beth Raisch

Charles Raisch had been getting together for dinner with other mystery writers for years. Often, he says, over the course of an evening, the conversation would turn into a lament. His colleagues complained there were hardly any publications open to American-style, contemporary mystery fiction and very few places where a new mystery writer could get a start.

Although Raisch counted 25 mystery magazines several years ago, today that number has dwindled to only two large publications and a handful of good, but very small, magazines. Of these outlets, he notes, the larger ones are devoted almost entirely to British-style "cozy" or "teacup" mysteries. Cozies are mysteries usually set in a small British town in a bygone era and feature a somewhat genteel, intellectual protagonist.

It became increasingly clear to Raisch and his friends that a new outlet was badly needed. The group decided to step in and fill the void by creating *New Mystery*, a magazine devoted to contemporary short mystery fiction. The new magazine was launched this winter with Raisch at the helm as editor.

The response to Raisch's call for manuscripts was overwhelming. "We definitely stumbled into a giant window of need." For the first issue, he says, he received 3,000 manuscripts. Of those, he accepted 91 before his first issue was published.

New Mystery features mysteries dealing with contemporary themes. Within that criteria Raisch is open to a wide variety of stories including hard-boiled detective, police procedurals, spy stories, psychological and "roman noir" (dark, moody mystery). "I've even accepted stories that are very close to horror, but these must have human situations, characters and solutions. I don't want anything dealing with supernatural elements."

Strong, sympathetic characterization is an important element in stories accepted for *New Mystery*, says Raisch. "One type of story very popular now is what I call the bickering team story. It offers the opportunity for interesting interplay and characterization." He looks for characters that the reader will care about—those that "take the reader on an emotional adventure."

Raisch finds personal or regional stories work best. "The old adage 'write what you know' still holds true. Interesting stories take place in small cities or towns." Good writers can capture the essence of these towns and make them personal and interesting to outsiders, he says.

Although many of the writers involved with the magazine are members of professional mystery writers groups, Raisch is very open to new, less experienced mystery writers. "A good manuscript stands out," he says, "and everyone will find it."

—Robin Gee

‡**NEW YORK RUNNING NEWS (IV)**, New York Road Runners Club, 9 East 89 St., New York NY 10128. Editor: Raleigh Mayer. Magazine: 8×11; 80+ pages; illustrations; b&w and color photos. "Regional running magazine, local event coverage and membership (NY Road Runners Club) profiles, for serious and recreational runners, and road racers." Bimonthly. Estab. 1958. Circ. 40,000.
Needs: "Only running-related" fiction. Receives "several dozen" unsolicited fiction mss/month. Accepts "one or less" ms/issue. Publishes ms 1-6 months after acceptance. Length: 1,000 words average; 500 words minimum; 1,500 words maximum. Publishes short shorts. Length: 500 words. Occasionally critiques rejected mss.
How to Contact: Send complete ms with cover letter. Reports in "a few" weeks. SASE. Photocopied and reprint submissions OK. Accepts computer printout submissions. Sample copy $3 and 2 first class stamps. Fiction guidelines for #10 SASE.
Payment: Pays $50-150; charges for extra copies.
Terms: Pays on publication for first rights.
Advice: "Anything well done is publishable. Be funny. Be sophisticated. Be natural."

THE NEW YORKER (III), The New Yorker, Inc., 25 W. 43rd St., New York NY 10036. (212)840-3800. Fiction Department. A quality magazine of interesting, well written stories, articles, essays and poems for a literate audience. Weekly. Estab. 1925.
How to Contact: Send complete ms with SASE. Reports in 2 months on mss. Publishes 2 mss/issue.
Payment: Varies.
Terms: Pays on acceptance.
Advice: "Be lively, original, not overly literary. Write what you want to write, not what you think the editor would like."

NOAH'S ARK (II, IV), A Newspaper for Jewish Children, Suite 250, 8323 Southwest Freeway, Houston TX 77074. (713)771-7143. Editors: Debbie Israel Dubin and Linda Freedman Block. Tabloid: 4 pages; newsprint paper; illustrations; photos. "All material must be on some Jewish theme. Seasonal material relating to Jewish holidays is used as well as articles and stories relating to Jewish culture (charity, Soviet Jewry, ecology), etc." for Jewish children, ages 6-12. Monthly Sept.-June. Estab. 1979. Circ. 450,000.
Needs: Juvenile (6-12 years); religious/inspirational; ages 6-12 Jewish children. "Newspaper is not only included as a supplement to numerous Jewish newspapers and sent to individual subscribers but is also distributed in bulk quantities to religious schools; therefore all stories and articles should have educational value as well as being entertaining and interesting to children." Receives 10 unsolicited mss/month. Buys "few mss but we'd probably use more if more appropriate mss were submitted." Published new writers within the last year. Length: 600 words maximum.
How to Contact: Send complete ms with SASE. "The cover letter is not necessary; the submission will be accepted or rejected on its own merits." Simultaneous, photocopied submissions and reprints OK. Accepts computer printouts. Sample copy for #10 envelope and 1 first class stamp. "The best guideline is a copy of our publication."
Payment: Varies; contributor's copies.
Terms: Pays on acceptance for one-time rights.
Advice: "Our newspaper was created by two writers looking for a place to have our work published. It has grown in only 10 years to nearly 1 million readers throughout the world. Beginners with determination can accomplish the impossible."

NORTHCOAST VIEW (II), Blarney Publishing, Box 1374, Eureka CA 95502. (707)443-4887. Editors: Scott K. Ryan and Damon Maguire. Magazine: 11 × 14½×; 56 pages; electrabrite, 38 lb. paper and cover; illustrations; photos. "Entertainment, recreation, arts and news magazine, open to all kinds of fiction." For Humboldt County, ages 18-75 and others. Monthly. Plans anthology in future. Estab. 1982. Circ. 22,500.
Needs: Open to most subjects. Adventure, condensed novel, contemporary, erotica, ethnic, experimental, fantasy, historical (local, general), horror, humor/satire, literary, psychic/supernatural/occult, regional, science fiction, suspense/mystery, translations. No romances. Receives 30-50 unsolicited mss/month. Buys 1-2 mss/issue; 12-20 mss/year. Publishes ms 1-3 months after acceptance. Length: 2,500 words average; 250 words minimum; 5,000 words maximum.
How to Contact: Send complete ms with cover letter (background info or bio if published). Reports in 3-6 months on mss. SASE. Simultaneous, photocopied submissions and reprints (sometimes) OK. Accepts computer printouts. Sample copy $2. Fiction guidelines for #10 SAE and 1 first class stamp.

Payment: Pays $5-150.
Terms: Pays on publication for all rights.

NORTHEAST, the Sunday Magazine of the Hartford Courant, 285 Broad St., Hartford CT 06115. (203)241-3700. Editor: Lary Bloom. Magazine: 10 × 11½; 32-100 pages; illustrations; photos. "A regional (New England, specifically Connecticut) magazine, we publish stories of varied subjects of interest to our Connecticut audience" for a general audience. Weekly. Published special fiction issue and a special college writing issue for fiction and poetry. Estab. 1981. Circ. 300,000.
Needs: Contemporary and regional. No children's stories or stories with distinct setting outside Connecticut. Receives 60 unsolicited mss/month. Buys 1 ms/issue. Publishes short shorts. Length: 750 words minimum; 3,500 words maximum.
How to Contact: Send complete ms with SASE. Reports in 3 weeks. Simultaneous and photocopied submissions OK. No reprints or previously published work. Accepts computer printout submissions. Prefers letter-quality. Free sample copy and fiction guidelines with 10 × 12 or larger SASE.
Payment: $250-1,000.
Terms: Pays on acceptance for one-time rights.

NORTHWEST MAGAZINE (I, II, IV), The Sunday Oregonian Magazine, 1320 SW Broadway, Portland OR 97210. (503)221-8228. Editor: Ellen Heltzel. Magazine: 10¼ × 11½; 24-36 pages; illustrations; photos. Weekly. Circ. 400,000.
Needs: Contemporary, experimental, fantasy, humor/satire, literary mainstream, prose poem, young adult and science fiction. Receives 20-30 mss/month. Buys 30-40 mss/year. "We don't run fiction every week. Publishes ms within 1-6 months of acceptance. Agented fiction 5%. Published new writers within the last year. Length: 2,000 words maximum. Publishes short shorts. Sometimes critiques rejected mss and recommends other markets.
How to Contact: Send complete mss with cover letter. Reports in 3-4 weeks. SASE. Photocopied submissions OK. Accepts computer printout submissions. Accepts electronic submission via disk or modem. Sample copy and fiction guidelines for SAE.
Payment: Pays $150-300 and contributor's copies.
Terms: Pays on acceptance for one-time rights. Offers kill fee. Sends galleys to author.

NUGGET (II), Dugent Publishing Corp., Suite 600, 2600 Douglas Rd., Coral Gables FL 33134. (305)443-2378. Editor: Jerome Slaughter. A newsstand magazine designed to have erotic appeal for a fetish-oriented audience. Bimonthly. Estab. 1956. Circ. 100,000.
Needs: Offbeat, fetish-oriented material should encompass a variety of subjects. Most of fiction includes several sex scenes. No fiction that concerns children or religious subjects. Buys 3 mss/issue. Approximately 5% of fiction is agented. Length: 2,000-3,500 words.
How to Contact: Send complete ms with SASE. Reports in 1 month on ms. Sample copy $5. Free guidelines with legal-sized SASE.
Payment: Pays $150-300. Free author's copy.
Terms: Pays on publication for first rights.
Advice: "Keep in mind the nature of the publication, which is fetish erotica. Subject matter can vary, but we prefer fetish themes."

‡OCEAN SPORTS INTERNATIONAL (II, IV), Box 1388, Soquel CA 95073. Editor: Susan Watrous. Magazine: 8 × 10¾; 84-96 pages; glossy paper and cover; illustrations; color/b&w photos. Articles on ocean sports of all kinds for ocean people and general audience. Quarterly. Estab. 1981. Circ. 45,000.
Needs: Adventure, historical (general), humor/satire, literary, sports, special interest: water related. No experimental. Plans to buy 1 every 2 issues. Publishes ms 3-6 months after acceptance. Published work by James Houston and Fred Van Dyke. Length: 2,000 words average; 1,000 words minimum; 4,000 words maximum. Occasionally comments on rejected mss if requested. Recommends other markets if requested.
How to Contact: "It's a good idea to query first." Send complete ms with cover letter with SASE. Reports in 6 weeks. SASE. Simultaneous, photocopied submissions and reprints OK with rights obtained. Accepts computer printouts. Sample copy $3. Fiction guidelines for #10 SAE and 1 first class stamp.

Payment: Pays 5¢-10¢/word, plus contributor's copies; $2.20 charge for extras.
Terms: Pays on publication for first rights within 2 months.
Advice: "There are many markets open to the right *kind* of fiction. Particularly fiction of specific readership: shorts, regional, parent/children, etc. A good query letter helps. Remember that we're looking for stories on ocean sports, risk and survival, high adventure and stories on relationships with the ocean/water. Remember also that editors have little time, so if you call or write, be prepared, conscious of time and specific."

‡OH! IDAHO (IV), The Idaho State Magazine, Peak Media, Box 925, Hailey ID 83333. Editor: Laurie Sammis. Magazine: 80-96 pages; high quality paper; some illustrations and photographs. Publishes material on "Idaho, for Idahoans and people across the nation." Quarterly. Estab. 1988. Circ. 20,000.
Needs: Humor/satire. "Must relate specifically to Idaho, without being denigrating to the potato state. Easy on the peeve, long on the humor. Adventure—stories with information in a fictional format." Receives 4-5 unsolicited mss/month. Publishes ms 6 months after acceptance. Length: 1,200 words preferred. Sometimes critiques rejected mss and recommends other markets.
How to Contact: Query with clips of published work. Include social security number with ms. Reports in 4-6 weeks on queries. SASE. Simultaneous, photocopied and reprint submissions OK. Accepts computer printouts. Accepts electronic submissions via Word Perfect or MS-DOS ASCII only. Sample copy for $3. Guidelines for #10 SAE and 1 first class stamp.
Payment: Pays 10¢/word.
Terms: Pays on publication. Purchases first North American serial rights.
Advice: "All articles must relate specifically to Idaho and should convey all or part of this idea: Idaho is a beautiful place to live and vacation in, there are many fun and interesting activities here and the people of Idaho are fascinating. Articles should be timeless, upscale and positive. The subject matter should focus on all facets of Idaho and/or her people."

OMNI (II), General Media, 1965 Broadway, New York NY 10023. Fiction Editor: Ellen Datlow. Magazine: 8½ × 11; 114-182 pages; 40-50 lb. stock paper; 100 lb. Mead off cover stock; illustrations; photos. "Magazine of science and science fiction with an interest in near future; stories of what science holds, what life and lifestyles will be like in areas affected by science for a young, bright and well-educated audience between ages 18-45." Monthly. Estab. 1978. Circ. 1,000,000.
Needs: Science fiction, contemporary fantasy and technological horror. No sword and sorcery or space opera. Buys 20 mss/year. Receives approximately 400 unsolicited fiction mss/month. Approximately 5% of fiction is agented. Recently published work by Joyce Carol Oates, Pat Cadigan and Michael Bishop. Length: 2,000 words minimum, 10,000 words maximum. Critiques rejected mss that interest me "when there is time." Sometimes recommends other markets.
How to Contact: Send complete ms with SASE. Accepts computer printout submissions. Reports within 3 weeks on mss. Publishes ms 3 months to two years after acceptance.
Payment: Pays $1,250-2,250; 3 free author's copies.
Terms: Pays on acceptance for first North American serial rights with exclusive worldwide English language periodical rights and nonexclusive anthology rights.
Advice: "Beginning writers should read a lot of the best science fiction short stories today. We are looking for strong, well written stories dealing with the next 100 years. Don't give up on a market just because you've been rejected several times. If you're good, you'll get published eventually. Don't ever call an editor on the phone and ask why he/she rejected a story. You'll either find out in a personal rejection letter (which means the editor liked it or thought enough of your writing to comment) or you won't find out at all (most likely the editor won't remember a form-rejected story)." Recent award winners and nominees: "At the Rialto," by by Connie Willis won the Nebula award for novelette and is up for a Hugo award. "Unidentified Objects," by James P. Blaylock was chosen for *the O'Henry Awards*: prize stories 1990.

ON OUR BACKS (II,IV), Entertainment for the Adventurous Lesbian, Blush Productions, 526 Castro St., San Francisco CA 94114. (415)861-4723. Editor: Susie Bright. Magazine: 8½ × 11; 50 pages; slick paper; illustrations; photos. "Lesbian erotica, short stories, nonfiction, commentary, news clips, photos." Quarterly. Estab. 1984. Circ. 15,000.
Needs: Erotica, fantasy, humor/satire, lesbian. No "non-erotic, heterosexual" fiction. Receives 20 mss/month. Buys 2-3 mss/issue. Publishes ms within 1 year of acceptance. Published new writers within the last year. Length: 3,500 words preferred; 2,500 words minimum; 5,000 words maximum.

How to Contact: Query with clips of published work or send complete ms with cover letter. Include Social Security number. Reports in 6 weeks. SASE. No simultaneous submissions. Accepts computer printout submissions. Accepts electronic submissions via disk. Sample copy for $5. Fiction guidelines for #10 SAE and 1 first class stamp.
Payment: Pays $20-100 and contributor's copies.
Terms: Pays on publication for first North American serial rights.
Advice: "Ask yourself—does it turn me on? Ask a friend to read it—does it turn her on as well? Is it as well-written as any well-crafted non-erotic story? We love to read things that we don't see all the time—originality is definitely a plus!" Sponsors awards for fiction writers.

ON THE LINE (II), Mennonite Publishing House, 616 Walnut Ave., Scottdale PA 15683-1999. (412)887-8500. Editor: Mary Meyer. Magazine: 7×10; 8 pages; illustrations; b&w photos. "A religious take-home paper with the goal of helping children grow in their understanding and appreciation of God, the created world, themselves and other people." For children ages 10-14. Weekly. Estab. 1970. Circ. 10,000.
Needs: Adventure and religious/inspirational for older children and young teens (10-14 years). Receives 50-100 unsolicited mss/month. Buys 1 ms/issue; 52 mss/year. Recently published work by Michael LaCross, Elizabeth Westra, Virginia Kroll; published new writers within the last year. Length: 750-1,000 words.
How to Contact: Send complete ms noting whether author is offering first-time or reprint rights. Reports in 1 month. SASE. Simultaneous, photocopied and previously published work OK. Accepts computer printout submissions. Sample copy and fiction guidelines free.
Payment: Pays on acceptance for one-time rights.
Advice: "We believe in the power of story to entertain, inspire and challenge the reader to new growth. Know children and their thoughts, feelings and interests. Be realistic with characters and events in the fiction. Stories do not need to be true, but need to *feel* true."

OPTIONS (I, II), The *Bi*-Monthly, AJA Publishing, Box 470, Port Chester NY 10573. Associate Editor: Diana Sheridan. Magazine: digest sized; 114 pages; newsprint paper; glossy cover stock; illustrations and photos. Sexually explicit magazine for and about bi-sexuals. 10 issues/year. Estab. 1982. Circ. 100,000.
Needs: Erotica, gay, lesbian. "First person as-if-true experiences." Accepts 5 unsolicited fiction mss/month. "Very little" of fiction is agented. Published new writers within the last year. Length: 2,000-3,000 words average; 2,000 words minimum. Sometimes critiques rejected mss.
How to Contact: Send complete ms with cover letter. Reports in approx. 3 weeks. SASE. Photocopied submissions OK, if clearly marked "not a simultaneous submission." Accepts computer printout submissions. Sample copy $2.95 and 6×9 SAE with 5 first class stamps. Fiction guidelines for SASE.
Payment: Pays $100.
Terms: Pays on publication for all rights.
Advice: "Read a copy of *Options* carefully and look at our spec sheet, before writing anything for us. We only buy 2 bi-woman/lesbian pieces per issue; need is greater for bi/gay male mss. Though we're a bi rather than gay magazine, the emphasis is on same-sex relationships. If the readers want to read about a male/female couple, they'll buy another magazine. Gay male stories sent to *Options* will also be considered for publication in *Beau*, our gay male magazine. *Most important: We only* publish stories that feature 'safe sex' practices unless the story is clearly something that took place pre-AIDS."

‡ORANGE COAST MAGAZINE (II), The Magazine of Orange County, Suite 8, 245-D Fischer, Coasta Mesa CA 92626. (714)545-1900. Editor: Palmer Thomason Jones. Managing Editor: Erik Himmelsbach. Magazine: 8½×11; 250 pages; 50 lb. Sonoma gloss paper; 10. Warrenflo cover; illustrations and photographs. *Orange Coast* publishes articles offering local insight to its affluent, well-educated Orange County readers. Monthly. Estab. 1974. Circ. 35,000.
Needs: Contemporary, humor/satire, regional, suspense/mystery. "We prefer Orange County setting." Receives 3 unsolicited mss/month. Buys 3 mss/year. Publishes ms 2-3 months after acceptance. Recently published work by Robert Ray. Length: 2,500 words average; 1,500 words minimum; 3,000 words maximum.
How to Contact: Query first, query with clips of published work or send complete manuscript with cover letter that includes Social Security number. Reports in 2 months. SASE. Simultaneous submissions OK. Sample copy for SAE. Free fiction guidelines.
Payment: Pays $100-250.
Terms: Pays on acceptance for first North American serial rights.

‡**ORGANICA QUARTERLY (II)**, Organica Press, 4419 N. Manhattan Ave., Tampa FL 33614. Editor: Susan Hussey. Fiction Editor: Silvia Curbelo. Tabloid: 28 pages. "Intelligent, literary." Quarterly. Circ. 200,000.

Needs: Contemporary, ethnic, experimental, humor/satire, literary. "Have strong aversion to 'New Age' genre; to self-indulgent writing of all kinds." Buys 1-2 mss/year. Time from acceptance to publishing varies. Recently published work by Ann Darby and Renée Ashley. Length: 2,500-3,000 words average; 5,000 words maximum. Publishes short shorts. Recommends other markets.

How to contact: Send complete manuscript with cover letter. "Not necessary; previous publications might be listed if cover letter is enclosed." Reports in 4-6 weeks on mss. Sample copy $1.

Payment: Varies.

Terms: Pays on publication for first North American serial rights. Sends galleys to author.

Advice: "Our only criteria is quality. We are looking for intelligent fiction and a fresh approach to language."

THE OTHER SIDE (III), 1225 Dandridge St., Fredericksburg VA 22401. (215)849-2178. Editor: Mark Olson. Fiction Editor: Barbara Moorman. Magazine: 8½ × 11; 55 pages, illustrations and photographs. Magazine of justice rooted in discipleship for Christians with a strong interest in peace, social and economic justice. Bimonthly. Estab. 1965. Circ. 14,000.

Needs: Contemporary, ethnic, experimental, feminist, humor/satire, literary, mainstream, spiritual and suspense/mystery. Receives 30 unsolicited fiction mss/month. Buys 6 mss/year. Published work by Laurie Skiba, Wilton Miller and Shirley Pendlebury. Length: 1,500 words minimum; 5,000 words maximum; 3,500 words average.

How to Contact: Send complete ms with SASE. No simultaneous submissions or pre-published material. Accepts computer printout submissions. Reports in 6-8 weeks on mss. Publishes ms 3-9 months after acceptance. Sample copy for $4.50.

Payment: Pays $50-250; free subscription to magazine; 5 free contributor's copies.

Terms: Pays on acceptance for all or first rights.

OUI MAGAZINE (II), 6th Floor, 300 W. 43rd St., New York NY 10036. (212)397-5200. Editor: Richard Kidd. Magazine: 8 × 11; 112 pages; illustrations; photos. Magazine for college-age males and older. Monthly. Estab. 1972. Circ. 1 million.

Needs: Contemporary, fantasy, lesbian, men's, mystery and humor. Buys 1 ms/issue; 12 mss/year. Receives 200-300 unsolicited fiction mss/month. Published new writers within the last year. Length: 1,500-3,000 words.

How to Contact: Cover letter with author background, previous publications, etc. Send complete ms with SASE. Accepts computer printout submissions. Prefers letter-quality. Reports in 6-8 weeks on mss.

Payment: Pays $250 and up.

Terms: Pays on publication for first rights.

Advice: "Many mss are rejected because writers have not studied the market or the magazine. We want writers to take chances and offer us something out of the ordinary. Look at several recent issues to see what direction our fiction is headed."

OUTLAW BIKER (II, IV), Outlaw Biker Enterprises, 450 7th Ave. #2305, New York NY 10123. (212)564-0112. FAX: (212)465-8350. Publisher/Editor: Casey Exton. Magazine: 8½ × 11; 96 pages; 50 lb. color paper; 80 lb. cover stock; illustrations; photos. Publication for hard-core bikers, their partners and for tattoo enthusiasts. Monthly. Special issue 5 times/year, *Tattoo Review*. Estab. 1984. Circ. 225,000.

Needs: Biker fiction and humor. Receives 20 unsolicited mss/month. Accepts 3 fiction mss/issue. Publishes ms 4 months after acceptance. Length: 1,000 words minimum; 2,500 words maximum.

How to Contact: Send complete ms with cover letter. SASE very important. Reports on queries in 1 month. Sample copy $3.50.

Payment: Pays $50-150.

Terms: Pays on publication for all rights.

Advice: "Timely biker events with photos used constantly. Photos do not have to be professionally taken. Clear snapshots of events with the short story usually accepted. Send to: Casey Exton, Attention."

PALOUSE JOURNAL (II, IV), North Country Book Express, Box 9632, Moscow ID 83843. (208)882-0888. Editors: Phil Druker, Ed Hughes. Tabloid: 11 × 17; 24-40 pages; 34 lb stock; illustrations; photos. "We are a regional general interest magazine, for an educated, literate audience." Bimonthly. Estab. 1981.
Needs: Regional. "We will consider good writing about our region." Buys 1 ms/issue at most; 2-6 mss/year. Recently published work by Jonathan Pitts, Linda Kittel and Robert Wrigley; published new writers within the last year. Length: 2,000 words maximum. Will consider short shorts as columns, up to 1,000 words. Occasionally critiques rejected mss.
How to Contact: Send complete ms with cover letter. Reports in 2-3 months on mss. SASE. Photocopied submissions OK. Accepts computer printout submissions. Sample copy $2. Writers' guidelines for SASE.
Payment: Pays $25-75 for a full feature story.
Terms: Pays on publication for first North American serial rights.
Advice: "We look for good clean writing, a regional relevance. Manuscripts are often rejected because writer is obviously not familiar with the magazine and story lacks regional flavor. We only publish work about the Pacific and Intermountain West."

‡PEN SYNDICATED FICTION PROJECT (I), P.O. Box 15650, Washington DC 20003. (203)543-6322. Editor: Caroline Marshall. "Fiction syndicate created to market quality short fiction to a broad, national audience via radio (The Sound of Writing, co-produced with NPR), newspaper Sunday magazines (a varying group) and a quarterly literary publication (*American Short Fiction* published by University of Texas Press.)"
Needs: Literary. Receives 2,500-3,000 submissions/year. Buys 50 mss/year. Only reads in January. Length: 2,500 maximum. Publishes short shorts.
How to Contact: Send complete ms with cover letter. Up to 10 stories may be submitted at one time, but no one story may exceed 2,500 words. Send two copies, brief bio and cover sheet. Reads in January only. Decisions made by April. SASE. Fiction guidelines for #10 SAE and 1 first-class stamp.
Payment: Pays $500 plus $100 per publication by participating newspapers and tearsheets. "Realistic possible potential: $1,000-1,500."
Terms: Pays $500 on return of contract, syndication fees paid on semiannual basis. Buys world-wide serial rights, audio and anthology rights.
Advice: "Newspaper and radio audiences prefer short pieces of general, topical or family interest. Submitters are encouraged to imagine seeing their work in a Sunday magazine with accompanying illustration or hearing it on the air to judge a story's suitability."

PENNYWHISTLE PRESS (II), Gannett Co., Inc., Box 500-P, Washington DC 20044. Editor: Anita Sama. Magazine: tabloid size; 8 pages; newsprint paper; illustrations; photos. Education and information for children ages 7-14. Weekly. Estab. 1981. Circ. 2.5 million.
Needs: Juvenile (7-9 years), (long) prose poem, young adult/teen (10-14 years). No talking animals. Receives "hundreds" of unsolicited fiction mss/month. Accepts 20 mss/year. Length: 450 words for 7-10 year olds; 850 words for older children.
How to Contact: Send complete ms with cover letter with SASE. *No* queries. No simultaneous submissions accepted. "We do not accept previously published manuscripts." Sample copy 50¢.
Payment: Varies.
Terms: Pays on acceptance.

PILLOW TALK (II), 801 2nd Ave., New York NY 10017. Editor: Asia Fraser. Magazine: digest-sized; 98 pages; photos. Bi-monthly erotic letters magazine.
Needs: "We use approximately 20 short letters of no more than five manuscript pages per issue, and five long letters of between seven and nine manuscript pages." Published new writers within the last year. Recommends other markets.
How to Contact: "We encourage unsolicited manuscripts. Writers who have proven reliable will receive assignments."
Terms: *Pillow Talk* pays $5 per page for short letters and a $75 flat rate for long letters and articles. Pays on acceptance.
Advice: "Keep it short and sensual. We buy many more short letters than long ones. This is a 'couples-oriented' book; the sex should be a natural outgrowth of a relationship, the characters should be believable, and both male and female characters should be treated with respect. No S&M, bondage, male homosexuality, incest, underage characters or anal sex—not even in dialog, not even in implica-

tion. No language that even implies sexual violence—not even in metaphor. No ejaculation on any part of a person's body. Romance is a big plus."

THE PLAIN DEALER MAGAZINE (II), 1801 Superior Ave., Cleveland OH 44114. (216)344-4546. Editor: Clint O'Connor. Magazine: 10×11½; 20-64 pages; color and b&w illustrations and photos. Regional magazine, Sunday supplement to The Plain Dealer newspaper for our readers (Cleveland and state). Weekly. Circ. 575,000.
Needs: Adventure, contemporary, ethnic, historical (general), humor/satire, literary, mainstream, psychic/supernatural/occult, regional, science fiction, sports, suspense/mystery. "Regional preferred." Publishes annual special summer fiction issue. Receives 10-20 unsolicited mss/month. Number of mss accepted per issue "depends on quality." Publishes ms 2-3 months after acceptance. Length: 2,000 words maximum. Occasionally comments on rejected mss.
How to Contact: Send complete ms with cover letter, include Social Security number. Reports in 1 month on mss. SASE for ms, not needed for query. Sample copy $1 and 7½×10½ SAE.
Payment: Pays $500 maximum; 2 contributor's copies.
Terms: Pays on publication for one-time rights.

PLAYBOY MAGAZINE (III), Playboy Enterprises, Inc., 919 N. Michigan Ave., Chicago IL 60611. (312)751-8000. Fiction Editor: Alice K. Turner. Magazine: 8½×11; 250 pages; glossy cover stock; illustrations; photos. Entertainment magazine for a male audience. Monthly. Estab. 1953. Circ. 4,250,342.
Needs: Literary, contemporary, science fiction, fantasy, horror, sports, western, mystery, adventure and humor. No pornography or fiction geared to a female audience. Buys 1-3 mss/issue; 25 mss/year. Receives approximately 1,200 unsolicited fiction mss each month. Recently published work by Tim O'Brien, Gustav Hasford and Robert Silverberg; published new writers within the last year. Length: 1,000-10,000 (average 6,000) words. Also publishes short shorts of 1,000 words. Critiques rejected mss "when there is time." Recommends other markets "sometimes."
How to Contact: Send complete ms with SASE and cover letter with prior publication information. Reports in 6-8 weeks on mss. Free guidelines with SASE.
Payment: Pays $5,000 minimum; $2,000 minimum for short shorts.
Terms: Pays on acceptance for all rights.

POCKETS (II), Devotional Magazine for Children, The Upper Room, Box 189, 1908 Grand Ave., Nashville TN 37202. (615)340-7333. Editor-in-Chief: Janet R. McNish. Magazine: 7×9; 32 pages; 50 lb. white econowrite paper; 80 lb. white coated, heavy cover stock; color and 2-color illustrations; some photos. Magazine for children ages 6-12, with articles specifically geared for ages 8 to 11. "The magazine offers stories, activities, prayers, poems—all geared to giving children a better understanding of themselves as children of God." Published monthly except for January. Estab. 1981. Estimated circ. 68,000.
Needs: Adventure, contemporary, ethnic, fantasy, historical (general), juvenile, religious/inspirational and suspense/mystery. "All submissions should address the broad theme of the magazine. Each issue will be built around several themes with material which can be used by children in a variety of ways. Scripture stories, fiction, poetry, prayers, art, graphics, puzzles and activities will all be included. Submissions do not need to be overtly religious. They should help children experience a Christian lifestyle that is not always a neatly wrapped moral package, but is open to the continuing revelation of God's will. Seasonal material, both secular and liturgical, is desired. No violence, horror, sexual and racial stereotyping or fiction containing heavy moralizing." Receives approximately 120 unsolicited fiction mss/month. Buys 2-3 mss/issue; 22-33 mss/year. Publishes short shorts. A peace-with-justice theme will run throughout the magazine. Approximately 50% of fiction is agented. Published work by Peggy King Anderson, Angela Gibson and John Steptoe; published new writers last year. Length: 600 words minimum; 1,500 words maximum; 1,200 words average.
How to Contact: Send complete ms with SASE. Photocopied and previously published submissions OK, but no simultaneous submissions. Accepts computer printout submissions. Reports in 2 months on mss. Publishes ms 1 year to 18 months after acceptance. Sample copy $1.70. Free fiction guidelines and themes with SASE. "Strongly advise sending for themes before submitting." Fiction-Writing Contest. Deadline August 1, 1991. 1,000-1,600 words.

Payment: Pays 12¢/word and up and 2-5 contributor's copies. $1.70 charge for extras; 25¢ each for 10 or more.
Terms: Pays on acceptance for newspaper and periodical rights. Buys reprints.
Advice: "Do not write *down* to children." Rejects mss because "we receive far more submissions than we can use. If all were of high quality, we still would purchase only a few. The most common problems are overworked story lines and flat, unrealistic characters. Most stories simply do not 'ring true', and children know that. Each issue is theme-related. Please send for list of themes. Include SASE."

PORTLAND MAGAZINE (II), 578 Congress St., Portland ME 04101. (207)773-5250. Editor: Colin Sargent. Magazine: 68 pages; 60 lb paper; 80 lb cover stock; illustrations and photographs. "City lifestyle magazine—style, business, real estate, controversy, fashion, cuisine, interviews, art." Estab. 1986. Circ. 22,000.
Needs: Contemporary, historical, literary. Receives 20 unsolicited fiction mss/month. Buys 1 mss/issue; 12 mss/year. Publishes short shorts. Recently published work by Frederick Barthelme, Diane Lefer, Dan Domench. Length: 3 double-spaced typed pages. Query first.
How to Contact: "Fiction below 700 words, please." Send complete ms with cover letter. Reports in 3 months. SASE. Accepts computer printout and electronic submissions. Sample copy $2.
Terms: Pays on publication for first North American serial rights.
Advice: "We publish ambitious short fiction featuring everyone from Frederick Barthelme to newly discovered fiction by Edna St. Vincent Millay."

‡PRIME TIME SPORTS AND FITNESS (IV), Prime Time Publishing, P.O. Box 6097, Evanston IL 60204. (708)864-8113. Editor: Dennis Dorner. Fiction Editor: Linda Jefferson. Magazine; 8½ × 11; 40-80 pages; coated enamel paper and cover stock; 10 illustrations; 42 photographs. "For active sports participants." Estab. 1975. Circ. 67,000.
Needs: Adventure, contemporary, erotica, fantasy, historical, humor/satire, mainstream, sports, young adult/teen (10-18 years). No gay, lesbian. Receives 30-40 unsolicited mss/month. Buys 1-2 mss/issue; 20/year. Publishes ms 3-8 months after acceptance. Agented fiction 10%. Recently published work by Dennis Dorner, Sally Hammill. Length: 2,000 words preferred; 250 words minimum; 3,000 words maximum. Publishes short shorts. Length: 250-500 words. Sometimes critiques rejected ms and recommends other markets.
How to Contact: Send complete ms with cover letter, include Social Security number. "Do *not* include credits and history. We buy articles, not people." Reports in 1 to 3 months on queries; 1 week to 3 months on mss. SASE. Simultaneous, photocopied and reprint submissions OK. Accepts computer printout submissions. Sample copy for 10 × 12 SAE and $1.40 postage. Fiction guidelines free for SAE.
Payment: Pays $25-500.
Terms: Pays on publication for all rights, first rights, first North American serial rights, one-time rights; "depends on manuscript."
Advice: "Be funny, ahead of particular sports season, and enjoy your story. Bring out some human touch that would relate to our readers."

PRIME TIMES (II), National Association for Retired Credit Union People, Inc., (NARCUP), Editorial Offices: Suite 120, 2802 International Ln., Madison WI 53704. (608)241-1557. Executive Editor: Rod Clark. Magazine: medium sized; 40 pages; illustrations and photos. Editorial slant is toward redefining the mid-life transition and promoting a dynamic vision of the prime-life years. Each edition revolves loosely around a theme—for example, stress management and preventive health help, second careers, unique problems of the midlife or "bridge" generation. The short story may sketch relational conflicts and resolutions between prime-life men and women, or with their children, parents, etc., or place them in situations that try their spirits and revalidate them. Fiction that is not targeted to this group but of excellent quality and broad general appeal is also very welcome. Staff will review adventure, ethnic, science fiction, fantasy, mainstream and humorous fiction as well. No sentimental romances or nostalgia pieces, please. Quarterly. Estab. 1979. Circ. 75,000.

 The double dagger before a listing indicates that the listing is new in this edition. New markets are often the most receptive to freelance contributions.

Needs: Literary, contemporary, romance, adventure, humor, ethnic, travel. Buys 2 mss/year. Approximately 10% of fiction is agented. Recently published work by Ethan Canin. Length: 1,000-2,500 words. Shorter lengths preferred.

How to Contact: Send complete ms. SASE always. Accepts computer printout submissions. Prefers letter-quality. Reports in 4-6 weeks on queries and mss. Publishes ms 6-12 months after acceptance. Free sample copy with 9×12 SASE (5 first class stamps). Free guidelines with SASE.

Payment: $150-750. 3 free author's copies; $1 charge for each extra.

Terms: Pays on publication for first North American serial rights and for second serial (reprint) rights.

Advice: "We may feature fiction only once or twice yearly, now, instead of regularly. Quality is *everything*. Readers favor the short stories we've featured on positive human relationships. We are very happy to feature second-serial work as long as it hasn't appeared in another *national* 'maturity market' publication. *Always* request a publication's writer's guidelines before submitting. Write with emotional integrity and imagination."

Jean Moss was the photographer for this cover of Prime Times *magazine. According to art director Marla Brenner, the photograph was chosen to highlight an article about women entrepreneurs. "The woman in the photo seems to convey the idea of a woman entrepreneur with a vision," she says. Copyright © 1989 Jean Moss.*

PRIVATE LETTERS (I, II), 801 2nd Ave., New York NY 10017. Editor: Asia Fraser. Magazine: digest-sized; 98 pages; illustrations; photographs. Bi-monthly letters magazine.

Needs: Erotica, written in letter form. No S&M, incest, homosexuality, anal sex or sex-crazed women and macho, women-conquering studs. "We use approximately 40 short letters per issue of no more than four double-spaced manuscript pages and five long letters of about 10 double-spaced manuscript pages." Recently published work by Diana Shamblin, Frank Lee and Shirley LeRoy; published new writers last year. Recommends other markets.

How to Contact: Send complete mss. "The majority of the material is assigned to people whose writing has proven consistently top-notch. They usually reach this level by sending us unsolicited material which impresses us. We invite them to send us some more on spec, and we're impressed again. Then a long and fruitful relationship is hopefully established. We greatly encourage unsolicited submissions. We are now printing two additional issues each year, so naturally the demand for stories is higher."

Payment: Pays $5 per page for short letters; $75 for long (7-10 page) letters.
Terms: Pays on acceptance.
Advice: "If you base your writing on erotic magazines other than our own, then we'll probably find your material too gross. We want good characterization, believable plots, a little romance, with sex being a natural outgrowth of a relationship. (Yes, it can be done. Read our magazine.) Portray sex as an emotionally-charged, romantic experience—not an animalistic ritual. *Never* give up, except if you die. In which case, if you haven't succeeded as a writer yet, you probably never will. (Though there have been exceptions.) Potential writers should be advised that each issue has certain themes and topics we try to adhere to. It would be greatly to one's benefit to write to ask for a copy of the writer's guidelines *and* a list of themes and topics for upcoming issues. Also, while the longer stories of more than 7 pages pay more, there are only about five of them accepted for each issue. We buy far more 4-6 page mss."

PURPOSE (II), Mennonite Publishing House, 616 Walnut Ave., Scottdale PA 15683-1999. (412)887-8500. Editor: James E. Horsch. Magazine: 5⅜ × 8⅜; 8 pages; illustrations; photos. "Magazine focuses on Christian discipleship—how to be a faithful Christian in the midst of tough everday life complexities. Use story form to present models and examples to encourage Christians in living a life of faithful discipleship." Weekly. Estab. 1969. Circ. 18,750.
Needs: Historical, religious/inspirational. No militaristic/narrow patriotism or racism. Receives 100 unsolicited mss/month. Buys 3 mss/issue; 40 mss/year. Publishes short shorts. Recently published work by Wynne Gillis, Maxine F. Dennis, Todd Lee and Louise Carroll. Length: 700 words average; 1,000 words maximum. Occasionally comments on rejected ms.
How to Contact: Prefers full manuscript. Reports in 6 weeks. Simultaneous, photocopied and previously published work OK. Accepts computer printout submissions. Sample copy free with 6 × 9 SAE and 2 first class stamps. Writer's guidelines free with sample copy only.
Payment: Pays up to 5¢/word for stories and up to $1 per line for poetry and 2 contributor's copies.
Terms: Pays on acceptance for one-time rights.
Advice: Many stories are "situational—how to respond to dilemmas. Write crisp, action moving, personal style, focused upon an individual, a group of people, or an organization. The story form is an excellent literary device to use in exploring discipleship issues. There are many issues to explore. Each writer brings a unique solution. Let's hear them. The first two paragraphs are crucial in establishing the mood/issue to be resolved in the story. Work hard on developing these."

ELLERY QUEEN'S MYSTERY MAGAZINE (II), Davis Publications, Inc., 380 Lexington Ave., New York NY 10017. (212)557-9100. Editor: Eleanor Sullivan. Magazine: Digest sized; 160 pages with special 288-page issues in March and October. Magazine for lovers of mystery fiction. Published 13 times/year. Estab. 1941. Circ. 350,000.
Needs: "We accept only mystery, crime and detective fiction." Buys 10-15 mss/issue. Receives approximately 250 unsolicited fiction mss each month. Approximately 50% of fiction is agented. Published work by Clark Howard, Robert Barnard and Ruth Rendell; published new writers within the last year. Length: up to 9,000 words. Critiques rejected mss "only when a story might be a possibility for us if revised." Sometimes recommends other markets.
How to Contact: Send complete ms with SASE. Cover letter should include publishing credits and brief biographical sketch. Reports in 1 month or sooner on mss. Publishes 6 months to 1 year after acceptance. Free fiction guidelines with SASE. Sample copy for $2.75.
Payment: Pays 3¢ per word and up.
Terms: Pays on acceptance for first North American serial rights. Occasionally buys reprints.
Advice: "We have a Department of First Stories and usually publish at least one first story an issue—i.e., the author's first published fiction. We select stories that are fresh and of the kind our readers have expressed a liking for. In writing a detective story, you must play fair with the reader re clues and necessary information. Otherwise you have a better chance of publishing if you avoid writing to formula."

R-A-D-A-R (II), Standard Publishing, 8121 Hamilton Ave., Cincinnati OH 45231. (513)931-4050. Editor: Margaret Williams. Magazine: 12 pages; newsprint; illustrations; a few photos. "*R-A-D-A-R* is a take-home paper, distributed in Sunday school classes for children in grades 3-6. The stories and other features reinforce the Bible lesson taught in class. Boys and girls who attend Sunday school make up the audience. The fiction stories, Bible picture stories and other special features appeal to their interests." Weekly. Estab. 1978.

Needs: Fiction—The hero of the story should be an 11- or 12-year-old in a situation involving one or more of the following: history, mystery, animals (preferably horses or dogs), prose poem, spiritual, sports, adventure, school, travel, relationships with parents, friends and others. Stories should have believable plots and be wholesome, Christian character-building, but not "preachy." No science fiction. Receives approximately 75-100 unsolicited mss/month. Published work by Betty Lou Mell, Betty Steele Everett and Alan Cliburn; published new writers within the last year. Length: 900-1,000 words average; 400 words minimum; 1,200 words maximum. Publishes short shorts.
How to Contact: Send complete ms. Reports in 2 weeks on queries; 6-8 weeks on mss. SASE for ms. No simultaneous submissions; photocopied and reprint submissions OK. Accepts computer printout submissions. Reports in 6-8 weeks. Free sample copy and guidelines.
Payment: Pays 3-7¢/word. Free contributor's copy.
Terms: Pays on acceptance for first rights, reprints, etc.
Advice: "Send for sample copy, guidesheet, and theme list. Follow the specifics of guidelines. Keep your writing current with the times and happenings of our world."

RADIANCE (II), The Magazine for Large Women, Box 31703, Oakland CA 94604. (415)482-0680. Editor: Alice Ansfield. Fiction Editors: Alice Ansfield and Carol Squires. Magazine: 8½ × 11; 48-52 pages; glossy/coated paper; 70 lb. cover stock; illustrations; photos. "Theme is to encourage women to live fully now, whatever their body size. To stop waiting to live or feel good about themselves until they lose weight. Health, emotional well-being, cultural views of body size, poetry/art, profiles, book reviews, lots of ads for services/products for large women, etc." Audience is "large women (size 16 and over) from all walks of life, all ages, ethnic groups, education levels and lifestyles. Feminist, fashion, emotionally supportive magazine." Quarterly. Estab. 1984. Circ. 35,000.
Needs: Adventure, contemporary, erotica, ethnic, fantasy, feminist, historical, humor/satire, mainstream, prose poem, science fiction, spiritual, sports, suspense, young adult/teen. "Would prefer fiction to have in it a larger-bodied character; living in a positive, upbeat way. Our goal is to empower women." Receives 30-50 mss/month. Buys 8 mss/year. Publishes ms within 1 year of acceptance. Recently published work by Marla Zarrow and Dan Davis. Length: 1,800 words preferred; 800 words minimum; 2,500 words maximum. Publishes short shorts. Sometimes critiques rejected mss and recommends other markets.
How to Contact: Query with clips of published work and send complete mss with cover letter. Reports in 1-2 months. SASE. Simultaneous, photocopied and reprint submissions OK. Accepts computer printout submissions. Sample copy for $2.50. Fiction guidelines for #10 SASE.
Payment: Pays $50-100 and contributor's copies.
Terms: Pays on publication for one-time rights. Sends galleys to the author if requested.
Advice: "Read our magazine before sending anything to us. Know what our philosophy and points of view are before sending a manuscript. Look around within your community for inspiring, successful and unique large women doing things worth writing about. We will do more fiction in the future, as we grow and have more space for it. At this time, prefer fiction having to do with a larger woman (man, child). Read our magazine. Know our point of view."

RANGER RICK MAGAZINE (II), National Wildlife Federation, 1400 16th St. NW, Washington DC 20036-2266. (703)790-4278. Editor: Gerald Bishop. Fiction Editor: Deborah Churchman. Magazine: 8 × 10; 48 pages; glossy paper; 60 lb cover stock; illustrations; photos. "*Ranger Rick* emphasizes conservation and the enjoyment of nature through full-color photos and art, fiction and nonfiction articles, games and puzzles, and special columns. Our audience ranges in ages from 6-12, with the greatest number in the 7 to 10 group. We aim for a fourth grade reading level. They read for fun and information." Monthly. Estab. 1967. Circ. 900,000+.
Needs: Fantasy, mystery, adventure, science fiction and humor. "Interesting stories for kids focusing directly on nature or related subjects. Fiction that carries a conservation message is always needed, as are adventure stories involving kids with nature or the outdoors. Moralistic 'lessons' taught children by parents or teachers are not accepted. Human qualities are attributed to animals only in our regular feature, 'Adventures of Ranger Rick.'" Receives about 75 unsolicited fiction mss each month. Buys about 6 mss/year. Recently published fiction by Judy Braus. Length: 900 words maximum. Critiques rejected mss "when there is time."

Market categories: (I) Beginning; (II) General; (III) Prestige; (IV) Specialized.

How to Contact: Query with sample lead and any clips of published work with SASE. Reports in 3 weeks on queries, 2 months on mss. Publishes ms 8 months to 1 year after acceptance, but sometimes longer. Free sample copy. Free guidelines with legal-sized SASE.
Payment: $550 maximum/full-length ms.
Terms: Pays on acceptance for all rights. Very rarely buys reprints. Sends galleys to author.
Advice: "For our magazine, the writer needs to understand kids and that aspect of nature he or she is writing about—a difficult combination! Mss are rejected because they are "contrived and/or condescending—often overwritten. Some mss are anthropomorphic, others are above our readers' level. We find that fiction stories help children understand the natural world and the environmental problems it faces. Beginning writers have a chance equal to that of established authors *provided* the quality is there."

REDBOOK (II), The Hearst Corporation, 224 W. 57th St., New York NY 10019. Editor: Dawn Raffel. Magazine: 8 × 10¾; 150-250 pages; 34 lb. paper; 70 lb. cover; illustrations; photos. "*Redbook's* readership consists of American women, ages 25-44. Most are well-educated, married, have children and also work outside the home." Monthly. Estab. 1903. Circ. 4,000,000.
Needs: "*Redbook* generally publishes two to three short stories per issue. We are looking for fiction that will appeal to active, thinking, contemporary women. Stories need not be about women exclusively; we also look for fiction reflecting the broad range of human experience. We are interested in new voices and buy up to a quarter of our stories from unsolicited submissions. Standards are high: Stories must be fresh, felt and intelligent; no straight formula fiction, pat endings, highly oblique or symbolic stories without conclusions." Receives up to 3,000 unsolicited fiction mss each month; published new writers within the last year. Length: up to 22 ms pages.
How to Contact: Send complete ms with 8 × 11 SASE. No queries, please. Reports in 8-10 weeks.
Terms: Pays on acceptance. Buys first North American serial rights.
Advice: "Superior craftsmanship is of paramount importance: Pay keen attention to character development and a strong and engaging storyline. Please read a few issues to get a sense of what we're looking for."

REFORM JUDAISM (II), Union of American Hebrew Congregations, 838 5th Ave., New York NY 10021. (212)249-0100, ext. 400. Editor: Aron Hirt-Manheimer. Managing Editor: Joy Weinberg. Fiction Editor: Steven Schnur. Magazine: 8½ × 11; 32 or 48 pages; illustrations; photos. "We cover subjects of Jewish interest in general and Reform Jewish in particular, for members of Reform Jewish congregations in the United States and Canada." Quarterly. Estab. 1972. Circ. 295,000.
Needs: Humor/satire, religious/inspirational. Receives 30 unsolicited mss/month. Buys 3 mss/year. Publishes ms 3 months after acceptance. Length: 1,000 words average; 700 words minimum; 2,000 words maximum. Sometimes recommends other markets.
How to Contact: Send complete ms with cover letter. Reports in 3 weeks. SASE for ms. Simultaneous and photocopied submissions OK. Accepts computer printout submissions. Sample copy for $1 and SAE. Fiction guidelines for SAE.
Payment: Pays 10¢/word.
Terms: Pays on publication for first North American serial rights.

ROAD KING MAGAZINE (I), William A. Coop, Inc., Box 250, Park Forest IL 60466. (708)481-9240. Magazine: 5¾ × 8; 48-88 pages; 60 lb. enamel paper; 60 lb. enamel cover stock; illustrations; photos. "Bi-monthly leisure-reading magazine for long-haul, over-the-road professional truckers. Contains short articles, short fiction, some product news, games, puzzles and industry news. Truck drivers read it while eating, fueling, during layovers and at other similar times while they are en route."
Needs: Truck-related, western, mystery, adventure and humor. "Remember that our magazine gets into the home and that some truckers tend to be Bible belt types. No erotica or violence." Buys 1 ms/issue; 6 mss/year. Receives 200 unsolicited fiction mss each year. Published work by Forrest Grove and Dan Anderson. Length: 1,200 words, maximum.
How to Contact: Send complete ms with SASE. Reports in 3-6 months on mss. Publishes ms 1-2 months after acceptance. Sample copy with 6 × 9 SASE.
Payment: Pays $400 maximum.
Terms: Pays on acceptance for all rights.
Advice: "Don't phone. Don't send mss by registered or insured mail or they will be returned unopened by post office. Don't try to get us involved in lengthy correspondence. Be patient. We have a small staff and we are slow." Mss are rejected because "most don't fit our format . . . they are too long; they do not have enough knowledge of trucking; there is too much violence. Our readers like fiction.

We are a leisure reading publication with a wide variety of themes and articles in each issue. Truckers can read a bit over coffee, in the washroom, etc., then save the rest of the magazine for the next stop. Know the trucker market. We are not interested in stereotypical image of truckers as macho, beer guzzling, women-chasing cowboys."

ST. ANTHONY MESSENGER (II), St. Anthony Messenger, 1615 Republic St., Cincinnati OH 45210. Editor: Norman Perry, O.F.M. Magazine: 8 × 10¾; 56 pages; illustrations; photos. *"St. Anthony Messenger* is a Catholic family magazine which aims to help its readers lead more fully human and Christian lives. We publish articles which report on a changing church and world, opinion pieces written from the perspective of Christian faith and values, personality profiles, and fiction which entertains and informs." Monthly. Estab. 1893. Circ. 380,000.
Needs: Contemporary, religious/inspirational, romance, senior citizen/retirement and spiritual. "We do not want mawkishly sentimental or preachy fiction. Stories are most often rejected for poor plotting and characterization; bad dialogue—listen to how people talk; inadequate motivation. Many stories say nothing, are 'happenings' rather than stories." No fetal journals, no rewritten Bible stories. Receives 70-80 unsolicited fiction mss/month. Buys 1 ms/issue; 12 mss/year. Recently published work by Marjorie Franco, Joseph Pici, Joan Savro and Philip Gambone. Length: 2,000-2,500 words. Critiques rejected mss "when there is time." Sometimes recommends other markets.
How to Contact: Send complete ms with SASE. Accepts computer printout submissions. Reports in 6 to 8 weeks on mss. Publishes ms up to 1 year after acceptance. Free sample copy and guidelines with #10 SASE.
Payment: Pays 14¢/word maximum; 2 free author's copies; $1 charge for extras.
Terms: Pays on acceptance for first North American serial rights.
Advice: "We publish one story a month and we get up to 1,000 a year. Too many offer simplistic 'solutions' or answers. Pay attention to endings. Easy, simplistic, deus ex machina endings don't work. People have to feel characters in the stories are real and have a reason to care about them and what happens to them. Fiction entertains but can also convey a point in a very telling way just as the Bible uses stories to teach."

ST. JOSEPH'S MESSENGER AND ADVOCATE OF THE BLIND (II), Sisters of St. Joseph of Peace, 541 Pavonia Ave., Jersey City NJ 07306. (201)798-4141. Magazine: 8½ × 11; 16 pages; illustrations; photos. For Catholics generally but not exclusively. Theme is "religious—relevant—real." Quarterly. Estab. 1903. Circ. 30,000.
Needs: Contemporary, humor/satire, mainstream, religious/inspirational, romance, and senior citizen/retirement. Receives 30-40 unsolicited fiction mss/month. Buys 3 mss/issue; 20 mss/year. Published work by Eileen W. Strauch; published new writers within the last year. Length: 800 words minimum; 1,800 words maximum; 1,500 words average. Occasionally critiques rejected mss.
How to Contact: Send complete ms with SASE. Simultaneous, photocopied and previously published submissions OK. Publishes ms an average of 1 year after acceptance. Free sample copy with #10 SAE and 1 first class stamp. Free fiction guidelines with SASE.
Payment: Pays $10-25 and 2 contributor's copies.
Terms: Pays on acceptance for one-time rights.
Advice: Rejects mss because of "vague focus or theme. Write to be read—keep material current and of interest. *Do not preach*—the story will tell the message. Keep the ending from being too obvious. Fiction is the greatest area of interest to our particular reading public."

SASSY MAGAZINE (II), Matilda Publications, 1 Times Square, New York NY 10036. (212)764-4860. Editor: Jane Pratt. Fiction Editor: Catherine Gysin. Magazine; 9½ × 11; 100-130 pages; glossy 40 lb. stock paper and cover; illustrations and photographs. "Lifestyle magazine for girls, ages 14-19, covering entertainment, fashion as well as serious subjects." Monthly. Estab. 1988. Circ. 650,000.
Needs: Contemporary, ethnic, experimental, feminist, gay, humor/satire, literary, mainstream, prose poem, regional, young adult/teen (10-18 years). "No typical teenage romance." Publishes annual special fiction issue. Receives 300 unsolicited mss/month. Buys 1 ms/issue; 12 mss/year. Publishes ms 3-6 months after publication. Published Christina Kelly, John Elder, Elizabeth Mosier. Length: 2,000

Read the Business of Fiction section to learn the correct way to prepare and submit a manuscript.

words; 1,000 words minimum; 3,500 words maximum. Sometimes critiques rejected mss and recommends other markets.
How to Contact: Send complete manuscript with cover letter. Include social security number and address, brief background, perhaps one sentence on what story is about or like. Reports in 3 months. SASE. Simultaneous and photocopied submissions OK. Computer printout submissions are acceptable. Sample copy for $2. Fiction guidelines are free.
Payment: Pays $1,000 and contributor's copies.
Terms: Pays on acceptance. Offers 20% kill fee. Buys all rights or first North American serial righs. Send galleys to author (if requested).
Advice: "We look for unusual new ways to write for teenagers. It helps if the story has a quirky, vernacular style that we use throughout the magazine. Generally our stories have to have a teenage protagonist but they are not typical teen fiction. In the end, our only real criterion is that a story is original, intelligent, well-crafted and moves us."

SCHOLASTIC SCOPE (II), Scholastic, Inc., 730 Broadway, New York NY 10003. Magazine: 8½×11; 22-28 pages; pulp paper stock; glossy cover; illustrations and photos. National publication on subjects of general and human interest; profiles of teenagers who have overcome obstacles or done something unusual; short stories and plays for teens. Weekly. Circ. 700,000.
Needs: Stories about the problems of teens (drugs, prejudice, runaways, failure in school, family problems, etc.); relationships between people in family, job and school situations. No crime stories. Recently published work by M.E. Kerr, Paul Zindel, Gloria D. Miklowitz and Walter Dean Myers; published new writers within the last year. Length: 400-2,000 words.
How to Contact: Send complete ms with SASE. Sample copy for $1.75 + 9×12 SASE.
Payment: Pays $125 minimum.
Terms: Buys all rights (negotiable).
Advice: "Strive for directness, realism and action in dialogue rather than narrative. Characters should have depth. Avoid too many coincidences and random happenings."

SEEK (II), Standard Publishing, 8121 Hamilton Ave., Cincinnati OH 45231. Editor: Eileen H. Wilmoth. Magazine: 5½×8½; 8 pages; newsprint paper; art and photos in each issue. "Inspirational stories of faith-in-action for Christian young adults; a Sunday School take-home paper." Weekly. Published special fiction issue last year; plans another. Estab. 1970. Circ. 75,000.
Needs: Religious/inspirational. Buys 150 mss/year. Published new writers within the last year. Length: 500-1,200 words.
How to Contact: Send complete ms with SASE. Accepts computer printout submissions. Reports in 4-6 weeks on mss. Publishes ms an average of 1 year after acceptance. Free sample copy and guidelines.
Payment: Pays 5-7¢/word.
Terms: Pays on acceptance. Buys reprints.
Advice: "Write a credible story with Christian slant—no preachments; avoid overworked themes such as joy in suffering, generation gaps, etc. Most mss are rejected by us because of irrelevant topic or message; unrealistic story; or poor character and/or plot development. We use fiction stories that are believable."

SENIOR LIFE MAGAZINE (IV), 1420 E. Cooley Dr., Suite 200L, Colton CA 92324. (714)824-6681. Editor: Bobbi Mason. Magazine: 8½×10¾; 48 pages; 47 lb. paper; 50 lb. cover; illustrations and photos. "For readers age 50+; subjects vary widely." Monthly. Estab. 1979. Circ. 30,000.
Needs: Adventure, condensed novel, historical, humor/satire, literary, inspirational, senior citizen/retirement, sports, suspense/mystery, western, nostalgia, holidays, family scenarios/reunions, RV camping, moving/relocating, trains (collectors or small steamers). No erotica, food, travel, health, political, gay/lesbian/feminist, psychic. Receives "too many" unsolicited fiction mss/month. Buys 6 fiction mss/year. Length: 400-1,800 words preferred. "The shorter the better; space is tight."
How to Contact: Query first; "please state 'up front' required/requested fee." Reporting time "depends on load." SASE. Simultaneous, photocopied (if clear) and reprint submissions OK. No dot-matrix computer printouts. Accepts electronic submissions via disk or modem; query for details. Sample copy $2.50.
Payment: Pays $10-$50 (with art and photos); 1 contributor's copy. Free subscription to magazine on request.
Terms: Pays on publication.
Advice: "Write tight. Space is limited. Prefer name, address and phone on all pieces sent, i.e. each page of manuscript, each sketch, graph or photo."

SEVENTEEN (II), News America, Inc., 850 3rd Ave., New York NY 10022. (212)759-8100. Fiction Editor: Adrian Nicole LeBlanc. Magazine: 8½×11; 125-400 pages; 40 lb. coated paper; 80 lb. coated cover stock; illustrations; photos. A service magazine with fashion, beauty care, pertinent topics such as trends in dating, attitudes, experiences and concerns during the teenage years. Monthly. Estab. 1944. Circ. 1.7 million.
Needs: High-quality literary fiction on topics of interest to teenage girls. The editors look for fresh themes and well paced plots. Buys 1 ms/issue. Receives 300 unsolicited fiction mss/month. Approximately 50% of fiction is agented. Recently published work by Margaret Atwood, Joyce Carol Oates; published new writers within the last year. Length: approximately 1,500-3,500 words. Also publishes short shorts.
How to Contact: Send complete ms with SASE and cover letter with relevant credits. Reports in 2 months on mss. Free guidelines when requested with SASE.
Payment: Pays $700-2,000.
Terms: Pays on acceptance for one-time rights.
Advice: "Respect the intelligence and sophistication of today's teenage reader. *Seventeen* remains open to the surprise of new voices. Our commitment to publishing the work of new writers remains strong; we continue to read every submission we receive. We believe that good fiction can move the reader toward thoughtful examination of her own life as well as the lives of others—providing her ultimately with a fuller appreciation of what it means to be human. While stories which focus on female teenage experience continue to be of interest, the less obvious possibilities are equally welcome. We encourage writers to submit literary short stories concerning subjects that may not be immediately identifiable as 'teenage,' with narrative styles that are experimental and challenging. Too often, unsolicited submissions possess voices and themes condescending and unsophisticated. Also, writers hesitate to send stories to *Seventeen* which they think too violent or risqué. Good writing holds the imaginable and then some, and if it doesn't find its home here, I'm always grateful for the introduction to a writer's work."

‡SHINING STAR (II), Practical Teaching Magazine for Christian Educators and Parents, Box 299, Carthage IL 62321. Editor: Becky Daniel. Magazine: 8½×11; 80 pages; illustrations. "Biblical stories only for teachers and parents of children K-8th graders." Quarterly. Estab. 1982. Circ. 20,000.
Needs: Looking for ideas to teach scripture to children age 4-12. Receives 100 unsolicited mss/month. Buys 3 mss/issue; 12 mss/year. Publishes ms 9-12 months after acceptance. Published new writers within the last year. Length: 500-1,000 words. Publishes short shorts.
How to Contact: Send complete ms with cover letter. Reports in 1 month. SASE for ms. Simultaneous and photocopied submissions OK. Accepts computer printouts. Sample copy $2. Fiction guidelines free with SASE.
Payment: Pays $20-50 and contributor's copies.
Terms: Pays on publication for all rights.
Advice: "Know the scriptures and be a teacher or person that has worked with and understands young children. Work should place emphasis on building positive self-concepts in children in Christian setting. Stories should be set in Biblical times and include characters and stories from the Bible."

THE SINGLE PARENT (IV), Journal of Parents Without Partners, Parents Without Partners, Inc., 8807 Colesville Rd., Silver Spring MD 20910. (301)588-9354. FAX: (301)588-9216. Editor: Allan Glennon. Magazine: 8½×11; 48 pages; 40 lb. glossy paper; illustrations; photos. Publication for divorced, separated, widowed or never-married parents and their children. Published 6 times/year. Estab. 1957. Circ. 120,000.
Needs: Short stories for *children only*, not adults. Stories should deal with issues that children from one-parent families might face. Buys 2 ms/issue. Recently published work by Terri Detmold, Doreen J. Tierman, Robert L. McGrath; published new writers within the last year. Length: 1,500 words maximum.
How to Contact: Send complete ms with SASE. Sample copy $1 or 10×12 manila SASE with 65¢ postage. Reports within 2 months.
Payment: Pays up to $75; 2 free contributor's copies.
Terms: Pays on publication.
Advice: "We still don't like anthropomorphic stories, even if they concern single-parent beaver kids. We do like stories about young children and teens learning to adjust to a single-parent household, coping with the breakup of their parents' marriage, or trying to get acquainted with a new step-parent."

SINGLELIFE MAGAZINE (II), Single Life Enterprises, Inc., 606 W. Wisconsin Ave., Suite 706, Milwaukee WI 53203. (414)271-9700. FAX: (414)271-5263. Editor: Leifa Butrick. Magazine: 8 × 11; 64 pages; slick paper; illustrations; photos. "Material deals with concerns of single persons of 24-60 age group." Primarily a nonfiction magazine. Bimonthly. Estab. 1982. Circ. 25,000.
Needs: Humor/satire, literary, travel, relationships, self-help, seasonal food and entertaining. Receives 50 unsolicited mss/month. Recently published work by Pamela Schweppe, Deborah Shouse and Christina Zawadiwsky. Publishes ms 2-4 months after acceptance. Length: 1,000 words minimum; 3,500 words maximum. Also publishes short shorts. Occasionally critiques rejected mss.
How to Contact: Send complete ms. Reports in 1 week, "depends on production schedule." SASE for ms. Simultaneous, photocopied and reprint submissions OK. Accepts computer printouts. Accepts electronic submissions via disc or modem. Sample copy $3.50. Fiction guidelines for SAE and 1 first class stamp.
Payment: Pays $50-150 and contributor's copies.
Terms: Pays on publication for one-time rights.

SPORTING TIMES (II,IV), (formerly *Equinews*), Whitehouse Publishing, Box 1778, Vernon, BC V1T 8C3 Canada. (604)545-9896. Editor: Geoff White. Tabloid: 10¼ × 12½; 24-28 pages; Electrabrite paper; illustrations and 85 screen photos. "For horsepersons." Estab. 1979. Circ. 17,000.
Needs: Adventure, juvenile (5-9 years), sports (horses) and young adult/teen (10-18). Receives 1-2 unsolicited mss/month. Buys 6-9 mss/year. Publishes ms 1-3 months after acceptance.
How to Contact: Send complete ms with cover letter. Reports in 1 month on queries. SASE. Sample copy for $1, 8 × 10 SAE. Fiction guidelines for #10 SAE.
Payment: Pay varies.
Terms: Pays on publication for first rights.

SPORTS AFIELD (II, IV), Hearst Magazine, 250 W. 55th St., New York 10019. (212)649-4000. Editor: Tom Paugh. Magazine: 8 × 11; 128 pages minimum; "the best paper"; 70 lb. cover stock; illustrations; photos. "This is an outdoor magazine: hunting, fishing, camping, boating, conservation, etc." for men and women who take an active interest in their sport. Monthly. Estab. 1887. Circ. 542,000.
Needs: Adventure, humor/satire when related to hunting and freshwater fishing, sports (fishing, hunting, camping). No old-fashioned me-and-Joe yarns. Receives 20 unsolicited mss/week. Buys a few mss each year. Publishes ms up to 2 years after acceptance. Agented fiction: 5%. Length: 2,500 words or less. Also publishes short shorts of 200-250 words.
How to Contact: Query first; include name, address, a little background and credits, *brief* synopsis of story. Reports in 1 month on queries and mss. SASE for query. Accepts computer printouts.
Payment: Pays $850.
Terms: Pays on acceptance for first rights.
Advice: "Fiction is a very tough market—and not just in the outdoor field. Know the market."

STANDARD (II, IV), Nazarene International Headquarters, 6401 The Paseo, Kansas City MO 64131. (816)333-7000. Editor: Beth A. Watkins. Magazine: 8½ × 11; 8 pages; illustrations; photos. Inspirational reading for adults. Weekly. Estab. 1936. Circ. 172,000.
Needs: Religious/inspirational, spiritual. Receives 350 unsolicited mss/month (both fiction and nonfiction). Accepts 60 mss/year. Publishes ms 9-24 months after acceptance. Published work by Todd Lee, Floyd Allen, Jeanne Hill and Mark Littleton; published new writers within the last year. Length: 1,000 words average; 300 words minimum; 1,500 words maximum. Also publishes short shorts of 300-350 words.
How to Contact: Send complete ms with name, address and phone number. Reports in 1-2 months on mss. SASE. Simultaneous submissions OK but will pay only reprint rates. Accepts computer printouts. Sample copy and guidelines for SAE and 1 first class stamp.
Payment: Pays 3.5¢/word; 2¢/word (reprint); contributor's copies.
Terms: Pays on acceptance for one-time rights.
Advice: "Too much is superficial; containing the same story lines. Give me something original, humorous, yet helpful. I'm also looking for more stories on current social issues. Make plot, characters realistic. Contrived articles are quick to spot and reject."

STORY FRIENDS (II), Mennonite Publishing House, 616 Walnut Ave., Scottdale PA 15683. (412)887-8500. Editor: Marjorie Waybill. Sunday school publication which portrays Jesus as a friend and helper. Nonfiction and fiction for children 4-9 years of age. Weekly.

Needs: Juvenile. Stories of everyday experiences at home, in church, in school or at play, which provide models of Christian values. Length: 300-800 words.
How to Contact: Send complete ms with SASE. Seasonal or holiday material should be submitted 6 months in advance. Free sample copy.
Payment: Pays 3-5¢/word.
Terms: Pays on acceptance for one-time rights. Buys reprints. Not copyrighted.
Advice: "It is important to include relationships, patterns of forgiveness, respect, honesty, trust and caring. Prefer exciting yet plausible short stories which offer different settings, introduce children to wide ranges of friends and demonstrate joys, fears, temptations and successes of the readers."

STRAIGHT (II), Standard Publishing Co., 8121 Hamilton Ave., Cincinnati OH 45231. (513)931-4050. Editor: Carla Crane. "Publication helping and encouraging teens to live a victorious, fulfilling Christian life. Distributed through churches and some private subscriptions." Magazine: 6½ × 7½; 12 pages; newsprint paper and cover; illustrations (color); photos. Quarterly in weekly parts. Estab. 1951. Circ. 75,000.
Needs: Contemporary, religious/inspirational, romance, spiritual, mystery, adventure and humor—all with Christian emphasis. "Stories dealing with teens and teen life, with a positive message or theme. Topics that interest teenagers include school, family life, recreation, friends, church, part-time jobs, dating and music. Main character should be a 15- or 16-year old boy or girl, a Christian and regular churchgoer, who faces situations using Bible principles." Buys 1-2 mss/issue; 75-100 mss/year. Receives approximately 100 unsolicited fiction mss/month. Less than 1% of fiction is agented. Published work by Alan Cliburn, Marian Bray, Teresa Cleary; published new writers within the last year. Length: 800-1,200 words. Recommends other markets.
How to Contact: Send complete ms with SASE and cover letter (experience with teens especially preferred from new writers). Accepts computer printout submissions. Reports in 1 month on mss. Publishes ms an average of 1 year after acceptance. Free sample copy and guidelines with SASE.
Payment: Pays 3-7¢/word.
Terms: Pays on acceptance for first and one-time rights. Buys reprints.
Advice: "Get to know us before submitting, through guidelines and sample issues (free with an SASE). And get to know teenagers. A writer must know what today's teens are like, and what kinds of conflicts they experience. In writing a short fiction piece for the teen reader, don't try to accomplish too much. If your character is dealing with the problem of prejudice, don't also deal with his/her fights with sister, desire for a bicycle, or anything else that is not absolutely essential to the reader's understanding of the major conflict."

THE STUDENT (I, II), A Christian Collegiate Magazine, Student Ministry Department of the Baptist Sunday School Board, 127 Ninth Ave., North, Nashville TN 37234. (615)251-2788. Editor: Milt Hughes. Magazine: 8¼ × 11; 50 pages; uncoated paper; coated cover stock; illustrations; photos. Magazine for Christians and non-Christians about life and work with Christian students on campus and related articles on living in dorm setting, dating life, missions activities, Bible study, and church ministry to students. Monthly. Estab. 1922. Circ. 40,000.
Needs: Adventure, humor, comics, confession, contemporary, ethnic, and religious/inspirational. Does not want to see mss "without purpose or without moral tone." Receives approximately 25 unsolicited fiction mss/month. Buys 1-2 mss/issue; 12-24 mss/year. Length: 300 words minimum (or less, depending on treatment); 1,500 words maximum; 750 words average.
How to Contact: Cover letter with bio and description of published works. Query first with SASE. Simultaneous, photocopied and previously published submissions OK. Reports in 3 weeks on queries; 6 weeks on mss. Sample copy 75¢. Free fiction guidelines with SASE.
Payment: 5¢/word and 3 contributor's copies.
Terms: Pays on publication for all rights, first rights, one-time rights, and assignments for work-for-hire basis.
Advice: "Fit writing to format and concept of the piece. View many issues of the magazine before you write. Our readers demand fiction which conveys our message in an interesting way."

STUDENT LAWYER (II, IV), American Bar Association, 750 N. Lake Shore Dr., Chicago IL 60611. (312)988-6048. Editor: Sarah Hoban. Managing Editor: Miriam Krasno. Magazine: 8½ × 10¾; 48 pages; glossy paper and cover; illustrations; photos. "Magazine for law students as part of their Law Student Division/ABA membership. Features legal aspects, trends in the law, social/legal issues, and lawyer profiles." Monthly (September-May). Circ. 35,000.

Needs: "All stories have to have a legal/law/lawyer/law-school element to them. No science fiction." Buys 1 full-length or 2-3 short humorous pieces/year. Length: 1,000-3,000 words. Sometimes recommends other markets.

How to Contact: Send complete ms with SASE. Accepts computer printout submissions. Reports in 1 month on mss. Publishes ms 1-6 months after acceptance. Sample copy $3; contact Order Fulfillment at above address.

Payment: Pays $75-500.

Terms: Pays on acceptance for first rights. Buys very few reprints.

Advice: Rejects mss because "usually, the stories are of mediocre quality. Because we favor nonfiction pieces, the fiction we do publish has to be outstanding or at least very original. Keep trying—and *know* the magazine you're submitting to."

‡STUDENT LEADERSHIP JOURNAL (IV), InterVarsity Christian Fellowship, 6400 Schroeder Rd., P.O. Box 7895, Madison WI 53707-7895. (608)274-9001. Managing Editor: Jeff Yourison. "The journal is a networking and leadership development tool for audience described below. We publish articles on leadership, spiritual growth and evangelism. We publish occasional poetry, short stories and allegories. The audience is Christian student leaders on secular college campuses." Quarterly. Estab. 1988. Circ. 8,000.

Needs: Religious/inspirational, prose poem. "The form of fiction is not nearly as important as its quality and content. Fiction published by *Student Leadership* will always reflect a Christian world view." No romance or children's fiction. Receives 10-15 unsolicited fiction mss/month. Buys up to 1 ms/issue; 4 ms/year. Publishes ms up to 2 years after acceptance. Recently published work by H. Edgar Hix. Length: 2,000 words preferred; 200 words minimum; 2,500 words maximum.

How to Contact: Query first with clips of published work. "A good cover letter will demonstrate familiarity with the magazine and its needs and will briefly describe the submission and any relevant information." Reports in up to 2 months on queries; up to 3 months on mss. SASE. Simultaneous, photocopied, reprint and computer printout submissions OK. Sample copy for $2, 9×12 SAE and $2.40 postage. Fiction quidelines for #10 SAE and 1 first-class stamp.

Payment: Pays $25-200.

Terms: Pays on acceptance for first or one-time rights. Sends pre-publication galleys to author.

‡SUN AND SONLIGHT CHRISTIAN NEWSPAPERS (I, II, IV), Neighbor News, Inc., 4118 10th Ave. N., Lake Worth FL 33461. (407)439-3509. Editor: Dennis Lombard. Newspaper: tabloid; 12-24 pages; newsprint; illustrations and photographs. "Interdenominational Christian news, views, fiction, poetry, sold to general public, *not* through churches." Monthly. ("May go weekly in late 1990-early 1991"). Estab. 1980. Circ. 13,000.

Needs: Adventure, historical (general), humor/satire, literary, mainstream, religious/inspirational, romance, sports. "All fiction needs to be related to the publication's religious content—we feel you must examine a sample issue because *Sonlight* is *different*." Nothing "preachy or doctrinal." Plans special fiction issue and other topical specials. Receives unsolicited mss/month. Buys 75 ms/issue. Publishes ms 1-6 months after acceptance. Recently published work by Michelle Starr. Length: 900 words average; 500 words minimum; 1,000 words maximum. "Will consider any length under 1,000."

How to Contact: Send complete manuscript with cover letter including Social Security number. "Absolutely no queries." "1-2 sentences on what the piece is and on who you are." Reports on mss in 1 week. SASE. Simultaneous, photocopied and reprint submissions OK. Accepts computer printout submissions. Sample copy for $1 and 9×12 SAE. Guidelines for #10 SAE and 1 first class stamp.

Payment: Pays $5-35.

Terms: Buys one-time rights.

Advice: "Read our newspapers—get the drift of our rather unusual interdenominational non-doctrinal content. Send $5 for a writer's 1-year subscription (12 issues, reg. $9)."

SUNDAY JOURNAL MAGAZINE, *The Providence Journal-Bulletin*, 75 Fountain St., Providence RI 02902. (401)277-7349. Editor: Elliot Krieger. Magazine: 10×11½; 28 pages; coated newsprint paper; illustrations; photos. "Magazine which has appeared weekly for 40 years in the *Providence Sunday Journal*." Circ. 280,000.

Needs: Regional. Recently published fiction by Paul Watkins and Ann Hood; published new writers within the last year.
How to Contact: Submit with SASE.
Payment: Pays $175 minimum; $400 maximum.
Terms: Buys one-time rights. Sponsors short-story contest for New England writers.
Advice: New England, especially Rhode Island, fiction only.

SUNSHINE MAGAZINE (II), Henrichs Publications, Box 40, Sunshine Park, Litchfield IL 62056. Magazine. 5¼ × 7¼; 48 pages; matte paper and cover stock; illustrations. "To promote good will for the betterment of our society. We publish short, non-denominational, inspirational material." Monthly. Estab. 1924. Circ. 60,000.
Needs: "Light" fiction, humor, juvenile (5-9 years), preschool (0-4 years), senior citizen/retirement. No fiction that is lengthy, fantasy, sexual, specifically religious, violent or dealing with death, drugs, divorce or alcohol. Receives 500 unsolicited fiction mss/month. Buys 12 mss/issue; 140 mss/year. Publishes ms within a year of acceptance. Recently published work by Robert Tefertillar, Gail Geddes, Joanna Captain; published new writers within the last year. Length: 750 words average; 100 words minimum; 1,250 words maximum. Publishes short shorts. Sometimes critiques rejected ms and recommends other markets.
How to Contact: Send complete ms with SASE and cover letter with name, address, rights offered. Reports in 2 months on mss. SASE. Photocopied submissions OK. Accepts computer printout submissions, including dot-matrix. Sample copy 50¢ or 6 × 8 SAE with 2 first class stamps. Fiction guidelines with #10 SASE.
Payment: $10-100, contributor's copies; charge for extras.
Terms: Pays on acceptance for first North American serial rights. Publication copyrighted.
Advice: "Beginning writers are more than welcome to submit to *Sunshine*. Don't get discouraged— just keep trying. We can use only about 5% of what we receive."

‡SURFING MAGAZINE (IV), Western Empire, Box 3010, San Clemente CA 92672. (714)492-7873. Editor: Bill Sharp. Editorial Director: David Gilovich. Magazine: 8 × 11; 140 pages; 45 lb. free sheet paper; 80 lb. cover stock; photos. Magazine covering "all aspects of the sport of surfing for young, active surfing enthusiasts." Monthly. Estab. 1964. Circ. 92,000.
Needs: Surfing-related fiction. Receives 2 unsolicited mss/month. Buys 3 mss/year. Length: 2,000-3,000 words average. Occasionally critiques rejected mss. Also publishes short shorts.
How to Contact: Cover letter with background on surfing. Query first. Reports in 2 weeks. SASE. Photocopied submissions OK. Accepts computer printout submissions. Free sample copy and fiction guidelines.
Payment: Pays 15-20¢/word.
Terms: Pays on publication for one-time rights.
Advice: "Establish yourself as a *Surfing* general contributor before tackling fiction."

SWANK MAGAZINE (II, IV), Broadway Publishing Company, 888 7th Ave., New York NY 10106. Editor: Michael Wilde. Magazine: 8½ × 11; 116 pages; 20 lb. paper; 60 lb. coated stock; illustrations; photos. "Men's sophisticate format. Sexually-oriented material. Presumably our reader is after erotic material." Monthly. Estab. 1952. Circ. 350,000.
Needs: High-caliber erotica. "Fiction always has an erotic or other male-oriented theme; also eligible would be mystery or suspense with a very erotic scene. Writers should try to avoid the clichés of the genre." Buys 1 ms/issue, 12 mss/year. Receives approximately 80 unsolicited fiction mss each month. Published new writers within the last year. Length: 1,500-2,750 words.
How to Contact: Send complete ms with SASE and cover letter, which should list previous publishing credits. No simultaneous submissions. Accepts high-quality computer printout submissions. Reports in 6 weeks on mss. Sample copy $5 with SASE.
Payment: Pays $250-400. Offers 25% kill fee for assigned ms not published.
Terms: Buys first North American serial rights.
Advice: "Research the men's magazine market." Mss are rejected because of "typical, overly simple storylines and poor execution. We're looking for interesting stories—whether erotic in theme or not— that break the mold of the usual men's magazine fiction. We're not only just considering strict erotica. Mystery, adventure, etc. with erotica passages will be considered."

'TEEN MAGAZINE (II), Petersen Publishing Co., 8490 Sunset Blvd., Los Angeles CA 90069. Editor: Roxanne Camron. Magazine: 100-150 pages; 34 lb paper; 60 lb. cover; illustrations and photos. "The magazine contains fashion, beauty and features for the young teenage girl. The median age of our readers is 16. Our success stems from our dealing with relevant issues teens face, printing recent entertainment news and showing the latest fashions and beauty looks." Monthly. Estab. 1957. Circ. 1.1 million.
Needs: Romance, adventure, mystery, humor and young adult. Every story, whether romance, mystery, humor, etc., must be aimed for teenage girls. The protagonist should be a teenager, preferably female. No experimental, science fiction, fantasy or horror. Buys 1 ms/issue; 12 mss/year. Publishes short shorts. Recently published work by Emily Ormand, Louise Carroll and Linda Bernson; published new writers within the last year. Length: 2,500-4,000 words.
How to Contact: Send complete ms and short cover letter with SASE. Reports in 10 weeks on mss. Generally publishes ms 3-5 months after acceptance. Sample copy for $2.50. Free guidelines with SASE.
Payment: Pays $100.
Terms: Pays on acceptance for all rights.
Advice: "Try to find themes that suit the modern teen. We need innovative ways of looking at the age-old problems of young love, parental pressures, making friends, being left out, etc. 'TEEN would prefer to have romance balanced with a plot, re: a girl's inner development and search for self. Handwritten mss will not be read."

TEEN POWER, Scripture Press Publications, Inc., Box 632, Glen Ellyn IL 60138. (312)668-6000. Editor: Amy Swanson. Magazine: 5⅜ × 8⅜; 8 pages; non-glossy paper and cover; illustrations and photographs. "Teen Power publishes true stories and fiction with a conservative Christian slant—must help readers see how principles for Christian living can be applied to everyday life; for young teens (11-14 years); many small town and rural; includes large readerships in Canada, England and other countries in addition to U.S." Estab. 1966.
Needs: Adventure, humor/satire, religious/inspirational, young adult/teen (10-18 years). "All must have spiritual emphasis of some sort." Receives approx. 50-75 unsolicited mss/month. Buys 1 ms/issue; about 50 mss/year. Publishes ms at least one year after acceptance. Recently published work by Alan Cliburn, Betty Steele Everett, Randy Southern and Michael La Cross; published new writers within the last year. Length: 1,000 words preferred; 250 words minimum; 1,100 words maximum. Publishes short shorts. Length: 300-500 words. Sometimes critiques rejected mss and recommends other markets.
How to Contact: Send complete ms with cover letter. Reports in 1 month. SASE. Simultaneous, photocopied and reprint submissions OK. Accepts computer printouts. Sample copy and fiction guidelines for #10 SAE and 1 first class stamp.
Payment: Pays $20 minimum; $120 maximum; contributor's copies.
Terms: Pays on acceptance. Purchases first rights and one-time rights.
Advice: "We look for spiritual emphasis (strong but not preachy); writing style; age appropriateness; creativity in topic choice and presentation. A writer for *Teen Power* must know something about young teens and what is important to them, plus have a working knowledge of basic principles for Christian living, and be able to weave the two together."

TEENS TODAY (II), Church of the Nazarene, 6401 The Paseo, Kansas City MO 64131. (816)333-7000. Editor: Karen DeSollar. Sunday school take-home paper: 8½ × 11; 8 pages; illustrations; photos. "For junior and senior high students involved with the Church of the Nazarene who find it interesting and helpful to their areas of life." Weekly. Circ. 60,000.
Needs: Contemporary, religious/inspirational, romance, humor, juvenile, young adult and ethnic. "Nothing that puts teens down or endorses lifestyles not in keeping with the denomination's beliefs and standards." Buys 1-2 mss/issue. Published new writers within the last year. Length: 1,000-1,500 words.
How to Contact: Send complete ms with SASE. Reports in 6 weeks on mss. Publishes ms 8-10 months after acceptance. Free sample copy and guidelines with SASE.
Payment: Pays 4¢/word and 3½¢/word on second reprint.
Terms: Pays on acceptance for first and second serial rights. Buys reprints.
Advice: "Don't be too juvenile."

TIKKUN (III), A Bimonthly Jewish Critique of Politics, Culture and Society, Institute for Labor and Mental Health, 5100 Leona St., Oakland CA 94619. (415)482-0805. Editor: Michael Lerner. Fiction Editor: Marcie Hershman. Magazine: 8 × 11; 96 pages; high quality paper. "*Tikkun* was created as the liberal alternative to *Commentary Magazine* and the voices of Jewish conservatism, but is not aimed just at a Jewish audience. Readers are intellectuals, political activists, Washington policy circles, writers, poets." Bimonthly.

Needs: Condensed/excerpted novel, contemporary, feminist, gay, historical (general), humor/satire, lesbian, literary, mainstream, translations, Jewish political. "No narrowly Jewish fiction. At least half of our readers are not Jewish. Or anything that is not of highest quality." Receives 150 unsolicited mss/month. Buys 1 ms/issue. Publishes ms 6-9 months after acceptance. Agented fiction 50%. Published work by Amos Oz, Lynne Sharon Schwartz, E.M. Broner. Length: 4,000 words preferred. Publishes short shorts. Almost always critiques rejected mss.

How to Contact: Send complete ms with cover letter. Reports in 2-3 months. SASE. Accepts computer printout submissions. Sample copy for $7.

Payment: Pays $100-250.

Terms: Pays on publication for first rights.

Advice: Looks for creativity, sensitivity, intelligence, originality, profundity of insight. "Read *Tikkun*, at least 3-4 issues worth, understand the kinds of issues that interest our readers, and then imagine yourself trying to write fiction that delights, surprises and intrigues this kind of an audience. Do not write what you think will feel sweet or appealing to this audience—but rather that which will provoke, bring to life and engage them."

TOUCH (II), Calvinettes, Box 7259, Grand Rapids MI 49510. (616)241-5616. Editor: Joanne Ilbrink. Magazine: 8½×11; 24 pages; 50 lb. paper; 50 lb. cover stock; illustrations and photos. "Our purpose is to lead girls into a living relationship with Jesus Christ. Puzzles, poetry, crafts, stories, articles, and club input for girls ages 9-14." Monthly. Circ. 15,000.

Needs: Adventure, ethnic, juvenile and religious/inspirational. "Articles must help girls discover how God is at work in their world and the world around them." Receives 50 unsolicited fiction mss/month. Buys 3 mss/issue; 30 mss/year. Usually does not read during February, March, September and October. Published work by Ida Mae Petsock; published new writers within the last year. Length: 900 words minimum; 1,200 words maximum; 1,000 words average.

How to Contact: Send complete ms with 8×10 SASE. Prefers no cover letter. Simultaneous, photocopied and previously published submissions OK. Reports in 1 month on mss. Free sample copy for 8×10 SASE. Free guidelines.

Payment: Pays 3¢/word.

Terms: Pays on acceptance for simultaneous, first or second serial rights.

Advice: "Write for guidelines and theme update and submit manuscripts in advance of deadline. In fiction often the truths we choose to convey can be done with short stories."

TQ (TEENQUEST) (II), Good News Broadcasting Co., Box 82808, Lincoln NE 68501. (402)474-4567. FAX: (402)474-4519. Managing Editor: Win Mumma. Magazine: 8×10¾; 48 pages; illustrations; photos. "*TQ* is designed to aid the spiritual growth of young teen Christian readers by presenting Biblical principles." 11 issues/year. Estab. 1946. Circ. 60,000.

Needs: Religious/inspirational, regional, romance, adventure, fantasy, science fiction and mystery. "Stories must be grounded in Biblical Christianity and should feature teens in the 14-17 year range." Buys 3-4 mss/issue; 35-40 mss/year. Receives 50-60 unsolicited fiction mss/month. Recently published work by Nancy Rue, Stephen Bly, Marian Bray, Scott Pinzon; published new writers within the last year. Length: up to 2,000 words.

How to Contact: Managing editor reads all query letters. All other mss screened. Send SASE and cover letter. Accepts computer printout submissions. Reports in 2 months. Publishes ms 6 months to 2 years after acceptance. Free sample copy and guidelines for 9×12 SASE.

Payment: Pays 7-10¢/word for unassigned fiction. More for assignments. Pays 3¢/word for reprints.

Terms: Pays on acceptance for first or reprint rights.

Advice: "The most common problem is that writers don't understand the limitations of stories under 2,500 words and try to cram a 6,000-word plot into 2,000 words at the expense of characterization, pacing, and mood. We feel that fiction communicates well to our teenage readers. They consistently rank fiction as their favorite part of the magazine. We get hundreds of stories on 'big issues' (death, drugs, etc). Choose less dramatic subjects, that are important to teenagers and give us a new storyline that has a Biblical emphasis, but isn't preachy. Although our magazine is based on Christian principles, we do not want fiction where the lesson learned is blatantly obvious. We're looking for subtlety. Before you try to write for teens, get to know some—talk to them, watch their TV shows, read their magazines. You'll get ideas for stories and you'll be able to write for our audience with accurate and up-to-date knowledge." Teen fiction writers under age 20 may enter annual contest.

TRAILER BOATS MAGAZINE (II, IV), Poole Publications Inc., 20700 Belshaw Ave., Carson CA 90246. Editor-in-Chief: Wiley Poole. Magazine: 100 pages; high paper quality; 100 lb. cover stock. "Our magazine covers boats of 26 feet and shorter, (trailerable size limits) and related activities; skiing, fishing, cruising, travel, racing, etc. We publish how-to articles on boat and trailer maintenance, travel, skiing, boat tests and evaluations of new products." Audience: owners and prospective owners of trailerable-size boats. Monthly. Estab. 1971. Circ. 80,000.
Needs: Adventure, contemporary, fantasy, humor/satire, science fiction, and suspense/mystery. "Must meet general guidelines of the magazine regarding boats and related activities." Receives very few unsolicited fiction mss/month. Buys 1-3 mss/year. Length: 200 words minimum; 1,000 words maximum. Publishes short shorts of 500 words. Occasionally critiques rejected mss. Sometimes recommends other markets.
How to Contact: Query first with SASE. Accepts computer printout submissions. Reports in 1 month on queries; 4-6 weeks on mss. Publishes ms 1-6 months after acceptance. Free general guidelines. Sample copy $1.50.
Payment: Pays 7-10¢/word.
Terms: Pays on publication for all rights.
Advice: "In our case, knowing the audience is of prime importance. Our readership and experience with fiction is limited. We are a consumer magazine with an audience of dedicated boaters. My suggestion is to know the audience and write for it specifically."

TURN-ON LETTERS (I, II), AJA Publishing, Box 470, Port Chester NY 10573. Editor: Julie Silver. Magazine: digest-size; 114 pages; newsprint paper; glossy cover; illustrations; photos. "Sexually explicit. Publishing first person 'letters' written as if true." Published 8 times/year. Estab. 1982. Circ. 100,000.
Needs: Erotica. Buys approx. 42 "letters"/issue; 400 "letters"/year. Publishes ms 4-8 months after acceptance. Very little agented fiction. Length: 2-3 typed, double-spaced pages average. Sometimes critiques rejected mss and occasionally recommends other markets.
How to Contact: Send complete ms with or without cover letter. Reports in an average of 3 weeks on mss. SASE. Photocopied submissions if clearly marked "not simultaneous submissions" OK. Accepts computer printout submissions. Sample copy for $2.95 and 6×9 SAE with 4 first class stamps. Fiction guidelines for #10 SAE with 1 first class stamp.
Payment: Pays $15.
Terms: Pays on publication for all rights.
Advice: "Letters must be hot and must 'read real.' We are very overstocked at present and buying relatively little material."

TURTLE MAGAZINE FOR PRESCHOOL KIDS (I, II), Children's Better Health Institute, Benjamin Franklin Literary & Medical Society, Inc., 1100 Waterway Blvd., Box 567, Indianapolis IN 46206. Executive Editorial Director: Beth Wood Thomas. Editorial Director: Christine French Clark. Magazine of picture stories and articles for preschool children 2-5 years old.
Needs: Juvenile (preschool). Receives approximately 100 unsolicited fiction mss/month. Length: 8-24 lines for picture stories; 500 words for bedtime or naptime stories. Special emphasis on health, nutrition, exercise and safety. Also has need for humorous and anthropomorphic animal stories. Recently published work by Ginny Winter, Robin Krautbauer and Ann Devendorf; published new writers within the last year.
How to Contact: Send complete ms with SASE. Reports in 8-10 weeks on mss. No queries. Send SASE for Editorial Guidelines. Sample copy 75¢.
Payment: Pays 10¢/word (approximate). Payment varies for poetry and activities.
Terms: Pays on acceptance for all rights.
Advice: "Keep it simple and easy to read. Vocabulary must be below first grade level. Be familiar with past issues of the magazine."

‡THE VANCOUVER CHILD (II), The Vancouver Child, 757 Union St., Vancouver, British Columbia V6A 2C3 Canada. (604)251-1760. Editor: Wendy Wilkins. Tabloid: 10¼×15½; 12 or 16 pages; newsprint paper; newsprint cover; illustrations and b&w photographs. "*The Vancouver Child* celebrates children and families, and we primarily publish nonfiction articles on issues affecting children's daily lives for parents in the Lower Mainland (Vancouver and suburbs); children also read our kids' pages but most of our readers are parents." Monthly. Estab. 1988. Circ. 18,000.

Needs: Feminist, juvenile (5-9 years), literary, mainstream, preschool (1-4 years), regional. "Short stories should have something to do with family life or children. It is possible that we would print a short story for children on our kids' pages, if the story were very short and of good quality. No foul language, please." No confession, erotica, romance, religious. Receives 1 or 2 unsolicited mss/month. Buys 2 or 3 mss/year. Publishes ms between 1 and 5 months after acceptance. Recently published work by Celia Challoner. Length: 750 words average; 1,000 words maximum. Publishes short shorts. Sometimes critiques rejected mss and recommends other markets.

How to Contact: Send complete manuscript with cover letter. "Complete manuscript more important than cover letter. We will read the story and judge it on its merits." Reports in 3-5 weeks. Send SAE with International Reply Coupon. Photocopied submissions OK. Accepts electronic submissions via disk. Sample copy free for 10 × 13 SAE and 2 first class stamps or IRC. Free fiction guidelines.

Payment: Pays 5¢/word.

Terms: Pays on publication for one-time rights.

Advice: "We prefer stories that have something to do with family life or children. Although stories do not have to have 'happy endings,' their tone should nonetheless be life-affirming and warm. Avoid the sentimental—please no Hallmark greeting card poems—but avoid despair and alienation as well. Although we do not have a policy to print only Canadian authors, we prefer stories which make reference to Canadian locations rather than American locations. In some stories, it's not a problem, but a manuscript may be rejected on those grounds."

VIRTUE (II), The Christian Magazine for Women, Virtue Ministries, Inc., Box 850, Sisters OR 97759. (503)549-8261. Editor: Marlee Alex. Magazine: 8⅛ × 10⅞; 80 pages; illustrations; photos. Christian women's magazine featuring food, fashion, family, etc., aimed primarily at homemakers—"real women with everyday problems, etc." Published 6 times/year. Estab. 1978. Circ. 150,000.

Needs: Condensed novel, contemporary, humor, religious/inspirational and romance. "Must have Christian slant." Buys 1 ms/issue; 6 mss/year (maximum). Publishes short shorts. Length: 1,200 words minimum; 2,500 words maximum; 2,000 words average.

How to Contact: Accepts computer printout submissions. Reports in 6-8 weeks on ms. Sample copy $3 with 9 × 13 SAE and 90¢ postage. Free fiction guidelines with SASE.

Payment: Pays 15-25¢/published word.

Terms: Pays on publication for first rights or reprint rights.

Advice: "Send us descriptive, colorful writing with good style. *Please*—no simplistic, unrealistic pat endings. There are three main reasons *Virtue* rejects fiction: 1) The stories are not believable, 2) writing is dull, and 3) the story does not convey a Christian message."

VISION (II,IV), Box 7259, Grand Rapids MI 45910. (616)241-5616. Editor: Dale Dieleman. Magazine: 8½ × 11; 16-20 pages; 60 lb. paper; 60 lb. cover; photos. *Vision*'s readers are young adults in their 20s in the U.S. and Canada. Bimonthly. Circ. 3,500.

Needs: Stories exploring values, lifestyles, relationships as young adults in workplace, campus, social settings—cultural, ethnic variety a plus. Christian perspective but no preachy, pious platitudes. Recently published work by Lonni Collins Pratt, Nancy Eastridge and Mark Littleton. Length: 1,500 words maximum.

How to Contact: Send ms plus SASE for return. Reports in 1 month on mss. Simultaneous submissions OK (specify other submission periodicals). Sample copy for 9 × 12 and 56¢ postage.

Payment: Pays $35-75.

Terms: Pays on publication.

VISTA (II), Wesley Press, Box 50434, Indianapolis IN 46953. (317)842-0444. Editor: Becky Higgins. Magazine: 8½ × 11; 8 pages; offset paper and cover; illustrations and photos. "*Vista* is our adult take-home paper and is published in conjunction with the Wesley Biblical Series adult Sunday school lesson." Weekly. Estab. 1906. Circ. 50,000.

Needs: Humor/satire, religious/inspirational, senior citizen/retirement, young adult/teen. "We are not looking for 'Sunday Soap Opera,' romance, stories with pat or easy outs, or incidents that wouldn't feasibly happen to members of your own church." Receives 100 unsolicited mss/month. Buys 4 mss/issue; 50 mss/year. Publishes ms 10 months after acceptance. Length: 500 words minimum; 1,300 words maximum.

How to Contact: Send complete ms with cover letter. Reports in 4-6 weeks. SASE. Simultaneous, photocopied and reprint submissions OK. Accepts computer printout submissions. Sample copy for 9 × 12 SAE.

Payment: Pays $10-60.
Terms: Pays on acceptance for one-time rights.
Advice: "Manuscripts for all publications must be in keeping with early Methodist teachings that people have a free will to personally accept or reject Christ. Wesleyanism also stresses a transformed life, holiness of heart and social responsibility."

THE WASHINGTONIAN (IV), Washington Magazine Co., Suite 200, 1828 L St. NW, Washington DC 20036. (202)296-3600. Editor: John A. Limpert. General interest, regional magazine. Magazine: 8¼ × 10⅞; 300 pages; 40 lb. paper; 80 lb. cover; illustrations; photos. Monthly. Estab. 1965. Circ. 166,000.
Needs: Short pieces that must be set in Washington. Receives 8-10 unsolicited fiction mss/month. Buys 3 fiction mss/year. Length: 1,000 words minimum; 10,000 words maximum. Occasionally critiques rejected mss.
How to Contact: Send complete ms with SASE. Simultaneous and photocopied submissions OK. Reports in 2 months on mss. Sample copy for $3.
Payment: $100-2,000. Negotiates kill fee for assigned mss not published.
Terms: Pays on publication for first North American rights.

WEE WISDOM MAGAZINE (II), Unity School of Christianity, Unity Villiage MO 64065. (816)524-3550-ext 3270. Editor: Judy Gehrlein. Magazine: 48 pages; 45 lb. pentair suede stock; 80 lb. Mountie matte cover; illustrations; photos (very seldom). "We publish material designed to meet needs of today's children in an entertaining, positive way. For children through age 12." Publishes 10 issues per year. Estab. 1893. Circ. 125,000.
Needs: Adventure, contemporary, fantasy, juvenile (5-9 years), preschool, (up to 4 years), young adult/teen (10-13). No violence or religious denominational. Receives 300 unsolicited mss/month. Buys 6 mss/issue; 60 mss/year. Publishes ms 6 months to 1 year after acceptance. Recently published work by Virginia L. Kroll, Julie Anne Peters and Julie Ann Matheson. "Many of our writers are previously unpublished." Length: 500-800 words.
How to Contact: Send complete ms with SASE and "short, informative" cover letter. Reports in 8-10 weeks on mss. Photocopied submissions OK. No simultaneous submissions or queries. Accepts computer printout submissions. Sample copy and fiction guidelines free.
Payment: Pays 6¢ per word.
Terms: Pays on acceptance for first rights.
Advice: "Grab the readers in the first few lines. Write with verbs—not adjectives. Help the child see the wisdom within himself and help him see how to use it."

WEIRD TALES (I,IV), The Unique Magazine, Terminus Publishing Company, Inc., Box 13418, Philadelphia PA 19101. Editors: George Scithers, Darrell Schweitzer and John Betancourt. Magazine: 6½ × 9½; 148 pages; acid-free book paper; pen and ink illustrations. "This is a professional fantasy-fiction and horror-fiction magazine." Quarterly. Estab. 1923. Circ. 10,000.
Needs: Fantasy, horror, supernatural/occult. "Writers should be familiar with the fantasy/horror genres; the three editors are well read in the field and want fresh ideas rather than tired old retreads. To paraphrase Ursula K. LeGuin, 'If you want to write it, you gotta read it!' " Receives 400-500 unsolicited fiction mss/month. Buys 3-4 fiction mss/month; 48-80 mss/year. Publishes ms usually less than 1 year after acceptance. Published work by Gene Wolfe, Ramsey Campbell and Nancy Springer; published new writers last year. Length: 20,000 words maximum. Publishes short shorts. Always comments on rejected mss.
How to Contact: Send complete ms, which should include return address. Reports within 1 month. SASE. Accepts photocopied submissions. Sample copy $5. Fiction guidelines for #10 SAE and 1 first class stamp.
Payment: Pays 3-5¢/word, depending on length of story, plus 3 contributor's copies.
Terms: Pays on acceptance for first North American serial rights. Sends galleys to author.
Advice: "*Weird Tales* is a revival of a famous old 'pulp' magazine, published in the original format, but with new fiction by many top writers and talented newcomers to the field. Basically, we're trying to make this *Weird Tales* as it would be today had it continued uninterrupted to the present. Know the field. Know manuscript format. Be familiar with the magazine, its contents and its markets. With the death of *Twilight Zone Magazine* and *The Horror Show*, *Weird Tales* has become the only profes-

sional horror and dark fantasy magazine in the U.S. So competition is fierce. Send only your best work."

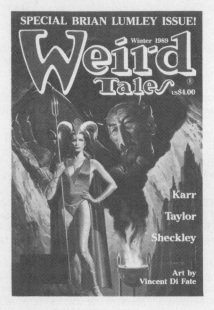

This cover illustration for Weird Tales magazine was rendered by illustrator Vincent DiFate. According to editor George Scithers, "this illustration doesn't illustrate any one story, but we felt it reflects the overall feeling of the magazine." Copyright © Terminus Publishing Company, Inc.

WESTERN PEOPLE (II), Western Producer Publications, Box 2500, Saskatoon, Saskatchewan S7K 2C4 Canada. (306)665-3500. FAX: (306)653-1255. Editor: Keith Dryden. Managing Editor: Liz Delahey. Magazine: 8½ × 11; 16 pages; newsprint paper and cover stock; illustrations and photos. *"Western People* is for and about western Canadians, a supplement of the region's foremost weekly agricultural newspaper. Includes fiction, nonfiction (contemporary and history) and poetry. Readership is mainly rural and western Canadian." Weekly. Published special fiction issue last year; plans another. Estab. 1978. Circ. 130,000.
Needs: Contemporary, adventure and humor. Buys 20 mss/year. Publishes short shorts. Published new writers within the last year. Length: 750-2,000 words.
How to Contact: Send complete ms with SAE, IRC (or $1 without IRC). Reports in 3 weeks on mss. Free sample copy with 9 × 12 SAE, IRC. Free general guidelines with legal-sized SAE, IRC.
Payment: $150 (Canadian) maximum (more for serials).
Terms: Pays on acceptance for first North American rights.
Advice: "The story should be lively, not long, related in some way to the experience of rural western Canadians. We believe our readers enjoy a good story, particularly when it has some relevance to their own lives. Although most of the stories in *Western People* are nonfictional, we offer variety to our readers, including fiction and poetry. Write about what could happen, not what did happen. We find that beginning writers try to fictionalize actual events with a result that is neither fish nor fowl."

WIGWAG (II), 73 Spring St., New York NY 10012. (212)941-7177. Editor: Alexander Kaplen. Fiction Editor: Nancy Holyoke. Magazine: 8 × 10; 80-100 pages; illustrations. "General interest magazine looking for the best fiction available." Published 10 times/year. Estab. 1989. Circ. 60,000.
Needs: "Serious literary fiction of any kind." Also short children's bedtime stories. Buys 1 mss/issue. Time between acceptance and publication varies. Published work by Jane Smiley, Richard Bausch. Length: up to 10,000. Comments on rejected manuscripts.
How to Contact: Send a complete ms. with a cover letter. Reporting time varies. SASE. Photocopied, reprinted and computer printout submissions are acceptable.
Payment: Payment is open; "competitive with other major magazines." Pays on publication.
Terms: Rights purchased vary.

WITH MAGAZINE (II, IV), Faith & Life Press and Mennonite Publishing House, Box 347, Newton KS 67114. (316)283-5100. Magazine: 8½×11; 24 pages; 60 lb. coated paper and cover; illustrations and photos. "Our purpose is to help teenagers understand the issues that impact them and to help them make choices that reflect Mennonite-Anabaptist understandings of living by the Spirit of Christ. We publish all types of material—fiction, nonfiction, poetry, prose poem, spiritual, sports, features, 'think' pieces, etc." Monthly. Estab. 1968. Circ. 6,000.
Needs: Contemporary, ethnic, humor/satire, literary, mainstream, religious, translations, young adult/teen (13-18 years). "We accept issue-oriented pieces as well as religious pieces. No religious fiction that gives 'pat' answers to serious situations." Receives about 50 unsolicited mss/month. Buys 1-2 mss/issue; 18-20 mss/year. Publishes ms up to 1 year after acceptance. Published work by Carol Gift Page, Katrina Cassel, Marian Flandrick Bray and Linda Evans; published new writers within the last year. Length: 1,500 words preferred; 1,000 words minimum; 2,000 words maximum. Publishes short shorts. Length: 800-1,000 words. Sometimes critiques rejected mss and recommends other markets.
How to Contact: Send complete ms with cover letter, which should include short summary of author's credits and what rights they are selling. Reports in 2-3 weeks on queries; 3 months on mss. SASE. Simultaneous, photocopied and reprint submissions OK. Accepts computer printout submissions. Accepts electronic submissions via DOS (IBM compatible) disk, preferably in Wordstar. Sample copy for $1.25 with 9×12 SAE and 85¢ postage. Fiction guidelines for #10 SAE and 1 first class stamp.
Payment: Pays 2¢/word for reprints; 4¢/word for first rights. Supplies contributor's copies; charge for extras.
Terms: Pays on acceptance for first or one-time rights.
Advice: "Write with a teenage audience in mind, but don't talk down to them. Treat the audience with respect. Don't expect to make a sale with the usual 'I've-got-a-problem-give-it-all-to-Jesus-and-everything-will-turn-out-fine' story. Real life isn't always like that and teens will perceive the story as unbelievable. Do include ethnic minorities in your stories; our audience is both rural and urban."

WOMAN'S DAY (II), 1633 Broadway, New York NY 10019. (212)767-6000. Editor-in-Chief: Ellen R. Levine. Fiction Editor: Eileen Herbert Jordan. A strong service magazine geared to women, with a wide variety of well written subjects (foods, crafts, beauty, medical, etc.). Publishes 15 issues/year. Estab. 1939. Circ. 7½ million; readership 17 million.
Needs: Literary, contemporary, fantasy, women's. No violence, crime or totally male-oriented stories. *Woman's Day* does not accept any unsolicited short fiction. Length: 2,000-3,000 words average.
How to Contact: Send complete ms with SASE. Free guidelines with SASE.
Payment: Pays top rates.
Terms: Pays on acceptance for first North American serial rights. Occasionally buys reprints.
Advice: "Read the magazine and keep trying."

‡WOMAN'S WORLD MAGAZINE (II), The Woman's Weekly, Heinrich Bauer North America, 270 Sylvan Ave., Englewood Cliffs NJ 07632. (201)569-0006. Editor: Dena Vane. Fiction Editor: Jeanne Muchnick. Magazine; 9½×11; 54 pages; newspaper quality. "The magazine for 'Mrs. Middle America.' We publish short romances and mini-mysteries for all women, ages 18-68." Weekly. Estab. 1980. Circ. 1.5 million.
Needs: Romance (contemporary), suspense/mystery. No humour, erotica. Receives 50 unsolicited mss/month. Buys 2 mss/issue; 104 mss/year. Publishes mss 6-10 weeks after acceptance. Agented fiction 2%. Recently published work by Tina Smith, P.J. Platz, Lisa Albert, Fay Thompson. Length: romances—2,600 words; mysteries—1,600 words. Publishes short shorts. Sometimes critiques rejected mss and recommends other markets.
How to Contact: Send complete manuscript with cover letter. *"No queries."* Reports in 6-8 weeks. SASE. Accepts computer printout submissions. Sample copy for $1. Fiction guidelines free.
Payment: Romances—$1,000, mysteries—$500.
Terms: Pays on acceptance. Buys first North American serial rights only.

WOMEN'S AMERICAN ORT REPORTER (II,IV), Women's American ORT, 315 Park Ave. S., New York NY 10010. (212)505-7700. Editor: Eve Jacobson. 8⅛×10⅞; glossy; photographs. "Jewish women's issues; education, for membership." Quarterly. Estab. 1968. Circ. 130,000.
Needs: Condensed/excerpted novel, ethnic, feminist, humor/satire and literary. Receives 2 unsolicited mss/month. Buys 2 mss/year. Publishes ms 3 months after acceptance. Agented fiction 50%. Length: 2,500 words. Published work by A.B. Yehoshua. Possibly publishes short shorts. Sometimes critiques rejected ms and recommends other markets.

How to Contact: Send complete ms with cover letter. Include Social Security number. Reports in 3 weeks. SASE. Photocopied submissions OK. Computer printout submissions are acceptable. Sample copy is free.
Payment: Pays 15¢/word.
Terms: Pays on publication for first North American serial rights.

WONDER TIME (II), Beacon Hill, Press of Kansas City, 6401 Paseo, Kansas City MO 64131. (816)333-7000. Editor: Evelyn Beals. Magazine: 8¼×11; 4 pages; self cover; color illustrations; photos. Handout story paper published through the Church of the Nazarene Sunday school; stories should follow outline of Sunday school lesson for 6-7 year olds. Weekly. Circ. 45,000.
Needs: Religious/inspirational and juvenile. Stories must have controlled vocabulary and be easy to read. No fairy tales or science fiction. Buys 1 ms/issue. Receives 50-75 unsolicited fiction mss/month. Approximately 25% of fiction is agented. Length: 300-550 words. Recently published works by Eleanor P. Anderson, Jane Landreth and Virginia Brossirt. Also publishes short shorts. Recommends other markets.
How to Contact: Send complete ms with SASE. Reports in 6 weeks on mss. Publishes ms an average of 1 year after acceptance. Free sample copy and curriculum guide with SASE.
Payment: Pays 3½¢/word.
Terms: Pays on acceptance for first rights. Buys reprints.
Advice: "Control vocabulary. Study children to know what children are interested in; stories should deal with children's problems of today and must be tastefully handled." Start with action—not description. Include an element of suspense. Don't just relate happenings."

‡XTRA MAGAZINE (IV), Church-Wellesley Review (Literary Supplement), Pink Triangle Press, Box 7289, Stn. A, Toronto, Ontario M5W 1X9 Canada. (416)925-6665. Editor: Ken Popert. Fiction Editor: Jeff Round. Tabloid: 11½×17; 44-60 pages; newsprint paper; illustrations and photographs. "Gay/lesbian magazine, but fiction/poetry does not have to be about sexual orientation." Fiction supplement is annual. Estab. 1990 (supplement only). Circ. 20,000.
Needs: Publishes annual special fiction issue. Receives 4-5 unsolicited mss/month. Buys up to 20 mss/year. Publishes mss spring after acceptance. Recently published work by Antler (American poet) Sky Gilbert (Canadian playwright). Length: 1,500 words maximum. Publishes short shorts. Sometimes critiques rejected mss and recommends other markets.
How to Contact: Send complete manuscript with cover letter. Reports in 1-2 months on mss. SASE. If notified, simultaneous, photocopied and reprint submissions OK. Accepts computer printout submissions. Sample copy free.
Payment: Pays 70¢/word (slightly more for poetry) up to $150 maximum.

YANKEE MAGAZINE (II, III), Yankee, Inc., Dublin NH 03444. Editor: Judson D. Hale. Fiction Editor: Edie Clark. Magazine: 6×9; 176+ pages; glossy paper; 4-color glossy cover stock; illustrations; 4-color photos. "Entertaining and informative New England regional on current issues, people, history, antiques and crafts for general reading audience." Monthly. Estab. 1935. Circ. 1,000,000.
Needs: Literary. Fiction is to be set in New England or compatible with the area. No religious/inspirational, formula fiction or stereotypical dialect, novels or novellas. Buys 1 ms/issue; 18 mss/year. Published work by Andre Dubus, H. L. Mountzovres and Fred Bonnie; published new writers within the last year. Length: 2,000-4,000 words. Publishes short shorts up to 1,500 words. Recommends other markets.
How to Contact: Send complete ms with SASE and previous publications. "Cover letters are important if they provide relevant information: previous publications or awards; special courses taken; special references (e.g. 'William Shakespeare suggested I send this to you . . . .')" Reports in 3-6 weeks on mss.
Payment: Pays $1,000.
Terms: Pays on acceptance; rights negotiable. Sends galleys to author.
Advice: "Read previous 10 stories in *Yankee* for style and content. Fiction must be realistic and reflect life as it is—complexities and ambiguities inherent. Our fiction adds to the 'complete menu'—the magazine includes many categories—humor, profiles, straight journalism, essays, etc. Listen to the advice of any editor who takes the time to write a personal letter. Go to workshops; get advice and other readings before sending story out cold." Fiction prize of $600 awarded to best story published in *Yankee* each year.

YOUNG AMERICAN (II), America's Newspaper for Kids, Box 12409, Portland OR 97212. (503)230-1895. Editor: Kristina T. Linden. Magazine: 10½ × 13. 16-32 pages; newsprint paper and cover; illustrations and photos. "Our focus is on children, and they are taken seriously. Articles are intended to inform and entertain. We are particularly interested in stories about newsworthy kids." Biweekly. Plans special fiction issue. Estab. 1983. Circ. 5.1 million in 1990.
Needs: Short (1,000 words) fiction pieces—fantasy, humor, mystery, prose poem and sports. No sex, violence, gore or religion. Receives more than 50 mss/week. Buys 4-6 mss/issue, 120 mss/year. Length: Up to 1,000 words.
How to Contact: Queries, clips, cover letters discouraged. Finished work encouraged. Reports within 4 months. No simultaneous submissions. SASE with mss. Sample copy available for $1.50. Guidelines available with SASE.
Payment: Pays minimum 7¢/word. Negotiable.
Terms: Pays on publication for first North American rights. May also purchase reprint rights of articles published in *Young American*.
Advice: "Speak to the kids, not down to them. Read some of the books that are popular with the younger set. You may be surprised of the level of sophistication of kids today. Now looking at longer fiction for serialization. Treat writing like a job, not a hobby."

THE YOUNG CRUSADER, National Woman's Christian Temperance Union, 1730 Chicago Ave., Evanston IL 60201. (708)864-1396. Editor-in-Chief: Mrs. Rachel Bubar Kelly. Managing Editor: Michael C. Vitucci. "Character building material showing high morals and sound values; inspirational, informational nature articles and stories for 6-12 year olds." Monthly. Estab. 1887. Circ. 10,000.
Needs: Juvenile. Stories should be naturally written pieces, not saccharine or preachy. Buys 3-4 mss/issue; 60 mss/year. Length: 600-650 words. Also prose and poetry. Recently published work by Nadine L. Mellott, William R. Barrow, Gloria L. Sollid and Veronica McClearin.
How to Contact: Send complete ms with SASE. Reports in 6 months or longer on mss. Free sample copy with SASE.
Payment: Pays ½¢/word and free author's copy. Pays ½¢/word for prose, 10¢ a line for poetry.
Terms: "If I like the story and use it, I'm very lenient and allow the author to use it elsewhere." Mss/prose/poetry, if used, pays on publication. If not used mss/prose/poetry will be destroyed.

YOUNG SALVATIONIST/YOUNG SOLDIER (II, IV), The Salvation Army, 799 Bloomfield Ave., Verona NJ 07044. (201)239-0606. Editor: Capt. Robert Hostetler. Magazine: 8 × 11; 16 pages (*Young Salvationist*), 8 pages (*Young Soldier*); illustrations and photos. Christian emphasis articles for youth members of the Salvation Army. Monthly. Estab. 1984. Circ. 50,000.
Needs: Religious/inspirational, young adult/teen. Receives 150 unsolicited mss/month. Buys 9-10 ms/issue; 90-100 mss/year. Publishes ms 3-4 months after acceptance. Length: 1,000 words preferred; 750 words minimum; 1,200 words maximum. Publishes short shorts. Sometimes critiques rejected mss and recommends other markets.
How to Contact: Send complete ms. Reports in 1-2 weeks on queries; 2-4 weeks on mss. SASE. Simultaneous, photocopied and reprint submissions OK. Accepts computer printout submissions. Sample copy free with 8½ × 11 SAE and 3 first class stamps. Fiction guidelines for #10 SAE with 1 first class stamp.
Payment: Pays 3-5¢/word.
Terms: Pays on acceptance for all rights, first rights, first North American serial rights and one-time rights.

Foreign commercial periodicals

The following commercial magazines located in the United Kingdom, Europe, Australia and Africa are paying markets for short fiction in English by North American writers. Query first for guidelines. Always enclose a return envelope with International Reply Coupons for a reply or for return of your manuscript. You might find it less expensive, when sending manuscripts, to send copies that do not need to be returned along with a self-addressed reply postcard and one IRC. IRCs are available at the main branch of your local post office.

ENCOUNTER, 44 Great Windmill St., London W1V 7PA England. Averages 10 stories/year. Sends 1 contributor's copy. "No mss returned unless accompanied by IRCs. Read the magazine first!"

FEAR, Newsfield Publications, Case Mill, Ludlow, Shropshire SY8 1JW England. Fiction Editor: David Western. Publishes fantasy, horror, science fiction and video film fiction. Pays minimum $100 for published fiction.

FORUM, Northern and Shell Building, Box 381, Mill Harbour, London E14 9TW England. Fiction Editor: Elizabeth Coldwell. Circ. 30,000. Publishes 13 stories/year. "Forum is the international magazine of human relations, dealing with all aspects of relationships, sexuality and sexual health. Fiction pieces are erotic short stories. No other type of fiction is accepted. Writers' fees are by arrangement with the editor. Writers are always sent one complimentary copy containing their story." Length: 3,000 words.

IKARIE, Radlicka 61, 150 02 Prague 6, Czechoslovakia. Editor-in-Chief: Ondřej Neff. Foreign Department Editors: Jaroslav Olša, Jr., Ivan Adamovič. Circ. 40-50,000. Publishes 100 short stories/year (50-70% translations). "We are interested in good quality SF, partly fantasy; no horror please. Ikarie is a newly-born (after the 'velvet' revolution) first Czechoslovak professional science fiction magazine published monthly. Each issue contains more than 80,000 words." Authors receive royalties in non-transferable Czechoslovak currency (since mid-1991 we will be, probably, able to send US dollars), which are at deposit on the special account, and a copy of their publication.

ISRAEL-AL, 17 Borgrashov St., Tel Aviv, Israel. Fiction Editor: Orna Fraser. Circ. 250,000. Publishes fiction related to tourism. Pays 15¢/word.

LONDON REVIEW OF BOOKS, Tavistock House S., Tavistock House Sth., London England. Deputy Editor: Susannah Clapp. Circ. 16,000. Publishes 3-6 stories annually. Publishes "book reviews with long essay-length reviews. Also publishes the occasional short story." Pays £150 per story and 5 contributor's copies.

MY WEEKLY, 80 Kingsway East, Dundee DD4 8SL Scotland. Editor: Sandy Monks. "*My Weekly* is a widely read magazine aimed at 'young' women of all ages. We are read by busy young mothers, active middle-aged wives and elderly retired ladies." Fiction (romance and humor) "should deal with real, down-to-earth themes that relate to the lives of our readers. Our rates compare favourably with other British magazines. Complete stories can be of any length from 1,500 to 4,000 words. Serials from 3 to 10 installments."

NOVA SF, Perseo Libri srl, Box 1240, I-40100 Bologna Italy. Fiction Editor: Ugo Malaguti. Circ. 5,000. "Science fiction and fantasy short stories and short novels." Pays $100-600 depending on length. "No formalities required, we read all submissions and give an answer in about 10 weeks. Buys first Italian serial rights on stories."

OVERSEAS! (II), Kolpingstr. 1, Leimen 6906 West Germany. Editorial Director: Charles L. Kaufman. "*Overseas!* is published for the US military personnel stationed in Europe. It is the leading military magazine in Europe, specifically directed to males ages 18-35." Needs very short tourist, travel-in-Europe, or military-related humor for Back Talk humor page. Also need cartoons.

‡PEOPLE'S FRIEND, 80 Kingsway East, Dundee Scotland. Fiction Editor: W. Balnave. Circ. 566,000. Averages 200 stories/year. Writers are paid for published fiction. "Writers should study the publication before submitting material. Stories can be anything from 1,000 up to 3,000 words in length."

R&R ENTERTAINMENT DIGEST (IV), R&R Werbe GmbH, Kolpingstrasse 1, 6906 Leimen, West Germany. Editor: Tory Billard. Monthly entertainment guide for U.S./Canadian military and government employees and their families stationed in Europe "specializing in travel in Europe, audio/video/photo, music and the homemaker scene. Generally we do not publish any fiction. However, best chances are with first-person stories with a tie to travel in Europe (with specifics on what to see, where to eat, shop and stay, etc.) or, better yet, celebrating American holidays in Europe." Sample copy for IRC.

REALITY MAGAZINE, 75 Orwell Rd., Rathgar, Dublin 6 Ireland. Fiction Editor: Fr. Kevin H. Donlon. Circ. 25,000. Publishes an average of 11 short stories annually. Pays £25/piece. "Be clear, brief, to the point and practical."

SUPERBIKE, Link House, Dingwall Ave., Croydon CR9 2TA England. Editor: John Cutts. Circ. 50,000. Publishes approximatley 6-8 fiction pieces/year. "Monthly motorcycle magazine — high-performance motorcycles only — tests and features. Will consider any fiction relating to this genre, preferably not death-wish/ghost/horror stories. 3,000 words max." Writers paid on publication. Looks for "Double-spaced type — neat manuscripts! Good spelling. Humorous!"

TODAY'S GUIDE, 17-19 Buckingham Palace Rd., London SW1W OPT England. Editor: Diana Wallace. Circ. 25,000. Publishes 12 short stories annually. "Magazine aimed at girls aged 10-14. The official magazine for the Girl Guides Association. Stories need to be 1,000-1,500 words long with a Guiding background." Payment is £40 per 1,000 words plus contributor copy. "We would be interested in stories with a North American Guiding background."

WOMAN'S REALM, IPC Magazines, King's Reach Tower, Stamford St., London SE1 9LS England. Fiction Editor: Sally Bowden. Circ. 530,000. Publishes 50-60 stories and 12-15 short serials/year. Appeals to practical, intelligent, family family-minded women, age 23 upwards. High standard of writing required. Originality important. Writers paid for published work. "Nearest US equivalent to our kind of fiction is probably *Redbook*. Length should be 1,200-4,000 words."

WOMAN'S WEEKLY, IPC Magazines, King's Reach, Stamford St., London SE1 9LS England. Fiction Editor: Gaynor Davies. Circ. 1.3 million. Publishes 2 serials and at least one short story per week. Fees individually negotiated. Complimentary copies given. "Short stories can be on any theme, but must have love as the central core of the plot, whether in a specific romantic context, within the family or mankind in general. Serials need not be written in installments. They are submitted as complete manuscripts and we split them up." To contact send first installment (8,000 words) and synopsis of the rest.

Other commercial periodicals

Most of the following commercial magazines appeared in the 1990 edition of *Novel and Short Story Writer's Market* but are not in the 1991 edition for a variety of reasons — they may be out of business, no longer taking fiction or overstocked with submissions. Those publications are listed below without further explanation. If we received information about why a publication would not appear, the explanation is included next to their name.

Ann Arbor (out of business)
Arete
Arthritis Today (no longer accepting fiction)
Bugle
Coastal Cruising (moved; no forwarding address)
Cobblestone (asked to be deleted)
Equilibrium
Esquire (declined listing)
Faces (not accepting fiction)
Fling

Hoof Beats
Latter-Day Woman Magazine (no longer publishing)
Lighted Pathway (asked to be deleted)
M.A. Training (not accepting fiction)
McCall's (asked to be deleted)
Maine
Meridian Magazine
Milwaukee Magazine
Monroe
Ms. (declined listing)

North Shore Magazine (no longer publishing)
Playgirl Magazine
Relix Magazine (asked to be deleted)
Shofar
Special Report: Fiction (asked to be deleted)
Tattoo Advocate Journal (out of business)
Texas Connection Magazine
Uncensored Letters

Other foreign commercial periodicals

Commando
Fantasy Tales

Interzone
Ireland's Own

Manushi
School Magazine

Only a decade ago, small and independent publishers faced insurmountable odds. They were neither financially nor structurally equipped to compete with the mega-publishers, conglomerates with billions of dollars in sales and marketing budgets to match. Unable to pay six-figure advances or promise large press-runs and lavish publicity, small presses lost successful authors to the "big guns." At the same time the independent bookseller, the lifeline between small publishers and the reading public, seemed doomed by competition from the powerful bookstore chains. The outlook for the small press industry was, at best, bleak. Or so it seemed.

Despite the predictions, however, things got better—much better. The small press industry not only beat the odds and survived the 1980s, but it flourished. While the larger houses got caught up in the "bestseller syndrome," putting energy, time and money behind big name authors and "major" mainstream books, the small press continued to do what it does best—publish and promote new authors, experimental, specialized and literary writing and books considered mid-list or backlist—alternatives all but ignored by the big houses.

Charles Wyrick, Jr., editor-in-chief of Wyrick & Company agrees. "Overemphasis by major houses and the media on blockbusters has created a greater, rather than a lesser, opportunity for small and medium-sized publishers to find and publish tomorrow's great books," he says.

The need for alternatives has not gone unnoticed by booksellers either. Independent booksellers have continued to stock the best of the small press and even the chains are beginning to recognize the selling strength of backlist titles. This year B. Dalton established the "Discover Great New Writers" program in about one-third of its 800 stores. The program is designed to promote little-known, but talented writers, a number of whom have been published in the small press.

Who are the small presses?

The term small press can be defined in many different ways. For our purposes, we define small press in the broadest sense—publishers who are not backed up by large corporations and who do not publish more than 10 or 15 titles each year. This section includes very small operations, nonprofit presses, university presses and small to mid-size independent commercial publishers.

Many of the very small presses are owned and operated by one or two people, usually family or friends. The publisher may have started by publishing his or her own books. These presses cannot handle more than one or two "outside" books each year and can easily become overwhelmed if swamped by submissions. Yet, writers published by very small houses will find they are treated as "one of the family." The publisher will have taken the book to heart and will take extra time and care with its production and promotion.

Nonprofit publishers depend on either public grants or private donations. If grant money is involved, the number of books published each year will depend on the grant money available. If the press is funded by a private organization, such as a church or club, it may look for books that reflect or promote the views of its backers.

University presses traditionally publish scholarly works and literature of little-known, but talented writers. Quite often the writer is affiliated with the university or with the state or region. The last decade brought hard times to some university-backed publishers and several have increased the number of general-interest titles to generate additional income from sales.

We've also included some larger independent commercial presses. These may publish up to 10 or 15 books. They tend to be well-known as literary or specialized presses. While they compete with the trade houses, these publishers are more apt to be open to new writers, translations and do a good share of business publishing reprints and reviving out-of-print books.

The small press alternative

Small presses won't offer you an all-expense paid publicity tour, a large advance or big royalties. Actually, you may be asked to contribute a great deal of time, energy and even money to the promotion of your book. Yet, small presses offer opportunities to writers who would otherwise have only slim chances at publication with large publishers. New writers have a better chance at smaller houses, as do writers whose work is experimental, regional or otherwise not mainstream.

Even though advances are small, publishing with a small press can be a profitable alternative. Successful small publishers tend to keep their books in stock and on bookstore shelves longer. Many belong to cooperative marketing and distribution networks, increasing their sales through group catalogs and advertising. This can actually mean more profits for writers in the long run.

Yet money is not the main reason most writers turn to small or independent publishers. Writers who have worked with the small press usually list a good, stable, editor/writer relationship as the greatest advantage. Editors at small presses tend to stay longer because they have more stake in the business — in fact, many are also the owner or publisher of the press. Many small press publishers, in turn, started as writers themselves.

Working with small presses

While most small publishers welcome unsolicited submissions, many editors say literary magazines are the first place they look for new talent. Publication, even in a small journal, gives the writer experience and demonstrates the writer is familiar with the publishing process.

Small presses succeed by identifying a niche or void in the market and creating books to fill that special need. That is why it is so important for writers interested in publishing with small presses to do research before submitting. Each press has its own special identity.

Visit local bookstores, especially independent operations and college bookstores. Check the library for books published by small presses. Write away for catalogs and guidelines. For small presses listed in this book, check the category index located just before the Markets Index at the back of the book. You will find the small press Category Index divided by subject. Find the subject or subjects best suited to your work and read each listing carefully to find the best match.

Another way to locate publishers suited to your work is to check the *Small Press Record of Books in Print*, published by Dustbooks, in your local library. The book contains titles of more than 2,000 small book publishers, indexed by subject, publisher, author and title. Look for presses that have published books similar to your own.

Even though most small presses are run by a handful of people and the atmosphere is less formal than that of larger houses, it is still important to submit professional-looking manuscripts. Submissions should be typed, double-spaced and relatively free of typos and cross-outs. Be sure to include a self-addressed, stamped envelope in a appropriate size for all correspondence.

Here are the codes we've used to classify small presses listed in this book:

I   **Publisher encourages beginning or unpublished writers to submit work for consideration and publishes new writers frequently;**

II **Publisher accepts work by established writers and by occasional new writers of unusual talent;**

III **Publisher does not encourage beginning, unagented writers; publishes mainly writers with extensive previous publication credits and a very few new writers:**

IV **Special-interest or regional publisher open only to writers on certain subjects or from certain geographic areas.**

‡ACADIA PUBLISHING CO. (II,IV), Subsidiary of World Three, Inc., Box 170, Bar Harbor ME 04609. (207)288-9025. President: Frank J. Matter. Fiction Editor: Christina Carter. Estab. 1980. "Small independent publisher." Publishes hardcover and paperback originals and reprints. Books: offset printing; case, paperback or spiral binding; line art, photo, illustrations; average print order: 2,500; first novel print order: 2,000. Published new writers within the last year. Plans 2 first novels this year. Averages 6 total titles, 4 fiction titles each year. Sometimes comments on rejected mss; $50 charge for critiques.
Needs: Historical, juvenile (5-9 yrs.) including: animal, historical and ethnic; young adult/teen (10-18 years). No erotica, gay, romance, science fiction. Published *My Dear Sarah Anne*, by T. Smedstad and *Aguahega*, by K. Snow.
How to Contact: Query first or submit complete ms with cover letter. SASE. Cover letter should include Social Security number. Reports on queries in 3 weeks; on mss in 3 months. Simultaneous and photocopied submissions OK, if good. Accepts computer printout submissions, including dot-matrix.
Terms: Pays standard royalties. Advance is negotiable. Sends galleys to author. Publishes within 12-18 months of acceptance. "We will produce a work under contract. Rate depends on condition of the manuscript, final quality required, etc. We are very selective (2-3 titles a year)." Subsidy titles "do not bear our imprint." Book catalog: for #10 SAE and 1 first class stamp.
Advice: "We like quality regardless of the author's past publishing history. Please, do not send a manuscript in its 'working stage.' We need to see what you *can do* — not what you only think you can do. Please be professional, neat and reasonable. Research, research, research. This is a very competitive business and each work we publish must be the best we can acquire. If the work is right we will work with the author."

ADVOCACY PRESS (IV), Box 236, Santa Barbara CA 93102. Publisher: Mindy Bingham. Estab. 1983. Small publisher with 3-5 titles/year. Hardcover and paperback originals. Books: perfect or Smythe-sewn binding; illustrations; average print order: 10,000 copies; first novel print order: 10,000. Plans 2 first novels this year; 2 children's fiction (32-48 pg.) titles per year.
Needs: Juvenile (5-9 years); preschool/picture book. New series: 32 page picturebook of stories of little known influential women in history. Wants only feminist/nontraditional messages to boys or girls — picture books; self-esteem issues. Published *Father Gander Nursery Rhymes*, by Dr. Doug Harch (picture book); *Berta Benz and the Motorwagon*, by Mindy Bingham (picture book).
How to Contact: Submit complete manuscript with SASE for return. Reports in 10 weeks on queries. Simultaneous submissions OK. No photocopies. Accepts computer printouts. Request editorial policy.
Terms: Pays in royalties of 5% minimum; 10% maximum. Sends pre-publication galleys to the author. Book catalog free on request with SASE.
Advice: "We are looking for fictional stories for children 4-8 years old that give messages of self sufficiency for little girls; little boys can nurture and little girls can be anything they want to be, etc. Looking for talented writers/artists. Please review some of our publications *before* you submit to us."

*AEGINA PRESS, INC. (I,II), 59 Oak Lane, Spring Valley, Huntington WV 25704. (304)429-7204. Imprint is University Editions, Inc. Managing Editor: Ira Herman. Estab. 1984. Independent small press. Publishes paperback originals and reprints. Books: 50 lb white text/10 point high gloss covers;

photo-offset printing; perfect binding, illustrations; average print order: 500-1,000. Published new writers within the last year. Plans 4-5 first novels this year. Averages 20 total titles, 10 fiction titles each year. Sometimes comments on rejected ms.

Needs: Adventure, contemporary, experimental, faction, fantasy, historical, horror, literary, mainstream, regional, science fiction, short story collections, suspense/mystery. No racist, sexist, or obscene materials. Recently published *The Golden Hour*, by Randolph Mains (novel); *Water Dancing*, by Pearl Duncan (short stories); and *New Beginnings*, by Cindy Degeyter (novel).

How to Contact: Accepts unsolicited mss. Query first, send outline/synopsis and 3 sample chapters or complete ms with cover letter. SASE. Agented fiction 5%. Reports in 3 weeks on queries; 1-2 months on mss. Simultaneous and photocopied submissions OK. Accepts computer printout submissions.

Terms: Pays 15% royalties. "If the manuscript meets our quality standards but is financially high risk, self-publishing through the University Editions imprint is offered. All sales proceeds go to the author until the subsidy is repaid. The author receives a 40% royalty thereafter. Remaining unsold copies belong to the author." *Subsidy publishes most new authors.* Sends galleys to author. Publishes ms 6 months after acceptance. Writer's guidelines for #10 SASE. Book catalog for 9×12 SASE, 4 first class stamps and $2.

‡ALASKA NATIVE LANGUAGE CENTER (IV), University of Alaska, Box 900111, Fairbanks AK 99775-0120. (907)474-6577. Editor: Tom Alton. Estab. 1972. Small education publisher limited to books in and about Alaska native languages. Generally nonfiction. Publishes hardcover and paperback originals. Books: 60 lb book paper; offset printing; perfect binding; photos, line art illustrations; average print order: 500-1,000 copies. Averages 6-8 total titles each year.

Needs: Ethnic. Publishes original fiction only in native language and English by Alaska native writers.

How to Contact: Does not accept unsolicited mss. Photocopied submissions OK. Accepts computer printout submissions, including dot-matrix. Electronic submissions via ASCII for modem transmissions or Macintosh compatible files on 3½" disk.

Terms: Does not pay. Sends galleys to author.

ALYSON PUBLICATIONS, INC. (II), 40 Plympton St., Boston MA 02118. (617)542-5679. Subsidiary is Carrier Pigeon Distributors. Fiction Editor: Sasha Alyson. Estab. 1977. Medium-sized publisher specializing in lesbian- and gay-related material. Publishes paperback originals and reprints. Books: paper and printing varies; trade paper, perfect bound binding; average print order: 8,000; first novel print order: 6,000. Published new writers within the last year; plans 4 first novels this year. Averages 15 total titles, 8 fiction titles each year. Average first novel print order 6,000 copies.

Needs: "We are interested in all categories; *all* materials must be geared toward lesbian and/or gay readers." Recently published *The Buccaneer*, by M. S. Hunter; *Behind the Mask*, by Kim Larabee; *Rapture and the Second Coming*, by Wendy Borgstrom.

How to Contact: Query first with SASE. Reports in 3 weeks on queries; 2 months on mss. Photocopied submissions OK but not preferable. Prefers letter-quality.

Terms: "We prefer to discuss terms with the author." Sends galleys to author. Book catalog for SAE and 45¢ postage.

AMERICAN ATHEIST PRESS (IV), Gustav Broukal Press, Box 140195, Austin TX 78714-0195. Editor: Robin Murray-O'Hair, Estab. 1960. Paperback originals and reprints. Books: bond and other paper; offset printing; perfect binding; illustrations "if pertinent." Averages 6 total titles/year. Occasionally critiques or comments on rejected mss.

Needs: Contemporary, humor/satire, literary, science fiction. No "religious/spiritual/occult."

How to Contact: Query with sample chapters and outline. SASE. Reports in 6 weeks on queries; 2 months on mss. Simultaneous and photocopied submissions OK. Accepts computer printout submissions. Accepts electronic submissions via IBM-PC/Word-Perfect on disk.

The asterisk indicates a publisher who sometimes offers subsidy arrangements. Authors are asked to subsidize part of the cost of book production. See the introduction to Commercial Publishers for more information.

Terms: Pays 6-11% royalties and subscription to magazine. Writers guidelines free for #9 SASE and 1 first class stamp. Book catalog free on request.
Advice: "We only publish fiction which relates to Atheism; we receive many queries for general interest fiction, which we do not publish."

‡**ANDROGYNE**, 930 Shields St., San Francisco CA 94132. (415)586-2697. Contact: Ken Weichel. Estab. 1971. "Independent press working within the cultural coincidence of San Francisco." Publishes books and a periodical, *Androgyne*. Publishes paperback originals. Averages 3 total titles, 1 fiction title each year. Average first novel print order 500 copies.
Needs: Contemporary, experimental, and literary.
How to Contact: Does not accept unsolicited mss. Query. Reports in 1 month on queries; 2 months on mss. Simultaneous and photocopied submissions OK. Accepts computer printout submissions.
Terms: Pays in author's copies (10%). See magazine for writer's guidelines. Free book catalog.

ANNICK PRESS LTD. (IV), 15 Patricia Ave., Willowdale, Ontario M2M 1H9 Canada. (416)221-4802. Publisher of children's books. Publishes hardcover and paperback originals. Books: offset paper; full-color offset printing; perfect and library binding; full-color illustrations; average print order: 9,000; first novel print order: 7,000. Plans 18 first picture books this year. Averages approximately 20 titles each year, all fiction. Average first picture book print order 2,000 cloth, 9,000 paper copies. Occasionally critiques rejected ms.
Needs: Children's books only.
How to Contact: "Annick Press publishes only work by Canadian citizens or residents." Does not accept unsolicited mss. Query with SASE. Free book catalog.
Terms: Sends galleys to author.
Advice: "Publishing more fiction this year, because our company is growing. But our publishing program is currently full."

ANOTHER CHICAGO PRESS (II), Box 11223, Chicago IL 60611. Senior Editor: Lee Webster. Estab 1976. Small literary press, non-profit. Books: offset printing; perfect binding, occasional illustrations; average print order 2,000. Averages 4 total titles, 3 fiction titles each year. Occasionally critiques or comments on rejected ms.
Needs: Literary. No inspirational religious fiction. Recently published *Private Acts*, by Robert Pope (short stories); *Margaret's Book*, by James Walton (novel); *The Bloodworth Orphan*, by Leon Forest (novel); published fiction by previously unpublished writers within the last year.
How to Contact: Does not accept or return unsolicited mss. Query first for books, then submit outline/synopsis and sample chapters. SASE. Agented fiction 10%. Reports in 3-6 weeks on queries; 8-12 weeks on mss. Simultaneous and photocopied submissions OK. Accepts computer printout submissions, but prefers letter.
Terms: Advance: $100 negotiable; honorarium depends on grant/award money. Sends galleys to author.
Advice: "We publish novels and collections of short stories and poetry as our funds and time permit— and then probably only by solicitation. We publish literary fiction and poetry of substance and quality. We publish books that will entertain, enlighten or disturb. Our books, our authors will be read well into the 21st Century."

ANOTHER WAY (IV), 400 East Las Palmas Dr., Fullerton CA 92635. (714)969-2346. President: Carrie Teasdale. Estab. 1985. Small, 2-person publisher. Publishes paperback originals. Plans 4 first novels this year. Averages about 4 total titles, 2 fiction titles each year.
Needs: Looking for practical new age fiction. Published new writers within the last year.
How to Contact: Does not accept or return unsolicited mss. Query first. SASE. Reports on queries in 1 month. Sends pre-publication galleys to author.
Advice: "Query only publishers with an expressed interest in your type of fiction. We get too many inappropriate submissions. We are *not* interested in descriptive, experiential works—we're looking for solutions, how-to's, *practical* writings."

 The double dagger before a listing indicates that the listing is new in this edition. New markets are often the most receptive to freelance contributions.

ANSUDA PUBLICATIONS (II), Box 158J, Harris IA 51345. Fiction Editor: Daniel Betz. Estab. 1978. One-man operation on part-time basis, "planning to someday expand into a full-time business." Publishes paperback originals. Books: mimeo paper; mimeo printing; index stock covers with square spine binding; illustrations on cover; average print order varies. Plans 1-2 first novels this year. Averages 3-5 total titles, 1 fiction title each year. Occasionally critiques rejected mss.
Needs: Fantasy, horror, literary, mainstream, psychic/supernatural, short story collections and suspense/mystery. "Interested mostly in fantasy, horror, psychic and supernatural. No romance, juvenile, experimental, translations or science fiction." Published *Motherland*, by Martin DiCarlantonio.
How to Contact: Query first or submit outline/synopsis and 1-2 sample chapters. SASE always. Photocopied submissions OK. Accepts computer printout submissions, prefers letter-quality. Reports in 1 day on queries, 1-8 weeks on mss. Publishes ms an average of 1 year after acceptance.
Terms: Pays in royalties by arrangement and 5 author's copies. Writer's guidelines and book catalog for #10 SASE.
Advice: "We appreciate neat copy. If photocopies are sent, we like to be able to read dark letters and to read all of the story. We try to work closely with the author through the period from first submission to publication."

APPLEZABA PRESS, Box 4134, Long Beach CA 90804. Editorial Director: Shelley Hellen. Estab. 1977. "We are a family-operated publishing house, working on a part-time basis. We plan to expand over the years." Publishes paperback originals. Averages 1 fiction title each year.
Needs: Contemporary, literary, experimental, feminist, gay, lesbian, fantasy, humor/satire, translations, and short story collections. No gothic, romance, confession, inspirational, satirical, black humor or slapstick. Recently published *Horse Medicine and Other Stories*, by Raephael Zepecha.
How to Contact: Accepts unsolicited mss. Submit complete ms with SASE. No simultaneous submissions; photocopied submissions OK. Accepts computer printout submissions, prefers letter-quality. Reports in 2 months. Publishes ms 2-3 years after acceptance.
Terms: Pays in author's copies and 8-15% royalties; no advance. Free book catalog.
Advice: "Cover letter with previous publications, etc. is OK. Each book, first or twentieth, has to stand on its own. If a first-time novelist has had shorter works published in magazines, it makes it somewhat easier for us to market the book. We publish only book-length material."

ARIADNE PRESS (I), 4817 Tallahassee Ave., Rockville MD 20853. (301)949-2514. President: Carol Hoover. Estab. 1976. Shoestring operation—corporation with 4 directors who also act as editors. Publishes hardcover and paperback originals. Books: 50 lb alkaline paper; offset printing; Smyth-sewn binding. Average print order 1,000; average first novel print order 1,000. Plans 1 first novel this year. Averages 1 total title each year; only fiction. Sometimes critiques rejected mss. "We comment on selected mss of superior writing quality, even when rejected."
Needs: Adventure, contemporary, feminist, historical, humor/satire, literary, mainstream, suspense, psychological, family relations and marital, mystery, war. Looking for "literary-mainstream" fiction. No short stories, no science fiction or horror. Published *How to Write an Uncommonly Good Novel*, (nonfiction).
How to Contact: Accepts unsolicited mss. *Query first.* SASE. 5% of fiction is agented. Reports in 1 month on queries; 2 months on mss. Simultaneous and photocopied submissions OK. Accepts computer printout submissions, no dot-matrix.
Terms: Pays royalties of 10%. No advance. Sends pre-publication galleys to author. Writer's guidelines not available. List of books in stock for #10 SASE.
Advice: "We exist primarily for non-established writers. Try large, commercial presses first."

ARTE PUBLICO PRESS (II, IV), University of Houston, Houston TX 77004. (713)749-4768. Publisher: Dr. Nicolas Kanellos. Estab. 1979. Small press devoted to the publication of contemporary U.S. Hispanic literature. Publishes paperback originals and occasionally reprints. Average print order 2,000-5,000; first novel print order 2,500-5,000. Sometimes critiques rejected mss.
Needs: Contemporary, ethnic, feminist, literary, short story collections. Published *A Shroud in the Family*, by Lionel Garcia (satire); *This Migrant Earth*, by Rolando Hinojosa; and *Taking Control*, by Mary Helen Ponce (short stories).
How to Contact: Accepts unsolicited mss. Submit outline/synopsis and sample chapters or complete ms with cover letter. 1% of fiction is agented. Accepts computer printout submissions.
Terms: $1,000 average advance; 20 author's copies. Sends pre-publication galleys to author. Book catalog free on request.
Tips: "All fiction, all paperback."

BANNED BOOKS (I, II), Subsidiary of Edward-William Publishing Co., Box 33280, #292, Austin TX 78764. Senior Editor: Tom Hayes. Estab. 1985. Small press with plans to expand. Publishes paperback originals. Books: 60 lb acid-free paper; sheet-fed offset printing; perfect binding; illustrations; average print order: 2,000; first novel print order: 2,000. Plans 10 first novels this year. Averages 12 total titles, 10 fiction titles each year.
Needs: "Must be written for the gay/lesbian market!" Erotica, fantasy, gay, humor/satire, lesbian, science fiction, short story collections. Looking for "all forms of fiction and nonfiction for the gay/lesbian market with the exception of poetry collections." Recently published *Syphilis As AIDS*, by Robert Ben Mitchell; *Free Fall*, by Marsha Zabarsky; and *Silverwolf*, by Roger Edmonson.
How to Contact: Query first. SASE. Reports in 3 weeks on queries. Simultaneous and photocopied submissions OK. Accepts computer printout submissions.
Terms: Pays in royalties of 10% minimum; 15% maximum; 10 author's copies. Sends galleys to author. Writer's guidelines free for SASE.
Advice: "Study the market before submitting. Much time and expense could be avoided if the author really read the entries in Novel & Short Story Writer's Market before sending it out."

BARLOW PRESS (I,II), Box 5403, Helena MT 59604. (406)449-7310. Fiction Editor: Russell B. Hill. Estab. 1987. One-person publishing/printing company which produces titles both by offset and letter-press (hand-set) printing. Publishes hardcover and paperback originals and reprints. Books: acid-free letterpress stock (i.e. Mohawk, Superfine); usually letterpress printing, occasionally offset, hand-sewn binding with end papers, heavier cover stock, sometimes leather; woodcuts, line-art plates or one-color artwork. Average print order: 500-1,000 letterpress; 2,000-3,000 offset. Publishes 2 total titles/year; plans 0-1 first fiction title this year. Sometimes critiques rejected mss.
Needs: Adventure, contemporary, historical, humor/satire, literary, mainstream, regional, short story.
How to Contact: Query first. Accepts unsolicited mss. Send complete mss with cover letter and SASE. Reports in 2 months. Simultaneous and photocopied submissions OK. Accepts computer printouts and electronic disk submissions.
Terms: Payment by individual arrangement, depending on the book. Publishes ms 6 months-2 years after acceptance. Rarely subsidy, but "publication by Barlow Press usually involves a joint effort—Barlow Press contributes the time and expenses, author contributes mss, with particular terms of reimbursement subject to negotiation."
Advice: "Frankly, a publisher like Barlow Press can't compete with larger publishers for manuscripts they want, and we encourage authors to submit material to potentially lucrative publishers first. But we are convinced too many manuscripts deserve one more reading, one more potential outlet. We don't publish most manuscripts we read, but we have never regretted reading a manuscript. And because Barlow Press handles every publication by individual arrangement with the author, we aren't shy about proposing to edit manuscripts to fit our needs."

FREDERIC C. BEIL, PUBLISHER, INC. (II), 414 Tattnall St., Savannah GA 31401. Imprints include The Sandstone Press. President: Frederic C. Beil III. Estab. 1983. General trade publisher. Publishes hardcover originals and reprints. Books: acid-free paper; letterpress and offset printing; Smyth-sewn, hardcover binding; illustrations; average print order: 2,000; first novel print order: 2,000. Plans 2 first novels this year. Averages 10 total titles, 2 fiction titles each year.
Needs: Historical, literary, regional, short story collections, translations. Published *A Woman of Means*, by Peter Taylor.
How to Contact: Does not accept unsolicited mss. Query first. Reports in 1 week on queries. Accepts computer printout submissions.
Terms: Payment "all negotiable." Sends galleys to author. Book catalog free on request.

‡BETHEL PUBLISHING (IV), 1819 S.Main, Elkhart IN 46516.(219)293-8585. Contact: Senior Editor. Estab. 1975. Mid-size Christian book publisher. Publishes paperback originals and reprints. Averages 3-5 total titles per year. Occasionally critiques or comments on rejected manuscripts.

Market categories: (I) Beginning; (II) General; (III) Prestige; (IV) Specialized.

Needs: Religious/inspirational,young adult/teen. No "workbooks, cookbooks, coloring books, theological studies, pre-school or elementary-age stories."
How to Contact: Accepts unsolicited manuscripts. Query first. Reports in 2 weeks on queries; 3 months on mss. Accepts simultaneous submissions. Publishes manuscripts 8-16 months after acceptance.
Terms: Pays royalties of 10% and 12 author's copies. Writer's guidelines and book catalog free on request.

BILINGUAL PRESS/EDITORIAL BILINGÜE (II, IV), Hispanic Research Center, Arizona State University, Tempe AZ 85287-2702. (602)965-3867. Editor: Gary Keller. Estab. 1973. "University affiliated." Publishes hardcover and paperback originals, hardcover and paperback reprints. Books: 60 lb acid free paper; single sheet or web press printing; casebound and perfect bound; illustrations sometimes; average print order: 4,000 copies (1,000 case bound, 3,000 soft cover). Published new writers within the last year. Plans 2 first novels this year. Averages 12 total titles, 6 fiction each year. Sometimes comments on rejected ms.
Needs: Ethnic, literary, short story collections and translations. "We are always on the lookout for Chicano, Puerto Rican, Cuban-American or other U.S. Hispanic themes with strong and serious literary qualities and distinctive and intellectually important themes. We have been receiving a lot of fiction set in Latin America (usually Mexico or Central America) where the main character is either an ingenue to the culture or spy, adventurer, or mercenary. We don't publish this sort of 'Look, I'm in an exotic land' type of thing. Also, novels about the Aztecs or other pre-Columbians are very iffy." Recently published *The Dream of Santa Maria de las Piedras*, by Miguel Méndez; *Sapogonia*, by Ana Castillo; *Voice-Haunted Journey*, by Eliud Martinez; and *The Devil in Texas/El diablo en Texas*, by Aristeo Brito (winner of Western States Book Award for fiction.).
How to Contact: Query first. SASE. Include Social Security number with submission. Reports in 3 weeks on queries, 2 months on mss. Simultaneous and photocopied submissions OK. Accepts computer printout submissions.
Terms: Pays royalties of 10%. Average advance $300. Provides 10 author's copies. Sends galleys to author. Publishes ms 1 year after acceptance. Writer's guidelines not available. Book catalog free.
Advice: "Writers should take the utmost care in assuring that their manuscripts are clean, grammatically impeccable, and have perfect spelling. This is true not only of the English but the Spanish as well. All accent marks need to be in place as well as diacritical marks. When these are missing it's an immediate first indication that the author does not really know Hispanic culture and is not equipped to write about it. We are interested in publishing creative literature that treats the U.S. Hispanic experience in a distinctive, creative, revealing way. The kinds of books that we publish we keep in print for a very long time (certainly into the next century) irrespective of sales. We are busy establishing and preserving a U.S. Hispanic canon of creative literature."

‡BLACK HERON PRESS (I, II), P.O. Box 95676, Seattle WA 98145. Publisher: Jerry Gold. Estab. 1984. One-person operation; no immediate plans to expand. Publishes paperback and hardback originals. Average print order: 1,000; first novel print order: 500-1,500. Averages 2 fiction titles each year. Occasionally critiques or comments on rejected mss.
Needs: Adventure, contemporary, experimental, humor/satire, literary, science fiction. Adventure/moral *dilemma*. Vietnam war novel—literary. "We don't want to see fiction written for the mass market. If it sells to the mass market, fine, but we don't see ourselves as a commercial press."
How to Contact: Will not accept unsolicited manuscripts until 1992. Reports in 2 months on queries, and 3 months on mss. Simultaneous and photocopied submissions OK.
Terms: Standard royalty rates. No advance.
Advice: "I prefer a query, but I'll look at an unsolicited ms anyway. A query letter should tell me: 1) number of words, 2) number of pages, 3) is ms available on floppy disk, 4) have parts of novel been published? 5) where? If you're going to submit to *Black Heron*, make the work as good as you can. I'm a good editor but I don't have the time to solve major problems with a manuscript."

BLACK MOSS PRESS (II), Box 143 Station A, Windsor ON N9V 6L7 Canada. (519)252-2551. Editorial Contact Person: Kristina Russelo. Fiction Editor: Marty Gervais. Estab. 1969. "Small independent publisher assisted by government grants." Publishes paperback originals. Books: Zephyr paper; offset printing; perfect binding; 4-color cover, b&w interior illustrations; average print order: 500. Averages 10-14 total titles, 7 fiction titles each year. Sometimes comments on rejected mss.

Needs: Humor/satire, juvenile (5-9 years, including easy-to-read, contemporary), literary, preschool/picture book, short story collections. "Usually open to children's material. Nothing religious, moralistic, romance." Published *Crossing the Snow Line*, by Elizabeth Hay (short story collection).
How to Contact: Accepts unsolicited mss. Submit outline/synopsis and 2 sample chapters. SASE. Reports in 1-3 months. Photocopied submissions OK. Accepts computer printout submissions.
Terms: Pays for children's in royalties; literary in author's copies. Sends galleys to author. Publishes ms 1 year after acceptance. Book catalog for SASE.
Advice: "Generally, originality, well developed plots, strong, multi-dimensional characters and some unusual element catch my interest. It's rare that we publish new authors' works, but when we do, that's what we want. (We do publish short story collections of authors who have had some stories in lit mags.) Because we are assisted by government grants which place certain restrictions on us, we are unable to publish any material by anyone other than a Canadian citizen or immigrant landed in Canada."

BLACK TIE PRESS (I, II), Box 440004, 12655 Whittington Dr., Houston TX 77244. (713)789-5119. Publisher/Editor: Peter Gravis. Estab. 1986. "We are a tiny press interested in contemporary poetry and short fiction." Publishes hardcover and paperback originals. Books: Mohawk vellum, Glatfelter paper; combination offset and letter press printing; Smythe sewn; illustrations; average print order: varies from 2,000 to 2,500. Publishes "two fiction anthologies each year."
Needs: Contemporary and experimental. "Our current aim is to publish an anthology of short fiction (4-6,000 words). No science fiction, romance, spiritual, religious, juvenile, historical."
How to Contact: Query or submit complete ms (with proper postage) with cover letter. SASE necessary for returns. Reports in 3-6 months on queries. Photocopied submission OK. Accepts computer printout submissions if letter quality.
Terms: Pays in royalties. "Payment will be determined on individual basis." Publishes ms one to two years after acceptance. Writer's guidelines free for SASE or IRC.

‡BLIND BEGGAR PRESS, Box 437, Bronx NY 10467. Imprint: LampLight Editions. Fiction Editors: Gary Johnston, C.D. Grant. Estab. 1975. Small press with plans to expand. Publishes paperback originals. Plans to publish first novels "dependent upon budget." Averages 2-3 total titles each year; "no fiction titles thus far." Average print order 2,000 copies. Occasionally critiques rejected ms.
Needs: Ethnic (Third World), experimental, juvenile (animal, easy-to-read, fantasy, historical), preschool/picture book, short story collections, translations and young adult/teen (historical).
How to Contact: Query first with SASE. Reports in 1 month on queries; 2 months on mss. Simultaneous and photocopied submissions OK. Publishes ms 12-18 months after acceptance.
Terms: Pays in author's copies (10-15% of run). "If author wishes to pay all or part of production costs, we work out individual arrangements directly." Book catalog free on request.
Advice: Recent trends include ethnic historical (biographies, political history, etc.). In first novels interested in high quality, relevancy to Third World readers. "Within two years we plan to publish children's books, short stories and *maybe* a small novel."

BOOKS FOR ALL TIMES, INC., Box 2, Alexandria VA 22313. Publisher/Editor: Joe David. Estab. 1981. One-man operation. Publishes hardcover and paperback originals. Books: 60 lb paper; offset printing; perfect binding; average print order: 1,000. "No plans for new writers at present." Has published 1 fiction title to date. Occasionally critiques rejected mss.
Needs: Contemporary, literary and short story collections. "No novels at the moment; hopeful, though, of someday soon publishing a collection of quality short stories. No popular fiction or material easily published by the major or minor houses specializing in mindless entertainment. Only interested in stories of the Victor Hugo or Sinclair Lewis quality." Published *The Fire Within*, by Joe David (literary); *Glad You Asked!*, by Joe David (non-fiction).
How to Contact: Query first with SASE. Simultaneous and photocopied submission OK. Reports in 1 month on queries.
Terms: Pays negotiable advance. "Publishing/payment arrangement will depend on plans for the book." Book catalog free on request.
Advice: Interested in "controversial, honest books which satisfy the reader's curiosity to know. Read Victor Hugo, Fyodor Dostoyevsky and Sinclair Lewis, for example."

Read the Business of Fiction section to learn the correct way to prepare and submit a manuscript.

BOREALIS PRESS (IV), 9 Ashburn Dr., Ottawa, Ontario K2E 6N4 Canada. Imprint includes *Journal of Canadian Poetry*. Editor: Frank Tierney. Fiction Editor: Glenn Clever. Estab. 1970. Publishes hardcover and paperback originals and reprints. Books: standard book-quality paper; offset printing; perfect and cloth binding; average print order: 1,000. Buys juvenile mss with b&w illustrations. Average number of titles: 4.
Needs: Contemporary, literary, adventure, historical, juvenile and young adult. "Must have a Canadian content or author; query first." Accepts short stories. Published *Sandy*, by Nancy Freeman; *Trouble with Heroes*, by Guy Vanderhaeghe (short stories); and *Windflower: Selected Poems of Bliss Carmans*, ed. by Richmand Souster.
How to Contact: Submit query with SASE (Canadian postage) or IRCs. No simultaneous submissions. Reports in 2 weeks on queries, 3-4 months on mss. Publishes ms 1-2 years after acceptance.
Terms: Pays 10% royalties and 3 free author's copies; no advance. Sends galleys to author. Free book catalog with SASE or IRC.
Advice: " Have your work professionally edited. We generally publish only material with a Canadian content or by a Canadian writer."

BOTTOM DOG PRESS (IV), Firelands College, Huron OH 44839. (419)433-5560. Editor/Publisher: Dr. Larry Smith. Estab. 1984. Four-person part-time operation assisted by grants from Ohio Arts Council. Publishes paperback originals. Books: fine paper; perfect binding; cover art illustrations; average print order: 1,500 fiction. Averages 3 total titles, 1-2 fiction titles each year. Always critiques or comments on rejected mss.
Needs: Literary, mainstream. Midwest life. Published *Best Ohio Fiction* collection (160 pages) with work by Jack Matthews, Robert Flanagan, Philip F. O'Connor, Robert Fox. Published new writers within the last year; *Loving Power:* Stories by Robert Flanagan this year.
How to Contact: Accepts unsolicited mss. Query first. Submit complete ms with cover letter. SASE. Reports on queries in 2 weeks; 2 months on mss. Accepts computer printout submissions, no dot-matrix.
Terms: Pays royalties of 10-15% minimum and 20 author's copies. Sends galleys to author. Has done 2 books co-operatively—50/50. Book catalog free on request.
Advice: "We do an 'Ohio Writers series' specializing in chapbook collection of stories or novellas— emphasis on sense of place and strong human characters." All submissions must fall within the 40,000 word limit. We also do a Contemporary Midwest Fiction series of stories or novel (160 pgs.).

BREITENBUSH BOOKS, INC. (II,III), Box 82157, Portland OR 97282. Managing Editor: Thomas Booth. Estab. 1977. Independent trade publisher with national distribution. Publishes hardcover and paperback originals and paperback reprints. Averages 12-15 total titles, 4-6 fiction titles each year.
Needs: Contemporary, ethnic, experimental, literary, regional, novels and short story collections. Recently published *In Memory of Hawks*, by Irving Warner; *East is West of Here*, by Joyce Thompson and *DeFord*, by David Shetzline (reprint).
How to Contact: Accepts unsolicited mss. Prefers published writers. Send outline/synopsis and 2 sample chapters or stories; SASE for query. Agented fiction 20%. Reports in 1 month on queries; 6-8 weeks on mss. Simultaneous and photocopied submissions OK.
Terms: Pays in royalties and author's copies. Offers advance. Sends galleys to author. Publishes ms 9 months to 1 year after acceptance. Book catalog for 4 first class stamps (we provide envelope).

■**BRYANS & BRYANS (I) (Book Packager and Editorial Consultant)**, Box 121, Fairfield CT 06430. (203)454-2051. President: John B. Bryans. Fiction Editor: James A. Bryans. Arranges publication of paperback originals (packages). Books: paperback/mass market. *Critiques mss: $100 charge* "for 2-page evaluation only when this has been agreed upon in advance. Often I will offer comments and criticism at no charge where we, based on a query, have encouraged submission."
Needs: Adventure, contemporary, historical, horror, humor/satire, literary, mainstream, romance (contemporary, historical). Titles (1990) include: *The Hucksters of Holiness*, by Ron Gorton (contemporary social thriller); *Cincinnati* (historical with romance elements); *Baton Rouge* (historical with romance elements); and *Portland*, by Lee Davis Willoughby.
How to Contact: Does not accept unsolicited mss. Query first. SASE. Agented fiction 50-90%. Reports in 2 weeks on queries; 1 month on mss. Electronic submissions OK via Microsoft Word on Macintosh disk.

Terms: Pays in royalties of 6% minimum; 10% maximum. Negotiable advance.

Advice: "Send us a letter, maximum 2 pages, describing the project and giving pertinent background info on yourself. Include an SASE and we will reply to let you know if we find the idea intriguing enough to see 3 sample chapters (the *first* three) and a detailed synopsis."

BURNING BOOKS (IV), 690 Market St., Suite 1501, San Francisco CA 94104. (415)788-7480. Publisher: Kathleen Burch, Michael Sumner, Melody Sumner. Estab. 1979. Three-person part-time operation. Publishes paperback originals. Books: acid-free paper; offset and letterpress printing; spiral or signature sewn binding; illustrations; average print order: 1,000-3,000. Averages 1 title/year; 1 fiction title every 2 years. *Will provide detailed critique of ms for $100.*

Needs: Literary. No "commercially inspired" fiction. Recently published *Moment of Silence*, by Toma Longinovic.

How to Contact: Does not accept unsolicited mss. Query first. Reports on queries in 6 weeks.

Terms: Pays in author's copies. Sends galleys to author. Book catalog free on request.

‡CACANADADADA (I, II, IV), 3350 West 21 Ave., Vancouver BC V6S 1G7 Canada. (604)738-1195. President: Ronald B. Hatch. Fiction Editor: J. Michael Yates. Estab. 1988. Publishes paperback originals. Books: 60 lb. paper; photo offset printing; perfect binding; average print order: 1,000; first novel print order: 1,000. Plans 1 first novel this year. Averages 6 total titles, 1 or 2 fiction this year. Sometimes comments on rejected ms.

Needs: Experimental and literary. Recently published *Torpor*, by J. Michael Yates (experimental, prose fiction).

How to Contact: Accepts unsolicited mss. Submit outline/synopsis and 1 or 2 sample chapters. SASE. Reports in 1 week on queries; 1 month on mss. Photocopied submissions OK. Accepts computer printout submissions.

Terms: Pays royalties of 10%. Provides author's copies. Sends galleys to author. Publishes ms 6 months after acceptance.

Advice: "We publish mostly poetry, but plan to do one or two fiction books each year. We are a Canadian publishing house and depend on a partial government subsidy to publish books. Thus, authors *must* be Canadian."

CADMUS EDITIONS (III), Box 687, Tiburon CA 94920. (707)431-8527. Editor: Jeffrey Miller. Estab. 1979. Emphasis on quality literature. Publishes hardcover originals and paperback originals. Books: Approximately 25% letterpress; 70% offset printing; perfect and case binding; average print order: 2,000; first novel print order: 2,000. Averages 3-5 total titles, 3 fiction titles each year.

Needs: Literary. Published *The Wandering Fool*, by Yunus Emre, translated by Edouard Roditi and Guzin Dino; *The Hungry Girls*, by Patricia Eakins; *Zig-Zag*, by Richard Thornley.

How to Contact: Does not accept or return unsolicited mss. Query first. SASE. Photocopied submissions OK.

Terms: Royalties negotiated per book. Sends galleys to author.

CALYX BOOKS (II,IV), Box B, Corvallis OR 97339. (503)753-9384. Editor: M. Donnelly. Estab. 1986. "We publish fine literature and art by women." Publishes hardcover and paperback originals. Books: offset printing; paper & cloth binding; average print order: 5,000-10,000 copies; first novel print order: 5,000. Published new writers within the last year. Plans 2 first novels this year. Averages 2-4 totals, 2 fiction, this year.

Needs: Contemporary, ethnic, experimental, feminist, lesbian, literary, short story collections and translations. Recently published *The Riverhouse Stories*, by Andrea Carlisle (literary); *The Forbidden Stitch*, by Shirley Geok-Lim, editor (anthology); and *Florilegia*, by Margarita Donnelly, editor (anthology).

How to Contact: Does not accept unsolicited mss. Query first or submit outline/synopsis and 3 sample chapters. Include SASE (IRC). *Note: Accepts mss only between January 15 and March 15 each year.* Reports in 1 month on queries; 6 months on mss. Photocopied submissions OK. Accepts computer printout submissions.

Listings marked with a solid box [■] are book packagers. See the introduction to Commercial Publishers for more information.

Terms: Pays royalties of 8% minimum, author's copies, (depends on grant/award money). Sends galleys to author. Publishes ms 1-2 years after acceptance. Writer's guidelines for #10 SASE or IRC and 1 first class stamp. Book catalog free on request.

CARLTON BOOKS (IV), Box 5052, Evanston IL 60204. (312)328-0400. Contact: Graham Carlton. Estab. 1985. Midsize independent publisher with plans to expand. Publishes hardcover and paperback originals and reprints.
Needs: Erotica, suspense/mystery.
How to Contact: Does not accept or return unsolicited ms. Query first. SASE.

*CAROLINA WREN PRESS (II,IV), Box 277, Carrboro NC 27510. (919)560-2738. Imprints are Lillipop Power Books. Editor-in-chief: Judy Hogan. Fiction Editor: Alisa Johnson. "Small non-profit independent publishing company which specializes in women's minority work and non-sexist, multi-racial children's books mainly from North Carolina." Publishes paperback originals. Books: off-set printing; perfect and saddle-stitching binding; illustrations mainly in children's; average print order: 1,000 adult, 3,000 children; first novel print order: 1,000. Published new writers within the last year. Plans 2 first novels this year. Averages 2-3 total titles each year. Sometimes comments on rejected mss (if Judy Hogan does it, $50 for 12 pages).
Needs: Contemporary, ethnic, experimental, feminist, gay, juvenile (east-to-read, fantasy, contemporary), lesbian, literary, preschool/picture book, regional, short story collections, translations. No standard clichéd stuff, romances, etc. No animals (children's books). Recently published *Love, Or a Reasonable Facsimile*, by Gloree Rogers (ethnic); *Brother and Keeper, Sister's Child*, by Margaret Stephens (literary).
How to Contact: Accepts unsolicited mss. Submit outline/synopsis and 1 or 2 sample chapters. SASE. Reports in 6 months. Photocopied submissions OK. Computer printout submissions are acceptable.
Terms: Pays in copies (10% of print run for adults. 5% for children's books). Pays cash advance and royalties if grants are available. Sends galleys to author. Publishes ms 2-3 years after acceptance. Writer's guidelines for #10 SAE and 1 first class stamp (for children's authors only). Book catalog for #10 SAE and 2 first class stamps.
Advice: "We would like to see work from more black women writers. We also have a minority editor— Alisa Johnson, who reads for all genres."

CARPENTER PRESS (I, II), Box 14387, Columbus OH 43214. Editorial Director: Robert Fox. Estab. 1973. One-man operation on part-time basis. Publishes paperback originals. Books: alkaline paper; offset printing; perfect or saddle stapled binding; illustrations sometimes; average print order: 500-2,500; first novel print order: 1,000.
Needs: Contemporary, literary, experimental, science fiction, and fantasy. "Literary rather than genre science fiction and fantasy." Published *Song for Three Voices*, by Curt Johnson (novel); and the 10th anniversary first novel contest winner, *The Three-Week Trance Diet*, by Jane Pirto. "Do not plan to publish more than one book/year including chapbooks, and this depends upon funding, which is erratic. Contemplating future competitions in the novel and short story."
How to Contact: Accepts unsolicited mss. Query. SASE. Simultaneous and photocopied submissions OK. Accepts computer printout submissions. Letter-quality only. Reports promptly.
Terms: Pays in author's copies or 10% royalties. "Terms vary according to contract." No cash advance. Free book catalog with #10 SASE.
Advice: "Don't try to impress us with whom you've studied or where you've published. Read as much as you can so you're not unwittingly repeating what's already been done. I look for freshness and originality. I wouldn't say that I favor experimental over traditional writing. Rather, I'm interested in seeing how recent experimentation is tying tradition to the future and to the work of writers in other countries. Our books should be read before submitting. We encourage first novelists."

*CATBIRD PRESS (II), 44 N. 6th Ave., Highland Park NJ 08904. Publisher: Robert Wechsler. Estab. 1987. Small independent trade publisher. Publishes hardcover and paperback originals and reprints. Books: acid-free paper; offset printing; cloth/paper binding; illustrations (where relevant). Average print order: 4,000; first novel print order: 3,000. Averages 5 total titles, 1-2 fiction titles each year.
Needs: Contemporary, humor (specialty); literary, mainstream, translations (specialty Czech, French and German read in-house). Recently published *Catapult*, by Vladimír Páral, translated by William E. Harkins (Czech, literary but popular).

How to Contact: Accepts unsolicited mss but no queries. Submit outline/synopsis with sample chapters. SASE. Reports in 4-6 weeks on mss. Simultaneous and photocopied submissions OK, but let us know if simultaneous.
Terms: Pays royalties of 7½% minimum; 15% maximum. Average advance: $1,000; offers negotiable advance. Pays in 10 author's copies. Sends prepublication galleys to author. Publishes ms approx. 1 year after acceptance. *Some subsidy publishing;* terms depend on particular book. Writer's guidelines for #10 SAE with 1 first class stamp.
Advice: "We are a new publisher interested in quality fiction particularly with a comic vision. We are definitely interested in unpublished novelists who combine a sense of humor with a true knowledge of and love for literature, a lack of ideology, care for craft and self-criticism."

CAVE BOOKS (IV), Subsidiary of Cave Research Foundation, 756 Harvard Ave., St. Louis MO 63130. (314)862-7646. Editor: Richard A. Watson. Estab. 1957. Small press. Publishes hardcover and paperback originals and reprints. Books: acid free paper; various methods printing; binding sewn in signatures; illustrations; average print order: 1,500; first novel print order: 1,500. Averages 4 total titles. Number of fiction titles varies each year. Critiques or comments on rejected ms.
Needs: Adventure (cave exploration). Needs any realistic novel with caves as central theme. "No gothic, romance, fantasy or science fiction. Mystery and detective OK if the action in the cave is central and realistic. (What I mean by 'realistic' is that the author must know what he or she is talking about.)"
How to Contact: Accepts unsolicited mss. Submit complete ms with cover letter. Reports in 1 week on queries; 1 month on mss. Simultaneous and photocopied submissions OK. Accepts computer printouts.
Terms: Pays in royalties of 10%. Sends galleys to author. Book catalog free on request.
Advice: Encourages first novelists. "We would like to publish more fiction, but we get very few submissions. Why doesn't someone write a historical novel about Mammoth Cave, Carlsbad Caverns, ...?"

CHELSEA GREEN PUBLISHING CO., Route 113, P.O. Box 130, Post Mills VT 05058. (802)333-9073. Editor: Ian Baldwin. Estab. 1985. "Small independent trade publisher with plans to expand." Publishes hardcover and paperback originals. Averages 8-10 total titles, 1-2 fiction titles each year.
Needs: Serious fiction only ... no genre fiction (ie. romance, spy, sci fi) or mainstream." Published *The Automotive History of Lucky Kellerman,* by Steve Heller (literary); *The Eight Corners of the World,* by Gordon Weaver (lit/comedy).
How to Contact: Query first. Prefers no unsolicited submissions. SASE.
Terms: Royalties to trade standards; small advances on royalties negotiable.

CHILD WELFARE LEAGUE OF AMERICA (IV), 440 First St. NW, Suite 310, Washington DC 20001. (202)638-2952. Director of Publications: Susan Brite. Estab. 1920. Nonprofit association with publishing arm. Publishes hardcover and paperback originals. Books: average print order 3,000. Publishes 1 or 2 fiction titles/year.
Needs: Published *Floating,* by Mark Krueger, PhD (stories about youth-care workers in residential homes for children).
How to Contact: Query first with SASE.
Terms: Payment varies. Book catalog free.

***CHINA BOOKS (IV),** 2929 24th St., San Francisco CA 94110. (415)282-2994. Senior Editor: Bob Schildgen. Estab. 1959. "Publishes books about China or things Chinese." Publishes hardcover and paperback originals. Books: letterpress, offset printing; perfect binding; b&w illustrations; average print order: 5,000. Published new writers within the past year. Averages 12 total titles, 3 fiction titles each year. Sometimes critiques rejected mss.
Needs: Ethnic, subjects relating to China and translations from Chinese. Recently published *The Piano Tuner,* by Cheng Naishan; *6 Tanyin Alley,* by Liu Zongren; *Old Well,* by Zheng Yi.
How to Contact: Query first or submit outline/synopsis and 2 sample chapters. Reports in 2 weeks on queries; in 1 month on mss. Simultaneous and photocopied submissions OK.
Terms: Pays royalties 5% minimum; 8% maximum. Sends galleys to author. Publishes ms 1 year after acceptance. *Subsidy publishes 1%/year.* Writer's guidelines and book catalog free on request.

CLARITY PRESS (I, II, IV), Suite 469, 3277 Roswell Rd NE, Atlanta GA 30505. Contact: Editorial Committee, Fiction. Estab. 1984. Small press publishing fiction and nonfiction on political, social, minority issues and human rights. Books: 120 M paper; offset printing; perfect binding; illustrations where necessary or enhancing; average print order: 3,000; first novel print order: 1,000. Plans 1 first novel this year. Averages 3 total titles/year. Occasionally critiques or comments on rejected ms.

Needs: Minority, literary, social commentary. Short stories for anthology. Published *The Invisible Women of Washington*, by Diana G. Collier, (social issues).

How to Contact: Accepts unsolicited mss. Query is a necessity. SASE. Reports in 6 weeks. Simultaneous and photocopied submissions OK. Accepts computer printout submissions.

Terms: Authors paid by individual arrangement.

Advice: "We are interested only in novels concerning political, minority or human rights issues. Mss not preceded by query letter will be returned."

CLIFFHANGER PRESS (II), Box 29527, Oakland CA 94604-9527. (415)763-3510. Editor: Nancy Chirich. Estab. 1986. Publishes hardcover originals. Books: 60 lb text stock paper; offset printing; case binding; average print order: 3,000; first novel print order: 3,000. Published new writers within the last year; goal is 10 novels a year.

Needs: Suspense/mystery. "Need mystery/suspense (75,000 words approximately); heavy on the American regional or foreign background. No grossly hardboiled detectives and no spies." (Send SASE for guidelines for specific needs.) Recently published *Beecher*, by Virginia O'Neal; *The Third Letter*, by Frank Ranieriz; and *The Druze Document*, by Gregory Fitzgerald and John Dillon.

How to Contact: Please first send for writer's guidelines and book catalog, free on request for SASE. Query first with outline/synopsis and first three chapters as sample. SASE. If sample appears to be our style, we will request complete ms. Reports in 2 weeks on queries; approx. 8 weeks on requested mss. Unsolicited mss are piled up until we can get to them; sometimes for over a year. Simultaneous and photocopied submissions OK, but please let us know. Accepts computer printout submissions, but no justified type.

Terms: No advances. Pays royalties of 10% minimum; 15% maximum. Sends galleys to author.

Advice: "Author must be able to accept editorial suggestions with grace. Our motto is 'we can work it out.' If manuscript is accepted, there is something there, so no *drastic* substantive changes would be anticipated."

*CLOTHESPIN FEVER PRESS (I), 5529 N. Figueroa, Los Angeles CA 90042. (213)254-1373. Publisher: Jenny Wrenn. Estab. 1986. Small two-person operation with plans to expand. Books: offset printing; perfect binding, comb or saddlestitched binding; graphics of 2 or 3 colors, photos etc., average print order: 2,000 copies. Averages 2 total titles, 0-1 fiction title each year.

Needs: Experimental, feminist, lesbian, literary, short story collections. "Looking for literary work by lesbian writers. No male stories by male writers." Recently published *Shitkickers and Other Texas Stories*, by Carolyn Weathers; *In A Different Light: An Anthology of Lesbian Writers*, by Jenny Wrenn and Carolyn Weathers; *Crazy*, by Carolyn Weathers (novel); published fiction by previously unpublished writers within the last year.

How to Contact: Accepts unsolicited mss. Query first with cover letter that includes summary or topic plus sample short story or chapter. SASE. Reports in 3 weeks on queries; 3 months on mss. Simultaneous and photocopied submissions OK. Accepts computer printout submissions.

Terms: Payment is negotiable. Sends galleys to author. Writer's guidelines free for SASE. Book catalog on request.

Advice: "A writer should be open to rewrite suggestions that a publisher might suggest without taking offense. Spelling and correct grammar should be strived for above all. Keep writing and rewriting but don't despair if you think your work is unmarketable. Keep in mind that the right publisher for you may be hard to find."

‡COFFEE HOUSE PRESS (II), 27 N. 4th St., Minneapolis MN 55401. (612)338-0125. Editorial Assistant: Michael L. Wiegers. Fiction Editor: Allan Kornblum. Estab. 1984. "Nonprofit publisher with a small staff. We publish literary titles: fiction and poetry." Publishes paperback originals. Books: acid-free paper; offset and letterpress printing; Smythe sewn binding; cover illustrations; average print order: 2,500; first novel print order: 3,000-4,000. Published new writers within the last year. Plans one first novel this year. Averages 10 total titles, 5-6 fiction titles each year. Sometimes critiques rejected mss.

Needs: Contemporary, ethnic, experimental, humor/satire, literary, short story collections. Looking for "Non-genre, contemporary, high quality, unique material." No westerns, romance, erotica, mainstream, sci-fi, mystery. Recently published *Through the Arc of the Rain Forest*, by Karen Tei Yamashita (first); *The Woman Who Read Novels & Peacetime*, by Constance Urdang (2 novellas); and *Dancers & the Dance*, by Summer Brenner (1st collection short stories).

How to Contact: Accepts unsolicited mss. Submit complete manuscript with cover letter. SASE. Agented fiction 10%. Reports in 3 months on queries; 9 months on mss. Photocopied submissions OK. Accepts computer printout submissions.
Terms: Pays royalties of 8%. Average advance $500. Provides 15 author's copies. Writer's guidelines for #10 SASE or IRC.
Advice: Be brilliant.

CONFLUENCE PRESS INC. (II), Spalding Hall, Lewis-Clark State College, Lewiston ID 83501. (208)799-2336. Imprint is Blue Moon Press. Fiction Editors: James R. Hepworth and Shirley Mc-Geoghegan. Estab. 1976. Small trade publisher. Publishes hardcover originals and reprints; paperback originals and reprints. Books: 60 lb paper; photo offset printing; Smythe-sewn binding; average print order: 1,500-5,000 copies. Published new writers this year. Averages 10 total titles/year. Critiques rejected mss for $25/hour.
Needs: Contemporary, historical, literary, mainstream, short story collections, translations. "Our needs favor serious fiction, 1 novel and 1 short fiction collection a year, with preference going to work set in the contemporary western United States." Published *A Charge of Angels*, by L.D. Clark (fiction); and *The Other Side of the Story*, by Richard Shelton (short fiction).
How to Contact: Query first. SASE for query and ms. Agented fiction 50%. Reports in 6-8 weeks on queries and mss. Simultaneous and photocopied submissions OK. Accepts computer printouts; letter-quality only.
Terms: Pays in royalties of 10%; advance is negotiable; 10 author's copies; payment depends on grant/award money. Sends galleys to author. Book catalog for 6x9 SASE.
Advice: "We are very interested in seeing first novels from promising writers emerging from writers' workshops who wish to break into serious print. We are also particularly keen to publish the best short story writers we can find."

COUNCIL FOR INDIAN EDUCATION (I,IV), 517 Rimrock Rd., Billings MT 59102. (406)252-7451. Editor: Hap Gilliland. Estab. 1963. Small, non-profit organization publishing Native American materials for schools. Publishes hardcover and paperback originals. Books: offset printing; perfect bound or saddle stitched binding; b&w illustrations; average print order: 1,500; first novel print order: 1,500. Published new writers within the last year; plans 3 first novels this year. Averages 5 total titles, 4 fiction titles each year. Usually critiques rejected ms.
Needs: Adventure, ethnic, historical, juvenile (historical, adventure and others), preschool/picture book, regional, western, young adult/teen (easy-to-read, and historical). Especially needs "short novels, and short stories accurately portraying American Indian life past or present—fast moving with high interest." No sex emphasis. Published *Sacajawea—A Native American Heroin*, by Martha F. Bryant; *Red Power on the Rio Grande* by Franklin Folsom; *Chief Stephen's Party*, by Ann Chandonnet.
How to Contact: Accepts unsolicited mss. Submit complete ms with SASE. Reports in 3 months. Simultaneous and photocopied submissions OK. Accepts computer printout submissions.
Terms: 10% of wholesale price or 1½¢/word. Sends galleys to author. Free writer's guidelines and book catalog.
Advice: Mostly publishes original fiction in paperback. "Be sure material is culturally authentic and good for the self-concept of the group about whom it is written. If you write about minorities, make sure they are true to the culture and way of life, and that you don't downgrade any group."

CREATIVE ARTS BOOK CO. (II), 833 Bancroft Way, Berkeley CA 94710. (415)848-4777. Imprints: Creative Arts Communications Books, Saturday Night Specials. Editorial Production Manager: Peg O'Donnell. Estab. 1975. Small independent trade publisher. Publishes hardcover originals and paperback originals and reprints. Average print order: 2,500-10,000; average first novel print order: 2,500-10,000. Published new writers within the last year. Plans 3 first novels this year. Averages 30-40 total titles; 20 fiction titles each year.
Needs: Contemporary, erotica (literary), feminist, historical, literary, regional, short story collections, suspense/mystery (Black Lizard Crime Fiction), translations, western. Recently published *Russia*, by Nikos Kazantzakis (first English translation, travel journal/literature); *A Butterfly Net And A Kingdom and other stories*, by Blair Fuller; *Driving Under the Carboard Pines*, by Colleen McElroy.
How to Contact: Accepts unsolicited ms. Submit outline/synopsis and 3 sample chapters (approx. 50 pages). SASE (IRC). 50% of fiction is agented. Reports in 2 weeks on queries; 1 month on mss. Simultaneous and photocopied submissions OK. Accepts computer printout submissions.
Terms: Pays royalties of 6-10%; average advance of $500-1,000; 10 author's copies. Sends galleys to author. Writers guidelines and book catalog for SASE or IRC.

CREATIVE WITH WORDS PUBLICATIONS (II, III), Box 223226, Carmel CA 93922. Editor-in-Chief: Brigitta Geltrich. Estab. 1975. One-woman operation on part-time basis. Books: bond and stock paper; mimeographed printing; saddle stitch binding; illustrations; average print order varies. Publishes paperback anthologies of new and established writers. Averages 2 anthologies each year. *Critiques rejected mss; $10 for short stories; $20 for longer stories, folklore items, $5 for poetry.*
Needs: Humor/satire, juvenile (animal, easy-to-read, fantasy). "Editorial needs center on folkloristic items (according to themes): tall tales and such for biannual anthologies." Needs seasonal short stories appealing to general public; "tales" of folklore nature, appealing to all ages, poetry and prose written by children. Recently published anthologies, "Rural America," "Native Americans" and "The Slavic People." Prose not to exceed 1,000 words.
How to Contact: Accepts unsolicited mss. Query first; submit complete ms with SASE and cover letter. Photocopied submissions OK. Accepts computer printout submissions, prefers letter-quality. Reports in 1 month on queries; 2 months on mss. Publishes ms 1-6 months after acceptance. Writer's guidelines and catalog sheet (2 oz.) for SASE. No simultaneous submissions.
Terms: Pays in 20% reduced author copies.
Advice: "Our fiction appeals to general public: children-senior citizens. Follow guidelines and rules of *Creative With Words* publications and not those the writer feels CWW should have. We only consider fiction along the lines of folklore or seasonal genres. Be brief, sincere, well-informed and proficient!"

CREATIVITY UNLIMITED PRESS (II), 30819 Casilina, Rancho Palos Verdes CA 90274. (213)377-7908. Contact: Rochelle Stockwell. Estab. 1980. One-person operation with plans to expand. Publishes paperback originals and self-hypnosis cassette tapes. Books: perfect binding; illustrations; average print order: 1,000. Averages 1 title (fiction) each year. Average first novel print order 1,000 copies.
Needs: Published *Insides Out*, by Shelley Stockwell (plain talk poetry); *Sex and Other Touchy Subjects*, (poetry and short stories).
Advice: Write for more information.

CROSS-CULTURAL COMMUNICATIONS (IV), 239 Wynsum Ave., Merrick NY 11566-4725. (516)868-5635. Editorial Director: Stanley H. Barkan. Estab. 1971. "Small/alternative literary arts publisher focusing on the traditionally neglected languages and cultures in bilingual and multimedia format." Publishes chapbooks, magazines, anthologies, novels, audio cassettes (talking books) and video cassettes (video books, video mags); hardcover and paperback originals. Number of titles in '89: 35. Publishes new women writers series, Holocaust series, Israeli writers series, Dutch writers series, Asian-American writers series.
Needs: Contemporary, literary, experimental, ethnic, humor/satire, juvenile and young adult folktales, and translations. "Main interests: bilingual short stories and children's folktales, parts of novels of authors of other cultures, translations; some American fiction. No fiction that is not directed toward other cultures. For an annual anthology of authors writing in other languages (primarily), we will be seeking very short stories with original-language copy (other than Latin script should be print quality 10/12) on good paper. Title: *Cross Cultural Review Anthology: International Fiction 1.* We expect to extend our *CCR* series to include 10 fiction issues: *Five Contemporary* (Dutch, Swedish, Yiddish, Norwegian, Danish, Yugoslav, Sicilian, Greek, Israeli, etc.) *Fiction Writers.*" Recently published *Sicilian Origin of the Odyssey*, by L.G. Pocock (bilingual English-Italian translations by Nat Scamacca) and *Sikano Americano!* by Nat Scammacca.
How to Contact: Accepts unsolicited mss. Query with SAE with 63¢ postage to include book catalog. "Note: Original language ms should accompany translations." Simultaneous and photocopied submissions "of good quality" OK. Accepts computer printout submissions. Prefers letter-quality. Reports in 1 month.
Terms: Pays "sometimes" 10-25% in royalties and "occasionally" by outright purchase, in author's copies—"10% of run for chapbook series," and "by arrangement for other publications." No advance.
Advice: "Write because you want to or you must; satisfy yourself. If you've done the best you can, then you've succeeded. You will find a publisher and an audience eventually. Generally, we have a greater interest in nonfiction novels and translations. Short stories and excerpts from novels written in one of the traditional neglected languages are preferred—with the original version (i.e., bilingual). Our kinderbook series will soon be in production with a similar bilingual emphasis, especially for folktales, fairy tales, and fables."

HARRY CUFF PUBLICATIONS LTD. (IV), 94 LeMarchant Rd., St. John's, Newfoundland A1C 2H2 Canada. (709)726-6590. Managing Editor: Douglas Cuff. Estab. 1981. "Small regional publisher specializing in Newfoundlandia." Publishes paperback originals. Books: offset printing; perfect binding;

average print order: 1,000; first novel print order: 800. Averages 12 total titles, 1 fiction each year.
Needs: "Either about Newfoundland, or by a Newfoundlander, or both. No mainstream or erotica."
Published *The Strange Things of the World*, by Alan Fisk (historical); *A Fresh Breeze from Pigeon Inlet*,
by Ted Russell (humorous short stories); and *Collected Works of A.R. Scammell* (short story collection).
How to Contact: Accepts unsolicited mss. Submit outline/synopsis and 3 sample chapters. SASE
(IRC) necessary for return of ms. Reports in 1 month on queries; 3-5 months on mss. Photocopied
submissions OK. Accepts computer printout submissions. Accepts electronic submissions via disk
(query first).
Terms: Pays royalties of 10% minimum. Sends galleys to author. Publishes ms 6-18 months after
acceptance. Writer's guidelines and book catalog free.
Advice: "I would like to see more good fiction, period, but it *has* to be about Newfoundland or by a
Newfoundlander (note that these are entirely discrete categories) I don't want any more mss about
the Vietnam War or running a radio station in Kansas City or the like! Our readers will not buy that
from us."

*DAN RIVER PRESS (I,II), Conservatory of American Letters, Box 88, Thomaston ME 04861. (207)354-
6550. President: Robert Olmsted. Fiction Editor: R.S. Danbury III. Estab. 1976. Publishes hardcover
and paperback originals. Books: 60 lb. offset paper; offset printing; perfect (paperback); hardcover
binding; illustrations; average print order: 1,000; first novel print order: 1,000. Published new writers
within the past year. Averages 10-12 total titles; 1 fiction title last year—3 planned for 1991.
Needs: Adventure, contemporary, experimental, fantasy, historical, horror, humor/satire, literary,
mainstream, military/war, psychic/supernatural/occult, regional, science fiction, short story collections,
western. "We want good fiction that can't find a home in the big press world. No mindless stuff written
flawlessly." Recently published *Looking for the Worm*, by Diana Azar (short stories); *Passengers and
Kings*, by Joe Fuoco (short stories); *Buono*, by William Hoffman, (novel).
How to Contact: Accepts unsolicited mss. Reports in 2 weeks. Simultaneous and photocopied submissions OK, plain paper only. Accepts computer printout submissions. "Guidelines help. Large SASE
please."
Terms: Royalties not paid on first $3,000 in sales, after that pays royalties of 10%. Sends galleys to
author. After acceptance, publication "depends on many things (funding, etc.). Probably in six months
once funding is achieved." Writer's guidelines for #10 SAE and 2 first class stamps. Book catalog for
6x9 SAE and 2 first class stamps.
Advice: "Submit to us (and any other small press) when you have exhausted all hope for big press
publication. Then, do not expect the small press to be a big press. We lack the resources to do things
like 'promotion,' 'author's tours.' These things either go undone or are done by the author. When you
give up on marketability of any novel submitted to small press, adopt a different attitude. Become
humble, as you get to work on your second/next novel, grow, correct mistakes and create an audience."

JOHN DANIEL AND COMPANY, PUBLISHERS (I, II), Box 21922, Santa Barbara CA 93121. (805)962-
1780. Fiction Editor: John Daniel. Estab. 1980/reestablished 1985. Small publisher with plans to expand. Publishes paperback originals. Books: 55-65 lb book text paper; offset printing; perfect bound
paperbacks; illustrations sometimes; average print order: 2,000; first novel print order: 2,000. Plans 2
first novels this year. Averages 10 total titles, 3-4 fiction titles each year. Critiques rejected ms.
Needs: "I'm open to all subjects (including nonfiction)." Literary, mainstream, short story collections.
No pornographic, exploitive, illegal, or badly written fiction. Recently published *Rats in the Trees*,
stories by Jess Mowry; and *Closer to Houston*, a novel by Richard Fagen; published new writers within
the last year.
How to Contact: Accepts unsolicited mss. Query first. SASE. Submit outline/synopsis and 2 sample
chapters. Reports in 3 weeks on queries; 2 months on mss. Simultaneous and photocopied submissions
OK. Accepts computer printouts.
Terms: Pays in royalties of 10% of net minimum. Sends galleys to author.
Advice: Encourages first novelists. "As an acquiring editor, I would never sign a book unless I were
willing to publish it in its present state. Once the book is signed, though, I, as a developmental editor,
would do hard labor to make the book everything it could become. Read a lot, write a lot, and stay in
contact with other artists so you won't burn out from this, the loneliest profession in the world."

*MAY DAVENPORT PUBLISHERS (I, II, IV), 26313 Purissima Rd., Los Altos Hills CA 94022. (415)948-
6499. Editor/Publisher: May Davenport. Estab. 1975. One-person operation with independent sub-
contractors. Publishes hardcover and paperback originals. Books: 65-80 lb paper; off-set printing;
perfect binding/saddle stitch/plastic spirals; line drawing illustrations; average print order 500-3,000;

average first novel print order: 3,000. Plans 1-3 first novels this year. Averages 3-5 total titles/year (including coloring books/reprints); 2-5 fiction titles/year. Sometimes critiques rejected mss.
Needs: "Overstocked with picture book mss. Prefer drama for junior and senior high students. Don't preach. Entertain!" Recently published *Creeps*, by Shelly Fredman; *The Chase of the Sorceress*, by Philip K. Johnson; *All About Turtles*, by Andrea Ross (coloring book with read-along cassette.)
How to Contact: Query first with SASE. 2% of fiction is agented. Reports in 2-3 weeks.
Terms: Pays royalties of 10-15%; no advance. Sends galleys to author. "Partial subsidy whenever possible in advance sales of 3,000 copies, which usually covers the printing and binding costs only. The authors are usually teachers in school districts who have a special book of fiction or textbook relating to literature." Writer's guidelines free with your SASE.
Advice: "If you are print-oriented, remember the TV-oriented are not literate. They prefer visuals and verbalizing to writing. Personal tip: Combat illiteracy by creating material which will motivate children/young adults to enjoy words and actions. Write a play for this junior/senior high age. They will read anything which they think they can participate in dramatically for themselves."

DAWNWOOD PRESS (II, IV), Fifth Floor, 387 Park Ave. South, New York NY 10016-8810. (212)532-7160. FAX: (212)213-2495. President: Kathryn Drayton. Fiction Editor: John Welch. Estab. 1984. Publishes hardcover originals. Books: 60 lb Lakewood-white paper; offset litho printing; adhesive case binding; average print order: 5,000. Averages 1 fiction title each year.
Needs: Contemporary. "Our needs are taken care of for the next 2 years." No experimental. Recently published 1990: *History's Trickiest Questions*, by Paul Kuttner (history); 1992: *Tough Questions . . . Amazing Answers*, by Paul Kuttner (non-trivia about science, sports, entertainment, places, literature, art, music); 1994: *Forget the Dog! (Beware of Owner!)*, by Paul Kuttner (satire). 1993: *Killing Love*, by Paul Kuttner; 1989: *The Iron Virgin*, by Paul Kuttner.
How to Contact: Does not accept unsolicited mss. Submit through agent only. Reports in 2 weeks on queries; 2 weeks on mss. Simultaneous and photocopied submissions OK.
Terms: Advance negotiable. Sends galleys to author.
Advice: "Same advice since Dickens's days: Tell a story from the opening sentence in easily understood English, and if you must philosophize do so through action and colloquial dialogue."

*DAYSPRING PRESS, INC. (I,II), Box 135, Golden CO 80401. (303)279-2462. Editor: John C. Brainerd. Estab. 1984. "One-person 'little literary' and 'religious' operation on part-time basis; 3 periodicals, tracts and paperbacks." Books: 20# Cascade Bond Xerographic; Photo offset printing; staple, spiral, perfect bound; b&w illustrations; average print order: 1,000; first novel print order: 500. Published new writers within the last year. Plans 2 first novels this year. Plans 3-4 fiction titles this year. Sometimes critiques rejected ms. "I would not reject any material categorically. Purposefully violent, scandalous and pejorative material would have to have very definite counter values."
Needs: Sci-fi, period, and contemporary genre. Published *The Final Love Story*, by Bea Halperin; *The Faerie Way*, by Josie Lightman and *The Incorrupti*, by Amanda Crannech.
How to Contact: Accepts unsolicited mss. Submit complete ms with cover letter. Include SASE and Social Security number with submission. Reports in 1 month. Photocopied submissions OK. Accepts computer printout submissions.
Terms: Usually payment, may negotiate. Subsidy publishes 30% of books. Sends galleys to author (books only). Publishes ms 90 days after acceptance. Writer's guidelines for #10 SAE and 1 first class stamp. Book catalog free for 6×9 SAE and 2 first class stamps.
Advice: "I would like to see more poignant trading in the hardcore human issues and less detraction in the trivial."

DOUBLE M PRESS (II), 16455 Tuba St., Sepulveda CA 91343. (818)360-3166. Publisher: Charlotte M. Stein. Estab. 1975. Small independent press with plans to expand. Publishes hardcover and trade paperback originals. Buys juvenile mss with illustrations. Books: 60 lb white or ivory paper; web press printing; perfect binding; graphics and photographs; average first novel print order 1,000 copies.
Needs: Juvenile (fantasy, historical, contemporary), preschool, inspirational, and young adult (fantasy, historical, problem novels). "We are interested in work that deals with the problems of growth and solving contemporary situations in a 'positive' manner. No degradation, violence, or exploitation of the characters. Strong in imagination."
How to Contact: Accepts unsolicited mss. Query first with outline/synopsis and 2 sample chapters. Reports in 2 weeks on queries; 2 months, if possible, on mss. Photocopied submissions OK. Publishes ms usually within 1 year after acceptance.

Terms: Pays in royalties of 8% minimum. "We do not pay advances."
Advice: "We are gearing up to publish at least 6 titles in 1991."

*DRAGON'S DEN PUBLISHING (II, IV), 11659 Doverwood Drive, Riverside CA 92505. President: G. Michael Short. Estab. 1988. Small, part-time press. Publishes hardcover and paperback originals, occasionally reprints. Books: usually paperback binding; cover artwork only; average print order 1,000; first novel print order 500-1,000. Plans 1 first novel this year. Sometimes comments on rejected mss; *charges $5.*
Needs: Fantasy, historical, horror, psychic/supernatural/occult, science fiction, short story collections, spiritual, suspense/mystery. Needs "novels dealing with the paranormal, extraordinary, etc.; also fantasy (especially sword and sorcery); historical novels dealing with the war periods; realistic horror (e.g. dealing with devil worshippers, witchcraft, voodoo, etc.)." No "fiction giving ESP a bad name; makeovers of Conan; unbelievable horror (such as *Nightmare on Elm Street* or *Friday the 13th*)."
How to Contact: Accepts unsolicited mss. Submit outline/synopsis and 3 sample chapters with SASE. Agented fiction 10%. Reports in 3-4 weeks on queries; 6-9 months on mss. Photocopied submissions OK.
Terms: Pays in royalties of 5-15%. Publishes ms 1 year after acceptance. *Subsidy publishes* "only at author's request upon receipt of rejection. Author pays 100% of production cost." Writer's guidelines free for #10 SASE.
Advice: "A cover letter is a must! We need to know the author's background. A résumé is not necessary for fiction. We encourage agented work. Keep cover letters short (no more than a page if possible) but sweet. Do not include your synopsis in your cover letter; keep it separate. Be patient."

‡THE DRAGONSBREATH PRESS (IV), 10905 Bay Shore Dr., Sister Bay WI 54234. Editor: Fred Johnson. Estab. 1973. One-man operation on part-time basis. Publishes paperback and hardback originals in small editions as handmade books. Books: varied paper; letterpress printing hand binding; illustrations.
Needs: Contemporary, literary, experimental, erotica, science fiction, fantasy, and humor/satire. "NO NOVELS, but rather single short stories."
How to Contact: "We are not currently accepting any unsolicited mss." Query and when requested send complete ms with SASE. Simultaneous and photocopied submissions OK. Accepts computer printout submissions. Reports in 1 month on queries, 2 months on mss. "Always include a cover letter and SASE."
Terms: Negotiates terms. No advance. "Since we are a small press, we prefer to work cooperatively, sharing the work and expenses between the author and the press. We are not a 'vanity press' ."
Advice: "This is a small press working with the book as an art form producing handmade limited-edition books combining original artwork with original writing. Since we work with hand-set type and have limited time and money, we prefer shorter writing suited to handwork and illustrating. We are not a typical publishing house; books would have limited distribution, mainly to art and book collectors. We are now also looking for regional (Wisconsin) writing for a regional magazine the press has begun publishing entitled *The Door County Alamanak*. Always include cover letter with brief description of story."

‡DUNDURN PRESS (II), 2181 Queen St. E., #301, Toronto, Ontario M4L 1I5 Canada. (416)698-0454. Editorial Contact Person: Kirk Howard. Estab. 1972. Midsize independent publisher with plans to expand. Publishes hardcover and paperback originals. "We do not as yet publish fiction, but intend to start in 1991 or 1992."
Needs: Contemporary.
How to Contact: Accepts unsolicited mss. Submit outline/synopsis and sample chapters. SASE for ms. Simultaneous and photocopied submissions OK. Accepts computer printout submissions. Accepts electronic submissions.
Terms: Pays royalties of 10-15%; $1,000 average advance; 10 author's copies. Sends galleys to author. Publishes ms 6-9 months after acceptance. Writer's guidelines not available. Book catalog free on request for SASE.

THE ECCO PRESS (II), 26 W. 17th St., New York NY 10011. (212)645-2214. Editor-in-Chief: Daniel Halpern. Estab. 1970. Small publisher. Publishes hardcover and paperback originals and reprints. Books: acid-free paper; offset printing; Smythe-sewn binding; occasional illustrations. Averages 25 total titles, 10 fiction titles each year. Average first novel print order 3,000 copies.

Needs: Literary and short story collections. "We can publish possibly one or two original novels a year." No science fiction, romantic novels, western (cowboy). Published: *The Assignation*, by Joyce Carol Oates (stories); *In the Music Library*, by Ellen Hunnicutt; *A Distant Episode*, by Paul Bowles.
How to Contact: Accepts unsolicited mss. Query first, especially on novels, with SASE. Photocopied submissions OK. Accepts computer printout submissions, prefers letter-quality. Reports in 2 to 3 months, depending on the season.
Terms: Pays in royalties. Advance is negotiable. Writer's guidelines for SASE. Book catalog free on request.
Advice: "We are always interested in first novels and feel it's important that they be brought to the attention of the reading public."

THE EIGHTH MT. PRESS (II), 624 SE 29th Ave., Portland OR 97214. (503)233-3936. Publisher: Ruth Gundle. Estab. 1984. One-person operation on full-time basis. Publishes paperback originals. Books: acid-free paper, perfect binding; average print order: 5,000. Averages 2 total titles, 1 fiction title, each year.
Needs: Ethnic, feminist, gay, lesbian, literary, short story collections. Published *Cows and Horses*, by Barbara Wilson (feminist/literary).
How to Contact: Accepts unsolicited mss. Query first. SASE. Reports on queries in 2 weeks; on mss in 3 weeks.
Terms: Pays royalties of 8% minimum; 10% maximum. Sends galleys to author. Publishes ms within 1 year of acceptance.

ESOTERICA PRESS (I, II, IV), Also publishes *Cuaderno: A Literary Journal*, Box 170, Barstow CA 92312-0170. Editor: Ms. Yoly Zentella. Estab. 1983. One-person operation on a part-time basis. Publishes paperback originals. Books: 50 lb white/neutral paper; offset printing; saddle stitch and perfect binding; black and white illustrations and photos; average print order: 200-300; first novel print order: 150-200. Plans more than 1 first novel this year. Averages 1-2 total titles each year. Sometimes comments on rejected ms.
Needs: Contemporary, ethnic (especially Chicano), historical, juvenile (5-9, including: historical), literary, short story collections, translations (Spanish-English/English-Spanish), young adult/teen (10-18 years, including: historical); women's issues. Recently published *Blood at the Root*, by Aisha Eshe (novella). Looking for "fiction, nonfiction based on Latino-American experience, Black-American, Arab-American, also humanist experience. No erotic, mystery, frivolity."
How to Contact: Accepts unsolicited mss with SASE and self addressed stamped postcard. Submit complete ms with cover letter. SASE (IRC) necessary for return of ms. Agented fiction 1%. Reports in 2-3 months on mss. Simultaneous and photocopied submissions OK. Accepts computer printout submissions.
Terms: Provides author's copies. Contract expenses paid first, then profits split between author/publisher. Sends pre-publication galleys to author. Publishes ms 6 months to 1 year after acceptance. Writer's guidelines and book catalog for #10 SAE and 1 first class stamp.

FABER AND FABER, INC. (I, II), 50 Cross St., Winchester MA 01890. Editor: Betsy Uhrig. Small trade house which publishes literary fiction and collections. Averages 5-10 total titles each year. Recently published *Life After Death and Other Stories*, by Susan Compo; *Summer of the White Peacock*, by Simon Burt; and *Holden's Performance*, by Murray Bail.
How to Contact: "Prefer query and one or two sample chapters with SASE for reply. Require synopsis/description—cannot consider ms without this. Many beginning writers make the mistake of submitting entire ms without even a cover letter."
Advice: Looking for "more fiction, more paperbacks due to increasing popularity/acceptance of paperback originals. Use a word processor if at all possible."

FASA CORPORATION (II, IV), 1026 West Van Buren, Chicago IL 60607. Editor: L. Ross Babcock III. "Company responsible for science fiction, adventure games, to include adventures, scenarios, game designs and novels, for an audience high school age and up." Published new writers within the last year.
Needs: Adventure, science fiction. Publishes ms an average of 9 months to 1 year after acceptance. Occasionally critiques or comments on rejected ms. Recommends other markets.
How to Contact: Query first. Reports in 2-6 weeks. Simultaneous and photocopied submissions OK. Accepts computer printout submissions. Accepts electronic submissions via IBM ASCII or MacIntosh disks.

Terms: Pays on publication for all rights. Sends galleys to author.
Advice: "Be familiar with our product and always ask about suitability before plunging into a big piece of work that I may not be able to use."

THE FEMINIST PRESS AT THE CITY UNIVERSITY OF NEW YORK, 311 East 94 St., New York NY 10128. (212)360-5790. Publisher: Florence Howe. Estab. 1970. "Nonprofit, tax-exempt, education organization interested in changing the curriculum, the classroom and consciousness." Publishes hardcover and paperback reprints. "We use a fine quality paper, perfect bind our books, four color covers; and some cloth for library sales if the book has been out of print for some time; we shoot from the original text when possible. We always include a scholarly and literary afterword, since we are introducing a text to a new audience; average print run: 4,000." Publishes no original fiction. Averages 12 total titles/year; 4-6 fiction titles/year (reprints of feminist classics only).
Needs: Contemporary, ethnic, experimental, feminist, gay, historical, lesbian, literary, regional, science fiction, short story collections, translations, women's.
How to Contact: Accepts unsolicited mss. Query first. Submit outline/synopsis and 1 sample chapter. SASE (IRC). Reports in 2 weeks on queries; 2 months on mss. Simultaneous and photocopied submissions OK. Accepts computer printout submissions.
Terms: Pays royalties of 10% of net sales; $100 advance; 10 author's copies. Sends galleys to author. Book catalog free on request.

‡FICTION COLLECTIVE TWO (II), c/o Department of English, Brooklyn College, Brooklyn NY 11210. Co-Directors: Ronald Sukenick and Curtis White. Estab. 1974. "The Fiction Collective has remained among the very few small presses devoted to the publication of quality fiction that is not considered in the commercial milieu of the large presses. We publish hardcover and paperback originals. We are looking for fiction that is radical in style, subject or tone." Publishes 6-8 books/year. Average first novel print order 2,000-2,500 copies.
Needs: Literary, innovative fiction. Recently published: *To Whom it May Concern*, by Raymond Federman; *Animal Acts*, stories by Cris Mazza; and *Trigger Dance*, Nilon-Award-winning collection of stories by Diane Glancy.
How to Contact: Query with SASE, brief synopsis and 2-3 stories or chapters. Photocopied submissions OK. Simultaneous submissions OK, except for the Nilon Award. (See information in Contests and Awards section. Reports in 2 months on queries, 9 months on mss. Send queries to Fiction Collective, Publications Center, Campus Box 494, University of Colorado, Boulder, Colorado 80309-0494.
Terms: Pays 10% royalties plus 35 copies of the book (upon publication). "The Collective is a nonprofit writers' cooperative. Some books are published with assistance from NEA and NYSCA. If a manuscript is accepted for publication, then the author shares in editorial decisions." No advance. Free book catalog available by writing to *Brooklyn* office.
Advice: "Now in its 16th year of successful operation, the Collective has entered a new stage. We are sounding the commercial possibilities of the expanding audience for quality innovative fiction we have helped to create. We have restructured our organization to compete more effectively in the marketplace. Replacing the diffuse authority of our more than forty author/members, the Collective has voted to concentrate decision-making in a smaller business and editorial group. To reflect this restructuring, the organization has been renamed Fiction Collective Two. The Collective will continue its established editorial policy—to publish books of high quality whose style, subject, or tone challenges the limits of quality publishing."

FIREBRAND BOOKS (II), 141 The Commons, Ithaca NY 14850. (607)272-0000. Contact: Nancy K. Bereano. Estab. 1985. Publishes quality trade paperback originals. Averages 8-10 total titles each year.
Needs: Feminist, lesbian. Recently published *Eye of A Hurricane* by Ruthann Robson (short stories); *Scuttlebutt*, by Jana Williams (novel).
How to Contact: Accepts unsolicited mss. Submit outline/synopsis and sample chapters or send complete ms with cover letter. SASE. Reports in 2 weeks on queries; 2 months on mss. Simultaneous and photocopied submissions OK with notification. Accepts computer printouts.
Terms: Pays royalties.

‡1st AMENDMENT PUBLISHERS INC. (IV), Suite H-3, 1505 Llano St., Santa Fe NM 87501. (505)988-4838. Editor: Allen A. Nysse. Fiction Editor: Dawn-Marie Peterson. Estab. 1989. New mid-size independent publisher with plans to expand. Publishes hardcover and paperback originals and paperback reprints. Books: 50 lb. Lakewood, 444PPI paper; belt press printing; adhesive case binding w/Kivar 5 cloth cover, .085 board, head and footbands; b&w illustrations; average print order: 3,000; first novel print order: 3,000. Published new writers within the last year. Plans 1 first novel this year. Averages 3 total titles, 2 fiction titles per year. Sometimes comments on rejected manuscripts.

Needs: Historical, literary, mainstream, military/war. Looking for novels that "encourage the reader to think about moral, social and philosophical problems; those that point out evils in society and challenge the reader to seek social and /or political reforms. Does not want to see "anything negative or with degenerating moral tendency, and all self-serving fiction." Recently published *America Within*, by Allen Nysse (psychological novel).

How to Contact: Accepts unsolicited manuscripts. Query first, then send outline/synopsis and 3 sample chapters. SASE. Reports in 6 weeks on queries; 3 months on mss. Accepts simultaneous and photocopied submissions.

Terms: Pays royalties of 2% minimum; 10% maximum; 100 contributor's copies. Publishes manuscripts 6-18 months after acceptance.

FOUR WALLS EIGHT WINDOWS, Box 548, Village Station, New York NY 10014. (212)226-4998. Co-Publishers: John Oakes/Dan Simon. Estab. 1986. "We are a small independent publisher." Publishes hardcover and paperback originals and paperback reprints. Books: quality paper; paper or cloth binding; illustrations sometimes; average print order: 3,000-5,000; first novel print order: 3,000-5,000. Averages 12 total titles/year; approximately 4-6 fiction titles/year.

Needs: Contemporary, experimental, literary, short story collections, translations. Recently published *Forgiveness: Contemporary Short Stories from Ireland*, edited by Augustine Martin; *A Stone of the Heart*, by Tom Grimes; and *Three Goat Songs*, by Michael Brodsky.

How to Contact: "Query letter accompanied by sample chapter and SASE is best. Useful to know if writer has published elsewhere, and if so, where." Accepts unsolicited mss. Submit outline/synopsis and 1 sample chapter. SASE (IRC). 30% of fiction is agented. Reports in 2 months on mss. Simultaneous and photocopied submissions OK. Accepts computer printout submissions.

Terms: Pays standard royalties; advance varies. Sends galleys to author. Book catalog free on request.

‡FROG IN THE WELL (I, II, IV), Box 170052, San Francisco CA 94117. (415)431-2113. Fiction Editor: Susan Hester. Estab. 1980. One-woman operation. Publishes paperback originals. Books: 50 lb off-white paper; web/offset printing; perfect binding; illustrations; average print order: 2,500; first novel print run: 2,500. Averages 2-3 total titles, 1-3 fiction titles each year. Occasionally critiques rejected mss.

Needs: Feminist, lesbian, regional, short story collections (about women), and women's. Recently published *The Honesty Tree*, by Carole Spearon McCauley; *For Nights Like This One*, by Becky Birtha; *The New Women's Broken Heart*, by Andrea Dworkin.

How to Contact: Submit outline/synopsis and 3 sample chapters with SASE. Simultaneous (if noted) and photocopied submissions OK. Accepts computer printout submissions. Reports in 2-3 months on mss.

Terms: Pays in royalties (varies); 12 author's copies. Sends galleys to author. Free book catalog on request.

Advice: "Write well—write from personal experience. Develop your own style. We like to publish first novels by serious writers. We consider our publishing house a place for writers to publish works which may not be placed elsewhere. We regard the author/editor relationship as very important. Go out and meet people in the book world, and do readings/events. Get known in your community—build a following."

‡FROMM INTERNATIONAL PUBLISHING CORPORATION (III), 560 Lexington Ave., New York NY 10022. (212)308-4010. Editorial Contact Person: Thomas Thornton, Managing Editor. Estab. 1981. "Small independent publisher of quality fiction, cultural history and history." Publishes hardcover originals and paperback reprints. Books: acid-free paper; burst-hardcover, 1-piece cloth binding; illustrations; average print order: 5,000; first novel print order: 4,000. Averages 10 total titles; 3-4 fiction titles each year. Usually comments on rejected ms.

Needs: Contemporary, faction, historical, literary, short story collections, translations. Recently published *Farewell Sidonia*, by Erich Hackl (literary); *Laura's Skin*, by J.F. Federspiel (literary); and *The Couple*, by Thomas Huerlimann (literary).

How to Contact: Query first, then submit outline/synopsis and sample chapters. SASE. Agented fiction 80%. Reports on queries in 6 weeks; on mss in 3 months. Photocopied submissions OK. Accepts computer printout submissions.

Close-up

John Oakes
Co-publisher
Four Walls Eight Windows

John Oakes, co-publisher of Four Walls Eight Windows, wasn't very happy working for major trade publishers. "I had a tiny room with a door—I'm sure it was illegal. It was like an oversized coffin with flourescent lighting," he says. He felt the environment was hierarchical, formal and business-like, and this frustrated him too. "Life is short and I don't believe in reincarnation," he says. "This is the only chance you get. I don't have time to worry about things like whether I'm going to wear a tie or office politics—all of those silly things. And going out to lunch with agents—I didn't want to do that." Yet what bothered him most was the way projects he was most excited about fell by the wayside because he couldn't convince his employers to approve them.

In 1986 Oakes met Dan Simon, who was equally unhappy with his job in commercial publishing and, like Oakes, felt he could do a better job on his own if given the chance. "We both found a kindred spirit," Oakes says. "What we immediately connected on was that we are both very interested in progressive politics of the left and the arts and literature. Generally, people tend to separate the two; both Dan and I feel they are very closely integrated and that it's a mistake to examine one without the other. I think that's reflected in all of our books—from the health books to the art books to the novels."

After planning for a year and pooling together $20,000 in savings, they presented their first books in the fall of 1987. Since then they have raised more than $100,000 from individual investors and have published an eclectic selection of 35 books which include: *The Best of Abbie Hoffman*, with an introduction by Norman Mailer; *Where is Home?*, a first-person account of life in a foster-care home, by E.P. Jones; Andrei Codrescu's anthology *Up Late: American Poetry Since 1970*; a few of Nelson Algren's works including *The Man with the Golden Arm*; and three novels by Michael Brodsky.

Their list has doubled, and there are now 18 books planned for 1991. For these it seems the co-publishers and the rest of the staff (two associate editors) will continue to commit themselves thoroughly to each project. If a book has been approved, it is because either Oakes or Simon is truly taken with and impassioned by it. Oakes says the advances are serious and competitive with other houses, he and Simon oversee all editorial and production, have print runs of 10,000, and keep the books in print.

"The packaging" (he hates to use that word) of the books also conveys the degree of care that goes into each. "I mean we promote them aggressively and that involves how we present the books," Oakes says. They employ a crew of professional freelance designers so the covers, for example, hint at the budget of a large corporate publisher rather than that of a small independent one, whose biggest problem (especially now that it has turned down a National Endowment for the Arts grant because of its stipulations) is lack of money. Their aim is to publish what they think people ought to be reading, and "few people," Oakes says, "want to pick up a book if it looks like you're part of some crazy, kooky minority. The only way to succeed is to present yourself as extraordinary but not something on the fringe."

In discussing some of their books, Oakes offers insight into what Four Walls Eight Windows seeks in a writer: a social critic, a voice for those who cannot speak for themselves, a defender of integrity, and an original thinker. "It's only worth hearing what someone has to say if it's going to shake people up," Oakes says, "if it's something different." He mentions *Where is Home?* as an example of articulation from the disenfranchised; he speaks of Michael Brodsky as "one who has enormous integrity and originality

John Oakes and Dan Simon

and has stuck to his path and made no compromises. I really believe when the history of 20th century literature is written, he's going to be the Herman Melville of this period." (Brodsky, he adds, was one of the writers he couldn't get his previous employers to publish.)

He mentions Tom Grime's *A Stone of the Heart* and the upcoming *Fire and Rain*, by Oswald Riviera, ("an amazing, very upsetting book about his experience in Vietnam") as books by first-time novelists. Oakes likes to publish such previously unpublished writers and says 60 to 70 percent of the books they put out originate as unsolicited manuscripts from writers and agents. Because he likes to be in direct contact and develop a personal relationship with his writers, he says he is not a big fan of agents. He receives about 1,000 unsolicited submissions a year. Of those he says, "maybe 300 are intriguing, of that maybe 100 are seriously intriguing, and of that we probably take about 20." Of the remaining 30 to 40 percent of the books published, some are actively sought by Oakes and Simon, and some are recommended by editors in other houses. On this Oakes muses, "The things that make people accept or reject books are very mysterious. It can be just that you have a headache and you don't want to look at this book today. You think, I just can't deal with this; get it off my desk. I mean this is sometimes all it amounts to. In trade publishing you're operating within such fuzzy parameters."

For those interested in submitting to Four Walls Eight Windows, it would be advantageous not to call, but to contact with a crisp query before sending anything else, to be familiar with Four Walls Eight Windows' list and to mention this in specific terms in the query. It would be to the writer's disadvantage, Oakes says, "if out of the context of the book, there is racism, sexism or jabs at the left wing. Beyond that," he says, "I'm open; I'm curious; I want to see what people come up with that's interesting and different. I would keep reading even if I thought the plot was a little shaky, if I thought, for example, the person was representing an alternative voice. That deserves a little extra attention."

— Lauri Miller

Terms: Pays negotiable royalties; advance is more for agented ms. Sends galleys to author. Publishes ms 9 months after acceptance. Writer's guidelines not available. Book catalog free on request.

GAY SUNSHINE PRESS AND LEYLAND PUBLICATIONS (IV), Box 40397, San Francisco CA 94140. (415)824-3184. Editor: Winston Leyland. Estab. 1970. Publishes hardcover and paperback originals. Books: natural paper; perfect bound binding; illustrations; average print order: 5,000-10,000.
Needs: Literary, experimental and translations—all gay material only. "We desire fiction on gay themes of *high* literary quality and prefer writers who have already had work published in literary magazines. We also publish erotica—short stories and novels." Recently published *Crystal Boys*, by Pai Hsien-yung (novel).
How to Contact: "Do not send an unsolicited manuscript." Query letter with SASE. Reports in 3 weeks on queries, 2 months on mss.
Terms: Negotiates terms with author. Sends galleys to author. Royalties or outright purchase.
Advice: "We continue to be interested in receiving queries from authors who have manuscripts of high literary quality. We feel it is important that an author know exactly what to expect from our press (promotion, distribution etc.) before a contract is signed. Before submitting a query or manuscript to a particular press, obtain critical feedback from knowledgeable people on your manuscript, e.g. a friend who teaches college English. If you alienate a publisher by submitting a manuscript shoddily prepared/typed, or one needing very extensive re-writing, you will surely not get a second chance with that press."

GOOSE LANE EDITIONS (I, II), 248 Brunswick St., Fredericton, New Brunswick E3B 1G9 Canada. (506)450-4251. Managing Editor: Susanne Alexander. Estab. 1957. Publishes hardcover and paperback originals and occasional reprints. Books: illustrations sometimes, average print run: 2,000; first novel print order: 1,500. Averages 12 total titles, 2-4 fiction, each year. Sometimes critiques rejected mss.
Needs: Contemporary, historical, literary, short story collections. "Not suitable for mainstream or mass-market submissions." Published *A View from the Roof*, by Helen Weinzweig (collected stories); *The Americans are Coming*, by Herb Curtis (first novel); *The Elephant Talks to God*, by Dale Estey, (stories).
How to Contact: Accepts unsolicited mss; complete work, no "samples." Query first. SASE. Reports in 8-10 weeks. Simultaneous and photocopied submissions OK. Accepts computer printout submissions.
Terms: *"Only mss from Canada considered at this time."* Pays royalties of 8% minimum; 12% maximum. Average advance: $100-200, negotiable. Sends galleys to author. Writers guidelines for 9x12 SASE and IRCs.

GRAYWOLF PRESS (III), 2402 University Ave., St. Paul MN 55114. (612)641-0077. Publisher: Randolph Jennings. Estab. 1974. Growing small press, nonprofit corporation. Publishes hardcover and paperback originals and paperback reprints. Books: acid-free quality paper; offset printing; hardcover and soft binding; illustrations occasionally; average print order: 3,000-10,000; first novel print order: 2,000-3,000. Averages 12-16 total titles, 6-8 fiction titles each year. Occasionally critiques rejected ms.
Needs: Literary, and short story collections. Published *Skywater*, by Melinda Worth Popham; *A Farm Under a Lake*, by Martha Bergland; and *A Gravestone Made of Wheat*, by Will Weaver.
How to Contact: Query with SASE. Reports in 2 weeks. Simultaneous and photocopied submissions OK.
Terms: Pays in royalties of 7½% minimum, 10% maximum; negotiates advance and number of author's copies. Sends galleys to author. Writer's guidelines for SASE. Free book catalog.

‡GREEN TIGER PRESS (II), 435 E. Carmel St., San Marcos CA 92069-4362. Contact: Editorial Committee. Estab. 1971. Publishes picture books, note cards and calendars. Published new writers within the last year. Buys 10% agented fiction. Averages 10-12 titles/year.
Needs: Specific interest in imaginative, short fiction for children which lends itself to illustration. Seeking manuscripts with "romantic, mythic or visionary qualities where fantasy and reality co-exist.We welcome nostalgia and 'the world of the child' themes. No science fiction. We are a visually-oriented house and want mss whose text readily conjures up a world of images full of magic and delight." Recently published *Shell of Wonder*, by Mary Belle Harwich and John Williams Hay.
How to Contact: Submit complete ms with SASE, or submit through agent. Simultaneous and photocopied submissions OK—do not sent original art. Reports in 6-8 months on mss. Publishes ms 12-18 months after acceptance.
Terms: Payment on royalty basis.

‡GRIFFON HOUSE PUBLICATIONS, Box 81, Whitestone NY 11357. (212)767-8380. President: Frank D. Grande. Estab. 1976. Small press. Publishes paperback originals and reprints.
Needs: Contemporary, literary, experimental, ethnic (open), translations, reprints, and multinational theory.
How to Contact: Query with SASE. No simultaneous submissions; photocopied submissions OK. Accepts computer printout submissions. Reports in 1 month on queries, 6 weeks on mss.
Terms: Pays in 6 free author's copies. No advance.

GUERNICA EDITIONS (III, IV), 3160 Avenue de Carignan, Montréal, Québec H1N 2Y5 Canada. Editor: Antonio D'Alfonso. Fiction Editor: Umberto Claudio. Estab. 1978. Publishes paperback originals. Books: offset printing; perfect/sewn binding; average print order: 1,000; average first novel print order: 1,000. Plans to publish 1 first novel this year. Publishes 8-10 total titles each year.
Needs: Contemporary, ethnic, literary. Looking for novels about women and ethnic subjects. No unsolicited works. Recently published *Toni* by Fiorella De Luca Calce; *The Sandwoman*, by Madeleine Ovellette-Michalska.
How to Contact: Does not accept or return unsolicited mss. Query first. IRC. 100% of fiction is agented. Reports in 6 months. Photocopied submissions OK. Accepts computer printout submissions. Electronic submissions via IBM WordPerfect disks.
Terms: Pays royalty of 10% and 10 author's copies. Book catalog for SAE and $1 postage. (Canadian stamps only).
Advice: Publishing "more pocket books."

*MAX HARDY—PUBLISHER (IV), Box 28219, Las Vegas NV 89126-2219. (702)368-0379. Contact: Max Hardy. Estab. 1976. Publishes paperback originals. Books: offset printing; perfect binding; illustrations; average print order: 2-3,000; first novel print order: 3,000. Averages 6 total titles each year. Occasionally critiques rejected ms.
Needs: Publishes fiction on bridge only. Published *The Mexican Contract*: by Allan De Serpa (novel); and *Everything's Jake with Me*, by Don Von Elsner (anthology).
How to Contact: Accepts unsolicited mss. Submit complete ms. Simultaneous and photocopied submissions OK.
Terms: Pays in royalties of 10% maximum. "Author pays all expenses; receives 80% of all returns until he recovers 150%—then revert to royalties." Free book catalog.
Advice: "We encourage first novelists. Of our 30+ titles we have 5 novels and 2 anthologies. We consider fiction on bridge only."

*HAYPENNY PRESS (I), 211 New St., West Paterson NJ 07424. Estab. 1988. "Small independent publisher with plans to expand." Publishes paperback originals. Books: offset and/or mimeo printing; perfect binding. Published new writers within the last year. Plans 2-4 first novels this year. Averages 2-3 titles (all fiction). Sometimes comments on rejected ms. "No charge for comments . . . *for detailed (separate) critique: $25 (for ms under 200 pages.)*"
Needs: Contemporary, ethnic, experimental, fantasy, humor/satire, literary, mainstream, military/war, regional, science fiction, short story collections, young adult/teen (10-18 years) easy-to-read and problem novels. No horror, pornography or formula stories. Published *Cooper Street*, by P.D. Jordan (Y/A).
How to Contact: Does not accept unsolicited mss. Query first (always!!). Include SASE. Reports in 2 weeks on queries; 1 month on ms. Photocopied submissions OK. Accepts computer printout submissions.
Terms: Pays by "individual arrangement. Cooperative situations possible." Sends galleys to author. Publishes ms up to 1 year after acceptance. Writer's guidelines for #10 SASE and 1 first class stamp.
Advice: "Prefer to work with authors who have a specific purpose/market/audience (ie: counselors at runaway shelters; teachers of literacy programs; etc.). The competition in 'general' markets is fierce and authors are expected to do all they can to help promote their work. We are open to suggestions/arrangements, if the work merits publication. Y/A writers: project something useful to your teen audience without being 'preachy.' Others: offbeat, unusual is fine . . . main criteria is to be good/original enough to stand out . . . Please no five-step plots or outlines."

*HERITAGE PRESS (II, IV), Box 18625, Baltimore MD 21216. (301)383-9330. President: Wilbert L. Walker. Estab. 1979. One-man operation, full-time basis; uses contractual staff as needed. Publishes hardcover originals. Books: 60 lb white offset paper; offset printing; sewn hardcover binding; average print order: 2,000; first novel print order: 1,000. Averages 2 total titles, 1-2 fiction titles each year.

Needs: Ethnic (black). Interested in "fiction that presents a balanced portrayal of the black experience in America, from the black perspective. No fiction not dealing with blacks, or which views blacks as inferior." Published *Stalemate at Panmunjon* (the Korean War), and *Servants of All*, by Wilbert L. Walker.
How to Contact: Does not accept unsolicited mss. Query first with SASE. Simultaneous and photocopied submissions OK. Reports in 2 weeks on queries, 2 months on mss. Publishes ms an average of 9 months after acceptance.
Terms: Must return advance if book is not completed or is unacceptable. *"We plan to subsidy publish only those works that meet our standards for approval.* No more than 1 or 2 a year. Payment for publication is based on individual arrangement with author." Book catalog free on request.
Advice: "Write what you know about. No one else can know and feel what it is like to be black in America better than one who has experienced our dichotomy on race." Would like to see new ideas with broad appeal. "First novels must contain previously unexplored areas on the black experience in America. We regard the author/editor relationship as open, one of mutual respect. Editor has final decision, but listens to author's views."

HERMES HOUSE PRESS (II), 39 Adare Place, Northampton MA 01060. (413)584-8402. Imprints include translations. Publisher: Richard Mandell. Estab. 1980. Small press, few-person operation. Publishes paperback originals and reprints. Books: 70 lb paper; offset printing; paper binding; illustrations; average print order: 1,000; first novel print order: 1,000. Plans 1-2 first novels this year. Averages 2 total titles, 1-2 fiction titles each year. Generally critiques rejected mss.
Needs: Contemporary, experimental, feminist, literary, short story collections, novellas and translations. No sexist, erotica, horror. Recently published *Three Stories*, by R.V. Cassill (short stories), *The Deadly Swarm & Other Stories*, by LaVerne Harrell Clark and *Bella B's Fantasy and Other Stories*, by Raymond Jean.
How to Contact: Not currently reading manuscripts. Reports in 3 weeks on queries; 2 months on mss. Photocopied submissions OK. Accepts computer printout submissions. Prefers letter-quality. Publishes ms within 1 year after acceptance.
Terms: Pays in author's copies plus percentage above costs. Sends galleys to author.
Advice: Encourages first novelists. "We regard the author/editor relationship as open communication/free dialogue. Be persistent."

*HOMESTEAD PUBLISHING (I, II), Box 227, Moose WY 83012. (406)538-8960. Editor: Carl Schreier. Estab. 1980. Regional publishers for the Rocky Mountains, midsize firm. Publishes hardcover and paperback originals and reprints. Books: natural stock to enamel paper; web, sheet-feed printing; perfect or smythe-sewn binding; b&w or 4-6 color illustrations; average print order: 10,000; first novel print order: 2,000-5,000. Plans 1-2 first novels this year. Averages 8-10 total titles; 1-2 fiction each year. Sometimes critiques rejected mss.
Needs: Historical, juvenile (wildlife, historical), literary, preschool/picture book, short story collection, western, young adult/teen (10-18 years, historical). Looking for "good quality, well written and contemporary" fiction. Published *The Great Plains: A Young Reader's Journal*, by Bullock (children's natural history-adventure).
How to Contact: Accepts unsolicited mss. Query first. SASE. Reports in 1 month. Sends galleys to author. Simultaneous and photocopied submissions OK. Accepts computer printout submissions.
Terms: Pays royalties of 6% minimum; 10% maximum. Provides 6 author's copies. Subsidy publishes "occasionally, depending on project."

HYPERION PRESS LIMITED, 300 Wales Ave., Winnipeg Manitoba R2M 2S9 Canada. President: Dr. Marvis Tutiah. Estab. 1977. "Well established small publisher with international distribution." Publishes hardcover and paperback originals. Published new writers within the last year. Plans 1 first novel this year. Averages 11 total titles, 4 fiction titles each year.
Needs: Young adult/teen (10-18 years) historical and spy/adventure. "We need adventure stories for young people." Published *The Mysterious Disk*, by Jim Prentice (juvenile adventure); *Sunken Treasure*, by Jim Prentice (juvenile adventure); *The Time Before Dreams*, by Stefan Czernecki and Timothy Rhodes (juvenile tale).
How to Contact: Accepts unsolicited mss. Submit outline/synopsis and sample 3 chapters. SASE. Reports in 1 month on queries; 3 months on mss.
Terms: Pays royalties. Sends galleys to author. Publishes ms 1-2 years after acceptance. Writer's guidelines for 9×4 SAE and 38¢ Canadian or IRC. Book catalog for 9×12 SAE and 76¢ Canadian or IRC.

INDEPENDENCE PUBLISHERS INC. (I, II), Box 29905, Atlanta GA 30359. (404)636-7092. Editorial Director: Stanley Beitler. Estab. 1987. Small press. Publishes hardcover originals. Books: offset, sheet-fed printing; case binding; halftone, line illustrations and drawings; first novel print order: 4,500. Published new writers within the last year. Rarely critiques rejected ms.
Needs: Contemporary, experimental, historical, humor/satire, literary, mainstream, regional, short story collections and translations. Looks for "novels that present the social scene." No horror. Published *Appalachian Patterns*, by Bo Ball (short-story collection).
How to Contact: Accepts unsolicited mss. Submit complete ms with cover letter. SASE (IRC) necessary for return of ms. Reports in 2 weeks on queries; 1 month on mss.
Terms: Pays royalties and author's copies.

INTERTEXT (III), 2633 E. 17th Ave., Anchorage AK 99508. Editor: Sharon Ann Jaeger. Estab. 1982. Independent publisher. Publishes hardcover and paperback originals. Books: pH-neutral paper; offset printing; smythe-sewn and perfect bound binding; illustrations sometimes; occasionally do 4-color covers; average print order: 1,000; first novel print order: 1,000. "We publish writers of excellence and accomplishment only." Averages 1-3 titles each year. No longer able to critique rejected mss. No longer takes on first-timers.
Needs: Literary, short story collections and translations. "We are presently concentrating on poetry, translations and literary criticism, together with selected (and solicited) titles in the fine arts."
How to Contact: Query by first-class mail with sample chapter and SASE. Do not send unsolicited complete mss. Reports in 2 months on queries; 6 months on mss. Simultaneous queries and photocopied submissions OK.
Terms: Pays 10% royalties after all costs of printing, promotion and distribution are met. Sends galleys to author. Writer's guidelines for SASE.
Advice: "A novel has to be very extraordinary indeed — truly compelling, with exquisite craftsmanship and a powerful and poetic style — for us to consider it. Get a variety of experience. Learn about people. Don't be (or at least sound) self-centered. Revise, revise, revise. We are not a market for the beginning writer, but would recommend to new writers to revise ruthlessly, to cut all unnecessary exposition — to make things *happen*, more 'show' than 'tell.'"

INVERTED-A, INC. (II), 401 Forrest Hill, Grand Prairie TX 75051. (214)264-0066. Editors: Amnon or Aya Katz. Estab. 1977. A small press which evolved from publishing technical manuals for other products. "Publishing is a small part of our business." Publishes paperback originals. Books: bond paper; offset printing; illustrations; average print order: 250; first novel print order: 250. Publishes 2 titles a year, in recent years mostly poetry, fiction is now about every other year. Also publishes a periodical *Inverted-A, Horn*, which appears irregularly and is open to very short fiction as well as excerpts from unpublished longer fiction. Comments on rejected mss.
Needs: "We are interested in justice and freedom approached from a positive and romantic perspective." Published *The Few Who Count*, by Aya Katz (novel); *Damned in Hell*, by A.A. Wilson (novella); *Inverted Blake* (collection); and *Inverted Blake #2* (collection).
How to Contact: Submit query with sample. SASE. Reports in 6 weeks on queries; 3 months on mss. Simultaneous and photocopied submissions OK. Accepts computer printouts. Accepts electronic submissions via modem or ASCII file on a PC MSDOS diskette. Electronic submission mandatory for final ms of accepted longer work.
Terms: We do not pay except for author copies. Sends galleys to author. For current list send SAE and 1 first class stamp.
Advice: "Deal with more than personal problems. Project hope."

ISLAND HOUSE (IV), 731 Treat Ave., San Francisco CA 94110. (415)826-7113. Imprints include Cottage Books. Senior Editor: Susan Sullivan. Fiction Editor: Pat Healy. Estab. 1987. "Small Press, four person, full time." Publishes paperback originals. Books: acid free paper; offset printing; perfect binding; average print order: 2-3,000. Published new writers within the last year. Averages 3 total titles, 2 fiction titles each year. Sometimes comments on rejected ms; *$75 charge for critiques*.
Needs: Ethnic, experimental, faction, literary and short story collections. Looking for Irish-Celtic themes and quality. Recently published *The West*, by Ed Stack (short stories).
How to Contact: No unsolicited mss. Query first. Agented fiction 50%. Reports in 2 weeks on queries; 3 months on mss. Simultaneous and photocopied submissions OK. Accepts computer printout submissions.
Terms: Pays royalties of 6% minimum; 10% maximum; offers negotiable advance. Sends galleys to author. Publishes ms 6-9 months after acceptance. Book catalog free.

ITALICA PRESS (IV), 595 Main St., #605, New York NY 10044. (212)935-4230. Publishers: Eileen Gardiner and Ronald G. Musto. Estab. 1985. Small independent publisher. Publishes paperback originals. Books: 50-60 lb natural paper; offset printing; smythe-sewn binding; illustrations; average print order: 1,000. "First time translators published. We would like to see translations of well-known Italian writers in Italy who are not yet translated for an American audience." Publishes 6 total titles each year; 2 fiction titles. Sometimes critiques rejected mss.
Needs: Translations from Italian. Looking for "4 novels over next two years—particularly translations of 20th Century Italian literature." Published *Woman at War,* by Dacia Maraini and *New Italian Women,* edited by Martha King (short story collection).
How to Contact: Accepts unsolicited mss. Query first. Reports in 3 weeks on queries; 2 months on mss. Simultaneous and photocopied submissions OK. Accepts computer printout submissions. Electronic submissions via Macintosh or IBM-PC disk.
Terms: Pays in royalties of 5-15% and 10 author's copies. Sends pre-publication galleys to author. Book catalog free on request.

JAYELL ENTERPRISES (IV), Box 2616, Dearborn MI 48124. (313)565-9687. President: James L. Limbacher. Estab. 1983. One-person operation on a part-time basis; also produces TV cable programs. Publishes paperback originals. Books: average print order: 500. Averages 1 fiction title each year. Sometimes comments on rejected mss; *$50 charge for critiques.*
Needs: Historical. No "badly written, amateurish works."
How to Contact: Does not accept unsolicited mss. Query first. Reports in 3 weeks on queries; in 1 month on mss. Photocopied submissions OK. Accepts computer printout submissions.
Terms: Pays royalties of 25% minimum. Provides 6 author's copies. Sends galleys to author.
Advice: Publishing "less fiction. Nonfiction sells better."

‡JESPERSON PRESS LTD. (I), 39 James Lane, St. John's, Newfoundland A1E 3H3 Canada. (709)753-0633. Trade Editor: Keith Pittman. Midsize independent publisher. Publishes hardcover and paperback originals. Published new writers within the last year. Averages 7-10 total titles, 1-2 fiction titles each year. Sometimes comments on rejected ms.
Needs: Adventure, fantasy, humor/satire, juvenile (5-9 yrs.) including: animal easy-to-read, fantasy, historical, sports, spy/adventure and contemporary. Recently published *Black Light,* by Ishmael Baksh (first novel).
How to Contact: Accepts unsolicited mss. Submit complete manuscript with cover letter. SASE. Reports in 3 months on mss. Photocopied submissions OK.
Terms: Pays negotiable royalties. Sends galleys to author. Book catalog free.

KAR-BEN COPIES, INC. (II), 6800 Tildenwood La., Rockville MD 20852. (301)984-8733. President: Judye Groner. Estab. 1974. Small publisher specializing in juvenile Judaica. Publishes hardcover and paperback originals. Books: 70-80 lb patina paper; offset printing; perfect and case binding; 2-4 color illustrations; average print order: 5,000-10,000. Averages 8-10 total titles, 6-8 fiction titles each year. Published new writers within the last year.
Needs: Juvenile (3-10 years). Recently published *Grandma's Soup,* by Nancy Karkowsky; *Mommy Never Went to Hebrew School,* by Mindy Portnoy; *Alef is One,* by Katherine Kahn.
How to Contact: Accepts unsolicited mss. SASE. Submit outline/synopsis and sample chapters or complete ms with cover letter. SASE. Reports in 1 week on queries; 1 month on mss. Simultaneous and photocopied submissions OK. Accepts computer printouts.
Terms: Pays in royalties of 5% minimum; 10% maximum; average advance: $1,000; 12 author's copies. Sends galleys to author. Writer's guidelines free for SASE. Book catalog free on request.

KITCHEN TABLE: WOMEN OF COLOR PRESS (II, IV), Box 908, Latham NY 12110. Publisher: Barbara Smith. Estab. 1981. "Independent press with several paid employees, very good distribution." Publishes paperback originals. Books: 50 lb stock paper; offset/web press printing; perfect binding; some b&w graphic elements/designs; average print order: 5,000; first novel print order: 3,000. "All of our books are trade paperbacks, a few of which are bound for libraries." Averages 2 total titles each year; 1 fiction title every two years. Occasionally critiques rejected ms.
Needs: Ethnic, feminist, lesbian, literary, short story collections. Needs for novels include novels by women of color—authors that reflect in some way the experiences of women of color. "We are looking for high quality, politically conscious writing and would particularly like to hear from American Indian women fiction writers." Has published *Cuentos: Stories by Latinas,* edited by Alma Gómez, Cherrie Moraga; Mariana Romo-Carmona (short story anthology with selections in both English and Spanish).

How to Contact: Accepts unsolicited mss. Query first. Submit outline/synopsis and 3 sample chapters. SASE. Reports in 1 month on queries; 6 months on mss. Simultaneous and photocopied submissions OK.

Terms: Pays in royalties of 8% minimum; 10% maximum and 10 author's copies. Sends galleys to author. Book catalog for 2 first class stamps.

Advice: "One of the most common mistakes that our press tries to address is the notion that the first work a writer publishes should be a book as opposed to a submission to a periodical. Periodicals serve as a very valuable apprenticeship for a beginning writer. They should submit work to appropriate literary and other kinds of journals that publish fiction. By appropriate I mean appropriate for the kind of writing they do. Getting published in periodicals gives the writer experience and also creates a 'track record' that may interest the prospective book publisher."

KNIGHTS PRESS (II, IV), P.O. Box 6737, Stamford CT 06901. (203)969-1699. Publisher: Elizabeth G. Gershman. Estab. 1983. Small press publishing only gay male fiction and non-fiction. Publishes trade paperback originals. Published new writers in the last year. Plans 4 first novels this year. Averages 12 total titles each year.

Needs: "Fiction must have a gay theme (not lesbian or non-gay). We publish on merit, not category." No erotica. Recently published *Boys In the Bars*, by Christopher Davis; *Some Dance to Remember*, by Jack Fritscher; and *Families*, by David Watmaugh.

How to Contact: Accepts unsolicited mss. Query first. SASE. Agented fiction: 50%. Reports in 3 weeks on queries; 3 months on mss. No simultaneous submissions. Photocopied submissions OK. Accepts computer printouts.

Terms: Pays in royalties of 10% minimum; average advance: $500. Sends galleys to author. Writer's guidelines free for #10 SASE and 1 first class stamp. Book catalog free on request, with #10 envelope, SAE, 25¢ stamp.

Advice: "Write about people, places, events you know. Then plot, plot, plot. Story must have a positive gay lifestyle or relationship. Consider that a book costs money to buy and to produce. Would *you* spend your money to read your submission? Would you spend thousands of dollars to produce it? If you wouldn't, neither would the book buyer or the publisher."

KRUZA KALEIDOSCOPIX, INC. (IV), Box 389, Franklin MA 02038. (508)528-6211. Editor/President: J.A. Kruza. Fiction Editor: R. Burbank. Estab. 1976. Publishes hardcover and paperback originals. Books: 60-80 lb coated paper; offset printing; saddle and perfect binding; illustrations; average print order: 10,000. Averages 12 total titles each year. Sometimes critiques rejected mss.

Needs: Historical (nautical); juvenile (5-9 yrs.) including: animal, lesson teachings about work ethic, historical. "Stories for children, ages 3-7, with problem and characters who work out solution to problem, i.e. work ethic."

How to Contact: Accepts and returns unsolicited mss. Submit complete ms with cover letter. SASE. Reports in 3 weeks on queries; 3 months on mss. Simultaneous and photocopied submissions OK. Accepts computer printout submissions; avoid dot-matrix if possible.

Terms: *Charges $3 reading fee.* Pays in royalties of 3% minimum; 5% maximum, "or flat fee, depending on strength of story. Length of royalties are usually limited to a specific time, usually 4 to 7 years." Provides 10 author's copies. Writer's guidelines for #10 SAE with 1 first class stamp.

KUBICEK & ASSOCIATES (I,II), Suite 202C, 3701 O St., Box 30269, Lincoln NB 68503-0269. (402)435-4607. President: David Kubicek. Estab. 1988. "We're a small company (3 people) with ambitious plans for expansion over the next few years." Publishes paperback originals. Books: normally 60 lb paper; photo offset printing; usually perfect binding; illustrations (depending on book); average print order: 1,000; first novel print order: 1,000 "unless it's an exceptional novel." Published new writers within the last year. Plans 1 first novel by previously unpublished writers this year. Plans 5 total titles, 3 fiction titles this year. Sometimes critiques rejected mss.

Needs: Fantasy, horror, psychic/supernatural/occult, regional (midwest), science fiction. No romance (the genre—we like to see some romance in our books, when it's done intelligently), pornography, sword and sorcery. Published *The Pelican in the Desert: And Other Stories of the Family Farm*, edited by David Kubicek (anthology of short stories); and *October Dreams*, edited by David Kubicek and Jeff Mason (anthology of horror/supernatural stories).

How to Contact: Accepts unsolicited mss. Query first with outline/synopsis and 1-3 sample chapters. Include social security number with submission. Reports on queries in 3-4 weeks; on mss in 6-8 weeks. Photocopied submissions OK. No dot-matrix computer printouts.

Terms: Pays royalties of 10-15%; at least 10 author's copies; discount on additional copies. Sends galleys to author. Publishes ms 9-18 months after acceptance. Writers guidelines for #10 SAE and 1 first class stamp.

Advice: "Our marketing program is flexible; if we find something we like and think we can sell it, we'll publish it. Our interests range from genre like science fiction to mainstream, but science fiction and horror have the best chance. We like writing that creates a strong mood and evokes an emotional reaction from the readers, writing by writers who enjoy working with the language."

*LIBRA PUBLISHERS, INC. (II), 3089C Clairemont Dr., Suite 383, San Diego CA 92117. (619)581-9449. President: William Kroll. Estab. 1960. Small independent publisher. Hardcover and paperback originals. Books: 60 lb offset paper; offset printing; hardcover—smyth sewn binding; paperback—perfect binding; illustrations occasionally; average print order 3,000; first novel print order 1,000+. Plans to publish 3 first novels this year. Averages approximately 15 titles/year; 3-4 fiction titles/year.

Needs: "We consider all categories." Published *All God's Children*, by Alex LaPerchia (inspirational); *Seed of the Divine Fruit*, by Enrico Rinaldi (multi-generational about founding of Atlantic City); and *Caveat Emptor*, by William Attias (racist takeover of a city).

How to Contact: Accepts unsolicited mss. Send complete ms with cover letter. SASE. Reports on queries in 1 week; on mss in 2-3 weeks. Simultaneous and photocopied submissions OK. Computer printout submissions OK.

Terms: Pays 10-40% royalties. Sends pre-publication galleys to author. Publishes ms an average of 6-12 months after acceptance. Book catalog for SASE with 5 first class stamps.

Advice: "Libra publishes nonfiction books in all fields, specializing in the behavioral sciences. We also publish two professional journals: *Adolescence* and *Family Therapy*. We have published fiction on a royalty basis but because of the difficulty in marketing works by unknown writers, we are not optimistic about the chances of offering a standard contract. However, we shall continue to consider fiction in the hope of publishing on a standard basis books that we like and believe have good marketing potential. In addition, our procedure is as follows: Manuscripts we do not consider publishable are returned to the author. When we receive manuscripts which we feel are publishable but are uncertain of the marketability, we suggest that the author continue to try other houses. If they have already done so and are interested in self-publishing, we offer two types of services: (1) we provide editing, proofreading, book and cover design, copyrighting and production of the book; copies are then shipped to the author. (2) We provide these services plus promotion and distribution. In all cases, the problems and risks are spelled out."

LIBRARY RESEARCH ASSOCIATES, INC. (IV), RD. 5, Box 41, Dunderberg Rd., Monroe NY 10950. Imprints include Lloyd-Simone Publishing Co., Willow Tree Press and Criminal Justice Press. Editorial Director: Matilda A. Gocek. Estab. 1968. Publishes hardcover and paperback originals. Books: 50 lb paper; narrow web offset printing; perfect bound hardcover binding; b&w half-tones, line drawings; average print order: 3,500; first novel print order: 1,500. Published 2 new writers within the last year.

Needs: New York State based, fictional biographies or historical events. Recently published *Tales from an Irish Wake* by Margaret Doar Armstrong; *The Hermes Project*, by John M. Friedman; and *Fugitive Deckhand*, by Fred G. Godfrey.

How to Contact: Accepts unsolicited mss. Submit outline/synopsis and sample chapters with SASE. No simultaneous submissions; photocopied submissions OK. Accepts computer printout submissions, prefers letter-quality. Reports in 10 weeks. Publishes ms 12-14 months after acceptance.

Terms: Pays in royalties; no advance. Sends galleys to author. Book catalog for #10 SASE.

Advice: "There is a gradual return to a good story line less dependent upon violence and explicit sex. I am looking to develop our line of Empire State Fiction. Fictionalized biographies based on fact would be welcomed, particularly of women in New York, any period. Prepare clean, double-spaced manuscripts—one-page outline or abstract is most helpful. I want to develop *new authors* so I work willingly with them." Publishing less fiction because it's "hard to generate sales."

‡LIGHTHOUSE PUBLICATIONS (II), P.O. Box 1377, Auburn WA 98071-1377. Editorial Contact Person: Tim Clinton, Editor/Publisher. Fiction Editor: Lynne Trindl. Estab. 1986. "Small family business printing bi-monthly fiction collection in magazine format." Published new writers within the last year. Averages 78 total titles, 60 fiction titles each year.

Needs: Adventure, contemporary, historical, humor/satire, juvenile (animal, easy-to-read, historical, sports, spy/adventure, contemporary), mainstream, military/war, regional, religious/inspirational, romance (contemporary, historical), science fiction, suspense/mystery, western, young adult/teen (easy-to-read, historical, romance/ya, sports, spy/adventure). "G-rated only; no murder mysteries."

How to Contact: Accepts unsolicited ms. Submit complete ms. SASE with sufficient postage for return of ms. Reports in 1-2 months. Photocopied submissions OK. Accepts computer printout submissions.

Terms: "Authors are paid upon publication in Lighthouse Fiction Collection." Publishes ms within two years after acceptance. Writer's guidelines free for letter size SASE and 1 first class stamp.

LINCOLN SPRINGS PRESS (II), Box 269, Franklin Lakes NJ 07417. Editor: M. Gabriel. Estab. 1987. Small, independent press. Publishes poetry, fiction, photography, high quality. Publishes paperback originals. Books: 65 lb paper; offset printing; perfect binding; average print order: 1,000. "Prefers short stories, but will publish first novels if quality high enough." Averages 4 total titles/year; 2 fiction titles.

Needs: Contemporary, ethnic, experimental, feminist, historical, literary, short story collections. No "romance, Janet Dailey variety." Published *Maybe It's My Heart*, by Abigail Stone (novel); *The KGB Solution at Katyn*, by Maurice Shainberg (memoir).

How to Contact: Accepts unsolicited mss. Query first with 1 sample chapter. SASE. Reports in 2 weeks-3 months. Simultaneous and photocopied submissions OK. Accepts computer printouts.

Terms: Authors receive royalties of 5% minimum; 15% maximum "after all costs are met." Provides 10 author's copies. Sends galleys to author. Book catalog for SASE.

LOLLIPOP POWER BOOKS (II), Box 277, Carrboro NC 27510. (919)376-8152. Editor: Elizabeth Core. Estab. 1970. New children's division of the Carolina Wren Press; publishes non-sexist, multi-racial "alternative" children's books. Publishes paperback originals. Buys juvenile mss with or without illustrations. Averages 1 title (fiction) each year. Average first book run 2,500 copies. Usually critiques rejected ms "unless completely inappropriate submission for our purpose."

Needs: Juvenile. "We are currently looking for well written stories with strong plots which deal with issues of race or sex-role stereotyping or with contemporary family problems, especially divorce. We would like to see ms about a realistic black child or family or ms dealing with handicapped children." Recently published *Brother's Keeper, Sister's Child* by Margaret Stephens; *Love, or a Reasonable Facsimile,* by Gloree Rogers; *The Boy Toy,* by Phyllis Johnson.

How to Contact: Query first for author guidelines and book catalog with SASE. Reports in 2 weeks on queries; 6 weeks on mss. Simultaneous and photocopied submissions OK. Publishes ms from 6 months to 1 year after acceptance.

Terms: Pays royalties of 10%.

Advice: "Know what the publisher's specialty is. Though we want books with a strong message, we also want strong and appealing characters, and plots which children will want to return to again and again."

HENDRICK LONG PUBLISHING CO. (IV), Box 25123, Dallas TX 75225. (214)358-4677. Vice President: Joann Long. Estab. 1969. "Independent publisher focusing on Texas material geared primarily to a young audience. (K through high school). Cornerstone of company is a Texas history seventh grade textbook (state adopted)." Publishes hardcover and paperback originals and hardcover reprints. Books: average print order: 2,000 (except textbooks which have a much longer run.) Published new writers within the last year. Averages 8 total titles, 4 fiction titles each year. Sometimes comments on rejected ms.

Needs: Historical, juvenile, Texas and historical, regional and young adult/teen (10-18 years) historical. "No material not suitable for junior high/high school audience." Recently published *Great Texas Scare*, by Jones (juvenile and YA); *Davy's Dawg* by Matthews/Hurlburt (juvenile and YA); *Tilli Comes to Texas*, by Oppenheimer (Christmas fantasy).

How to Contact: Accepts unsolicited queries, (but prefer query. Query first or submit outline/synopsis and sample chapters (at least 2—no more than 3). SASE necessary for return of ms. Reports in 2 weeks on queries; 2 months on ms. Photocopied submissions OK. Accepts computer printout submissions.

Terms: Offers negotiable advance. Sends galleys to author. Publishes ms 18 months after acceptance. Writer's guidelines for SASE. Book catalog for $1.

‡LONGSTREET PRESS (II), Suite 102, 2150 Newmarket Parkway, Marietta GA 30067. (404)980-1488. Editorial Contact Person: John Your, Associate Editor. Fiction Editor: Jane Hill/Senior Editor. Estab. 1988. "Small independent publisher with plans to grow." Publishes hardcover and paperback originals. Published new writers within the last year. Plans 2 first novels this year. Averages 20-25 total titles, 4-5 fiction titles each year. Sometimes comments on rejected ms.

Needs: Literary, mainstream, short story collections. "Quality fiction." No "genre fiction, highly experimental work, Y/A, juvenile." Recently published *Crazy Ladies*, by Michael Lee West (literary); *Unheard Melodies*, by Warren Leamon (literary); and *Street Songs 1: New Voices in Fiction*, by Jane Hill, ed. (anthology of stories).
How to Contact: Accepts unsolicited mss. Submit outline/synopsis and sample chapters. SASE. Agented fiction 50%. Reports on queries in 6 weeks; on mss in 3 months. Simultaneous (if told) and photocopied submissions OK. Accepts computer printout submissions.
Terms: Pays in royalties; advance is negotiable; author's copies. Sends galleys to author. Publishes ms 6 months-1 year after acceptance. Writer's guidelines free for #10 SASE and 1 first class stamp. Book catalog free on request.
Advice: "Read good contemporary literary fiction – know the field."

LOS HOMBRES PRESS (II,IV), Box 632729, San Diego CA 92163-2729. (619)234-6710. Publisher: James D. Kitchen. Estab. 1989. Small publisher-plan to do 6 books in 1991. Publishes paperback originals. Books: 60# paper; offset printing; perfect binding; average print order: 2,000; first novel print order: 2,000. Published new writers within the last year. Plans 2 first novels this year. Averages 4-5 total titles, 3-4 fiction titles each year. Sometimes comments on rejected mss.
Needs: Gay and lesbian. "Novels including mainstream, literary, science fiction, mystery, fantasy, futuristic, adventure. Open to most categories with a gay theme; short story collections." No men's action, pornography. Recently published *Triple Fiction*, by Richard L. Stone, Marsh Cassady, Stephen Richard Smith (gay short stories); and *The Search for Sebastion* by Judston Crown (gay-comedy-adventure).
How to Contact: Accepts unsolicited mss. Query first or submit 3 sample chapters. SASE; include social security number with submission. Agented fiction 50%. Reports in 2 weeks; mss in 2 months. Simultaneous and photocopied submissions OK. Computer printout submissions are acceptable.
Terms: Pays 10-15% royalties and 10 author's copies. Sends galleys to author. Publishes ms 1 year after acceptance. Writer's guidelines for #10 SASE and 1 first class stamp.

LUCKY HEART BOOKS (I), Subsidiary of Salt Lick Foundation, 1804 E. 38½ St., Austin TX 78722. Editor/Publisher: James Haining. Estab. 1969. Small press with significant work reviews in several national publications. Publishes paperback originals and reprints. Books: offset/bond paper; offset printing; stitch, perfect bound; illustrations; average print order: 500; first novel print order: 500. Sometimes comments on rejected mss.
Needs: Open to all fiction categories.
How to Contact: Accepts unsolicited mss. SASE. 1% of fiction is agented. Reports in 2 weeks on mss. Photocopied submissions OK. Accepts computer printout submissions.
Terms: Pays 10 author's copies. Sends pre-publication galleys to author.

‡MARRON PUBLISHERS, INC. (II), Dark Secrets, Romance In Black, P.O. Box 756, Yonkers NY 10703. (718)481-9599. Editorial Contact Person: Marquita Guerra, Co-Owner. Fiction Editor: Sharon A. Ortiz. Estab. 1988. "Marron Publishers is a small, growing independent publisher dedicated to printing quality works which celebrate ethnic and cultural diversity." Publishes hardcover and paperback originals. Books: illustrations on newsletter (Dark Secrets); average print order: 10,000; first novel print order: 10,000. Plans 8 first novels this year. Averages 8-10 total titles, 8-10 fiction titles each year. Sometimes comments on rejected mss.
Needs: Adventure, contemporary, ethnic, fantasy, historical, literary, mainstream, romance (contemporary, historical), suspense/mystery, young adult/teen (historical, romance/ya). Looking for "romance for the *Romance In Black* line."
How to Contact: Accepts unsolicited mss. Submit outline/synopsis and 3 sample chapters, or complete ms with cover letter. SASE. Agented fiction 25%. Reports on queries in 2 weeks; on mss in 4 weeks. Photocopied submissions OK. Accepts letter quality computer printout submissions. Accepts electronic submissions with prior approval.
Terms: Depends on experience of author and previous track record. "Individual arrangement with author depending on the book." Sends galleys to author. Publication time "depends on the book" (approximately 2 to 18 months). Writer's guidelines free for 8½ × 11 SASE and 45¢ postage. Book catalog for SASE.
Advice: "Be honest and forthright in your cover letters without gushing. State your case – don't be shy about what you feel are your positive points. Always remember that you have to sell yourself to the publisher and don't back down on questions of quality – your name will appear on the book or the

Close-up

Melissa Pritchard
Writer

In 1978, Melissa Pritchard turned 30, gave birth to her first child, and, as a result of these events, realized that someday she was going to die. It was then she began to take her fiction writing seriously. "Mortality, acute awareness of mortality, seized me, and despite considerable fears and doubts about being a writer, I made a commitment to write at least one hour each day."

And that she does. In addition to writing three to four hours each morning, she teaches part-time and serves as an advisory editor for *StoryQuarterly*, which she co-edited from 1984-88.

The existence of small presses and literary magazines is vital to serious writers, she says. "They take risks more commercial magazines can or will not take. Editors of small magazines are often writers themselves, and gladly reward and recognize literary effort as opposed to marketplace saleability. They are idealists, often rich in encouragement, notoriously poor in monetary payment. Yet publishers, agents and editors continually fish these waters for fresh voices.

"I would probably have had no career without these small literary magazines," says Pritchard, whose acclaim has been achieved mostly through small press media.

Today she is relishing her success, saying that winning the Flannery O'Connor Award For Short Fiction (for her collection of short stories, *Spirit Seizures*) was "emotionally gratifying, validating years of work on these stories." *Spirit Seizures* also received the Carl Sandburg Literary Arts Award. Pritchard is currently completing a second short story collection, *Sweet Feed*.

In addition to being a short story writer, Pritchard is also a novelist. *Phoenix*, her first published novel, is due out in 1991 by Cane Hill Press. She says she found the transition from short stories to novels quite difficult. "A short story is a compressed, urgent form. (It) is like laps in a pool, swimming deliberate strokes in a confined space. A novel is like floating on a dark sea, one's only steering the faintest stars. My first novel was utterly clumsy. I was afraid of the form, so I overcontrolled my material and strangled it, in effect. That novel remains and shall ever remain unpublished. It was a long, painful lesson in how not to write a novel. My second novel, *Phoenix*, was written with more confidence, benefitting from the failures of the first."

Pritchard's prescription for success is a mixture of practical and idealistic elements. Try not to send out a story before it's polished and perfected, she says. Then, send to the regional, lesser known literary magazines as well as to the more widely known ones. "They are often your first entry into publication." Finally, Pritchard says, "Try not to judge others in your writing. Cultivate courage, humility and a boundless empathy for humanity."

—Lisa Carpenter

publication. Be open to criticism and flexible when it comes to certain changes. But be wary of changing your original concept to one that is foreign to your creative intent."

‡MERCURY HOUSE (III), Suite 400, 201 Filbert St.,San Francisco CA 94133. Executive Editor: Tom Christensen. Publisher: William Brinton. Submissions Editor: Alison Macondray. Small, independent publisher of quality fiction and nonfiction. Publishes hardcovers and some paperback originals and reprints. Averages 20 titles annually. 25% of books from first-time authors.
Needs: Literary adult fiction, nonfiction and translations.
How to Contact: No unsolicited mss. Submit query letter, 3 sample chapters, synopsis and SASE. Reports in 3 months. Book catalog for 8½×11 SAE and 65¢. Simultaneous submissions OK.

*MEY-HOUSE BOOKS (II), Box 794, Stroudsburg PA 18360. (717)646-9556. Editorial contact person: Ted Meyer. Estab. 1983. One-person operation part-time with plans for at least two novels shortly. Publishes hardcover and paperback originals. Averages 1 title/year. Occasionally critiques or comments on rejected ms, "cost varies."
Needs: Adventure, contemporary, ethnic, science fiction. "No gay, erotic or lesbian fiction."
How to Contact: Accepts unsolicited mss. Query first. SASE. Reports in 1 month on queries. Simultaneous, photocopied submissions OK.
Terms: Payment "varies." Sends galleys to author. *Subsidy publishes "on an individual basis."*

MILKWEED EDITIONS, Box 3226, Minneapolis MN 55403. (612)332-3192. Editor: Emilie Buchwald. Estab. 1980—*Milkweed Chronicle*/1984—*Milkweed Editions*. Small press with emphasis on literary and visual arts work. Publishes hardcover and paperback originals. Books: book text quality—acid free paper; offset printing; perfect or hardcover binding; illustrations in all books; average print order: 2,000; first novel print order depends on book. Averages 8 total titles/year. Number of fiction titles "depends on mss."
Needs: Contemporary, experimental, literary. Looking for excellent writing. No romance, mysteries, science fiction. Recently published *Tokens of Grace*, by Sheila O'Connor; *Circe's Mountain*, by Marie Luise Kaschnitz, translated by Lisa Mueller; and *Blue Taxis*, by Eileen Drew.
How to Contact: Accepts unsolicited mss. Submit outline/synopsis and 2 sample chapters. SASE. Reports in 4 weeks on queries; 2 months on mss. Simultaneous and photocopied submissions OK. Accepts computer printouts. No dot-matrix. "Please send for guidelines. Must enclose SASE."
Terms: Authors are paid in royalties of 10%; advance is negotiable; 10 author's copies. Sends galleys to author. Book catalog for 3 first class stamps.
Advice: "Read good contemporary fiction; find your own voice. Do not send us pornographic work, or work in which violence is done to women or children or men."

MISTY HILL PRESS (II), 5024 Turner Rd., Sebastopol, CA 95472. (707)823-7437. Managing Editor: Sally S. Karste. Estab. 1985. One person operation on a part-time basis. Publishes paperback originals. Books: illustrations; average print order: 2,000; first novel print order: 500-1,000. Plans 1 first novel this year. Publishes 1 title each year. Sometimes critiques rejected mss; *$15/hour charge for critiques.*
Needs: Juvenile (historical). Looking for "historical fiction for children, well researched for library market." Recently published *Trails to Poosey*, by Olive R. Cook (historical fiction); *Tales Fledgling Homestead*, by Joe Armstrong (nonfiction portraits).
How to Contact: Accepts unsolicited mss. Submit outline/synopsis and sample chapters. Reports within weeks. Simultaneous and photocopied submissions OK. Accepts computer printout submissions, no dot-matrix.
Terms: Pays royalties of 5%. Sends prepublication galleys to author. Writer's guidelines and book catalog for SASE.

*MOSAIC PRESS (II, IV), Fine Miniature Books, 358 Oliver Rd., Cincinnati OH 45215. (513)761-5977. Publisher: Miriam Irwin. Estab. 1977. Publishes hardcover originals in miniature format. Books: acid-free archival paper; litho or letter press printing; hardbound, cloth, leather or half-leather binding; illustrations; average print order: 2,000. Plans to publish 2 new authors this year. Averages 6 total titles, 1 fiction title each year. Occasionally buys juvenile mss with or without illustrations.
Needs: Comics, historical, humor/satire, literary, regional, religious/inspirational, romance, and young adult (historical, sports). "Our books are short (3,500 words maximum). No fantasy, science fiction or occult." Published *Scrimshaw*, by Carolyn G. Orr.

How to Contact: Accepts unsolicited mss. Query first or submit complete ms. SASE always. Simultaneous and photocopied submissions OK. Accepts computer printout submissions. Reports in 2 weeks on queries; 2 weeks on mss. Publishes ms an average of 2 years after acceptance.
Terms: Pays in outright purchase of $50 and 5 author's copies. "We also do subsidy publishing of private editions. Negotiable arrangements." Book catalog $3. Free writer's guidelines with SASE.
Advice: "We want a good topic, beautifully written, in very few words; no full-length novel submissions. Regarding the author/editor relationship, the writer should trust editor; editor should trust designer. Read the publisher's stated purpose carefully."

MOTHER COURAGE PRESS (II), 1533 Illinois St., Racine WI 53405. (414)634-1047. Executive Editor: Barbara Lindquist. Estab. 1981. Small feminist press. Publishes paperback originals. Books: perfect binding; sometimes illustrations; average print order: 3,000; first novel print order: 3,000. Plans 3 first novels 1991. Averages 4 total titles, 1 fiction title each year.
Needs: Lesbian adventure, lesbian feminist/humor/satire, lesbian romance, lesbian science fiction, lesbian suspense/mystery. "Need strongly feminist, lesbian or women oriented, nothing written by men." Recently published *News*, by Heather Conrad (political, humanist feminist); and *Night Lights*, by Bonnie Arthur (lesbian romance).
How to Contact: Accepts unsolicited mss. Query first then submit outline/synopsis and 2 sample chapters. SAE. Reports in 6 weeks on queries; 3 months on mss. Simultaneous and photocopied submissions OK. Accepts computer printout submissions. Accepts electronic submissions via Macintosh.
Terms: Pays in royalties of 10% minimum; 15% maximum. Average advance: $250. Sends galleys to author. Book catalog free on request.
Advice: "Write a good query letter, including, the plot of the novel, main characters, possible markets, etc."

MOYER BELL LIMITED, Colonial Hill, RFD #1, Mt. Kisco NY 10549. (914)666-0084. President: Jennifer Moyer. Fiction Editor: Britt Bell. Estab. 1984. "Small publisher established to publish literature, reference and art books." Publishes hardcover and paperback originals and hardcover and paperback reprints. Books: average print order 2,500; first novel print order: 2,500. Averages 14 total titles, 1 fiction title each year. Sometimes comments on rejected ms.
Needs: Serious literary fiction. No genre fiction. Recently published *The Other Garden*, by Francis Wyndham (literary).
How to Contact: Accepts unsolicited mss. Submit outline/synopsis and 2 sample chapters. SASE. Reports in 2 weeks on queries; 2 months on mss. Simultaneous submissions OK. Accepts electronic submissions.
Terms: Pays royalties of 10% minimum. Average advance $1,000. Sends galleys to author. Publishes ms 9-18 months after acceptance. Book catalog free.

THE NAIAD PRESS, INC. (I, II, IV), Box 10543, Tallahassee FL 32302. (904)539-5965. FAX: (904)539-9731. Editorial Director: Barbara Grier. Estab. 1973. Books: 55 lb offset paper; sheet-fed offset; perfect binding; illustrations seldom; average print order: 12,000; first novel print order: 12,000. Published new writers within the last year. Publishes 24 total books/year.
Needs: Lesbian fiction, all genres. Published *After the Fire*, by Jane Rule; *The Beverly Malibu* (A Kate Delafield Mystery), by Katherine V. Forrest; *Rose Penski*, by Roz Perry; published fiction by previously unpublished writers within the last year.
How to Contact: Query first only. SASE for query, ms. No simultaneous submissions; photocopied submissions OK "but we prefer original mss." Reports in 3 week on queries, 3 months on mss. Publishes ms 1-2 years after acceptance.
Terms: Pays 15% royalties using a standard recovery contract. Occasionally pays 7½% royalties against cover price. "Seldom gives advances and has never seen a first novel worthy of one. Believes authors are investments in their own and the company's future—that the best author is the author that produces a book every 12-18 months forever and knows that there is a *home* for that book." Book catalog for legal-sized SASE.
Advice: "We publish lesbian fiction primarily and prefer honest work (i.e., positive, upbeat lesbian characters). Lesbian content must be accurate . . . a lot of earlier lesbian novels were less than honest. No breast beating or complaining." New imprint will publish reprints and original fiction. "Our fiction titles are becoming increasingly *genre* fiction, which we encourage. Original fiction in paperback is our main field, and its popularity increases. First novels are where the world is . . . really. Don't be a smart aleck. Send a simple letter, who, what, why, where, when, about yourself and a single page with

at most a 2 paragraph precis of your book . . . not how good but WHAT IT IS ABOUT. Remember that no editor has time to waste, and the more accurate your self-description is, the more chance you have of getting a reader who will READ your book. Include telephone numbers, day and evening if possible. Get your homework done, be sure you are sending out the best book you can produce. Publishers are not sitting around waiting to help you write your book. Make it VERY easy for the editor to deal with you. The concise, smart, savvy, self-serving author wins the glass doughnut . . . every time."

THE NAUTICAL & AVIATION PUBLISHING CO. OF AMERICA INC. (II), Suite 314, 101 W. Read St., Baltimore MD 21203. (301)659-0220. Editor: Jan Snouck-Hurgronje. Estab. 1979. Small publisher interested in quality military history and literature. Publishes hardcover originals and reprints. Averages 10 total titles, 1-4 fiction titles each year. Sometimes comments on rejected mss.
Needs: Military/war. Looks for "novels with a strong military history orientation." Published *South to Java*, by Adm. William P. Mack and William Mack, Jr., (historical fiction); *The Captain*, Hartog (reprint); *Greenmantle*, John Buchan (reprint).
How to Contact: Accepts unsolicited mss. Query first or submit complete mss with cover letter, SASE necessary for return of mss. Agented fiction "miniscule." Reports on queries in 2-3 weeks, on mss in 3 weeks. Simultaneous and photocopied submissions OK. Accepts computer printout submissions.
Terms: Pays royalties of 15%. Advance negotiable. After acceptance publishes ms "as quickly as possible—next season." Book catalog free on request.
Advice: Publishing more fiction. Encourages first novelists. "We're interested in good writing—first novel or last novel. Keep it historical, put characters in a historical context. Professionalism counts. Know your subject. *Convince us.*"

NEW DIRECTIONS (I, II), 80 Eighth Ave., New York NY 10011. (212)255-0230. Editor-in-Chief: Peter Glassgold. Midsize independent publisher with plans to expand. Publishes hardcover and paperback originals and reprints. Average print order: 1,000 hardback; 3,000 paperback. Sometimes critiques rejected ms.
Needs: "Mostly avant-garde; look at everything, including poetry." Published *The Hedgehog*, by H.D.; *A Tree Within*, by Octavio Paz.
How to Contact: Query first with outline/synopsis and sample chapters. Accepts unsolicited mss. SASE. Reports in 6-8 weeks on queries; 3-4 months on mss. Photocopied submissions OK. Accepts computer printout submissions.
Terms: Pays in royalties. Offers advance. Sometimes sends pre-publication galleys to author. Publishes ms at least 1 year after acceptance, "depends on type of book."
Advice: "Try to get published in a literary magazine first to establish a writing reputation and for the experience."

NEW RIVERS PRESS, Suite 910, 420 North 5th St., Minneapolis MN 55401. Publisher: C.W. Truesdale. Fiction Editor: C.W. Truesdale. Estab. 1968. Plans 4 fiction titles in 1989 (1990 as well).
Needs: Contemporary, literary, experimental, translations. "No popular fantasy/romance. Nothing pious, polemical (unless very good other redeeming qualities). We are interested in only quality literature and always have been (though our concentration in the past has been poetry)." Recently published *Out Far, in Deep*, by Alvin Handleman (short stories); *Borrowed Voices*, by Roger Sheffer (short stories); and *Suburban Metaphysics*, by Ronald J. Rindo (short stories).
How to Contact: Query. SASE for query, ms. Photocopied submissions OK. Reports in 2 months on queries, within 2 months of query approval on mss. "No multiple submissions tolerated."
Terms: Pays in 100 author's copies; also pays in royalties; no advance. Minnesota Voices Series pays authors $500 cash plus 15% royalties on list price for second and subsequent printings. Free book catalog.
Advice: "We are not really concerned with trends. We read for quality, which experience has taught can be very eclectic and can come sometimes from out of nowhere. We are interested in publishing short fiction (as well as poetry and translations) because it is and has been a great indigenous American form and is almost completely ignored by the commercial houses. Find a *real* subject, something that belongs to you and not what you think or surmise that you should be doing by current standards and fads."

NEW SEED PRESS (II, IV), Box 9488, Berkeley CA 94709. (415)540-7576. Editor: Helen Chetin. Estab. 1971. Publishes paperback originals in Spanish/English, Chinese/English and English only. Books: 70 lb paper; typeset printing; saddle-stitched, perfect and spiral binding; b&w line art or halftone. Average print order: 2,000-3,000. Encourages new writers.
Needs: Feminist, ethnic, regional, juvenile (historical, contemporary), and young adult (historical, problem novels, easy-to-read teen). "No adult fiction that is not appropriate for children." Recently published *The Girls of Summer*, by Anita Cornwell; and *The Good Bad Wolf*, by Lynn Rosengarten Horowitz; published fiction by previously unpublished writers within the last year.
How to Contact: Query only. SASE always, but not considering new mss until 1992. Simultaneous and photocopied submissions OK. Accepts computer printout submissions. Reports in 2 weeks.
Terms: Pays in royalties and by outright purchase. Sends galleys to author. Book catalog for letter-sized SASE.
Advice: "We publish children's books free from stereotyping with content that is relative to today's happenings—stories with active female characters who take responsibility for their lives, stories that challenge assumptions about the inferiority of women and Third World peoples."

NEW VICTORIA PUBLISHERS, Box 27, Norwich VT 05055. (802)649-5297. Editor: Claudia Lamperti. Publishes trade paperback originals. Averages 4-5 titles/year.
Needs: Adventure, erotica, ethnic, fantasy, lesbian, historical, humor, feminist, mystery, romance, science fiction and western. Looking for "strong feminist characters, also strong plot and action. We will consider most anything if it is well written and appeals to a lesbian/feminist audience." Recently published *Scrects*, Lesleä Newman (short stories); and *A Captive in Time*, by Sarah Dreher.
How to Contact: Submit outline/synopsis and sample chapters. SASE. Reports in 2 weeks on queries; 1 month on mss. Photocopied and disk submissions OK.
Terms: Pays royaltics of 10%.
Advice: "We would particularly enjoy a humorous novel."

NEWEST PUBLISHERS LTD. (IV), #310, 10359 Whyte Ave., Edmonton, Alberta T6E 1Z9 Canada. General Manager: Liz Grieve. Estab. 1977. Publishes paperback originals. Published new writers within the last year. Plans 1 first novel this year. Averages 7 total titles, 2 fiction titles each year. Sometimes offers brief comments on rejected ms.
Needs: Literary. "Our press is most interested in western Canadian literature." Recently published *Winter of the White Wolf*, by Byrna Barclay (literary); *Breathing Water*, by Joan Crate (literary); *Last One Home*, by Fred Stenson (literary); *Grace Lake*, by Glen Huser (literary).
How to Contact: Accepts unsolicited mss. Query first or submit outline/synopsis and 3 sample chapters. SASE (IRC) necessary for return of manuscript. Reports in 2 weeks on queries; 3 months on mss. Accepts computer printouts, photocopied and electronic submissions.
Terms: Pays royalties of 10% minimum. Sends galleys to author. Publishes ms at least one year after acceptance. Book catalog for 9 × 12 SASE or IRC.

OMMATION PRESS (II, IV), 5548 N. Sawyer, Chicago IL 60625. Imprints include *Mati Magazine*, *Ditto Rations Chapbook Series*, *Offset Offshoot Series*, *Salome: A Literary Dance Magazine*, *Dialogues on Dance Series*, Editorial Director: Effie Mihopoulos. Estab. 1975. Rarely comments on rejected mss.
Needs: Contemporary, literary, experimental, feminist, prose poetry. "For the Dialogues on Dance Series, dance-related fiction; for the Offset Offshoot Series, poetry mss, including prose poems." Published *Victims Of The Latest Dance Craze*, by Cornelius Eady (1985 Lamont Selection by Academy of American Poets); *Invisible Mirror*, by Michael Cadnum.
How to Contact: Submit complete ms with SASE. Simultaneous, if so indicated, and photocopied submissions OK. Reports in 1 month.
Terms: Pays 50 author's copies (and $100 honorarium if grant money available). Book catalog for #10 SASE.

‡OPEN HAND PUBLISHING, INC., P.O. Box 22048, Seattle WA 98122. (206)323-3868. Manuscript Editor: Pat Andrus. Estab. 1981. Small publisher of books. Publishes hardcover and paperback originals and reprints. Books: 55 or 60 lb. paper; offset printing; perfect bound and case bound; average print order: 5,000; first novel print order: 3,500. Published new writers within the last year. Plans 1 first novel this year. Averages 4 total titles/year. Sometimes comments on rejected mss.

Needs: Ethnic, juvenile (historical), young adult/teen (historical). Recently published *Love, Debra*, by Fritz Hamilton (human interest).
How to Contact: Accepts unsolicited mss. Query letter first or submit outline/synopsis and 2 sample chapters. SASE. Reports in 3 weeks on queries; 6 weeks on mss. Simultaneous and photocopied submissions OK. Accepts computer printout submissions. Must be double spaced.
Terms: Pays in royalties (negotiable). "Reports in sales and royalty sent out at 6-month intervals." Sends galleys to author. Publishes ms 1-2 years after acceptance. Writer's guidelines available upon request.

‡ORCA BOOK PUBLISHERS LTD. (I), P.O. Box 5626, Sta. B, Victoria, British Columbia V8R 6S4 Canada. (604)380-1229. Editorial Contact Person: R.J. Tyrrell, Publisher. Estab. 1984. "Regional publisher of west coast-oriented titles." Publishes hardcover and paperback originals. Books: quality 60lb. book stock paper; illustrations; average print order: 3,000-5,000; first novel print order: 2,000-3,000. Plans 1-2 first novels this year. Averages 12 total titles, 2-3 fiction titles each year. Sometimes comments on rejected ms.
Needs: Contemporary, juvenile (5-9 years), literary, mainstream, young adult/teen (10-18 years). Looking for "contemporary fiction—West Coast." No "romance, science fiction."
How to Contact: Query first, then submit outline/synopsis and 1 or 2 sample chapters. SASE. Agented fiction 20%. Reports in 2 weeks on queries; 1-2 months on mss. Photocopied submissions OK. Accepts computer printout submissions.
Terms: Pays royalties of 10%; $500 average advance. Sends galleys to author. Publishes ms 6 months-1 year after acceptance. Writer's guidelines free for SASE. Book catalog for 8½×11 SASE.
Advice: "We are looking to promote and publish new west coast writers, especially Canadians."

OUR CHILD PRESS, 800 Maple Glen Lane, Wayne PA 19087. (215)964-0606. CEO: Carol Hallenbeck. Estab. 1984. Publishes hardcover and paperback originals and hardcover and paperback reprints. Published new writers within the last year. Plans 2 first novels this year. Plans 2 titles, both fiction, this year. Sometimes comments on rejected ms.
Needs: Adventure, contemporary, fantasy, juvenile (5-9 yrs.), preschool/picture book and young adult/teen (10-18 years). Especially interested in books on adoption or learning disabilities. Published *Don't Call me Marda*, by Sheila Welch (juvenile); and *Oliver—An Adoption Story*, by Lois Wickstrom.
How to Contact: Does not accept unsolicited mss. Query first. Reports in 2 weeks on queries; 2 months on mss. Simultaneous and photocopied submissions OK. Accepts computer printout submissions.
Terms: Pays royalties of 5% minimum. Publishes ms up to 6 months after acceptance. Book catalog free.

‡THE OVERLOOK PRESS, 12 W. 21st St., New York NY 10010. (212)675-0585. Estab. 1972. Small-staffed, full-time operation. Publishes hardcover and paperback originals and reprints. Averages 30 total titles; 7 fiction titles each year. Occasionally critiques rejected mss.
Needs: Fantasy, humor/satire, juvenile (fantasy, historical, sports, contemporary), literary, psychic/supernatural/occult, science fiction, translations. No romance or horror. Recently published *The Book of Rowing*, by D. C. Churbuck (sports); *The Corn King and the Spring Queen*, by Naomi Mitchison (novel); *The Universe, and Other Fictions*, by Paul West (short stories).
How to Contact: Query first or submit outline/synopsis and 3 sample chapters with SASE. Allow up to 6 months for reports on queries and mss. Simultaneous and photocopied submissions OK.
Terms: Vary.

‡OWL CREEK PRESS (III), 1620 N. 45th St., Seattle WA 98103. (206)633-5929. Editor: Rich Ives. Estab. 1979. Small independent literary publisher with plans to expand. Publishes hardcover and paperback originals. Books: photo offset printing; case or perfect binding; illustrations sometimes; average print order: 1,000; first novel print order: 1,000. Plans 3-4 short fiction collections/novels in next year or two. Averages 7 total titles, 0-3 fiction titles each year. Occasionally critiques rejected ms.
Needs: Contemporary, literary, short story collections, and translations. "Literary quality is our only criteria." No formula fiction.
How to Contact: Accepts unsolicited mss. "We recommend purchase of sample issue ($3 back issue, $5 current) of *The Montana Review* to determine our interests." Submit 1-3 sample chapters with SASE. Reports in 2 months. Simultaneous (if stated) and photocopied submissions OK. Accepts computer printout submissions (if clear copy). Publishes ms 3-18 months after acceptance.

Terms: Payment depends on grant/award money. Possible payment in royalties of 10% minimum, 20% maximum; author's copies, 10% of run minimum. Book catalog for SASE.
Advice: "We are expanding in all areas. The number of fiction titles in the next 2-3 years will depend on grants, sales and the quality of submissions. We ignore trends. Subject is irrelevant. Our *only* criterion is quality of the writing itself. Write to last—ignore fads and 'market advice'; good writers create their own markets."

PADRE PRODUCTIONS (II), Box 840, Arroyo Grande CA 93421-0840. (805)473-1947. Accepts fiction and poetry. See The Press of MacDonald and Reinecke.

PANDO PUBLICATIONS (II), 540 Longleaf Dr., Roswell GA 30075. (404)587-3363. Editorial Contact Person: Andrew Bernstein. Estab. 1987. "Two person, full-time book publisher." Publishes hardcover and paperback originals. Books: 60 pound paper; perfect bound, smythe sewn or hardcover binding; average print order: 3,000-9,000. Averages 6-10 total titles each year. Rarely comments on rejected mss.
Needs: Adventure, historical, humor/satire, juvenile (animal, easy-to-read, historical, sports, spy/adventure, contemporary), mainstream, military/war, regional, science fiction, suspense/mystery, young adult/teen (easy-to-read, fantasy/science fiction, historical, problem novels, sports, spy/adventure).
How to Contact: Accepts unsolicited mss. Submit outline/synopsis and 3 sample chapters. SASE for ms. Reports in 1 month on queries; 2 months on ms. Simultaneous and photocopied submissions OK. Computer printout submissions are acceptable. Accepts electronic submissions via WordPerfect.
Terms: Pays royalties of 6% minimim; 12½% maximum. Average advance is about ⅓ of royalty of 1st run; negotiable. Sends galleys to author. Publishes ms 6 months after acceptance. Book catalog free on request.
Advice: Would like to see "more children's stories based on myth and legend, current happenings (world events, politics, demogrpahic movements, social problems, ecological concerns, medical problems, growing up in a TV-VCR-cable-computer world, and so on)."

‡THE PAPER BAG PRESS (I, II), P.O. Box 268805, Chicago IL 60626-8805. (312)285-7972. Editor: Michael H. Brownstein. Estab. 1988. "Small press with a small staff." Publishes paperback originals. Books: regular paper; Xerox printing; saddle stapled binding; photocopy illustrations; average print order: 200. Published new writers within the last year. Averages 2 total titles, 1 fiction title each year. Always comments on rejected mss.
Needs: Adventure, contemporary, erotica, ethnic, experimental, fantasy, feminist, historical, horror, humor/satire, literary, mainstream, military/war, science fiction, short story collection, suspense/mystery, western. "We will only consider collections of short fiction. We never take short stories longer than 500 words."
How to Contact: Accepts unsolicited mss. Submit complete manuscript with cover letter. SASE. Reports in 1 week to 2 months on queries; 1 week to 3 months on mss. Photocopied submissions OK. Accepts computer printout submissions.
Terms: Provides author's copies "depends on press run;" honorarium; payment depends on grant/award money. Sometimes sends galleys to author. Writer's guidlines free for SASE.
Advice: "Too often the fiction we get is sloppy, needs tremendous editing and does not follow our guidelines that all short stories be under 500 words."

PAPIER-MACHE PRESS (IV), 795 Via Manzana, Watsonville CA 95076. (408)726-2933. Editor/Publisher: Sandra Martz. Estab. 1984. Two person operation on a full-time basis. Publishes anthologies and paperback originals. Books: 60-70 lb offset paper; perfect binding; photographs; average print order: 3,000-6,000 copies. Published new writers within the last year. Publishes 4-6 total titles/year; 4-6 fiction/poetry titles/year.
Needs: Contemporary, feminist, short story collections, women's. Recently published fiction by Mary Ann Ashley, Molly Martin, Ric Masten and Ruthann Robson.
How to Contact: Query first. SASE. Reports in 2 months on queries; 6 months on mss. Simultaneous and photocopied submissions OK. Accepts computer printouts.
Terms: Standard royalty agreements for novels/fiction collections. Complimentary copies for anthology contributors; honorarium for contributors when anthologies go into second printings.
Advice: "Indicate with your manuscript whether or not you are open to revision suggestions. Always indicate on original submission if this is a simultaneous submission or a previously published work. We can handle either, but only if we know in advance. Absolutely essential to query first."

PAPYRUS PUBLISHERS (III), Box 466, Yonkers NY 10704. (914)664-0840. Editor-in-Chief: Geoffrey Hutchison-Cleaves. Fiction Editor: Jessie Rosé. Estab. London 1946; USA 1982. Small publisher. Publishes hardcover originals and reprints. Audio books; average print order 2,500. Averages 3 total titles each year (all fiction).
Needs: Suspense/Mystery. "No erotica, gay, feminist, children's, spiritual, lesbian, political." Published *Wilderness*, by Tony Dawson (suspense); *Curse of the Painted Cats*, by Heather Latimer (romantic suspense); *Louis Wain—King of the Cat Artists 1860-1939*, by Heather Latimer (dramatized biography).
How to Contact: Query first. SASE. Reports on queries in 6 weeks."Not accepting right now."
Terms: Pays royalties of 10% minimum. Advance varies. Publishes ms 1 year after acceptance. Book catalog for SASE or IRC.

PATH PRESS, INC. (II), Suite 724, 53 W. Jackson, Chicago IL 60604. (312)663-0167. FAX: (312)663-0318. Editorial Director: Herman C. Gilbert. "Small independent publisher which specializes in books by, for and about Black Americans and Third World Peoples." Averages 6 total titles, 3 fiction titles each year. Occasionally critiques rejected ms.
Needs: Ethnic, historical, sports, and short story collections. Needs for novels include "black or minority-oriented novels of any genre, style or subject." Published *Brown Sky*, by David Covin (a novel of World War II); *Congo Crew*, by William Goodlett (a novel set in Africa during 1960-61); published new writers within the last year.
How to Contact: Accepts unsolicited mss. Query first or submit outline/synopsis and 5 sample chapters with SASE. Reports in 2 months on queries; 4 months on mss. Simultaneous and photocopied submissions OK. Accepts computer printout submissions.
Terms: Pays in royalties.
Advice: "Deal honestly with your subject matter and with your characters. Dig deeply into the motivations of your characters, regardless how painful it might be to you personally."

PAYCOCK PRESS (II), Box 30906, Bethesda MD 20814. (301)656-5146. Imprint: *Gargoyle Magazine*. Editor/Publisher: Richard Peabody, Jr. Estab. 1976. Small independent publisher with international distribution. Publishes paperback originals and reprints. Books: 55 lb natural paper; offset printing; perfect binding; illustrations sometimes; average print order: 1,000; first novel print order: 1,000. Number of titles: 1 in 1988. Encourages new writers. Occasionally comments on rejected mss. "Recently started producing audio tapes of music/spoken-word material."
Needs: Contemporary, literary, experimental, humor/satire and translations. "No tedious AWP résumé-conscious writing or NEA-funded minimalism. We'd be interested in a good first novel that deals with the musical changes of the past few years." Published *The Love Letter Hack*, by Michael Brondoli (contemporary/literary); *Natural History*, by George Myers, Jr. (poems and stories). Over 15,000 submissions were considered for those 3 volumes."
How to Contact: Accepts unsolicited mss. Query with SASE. No simultaneous submissions; photocopied submissions OK. Accepts computer printout submissions. Prefers letter-quality. Reports in 1 week on queries, 1 month on mss.
Terms: Pays in author's copies—10% of print run plus 50% of all sales "after/if we break even on book." Sends galleys to author. No advance.
Advice: "Keep trying. Many good writers simply quit. Many mediocre writers keep writing, eventually get published, and become better writers. If the big magazines won't publish you, try the small magazines, try the local newspaper. Always read your fiction aloud. If you think something is *silly*, no doubt we'd be embarrassed too. Write the kind of stories you'd like to read and can't seem to find. We are more concerned with *how* a novelist says what he/she says, than with *what* he/she says. We are more interested in *right now* than in books about the '50s, '60s, '70s, etc. We are publishing more in anthology format, and encourage first novelists."

‡PEACHTREE PUBLISHERS, LTD. (II), 494 Armour Circle NE, Atlanta GA 30324. (404)876-8761. President: Margaret Quinlin. Estab. 1977. Small, independent publisher specializing in general interest publications, particularly of Southern origin. Publishes hardcover and paperback originals and hardcover reprints. Averages 20 total titles, 4 fiction titles each year. Average first novel print order 10,000-15,000 copies.
Needs: Contemporary, literary, mainstream, regional, and short story collections. "We are primarily seeking Southern fiction: Southern themes, characters, and/or locales." No science fiction/fantasy, children's/young adult, horror, religious, romance, historical or mystery/suspense. Recently published *The Blue Valleys*, by Robert Morgan (stories); *The Song of Daniel*, by Philip Lee Williams; and *To Dance with the White Dog*, by Terry Kay.

How to Contact: Accepts unsolicited mss. Query, submit outline/synopsis and 50 pages, or submit complete ms with SASE. Reports in 1 month on queries; 3 months on mss. Simultaneous and photocopied submissions OK. Accepts computer printout submissions.
Terms: Pays in royalties. Sends galleys to author. Free writer's guidelines and book catalog.
Advice: "We encourage original efforts in first novels."

PERSPECTIVES PRESS (II, IV), Box 90318, Indianapolis IN 46290-0318. (317)872-3055. Publisher: Pat Johnston. Estab. 1981. Small operation expanding to become *the* publisher of fiction and nonfiction materials related to adoption and infertility. Publishes hardcover originals and paperback originals. Books: offset printing; smythe sewn cloth, perfect bound and saddle stitched binding; average print order: 3,000; first novel print order: 2,000. Published new writers within the last year; plans 1 first novel this year. Averages 2-6 total titles, 1 fiction title each year.
Needs: Submissions for adults or children but must have adoption or infertility as the theme. Published *The Miracle Seekers*, by Mary Martin Mason.
How to Contact: Query first. SASE. Reports in 2 weeks on queries; 1 month on mss. Simultaneous and photocopied submissions OK. Accepts computer printouts.
Terms: Pays in royalties of 5% minimum; 15% maximum. Advance negotiable. Sends galleys to author. Book catalog for #10 SAE and 45¢ postage.

PIKESTAFF PUBLICATIONS, INC. (I, II), Box 127, Normal IL 61761. (309)452-4831. Imprints include The Pikestaff Press: Pikestaff Fiction Chapbooks; *The Pikestaff Forum*, general literary magazine. Editorial Directors: Robert D. Sutherland and James R. Scrimgeour. Estab. 1977. Small independent publisher with plans to expand gradually. Publishes hardcover and paperback originals. Books: paper varies; offset printing; b&w illustrations; average print order: 500-2,000. "One of the purposes of the press is to encourage new talent." Occasionally comments on rejected mss.
Needs: Contemporary, literary, and experimental. "No slick formula writing written with an eye to the commercial mass market or pure entertainment that does not provide insights into the human condition. Not interested in heroic fantasy (dungeons & dragons, swords & sorcery); science-fiction of the space-opera variety; westerns; mysteries; love-romance; gothic adventure; or pornography (sexploitation)." Published fiction by Constance Pierce and Linnea Johnson.
How to Contact: Query or submit outline/synopsis and sample chapters (1-2 chapters). SASE always. "Anyone may inquire; affirmative responses may submit ms." No simultaneous or photocopied submissions. Accepts computer printout submissions. Reports in 1 month on queries, 3 months on mss. Publishes ms within 1 year after acceptance.
Terms: Negotiates terms with author. Sends galleys to author.
Advice: "Have fictional characters we can really *care* about; we are tired of disembodied characters wandering about in their heads unable to relate to other people or the world about them. Avoid too much TELLING; let the reader participate by leaving something for him or her to do. Yet avoid vagueness, opaqueness, personal or 'private' symbolisms and allusions. Here we regard the relationship between the writer and editor as a cooperative relationship—we are colleagues in getting the book out. The writer has an obligation to do the best self-editing job of which he or she is capable; writers should not rely on editors to make their books presentable. Don't give up easily; understand your reasons for wanting the work published (personal satisfaction? money? fame? to 'prove' something? to 'be a novelist'? etc.) Ask yourself honestly, Should it be published? What can it provide for a reader that makes it worth part of that reader's *lifetime* to read? Be prepared for shocks and disappointments; study contracts carefully and retain as many rights and as much control over the book's appearance as possible. Be prepared to learn how to be your own best promoter and publicist."

PINEAPPLE PRESS (II), P.O. Drawer 16008, Southside Station, Sarasota FL 34239. (813)952-1085. Executive Editor: June Cussen. Estab. 1982. Small independent trade publisher. Publishes hardcover and paperback originals and paperback reprints. Books: book quality paper; offset printing; smythe sewn hardcover perfect bound paperback binding; illustrations occasionally; average print order: 5,000; first novel print order: 2,000-5,000. Published new writers within the last year. Averages 12 total titles each year. Occasionally critiques rejected ms.
Needs: Contemporary, experimental, historical, environmental, regional, how-to and reference. Recently published *A Court for Owls*, by Richard Adicks (novel).
How to Contact: Prefers query, outline or one-page synopsis with sample chapters (including the first) and SASE. Then if requested, submit complete ms with SASE. Reports in 6 weeks. Simultaneous and photocopied submissions OK. Accepts computer printout submissions.

Terms: Pays in royalties of 7½% minimum; 15% maximum. Sends galleys to author. Advance is not usually offered. "Basically, it is an individual agreement with each author depending on the book." Book catalog sent if label and 45¢ stamp enclosed.

Advice: "We publish both Florida regional books and general trade fiction and nonfiction. Quality first novels will be published. We regard the author/editor relationship as a trusting relationship with communication open both ways. Learn all you can about the publishing process and about how to promote your book once it is published."

PIPPIN PRESS 229 East 85th Street, Gracie Station Box 92, New York NY 10028. (212)288-4920. Publisher: Barbara Francis. Estab. 1987. "Small, independent children's book company, formed by the former editor-in-chief of Prentice Hall's juvenile division." Publishes hardcover originals. Books: 135-150 GSM offset-semi-matte (for picture books) paper; offset, sheet-fed printing; smythe-sewn binding; full color, black and white line illustrations and half tone, b&w and full color photographs. Averages 8-10 titles for first 2 years; will average 10-12. Sometimes comments on rejected mss.

Needs: Juvenile (5-9 yrs. including animal, easy-to-read, fantasy, science, humorous, spy/adventure). "I am interested in humorous novels for children of about 7-12 and in picture books with the focus on humor."

How to Contact: Accepts unsolicited mss. Query first or submit outline/synopsis and 2 sample chapters. SASE. Reports in 2-3 weeks on queries; 3 months on mss. Simultaneous submissions OK. Accepts computer printout submissions, no dot-matrix.

Terms: Pays royalties. Sends galleys to author. Publication time after ms is accepted "depends on the amount of revision required, type of illustration, etc."

*POCAHONTAS PRESS, INC. (II, IV), Manuscript Memories, 2805 Wellesley Court, Blacksburg VA 24060-4126. (703)951-0467. Editorial contact person: Mary C. Holliman. Estab. 1984. "One-person operation on part-time basis, with several part-time colleagues. Subjects not limited, but stories about real people are almost always required. Main intended audience is youth—young adults, ages 10-18." Books 70 lb white offset paper; offset litho printing; perfect binding; illustrations; average print order 3,000-5,000. Averages 4 total titles, 2-3 fiction and 2 poetry titles each year. Usually critiques or comments on rejected mss.

Needs: "Stories based on historical facts about real people." Contemporary, ethnic, historical, sports, regional, translations, western. "I will treat a short story as a book, with illustrations and a translation into Spanish or French and also Chinese someday." No fantasy or horror. Published *From Lions to Lincoln*, by Fran Hartman; and *Mountain Summer*, by Bill Mashburn.

How to Contact: Accepts unsolicited mss. "I don't expect to be considering any new material until mid-1991. I need to complete current projects first." Query first. Reports in 1 month on queries; 1-2 months on manuscripts. Simultaneous, photocopied submissions OK. "If simultaneous, I would need to know up front what other options the author is considering." Accepts computer printout submissions.

Terms: Pays royalties of 10% maximum. $50 advance negotiable. Sends galleys to author. "I will subsidy publish—but expect book and author to meet the same qualifications as a regular author, and will pay royalties on all copies sold as well as pay back the author's investment as books are sold."

Advice: "Get an unbiased, non-friend editor and follow his or her suggestions. Understand that the author *must* be involved in selling the book; if he/she is not willing to help sell, don't expect too much from publisher. Beginning writers seem to think that all they have to do is get the book into bookstores—and they have no conception at all as to how hard that is, and that that's only the *beginning* of selling the book. I'm really looking for long short stories about real people and places, to be published with copious illustrations."

PORCUPINE'S QUILL, INC. (III), 68 Main St., Erin, Ontario, N0B 1T0 Canada. (519)833-9158. Contact: April Simone Hall. Estab. 1974. Small press. Publishes hardcover and paperback originals. Books: 70 lb Zephyr antique paper; offset on Heidelberg Kord 64 printing; paper, occasional hand hardcover binding; illustrations; average print order: 750; first novel print order: 750. Averages 9 total titles, 4 fiction titles each year.

Needs: Contemporary, fantasy, historical, literary, and young adult/teen (historical). Recently published *A Short Walk in the Rain*, by Hugh Hood.

How to Contact: Accepts unsolicited mss, but prefers query first. Reports in 1 month. Simultaneous and photocopied submissions OK. Accepts computer printout submissions.

Terms: Pays in royalties of 5% minimum; 10% maximum; 10 author's copies. Sends proofs to author. Free book catalog.

THE POST-APOLLO PRESS (I), 35 Marie St., Sausalito CA 94965. (415)332-1458. Publisher: Simone Fattal. Estab. 1982. Publishes paperback originals. Book: acid free paper; lithography printing; perfect binding; average print order: 3,000. First novel print order: 3,000. Published new writers within the last year. Averages 2 total titles, 1 fiction title each year. Sometimes comments on rejected ms.
Needs: Feminist, lesbian, literary, short story collections, spiritual and translations. No juvenile, horror, sports or romance. Recently published *Sitt Marie-Rose*, by Etel Adnan; *Home For The Summer*, by Georgina Kleege (psychological thriller).
How to Contact: Send query or complete ms with SASE. Reports in 3 months.
Terms: Pays royalties of 6½% minimum or by individual arrangement. Sends galleys to author. Publishes ms 1½ years after acceptance. Book catalog free.

PRAIRIE JOURNAL PRESS (II, IV), Prairie Journal Trust, Box 997, Station G, Calgory, Alberta T3A 3G2 Canada. Estab. 1983. Small-press non-commercial literary publisher. Publishes paperback originals. Books: bond paper; offset printing; stapled binding; b&w line drawings. Average 2 total titles or anthologies/year. Occasionally critiques or comments on rejected ms if requested.
Needs: Literary. No romance, horror, pulp, erotica, magazine type, children's, adventure, formula, "western." Published *Prairie Journal Fiction*, *Prairie Journal Fiction II* (anthologies of short stories) and *Solstice*, (short fiction on the theme of aging).
How to Contact: Accepts unsolicited mss. Query first and send IRCs and $3 for sample copy, then submit 1 or 2 stories. Submit outline/synopsis and 1-2 stories with SASE (IRC). Reports in 2 weeks. Photocopied submissions OK. Accepts computer printout submissions.
Terms: Pays 1 author's copy; honorarium depends on grant/award provided by the government or private/corporate donations. Sometimes sends galleys to author. Book catalog free on request to institutions; SAE with IRC for individuals. "No U.S. stamps!"
Advice: "We wish we had the means to promote more new writers. We often are seeking theme-related stories. We look for something different each time and try not to repeat types of stories."

THE PRAIRIE PUBLISHING COMPANY, Box 2997, Winnipeg, Manitoba R3C 4B5 Canada. (204)885-6496. Publisher: Ralph Watkins. Estab. 1969. Buys juvenile mss with illustrations. Books: 60 lb high-bulk paper; offset printing; perfect binding; line-drawings illustrations; average print order: 2,000; first novel print order: 2,000.
Needs: Open. Recently published: *The Homeplace*, (historical novel); *My Name is Marie Anne Gaboury*, (first French-Canadian woman in the Northwest); and *The Tale of Jonathan Thimblemouse*. Published work by previously unpublished writers within the last year.
How to Contact: Query with SASE or IRC. No simultaneous submissions; photocopied submissions OK. Reports in 1 month on queries, 6 weeks on mss. Publishes ms 4-6 months after acceptance.
Terms: Pays 10% in royalties. No advance. Free book catalog.
Advice: "We work on a manuscript with the intensity of a Max Perkins of Charles Scribner's Sons of New York. A clean, well-prepared manuscript can go a long way toward making an editor's job easier. On the other hand, the author should not attempt to anticipate the format of the book, which is a decision for the publisher to make. In order to succeed in today's market, the story must be tight, well written and to the point. Do not be discouraged by rejections."

PRESS GANG PUBLISHERS (II, IV), 603 Powell St., Vancouver, British Columbia V6A 1H2 Canada. (604)253-2537. Estab. 1974. Feminist press, 2 full-time staff, 1 half-time staff. Publishes paperback originals and reprints. Books: paperback paper; offset printing; perfect binding; average print order: 3,500; first novel print order: 2,500. Sometimes critiques rejected mss.
Needs: Contemporary, erotica, ethnic (native women especially), feminist, humor/satire, lesbian, literary, regional (priority), science fiction, short story collections, suspense/mystery. Looking for "feminist, mystery/suspense, short stories." No children's/young adult/teen.
How to Contact: Accepts unsolicited mss. Query first. SASE (IRC). Reports in 1 month on queries; 2-3 months on mss. Simultaneous and photocopied submissions OK. Accepts computer printout submissions. Accepts AT compatible discs.
Terms: Pays 10% royalties. Sends galleys to author. Book catalog free on request.

THE PRESS OF MACDONALD AND REINECKE (II,III), Padre Productions, Box 840, Arroyo Grande CA 93420. (805)473-1947. Publisher: Lachlan P. MacDonald. Fiction Editor: Mack Sullivan. Estab. 1974. "Literary imprint of a small independent press." Publishes hardcover and paperback originals. Books: book paper; offset printing; Smyth casebound and perfect binding; illustrations; average print order: 3,000; first novel print order: 500-3,000. Publishes fiction by a previously unpublished writer "every 2-3 years." Plans 1 first novel this year. Averages 6 total titles, 1-2 fiction titles each year. Sometimes comments on rejected mss.

Needs: Historical, humor/satire, literary, mainstream, short story collections. Currently overstocked. No mystery, suspense, western, religious, military, adventure, fantasy, romance categories. Published *Joel in Tananar*, by Robert M. Walton (juvenile); *Contemporary Insanities*, by Charles Broshew (short fiction).

How to Contact: Accepts unsolicited mss. Submit outline/synopsis and sample chapters (1-2). SASE. Agented fiction 5%. Reports on queries in 2 weeks; on mss in 2 months. Simultaneous and photocopied submissions OK.

Terms: Pays in royalties. Sends galleys to author. "Unfortunately, it may be 2 years" before publication after acceptance. Writer's guidelines for SASE. Book catalog for 6×9 SAE.

Advice: "Publishing less fiction than in the past. Demonstrate a following by documenting publication in literary magazines, general magazines or anthologies."

‡PRIMAL PUBLISHING (I,II), 107 Brighton Ave., Allston MA 02134. (617)787-0203. Publisher: Michael McInnis. Editor: Geary Kaczorowski. Estab. 1986. Publishes paperback originals. Books: standard 50 lb paper; offset printing; perfect bound; some illustrations; color cover; average print order 1,000-2,500; first novel print order: 1,000. Averages 10 total titles, 7 fiction titles each year.

Needs: Contemporary, erotica, experimental, gay, lesbian, literary, speculative fiction. No "cliché romance, soap opera lifestyles or new age spiritualism."

How to Contact: Accepts unsolicited mss. Submit complete ms with cover letter. SASE. Reports in 1-3 months. Simultaneous submissions OK. Accepts computer printout submissions, including dot-matrix.

Terms: Pays 10% royalties or 10% print run in author's copies. Sends galleys to author. Publishes ms 1 year after acceptance.

Advice: "Keep it tight. It's gotta hit in the gut, but keep the brain active as well. Violence and sex are okay. Definitely look for things with an edge."

PUCKERBRUSH PRESS (I,II), 76 Main St., Orono ME 04473. (207)581-3832. Publisher/Editor: Constance Hunting. Estab. 1979. One-person operation on part-time basis. Publishes paperback originals. Books: laser printing; perfect binding; sometimes illustrations; average print order: 5,000; first novel print order: 1,000. Published new writers within the last year. Plans 1 first novel this year. Averages 3 total titles, 2 fiction titles each year. Sometimes comments on rejected ms. *If detailed comment, $500.*

Needs: Contemporary, experimental, literary.

How to Contact: Accepts unsolicited mss. Submit complete ms with cover letter. SASE. Reports in 1 week on queries; 2 months on mss.

Terms: Pays royalties of 10%; 10 author's copies. Sends galleys to author. Publishes ms usually 1 year after acceptance. Writer's guidelines for #10 SASE and 1 first class stamp. "I have a book list and flyers."

QUARRY PRESS (I,II), Box 1061, Kingston, Ontario, K7L 4Y5 Canada. (613)548-8429. Managing Editor: Cheryl Sutherland. Estab. 1965. Small independent publisher with plans to expand. Publishes paperback originals. Books: Rolland tint paper; offset printing; perfect binding; illustrations; average print order: 1,200; first novel print order: 1,200. Published new writers within the past year. Plans 1 first novel this year. Averages 12 total titles, 2-4 fiction titles each year. Sometimes comments on rejected mss.

Needs: Experimental, feminist, historical, literary, short story collections. Published *Ritual Slaughter,* by Sharon Drache; *Engaged Elsewhere,* edited by Kent Thompson (includes work by Mavis Gallant, Margaret Laurence, Dougles Glover, Ray Smitz, Keath Fraser and others); published fiction by previously unpublished writers within the last year.

How to Contact: Accepts unsolicited mss. Query first. SASE for query and ms. Reports in 4 months. Simultaneous and photocopied submissions OK. Accepts computer printout submissions.

Terms: Pays royalties of 7% minimum; 10% maximum. Advance: negotiable. Provides 5-10 author's copies. Sends galleys to author. Publishes ms 6-8 months after acceptance. Book catalog free on request.

Advice: Publishing more fiction than in the past. Encourages first novelists. Canadian authors only for New Canadian Novelists Series.

‡RAMALO PUBLICATIONS (I,II), 2107 N. Spokane St., Post Falls ID 83854-9192. (208)773-9416. Editor-Publisher: Marie B. Fish, Estab. 1988. "One person operation." Publishes laminated softcover books. Books: 50 lb., 60 lb, 70 lb, also some 20 lb. paper; perfect and spiral bound; b&w and pen & ink illustrations; average print order: 500-1,000 copies. Published new writers within the last year. Averages 2 total titles, 2 fiction titles each year. Sometimes critiques rejected mss.
Needs: Contemporary, humor/satire, literary, regional, short story collections, western. "Nothing grotesque, unnecessarily violent, obscene. We do not read science fiction, or material so obtuse that we do not get the point."
How to Contact: Accepts unsolicited mss. Submit complete manuscript with cover letter. SASE. Reports in 6 weeks. Simultaneous and photocopied submissions OK. Accepts computer printout submissions.
Terms: "Our publishing/payment arrangements are still evolving." Publishes ms within 1 year after acceptance.

*READ 'N RUN BOOKS (I), Subsidiary of Crumb Elbow Publishing, Box 294, Rhododendron OR 97049. (503)622-4798. Imprints are Elbow Books, Research Centrex. Publisher: Michael P. Jones. Estab. 1978. Small independent publisher with three on staff. Publishes hardcover and paperback originals and reprints. Books: special order paper; offset printing; "usually a lot" of illustrations; average print order: varies. Published new writers within the last year. Plans 1 first novel this year. Averages 10 titles, 2 fiction titles each year. Sometimes comments on rejected ms; *$75 charge for critiques depending upon length. May be less or more.*
Needs: Adventure, contemporary, ethnic, experimental, fantasy, feminist, historical, horror, humor/satire, juvenile (animal, easy-to-read, fantasy, historical, sports, spy/adventure, contemporary), literary, mainstream, military/war, preschool/picture book, psychic/supernatural/occult, regional, religious/inspirational, romance (contemporary, historical), science fiction, short story collections, spiritual, suspense/mystery, translations, western, young adult/teen (easy-to-read, fantasy/science fiction, historical, problem novels, romance, sports, spy/adventure). Looking for fiction on "historical and wildlife" subjects. "Also, some creative short stories would be nice to see for a change. No pornography."
How to Contact: Accepts unsolicited ms. Query first. Submit outline/synopsis and complete ms with cover letter. SASE. Reports in 2 weeks on queries; 1-2 months on mss. Simultaneous and photocopied submissions OK. Accepts computer printout submissions.
Terms: Provides 5+ author's copies (negotiated). Sends galleys to author. Publishes ms 6-12 months after acceptance. Subsidy publishes two books or more/year. Terms vary from book to book. Writer's guidelines for 45¢ postage. Book catalog for SASE or IRC and $1.25 postage.
Advice: Publishing "more hardcover fiction books based on real-life events. They are in demand by libraries. Submit everything you have — even artwork. Also, if you have ideas for layout, provide those also. If you have an illustrator that you're working with, be sure to get them in touch with us."

RED ALDER BOOKS (IV), Box 2992, Santa Cruz CA 95063. (408)426-7082. Editorial Contact Person: David Steinberg, owner. Imprint: Pan-Erotic Review. Estab. 1974. Small, independent publisher. Publishes hardcover and paperback originals. Books: offset printing, case/perfect binding; some illustrations; average print order: 5,000. Averages 1 total title, 1 fiction title each year.
Needs: "Quality-conscious, provocative erotica." Erotica, feminist, lesbian, literary, short story collections. "Short stories only. No pornography, cliché sexual stories." Published *Erotic by Nature*, by Steinberg, editor (collection of erotic stories, poems, photographs).
How to Contact: Accepts and returns unsolicited mss. Query first. SASE for query and ms. Reports on queries in 6-8 weeks. Simultaneous and photocopied submissions OK. Accepts computer printout submissions.
Terms: Pays royalties of 8% minimum. Sends galleys to author.

RED DEER COLLEGE PRESS (I,IV), Box 5005, Red Deer, Alberta T4N 5H5 Canada. (403)342-3321. Managing Editor: Dennis Johnson. Estab. 1975. Publishes hardcover and paperback originals. Books: offset paper; offset printing; hardcover/perfect binding; average print order: 1,000-4,000; first novel print order 2,500. Plans 1 first novel this year. Averages 8-10 total titles, 1 fiction title each year. Sometimes comments on rejected mss.
Needs: Contemporary, experimental, literary, short story collections. No romance, sci-fi, gay.
How to Contact: Does not accept unsolicited mss. Query first or submit outline/synopsis and 2 sample chapters. SASE for query and for ms. Agented fiction 10%. Reports in 1 month on queries; in 3 months on mss. Simultaneous and photocopied submissions OK. Accepts computer printout submissions.

Terms: Pays royalties of 8% minimum; 10% maximum. Advance is negotiable. Sends galleys to author. Publishes ms 1 year after acceptance. Book catalog for 8½×11 SASE and IRC.
Advice: "Final manuscripts must be submitted on Mac disk in MS Word. Absolutely *no* unsolicited mss. Query first. Canadian authors only."

REFERENCE PRESS (IV), Box 70, Teeswater, Ontario N0G 2S0 Canada. (519)392-6634. Imprints are RP Large Print Books. Editor: Gordon Ripley. Estab. 1982. Small independent Canadian publisher of library reference material, computer software and large print books. Hardcover and paperback originals and hardcover reprints. Books: 70 lb Zepher laid paper; offset printing; casebound, some perfect-bound; average print order: 1,000. Published new writers within the last year. Averages 10 total titles, 4 fiction titles each year. Always comments on rejected mss.
Needs: Sports. Published *Canadian Sports Stories* (fiction, anthology); *Dance Me Outside* and *Born Indian*, by W.P. Kinsella (large print).
Terms: Pays in royalties of 10%; 5 author's copies. Writer's guidelines and book catalog free. Accepts unsolicited mss. Accepts electronic submissions.

RE/SEARCH PUBLISHING (I,II), 20 Romolo, Suite B, San Francisco CA 94133. (415)362-1465. Editors: V. Vale and A. Juno. Estab. 1980. Two-person operation, small independent publisher. Publishes paperback originals of non-fiction and paperback reprint classics. Books: 50 lb paper; sewn & stitched binding; photos and other illustrations; average print order: 5,000-7,000. Averages 3-5 total titles per year. Occasionally critiques or comments on rejected ms.
Needs: Experimental, science fiction or *roman noir*. No realism.
How to Contact: Accepts unsolicited mss. Query first. SASE. Reports in 1 month on queries; 1 month on mss. Simultaneous and photocopied submissions OK. Accepts computer printout submissions.
Terms: Pays 8% of press run. Book catalog on request.

‡RISING TIDE PRESS (II), 5 Kivy St., Huntington Station NY 11746. (516)427-1289. Editor: Lee Boojamra. Estab. 1988. "Small, independent press, publishing lesbian fiction—novels only—no short stories." Publishes paperback trade originals. Books: 50-60 lb. offset paper; web printing; perfect binding; average print order: 5,000; first novel print order: 4,000-6,000. Plans 4 first novels this year. Averages 4-6 total titles. Sometimes comments on rejected ms.
Needs: Lesbian adventure, contemporary, erotica, fantasy, feminist, lesbian, romance, science fiction, suspense/mystery, western. Looking for romance and mystery. "Nothing with heterosexual content."
How to Contact: Accept unsolicited mss. with SASE. Photocopied submissions OK. Reports in 1 week on queries; 6-8 months on mss. Accepts computer printout submissions.
Terms: Pays 10-12% royalties. "We will assist writers who wish to self-publish for a nominal fee." Sends galleys to author. Publishes ms 6-18 months after acceptance. Writer's guidelines free for #10 SAE and 1 first class stamp.

*SAMISDAT (II), 456 Monroe Turnpike, Monroe CT 06468. Imprint: *Samisdat Magazine.* Editor/Publisher: Merritt Clifton. Estab. 1973. Publishes paperback originals. Books: standard bond paper; offset printing; saddle-stitch or square back binding; illustrations sometimes; average print order: 300-500. Encourages new writers. "Over 60% of our titles are first books—about 1 first novel per year." Comments on rejected mss.
Needs: Literary, feminist, gay, lesbian, and regional. Published *An American Love Story*, by Robert Swisher (novel).
How to Contact: Query or submit complete ms. SASE always. Reports in 1 week on queries; time varies on mss.
Terms: No advance. Free book catalog with SASE. "Our author payments for books are a paradox: At this writing, we've published over 200 titles over the past 15 years, about 85% of which have earned the authors a profit. On the other hand, we've relatively seldom issued royalty checks—maybe 20 or 30 in all this time, and all for small amounts. We're also paradoxical in our modus operandi: *Authors cover our cash expenses* (this comes to about a third of the total publishing cost—we're supplying equipment and labor) in exchange for half of the press run, but we make no money from authors, and if we don't promote a book successfully, we still lose." Publishes ms from 2-6 months after acceptance.
Advice: "We do not wish to see *any* book-length ms submissions from anyone who has not already either published in our annual magazine, *Samisdat,* or at least subscribed for about a year to find out who we are and what we're doing. We are not a 'market' engaged in handling books as commodities. Submissions are getting much slicker, with a lot less guts to them. This is precisely the opposite of what we're after. Read the magazine. Submit stories or poems or chapters to it. When familiar with

us, and our subscribers, query about an appropriate book ms. We don't publish books except as special issues of the magazine, and blind submissions stand absolutely no chance of acceptance at all. Go deep. Involve your characters with the outside world, as well as with each other. Use the most compact structure possible, bearing in mind that fiction is essentially drama without a stage. I no longer wish to see novels or queries about novels at all. My patience has been too severely abused by would-be novelists. I am still interested in the occasional chapbook-length short story or novella (up to about 10,000 words)."

SANDPIPER PRESS (IV), Box 286, Brookings OR 97415. (503)469-5588. Owner: Marilyn Reed Riddle. Estab. 1979. One person operation specializing in low-cost large-print 18 pt. books. Publishes paperback originals. Books: 70 lb paper; saddle stitch binding, perfect bound, 80 page maximum; leatherette cover binding; b&w sketches or photos; average print order 2,000; no novels. Averages 1 title every 2 years. Occasionally critiques or comments on rejected mss.
Needs: From Native American "Indian" writers only, *true* visions and prophesies; from general public writers, unusual quotations, sayings.
How to Contact: Does not accept unsolicited mss. Query first or submit outline/synopsis. SASE. Reports in 1 month on queries; 1 month on mss. Simultaneous and photocopied submissions OK. Accepts computer printout submissions.
Terms: Pays 2 author's copies and $10 Native American. Publisher buys true story and owns copyright. Author may buy any number of copies at 40% discount and postage. Book catalog for #10 SAE and 1 first class stamp.
Advice: Send SASE for more information.

SATCHELL'S PUBLISHING (II), Adams Press, 3124 5th Ave., Richmond VA 23222. (804)329-6740. President: Alexis Satchell. Fiction Editor: Kim D. Gaines. Estab. 1983. "Midsize independent publisher with plans to expand." Publishes paperback originals. Books: 70 lb wt. paper; typeset printing; saddle stitch, spiral binding, perfect binding; b&w and color illustrations; average print order: 500-250; first novel print order: 500. Plans 20-35 first novels this year. Averages 10 total titles, 3-4 fiction titles each year. Sometimes comments on rejected ms; charges for critiques.
Needs: Adventure, ethnic, faction, fantasy, juvenile (easy-to-read, fantasy), religious/inspirational, romance, spiritual, young adult (fantasy/science fiction). "We will not except obscene novels of any type. We would like to see more poetry-spiritual-text." Recently published *The Calling of Cable*, by Brian Tinsley (spiritual); *Peter Pan Boy*, by Jim Kirby (fiction); and *The Other You*, by Venor Johnson (humor/satire); published new writers within the last year.
How to Contact: Does not accept unsolicited mss. Query first or submit complete ms with cover letter. SASE. Reports in 1 month on mss. Simultaneous and photocopied submissions OK. Accepts computer printout submissions.
Terms: Does not pay. Publishes ms 8-10 weeks after acceptance. Writer's guidelines free.

‡SCARE WARE (I,IV), P.O. Box 705, Salem OR 97308. Editorial Contact Person: Michelle Marr. Estab. 1990. "One-person operation publishing books on disks." Books: 5¼" computer disks for IBM and compatible computers. Plans 10 first novels this year. Plans for 12+ total titles, 12+ fiction titles each year. Sometimes comments on rejected ms.
Needs: Horror, psychic/supernatural/occult. "I plan to use horror novels and story collections, probably none over 75,000 words. No juvenile, romance, science fiction, etc."
How to Contact: Accepts unsolicited mss. Query first, then submit outline/synopsis and sample chapters or completed ms. SASE. Reports in 2 weeks on queries; 2 months on mss. Photocopied submissions OK. Accepts computer printouts. Accepts electronic submissions.
Terms: Pays royalties of 25%, and 1 author's copy. No advances at this time. Sends galleys to author. Publishes ms 2 months after acceptance. Writer's guidelines free for #10 SASE and 25¢ postage. Book catalog free on request (when available).
Advice: "I would like to work with new novelists; I feel that the electronic market is easier to break into as there is less expense involved."

*SCOJTIA, PUBLISHING COMPANY (II), 6457 Wilcox Station, Box 38002, Los Angeles CA 90038. Imprint: The Lion. Managing Editor: Patrique Quintahlen. Estab. 1990. "Small independent publisher plans to expand, ten-member operation on full-time basis." Publishes hardcover and paperback originals and reprints. Books: 50-60 lb weight paper; perfect bound; artists on staff for illustrations; average print order: 1,000-15,000; first novel print order: 1,000. Averages 5 total titles/year; 2 fiction titles/

year. Offers editorial/publishing services for a fee. Query for details. (Direct all fiction to Jordan Enterprises Pub. Co.-Subsidiary).

Needs: Adventure, contemporary, ethnic, experimental, fantasy, historical, juvenile (animal, easy-to-read, fantasy, historical, contemporary), literary, mainstream, preschool/picture book, romance (contemporary, historical), science fiction, young adult/teen (easy-to-read, fantasy/science fiction, historical, problem novels, romance). "Looking for contemporary juvenile novels, interesting settings." No horror, gore, erotica, gay, occult, novels. No sexism, racism, or pornography. Published *The Boy Who Opened Doors* (novel for intermediate readers 7-14), *The Boy Who Opened Doors* (the musical) and *The Boy And the Boss' Breakfast,* by Prentiss Van Daves.

How to Contact: Accepts unsolicited mss. Query first. Submit outline/synopsis with 3 sample chapters. SASE (IRC). 50% of fiction is agented. Reports in 4 months on queries; in 6 months on mss. Photocopied submissions OK. Accepts computer printout submissions, no dot-matrix. Accepts disk submissions from Macintosh Plus.

Terms: Pays royalties of 7-10%; average advance $1,000-$3,000; advance is negotiable; advance is more for agented ms; 50 author's copies. Sends galleys to author. *Subsidy publishes 1% of books each year.* Subsidy publishes books of poetry only, 50-150 pages. Subjects: love, psychology, philosophy, new male/female relationships, family.

Advice: "To save time and expense, it is recommended that authors learn as much as possible about not simply their writing craft, but also the very art of publishing. I recommend studying self publishing at some point after the author has completed several works, learning the actual book making process, book design, marketing, sales, distribution, and publishing and the money saving typesetting advantages of today's word processing and computer options. This advice is to speed the 'submission-to-publication' process between author and small press operations. This is valuable in respect to new unpublished authors, but the classical submissions methods of ms to major publishers still remains an important option to the author with a book with commercial value, for literary works of the highest quality small presses are the proven markets for success to the literary author."

SEAL PRESS (IV), 3131 Western Ave., Seattle WA 98121. (206)283-7844. President: Faith Conlon. Estab. 1976. Publishes hardcover and paperback originals. Books: acid-free paper; offset printing; perfect or cloth binding; average print order: 4,000. Averages 8-12 total titles, including 5-6 fiction, each year. Sometimes critiques rejected ms "very briefly."

Needs: Ethnic, feminist, lesbian, literary, short story collections. "We publish women only. Work must be feminist, non-racist, non-homophobic." Recently published *The Haunted House,* by Rebecca Brown; *The Dog Collar Murders,* by Barbara Wilson; *Nervous Conditions,* by Tsitsi Dangarembga; *Words of Farewell Stories by Korean Women Writers*; and *Voyages Out 1: Lesbian Short Fiction,* by Paula Martinac and Carla Tomasco. "A recent development is 'International Women's Crime'—a feminist mystery series translated from other languages."

How to Contact: Query first. SASE. Reports in 1-2 months. Accepts "readable" computer printouts.

Terms: "Standard publishing practices; do not wish to disclose specifics." Sends galleys to author. Book catalog for SAE and 45¢ postage.

SECOND CHANCE PRESS AND THE PERMANENT PRESS (II), Noyac Rd., Sag Harbor NY 11963. (516)725-1101. Co-publisher: Judith Shepard. Estab. 1977. Mid-size, independent publisher. Publishes hardcover originals and reprints. Books: hardcover; average print order: 1,500-2,000; first novel print order: 1,500-2,000. Plans to publish 4 first novels this year. Averages 10 total titles; 10 fiction titles each year.

Needs: Contemporary, humor/satire, literary, supsense/mystery. "I like novels that have a unique point of view and have a high quality of writing." No gothic, romance, horror, science fiction, pulp. Recently published *Dies Irae,* by Ruby Spinell, (literary/mystery); *The Affair at Honey Hill,* by Berry Fleming, (literary/historical); and *Zulus,* by Percival Everett (literary/futuristic);published new writers within the last year.

How to Contact: Query first. Submit outline and no more than two chapters. SASE. Agented fiction: 15%. Reports in 4 weeks on queries; 6 weeks on mss. Photocopied submissions OK.

Terms: Pays in royalties of 10% minimum; 15% maximum. Sends galleys to author. Advance to $1,000. Sends galleys to author. Book catalog for $2.

Advice: "We are looking for good books, be they tenth novels or first novels, it makes little difference. The fiction is more important than the track record."

SEVEN BUFFALOES PRESS (II), Box 249, Big Timber MT 59011. Editor/Publisher: Art Cuelho. Estab. 1975. Publishes paperback originals. Averages 4-5 total titles each year.
Needs: Contemporary, short story collections, "rural, American Hobo, Okies, American Indian, Southern Appalachia, Arkansas and the Ozarks. Wants farm and ranch based stories." Published *Rig Nine*, by William Rintoul (collection of oilfield short stories).
How to Contact: Query first with SASE. Photocopied submissions OK. Reports in 1 week on queries; 2 weeks on mss.
Terms: Pays in royalties of 10% minimum; 15% on second edition or in author's copies (10% of edition). No advance. Free writer's guidelines and book catalog for SASE.
Advice: "There's too much influence from TV and Hollywood; media writing I call it. We need to get back to the people; to those who built and are still building this nation with sweat, blood, and brains. More people are into it for the money; instead of for the good writing that is still to be cranked out by isolated writers. Remember, I was a writer for 10 years before I became a publisher."

‡HAROLD SHAW PUBLISHERS (II), Box 567, 388 Gundersen Dr., Wheaton IL 60189. (708)665-6700. Director of Editorial Services: Ramona Cramer Tucker. Estab. 1968. "Small, independent religious publisher with expanding fiction line." Publishes paperback originals and reprints. Books: 35 lb. Mando Supreme paper; sheet-fed printing; perfect binding; average print order: 5,000. Published new writers within the last year. Plans 1 novel per year in Northcote Books (our literary/academic fiction subsidiary). Averages 30 total titles, 3-4 fiction titles each year. Sometimes critiques on rejected mss.
Needs: Literary, religious/inspirational, young adult/teen (13-18 years) problem novels. Looking for religious literary novels or young adult fiction (religious). No short stories, romances, children's fiction. Recently published *All the King's Horses*, by Jeffrey Asher Nesbit (young adult); and *Dark Is a Color*, by Fay Lapka (young adult).
How to Contact: Accepts unsolicited mss. Query first. Submit outline/synopsis and 2-3 sample chapters. SASE. Reports in 2 weeks on queries; 2-4 weeks on mss. Simultaneous and photocopied submissions OK. Accepts computer printout submissions.
Terms: Pays royalties of 10%, Average advance $1,000. Provides 10 author's copies. Sends pages to author. Publishes ms 12-18 months after acceptance. Free writer's guidelines. Book catalog for 9×12 SASE or IRC and $1.25 postage.
Advice: "Character and plot development are important to us. We look for quality writing in word and in thought. 'Sappiness' and 'pop-writing' don't go over well at all with our editorial department."

SHOE TREE PRESS, Box 219, Crozet VA 22932. An Imprint of Betterway Publications Inc. Editor: Susan Lewis. Estab. 1984. Publishes juvenile hardcover and paperback original and reprints. Books: generally 70 lb vellum paper; offset printing; reinforced binding; and perfect for softcover; occasionally uses illustrations for middle years books; average print order: 5,000. First novel print order: 5,000. Plans 3 novels this year. Averages 5 fiction titles each year. Rarely critiques or comments on rejected mss.
Needs: Young adult, middle years fiction. No formula or genre fiction please. Published *Summer Captive*, by Penny Pollock (young adult); published new writers within the last year.
How to Contact: We no longer accept unsolicited manuscripts. Please query. SASE. Agented fiction 33%. Reports in 2-4 weeks on queries; 10-12 weeks on mss. Simultaneous and photocopied submissions OK. Accepts computer printout submissions.
Terms: Pays royalties on graduating scale, beginning at 12% of wholesale price. Advance varies and is negotiable. Sends galleys to author.
Advice: "We publish juvenile fiction and nonfiction only. Our primary focus is on historical fiction for middle years and on nonfiction. We do *not* publish picture books. Don't get caught up in trying to follow 'market trends.' Write about what you know, and write it from the heart. We publish books that children, ages 10 and up, will enjoy but also learn from. We are also interested in 'problem' novels that confront issues kids must deal with today."

 The double dagger before a listing indicates that the listing is new in this edition. New markets are often the most receptive to freelance contributions.

SILVERLEAF PRESS, INC. (I, II), Box 70189, Seattle WA 98107. Editor: Ann Larson. Estab. 1985. Publishes paperback originals. Books: 50 lb book stock; offset printing; perfect binding; no illustrations; average print order: 1,600; first novel print order: 1,600. Plans 1-2 first novels this year. Averages 2 total titles/year; 2 fiction titles/year. Sometimes critiques or comments on rejected mss.
Needs: Feminist, humor/satire, lesbian, short story collections. "Must be feminist or lesbian." Published *Three Glasses of Wine Have Been Removed From This Story,* by Marian Michener; published new writers within the last year.
How to Contact: Accepts unsolicited mss. Submit complete ms with cover letter. SASE (IRC). Reports in 2-3 months. Photocopied submissions OK. Accepts computer printout submissions.
Terms: Pays negotiable royalties and advance; author's copies. Sends galleys to author. Book catalog free on request.
Advice: "Try the small presses—they are more likely to give you a chance."

SIMON & PIERRE PUBLISHING COMPANY LIMITED (II), Box 280, Adelaide St. Postal Stn., Toronto, Ontario M5C 2J4 Canada. Imprints includes Bastet Books, Canplay Series, Canadian Theatre History Series and The Canadian Dramatist. Contact: Editors. Estab. 1972. Publishes hardcover and paperback originals. Published new writers last year. Books: 55 lb hi bulk web printing; perfect binding; line drawings; average print order 2,000. Averages 10-12 titles/year.
Needs: Contemporary, literary, mystery, spy, historical, humor/satire, juvenile, young adult and translations. No romance, erotica, horror, science fiction. Recently published *The Blackbird's Song,* by Pauline Holdstock; and *Sherlock Holmes & The Mark of the Beast,* by Ronald C. Weyman.
How to Contact: Query, submit complete ms, submit outline/synopsis and sample chapter or submit through agent with SASE (Canadian stamps) or IRCs. Simultaneous and photocopied submissions OK. Reports in 1 month on queries, 4 months on mss.
Terms: Pays in royalties; small advance. Sends galleys to author. Free book catalog.
Advice: "We publish only Canadian authors. Include with submissions: professional résumé listing previous publications, detailed outline of proposed work and sample chapters. We publish novelists who are good at proofing themselves and not afraid of being involved in their own marketing, but the fiction must be based on a current topics or themes."

‡THE SMITH (III), 69 Joralemon St., Brooklyn NY 11201. Editor: Harry Smith. Estab. 1964. Books: 70 lb vellum paper for offset and 80 lb vellum for letterpress printing; perfect binding; often uses illustrations; average print order: 1,000; first novel print order: 1,000. Plans 2 fiction titles this year.
Needs: *Extremely* limited book publishing market—currently doing only 4-6 books annually, and these are of a literary nature, usually fiction or poetry.

SOHO PRESS, 1 Union Square, New York NY 10003. (212)243-1527. Publisher: Juris Jurjevics. Publishes hardcover and trade paperback originals. Averages 14 titles/year.
Needs: Adventure, ethnic, historical, mainstream, mystery/espionage, suspense. "We do novels that are the very best in their genres." Recently published *Exit Wounds,* by John Westermann; *Falling ,* by Barbara Gowdy; and *Spook,* by Steve Vance; published new writers within the last year.
How to Contact: Submit query or complete ms with SASE. Reports in 2 weeks on queries; 1 month on mss. Photocopied and simultaneous submissions OK.
Terms: Pays royalties of 10% minimum; 15% maximum on retail price. For trade paperbacks pays 7½% royalties to 10,000 copies; 10% after. Offers advance. Book catalog free on request.
Advice: "There aren't any tricks (to writing a good query letter)—just say what the book is. Don't analyze the market for it. Don't take writing courses too seriously, and *read* the best people in whatever genre you are working. We are looking for those who have taught themselves or otherwise mastered the craft."

‡SOLEIL PRESS (IV), R.F.D. #1, Box 452, Lisbon Falls ME 04252. (207)353-5454. Editorial Contact Person: Denis Ledoux, Editor. Estab. 1988. "Soleil Press publishes writing by and/or about Franco-Americans (French-Canadian-American). SP has no interest in the European French experience." Publishes paperback originals. Books: average print order: 2,000. Publishes new writers within the last year. Averages 1-2 total titles, 0-1 fiction title/year. Occasionally comments on rejected ms.
Needs: Ethnic (Franco-American). "No interest at all in exploring the French of France."
How to Contact: Accepts unsolicited mss. SASE. Reports in 1 month on queries; 1-2 months on mss. Simultaneous and photocopied submissions OK. Accepts computer printout submissions.
Terms: Pays in author's copies. Writer's guidelines free for SASE or IRC. Book catalog for SASE or IRC and 25¢ postage.

‡**SPACE AND TIME (IV)**, 138 W. 70th St. (4-B), New York NY 10023-4432. Book Editor: Jani Anderson. Estab. 1966—book line 1984. Two-person operation on part-time basis. Publishes paperback originals. Books: 50 lb Lakewood white 512PPi paper; offset Litho printing; perfect binding; illustrations on cover and frontispiece; average print order: 1,000; first novel print order: 1,000. Averages 8 total titles; 1 fiction title each year. Critiques or comments on rejected ms.
Needs: Fantasy, horror, psychic/supernatural/occult, science fiction. Wants to see cross-genre material, such as horror-western, sf-mystery, occult-spy adventure, etc. Does not want anything *without* some element of fantasy or sf (or at least the 'feel' of same). Recently published *The Wall*, by Ardath Mayhar (horror-mystery); *Vanitas*, by Jeffrey Ford (sci-fantasy-horror); *The Gift*, by Scott Edelman (gay-horror).
How to Contact: *No unsolicited mss.* Query first or submit outline/synopsis and 2 sample chapters. Reports in 4-6 weeks on queries; 3-4 months on mss. Simultaneous and photocopied submissions OK. Prefer photocopies. Prefer around 50,000 words.
Terms: Pays in royalties of 10% based on cover price and print run, within 60 days of publication (additional royalties, if going back to press). Average advance $100, negotiable. Sends galleys to author. Book catalog free on request.
Advice: "We are actively interested in publishing new authors, though at present have enough on hand to last us through 1992."

THE SPEECH BIN, INC. (IV), 1766 20th Ave., Vero Beach FL 32960. (407)770-0007. FAX: (407)770-0006. Senior Editor: Jan J. Binney. Estab. 1984. Small independent publisher and major national and international distributor of books and material for speech-language pathologists, audiologists, special educators and caregivers. Publishes hardcover and paperback originals. Averages 6-10 total titles/year. "No fiction at present time, but we are very interested in publishing fiction relevant to our specialties."
Needs: "We arc most intcrcstcd in sccing fiction, including books for children, dealing with individuals experiencing communication disorders, other handicaps, and their families and caregivers, particularly their parents, or family members dealing with individuals who have strokes, physical disability, hearing loss, Alzheimer's and so forth."
How to Contact: Accepts unsolicited mss. Query first. SASE (IRC). 10% of fiction is agented. Reports in 4-6 weeks on queries; 1-3 months on mss. Simultaneous and photocopied submissions OK. Accepts computer printout submissions.
Terms: Pays royalties of 8%+. Sends galleys to author. Writer's guidelines for #10 SASE. Book catalog for 9×12 SAE with 3 first class stamps.
Advice: "We are most interested in publishing fiction about individuals who have speech, hearing and other handicaps."

*****STAR BOOKS, INC.**, 408 Pearson St., Wilson NC 27893. (919)237-1591. President: Irene Burk Harrell. Estab. 1983. "Small but growing" publisher. Publishes paperback originals. Books: offset paper; offset printing; perfect binding. some illustrations; average print order: 1,000; first novel print order: 1,000. Plans 1 first novel this year. Expects to publish 20 titles this year. Published 3 novels in 1989. Published one book of short stories in 1990. One novel—so far—scheduled for 1991. Sometimes comments on rejected mss, "comment no charge; critique $1 per ms page, $25 minimum."
Needs: Religious/inspirational, young adult/teen. "Strongly and specifically Christian." Published *The Bridge*, by Ralph Filicchia (contemporary inner-city); *And Now I See*, by Clyde Bolton (Biblical novel); and *Mory*, by Marie Denison (contemporary).
How to Contact: Accepts unsolicited mss. Submit complete ms with cover letter. SASE for ms. Reports on queries in 2 weeks. Photocopied submissions OK. Accepts computer printout submissions. No simultaneous submissions.
Terms: Pays royalties of 10% minimum; 15% maximum. Sends page proofs to author. Publishing of ms after acceptance "depends on our situation." "*Sometimes*, (not always) we need author to buy prepub copies (at 50% off list) to help with first printing costs." Guidelines and book catalog for #10 SAE and 2 first class stamps.
Advice: "Make sure that for us the book is in line with Biblical principles and powerful enough to cause the reader to make an initial commitment of his/her life to Jesus Christ, or if the reader is already a Christian, to strengthen his/her walk with Him."

Market categories: (I) Beginning; (II) General; (III) Prestige; (IV) Specialized.

‡*STARBURST PUBLISHERS (IV), P.O. Box 4123, Lancaster PA 17604. (717)293-0939. Managing Editor: Ellen. Estab. 1977. Corporation. Publishes paperback and hardcover originals. Books: paper varies; offset printing; perfect binding; line art(text), full color cover. Average print order 10,000; first novel print order 5,000 to 10,000. Published new writers within the last year. Plans 4-6 new novels this year. Averages 12-15 total titles, 6-7 fiction tiles per year. Charges for critique of rejected manuscript.

Needs: Adventure, contemporary, fantasy, historical, horror, military/war, psychic/supernatural/occult (with Judeo-Christian solution), religious/inspirational, romance (contemporary, historical), spiritual, suspense/mystery, western. Wants "inspirational material similar to Frank Peretti's *This Present Darkness.*" Recently published *A Candle in Darkness* and *While They Sleep*, by June Livesay and *The Quest for Truth*, by Ken Johnson.

How to Contact: Query first, then submit outline/synopsis and 3-4 sample chapters. SASE. Include Social Security number with submission. Agented fiction less that 10%. Reports in 6-8 weeks on manuscripts. Accepts computer printouts and electronic submissions via disk and modem, "but also wants clean double-spaced typewritten or computer printout manuscript."

Terms: Pays in variable royalties. "Individual arrangement with writer depending on the manuscript as well as writer's experience as a published author." *Subsidy publishes "occasionally."* Sends galleys to author. Publishes ms up to one year after acceptance. Writer's guidelines for SAE and 1 first class stamp.

*STATION HILL PRESS (II, III), Barrytown NY 12507. (914)758-5840. Imprints include Open Book, Pulse, Artext, Clinamen Studies and Contemporary Artists Series. Publishers: George Quasha and Susan Quasha. Estab. 1978. Publishes paperback and cloth originals. Averages 10-15 total titles, 5-7 fiction titles each year.

Needs: Contemporary, experimental, literary, translations, and new age. Published *Operas and Plays*, by Gertrude Stein; *Narrative Unbound*, by Donald Ault.

How to Contact: Query first with SASE before sending ms. No unsolicited mss.

Terms: Pays in author's copies (10% of print run) or by standard royalty, depending on the nature of the material. *Occasional subsidy publishing.* "Co-venture arrangements are possible with higher royalty." Book catalog free on request.

STORMLINE PRESS, INC. (I,II, IV), Box 593, Urbana IL 61801. (217)328-2665. Publisher: Raymond Bial. Estab. 1985. Independent literary press. Publishes hardcover and paperback originals. Books: best quality, usually acid-free paper; commercial printing—all graphics in duotone printing; perfect bound and clothbound binding; illustrations photographs and original artwork; average print order: 1,000-1,500; first novel print order: 1,000-1,500. Averages 2-3 total titles; 1 fiction title each year. Occasionally critiques or comments on rejected ms "on serious works only."

Needs: Ethnic, humor/satire, literary, short story collections. "Serious literary works only. No genre fiction, or anything that was written primarily for its commercial value." Published *People of Gumption and Other Stories*, by Fran Lehr (short stories).

How to Contact: Accepts mss during November and December only. Query first with SASE. Does not read unsolicited mss. Reports in 2 weeks on queries. Accepts computer printout submissions.

Terms: Pays royalties of 10% minimum; 15% maximum. Pays 25 author copies. Payment depends on grant/award money. Authors are generally paid 15% royalties once the production costs of the book have been met. Book catalog free on request.

Advice: "We are interested in works of the highest literary quality only."

SUNSTONE PRESS (IV), Box 2321, Santa Fe NM 87504-2321. (505)988-4418. Contact: James C. Smith, Jr. Estab. 1971. Midsize publisher. Publishes paperback originals. Plans 2 first novels this year. Averages 16 total titles; 2-3 fiction titles each year. "Sometimes" buys juvenile mss with illustrations. Average first novel print order: 2,000 copies.

Needs: Western. "We have a Southwestern theme emphasis." No science fiction, romance or occult. Published *Apache: The Long Ride Home*, by Grant Gall (Indian/Western); *Border Patrol*, by Cmdr. Alvin E. Moore; and *The Last Narrow Gauge Train Robbery*, by Robert K. Swisher, Jr.; published new writers within the last year.

How to Contact: Accepts unsolicited mss. Query first or submit outline/synopsis and 2 sample chapters with SASE. Reports in 2 weeks. Simultaneous and photocopied submissions OK. Accepts computer printout submissions. Publishes ms 9 months to 1 year after acceptance.

Terms: Pays in royalties, 10% maximum, and 10 author's copies.

TEAL PRESS (II), Box 4098, Santa Fe NM 87502-4098. (505)989-7861. Editor: Jeanne Jebb. Estab. 1983. Small press publishing 2-4 titles per year. Publishes paperback originals. Books: acid-free paper; offset printing; Smyth-sewn binding; average print order: 1,500.
Needs: Contemporary and literary. Recently published *The Testimony of Mr. Bones,* by Olive Ghiselin (short stories); published new writers within the last year. "Looking for short fiction only, either novellas of around 70 to 100 pages or collections of short stories. No full length novels will be considered. Not interested in science fiction, mysteries, romance or adventure."
How to Contact: Mss without SASE will not be responded to or returned.
Terms: Pays in royalties of 10% minimum.

TEXTILE BRIDGE PRESS (II), Subsidiary of Moody Street Irregulars, Inc., Box 157, Clarence Center NY 14032. (716)741-3393. Imprints include The Jack Kerouac Living Writers Reading Series. President/Editor: Joy Walsh. Fiction Editor: Marion Perry. Estab. 1978. "We publish a magazine on and about the work of Jack Kerouac. We also publish book length manuscripts in the spirit of Kerouac when available." Publishes paperback originals. Books: bond paper; offset printing; saddle or perfect binding; average print order: 300-500; first novel print order: 500. Plans 1 first novel this year. Averages 5 total titles each year, 2 fiction titles each year. Sometimes comments on rejected ms; charges for critiques.
Needs: Experimental, literary, short story collections. No romance, gothic. Published *Big Ben Hood,* by Emmanual Freed (literary); *Links of the Chain,* by William Harnock (short story collection); and *Walk With Me,* by Dorothy Smith (literary); published new writers within last year.
How to Contact: Accepts unsolicited mss. Submit complete ms with cover letter. SASE. Agented fiction 1%. Reports in 1 week on queries; 1 month on mss. Simultaneous and photocopied submissions OK. Accepts computer printout submissions.
Terms: Pays in author's copies "if run 300, 30 copies/if 500, 50 copies." Sends galleys to author. Publishes ms 1 year after acceptance. Writers guidelines not available. Book catalog free, if available.

THIRD WOMAN PRESS (II), Chicano Studies, Dwinelle Hall 3412, University of California, Berkeley, CA 94720. (415)642-0240. Editor and Publisher: Norma Alarcón. Estab. 1981. Publishes paperback originals and annual journal *Third Woman.* Books and journal: 5½×8½ paper; offset printing; perfect binding; illustrations and photos; average print order 1,000. Publishes 2-3 titles each year; fiction, poetry, criticism.
Needs: U.S. Hispanic women primarily, Chicanas in particular. Recent books include poetry by Barbara Brinson Curiel and Lucha Corpi and interviews with Chicana writers.
How to Contact: Accepts unsolicited mss. Submit complete ms with cover letter. SASE. Reports in 2 months. Simultaneous and photocopied submissions OK. Accepts computer printouts.
Terms: Pays in author's copies. Sends pre-publication galleys to author. Catalog on request.
Advice: "Read."

THISTLEDOWN PRESS (II, IV), 668 East Place, Saskatoon, Saskatchewan S7J 2Z5 Canada. (306)244-1722. Editor-in-Chief: Patrick O'Rourke. Estab. 1975. Publishes hardcover and paperback originals. Books: quality stock paper; offset printing; Smythe-sewn binding; occasionally illustrations; average print order 1,500-2,000; first novel print order: 1,250-1,500. Plans 1 first novel and 3 collections of stories. Publishes 12 titles/year, 4 or 5 fiction. Occasionally critiques rejected mss.
Needs: Literary, experimental, short story collections and novels. "We *only* want to see Canadian-authored submissions. We will *not* consider multiple submissions."
How to Contact: No unsolicited mss. Query first with SASE. Photocopied submissions OK. Reports in 2 months on queries. Recently published *The Second Season of Jonas MacPherson,* by Lesley Choyce; *In Light of Chaos,* by Bela Szabados; *The Love Song of Romeo Paquette,* by Cecelia Frey; and *The Eleventh Commandment,* by Andreas Schroeder and Jack Thiessen.
Advice: "We are primarily looking for quality writing that is original and innovative in its perspective and/or use of language. Thistledown would like to receive queries first before submission—perhaps with novel outline, some indication of previous publications, periodicals your work has appeared in.

Read the Business of Fiction section to learn the correct way to prepare and submit a manuscript.

We publish Canadian authors only. We are continuing to publish more fiction and are looking for new fiction writers to add to our list. Familiarize yourself with some of our books before submitting a query or manuscript to the press."

THREE CONTINENTS PRESS (II, IV), 1901 Pennsylvania Ave. N.W., Suite 407, Washington DC 20006. (202)223-2554. Fiction Editor: Donald Herdeck. Estab. 1973. Small independent publisher with expanding list. Publishes hardcover and paperback originals and reprints. Books: library binding; illustrations; average print order: 1,000-1,500; first novel print order: 1,000. Averages 15 total titles, 6-8 fiction titles each year. Average first novel print order: 1,000 copies. Occasionally critiques ("a few sentences") rejected mss.
Needs: "We publish original fiction only by writers from Africa, the Caribbean, the Middle East, Asia and the Pacific. No fiction by writers from North America or Western Europe." Published *Kaidara*, by Mamadou Bah, translated by Daniel Whitman; *Fountain and Tomb* by Naguib Mahfous, translated by James Kennison. Also, short-story collections by established writers.
How to Contact: Query with outline/synopsis and sample pages and SAE, IRC. State "origins (non-Western), education and previous publications." Reports in 1 month on queries; 2 months on mss. Simultaneous and photocopied submissions OK. Computer printout submissions OK.
Terms: "We are not a subsidy publisher, but do a few specialized titles a year with subsidy. In those cases we accept grants or institutional subventions. Foundation or institution receives 20-30 copies of book and at times royalty on first printing. We pay royalties twice yearly (against advance) as a percentage of net paid receipts." Royalties of 5% minimum, 10% maximum; 10 author's copies; offers negotiable advance, $300 average. Depends on grant/award money. Sends galleys to author. Free book catalog.

‡THRESHOLD BOOKS, RD 4, Box 600, Dusty Ridge Rd., Putney VT 05346. (802)254-8300. Director: Edmund Helminski. Estab. 1981. Small independent publisher with plans for gradual expansion. Publishes paperback originals. Books: 60 lb natural paper; offset litho printing; sew-wrap binding; average print order: 2,500. Averages 2-3 total titles each year. Occasionally critiques rejected ms.
Needs: Spiritual literature and translations of sacred texts. Recently published *Lineage*, by Bo Lozzoff (short stories); and *Toward the Fullness of Life, The Fullness of Love*, by Arnaud Desjardin (nonfiction on male female relationships).
How to Contact: Accepts unsolicited mss. Query first, submit outline/synopsis and sample chapters or complete ms with SASE. Reports in 8 weeks. Simultaneous and photocopied submissions OK. Accepts computer printout submissions. Publishes ms an average of 18 months after acceptance.
Terms: Pays in royalties of 10% of net. Sometimes sends galleys to author. Book catalog free on request.
Advice: "We are still small and publishing little fiction." Publishing "less fiction, more paperbacks due to our particular area of concentration and our size."

TIMES EAGLE BOOKS (IV), Box 7461, Berkeley CA 94707. Fiction Editor: Mark Hurst. Estab. 1971. "Small operation on part-time basis." Specialized publisher limited to contributors from West Coast region. First novel print order: 2,500. Plans 2 first novels this year. Averages 2 titles/year, all fiction.
Needs: Contemporary. "Graphic descriptions of teenage life by West Coast youth, such as Bret Easton Ellis's *Less than Zero*." Recently published *Equator: The Story and the Letters*, by V.O. Blum (erotic/philosophical novel).
How to Contact: Does not accept or return unsolicited mss. Query first in one paragraph. Reports in 2 weeks.
Terms: Pays 10-15% royalties.
Advice: "Times Eagle Books prefers first novelists."

THE TRANSLATION CENTER (II), 412 Dodge Hall, Columbia University, New York NY 10027. (212)854-2305. Editors: Frank MacShane, William Jay Smith, Lane Dunlop. Estab. 1972. Publishes paperback originals. Books: 6×9; perfect bound; high-quality paper. Averages 2 total titles/year.
Needs: Translations.
How to Contact: Accepts unsolicited ms. Submit complete ms with cover letter and SASE. Photocopied submissions OK. Accepts computer printouts.
Terms: Pays in 2 translator's copies.

TUDOR PUBLISHERS, INC. (II), P.O. Box 38366, Greensboro NC 27438. (919)282-5907. Editor: M.L. Hester. Estab. 1986. Small independent press. Publishes hardcover and paperback originals. Book: offset; Smythe sewn hardcover/trade paperback; occasional illustrations; average print order: 3,000; first novel print order: 1,000-2,000. Plans 1 first novel this year. Averages 3-5 total titles, 1-2 fiction titles each year. Sometimes comments on rejected ms.
Needs: Contemporary, historical, literary, mainstream, regional (Southeast), suspense/mystery, young adult/teen (10-18 years). "Especially needs suspense; literary; YA suspense. No romance, western." Recently published *Statutory Murder*, by Dicey Thomas (mystery/suspense); published new writers within the last year.
How to Contact: Accepts unsolicited mss. "Outline and query first, please." Submit outline/synopsis and 3 sample chapters. SASE. Reports on queries in 2 weeks; 6 weeks on mss. Accepts computer printouts and photocopied submissions.
Terms: Pays royalties of 10%. Sends galleys to author. Publishes ms 1 year to 18 months after acceptance. Book catalog for # 10 SASE or IRC and one 1st class stamp.
Advice: "Tell us of any publishing done previously. Send a clear summary or outline of the book with a cover letter. Interested in suspense in both adult and young adult; also literary fiction of high quality. Send only your best work. No romance, science fiction, western; no multigenerational sagas unless of extremely high quality."

TURNSTONE PRESS (II), 607-100 Arthur St., Winnipeg, Manitoba R3B 1H3 Canada. (204)947-1555. Managing Editor: Marilyn Morton. Books: offset paper; usually photo direct printing; perfect binding; average first novel print order: 2,000. Estab. 1976. Publishes paperback originals. Averages 8 total titles/year. Occasionally critiques rejected ms.
Needs: Experimental and literary. "We will be doing only 2-3 fiction titles a year. Interested in new work exploring new narrative/fiction forms." Recently published *The Pumpkin-Eaters*, by Lois Braun; and *Older Than Ravens*, by Douglas Reimer; published fiction by previously unpublished writers within the last year.
How to Contact: Send SASE or SAE and IRC. Photocopied submissions OK. Reports in 1 month on queries; 2-4 months on mss.
Terms: "Like most Canadian literary presses, we depend heavily on government grants which are not available for books by non-Canadians. Do some homework before submitting work to make sure your subject matter/genre/writing style falls within the publishers area of interest." Pays in royalties of 10%; 10 (complimentary) author's copies. Book catalog free on request.

ULTRAMARINE PUBLISHING CO., INC. (III), Box 303, Hastings-on-the-Hudson NY 10706. (914)478-2522. Publisher: Christopher P. Stephens. Estab. 1973. Small publisher. "We have 150 titles in print. We also distribute for authors where a major publisher has dropped a title." Encourages new writers. Averages 15 total titles, 12 fiction titles each year. Buys 90% agented fiction. Occasionally critiques rejected ms.
Needs: Experimental, fantasy, mainstream, science fiction, and short story collections. No romance, westerns, mysteries.
How to Contact: Does not accept unsolicited mss. Submit outline/synopsis and 2 sample chapters with SASE. Prefers agented ms. Reports in 6 weeks. Simultaneous, photocopied submissions OK. Accepts computer printout submissions. Publishes ms an average of 8 months after acceptance.
Terms: Pays in royalties of 10% minimum; advance is negotiable. Free book catalog.

*UNIVERSITY EDITIONS (I, II), 59 Oak Lane, Spring Valley, Huntington WV 25704. Imprint of Aegina Press. Managing Editor: Ira Herman. Estab. 1983. Independent publisher presently expanding. Publishes paperback originals and reprints. Books: 50 lb library-weight paper; litho offset printing; most are perfect bound; illustrations; average print order: 500-1,000; first novel print order: 500-1,000. Plans 10 first novels this year. "We strongly encourage new writers." Averages 20 total titles, approximately 12 fiction titles each year. Often critiques rejected ms.
Needs: Adventure, contemporary, ethnic, experimental, faction, fantasy, feminist, historical, romance, horror, humor/satire, juvenile (all types), literary, mainstream, regional, science fiction, short story collections, translations and war. "Historical, literary, and regional fiction are our main areas of emphasis." Recently published *The Power Players*, by Bonnie Huval (novel); *Living Legends*, by John Randall Brown (novel); *The Anguish of the Earth*, by Franklin Richardson; and *Moose*, by Gloria Ladd.
How to Contact: Accepts unsolicited mss. "We depend upon manuscripts that arrive unsolicited." Query or submit outline/synopsis and 3 or more sample chapters or complete ms. "We prefer to see entire manuscripts; we will consider queries and partials as well." SASE for queries, mss. Reports in

1 week on queries; 1 month on mss. Simultaneous and photocopied submissions OK. Accepts computer printout submissions.
Terms: Payment is negotiated individually for each book. Sends galleys to author. Depends upon author and subject. *Subsidy publishes most new titles.*
Advice: "We attempt to encourage and establish new authors. Editorial tastes in fiction are eclectic. We try to be open to any type of fiction that is well written. We are publishing more fiction now that the very large publishers are getting harder to break into. We publish softcovers primarily, in order to keep books affordable. We hope to publish more first novels in 1991."

THE UNIVERSITY OF ARKANSAS PRESS (I), Fayetteville AR 72701. (501)575-3246. Director: Miller Williams. Acquisitions Editor: James Twiggs. Estab. 1980. Small university press. Publishes hardcover and paperback originals. Averages 40 total titles, 2 short fiction titles (rarely a novel) each year. Average print order 750 cloth and 2,000 paper copies.
Needs: Literary, mainstream, novels and short story collections, and translations. Published *Long Blues in a Minor*, by Gerard Herzhaft (novel); *The Blacktop Champion of Ickey Honey and Other Stories*, by Robert Sorrells; *Power Lines and Other Stories*, by Jane Bradley; published fiction by previously unpublished writers within the last year.
How to Contact: Accepts unsolicited mss. Query first with SASE. Simultaneous and photocopied submissions OK "if very clean." Accepts computer printout submissions. Reports in 2 weeks on queries. Publishes ms an average of 1 year after acceptance.
Terms: Pays in royalties of 10%; 10 author's copies. Writer's guidelines and book catalog free for 9 × 12 SASE.
Advice: "We are looking for fiction written with energy, clarity and economy. Apart from this, we have no predisposition concerning style or subject matter. The University of Arkansas Press does not respond to queries or proposals not accompanied by SASE."

UNIVERSITY OF IDAHO PRESS (IV), 16 Brink Hall, University of Idaho, Moscow ID 83843. (208)885-7564. Director: James J. Heaney. Estab. 1972. "Small university press with combined scholarly and regional emphasis." Publishes hardcover and paperback originals and paperback reprints. Averages 7 total titles, 1-2 fiction titles each year. Sometimes comments on rejected ms.
Needs: Regional, short story collections. "We would like to publish some Western fictional works of suitable stylistic competence for a primarily regional market in Idaho and the inland Northwest. No fictionalized memoirs of pioneers, pony express riders, and so on." Recently published *Unearned Pleasures*, by Ursula Hegi (short story collection).
How to Contact: Accepts unsolicited mss. Query first. Reports in 1 month on queries; 4 months on ms. Photocopied submissions OK. Accepts computer printout submissions. Accepts electronic submissions via disk.
Terms: Pays in royalties. "Contracts are always negotiated individually. The small size of the regional fiction market makes less than luxurious terms a necessity for the publisher." Sends galleys to author. Writer's guidelines and book catalog free.

UNIVERSITY OF ILLINOIS PRESS (I), 54 E. Gregory, Champaign IL 61820. (217)333-0950. Senior Editor: Ann Lowry. Estab. 1918. Not-for-profit university press. Publishes clothbound originals. Books: acid free paper; cloth binding; average print order: 1,500-2,000. Number of titles: 2-4 per year. Encourages new writers who have journal publications. Occasionally comments on rejected mss.
Needs: Contemporary, literary, and experimental. Story collections only. "No novels." Published *Man Without Memory*, by Richard Burgin; *The People Down South*, by Cary C. Holladay; *Bodies at Sea*, by Erin McGraw.
How to Contact: Accepts unsolicited mss. Query or submit complete ms. SASE. Simultaneous and photocopied submissions OK. Accepts computer printout submissions. Reports in 1 week on queries, 2-4 months on mss.
Terms: Pays 7½% net of all copies sold. No advance. Free book catalog.
Advice: "We do not publish novels, and we have no outlet for individual short stories. We publish collections of short fiction by authors who've usually established their credentials by being accepted for publication in periodicals, generally literary periodicals."

UNIVERSITY OF UTAH PRESS (IV), 101 University Services Bldg., Salt Lake City UT 84112. (801)581-6771. Director: David Catron. Estab. 1949. "Small university press." Publishes hardcover originals. Books: 60# paper; offset printing; sewn binding; average print order: 2,000; first novel print order:

2,000. Plans 2 first novels this year. Averages 25 total titles, 2 fiction titles each year. Sometimes comments on rejected ms.

Needs: Literary, western. Recently published *The School of Love*, by Barber; *Bones*, by Fisher.

How to Contact: Accepts unsolicited mss. Query first. SASE. Reports in 1-2 weeks on queries; 2 months on mss. Simultaneous and photocopied submissions OK. Accepts computer printout submissions. Accepts electronic submissions.

Terms: Pays 10% royalties. Publishes ms 1 year after acceptance. Writer's guidelines and book catalog free.

Advice: "We particularly want to provide a publishing venue for authors whose material tends to be ignored by the large eastern houses."

‡VÉHICULE PRESS (IV), Box 125, Place du Parc Station, Montréal, Québéc H2W 2M9 Canada. Imprint: Signal Editions for poetry. Publisher/Editor: Simon Dardick. Estab. 1973. Small publisher of scholarly, literary and cultural books. Publishes hardcover and paperback originals. Books: good quality paper; offset printing; perfect and cloth binding; illustrations; average print order: 1,000-3,000. Averages 13 total titles/year.

Needs: Feminist, literary, regional, short story collections, translations—"*by Canadian residents only.*" No romance or formula writing. "We do not accept novels at this point."

How to Contact: Query first or send sample chapters; SASE or SAE and IRC ("no US stamps, please"). Reports in 2 weeks on queries, 2 months on mss. Attention: Linda Leith, Fiction ed.

Terms: Pays in royalties of 10% minimum, 12% maximum; "depends on press run and sales. Sends galleys to author. Translators of fiction can receive Canada Council funding, which publisher applies for." Book catalog for 9x12 SASE.

Advice: "Our only fiction titles at this point are short story collections. Quality in almost any style is acceptable. We believe in the editing process."

W.W. PUBLICATIONS (IV), Subsidiary of A.T.S., Box 373, Highland MI 48357-0373. (313)887-4703. Also publishes *Minas Tirith Evening Star*. Editor: Philip Helms. Estab. 1967. One-man operation on part-time basis. Publishes paperback originals and reprints. Books: typing paper; offset printing; stapled binding; black ink illustrations; average print order: 500+; first novel print order: 500. Averages 1 title (fiction) each year. Occasionally critiques rejected ms.

Needs: Fantasy, science fiction, and young adult/teen (fantasy/science fiction). Novel needs: "Tolkien-related mainly, some fantasy."

How to Contact: Accepts unsolicited mss. Submit complete ms with SASE. Reports in 1 month. Simultaneous and photocopied submissions OK. Accepts computer printout submissions.

Terms: Individual arrangement with author depending on book, etc.; provides 5 author's copies. Free book catalog.

Advice: "We are publishing more fiction and more paperbacks. The author/editor relationship: a friend and helper."

*WATERFRONT PRESS (IV), 52 Maple Ave., Maplewood NJ 07040. (201)762-1565. President: Kal Wagenheim. Estab. 1982. Two persons, active part-time small press. Hardcover originals and reprints; paperback originals and reprints. Books: standard trade and textbook formats, illustrations occasionally; average print order: 1,000-1,500; first novel print order: 500-1,000. Averages 4 total titles/year; 1 or 2 fiction titles/year. Occasionally critiques rejected mss.

Needs: Ethnic, translations. "Our main focus is Puerto Rico and Hispanics in the US. We may consider other Caribbean nations." Published *The Labyrinth*, by Enrique A. Laguerre (translation from Spanish of book first published 1959); and *La Charca*, by Manuel Zeno-Gandia (translation from Spanish of 19th century novel).

How to Contact: Does not accept unsolicited mss. Query first or submit outline/synopsis and sample chapters. SASE for query and ms. Reports in 1 month on queries; 2 months on mss. Simultaneous and photocopied submissions OK. Accepts computer printouts.

Terms: Pays in royalties of 10% minimum; 15% maximum; $250-500 advance; advance is negotiable. Sends galleys to author. "On a few occasions, with books of great merit, *we have co-published with author*, who provided part of costs (in cases where our budget did not permit us to proceed quickly with the project)."

Advice: "We will endorse or support grant applications made by writers to foundations, if we believe the work has merit."

WATERMARK PRESS, INC. (I,II,IV), 149 N. Broadway, Suite 201, Wichita KS 67202. (316)263-8951. Editor: Gaylord L. Dold. Estab. 1988. Regional independent publisher, planning to expand. Publishes hardcover originals. "New line in spring, 1989, high quality cover." Plans to publish 2 first novels this year.
Needs: Literary. "We need quality literary manuscripts, short story collections, with a regional theme, novels but no genre work, mystery etc."
How to contact: Accepts unsolicited mss. Query first. Reports on queries in 3 month. Simultaneous and photocopied submissions OK.
Terms: Sends prepublication galleys to author. Publishes ms an average of 1 year after acceptance.
Advice: "We are currently planning to publish four works of fiction for fall 1989. Two of the manuscripts are from new writers who have never before published fiction. These manuscripts were received through previous contacts. We encourage absolutely new writers, established—in fact, the only criterion is the quality of the manuscript itself. No computer printouts."

‡WILLOWISP PRESS, INC. (II), subsidiary of SBF Services, Inc. 10100 SBF Dr., Pinellas Park FL 34666. (813)578-7600. Imprints include Worthington Press, Hamburger Press. Editorial contact person: Eileen Haley. Estab. 1984. Publishes paperback originals. Published new writers within the last year. Sometimes critiques rejected mss.
Needs: "Children's fiction and nonfiction, K-middle school." Adventure, contemporary, horror, juvenile (5-9 yrs.), preschool/picture book, young adult. No "Violence, sexual; romance must be very lightly treated."
How to Contact: Accepts unsolicited mss. Query (except picture books) with outline/synopsis and 3 sample chapters. SASE. Report on queries varies; 2 months on mss. Simultaneous and photocopied submissions OK. Accepts computer printout submissions. "Prefer hard copy for original submissions; might require disk for publication."
Terms: Pay "Varies." Publishes ms 6 months to 1 year after acceptance. Writer's guidelines for #10 SAE and 1 first class stamp. Book catalog for 9 × 12 SAE or IRC with $1.25 postage.
Advice: "We publish what *kids* want to read, so tell your story in a straightforward way with 'kid-like' language that doesn't convey an adult tone or sentence structure."

WOMAN IN THE MOON PUBLICATIONS (I,IV), 2215-R Market St., San Francisco, CA 94110. (209)667-0966. Publisher: Dr. S. Diane A. Bogus. Estab. 1979. "We are a small press with a primary publishing agenda for poetry. We accept short story manuscripts infrequently but are open to them." Publishes paperback originals. Books: 60 lb non-acidic paper; off-set/web press printing; perfect binding preferred, sometimes saddle, smythe sewn; occasionally illustrations; average print order: 1,000. Averages 2-4 total titles each year. Sometimes comments on rejected mss.
Needs: Contemporary, ethnic, fantasy, gay, lesbian, psychic/supernatural/occult, prisoner's stories, short story collections.
How to Contact: Accepts unsolicited mss between April and June only up to 100 mss.. Query first or submit outline/synopsis and sample chapters. SASE for query. Reports in 3 months on queries. Simultaneous submissions OK.
Terms: Pays in author's copies (half of press run). Publishes ms within 2 years after acceptance. Writer's guidelines for #10 SASE and 1 first class stamp. Book catalog for 6 × 9 SASE and 45¢ postage.
Advice: "To the short story writer, write us a real life lesbian gay set of stories. Tell us how life is for a Black person in an enlightened world. Create a possibility, an ideal that humanity can live toward. Write a set of stories that will free, redeem and instruct humanity. We've been publishing poetry and nonfiction directories. We have wanted to do fiction, but have accepted none yet, because our priority is poetry."

THE WOMAN SLEUTH MYSTERY SERIES (II), A specialized series within The Crossing Press, Freedom, CA. Contact series editor directly at 307 W. State St., Ithaca NY 14850. (607)273-4675. Series Editor: Irene Zahava. Publishes paperback originals and reprints. Books: 5½x8½ inch trade paperbacks; average print order: 5,000. Publishes 2-4 total titles/year.
Needs: Feminist, lesbian, suspense/mystery. Looking for "mystery novels, written by women, featuring strong female main character(s)—a womansleuth who is either a professional or amateur detective." No romance/mystery, if it's primarily romance. Published *Footprints*, by Kelly Bradford; *Clio Browne*, by Dolores Komo; *Shadow Dance*, by Agnes Bushell.
How to Contact: Accepts unsolicited material. Submit detailed outline/synopsis and 3-4 sample chapters. Do not send complete ms. SASE (IRC). Reports in 1 month. Photocopied submissions OK. Accepts computer printout submissions. Also send short stories for forthcoming volumes of *Woman*

Sleuth Anthology — open deadline for stories. Subject requirements the same as for novels (see "Needs" above).

Terms: Pays 7-10% royalties on novels; negotiable advance. Sends galleys to author. Book catalog free on request (write to Crossing Press, Box 1048, Freedom CA 95019).

Advice: "Contemporary subjects, settings, characters preferred. Not interested in gothic or romantic subjects/styles. Don't feel you need to 'tack on' romance and/or sexuality if it isn't integral to the plot."

WOMEN'S PRESS (I, II, IV), Suite 233, 517 College St., Toronto, Ontario M6G 4A2 Canada. (416)921-2425. Estab. 1972. Publishes paperback originals. Books: web coat paper; web printing; perfect binding; average print order: 2,000; first novel print order: 1,500. Plans 2 first novels this year. Averages 8 total titles each year. Sometimes "briefly" critiques rejected ms.

Needs: Contemporary, experimental, feminist, historical, juvenile and adolescent (fantasy, historical, contemporary), lesbian, literary, preschool/picture book, short story collections, mysteries, women's and young adult/teen (problem novels). Nothing sexist, pornographic, racist. Published *S.P. Likes A.D.*, by Catherine Brett; *Patternmakers*, by Frances Sandy Duncan; *Harriet's Daughter*, by Marlene Nourbese Philip; published fiction by previously unpublished writers within the last year.

How to Contact: Submit complete ms with SAE and "Canadian NB. stamps or a check. Our mandate is to publish Canadian women or landed immigrants." Reports in 3 months. Simultaneous or photocopied submissions OK. Accepts computer printout submissions; prefers letter-quality.

Terms: Pays in royalties of 10% maximum. Sends galleys to author. Advance is negotiable. Free book catalog.

Advice: "We have so far published over 6 novels and over 4 collections of short stories. Our three adult novels have all been first novels. A translated work of fiction from Québec was published in 1985 and we plan more translations. We encourage first novelists. We edit very carefully. We can sometimes suggest alternative publishers."

WOODLEY MEMORIAL PRESS (IV), English Dept., Washburn University, Topeka KS 66621. (913)295-6448. Editor: Robert Lawson. Estab. 1980. "Woodley Memorial Press is a small press organization which publishes book-length poetry and fiction collections by Kansas writers only; by 'Kansas writers' we mean writers who reside in Kansas or have a Kansas connection." Publishes paperback originals. Averages varying number of total titles each year. Sometimes comments on rejected ms.

Needs: Contemporary, experimental, literary, mainstream, short story collection. "We do not want to see genre fiction, juvenile, or young adult."

How to Contact: *Charges $5 reading fee.* Accepts unsolicited mss. Submit outline/synopsis and 2 sample chapters. SASE. Reports in 2 weeks on queries; 2 months on mss. Photocopied submissions OK. Accepts computer printout submissions.

Terms: "Terms are individually arranged with author after acceptance of manuscript." Sends galleys to author. Publishes ms one year after acceptance. Writer's guidelines free for #10 SASE and 1 first class stamp. Book catalog for #10 SASE and 2 first class stamps.

WOODSONG GRAPHICS INC. (II), Box 238, New Hope PA 18938. (215)794-8321. Editor: Ellen Bordner. Estab. 1977. "Small publishing firm dedicated to printing quality books and marketing them creatively." Publishes paperback and hardcover originals. Books: standard or coated stock paper; photo offset printing; GBC or standard binding; illustrations; average print order: 5,000; first novel print order; 2,500. Averages 6-8 total titles each year. "Sometimes" buys juvenile mss with illustrations. Occasionally critiques rejected mss.

Needs: Adventure, contemporary, gothic/historical and contemporary romance, historical (general), humor/satire, juvenile (animal, easy-to-read, fantasy, historical, picture book, spy/adventure, contemporary), literary, mainstream, psychic/supernatural/occult, science fiction, suspense/mystery, war, western, and young adult (easy-to-read/teen, fantasy/science fiction, historical, problem novels, spy/adventure). No deviant sex of any kind or pornography.

How to Contact: Accepts unsolicited mss. Query first or submit complete ms. SASE always. Simultaneous and photocopied submissions OK. Accepts computer printout submissions, prefers letter-quality. Reports in 3 weeks on queries, longer on mss. "We do everything possible to get replies out promptly, but do read everything we're sent . . . and that takes time." Publishes ms 6-12 months after acceptance.

Terms: Pays in royalties; negotiates advance. Sends galleys to author. "Arrangements will depend totally on the author and manuscript."
Advice: "If first novels are good, we have no problem with them, and we're always happy to look. Along with queries, send at least a few pages of actual ms text, since quality of writing is more important than topic where fiction is concerned. If you believe in what you've written, stick with it. There is so much good material that we must reject simply because we can't afford to do everything. Others must have the same problem, and it's a matter of being on the right desk on the right day to finally succeed."

WYRICK & COMPANY, 12 Exchange St., Box 89, Charleston SC 29402. (803)772-0881. Editor-in-Chief: Charles L. Wyrick, Jr. Publishes hardcover and trade paperback originals and reprints. Averages 8-12 titles/year.
Needs: Adventure, southern regional, experimental, humor, mainstream. "We seek exemplary works of fiction, particularly those by southern writers. We welcome submissions by unpublished authors. We are not normally interested in sci-fi, western or romance." Published *Things Undone*, by Max Childers; published new writers within the last year.
How to Contact: Submit outline/synopsis with a "clear, concise" cover letter and sample chapters or complete ms. SASE. Reports in 2-3 weeks on queries; 8-12 weeks on mss. Simultaneous and photocopied submissions OK.
Terms: Pays royalties of 8-12% on retail price. Average advance: $500.
Advice: "By publishing quality works of fiction and nonfiction, Wyrick & Company hopes to sell to knowledgeable readers of all ages—those who seek well written, well designed and well produced books of all types. Overemphasis by major houses and the media on blockbusters has created a greater, rather than a lesser, opportunity for small and medium-sized publishers to find and publish tomorrow's great books."

YITH PRESS (I, IV), 1051 Wellington Rd., Lawrence KS 66044. (913)843-4341. Subsidiary: *Eldritch Tales Magazine*. Editor/Publisher: Crispin Burnham. Estab. 1984. One-man operation on part-time basis. Publishes paperback originals and reprints. Books: offset printing; perfect binding; illustrations; average print order: 500-1,000. Averages 1-2 titles each year. Average first novel print order: 500-1,000 (depending pre-publication orders). Occasionally critiques rejected ms.
Needs: Fantasy and horror. Accepts short stories for collections only. Novel needs include "anything in the supernatural horror category." No "mad slasher or sword and sorcery."
How to Contact: Accepts unsolicited mss. Submit complete ms with SASE. Reports in 2 months. Simultaneous and photocopied submissions OK. Accepts computer printout submissions. Prefers letter-quality. Disk submissions OK with MacIntosh II system.
Terms: Individual arrangement with author depending on the book. Sends galleys to author. Pays in royalties of 25% minimum; 35% maximum.
Advice: "Be original, don't try to be the next Lovecraft or Stephen King. Currently, I plan to publish one or two books/year, along with *Eldritch Tales*. The author/editor relationship should be give and take on both sides. I will try *not* to rewrite the author's work. If I feel that it needs some changes then I'll suggest them to the author. We are currently on hold with the book line as we are trying to get *Eldritch Tales* out on a quarterly schedule. Any potential submitter should send a card to inquire as to status."

YORK PRESS, Box 1172, Fredericton, New Brunswick E3B 5C8 Canada. (506)458-8748. Editorial Director: Dr. S. Elkhadem. Estab. 1975. Midsize independent publisher with plans to expand. Publishes hardcover and paperback originals. Publishes in English and other languages. Number of titles: 60 in 1988. Average first novel print order 1,000 copies.
Needs: Contemporary, experimental, and translations by established writers. "No mss written mainly for entertainment, i.e., those without literary or artistic merit." Recently published *Three Pioneering Egyptian Novels*, translated and edited by Saad El-Gabalawy; and Michel Butor's *Description of San Marco*, translated by Barbara Mason; and *Missing in Action* by W. Van Wert.
How to Contact: Accepts unsolicited mss, "although an initial query is appreciated." Query with SASE or SAE and IRC. No simultaneous submissions; photocopied submissions OK. Reports in 1 week on queries, 1 month on mss.
Terms: Pays 10% in royalties; no advance. Free book catalog.
Advice: "We are devoted to the promotion of scholarly publications; areas of special interest include general and comparative literature, literary criticism, translations of important works of fiction and creative writing of an experimental nature."

Close-up

Roland Pease
Publisher
Zoland Books

Roland Pease has seen the publishing business from both sides. A published poet, Pease had been writing for 15 years before he started his own publishing company in 1987. Located in Cambridge near Harvard Square, Zoland Books is a small, but growing, literary press. The name is in part a tribute to one of Pease's favorite writers, Émile Zola. "I admire his crisp prose and the simple, but strong language he used," says Pease.

He came into the business not only with a love of fine writing and books, but also with an understanding that can only come from being there. "I don't take the manuscripts I receive lightly," he says. "I get lots of manuscripts but I look at each one carefully. I respect the writers and try to respond as quickly as possible."

In fact Pease received some 400 submissions last year. Of these, he published four books. The odds are steep, as they are in many small publishing operations, but Pease encourages writers to be persistent in sending out their work.

"I've seen a lot of quality work and I'm encouraged by that," he says. "Sometimes it's just a matter of finding the right publisher at the right time."

When Pease started, he found it very different and sometimes difficult to make decisions on the economic side of publishing. "I've heard some publishers have accountants sitting on their editorial boards. Not us. I tend to go with my heart anyway.

"Yet I do see it as my responsibility not just to publish books of quality, but to follow up on them—to make sure they are marketed properly. Marketing is a challenge."

One way Pease has answered the marketing challenge is to come up with innovative ways to publish poetry. He has combined poetry with artwork in a book of days and has published a book of tear-out poetry postcards. But, although he began publishing poetry, he has published fiction, photography books and a translation by Denise Levertov of a French children's book. He plans two novels for next spring and is looking for more.

"I get a fair amount of manuscripts from agents and some are very good, but some are no better than those I receive unsolicited. I really get very few poor manuscripts."

Pease appreciates the effort most writers put into their work. "Writing can be an act of faith," he says. "You may have to revise the same page 30 times to make it good."

Once you feel your manuscript is ready, he says, get feedback. "It's hard to work in a vacuum. Workshops can be extremely helpful. While it's important to get feedback from friends, there's no better validation than to have a stranger excited by what you wrote."

Once you are ready to submit, he says, study the market and "know what's out there. And read, of course—it's almost an obligation. We must support one another."

—Robin Gee

ZEPHYR PRESS (I), 13 Robinson St., Somerville MA 02145. Subsidiary of Aspect, Inc. Editors: Ed Hogan, Leora Zeitlin, Hugh Abernethy. Estab. 1980. Publishes hardcover and paperback originals. Books: acid free paper; offset printing; Smythsewn binding; illustrations sometimes; average print order: 1000-1,500; first novel print order: 1,000-1,500. Averages 2 total titles, 1-2 fiction titles each year.
Needs: Contemporary, ethnic, experimental, feminist/lesbian, gay, historical, humor/satire, literary, mainstream, regional, short story collections. Published *Two Novels*, by Philip Whalen, and *The St. Veronica Gig Stories*, by Jack Pulaski.
How to Contact: "We no longer read unsolicited mss. We read small press and literary magazines to find promising writers. We accept queries from agents, and from authors whose previous publications and professional credits (you must include a summary of these) demonstrate work of exceptional talent and vision. Queries that do not meet these standards will be returned without comment. If we are interested, we will request the full manuscript, *accompanied by a $15 reader fee*, and will provide a critique with the returned manuscript, if we decide against publication."
Terms: Pays in author's copies of 10% of print (1st edition); 20% royalties on publisher's net (subsequent editions, if any). Sends galleys to author by arrangement. "There can be some flexibility of terms, based on mutual arrangements, if desired by author and publisher." Book catalog for SASE.
Advice: "Seek well qualified feedback from press and/or professionally established writers before submitting manuscripts to publishers. We regard the author/editor relationship as one of close cooperation, from editing through promotion."

ZOLAND BOOKS, INC. (II), Box 2766, Cambridge MA 02238. (617)864-6252. Publisher: Roland Pease. Estab. 1987. "We are a literary press, publishing poetry, fiction, photography, and other titles of literary interest." Publishes hardcover and paperback originals. Books: acid-free paper; sewn binding; some with illustrations; average print order: 1,000-5,000. Averages 4 total titles each year. Sometimes comments on rejected mss.
Needs: Contemporary, experimental, feminist, gay, humor/satire, lesbian, literary, short story collections, translations.
How to Contact: Accepts unsolicited mss. Query first, then send complete ms with cover letter. SASE. Reports in 2-4 weeks on queries; 4-6 weeks on mss. Photocopied submissions OK. Computer printout submissions are acceptable.
Terms: Pays royalties of 5-10%. Average advance: $500; negotiable (also pays 5 author's copies). Sends galleys to author. Publishes ms 1-2 years after acceptance. Book catalog for #10 SASE and 2 first class stamps.

Foreign small press

The following small presses in countries outside the U.S. and Canada will consider novels or short stories in English from North American writers. Most of these markets do not pay. Always include a self-addressed envelope with International Reply Coupons to ensure a response or the return of your manuscript. International Reply Coupons are available at the main branch of your local post office. To save the cost of return postage on your manuscript, you may want to send a copy of your manuscript for the publisher to keep or throw away and enclose a return postcard with one IRC for a reply.

ASHTON SCHOLASTIC LTD., Private Bag 1, Penrose, Auckland, New Zealand. Fiction Editor: Penny Scown. Publishes 20 fiction titles annually. "Educational publishing with a focus on books for the teaching of language arts and children's literature for all ages from picture books to teen novels." Pays royalties. "Do not 'write down' to children—write the story you want to tell using the best language—i.e., most appropriate vocabulary, letting the story only dictate the length."

BIBLIOTECA DI NOVA SF, FUTURO, GREAT WORKS OF SF, Perseo Libri srl, Box 1240, I-40100 Bologna Italy. Fiction Editor: Ugo Malaguti. "Science fiction and fantasy; novels and/or collections of stories." Pays 7% royalties on cover price; advance: $800-1,000 on signing contract. Buys Italian book rights; other rights remain with author. "While preferring published writers, we also consider new writers."

EASTERN CARIBBEAN INSTITUTE (ECI) (IV), Box 1338, Frederiksted, Virgin Islands 00841. Editor/ President: S.B. Jones-Hendrickson, PhD. Estab. 1982. Small press with plans to expand. Publishes hardcover originals and paperback originals. Regional. Needs for novels include Caribbean issues and settings. No religious. Query with SASE. Reports in 1 week on queries; 1 month for mss.

GMP PUBLISHER LTD., Box 247, London N17 9QR England. Editors: Ben Goldstein, Richard Dipple. Publishes 12-13 story collections or novels yearly. "Principally publishing works of gay interest—both popular and literary." Pays royalties. Send synopsis and/or sample chapters first. "We're particularly interested in authors who use a word processor and can supply material on disk. This is particularly true with writers sending in work from abroad."

‡HANDSHAKE EDITIONS, Atelier A2, 83 rue de la Tombe Issoire, 75014 Paris France. Editor: Jim Haynes. Publishes 4 story collections or novels/year. "Only face-to-face submissions accepted. More interested in 'faction' and autobiographical writing." Pays in copies. Writers interested in submitting a manscript should "have lunch or dinner with me in Paris."

HEMKUNT, Publishers A-78 Naraina Industrial Area Ph.I, New Delhi India 110028. Managing Director: G.P. Singh. "We would be interested in novels, preferably by authors with a published work. Would like to have distribution rights for US, Canada and UK beside India."

KARNAK HOUSE, 300 Westbourne Park Road, London W11 1EH England. Fiction Editor: Amon Saba Saakana. Publishes 3-4 fiction titles annually. "An Afro-Caribbean publishing company concerned with global literary concerns of the Afrikan community, whether in North and South America, the Caribbean, Afrika or Europe. We rarely pay advances, and if so, very small, but pay a royalty rate of 8-10% on the published price of the book. We look for innovative work in the areas outlined above and work which attempts to express the culture, language, mythology—ethos—of the people. We look for work which tries to break away from standard English as the dominant narrative voice."

‡KAWABATA PRESS (II), Knill Cross House, HR Anderton Rd., Millbrook, Torpoint, Cornwall PL10 1DX England. Fiction Editor: C. Webb. "Mostly poetry—but prose should be realistic, free of genre writing and clichés and above all original in ideas and content." Writers receive half of profits after print costs are covered. "Write first with outline."

KINGSWAY PUBLICATIONS, 1 St. Anne's Road, Eastbourne, E. Sussex BN21 3UN England. Managing Editor: Elizabeth Gibson. Publishes 10-12 fiction titles annually. Publishes "Christian books; children's books. Books on leadership, discipleship, devotional, biography, music, the church, currrent issues from a Christian perspective. A few works of children's fiction." Payment varies "according to whether writer has an agent or not, and whether we negotiate contract directly or through a US publisher. Submit one sample chapter, double-spaced, typed with adequate margins and a synopsis. Allow 6-8 weeks for response. The writer should understand the international market. Do not send anything on millenium, new age or astrology."

MAROVERLAG, Riedingerstrasse 24, D-8900, Augsburg West Germany. Editor: Benno Käsmayr. Publishes 4-6 novels or story collections/year. Publishes "exciting American authors in excellent translations; e.g. Charles Bukowski, Jack Kerouac, William Burroughs, Paul Bowles, Gerald Locklin, Keith Abbott and Gilbert Sorrentino." Writers paid for published fiction. "Please include SAE and postage."

MONARCH PUBLICATIONS LIMITED, 1 St. Anne's Road, Eastbourne, E. Sussex, BN21 3UN England. Contact: Managing Editor. Publishes up to 12 novels per year. "We are Christian publishers and therefore only interested in full-length works of fiction with a religious slant. Christian characters and conversions not cssential, but a Christian world view on the part of the author is." Pays in advanced royalty and standard royalties based on sales. "Address a synopsis and two sample chapters to the Managing Editor. Please do not send entirc manuscripts. International reply coupons are not essential but appreciated. Manuscripts should be typed double-spaced with generous margins. Authors should keep a copy of any material sent. US writers should be aware of barriers created by the use of what is strictly US idiom, and of fiction which is exclusive to the US culture. They should also understand that readers' tastes differ enormously in the UK!"

SETTLE PRESS, 10 Boyne Terrace Mews, London W11 3LR England. Fiction Editors: Mrs. M. Carter, Mr. D. Settle. "Publishing interest: contemporary thrillers (film potential), strong storyline books from romance to animal subjects." Writers paid on royalty basis. "Send solely a synopsis plus information on author."

THE VANITAS PRESS, Plaatslagarevägen 4 E 1, 22230 Lund Sweden. Fiction Editor: Mr. March Laumer. "One-person full-time operation publishing for prestige, not cash profit motives." Publishes fantasy, historical, satire, mainstream, romance (historical), short story collections. "At present exclusively interested in promising 'Oz' novels. Very actively interested in attracting writers/illustrators who would care to *collaborate* in the creation of 'latter-day' Oz novels."

Other small press

The following small presses appeared in the 1990 edition of *Novel and Short Story Writer's Market* but are not in the 1991 edition. Those presses whose editors did not respond to our request for an update are listed below without further explanation. There are several reasons why a small press did not respond—they may be out of business, for example, or they may be overstocked with submissions. If an explanation was given, it is included next to the listing name. Note that small presses from outside of the U.S. and Canada appear at the end of the list.

Alaska Nature Press-Publishers (out of business)
Arsenal Pulp Press (moved; no forwarding address)
BkMk Press
Blood & Guts Press (asked to be deleted)
Bookmakers Guild Inc.
Bright Ring Publishing (accepts no fiction)
Canadian Stage & Arts Publications
Cleis Press
Corkscrew Press
Coteau Books
The Crossing Press (asked to be deleted)
Curbstone Press
Devonshire Publishing Co.
The Galileo Press, Ltd. (asked

to be deleted)
The Green Street Press
Heart of the Lakes Publishing (asked to be deleted)
Knoll Publishing Co.,Inc. (too much subsidy)
Lintel
Ltd. Edition Press (asked to be left out this year)
Mainspring Press (out of business)
Melior Publications
Metamorphous Press (accepts no fiction)
Mina Press (asked to be left out this year)
Night Tree Press (asked to be deleted)
Pentagram (accepts no fiction)
Perseverence Press (asked to

be deleted)
Pulp Press Book Publishers (moved; no forwarding address)
Q.E.D. Press of Ann Arbor
Ranger Associates
Rowan Tree Press (out of business)
Sea-Fog Press, Inc. (asked to be left out this year)
The Sheep Meadow Press (asked to be deleted)
Spinsters/Aunt Lute Book Co.
Spiritual Fiction Publications
Tide Book Publishing Company
Tiptoe Literary Service (asked to be left out this year)
Vardaman

Other foreign small press

Excess Press
Fourth Estate
Hard Echo Press

McPhee Gribble Publishers
The Malvern Publishing Co. Ltd.

Prospice Publishing (UK) Ltd. (out of business)
Ravan Press (PTY) Ltd.

Commercial Publishers

Now that the dust from the many mergers, takeovers and buy-outs of the last decade is settling, the book publishing industry is going through a period of internal change. Last year was not a very good year for editors as new owners began to pare away and regroup newly-purchased properties. For writers, this was a sad turn of events. Many lost editors with whom they had established good working relationships and even friendships. Others found the publication dates for their books pushed back again and again as publishers reorganized departments and redefined their lines.

Despite increased competition and consolidation of the market, however, industry experts predict a more than 10 percent increase in sales this year. Many publishers are developing new imprints and several are paying more attention to literary fiction and short story collections from new writers and writers who have built a reputation in literary magazines and small presses. The market is particularly strong for children's books, mystery, science fiction, as well as mainstream novels.

Hardcover houses

Although the media is full of reports of record deals and six-figure advances, book publishers are proceeding with caution. Most fiction titles that made the bestseller lists were either by celebrities or well-known authors. For most writers, especially those whose work is previously unpublished, advances are modest and royalties are usually around 5-10 percent. Yet publishers continue to look for writers who show potential.

Mergers have enabled publishers to secure rights to both hardcover and paperback editions, published simultaneously by different subsidiaries of the same company. This means more money for the publisher from a single book deal. Publishers are also purchasing more foreign rights and selling rights to publishers abroad. With all the changes in Eastern Europe this year, many are watching eagerly for new markets and publishing opportunities outside North America.

Mainstream books with contemporary themes continue to do well. Series novels seem to be making a comeback. One of the best recent examples of this trend is Jean Auel's series about the life of the prehistoric woman, Ayla. If you are considering a series involving one place, character or family, be sure to mention this in your cover letter. Editors look for writers who are not "one book" authors. Even if your work is not suited to a series, it helps to let agents and editors know you are have other work in mind or available.

With the success of small publishers, large houses are beginning to pay more attention to literary writers and writers whose work is good, but not blockbuster material. This has opened more opportunities for literary and special-audience writers. Short story collections are also easier to sell to big houses now, especially if many of the stories have been previously published in quality literary journals. Another trend is more publishing of short novels or novellas. Sometimes novellas are included with a few short stories by a popular author.

Although most publishers say they accept unsolicited submissions, many will give top priority to solicited submissions and manuscripts submitted through an agent. Agents are becoming "first readers" in many cases and publishers rely on them to weed out the unpublishable or inappropriate manuscripts. For more information about working with agents see both the introduction to the Literary Agents section and the "Agents' Roundtable" beginning on page 59. Having an agent will help you get a foot in the door and may provide the career stability once provided by editors.

Mass market paperbacks

Mass market paperbacks have traditionally been cheaper editions (reprints) of hard-bound books. They take their name from the type of mass distribution methods started by such industry pioneers as Ian Ballantine. While years ago publishers were divided between those who publish hardback editions and those who publish paperbacks, today that line is completely blurred. Thanks to mergers and the like, many publishers own both hardcover and paperback houses. Paperback houses are publishing more original titles in paper and even venturing into publishing their own mass-market hardback books, heavily discounted.

Another, more recent, change comes from the new economic atmosphere in Europe. In fact, according to a report in *Publishers Weekly* (April 27, 1990), Harlequin, one of the largest mass-market publishers, posted representatives at border crossings along the Berlin Wall. The publisher greeted East Europeans with their first taste of the West—a paperback Harlequin romance.

Better distribution is another welcome change. Mass market paperbacks are no longer confined to a few revolving racks at the back of drug stores. Today they are prominently displayed and available in grocery stores, discount department stores, drug stores and specialized retail outlets.

Despite the improvements, however, the industry's growth has slowed recently, because of high competition. Returns on books are a major problem and some firms are cutting back on the number of titles published each month. Yet mass market paperback publishers remain very open to new writers and rely more on the strength of their category lines than on "big names."

Trade paperbacks

Trade paperbacks can be either original or reprint titles and are marketed through bookstores. The paper quality is higher than that of mass market paperbacks and so is the price. Many publishers are bringing new authors out in this form instead of expensive hardbound editions.

This type of paperback publishing is a relatively new concept for the publishing industry. Trade paperback editions have become an option for most publishers only in the last 15 to 20 years. The challenge to publishers is to produce books strong enough to compete with mass market paperbacks, while keeping their "respectable" place next to hardbound editions. Despite the difficulties, both hardcover and mass market paperback houses have recently developed trade paperback lines.

For fiction, the market for trade paperbacks is tight—some experts say it is the result of market saturation. Others feel publishers are taking fewer risks in fiction because of competition from mass market paperbacks, hardbound and discounted hardbound editions. Many publishers are sticking with classics and tried-and-true authors.

But this new type of book appears to be here to stay. Although there has been a slump in original fiction publishing, the pendulum may indeed swing back—trade paperbacks offer less financial risk to publishers. In turn publishers may be more willing to risk publishing trade paperback editions of fiction by new or less well-known authors in the future.

The genres

It remains true that category fiction offers more opportunities for new writers than any other type of fiction book publishing. Writers interested in particular genres should, however, be well-read within the genre. Study the market carefully and read both new titles and classics within the field. While each genre has its own established set of conventions, publishers are constantly looking for something new.

Genre publishing tends to go in cycles with up and down fluxes in the market normal. Mysteries, westerns and romances continue to do well, but only certain subgenres within each field are flourishing. Science fiction — especially series — seem to be on the upswing again as are detective and police thrillers.

Unlike other fields, most genres provide a strong level of support for writers. There are branches of clubs for science fiction, romance and mystery writers in most major cities and regions. Groups such as the Romance Writers of America, Mystery Writers of America and Horror Writers of America, provide their members with a wide-range of opportunities — newsletters, awards, conventions and workshops, as well as a strong network of other writers within the field.

Some other trends to note:
- Another result of the changes in Europe and the Soviet Union has been an immediate change in the nature of thrillers. It quickly became clear the Soviet-backed spies and Eastern-bloc "bad guys" were outdated. Yet thriller writers agree there's plenty of "badness" left to choose from. New/old bad guys may come from terrorist gangs, drug rings and organized crime. Some predict more books focusing on industrial espionage.
- Police thrillers continue to be popular. Technology plays an increased role in many of these books, as crime detection methods advance rapidly. Writers in this genre have little need for fantasy — they can get hundreds of ideas everyday from newspaper and television reports. Many real crimes have been fictionalized in recent months.
- Some romance writers and editors predict the return of the gothic romance in the next few years. New age romances — those with fantastic plot elements — were off to a very slow start, but with the popularity of the on-screen metaphysical romance, *Ghost*, we may see more of this subgenre.
- Although popular since the 1950s, traditional westerns have experienced a resurgence. The successes of Louis L'Amour's books and more recently Larry McMurtry's *Lonesome Dove* as well as the "Young Guns" television series and movies have led to a revival of the genre.
- Historical novels — frontier-era and those focusing on early immigrants — are also very popular. These novels require accurate research as well as crisp characterization and prose.

Book packagers

Book packagers are indicated by a filled-in square (■) next to the listing. Although new to the fiction field, the use of book packagers has become a common practice for large book publishers. Packagers are hired by publishers to fill the needs of particular lines. Rather than locating a book and fitting it into one of their lines, publishers develop ideas for lines of books and look for authors to write books for them. Usually they turn to packagers for help.

Packagers actually produce books for publishers. They will also sometimes develop ideas on their own and attempt to sell them to publishers. Then the packager will handle all the production details — from hiring writers to overseeing the printing. Writers are usually used on a work-for-hire basis to write books already developed. They are supplied with a "bible" or series outline describing the main characters, setting and overall story. Sometimes more than one writer will write a series of books, but one pseudonym will be used throughout.

Work-for-hire arrangements mean the publisher or packager owns all rights—even the copyright—to the material. Writers are usually not credited and are paid in one lump sum instead of royalties. This sounds like a bad deal at first, but for new writers, it can be an excellent opportunity. Fees paid to writers can be fairly high. Editors at book packagers often act as co-writers and work very closely with authors. For some, the opportunity for publication may offset the sale of all rights.

Subsidy publishing

Markets listed in this book that offer some subsidy arrangements, but do not publish more than 50 percent of their books under subsidy agreements, are marked with an asterisk (*). For our purposes we consider subsidy any arrangement where the author is asked to pay part or all of the costs for producing the book.

Some publishers feel the financial risks for new writers or experimental works are too high, so they offer marketing and sales help in exchange for publishing the books for a fee. Writers should consider such an arrangement only after exhausting more conventional publishing routes. Beware of publishers who ask for large sums. To find out if a price is fair, ask how many books will be published and what type of paper, printing and binding will be used. Then check these figures with a local printer to find out how much it would cost you to print the same number and type of book. If the publisher's fee is considerably higher, you may want to consider carefully if the marketing and distribution offered will be worth the additional cost.

While some subsidy publishers are legitimate, problems continue. Last year a group of writers won a $3.5 million lawsuit against Vantage Press, a subsidy publisher. Writers charged that the publisher defrauded them by not following through on promised distribution and marketing plans. Make sure you can find the publisher's books at local bookstores before making a big monetary commitment. After all, if you can't find them, how will readers?

Submitting to commercial publishers

Before sending out your manuscript read the Business of Fiction for particulars on mailing and other procedures. For the most part, publishers looking for fiction want to see how you write. Querying is fine if you are checking to make sure a publisher is accepting unsolicited manuscripts or if you are asking for submission guidelines, but publishers will want to see your work before making a decision on publication.

On the other hand, most do not want to see the entire manuscript. It's best to query first to find out what to send. Many ask for a cover letter and about three sample chapters. Resist the urge to send your "best" three—most want three *consecutive* chapters, preferably the first three chapters. Some publishers will ask for a brief one or two page summary or a chapter-by-chapter outline. Some use the terms summary and outline interchangeably— make sure you find out exactly what they mean.

While you should avoid telling too much in your proposal or cover letter, do take time crafting it. You must spark some interest from the publisher within the first few lines. Show you've done your homework by describing just how the manuscript will fit into the publisher's line. Mention previous publishing credits, but try to keep the letter to one or two pages. Limit the amount of personal information you give, unless it lends credibility to your story. If your manuscript is set in Mexico and you lived there three years, by all means mention it.

Previous publication can help you get a foot in the publisher's door. Build publication credits by submitting first to magazines. If you do not write short stories, don't despair. Many magazines are also interested in novel excerpts and your novel need not be previously published. Another way to gain publication credits is to submit to contests, a source of recognition and sometimes payment. Either way can demonstrate your work is publishable and you are familiar with the publishing process.

Check the Category Index located just before the Markets Index to get an idea of possible publishers for your type of work. We've used the following ranking system to help you find appropriate markets:

I **Publisher encourages beginning or unpublished writers to submit work for consideration and publishes new writers frequently;**

II **Publisher accepts work by established writers and by occasional new writers of unusual talent;**

III **Publisher does not encourage beginning or unagented writers, publishes mainly writers with previous credits;**

IV **Special-interest or regional publisher open only to writers on certain subjects or from certain geographical areas.**

ABINGDON PRESS (III), The United Methodist Publishing House, 201 8th Ave. S., Nashville TN 37202. (615)749-6403. General Manager and Editorial Director: Neil Alexander. Estab. 1789. Large religious publisher. Publishes hardcover and paperback originals and paperback reprints. Averages 100-120 total titles each year. "We publish no fiction for adults."
Needs: Religious/Bible stories.
How to Contact: Submit outline/synopsis and 2-3 sample chapters with SASE. Accepts unsolicited mss. Reports in 2 weeks. Photocopied submissions OK. Accepts computer printout submissions. Prefers letter-quality. Publishes ms 1-2 years after acceptance.
Terms: Pays in royalties of 2.5% minimum; 15% maximum; average advance $500.

ACADEMY CHICAGO PUBLISHERS (I), 213 W. Institute Place, Chicago IL 60610. (312)751-7302. Imprints carrying fiction include Cassandra Editions, Academy Mystery, Academy Travel Classic and Academy Firsts. Editor: Anita Miller. Estab. 1975. Midsize independent publisher. Publishes hardcover and paperback originals and paperback reprints. Books: 55 lb. Glatfelter; mostly sheet fed; perfect, sometimes Smyth-sewn for hardcovers; b&w illustrations; average print order for paperback 5,000; for hardcover 1,500-3,000. Buys 20% agented fiction for reprints only. Average first novel print order 5,000 copies paper, 1,500 copies hardbound. Occasionally comments on rejected mss.
Needs: Mystery, historical, feminist and translations. No experimental, religious, romance or children's. Recently published *The Scarlet City: A Novel of 16th-Century Italy*, by Hella S. Haasse; *Tales for a Winter's Night*, by Arthur Conan Doyle; and *Miss Read's Christmas*, by Miss Read (psuedonym).
How to Contact: Accepts unsolicited mss. Query and submit first three chapters with SASE. No simultaneous submissions; photocopied submissions OK. Reports in 2 weeks on queries, 6 weeks on mss. "*No* micro-dot printer. Manuscripts without envelopes will be discarded. *Mailers* are a *must*." Publishes ms an average of 1 year after acceptance.
Terms: Pays 5-10% on net in royalties; no advance. Sends galleys to author.
Advice: "The relationship between novelist and editor should be close; the manuscript is gone over line by line, word by word. An aspiring novelist should submit manuscripts directly to publishers and avoid agents. If the big houses turn it down there are many smaller independent presses which will read everything that comes in a bound manuscript. We do not like to receive postage and label *without* a mailing envelope—it prejudices us against the work from the outset."

ACCENT BOOKS (II), A Division of Accent Publications, Box 15337, Denver CO 80215. (303)988-5300. Executive Editor: Mary B. Nelson. Estab. 1975. Growing midsize independent publisher of Christian books. Publishes paperback originals. Books: type of paper varies; established book printers; average print order varies. Will publish new writers this year. Averages 10-12 total titles, 4 fiction titles per year. Occasionally critiques rejected mss.
Needs: "Only Christian novels in these categories: contemporary, mystery/romance and frontier romance. All must have strong, evangelical, Christian storylines showing how Christ makes a difference in a person's life." Recently published *Shadow Wind*, by Diane Todd; *Dark Riber Legacy*, by B.J. Hoff; *Walk in Deep Shadows*, by Sara Mitchell; and *Touch of the Black Widow*, by Bea Carlton.
How to Contact: Submit outline/synopsis and 3-4 sample chapters with SASE. Reports in 5 weeks on queries, 3 months on proposals. Simultaneous submissions and clear photocopied submissions accepted. Accepts computer printout submissions if letter-quality. No dot-matrix.
Terms: Pays royalties. Sends galleys to author. Writer's guidelines for SASE; book catalog for 9 × 12 SASE with $1.25 postage.
Advice: "We are looking for fiction with a solid evangelical message. People are realizing that important truths as well as clean entertainment can be provided through quality Christian fiction. Know the publishing house standards. Be sure to enclose SASE with every submission. Don't take shortcuts. Write it, then re-write it. Be willing to keep re-working the same proposal until it is absolutely tight, top-notch entertainment. Be unique, not trite. Be aware of the world and people around you."

ACE CHARTER BOOKS, Berkley Publishing Group, 200 Madison Ave., New York NY 10016. (212)951-8800. Estab. 1977. Publishes paperback originals and reprints. See Berkley Publishing Group.

APPLE BOOKS, Scholastic, Inc., 730 Broadway, New York NY 10003. (212)505-3000. Senior Editor: Regina Griffin. Children's imprint. See Scholastic Inc.
Needs: "Apple books are generally contemporary. There are no restrictions as to length or subject matter, but all Apple Books are geared toward the capacities and interests of 8-12 year olds." Recently published *Fourth Graders Don't Believe in Witches*, by Terri Fields; *I Spent My Summer Vacation Kidnapped Into Space*, by Martyn Godfrey; and *The Broccoli Tapes*, by Jan Slepian.
How to Contact: Accepts unsolicited mss. Submit outline/synopsis and 3 sample chapters. Reports in 3 weeks on queries; 8 weeks on mss. Single submissions only. Accepts computer printout submissions. Prefers letter-quality.
Terms: Pays an advance against royalties.

ARCHWAY PAPERBACKS, 1230 Avenue of the Americas, New York NY 10020. (212)698-7000. Executive Editor: Patricia MacDonald. Published by Pocket Books. Imprints: Minstrel Books (ages 7-11); and Archway (ages 11 and up). Publishes paperback originals and reprints.
Needs: Young adult (mystery, suspense/adventure, thrillers, young readers (short, 64 pages and up), animals, themes: friends, adventure, mystery, school, fantasy family, etc.). Recently published *My Heart Belongs to That Boy*, by Linda Lewis; *Scavenger Hunt*, by Christopher Pike; and the *Fear Street Series*, by R.L. Stine. Published new writers this year.
How to Contact: Submit query first with outline; SASE "mandatory. If SASE not attached, query letter will not be answered."

ATHENEUM BOOKS FOR CHILDREN (II), Imprint of the Macmillan Children's Book Group, 866 Third Ave., New York NY 10022. (212)702-7894. Editorial Director: Jonathan J. Lanman. Fiction Editors: Gail Paris or Marcia Marshall (especially sf/fantasy). Midsize imprint of large publisher/corporation. Publishes hardcover originals. Books: illustrations for picture books, some illustrated short novels; average print order: 6,000-7,500; first novel print order: 6,000. Averages 70 total titles, 55 fiction titles each year. Very rarely critiques rejected mss.
Needs: Juvenile (animal, fantasy, historical, sports, adventure, contemporary), preschool/picture book, young adult/teen (fantasy/science fiction, historical, problem novels, sports, spy/adventure, mystery). No "paperback romance type" fiction. Published books include *The Good-bye Book*, by Judith Viorst (3-6, picture book); *Tree by Leaf*, by Cynthia I. Voigt (9-13, pre-teen "problem"); and *Maudie in the Middle*, by Phyllis Reynolds Naylor (7-11, pre-teen illustrated novel).
How to Contact: Accepts unsolicited mss "if novel length; we want outline and 3 sample chapters." SASE. Agented fiction 40%. Reports in 3-4 weeks on queries; 6-8 weeks on mss. Simultaneous submissions OK "if we are so informed"; photocopied submissions OK "if clear and legible." Accepts computer printout submissions.

Terms: Pays in royalties of 10% minimum; 12% maximum. Average advance: $3,000 "along with advance and royalties, authors standardly receive ten free copies of their book and can purchase more at a special discount." Sends galleys to author. Writer's guidelines for #10 SAE and 1 first class stamp. Book catalog for 9 × 12 SAE and 6 first class stamps.

Advice: "We publish all hardcover originals, occasionally an American edition of a British publication. Our fiction needs have not varied in terms of quantity—of the 60-70 titles we do each year, 50-60 are fiction in different age levels. Our Spring 1989 list consisted of approximately 12 books for those between 3 and 8, one of which was nonfiction; 11 books for ages 7-12 (4 nonfiction); 4 for the 10-14 level (2 nonfiction); and 5 for 10, 11 and up (1 nonfiction). We are less interested in specific topics or subject matter than in overall quality of craftsmanship. First, know your market thoroughly. We publish only children's books, so caring for and *respecting* children is of utmost importance. Also, fad topics are dangerous, as are works you haven't polished to the best of your ability. (Why should we choose a 'jewel in the rough' when we can get a manuscript a professional has polished to be ready for publication.) The juvenile market is not one in which a writer can 'practice' to become an adult writer. In general, be professional. We appreciate the writers who take the time to find out what type of books we publish by visiting the libraries and reading the books. Neatness is a pleasure, too."

‡AVALON BOOKS (II, IV), 401 Lafayette St., New York NY 10003. Vice President/Publisher: Barbara J. Brett. Subsidiary of Thomas Bouregy Company, Inc. Publishes hardcover originals. Average print order for all books (including first novels): 2,100. Averages 60 titles/year. Buys very little agented fiction. Recently published *Where the Heart Seeks Shelter*, by Anne Ladley (career romance); *A Storybook Love*, by Alice Sharpe (romance); *Dangerous Odyssey*, by Jane Edwards (mystery romance).

Needs: "Avalon Books publishes wholesome romances, adventures and westerns that are sold to libraries throughout the country. Intended for family reading, our books are read by adults as well as teenagers, and their characters are all adults: The heroines of the romances are all young (mid-twenties) single (no divorcees or widows, please!) women, and the heroes of the westerns range in age from late twenties to early thirties. There is no graphic sex in any of our novels; kisses and embraces are as far as our characters go. The heroines of the romances and the heroes of the westerns and adventures should all be looking forward to marriage at the end of the book. Currently, we publish five books a month: two romances, one mystery romance, one career romance and one western; we publish only thre adventures a year. All the romances and adventures are contemporary; all the westerns are historical. The important action in all our novels takes place over a short period of time, ranging from days to no longer than a year." Books range in length from a minimum of 40,000 words to a maximum of 50,000 words.

How to Contact: Submit the first chapter and a brief, but complete, summary of the book, or submit complete manuscript. Publishes many first novels and very little agented fiction. Enclose ms-size SASE. Reports in about three months. "Send SASE for a copy of our tip sheet."

Terms: $500 for the first book and $600 thereafter, against the first 3,500 copies sold. (Initial run is 2,100.) A royalty of 10% is paid on any additional sales. The first half of the advance is paid upon signing of the contract; the second within 30 days after publication. Usually publishes within six to eight months.

AVON BOOKS (II), The Hearst Corporation, 105 Madison Ave., New York NY 10016. (212)481-5600. Imprints include Avon, Camelot and Flare. Estab. 1941. Large paperback publisher. Publishes paperback originals and reprints. Averages 300 titles a year.

Needs: Fantasy, historical romance, mainstream, occult/horror, science fiction, medical thrillers, intrigue, war, western and young adult/teen. No poetry, mystery, short story collections, religious, limited literary or esoteric nonfiction. Recently published *Butterfly*, by Kathryn Harvey; *So Worthy My Love*, by Kathleen Woodiwiss.

How to Contact: Query letters only. SASE to insure response.

Terms: Vary. Book catalog for SASE. Sponsors Flare Novel competition.

 The double dagger before a listing indicates that the listing is new in this edition. New markets are often the most receptive to freelance contributions.

BAEN BOOKS (II), P.O.Box 1403, Riverdale NY 10471. (212)548-3100. Baen Science Fiction, Baen Fantasy. Publisher and Editor: Jim Baen. Editor: Toni WeisKopf. Consulting Editor: Josepha Sherman. Estab. 1983. Independent publisher; books are distributed by Simon & Schuster. Publishes hardcover and paperback originals and paperback reprints. Published new writers within the last year. Plans 8-12 first novels this year. Averages 60 fiction titles each year. Occasionally critiques rejected mss.
Needs: Fantasy and science fiction. Interested in science fiction novels (generally "hard" science fiction) and fantasy novels "that are not rewrites of last year's bestsellers." Recently published *Sassinak*, by Anne McCaffrey and Elizabeth Moon (science fiction); *The Man-Kzin Wars III*, by Larry Niven (science fiction); and *The Wizardry Compiled*, by Rick Cook (fantasy).
How to Contact: Accepts unsolicited mss. Submit ms or outline/synopsis and 3 consecutive sample chapters with SASE. Reports in 2-3 weeks on partials; 4-8 weeks on mss. Will consider simultaneous submissions, "but grudgingly and not as seriously as exclusives." Accepts letter-quality computer printout submissions.
Terms: Pays in royalties; offers advance. Sends galleys to author. Writer's guidelines for SASE.
Advice: "Keep an eye and a firm hand on the overall story you are telling. Style is important but less important than plot. We like to maintain long-term relationships with authors."

BALLANTINE BOOKS, 201 E. 50th St., New York NY 10022. Subsidiary of Random House. Vice Pres. and Senior Editor: Pamela D. Strickler. Publishes originals (general fiction, mass-market, trade paperback and hardcover). Averages over 120 total titles each year.
Needs: Major historical fiction, women's mainstream and general contemporary fiction. Manuscripts can be submitted unsolicited to Pamela D. Strickler. Recently published *Panther In The Sky*, by James Alexander Thom; *Sins of Omission*, by Fern Michaels; and *The Hill*, by Leonard B. Scott. Published new writers this year.
How to Contact: Submit outline/synopsis and complete ms. SASE required. Photocopied submissions OK. Reports in 2 months on queries; 4-5 months on mss.
Terms: Pays in royalties and advance.

BALLANTINE/EPIPHANY BOOKS (II), 201 E. 50th St., New York NY 10022. (212)751-2600. Division of Random House. Director of Publicity: Carol Fass. Estab. 1983. Imprint includes Ballantine/Epiphany Hardcover. Publishes hardcover and paperback originals and paperback reprints. Books: offset printing; average print order: 30,000. Averages 13 total titles, 20% fiction titles each year. Average first novel print order 30,000 copies.
Needs: Religious/inspirational. "Novels must have inspirational qualities of a Christian nature." No fantasies. No Christian romances. Published *The River Line*, by Charles Morgan; *Poppy*, by Barbara Larriva.
How to Contact: Query; submit outline/synopsis, 3 sample chapters and SASE. Reports in 4-6 weeks. Simultaneous and photocopied submissions OK. Accepts computer printout submissions; prefers letter-quality.
Terms: Offers negotiable advance. Sends galleys to author. Writer's guidelines for #10 SASE. Book catalog for 9x12 SAE and 40¢ postage.
Advice: "Read some novels published by the publishing company to which you intend to submit a manuscript. Find an author you particularly admire and read all of his/her books! Common mistake is to try to describe a lengthy novel in a brief query letter without including a synopsis! It's impossible to assess a novel from a writer's brief description. It also looks amateurish when a writer states that he/her work is copywritten and when he/she states an expected advance. And *never* call an editor to query him/her about your manuscript!"

BANTAM SPECTRA BOOKS/FOUNDATION BOOKS (II, IV), Subsidiary of Bantam Doubleday Dell Publishing Group, 666 5th Ave., New York NY 10103. (212)765-6500. Vice-President and Publisher: Lou Aronica; Executive Editor: Amy Stout. Associate Publisher: Betsy Mitchell. Editor: Janna Silverstein. Estab. 1985. Large science fiction, fantasy and speculative fiction line. Publishes hardcover originals and paperback originals and reprint trade paperbacks. Averages 66 total titles each year, all fiction.

Market categories: (I) Beginning; (II) General; (III) Prestige; (IV) Specialized.

Close-up

Cameron Judd
Writer

When Cameron Judd decided to write his first western, he did what he says a lot of new writers do—he kept it a secret. "People think you're crazy when trying to do something like that. I guess the odds are against you, but, as in a job interview, when the odds are against you, you can't let that stop you." However, unlike most beginning writers with their first books, Judd beat the odds. The then 22-year-old sold *Beggar's Gulch* to Leisure Books within two weeks of mailing it.

Today, 12 years and 11 westerns later, he has one million westerns in print and writes full time for Bantam. "I consider my westerns to be traditional ones, but I try to avoid predictable plot formulas and overdone character types." He says he writes about "common folks thrown into uncommon situations. I like western characters who have a little humanity about them, who make a few mistakes along the way, don't always know the right thing to do, and don't always have the fastest draw or the hardest fist."

Currently he is working on a three-part frontier series for Bantam. The first book, *The Overmountain Men*, due out in June 1991, is set primarily on the East Tennessee frontier from 1757-1777. Judd admits the longer frontier novels are a new challenge for him, but adds he enjoys the change of pace and invites the broader characterization the term 'frontier novel' promotes. "There are stories out of the frontier history of 'unwestern' places like Florida that have all the basic elements of traditional westerns and could appeal to western readers, but you'd probably never see a book like that published as a traditional western.

"Having said that, though, I still would have to advise writers trying to break specifically into the western writing field to start out by sticking very close to the traditional categories. Set your stories west of the Mississippi in the period between the Civil War and the turn of the century. Use strong characters, lots of encounter and action, terse writing, and all the familiar western trappings; but within that framework, let your imagination run free."

Judd says the amount of research he does depends on the story, and his methods include reading history, original writers from the period, and reading old diaries and journals. Also, it helps to occasionally travel the West. Living in East Tennessee, though, does make it difficult sometimes for him to research the West. It also presents other interesting challenges. He relays this anecdote: "A photographer was coming to shoot a cover photo, and I needed to wear a western hat in the picture. So I started looking around for one, and called up a western store and asked what styles of hats were in stock. The man said, 'Well, we've just got the one hat.' I said, 'You've just got one style of hat?,' and he said, 'Not one style, just the one hat.' That was his whole hat inventory. I don't know if he ever sold it."

—Lisa Carpenter

Needs: Fantasy, literary, science fiction. Needs for novels include novels that attempt to broaden the traditional range of science fiction and fantasy. Strong emphasis on characterization. Especially well written traditional science fiction and fantasy will be considered. No fiction that doesn't have at least some element of speculation or the fantastic.
How to Contact: Query first. No unsolicited manuscripts accepted. SASE. Agented fiction 90%. Reports in 3-4 weeks on queries; 6-8 weeks on mss. Photocopied submissions OK. Accepts computer printouts, including dot-matrix, "only very dark and very readable ones."
Terms: Pays in royalties; negotiable advance. Sends galleys to author.

THE BERKLEY PUBLISHING GROUP (III), Subsidiary of G.P. Putnam's Sons, 200 Madison Ave., New York NY 10016. (212)951-8800. Imprints are Berkley, Jove, Charter/Diamond, Ace, Pacer. Editor-in-Chief: Leslie Gelbman. Fiction Editors: Natalee Rosenstein, Judith Stern, John Talbot, Melinda Metz, Susan Allison, Peter Heck, Ginger Buchanan, Carrie Feron, Hillary Cige, Jim Morris. Nonfiction: Open. Large commercial category line. Publishes paperback originals and hardcover and paperback reprints. Books: paperbound printing; perfect binding; average print order: "depends on position in list." Plans approx. 10 first novels this year. Averages 1,180 total titles, 1,000 fiction titles each year. Sometimes critiques rejected mss.
Needs: Fantasy, horror, humor/satire, literary, mainstream, psychic/supernatural/occult, religious/inspirational, romance (contemporary, historical), science fiction, short story collections (by established authors, but rarely), suspense/mystery, war, western, young adult/teen (problem novels). We are looking for strong horror and contemporary romance/mainstream fiction titles. "Because we are a mass market publishing house, we publish a vast array of genres. We do short story collections, except for the rare collection by an established author." Recently published *Springfancy*, by LaVyrle Spencer (historical romance); *The Cardinal and the Kremlin*, by Tom Clancy (fiction/military); and *Midnight*, by Dean Koontz (horror).
How to Contact: Accepts no unsolicited mss. Submit through agent only. Agented fiction 98%. Reports in 1 month on mss. Simultaneous and photocopied submissions OK. Accepts computer printout submissions.
Terms: Pays royalties of 4% minimum; 10% maximum. Provides 25 author's copies. Writer's guidelines and book catalog not available.
Advice: "Aspiring novelists should keep abreast of the current trends in publishing by reading the New York Times Bestseller Lists, trade magazines for their desired genre and *Publishers Weekly*."

BERKLEY/ACE SCIENCE FICTION (II), Berkley Publishing Group, 200 Madison Ave., New York NY 10016. (212)951-8800. Editor-in-Chief: Susan Allison. Estab. 1948. Publishes paperback originals and reprints. Number of titles: 10/month. Buys 85-95% agented fiction.
Needs: Science fiction and fantasy. No other genre accepted. No short stories. Published *The Cat Who Walks Through Walls*, by Robert Heinlein; *Neuromancer*, by William Gibson.
How to Contact: Submit outline/synopsis and 3 sample chapters with SASE. No simultaneous submissions; photocopied submissions OK. Reports in 2 months minimum on mss. "Queries answered immediately if SASE enclosed." Publishes ms an average of 18 months after acceptance.
Terms: Standard for the field. Sends galleys to author.
Advice: "Good science fiction and fantasy are almost always written by people who have read and loved a lot of it. We are looking for knowledgeable science or magic, as well as sympathetic characters with recognizable motivation. We need less fantasy and more science fiction. We are looking for solid, well-plotted SF: good action adventure, well-researched hard science with good characterization and books that emphasize characterization without sacrificing plot. In fantasy, again, we are looking for all types of work, from high fantasy to sword and sorcery." Submit fantasy and science fiction to Susan Allison, Ginjer Buchanan and Beth Fleisher.

BETHANY HOUSE PUBLISHERS (II), 6820 Auto Club Rd., Minneapolis MN 55438. (612)829-2500. Fiction lines include: Prairie Love Stories, The Stonewyck Trilogy, The Starlight Trilogy, George MacDonald Classics, Canadian West, The Zion Chronicles. Editorial Director: Carol Johnson. Manuscript Reviews: Sharon Madison. Estab. 1956. Midsize independent religious publisher with plans to expand; publishing in a variety of categories from theological to fiction. Publishes paperback and

Read the Business of Fiction section to learn the correct way to prepare and submit a manuscript.

hardcover originals. Books: type of paper varies; offset printing; average print order: 20,000; first novel print order average: 15,000.

Needs: Religious/inspirational, adventure, mystery, regional, romance (historical and young adult), gothic and juvenile. Published *Love Takes Wing*, by Janette Oke (prairie romance); *Key to Zion*, by Bodie Thoene (historical); *Code of Honor*, by Sandy Dengler (historical).

How to Contact: Query or submit outline/synopsis and 2-3 sample chapters with SASE. Simultaneous and photocopied submissions OK. Accepts computer printout submissions. Prefers letter-quality. No disks. Reports in 1 month on queries, 6 weeks on mss. Publishes ms an average of 1 year after acceptance.

Terms: Pays in royalties. Sends galleys to author. Free book catalog and fiction guidelines with 8½x11 SASE.

Advice: "Prairie romances are *very* strong in our line; next are gothic romances, then historical fiction. We look at everything that is submitted; a first novel has a chance with us, especially if it has series possibilities. We do *not* recommend an agent—this puts an unnecessary barrier between publisher and author (chances for misunderstanding, mistrust). Send queries and proposals around till you have raised some interest; work with the editor to fit it to a publisher's needs."

JOHN F. BLAIR, PUBLISHER (II, IV), 1406 Plaza Dr., Winston-Salem NC 27103. (919)768-1374. President: Margaret Couch. Editor: Stephen Kirk. Estab. 1954. Small independent publisher. Publishes hardcover and paperback originals. Books: acid free paper; offset printing; casebound or softbound; illustrations; average print order 2,500-5,000. Number of titles: 6 in 1990. Encourages new writers. Occasionally comments on rejected mss.

Needs: Contemporary, literary and regional. Generally prefers regional material dealing with southeastern U.S. No confessions or erotica. "We do not limit our consideration of manuscripts to those representing specific genres or styles. Our primary concern is that anything we publish be of high literary quality." Published works include *Blackbeard's Cup and Stories of the Outer Banks*, by Charles Harry Whedbee (folklore); and *The Hatterask Incident*, by John D. Randall (novel).

How to Contact: Query or submit with SASE. Simultaneous and photocopied submissions OK. Accepts computer printout submissions. Prefers letter-quality. Reports in 1 month on queries, 3 months on mss. Publishes ms 1-2 years after acceptance. Free book catalog.

Terms: Pays 10% standard royalties, 7% on paperback royalties.

Advice: "We are primarily interested in serious adult novels of high literary quality. Most of our titles have a tie-in with North Carolina or the southeastern United States. Please enclose a cover letter and outline with the manuscript. We prefer to review queries before we are sent complete manuscripts. Queries should include an approximate word count."

BOOKCRAFT, INC., 1848 W. 2300 South, Salt Lake City UT 84119. (801)972-6180. Editorial Manager: Cory H. Maxwell. Publishes hardcover originals. Books: #60 stock paper; sheet-fed and web press; average print order: 5,000-7,000; 3,000 for reprints. Published new writers within the last year. Encourages new writers. "We are always open for creative, fresh ideas."

Needs: Contemporary, historical, western, romance and religious/inspirational. Recently published *Choices*, by Dorothy W. Peterson; *On the Side of the Angels*, by Kristen D. Randle; and *The Falcon Heart*, by Jaroldeen Edwards.

How to Contact: Query, submit outline/synopsis and sample chapters, or submit complete ms with SASE. Photocopied submissions OK. Reports in 2 months on both queries and mss.

Terms: Pays royalties; no advance. Sends galleys to author. Free book catalog and writer's guidelines.

Advice: "Read our fiction. Our market is the membership of The Church of Jesus Christ of Latter-Day Saints (Mormons), and all stories must be related to the background, doctrines or practices of that church. No preaching, but tone should be fresh, positive and motivational. No anti-Mormon works. The amount of fiction we publish has remained the same the last three or four years. We publish little in the way of paperback; given regional nature of our market, it is difficult to price paperbacks competitively."

THOMAS BOUREGY & COMPANY, INC., 401 Lafayette St., New York, NY 10003. See Avalon Books. Small category line.

‡BOYDS MILLS PRESS (II, IV), Subsidiary of Highlights for Children, 910 Church St., Honesdale PA 18431. (717)253-1164. Manuscript Coordinator: Juanita Galuska. Estab. 1990. "New independent publisher of quality books for children of all ages." Publishes hardcover and paperback originals. Books: coated paper; offset printing; case binding; 4-color illustrations; average print order: 8,000.

Plans 24 titles in first season, 18 fiction titles. Critiques or comments on rejected mss.
Needs: Juvenile, young adult (adventure, contemporary, ethnic, fantasy, historical, animal, easy-to-read, sports, preschool/picture book, science fiction).
How to Contact: Accepts unsolicited mss. Send complete ms with cover letter. Reports in 1 month. Simultaneous and photocopied submissions OK.
Terms: Pays standard rates. Sends pre-publication galleys to author. Time between acceptance and publication depends on "what season it is scheduled for." Writer's guidelines for #10 SAE and 1 first-class stamp.
Advice: "We're interested in young adult novels of real literary quality as well as middle grade fiction that's imaginative with fresh ideas. Getting into the mode of thinking like a child is important."

BRADBURY PRESS, INC. (I, II), Affiliate of Macmillan, Inc., 866 3rd Ave., New York NY 10022. (212)702-9809. Editor: Barbara Lalicki. Publishes juvenile hardcover originals. Books: excellent quality paper printing and binding; full color or black-and-white illustrations—depends on what the book needs. Number of titles: 34 in 1989. Encourages new writers. Seldom comments on rejected mss.
Needs: Juvenile and young adult: contemporary, adventure, science fiction. Recently published *Mariah Keeps Cool*, by Mildred Pitts Walter; *Ginger Jumps*, by Lisa Campbell Ernst; and *Aurora Means Dawn*, by Scott Russell Sanders.
How to Contact: Query first on novels. Send complete picture book ms with SASE. Specify simultaneous submissions; photocopied submissions OK. Reports in 3 months on mss.
Terms: Pays royalty based on retail price. Advance negotiable.

BRANDEN PUBLISHING CO. (I, II), Subsidiary of Branden Press, 17 Station St., Box 843, Brookline Village MA 02147. (617)734-2045. Imprint: I.P.L. President: Adolpho Caso. Estab. 1967. Publishes originals and hardcover and paperback originals and reprints. Books: 55-60 lb acid free paper; case or perfect binding; illustrations; average print order: 5,000. Published new writers within the last year. Plans 5 first novels this year. Averages 15 total titles, 5 fiction titles each year.
Needs: Adventure, contemporary, ethnic, historical, literary, mainstream, military/war, romance, short story collections, suspense/mystery and translations. Looking for "contemporary, fast pace, modern society." No porno, experimental or horror. Published *Payola!*, by Gerry Cagle; *Miss Emily Martine*, by Lynn Thorsen; *Tales of Suicide*, by Luigi Pirandello; and *The Saving Rain*, by Elsie Webber.
How to Contact: Does not accept unsolicited mss. Query first with vita. SASE. Reports in 1 week on queries. Accepts computer printout submissions.
Terms: Pays royalties of 10% minimum. Advance negotiable. Provides 10 author's copies. Sends galleys to author. Publishes ms "several months" after acceptance.
Advice: "Publishing more fiction because of demand. Do not oversubmit; try single submissions; do not procrastinate if contract is offered."

GEORGE BRAZILLER, INC. (III), 60 Madison Ave., New York NY 10010. (212)889-0909. Literary and Nonfiction Editor: Caroline Baumann. Estab. 1955. Publishes hardcover originals and paperback reprints. Books: cloth binding; illustrations sometimes; average print order: 4,000. Average first novel print order: 3,000. Buys 10% agented fiction. Averages 25 total titles, 6 fiction titles each year. Occasionally critiques rejected mss.
Needs: Art, feminist, literary, short story collections and translations. Published *Confessions of a Good Arab*, by Yoram Kaniuk (literary); *The Carpanthians*, by Janet Frame (literary); and *A Revolutionary Woman*, by Sheila Fugard.
How to Contact: Query first with SASE. Photocopied submissions OK. Reports in 2 weeks on queries. Publishes ms an average of 1 year after acceptance.
Terms: Negotiates advance. Must return advance if book is not completed or is not acceptable. Sends galleys to author. Free book catalog on request with oversized SASE.

BROADMAN PRESS (II), 127 9th Ave. N., Nashville TN 37234. (615)251-2433. Editorial Director: Harold S. Smith. Religious publisher associated with the Southern Baptist Convention. Publishes hardcover and paperback originals. Books: offset paper stock; offset printing; perfect Smyth sewn binding; illustrations possible; average print order: depends on forecast. Average number of titles: 3/year.
Needs: Adventure, historical, religious/inspirational, humor/satire, juvenile, and young adult. Will accept no other genre. Published: *Recovery of the Lost Sword*, L.L. Chaikin; and *Mary of Magdala*, by Anne C. Williman.

How to Contact: Query, but decision is not made until ms is reviewed. No simultaneous submissions; photocopied submissions OK. Reports in 2 months on queries and mss.
Terms: Pays 10% in royalties; no advance. Sends galleys to author if requested.
Advice: "We publish very few fiction works, but we encourage first novelists. We encourage a close working relationship with the author to develop the best possible product."

CAMELOT BOOKS (II), Imprint of Avon Books, (Division of the Hearst Corporation), 105 Madison Ave., New York NY 10016. (212)481-5609. Editorial Director: Ellen E. Krieger. Estab. 1961. Publishes paperback originals and reprints for middle-grade juvenile list. Books: 6-10 line drawings in a few of the younger books. No color.
Needs: Juvenile (fantasy—"very selective," contemporary—"selective"). Looking for "contemporary, humorous books about real kids in real-life situations." No "science fiction, animal stories, picture books." Published *Haunting in Williamsburg*, by Lou Kassem; *The Return of the Plant that Ate Dirty Socks*, by Nancy McArthur; and *The Secret of the Indian*, by Lynne Reid Banks.
How to Contact: Accepts unsolicited mss. Submit complete ms with cover letter (preferred) or outline/synopsis and 3 sample chapters. Agented fiction 75%. Reports in 3-4 weeks on queries; 6-10 weeks on mss. Simultaneous and photocopied submissions OK. Accepts computer printout submissions.
Terms: Royalties and advance negotiable. Sends galleys to author. Writer's guidelines for #10 SAE and 1 first class stamp. Book catalog for 9×11 SAE and 98¢ postage.

CARROLL & GRAF PUBLISHERS, INC. (III), 260 5th Ave., New York NY 10001. (212)889-8772. Contact: Editor. Estab. 1983. Publishes hardcover and paperback originals and paperback reprints. Plans 5 first novels this year. Averages 80 total titles, 45 fiction titles each year. Average first novel print order 20,000 copies. Occasionally critiques rejected mss.
Needs: Contemporary, erotica, fantasy, science fiction, literary, mainstream and suspense/mystery. No romance.
How to Contact: Does not accept unsolicited mss. Query first or submit outline/synopsis and sample chapters. SASE. Reports in 2 weeks. Photocopied submissions OK. Accepts computer printout submissions, no dot-matrix. Prefers letter-quality.
Terms: Pays in royalties of 6% minimum; 15% maximum; advance negotiable. Sends galleys to author. Free book catalog on request.

*CHILDRENS PRESS (II), Division of Regensteiner Publishing Enterprises, Inc., 544 N. Cumberland Ave., Chicago IL 60656. (312)693-0800. Vice President, Editorial: Fran Dyra. Estab. 1946. Publishes hardcover originals. Published new writers within the last year. Averages 125-150 total titles, 40 fiction titles each year.
Needs: Juvenile (easy-to-read, picture books, biographies (historical and contemporary) for middle and Junior high grades.
How to Contact: Query first if long ms (more than 5 ms pages or series idea); or submit outline/synopsis and sample chapters or complete ms with SASE. Simultaneous submissions and photocopied submissions OK. Do not send original artwork. Reports in 3 months.
Terms: Occasionally pays in royalties of 5% minimum; negotiates advance. Generally makes outright purchase of $500 minimum; 6 author's copies. Occasionally subsidy publishes. Offers 25% of sale price for subsidiary rights. Free writer's guidelines; free book catalog on request.
Advice: "Have started trade sales primarily to museums and teacher-supply bookstores. Need authors who can write social studies materials for our Enchantment of the World series (128 page books, 6th-grade reading level). Also need writers for our Cornerstones of Freedom series (48 pages, 4th grade reading level). Looking for action-packed stories for young readers who have second- or third-grade reading skills."

CITADEL PRESS (II), Lyle Stuart Inc., 120 Enterprise Ave., Secaucus NJ 07094. (201)866-4199. Vice President: Allan J. Wilson. Estab. 1942. Publishes hardcover and paperback originals and paperback reprints. Averages 65 total titles, 4-7 fiction titles each year. Occasionally critiques rejected mss.
Needs: No religious, romantic or detective. Published *The Rain Maiden*, by Jill M. Phillips and *Human Oddities*, by Martin Monestiere.
How to Contact: Accepts unsolicited mss. Query first with SASE. Reports in 6 weeks on queries; 2 months on mss. Simultaneous and photocopied submissions OK.
Terms: Pays in royalties of 10% minimum; 15% maximum; 12-25 author's copies. Advance is more for agented ms; depends on grant/award money.

CLARION BOOKS (II): A Houghton Mifflin Company, 215 Park Ave., South, New York NY 10003. (212)420-5800. Editor/Publisher: Dorothy Briley. Executive Editor: Dinah Stevenson. Estab. 1965 "as the children's book division of Seabury Press; 1979 as a new children's book imprint of Houghton Mifflin Company." Midsize children's book imprint of a major publishing company. Publishes hardcover originals and paperback reprints from its own backlist. Number of titles: 30 in 1989; 30 in 1990. Average print order: 6,000-7,000. Published new writers within the last year. Buys 10-15% agented fiction. Comments on rejected mss "only if we're encouraging a revision."
Needs: Juvenile and young adult: adventure, suspense and humorous contemporary stories for ages 8-12 and 10-14; "fresh, personal stories that capture our attention, and that we think young readers would enjoy." Published *Always and Forever Friends*, by C. S. Adler; *Saying Good-bye to Grandma*, by Jane Resh Thomas; *December Stillness*, by Mary Downing Hahn. Especially interested in humorous stories for ages 8 to 12.
How to Contact: Accepts unsolicited mss. Query on mss of more than 50 pages. SASE. "We like queries to be straightforward—no dramatic teaser openings—and to contain a description of the story, plus any relevant writing credits. It's good if they can be kept to a page, or at most two pages." Reluctantly considers simultaneous submissions; photocopied submissions OK. Accepts computer printout submissions. Reports in 2 weeks on queries, 8 weeks on mss. Publishes ms 1-1½ years after acceptance.
Terms: Pays 5% royalties on picture books; 10% on other books; offers $2,000-$3,500 advances. Writer must return advance if book is not completed or is not acceptable. Free book catalog and guidelines.
Advice: "I really believe that the best novels come out of the author's self-knowledge of his or her own experience and background. Don't send us imitations of other writers' successes. We're always open to first novelists in the hope that they'll become regular contributors to our list. We've noticed a return to lighter stories from the heavier problem novels of recent years. Attend a writer's workshop or critique group in order to study the structure of successful novels." Publishing "more middle grade fiction, less young adult fiction, because paperback originals seem to have covered that market. More paperback reprints from our backlist because bookstores like them."

■**CLOVERDALE PRESS INC. (II).** 96 Morton St., New York NY 10014. (212)727-3370. Executive Editor: Robin Hardy. Estab. 1980. Book packager. Publishes paperback originals. Published new writers within the last year. Plans 2-5 first books this year. Averages 200 total titles; fiction and nonfiction. Sometimes comments on rejected ms.
Needs: Juvenile and young adult fantasy/science fiction, historical, adventure, and coming-of-age stories. No mainstream material. Recently published *Nowhere High*, by Jesse Maguire; *Animal Inn*, by Virginia Vail ; and nonfiction sports titles for Y/A and juvenile.
How to Contact: Accepts unsolicited mss. Query first and submit outline/synopsis and 2-3 sample chapters (30 pages). Agented fiction 50%. Reports in 3 months. Simultaneous and photocopied submissions OK. Accepts computer printout submissions.
Terms: Average advance $2,000-$4,000 and 10 author's copies. Publishes ms 6-9 months after acceptance.
Advice: "Write to category. Submit 30 pages—if it doesn't happen in 30 pages it's not going to happen."

CONTEMPORARY BOOKS (IV), 180 N. Michigan Ave., Chicago IL 60601. (312)782-9181. Imprint: Congdon & Weed. Associate Publisher: Nancy J. Crossman. Estab. 1977. Mostly nonfiction adult trade publisher. Publishes hardcover and paperback originals and reprints. Recently published *Elements of Chance*, by Louisa Elliott; published new writers within the last year (agented only). Averages 120 total titles, 1-2 fiction titles each year.
How to Contact: Accepts unsolicited mss. Send 2-3 sample chapters. SASE. Reports in 3 weeks on queries; 3 months on mss. Simultaneous and photocopied submissions OK.
Terms: Pays royalties.

Listings marked with a solid box [■] are book packagers. See the introduction to Commercial Publishers for more information.

CROSSWAY BOOKS (II, IV), Division of Good News Publishers, 1300 Crescent, Wheaton IL 60187. (312)345-7474. Managing Editor: Ted Griffin. Estab. 1938. Midsize independent religious publisher with plans to expand. Publishes paperback originals. Book: average print order 5,000. Buys 10% agented fiction. Averages 35 total titles, 8-10 fiction titles each year.
Needs: Contemporary, adventure, fantasy, juvenile (fantasy), literary, religious/inspirational, science fiction and young adult (fantasy/science fiction). "All fiction published by Crossway Books must be written from the perspective of historic orthodox Christianity. It need not be *explicitly* Christian, but it must understand and view the world through Christian principle. For example, our books *Taliesin* and *Merlin* take place in a pre-Christian era, but Christian themes (e.g., sin, forgiveness, sacrifice, redemption) are present. We are *eager* to discover and nurture Christian novelists." No sentimental, didactic, "inspirational" religious fiction; heavy-handed allegorical or derivative (of C.S. Lewis or J.R.R. Tolkien) fantasy. Recently published *The Throne of Tara* by John Desjarlais; *In the Midst of Wolves*, by Barry McGuire and Logan White; and *The Power of Charles Street*, by Jean Harmeling.
How to Contact: Send query with synopsis and sample chapters. Accepts computer printout submissions. Prefers letter-quality. Reports in 5 weeks to 4 months on queries. Publishes ms 1-2 years after acceptance.
Terms: Pays in royalties and negotiates advance. Book catalog for 9×12 SAE and $1.25.
Advice: "Publishing a higher quality of writing as we develop a wider reputation for excellent Christian fiction. Christian novelists—you must get your writing *up to standard*. The major reason novels informed by a Christian perspective do not have more presence in the market is because they are inferior. Sad but true. I believe Crossway can successfully publish and market *quality* Christian novelists. Also read John Gardner's *On Moral Fiction*. The market for fantasy/science fiction continues to expand (and genre fiction in general). There are more attempts lately at Christian science fiction and fantasy, though they generally fail from didacticism or from being overly derivative."

CROWN PUBLISHING GROUP (II), 201 E. 50th St., New York NY 10022. (212)572-6190. Imprints include Crown, Harmony Books, Orion Books, Clarkson N. Potter, Inc. Executive Vice Pres., Editor-in-Chief: Betty A. Prashker. Crown Executive Editor: James O'Shea Wade. Sr. Editors: Editorial Director, Harmony Books: Peter Guzzardi. Executive Editor: Michael Pietsch. Executive Editor: Lauren Shakely. Editorial Director, Orion Books: James O'Shea Wade. Executive Managing Editor: Laurie Stark. Estab. 1936. Large independent publisher of fiction and nonfiction. Publishes hardcover and paperback originals and reprints. Magazine: 50 lb paper; offset printing; hardcover binding; sometimes illustrations; average print order: 15,000. Plans 4 first novels this year. Averages 250 total titles, 20 fiction titles each year. Average first novel print order: 15,000 copies. Occasionally critiques rejected mss.
Needs: Adventure, contemporary, historical, horror, humor/satire, literary, mainstream, science fiction, war. Recently published *Plains of Passage*, by Jean Avel; *Dave Barry Turns 40*, by Dave Barry; and *American Country Classics*, by Mary Emmerling.
How to Contact: "Query letters only addressed to the Editorial Department. Complete mss are returned unread . . ." SASE. Reports in 3-4 months. Photocopied submissions OK.
Terms: Pays advance against royalty; terms vary and are negotiated per book. Book catalog for SASE.

DAW BOOKS, INC. (I, IV), 375 Hudson St., New York NY 10014. President/Editor-in-Chief: Betsy Wollheim. Executive Editor: Sheila Gilbert. Estab. 1971. Publishes paperback originals, hardcover reprints and hardcover originals. Books: illustrations sometimes; average print and first novel order vary widely. May publish as many as 6 or more first novels a year. Averages 60 total titles, all fiction, each year. Occasionally critiques rejected mss.
Needs: Fantasy, science fiction and horror only.
How to Contact: Submit complete ms with SASE. Usually reports in 2-3 months on mss, but in special cases may take longer.
Terms: Pays an advance against royalties. Sends galleys to author (if there is time).
Advice: "We strongly encourage new writers. We like a close and friendly relationship with authors. We are publishing more fantasy than previously, but we are looking for more *serious* fantasy and especially need science fiction. To unpublished authors: Try to make an educated submission and don't give up."

DEL REY BOOKS, Subsidiary of Ballantine Books, 201 E. 50 St., New York NY 10022. (212)572-2677. Estab. 1977. Publishes hardcover originals and paperback originals and reprints. Plans 6-7 first novels this year. Publishes 120 titles each year, all fiction. Sometimes critiques rejected mss.

Needs: Fantasy and science fiction. Fantasy must have magic as an intrinsic element to the plot. No flying-saucer, Atlantis or occult novels. Recently published *Renegades of Pern*, by Anne McCaffrey (science fiction/hardcover original); *The Diamond Throne*, by David Eddings (fantasy/hardcover original); and *The Metaconcert*, by Julian May (science fiction/paperback reprint).

How to Contact: Accepts unsolicited mss. Submit complete manuscript with cover letter or outline/synopsis and first 3 chapters. Address science fiction to SF editor; fantasy to fantasy editor. Reports in 2 weeks on queries; 10 months on ms. Photocopied submissions OK. Computer printout submissions OK.

Terms: Pays in royalties; "advance is competitive." Sends pre-publication galleys to author. Writer's guidelines for #10 SAE and 1 first class stamp.

Advice: Has been publishing "more fiction and more hardcovers, because the market is there for them. Read a lot of science fiction and fantasy, such as works by Anne McCaffrey, David Eddings, Larry Niven, Arthur C. Clarke, Terry Brooks, Frederik Pohl, Barbara Hambly. When writing, pay particular attention to plotting (and a satisfactory conclusion) and characters (sympathetic and well-rounded) — because those are what readers look for."

DELACORTE/DELL BOOKS FOR YOUNG READERS (II, III, IV), Division of Bantam Doubleday Dell Publishing Group, Inc., 666 5th Ave., New York NY 10103. (212)765-6500. Imprints include Yearling and Laurel-Leaf Books and Yearling Classics. New imprint: Young Yearling Books, for readers 5-8 years old. Vice President/Publisher: George Nicholson. Vice President and Associate Publisher: Craig Virden. Exec. Editor: Michelle Poploff. Large publisher specializing in young adult and middle-age fiction. Occasionally critiques or comments on rejected ms.

Needs: Fantasy, juvenile, young adult. "We are looking for quality fiction — all categories possible." No romance of the formula type. Published *Fade*, by Robert Cormier; *Beans on the Roof*, by Betsy Byars; *Cal Cameron by Day, Spiderman by Night*, by Ann Cosum (winner of Delacorte fiction contest).

How to Contact: Query first. Unsolicited manuscripts not accepted. Fiction is agented.

Terms: Pays in royalties; advance is negotiable. Send galleys to author. Book catalog free on request.

Advice: "We are publishing more fiction than in the past. The market is good."

DELL PUBLISHING, 666 Fifth Avenue, New York NY 10103. (212)765-6500. Imprints include Delacorte Press, Delacorte Juvenile, Delta, Dell, Laurel, Laurel-Leaf and Yearling. Estab. 1922. Publishes hardcover and paperback originals and paperback reprints.

Needs: See below for individual imprint requirements.

How to Contact: Reports in 3 months. Photocopied and simultaneous submissions OK. Please adhere strictly to the following procedures: 1. Send *only* a 4-page synopsis or outline with a cover letter stating previous work published or relevant experience. Enclose SASE. 2. *Do not* send ms, sample chapters or artwork. 3. *Do not* register, certify or insure your letter. Dell is comprised of several imprints, each with its own editorial department. Please review carefully the following information and direct your submissions to the appropriate department. Your envelope must be marked: Attention: (One of the following names of imprints), Editorial Department — Proposal.

DELACORTE: Publishes in hardcover; looks for top-notch commercial fiction; historical romance. Recently published *Firefly Summer*, by Maeve Binchy; and *Daddy*, by Danielle Steel. 35 titles/year.

DELTA: Publishes trade paperbacks; will be publishing original fiction; looks for useful, substantial guides (nonfiction). 20 titles/year.

DELL: Publishes mass-market paperbacks; rarely publishes original nonfiction; looks for family sagas, historical romances, sexy modern romances, adventure and suspense thrillers, psychic/supernatural, horror, war novels, fiction and nonfiction. Not currently publishing original mysteries or science fiction. 200 titles/year.

DELACORTE JUVENILE: Publishes in hardcover for children and young adults, grades K-12. 40 titles/year. "We prefer complete mss for fiction."

LAUREL-LEAF: Publishes originals and reprints in paperback for young adults, grades 7-12. 48 titles/year.

YOUNG YEARLING: pre K to 4th grade. Publishes originals and reprints in paperback for children.

YEARLING: Publishes originals and reprints in paperback for children, grades 1-6. 75 titles/year.

Terms: Pays 6-15% in royalties; offers advance. Sends galleys to author. Book catalog for 8½×11 SASE plus $1.30 postage (Attention: Customer Service).

Advice: "Don't get your hopes up. Query first only with 4-page synopsis plus SASE. Study the paperback racks in your local drugstore. We encourage first novelists. We also encourage all authors to seek agents."

DEMBNER BOOKS (II), Division of Red Dembner Enterprises, 80 8th Ave., New York NY 10011. Editor: S. Arthur Dembner. Publishes hardcover originals. Books: quality consignment stock paper; sheet and web printing; hardcover binding; illustrations rarely; average print order: 5,000-10,000; first novel print order: 3,000-5,000.
Needs: Mystery/suspense and literary. "We are prepared to publish a limited number of well-written, nonsensational works of fiction." Recently published *The Dividing Line*, by Kjell-Olof Bornemark (a spy thriller); and *Wolf in Sheep's Clothing*, by John R. Riggs.
How to Contact: Not accepting unsolicited ms. Simultaneous and legible photocopied submissions OK.
Terms: Offers negotiable advance. Sends galleys to author.
Advice: "Library sales are up; general sales to bookstores are down. Have patience and forbearance. Those who make it big on a first novel are a very not-so-select few. The randomness of publishing success stories is one of the hardest things about being a writer (and editor, I must add)."

DIAL BOOKS FOR YOUNG READERS (II), Subsidiary of Penguin Books U.S.A. Inc., 375 Hudson St., New York NY 10014. (212)366-2000. Imprints include Pied Piper Books, Easy-to-Read Books. Editor-in-Chief/Pres./Publisher: Phyllis Fogelman. Estab. 1961. Trade children's book publisher, "looking for picture book mss and novels." Publishes hardcover originals. Plans 1 first novel this year. Averages 50-60 titles, all fiction. Occasionally critiques or comments on rejected ms.
Needs: Juvenile (1-9 yrs.) including: animal, fantasy, spy/adventure, contemporary and easy-to-read; young adult/teen (10-18 years) including: fantasy/science fiction, literary fiction, sports and spy/adventure. Recently published *Lionel in the Spring*, by Stephen Krensky (easy-to-read); *The Tale of Caliph Stork*, by Lenny Hort (picture book); and *Bailey's Bones*, by Victor Kelleher (novel).
How to Contact: Accepts unsolicited mss. Submit outline/synopsis and sample chapters or complete ms with cover letter. SASE. Agented fiction 50%. Reports in 3-4 weeks on queries. Simultaneous and photocopied submissions OK. Accepts computer printout submissions.
Terms: Pays in royalties. Writer's guidelines free for #10 SAE and 1 first class stamp. Book catalog for 9×12 SAE and $1.92 postage.
Advice: "We are publishing more fiction books than in the past, and we publish only hardcover originals, most of which are fiction. At this time we are particularly interested in both fiction and nonfiction for the middle grades, and innovative picture book manuscripts. We also are looking for easy-to-reads for first and second graders. Plays, collections of games and riddles, and counting and alphabet books are generally discouraged. Before submitting a manuscript to a publisher, it is a good idea to request a catalog to see what the publisher is currently publishing. As the 'Sweet Valley High' phenomenon has loosened its stranglehold on YA fiction, we are seeing more writers able to translate traditional values of literary excellence and contemporary innovation into the genre. Make your cover letters read like jacket flaps—short and compelling. Don't spend a lot of time apologizing for a lack of qualifications. In fact, don't mention them at all unless you have publishing credits, or your background is directly relevant to the story. 'I found this folktale during a return trip to the Tibetan village where I spent the first ten years of my life.'"

DORCHESTER PUBLISHING CO., INC. (II), Leisure Books, 276 Fifth Ave., New York NY 10001. (212)725-8811. Imprint: Leisure Books. Submissions Editor: Frank Walgren. Estab. 1970. Publisher of mass market paperbacks. Publishes paperback originals and reprints. Books: photo offset printing; average print order varies. Receptive to first novels. Published new writers within the last year. Averages 150 total titles, mostly fiction. Buys 40% agented fiction.
Needs: "At present, Dorchester publishes an occasional science fiction or nonfiction book, but these are usually agented." Recently published *Sweet Fury*, by Catherine Hart (historical romance); and *The Devil's Auction*, by Robert Weinberg. No juvenile, young adult, contemporary romance, romantic suspense, or original mysteries. Romance (historical, 90,000 words; futuristic, timeswept, gothic, 75,000 words), horror (80,000 words).
How to Contact: Query first or submit outline/synopsis and 3 sample chapters with SASE. Nothing will be returned without an SASE. Reports in 3 weeks on queries; 8-10 weeks on mss. No simultaneous submissions accepted. Letter-quality computer printouts only. Publishes ms usually within 2 years after acceptance.
Terms: Pays in royalties of 4%. Advance is negotiable. Sends galleys to author.
Advice: We are concentrating on romance. Learn to spell and know your grammar! Most importantly, don't get discouraged by all those rejection slips—if you're good, you'll get published sooner or later. We encourage first novelists. Our relationship with authors is "a limited partnership with limitless possibilities."

DOUBLEDAY BOOKS, Division of Bantam Doubleday Dell Publishing Group, 666 Fifth Ave., New York NY 10103. (212)765-6500. Estab. 1897. Publishes hardcover originals and paperback reprints.
Needs: Doubleday is not able to consider unsolicited queries, proposals or manuscripts unless submitted through a bona fide literary agent, except that we will consider fiction for crime club, science fiction and western imprints.
How to Contact: Send copy of complete ms (60,000-80,000 words) to Crime Club Editor, Science Fiction Editor or Western Editor as appropriate. Sufficient postage for return via fourth class mail must accompany ms. Reports in 2-6 months.
Terms: Pays in royalties; offers advance.

DOUBLEDAY CANADA LIMITED (III,IV), 105 Bond St., Toronto, Ontario M5B 1Y3 Canada. (416)340-0777. Imprint: Dell Distributing. Editorial Department: Jill Lambert. Estab. 1936. Large commercial *Canadian* publisher. Publishes hardcover originals (Doubleday) and paperback reprints (Dell). Book: offset or high bulk paper; offset printing; perfect or sewn binding. Plans "one at most" first novels this year. Publishes 20-40 total titles each year, 10-15 fiction titles.
Needs: Mainstream, humor/satire, literary, mysteries, commercial fiction, literary fiction, suspense, science fiction, juvenile. Published *Road to the Top*, by Aird, Novack and Westcott (business); *Death on Prague*; by John Reeves (mystery); *My Father's House*, by Sylvia Fraser (autobiography).
How to Contact: Accepts unsolicited mss. Query or send outline and chapters with cover letter. SASE (IRC) necessary for return of mss. "Please do *not* send SASE with US stamps!" 90% of fiction is agented. Reports on queries in up to 3 weeks; on ms in up to 2 months. Simultaneous and photocopied submissions OK. Accepts computer printout submissions, no dot-matrix.
Terms: Pays standard royalties, negotiable advance and 10 author's copies. Sends prepublication galleys to author.
Advice: "Think about marketability. Research the publishing house you plan to submit your work to."

DOUBLEDAY-FOUNDATION BOOKS (II), Subsidiary of Bertelsmann, 666 Fifth Ave., New York NY 10103. (212)492-8971. Editors: Amy Stout and Lou Aronica. Estab. 1987. Publishes hardcover originals and reprints. Published new writers within the last year. Plans 1 first novel this year. Averages 18 total titles, all fiction each year. Sometimes critiques rejected mss.
Needs: Fantasy, horror, science fiction and short story collections. Needs "SF, fantasy mainly. Horror in very limited amounts. No unimaginative, lousy fiction." Recently published *Prince of the Blood*, by Ray Feist (fantasy); and *Reach*, by Edward Gibson (SF 1st novel).
How to Contact: Accepts unsolicited mss. Query first. SASE. Agented fiction 80-90%. Reports in 2 months. Simultaneous and photocopied submissions OK.
Terms: Pays royalties of 6-10%; offers negotiable advance. Sends galleys to author. Publishes ms within 1½-2 years after acceptance. Writer's guidelines and book catalog free.

EAKIN PRESS (II, IV), Box 90159, Austin TX 78709-0159. (512)288-1771. Imprint: Nortex. Editor: Edwin M. Eakin. Estab. 1978. Publishes hardcover originals. Books: old style (acid free); offset printing; case binding; illustrations; average print order 2,000; first novel print order 5,000. Plans 2 first novels this year. Averages 80 total titles each year.
Needs: Juvenile. Specifically needs historical fiction for school market, juveniles set in Texas for Texas grade schoolers. Recently published *Wall Street Wives*, by Ande Ellen Winkler; *Jericho Day*, by Warren Murphy; and *Blood Red Sun*, by Stephen Mertz. Published new writers within the last year.
How to Contact: Accepts unsolicited mss. First send query or submit outline/synopsis and 2 sample chapters. SASE. Agented fiction 5%. Simultaneous and photocopied submissions OK. Accepts computer printout submissions. Prefers letter quality. Reports in 3 months on queries.
Terms: Pays royalties; average advance: $1,000. Sends galleys to author. Publishes ms 1-1½ years after acceptance. Writers guidelines for #10 SAE and 1 first class stamp. Book catalog for 75¢.
Advice: "Juvenile fiction only with strong Texas theme. Just beginning category of adult fiction. We receive around 600 queries or unsolicited mss a year."

‡ECLIPSE BOOKS/ECLIPSE COMICS (II, IV), P.O. Box 1099, Forestville CA 95460. (707)887-1521. Editor-in-Chief: Catherine Yronwode. Estab. 1978. Books: white or coated stock, up to 200 pages, every page illustrated. "Publishes 10-20 titles—comics and graphic novels each month."
Needs: Comics and graphic novels: adventure, condensed/excerpted novel, contemporary, ethnic, experimental, fantasy, feminist, gay, historical, horror, juvenile, lesbian, literary, mainstream, psychic/supernatural/occult, romance, science fiction, serialized novel, suspense/mystery, translations, westerns, young adult. "No religious, nationalistic, racist material." Receives "hundreds" of unsolicited

fiction mss/year. Recently published *The Hobbit*, by J.R.R. Tolkien, adapted by Chuck Dixon, Sean Deming and David Wenzel; *The Complete Alec*, by Eddie Campbell; *The Magic Flute*, by W.A. Mozart, adapted by P. Craig Russell.
How to Contact: Send a cover letter, proposal, sample of script for artist to draw from. Reports in 3 months. SASE. Simultaneous, photocopied and reprint submissions (especially adaptations of well-known prose fiction). Sample copy for $3. Fiction guidelines for #10 SAE.
Terms: Pays $35-50 per page (for a screenplay type of comics script, not a page of prose) advance against royalties (royalties are about 8%, but must be shared with the artist). Also pays 2-5 contributor's copies and discount on extras.
Advice: Looks for "interesting, original stories with in-depth characterization."

PAUL S. ERIKSSON, PUBLISHER (II), 208 Battell Bldg., Middlebury VT 05753. (802)388-7303. Editor: Paul S. Eriksson. Estab. 1960. Publishes hardcover and paperback originals.
Needs: Mainstream. Published *Zachary*, by Ernest Pintoff; and *A Season of Dreams*, by Laurence Dean Hill.
How to Contact: Query first. Photocopied submissions OK. Publishes ms an average of 6 months after acceptance.
Terms: Pays 10-15% in royalties; advance offered if necessary. Free book catalog.
Advice: "Our taste runs to serious fiction."

M. EVANS & CO., INC. (II), 216 E. 49th St., New York NY 10017. (212)688-2810. Contact: Editors. Westerns Editor: Patrick La Brutto. Publishes hardcover and trade paper fiction and nonfiction. Publishes 40-50 titles each year.
Needs: Western, young adult/teen (10-18 years).
How to Contact: Accepts unsolicited mss. Query first with outline/synopsis and 3 sample chapters. SASE. Agented fiction: 100%. Reports on queries in 3-5 weeks. Simultaneous and photocopied submissions OK. Accepts computer printout submissions, no dot-matrix.
Terms: Pays in royalties and offers advance; amounts vary. Sends galleys to author. Publishes ms 6-12 months after acceptance.

‡FANTAGRAPHICS BOOKS, (II,IV), 7563 Lake City Way, Seattle WA 98115. (206)524-1967. Publisher: Gary Groth. Estab. 1976. Publishes comic books, comics series and graphic novels. Books: offset printing, saddlestitch binding; heavily illustrated. Publishes originals and reprints. Publishes 20 titles/year.
Needs: Comic books and graphic novels (adventure, fantasy, romance, mystery, horror, science, social parodies). "We look for subject matter that is more or less the same as you would find in mainstream fiction." Recently published *Blook of Palomar*, by Gilbert Hernandez; *The Dragon Bellows Saga*, by Stan Sakai; *Barney and the Blue Note*, by Loustal and Paringaux.
How to Contact: Send a plot summary, pages of completed art (photocopies only) and character sketches. Include cover letter and SASE. Reports in 1 month.
Terms: Pays in royalties of 8% (but must be split with artist) and advance.

‡FARRAR, STRAUS & GIROUX (III), 19 Union Sq. W., New York NY 10003. (212)741-6900. Imprints include Michael di Capua Books, Hill & Wang, The Noonday Press. Editor-in-Chief: Jonathan Galassi. Midsized, independent publisher of fiction, nonfiction, poetry. Publishes hardcover originals. Published new writers within the last year. Plans 2 first novels this year. Averages 100 total titles, 30 fiction titles each year. No genre material. Recently published *The Mambo Kings Play Songs of Love*, by Oscar Hijuelos; *My Son's Story*, by Nadine Gordimer; *The Burden of Proof*, by Scott Turow.
How to Contact: Does not accept unsolicited mss. Query first. "Vast majority of fiction is agented." Reports in 2 months. Simultaneous and photocopied submissions OK. Accepts computer printout submissions.
Terms: Pays royalties (standard, subject to negotiation). Advance. Sends galleys to author. Publishes ms one year after acceptance. Writer's guidelines for #10 SAE and 1 first class stamp.

FARRAR, STRAUS & GIROUX/CHILDREN'S BOOKS (II), 19 Union Sq. W., New York NY 10003. FAX: (212)633-2427. Imprints include Michael DiCapua Books, Sunburst Books. Children's Books

Publisher: Stephen Roxburgh. Editor-in-Chief: Margaret Ferguson. Number of titles: 40 in 1989. Published new writers within the last year. Buys juvenile mss with illustrations. Buys 50% agented fiction.

Needs: Children's picture books, juvenile novels, nonfiction. Recently published *Celine*, by Brock Cole; *The Abduction*, by Mette Newth; and *The Shining Company*, by Rosemary Sutcliff (all young adult).

How to Contact: Submit outline/synopsis and 3 sample chapters, summary of ms and any pertinent information about author, author's writing, etc. No simultaneous submissions; photocopied submissions OK. No unsolicited submissions during the month of August. Reports in 1 month on queries, 3 months on mss. Publishes ms 18 months to 2 years after acceptance.

Terms: Pays in royalties; offers advance. Free book catalog with 6½ × 9½ SASE.

Advice: "Study our list before sending something inappropriate. Publishing more hardcovers – our list has expanded."

FEARON/JANUS/QUERCUS (II), Subsidiary of Simon & Schuster, Supplementary Education Group, 500 Harbor Blvd., Belmont CA 94002. (415)592-7810. Publisher and Editorial Director: Carol Hegarty. Estab. 1954. Special-education publishers with a junior high, high school, and adult basic education audience – publishing program includes high interest/low level fiction, vocational and life skills materials, and low reading level secondary textbooks in all academic areas. Publishes paperback originals and reprints. Books: 3 lb book set paper; offset printing; perfect or saddlewired binding, line art illustrations, average print order: 5,000. Published only academic texts in 1989 but plans to publish 30 fiction titles in 1990.

Needs: Adventure, contemporary, ethnic, historical, regional, romance, science fiction, short story collections, suspense/mystery, western, young adult/teen. "Our fiction appears in series of short novellas, aimed at new literates and high school students reading no higher than a fifth-grade level. All are written to specification. It's a hard market to crack without some experience writing at low reading levels. Manuscripts for specific series of fiction are solicited from time to time, and unsolicited manuscripts are accepted occasionally." Published *A Question of Freedom*, by Lucy Jane Bledsoe (adventure novella – one of series of eight); *Just for Today*, by Tana Reiff (one novella of series of seven life-issues stories); and *The Everett Eyes*, by Bernard Jackson & Susie Quintanilla (one of twenty in a series of extra-short thrillers).

How to Contact: Submit outline/synopsis and sample chapters. SASE. Reports in 1 month. Simultaneous and photocopied submissions OK.

Terms: Authors usually receive a predetermined project fee. Book catalog for 9 × 12 SAE with 4 first class stamps.

FLARE BOOKS (II), Imprint of Avon Books, Div. of the Hearst Corp., 105 Madison Ave., New York NY 10016. (212)481-5609. Editorial Director: Ellen Krieger. Estab. 1981. Small, young adult line. Publishes paperback originals and reprints. Plans 2-3 first novels this year. Averages 30 titles, all fiction each year.

Needs: Young adult (easy-to-read [hi-lo], problem novels, romance, spy/adventure) "very selective." Looking for contemporary fiction. No historical, science fiction/fantasy, heavy problem novels. Published *Show Me the Evidence*, by Alane Ferguson; *One Step Short*, by Jane McFann; and *So Long at the Fair*, by Hadley Irwin.

How to Contact: Accepts unsolicited mss. Submit complete ms with cover letter (preferred) or outline/synopsis and 3 sample chapters. Agented fiction 75%. Reports in 3-4 weeks on queries; 6-10 weeks on mss. Simultaneous and photocopied submissions OK. Accepts computer printout submissions.

Terms: Royalties and advance negotiable. Sends galleys to author. Writer's guidelines for #10 SAE and 1 first class stamp. Book catalog for 9 × 12 SAE with 98¢ postage. "We run a young adult novel competition each year."

FOUR WINDS PRESS (II), Subsidiary of Macmillan Publishing Co., 866 Third Ave., New York NY 10022. Editor-in-Chief: Cindy Kane. Estab. 1966. A children's trade book imprint. Publishes hardcover originals. Books: 3 piece binding for older reading books, 1 piece binding for picture books. Books for children ages 3-12 usually illustrated; average print order 6,000-10,000; first novel print order: 6,000. Published new writers within the last year. Publishes 18 total titles each year, 10 fiction titles. No longer publishing young adult fiction.

Needs: Picture book manuscripts for ages 2-4 and 5-8. Recently published *Mrs. Toggle's Zipper*, by Robin Pulver and *Crow Moon, Worm Moon*, by James Skofield (picture books).
How to Contact: Accepts unsolicited mss. Submit complete ms with cover letter. SASE required. 75% of fiction is agented. Reports in 12 weeks. Photocopied submissions OK. Accepts computer printout submissions. No simultaneous submissions.
Terms: Pays royalties, negotiable advance and author's copies. Book catalogs *not* available. Manuscript guidelines and portfolio guidelines are available on request with #10 SAE and 1 first class stamp. "No calls, please."
Advice: "The majority of the fiction manuscripts accepted by Four Winds Press are picture book texts; we publish very little older fiction. Due to volume of submissions received, we cannot guarantee a quick response time or answer queries about manuscript status."

‡**GARETH STEVENS, INC (II,IV),** 1555 N. River Center Dr., Milwaukee WI 53212. (414)225-0333. Creative Director: Paul Humphrey. Estab. 1986. "Midsize independent children's book publisher determined to expand." Publishes hardcover originals. Books: Matte paper; sheet feed printing; reinforced binding; several 4-color illustrations; average print order: 6,000; first novel print order: 4,000-5,000. Published new writers within the last year. Plans 3 first novels this year. Publishes total of 120 titles, 30 fiction titles/year.
Needs: Juvenile (animal, easy-to-read, fantasy, historical, sports, spy/adventure, contemporary). Especially needs picture books and very juvenile fiction.
How to Contact: Accepts unsolicited mss. Send outline/synopsis and sample chapters or complete ms with cover letter. SASE. Reports in 3 weeks on queries; 6 months on mss. Simultaneous, photocopied, computer printout submissions OK. Accepts electronic submissions.
Terms: Pays royalties of 3% mimimum, 7% maximum. Average advance: $750. Advance is negotiable. Sends pre-publication galleys to author. Publishes ms 1 year to 18 months after acceptance. Book catalog for 9×12 SAE and 1 first-class stamp.

GEMSTONE BOOKS (I, II), Imprint of Dillon Press, 242 Portland Ave. S., Minneapolis MN 55415. (612)333-2691. Fiction Reader: Shelley Saterem. Estab. 1966. "Dillon Press is a juvenile book publisher, both of fiction and educational nonfiction titles." Publishes hardcover and paperback originals. Books: type of paper varies; offset lithography; Smythe and sidesewn binding; illustrations; average print order: 5,000. Averages 40 total titles, 5 fiction titles each year.
Needs: Juvenile (8-14): historical, adventure, contemporary and science fiction/fantasy; juvenile (7-9) 2,000-3,000 words, stories about Hispanics, Asians and Blacks; juvenile (8-11) historical fiction based on actual events. No picture books. Published *Mr. Z and the Time Clock*, by Bonnie Pryor and *A Gift for Tia Rosa*, by Karen Taha.
How to Contact: Not accepting unsolicited mss; send query. Prefer complete ms with SASE. Reports in 6 weeks. Simultaneous and photocopied submissions OK. Accepts computer submissions, prefers letter-quality.
Terms: Negotiable. Sends galleys to author. Book catalog for 9×12 SAE with 90¢ postage.
Advice: "We are expanding our fiction imprint, Gemstone Books."

‡**GESSLER PUBLISHING COMPANY,** 55 W. 13th St., New York NY 10011. (212)627-0099. Editorial Contact Person: Seth C. Levin. Estab. 1932. "Publisher/distributor of foreign language educational materials (primary/secondary schools)." Publishes paperback originals and reprints. Averages 75 total titles each year. Sometimes comments on rejected ms.
Needs: "Foreign language or English as a Second Language." Needs juvenile, literary, preschool/picture book, short story collections, translations. Recently published *Don Quijote de la Mancha, (cartoon version of classic, in Spanish); El Cid,* (prose and poetry version of the classic in Spanish); and *Les Miserables* (simplified versions of Victor Hugo classic, in French).
How to Contact: Query first, then send outline/synopsis and 2-3 sample chapters; complete ms with cover letter. Agented fiction 40%. Reports on queries in 4 weeks; on mss in 6 weeks. Simultaneous and photocopied submissions OK. Accepts computer printout submissions.
Terms: Pay varies with each author and contract. Sends galleys to author. "Varies on time of submissions and acceptance relating to our catalogue publication date." Writer's guidelines not available. Book catalog free on request.
Advice: "We specialize in the foreign language market directed to teachers and schools—a book that would interest us has to be attractive to that market—a teacher would be most likely to create a book for us."

DAVID R. GODINE, PUBLISHER, INC. (I, II), 300 Massachusetts Ave., Boston MA 02115. (617)536-0761. Imprint: Nonpareil Books (trade paperbacks). President: David R. Godine. Manuscript submissions: Thomas Frick. Juvenile ms submissions: Audrey Bryant. Estab. 1970. Books: acid free paper; sewn binding; illustrations; average print order: 4,000-5,000; first novel print order: 3,500-6,500. Small independent publisher (12-person staff). Publishes hardcover and paperback originals and reprints. Comments on rejected mss "only if of particular interest."
Needs: Literary, mystery, collecting, historical, food and wine and juvenile. Recently published *Things. A Story of the Sixties* and *A Man Asleep*, by Georges Perec; *Neons*, by Denis Belloc; *The Empty Notebook*, by William Kotzwinkle; and *Henry in Shadowland*, by Laszlo Varvasovsky.
How to Contact: Accepts unsolicited mss with self-addressed, stamped book envelope. Query with outline/synopsis. "We prefer query letters—include publishing history, complete outline of story and SASE. Do not call to follow up on submission." Simultaneous and photocopied submissions OK. Accepts computer printout submissions; letter-quality only.
Terms: Standard royalties; offers advance. Sends galleys to author. Free book catalog.
Advice: "Keep trying. Remember that every writer now published has been rejected countless times at the beginning."

GROSSET & DUNLAP, INC. (III), A Division of the Putnam & Grosset Group, 200 Madison Ave., 11th Floor, New York NY 10016. (212)951-8700. Editor-in-Chief: Jane O'Connor.
Needs: Juvenile, preschool/picture book. Queries only. "Include such details as length and intended age group and any other information that you think will help us to understand the nature of your material. Be sure to enclose a stamped, self-addressed envelope for our reply. We can no longer review manuscripts that we have not asked to see, and they will be returned unread."

HARCOURT BRACE JOVANOVICH (III), 1250 Sixth Ave., San Diego CA 92101. (619)699-6810. FAX: (619)699-6777. Imprints include HBJ Children's Books, Gulliver Books and Jane Yolen Books. Director: Louise Howton. Executive Editor: Bonnie V. Ingber. Senior Editors: Diane D'Andrade and Elizabeth Van Doren. Editors: Allyn Johnston and Karen Grove. *All serve the HBJ Children's Books Divisions, no longer specifically one imprint or another. Publishes hardcover originals and paperback reprints. Averages 75 titles/year. Published new writers within the last year.
Needs: Young adult fiction, nonfiction for all ages, picture books for very young children, mystery. Published *Baseball in April*, by Gary Soto; *Ghost Cave*, by Barbara Steiner; and *Dixie Storms*, by Barbara Hall.
How to Contact: Unsolicited mss currently accepted *only* by HBJ Children's Books, not by Gulliver Books, Jane Yolen Books or Voyager Books. Send to "Manuscript Submissions, HBJ Children's Books." SASE. For picture books, send complete ms; for novels, send outline/synopsis and 2-4 sample chapters. Photocopied submissions OK. No simultaneous submissions. No phone calls. Responds in 6-8 weeks.
Terms: Terms vary according to individual books; pays on royalty basis. Writers' guidelines for #10 SASE; catalog for 9×12 SASE.
Advice: "Familiarize yourself with the type of book published by a company before submitting a manuscript; make sure your work is in line with the style of the publishing house. Research the market your work will reach; make yourself familiar with the current children's book field."

HARLEQUIN ENTERPRISES, LTD. (II, IV), 225 Duncan Mill Rd., Don Mills, Ontario M3B 3K9 Canada. (416)445-5860. Imprints include Harlequin Romances, Harlequin Presents, Harlequin American Romances, Superromances, Temptation, Intrigue and Regency, Silhouette, Worldwide Mysteries, Gold Eagle. Editorial Manager: Karin Stoecker. Estab. 1949. Publishes paperback originals and reprints. Books: newsprint paper; web printing; perfect binding. Published new writers within the last year. Number of titles: averages 670/year. Buys agented and unagented fiction.
Needs: Romance and heroic adventure. Will accept nothing that is not related to the desired categories.
How to Contact: Send query letter or send outline and first 50 pages (2 or 3 chapters) or submit through agent with IRC and SASE (Canadian). Absolutely no simultaneous submissions; photocopied submissions OK. Reports in 1 month on queries; 2 months on mss.
Terms: Offers royalties, advance. Must return advance if book is not completed or is unacceptable. Sends galleys to author.
Advice: "The quickest route to success is to follow directions for submissions: query first. We encourage first novelists. Before sending a manuscript, read as many Harlequin titles as you can get your hands on. It's very important to study the style and do your homework first." Authors may send

Close-up

Thomas Frick
Editor
David Godine, Publisher, Inc.

It's hard to put into words exactly what a David Godine book is, says Editor Thomas Frick. "We're quirky. We're eclectic. It makes our identity hard to pinpoint," he says. The company publishes many different kinds of books, from children's books to literary fiction to natural science topics. Yet, he adds, there are certain characteristics that all the books in the publisher's line share, including a unique approach to the subject, as well as quality writing.

Established in 1970, the company has become known for publishing serious literary fiction and poetry as well as books on natural history, sport fishing and typography. Based in Boston, the publisher also looks for books with New England interest.

Frick says the company receives about 125 manuscripts each week. Of these, the company publishes about 35 titles per year, but only three or four are adult fiction books and this small number includes translations.

Translations are an important part of the Godine line, says Frick. He looks for translations of writers whose work is popular elsewhere but relatively unknown in the United States. Writers interested in translating foreign works should send him samples.

"So many good foreign books are out there, including those by British, Canadian and Australian writers," says Frick. With the changes in Eastern Europe, he expects more previously unavailable works to be made accessible—and ripe for translation.

David Godine also publishes several reprints each year. Although the company has been very successful with its line of original juvenile literature, children's books also make very popular reprints, says Frick. Often a book is repackaged with better printing, binding and striking artwork. For example, the company recently repackaged *The Secret Garden*, a well-loved children's classic, in a high-quality, hardbound edition with new illustrations.

"For original fiction I like to see a good query," he says. "Describe the project and send a few good chapters. An outline or synopsis is no good, however. I need to see *how* you write."

Frick advises writers to study the market. "Spend time with other writers. Go to writers' lectures at universities; go to readings. Talking to other writers makes you more realistic about your own work." A lot of new writers neglect submitting to literary magazines, says Frick. These can help you develop a publication record and the whole process of publication, he says, will help mature your writing.

"We always read and try to respond to unsolicited manuscripts," says Frick. "And we're always looking for new, original material. We want the writer to take us somewhere we haven't been before."

—Robin Gee

manuscript for Romances and Presents to Paula Eykelhof, editor. Superromances: Marsha Zinberg, senior editor; Temptation: Birgit Davis-Todd, senior editor, Regencys: Marmie Charndoff, editor to the Canada address. American Romances and Intrigue: Debra Matteucci, senior editor and editorial coordinator, Harlequin Books, 300 E. 42 Street, 6th Floor, New York, NY 10017. Silhouette submissions should also be sent to the New York office, attention Isabel Swift. Gold Eagle query letters should be addressed to Feroze Mohammed, senior editor, at the Canada address. "The relationship between the novelist and editor is regarded highly and treated with professionalism."

HARMONY BOOKS (II), Subsidiary of Crown Publishers, 201 E. 50th St., New York NY 10022. (212)572-6121. Contact: General Editorial Department. Publishes hardcover and paperback originals.
Needs: Literary fiction. Also publishes in serious nonfiction, history, biography, personal growth, media and music fields.
How to Contact: Accepts unsolicited mss. Query first with outline/synopsis and 2-3 sample chapters. SASE. Agented fiction: 75%. Simultaneous and photocopied submissions OK. Accepts computer printouts.
Terms: Pays royalties and advance; amounts negotiable. Sends galleys to authors.

HARPERCOLLINS CHILDREN'S BOOKS (II), (formerly Harper & Row Junior Books Group), 10 E. 53rd St., New York NY 10022. (212)207-7044. Publisher: Marilyn Kriney. Editors: Charlotte Zolotow, Nina Ignatowicz, Barbara Fenton, Laura Geringer, Robert O. Warren, Antonia Markiet, David Allender, Joanna Cotler. Publishes hardcover originals and paperback reprints. Number of titles: *Harper—Cloth*: 80 in 1989; *Harper—Trophy* (paperback): 74 in 1989; *Crowell*: 29 in 1989; *Lippincott*: 37 in 1989.
Needs: Picture books, easy-to-read, middle-grade, teenage and young adult novels; fiction, fantasy, animal, sports, spy/adventure, historical, science fiction, problem novels and contemporary. Recently published Harper/Charlotte Zolotow Books: *Fell Back*, by M.E. Kerr (ages 12 and up); Harper: *My Daniel*, by Pam conrad (ages 10 and up); Crowell: *Lucie Babbidge's House*, by Sylvia Cassedy (ages 9-12); Lippincotte: *Yours Till Forever*, by David Gifaldi (ages 12 and up).
How to Contact: Query; submit complete ms; submit outline/synopsis and sample chapters; submit through agent. SASE for query, ms. Please identify simultaneous submissions; photocopied submissions OK. Reports in 2-3 months.
Terms: Average 10% in royalties. Royalties on picture books shared with illustrators. Offers advance. Book catalog for self-addressed label.
Advice: "Write from your own experience and the child you once were. Read widely in the field of adult and children's literature. Realize that writing for children is a difficult challenge. Read other young adult novelists as well as adult novelists. Pay attention to styles, approaches, topics. Be willing to rewrite, perhaps many times. We have no rules for subject matter, length or vocabulary but look instead for ideas that are fresh and imaginative. Good writing that involves the reader in a story or subject that has appeal for young readers is also essential. One submission is considered by the four imprints."

HARVEST HOUSE PUBLISHERS (IV), 1075 Arrowsmith, Eugene OR 97402. (503)343-0123. Manuscript Coordinator: LaRae Weikert. Editor-in-Chief: Eileen L. Mason. Estab. 1974. Midsize independent publisher with plans to expand. Publishes hardcover and paperback originals and reprints. Books: 40 lb ground wood paper; offset printing; perfect binding; average print order 10,000; first novel print order: 10,000-15,000. Averages 50 total titles, 4 fiction titles each year.
Needs: Christian living, contemporary issues, humor, Christian preschool/picture books, religious/inspirational and Christian romance (contemporary, historical). Especially seeks inspirational, romance/historical and mystery. Recently published *A Place Called Home*, by Lori Wick; *Love's Enduring Hope*, by June Masters Bacher; *A Song for Silas*, by Lori Wick; and *Moses*, by Ellen Gunderson Traylor.
How to Contact: Accepts unsolicited mss. Query first or submit outline/synopsis and 2 sample chapters with SASE. Reports on queries in 2-8 weeks; on mss in 6-8 weeks. Simultaneous and photocopied submissions OK.
Terms: Pays in royalties of 14-18%; 10 author's copies. Sends galleys to author. Writer's guidelines for SASE. Book catalog for 8½×11 SASE.

HEARTFIRE ROMANCE (I), Subsidiary of Zebra Books, 475 Park Ave. So., New York NY 10016. (212)889-2299. Editorial Director: Carin Ritter. Publishes paperback originals and reprints. Publishes 48 fiction titles each year.

Needs: Romance. Recently published *Blood Wings*, by Stephen Gresham; *Lovers' Masquerade*, by Robin St. Thomas; and *Last of the California Girls*, by Pamela Jekel. Ms length ranges from 125,000 to 150,000 words.
How to Contact: Submit short (no more than 3 page) synopsis and first several chapters. SASE. Reports on queries in 6 weeks; on mss in 3 months. Simultaneous and photocopied submissions OK. Accepts computer printout submissions, no dot-matrix.
Terms: Pays royalties and negotiable advance. Writer's guidelines and book catalog free for SASE.
Advice: Send for tip sheet. "Don't use all the fancy fonts available to you; we're not impressed and it often works against you. Don't tell me my business in your cover letter; just give me the basic facts and let your ms sell itself."

HERALD PRESS (II), Division of Mennonite Publishing House, Imprints include Congregational Literature Division; Herald Press. 616 Walnut Ave., Scottdale PA 15683. (412)887-8500. Book Editor: S. David Garber. Fiction Editor: Michael A. King. Estab. 1908. "Church-related midsize publisher." Publishes paperback originals. Books: recycled, acid-free Glatfelter thor paper; offset printing; adhesive binding; illustrations for children; average print order: 4,000; first novel print order: 3,500. Published new writers in the last year. Company publishes 30 titles/year. Number of fiction titles: 5 per year. Sometimes critiques rejected mss.
Needs: Adventure, historical, juvenile (historical, spy/adventure, contemporary), literary, religious/inspirational, young adult/teen (historical, problem novels and spy/adventure). "Does not want to see fantasy, picture books." Recently published *Fear Strikes at Midnight*, by Jones (juvenile); *Leah*, by Schott (adult, biblical); and *The Deserter*, by Koch (historical, peace/Civil War).
How to Contact: Accepts unsolicited mss. Submit outline/synopsis and 2 sample chapters with SASE. Agented fiction 2%. Reports in 1 month on queries, 2 months on mss. Photocopied submissions OK. Accepts computer printout submissions. Accepts electronics submissions (only *with* paper copy).
Terms: Pays 10-12% in royalties; 12 free author's copies. Pays after first 3 months, then once a year payment. Sends galleys to author. Publishes ms 10 months after acceptance. Writer's guidelines free. Book catalog 50¢.
Advice: "Need more stories with Christian faith integrated smoothly and not as a tacked-on element."

HOLIDAY HOUSE, INC. (I, II), 425 Madison, New York NY 10017. (212)688-0085. Editor: Margery Cuyler. Estab. 1935. Independent publisher. Books: high quality printing; occasionally reinforced binding; illustrations sometimes. Publishes hardcover originals and paperback reprints. Published new writers within the last year. Number of titles: 52 hardcovers in 1990; 14 paperbacks in 1990.
Needs: Contemporary, judaica and holiday, literary, adventure, humor and animal stories for young readers—preschool through middle grade. Recently published *Awfully Short for the Fourth Grade*, by Elvira Woodruff; *Glass Slippers Give You Blisters*, by Mary Jane Auch. "We're not in a position to be too encouraging, as our list is tight, but we're always open to good 'family' novels and humor."
How to Contact: "We prefer query letters for novels; complete manuscripts for shorter books and picture books." Simultaneous and photocopied submissions OK as long as a cover letter mentions that other publishers are looking at the same material. Accepts computer printout submissions. Prefers letter-quality. Reports in 1 month on queries, 6-8 weeks on mss.
Terms: Advance and royalties are flexible, depending upon whether the book is illustrated.
Advice: "We have received an increasing number of manuscripts, but the quality has not improved vastly. This appears to be a decade in which publishers are interested in reviving the type of good, solid story that was popular in the '50s. Certainly there's a trend toward humor, family novels, novels with school settings, biographies and historical novels. Problem-type novels and romances seem to be on the wane. We are always open to well-written manuscripts, whether by a published or nonpublished author. Submit only one project at a time."

HOLLOWAY HOUSE PUBLISHING COMPANY (II), 8060 Melrose Ave., Los Angeles CA 90046. (213)653-8060. Imprints include Mankind Books, Melrose Square and Heartline Books. Editor: Peter Stone. Estab. 1960. Midsize independent publisher of varying interests, publishes black experience books, history, games and gambling books. Publishes paperback originals and reprints. Book: offset printing; paper binding; some illustrations; average print order: 20,000 to 30,000; first novel print order: 15,000. Published new writers within last year. Plans 6 first novels this year. Publishes 30-40 titles each year, 6 fiction titles.
Needs: Adventure, contemporary, ethnic, experimental, fantasy, historical, horror, literary, mainstream, romance (historical), science fiction, suspense/mystery, war, western. "We are looking for more 'literary' type books than in the past; books that appeal to young professionals. No books dealing

with 'street action' about pimps, whores, dope dealing, prisons, etc." Published *A Mississippi Family*, by Barbara Johnson (fiction); *Diva*, a first novel by the award-winning playright Stanley Bennet Clay; *Secret Music*, by Odie Hawkins (memoirs); also a Jessie Jackson bio, by Eddie Stone.
How to Contact: No unsolicited mss.
Advice: Publishing fewer Heartline Romances "as the contemporary romance market seems to have bottomed out, at least for us. Study the market; we do not publish poetry, short story collections, juvies, etc. but not a week goes by that we don't get at least one submission of each. If you send second-generation copies or dot-matrix check and see if *you* can read it before you expect us to. Neatness, spelling, etc. counts!"

HENRY HOLT & COMPANY (II), 115 W 18th St., 6th Floor, New York NY 10011. (212)886-9200. Imprint includes Owl (paper). Publishes hardcover originals and reprints and paperback originals and reprints. Averages 50-60 total original titles, 20% of total is fiction each year.
Needs: Adventure, contemporary, feminist, historical, humor/satire, juvenile (5-9 years, including animal, easy-to-read, fantasy, historical, sports, spy/adventure and contemporary), literary, mainstream, suspense/mystery, translations and young adult/teen (10-18 years including easy-to-read, fantasy/science fiction, historical, problem novels, romance, sports and spy/adventure). Recently published *Fool's Progress*, by Edward Abbey; *Tracks*, by Louise Erdrich; *Trust*, by George V. Higgins; and *Frank Furbo*, by Wm. Wherton.
How to Contact: Accepts queries; no unsolicited mss. Agented fiction 95%.
Terms: Pays in royalties of 10% minimum; 15% maximum; advance. Sends galleys to author. Book catalog free on request.

■**HORIZON PUBLISHERS & DIST., INC. (III, IV)**, 50 S. 500 West, Box 490, Bountiful UT 84011-0490. (801)295-9451. President: Duane S. Crowther. Estab. 1971. "Midsize independent publisher with in-house printing facilities, staff of 30+." Publishes hardcover and paperback originals and reprints. Books: 60 lb offset paper; hardbound, perfect and saddlestitch binding; illustrations; average print order: 3,000; first novel print order: 3,000. Plans 2 first novels this year. Averages 25-30 total titles; 1-3 fiction titles each year.
Needs: Adventure, historical, humor/satire, juvenile, literary, mainstream, military/war, religious/inspirational, romance (contemporary and historical), science fiction, spiritual and young adult/teen (romance and spy/adventure). "Religious titles are directed only to the LDS (Latter Day Saints) market. General titles are marketed nationwide." Looking for "good quality writing in salable subject areas. Will also consider well-written books on social problems and issues, (divorce, abortion, child abuse, suicide, capital punishment and homosexuality)." Recently published *The Couchman and the Bells*, by Ted C. Hindmarsh.
How to Contact: Accepts unsolicited mss. Query first. SASE. Include social security number with submission. Reports in 2-4 weeks on queries; 10-12 weeks on mss. Simultaneous and photocopied submissions OK if identified as such. Accepts computer printout submissions. Accepts electronic submissions.
Terms: Pays royalties of 6% minimum; 12% maximum. Provides 10 author's copies. Sends page proofs to author. Publishes ms 3-9 months after acceptance. "We are not a subsidy publisher but we do job printing, book production for private authors and book packaging." Writer's guidelines for #10 SAE and 1 first class stamp.
Advice: Encourages "only those first novelists who write very well, with salable subjects. Please avoid the trite themes which are plaguing LDS fiction such as crossing the plains, conversion stories, and struggling courtships that always end in temple marriage. While these themes are important, they have been used so often that they are now frequently perceived as trite and are often ignored by those shopping for new books. In religious fiction we hope to see a process of moral, spiritual, or emotional growth presented. Some type of conflict is definitely essential for good plot development. Watch your vocabulary too—use appropriate words for the age group for which you are writing. We don't accept elementary children's mss for elementary grades."

INTERLINK PUBLISHING GROUP, INC. (IV), Imprints include: Interlink Books, Olive Branch Press and Crocodile Books USA. 99 Seventh Ave., Brooklyn NY 11215. (718)797-4292. Publisher: Michel Moushabeck. Fiction Editor: Phyllis Bennis. Estab. 1987. "Midsize independent publisher." Publishes hardcover and paperback originals. Books: 55 lb Warren Sebago Cream white paper; web offset printing; perfect binding; average print order: 5,000; first novel print order: 5,000. Published new writers within the last year. Plans 3-5 first novels this year. Averages 30 total titles, 3-5 fiction titles each year.

WOULD YOU USE THE SAME CALENDAR YEAR AFTER YEAR?

Of course not! If you scheduled your appointments using last year's calendar, you'd risk missing important meetings and deadlines, so you keep up-to-date with a new calendar each year. Just like your calendar, *Novel & Short Story Writer's Market* changes every year, too. Many of the editors move or get promoted, rates of pay increase, and even editorial needs change from the previous year. You can't afford to use an out-of-date book to plan your marketing efforts!

So save yourself the frustration of getting manuscripts returned in the mail, stamped MOVED: ADDRESS UNKNOWN. And of NOT submitting your work to new listings because you don't know they exist. Make sure you have the most current writing and marketing information by ordering *1992 Novel & Short Story Writer's Market* today. All you have to do is complete the attached post card and return it with your payment or charge card information. Order now, and there's one thing that won't change from your *1991 Novel & Short Story Writer's Market* - the price! That's right, we'll send you the 1992 edition for just $18.95. *1992 Novel & Short Story Writer's Market* will be published and ready for shipment in February 1992.

Let an old acquaintance be forgot, and toast the new edition of *Novel & Short Story Writer's Market*! Order today!

(See other side for more helpful writing books)

To order, drop this postpaid card in the mail.

☐ **Yes!** I want the most current edition of *Novel & Short Story Writer's Market*. Please send me the 1992 edition at the 1991 price - $18.95.* (NOTE: *1992 Novel & Short Story Writer's Market* will be ready for shipment in February 1992.) #10224

Also send me these books to help me get published:

____ (#10099) Dialogue, $13.95*   ____ (#10067) Characters & Viewpoint, $13.95*
____ (#10100) Revision, $13.95*   ____ (#10155) Theme & Strategy, $13.95*
____ (#10044) Plot, $13.95*   ____ (#10156) Manuscript Submission, $13.95*

*Plus postage and handling: $3.00 for one book, $1.00 for each additional book. Ohio residents add 5 1/2% sales tax.

☐ Payment enclosed (Slip this card and your payment into an envelope)
☐ Please charge my: ☐ Visa ☐ MasterCard

Account # _____ Exp. Date _____

Signature _____

Name _____

Address _____

City _____ State _____ Zip _____

(This offer expires August 1, 1992)

Writer's Digest Books
Writer's Digest Books
1507 Dana Avenue
Cincinnati, OH 45207

Credit card orders call toll-free 1-800-289-0963

5916

More Books to Help You Get Published!

The Elements of Fiction Writing Series

Dialogue
Lewis Turco
128 pages/$13.95

Revision
Kit Reed
176 pages/$13.95

Plot
Ansen Dibell
170 pages/$13.95

Characters & Viewpoint
Orson Scott Card
182 pages/$13.95

Theme & Strategy
Ronald B. Tobias
160 pages/$13.95

Manuscript Submission
Scott Edelstein
176 pages/$13.95

Use coupon on other side to order today!

- -

Needs: Juvenile (5-9 yrs.), preschool/picture book and translations. Needs adult ficiton—relating to the Middle East, Africa or Latin America; translations accepted. Also needs juvenile (5-9 yrs)—illustrated picture books. Published *Wild Thorns*, by Sahar Khalifeh; *Crocodile, Crocodile*, by Peter Nickl, Binette Shroeder (illus.); and *The Elephant's Child*, by Rudyard Kipling, Jan Mogensen (illus.).
How to Contact: Accepts unsolicited mss. Submit outline/synopsis and 2 sample chapters. SASE. Reports in 2 weeks on queries; 3 months on mss. Photocopied submissions OK. Accepts computer printout submissions.
Terms: Pays royalties of 5% minimum; 8% maximum. Sends galleys to author. Publishes ms 1-1½ years.

IRON CROWN ENTERPRISES, INC., P.O. Box 1605, Charlottesville VA 22902. (804)295-3918. Editor: John D. Ruemmler. Estab. 1980. "Growing independent publishers of gamebooks expanding into sci fi and fantasy fiction." Publishes paperback originals. Books: offset printing; adhesive paper binding; 4-color covers, 1-color illustrations inside; average print order: 5,000-10,000 (some up to 50,000); first novel print order: 25,000-50,000. Plans 2 first novels this year. Averages 60 total titles, 2-10 fiction titles each year. Sometimes comments on rejected mss.
Needs: Fantasy and science fiction. Published *Murder at The Diogenes Club*, by G. Lientz (interactive mystery); *Return to Deathwater*, by C. Norris (interactive fantasy); and *A Spy in Isengard*, by Terry Amthor (interactive fantasy).
How to Contact: Accepts unsolicited mss. Query first. SASE. Reports in 2-4 weeks on queries; 1-2 months on mss. Simultaneous and photocopied submissions OK. Computer printout submissions OK. Accepts electronic submissions.
Terms: Pays royalties of 4% minimum; 8% maximum. Average advance: $1,000. Provides 25 author's copies. Publishes ms 2-8 months after acceptance. Writer's guidelines for #10 SASE with 1 first class stamp.
Advice: "We publish only paperback originals, most of it either FRP (gaming) oriented or interactive fiction. We plan to begin publishing paperback originals in fantasy in 1990; science fiction in 1991. We still get a lot of letters and manuscripts from writers who have no idea what we're looking for. Take courses and join a club or group if they help to keep you writing. And hang on to your job until you make your first million!"

JAMESON BOOKS (I, II, IV), Jameson Books, Inc., The Frontier Library, 722 Columbus St., Ottawa IL 61350. (815)434-7905. Editor: Jameson G. Campaigne, Jr. Estab. 1986. Publishes hardcover and paperback originals and reprints. Books: free sheet paper; offset printing; average print order: 10,000; first novel print order: 5,000. Plans 6-8 novels this year. Averages 12-16 total titles, 4-8 fiction titles each year. Occasionally critiques or comments on rejected mss.
Needs: Very well-researched western (frontier pre-1850). No romance, sci-fi, mystery, et al. Published *Wister Trace*, by Loren Estelman; *Buckskin Brigades*, by L. Ron Hubbard; *One-Eyed Dream*, by Terry Johnston.
How to Contact: Does not accepted unsolicited mss. Submit outline/synopsis and 3 consecutive sample chapters. SASE. Agented fiction 50%. Reports in 2 weeks on queries; 2-5 months on mss. Simultaneous and photocopied submissions OK. Accepts computer printouts.
Terms: Pays royalties of 5% minimum; 15% maximum. Average advance: $1,500. Sends galleys to author. Book catalog for 6×9 SASE.

JOY STREET BOOKS, 34 Beacon St., Boston MA 02108. (617)227-0730. Imprint of Little, Brown and Co. Children's Books Editor-in-chief: Melanie Kroupa. Publishes hardcover and quality paperback originals. Number of titles: 40 in 1989. Sometimes buys juvenile mss with illustrations.
Needs: General fiction, juvenile: sports, animal, mystery/adventure, realistic contemporary fiction, picture books and easy-to-read. Published *The Arizona Kid*, by Ron Koertge; *The Girl in the Box*, by Ouida Sebestyen; *Alias Madame Doubtfire*, by Anne Fine. Very interested in first novels.
How to Contact: Prefers query letter with sample chapters. SASE. Accepts simultaneous submissions; photocopied submissions OK.
Terms: Pays variable advances and royaltics.

ALFRED A. KNOPF (II), 201 E. 50th St., New York NY 10022. Senior Editor: Ashbel Green. Estab. 1915. Publishes hardcover originals. Number of titles: 47 in 1989. Buys 75% agented fiction. Published 16 new writers within the last year.

Needs: Contemporary, literary, mystery and spy. No western, gothic, romance, erotica, religious or science fiction. Recently published *Like Life*, by Lorrie Moore; *The Gift of Asher Lev*, by Chaim Potok; and *Blossom*, by Andrew Vachss. Published work by previously unpublished writers within the last year.

How to Contact: Submit complete ms with SASE. Simultaneous and photocopied submissions OK. Reports in 1 month on mss. Publishes ms an average of 1 year after acceptance.

Terms: Pays 10-15% in royalties; offers advance. Must return advance if book is not completed or is unacceptable.

Advice: Publishes book-length fiction of literary merit by known and unknown writers. "Don't submit manuscripts with matrix type."

KNOPF BOOKS FOR YOUNG READERS (II), 225 Park Ave. South, New York NY 10003. Subsidiary of Random House, Inc. Editor-in-Chief: Janet Schulman. Publishes hardcover and paperback originals and reprints. New paperback imprints include Dragonfly Books (picture books), Bullseye (middle-grade fiction) and Borzoi Sprinters (Young Adult fiction). Averages 50 total titles, approximately 20 fiction titles each year.

Needs: "High-quality" contemporary, humor and nonfiction. "Young adult novels, picture books, middle group novels." Recently published *No Star Nights*, by Anna Smucker; *Mirandy and Brother Wind*, by Patricia McKissoch; *The Boy Who Lost His Face*, by Lewis Sachar.

How to Contact: Query with outline/synopsis and 2 sample chapters with SASE. Simultaneous and photocopied submissions OK. Reports in 6-8 weeks on mss.

Terms: Sends galleys to author.

LARKSDALE (II), Subsidiary of Houston Printing & Publishing, Inc. Imprints include Lindahl Books, Harle House, The Linolean Press and Post Oak Press. Suite 190, 10661 Haddington, Houston TX 77043. (713)861-6214. Publisher: James Goodman. Fiction Editor: Charlotte St. John. Estab. 1978. General trade line—national in scope. Publishes hardcover and paperback originals and hardcover and paperback reprints. Books: 60 lb natural Glatfelter paper; web printing; case/perfect binding; illustrations; average print order: 5,000; first novel print order: 2,000. Published new writers within the last year. Plans 4-5 first novels this year. Averages 30 total titles, 2-5 fiction titles each year. Sometimes comments on rejected ms; *charges "nothing if we initiate, $50 fee if requested by author."*

Needs: Humor/satire, juvenile (5-9 yrs.) animal, easy-to-read, literary, mainstream, military/war, religious/inspirational and young adult/teen (10-18 years) easy-to-read, historical, problem novels, romance (young adult) and sports. Recently published *Mending of the Heart*, by Mary Wyche Estes (romance); *Way of the Child*, by Dr. David Patterson (child abuse); and *Angel On The Bridge*, by Kitty Ellis.

How to Contact: Accepts unsolicited mss. Submit complete ms with cover letter. SASE (must include *container, not* just postage). Reports in 4-6 weeks on mss. Simultaneous and photocopied submissions OK. Accepts computer printout submissions.

Terms: Pays royalties of 10% minimum. Provides 10 author's copies. Publishes ms up to 18 months after acceptance.

Advice: (1) Don't be cute; (2) Never make a submission w/o a cover letter; (3) Don't drop names; (4) Don't oversell; (5) The more info on the author, the better.

LEISURE BOOKS (II), A Division of Dorchester Publishing Co., Inc., Suite 1008, 276 Fifth Ave., New York NY 10001. (212)725-8811. Senior Editor: Alicia Convon. Editor: John Littell. Address submissions to Audrey LaFehr, Editor. Mass-market paperback publisher—originals and reprints. Books: newsprint paper; offset printing; perfect binding; average print order: variable; first novel print order: variable. Published new writers within the last year. Plans 25 first novels this year. Averages 150 total titles, 145 fiction titles each year. Comments on rejected ms "only if requested ms requires it."

Needs: Techno-thriller, historical, horror, romance (historical), western. Looking for "historical romance (90,000 words), horror novels (80,000 words), western series books." Recently published *Fortune's Lady*, by Patricia Gaffney (romance); *The Sisterhood*, by Florence Stevenson (horror); and *Tough Bullet/The Killers*, by Peter McCurtin.

How to Contact: Accepts unsolicited mss. Query first. SASE. Agented fiction 70%. Reports in 4 weeks on queries; 2 months on mss. Simultaneous and photocopied submissions OK.

Terms: Offers negotiable advance. Payment depends "on category and track record of author." Sends galleys to author. Publishes ms 18 months after acceptance. Writer's guidelines and book catalog for #10 SASE.

Advice: Encourages first novelists "if they are talented and willing to take direction, *and* write the kind of category fiction we publish. The horror market is seriously declining. Too many bad books are being written. We, like other publishers, are cutting back this category. Please include a brief synopsis if sample chapters are requested."

LION PUBLISHING CORPORATION (II). Subsidiary of Lion Publishing plc, Oxford, England. 1705 Hubbard Ave., Batavia IL 60510. (708)879-0707. Editor: R.M. Bittner. Estab. 1971 (Oxford offices); 1984 (US). "Christian book publisher publishing books for the *general* market." Publishes hardcover and paperback originals and paperback reprints. Books: average print order 7,500; first-novel print order 5,000. Plans 1-3 first novels this year. Averages 15 total titles, 2-5 fiction titles each year. Sometimes comments on rejected ms.
Needs: Open. "Because we are a Christian publisher, all books should be written from a Christian perspective." Recently published *The Breaking of Ezra Riley*, by John L. Moore (contemporary western); *The Tale of Jeremy Vale*, by Stephen Lawhead (middle-reader fiction); and *Missing!*, by Janice Brown (young adult suspense).
How to Contact: Accepts unsolicited mss. Submit complete ms with cover letter. SASE. Agented fiction 5%. Reports in 2 weeks on queries; 1-3 months on mss. Photocopied submissions OK. Accepts computer printout submissions.
Terms: Pays negotiable royalties. Sends galleys to author. Publishes ms 1 year after acceptance. Writer's guidelines and book catalog free.
Advice: "Seriously study our author guidelines—they're 6 pages of essential information. We're looking for interesting, important stories that show how God can work in the world today—and that applies whether you're exploring the effects of divorce on a teenage girl, retelling the Celtic legends, or creating adventure-packed future worlds."

LITTLE, BROWN AND COMPANY CHILDREN'S BOOKS (II), Trade Division; Children's Books, 34 Beacon St., Boston MA 02108. Editorial Department. Contact: John G. Keller, publisher; Maria Modugno, editor-in-chief; Stephanie Owens Lurie, editor. Books: 70 lb paper; sheet-fed printing; illustrations. Published new writers within the last year. Sometimes buys juvenile mss with illustrations "if by professional artist." Buys 60% agented fiction.
Needs: Middle grade fiction and young adult. Recently published *Maniac Magee*, by Jerry Spinelli; *The Day that Elvis Came to Town*, by Jan Mavino.
How to Contact: Will accept unsolicited mss. "Query letters for novels are not necessary."
Terms: Pays on royalty basis. Sends galleys to author. Publishes ms 1-2 years after acceptance.
Advice: "We are looking for trade books with bookstore appeal. Young adult 'problem' novels are no longer in vogue, but there is now a dearth of good fiction for that age group. We are looking for young children's (ages 3-5) books and first chapter books. We encourage first novelists. New authors should be aware of what is currently being published. I recommend they spend time at the local library familiarizing themselves with new publications."

LITTLE, BROWN AND COMPANY, INC. (II, III), 34 Beacon St., Boston MA 02108. (617)227-0730. Imprints include Little, Brown, Joy Street, Bulfinch Press, Arcade Publishing. Medium-size house. Publishes adult and juvenile hardcover and paperback originals. Averages 200-225 total adult titles/year. Number of fiction titles varies.
Needs: Open. No science fiction. Recently published *Vineland*, by Thomas Pynchon; *Old Silent*, by Martha Grimes; *The Truth About Lorin Jones*, by Alison Lurie; published new writers within the last year.
How to Contact: Does not accept unsolicited mss. Query editorial department first; "we accept submissions from authors who have published before, in book form, magazines, newspapers or journals. No submissions from unpublished writers." Reports in 4-6 months on queries. Simultaneous and photocopied submissions OK.
Terms: "We publish on a royalty basis, with advance." Writer's guidelines free.

LODESTAR BOOKS (II), An affiliate of Dutton Children's Books; A division of Penguin Books U.S.A., 375 Hudson St., New York NY 10014. (212)366-2000. Editorial Director: Virginia Buckley. Senior Editor: Rosemary Brosnan. Books: 50 or 55 lb antique cream paper; offset printing; hardcover binding; illustrations sometimes; average print order: 5,000-6,500; first novel print order 5,000. Published new writers within the last year. Number of titles: approximately 30 annually, 12-15 fiction titles annually. Buys 50% agented fiction.

Needs: Contemporary, humorous, sports, mystery, adventure, for middle-grade and young adult. Recently published *For Love of Jeremy*, by Hazel Krantz (ages 10-14 yrs.); *The Mind Trap*, by G. Clifton (ages 10-14 yrs.); and *Park's Quest*, by Katherine Paterson (young adult contemporary).
How to Contact: "Can query, but prefer complete ms." SASE. Simultaneous and photocopied submissions OK. Accepts computer printout submissions. Reports in 2-4 months. Publishes ms an average of 1 year after acceptance.
Terms: Pays 8-10% in royalties; offers negotiable advance. Sends galleys to author. Free book catalog.
Advice: "We are looking to add to our list more books about black, Hispanic, Native American, and Asian children, in particular. We encourage first novelists. Publishing fewer young adult novels. They are difficult to find and difficult to sell reprint rights. Middle grade does better in terms of subsidiary rights sales."

LOUISIANA STATE UNIVERSITY PRESS (II), French House, Baton Rouge LA 70893. (504)388-6294. Editor-in-Chief: Margaret Fisher Dalrymple. Fiction Editor: Martha Hall. Estab. 1935. University press—medium size. Publishes hardcover originals. Average print order: 1,500-2,500; first novel print order: 2,000. Averages 60 total titles, 4 fiction titles/year.
Needs: Contemporary, literary, mainstream, short story collections. No science fiction and/or juvenile material. Recently published *The Apple-Green Triumph*, by Martha Lacy Hall; *The Knight Has Died*, by Cees Nooteboom; *Family Men*, by Steve Yarbrough; and *Furors Die*, by William Hoffman.
How to Contact: Does not accept unsolicited mss. Query first. Reports in 2-3 months on queries and mss. Simultaneous and photocopied submissions OK. No computer printouts.
Terms: Pays in royalties, which vary. Sends pre-publication galleys to the author.

LOVESWEPT (I, II), Bantam Books, 666 5th Ave., New York NY 10103. (212)765-6500. Associate Publisher: Carolyn Nichols. Senior Editor: Susann Brailey. Imprint estab. 1982. Publishes paperback originals. Plans several first novels this year. Averages 72 total titles each year.
Needs: "Contemporary romance, highly sensual, believable primary characters, fresh and vibrant approaches to plot. No gothics, regencies or suspense."
How to Contact: Query with SASE; no unsolicited mss or partial mss. "Query letters should be no more than two to three pages. Content should be a brief description of the plot and the two main characters."
Terms: Pays in royalties of 6%; negotiates advance.
Advice: "Read extensively in the genre. Rewrite, polish, and edit your own work until it is the best it can be—before submitting."

■**LUCAS/EVANS BOOKS (II)**, 1123 Broadway, New York NY 10010. (212)929-2583. Editorial Director: Barbara Lucas. Projects Director: Jill Kastner. Estab. 1984. "Book packager—specializes in children's books." Publishes hardcover and paperbook originals. Published new writers within the last year. Plans 1 first novel this year. Averages 17 total titles, 11 or 12, many of which are children's picture books. Sometimes comments on rejected ms; sometimes charge for critiques.
Needs: Juvenile (5-9 yrs.) animal, easy-to-read, fantasy, historical, sports, spy/adventure and contemporary; young adult/teen (10-18 years) easy-to-read, fantasy/science fiction, historical, romance (young adult) and sports and spy/adventure. "Novels are not our specialty. If we come across something really spectacular, we'll try to sell it. Usually publishers handle individual novels themselves." Published *Sing for a Gentle Rain*, by J. Alison James (Atheneum); *The Trouble with Buster*, by Janet Lorimer (Scholastic); and *The Glass Salamander*, by Ann Downer (Atheneum).
How to Contact: No unsolicited mss. Query first or submit outline/synopsis and 1 or 2 sample chapters. SASE. Agented fiction 15 to 25%. Reports in 2 weeks on queries; 4-6 weeks on mss. Photocopied submissions OK. Accepts computer printout submissions.
Terms: Pays royalties; variable advance. Provides 5-10 author's copies. Sends galleys to author. Writer's guidelines for SASE. Brochure available.

MARGARET K. McELDERRY BOOKS (I, II), Imprint of the Macmillan Children's Book Group, 866 3rd Ave., New York NY 10022. (212)702-7855. Publisher: Margaret K. McElderry. Publishes hardcover originals. Books: high quality paper; offset printing; cloth and three-piece bindings; illustrations; average print order: 15,000; first novel print order: 6,000. Published new writers within the last year. Number of titles: 22 in 1990 for picture books. Buys juvenile and young adult mss, agented or non-agented.

Needs: All categories (fiction and nonfiction) for juvenile and young adult: picture books, early chapter books, contemporary, literary, adventure, mystery, science fiction and fantasy. "We will consider any category. Results depend on the quality of the imagination, the artwork and the writing." Recently published *We're Going on a Bear Hunt*, by Michael Rosui and Helen Openry; *Next-Door Neighbor*, by Sarah Ellis; *Roommates*, by Kathryn O. Galbraith; *Rain Talk*, by Mary Sorfoza and Keiko Narahashi; *Charlie Quadorum*, by Barbara Abercrombie and Mark Graham.
How to Contact: Accepts unsolicited mss. Prefers complete ms. SASE for queries and mss. Simultaneous submissions OK is so indicated; photocopied submissions must be clear and clean. Accepts computer printout submissions. Prefers letter-quality. Reports in 4 weeks on queries, 12-14 weeks on mss. Publishes ms an average of 1 year after acceptance.
Terms: Pays in royalties; offers advance.
Advice: "Imaginative writing of high quality is always in demand; also picture books that are original and unusual. We are looking especially for nonfiction and for easy-to-read books for beginners. Beginning picture-book writers often assume that texts for the very young must be rhymed. This is a misconception and has been overdone. Picture-book manuscripts written in prose are totally acceptable. We continue to publish for a wide age range."

MACMILLAN CHILDREN'S BOOKS, Macmillan Publishing Co., 866 Third Ave., New York NY 10022. (212)702-4299. Imprint of Macmillan Publishing/Children's Book Group. Contact: Attention Submissions Editor. Estab. 1919. Large children's trade list. Publishes hardcover originals.
Needs: Juvenile submissions. Not interested in series. We generally are not interested in short stories as such, unless intended as the basis for a picture book. As the YA market is weak, only extremely distinctive and well-written YA novels will be considered (and must be preceded by a query letter). Recently published *Weasel*, by Cyntha De Felice; *Dynamite Dinah*, by Claudia Mills; *Borgel*, by Daniel Pinkwater.
How to Contact: Accepts unsolicited mss or for novel send query letter with outline, sample chapter and SASE. Response in 6-8 weeks. No simultaneous submissions; photocopied submissions OK. Accepts computer printout submissions; prefers letter-quality.
Terms: Pays in royalties; negotiates advance. For catalog, send 7½ × 10½ envelope with 4 oz. postage.

MACMILLAN OF CANADA (II), A Division of Canada Publishing Corporation, 29 Birch Ave., Toronto, Ontario M4V 1E2 Canada. (416)963-8830. Editor-in-Chief: Philippa Campsie. Estab. 1905. Publishes hardcover and trade paperback originals and paperback reprints. Published new writers within the last year. Books: average print order: 4,000-5,000; first novel print order: 2,000. Averages 35 total titles, 8-10 fiction titles each year. Rarely comments on rejected mss.
Needs: Literary, mainstream, short story collection and suspense/mystery. Recently published *Last Rights*, by David Laing Dawson; *Tall Lives*, by Bill Gaston and *Swimming Toward the Light*, by Joan Clark.
How to Contact: No longer accepts unsolicited mss. Agented material only. SASE for return of ms. Reports in 1-2 months on mss. Simultaneous and photocopied submissions OK. Accepts computer printout submissions.
Terms: Pays royalties of 8% minimum; 15% maximum; advance negotiable. Provides 10 author's copies. Sends galleys to author. Book catalog for 9 × 12 SASE.
Advice: "Canadian material only."

MACMILLAN PUBLISHING CO., INC. (III), 866 3rd Ave., New York NY 10022. (212)702-2000. Contact: Fiction Editor. Fiction imprints include Collier Books, Charles Scribner's Sons, The Free Press, Bradbury and Schimer. Publishes hardcover and paperback originals and paperback reprints. Recently published *Good Hearts*, by Reynolds Price; *The Mustache*, by Emmanuel Carrére; *Spirit Lost*, by Nancy Thayer.
How to Contact: Submit through agent or brief query.
Terms: Pays in royalties; offers advance. Free book catalog.

‡MODERN PUBLISHING (II), A Division of Unisystems, Inc., 155 East 55th St., New York NY 10022. (212)826-0850. Imprint: Honey Bear Books. Contact: Kathy O'Hehir, Editorial Director. Fiction Editors: Susan Kantor, Mandy Rubenstein; Art Director: Paul Matarazzo. Estab. 1973. "Mass-market juvenile publisher; list mainly consists of picture, coloring and activity, and novelty books for ages 2-8 and board books." Publishes hardcover and paperback originals, and Americanized hardcover and paperback reprints from foreign markets. Average print order: 50,000-100,000 of each title within a series. "85% of our list first novels this year." Averages 100+ total titles each year. Sometimes comments on rejected mss.

Needs: Juvenile (5-9 yrs, including animal, easy-to-read, fantasy, historical, sports, spy/adventure and contemporary), preschool/picture book, young adult/teen (easy-to-read). Published new writers within the last year.

How to Contact: Accepts unsolicited mss. Submit complete ms. SASE. Agented fiction 5%. Reports in 2 months. Simultaneous and photocopied submissions OK.

Terms: Pays by work-for-hire or royalty arrangements. Advance negotiable. Publishes ms 7-12 months after acceptance.

Advice: "We publish picture storybooks, board books, coloring and activity books, bath books, shape books and any other new and original ideas for the children's publishing arena. We gear our books for the preschool through third-grade market and publish series of four to six books at a time. Presently we are looking for new material as we are expanding our list and would appreciate receiving any new submissions. We will consider manuscripts with accompanying artwork or by themselves, and submissions from illustrators who would like to work in the juvenile books publishing genre and can adapt their style to fit our needs. However, we will only consider those projects that are written and illustrated for series of four to six books. Manuscripts must be neatly typed and submitted either as a synopsis of the series and broken-down plot summaries of the books within the series, or full manuscripts for review with a SASE."

WILLIAM MORROW AND COMPANY, INC. (II), 1350 Avenue of the Americas, New York, NY 10019 (*After May 1*). Before May send to old address: 105 Madison Ave., New York NY 10016. Imprints include Hearst Books, Hearst Marine Books, Mulberry Books, Tambourine Books, Beech Tree Books, Quill, Perigord, Greenwillow Books, Lothrop, Lee & Shepard and Fielding Publications (travel books), and Morrow Junior Books. Publisher, Morrow Adult: James D. Landis. Estab. 1926. Approximately one fourth of books published will be fiction.

Needs: "Morrow accepts only the highest quality submissions" in contemporary, literary, experimental, adventure, mystery, spy, historical, war, feminist, gay/lesbian, science fiction, horror, humor/satire and translations. Juvenile and young adult divisions are separate. Recently published *Death in a Serene City*, by Edward Sklepowich; *Firefly*, by Piers Anthony; and *Walls of Fear*, edited by Kathryn Cramer. Published work by previously unpublished writers within the last year.

How to Contact: Submit through agent. All unsolicited mss are returned unopened. "We will accept queries, proposals or mss only when submitted through a literary agent." Simultaneous and photocopied submissions OK. Accepts double-spaced computer printout submissions; prefers letter-quality. Reports in 2-3 months.

Terms: Pays in royalties; offers advance. Sends galleys to author. Free book catalog.

Advice: "The Morrow divisions of Morrow Junior Books, Greenwillow Books, Tambourine Books, Mulberry Books, Beech Tree Books, and Lothrop, Lee and Shepard handle juvenile books. We do five to ten first novels every year and about one-fourth titles are fiction. Having an agent helps to find a publisher. Morrow Junior Books not accepting unsolicited mss."

MORROW JUNIOR BOOKS (III), 105 Madison Ave., New York NY 10016. (212)889-3050. Editor-In-Chief: David L. Reuther. Plans 1 first novel this year. Averages 55 total titles each year.

Needs: Juvenile (5-9 years, including animal, easy-to-read, fantasy (little), spy/adventure (very little), preschool/picture book, young adult/teen (10-18 years, including historical, sports). Published new writers within the last year.

How to Contact: Does not accept unsolicited fiction mss.

Terms: Authors paid in royalties. Books published 12-18 months after acceptance. Book catalog free on request.

Advice: "Our list is very full at this time. No unsolicited manuscripts."

MULTNOMAH (II, IV), 10209 SE Division, Portland OR 97266. (503)257-0526. Editor: Al Janssen. Estab. 1969. Midsize publisher of religious and inspirational books. Publishes hardcover and paperback originals. Books: average print order: 10,000. Averages 25-35 total titles a year. "We are just getting into publishing fiction and our first books will be for children (8-12 yrs.)."

Needs: Juvenile (5-9 yrs.) easy-to-read and fantasy, historical, sports, humorous spy/adventure and contemporary, preschool/picture book, religious/inspirational and spiritual. Young adult/teen (10-18 years), religious/inspirational, fantasy, historical, problem novels, sports and spy/adventure. "We're looking for children's (juvenile) 8-12 yrs. and short chapter books for 7-9 yr. olds—both in series. No adult romance, science fiction."

How to Contact: Accepts unsolicited mss. Submit outline/synopsis and 3 sample chapters. SASE. Simultaneous and photocopied submissions OK. Accepts computer printout submissions.
Terms: Pays royalties of 8-12% net with possible escalation depending on type of children's book, amount of illustrations and stature of author; offers negotiable advance. Provides 15 author's copies. Sends galleys to author. Publishes ms 9-12 months after acceptance. Writer's guidelines free. Book catalog for 9 × 12 SASE.

THE MYSTERIOUS PRESS (III), 129 W. 56th St., New York NY 10019. (212)765-0923. Imprint: Penzler Books. Publisher: Otto Penzler. Editor-in-Chief: William Malloy. Editor: Sara Ann Freed. Estab. 1976. Small independent publisher, publishing only mystery and suspense fiction. Publishes hardcover originals and paperback reprints. Books: hardcover (some Smythe sewn) and paperback binding; illustrations rarely. 76 titles scheduled for 1990. Average first novel print order 5,000 copies. Critiques "only those rejected writers we wish particularly to encourage."
Needs: Suspense/mystery. Recently published *The Fourth Durango*, by Ross Thomas; *The Bridesmaid*, by Ruth Rendell; *Tomorrow's Crimes*, by Donald E. Westlake; published new writers within the last year.
How to Contact: Agented material only.
Terms: Pays in royalties of 10% minimum; offers negotiable advance. Sends galleys to author. Buys hard and softcover rights. Book catalog for SASE.
Advice: "We have a strong belief in the everlasting interest in and strength of mystery fiction. Don't talk about writing, do it. Don't ride band wagons, create them. Our philosophy about publishing first novels is the same as our philosophy about publishing: the cream rises to the top. We are looking for writers with whom we can have a long term relationship. *Sea of Green*, by Thomas Adcock is a first novel published this year. A good editor is an angel, assisting according to the writer's needs. My job is to see to it that the writer writes the best book he/she is capable of, *not* to have the writer write *my* book. Don't worry, publishing will catch up to you; the cycles continue as they always have. If your work is good, keep it circulating and begin the next one, and keep the faith. Get an agent."

NAVAL INSTITUTE PRESS (II, IV), Book publishing arm of US Naval Institute, Annapolis MD 21402. Fiction Editor: Paul W. Wilderson. Estab. 1873. Nonprofit publisher with area of concentration in naval and maritime subjects. Publishes hardcover originals. Averages 35 total titles each year. Fiction only occasionally. Average first novel print order: 15,000 copies.
Needs: Historical (naval), war (naval aspects) and adventure (naval and maritime). "We are looking for exceptional novels written on a naval or maritime theme." Published *Hunt for Red October*, by T. Clancy (naval adventure, contemporary); *Flight of the Intruder*, by Stephen Coonts.
How to Contact: Accepts unsolicited mss. Prefers to receive outline/synopsis and 2 sample chapters. Reports in 8 weeks. Discourages simultaneous submissions. Accepts computer printout submissions; prefers letter-quality.
Terms: Pays in royalties of 14% of net sales minimum; 21% maximum; 6 author's copies; offers negotiable advance. Sends galleys to author. Free writer's guidelines and book catalog.

NEW AMERICAN LIBRARY (III), A division of Penguin USA, 375 Hudson St., New York NY 10014. (212)366-2000. Imprints include Onyx, Signet, Mentor, Signet Classic, Plume, Plume Fiction, DAW, Meridian. Contact: Michaela Hamilton, executive/director (mass market books); Arnold Dolin, associate publisher, Plume (trade paperback); Maureen Baron, editor-in-chief, Signet/Onyx Books (mass-market). Estab. 1948. Publishes hardcover and paperback originals and paperback reprints.
Needs: "All kinds of commercial and literary fiction, including mainstream, historical, Regency, New Age, western, thriller, science fiction, fantasy, gay. Full length novels and collections." Published *Misery*, by Stephen King; *Small Sacrifices*, by Ann Rule; and *Blood Run*, by Leah Ruth Robinson; published new writers within the last year.
How to Contact: Queries accepted with SASE. "State type of book and past publishing projects." Agented mss only. Simultaneous and photocopied submissions OK. Reports in 3 months.
Terms: Pays in royalties and author's copies; offers advance. Sends galleys to author. Free book catalog.
Advice: "Write the complete manuscript and submit it to an agent or agents."

‡NEW READERS PRESS (IV), Publishing division of Laubach Literacy International, Box 131, Syracuse NY 13210. (315)422-9121. Editor-in-Chief: Laura Martin. Estab. 1959. Publishes paperback originals. Books: 55A Warner's Old Style paper; offset printing; paper binding; 6-12 illustrations per fiction book; average print order: 7,500; first novel print order: 5,000. Fiction titles may be published both in

book form and as read-along audio tapes. Averages 30 total titles, 4-8 fiction titles each year.
Needs: High-interest, low-reading-level materials for adults and older teens with limited reading skills. Short novels of 12,000-15,000 words, written on 3rd-grade level, "Can be mystery, romance, adventure, science fiction, sports or humor. Characters are well-developed, situations realistic, and plot developments believable." Accepts short stories only in collections of 8-20 very short stories of same genre. Will accept collections of one-act plays that can be performed in a single class period (45-50 min.) with settings than can be created within a classroom. Short stories and plays can be at 3rd-5th grade reading level. All material must be suitable for classroom use in public education, i.e., little violence and no explicit sex. "We will not accept anything at all for readers under 18 years of age."
How to Contact: Accepts unsolicited mss. Query first or submit outline/synopsis and 3 sample chapters. SASE. Reports in 1 month on queries; 3 months on mss. Photocopied submissions OK. Accepts computer printout submissions.
Terms: Pays royalties of 5% minimum, 7.5% maximum on gross sales. Average advance: $200. "We may offer authors a choice of a royalty or flat fee. The fee would vary depending on the type of work." Book catalog, authors' brochure and guidelines for short novels free.
Advice: "Most of our fiction authors are being published for the first time. It is necessary to have a sympathetic attitude toward adults with limited reading skills and an understanding of their life situation. Direct experience with them is helpful."

W.W. NORTON & COMPANY, INC. (II), 500 5th Ave., New York NY 10110. (212)354-5500. For unsolicited mss contact: Liz Malcolm. Estab. 1924. Midsize independent publisher of trade books and college textbooks. Publishes hardcover originals. Occasionally comments on rejected mss.
Needs: High-quality fiction (preferably literary). No occult, science fiction, religious, gothic, romances, experimental, confession, erotica, psychic/supernatural, fantasy, horror, juvenile or young adult. Published *God's Snake*, by Irini Spanidou (literary); *Agents of Innocence*, by David Ignatius (suspense); published new writers within the last year.
How to Contact: Submit outline/synopsis and sample chapters (of which one is the first). Simultaneous and photocopied submissions OK. Accepts computer printout submissions prefers letter-quality. Reports in 6-8 weeks. Packaging and postage must be enclosed to ensure safe return of materials.
Terms: Graduated royalty scale starting at 7½% or 10% of net invoice price, in addition to 25 author's copies; offers advance. Free book catalog.
Advice: "We will occasionally encourage writers of promise whom we do not immediately publish. We are principally interested in the literary quality of fiction manuscripts. A familiarity with our current list of titles will give you an idea of what we're looking for. Chances are, if your book is good and you have no agent you will eventually succeed; but the road to success will be easier and shorter if you have an agent backing the book. We encourage the submission of first novels."

PANTHEON BOOKS (III), Subsidiary of Random House, 201 E. 50th St., New York NY 10022. (212)572-2404. Estab. 1950. "Small but well established imprint of well known large house." Publishes hardcover and trade paperback originals and trade paperback reprints. Plans 1-2 first novels this year. Averages 90 total titles, 25 fiction titles each year.
Needs: Pantheon no longer accepts unsolicited fiction. Published *Blue Eyes, Black Hair*, by Marguerite Duras; *A Friend From England*, by Anita Brookner; and *Once in Europa*, by John Berger.
How to Contact: Agented fiction 100%.

PELICAN PUBLISHING COMPANY (IV), Box 189, 1101 Monroe St., Gretna LA 70053. Editor: Nina Kooij. Estab. 1926. Publishes hardcover reprints and originals. Books: hardcover and paperback binding; illustrations sometimes. Published new writers within the last year. Buys juvenile mss with illustrations. Comments on rejected mss "infrequently."
Needs: Juvenile and young adult fiction, especially with a regional focus. "Our adult fiction is *very* limited." Recently published *A Bullet for Stonewall*, by Benjamin King; and *The Magic Box*, by Olga Cossi.
How to Contact: Prefers query. May submit outline/synopsis and 2 sample chapters with SASE. No simultaneous submissions; photocopied submissions only. "Not responsible if writer's only copy is sent." Reports in 4 weeks on queries; 12 weeks on mss. Publishes ms 12-18 months after acceptance.
Terms: Pays 10% in royalties; 10 free author's copies; advance considered. Sends galleys to author. Catalog of titles and writer's guidelines with SASE.
Advice: "Research the market carefully. Order and look through publishing catalogs to see if your work is consistent with their lists."

POCKET BOOKS (II), Division of Simon & Schuster, 1230 Avenue of the Americas, New York NY 10020. (212)698-7000. Imprints include Washington Square Press and Star Trek. Vice President/Editorial Director: William Grose. Publishes paperback and hardcover originals and reprints. Averages 300 titles each year. Buys 90% agented fiction. Sometimes critiques rejected mss.
Needs: Contemporary, literary, faction, adventure, mystery, spy, historical, western, gothic, romance, literary, military/war, mainstream, suspense/mystery, feminist, ethnic, erotica, psychic/supernatural, fantasy, horror and humor/satire. Recently published *Dalva*, by Jim Harrison; *The Wolf's Hour*, by Robert R. McCammon (horror); *A Question of Guilt*, by Frances Fyrield (hardcover); published new writers within the last year.
How to Contact: Query with SASE. No unsolicited mss. Reports in 6 months on queries only. Publishes ms 12-18 months after acceptance.
Terms: Pays in royalties and offers advance. Sends galleys to author. Writer must return advance if book is not completed or is not acceptable. Free book catalog.

POINT BOOKS, Scholastic, Inc., 730 Broadway, New York NY 10003. (212)505-3000. Senior Editor: Regina Griffin. Estab. 1984. Young adult imprint. Publishes paperback originals and reprints.
Needs: Young adult/teen (12-18 years). Published *Fallen Angels*, by Walter Dean Myers; *Born into Light*, by Paul Samuel Jacobs; *The Babysitter*, by R.L. Stine; and *April Fools*, by Richard Cusick.
How to Contact: Query first. SASE.
Advice: "Query letters should describe the genre of the book (mystery, sci-fi, etc.), give a brief plot description, and tell about the writer's background (i.e. have they published anything; taken writing courses, etc.). One common mistake I see is that I get letters that go on and on about the marketing possibilities, but neglect to describe the book at all. That makes me feel I'm dealing with someone who wants to be a 'writer,' but doesn't really take writing seriously enough. We like to publish fiction by previously unpublished writers, if we can. We are expanding our hardcover program and our paperback middle-reader line."

POSEIDON PRESS (II), 1230 Avenue of the Americas, New York NY 10020. (212)698-7290. Distributed by Simon & Schuster. Publisher: Ann E. Patty. Senior Editor: Elaine Pfefferbilt. Estab. 1981. Hardcover and quality trade paper. Books: paper varies; offset printing; illustrations; average print order varies; first novel print order: 5,000-7,500. Averages 20 total titles, 10-12 fiction titles (3 first novels) each year. Does "not critique rejected ms by unsolicited authors unless work merits it."
Needs: General fiction and nonfiction, commercial and literary. Published *Inheritance*, by Judith Michael; and *Bad Behavin*, by Mary Gaitskill.
How to Contact: Query first. No unsolicited manuscripts or sample chapters. Photocopied submissions OK. Reports in 2 months.
Terms: Payment varies, according to content of book.

CLARKSON N. POTTER, INC., 201 E. 50th St., New York NY 10022. (212)572-6121. Distributed by Crown Publishers, Inc. Vice President Editor-in-Chief: Carol Southern.
Needs: Illustrated fiction, biography, humor/satire and juvenile. Recently published *Black Water: The Book of Fantastic Literature*, by Alberto Manguel.
How to Contact: Prefers submissions through an agent. Simultaneous and photocopied submissions OK. Accepts computer printout submissions.
Terms: Pays 6-12% in royalties on hardcover; 6-7½% in royalties on paperback; offers $5,000 up in advance.

PRENTICE-HALL BOOKS FOR YOUNG READERS (II), A Division of Simon & Schuster, Inc., Juvenile Publishing Division, 1230 Avenue of the Americas, New York NY 10020. (212)698-7000. Manuscript Coordinator: Rose Lopez. Publishes hardcover originals and paperback originals and reprints. Books: offset printing; illustrations on most titles; average print order: 10,000. Number of titles: 30 hardcover children's books and 15 children's paperbacks/year.
Needs: Juvenile, picture books, humor, mystery, "high-quality middle-grade fiction," and "imaginative nonfiction." Published *Over in the Meadow*, by Paul Galdone (picture book); *Waiter, There's a Fly In My Soup!*, by Charles Keller, illustrations by Lee Lorenz (humor); *Who Let Muddy Boots Into The White House?*, by Robert Quackenbush (biography); published new writers within the last year.
How to Contact: Agented or solicited mss only.
Terms: Pays in royalties; offers advance. Sends galleys to author.

PRESIDIO PRESS (IV), 31 Pamaron Way, Novato CA 94949. (415)883-1373. Editors: Robert Kane, Joan Griffin and Robert Tate. Estab. 1976. Small independent general trade—specialist in military. Publishes hardcover originals. Books: 20 lb regular paper, average print order: 5,000. Published new writers within the last year. Publishes at least one military fiction book per list. Averages 20 total titles each year. Critiques or comments on rejected mss.
Needs: Historical with military background, war. Recently published *Shadow Flight*, by Joe Weber; *HMS Marathon*, by A.E. Langsford; and *Feast of Bones*, by Dan Bolger.
How to Contact: Accepts unsolicited mss. Query first or submit 4 sample chapters. SASE. Reports in 2 weeks on queries; 3 months on mss. Simultaneous and photocopied submissions OK. Accepts computer printouts.
Terms: Pays in royalties of 15% of net minimum; advance: $1,000 average. Sends galleys to author. Book catalog free on request.
Advice: "Think twice before entering any highly competitive genre; don't imitate; do your best. Have faith in your writing and don't let the market disappoint or discourage you."

PRICE STERN SLOAN, INC. (II), 360 N. La Cienega Blvd., Los Angeles CA 90048. (213)657-6100. Subsidiaries/Divisions are Wonder Books, Troubador, Serendipity, Doodle Art and HPBooks. Contact: Editorial Dept. Estab. 1962. Midsize independent, expanding. Publishes hardcover originals, paperback originals and reprints. Books: perfect or saddle-stitched binding; illustrations. Averages 200 total titles each year.
Needs: Humor/satire, juvenile (series, easy-to-read, humor, educational) and adult trade nonfiction. No adult fiction. Published *Shopaholics* (adult trade); *My Grandmother's Cookie Jar* (juvenile fiction); and *Where Fish Go in Winter*, (juvenile nonfiction). Also publishes "self-help, cookbooks, automotive books, photography and gardening."
How to Contact: Query only. Submit outline/synopsis and sample pages. SASE required. Reports in 2 months on queries. Simultaneous and photocopied submissions OK. Accepts computer printouts.
Terms: Terms vary.

G.P. PUTNAM'S SONS (III), The Putnam Publishing Group, 200 Madison Ave., New York NY 10016. (212)951-8400. Imprints include Perigee, Philomel, Platt and Munk, Coward McCann, Grosset and Dunlap Pacer. Publishes hardcover originals.
Needs: Published fiction by Stephen King, Lawrence Sanders, Alice Hoffman; published new writers within the last year.
How to Contact: Does not accept unsolicited mss.

RANDOM HOUSE, INC., 201 E. 50th St., New York NY 10022. (212)751-2600. Imprints include Pantheon Books, Panache Press at Random House, Vintage Books, Times Books, Villard Books and Knopf. Contact: Adult Trade Division. Publishes hardcover and paperback originals. Encourages new writers. Rarely comments on rejected mss.
Needs: Adventure, contemporary, historical, literary, mainstream, short story collections, suspense/mystery. "We publish fiction of the highest standards." Authors include James Michener, Robert Ludlum, Mary Gordon.
How to Contact: Query with SASE. Simultaneous and photocopied submissions OK. Reports in 4-6 weeks on queries, 2 months on mss.
Terms: Payment as per standard minimum book contracts. Free writer's guidelines.
Advice: "Please try to get an agent because of the large volume of manuscripts received, agented work is looked at first."

RESOURCE PUBLICATIONS, INC. (I, IV), Suite 290, 160 E. Virginia St., San Jose CA 95112. (408)286-8505. Book Editor: Kenneth Guentert. Estab. 1973. "Independent book and magazine publisher focusing on imaginative resources for celebration." Publishes paperback originals. Averages 12-14 total titles, 2-3 fiction titles each year.
Needs: Story collections for storytellers, "not short stories in the usual literary sense." No novels. Recently published *Jesus on the Mend: Healing Stories for Ordinary People*, by Andre Papineau; and *The Magic Stone: Stories for Your Faith Journey*, by James Henderschedt.
How to Contact: Query first or submit outline/synopsis and 1 sample chapter with SASE. Reports in 2 weeks on queries; 6 weeks on mss. Photocopied submissions OK "if specified as *not* simultaneous." Accepts computer printout submissions. Prefers letter-quality. Accepts disk submissions compatible with CP/M, IBM system. Prefers hard copy with disk submissions.

Terms: Pays in royalties of 8% minimum, 10% maximum; 10 author's copies. "We require first-time authors purchase a small portion of the press-run, but we do not subsidy publish under the Resource Publications imprint. However, our graphics department will help authors self-publish for a fee."

ST. MARTIN'S PRESS, 175 5th Ave., New York NY 10010. (212)674-5151. Imprint: Thomas Dunn. Chairman and CEO: Thomas J. McCormack. President: Roy Gainsburg. Publishes hardcover and paperback reprints and originals.
Needs: Contemporary, literary, experimental, faction, adventure, mystery, spy, historical, war, gothic, romance, confession, feminist, gay, lesbian, ethnic, erotica, psychic/supernatural, religious/inspirational, science fiction, fantasy, horror and humor/satire. No plays, children's literature or short fiction. Published *The Silence of the Lambs*, by Thomas Harris; *Little Saigon*, by T. Jefferson Parker; *The Shell Seekers*, by Rosamunde Pilcher.
How to Contact: Query or submit complete ms with SASE. Simultaneous (if declared as such) and photocopied submissions OK. Reports in 2-3 weeks on queries, 4-6 weeks on mss.
Terms: Pays standard advance and royalties.

ST. PAUL BOOKS AND MEDIA (I), Subsidiary of Daughters of St. Paul, 50 St. Paul's Ave., Jamaica Plain, Boston MA 02130. (617)522-8911. Children's Editor: Sister Anne Joan, fsp. Estab. 1934. Roman Catholic publishing house. Publishes hardcover and paperback originals. Averages 20 total titles, 5 fiction titles each year.
Needs: Juvenile (animal, easy-to-read, fantasy, historical, religion, contemporary), preschool/picture book and young adult/teen (historical, religion, problem novels). All fiction must communicate high moral and family values. "Our fiction needs are entirely in the area of children's literature. We are looking for bedtime stories, historical and contemporary novels for children. Would like to see characters who manifest faith and trust in God." Does not want "characters whose lifestyles are not in conformity with Catholic teachings."
How to Contact: Does not accept unsolicited mss. Query first. SASE. Reports in 2 weeks.
Terms: Pays royalties of 8% minimum; 12% maximum. Provides negotiable number of author's copies. Publishes ms approx 2 or 3 years after acceptance. Writer's guidelines for #10 SAE and 1 first class stamp.
Advice: "There is a dearth of juvenile fiction appropriate for Catholics and other Christians."

SCHOLASTIC, Scholastic, Inc., 730 Broadway, New York NY 10003. (212)505-3000. Publishes a variety of books (hardcovers, paperback originals and reprints) for children and young adults under the following imprints: Scholastic Hardcover: Senior Editor: Regina Griffin. Estab. 1985. A hardcover line of high quality fiction. No multiple submissions. Include SASE.
POINT BOOKS: Senior Editor: Regina Griffin. Estab. 1984. A paperback line of young adult fiction for readers aged 12-up. Most Point novels have contemporary settings, and take as their central characters young adults between the ages of 13-18. No multiple submissions. Scholastic also publishes original paperback books for its school book clubs: Tab Book Club (Teen Age Book Club): Editor: Greg Holch. Especially interested in humorous novels and novels about friendship for readers 12-14. APPLE BOOKS: Senior Editor: Regina Griffin. Estab. 1981. A paperback line of juvenile fiction for readers aged 8-12. No multiple submissions. include SASE. Executive Editor: Ann Reit. Publishes novels dealing with family, romance and school. Paper and hardcover. Ages 9-11; 12-14.
How to Contact: Query first or submit outline/synopsis and 3 sample chapters with SASE. Accepts computer printout submissions.

CHARLES SCRIBNER'S SONS (II), Subsidiary of Macmillan, 866 3rd Ave., New York NY 10022. (212)702-2000. Editors: Edward Chase, Susanne Kirk. Publisher and Editor-in-Chief: Barbara Grossman. Estab. 1846. Publishes hardcover originals and paperback reprints of its own titles. Number of titles: over 100 last year. Does not comment on rejected mss.
Needs: Contemporary, adventure, mystery, spy, feminist, horror, humor/satire.
How to Contact: Submit outline/synopsis and sample chapter with SASE or submit through agent. "Go to writing workshops. Most important, find an agent." Reports in 2 months on queries. Does not accept unsolicited mss, only queries.
Terms: Pays in royalties; offers advance. Sends galleys to author.

CHARLES SCRIBNER'S SONS, BOOKS FOR YOUNG READERS, Division of Macmillan Publishing Co., 866 Third Ave., New York NY 10022. (212)702-7885. Editorial Director: Clare Costello. Publishes hardcover originals. Averages 20-25 total titles, 8-13 fiction titles each year.

Close-up

Laura Resnick
Romance Writer

Laura Resnick never wanted to be a writer. She grew up with a writer in the house—her father, Mike Resnick, who routinely cranks out award-winning science fiction stories and novels. Having seen what the life of a writer is like convinced her that writing was the last thing she wanted to do for a living.

But fate, it would seem, willed otherwise. Laura Resnick became a writer. A romance novelist, to be exact. And in the kind of fine irony one rarely finds outside fiction, a bestselling romance novelist. And, to top things off, she received the *Romantic Times* Award for Best New Series Author, 1989. This, only a year after her first novel, *One Sultry Summer*, was published as a Silhouette Desire romance.

When she graduated from Georgetown University (where she majored in languages) Resnick had in mind to travel and perhaps do some acting. And travel she did, living in and working her way through several countries, including Italy, France, Israel and England. She worked all sorts of jobs, went to drama school in London, and when in the U.S. she taught and waited tables.

Throughout four years of travel, friends and acquaintances frequently urged her to write, either because of her traveling experiences, the fact that her father had published more than 200 books, or both. But she resisted—until she saw an ad for Kathryn Falk's book, *How to Write a Romance and Get it Published*. At the time she was living in Sicily, teaching English, and the decision to write a romance novel was heavily driven by economic concerns. She read the book and started writing a romance novel, even though she wasn't really a romance reader. "If you're disciplined and do a good job, you don't have to be a big romance fan," she says.

She credits *How to Write a Romance and Get it Published* for much of her success. "Everything you need to know is in this book," Resnick says. "I wrote my first two novels with my nose buried in this book."

Resnick carefully targeted her market, selecting the steamy 60,000-word category as the best place to break in. Then she went to work.

Her novels were published under the name "Laura Leone." "Since Leone was the word for my astrological sign in Italian, and friends said it would be lucky for me, I used that."

Eight novels later (her latest are *A Woman's Work* and *Upon a Midnight Clear*, both Silhouette Desire novels), it would seem her choice was luck, indeed. But Resnick doesn't count on luck. Hard work and craftsmanship are what's important. "I can't see just grinding them out," she says. "I do my best work on every novel."

But doing her best work doesn't mean taking years to "polish" a novel, as some writers do. She takes a practical approach and it shows in the length of time it takes her to turn out quality fiction. "I wrote *Guilty Secrets* (her fourth romance) in 16 days, start to finish."

"On the other hand," she admits, "some books take six to eight weeks."

Resnick's schedule is erratic. "When I'm getting ready to write, I pace my work for two or three weeks. During this time, I run errands as an excuse to get away, to socialize. When I'm ready, I sit down and write. I don't do anything but write and sleep until the book is done. My best hours for writing are between 10:00 p.m. and 6:00 a.m."

When asked for advice for beginning writers, Resnick gets right to the point. "They need to start a book, they need to finish a book, and treat it like a product for sale. Of the people who bother to start a book, only one in a hundred tries to write for the market."

As you might expect, Resnick's background shows up in her novels. Characterizing herself as "a travel bum," she credits living and working in other countries as a source of inspiration. "A lot of my background goes into my books. I write from experience — things I've done, people I've met, my jobs, and so forth."

Resnick hired an agent — her first — to handle this book. The process took months of research, telephone calls, and a trip to New York for personal interviews. She was in no hurry to get an agent, for practical reasons. "Most writers make the mistake of acquiring an agent before they're ready. I worked two years in the business before I went looking. By then, I knew what I wanted and what I deserved in an agent." From an author who has sold eight novels without an agent, this is sound advice.

Resnick is now working on a mainstream novel — "a contemporary ghost story set in a kennel." She isn't ready to forsake romance novels, but prefers not to limit herself to one kind of writing. Which is what you would expect from a self-professed "travel bum." "I'm probably most alive when I'm on the road with my backpack." And, no doubt, filing away ideas and experiences and characters for when she's not on the road.

—Michael A. Banks

❝I can't see just grinding them out. I do my best work on every novel.❞

—Laura Resnick

Needs: Juvenile (animal, easy-to-read, fantasy, historical, picture book, sports, spy/adventure, contemporary, ethnic and science fiction) and young adult (fantasy/science fiction, romance, historical, problem novels, sports and spy/adventure). Published *The Giver*, by Lynn Hall (young adult contemporary fiction); *How Do You Know It's True?*, by David and Marymae Klein (young adult nonfiction); and *Welcome to Grossville*, by Alice Fleming (intermediate contemporary fiction).
How to Contact: Submit complete ms with SASE. Simultaneous and photocopied submissions OK. Reports in 8-10 weeks on mss.
Terms: Free book catalog free on request. Sends galleys to author.

SIERRA CLUB BOOKS, 100 Bush St., San Francisco CA 94104. (415)291-1617. FAX: (415)291-1602. Editor-in-Chief: D. Moses. Estab. 1892. Midsize independent publisher. Publishes hardcover and paperback originals and paperback reprints. Averages 20-25 titles, 1-2 fiction titles each year.
Needs: Contemporary (conservation, environment).
How to Contact: Query only with SASE. "We will only deal with queries; we are not staffed to deal with mss." Simultaneous and photocopied submissions OK. Accepts computer printout submissions; prefers letter-quality. Reports in 6 weeks on queries.
Terms: Pays in royalties. Free book catalog for SASE.
Advice: "Only rarely do we publish fiction. We will consider novels on their quality and on the basis of their relevance to our organization's environmentalist aims."

SILHOUETTE BOOKS (II, IV), 6th Floor, 300 E. 42nd St., New York NY 10017. (212)682-6080. Imprints include Silhouette Romance, Silhouette Special Edition, Silhouette Desire, Silhouette Intimate Moments, Harlequin Historicals; also Silhouette Christmas Stories, Silhouette Summer Sizzlers, Harlequin Historical Christmas Stories. Editorial Manager: Isabel Swift. Senior Editor & Editorial Coordinator (SIM, HH): Leslie J. Wainger. Seniors Editors: (SE) Tara Hughes Gavin, (SD) Lucia Macro, (SR) Valerie Hayward. Editor: Mary Clare Kersten, Beth de Guzman. Historicals: Editors: Tracy Farrell, Eliza Shallcross. Estab. 1979. Publishes paperback originals. Published 10-20 new writers within the last year. Buys agented and unagented adult romances. Number of titles: 316/year. Occasionally comments on rejected mss.
Needs: Contemporary romances, historical romances. Recently published *Connal*, by Diana Palmer; *Without a Trace*, by Nora Roberts; *Glory, Glory*, by Linda Lael Miller.
How to Contact: Submit query letter with brief synopsis and SASE. No unsolicited or simultaneous submissions; photocopied submissions OK. Accepts computer printout submissions. Prefers letter-quality. Publishes ms 9-24 months after acceptance.
Terms: Pays in royalties; offers advance (negotiated on an individual basis). Must return advance if book is not completed or is unacceptable.
Advice: "Study our published books before submitting to make sure that the submission is a potential Silhouette. Added new line of historical romances. Looking for new authors in all lines. Interested in fresh, original ideas and new directions within the romance genre."

SIMON & SCHUSTER, 1230 Avenue of the Americas, New York NY 10020. (212)698-7000. Imprints include Pocket Books, Linden Press.
Needs: General adult fiction, mostly commercial fiction.
How to Contact: Agented material 100%.

GIBBS SMITH, PUBLISHER (II), Box 667, Layton UT 84041. (801)544-9800. FAX: (801)544-5582. Imprints: Peregrine Smith Books. Editorial Director: Madge Baird. Fiction Editor: Steve Chapman. Estab. 1969. Publishes hardcover and paperback originals and reprints. Books: illustrations as needed; average print order 5,000. Publishes 25+ total titles each year, 5-6 fiction titles.
Needs: Contemporary, experimental, humor/satire, literary, short story collections, translations and nature. Literary works exhibiting the social consciousness of our times. Recently published *Relative Distances*, by Victoria Jenkins; *The Tennessee Waltz and Other Stories*, by Alan Cheuse; and *The Light Possessed*, by Alan Cheuse.
How to Contact: Query first. SASE. 60% of fiction is agented. Reports in 3 weeks on queries; 10 weeks on mss. Simultaneous and photocopied submissions OK. Accepts computer printout submissions.
Terms: Pays 7-15% royalties. Sends galleys to author. Writer's guidelines for #10 SASE; book catalog for 9×6 SAE and 56¢ postage.
Advice: "Our foremost criteria is the literary merit of the work."

STANDARD PUBLISHING (II, IV), 8121 Hamilton Ave., Cincinnati OH 45231. (513)931-4050. Director: Mark Plunkett. Estab. 1866. Independent religious publisher. Publishes paperback originals and reprints. Books: offset printing; paper binding; b&w line art; average print order: 7,500; first novel print order: 5,000-7,500. Number of titles: averages 18/year. Rarely buys juvenile mss with illustrations. Occasionally comments on rejected mss.
Needs: Religious/inspirational and easy-to-read. "Should have some relation to moral values or Biblical concepts and principles." Katie Hooper Series, by Jane Sorenson; Julie McGregor Series, by Kristi Hall.
How to Contact: Query or submit outline/synopsis and 2-3 sample chapters with SASE. "Query should include synopsis and general description of perceived market." Accepts computer printout submissions. Prefers letter-quality. Reports in 1 month on queries, 12 weeks on mss. Publishes ms 12-24 months after acceptance.
Terms: Pays varied royalties and by outright purchase; offers varied advance. Sends galleys to author. Free catalog with SASE.
Advice: Publishes fiction with "strong moral and ethical implications." First novels "should be appropriate, fitting into new or existing series. We're dealing more with issues."

STODDART (III), Subsidiary of General Publishing, 34 Lesmill Rd., Toronto, Ontario M3B 2T6 Canada. (416)445-3333. Managing Editor: Donald G. Bastian. "Largest Canadian-owned publisher in Canada, with a list that features nonfiction primarily." Publishes hardcover and paperback originals and reprints. Plans 2 first novels this year. Averages 50-60 total titles, 8 fiction each year.
Needs: Adventure, suspense/mystery, young adult/teen (10-18 years). Looking for "quality commercial fiction with international potential." Recently published *A Man Wanders Sometimes*, by Kent Baker; *The First Garden*, by Anne Hebert; and *The Leaving*, by Budge Wilson.
How to Contact: Submit outline/synopsis and 2-3 sample chapters. SASE. Agented fiction 50%. Reports in 4-6 weeks on queries; 2-3 months on mss. Simultaneous and photocopied submissions OK. Accepts computer printout submissions, including dot-matrix.
Terms: Pays royalties of 10% minimum; 25% maximum for hardcover. Advance is negotiable. Sends galleys to author. Publishes ms up to 2 years after acceptance.
Advice: "Fiction accounts for about 10% of the list. The amount we do depends on quality and marketability, co-publishing arrangements in US etc., and foreign language sales potential." Encourages first novelists, "but they should be realistic. Don't expect to make a living on it. Presentation is very important. Clear-typed, open spacing. Typos can easily turn readers away from a potentially good book."

‡TAB BOOK CLUB (TEEN AGE BOOK CLUB) (II), Scholastic Inc., 730 Broadway, New York NY 10003. Contact: Greg Holch. See listing for Scholastic Inc. Published new writers within the last year.
Needs: "Scholastic and the TAB Book Club publish novels for young teenagers in seventh through ninth grades. We do no publish short stories or standard teenage romances. A book has to be unique, different, and of high literary quality."
How to Contact: Send "a query letter and the first 20 pages of the manuscript."
Advice: "I personally prefer humorous, light novels that revolve around a unique premise, such as *A Royal Pain*, by Ellen Conford. We publish mass-market entertainment reading, not educational books."

THORNDIKE PRESS (IV), Subsidiary of Senior Service Corp., Box 159, Thorndike ME 04986. (800)223-6121. Editorial Assistant: Barbara Libby. Estab. 1979. Midsize publisher, a division of Macmillan, Inc., of large print reprints. Publishes hardcover and paperback large print *reprints*. Books: alkaline paper; offset printing; Smythe-sewn library binding; average print order: 4,000. Publishes 132 total titles each year, 120 fiction titles.
Needs: *No fiction that has not been previously published*. Recently published *First Salute*, by Barbara Tuchman; *Temple of My Familiar*, by Alice Walker.
How to Contact: Does not accept unsolicited mss.
Terms: Pays 10% in royalties.

The double dagger before a listing indicates that the listing is new in this edition. New markets are often the most receptive to freelance contributions.

TICKNOR & FIELDS (I, II), Affiliate of Houghton-Mifflin, 215 Park Ave. South, New York NY 10003. (212)420-5800. Estab. 1979. Publishes hardcover originals.
Needs: Open to all categories, but selective list of only 30 titles a year. Recently published *The Kneeling Bus*, by Beverly Coyle; *Julian's House*, by Judith Hawkes; *Homesick*, by Guy Vanderhaeghe; and *Barking Man*, by Madison Smartt Bell.
How to Contact: Query letters only; no unsolicited mss accepted. No simultaneous submissions (unless very special); photocopied submissions OK. Reports in 2 months on ms.
Terms: Pays standard royalties. Offers advance depending on the book. Free book catalog with SAE and first class stamps.

TOR BOOKS (II), 49 W. 24th St., New York NY 10010. Imprints include Tor Horror, Tor SF, Tor Fantasy and Aerie Books. Managing Editor: Maria Melilli. Estab. 1980. Publishes paperback originals and reprints; also has hardcover trade list of approximately 30 titles a year. Books: 5 point Dombook paper; offset printing; Bursel and perfect binding; few illustrations. Averages 200 total titles, all fiction, each year. Some nonfiction titles.
Needs: Fantasy, science fiction, westerns, suspense and mainstream. Recently published *Prentice Alvin*, by Orson Scott Card; *Necroscope*, by Brian Lumley; *Angel Fire*, by Andrew M. Greely; and *Araminta Station*, by Jack Vance.
How to Contact: Agented mss preferred. Buys 90% agented fiction. Photocopied submissions OK. No simultaneous submissions. Address manuscripts to "editorial," *not* to the Managing Editor's office.
Terms: Pays in royalties and advance. Writer must return advance if book is not completed or is unacceptable. Sends galleys to author. Free book catalog on request.

TRILLIUM PRESS I, II), Box 209, Monroe NY 10950. (914)783-2999. Vice President: Thomas Holland. Fiction Editor: William Neumann. Estab. 1978. "Independent educational publisher." Publishes hardcover and paperback originals and paperback reprints. Published new writers within the last year. Plans 40 first novels this year. Averages 150 total titles, 70 fiction titles each year.
Needs: Juvenile (5-9 yrs.) animal, easy-to-read, fantasy, historical, sports, spy/adventure and contemporary, young adult/teen (10-18 years) easy-to-read, fantasy/science fiction, historical, problem novels, romance (ya), sports and spy/adventure, middle school/young adult (10-18) series. Recently published the following young adult series: Mystery & Adventure (including historical novels); Growing Up Right (values, relationships, adult development); science fiction. Also published *Eerie Canal*, by Jack Reber; *Taking Control*, by Ann Love; and *Echo Summer*, by Jean Blackie.
How to Contact: Accepts unsolicited mss. SASE. Reports in 3 months on mss. Photocopied submissions OK. Accepts computer printouts.
Terms: Negotiated "as appropriate." Sends galleys to author. Writer's guidelines for #10 SAE and 1 first class stamp. Book catalog for 9 × 12 SAE and first class stamps.

TROLL ASSOCIATES (II), Watermill Press, 100 Corporate Drive, Mahwah NJ 07430. (201)529-4000. Editorial Contact Person: M. Frances. Estab. 1968. Midsize independent publisher. Publishes hardcover originals, paperback originals and reprints. Averages 100-300 total titles each year.
Needs: Adventure, historical, juvenile (5-9 yrs. including: animal, easy-to-read, fantasy), preschool/picture book, young adult/teen (10-18 years) including: easy-to-read, fantasy/science fiction, historical, romance (ya), sports, spy/adventure. Published new writers within the last year.
How to Contact: Accepts and returns unsolicited mss. Query first. Submit outline/synopsis and sample chapters. Reports in 2-3 weeks on queries. Accepts dot-matrix computer printout submissions.
Terms: Pays royalties. Sometimes sends galleys to author. Publishes ms 6-18 months after acceptance.

TSR, INC., Box 756, Lake Geneva WI 53147. (414)248-3625. Imprints include the Dragonlance® series, Forgotten Realms™ series, Buck Rogers® books, TSR® Books. Contact: Mary Kirchoff, Managing Editor. Estab. 1974. "We publish original paperback novels and "shared world" books. TSR publishes games as well, including the Dungeons & Dragons® role-playing game. Books: standard paperbacks; offset printing; perfect binding; b&w (usually) illustrations; average first novel print order: 75,000. Averages 20-30 titles each year, mostly fiction.
Needs: "We most often publish character-oriented fantasy and science fiction, and some horror. We work with authors who can deal in a serious fashion with the genres we concentrate on and can be creative within the confines of our work-for-hire contracts." Recently published *Homeland*, by R.A. Salvatore; *Warsprite*, by Jefferson Swycaffer; and *The Gates of Thorbardin*, by Dan Parkinson.

How to Contact: "TSR seldom accepts unsolicited manuscripts. Because most of our books are strongly tied to our other products, we expect our writers to be very familiar with those products."
Terms: Pays royalties of 3%-4% of cover price. Offers advances. Always sends galleys to authors. "Commissioned work, with the exception of our TSR® Books line, are written as work-for-hire, with TSR, Inc., holding all copyrights.
Advice: "With the huge success of our Dragonlance® series and Forgotten Realms® books, we expect to be working even more closely with TSR-owned fantasy worlds. Be familiar with our line and query us regarding a proposal."

TYNDALE HOUSE PUBLISHERS (II, IV), 351 Executive Drive, P.O. Box 80, Wheaton IL 60189. (708)668-8300. Vice President of Editorial: Ron Beers. Estab. 1960. Privately owned religious press. Publishes hardcover and mass paperback originals and paperback reprints. Plans 6 first novels this year. Averages 100 total titles, 6 fiction titles each year. Average first novel print order: 5,000-10,000 copies.
Needs: Religious/inspirational. Recently published *Grace Livingston Hill Series* and *Mark: Eyewitness*, by Ellen Traylor (biblical novel).
How to Contact: Accepts unsolicited mss. Submit complete ms. Reports in 6-10 weeks. Simultaneous and photocopied submissions OK. Publishes ms an average of 18 months after acceptance.
Terms: Pays in royalties of 10% minimum; negotiable advance. Must return advance if book is not completed or is unacceptable. Free writer's guidelines and book catalog on request; send 9×12 SAE and $2 for postage.

UNIVERSITY OF GEORGIA PRESS (II), Terrell Hall, Athens GA 30602. (404)542-2830. Flannery O'Connor Short Fiction Award Editor: Charles East. Estab. 1938. Midsize university press with editorial program focusing on scholarly nonfiction. Publishes hardcover and paperback originals and reprints.
Needs: Short story collections. No novellas or novels. Recently published *The Source of Trouble*, by Debra Monroe; and *Ghost Traps*, by Robert Abel.
How to Contact: Short story collections are considered only in conjunction with the Flannery O'Connor award competition. Next submission period is June 1-July 31. *Manuscripts cannot be accepted at any other time. Manuscripts will not be returned. Competition information for SASE.*
Terms: The Flannery O'Connor Award carries a $1,000 cash award plus standard royalties. Free book catalog.

*UNIVERSITY OF MINNESOTA PRESS (I, II), 2037 University Ave. SE, Minneapolis MN 55414. (612)624-2516. Director: Lisa Freeman. Estab. 1925. "We are a midsize academic publisher." Publishes hardcover and paperback originals and hardcover and paperback reprints. Books: acid-free paper; offset printing; simultaneous hardcover/paperback binding; b&w, 4-color illustrations and line drawings; average print order: 500 hardcovers; 3,000 paperbacks; first novel print order: 500 hardcovers; 5,000 paperbacks. Averages 55 total titles, 4 fiction titles each year. Sometimes comments on rejected ms; charges for critiques.
Needs: Contemporary, ethnic, experimental, fantasy, feminist, gay, historical, lesbian, literary, science fiction, short story collections and translations. "We are especially interested in submissions from Third-World/minority writers." Published *The Stream of Life*, by Clarice Lispector (Brazilian); *The Trickster of Liberty*, by Gerald Vizenor (American Indian); and *Little Mountain*, by Elias Khoury (Lebanese).
How to Contact: Accepts unsolicited mss. Query first. Outline/synopsis and 2 sample chapters. Agented fiction 10%. Reports in 1 month. Simultaneous and photocopied submissions OK. Accepts computer printout submissions. Accepts electronic submissions.
Terms: Pays royalties of 2% minimum; 12% maximum (on net price). Average advance $750-$1,000. Provides 10 author's copies. Subsidy publishes 10%. Book catalog free.
Advice: "We began a fiction series approximately one year ago and plan to continue publishing approximately two new fiction titles per season for the foreseeable future. We are looking for writers with a unique voice that is not usually represented by other U.S. publishers; their number of publications does not enter into our consideration."

Market categories: (I) Beginning; (II) General; (III) Prestige; (IV) Specialized.

*VESTA PUBLICATIONS, LTD (II), Box 1641, Cornwall, Ontario K6H 5V6 Canada. (613)932-2135. Editor: Stephen Gill. Estab. 1974. Midsize publisher with plans to expand. Publishes hardcover and paperback originals. Books: bond paper; offset printing; paperback and sewn hardcover binding; illustrations; average print order: 1,200; first novel print order: 1,000. Plans 7 first novels this year. Averages 18 total titles, 5 fiction titles each year. Negotiable charge for critiquing rejected mss.
Needs: Adventure, contemporary, ethnic, experimental, faction, fantasy, feminist, historical, humor/satire, juvenile, literary, mainstream, preschool/picture book, psychic/supernatural/occult, regional, religious/inspirational, romance, science fiction, short story collections, suspense/mystery, translations, war and young adult/teen. Published *Sodom in her Heart*, by Donna Nevling (religious); *The Blessings of a Bird*, by Stephen Gill (juvenile); and *Whistle Stop and Other Stories*, by Ordrach.
How to Contact: Accepts unsolicited mss. Submit complete ms with SASE or SAE and IRC. Reports in 1 month. Simultaneous and photocopied submissions OK. Accepts computer printout submissions. Disk submissions OK with CPM/Kaypro 2 system.
Terms: Pays in royalties of 10% minimum. Sends galleys to author. "For first novel we usually ask authors from outside of Canada to pay half of our printing cost." Free book catalog.

VILLARD BOOKS (II, III), Random House, Inc., 201 E. 50th St., New York NY 10022. (212)572-2720. Editorial Director: Peter Gethers. Fiction Editors: Diane Reverand, Stephanie Long, Emily Bestler. Estab. 1983. Imprint specializes in commercial fiction and nonfiction. Publishes hardcover and trade paperback originals. Published new writers within the last year. Plans 2 first novels this year. Averages 40-45 total titles, approx. 10 fiction titles each year. Sometimes critiques rejected mss.
Needs: Strong commercial fiction and nonfiction. Adventure, contemporary, historical, horror, humor/satire, literary, mainstream, romance (contemporary and historical), suspense/mystery. Special interest in mystery, thriller, and literary novels. Recently published *All I Need to Know I Learned in Kindergarten* (inspirational); and *North Dallas After Forty* (commercial fiction).
How to Contact: Does not accept unsolicited mss. Submit outline/synopsis and 1-2 sample chapters to a specific editor. Agented fiction: 95%. Reports in 2-3 weeks. Simultaneous and photocopied submissions OK. Accepts electronic submissions, no dot-matrix.
Terms: "Depends upon contract negotiated." Sends galleys to author. Writer's guidelines for 8½x11 SAE with 1 first class stamp. Book catalog free on request.
Advice: "Most fiction published in hardcover."

WALKER AND COMPANY (II), 720 5th Ave., New York NY 10019. Editors: Jacqueline Johnson, Janet Hutchings, Mary Elizabeth Allen, Peter Rubie, Amy Shields, Mary Kennan Herbert. Midsize independent publisher with plans to expand. Publishes hardcover and trade paperback. Average first novel print order: 4,000-5,000. Number of titles: averages 200/year. Published many new writers within the last year. Occasionally comments on rejected mss.
Needs: Nonfiction, sophisticated, quality mystery, regency romance, quality thrillers and adventure, western and young adult nonfiction.
How to Contact: Submit outline and chapters as preliminary. Query letter should include "a concise description of the story line, including its outcome, word length of story, writing experience, publishing credits, particular expertise on this subject and in this genre. Common mistakes: sounding unprofessional (i.e. too chatty, too braggardly). Forgetting SASE." Buys 50% agented fiction. Photocopied submissions OK, "but must notify if multiple submissions." Accepts computer printout submissions; must be letter-quality. Reports in 1-2 months. Publishes ms an average of 1 year after acceptance.
Terms: Negotiable (usually advance against royalty). Must return advance if book is not completed or is unacceptable.
Advice: Publishing more fiction than previously, "exclusively hardcover. Manuscripts should be sophisticated. As for mysteries, we are open to all types, including suspense novels and offbeat, cross genre books. We are always looking for well written western novels and Thrillers that are offbeat and strong on characterization. Character development is most important in all Walker fiction. We have been actively soliciting submissions to all divisions."

WARNER BOOKS (II), Subsidiary of Warner Publishing, Inc., 666 Fifth Ave., New York NY 10103. (212)484-2900. Imprints include Questor Science Fiction/Fantasy, Mysterious Press. Contact: Editorial dept. for specific editors. Estab. 1961. Publishes hardcover and paperback originals. Published new writers within the last year. Averages approx. 500 titles/year. Sometimes critiques rejected mss.
Needs: Adventure, contemporary, fantasy, horror, mainstream, preschool/picture book, romance (contemporary, historical, regency), science fiction, suspense/mystery, war, western, "We are continuing to publish romances, mainstream novels, science fiction, men's adventure, etc. No historicals that

are not romances, Civil War novels, young adult." Recently published *Red Phoenix*, by Larry Bond (military thriller); *Mirror Image*, by Sandra Brown (commercial women's fiction).

How to Contact: Does not accept unsolicited mss. Query first. Agented fiction 85-90%. Reports in 6-8 weeks on mss. Simultaneous submissions accepted "but we prefer exclusive submissions"; and photocopied submissions "of high quality" OK.

Terms: Varies for each book.

Advice: "Continuing a strong, varied list of fiction titles. We encourage first novelists we feel have potential for more books and whose writing is extremely polished. Be able to explain your work clearly and succinctly in query or cover letter. Read books a publisher has done already—best way to get a feel for publisher's strengths. Read *Publisher's Weekly* to keep in touch with trends and industry news."

WASHINGTON SQUARE PRESS (III), Subsidiary of Pocket Books/Simon & Schuster, 1230 Ave. of the Americas, New York NY 10020. Senior Fiction Editor: Jane Rosenman. Estab. 1962. Quality imprint of mass-market publisher. Publishes paperback originals and reprints. Recently published *Dalva* and *Sun Dog*, by Jim Harrison (reprints); *The Pigeon*, by Patrick Susskind (reprint); and *Men*, by Margaret Diehl (reprint). Books: trade paperbacks. Averages 26 titles, mostly fiction, each year.

Needs: Literary, high quality novels; serious nonfiction.

How to Contact: Accepts unsolicited mss. Query first. Agented fiction nearly all. Reports in 2 months on queries. Simultaneous and photocopied submissions OK.

■**DANIEL WEISS ASSOCIATES, INC. (II)**, 33 W. 17th St., New York NY 10011. Editor-in-Chief: Elise Howard. Estab. 1987. "Packager of 75 titles a year including juvenile and adult fiction as well as nonfiction titles. We package for a range of publishers within their specifications." Publishes hardcover and paperback originals. All titles by first-time writers are commissioned for established series. Averages 120 total titles, 100 fiction titles each year. Sometimes critiques rejected mss.

Needs: Juvenile (animal, easy-to-read, historical, sports, spy/adventure, contemporary), mainstream, preschool/picture book, young adult (easy-to-read, fantasy/science fiction, historical, problem novels, romace, sports, spy/adventure). "We cannot acquire single-title manuscripts that are not part of a series the author is proposing or submitted specifically according to our guidelines for an established series." Recently published *Sweet Valley High*, by Francine Pascal (young adult series); *Hollywood Daughters*, by Joan Lowery Nixon (young adult historical trilogy); *Pets, Inc.*, by Jennifer Armstrong (elementary fiction series).

How to Contact: Accepts unsolicited mss. Query first with outline and 3-5 sample chapters. SASE. Agented fiction 75%. Reports in 2 months. Simultaneous and photocopied submissions OK. Accepts computer printout submissions.

Terms: Pays flat fee plus royalty. Advance is negotiable. Sends galleys to author. Publishes ms 1 year after acceptance. Writer's guidelines for #10 SAE and 1 first class stamp.

Advice: "We are always happy to work with and encourage first time novelists. Being packagers, we often create and outline books by committee. This system is quite beneficial to writers who may be less experienced. Usually we are contacted by agent rather than writer directly. Occasionally, however, we do work with writers who send in unsolicited material. I think that a professionally presented manuscript is of great importance."

WESTERN PRODUCER PRAIRIE BOOKS (II), Subsidiary of Saskatchewan Wheat Pool, 2310 Millar Ave., Box 2500, Saskatoon, Saskatchewan S7K 2C4 Canada. (306)665-3548. Imprint: Concordia International Youth Fiction Series (translations of foreign young adult novels). Editorial Director: Jane McHughen. Estab. 1954. Midsize publisher with plans to expand line of juvenile and young adult fiction. Publishes hardcover and paperback originals and reprints. Books: 60 lb hi-bulk paper; traditional offset printing; perfect bound hardcover and paperback binding; b&w illustrations (if warranted); average print order: 5,000; first novel print order: 3,000. Published new writers within the last year. Plans 1 first novel this year. Averages 20 total titles, 3 fiction titles each year. Sometimes critiques rejected mss.

Needs: Young adult/teen (historical, problem novels, sports). Recently published *A Question of Courage*, by Irene Morck; *A Gift of Sky*, by Linda Ghan; *Dog Runner*, by Don Meredith; and *The Ghost of Peppermint Flats and Other Stories*, by Ted Stone.

Read the Business of Fiction section to learn the correct way to prepare and submit a manuscript.

Close-up

Barbara Mertz
(Elizabeth Peters, Barbara Michaels)
Writer

Sigrid Estrada

"Don't use a pseudonym," says mystery writer Barbara Mertz. This piece of advice comes from a woman who has written more than 40 novels with two of them. Suspense enthusiasts may know her better by one of her pen names: Elizabeth Peters or Barbara Michaels.

Mertz explains that when her first novel, a gothic suspense story entitled *The Master of Blacktower*, was purchased in 1967, her agent, feeling a pen name was necessary, bestowed the Michaels name upon her. At the time, her attitude was "call me Genghis Kahn, just sell the book!"

Today, she is adamant about her discontent with pseudonyms. "I think they are a terrible waste of time and energy. They're confusing and unnecessary." However, Mertz says, she understands the theory behind having two of them. She contends publishers fear writers will be perceived as too prolific if too many of their books are published within a short time, resulting in readers not taking them seriously. On a lighter note, she mentions that writing "something that would embarrass your mother" might be one valid reason to use a pen name.

Not long after receiving her Ph.D in Egyptology in 1950, Mertz married and had children. Thus, her career options in those days seemed limited. She credits boredom as the reason she started writing mysteries, saying that when she started, " I hadn't been using my brains at all, so it was kind of exciting to be able to sit down and think."

Mertz knows about the cycle so familiar to writers—repeatedly sending submissions out and getting them back. She herself at one time suffered that plight. But acquiring an agent was one thing she did that helped her (which, she notes, was easier in those days). At that time spy stories were hot, says Mertz, who admits she has never been able to write spy mysteries. Therefore, it was the agent that suggested she use her archaeological knowledge by writing nonfiction archaeological books. So before her first novel was ever published, she wrote three nonfiction books on Egyptian and Roman civilization.

Today she mostly writes romantic mysteries with archaeological settings and has no problem getting them published. Reflecting, she says, "I was very naive about how difficult it was to publish a book. I knew nothing whatsoever about the market. I thought you just wrote what you wanted to write and then sent it out and sold it." Instead, she found "just spelling the words right, turning out the typewritten pages and making it coherent is very hard work, which is why there are so few people who actually finish the book they talk about writing." She says people who are not writers don't realize how tiring writing actually is. "Eight hours of writing just knocks me out," she says. "I did develop a great deal of respect for writing and I am still learning my craft. There are still things I discover every time I do a book."

Even after all the years and all the books, she says for her the writing doesn't ever get any easier. "I don't know whether it's because I make more demands upon myself or because I actually realize writing a book is not easy. With every book I write I see more challenges and struggle more." An additional challenge after over 40 books is avoiding blatantly replicating plots from past books. But, she says, a little similarity doesn't hurt. "I steal from myself all the time. What you want is a fresh twist on an old idea."

To ensure historical accuracy, Mertz spends months researching her books, and that suits her just fine. "I love the research almost better than the writing," she says. Keeping a close eye on history is essential, considering the historical settings of her books, and since she writes in series, the chronology of her books in each series is also pertinent. Her current book, *The Last Camel Died at Noon*, the sixth book featuring eccentric female archaeologist Amelia Peabody, is set in the Sudan in 1897.

Mertz feels that right now is the Golden Age of traditional mysteries and the trend is for stories with more interesting characters. "Don't go too heavy on violence or on thought; I think character is the way to go these days. The old days where an intricately worked out plot was enough is no longer true. People demand more. I'm not saying go without a plot, but if you have to go for one or the other, go for character."

Giving away the "whodunit" in the middle of the book is a stupid mistake, says Mertz. Yet she says writing this type of suspense is a challenge. "It's hard to get a medium line. You have to make the story clear enough so the reader doesn't think you're cheating. You also have to be careful not to give it away. But if you do it right, they (the readers) aren't going to care as much. My classic line is 'I don't give a damn whodunit.' I read the book for the fun of watching the detective or the other characters who are around."

Getting ideas for stories has never been a problem for Mertz. In fact, she has never been able to understand why writers have a hard time getting ideas. Though she says casual reading is most effective in sparking the imagination, she says ideas "come from everything I see and do; it's a question of training yourself to be on the alert for them. I've got thousands of ideas. The problem is how you develop a one-liner into a book. That's where the fun begins."

—Lisa Carpenter

❝I steal from myself all the time. What you want is a fresh twist on an old idea.❞

—Barbara Mertz

How to Contact: Accepts unsolicited mss. Submit outline/synopsis and 3-4 sample chapters. SASE. Agented fiction: very little. Reports in 1 month on queries; 2-3 months on mss. Simultaneous (as long as we are notified) and photocopied submissions OK. Accepts computer printout submissions.
Terms: Pays in royalties of 8% minimum; 12.5% maximum. Offers average advance: $1,000. Sends galleys to author. Writer's guidelines and book catalog free on request.
Advice: "Interested in expanding paperback juvenile and young adult fiction list. We have published a greater number of young adult fiction titles, probably because we receive more manuscripts in this area now that we are recognized by authors as a publisher of high-quality young adult fiction."

WESTERN PUBLISHING COMPANY, INC., 850 3rd Ave., New York NY 10022. (212)753-8500. Imprint: Golden Books. Juvenile Editor-in-Chief: Thelma Lanes. Estab. 1907. High-volume mass market and trade publisher. Publishes hardcover and paperback originals. Number of titles: averages 160/year. Buys 20-30% agented fiction.
Needs: Juvenile: adventure, mystery, humor, sports, animal, easy-to-read picture books, and "a few" nonfiction titles. Published *Little Critter's Bedtime Story*, by Mercer Mayer; *Cyndy Szokeves' Mother Goose Rhymes*; and *Spaghetti Manners*, by Stephanie Calmsenson, illustrated by Lisa MaCue Karsten.
How to Contact: Send a query letter with a description of the story and SASE. Unsolicited mss are returned unread. Publishes ms an average of 1 year after acceptance.
Terms: Pays by outright purchase or royalty.
Advice: "Read our books to see what we do. Call for appointment if you do illustrations, to show your work. Do not send illustrations. Illustrations are not necessary; if your book is what we are looking for, we can use one of our artists."

ALBERT WHITMAN & COMPANY (II), 6043 Oakton St., Morton Grove Il 60053. (708)647-1358. Senior Editors: Judith Mathews and Abby Levine. Editor-in-Chief: Kathleen Tucker. Estab. 1919. Small independent juvenile publisher. Publishes hardcover originals. Books: paper varies; printing varies; library binding; most books illustrated; average print order: 7,500. Average 20-26 total titles/year. Number of fiction titles varies.
Needs: Juvenile (2-12 years including easy-to-read, fantasy, historical, adventure, contemporary, mysteries, picture-book stories). Primarily interested in picture book manuscripts. Recently published *All About Asthma*, by William Ostrow and Vivian Ostrow; *You Push, I Ride*, by Abby Levine; published new writers within the last year.
How to Contact: Accepts unsolicited mss. Submit outline/synopsis and 1-3 sample chapters; complete ms for picture books. SASE. "Half or more fiction is not agented." Reports in 3 weeks on queries; 2 months on mss. Simultaneous and photocopied submissions OK. ("We prefer to be told.") Accepts computer printouts including dot-matrix.
Terms: Payment varies. Royalties, advance; number of author's copies varies. Some flat fees. Sends galleys to author. Writer's guidelines free for SASE. Book catalog for 9 × 12 SASE and 85¢ postage.

■**WILDSTAR BOOKS/EMPIRE BOOKS (II, IV)**, Subsidiary of The Holy Grail Co., Inc., 26 Nantucket Pl., Scarsdale NY 10583. (914)961-2965. Vice President: Ralph Leone. Estab. 1986. Packager of Empire Books. Imprint: Wildstar (with Lynx Communications). Publishes paperback originals. Averages 40 fiction titles each year. Sometimes critiques rejected mss.
Needs: Horror, biography, psychic/supernatural/occult, romance (contemporary, historical), suspense/mystery, western. Looking for romance, horror, new age, occult, western, mystery and thriller. Recently published 22-book series *American Regency*; *Wildstar* for Warner Books (romance); 12-book series, *Americans Abroad, Empire* for St. Martin's (romance); 18-book series, *Horror, Empire* for Pageant Books (horror).
How to Contact: Accepts unsolicited mss. Query first. SASE. Agented fiction 80%. Reports in 3 weeks on queries; 3 months on mss. Photocopied submissions OK. Accepts computer printout submissions, including dot-matrix.
Terms: Pays in royalties: "depends on deal we make with publisher." Advance negotiable. Provides author's copies. Sends galleys to author. Publishes ms generally within 18 months after acceptance.
Advice: "Short and to the point—not cute or paranoid—is best tone in a query letter."

*Listings marked with a solid box [■] are book packagers.
See the introduction to Commercial Publishers for more
information.*

‡WINDSONG BOOKS (II,IV), Subsidiary of St. Paul Books and Medis, 50 St. Paul's Ave., Boston MA 02130. Children's Editor: Sister Anne Joan, fsp. Estab. 1932. "Midsize Roman Catholic publishing house." Publishes paperback originals. Plans 2 first novels this year. Company publishes 20 total titles/ year.

Needs: Juvenile (contemporary, religious/inspirational) and young adult (historical, problem novels, romance (Christian), religious/inspirational). Especially needs "young adult/teen novels with a Christian (and Catholic) focus. Religion should be vital in the plot and outcome."

How to Contact: No unsolicited mss. Send an outline/synopsis with 3 sample chapters. SASE. Reports in up to 2 months. Photocopied submissions OK.

Terms: Pays in royalties of 4-8%. Also pays author's copies (amount varies). Publishes ms 2 years after acceptance. Writer's guidelines for #10 SAE and 1 first-class stamp. Catalog for 9 × 12 SAE and 1 first-class stamp.

Advice: Looks for "characters and plots in which religion, faith, convictions are not just written it, but essential to the person or story."

*WINSTON-DEREK PUBLISHERS (II), Box 90883, Nashville TN 37209. (615)321-0535, 329-1319. Imprints include Scythe Books. Senior Editor: Marjorie Staton. Estab. 1978. Midsize publisher. Publishes hardcover and paperback originals and reprints. Books: 60 lb old Warren style paper; litho press; perfect and/or sewn binding; illustrations sometimes; average print order: 3,000-5,000 copies; first novel print order: 2,000 copies. Published new writers within the last year. Plans 10 first novels this year. Averages 55-65 total titles, 20 fiction titles each year; "90% of material is from freelance writers; each year we add 15 more titles."

Needs: Gothic, historical, juvenile (historical), psychic, religious/inspirational, and young adult (easy-to-read, historical, romance) and programmed reading material for middle and high school students. "Must be 65,000 words or less. Novels strong with human interest. Characters overcoming a weakness or working through a difficulty. Prefer plots related to a historical event but not necessary. No science fiction, explicit eroticism, minorities in conflict without working out a solution to the problem. Downplay on religious ideal and values." Recently published *A Gentle Wind Came with Us*, by George T. McGuire, Jr.; *The Mengele Hoax*, by Ray V. Waymire; and *From Kathmandu to Timbuctu*, by Juanita Owen Fleming.

How to Contact: Submit outline/synopsis and 3-4 sample chapters with SASE. Simultaneous and photocopied submissions OK. Accepts computer printout submissions. Prefers letter-quality. Reports in 4-6 weeks on queries; 6-8 weeks on mss. Must query first. Do not send complete ms.

Terms: Pays in royalties of 10% minimum, 15% maximum; negotiates advance. *Offers some subsidy arrangements.* Book catalog on request for $1 postage.

Advice: "Stay in the mainstream of writing. The public is reading serene and contemplative literature. Authors should strive for originality and a clear writing style, depicting universal themes which portray character building and are beneficial to mankind. Consider the historical novel; there is always room for one more."

WORLDWIDE LIBRARY (II), Division of Harlequin Books, 225 Duncan Mill Rd., Don Mills, Ontario M3B 3K9, Canada. (416)445-5860. Imprints are Worldwide Library Science Fiction; Worldwide Library Mystery; Gold Eagle Books. Senior Editor: Feroze Mohammed. Est. 1979. Large commercial category line. Publishes paperback originals and reprints. Published new writers within the last year. Averages 60 titles, all fiction, each year. Sometimes critiques rejected ms. Mystery program is largely reprint; no originals please.

Needs: "We are looking for action-adventure series and writers; future fiction." Recently published *Horn*; soon to be published: *Survival 2000; Soldiers of War; Time warriors; Agents* — all action series.

How to Contact: Query first or submit outline/synopsis/series concept or overview and sample chapters. SAE. U.S. stamps do not work in Canada; use International Reply Coupons or money order. Agented fiction 95%. Reports in 10 weeks on queries. Simultaneous submissions OK.

Terms: Advance and royalties; copyright buyout. Publishes ms 1-2 years after acceptance.

Advice: "Publishing fiction in very selective areas. As a genre publisher we are always on the lookout for new writing talent and innovative series ides, especially in the men's adventure area."

YEARLING (II, III), 666 5th Ave., New York NY 10103. (212)765-6500. See Dell Publishing Co., Inc. Publishes originals and reprints for children grades K-6. Most interested in humorous upbeat novels, mysteries and family stories. 60 titles a year. "Will, regrettably, no longer consider unsolicited material at this time."

Terms: Sends galleys to author.

ZEBRA BOOKS (II), 475 Park Ave. S, New York NY 10016. (212)889-2299. Contact: Editorial Director. Estab. 1975. Publishes hardcover reprints and paperback originals. Averages 400 total titles/year.

Needs: Contemporary, adventure, English-style mysteries, historical, war, gothic, saga, romance, true crime, nonfiction, women's, erotica, thrillers and horror. No science fiction. Recently published *Missing Beauty*, by Teresa Carpenter; *Kiss of the Night Wind*, by Janelle Taylor; *Stardust*, by Nan Ryan; and *Wolf Time*, by Joe Gores.

How to Contact: Query or submit complete ms or outline/synopsis and sample chapters with SASE. Simultaneous and photocopied submissions OK. Address women's mss to Carin Cohen Ritter and male adventure mss to Editorial Director. Reports in 3-5 months.

Terms: Pays royalties and advances. Free book catalog.

Advice: "Put aside your literary ideals and be commercial. We like big contemporary women's fiction; glitzy career novels, high-tech espionage and horror. Work fast and on assignment. Keep your cover letter simple and to the point. Too many times, 'cutesy' letters about category or content turn us off some fine mss. We are more involved with family and historical sagas. But please do research. We buy many unsolicited manuscripts, but we're slow readers. Have patience."

CHARLOTTE ZOLOTOW BOOKS (II), 10 E. 53rd St., New York NY 10022. (212)207-7044. FAX: (212)207-7192. "Editor works mainly with authors she has edited over the years." See HarperCollins Children's Books Group.

ZONDERVAN, 1415 Lake Dr. SE, Grand Rapids MI 49506. (616)698-6900. Imprints include Academie Books, Daybreak Books, Francis Asbury Press, Lamplighter Books, Ministry Resources Library, Pyranee Books, Regency Reference Library, Youth Specialties and Zondervan Books. Publishers: Stan Gundry, Scott Bolinder. Estab. 1931. Large evangelical Christian publishing house. Publishes hardcover and paperback originals and reprints, though fiction is generally in paper only. Published new writers in the last year. Averages 150 total titles, 5-10 fiction titles each year. Average first novel: 5,000 copies.

Needs: Adult fiction, (mainstream, biblical, historical, adventure, sci-fi, fantasy, mystery), "Inklings-style" fiction of high literary quality and juvenile fiction (primarily mystery/adventure novels for 8-12-year-olds). Christian relevance necessary in all cases. Will *not* consider collections of short stories or inspirational romances. Recently published *Men of Kent*, by Elizabeth Gibson; *Nightwatch*, by John Leax; and *Morning Morning True*, by Ernest Herndon.

How to Contact: Accepts unsolicited ms. Write for free writer's guidelines first with #10 SASE. Query or submit outline/synopsis and 2 sample chapters. Reports in 4-6 weeks on queries; 3-4 months on mss. Photocopied submissions OK. Accepts computer printout submissions.

Terms: "Standard contract provides for a percentage of the net price received by publisher for each copy sold, usually 14-17% of net."

Advice: "There has been a revival of Christian fiction in last year. The renewed reader interest is exciting. There is great room for improvement of writing quality, however. Send plot outline and one or two sample chapters. Most editors will *not* read entire mss. Your proposal and opening chapter will make or break you."

Foreign commercial publishers

The following commercial publishers buy novel and short story manuscripts in English from U.S. and Canadian writers. Query first for submission guidelines and a catalog, if available. Always include a self-addressed envelope with International Reply Coupons for catalogs, guidelines and manuscript return. Be sure to include the correct number of IRC's (available from the main branch of your local post office) and an envelope of the appropriate size. To save on the cost of return postage on your manuscript, you may want to send a copy for the publisher to keep along with a return postcard and IRC for reply.

THE BLACKSTAFF PRESS (I), 3 Galway Park, Dundonald BT16 0AN Northern Ireland. Editor: Hilary Parker. Midsize, independent publisher, wide range of subjects. Publishes hardcover and paperback originals and reprints. Contemporary, ethnic (Irish), historical, humor/satire, literary, short story collections, political thrillers and feminist.

ROBERT HALE LIMITED (II), Clerkenwell House, 45/47 Clerkenwell Green, London EC1R 0HT England. Publishes hardcover and trade paperback originals and hardcover reprints. Historical, mainstream, romance and western.

*HALLMARK PUBLISHING LTD., Gopala Prabhu Rd., Box 3541 Cochin-682 035 India. President: Prof. Dr. M. V. Pylee. Managing and Editorial Director: C. I. Oommen. Publishers of trade paperbacks and educational books. Looking for folktales, adventure, novel and short fiction anthologies. Accepts unsolicited mss, simultaneous and photocopied submissions and computer printouts (prefers letter quality). Reports in 2 months. Pays in royalties of 10% maximum. No advance. "We also produce books for self publishers and small press with marketing and distribution support."

HAMISH HAMILTON LTD., 27 Wrights Lane, London W8 5TZ England. Fiction Editors: Andrew Franklin, Kate Toner and Alexandra Pringle. General trade hardback publisher quality fiction—literary plus some crime and thrillers. Advance on delivery of accepted book or on accepted commission. Send first chapter with synopsis before submitting whole manuscript.

HEADLINE BOOK PUBLISHING PLC, 79 Great Titchfield St., London W1P 7FN England. Editorial Director: Susan J. Fletcher. Averages approximately 300 titles/year. Mainstream publisher of popular fiction and nonfiction in hardcover and mass-market paperback. Pays advance against royalties. "Send a synopsis and *curriculum vitae* first, and return postage."

HODDER & STOUGHTON PUBLISHERS, 47 Bedford Square, London WC1B 3DP, England, U.K. Imprints: Coronet, NEL, Sceptre. Editorial Director: Nick Sayers. Fiction Editors: Humphrey Price (NEL); Anna Powell (Coronet); Carole Welch (Sceptre). Coronet: intelligent, mainstream romantic fiction; humour; historical novels/crime; Sceptre: literary—fiction and nonfiction; NEL: horror, SF, fantasy, humour, serious nonfiction. "We do not consider short stories." Payment is made "usually by an advance and then final payment on publication." Send a cover letter, synopsis and sample chapters. "If you can't get an agent to represent you, then do make enquiries to the editorial departments first, before sending off complete manuscripts."

MICHAEL JOSEPH LTD., The Penguin Group, 27 Wrights Lane, London W8 5TZ England. Contact: Fiction Editor. General publisher of adult fiction and nonfiction. Publishes hardcover originals and some trade paperback originals and reprints, not mass market. Needs: Adventure, contemporary, historical, humor, literary, mainstream, regional, suspense/mystery and war.

MILLS & BOON, Eton House, 18-24 Paradise Road, Richmond, Surrey TW9 1SR England. Publishes 250 fiction titles/year. Modern romantic fiction, historical romances and medical romances. "We are happy to see the whole manuscript or 3 sample chapters and synopsis."

MY WEEKLY STORY LIBRARY, D.C. Thomson and Co., Ltd., 22 Meadowside, Dundee DD19QJ, Scotland. Fiction Editor: Mrs. D. Hunter. Publishes 48, 35,000-word romantic novels/year. "Cheap paperback story library with full-colour cover. Material should not be violent, controversial or sexually explicit." Writers are paid on acceptance. "Send the opening two chapters and a synopsis."

ORIENT PAPERBACKS, A division of Vision Books Pvt Ltd., Madarsa Rd., Kashmere Gate, Delhi 110 006 India. Editor: Sudhir Malhotra. Publishes 10-15 novels or story collections/year. "We are one of the largest paperback publishers in S.E. Asia and publish English fiction by authors from this part of the world." Pays royalty on copies sold.

 The asterisk indicates a publisher who sometimes offers subsidy arrangements. Authors are asked to subsidize part of the cost of book production. See the introduction to Commercial Publishers for more information.

QUARTET BOOKS LIMITED, 27-29 Goodge Street, London W1P1FD England. Fiction Editor: Stephen Pickles. Publishes 50 stories/year. "Middle East fiction, European classics in translation, original novels." Payment is: advance—half on signature, half on delivery and publication. "Send brief synopsis and sample chapters. *No* romantic fiction, historical fiction, crime, science fiction or thrillers."

VISION BOOKS PVT LTD., Madarsa Rd., Kashmere Gate, Delhi 110006 India. Fiction Editor: Sudhir Malhotra. Publishes 25 titles/year. "We are a large multilingual publishing house publishing fiction and other trade books." Pays royalties. "A brief synopsis should be submitted initially. Subsequently, upon hearing from the editor, a typescript may be sent."

WEIDENFELD AND NICOLSON LTD., 91, Clapham High St., London SW4 7TA England. Fiction Editors: Allegra Huston, David Roberts. Publishes approx. 30 titles/year. "We are an independent publisher with a well established fiction list. Authors include, or have included, V. Nabokov, J.G. Farrell, Olivia Manning, Edna O'Brien, Margaret Drabble, Richard Powers, John Hersey, Penelope Gilliatt, Charlotte Vale Allen. We publish literary and commercial fiction: sagas, historicals, crime." Pays by advance. Royalties are set against advances. "Send a covering letter, a detailed synopsis and some sample pages such as the first chapter. Do not send the whole typescript unless invited. Please enclose return postage and retain photocopies of all material sent."

THE WOMEN'S PRESS, 34 Great Sutton St., London EC1V 0DX England. Publishes approx. 50 titles/year. "Women's fiction, written by women. Centered on women. Theme can be anything—all themes may be women's concern—but we look for political/feminist awareness, originality, wit, fiction of ideas. Includes genre fiction, sf, crime, and teenage list *Livewire*." Writers receive royalty, including advance. Writers should ask themselves, "is this a manuscript which would interest a feminist/political press?"

Other commercial publishers

The following commercial publishers appeared in the 1990 edition of *Novel and Short Story Writer's Market* but do not appear in the 1991 edition. Those listings that did not respond to our request for an update are listed without further explanation below. There are several reasons why a publisher did not return an update—they could be overstocked, no longer taking fiction or have been recently sold. If a reason for the omission is known, it is included next to the publisher's name. Additional foreign commercial publishers appear at the end of the list.

Bantam/Doubleday Books
The Child's World, Inc. (asked to be left out this year)
T.Y. Crowell Junior Books (see HarperCollins)
Fawcett
Field Publications (asked to be left out this year)
Gospel Publishing House (not accepting fiction)
Houghton Mifflin Company (asked to be left out this year)
J.B. Lippincott Junior Books (see HarperCollins)
Newmarket Press (accepts no fiction)
Orchard Books (asked to be deleted)
Philomel Books (moved; no forwarding address)
Popular Library (out of business)
Stemmer House Publishers, Inc. (asked to be deleted)
Summit Books
Texas Monthly Press (press has been sold)

Other foreign commercial publishers

Angus & Robertson/Collins Publishers Australia
Atma Ram and Sons
Grafton Books
The Macmillan Company of Australia (asked to be deleted)
Sidgwick & Jackson Ltd.
Transworld Publishers
Walker Books/Julia MacRae Books/Nick Hern Books

Contests and Awards

Contests and awards serve as important alternative markets for both beginning and established writers. The possibility of attaining recognition, as well as possible financial reward, is a tempting challenge for the writer seeking a change of pace from submitting work for publication only. This section continues to grow rapidly, and we have included new listings for contests, awards, fellowships and grants.

One of the benefits of entering a contest is that your work will be judged on the basis of quality alone and in comparison with the work of other writers whose submissions focus on the same theme and are subject to identical conditions. Thus, in contest judging, the regular restrictions involved in publishing decisions, i.e., the weighing of tone, length and timing against the quality of the work itself, are eliminated.

There are contests for almost every type of fiction (and nonfiction) writing. While some focus on form, such as those for novels, short stories or novellas, others require writers to handle a particular theme or subject. This year, we have included contests for fiction with unique, highly-specific themes such as the best first "malice domestic novel," the funniest/most overdone horror story, and the best story set in Southwest Florida. Chances are, you will be able to find a contest that sparks your interest.

The majority of contest and award programs listed here do offer prizes, which may range from plaques or certificates of recognition to monetary awards of a few dollars to a few thousand dollars. Certain highly prestigious awards such as the Pushcart Prize do not actually offer prizes, but the attainment of them creates significant exposure for a writer.

For the writer who is working on a manuscript or other long-term project and seeks freedom from financial pressures, there are fellowship, residency and grant opportunities. These generally provide money, time and sometimes work space and lodging. This year, we have added several new listings in each category, including The National Endowment for the Arts Creative Writing Fellowships, The Houghton Mifflin Literary Fellowship, the North Carolina Arts Council Residencies, and the Money for Women grants sponsored by the Barbara Deming Memorial Fund. Due to new NEA restrictions, some state arts councils and literary magazines may be forced to reduce contest and award funding.

Choosing and submitting

Certain contests are open to previously unpublished submissions, while others require that work be published. If the latter applies, be sure to check out the acceptable publication dates. In some cases, a competition will only accept work from a nominating body, rather than the actual author. Nominating bodies can be teachers, publishers or a contest sponsor's own ad-hoc committee.

It is important to obtain a copy of a contest's submission requirements, which frequently include filling out entry forms and paying an entry fee. Entry fees generally range from $5 to $25. Beware of entry fees that are disproportionate to the actual amount of the prize.

If a contest requires that a piece be nominated through a publisher, just ask. However, give the publisher sufficient time to do the job.

Coding system for contests and awards

The Roman numeral coding system in this section is different from that used in other parts of the book. A new or unpublished writer is eligible to enter those contests ranked I (and some IVs), while a writer with a published (usually including self-published) book may enter most contests ranked I and II (and again, some IVs). Entrants for contests ranked III must be nominated by someone who is not the writer (usually the publisher or editor).

I **Contest for unpublished fiction, usually open to both new and experienced writers;**

II **Contest for published (usually including self-published) fiction, which may be entered by the author;**

III **Contest for published fiction, which must be nominated by an editor, publisher or other nominating body;**

IV **Contest limited to residents of a certain region, of a certain age or to writing on certain themes or subjects.**

ACT 1 CREATIVITY CENTER FELLOWSHIPS (I), ACTS Institute, Inc., Box 10153, Kansas City MO 64111. (816)753-0208 or (816)753-0383. Contact: Charlotte Plotsky. Award: Residency at the ACT 1 Writers/Artists Colony at the ACT 1 Creativity Center, Lake of the Ozarks, MO. Receives approx. 25 applications/year. Judge: "a professional." Application fee $10. No deadlines—open admissions policy. Send SASE for kit.

‡JANE ADDAMS CHILDREN'S BOOK AWARD, Jane Addams Peace Association/Women's International League for Peace and Freedom, Jean Gore. Chair: Contact her at: 980 Lincoln Place, Boulder CO 80302. "To honor the writer of the children's book that most effectively promotes peace, social justice, world community and the equality of the sexes and all races." Annual competition for short stories, novels and translations. Award: Certificate. Competition receives approx. 100 submissions. Judges: committee. Guidelines for SASE. Deadline April 1, for books published during previous year.

AIM MAGAZINE SHORT STORY CONTEST (I), Box 20554, Chicago IL 60620. (312)874-6184. Contact: Ruth Apilado and Mark Boone, publisher and fiction editor. Estab. 1984. Contest likely to be offered annually if money is available. "To encourage and reward good writing in the short story form. The contest is particularly for new writers." Unpublished submissions. Award: $100 plus publication in fall issue. "Judged by *Aim*'s editorial staff." Contest rules for SASE. "We're looking for compelling, well-written stories with lasting social significance." Sample copy $3.50.

ALABAMA STATE COUNCIL ON THE ARTS INDIVIDUAL ARTIST FELLOWSHIP (II, IV), #1 Dexter Ave., Montgomery AL 36130. (205)242-4076. Randy Shoults. "To provide assistance to an individual artist." Annual grant/fellowship. Award: $2,500 and $5,000 grants. Competition receives approximately 30 submissions annually. Judges: independent peer panel. Entry forms or rules for SASE. Deadline: May 1. Two-year Alabama residency required.

ALASKA STATE COUNCIL ON THE ARTS LITERARY ARTS FELLOWSHIPS (I, IV), Alaska State Council on the Arts, 619 Warehouse Ave., #220, Anchorage AK 99501-1682. (907)279-1558. Contact: Christine D'Arcy. "Open-ended grant award, non-matching, to enable creative writers to advance their careers as they see it." Biannual competition for short stories and novels. Award: $5,000 per writer. Competition receives approx. 45 submissions. Judges: panel of Alaskan writers. Next award offered in October, 1990. "Alaskan writers only are eligible to apply."

EDWARD F. ALBEE FOUNDATION FELLOWSHIP (I), Edward F. Albee Foundation, Inc., 14 Harrison St., New York NY 10013. (212)226-2020. Provides one-month residencies for writers and artists at the William Flanagan Memorial Creative Persons Center (better known as "The Barn") in Montauk, on Long Island, New York. 24 residencies per year, June-September. Award for writers of fiction, nonfiction, poetry and plays. Judges: several writers. Applications are accepted from January 1 through April 1. Write for official guidelines.

‡ALBERTA NEW FICTION COMPETITION (I, IV), Alberta Culture and Multiculturalism in cooperation with Doubleday Canada Ltd. of Toronto, 12th Floor, CN Tower, Edmonton, Alberta T5J 0K5 Canada. Contact: Ruth B. Bertelsen, director. Biennial award. To encourage the development of fiction writers living in the province of Alberta. The competition is open to all writers who are residents of the province of Alberta. Deadline December 31, 1989. No SASE is necessary. Brochures and further information available. Award: $4,000; of this, $2,500 is an outright award given by Alberta Culture and $1,500 is an advance against royalties given by Doubleday. Three categories of submission: full-length novel from 60,000-100,000 words; short story collection totalling approximately 60,000 words; novella/short story combination totalling 60,000 words.

THE ALBERTA WRITING FOR YOUNG PEOPLE COMPETITION (I, IV), Alberta Culture and Multiculturalism in cooperation with Doubleday Canada Ltd. and Allarcom/Superchannel. 12th Floor, CN Tower, 10004-104 Avenue, Edmonton, Alberta T5J 0K5 Canada. Contact: Film and literature art branch director. Bienniel award (even years). The competition is designed to direct Alberta's writers to the challenging world of writing for juveniles. Unpublished submissions. Entry deadline: Dec. 31. The competition brochure and/or further information will be sent upon request. Award: $4,500 prize; an outright award of $2,000 from Alberta Culture and Multiculturalism, a $1,000 advance against royalties from Doubleday Canada Ltd. and a $1,500 12-month option for motion picture/television rights from Allarcom/Superchannel. "We have 2 categories: book mss for young adults (up to age 16) averaging 40,000 words in length; and book mss suitable for younger readers (8-12 years) running between 12,000 and 20,000 words."

THE NELSON ALGREN AWARD FOR SHORT FICTION (I), *Chicago Tribune*, 435 N. Michigan Ave., Chicago IL 60611. (312)222-3232. Annual award. To recognize an outstanding, unpublished short story, minimum 2,500 words; maximum 10,000 words. Awards: $5,000 first prize; three runners-up receive $1,000 awards. Publication of four winning stories in the *Chicago Tribune*. Deadline: Entries are accepted only from November 30-January 1. No entry fee. A poster bearing the rules of the contest will be sent to writers who inquire in writing.

ALLEGHENY REVIEW AWARDS (I), Box 32, Allegheny College, Meadville PA 16335. Contact: Richardson Prouty and Vern Maczuzak, editors. Annually. Award for unpublished short stories. U.S. undergraduate students only. Deadline: January 31. SASE for rules.

AMBERGRIS ANNUAL FICTION CONTEST (I,IV), *Ambergris* Magazine, P.O. Box 29919, Cincinnati OH 45229. Editor: Mark Kissling. Award "to promote and reward excellence in fiction writing." Annual competition for short stories. Award: $100 first prize. Competition receives 300 mss/contest. Judges: editorial staff. Guidelines for #10 SASE. Previously unpublished submissions. "We give special but not exclusive consideration to works by Ohio writers or about the Midwest in general. We prefer works under 5,000 words. Writers may want to review the results of previous contests. Sample copies are $4 and back issues are available for $3."

AMELIA MAGAZINE AWARDS (I), The Reed Smith Fiction Prize; The Willie Lee Martin Short Story Award; The Cassie Wade Short Fiction Award; The Patrick T. T. Bradshaw Fiction Award; and four annual genre awards in science fiction, romance, western and fantasy/horror. 329 "E" St., Bakersfield CA 93304. (805)323-4064. Contact: Frederick A. Raborg, Jr., editor. Estab. 1984. Annually. "To publish the finest fiction possible and reward the writer; to allow good writers to earn some money in small press publication. *Amelia* strives to fill that gap between major circulation magazines and quality university journals." Unpublished submissions. Length: The Reed Smith—3,000 words max.; The Willie Lee Martin—3,500-5,000 words, The Cassie Wade—4,500 words max.; The Patrick T. T. Bradshaw—10,000 words; the genre awards—science fiction, 5,000 words; romance, 3,000 words; western, 5,000 words; fantasy/horror, 5,000 words. Award: "Each prize consists of $200 plus publication and two contributor's copies of issue containing winner's work. The Reed Smith Fiction Prize offers two

Market categories: (I) Unpublished entries; (II) Published entries nominated by the author; (III) Published entries, nominated by the editor, publisher or nominating body; (IV) Specialized entries.

additional awards of $100 and $50, and publication; Bradshaw Book Award: $300 plus publication, 2 copies. Deadline: The Reed Smith Prize—September 1; The Willie Lee Martin—March 1; The Cassie Wade—June 1; The Patrick T. T. Bradshaw—February 15; Amelia fantasy/horror—February 1; Amelia western—April 1; Amelia romance—October 1; Amelia science fiction—December 15. Entry fee: $5. Bradshaw Award fee: $7.50. Contest rules for SASE. Looking for "high quality work equal to finest fiction being published today."

‡AMERICAN ACADEMY AND INSTITUTE OF ARTS AND LETTERS LITERARY AWARDS (III), 633 W. 155th St., New York NY 10032. Contact: Jeanie Kim, assistant to the executive director. Annual awards for previously published books. To honor authors for excellence in literature and encourage them in their creative work. Selection is by the Academy-Institute. *Applications not accepted.* Award: Prizes vary. Seven $7,500 Academy-Institute awards. Special awards include: The Richard & Hinda Rosenthal Foundation Award: $5,000 for "an American work of fiction published during the preceding 12 months"; The Sue Kaufman Prize for First Fiction: $2,500; and The William Dean Howells Medal for Fiction (every 5 years). Also the Award of Merit Medal for the Novel and $5,000 prize (every 6 years); the Award of Merit Medal for The Short Story and $5,000 prize (every 6 years); and The Gold Medal for Fiction (every 6 years). The Harold D. Vursell Memorial Award: $5,000 to single out recent writing in book form that merits recognition for the quality of its prose style. The Morton Dauwen Zabel Award: $2,500 for a writer of fiction of progressive, original and experimental tendencies (every 3 years). The Rome Fellowship in Literature (periodically) for a year's residence at the American Academy in Rome.

AMERICAN FICTION VOL II (I), Birch Lane Press/American Fiction, English Dept., Springfield College, 263 Alden St., Springfield MA 01109. (413)788-3000. Editors: Michael C. White and Alan Davis. To "recognize unpublished stories by both *known* and *unknown* writers." Annual competition for short stories. Award: $1,000 first prize; $500 second; $250 third, publication, 2 copies. Competition received 650 submissions in 1989. Entry fee: $7.50. Deadline: April 1. Guidelines in *AWP Newsletter* and in *Poets and Writers*. Unpublished submissions. 10,000 word limit.

‡*ANALECTA* COLLEGE FICTION CONTEST (I,IV), The Liberal Arts Council, FAC 19, Austin TX 78712. (512)471-6563. Awards Coordinator: Lisa Barnett. Award to "give student writers, at the Univ. of Texas and universities across the country, a forum for publication. We believe that publication in a magazine with the quality and reputation of *Analecta* will benefit student writers." Annual competition for short stories. Award: $65.Competition receives approx. 80 submissions. Judges: student editorial board of approx. 15 people. No entry fee. Guidelines for SASE. Deadline: October 22, 1991. Previously unpublished submissions. Limited to college students. Word length: 3,500 words or less. "We also accept poetry, drama and art submissions."

SHERWOOD ANDERSON SHORT FICTION PRIZE (I), *Mid-American Review*, Dept. of English, Bowling Green State University, Bowling Green OH 43403. (419)372-2725. Contact: Robert Early, fiction editor. Award frequency is subject to availability of funds. "To encourage the writer of quality short fiction." Unpublished material. No deadline. No entry fee. "Winners are selected from stories published by the magazine, so submission for publication is the first step."

‡*ANIMAL TALES* HOLIDAY CONTEST, 2113 W. Bethany Home Rd., Phoenix AZ 85015. (602)246-7144. "To provide us with short stories with a holiday theme." Competition for short stories. Award: $25-100. Competition receives approx. 50-100 submissions. Judges: Two judges and editor. Entry fee: $5. Guidelines for SASE. Previously unpublished submissions. Word length: 6,000 words or less. "All entries must be about animals and the people who love them."

‡THE ANNUAL/ATLANTIC WRITING COMPETITIONS, Writers' Federation of Nova Scotia, 5516 Spring Garden Rd., Suite 203, Halifax, Nova Scotia B3J 1G6 Canada. (902)423-8116. "To recognize and encourage unpublished writers in the region of Atlantic Canada. (Competition only open to residents of Nova Scotia, Newfoundland, Prince Edward Island and New Brunswick, the four Atlantic Provinces.)" Annual competition for short stories, novels, poetry, nonfiction, children's writing, drama, magazine feature/essay. Award: various cash awards. Competition receives approximately 10-12 submissions for novels; 75 for poetry; 75 for children's; 75 for short stories; 10 for nonfiction. Judges: professional writers, librarians, booksellers. Entry fee $15/entry. Guidelines for SASE. Previously unpublished submissions.

ANTIETAM REVIEW LITERARY AWARD (I, IV), *Antietam Review*, 82 W. Washington St., Hagerstown MD 21740. (301)791-3132. Contact: Ann B. Knox, editor. Annual award, to encourage and give recognition to excellence in short fiction. Open to writers from Maryland, Pennsylvania, Virginia, West Virginia, Washington DC and Delaware. "We consider only previously unpublished work. We read manuscripts between October 1 and March 1." Award: $100 plus $100 for the story; the story is printed as lead in the magazine. "We consider all fiction mss sent to *Antietam Review* as entries for the prize. We look for well crafted, serious literary prose fiction under 5,000 words."

ARIZONA AUTHORS' ASSOCIATION ANNUAL LITERARY CONTEST (I), Annual Literary Contest, 3509 E. Shea Blvd., Suite 117, Phoenix AZ 85028. (602)996-9706. Contact: Velma Cooper. Estab. 1981. Annually. "To encourage AAA members and all other writers in the country to discipline themselves to write regularly, steadily for competition and publication." Unpublished submissions. Award: "Cash prizes totalling $1,000 for winners and honorable mentions in short stories, essays and poetry. Winning entries are published in the *Arizona Literary Magazine*." Deadline: July 29. Entry fee: $4 for poetry, $6 for essays and short stories. Contest rules for SASE. Looking for "strong concept; good, effective writing, with emphasis on the subject/story."

ARIZONA COMMISSION ON THE ARTS CREATIVE WRITING FELLOWSHIPS (I,IV), 417 West Roosevelt St., Phoenix AZ 85003. (602)255-5882. Literature Director: Tonda Gorton. Fellowships awarded in alternate years to fiction writers and poets. Four awards of $5,000-7,500. Judges: out-of-state writers/editors. Next deadline for fiction writers: 1991. Arizona poets and writers over 18 years of age only.

‡ARTIST TRUST ARTIST FELLOWSHIPS; GAP GRANTS (I,II,IV), Artist Trust, 1331 3rd Ave. #512, Seattle WA 98101. (206)467-8734. Awards Coordinator: Gabrielle Dean. Awards to "offer direct support to individual artists in all disciplines in Washington state: The Fellowship Program and the GAP (Grants for Artist Projects) Program. Our goal is to offer financial support for an artist's creative process, therefore grants are made to generative, rather than interpretive, artists." Annual fellowships and biannual grants for short stories, novels and story collections. Awards: $5,000 fellowship; up to $750 GAP. Competition receives approx. 200-300 submissions. Judges: peer panel of 3 professional artists and arts professionals in each discipline. Guidelines available for SASE. Deadlines: Nov.1-GAP; Dec. 1 fellowships. Limited to Washington state artists only. Students not eligible.

ASF TRANSLATION PRIZE (I, IV), American-Scandinavian Foundation, 725 Park Ave., New York NY 10021. Contact: Publishing office. Estab. 1980. Annual award. Competition includes submissions of poetry, drama, literary prose and fiction translations. To encourage the translation and publication of the best of contemporary Scandinavian poetry and fiction and to make it available to a wider American audience. Submissions must have been previously published in the original Scandinavian language. No previously translated material. Original authors should have been born within past 100 years. Deadline for entry: June 3, 1991. Competition rules and entry forms available with SASE. Award: $1,000, a bronze medallion and publication in *Scandinavian Review*.

ASTED/GRAND PRIX DE LITTERATURE JEUNESSE DU QUEBEC-ALVINE-BELISLE (III,IV), Association pour l'avancement des sciences et des techniques de la documentation, 1030 rue Cherrier, Bureau 505, Montréal, Québec Canada. (514)521-9561. President: Jean Pierre Leduc. "Prize granted for the best work in youth literature edited in French in the Quebec Province. Authors and editors can participate in the contest." Annual competition for fiction and nonfiction for children and young adults. Award: $500. Deadline: June 1. Contest entry limited to editors of books published during the preceding year. French translations of other languages are not accepted.

THE ATHENAEUM LITERARY AWARD (II, IV), The Athenaeum of Philadelphia, 219 S. 6th St., Philadelphia PA 19106. Contact: Literary Award Committee. Annual award. To recognize and encourage outstanding literary achievement in Philadelphia and its vicinity. Submissions must have been published during the preceding year. Deadline: December. Nominations shall be made in writing to the Literary Award Committee by the author, the publisher or a member of the Athenaeum, accompanied

 The double dagger before a listing indicates that the listing is new in this edition. New markets are often the most receptive to freelance contributions.

by a copy of the book. Judged by committee appointed by Board of Directors. Award: A bronze medal bearing the name of the award, the seal of the Athenaeum, the title of the book, the name of the author and the year. The Athenaeum Literary Award is granted for a work of general literature, not exclusively for fiction. Juvenile fiction is not included.

AVON FLARE YOUNG ADULT NOVEL COMPETITION (I, IV), *Avon Books*, 105 Madison Ave., New York NY 10016. (212)481-5609. Ellen E. Krieger, Editorial Director, Books for Young Readers. "To discover, encourage, and develop young writing talent." Biannual award for novels "about 30,000 to 50,000 words." Award: Publication of the novel under the Avon/Flare imprint for an advance against royalties. Competition receives approximately 400-500 submissions annually. Judges are the Avon editorial staff. Entry forms or rules for SASE. Deadline August 31, 1991. Contest restricted to writers who were no younger than 12 and no older than 18 years of age as of December 31, 1990. With your manuscript include letter with your name, address, telephone number, age and short description of your novel."

AWP AWARD SERIES IN SHORT FICTION (I), The Associated Writing Programs, c/o Old Dominion University, Norfolk VA 23529-0079. Annual award. The AWP Award Series was established in cooperation with several university presses in order to make quality short fiction available to a wide audience. It is an anonymous competition and only book-length (150-300 pp.) manuscripts are eligible. Manuscripts previously published in their entirety, including self-publishing, are not eligible. Submissions dates: manuscripts postmarked between January 1-February 29. Awards judged by distinguished writers in each genre. Contest/award rules and entry forms available for SASE. Award: The winning manuscript in short fiction is published by the University of Missouri Press. Carries a $1,000 honorarium. $10 submission fee with ms. No mss returned.

AWP AWARD SERIES IN THE NOVEL AND SHORT FICTION (I), The Associated Writing Programs, c/o Old Dominion University, Norfolk VA 23529-0079. Annual award. The AWP Award Series was established in cooperation with several university presses in order to publish and make fine fiction available to a wide audience. Only book-length mss in the novel and short story collections are eligible. Manuscripts previously published in their entirety, including self-publishing, are not eligible. Submission dates: manuscript postmarked between January 1-February 29. Awards judged by distinguished writers in each genre. Contest/award rules available for SASE. Carries a $1,000 honorarium and publication with a university press. In addition, AWP tries to place mss of finalists with participating presses. $10 submission fee with ms.

‡AWP INTRO JOURNALS PROJECT (IV), Old Dominion University, Norfolk VA 23529-0079. (804)683-3840. Contact: Tony Ardizzone. "This is a prize for students in AWP member university creative writing programs only. Authors are nominated by the head of the creative writing department. Each school may send 2 nominated short stories." Annual competition for short stories. Award: $25 plus publication in participating journal. 1991 journals include *New England Review*, *Puerto del Sol*, *Indiana Review*, *Quarterly West*, *The Iowa Review* and *Black Warrior Review*. Judges: AWP. Deadline December 15. Unpublished submissions. Writers must be students in an AWP member creative writing program.

‡EMILY CLARK BALCH AWARDS (I), *The Virginia Quarterly Review*, 1 West Range, Charlottesville VA 22903. Editor: Staige D. Blackford. Annual award. To recognize distinguished short fiction by American writers. For stories published in *The Virginia Quarterly Review* during the calendar year. Award: $500.

BANFF WRITING RESIDENCY (I), The Banff Centre for Continuing Education, Box 1020, Banff, Alberta T0L 0C0 Canada. (403)762-6186. Writing residency. Annual competition for short stories, novels, story collections and poetry. Competition receives over 100 applicants for 20 residencies. Judges: Faculty of Writing. Entry fee $43 (Canadian Funds). Guidelines for SASE. Deadline: January 14.

Read the Business of Fiction section to learn the correct way to prepare and submit a manuscript.

MILDRED L. BATCHELDER AWARD (II), Association for Library Service to Children/American Library Association, 50 E. Huron St., Chicago IL 60611. (312)944-6780. To encourage international exchange of quality children's books by recognizing U.S. publishers of such books in translation. Annual competition for translations. Award: citation. Judge: Mildred L. Batchelder award committee. Guidelines for SASE. Deadline: December. Books should be U.S. trade publications for which children, up to and including age 14 are potential audience.

H.E. BATES SHORT STORY COMPETITION (I), Northampton Borough Council, Bedford Rd., Northampton England. Contact: Marketing & Development Officer. "An arts service." Annual competition for short stories. Award: £100. Competition receives approx. 200 submissions. Entry fee £1.20. Guidelines for SASE. Deadline: August. Word length: 2,000 words.

BELLAGIO CENTER RESIDENCY (I), Rockefeller Foundation, 1133 Avenue of the Americas, New York NY 10036. (212)869-8500. Manager: Susan E. Garfield. Award 4- to 5-week residency in northern Italy for scholars and artists (including writers). Residencies for authors of short stories, novels and story collections. Judges: committee of Foundation officers. Guidelines for SASE. Writers should submit applications 1 year prior to preferred dates. "Competition is most intense for May through September. Each scholar or artist is provided with a private room and a bath, and with a study in which to work. At dinner and over aperitivi, scholars in residence occasionally have the opportunity to meet participants in international conferences that are scheduled concurrently. The Foundation does not provide financial assistance to scholars in residence, nor does it contribute ordinarily to travel expenses. Write for application."

GEORGE BENNETT FELLOWSHIP (I), Phillips Exeter Academy, Exeter NH 03833. (603)772-4311. Coordinator, Selection Committee: Charles Pratt. "To provide time and freedom from monetary concerns to a person contemplating or pursuing a career as a professional writer." Annual award for writing residency. Award: A stipend ($5,000 at present), plus room and board for academic year. Competition receives approximately 100 submissions. Judges are a committee of the English department. Entry fee $5. SASE for application form and guidelines. Deadline: December 1.

‡BEST FIRST MALICE DOMESTIC NOVEL (I, IV), Thomas Dunne Books, St. Martin's Press and MacMillan London Ltd., St. Martin's Press, 175 Fifth Ave., New York NY 10010. "To publish a writer's first 'malice domestic novel.'" Annual competition for novels. Award: Publication by St. Martin's Press in the US and MacMillan London in the UK. Advance: $10,000 (and standard royalties). Judges are selected by sponsors. SASE. Deadline: November 1. Unpublished submissions. "Open to any professional or nonprofessional writer who has never published a malice domestic novel and who is not under contract with a publisher to publish one. Malice domestic is a traditional mystery novel that is not hardboiled; emphasis is on the solution rather than the details of the crime. Suspects and victims know one another. In marginal cases, judges will decide whether entry qualifies."

BEST FIRST PRIVATE EYE NOVEL CONTEST (I, IV), Private Eye Writers of America, St. Martin's Press and Macmillan London Ltd., Thomas Dunne Books, St. Martin's Press, 175 Fifth Ave., New York NY 10010. To publish a writer's first "private eye" novel. Annual award for novels. Award: Publication of novel by St. Martin's Press in the US and Macmillan London in the UK. Advance: $10,000 against royalties (standard contract). Judges are selected by sponsors. Guidelines for SASE. Deadline: September 30. Unpublished submissions. "Open to any professional or non-professional writer who has never published a 'private eye' novel and who is not under contract with a publisher for the publication of a 'private eye' novel. As used in the rules, private eye novel means: a novel in which the main character is an independent investigator who is not a member of any law enforcement or government agency."

IRMA SIMONTON BLACK CHILDREN'S BOOK AWARD (II), Bank Street College, 610 W. 112th St., New York NY 10025. (212)663-7200, ext. 587. Children's Librarian: Linda Greengrass. Annual award. "To honor the young children's book published in the preceding year judged the most outstanding in text as well as in art. Book must be published the year preceding the May award." Award: Press luncheon at Harvard Club, a scroll and seals by Maurice Sendak for attaching to award book's run. Entry deadline: January 15. No entry fee. "Write to address above. Usually publishers submit books they want considered, but individuals can too. No entries are returned."

JAMES TAIT BLACK MEMORIAL PRIZES (III, IV), Department of English Literature, University of Edinburgh, Edinburgh EH8 9JX Scotland. Contact: Professor R.D.S. Jack. "Two prizes are awarded: one for the best work of fiction, one for the best biography or work of that nature, published during the calendar year." Annual competition for short stories, novels and story collections. Award: £1,500 each. Competition receives approx. 200 submissions. Judge: Professor R.D.S. Jack, Chairman, Dept. of English Literature. Guidelines for SASE. Deadline: December 31. Previously published submissions. "Eligible works are those written in English, originating with a British publisher, and first published in Britain in the year of the award. Works should be submitted by publishers."

THE BLACK WARRIOR REVIEW LITERARY AWARD (II, III), Box 2936, Tuscaloosa AL 35486. (205)348-4518. Editor: Alicia Griswold. "Award is to recognize the best fiction published in *BWR* in a volume year." Competition is for short stories and novel chapters. Award: $500. Competition receives approximately 1,500 submissions. Prize awarded by an outside judge. SASE.

‡THE BLUE MOUNTAIN CENTER (I), Blue Mountain Lake NY 12812. (518)352-7391. Director: Harriet Barlow. "To provide a peaceful and comfortable environment in which guests are able to work, free from the distractions and demands of normal daily life." Residencies for established writers. Award: residencies are for 1 month between June 15 and October 15. Send SASE for guidelines. Application deadline. March 1. Write for brochure.

BOARDMAN TASKER PRIZE (III, IV), 14 Pine Lodge, Dairyground Rd., Bramhall, Stockport, Cheshire SK7 2HS United Kingdom. Contact: Mrs. D. Boardman. "To reward a book which has made an outstanding contribution to mountain literature. A memorial to Peter Boardman and Joe Tasker, who disappeared on Everest in 1982." Award: £1,000. Competition receives approx. 15 submissions. Judges: a panel of 3 judges elected by trustees. Guidelines for SASE. Deadline: August 1. Limited to works published or distributed in the UK for the first time between November 1, 1990 and October 31, 1991. Publisher's entry only. "May be fiction, nonfiction, poetry or drama. Not an anthology. The prize is not primarily for fiction though that is not excluded. Subject must be concerned with mountain environment. Previous winners have been books on expeditions, Himalayan experiences; a biography of a mountaineer; a novel."

BOOTS ROMANTIC NOVEL OF THE YEAR (II, IV), Dove House Farm, Potter Heigham, Norfolk NR29 5LJ England. Contact: Olga Sinclair, Award Organiser, Romantic Novelists' Association. "To publish good romantic fiction and therefore raise the prestige of the genre." Annual competition for novels. Award £5,000. Competition receives approx. 100 submissions. Judges: a panel of experienced writers. Deadline: September 1-December 1. Previously published submissions. For novels "published in the U.K. only." A modern or historical (before 1950) romantic novel. "Three copies of each entry are required. They may be hardback or paperback. Only novels written in English and published in the U.K. during the relevant year are eligible. Authors must be domiciled in UK or temporarily living abroad whilst in possession of British passport."

BOSTON GLOBE-HORN BOOK AWARDS (II), *Boston Globe* Newspaper, Horn Book Awards, *Horn Book* Magazine, 14 Beacon St., Boston MA 02108. Annual award. "To honor most outstanding children's fiction, picture and nonfiction books published within the U.S." Previously published material from July 1-June 30 of previous year. Award: $500 first prize in each category; silver plate for the 2 honor books in each category. Entry deadline: May 1. No entry fee. Entry forms or rules for SASE.

BRANDEIS UNIVERSITY CREATIVE ARTS AWARDS (III), Brandeis University, Irving Enclave, Commission Office, Waltham MA 02254-9110. (617)736-3007. Special Assistants to the President: Mary R. Anderson and Suzanne Yates. Awards "medal to an established artist in celebration of a lifetime of achievement, and a citation to an individual in an earlier stage of his or her career. From time to time the Creative Arts Awards Commission bestows the Notable Achievement Award, when in the Commission's judgment there is someone whose accomplishments so transcend the normal categories that special recognition is due." Awards are made by internal selection only.

‡BRAZOS BOOKSTORE (HOUSTON) AWARD (SINGLE SHORT STORY) (II,IV), The Texas Institute of Letters, P.O. Box 9032, Wichita Falls TX 76308. (817)692-6611 ext.4123. Awards Coordinator: James Hoggard. Award to "honor the writer of the best short story published for the first time during the calendar year before the award is given." Annual competition for short stories. (Translations of published book-length works come under the Soeurette Diehl Fraser Award in Translation.) Award for short story: $500. Competition receives approx. 30-40 submissions. Judges: panel selected by TIL Council. Guidelines available for SASE. Deadline: January 4. Previously published submissions. Published entries must have appeared in print between Jan.1, 1991 and Dec.31, 1991. "Award available to writers who, at some time, have lived in Texas at least two years consecutively or whose work has a significant Texas them."

BUMBERSHOOT WRITTEN WORKS COMPETITION (I), Seattle's Arts Festival, Box 9750, Seattle WA 98109-0750. (206)622-5123. Annual award for short stories. Award: Six awards of $150 for poetry or literary prose. Winners published in Bumbershoot arts magazine, *Ergo!* and invited to read at Bumbershoot Festival. Judges are professional writers/publishers. Entry forms or rules for SASE. Deadline: late February.

BUNTING INSTITUTE FELLOWSHIP (I), Mary Ingraham Bunting Institute of Radcliffe College, 34 Concord Ave., Cambridge MA 02138. (617)495-8212. Deadline: October 15, 1991. Women scholars, creative writers, and visual and performing artists are eligible. Scholars must have held the Ph.D. or appropriate terminal degree at least two years prior to appointment (July 1, 1991). Non-academic applicants, such as artists, writers, social workers, lawyers, journalists, etc., need to have a significant record of accomplishment and professional experience equivalent to a doctorate and some post-doctoral work. For example, artists must have participated in some group and/or one-person shows; writers must have some published work; other professionals must have some years of work in their respective fields after the appropriate degree. $21,500 stipend for a one-year appointment, July 1, 1991-June 30, 1992. Private office or studio space is provided, along with access to most Harvard/Radcliffe resources. Fellows are required to present a public lecture or reading in the Institute Collo-quium Series or an exhibition in the Institute gallery. Bunting fellows are required to be in residence in teh Cambridge/Boston area for the entire terms of appointment. We do not provide housing. Number of fellowships awarded: 10. Applications go through three-stage selection process. In the first stage applications are reviewed by an individual reader in teh applicant's field. (Creative writing and visual arts applications go to a relevant first stage committee—i.e., fiction, sculpture, etc.) All applications then go to a second stage committee in the applicant's field (i.e., psychology, literature, etc.), which chooses a small number of finalists. Fellows are chosen from the finalist group by an interdisciplinary final selection committee. Applications are judged on the significance and quality of the project proposal, the applicant's record of accomplishment, and on the difference the fellowship might make in advancing the applicant's career. Rejection letters are send on a rolling basis, but should be received no later than the beginning of March. Finalists will be notified during the months of January and February. Fellows and alternates will be notified in the beginning of April. We request that you provide us with the names of your three intended recommenders on the Summary Application Information sheet. In December and January we will solicit three letters of recommendation from finalists. We will send you the required forms with your letter of notification and you are requested to have your recommenders send their letters directly to us. We will not contact your recommenders.

‡BURNABY WRITERS' SOCIETY ANNUAL COMPETITION (I, IV), 6450 Gilpin St., Burnaby, British Columbia V5G 2J3 Canada. (604)435-6500. Annual competition to encourage creative writing in British Columbia. "Category varies from year to year." Award: $100, $50 and $25 prizes. Receives 400-600 entries for each award. Judge: "independent recognized professional in the field." Entry fee $5. Contest requirements for SASE. Deadline April 30. Open to British Columbia authors only.

BUSH ARTIST FELLOWSHIPS (I, IV), The Bush Foundation, E-900 First Nat'l Bank Building, 332 Minnesota St., St. Paul MN 55101. (612)227-5222. Contact: Sally Dixon, Program Director. To provide artists of exemplary talent time to work in their chosen art forms. Annual grant. Award: Stipend maximum of $26,000 for 6-18 months, plus a production and travel allowance of $7,000. Competition receives approximately 450 submissions. Judges are writers, critics and editors from outside MN, SD, ND or WI. Applicants must be at least 25 years old, and Minnesota, South Dakota, North Dakota or Western Wisconsin residents. Students not eligible.

***BYLINE* MAGAZINE LITERARY AWARDS (I,IV)**, Box 130596, Edmond OK 73013. (405)348-5591. Exec. editor/publisher: Marcia Preston. "To encourage our subscribers in striving for high quality writing." Annual award for short stories. Award: $250 cash in each category—fiction and poetry. Judges are published writers not on the *Byline* staff. Entry fee $5 for stories; $2 for poems. Postmark Deadline: December 1. "Entries should be unpublished and not have won money in any previous contest. Winners announced in February issue and published in March issue with photo and short bio. Open to subscribers only."

‡**CALIFORNIA WRITERS' CLUB CONTEST**, California Writers' Club, 2214 Derby St., Berkeley CA 94705. (415)841-1217. Awards "to encourage writing." Awards: First prize in each category is tuition to our biennial writers' conference. Second prize cash, third certificate. Competition receives varying number of submissions. Judges: professional writers, members of California Writers' Club. Entry fee $5. Guidelines for SASE. Deadline is mid-April. Previously unpublished submissions. "Open to anyone who is not, nor has ever been, a member of California Writers' Club." For the contest rules, write to the Secretary.

JOHN W. CAMPBELL MEMORIAL AWARD FOR THE BEST SCIENCE-FICTION NOVEL OF THE YEAR; THEODORE STURGEON MEMORIAL AWARD FOR THE BEST SF SHORT FICTION (II, III), Center for the Study of Science Fiction, English Dept., University of Kansas, Lawrence KS 66045. (913)864-3380. Professor and Director: James Gunn. "To honor the best novel and short science fiction of the year." Annual competition for short stories and novels. Award: Engraved trophy and a certificate. Competition receives approx. 50-100 submissions. Judges: two separate juries. Deadline: May 1. For previously published submissions. "Ordinarily publishers should submit work, but authors have done so when publishers would not. Send for list of jurors."

‡**CANADA COUNCIL AWARDS (III, IV)**, Canada Council, 99 Metcalfe St., Box 1047, Ottawa, Ontario K1P 5V8 Canada. (613)598-4365. The Canada Council sponsors the following awards, for which no applications are accepted. *Canada-Australia Literary Prize*: 1 prize of $3,000, awarded in alternate years to an Australian or Canadian writer for the author's complete work; *Canada-French Community of Belgium Literary Prize*: 1 prize of $2,500, awarded in alternate years to a Canadian or Belgian writer on the basis of the complete works of the writer; *Canada-Switzerland Literary Prize*: 1 prize of $2,500, awarded in alternate years to a Canadian or Swiss writer for a work published in French during the preceding 8 years.

CANADA COUNCIL GOVERNOR GENERAL'S LITERARY AWARDS (IV), Canada Council, Box 1047, 99 Metcalfe St., Ottawa, Ontario K1P 5V8 Canada. (613)598-4376. Contact: writing and publishing section. "Awards of $10,000 each are given annually to the best English-language and best French-language Canadian work in each of the six categories: children's literature (text and illustration), drama, fiction, poetry, nonfiction and translation." All literary works published by Canadians between 1 December 1989 and 31 October 1990 are considered. Canadian authors, illustrators and translators only.

CANADIAN AUTHOR & BOOKMAN STUDENT'S CREATIVE WRITING CONTEST, 121 Avenue Rd., #104, Toronto, Ontario M5R 2G3 Canada. (416)926-8084. "To encourage writing among secondary school students." Annual competition for short stories. Award: $100 plus $100 to the nominating teacher; $500 to pay for undergraduate education to a worthy student enrolled at a college. Receives 100-120 submissions. Judge: Magazine editor. "Entry form in Winter issue." Deadline: March. Previously unpublished submissions. Word length: 2,500 words. Writer must be nominated by teacher.

CANADIAN AUTHORS ASSOCIATION LITERARY AWARDS (FICTION) (II, IV), Canadian Authors Association, 121 Avenue Road, #104, Toronto M5R 2G3 Ontario, Canada. (416)926-8084. Contact: Executive Director. Annual award. "To honor writing that achieves literary excellence without sacrificing popular appeal." For novels published during the previous calendar year. Award: $5,000 plus silver medal. Entry deadline: December 31. No entry fee. Entry forms or rules for SASE. Restricted to full-length English language novels. Author must be Canadian or Canadian landed immigrant. CAA also sponsors the Air Canada Award, literary awards as above in poetry, nonfiction and drama, and the Vicky Metcalf Awards for children's literature.

CANADIAN FICTION MAGAZINE **CONTRIBUTOR'S PRIZE (IV)**, Box 946, Station F, Toronto, Ontario M4Y 2N9 Canada. Contact: Geoffrey Hancock, editor-in-chief. Annual award. To celebrate the best story published by *CFM* in either French or English during the preceding year. Contributors must reside in Canada or be Canadians living abroad. All manuscripts published in *CFM* are eligible. Deadline: August 15. Award: $500, public announcement, photograph. "Looking for contemporary creative writing of the highest possible literary standards."

CANADIAN LIBRARY ASSOCIATION BOOK OF THE YEAR FOR CHILDREN AWARD (III,IV), Canadian Library Association, 200 Elgin Street, Ottawa, Ontario K2P 1L5 Canada. (613)232-9625. To encourage the writing in Canada of good books for children up to and including age 14. Annual competition for short stories and novels for children. Award: a specially designed medal. Competition receives approx. 10-20 submissions/year. Judging: CLA Book of the Year Award Committee. Guidelines for SASE. Deadline Februrary 1. Book must have been published in Canada during the last year and its author must be Canadian citizen or a landed immigrant. Nominations are generally made by CLA membership—a call for nominations is posted in the Association's newsletter in October. "Although the award is sponsored by the Canadian Library Association, it is the Canadian Association of Children's Librarians (a section of Canadian Association of Public Libraries which in turn is a division of CLA) which staffs the Award Committee, selects the winner and administers the award."

RAYMOND CARVER SHORT STORY CONTEST (I), Dept. of English, Humboldt State University, Arcata CA 95521-4957. Contact: Coordinator. Annual award for previously unpublished short stories. First prize: $500 and publication in *Toyon 91*. Second Prize: $250. For authors living in United States only. Deadline: November. Entry fee $7.50 per story. SASE for rules. Send 2 copies of story; author's name, address, phone number and title of story on separate cover page only. Story must be no more than 25 pages. Title must appear on first page. For notification of receipt of ms, include self-addressed stamped postcard. For Winners List include SASE.

CCL STUDENT WRITING CONTEST (I,IV), Conference on Christianity and Literature. Dept. of English, Seattle Pacific University, Seattle WA 98119. Contact: Daniel Taylor, Dept. of English, Bethel College, 3900 Bethel Drive, St Paul MN 55112. Annual award. "To recognize excellence in undergraduate writing." Unpublished submissions. Award: $75, $50 and $25 awarded in book certificates. Deadline: February 15. Looking for "excellence in artistic achievement and reflection of writer's Christian premises." Contest open to all regularly enrolled undergraduate students. Entries will not be returned. Winners will be announced in summer issue of *Christianity and Literature*.

‡CENTRUM RESIDENCY PROGRAM (I,II), Centrum, P.O. Box 1158, Port Townsend WA 98368. (206)385-3102. Program Coordinator: Sarah Muirhead. Award to "offer one month retreat for writers to concentrate on their work. "Biannual competition for short stories, novels, story collections and translations." Award: cottage and small stipend for one month. Competition receives approx. 6 submissions. Judges: peer panels. Guidelines for SASE. Deadline: April 1,1991 for fall residencies; Oct.1 for spring. Previously published submissions. Unpublished submissions. Length: 10 pages max. for poetry; 30 pages max. for prose.

CHILD STUDY CHILDREN'S BOOK AWARD (III, IV), Child Study Children's Book Committee at Bank St. College, 610 W. 112th St., New York NY 10025. Contact: Anita Wilkes Dore, Committee Chair. Annual award. "To honor a book for children or young people which deals realistically with problems in their world. It may concern social, individual and ethical problems." Only books sent by publishers for review are considered. No personal submissions. Books must have been published within current calendar year. Award: Certificate and cash prize.

THE CHILDREN'S BOOK AWARD (II), Federation of Children's Book Groups, 30 Senneleys Park Rd., Northfield, Birmingham B31 1AL England. Award "to promote the publication of good quality books for children." Annual award for short stories, novels, story collections and translations. Award: "portfolio of children's writing and drawings and a magnificent trophy of silver and oak." Competition received 600 submissions in 1989. Judges: thousands of children from all over the United Kingdom. Guidelines for SASE. Deadline: December 31. Published and previously unpublished submissions (first publication in UK). "The book should be suitable for children."

THE CHRISTOPHER AWARD (II), The Christophers, 12 E. 48th St., New York NY 10017. Contact: Ms. Peggy Flanagan, awards coordinator. Annual award. "To encourage creative people to continue to produce works which affirm the highest values of the human spirit in adult and children's books." Published submissions only. "Award judged by a grassroots panel and a final panel of experts. Juvenile works are 'children tested.' " Award: Bronze medallion. Examples of books awarded: *Dear Mr. Henshaw*, by Beverly Cleary (ages 8-10); *Sarah, Plain and Tall* by Patricia MacLachlan (ages 10-12).

CINTAS FELLOWSHIP (I, IV), Cintas Foundation/Arts International Program of I.I.E., 809 U.N. Plaza, New York NY 10017. (212)984-5564. Contact: Rebecca A. Sayies. "To foster and encourage the professional development and recognition of talented Cuban creative artists. *Not* intended for furtherance of academic or professional study, nor for research or writings of a scholarly nature." Annual competition for authors of short stories, novels, story collections and poetry. 10 awards of $10,000 each. Fellowship receives approx. 40 literature applicants/year. Judges: selection committees. Guidelines for SASE. Deadline: March 1. Previously published or unpublished submissions. Limited to artists of Cuban lineage *only*. "Awards are given to artists in the following fields: visual arts, literature, music composition and architecture."

CITY OF REGINA WRITING AWARD (I, IV), City of Regina Arts Commission, Saskatchewan Writers Guild, Box 3986, Regina, Saskatchewan S4P 3R9 Canada. (306)757-6310. "To enable a writer to work for 3 months on a specific writing project; to reward merit in writing." Annual competition for short stories, novels and story collections. Award: $3,300. Competition receives approx. 21 submissions. Judges: selection committee of SWG. Guidelines for SASE. Deadline: March. Unpublished submissions. "Grant available only to residents of Regina for previous year."

COLORADO COUNCIL ON THE ARTS & HUMANITIES CREATIVE FELLOWSHIP (I, II, IV), 770 Pennsylvania Street, Denver CO 80203. (303)866-2617. Director, Individual Artist Programs: Daniel Salazar. To provide both recognition and significant financial support to Colorado's outstanding individual artists and to provide a forum and secure an audience for the promotion of their work. Award presented on rotating basis (in 1992, 1995 and 1998). Award: 16 fellowships of $4,000 each. Competition receives 350 entries/year. Judges: peer panels. Guidelines available for SASE. For either previously published or unpublished manuscripts. Colorado residents only.

‡*COLUMBIA MAGAZINE* EDITORS AWARDS (I), *Columbia; a Magazine of Poetry and Prose*, Writing Division, 404 Dodge Hall, Columbia University NY 10027. Contact: Fiction Editors. Semiannually. Short stories and sections of novels, unpublished. Deadlines: Spring: December 15; Fall: April 15. Entry fee $6, made payable to *Columbia Magazine*. SASE for rules/entry forms. "Submissions can be no more than 25 pages; include SASE. First prize is $350; second prize is $150; both include publication."

COMMONWEALTH CLUB OF CALIFORNIA (II, IV), California Book Awards, 595 Market St., San Francisco CA 94105. (415)543-3353. Contact: James D. Rosenthal, Executive Director. Main contest established in 1931. Annually. Purpose: "To encourage California writers and honor literary merit." Requirements: For books published during the year of the particular contest. Three copies of book and a completed entry form required. Awards: Gold and silver medals. Judged by jury of literary experts. "Write or phone asking for the forms. Either an author or publisher may enter a book. We usually receive over 200 entries."

CONNECTICUT COMMISSION ON THE ARTS ARTIST GRANTS (I, II, IV), 227 Lawrence St., Hartford CT 06106. (203)566-4770. Senior Program Associate: Linda Dente. To support the creation of new work by a creative artist *living in Connecticut*. Biannual competition for the creation or completion of new works in literature, i.e. short stories, novels, story collections, poetry and playwriting. Award: $5,000. Judges: peer professionals (writers, editors). Guidelines available in August. Deadline: January. Writers may send either previously published or unpublished submissions. Writers may submit up to 25 pages of material. Connecticut residents only.

CONSEIL DE LA VIE FRANCAISE EN AMÉRIQUE/PRIX CHAMPLAIN (The Champlain Prize) (II, IV), Conseil de la vie française en amérique, 56 rue St-Pierre 3e Étage, Québec, Québec Q1K 4A1 Canada. Prix Champlain estab. 1957. Annual award. To encourage literary work in novel or short story in French by Francophiles living outside Québec and in the US or Canada. "There is no restriction as to the subject matter. If the author lives in Quebec, the subject matter must be related to French-speaking people living outside of Quebec." For previously published or contracted submissions, published no more than 3 years prior to award. Deadline: December 31. Author must furnish 4 examples of work, curriculum vita, address and phone number. Judges: 3 different judges each year. Award: $1,500 in Canadian currency. The prize will be given alternately; one year for fiction, the next for nonfiction. Next fiction award in 1991.

COUNCIL FOR WISCONSIN WRITERS ANNUAL WRITING CONTEST (II, IV), Box 55322, Madison WI 53705. President: Ray Helminiak. "To recognize excellence in Wisconsin writing published during the year in 10 categories." Annual competition. Award: $500 in 8 categories; $1,000 for first place short nonfiction category; and $1,500 for the Paulette Chandler Poetry Award. Competition receives between 5 and 80 entries, depending on category. Judges: qualified judges from other states. Entry fee $10/member; $15/nonmember. Guidelines for SASE. Previously published submissions. Wisconsin residents only. Official entry form (available in November) required. Deadline: mid-January.

CREATIVE ARTIST GRANT (I,IV), Michigan Council for the Arts, 1200 Sixth St., Detroit MI 48226. (313)256-3719. Award "to create new works of art or complete works in progress." Annual competition for short stories, novels, story collections, poetry and nonfiction. Award: up to $10,000. Competition receives approximately 125 submissions. Judges: out-of-state evaluators—different every year. Guidelines for SASE. Deadline April 5. *Michigan residents only.*

CRIME WRITERS' ASSOCIATION AWARDS (III, IV), Box 172, Tring Herts HP23 5LP England. Six awards. Annual award for crime novels. Competition receives varied amount of submissions. Deadline: October 1. Published submissions in UK in current year. Writer must be nominated by UK publishers.

‡CUMMINGTON COMMUNITY OF THE ARTS ARTIST'S COLONY (I,II), Cummington Community of the Arts, RR 1, Box 145, Cummington MA 01026. (413)634-2172. Admissions Coordinator: Gloria Gowdy. "Cummington is an artist's colony where artists come for 1 to 3 months to work on their art." Award: residencies. Competition receives approximately 200 applications. Judges: Juried professionals in their respective fields. Application fee: $10 (subject to change.) Application for SASE. Deadlines: January 1 for May and June residencies; March 1 for July and August residencies; June 1 for September, October and November residencies. Either previously published or unpublished submissions. Award available to all writers, "fiction preferred over nonfiction." Submit a maximum of 10 poems, or 20 pages of prose. "Cummington accepts writers, flimmakers, performance artists, sculptors, visual artists, composers and photographers."

DEEP SOUTH WRITERS CONFERENCE ANNUAL COMPETITION (I), DSWC Inc., English Dept., University of Southwestern Louisiana, Box 44691, Lafayette LA 70504. (318)231-6908. Contact: John Fiero, director. Annual awards. "To encourage aspiring, unpublished writers." Unpublished submissions. Award: Certificates and cash plus possible publication of shorter works. Contest rules for SASE and addition to mailing list. Deadline: July 15.

DELACORTE PRESS ANNUAL PRIZE FOR FIRST YOUNG ADULT NOVEL (I), Delacorte Press, Department BFYR (Books for Young Readers), 666 Fifth Ave., New York NY 10103. (212)765-6500. Contact: Lisa T. Oldenburg, Contest Director. Estab. 1983. Annual award. "To encourage the writing of contemporary young adult fiction." Unpublished submissions; fiction with a contemporary setting in the United States or Canada that will be suitable for ages 12-18. Award: Contract for publication of book; $1,500 cash prize and a $6,000 advance against royalties. Judges are the editors of Delacorte Press Books for Young Readers. Deadline: December 31 (no submissions accepted prior to Labor Day). Contest rules for SASE.

DELAWARE STATE ARTS COUNCIL (I, IV), 820 N. French St., Wilimington DE 19801. (302)571-3540. Barbara R. King, coordinator. "To help further careers of established, professional and emerging artists." Annual award for Delaware residents only. Award: $5,000 for established professional; $2,000 for emerging professional. Judges are out-of-state professionals in each division. Entry forms or rules for SASE. Deadline March 22, 1991.

DJERASSI FOUNDATION RESIDENT ARTISTS PROGRAM (I, II), Djerassi Foundation, 2325 Bear Gulch Road, Woodside CA 94062. (415)851-8395. "To provide international working community for emerging mature artists able to work in isolation." Biannual award for short stories, novels, story collections and translations. Award: residency at Foundation. Judges: professional review panel. Guidelines for SASE. Deadline: February 1. Previously published or unpublished submissions.

DORLAND MOUNTAIN ARTS COLONY, INC. (I), P.O. Box 6, Temecula CA 92390. (714)676-5039. Contact: Admissions committee. "To provide uninterrupted time for creativity in a natural environment. The Colony is located on a 300-acre nature preserve." Residencies for authors of short stories, novels, translations and story collections. Award: residency for 1-2 months. Judges: admissions committee review panel. $150/month cottage fee requested. Guidelines for SASE. Deadline: March 1 and September 1 annually. "Four to seven residents can be accommodated at one time. Composers, writers and painters live in studio cottages of simple construction, consisting of kitchen, bathroom, living- and work-area. Residents learn to use woodstoves and kerosene lamps for their heat and evening light."

JOHN DOS PASSOS PRIZE FOR LITERATURE (III, IV), Longwood College, Farmville VA 23901. (804)395-2155. "The John Dos Passos Prize for Literature, annually commemorates one of the greatest of 20th-century American authors by honoring other writers in his name." Award: a medal and $1,000 cash. "The winner, announced each fall in ceremonies at the college, is chosen by an independent jury charged especially to seek out American creative writers in the middle stages of their careers—men and women who have established a substantial body of significant publication, and particularly those whose work demonstrates one or more of the following qualities, all characteristics of the art of the man for whom the prize is named: an intense and original exploration of specifically American themes; an experimental tone; and/or writing in a wide range of literature forms." Application for prize is by nomination only.

DREAMS & VISIONS: BEST SHORT STORY OF THE YEAR (I, IV), Skysong Press, RR1, Washago, Ontario L0K 2B0 Canada. Contact: Steve Stanton. The "competition serves the dual purpose of rewarding literary excellence among the authors published in *Dreams & Visions*, and of providing feedback from subscribers as to the type of literature they prefer." Annual award for short stories. Award: $100. "Only the 28 stories published in *Dreams & Visions* each year are eligible for the award." Judges: subscribers to *Dreams & Visions*. Guidelines for SASE. Previously unpublished submissions.

EATON LITERARY ASSOCIATES' LITERARY AWARDS PROGRAM (I), Eaton Literary Associates, Box 49795, Sarasota FL 34230. (813)366-6589. Richard Lawrence, Vice President. Biannual award for short stories and novels. Award: $2,500 for best book-length ms, $500 for best short story. Competition receives approximately 2,000 submissions annually. Judges are 2 staff members in conjunction with an independent agency. Entry forms or rules for SASE. Deadline is March 31 for short stories; August 31 for book-length mss.

‡EDMONTON JOURNAL'S LITERARY AWARDS (I,IV), *Edmonton Journal*, Box 2421, Edmonton, Alberta T5J 2S6 Canada. (403)429-5174. Contact: Dennis L. Skulsky, manager, human resources and community relations. Annual award "to recognize novice writers in our circulation area; promote writing and reading; establish good-will in the community." SASE for guidelines. Unpublished submissions. Award changes annually.

EYSTER PRIZES (II), *The New Delta Review*, LSU/Dept. of English, Baton Rouge LA 70803. (504)388-5922. Kathleen Fitzpatrick, editor. "To honor author and teacher Warren Eyster, who served as advisor to *New Delta Review* predecessors *Manchac* and *Delta*." Semiannual award for short stories. Award: $50 and 2 free copies of our publication. Competition receives approximately 400 submissions/issue. Judges are published authors. Deadline: October 15 for fall, April 15 for spring.

FINE ARTS WORK CENTER IN PROVINCETOWN FELLOWSHIP (I), Box 565, Provincetown MA 02657. (508)487-9960. Contact: Writing Coordinator. "7-month residency for writers who have received some recognition but have yet to firmly establish their careers." Writing residency offered annually. Award: An apartment and stipend, from October 1 to May 1. "We choose 8 fellows out of 400 applicants yearly." Judged by writing committee of the Fine Arts Work Center. Entry fee $20. Entry forms for SASE.

ROBERT L. FISH MEMORIAL AWARD (II), Mystery Writers of America, 236 West 27th St. #600, New York NY 10001-5906. (212)255-7005. Estab. 1984. Annual award. "To encourage new writers in the mystery/detective/suspense short story—and, subsequently, larger work in the genre." Previously published submissions published the year prior to the award. Award: $500. Judged by the MWA committee for best short story of the year in the mystery genre. Deadline: December 1. Looking for "a story with a crime that is central to the plot that is well written and distinctive."

DOROTHY CANFIELD FISHER AWARD (III), Vermont Congress of Parents and Teachers, % Southwest Regional Library, Pierpoint Avenue, Rutland VT 05701. Contact: Gail Furnas, chairperson. Estab. 1957. Annual award. "To encourage Vermont schoolchildren to become enthusiastic and discriminating readers and to honor the memory of one of Vermont's most distinguished and beloved literary figures." Publishers send the committee review copies of books to consider. Only books of the current publishing year can be considered for next year's award. Master list of titles is drawn up in late February or March each year. Children vote each year in the spring and the award is given before the school year ends. Award: illuminated scroll. Submissions must be "written by living American authors, be suitable for children in grades 4-8, and have literary merit. Can be nonfiction also."

FLORIDA ARTS COUNCIL/LITERATURE FELLOWSHIPS (I,IV), Division of Cultural Affairs, Dept. of State, The Capitol, Tallahassee FL 32399-0250. (904)487-2980. Director: Ms. Peyton C. Fearington. "To allow Florida artists time to develop their artistic skills and enhance their careers." Annual award for fiction or poetry. Award: $5,000. Competition receives approximately 100 submissions/year. Judges are review panels made up of individuals with a demonstrated interest in literature. Entry forms for SASE. Entry restricted to practicing, professional writers who are legal residents of Florida and have been living in the state for 12 consecutive months at the time of the deadline.

FLORIDA STATE WRITING COMPETITION (I), Florida Freelance Writers Association, Box 9844, Fort Lauderdale FL 33310. (305)485-0795. "To offer additional opportunities for writers to earn income from their stories." Annual competition for short stories and novels. Award: varies from $50-150. Competition receives approx. 300 short stories; 125 novels. Judges: authors, editors and teachers. Entry fee from $5-15. Guidelines for SASE. Deadline: March 15. Unpublished submissions. Literary: 3,000 words maximum; SF/Fantasy: 7,500 words maximum; Genre: 3,000 words maximum; and novel chapter: 7,500 words maximum. "Guidelines are revised each year and subject to change."

FOLIO (I), Dept. of Literature, American University, Washington DC 20016. Competition "to recognize outstanding poetry and short fiction submitted to *Folio*." Annual competition for short stories and poetry. Award: $75 in each category, plus a year's subscription. Competition receives 300 submissions. Judges: prominent Washington DC authors. Guidelines for SASE. Deadline: March 1. Previously unpublished submissions. Prefer stories under 3,000 words. "There is no separate submission procedure for the contest. Winners are selected by the judges from work accepted for publication by the editors."

‡FOSTER CITY ANNUAL WRITERS CONTEST (I), Foster City Committee for the Arts, 650 Shell Blvd., Foster City CA 94404. Contact: Ted Lance, contest chairman. Annually. "To foster and encourage aspiring writers." Unpublished submissions. Award: 1st prize in each of five categories $300. Ribbons for honorable mention in each category. The five categories are short stories, blank verse, rhymed verse, humor and children's stories. "Contest begins April 1 and usually closes August 31." Entry fee: $5. Contest rules for SASE. Looking for short stories (3,000 words maximum).

FOUNDATION FOR THE ADVANCEMENT OF CANADIAN LETTERS AUTHOR'S AWARDS (II,IV), In conjunction with Periodical Marketers of Canada (PMC), 20 Toronto St., Ste 400, Toronto, Ontario M5C 2B8 Canada. (416)363-4549. Award Coordinators: Ray Argyle, Marjory Dunstan. "To recognize outstanding Canadian writing and design." Annual award for short stories, novels. 1990 competition judged by an independent panel. Deadline: July 15. "Must be published in a Canadian 'mass market' publication."

‡FRIENDS OF AMERICAN WRITERS AWARDS (III, IV), Mrs. Sean O'Connor, 15237 W. Redwood Ln., Libertyville IL 60048. Chairman: Mrs. Sean O'Connor. "To encourage high standards and to promote literary ideals among American writers." Annual award for prose writing. Awards: $1,200 (1st prize) and $750 (2nd prize). Competition receives 50 entries. Judges: a committee of 14. Deadline: December 31. Manuscripts must have been published during current year. Limited to midwestern authors who have previously published no more than 3 books; or to authors of books set in the midwest and have not published more than 3 books previously. Two copies of the book are to be submitted to awards chairman by the publisher of the book. Young Peoples' books awards judged by committee of 9. Awards: $700 (1st prize); $400 (2nd prize). Same limitations.

GESTALT MAGAZINE FICTION AWARD (I,II), Anti-Matter Publishing, Inc., 516 W. Wooster, Bowling Green OH 43402. (419)352-2425. Annual competition for short fiction. Award: $50. Judges: the staff of Gestalt Magazine. Guidelines for SASE. No deadline. Published or previously unpublished submissions. "Any story, published or unpublished, is acceptable, as long as previously published stories are submitted with permission of right's owner. We want our contest to be as open as possible. We are looking for less traditional fiction, and fiction with a social consciousness."

GOLD MEDALLION BOOK AWARDS (III,IV), Evangelical Christian Publishers Association, Suite 106-B, 950 W. Southern Ave., Tempe AZ 85282. Executive Director of ECPA: Doug Ross. Award to "encourage excellence in evangelical Christian book publishing in 20 categories." Annually. Judges: "at least eight judges for each category chosen from among the ranks of evangelical leaders and book-review editors." Entry fee $75 for ECPA member publishers; $175 for non-member publishers.

Deadline December 1, 1991. For books published in 1990. Publishers submit entries. Contest breaks down into 20 categories.

GOODMAN FIELDER WATTIE BOOK AWARD (III, IV), Goodman Fielder Wattie Industries/Ltd., Book Publishers Association of New Zealand (BPANZ), Box 44146, Auckland 2, New Zealand. Contact: Gerard Reid, executive director. "To recognize excellence in writing and publishing books by New Zealanders. This is not a category award. Fiction/nonfiction/childen's etc. are all included." Award: 1st NZ$20,000; 2nd: NZ$10,000; 3rd: NZ$5,000. Competition receives approx. 80-90 submissions. Judges: panel of 3 selected annually by the BPANZ—1 writer, 1 book trade person and 1 other. Entry fee NZ$65. Guidelines for SASE. Deadline: April 5. "Writer must be New Zealander or resident of New Zealand and its former Pacific territories. Must be submitted by publisher. Fuller details available from BPANZ."

LES GRANDS PRIX DU *JOURNAL DE MONTRÉAL* (I,IV), Union des écrivaines et écrivains Québécois, 1030 rue Cherrier, #510, Montréal, Québec H2L 1H9 Canada. (514)526-6653. "To support the development of the literature of Québec and assure the public recognition of its authors." Annual award for novels and story collections. Award: $1,500 (Canadian). Judges: 5 judges, nominated by the *Journal de Montréal*. Guidelines for SASE. Deadline: June 10. For books published within the 12 months preceding June 1. Writers must have published at least 3 books including the one already submitted and must submit 6 copies of the work to be considered. Write for rules and entry form (in French).

GREAT LAKES COLLEGES ASSOCIATION NEW WRITERS AWARDS (III), Great Lakes Colleges Association, Albion College, Albion MI 49224. Contact: Paul Loakides, Director. Annual award. "To recognize new young writers, promote and encourage interest in good literature." For books published "during the year preceding each year's February 28 deadline for entry, or the following spring." Award judged by critics and writers in residence at Great Lakes Colleges Association colleges and universities. Entry form or rules for SASE. Award: "Invited tour of up to 12 Great Lakes Colleges (usually 7 or 8) with honoraria and expenses paid. Entries in fiction (there is also a poetry section) must be first novels or first volumes of short stories already published, and must be submitted (four copies) *by publishers only*—but this may include privately published books."

GREAT PLAINS STORYTELLING & POETRY READING CONTEST (I,II), Box 438, Walnut IA 51577. (712)784-3001. Contact: Robert Everhart, director. Estab. 1976. Annual award. "To provide an outlet for writers to present not only their works, but also to provide a large audience for their presentation *live* by the writer." Attendance at the event, which takes place annually in Avoca, Iowa, is *required*. Previously published or unpublished submissions. Award: 1st prize $75; 2nd prize $50; 3rd prize $25; 4th prize $15; and 5th prize $10. Entry deadline: day of contest, which takes place over Labor Day Weekend. Entry fee: $5. Entry forms or rules for SASE.

THE GREENSBORO REVIEW LITERARY AWARDS (I), Dept. of English, UNC-Greensboro, Greensboro NC 27412. (919)334-5459. Editor: Jim Clark. Annual award. Unpublished submissions. Award: $250. Deadline: September 15. Contest rules for SASE.

GUARDIAN CHILDREN'S FICTION AWARD (III, IV), The Guardian, 119 Farringdon Rd., London EC1R 3ER England. Contact: Stephanie Nettell, children's books editor. "To recognize an outstanding work of children's fiction—and gain publicity for the field of children's books." Annual competition for fiction. Award: £500. Competition receives approx. 100 submissions. Judges: four eminent children's writers plus children's books editor of the *Guardian*. Deadline: December 31. "British or Commonwealth authors only; published in UK; no picture books. Awarded every March for book published in previous year."

‡GULFSHORE LIFE FICTION WRITER'S CONTEST, Suite 800, 2975 S. Horseshoe Dr., Naples FL 33942. (813)643-3933. Annual competition for short stories. First prize: $200 plus publication in April edition of *Gulfshore Life*; second prize: $100. Judges: the editors of *Gulfshore Life*. Guidelines for SASE. Deadline Dec. 29. Unpublished submissions. Open to all writers. Story must be set in southwest Florida (Sarasota to the Florida Keys). Length: 3,000 words maximum.

HACKNEY LITERARY AWARDS (I), Birmingham Southern College, Box A-3, Birmingham AL 35254. (205)226-4921. Contact: Special Events Office. Annual award for previously unpublished short stories, poetry and novel. Deadline for submitting a novel—must be postmarked on or before November 24.

Deadline for submitting short stories or poetry—must be postmarked on or before December 31. No entry fee. Rules/entry form for SASE.

HAMBIDGE CENTER FOR CREATIVE ARTS AND SCIENCES (I), Box 339, Rabun Gap GA 30568. (404)746-5718. Executive Director: J. Barber. Two-week to two-month residencies are offered to writers, visual artists, composers, historians, humanists and scientists. "Center is open from May through October. It is located on 600 acres of quiet woods and streams in north Georgia. Private cottages as well as communal housing available for those who qualify. For application forms send SASE to Executive Director. Once application forms are returned to the Center it takes about 2 months processing time. No deadline."

DRUE HEINZ LITERATURE PRIZE (II), University of Pittsburgh Press, 127 North Bellefield Ave., Pittsburgh PA 15260. (412)624-4110. Annual award. "To support the writer of short fiction at a time when the economics of commercial publishing make it more and more difficult for the serious literary artist working in the short story and novella to find publication." Manuscripts must be unpublished in book form. The award is open to writers who have published a book-length collection of fiction or a minimum of three short stories or novellas in commercial magazines or literary journals of national distribution. Award: $7,500 and publication by the University of Pittsburgh Press. Request complete rules of the competition before submitting a manuscript. Entry deadline: August 31. Submissions will be received only during the months of July and August.

HEMINGWAY DAYS SHORT STORY COMPETITION (I), Hemingway Days Festival, Box 4045, Key West FL 33041. (305)294-4440. "To honor Nobel laureate Ernest Hemingway, who was often pursued during his lifetime by young writers hoping to learn the secrets of his success." Annual competition for short stories. Award: $1000—1st; $500—2nd; $500—3rd. Competition receives approx. 600 submissions. Judges: panel lead by Lorian Hemingway, granddaughter of Ernest Hemingway and writer based out of Seattle, WA. Entry fee $10/story. Guidelines for SASE. Deadline: July 8, 1991. Unpublished submissions. "Open to anyone so long as the work is unpublished. No longer than 2,500 words."

ERNEST HEMINGWAY FOUNDATION AWARD (II), PEN American Center, 568 Broadway, New York NY 10012. Contact: John Morrone, coordinator of programs. Annual award. "To give beginning writers recognition and encouragement and to stimulate interest in first novels among publishers and readers." Novels must have been published during calendar year under consideration. Deadline: December 31. Entry form or rules for SASE. Award: $7,500. "The Ernest Hemingway Foundation Award is given to an American author of the best first-published book length work of fiction published by an established publishing house in the US each calendar year."

THE O. HENRY AWARDS (III), Doubleday, 666 Fifth Avenue, New York NY 10103. Contact: Heidi Von Schreiner, senior editor. Annual award. To honor the memory of O. Henry with a sampling of outstanding short stories and to make these stories better known to the public. These awards are published by Doubleday in hardcover and by Anchor Books in paperback every spring. Previously published submissions. "All selections are made by the editor of the volume, William Abrahams. No stories may be submitted."

‡GEORGETTE HEYER HISTORICAL NOVEL PRIZE (I), The Bodley Head and Transworld Publishers, (Corgi Books). The Bodley Head, Random Century House, 20 Vauxhall Bridge Rd., London SW1V 2SA England. Jill Black, editor. For an outstanding full-length historical novel, which should be set pre-1939 and have a minimum length of 40,000 words. Annual award for novels. Award: £5,000 and hardback and paperback publication plus royalties. Judges are appointed by The Bodley Head and Corgi Books. Entry forms for SASE.

HIGHLIGHTS FOR CHILDREN **(I,IV)**, 803 Church St., Honesdale PA 18431. Editor: Kent L. Brown, Jr. "To honor quality stories (previously unpublished) for young readers." Stories: up to 600 words for beginning readers (to age 8) and 900 words for more advanced readers (ages 9 to 12). No minimum word length. No entry form necessary. To be submitted between January 1 and February 28 to "Fiction Contest" at address above. Three $1,000 awards. No violence, crime or derogatory humor. Non-winning entries returned in June if SASE is included with manuscript. "This year's category is mystery stories." Write for information.

HILAI RESIDENCIES, The Israeli Center for the Creative Arts, P.O. Box 53007, Tel-Aviv 61530 Israel. (03)478704. Two centers for residencies which are international and interdisciplinary—in the Galilee and in the Negev. "To provide tranquil atmosphere for visiting writers and the opportunity to interact with the local community in cultural activities. Provides publicity, organizes and coordinates the meetings and activities with the community. Possibility for a writer and translator to work together to translate a work from Hebrew into English and vice versa." Each residency lasts from two weeks to two months. Award: residency at Hilai Center for up to two months; studio apartment with work and living space. Judges: admission committee. Guidelines for SASE. Contact: Hilai, Admission Committee, P.O. Box 119 Ma'alot-Tarshiha, 24953 Israel. Deadline ongoing.

THE ALFRED HODDER FELLOWSHIP (II), The Council of the Humanities, Princeton University, 122 E. Pyne, Princeton NJ 08544. "This fellowship is awarded for the pursuit of independent work in the humanities. The recipient is usually a writer or scholar in the early stages of his or her career, a person "with more than ordinary learning" and with "much more than ordinary intellectual and literary gifts." Traditionally, the Hodder Fellow has been a humanist outside of academia. Candidates for the Ph.D. are not eligible. Annual competition for short stories, novels, story collections and translations. Award: $37,000. The Hodder fellow spends an academic year in residence at Princeton working independently. Judges; Princeton Committee on Humanistic studies. Guidelines for SASE. Deadline November 15, 1990. "Applicants must submit a résumé, a sample of previous work (10 page maximum, not returnable), and a project proposal of 2 to 3 pages. Letters of recommendation are not required."

‡THEODORE CHRISTIAN HOEPFNER AWARD (I), *Southern Humanities Review*, 9088 Haley Center, Auburn University AL 36849. Contact: Thomas L. Wright or Dan R. Latimer, co-editors. Annual award. "To award the authors of the best essay, the best short story and the best poem published in *SHR* each year." Unpublished submissions to the magazine only. Award judged by editorial staff. Award: $100 for the best short story. Only published work in the current volume.(4 issues) will be judged.

HONOLULU MAGAZINE/PARKER PEN COMPANY FICTION CONTEST (I,IV), *Honolulu* Magazine, 36 Merchant St., Honolulu HI 96813. (808)524-7400. Ed Cassidy, editor. "We do not accept fiction except during our annual contest, at which time we welcome it." Annual award for short stories. Award: $1,000 and publication in the March issue of *Honolulu* Magazine. Competition receives approximately 400 submissions. Judges: panel of well-known Hawaii-based writers. Rules for SASE. Deadline: December 9. "Stories must have a Hawaii theme, setting and/or characters. Author should enclose name and address in separate small envelope. Do not put name on story."

‡HOUGHTON MIFFLIN LITERARY FELLOWSHIP (I,IV), Houghton Mifflin Co., 2 Park St., Boston MA 02108. Contact: Fellowship Coordinator. Fellowship "to reward American authors for a first adult trade book (fiction or nonfiction) of outstanding literary merit. Only books accepted for publication by Houghton Mifflin Co. are eligible." For novels and story collections, granted when an acquisition is adjusted suitable. Award: $10,000. Judges: Houghton Mifflin editors. Guidelines for SASE. Deadline: none. Previously unpublished submissions. Open to U.S. authors only. "We ask that applicants follow our standard submission procedure. Please provide:(1) a letter describing the project and your background;(2) a sample chapter;(3) a stamped, self-addressed envelope for the return of the material if necessary." (Note: Poetry and drama are not eligible and will not be read. Queries regarding juvenile submissions should be directed to the Children's Department; textbook proposals, to the School or College Division.)

L. RON HUBBARD'S WRITERS OF THE FUTURE CONTEST (I,IV), P.O. Box 1630, Los Angeles CA 90078. Estab. 1984. Quarterly. "To find, reward and publicize new speculative fiction writers, so that they may more easily attain to professional writing careers." Competition open to new and amateur writers of short stories or novelettes of science fiction or fantasy. Unpublished submissions. Awards: 1st prize, $1,000; 2nd prize, $750; 3rd prize, $500. Annual grand prize $4,000. SASE for contest rules. Contest deadline: September 30, 1991.

THE 'HUGO' AWARD (Science Fiction Achievement Award) (III, IV), The World Science Fiction Convention, c/o Howard DeVore, 4705 Weddel St., Dearborn Heights MI 48125. Temporary; address changes each year. "To recognize the best writing in various categories related to science fiction and fantasy." The award is voted on by ballot by the members of the World Science Fiction Convention from previously published material of professional publications. Writers may not nominate their own work. Award: Metal spaceship 15 inches high. "Winning the award almost always results in reprints of the original material and increased payment. Winning a 'Hugo' in the novel category frequently results in additional payment of $10,000-20,000 from future publishers."

HUTTON FICTION CONTEST, Hutton Publications, Box 1870, Hayden ID 83835. (208)772-6184. "To encourage beginning short story writers." Granted five times per year; more often if interest warrants for short stories. Award: cash up to $50; publication of winners. Competition receives no more than 50 submissions. Judges: Linda Hutton, editor of Hutton Publications. Entry fee $1-3. (December contest has no fee.) Guidelines and entry form for #10 SASE. Deadline: First of March, June, August, November and December. Unpublished submissions.

ILLINOIS STATE UNIVERSITY NATIONAL FICTION COMPETITION (I), Illinois State University/Fiction Collective, English Dept., Illinois State University, Normal IL 61761. Curtis White, series editor. Annual award for novels, novellas and story collections. Award: publication. Competition receives approximately 150 submissions each year. Judges different each year. Entry fee $10. Entry forms or rules for SASE.

INTERNATIONAL JANUSZ KORCZAK LITERARY COMPETITION (II, IV), Joseph H. and Belle R. Braun Center for Holocaust Studies Anti-Defamation League of B'nai B'rith, 823 United Nations Plaza, New York NY 10017. (212)490-2525. Contact: Dr. Dennis B. Klein, director. For published novels, novellas, translations, short story collections. "Books for or about children which best reflect the humanitarianism and leadership of Janusz Korczak, a Jewish and Polish physician, educator and author." Deadline: inquire.

INTERNATIONAL READING ASSOCIATION CHILDREN'S BOOK AWARDS (II), Sponsored by IRA/ Institute for Reading Research, 800 Barksdale Rd., Box 8139, Newark DE 19714-8139. (302)731-1600. Annual award. To encourage an author who shows unusual promise in the field of children's books. Two awards will be given for a first or second book in two categories: one for literature for older children, 10-16 years old; one for literature for younger children, 4-10 years old. Submissions must have been published during the calendar year prior to the year in which the award is given. Award: $1,000 stipend. Entry deadline: December 1. No entry fee. Contest/award rules and awards flyer available from IRA.

IOWA ARTS COUNCIL LITERARY AWARDS (I, IV), Iowa Arts Council, State Capitol Complex, Des Moines IA 50319. (515)281-4451. Director of Partnership Programs: Julie Bailey. Estab. 1984. "To give exposure to Iowa's fine poets and fiction writers." Unpublished submissions by legal residents of Iowa only. Award: 1st prize, $1,000; 2nd prize, $500. Deadline: January 15. Contest rules for SASE.

‡**IOWA SCHOOL OF LETTERS AWARD FOR SHORT FICTION, THE JOHN SIMMONS SHORT FICTION AWARD (I),** Iowa Writers' Workshop, 436 English-Philosophy Building, The University of Iowa, Iowa City IA 52242. Annual award for short story collections. To encourage writers of short fiction. Entries must be at least 150 pages, typewritten, and submitted between Aug. 1 and Sept. 30. Stamped, self-addressed return packaging must accompany the manuscript. Rules for SASE. Two awards: $1,000 each, plus publication of winning collections by University of Iowa Press the following fall. Iowa Writer's Workshop does initial screening of entries; finalists (about 6) sent to outside judge for final selection. "A different well known writer is chosen each year as judge. Any writer who has not previously published a volume of prose fiction is eligible to enter the competition for these prizes. Revised manuscripts which have been previously entered may be resubmitted."

‡*IOWA WOMAN* **CONTEST, INTERNATIONAL WRITING CONTEST,** P.O. Box 2938, Waterloo IA 50704. Annual award for short fiction, poetry and essays. Award: first place of $150 in each category. Judges: anonymous, women writers who have published work in the category. Entry fee: (Subscriber)— $3 for one story, essay or up to 3 poems. (Non-subscriber)—$7 for one story, essay, or up to 3 poems. Guidelines available for SASE. Deadline is December 31, 1990. Previously unpublished submissions. Limited to women writers, with a 5,000 words limit on fiction and essays. "Submit typed or computer printed manuscripts with a cover sheet listing category, title, name, address and phone number. A single cover sheet per category is sufficient. Identify actual entry by title only. Do not identify author on the manuscript. Manuscripts cannot be returned; do not send SASE for return."

JAB PUBLISHING FICTION CONTEST, Box 4086, Cary NC 27519-4086. (919)460-6668. Competition held yearly. First place: $100; second place: $75; third place: $50. Competition receives 100-200 short story submissions. Judges: editor/co-publisher. Entry fee: $5/story. Guidelines for SASE. Deadline Dec. 31. Previously unpublished submissions only. Length: 4,000 words maximum. Writers may submit their own fiction.

JOSEPH HENRY JACKSON AWARD (I, IV), The San Francisco Foundation, 685 Market St., Suite 910, San Francisco CA 94105. Contact: Awards Program Coordinator. Annual competition "to award the author of an unpublished work-in-progress of fiction (novel or short stories), nonfiction or poetry." Unpublished submissions only. Applicant must be resident of northern California or Nevada for 3 consecutive years immediately prior to the deadline date. Age of applicant must be 20 through 35. Deadline: January 15. Entry form and rules available after November 1 for SASE. Award: $2,000 and award certificate.

JAPANOPHILE **SHORT STORY CONTEST (I, IV)**, *Japanophile*, Box 223, Okemos MI 48864. (517)349-1795. Contact: Earl R. Snodgrass, editor. Estab. 1972. Annual award. "To encourage quality writing on Japan-America understanding." Prefers unpublished submissions. Stories should involve Japanese and non-Japanese characters. Award: $100 plus possible publication. Deadline: December 31. Entry fee: $5. Send $4 for sample copy of magazine. Contest rules for SASE.

JAPAN-UNITED STATES FRIENDSHIP COMMISSION PRIZE FOR THE TRANSLATION OF JAPANESE LITERATURE (I, IV), The Donald Keene Center of Japanese Culture, Columbia University, 407 Kent Hall, Columbia University, New York NY 10027. (212)854-5036. Contact: Victoria Lyon-Bestor. "To encourage fine translations of Japanese literature and to award and encourage young translators to develop that craft." Annual competition for translations only. Award: $2,000. Competition receives approx. 15 submissions. Judges: a jury of writers, literary agents, critics and scholar/translators. Guidelines for SASE. Previously published or unpublished submissions. "Translators must be American citizens."

‡JESSE JONES AWARD FOR FICTION (BOOK) (I,IV), The Texas Institute of Letters, P.O. Box 9032, Wichita Falls TX 76308. (817)692-6611 ext.211. Awards Coordinator: James Hoggard. Award "to honor the writer of the best novel or collection of short fiction published during the calendar year before the award is given." Annual award for novels, translations and story collections. Award: $6,000. Competition receives approx. 30-40 entries per year. Judges: panel selected by TIL Council. Guidelines for SASE. Deadline: January 4. Previously published fiction, which must have appeared in print between January 1, 1991 and December 31, 1991. "Award available to writers who, at some time, have lived in Texas at least two years consecutively or whose work has a significant Texas theme."

THE JANET HEIDINGER KAFKA PRIZE (II,IV), University of Rochester, Susan B. Anthony Center and English Dept., 538 Lattimore Hall, Rochester NY 14627. (716)275-8318. Award for fiction by an American woman. Annual competition for short stories and novels. Award: $1,000. Judges: Kafka Committee. Guidelines for SASE. Deadline: December 31. Recently published submissions. American women only.

KANSAS QUARTERLY/**KANSAS ARTS COMMISSION AWARDS (I)**, *Kansas Quarterly*, 122 Denison Hall, Dept. of English, Kansas State University, Manhattan KS 66506-0703. Contact: Editors. Annual awards. "To reward and recognize the best fiction published in *Kansas Quarterly* during the year from authors anywhere in the US or abroad. Anyone who submits unpublished material which is then accepted for publication becomes eligible for the awards." No deadline; material simply may be submitted for consideration at any time. To submit fiction for consideration, send it in with SASE. Award: Recognition and monetary sums of $250, $200, $100, $50. "Ours are not 'contests'; they are monetary awards and recognition given by persons of national literary stature." Fiction judges recently have included David Bradley, James B. Hall, Gordon Weaver and Mary Morris.

ROBERT F. KENNEDY BOOK AWARDS (II, IV), 1031 31st St., NW, Washington DC 20007. (202)333-1880. Contact: Mr. Frederick Grossberg. Endowed by Arthur Schlesinger, Jr., from proceeds of his biography, *Robert Kennedy and His Times*. Annual award. "To award the author of a book which most faithfully and forcefully reflects Robert Kennedy's purposes." For books published during the calendar year. Award: $2,500 cash prize awarded in the spring. Looking for "a work of literary merit in fact or fiction that shows compassion for the poor or powerless or those suffering from injustice." Deadline: January 4.

KENTUCKY ARTS COUNCIL, AL SMITH ARTISTS FELLOWSHIPS (I, IV), Berry Hill, Frankfort KY 40601. (502)564-3757. "To encourage and support the professional development of Kentucky artists." Writing fellowships offered every other year in fiction, poetry, playwriting. Award: $5,000. Competition received approximately "110 submissions in 1990 in all writing categories." Judges are out-of-state panelists (writers, editors, playwrights, etc.) of distinction. Open only to Kentucky residents (minimum one year). Entry forms or rules available "even without SASE." Next appropriate deadline for writers is July 1.

‡JACK KEROUAC LITERARY PRIZE, Lowell Historic Preservation Commission, 222 Merrimack St., Lowell MA 01852. (508)458-7653. Award "to promote cultural activities in Lowell, a pivotal event in annual 'Lowell Celebrates Kerouac' festival." Annual award for short stories, poems and essays. Award: $500 and plaque. Competition receives approximately 200 submissions. Judges: local authors. Guidelines available for SASE. Deadline is May 1. Previously unpublished submissions. Limited to: fiction—30 pages or less; nonfiction—30 pages or less; poetry—15 pages or less.

AGA KHAN PRIZE (I), Address entry to Aga Khan Prize, *Paris Review*, 541 E. 72nd St., New York NY 10021. Annual award. For the best short story received during the preceding year. Unpublished submissions with SASE. One submission per envelope. Work should be submitted between May 1-June 1. Award judged by the editors. Award: $1,000 and publication. Unpublished short story (1,000-10,000 words). Translations acceptable.

‡KILLER FROG CONTEST (I, II), Scavenger's Newsletter, 519 Ellinwood, Osage City KS 66523. (913)528-3538. Contact: Janet Fox. Competition "to see who can write the funniest/most overdone horror story, or poem, or produce the most outrageous artwork on a horror theme." Annual award for short stories, poems and art. Award: $20 for each of 4 categories and "coveted froggie statuette." Judge: editor of Scavenger: Janet Fox. Entry fee $2 for initial entry, $1 for each thereafter. Guidelines available for SASE. Deadline is April 1 to July 31 (postmarked). Published or previously unpublished submissions. Limited to horror/humor. Length: up to 1,500 words.

***LANGUAGE BRIDGES* CONTEST**, Box 850792, Richardson TX 75086-0792. (214)530-2782. Competition "to disseminate Polish literature and writing in the US." Quarterly competition for short stories, novels, story collections and translations. Award: $25 and a certificate and an announcement in *Language Bridges Quarterly*. Competition receives 10 (all works published in the issue) submissions. Judges: the readers send their votes. Guidelines for SASE. No deadline—ongoing. Previously unpublished submissions. "All works in every issue of *Language Bridges Quarterly* are subject to selection for the award by the readers. But applies *only* to previously unpublished works."

‡LATIN AMERICAN WRITERS INSTITUTE SHORT STORY CONTEST (I,IV), The Latin American Writers Institute, Division of Humanities NAC6293, The City College of New York, New York NY 10031. (212)650-7382/7383. Competition "to promote the work of Latin American and Hispanic writers who write in Spanish and live in New York, Connecticut or New Jersey." Awarded every three years for short stories. Award: $300 first prize; $200 second; $100 third. Competition receives approximately 35 submissions. Judges: three prominent Latin American writers and/or critics. Guidelines available for SASE. "Next contest in 1992." Previously unpublished fiction. Open to writers from New York, New Jersey and Connecticut. Length: less than 20 pages.

LAWRENCE FELLOWSHIP (I), University of New Mexico, Dept. of English Language and Literature, Albuquerque NM 87131. (505)277-6347. Contact: Prof. Gene Frumkin, chairperson. Annual award. Fellowship for writers of unpublished or previously published fiction, poetry, drama. (June-August residency at D.H. Lawrence Ranch, $2,100 stipend). Deadline: January 31. $10 processing fee. SASE for return of materials. Write for rules, application form.

STEPHEN LEACOCK MEDAL FOR HUMOUR (II,IV), Stephen Leacock Associates, Box 854, Orillia, Ontario L3V 6K8 Canada. (705)325-6546. Award "to encourage writing of humour by Canadians." Annual competition for short stories, novels and story collections: Receives 25-40 entries. Award: Stephen Leacock (silver) medal for humour and J.P. Wiser cash award $3,500 (Canadian). Five judges selected across Canada. Entry fee $25 (Canadian). Guidelines for SASE. Deadline December 30.

Submissions should have been published in the previous year. Open to Canadian citizens or landed immigrants only.

‡THE LEADING EDGE MAGAZINE FICTION CONTEST, 3163 JKHB, Provo UT 84602. (801)378-2456. Competition "to generate interest in the magazine; to increase the quality of submissions to the magazine; to reward excellence in story-telling among new and upcoming authors." Annual award for short stories. Award: $100 first prize, $60 second prize, $40 third prize. Competition receives approximately 500 submissions each year. Judges: editorial staff of the Leading Edge. Guidelines available for SASE. Deadline is December 15, 1991. Previously unpublished fiction. "The contest is open to all writers of science fiction and fantasy, whether they be pro, semi-pro, or first timer. Word length should be under 20,000 words unless story absolutely requires more—whatever it takes to tell the story right. No novels." Writers may submit their own fiction. "The Leading Edge is a semi-professional magazine of science fiction and fantasy that caters to the new and upcoming author, artist and poet. It is our goal to be the magazine that the professionals look to to find the next generation of writers."

LETRAS DE ORO SPANISH LITERARY PRIZES (I, IV), The Graduate School of International Studies, University of Miami, Box 248123, Coral Gables FL 33124. (305)284-3266. "The *Letras de Oro* Spanish Literary Prizes were created in order to reward creative excellence in the Spanish language and to promote Spanish literary production in this country. *Letras de Oro* also serves to recognize the importance of Hispanic culture in the United States." Annual award for novels, story collections, drama, essays and poetry. The prizes are $2,500 cash. Deadline: October 12.

LITERATURE AND BELIEF WRITING CONTEST (I,IV), Center for the Study of Christian Values in Literature, 3134 JKHB, Brigham Young University, Provo UT 84602. (801)378-2304. Director: Jay Fox. Award to "encourage affirmative literature in the Judeo-Christian tradition." Annual competition for short stories. Award $150 (1st place); $100 (2nd place). Competition receives 200-300 entries. Judges: BYU faculty. Guidelines for SASE. Deadline: May 15. Unpublished submissions, up to 30 pages. All winning entries are considered for publication in the annual journal *Literature and Belief*.

LOFT-MCKNIGHT WRITERS AWARDS (I,IV), The Loft, 2301 E. Franklin Ave., Minneapolis MN 55406. (612)341-0431. Susan Broadhead, executive director. "To give Minnesota writers of demonstrated ability an opportunity to work for a concentrated period of time on their writing." Annual award for creative prose. $7,500 per award; four awards. Competition receives approximately 275 submissions/year. Judges are out-of-state judges. Entry forms or rules for SASE. "Applicants must be Minnesota residents and must send for and observe guidelines."

LOS ANGELES TIMES BOOK PRIZES (III), *L.A. Times, Book Review*, Times Mirror Square, Los Angeles CA 90053. Contact: Jack Miles, book editor. Annual award. "To recognize finest books published each year." For books published between August 1 and July 31. Award: $1,000 cash prize plus a handmade, leather-bound version of the winning book. Entry is by nomination; *Times* reviewers nominate. No entry fee.

LOUISIANA LITERARY AWARD (II, IV), Louisiana Library Association (LLA), Box 3058, Baton Rouge LA 70821. (504)342-4928. Contact: Chair, Louisiana Literary Award Committee. Annual award. "To promote interest in books related to Louisiana and to encourage their production." Submissions must have been published during the calendar year prior to presentation of the award. (The award is presented in March or April.) Award: Bronze medallion and $250. Entry deadline: publication by December 31. No entry fee. "All Louisiana-related books which committee members can locate are considered, whether submitted or not. Interested parties may correspond with the committee chair at the address above. All books considered *must* be on subject(s) related to Louisiana or be written by a Louisiana author. Each year, there may be a fiction *and/or* nonfiction award. Most often, however, there is only one award recipient, and he or she is the author of a work of nonfiction."

MACDOWELL COLONY RESIDENCIES (I), The MacDowell Colony, 100 High St., Peterborough NH 03458. (603)924-3886 or (212)966-4860. Admissions Coordinator: Shirley Bewley. "Private studios plus board and room at the MacDowell Colony are provided to competitively selected writers, composers, visual artists and filmmakers, allowing up to 8 weeks of uninterrupted time for creative projects." Colony operates year-round for writers of short stories, novels and story collections, as well as poets and playwrights. Colony helps support costs of residencies for accepted applicants. Colony receives

INTRODUCING . . . . . . THE NEW . . . . . .

STORY

The magazine that first published J.D. Salinger, Tennessee Williams, William Saroyan, Carson McCullers, Erskine Caldwell......is back!

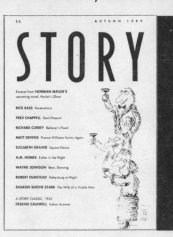

Share in the discovery of great short fiction by today's unknown writing talents with the revival of STORY magazine. The legendary magazine that once helped struggling writers like Truman Capote and Norman Mailer break into print has returned with captivating stories by today's most promising new authors.

As a subscriber to STORY, you'll count yourself among the first to enjoy brilliant short fiction by new writers destined for literary acclaim. Every issue features an assemblage of gripping, spellbinding, humorous, tantalizing tales you'll cherish for years to come. Become a part of literary history, and accept our Introductory Subscription Invitation today!

STORY INTRODUCTORY SUBSCRIPTION INVITATION

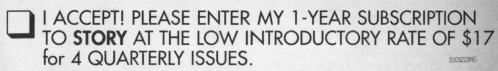

ONE OF THE MOST TALKED-ABOUT REVIVALS IN MAGAZINE PUBLISHING.....

STORY

The first issues of STORY were cranked out on an old mimeograph machine in 1931 by two American newspaper correspondents in Vienna. Editors Whit Burnett and his wife Martha Foley had no money—just a vision to create a forum for outstanding short stories, regardless of their commercial appeal. The magazine was an instant literary success, and was hailed "the most distinguished short story magazine in the world."

Now STORY returns with the same commitment to publishing the best new fiction written today. It will also provide a workshop for new material from today's more established writers, as well as feature at least one piece reprinted from an original issue of STORY. Printed on heavy premium paper, each issue is meant to be read and cherished for years to come. (Those first mimeographed copies of STORY are collectors' items today!)

Share in the rebirth of a literary legend. Become a subscriber to STORY today!

BUSINESS REPLY MAIL

FIRST CLASS MAIL   PERMIT NO. 125   MT. MORRIS, IL

POSTAGE WILL BE PAID BY ADDRESSEE

STORY

PO BOX 396
MOUNT MORRIS IL 61054-7910

No Postage
Necessary
If Mailed
In The
United States

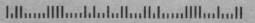

approx. 5-6 applicants for each residency. Judges: panels of professionals in each creative field. Entry fee: $20. Guidelines for SASE. Deadline: April 15 for September-December; September 15 for January-April; January 15 for May-August. Submissions may be either unpublished or previously published. "Open to all professionally qualified writers. See application instructions for length of work sample. Accepted applicants are asked to contribute as much as they are able toward residency costs, but no applicant is rejected for financial reasons. Residencies average 6 weeks. Applications from fiction writers are pooled for review with writers of poetry, plays and nonfiction. Over 200 artists are accepted each year, of whom approx. 90 are writers. The Colony has 31 studios open in summer, 24 in spring and fall, 19 in winter."

THE JOHN H. MCGINNIS MEMORIAL AWARD (I), *Southwest Review*, 6410 Airline Road, Southern Methodist University, Dallas TX 75275. Contact: Elizabeth Mills, associate editor. Annual award. (fiction and nonfiction). Stories or essays must have been published in the *Southwest Review* prior to the announcement of the award. Award: $1,000. Pieces are not submitted directly for the award, but simply for publication in the magazine.

THE ENID MCLEOD LITERARY PRIZE (II, IV), Franco-British Society, Room 636, Linen Hall, 162-168 Regent St., London W1R 5TB England. Executive Secretary: Mrs. Marian Clarke. "To recognize the work of the author published in the UK which in the opinion of the judges has contributed most to Franco-British understanding." Annual competition for short stories, novels and story collections. Award: copy of Enid McLeod's memoirs. Competition receives approx. 6-12 submissions. Judges: Lord Lansdowne (FBS President), Martyn Goff and Terence Kilmartin. Guidelines for SASE. Deadline: December 31. Previously published submissions. "Writers, or their publishers, may submit 4 copies to the London Office. No nominations are necessary."

MADEMOISELLE FICTION WRITERS CONTEST (I), *Mademoiselle Magazine*, 350 Madison Ave., New York NY 10017. Send entries to Fiction Writers Contest. Each entry must be accompanied by the entry coupon or a 3x5 card with name, age, home address. Award: 1st prize: $2,500 and publication in *Mademoiselle*; 2nd prize: $500 cash. Open to all short story writers, male and female, age 18-30, who have not published fiction in a magazine with a circulation over 25,000. Entries will not be returned.

MAGGIE AWARD (I, IV), Georgia Romance Writers, Inc., Box 142, Acworth GA 30101. (404)974-6678. "To encourage and instruct unpublished writers in the romance genre." Annual competition for novels. Award: silver pendant (1st place), certificates (2nd-4th). 4 categories—short contemporary romance; long contemporary romance, historical, mainstream. Judges: published romance authors. Entry fee $25. Guidelines for SASE. Deadline: on or about June 1, 1991 (deadline not yet final). Unpublished submissions. Writers must be members of Romance Writers of America. Entries consist of 3 chapters plus synopsis. "We welcome a variety of fiction types in our mainstream category, since romance has achieved such a broad and sophisticated scope."

‡MANITOBA ARTS COUNCIL SUPPORT TO INDIVIDUAL ARTISTS (II,IV), Manitoba Arts Council, 525-93 Lombard Ave., Winnipeg, Manitoba R3B 3B1 Canada. (204)945-2237. Grants "to encourage and support Manitoba writers." Two annual awards: Writer's Grants "A" ($7,500 Canadian) for practicing writers who have had previous work published or produced and are recognized as professionals in their field. Writer's Grants "B" ($4,000 Canadian) for emerging writers who have had some previous work published or produced. Guidelines for SASE. Deadlines: May 1, September 1 and February 1. Open only to Manitoba writers.

WALTER RUMSEY MARVIN GRANT (I, IV), Ohioana Library Association, 1105 State Department Building, 65 S. Front St., Columbus OH 43215. (614)466-3831. Contact: Linda Hengst. "To encourage young writers (under age 30)." Biannual competition for short stories. Award: $1,000. Guidelines for SASE. Deadline January 31, 1992. Unpublished submissions. Open to unpublished authors born in Ohio or who have lived in Ohio for a minimum of five years. Must be under 30 years of age. Up to six pieces of prose may be submitted.

MARYLAND STATE ARTS COUNCIL FELLOWSHIP (I, IV), 15 West Mulberry St., Baltimore MD 21201. (301)333-8232. Fellowships given to reward artistic excellence and to promote career development. Annual grant for writers of stories, novels, novellas and story collections. Award: $6,000. Competition receives 200 applications for fellowships; 120 for work-in-progress grants annually. Judge: out-of-state selection panel. Further information available for SASE. Applicants must be Maryland residents over 18. Students are not eligible. Writers are required to submit a body of work demonstrating artistic accomplishment and skill.

MASSACHUSETTS ARTISTS FELLOWSHIP PROGRAM (I, IV), Artists Foundation—Artists Fellowship Program, 8 Park Plaza, Boston MA 02116. (617)227-ARTS. Contact: Kathleen Brandt, Fellowship Director. Biannual award. "To encourage artists who live and work in Massachusetts." Categories include playwriting, fiction, nonfiction, poetry. Massachusetts residents 18 years of age or older are eligible to apply as long as resident is not enrolled as a student in an undergraduate program or a graduate program in their field. "Specific instructions are detailed in the entry form which is available upon request." Previous publication is not necessary, but any published work must be submitted in typewritten form. Entry forms available upon request. Award: $10,000 for fellows; $1,000 for finalists. "Looking for artistic excellence. Work is judged anonymously by a panel of professional working writers and experts in the field who live outside Massachusetts." Next deadline is December 1991.

THE VICKY METCALF BODY OF WORK AWARD (II, IV), Canadian Authors Association, #104 Avenue Rd., Toronto, Ontario M5R 2G3 Canada. (416)926-8084. Contact: Executive Director. Annual award. "The prize is given solely to stimulate writing for children, written by Canadians, for a *number* of strictly children's books—fiction, nonfiction or even picture books. No set formula." To be considered, a writer must have published at least 4 books. Award: $2,000 for a body of work inspirational to Canadian youth. Entry deadline: December 31. No entry fee. "Nominations may be made by any individual or association by letter *in triplicate* listing the published works of the nominee and providing biographical information. The books are usually considered in regard to their inspirational value for children. Entry forms or rules for SASE."

VICKY METCALF SHORT STORY AWARD (II, IV), Canadian Authors Association, Suite 104, 121 Avenue Rd., Toronto, Ontario M5R 2G3 Canada. (416)926-8084. Contact: Executive Director. "To encourage Canadian writing for children (open only to Canadian citizens)." Submissions must have been published during previous calendar year in Canadian children's magazine or anthology. Award: $1,000 (Canadian). Matching award of $1,000 to editor of winning story if published in a Canadian journal or anthology. Entry deadline: December 31. No entry fee. Entry forms or rules for SASE. Looking for "stories with originality, literary quality for ages 7-17."

MIDLAND AUTHORS' AWARD (II, IV), Society of Midland Authors, 220 N. Harvey, Oak Park IL 60302. (708)383-7568. Attn: Jim Bowman. "To honor outstanding works published during the previous year by Midwestern authors." Biannual Summit award for previously published novels or story collections. Award: $400, and plaque. Competition receives approximately 30-50 submissions. Judges are usually members of Society of Midland Authors. Entry forms or rules for SASE. Authors must be residents of IL, IN, IA, KS, MI, MN, MO, NE, OH, SD or WI. Send for entry form.

MILITARY LIFESTYLE **SHORT STORY CONTEST,** 1732 Wisconsin Ave. NW, Washington DC 20007. (202)944-4000. "To publish the work of previously unpublished writers; to encourage those of our readers who are military to send us short stories about a lifestyle they know very well." Annual competition for short stories. First Prize: $500; Second Prize: $250; Third Prize: $100. "Also, all three are published in the July/August issue of *Military Lifestyle*." Competition receives 700 submissions. Judges: editorial staff of *Military Lifestyle*. Guidelines for SASE. Deadline: March 31. Previously unpublished submissions. "Theme of contest changes annually. Contact magazine for details and contest rules."

MILKWEED EDITIONS NATIONAL FICTION PRIZE (I), Milkweed Editions, Box 3226, Minneapolis MN 55403. (612)332-3192. Editor: Emilie Buchwald. Annual award for three short stories, a short novel or a novella. Award: publication, $3,000 advance against royalties. Entry fee $5. Guidelines for SASE. Deadline: September 10. "Please look at *Ganado Red*, by Susan Lowell, our first winning NFP book, or at *Backbone*, by Carol Bly, or *The Country I Come From*, by Maura Stanton—this is the caliber of fiction we are searching for. Catalog available for 3 first class stamps, if people need a sense of our list."

MILLAY COLONY FOR THE ARTS (I), Steepletop P.O. Box 3, Austerlitz, NY 12017-0003. (518)392-3103. Executive Director: Ann-Ellen Lesser. "The Millay Colony gives residencies to writers, composers and visual artists. Residencies are for one month and usually cover a period from the first to the

Close-up
Kathleen Brandt
Massachusetts Artists Fellowship Program

It has not been a good year for many state art programs. Forced with economic slowdown or worse, several states have slashed all but the most necessary programs. Budgets for arts programs have been trimmed and, in some cases, cut drastically.

Kathleen Brandt heads up the Massachusetts Artist Foundation, the group that administers a number of arts programs funded by the state arts council. She directs the only program in the state to fund individual artists and writers.

Both her staff and her budget have been cut. "My program has been cut 62 percent in the past two years. But we're not the only program—there have been major cuts across the state."

Despite the cuts, however, Brandt is somewhat optimistic. "The fact that it was not cut entirely shows a commitment to the program."

The program for writers, she says, has been very successful. In the literature program last year six writers were awarded fellowships of $10,000 each. Nine or 10 others received finalist awards of $1,000 each.

The purpose of the program is to help eliminate some of the financial burden on writers in the state. While for many writers the money is important, the recognition is also valued. The recognition comes from a panel of peers, professional writers from outside the state.

Brandt attributes much of the program's success to its openness. There are few restrictions, except for a requirement that the individual must be a Massachusetts resident six months prior to the deadline and be a resident at the time of the award. Writers may submit published work or works-in-progress and writers of all levels of experience are encouraged to submit.

Writers are asked to submit up to 30 pages of either short stories or a novel excerpt. Published material is acceptable as long as it has been published in the last five years and is presented typed as any manuscript.

A panel reviews the submissions and makes the final (and only) decision, explains Brandt. Panels include writers from all genres—nonfiction, poetry, playwriting and fiction. The fellowship committee also tries to choose panelists from varying social backgrounds.

The process, says Brandt, helps to ensure a fair selection. Each panelist receives one-fifth of the submission. From these each selects a "top ten." Then panelists read all of the 50 manuscripts nominated and from these select finalists and fellowship recipients.

The best way to make sure the program remains intact, says Brandt, is to demonstrate that it fills a need in the community. Participation, therefore, is the key. Take advantage of these opportunities for both funding and recognition, she says. In turn, your involvement may help guarantee that public support for individual artists will continue.

—Robin Gee

28th of each month." Judges: professional artists on admissions committee. Deadline: February 1 (for June-September residencies); May 1 (for October-January residencies); September 1 (for February-May residencies).

THE MILNER AWARD (III), Friends of the Atlanta-Fulton Public Library, 1 Margaret Mitchell Square, Atlanta GA 30303. (404)730-1710. Executive Director: Rennie Davant. Award to a living American author of children's books. Annual competition for novels and story collections. Award: $1,000 honorarium and specially commissioned glass sculpture by Hans Frabel. Judges: children of Atlanta vote during children's book week. Prior winners not eligible. Children vote at will—no list from which to select. Winner must be able to appear personally in Atlanta to receive the award at a formal program.

MIND BOOK OF THE YEAR—THE ALLEN LAND AWARD (II, IV), MIND, 22 Harley St., London W1N 2ED England. Contact: Ms. A. Brackx. "To award a prize to the work of fiction or nonfiction which outstandingly furthers public understanding of the causes, experience or treatment of mental illness." Annual competition for novels and works of nonfiction. Award: £1,000. Competition receives approx. 50-100 submissions. Judges: a panel of judges drawn from MIND's Council of Management. Deadline: December. Previously published submissions. Author's nomination is accepted.

MINNESOTA STATE ARTS BOARD/ARTISTS ASSISTANCE FELLOWSHIP (I, IV), 432 Summit Ave., St. Paul MN 55407. (612)297-2603. Artist Assistance Program Associate: Karen Mueller. "To provide support and recognition to Minnesota's outstanding literary artists." Annual award for fiction, creative nonfiction writers and poets. Award: $6,000. Competition receives approx. 150 submissions/year. Deadline: January. Previously published or unpublished submissions. Send request or call the above number for application guidelines. *Minnesota residents only.*

MINNESOTA VOICES PROJECT (IV), New Rivers Press, 420 N. 5th St., #910, Minneapolis MN 55401. Contact: C.W. Truesdale, editor/publisher. Annual award. "To foster and encourage new and emerging regional writers of short fiction, novellas, personal essays and poetry." Requires bibliography of previous publications and residency statement. Awards: $500 to each author published in the series plus "a generous royalty agreement if book goes into second printing." Send request with SASE for guidelines in December. Entry deadline: April 1. No entry fee. Send two copies of each manuscript of 125-200 pages; restricted to writers from Minnesota, Wisconsin, North and South Dakota and Iowa.

MISSISSIPPI ARTS COMMISSION ARTIST FELLOWSHIP GRANT (I, IV), Suite 207, 239 N. Lamar St., Jackson MS 39201. (601)359-6030. Contact: Program Administrator. "To encourage and support the creation of new artwork, and to recognize the contribution that artists of exceptional talent make to the vitality of our environment. Awards are based upon the quality of previously created work." Award granted every 3 years on a rotating basis. Award for writers of short stories, novels and story collections. Grant: up to $5,000. Competition receives 10+ submissions/year. Judging: peer panel. Guidelines for SASE. "The next available grants for creative writing, including fiction, nonfiction and poetry will be in 1993-94." Applicants should request guidelines. Application deadline: March 1. Applicants must be Mississippi residents. "The Mississippi Arts Commission's Art in Education Program contains a creative writing component. For more information, contact the AIE Coordinator. The Mississippi Touring Arts program offers writers the opportunity to give readings and workshops and have the Arts Commission pay part of the fee." For more information, contact the Program Administrator.

MISSOURI WRITERS' BIENNAL (I, IV), Suite 105, Missouri Arts Council, 111 N. 7th St., St. Louis MO 63101-2188. (314)444-6845. Award to support and promote Missouri writers. Every 2 years competition for short stories, essays and poetry. Award: $5,000 each to 5 writers. Competition receives approx. 400 submissions. Judges: panel of national judges. Guidelines for SASE. Deadline "approx." July 30. Unpublished submissions. "Writers must have lived in Missouri for at least 2 years immediately preceding submission. Writers *must* request complete written guidelines."

Market categories: (I) Unpublished entries; (II) Published entries nominated by the author; (III) Published entries, nominated by the editor, publisher or nominating body; (IV) Specialized entries.

‡**MONEY FOR WOMEN**, Money for Woman/Barbara Deming Memorial Fund, Inc., Box 40-1043, Brooklyn NY 11240-1043. "Small grants to individual feminists in the arts." Biannual competition. Award: $200-1,000. Competition receives approx. 130 submissions. Judges: Board of Directors. Guidelines for SASE. Deadline Feb. 1, July 1. Limited to U.S. and Canadian citizens. Word length: 6-25 pages. May submit own fiction. "Only for feminists in the arts. Subject matter must be feminist-related."

MONTANA ARTS COUNCIL FIRST BOOK AWARD (IV), New York Block, 48 North Last Chance Gulch, Helena MT 59620. (406)444-6430. Director of Artists Services: Julia Smith. Biannual award for publication of a book of poetry or fiction—the best work in Montana. Submissions may be short stories, novellas, story collections or poetry. Award: publication. Competition receives about 35 submissions/year. Judges are professional writers. Entry forms or rules for SASE. Deadline: April 20 (1992). Restricted to residents of Montana; not open to degree-seeking students.

MONTANA ARTS COUNCIL INDIVIDUAL ARTIST FELLOWSHIP (IV), New York Block, 48 North Last Chance Gulch, Helena MT 59620. (406)444-6430. Director of Artists Services: Julia Smith. Biannual award of $2,000. Competition receives about 35 submissions/year. Panelists are professional writers. Contest requirements avialable for SASE. Deadline May 1, 1991. Restricted to residents of Montana; not open to degree-seeking students.

MYTHOPOEIC FANTASY AWARD (III), The Mythopoeic Society, Box 6707, Altadena CA 91001. Chair, awards committee: Christine Lowentrout. Annual award for novels. "A statue of a lion is given to the author; magazines and publishers are notified, plus we announce the award in our publications." Judges: members of the Mythopoeic Society who volunteer for the selection committee. Guidelines for SASE. Deadline: February. Fantasy novels only. "Books are nominated by Society members. If an author has published his/her work during the previous year, and is a member of the Society, he/she can nominate his/her own work."

NATIONAL BOOK AWARDS, INC. (III), 260 5th Ave., Rm. 904, New York NY 10001. (212)685-0261. Executive Director: Neil Baldwin. Assistant: Lucy Logsdon. Annual award to honor distinguished literary achievement in two categories, nonfiction and fiction. Books published Nov. 1 through Oct. 31 are eligible. Deadline is July 15. Awards judged by panels of critics and writers. November ceremony. Award: $10,000 award to each winner. $1,000 to four runners-up in each category. Selections are submitted by publishers only, or may be called in by judges. A $100 fee is required for entry. Read *Publishers Weekly* for additional information.

NATIONAL BOOK COUNCIL/BANJO AWARDS (III, IV), National Book Council, Suite 3, 21 Drummond Place, Carlton, Victoria 3053 Australia. "For a book of highest literary merit which makes an outstanding contribution to Australian literature." Annual competition for creative writing. Award: $10,000 each for a work of fiction and nonfiction. Competition receives approx. 100-140 submissions. Judges: 4 judges chosen by the National Book Council. Entry fee $30. Guidelines for SASE. Deadline: mid-April. Previously published submissions. For works "written by Australian citizens and published in Australia during the qualifying period." Books must be nominated by the publisher.

NATIONAL ENDOWMENT FOR THE ARTS FELLOWSHIP (I), Nancy Hanks Center, 1100 Pennsylvania Ave. N.W., Washington DC 20506. (202)682-5732. Program Specialist, Literature Program: Christine Prickett. For fiction contact Susan Campbell. "The mission of the NEA is to foster the excellence, diversity and vitality of the arts in the United States, and to help broaden the availability and appreciation of such excellence, diversity and vitality." The purpose of the fellowship is to enable creative writers "to set aside time for writing, research or travel and generally to advance their careers." Annual award: $20,000. All mss are judged anonymously. Entry forms and guidelines available upon request. Competition open to fiction writers who have published a novel or novella, a collection of stories or at least 5 stories in magazines since 1980. Deadline: March 5.

 The double dagger before a listing indicates that the listing is new in this edition. New markets are often the most receptive to freelance contributions.

NATIONAL FOUNDATION FOR ADVANCEMENT IN THE ARTS, ARTS RECOGNITION AND TALENT SEARCH (ARTS) (I, IV), 3915 Biscayne Blvd., Miami FL 33137. (305)573-0490. President: Dr. Grant Beglarian. "To encourage 17- and 18-year-old writers and put them in touch with institutions which offer scholarships." Annual award for short stories, novels, "fiction, essay, poetry, scriptwriting." Award: $3,000, $1,500, $500, and $100 awards. Judges: nationally selected panel. Entry fee $25 by May 15; $35 until October 1. Guidelines for SASE. 17- and 18-year-old writers only.

NATIONAL NOVELLA AWARD (I), Arts and Humanities Council of Tulsa, 2210 S. Main St., Tulsa OK 74114. (918)584-3333. Literary Arts Program Coordinator: Elizabeth Thompson. "To provide fiction writers with an opportunity to be awarded for work in a somewhat unrecognized field and to provide a publishing opportunity for a genre that is becoming increasingly important to contemporary literature." Biennial (every other year) award for novellas. Award: $2,500, publication in quality trade paperback and royalties. Publication by local trade publisher, Council Oak Books. Judge: nationally recognized fiction writer. Entry fee $10. Guidelines for #10 SASE. Deadline: September 1. Previously unpublished submissions. Word length: 18,000 to 40,000 words.

NATIONAL WRITERS CLUB ANNUAL NOVEL WRITING CONTEST (I), National Writers Club, Suite 620, 1450 S. Havana, Aurora CO 80012. (303)751-7844. Contact: James L. Young, director. Annual award to "recognize and reward outstanding ability and to increase the opportunity for publication." Unpublished submissions, any gentre or category. Entry deadline: April 29. Opens December 1. Length: 20,000-100,000 words. Award judged by successful writers. Contest/award rules and entry forms available with SASE. Charges $25 entry fee. Award: $500 first prize, $300 second prize; $100 third prize.

NATIONAL WRITERS CLUB ANNUAL SHORT STORY CONTEST (I), National Writers Club, 1450 S. Havana, Aurora CO 80012. (303)751-7844. Contact: James L. Young, director. Annual award. To encourage and recognize writing by freelancers in the short story field. Opens March 1, 1990. All entries must be postmarked by July 1, 1990. Length: No more than 5,000 words. Unpublished submissions. Write for entry form and rule sheet. Charges $10 entry fee. Award: $200 first prize; $100 second prize; $50 third prize.

THE NATIONAL WRITTEN & ILLUSTRATED BY ... AWARDS CONTEST FOR STUDENTS (I, IV), Landmark Editions, Inc., Box 4469, Kansas City MO 64127. (816)241-4919. Contact: Nan Thatch. "Contest initiated to encourage students to write and illustrate original books and to inspire them to become published authors and illustrators." Annual competition. "Each student whose book is selected for publication will be offered a complete publishing contract. To insure that students benefit from the proceeds, royalties from the sale of their books will be placed in an individual trust fund, set up for each student by his or her parents or legal guardians, at a bank of their choice. Funds may be withdrawn when a student becomes of age, or withdrawn earlier (either in whole or in part) for educational purposes or in case of proof of specific needs due to unusual hardship. Reports of book sales and royalties will be sent to the student and the parents or guardians annually." Winners also receive an all-expense-paid trip to Kansas City to oversee final reproduction phases of their books. Books by students may be entered in one of three age categories: A—6 to 9 years old; B—10 to 13 years old; C—14 to 19 years old. Each book submitted must be both written and illustrated by the same student. Any books that are written by one student and illustrated by another will be automatically disqualified." Book entries must be submitted by a teacher or librarian. Deadline: May 1 of each year. For a free copy of the rules and guidelines, send a #10 SASE envelope to the above address.

NEBULA® AWARDS (III, IV), Science Fiction Writers of America, Inc., Box 4335, Spartanburg SC 23305-4335. Contact: Peter Dennis Pautz, executive secretary. Annual awards for previously published short stories, novels, novellas, novelettes. SF/fantasy only. "No submissions; nominees upon recommendation of members only." Deadline: December 31. "Works are nominated throughout the year by active members of the SFWA."

NEGATIVE CAPABILITY **SHORT FICTION COMPETITION (I)**, *Negative Capability*, 62 Ridgelawn Dr. E., Mobile AL 36608. (205)343-6163. Contact: Sue Walker. "To promote and publish excellent fiction and to promote the ideals of human rights and dignity." Annual award for short stories. Award: $1,000 best story award. Judge: Leon Driskell. Reading fee $10, "includes copy of journal publishing the award." Guidelines for SASE. Deadline: December 15. Length: 1,500-4,500 words. "Award honors an outstanding author each year, and the award is given his or her name."

THE NENE AWARD (II), School Library Services, Dept. of Education, 641 18th Ave., Honolulu HI 96816. Contact: Linda Reser, chairperson (chairperson changes annually). Annual award. "To help the children of Hawaii become acquainted with the best contemporary writers of fiction for children; to become aware of the qualities that make a good book; to choose the best rather than the mediocre; and to honor an author whose book has been enjoyed by the children of Hawaii." Award: Koa plaque. Judged by the children of Hawaii. No entry fee.

NEUSTADT INTERNATIONAL PRIZE FOR LITERATURE (III), *World Literature Today*, 110 Monnet Hall, University of Oklahoma, Norman OK 73019. Contact: Dr. Ivar Ivask, director. Biennial award. To recognize distinguished and continuing achievement in fiction, poetry or drama. Awards: $25,000, an eagle feather cast in silver, an award certificate and a special issue of *WLT*. "We are looking for outstanding accomplishment in world literature. The Neustadt Prize is not open to application. Nominations are made only by members of the international jury, which changes for each award. Jury meetings are held in February of even-numbered years. Unsolicited manuscripts, whether published or unpublished, cannot be considered."

THE NEW ERA WRITING, ART, PHOTOGRAPHY AND MUSIC CONTEST (I, IV), *New Era Magazine* (LDS Church), 50 E. North Temple, Salt Lake City UT 84150. (801)240-2951. "To encourage young Mormon writers and artists." Annual competition for short stories. Award: Scholarship to Brigham Young University or Ricks College or cash awards. Competition receives approx. 300 submissions. Judges: *New Era* editors. Guidelines for SASE. Deadline: January 3. Unpublished submissions. Contest open only to members of the Church of Jesus Christ of Latter-Day Saints.

NEW HAMPSHIRE STATE COUNCIL ON THE ARTS INDIVIDUAL ARTIST FELLOWSHIP (I, IV), 40 N. Main St., Concord NH 03301-4974. (603)271-2789. Contact: assistant director, Rebecca Lawrence. Fellowship "for career development to professional artists who are legal/permanent residents of the state of New Hampshire." Annual award: up to $2,000. Competition receives 150 entries for 10 awards in all disciplines. Judges: panels of in-state and out-of-state experts (music, theater, dance, literature, film, etc.). Guidelines for SASE. Deadline May 1. Submissions may be either previously published or unpublished. Applicants must be over 18 years of age, not enrolled as full-time students, permanent, legal residents of New Hampshire. Application form required.

NEW JERSEY AUTHOR AWARDS (II, IV), NJIT Alumni Association, New Jersey Institute of Technology, 323 King Blvd., Newark NJ 07102. (201)889-7336. Contact: Dr. Herman A. Estrin, professor of English-Emeritus. Annual award. "To recognize New Jersey writers." Previously published submissions. Award: Citation inscribed with the author's name and the title of his work. Author is an invited guest at the author's luncheon, and a photograph of author receiving the citation is sent to the author's hometown newspaper. Entry deadline: February. No entry fee. Entry forms or rules for SASE.

NEW JERSEY STATE COUNCIL ON THE ARTS PROSE FELLOWSHIP (I, IV), 4 North Broad St., Trenton NJ 08625. (609)292-6130. Annual award for writers of short stories, novels, story collections. Award: maximum is $15,000; other awards are $8,000 and $5,000. Judges: a peer panel. Guidelines for SASE. Deadline February. For either previously published or unpublished submissions. "Previously published work must be submitted as a manuscript." Applicants must be New Jersey residents. Submit several copies of short fiction, short stories or prose not exceeding 15 pages and no less than 10 pages. For novels in progress, a synopsis and first chapter should be submitted.

NEW LETTERS LITERARY AWARD (I), *New Letters*, UMKC 5100 Rockhill, Kansas City MO 64110. (816)276-1168. Adm. Assistant: Glenda McCrary. Award to "discover and reward good writing." Annual competition for short stories. Award: $750. Competition receives 350 entries/year. Entry Fee $10. Guidelines for SASE. Deadline May 15. Submissions must be unpublished. Length requirement: 5,000 words or less.

‡NEW WRITING AWARD, *New Writing Magazine*, 165 Calvin Ct. S., Tonawanda NY 14150. "To seek out and reward *new* writing. We want to see originality in form and content. Awarding those who find the current literary scene a hard market because it is too confining." Annual competition for stories.

Read the Business of Fiction section to learn the correct way to prepare and submit a manuscript.

Award: Varies, but should be $1,000 or more. Additional awards for finalists. Possible publication. Judges: Panel of editors. Entry fee $10, $5 for additional. Guidelines for SASE. Unpublished submissions.

NEW YORK FOUNDATION FOR-THE-ARTS FELLOWSHIP (I, IV), New York Foundation for the Arts, #600, 5 Beekman St., New York NY 10038. (212)233-3900. Contact: D. Green. Annual competition for short stories and novels. Award: $7,000. Competition receives approx. 450 submissions. Judges: fiction writers. Call for guidelines (send SASE). Deadline: September 4. Previously published or unpublished submissions. "Applicants must have lived in New York state at least 2 years immediately prior to application deadline."

NEW YORK STATE EDITH WHARTON CITATION OF MERIT (State Author) (III, IV), NYS Writers Institute, Humanities 355, University at Albany/SUNY, Albany NY 12222. (518)442-5620. Contact: Thomas Smith, associate director. Awarded biennially to honor a New York State fiction writer for a lifetime of works of distinction. Fiction writers living in New York State are nominated by an advisory panel. Recipients receive an honorarium of $10,000 and must give two public readings a year, for two years.

JOHN NEWBERY AWARD (III), American Library Association (ALA) Awards and Citations Program, Association for Library Service to Children, 50 E. Huron St., Chicago IL 60611. Annual award. Entry restricted to US citizens-residents. Only books for children published during the preceding year are eligible. Award: Medal.

CHARLES H. AND N. MILDRED NILON EXCELLENCE IN MINORITY FICTION AWARD (I, IV), University of Colorado at Boulder and the Fiction Collective Two, English Dept. Publications Center, University of Colorado, Campus Box 494, Boulder CO 80309-0494. "We recognize excellence in new minority fiction." Annual competition for novels; story collections and novellas. Award: $1,000 cash prize; joint publications of mss by CU-Boulder and Fiction Collective Two. Competition receives approx. 50 submissions. Judges: well-known minority writers. Guidelines for SASE. Deadline: November 30. Unpublished submissions. "Only specific recognized U.S. racial and ethnic minorities are eligible. The definitions are in the submission guidelines. The ms must be book length (a minimum of 250 pages)."

NORTH CAROLINA ARTS COUNCIL FELLOWSHIP (IV), 221 E. Lane St., Raleigh NC 27611. (919)733-2111. Contact: Literature Director: Deborah McGill. Competition "to recognize and encourage North Carolina's finest creative writers." Annual award: $8,000. Competition receives approximately 200 submissions. Judges are a panel of editors and published writers from outside the state. Writers must be over 18 years old, not currently enrolled in degree-granting program on undergraduate or graduate level, and must have been a resident of North Carolina for 1 full year prior to applying. Writers may apply in either poetry or fiction. Deadline: February 1.

‡NORTH CAROLINA ARTS COUNCIL RESIDENCIES (IV), 221 E. Lane St., Raleigh NC 27611. (919)733-2111. Literature Director: Deborah McGill. "To recognize and encourage North Carolina's finest creative writers." Annual competition. "We offer a three-month residency at the LaNapoule Foundation in southern France and a two-to-three month residency at Headlands Center in Northern California." Judges: Editors and published writers from outside the state. Deadline for France, February 1; for California, mid-August. Writers must be over 18 years old, not currently enrolled in degree granting program on undergraduate or graduate level and must have been a resident of North Carolina for 1 full year prior to applying.

‡NORTH CAROLINA ARTS COUNCIL SCHOLARSHIPS (IV), 221 E. Lane St., Raleigh NC 27611. (919)733-2111. Literature Director: Deborah McGill. To provide writers of fiction with opportunities for research or enrichment. Available on a six-weeks basis throughout the year. Award up to $500. "To be eligible writers must have lived in the state for at least a year and must have published at least five works of fiction in two or more literary journals, a volume of short fiction or collection of short stories, a novel or a novella. Self-published or vanity press published work is ineligible."

NORTHWOOD INSTITUTE ALDEN B. DOW CREATIVITY CENTER FELLOWSHIP (I), Midland MI 48640-2398. (517)832-4478. Carol B. Coppage, director. Annual fellowship: 10-week residency, including travel, housing and food, small stipend and project costs. Competition receives approx. 100 submissions each year from all fields (arts, humanities and sciences). Four awards annually. Judges: board, staff and evaluators. Write or call for entry forms. Deadline: December 31.

NUTS TO US!, New Hope Press, 304 S. Denton St., Dothan AL 36301. (205)792-2331. Annual short story competition. Award: $100 (first place) and royalties on books sold. Receives 120 submissions. Judges: Professional writers and poets. $12 entry fee for first submission; $5 for each additional submission. Deadline: July 31, 1990. Previously unpublished fiction. Length: 3,000 words. Must mention peanuts in some way. "Contest open to both new and experienced writers. All manuscripts must be accompanied by SASE."

THE FLANNERY O'CONNOR AWARD FOR SHORT FICTION (I), The University of Georgia Press, Terrell Hall, Athens GA 30602. (404)542-2830. Contact: award coordinator. Annual award, "to recognize outstanding collections of short fiction. Published and unpublished authors are welcome." Award: $1,000 and publication by the University of Georgia Press. Deadline: June 1-July 31. "Manuscripts cannot be accepted at any other time." Entry fee: $10. Contest rules for SASE. Ms will not be returned.

FRANK O'CONNOR FICTION AWARD (I), *Descant*, Dept. of English, Texas Christian University, Fort Worth TX 76129. (817)921-7240. Contact: Betsy Colquitt, editor. Estab. 1979 with *Descant*; earlier awarded through *Quartet*. Annual award. To honor achievement in short fiction. Submissions must be published in the magazine during its current volume. Award: $300 prize. No entry fee. "About 12 to 15 stories are published annually in *Descant*. Winning story is selected from this group."

‡THE SCOTT O'DELL AWARD FOR HISTORICAL FICTION (II, IV), Scott O'Dell (personal donation), c/o Houghton Mifflin, 2 Park St., Boston MA 02108. (617)725-5000. Contact: Mrs. Zena Sutherland, professor, 1100 E. 57th St., Chicago IL 60637. Annual award. "To encourage the writing of good historical fiction about the New World (Canada, South and Central America, and the United States) for children and young people." For books published during the year preceding the year in which the award is given. To be written in English by a U.S. citizen and published in the U.S. Award: $5,000. Entry deadline: December 31. Entry forms or rules for SASE. Looking for "accuracy in historical details, and all the standard literary criteria for excellence: style, setting, characterization, etc."

OHIO ARTS COUNCIL AID TO INDIVIDUAL ARTISTS FELLOWSHIP (I, IV), 727 E. Main St., Columbus OH 43205-1796. (614)466-2613. Susan Dickson, coordinator. "To recognize and support Ohio's outstanding creative artists." Annual grant/fellowship. Award: cash awards of $5,000 or $10,000. Competition receives approx. 200-300 submissions/year. Judges: panel of experts. Contact the OAC office for guidelines. Writers must be residents of Ohio and must not be students.

‡OHIOANA AWARD FOR CHILDREN'S LITERATURE, ALICE WOOD MEMORIAL, Ohioana Library Association, 1105 Ohio Department Bldg., 65 S. Front St., Columbus OH 43215. (614)466-3831. Competition "to honor an individual whose body of work has made, and continues to make, a significant contribution to literature for children or young adults." Annual award for body of work. Award: $1,000. Guidelines available for SASE. Deadline is December 31 prior to year award is given. Published fiction. "Open to authors born in Ohio or who have lived in Ohio for a minimum of five years."

OHIOANA BOOK AWARD (II, IV), Ohioana Library Association, 1105 Ohio Departments Bldg., 65 S. Front St., Columbus OH 43266-0334. Contact: Linda R. Hengst, director. Annual award (only if the judges believe a book of sufficiently high quality has been submitted). To bring recognition to outstanding books by Ohioans or about Ohio. Criteria: Book written or edited by a native Ohioan or resident of the state for at least 5 years; Two copies of the book MUST be received by the Ohioana Library by December 31 prior to the year the Award is given; Literary quality of the book must be outstanding. Each spring a jury considers all books received since the previous jury. Award judged by a jury, selected from librarians, book reviewers, writers, and other knowledgeable people. No entry forms are needed, but they are available. "We will be glad to answer letters asking specific questions." Award: Certificate and glass sculpture.

THE OKANAGAN SHORT FICTION AWARD (I,IV), *Canadian Author & Bookman*, #104, 121 Avenue Rd., Toronto, Ontario M5R 2G3 Canada. Contact: Geoff Hancock, fiction editor. Award offered 4 times a year. To present good fiction "in which the writing surpasses all else" to an appreciative literary readership, and in turn help Canadian writers retain an interest in good fiction. Unpublished submissions. Entries are invited in each issue of our quarterly *CA&B*. Sample copy $5; guidelines printed in the magazine. "Our award regulations stipulate that writers must be Canadian, stories must not have been previously published, and be under 3,000 words. Mss should be typed double-spaced on 8½×11 bond. SASE with Canadian postage or mss will not be returned. Award: $125 to each author whose story is accepted for publication. Looking for superior writing ability, stories with good plot, movement, dialogue and characterization. A selection of winning stories has been anthologized as *Pure Fiction: The Okanagan Award Winners*, and is essential reading for prospective contributors."

OMMATION PRESS BOOK AWARD (I, II), Ommation Press 5548 N. Sawyer, Chicago IL 60625. (312)539-5745. Annual competition for short stories, novels, story collections and poetry. Award: book publication, $50 and 50 copies of book. Competition receives approx. 60 submissions. Judge: Effie Mihopoulos (editor). Entry fee $12 includes copy of form award book winner. Guidelines for SASE. Deadline: December 30. Either previously published or unpublished submissions. Submit no more than 50 pages.

OPEN VOICE AWARDS (I, II), Westside YMCA—Writer's Voice, 5 W. 63rd St., New York NY 10023. (212)787-6557. Biannual (twice a year) competition for short stories. Award: $50 honorarium and featured reading. Semi-annual deadlines: January 1 and June 1. "Submit 10 double-spaced pages in a single genre. Nonmembers enclose $5 entry fee."

OREGON INDIVIDUAL ARTIST FELLOWSHIP (I,IV), Oregon Arts Commission, 835 Summer St. NE, Salem OR 97301. (503)387-3625. Artist Services Coordinator: Nancy Lindburg. "Award enables professional artists to undertake projects to assist their professional development." Biennial competition for short stories, novels, poetry and story collections. Award: $3,000 and $10,000. (Please note: 8 $3,000 awards and 2 $10,000 Master Fellowship Awards are spread over 5 disciplines—literature, music/opera, media arts, dance and theatre awarded in even-numbered years.) Competition receives approx. 50 entries/year. Judges: professional advisors from outside the state. Guidelines and application available for SASE. Deadline: September 1. Competition limited to Oregon residents.

THE OTHER SIDE SHORT FICTION AWARD (I), 1225 Dandridge St., Fredericksburg VA 22401. (703)371-7416. Mark Olson, editor. "To recognize excellence in short fiction writing among people who have a commitment to Christian faith and an active concern for peace and justice." Annual award for short stories. Award: $250 plus a year's subscription to *The Other Side*. Winning story is published in *The Other Side*. Competition receives approx. 70 submissions/year. Judges are the magazine's editors. Entry forms for SASE. Deadline: May 1.

DOBIE PAISANO FELLOWSHIPS (IV), Texas Institute of Letters/University of Texas at Austin, Office of Grad. Studies, University of Texas at Austin, Austin TX 78712. (512)471-7213. Annual fellowships for creative writing (includes fellowships/short stories, novels and story collections. Award: 6 months residence at ranch; $7,200 stipend. Competition receives approx. 100 submissions. Judges: faculty of University of Texas and members of Texas Institute of Letters. Entry fee: $5. Guidelines on request. "Open to writers with a Texas connection—native Texans, people living in Texas now or writers whose work focuses on Texas and Southwest." Deadline: January 21.

‡**PALENVILLE INTERARTS COLONY (I,II)**, P.O. Box 59, Palenville NY 12463. (518)678-3332 (June-September); (212)254-4614 (October-May.) Contact: Admissions Director. Artists residencies for professional and emerging literary artists. Annual awards for short stories, novels, story collections and translations. Competition receives approx. 24 applications. Judges: panel of 8 distinguished artists. Application fee: $10. Guidelines for SASE. Deadline: April 1. Either previously published or unpublished submissions.

‡**PALM COUNCIL PHILIPPINE AMERICAN SHORT STORY CONTEST**, Philippine Arts, Letters and Media Council, Washington DC, 10829 Split Oak Lane, Burke VA 22015. (703)503-9012. Competition "to encourage and recognize fiction writing talent in the Philippine American community and promote the writing of Philippine American fiction." Annual award for short stories (when money is available). Award: $300 for first prize, $200 for second, $100 for third. Competition receives approximately 25 submissions. Judges: screening committee selects 10 best entries which are sent to a panel of judges (3) who select the winners. Guidelines available for SASE. Deadline is May 3. Previously unpublished fiction. Limited to Philippine American themes by writers of Philippine American ancestry. No more than 5,000 words.

PAPER BAG Short, Shorts (I), Paper Bag Press, P.O. Box 268805, Chicago IL 60626-8805. (312)285-7972. Award "to find quality short, short works of fiction (under 500 words)." Annual award for short stories (under 500 words). Award: publication and $25. Competition receives approx. 50 submissions. Judges: editors of *Paper Bag*. Guidelines for SASE. Deadline is ongoing. Unpublished submissions. Nothing over 500 words.

JUDITH SIEGEL PEARSON AWARD (I), Wayne State University, Detroit MI 48202. Contact: Chair, English Dept. Competition "to honor writing about women." Annual award. Short stories up to 20 pages considered every third year (poetry and drama/nonfiction in alternate years). Plays and nonfictional prose in 1989. Award: up to $400. Competition receives up to 100 submissions/year. Submissions are internally screened; then a noted writer does final reading. Entry forms for SASE.

WILLIAM PEDEN PRIZE IN FICTION (I), *The Missouri Review*, 1507 Hillcrest Hall University of Missouri, Columbia MO 65211. (314)882-4474. Contact: Speer Morgan, Gregg Michalson, editors. Annual award. "To honor the best short story published in *The Missouri Review* each year." Submissions are to be previously published in the volume year for which the prize is awarded. Award: $1,000 cash. No deadline entry or entry fee. No rules; all fiction published in *MR* is automatically entered.

PEN/BOOK-OF-THE-MONTH CLUB TRANSLATION PRIZE (II, IV), PEN American Center, 568 Broadway, New York NY 10012. (212)334-1660. Awards Coordinator: John Morrone. Award "to recognize the art of the literary translator." Annual competition for translations. Award: $3,000. Deadline: December 31. Previously published submissions within the calendar year. "Translators may be of any nationality, but book must have been published in the U.S. and must be a book-length literary translation." Writer must be nominated by publishers, agents or translators. No application form. Send three copies. "Early submissions are strongly recommended."

THE PEN/FAULKNER AWARD (II, III), c/o The Folger Shakespeare Library, 201 E. Capitol St. SE, Washington DC 20003. (202)544-4600. Attention: Janice Delaney, PEN/Faulkner executive director. Annual award. "To award the most distinguished book-length work of fiction published by an American writer." Published submissions only. Writers and publishers submit four copies of eligible titles published the current year. Deadline for submissions, December 31. No juvenile. Authors must be American citizens. Book award judged by three writers chosen by the Trustees of the Award. Award: $7,500 for winner; $2,500 for nominees.

PENNSYLVANIA COUNCIL ON THE ARTS, FELLOWSHIP PROGRAM (I, IV), 216 Finance Bldg. Harrisburg PA 17120. (717)787-6883. Peter M. Carnahan, Literature Program director. Annual awards to provide fellowships for creative writers. Award: up to $5,000. Competition receives approx. 175 submissions for 12 to 15 awards/year. Six judges: three poetry, three fiction, different each year. Guidelines mailed upon request. Deadline: October 1. Applicants must be Pennsylvania residents.

JAMES D. PHELAN AWARD (I,IV), The San Francisco Foundation, 685 Market St., Suite 910, San Francisco CA 94105. Contact: Awards Program Coordinator. Annual award "to author of an unpublished work-in-progress of fiction, (novel or short story), nonfictional prose, poetry or drama." Unpublished submissions. Applicant must have been born in the state of California and be 20-35 years old. Entry deadline: January 15. Rules and entry forms available after November 1 for SASE. Award: $2,000 and a certificate.

PLAYBOY COLLEGE FICTION CONTEST (I), *Playboy* Magazine, 919 North Michigan Ave., Chicago IL 60611. (312)751-8000. Fiction Editor: Alice K. Turner. Award "to foster young writing talent." Annual competition for short stories. Award: $3,000 plus publication in the magazine. Judges: staff. Guidelines available for SASE. Deadline: January 1. Submissions should be unpublished. No age limit; college affiliation required. Stories should be 25 pages or fewer. "Manuscripts are not returned. Results of the contest will be sent via SASE."

EDGAR ALLAN POE AWARDS (II), Mystery Writers of America, Inc., 236 West 27th St., New York NY 10001. Annual award. To enhance the prestige of the mystery. For manuscripts published during the calendar year. Entry deadline: December 1. Contact above address for specifics. Award: Ceramic bust of Poe. Awards for best mystery novel, best first novel by an American author, best softcover original novel, best short story, best critical/biographical work, best fact crime, best young adult, best juvenile novel, best screenplay, best television feature and best episode in a series.

THE RENATO POGGIOLI TRANSLATION AWARD (I, IV), PEN American Center, 568 Broadway, New York NY 10012. (212)334-1660. Awards Coordinator: John Morrone. Award "to encourage beginning and promising translator who is working on a book-length translation from Italian to English." Annual competition for translations. Award: $3,000. Competition receives approx. 30-50 submissions. Judges: A panel of three translators. Guidelines for SASE. Deadline: January 15. Unpublished submissions. "Letters of application should be accompanied by a curriculum vitae, including Italian studies and samples of translation-in-progress."

KATHERINE ANNE PORTER PRIZE FOR FICTION (I), *Nimrod*, Arts and Humanities Council of Tulsa, 2210 S. Main St., Tulsa OK 74114. (918)584-3333. Editor: Francine Ringold. "To award promising young writers and to increase the quality of manuscripts submitted to *Nimrod*." Annual award for short stories. Award: $1,000 first prize; $500 second prize. Receives approx. 650 entries/year. Judge varies each year. Past judges have been Rosellen Brown, Alison Lurie and Gordon Lish, George Garrett, Toby Olson and John Leonard. Entry fee: $10. Guidelines for #10 SASE. Deadline for submissions: April 1. Previously unpublished manuscripts. Word length: 7,500 words maximum. "Must be typed, double spaced. Our contest is judged anonymously, so we ask that writers take their names off of their manuscripts (need 2 copies total). Include a cover sheet containing your name, full address, phone and the title of your work. Finally, include a SASE for notification of the results."

***PRAIRIE SCHOONER* THE LAWRENCE FOUNDATION AWARD (I)**, 201 Andrews Hall, University of Nebraska, Lincoln NE 68588-0334. (402)472-1812. Contact: Hilda Raz, editor. Annual award. "The award is given to the author of the best short story published in *Prairie Schooner* during the preceding year." Award $500. "Only short fiction published in *Prairie Schooner* is eligible for consideration."

***PRISM INTERNATIONAL* SHORT FICTION CONTEST (I)**, *Prism International*, Dept. of Creative Writing, University of British Columbia, E455-1866 Main Mall, Vancouver, British Columbia V6T 1W5 Canada. (604)228-2514. Contact: Publicity Manager. Award: $2,000 first prize and 5 $200 consolation prizes. Entry fee $10 plus $5 reading fee for each story. SASE for rules/entry forms.

LE PRIX MOLSON DE L'ACADÉMIE CANADIENNE-FRANÇAISE (II,IV), Union des écrivainesi québécois, 1030 rue Cherrier #510, Montréal, Québec H2L 1H9 Canada. (514)526-6653. Prize for a novel in French by a writer from Québec or another province in Canada. Annual award for novels. Award: $5,000 (Canadian). Judges: 5 persons, members of the Académie canadienne française. Guidelines for SASE. Deadline: June 10. Five copies of the work must be submitted. Write for guidelines and entry forms (in French).

PUBLISHED SHORT-STORY CONTEST (II), Hutton Publications, P.O. Box 1870, Hayden ID 83835. (208)772-6184. Award "to recognize good literature already published." Annual competition for short stories. Award: cash/subscriptions/books. Competition receives approx. 50-75 submissions. Judge: Linda Hutton, Editor of Hutton Publications. Guidelines and entry form for #10 SASE. Deadline: December 1. Previously published submissions.

PULITZER PRIZE IN FICTION (III), Columbia University, Graduate School of Journalism, 702 Journalism Bldg., New York NY 10027. Contact: Robert C. Christopher. Annual award for distinguished fiction *first* published in book form during the year by an American author, preferably dealing with American life. Submit 4 copies of the book, entry form, biography and photo of author and $20 handling fee. Open to American authors. Deadline: Beginning in 1990, books published between January 1 and June 30 must be submitted by July 1. Books published between July 1 and December 31 must be submitted by November 1. Award: $3,000.

PURE BRED DOGS/AMERICAN KENNEL GAZETTE (I), 51 Madison Ave., New York NY 10010. (212)696-8331. Executive Editor: Marion Lane. Annual contest for short stories under 2,000 words. Award: Prizes of $500, $250 and $150 for top three entries. Certificate and complimentary one-year subscription for nine honorable mention winners. Top 3 entries published in magazine; all 12 published in separate anthology. Judge: panel. Contest requirements available for SASE. "The *Gazette* sponsors an annual fiction contest for short short stories on some subject relating to pure-bred dogs. Three winning entries are published one per month. Fiction for our magazine needs a slant toward the serious fancier with real insight into the human/dog bond and breed-specific pure-bred behavior."

PUSHCART PRIZE (III), Pushcart Press, Box 380, Wainscott NY 11975. (516)324-9300. Contact: Bill Henderson, editor. Annual award. To publish and recognize the best of small press literary work. Previously published submissions, short stories, poetry or essays on any subject. Must have been published during the current calendar year. Deadline: Dec. 1. Nomination by small press publishers/ editors only. Award: Publication in *Pushcart Prize: Best of the Small Presses*.

QUARTERLY WEST NOVELLA COMPETITION (I), University of Utah, 317 Olpin Union, Salt Lake City UT 84112. Biennial award for novellas. Award: 2 prizes of $300+. Deadline postmarked by December 31. Send SASE for contest rules.

RAGDALE FOUNDATION RESIDENCIES FOR WRITERS AND VISUAL ARTISTS (I), 1260 N. Green Bay Rd., Lake Forest IL 60645. (708)234-1063. Director: Michael Wilkerson. Award "to provide living and work space, as well as uninterrupted time to writers and visual artists for a modest weekly fee ($70/week). Financial assistance is available." The Foundation is open year-round, except for the last two weeks of June and December. Award: includes work and sleeping space, and food for all meals. Residencies for 12 artists and writers for periods of two weeks to two months. Applicants are reviewed by a selection committee composed of professionals in the arts. Guidelines available. Application deadlines: January 15th for May, June, July, August residencies; May 15th for September through December; September 15th for January-April. Late applications will be considered if space is available. Submissions may either be previously published or unpublished.

SIR WALTER RALEIGH AWARD (II, IV), North Carolina Literary and Historical Association, 109 E. Jones St., Raleigh NC 27601-2807. (919)733-7305. Secretary-Treasurer: Jeffrey J. Crow. Award "to promote among the people of North Carolina an interest in their own literature." Annual award for novels. Award: statue of Sir Walter Raleigh. Judges: University English and history professors. Guidelines for SASE. Book must be published between July 1, 1990 and June 30, 1991. Writer must be a legal or physical resident of North Carolina. Authors or publishers may submit 3 copies of their book to the above address. "(1)Must be an original work published during the twelve months ending June 30 of the year for which the award is given. (2)Its author or authors must have maintained either legal or physical residence, or a combination of both, in North Carolina for the three years preceding the close of the contest period."

RAMBUNCTIOUS REVIEW, ANNUAL FICTION CONTEST (I), 1221 W. Pratt, Chicago IL 60626. Contact: Nancy Lennon, co-editor. Annual award. Short stories. Requirements: Typed, double-spaced, maximum 12 pages. SASE for deadline, rules/entry forms.

REGINA MEDAL AWARD (III), Catholic Library Association, 461 W. Lancaster Ave., Haverford PA 19041. Contact: Natalie A. Logan, Executive Director. Annual award. To honor a continued distinguished contribution to children's literature. Award: Silver medal. Award given during Easter week. Selection by a special committee; nominees are suggested by the Catholic Library Association Membership.

RHODE ISLAND STATE ARTS COUNCIL (I,IV), Individual Artist's Fellowship in Literature, 95 Cedar St., Suite 103, Providence RI 02903-1034. (401)277-3880. Contact fellowship program director, Edward Holgate. Annual fellowship. Award: $3,000. Competition receives approximately 50 submissions. In-state panel makes recommendations to an out-of-state judge, who makes the final award. Entry forms for SASE. Deadline: April 1. Artists must be Rhode Island residents and not undergraduate or graduate students.

HAROLD U. RIBALOW PRIZE (II, IV), *Hadassah Magazine*, 50 W. 58th St., New York NY 10019. (212)355-7900. Contact: Alan M. Tigay, Executive Editor. Estab. 1983. Annual award. "For a book of fiction on a Jewish theme. Harold U. Ribalow was a noted writer and editor who devoted his time to the discovery and encouragement of young Jewish writers." Book should have been published the year preceding the award. Award: $500 and excerpt of book in *Hadassah Magazine*. Deadline: December 31.

THE MARY ROBERTS RINEHART FUND (III), *George Mason University*, 4400 University Dr., Fairfax VA 22030. (703)323-2221. Roger Lathbury, director. Biennial award for short stories, novels, novellas and story collections by unpublished writers (that is, writers ineligible to apply for NEA grants). Award: Two grants whose amount varies depending upon income the fund generates. 1989 awards were $950 each. Competition receives approx. 75-100 submissions annually. Entry forms or rules for SASE. Next fiction period and deadline: December 1990-November 30, 1991. Writers must be nominated by a sponsoring writer or editor.

‡*RIVER CITY* WRITING AWARDS IN FICTION, *River City* (formerly Memphis State Review), Dept. of English/Memphis State U., Memphis TN 38152. (901)678-8888. Awards Coordinator: Sharon Bryan. "Annual award to reward the best short stories." Award: $2,000 first prize; $500 second; $300 third. Competition receives approximately 280 submissions. Judge: James Welch. Entry fee $6; waived for subscribers to *River City*. Guidelines available for SASE. Deadline: Dec. 5, 1990. Previously unpublished fiction. Open to all writers. Word length: 7,500 maximum.

SUMMERFIELD G. ROBERTS AWARD (IV), The Sons of the Republic of Texas, Suite 222, 5942 Abrams Rd., Dallas TX 75231. "Given for the best book or manuscript of biography, essay, fiction, nonfiction, novel, poetry or short story that describes or represents the Republic of Texas, 1836-1846." Annual award of $2,500. Deadline: January 31. "The manuscripts must be written or published during the calendar year for which the award is given. Entries are to be submitted in quintuplicate and will not be returned."

ROBERTS WRITING AWARDS (I), H. G. Roberts Foundation, Box 1868, Pittsburg KS 66762. (316)231-2998. Awards Coordinator: Stephen E. Meats. "To reward and recognize exceptional fiction writers with money and publication." Annual competition for short stories. Award: $500 (first place); $200 (second place); $100 (third place); publication for prize winners and honorable mention receipts. Competition receives approx. 600 submissions. Judges: established fiction writer, different each year. Entry fee $5/story. Guidelines and entry form for SASE. Deadline: September 1. Previously unpublished submissions. "Open to any type of fiction, up to 15 typed pages."

‡ROCKLAND CENTER FOR THE ARTS WRITER-IN-RESIDENCE (II, IV), 5 Old Farm Ct., West Nyack NY 10994. (914)358-0877. Executive Director: Julianne Ramos. "Provides residencies to write and perform community service (e.g. workshops, readings, etc.)." Award: up to $3,750 for 4 month residency. Judges: literary committee. Guidelines for SASE. Deadline December 1. Applicants "must be previously published writers of fiction or poetry. Award does not include additional room and board. Therefore, we prefer applicants from New York, New Jersey and Connecticut in commuting distance."

ROCKY MOUNTAIN WOMEN'S INSTITUTE ASSOCIATESHIP (I, II), 7150 Montview Blvd., Foote Hall 317, Denver CO 80220. (303)871-6923. "Each year RMWI receives project proposals, selects those most promising and invites seven to ten to become Associates. These are artists, writers and scholars who are given office/studio space, stipends, support services and promotional events for a one year." Competition receives approx. 100 submissions with selection based on excellence, project feasibility, group dynamics and need. Selection committees composed of experts in arts/humanities. Entry fee $5. SASE for returns. Deadline: March 15 of each year for following September. Located at the University of Denver Law campus, work space provided but not residence. Part-time committee per week and Associates meet as group once each week.

ROMANCE WRITERS OF AMERICA GOLDEN HEART/GOLDEN MEDALLION AWARDS (I, II, IV), 13700 Veterans Memorial, #315, Houston TX 77014. (713)440-6885. "To recognize best work in romantic fiction in 7 categories by members of RWA, both published and not-published." Annual award for novels. Golden Heart Award: heart and certificate; Golden Medallion Award: etched plaque. Golden Heart award receives 600+ submissions/year; Golden Medallion Award receives 250+ submissions/year. Judges: published writers, editors. Entry fee for Golden Heart is now $25; Golden Medallion fee is $15. Guidelines for SASE. Deadline: November 30. Previously published submissions for Golden Medallion; unpublished for Golden Heart. Categories are "traditional, short and long contemporary, historical, single title (historical and contemporary), young adult."

SACRAMENTO PUBLIC LIBRARY FOCUS ON WRITERS CONTEST (I, IV), 1010 8th St., Sacramento CA 95814. (916)440-5926. Contact: Debbie Runnels. Award "to support and encourage aspiring writers." Annual competition for short stories and novels. Awards: $100 (first place); $50 (second place); $25 (third place). Competition receives approx. 147 short story; 78 novel chapters; 71 children's stories. Judges: local teachers of English, authors and librarians. Entry fee $5/entry. Guidelines for SASE. Deadline February 1. Previously unpublished submissions. Length: 2,500-word short story; 1,000-word story for children. Open to all writers in northern California. Send for guidelines.

SAN JOSE STUDIES **BEST STORY AWARD (I)**, Bill Casey Memorial Fund, 1 Washington Square, San Jose CA 95192. Contact: Fauneil J. Rinn. Winning author receives a year complimentary subscription to journal, which prints notice of award, and is also considered for the Bill Casey Memorial Award of $100 for the best contribution in each year's volume of *San José Studies* in essay, fiction or poetry.

‡**CARL SANDBURG AWARDS (I, IV)**, Friends of the Chicago Public Library, 78 E. Washington, Chicago IL 60602. (312)269-2922. Annually. To honor excellence in Chicago or Chicago area authors (including 6 counties). Books published between May 31 and June 1 (the following year). $1,000 cash honorarium for fiction, nonfiction, poetry and children's literature. Medal awarded also. Deadline: September 1. All entries become the property of the Friends.

‡**SASSY FICTION CONTEST**, *Sassy*, 1 Times Square, New York NY 10036. (212)764-4860. Competition "to recognize promise in fiction writers aged 13-19 and to encourage teenagers to write." Annual award for short stories. Award: 1st prize $1,000, a Smith Corona PWP 2100, and the story printed. 2nd prize: $500, a Smith Corona 1XO7700. Competition receives approximately 5,000 submissions. Judges: Christina Kelly, Mary Kay Schilling, Jane Pratt. No entry fee. Guidelines available for SASE. Deadline is November 30, 1990. Previously unpublished fiction. Only aged 13-19.

SCHOLASTIC WRITING AWARDS (I, IV), Scholastic Inc., 730 Broadway, New York NY 10003. (212)505-3440. Contact: Director of Awards Program, Chuck Wentzel. To provide opportunity for recognition of young writers. Annual award for short stories. Award: Cash awards, scholarships and grants. Competition receives 22,000 submissions/year. Judges vary each year. Deadline: January 9. Previously unpublished submissions. Contest limited to junior high and senior high school students; grades 7-12. Entry blank must be signed by teacher. "Program is run through school and is only open to students in grades 7 through 12, regularly and currently enrolled in public and non-public schools in the United States and its territories, U.S.-sponsored schools abroad or any schools in Canada."

SCIENCE FICTION WRITERS OF EARTH (SFWoE) SHORT STORY CONTEST, Science Fiction Writers of Earth, Box 121293, Fort Worth TX 76121. (817)451-8674. SFWoE Administrator: Gilbert Gordon Reis. Purpose "to promote the art of science fiction/fantasy short story writing." Annual award for short stories. Award: $100 (1st prize); $50 (2nd prize); $25 (3rd prize). Competition receives approx. 75 submissions/year. Judge: author Edward Bryant. Entry fee: $5 for 1st entry; $2 for additional entries. Guidelines for SASE. Deadline: October 30. Submissions must be unpublished. Stories should be science fiction or fantasy, 2,000-7,500 words. "Although many of our past winners are now published authors, there is still room for improvement. The odds are good for a well written story."

‡*SE LA VIE WRITER'S JOURNAL* **CONTEST (I)**, Rio Grande Press, P.O. Box 371371, El Paso TX 79937. (915)595-2625. Contact: Rosalie Avara, editor. Competition offered quarterly for short stories. Award: Publication in the *Se La Vie Writer's Journal* plus up to $10 and contributor's copy. Judge: Editor. Entry fee $4 for each or $7 for two. Guidelines for SASE. Deadline March 31, June 30, September 30, December 31. Unpublished submissions. Theme is "life" or "the writing life." Length: 500 words maximum.

THE SEATON AWARDS (I,IV), *Kansas Quarterly*, 122 Denison Hall, Kansas State University, KS 66506-0703. Annual awards. To reward and recognize the best fiction published in *KQ* during the year from authors native to or resident in Kansas. Submissions must be previously unpublished. Anyone who submits unpublished material which is then accepted for publication becomes eligible for the awards. No deadline. Material simply may be submitted for consideration at any time with SASE. Award: Recognition and monetary sums of $250, $150, $100 and $50. "Ours are not contests. We give monetary awards and recognition to Kansas writers of national literary stature."

SEVENTEEN MAGAZINE FICTION CONTEST/ **SMITH CORONA FICTION CONTEST (I,IV)**, *Seventeen Magazine*, 850 3rd Ave., New York NY 10022. Contact: Adrian Nicole LeBlanc. To honor best short fiction by a young writer. Rules are found in the November issue. Contest for 13-21 year olds. Deadline: January 31. Submissions judged by a panel of outside readers and *Seventeen*'s editors.

SHORT STORY SCIENCE FICTION/FANTASY COMPETITION (I, IV), Maplecon SF/F Convention (O.F.I.), 2105 Thistle Crescent, Ottawa, Ontario K1H 5P4 Canada. "To offer incentive and encouragement for amateur writers." Annual competition for short stories. Award: certificates and varying prizes. Competition receives approx. 25-35 submissions. Judges: professional authors. Guidelines for

SASE. Deadline: May 21. Unpublished submissions. Available to any writer, anywhere, in amateur standing, i.e. has *not* had *more* than 3 short stories published professionally in the SF/F field or not had a novel published in the SF/F field. Maximum word length: 11,000 words. "Name must not appear on ms itself—should be included on a separate sheet. Please include a SASE. Use *Canadian* stamps or IRC's or include *loose* U.S. stamps as trade."

CHARLIE MAY SIMON BOOK AWARD (III, IV), Arkansas Department of Education, Elementary School Council, State Education Building, Capitol Mall, Division of Instruction, Room 305B, Little Rock AR 72201. (501)682-4361. Contact: James A. Hester, Secretary/Treasurer, Arkansas Elementary School Council. Annual award. "To encourage reading by children in quality children's literature." Previously published submissions. Award: Medallion. No entry fee. "The committee doesn't accept requests from authors. They will look at booklists of books produced during the previous year and check recommendations from the following sources: *Booklist, Bulletin of the Center for Children's Books, Children's Catalog, Elementary School Library Collection, Hornbook, Library of Congress Children's Books, School Library Journal.*"

W.H. SMITH/BOOKS IN CANADA AWARD FOR FIRST NOVELS (III, IV), Books in Canada, 366 Adelaide St. E, Toronto, Ontario M5A 3X9 Canada. (416)363-5426. Contact: Paul Stuewe, editor. Annual award. "To promote and recognize Canadian writing." Award: $5,000. No entry fee. Submissions are made by publishers. Contest is restricted to first novels in English published in Canada in the previous calendar year.

SOCIETY OF CHILDREN'S BOOK WRITERS GOLDEN KITE AWARDS (II), Society of Children's Book Writers, Box 296, Mar Vista Station, Los Angeles CA 90066. Contact: Sue Alexander, chairperson. Annual award. "To recognize outstanding works of fiction, nonfiction and picture illustration for children by members of the Society of Children's Book Writers and published in the award year." Published submissions should be submitted from January to December of publication year. Deadline entry: December 15. Rules for SASE. Award: Statuette and plaque. Looking for quality material for children. Individual "must be member of the SCBW to submit books."

SOCIETY OF CHILDREN'S BOOK WRITERS WORK-IN-PROGRESS GRANTS (I,IV), Box 66296, Mar Vista, Los Angeles CA 90066. (818)347-2849. Contact: SCBW. Grant for contemporary novel for young people; also, nonfiction research grant and grant for work whose author has never been published. Annual competition for novels. Award: 1st-$1,000; 2nd-$500 (work-in-progress). 1st-$1,000; 2nd-$400 (Judy Blume/SCBW contemporary novel grant). Competition receives approx. 80 submissions. Judges: members of children's book field—editors, authors, etc. Guidelines for SASE. Unpublished submissions. Deadline: Feb. 1-May 1. Applicants must be SCBW members only.

SONORA REVIEW FICTION CONTEST (I), Dept. of English, University of Arizona, Tucson AZ 85721. (602)621-8077. Contact: fiction editor. Annual award. "To encourage and support quality short fiction." Unpublished submissions. Award: $150 first prize, plus publication in *Sonora*; $50 second prize, plus publication in *Sonora*. "We accept manuscripts all year, but manuscripts received during the summer (May-August) will not be read until fall." Contest rules for SASE.

SOUTH CAROLINA ARTS COMMISSION AND *THE STATE NEWSPAPER* SOUTH CAROLINA FICTION PROJECT (I,IV), 1800 Gervais St., Columbia SC 29201. (803)734-8696. Steve Lewis, director, Literary Arts Program. The purpose of the award is "to get money to fiction writers and to get their work published and read." Annual award for short stories. Award: $500 cash and publication in *The State Newspaper*. Competition receives approximately 400 submissions for 12 awards (up to 12 stories chosen). Judges are a panel of professional writers and senior writer for *The State Newspaper*. Entry forms or rules for SASE. Deadline November 19. South Carolina residents only.

SOUTH CAROLINA ARTS COMMISSION LITERATURE FELLOWSHIP AND LITERATURE GRANTS (I, IV), 1800 Gervais St., Columbia SC 29201. (803)734-8696. Steve Lewis, director, Literary Arts Program. "The purpose of the fellowships is to give a cash award to two deserving writers (one in poetry, one in creative prose) whose works are of the highest caliber." Award: $7,500 fellowship. Matching grants up to $7,500. Competition receives approximately 40 submissions per fellowship. Judges are out-of-state panel of professional writers and editors for fellowships, and in-state panels and SCAC staff for grants. Entry forms or rules for SASE. Fellowship deadline September 15. Grants deadline January 15. South Carolina residents only.

SOUTH DAKOTA ARTS COUNCIL, ARTIST FELLOWSHIP (IV), 108 West 11th, Sioux Falls SD 57102. (605)339-6646. Award "to assist artists with career development. Grant can be used for supplies or to set aside time to work, but cannot be used for academic research or formal study toward a degree." Annual competition for writers. Award: $1,000 for emerging artists; $5,000 for established artists. Competition receives approx. 80 submissions. "Grants are awarded on artists' work and *not* on financial need." Judges: panels of in-state and out-of-state experts in each discipline. Guidelines for SASE. Deadline February 1. Previously published or unpublished submissions. Fellowships are open only to residents of South Dakota. "Writers with specific projects may apply for a Project Grant. They would not be eligible for fellowship grants in that case. Deadline is Feb. 1 and guidelines are available by writing SDAC."

‡SOUTHERN ARTS LITERATURE PRIZE (IV), 13 St. Clement St., Winchester, Hampshire S023 9DQ England. Award "to recognize good works by authors (known or unknown) in the southern region (of the U.K.)." Annual competition for short stories, novels and poetry. Award £1,000. Competition receives approx. 20-30 submissions. Judges: 3 people (involved in literature or authors themselves), different each year. Guidelines for SASE. Southern arts region covers Hampshire, Berkshire, Wiltshire, Oxfordshire, West Sussex, Isle of Wight and East Dorset. Awards for fiction and poetry alternate each year. Check for details.

THE SOUTHERN REVIEW/**LOUISIANA STATE UNIVERSITY ANNUAL SHORT FICTION AWARD (II)**, *The Southern Review*, 43 Allen Hall, Louisiana State University, Baton Rouge LA 70803. (504)388-5108. Contact: Editors, *The Southern Review*. Annual award. "To encourage publication of good fiction." For a first collection of short stories by an American writer appearing during calendar year. Award: $500 to author. Possible campus reading. Deadline: a month after close of each calendar year. The book of short stories must be released by a U.S. publisher. Two copies to be submitted by publisher or author. Looking for "style, sense of craft, plot, in-depth characters."

SPUR AWARD CONTEST (II, IV), Western Writers of America, P.O. Box 823, Sheridan WY 82801. Contact: Barb Ketcham, secretary-treasurer. Annual award. To encourage excellence in western writing. Entries are accepted only from the current calendar year for each year's award; that is, books can only be entered in the year they are published. Entry deadline: December 31. Award judged by a panel of experienced authors appointed by the current Spur Awards Chairman. Contest/award rules and entry forms available with SASE. Award: A wooden plaque shaped like a W with a bronze spur attached. "A special Medicine Pipe Bearer Award, is offered in the Best First Western Novel competition. First novels may be entered in both Spur and Medicine Pipe Bearer competition. Books must be of the traditional or historical western theme, set anywhere west of the Mississippi River before the 20th century, ideally from 1850 to 1900." A spur is awarded for Best Historical Fiction, Best Juvenile Fiction and Best Short Fiction works.

STAND MAGAZINE **SHORT STORY COMPETITION (I)**, *Stand Magazine*, 179 Wingrove Road, Newcastle upon Tyne NE4 9DA England. Biennial award for short stories. Award: 1st prize £1,250; 2nd prize £500; 3rd prize £250; 4th prize £150; 5th prize £100 (or U.S. $ equivalent). 1991 judges are Emma Tennant, Ian and Corchron Smith. Entry fee $6. Deadline: March 31, 1991. Send 2 IRC's and SAE.

WALLACE E. STEGNER FELLOWSHIP (I, IV), Creative Writing Program, Stanford University, Stanford CA 94305-2087. (415)723-2637. Contact: Gay Pierce, program coordinator. Annual award. Five two-year fellowships in fiction ($9,000 stipend plus required tuition or $3,500 annually). For unpublished or previously published fiction writers. Residency required. Deadline: January 1. Entry fee $20.

STORY TIME **SHORT-STORY CONTEST (I)**, Hutton Publications, Box 1870, Hayden, ID 83835. (208) 772-6184. Contact: Linda Hutton, editor. Estab. 1982. Annual award. "To encourage short-story writers." For previously published or unpublished submissions. Award: $15 first prize; $10 second prize; $7.50 third prize. Entry deadlines: March 1, June 1, August 1, December 1. Send #10 SASE for entry form and rules. Looking for "tightly written plot and well developed characters."

SWG LITERARY AWARDS (I, IV), Saskatchewan Writers Guild, Box 3986, Regina, Saskatchewan S4P 3R9 Canada. (306)757-6310. Awards "to recognize excellence in work by Saskatchewan writers." Annual competition for short stories, dramas, humor, poetry, nonfiction, children's literature. Awards: Major awards (3) are $1,000; 3 awards of $100. In 1989 SWG received 118 entries for short fiction. Judges: Writers from outside the Province. Entry fee: $15 for (one ms allowed); $4 for other categories (multiple submissions allowed). Guidelines for SASE. Deadline: February 28. Unpublished submissions. Available only to Saskatchewan citizens.

‡THE SYVENNA FOUNDATION WRITERS-IN-RESIDENCE (I,II), The Syvenna Foundation, Route 1, Box 193, Linden TX 75563. (903)835-8252. Award "to encourage and support beginning and intermediate women writers of all ages." Awards granted quarterly, four terms each year; two residents per term; for short stories, novels, story collections and translations. Award: 2 or 3 month residency, with private cottage and $300/month stipend. Competition receives approx. 30-40 applications per term. Judges: "Two panels of female writers and academicians; one panel in Winston-Salem NC and another in Tulsa OK." Guidelines for SASE. Deadlines: April 1 for fall (September-November); August 1 for winter (January -March); October 1 for Spring (April-May); December 1 for summer (June-August). Either previously published or unpublished submissions. Length: Prose, 12 pages (typed, double-spaced) or first chapter of book, whichever is shorter; Poetry, 5 poems; Drama, 1 act, or 12 pages, whichever is shorter.

TENNESSEE ARTS COMMISSION INDIVIDUAL ARTISTS FELLOWSHIP (I,IV), Suite 100, 320 6th Ave. N., Nashville TN 37243-0780. (615)741-1701. Contact: Alice Swanson, director of literary arts. Competition "recognizes outstanding writers in the state." Annual award for fiction in 1991-1992. Award: up to $5,000 ($2,500 minimum). Competition receives approximately 40 submissions. Judges are 2 out-of-state jurors. Entry forms available. Writers must be residents of Tennessee.

‡TEXAS-WIDE WRITERS CONTEST, Byliners, P.O. Box 6218, Corpus Christi TX 78413. (512)991-1442. Awards Coordinator: Deborah Ferguson. "Award to fund a scholarship in journalism or creative writing." Annual award for adult and children's short stories, novels and poems. Award: novels—1st $100, 2nd $75, 3rd $50; short stories—1st $75, 2nd $50, 3rd $25. Competition receives approximately 50 novel, 125 short story and 62 children's story submissions. Judges: varies each year. Entry fee $5/story, $10/novel. Guidelines available for SASE. Deadline is March 1, (deadline date remains same each year). Previously unpublished submissions. Limited to Texas resident and Byliner members. Word Length: children story limit 2,000 words; short story limit 3,000 words; novel 3 page synopsis plus chapter one. "Contest also has nostalgia, article and nonfiction book categories."

THURBER HOUSE RESIDENCIES (II), The Thurber House, 77 Jefferson Ave., Columbus OH 43215. (614)464-1032. Literary Director: Michael J. Rosen. "Four writers/year are chosen as writers-in-residence, one for each quarter." Award for writers of novels and story collections. $5,000 stipend and housing for a quarter in the furnished third-floor apartment of James Thurber's boyhood home. Judges: advisory panel. Guidelines for SASE. Deadline: January 1. "The James Thurber Writer-in-Residence will teach a class in the Creative Writing Program at The Ohio State University in either fiction or poetry, and will offer one public reading and a short workshop for writers in the community. Significant time outside of teaching is reserved for the writer's own work in progress. Candidates should have published at least one book with a major publisher, in any area of fiction, nonfiction or poetry, and should possess some experience in teaching."

TOWSON STATE UNIVERSITY PRIZE FOR LITERATURE (I, IV), Towson State University Foundation, Towson State University, Towson MD 21204. (301)830-2128. Contact: Annette Chappell, dean, College of Liberal Arts. Annual award. Novels or short story collections, previously published. Requirements: writer must not be over 40; must be a Maryland resident. Deadline: May 15. SASE for rules/entry forms.

JOHN TRAIN HUMOR PRIZE (I), *The Paris Review*, 541 E. 72nd St., New York NY 10021. Fiction Editor: George Plimpton. Award for the best previously unpublished work of humorous fiction, nonfiction or poetry. One submission per envelope. Annual competition for short stories. Award: $1,500 and publication in *The Paris Review*. Guidelines for SASE. Deadline March 31. Submissions should be unpublished. Manuscripts must be less than 10,000 words. No formal application form is required; regular submissions guidelines apply.

TRANSLATION CENTER AWARDS (I, II, IV), The Translation Center, 412 Dodge Hall, Columbia University, New York NY 10027. (212)854-2305. Contact: Award Secretary. Annual awards. "For outstanding translation of a substantial part of a book-length *literary* work." Award: Cash grant (varies). Entry deadline: January 15. No entry fee. Write for application form.

TRANSLATORS ASSOCIATION AWARDS (III, IV), 84 Drayton Gardens, London SW10 9SB England. Scott Moncrieff Prize for best translation into English of 20th century French work; Schlegel Tieck Prize for translations from German; John Florio Prize for translations from Italian into English. Annual competition for translations. Award: Scott Moncrieff Prize: £1,500; Schlegel-Tieck Prize: £2,000; John Florio Prize (biannual): £900. Judges: 3 translators. Deadline December 31. Previously published submissions. Awards for translations published in U.K. during year of award. U.K. publishers submit books for consideration.

UCROSS FOUNDATION/RESIDENCY (I), Residency Program/Ucross Foundation, 2836 U.S. Highway 14-16 East, Clearmont WY 82835. (307)737-2291. Award "to allow artists uninterrupted time to work in their field creatively." Biannual competition for short stories, novels, story collections and translations. Award: time to spend at Ucross to accomplish their works and ideas. Competition receives approx. 150 submissions per session. Judges: three-member selection committee. Guidelines for SASE. Deadline: March 1 and October 1. Previously published or unpublished submissions.

UTAH ORIGINAL WRITING COMPETITION (I,IV), Utah Arts Council. 617 East South Temple, Salt Lake City UT 84012. (801)533-5895. Literary Arts Coordinator: G. Barnes. "An annual writing competition, now entering its 33rd year." Annual competition for poetry, essays, nonfiction books, short stories, novels and story collections. Awards: vary; last year between $200-$1,000. Competition receives 700 entries. Judges: "published and award-winning judges from across America." Guidelines available, no SASE necessary. Deadline: mid-February or later. Submissions should be unpublished. *Limited to Utah residents.* "Some limitation on word-length. See guidelines for details."

VERMONT COUNCIL ON THE ARTS FELLOWSHIP (I, II, IV), Vermont Council on the Arts, 136 State Street, Montpelier VT 05602. (802)828-3291. "To support creative development." Annual competition for short stories, novels, story collections and translations. Award: $3,500 with $500 Finalist Awards. The VCA awards approximately 17-20 Fellowships annually. There is no pre-determined number of Fellowships by discipline. Judges: a peer panel makes recommendations to the VCA Board of Trustees. Guidelines for SASE after December 1. Deadline: March 15. Previously published and unpublished submissions. Applicants must be legal residents of Vermont and must have lived in VT at least 6 months prior to date of application. Word length: 10-12 pages poetry, 10-20 pages fiction. Applicants may include a synopsis or summary of longer works in addition to submitted excerpts. Applicants must be 18 or older, may not be enrolled as full-time students, and must have submitted all reports on past council grants. Grant money may not be used for foreign travel, tuition applied to academic programs, or purchase of permanent equipment. *Manuscripts should be unsigned and should indicate completion date.* Manuscripts must be send with completed application.

‡VERMONT STUDIO CENTER RESIDENCY FELLOWSHIPS (I,II), Vermont Studio Center, P.O. Box 613, Johnson VT 05656. (802)635-2727. Residency Coordinator: Roger J. Kowalsky. Purpose of fellowships is "to reduce Residency fee by 25% or 50%. Awards granted as applications for Residency are received. For 'any writing project.' " Judges: internal review committee. Application fee: $15. Guidelines for SASE. Either previously published or unpublished fiction.

VICTORIAN FELLOWSHIP OF AUSTRALIAN WRITERS ANNUAL NATIONAL LITERARY AWARDS (I, II, IV), 1/317 Barkers Rd., Kew (Melbourne) Victoria 3101 Australia. Contact: J.S. Hamilton, president, Victorian FAW. Sponsors 20 awards for Australian writers, both published and unpublished. Annual competition for shorts stories, novels and story collections. Award varies: largest award is $1,000. Competition receives over 50 entries for books, at least 100 for manuscripts. Judges: writers and critics appointed by the organizer. Guidelines for SASE. Deadline: December 31. Published or previously unpublished submissions, depending on award. Awards offered to Australians (including those living overseas) or residents of Australia. Send for guidelines, but only from October each year.

VIRGINIA CENTER FOR THE CREATIVE ARTS RESIDENCY FELLOWSHIP (I), Mt. San Angelo, Sweet Briar VA 24595. (804)946-7236. Director: William Smart. Award to "provide residencies to writers, visual artists and composers in order that they may work without interruption on their own projects." Approximately 250 fellowships awarded annually. Periodic deadlines. Award: 1 to 3 month residencies. Receives 1,000 applications/year. Judges: writers, visual artists and composers established in their fields. Application fee $15. Write for application form.

THE VIRGINIA PRIZE FOR FICTION (I,IV), Virginia Commission for the Arts, 101 N. 14th St., 17th Floor, Richmond VA 23219. (804)225-3132 Voice/TDD. "The Commission has established these awards to support and encourage the work of Virginia's professional writers, and in recognition of exceptional talent. The prizes are intended to assist writers in the creation of new works and to support writers' efforts to advance their careers." Annual competition for novels and story collections (150-page minimum submission). Award: 1st: $10,000; 2nd: $5,000; 3rd: $2,500. Competition receives approx. 175 submissions. Judges: a different out-of-state judge each year. Deadline: March 1. Unpublished submissions (short stories may have been published individually, but the collection unpublished). Virginia residents only. Program administered by Virginia Center for the Creative Arts, Sweet Briar, VA. Funded by VA. Commission for the Arts, a state agency.

VOGELSTEIN FOUNDATION GRANTS (II), The Ludwig Vogelstein Foundation, Inc., Box 4924, Brooklyn, NY 11240-4924. Executive Director: Frances Pishny. "A small foundation awarding grants to individuals in the arts and humanities." Criteria are merit and need. No student aid given. Send SASE for complete information.

HAROLD D. VURSELL MEMORIAL AWARD (III), American Academy and Institute of Arts and Letters, 633 W. 155th St., New York NY 10032. (212)368-5900. Annual award. "To single out recent writing in book form that merits recognition for the quality of its prose style. It may be given for a work of fiction, biography, history, criticism, belles lettres, memoir, journal or a work of translation." Award: $5,000. Judged by 7-member jury composed of members of the Department of Literature of the American Academy and Institute of Arts and Letters. *No applications accepted.*

EDWARD LEWIS WALLANT MEMORIAL BOOK AWARD (II, IV), 3 Brighton Rd., West Hartford CT 06117. Sponsored by Dr. and Mrs. Irving Waltman. Contact: Mrs. Irving Waltman. Annual award. Memorial to Edward Lewis Wallant, which offers incentive and encouragement to beginning writers, for books published the year before the award is conferred in the spring. Books may be submitted for consideration to Irving Malin, 96-13 68 Avenue, Forest Hills NY 11375. Award: $250 plus award certificate. "Looking for creative work of fiction by an American which has significance for the American Jew. The novel (or collection of short stories) should preferably bear a kinship to the writing of Wallant. The award will seek out the writer who has not yet achieved literary prominence."

WASHINGTON PRIZE FOR FICTION (I), 1301 S. Scott St., Arlington VA 22204. (703)920-3771. Larry Kaltman, Director. Award: $300 (1st prize), $200 (2nd prize), $100 (3rd prize). Judges: Hank Burchard (The Washington Post), Ethelbert Miller (Howard University), Elisavietta Ritchie (Thrice winner PEN/NEA Syndicated Fiction). Entry fee $25. Deadline: November 30. Unpublished submissions. Word length: 75,000 words minimum.

WASHINGTON STATE ARTS COMMISSION ARTIST FELLOWSHIP AWARD (I,IV), 110 9th and Columbia, Olympia WA 97504-4111. (206)753-3860. Arts Program Manager: Karen Kamara Gose. "Unrestricted award to a mid-career artist." Biannual award for writers of short stories, novels and literary criticism. Washington residents only. Award: $5,000. Competition receives 80 entries. Judges: peer panel. Guidelines upon request. Deadline: Spring/Summer. Literary arts award made in even-numbered years. Submissions can be either previously published or unpublished. "Applicant must be 5 years out of school in field they're applying to and have 5 years of professional experience. No emerging artists."

‡WEST VIRGINIA DIVISION OF CULTURE AND HISTORY, ARTS AND HUMANITIES SECTION, ARTIST-IN-RESIDENCE PROGRAM (I), The Cultural Center, Capitol Complex, Charleston WV 25305. (304)348-0240. Director: Lakin Ray Cook. Awards to "assist with artist-in-residence programs in West Virginia." Three deadlines per year. Award: financial support for residencies. Judges: West Virginia Commission on the Arts. Write or call for guidelines. Deadlines February 1, April 1, and August 1 of each year. In-state and out-of-state writers are eligible.

WESTERN CANADIAN MAGAZINE AWARDS (II,IV), 3898 Hillcrest Ave., North Vancouver, British Columbia V7R 4B6 Canada. (604)984-7525. "To honour and encourage excellence." Annual competition for short stories (fiction articles in magazines). Award: $500. Entry fee: $15-20 (depending on circulation of magazine). Deadline: January. Previously published submissions (between January and December). "Must be Canadian or have earned immigrant status and the fiction article must have appeared in a publication (magazine) that has its main editorial offices located in the 4 Western provinces, the Yukon or NW territories."

WESTERN HERITAGE AWARDS (II, IV), National Cowboy Hall of Fame, 1700 NE 63rd St., Oklahoma City OK 73111. (405)478-2250. Contact: Dana Sullivant, public relations director. Annual award. "To honor outstanding quality in fiction, nonfiction and art literature." Submissions are to have been published during the previous calendar year. Award: The Wrangler, a replica of a C.M. Russell Bronze. Entry deadline: December 31. No entry fee. Entry forms and rules available November 1 for SASE. Looking for "stories that best capture the spirit of the West."

WESTERN STATES BOOK AWARDS, Western States Arts Federation, 236 Montezuma, Santa Fe NM 87501. (505)988-1166. Contact: Violetta Romero, Special Project Administrator. Estab. 1984. Biannual award. "Recognition for writers living in the West; encouragement of effective production and marketing of quality books published in the West; increase of sales and critical attention." For unpublished manuscripts submitted by publisher. Award: $2,500 for authors; $5,000 for publishers. Write for information on deadline. Contest rules for SASE.

WILLIAM ALLEN WHITE CHILDREN'S BOOK AWARD (III), Emporia State University, 1200 Commercial, Emporia KS 66801. Contact: Mary E. Bogan, executive secretary. Estab. 1952. Annual award. To honor the memory of one of the state's most distinguished citizens by encouraging the boys and girls of Kansas to read and enjoy good books. "We do not accept submissions from authors or publishers." Award: bronze medal. The White Award Book Selection Committee looks for excellence of literary quality in fiction, poetry and nonfiction appropriate for 4th through 8th graders. All nominations to the annual White Award master list must be made by a member of the White Award Book Selection Committee.

WHITING WRITER'S AWARDS (III), Mrs. Giles Whiting Foundation, Rm 3500, 30 Rockefeller Pl., New York NY 10112. Director: Dr. Gerald Freund. To encourage the work of emergent writers and to recognize the work of older, proven writers. Annual award for writers of fiction, poetry, nonfiction and plays. Award: $25,000 (10 awards). Writers are submitted by appointed nominators and chosen for awards by an appointed selection committee. Direct applications and informal nominations not accepted by the foundation.

LAURA INGALLS WILDER AWARD (III), American Library Association/Association for Library Service to Children, 50 E. Huron St., Chicago IL 60611. Award offered every 3 years; next year 1992. "To honor a significant body of work for children, for illustration, fiction or nonfiction." Award: bronze medal.

LAURENCE L. WINSHIP BOOK AWARD (III, IV), *The Boston Globe*, Boston MA 02107. (617)929-2649. Contact: Marianne Callahan, public affairs department. Annual award. "To honor *The Globe*'s late editor who did much to encourage young talented New England authors." Previously published submissions from July 1 to July 1 each year. To be submitted by publishers. Award: $2,000. Deadline: June 30. Contest rules for SASE. Book must have some relation to New England—author, theme, plot or locale.

WISCONSIN ARTS BOARD INDIVIDUAL ARTIST PROGRAM (II,IV), 131 W. Wilson St., Suite 301, Madison WI 53703. (608)266-0190. Contact: Elizabeth Malner. Annual award for short stories, poetry, novels, novellas, drama, essay/criticism. Awards: 3 awards of $5,000; 4 awards of $3,500; 6 awards of $1,000. Competition receives approx. 175 submissions. Judges are 3 out-of-state jurors. Entry forms or rules for SASE. Deadline: September 15. Wisconsin residents only. Students are ineligible.

‡WISCONSIN INSTITUTE FOR CREATIVE WRITING FELLOWSHIP, University of Wisconsin—Creative Writing, English Department, Madison WI 53705. Competition "to provide time, space and an intellectual community for writers working on first books." Annual award for short stories, novels and story collections. Award: $17,000 per nine month appointment. Competition receives approximately 300 submissions. Applicants must have received an M.F.A. or comparable graduate degree in creative writing. Judges: English Department faculty. Guidelines available for SASE; write to Ron Kuka. Deadline is month of February. Published, unpublished submissions. Published submissions must be typed. Limit one story up to 30 pages in length.

WORLD'S BEST SHORT SHORT STORY CONTEST (I), English Department Writing Program, Florida State University, Tallahassee FL 32306. (904)644-4230. Contact: Jerome Stern, director. Annual award for short-short stories, unpublished, under 250 words. Prize-winning story gets $100, 1 box of Florida oranges, and broadside publication; winner and finalists are published in *Sun Dog: The Southeast Review*. Open to all. Deadline: February 15. SASE for rules.

WRITERS AT WORK FELLOWSHIP COMPETITION (I), Writers At Work, Box 8857, Salt Lake City UT 84108. (801)355-0264. Contact: Director. "To award new talent—and in addition to the prizes listed below, winners are invited to attend the Writers at Work Conference (June 12-18) free of charge. Award: first: $500 and publication in *Quarterly West*; second: $200. Competition receives approx. 600 submissions. Judges: preliminary judges *Quarterly West* staff; final judges Francois Camoin, W. D. Wetherell and Peggy Schumaker. Entry fee $6. Guidelines for SASE. Unpublished submissions.

WRITER'S DIGEST ANNUAL WRITING COMPETITION (Short Story Division) (I,II), *Writer's Digest*, 1507 Dana Ave., Cincinnati OH 45207. (513)531-2222. Entry deadline: May 31. Entry fee: $5. All entries must be original, unpublished and not previously submitted to a *Writer's Digest* contest. Length: 2,000 words maximum, one entry only. No acknowledgment will be made of receipt of mss nor will mss be returned. Grand Prize is a trip to New York City with arrangements to meet editors in writer's field. Other awards include electronic typewriters, reference books, plaques and certificates of recognition. Names of grand prize winner and top 100 winners are announced in the October issue of *Writer's Digest*. Top two entries published in booklet ($4.50). Send SASE to *WD* Writing Competition for rules or see January-May issues of *Writer's Digest*.

WRITERS GUILD OF ALBERTA LITERARY AWARD (II,IV), Writers Guild of Alberta, 10523-100 Avenue, Edmonton Alberta T5J 0A8 Canada. (403)426-5892. "To recognize, reward and foster writing excellence." Annual competition for novels and story collections. Award: $500 cash, plus leatherbound copy of winning work. Short story competition receives 5-10 submissions; novel competition receives about 20; children's literature category up to 40. Judges: three published writers. Guidelines for SASE. Deadline December 31. Previously published submissions (between January and December). Open to Alberta authors, resident for previous 18 months. Entries must be book-length and published within the current year.

WRITERS' JOURNAL ANNUAL FICTION CONTEST (I), Box 9148, N. St. Paul MN 55109. (612)433-3626. Publisher/Managing Editor: Valerie Hockert. Annual award for short stories. Award: 1st place: $200; 2nd place: $75; 3rd place: $25. Also give honorable mentions. Competition receives approximately 400 submissions/year. Judges are Valerie Hockert, Anne Miller and others. Entry fee $5 each. Maximum of 2 entries/person. Entry forms or rules for SASE. Maximum length is 3,000 words. Two copies of each entry are required—one *without* name or address of writer.

WYOMING COUNCIL ON THE ARTS, LITERARY FELLOWSHIPS (I, IV), Wyoming Council on the Arts, 2320 Capitol Ave., Cheyenne WY 82002. (307)777-7742. Contact: literature consultant. Award to "honor the most outstanding new work of Wyoming writers—fiction, nonfiction, drama, poetry." Annual competition for short stories, novels, awards, story collections, translations, poetry. Award: 4 awards $25,000 each. Competition receives approx. 120 submissions. Judges: panel of writers selected each year from outside Wyoming. Deadline: Fall. Applicants "must be Wyoming resident for one year prior to application deadline. Must not be a full-time student *or* a full-time tenured faculty member." No genre exclusions; combined genres acceptable. 25 pages double spaced maximum; 10 pages maximum for poetry. Guidelines for SASE. Winners may not apply for 4 years after receiving fellowships.

YADDO RESIDENCIES (I, II), Box 395, Saratoga Springs NY 12866-0395. President: Myra Sklarew. To provide undisturbed working time for writers and artists. Prefer authors of short stories, novels, translations, story collections. Award: one to two month residency at Yaddo. Judges: advisory committee. Filing fee $20. Guidelines for SASE. Deadlines: January 15 and August 1. "Those qualified for invitation to Yaddo are writers, visual artists and composers who have already published (or exhibited or had performed) work of high artistic merit. Unpublished work may serve as the sole basis for admission, if the judges panels feels that it shows unusual promise."

YOUNG ADULT CANADIAN BOOK AWARD (II, IV), Young Adult Services Interest Group, c/o Unionville Library, 15 Library Lane, Unionville, Ont L3R 5C4 Canada. Contact: Nancy E. Black, convener of book award committee. Established 1980 by the Young Adult Caucus of the Saskatchewan Library

Association. Transfered to YASIG 1988. Annual award given when merited. To recognize an outstanding Canadian work of fiction written for young adults. Submissions should have been published during the previous calendar year. Award: Recognition through media press releases; leatherbound copy of book; "usually an author tour." Judged by Young Adult Services Group of the Canadian Library Association.

YOUNG READER'S CHOICE AWARD (III), Pacific Northwest Library Association, Graduate School of Library and Information Sciences, 133 Suzzallo Lib., FM-30 University of Washington, Seattle WA 98195. (206)543-1897. Contact: Carol A. Doll. Award "to promote reading as an enjoyable activity and to provide children an opportunity to endorse a book they consider an excellent story." Annual award. Award: silver medal. Judges: Children's librarians and teachers nominate; children in grades 4-8 vote for their favorite book on the list. Guidelines for SASE. Deadline: February 1. Previously published submission. Writers must be nominated by children's librarians and teachers.

Other contests

The following contests, grants and awards appeared in the 1990 edition of *Novel and Short Story Writer's Market* but do not appear in the 1991 edition. Those contests, grants and awards that did not respond to our request for an update appear below without further explanation. If a reason for the omission was available, it was included next to the listing name. There are several reasons why a contest may not appear—the contest may not be an annual event, for example, or last year's listing might have resulted in too many unsuitable manuscripts.

American Health Body Story contest (discontinued)
Charles Angoff Awards (asked to be deleted)
Best of Blurbs Contest (asked to be deleted)
Best of Housewife-Writer's Forum (asked to be left out this year)
Black Ice Margaret Jones Fiction Award
The F.G.Bressani Prize
California Writers' Roundtable Annual Writing Contests
The Chattahoochee Prize
Connecticut Writers League Annual Writing Contest
Cross-Canada Writers' Magazine Editors' Prize
Fiction Network Competition
Miles Franklin Literary Award
Georgia State Writing Competition

Illinois Arts Council Special Assistance Grant and Artist's Fellowship
International Literary Contest
Louisa Kern Fund Grant (discontinued)
Literary Lights Short Story Contest
Lyra Short Fiction Contest
McDonald's Literary Achievement Awards for Writing on the Black Experience (discontinued)
The Marten Bequest Award
National Jewish Book Awards
The Noma Award for Publishing in Africa
Nordmanns-Forbundet Translation Grant
Ploughshares Denise and Mel Cohen Award (asked to be deleted)
Pulp Press International, 3 Day

Novel-Writing Competition
Pushcart Press Editors Book Award (asked to be left out this year)
Kay Snow Contest
Suntory Awards for Mystery Fiction
Texas State Writing Competition
Mark Twain Award
University of Missouri Breakthrough Series (discontinued)
James F. Victorin Memorial Award
Wyoming Council on the Arts Frank Nelson Doubleday Memorial Award (asked to be deleted)
Wyoming Council on the Arts Neltje Blanchan Memorial Award (asked to be deleted)

Literary Agents

Every year we visit a number of writers' conferences to try to learn what kinds of information writers need. Fiction writers in particular want to know about agents. They are aware the market for unsolicited manuscripts is narrow—more and more publishers are saying "no unsolicited submissions." And even though a few do say they are open, writers wonder how many unagented manuscripts really get past the "slush pile."

The answer is "fewer and fewer each year." It is basically a matter of economics. As more publishers are merged or sold and reorganized to cut costs, valuable staff members are lost. Many of the first to go are the front lines of the editorial offices—those first readers and young editors whose job it has been to read through the hundreds of unsolicited manuscripts the publisher receives each week. Overwhelmed by the workload, publishers are turning to agents to provide that first screening step.

Should I get an agent?

If you are a mainstream fiction writer, you will want to seriously consider getting an agent. There are several agents interested in category and juvenile fiction, but these fields remain fairly open to unagented writers. Most novelists and short story writers who are looking to market a collection will want to at least consider getting an agent.

If you are submitting short fiction to literary journals or magazines, you do not need an agent. In fact, payment for most magazine fiction is just not enough to cover the added expense of an agent and most agents will not represent short fiction unless they already handle a writer's novels.

You do not need an agent to approach most small press publishers and, if your work is experimental or has a limited specialized audience, you may want to send manuscripts to small press publishers rather than large, commercial markets. If you are a new writer, you may also want to try to get published in a literary journal or small press before approaching an agent and a larger publisher.

How do I find an agent?

Shop around for your agent. Examine the agents in this section and check the Category Index before the Markets Index to find an agent interested in the type of work you do. It is usually better to query an agency first to find out if they are accepting new clients. It is usually all right to query more than one agent at a time, but, when sending a manuscript, it is courteous to avoid simultaneous submission to agents.

Agents find writers through directory listings, such as ours, but there are other ways. Some like to frequent writers' conferences and meet writers in person. In fact most writers' conferences include at least one resident agent or agent on a panel.

Another way to get noticed by agents is through referrals. Whenever you meet published writers ask who their agents are. If your work is very similar to that of another writer, you may try writing to that writer and asking for a referral. Agents pay close attention to writers referred to them by those whose literary judgment they respect.

Make sure your query letter is as carefully written as your manuscript. If your work can be classified as a particular genre or category, a brief plot description (one or two paragraphs) may be all you need. But if your manuscript is a mainstream novel, you will want to include a detailed outline and sample chapters.

Choose an agent who is familiar with and handles work similar to your own. Agents based on the West Coast usually have experience handling scripts and know the movie business. New York area agents probably have more contacts within the large publishing houses. Although some writers choose these agents because of their close proximity to publishers, don't ignore agencies located in the South or Midwest. These agents are more in tune with regional publishers, and with fax machines, express mail and other advances in office technology, location has become a secondary consideration.

Read listings carefully. Note if the agent charges a fee and check the list of "recent sales." This list will give you some idea of the type of work the agent handles. If you have last year's copy of *Novel & Short Story Writer's Market*, check to see if the titles listed under the Recent Sales have changed from previous years. Agents who sell new fiction titles every year to different publishers are obviously a good bet.

How do agents work?

Agents are not required to have licenses or formal training. In fact, anyone can call himself an agent. That is why agents listed in this book must answer a detailed questionnaire. We want to let writers know as much as possible about an agent's operation and fees. Before selecting an agent, meet with him and feel free to ask questions before making a decision.

Even though anyone can open an agency, it takes a combination of skills to be a successful agent. A few agents are also lawyers and some lawyers will act as agents, but an understanding of publishing law and contracts is essential, whether or not the agent has a law degree. Agents must be good sales people and negotiators. Many agents come from editing backgrounds and should have a working knowledge of the publishing industry. Agents should know how to get the best deal for you and have a good amount of business savvy.

Most agents charge a standard commission of 10-15 percent earned on the domestic sales of your book. For foreign sales, the agent may pay a foreign agent, so commissions are higher—about 20 percent. In addition to the commission, authors are often required to cover the costs of handling their work such as photocopying, express mail and phone calls.

Some agents also charge a reading fee. A fee of $50 to $100 is not unreasonable. The money is used to pay an outside reader. Some agents will return the reading fee if they decide to represent the author, but payment of the fee rarely insures representation.

A few agents also offer criticism or editorial services. Fees can vary widely and most writers we've talked to who used such a service did not feel the critiques were worth the money spent. Be sure to check an agent's credentials and ask for a fee schedule if you are interested in a such a service. Many writers find they get better and less expensive feedback from writers' groups and workshops.

We advise writers to try agents who do not charge fees or who charge very modest fees, before contacting those that charge more. After all, an agency that receives most of its money from fees has little incentive to sell your book for commission.

It's best to think of an agent as a business partner rather than a teacher or editor. Most agents expect your work to be in publishable form before you submit to them. Their job is to sell what you've written, to get the best deal and to advise you on your career. A good agent today provides much of the career stability once provided by editors.

Other sources of information

This year we've included an "Agents' Roundtable" along with our assortment of articles on writing and publishing. We asked three well-known agents many of the questions writers ask us. Their answers begin on page 59.

There are a number of directories listing agents. Check the annual publishing industry directory, *Literary Market Place*, often referred to as the *"LMP."* It's published by R.R. Bowker (245 West 17th St., New York NY 10011) and lists many agents in its "Literary Agents" section. Additional listings may also be found in *Literary Agents of North America*, published by Author Aid/Research Associates International (340 East 52nd St., New York NY 10019).

Other useful books on agents include *Literary Agents: How to Get and Work with the Right One for You*, by Michael Larsen and published by Writer's Digest Books (1507 Dana Ave., Cincinnati OH 45207). Another Writer's Digest Book, *A Writer's Guide to Contract Negotiations* by Richard Balkin may also be helpful.

Another way to find successful agents is to look in the *Poets and Writers* annual *Directory of Poets and Fiction Writers* (c/o *Poets and Writers*, 201 West 54th St., New York NY 10019). This directory contains the names and addresses of successful writers, but many can be contacted through their agents also listed. Check to see who is handling the work of the writers you admire. *Poets and Writers* also does a book on working with agents, *Literary Agents: A Writer's Guide*, by Debby Mayer.

Some of the agents listed in this section belong to professional agent organizations. The Independent Literary Agents Association (I.L.A.A.) and the Society of Authors' Representatives (S.A.R.) offer brochures and lists of members for an SASE. Membership in these organizations is voluntary, but agents who are members are expected to follow the groups' codes of ethics and standards. The I.L.A.A. is located in Suite 1205, 432 Park Ave. S., New York NY 10016. S.A.R. may be contacted at 10 S. Portland Ave., Brooklyn NY 11217.

DOMINICK ABEL LITERARY AGENCY, INC., 146 W. 82nd St., #1B, New York NY 10024. (212)877-0710. Agency estab. 1975. Adult fiction and nonfiction only. Adult fiction specialty: mystery and suspense. Usually obtains new clients via recommendations. Currently represents 75 authors. Occasionally accepts new clients. Query with SASE. Reports to queries in 1 week; to mss in 3 weeks. New/unpublished writers: 10%. Member of I.L.A.A.
Terms: Agent's commission: 10% on domestic sales; 20% on foreign sales. Charges for photocopying expenses, overseas mailing and authors' books.

ACTON AND DYSTEL INC., 928 Broadway, New York NY 10010. (212)473-1700. Agent contact: Ed Novak. Agency estab. 1975. Novels. Also reviews nonfiction (40%-60% fiction to nonfiction). Special interests: Commercial works. Usually obtains new clients via author references. Currently represents 100 authors. Presently accepting limited number of new clients. Query letter first. No unsolicited mss. Responds to queries in 1 month. New/unpublished writers: 10%. Member of I.L.A.A.
Recent Sales: *Seconds*, by Lois Wyse (Crown); *China Boy*, by Gus Lee (NAL).
Terms: Agent's commission: 15% on domestic sales; 19% on foreign sales.

LEE ALLAN AGENCY, Box 18617, Milwaukee WI 53218. (414)357-7708; call for our Fax number. Agent contact: Lee A. Matthias. Estab. 1983. Novels and feature film screenplays. Also reviews nonfiction (95%-5% fiction to nonfiction). Special interests: genre fiction, including mystery, thriller, horror, science fiction, western. Usually obtains new clients via "market directory listings, such as *L.M.P.*, *L.A.N.A.*, *Writer's Market*, Writer's Guild List, and various other directories and lists; also recommendations and writer conferences. Currently represents 20 authors. Presently accepting new clients. Send query. Responds to queries in 3-4 weeks; to mss in 4-6 weeks. New/unpublished writers: 80%. Member of WGA; Horror Writers of America. Foreign rights handled by Mildred Hird, NYC.
Recent Sales: *Fire Arrow, The Fire Dream* and *Valley of the Shadow*, by Franklin Allen Leib (Presidio Press); *Shadowdale* and *Tantras*, by Richard Awlinson (aka Scott Ciencin) (TSR); *Hollow Pursuits* (episode, *Star Trek: The Next Generation*), by Sally Caves.
Terms: Agent's commission: 10% on domestic sales; higher on foreign sales. 100% of income derived from commission on ms sales. "From new, unpublished writers, we are most interested in material directed toward an established market. If a novel, we prefer fresh, innovative and strong mysteries, thrillers and horror stories. If a feature theatrical-release type screenplay, we prefer low-to medium-budgeted contemporary genre scripts of high quality—no exploitation or trend-followers—written

with an immediately compelling, hook-type premise, engaging characters, and a strong point of view. Scripts need to be quite distinctive to get serious consideration. No articles, poetry, or short stories considered. Proper length and format essential. Return postage and/or SASE must accompany all correspondence until we represent the prospective writer. If you do not hear from us soon enough, call during business hours; be a friendly squeaky wheel. Updates when no substantive news is in the offing should be initiated by the author. Otherwise, we'll call when we have something."

JAMES ALLEN LITERARY AGENCY, 538 E. Harford St., P.O. Box 278, Milford PA 18337. Agency estab. 1974. Novels. Also reviews nonfiction (90%-10% fiction to nonfiction). Special interests: "genre fiction, especially SF, fantasy, historicals, mysteries, horror and high quality mainstream." Obtains new clients "most happily through recommendation by people whose opinion I respect; secondarily by unsolicited queries." Currently represents 40 authors. Presently accepting hardly any new clients "and *only* if previously published." Query first with descriptive letter, 2-3 page synopsis and SASE. Responds to queries in 1 week; to mss in 3 months. New/unpublished writers: 5%.
Recent Sales: *Shadow Leader*, plus two unnamed books by Tara K. Harper (Del Rey Books); *The Veiled Vixen*, by Virginia Brown (Walker and Company); *The Circle*, by David C. Poyer (St. Martin's Press).
Terms: Agent's commission: 10% on domestic sales; 20% on dramatic-rights sales; 20% on foreign sales. Charges for extraordinary expenses: "copying of full length mss, intercontinental phone calls on client's behalf—not billed; rather, deducted from future income. I am turning away just about all of the people who approach me; I feel that my list is comfortably full and it takes something really extraordinary to inspire my interest. And absolutely *no* response is given to anyone who queries without a SASE. When I mention commissions on dramatic rights, this reflects that I market film rights to published books that I have sold—I am *not* representing original screenplays or filmscripts."

‡AMERICAN PLAY CO. INC., 19 W. 44th St., New York NY 10036. (212)921-0545. Agent contact: Sheldon Abend. Estab. 1889. Novels, novellas and story collections. Also reviews nonfiction (80-20% fiction to nonfiction). Special interests: "Mysteries, action stories or mss that would make good motion pictures as well as published book." Usually obtains new clients via recommendations and solicitations. Currently represents 20 authors plus 200 estates. Presently accepting new clients. Query with outline. Responds to queries in 1 week; to mss in 4-5 weeks. New/unpublished writers: 15%.
Recent Sales: *Into-the-Night*, by Conrell-Woolrich and Lawrence Block (Mysterious Press); *The Best of Conrell-Woolrich*, by Conrell-Woolrich (Editions General, France); and *The World of Damon-Runyon*, by Tom Clark (Avon).
Terms: Agent's commission: 15% on domestic sales; 20% on foreign sales. "*We charge $100 reading fee and provide author with written critique*. We refund the critiquing fee out of our commission." "Two people who are literary veterans in this business." 75% of income derived from commission on ms sales.

MARCIA AMSTERDAM AGENCY, 41 W. 82nd St., New York NY 10024. (212)873-4945. Agency estab. 1969. Novels. Also reviews nonfiction (90%-10% fiction to nonfiction). Special interests: young adult, horror, humor, mainstream, science fiction, romance, men's adventure, mysteries. Usually obtains new clients via recommendations and query letters. Presently accepting new clients. Query with first three sample chapters and outline. SASE. Responds to queries in 2 weeks; to mss in 1 month. Member of WGA.
Recent Sales: *The Paratwa*, by Christopher Hinz (St. Martin's); *Killing Suki Flood*, by Robert Leininger (St. Martin's); *Face The Dragon*, by Joyce Sweeney (Delacorte Press).
Terms: Agent's commission: 15% on domestic and foreign sales. Charges for legal fees when agreed upon, occasional cable, telex, etc. 100% of income derived from commissions on sales. "If there is no SASE, we do not return queries or submissions."

AUTHORS' MARKETING SERVICES LTD., 217 Degrassi St., Toronto, Ontario M4M 2K8 Canada. (416)463-7200. FAX: (416)469-4494. Agency estab. 1978. Novels. Also reviews nonfiction (60%-40% fiction to nonfiction). Special interests: mainstream, male-adventure/thriller, horror, contemporary, regency. Usually obtains new clients via recommendations, word of mouth and advertising. Currently represents 25 authors. Presently accepting new clients. *Fiction*: We require a query letter first and then, from unpublished authors, the entire manuscript. *Nonfiction*: We require a query letter and then a proposal containing outline and two sample chapters. Responds to queries in 1 week; to mss in 6 weeks. New/unpublished writers: 35%.

Recent Sales: *Minstral Boy,* by Dennis Jones (Random House); *To Live Again,* by Martyn Kendrick (Random House); *One Step Beyond,* by John Amatt (Macmillan).
Terms: Agent's commission: 15% on Canadian/US sales; 20% on foreign sales. *Charges $225 to review full mss by unpublished authors.* "Fee includes a detailed critique and evaluation, which will indicate the weaknesses of the work, and offer specific suggestions as to how they can be eliminated." 95% of income derived from commission on ms sales; 5% from criticism service.

THE AXELROD AGENCY, INC., Room 5805, 350 Fifth Ave., New York NY 10118. (212)629-5620. Agency estab. 1983. Novels. Also reviews nonfiction (50%-50% fiction to nonfiction). Special interests: mainstream, mysteries. Usually obtains new clients via recommendations from others; at conferences. Currently represents 30 authors. Presently accepting new clients. Query. Responds to queries in 1 week; to mss in 1 month. New/unpublished writers: 20%.
Terms: Agent's commission: 10% on domestic sales; 20% on foreign sales. Charges extra for photocopying expenses. 100% of income derived from commission on ms sales.

‡MALAGA BALDI LITERARY AGENCY INC., P.O. Box 591, Radio City Station, New York NY 10101. (212)222-1221. Agent contact: Malaga Baldi. Estab. 1985. Novels, novellas, story collections (if previously published in magazine). Also review nonfiction (60%-40% fiction to nonfiction). Special interests: literary, mainstream, commercial, some mysteries. Usually obtains new clients via "Clients and editors recommend me. I write fan letters." Currently represents 40-50 authors. Presently accepting new clients. Responds to queries in *at least* 2 months; to mss in 2 months. New/unpublished writers: 95%.
Recent Sales: *Wild Again,* by Kathrin King Segal (Dutton); *International Writers Selections,* Charles Carson, editorial consultant (Anchor/Doubleday); *Henfield Prize Stories,* edited by the Henfield Foundation (Warner Books).
Terms: Agent's commission: 15% on domestic sales; 20% on foreign sales. "I keep track of photocopying of manuscript changes and overseas mailing. I ask new clients for $50 up front for photocopying of manuscripts *or* several duplicates of manuscript." 100% of income derived from commission on ms sales.

MAXIMILIAN BECKER, 115 E. 82nd St., New York NY 10028. (212)988-3887. Agent contact: Maximilian Becker and Aleta M. Daley. Agency estab. 1950. Novels. Also reviews nonfiction (75%-25% fiction to nonfiction). Special interests: adventure, mainstream, science fiction, suspense. Usually obtains new clients by recommendations from others. Currently represents 50 authors. Presently accepting new clients. Query. Responds to queries in 2 weeks; to mss in 3 weeks. 20% of clients are new/unpublished writers.
Sales: *Goering,* by David Irving (William Morrow); *Time to Choose,* by Janine Boissard (Little, Brown); *The Enigma,* by David Kahn (Houghton Mifflin).
Terms: Agent's commission: 15% on domestic sales; 19% on foreign sales. 100% of income is derived from commission on ms sales and film rights.

MEREDITH BERNSTEIN LITERARY AGENCY, Suite 503A, 2112 Broadway, New York NY 10023. (212)799-1007. Agent Contact: Meredith Bernstein. Agency estab. 1981. Fiction, nonfiction, science fiction and creative endeavors. Usually obtains new clients via recommendations from others, solicitation, at conferences. "Some, I go out and seek, if I have a prospect in mind." Currently represents 75-100 authors. Presently accepting new clients. Query first. Responds to mss within 3 weeks. Member of I.L.A.A.
Terms: Agent's commission: 15% on domestic sales; 20% on foreign sales. *Charges $45 reading fee to unpublished authors for outline and 3 sample chapters.* Offers criticism service: "My assistant and I collaborate on our suggested ideas."

THE BLAKE GROUP LITERARY AGENCY, One Turtle Creek Village, Suite 600, Dallas TX 75219. Director/Agent: Ms. Lee B. Halff. Agency estab. 1979. Novels, novellas, story collections. Also reviews nonfiction (50%-50% fiction to nonfiction). Special interest: general. Usually obtains new clients via recommendations from others and publications. Currently represents 40 authors. Presently accepting new clients. Query first with sample chapters. Responds to queries within 1 month, to mss or chapters in 3 months, "depending on workload." New/unpublished writers: 50%.
Sales: *Captured on Corregidor,* by John M. Wright, Jr. (McFarland & Co.); *Modern Languages for Musicians,* by Julie Yarbrough (Pendragon Press); *Linda Richards* article, by Katherine Kelly (*Cricket* magazine).

Terms: Agent's commission: 10% on domestic sales; 20% on foreign sales. Will read at no charge query letter and two sample chapters. Offers criticism service "if author wants a critique": *$100 for book-length manuscript (400 page maximum); $75 for less than 100 pages.* "Written critique done by a qualified consulting editor." 95% of income derived from commission on ms sales; 5% from criticism service. "No submissions read unless accompanied by a self-addressed, pre-stamped return mailer or envelope."

HARRY BLOOM AGENCY, 16272 Via Embeleso, San Diego CA 92128. (619)487-5531. Agent Contact: Patrice Dale. Estab. 1956. Novels. Also reviews nonfiction (80%-20% fiction to nonfiction). Special interest: mainstream. Usually obtains new clients via recommendations from others. Presently accepting new clients. Send in query. Responds to queries in 2 weeks; to mss in 3-4 weeks. New/unpublished writers: 10%.
Terms: Agent's commission: 10% on domestic sales; 10% on foreign sales. 100% of income derived from commission on ms sales.

REID BOATES LITERARY AGENCY, P.O. Box 328, 274 Cooks Crossroad, Pittstown NJ 08867. Contact: Reid Boates. Novels. Also reviews nonfiction (15%-85% fiction to nonfiction). Special interests: mainstream, literary and popular. Usually obtains new clients via referral. Currently represents 45 authors. Presently accepting new clients. Query first. Responds to queries in 1 month. New/unpublished writers: 20%.
Recent Sales: *Japanese Power Game,* by Bill Holstein (Scribners); *Autobiography of Ava Gardner,* (Bantam); *Love You To Death,* by Stephen Singular (Morrow).
Terms: Agent's commission: 15% on domestic and movie sales; 20% on foreign sales. Charges for photocopying complete ms. 100% of income derived from commission on ms sales.

‡ALISON M. BOND LTD., 171 West 79th St., New York NY 10024. (212)362-3350. Agent contact: Rebecca Gleason. Estab. 1977. Reviews novels (30%-70% fiction to nonfiction). Special interests: adult literary and commercial fiction. "No children's books." Usually obtains new clients via recommendations. Currently represents 30 authors. Presently accepting new clients. Send outline plus 2 sample chapters. Reports in 2 weeks on queries; 8 weeks on ms. New/unpublished writers; 20%.
Sales: *Behind the Waterfall,* by Chinatsu Nakayama (Atheneum); *Gallow's View,* by Peter Robinson (Scribners); and *The Snake Tree,* by Uwe Timm (New Directions).
Terms: Agent's commission: 10% on domestic sales; 15% on foreign sales. 100% of income derived from commission on ms.

GEORGES BORCHARDT INC., 136 E. 57th St., New York NY 10022. (212)753-5785. Agency estab. 1967. Novels, novellas, short stories, story collections. Also reviews nonfiction (35%-65% fiction to nonfiction). Special interest: literary. Usually obtains new clients via recommendations from others. Currently represents 200 authors. Presently accepting "very few" new clients. Query. No unsolicited mss.
Sales: *Lust and Other Stories,* by Susan Minot (Seymour Lawrence); *Walking the Tightrope,* by Francine du Plessix Gray (Doubleday).
Terms: Agent's commission: 10% on domestic sales; 20% on foreign sales. Charges for photocopying expenses. 100% of income derived from commission on ms sales.

THE BARBARA BOVA LITERARY AGENCY, 207 Sedgwick Rd., West Hartford CT 06107. (203)521-5915. Agent contact: Barbara Bova. Agency estab. 1978. Novels. Also reviews nonfiction (40%-60% fiction to nonfiction). Special interests: science and health, mysteries, science fiction. Usually obtains new clients via "recommendations from others, occasionally over-the-transom mss." Currently represents 20 authors. Presently accepting new clients. Send query first, don't send mss to read. Responds to queries in 2 weeks; to mss in 2 months. New/unpublished writers: 20%.
Recent Sales: *Ozone Crisis,* by Sharon Roan (Wiley); *Cyberbooks,* by Ben Bova (TOR); *Nicoti,* by M. Shayne Bell (Baen Books); *Xenicide,* by Orson Scott Card (St. Martin's).
Terms: "I do not accept anything without a letter of inquiry first, with a self-addressed, stamped return envelope included."

BRANDT & BRANDT LITERARY AGENTS, INC., 1501 Broadway, New York NY 10036. (212)840-5760. Agency Contact: Carl Brandt. Agency estab. 1913. Novels, novellas, short stories, story collections, nonfiction. Usually obtains new clients via recommendations by editors and current clients. Currently represents 150 authors. Accepting new clients. Query first. Responds in 1 week. Member of S.A.R.

Terms: Agent's commission: 10% on domestic sales; 20% on foreign sales. 100% of income derived from commissions on ms sales.

RUTH HAGY BROD LITERARY AGENCY, 15 Park Ave., New York NY 10016. (212)683-3232 or 674-0403. Agent contact: Ann Hawwood-Burton. Agency estab. 1977. Novels, story collections. Also reviews nonfiction (60%-40% fiction to nonfiction). Special interests: mainstream, mystery. Usually obtains new clients via solicitation. Presently accepting new clients. Query. Responds to queries in 1-2 weeks; to mss in 1-2 months.
Terms: Agent's commission: 15% on domestic sales. 100% of income derived from commissions on ms sales.

CURTIS BROWN, LTD., 10 Astor Pl., New York NY 10003. (212)473-5400. West Coast office: Suite 309, 606 North Largemont Ave., Los Angeles CA 90004, (213)461-8365; Canadian office: Suite 400, 1235 Bay St., Toronto M5R 3K4 Canada. (416)923-9111. Contacts: Perry Knowlton (Chairman/Chief Executive), Peter Ginsberg (President), Emilie Jacobson, Marilyn Marlow, Henry Dunow, Irene Skolnick, Maureen Walters, Clyde Taylor or Ginger Knowlton. Fiction and nonfiction (50%-50% fiction to nonfiction). Presently accepting new clients. Query by letter with SASE. No reading fee. Responds to queries in 2 weeks; to mss in 1 month. Member of S.A.R. and I.L.A.A.
Terms: Charges for special postage (e.g., express mail), telexes, book purchases for subsidiary-rights sales. 100% of income derived from commissions on ms sales.

PEMA BROWNE LTD., Box 104B Pine Road HCR, Neversink NY 12765. (914)985-2936. FAX: (914)985-7635. Agent contact: Pema Browne, Perry J. Browne. Novels. Also reviews nonfiction (60%-40% fiction to nonfiction). Special interests: mass-market romance, thrillers, horror, young adult, picture books, mainstream. Usually obtains new clients via agencies, listings, word-of-mouth. Currently represents 40 authors. Presently accepting new clients. Send synopsis plus sample chapters and SASE. Responds to queries in 1 week; to mss in 1 month. New/unpublished writers: 50%. *Reading fee for unpublished book authors.*
Recent Sales: *Over 40 and Looking for Work?,* by Rebecca Jesperson Anthony and Gerald Roe (Bob Adams, Inc.); and *The Deer Killers,* by Gunnard Landers (Walker & Co.).
Terms: Agent's commission: 15% on domestic sales; 20% on foreign sales. 100% of income derived from commissions on ms sales. "We only review manuscripts not sent out to publishers or other agents."

JANE BUTLER, ART & LITERARY AGENT, 212 Third St., Milford PA 18337. (717)296-2629. Agency estab. 1980. Novels. Also reviews nonfiction (75%-25% fiction to nonfiction). Special interests: science fiction, fantasy, horror, historicals and mystery. Usually obtains new clients by recommendations. Query only, no sample chapters. "NO SASE NO RESPONSE!" Responds to queries in 3 weeks.
Sales: *The Horns of Hattin,* by Judith Tarr (Doubleday Foundation); *Goblin Moon,* by Teresa Edgerton (Berkley Books); *Brother Lowdown,* by Sharon Epperson (St. Martin's).
Terms: Agent's commission: 10% on domestic sales; 20% on foreign sales.

‡RUTH CANTOR, Rm. 1133, 156 5th Ave., New York NY 10010. (212)243-3246. Agency estab. 1952. Novels. Also reviews nonfiction. Special interests: mainstream, workmanlike novels, mysteries, psychological novels, anything that sells in the marketplace. Usually obtains new clients via recommendations from others. Currently represents 40-50 authors. Presently accepting new clients. Query with outline plus sample chapters.
Recent Sales: *Golf Humor,* by Blumenfield (Price/Stern/Sloan); *The Hurry Up Summer,* by Mary Mahoney (Putnam); *Mary,* by Mary Sherrod (Warner Paperback).
Terms: Agent's commission: 10% on domestic sales; 20% on foreign sales. 100% of income derived from commissions on ms sales.

MARIA CARVAINIS AGENCY, INC., 235 West End Ave., New York NY 10023. (212)580-1559. Contact: Maria Carvainis. Agency estab. 1977. Novels, story collections. Also reviews nonfiction (65%-35% fiction to nonfiction). Special interests: general fiction, mainstream, suspense, mysteries, westerns, historicals, Regencies, category romance and young adult novels. Obtains new clients through the recommendations of clients, editors, attendance of conferences and letters of query. Currently represents 60 clients. Accepting new clients. Query with SASE. Responds to queries in 2-3 weeks "if not earlier"; to mss in 4-12 weeks. New/unpublished writers: 15%. Member of Independent Literary Agents Association, Writers Guild of America, The Authors Guild, Romance Writers of America.

Recent Sales: *Alchemy Unlimited*, by Douglas W. Clark; *Stonewords*, by Pam Conrad; *Tempest Born*, by Catherine Hart; *Secret Sins*, by Joann Ross.
Terms: Agent's commission: 15% on domestic sales; 20% on foreign sales. 100% of income derived from commissions on ms sales. "I view the project's editorial needs and the author's professional and career development as integral components of the literary agent's role, in addition to the negotiation of intricate contracts and the maintenance of close contact with the New York City publishing industry."

MARTHA CASSELMAN LITERARY AGENCY, Box 342, Calistoga CA 94515-0342. (707)942-4341. Agency estab. 1979. Novels, nonfiction (20%-80% fiction to nonfiction). Special interests: mainstream; food-related books; biography; children's. Usually obtains new clients via referrals from clients and editors. Currently represents 25 authors. Query with outline/proposal. No multiple submissions. No unsolicited mss. Responds to queries in 2-4 weeks. New/unpublished writers: 40-60%. Member of I.L.A.A. "I regret I cannot return long-distance phone queries; send written query, please."
Terms: Agent's commission: 15% on domestic sales; 10% for foreign agent and other sub agents. Charges for copying and overnight mail expenses.

THE LINDA CHESTER LITERARY AGENCY, 265 Coast, La Jolla CA 92037. (619)454-3966. Agent contact: Linda Chester. Estab. originally 1977-1984; reopened 1987. Novels, novellas, short story collections. Also reviews nonfiction (40%-60% fiction to nonfiction). Special interest: mainstream and literary fiction. Usually obtains new clients via recommendations from others, solicitation, at conferences. Currently represents 50 authors. Presently accepting new clients. Send query first. Reports on queries in 2 weeks; on mss in 3 weeks. New/unpublished writers: 50%.
Recent Sales: "I am constantly on the lookout for gifted fiction writers." Recent sales include: *Night Driving and Other Stories*, by John Vande Zande (Arbor House); and *Two Halves of New Haven*, by Martin Schecter (Crown Publishers).
Terms: Agent's commission: 15% on domestic sales; 25% on foreign sales. "I charge a nonrefundable deposit to cover ordinary expenses incurred (phone calls, postage, etc.)." 99% of income derived from commission on sales; 1% reading fees.

CINEMA TALENT INTERNATIONAL, Suite 808, 8033 Sunset Blvd., Hollywood CA 90046. Agent contact: George Kriton. Agency estab. 1979. Motion picture and television scripts and stories. Also reviews nonfiction. Special interests: motion picture and television. Usually obtains new clients via solicitation and recommendations. Currently represents 25 authors. Presently accepting new clients. Send query. Responds to queries in 3 weeks. New/unpublished writers: 35%.
Recent Sales: Motion picture and TV scripts on assignment to my clients.
Terms: Agent's commission: 10% on domestic sales. 100% of income derived from commission on ms sales.

SJ CLARK LITERARY AGENCY, 101 Randall St., San Francisco CA 94131. (415)285-7401. Agent Contact: Sue Clark. Novels. Also reviews nonfiction (75%-25% fiction to nonfiction). 90% mystery/10% suspense. Special interests: mystery, psychic, children's. Usually obtains new clients by word of mouth. Represents 15 writers. Presently accepting new clients. Query, then send entire ms. New/unpublished writers: 90%.
Terms: Agent's commission: 15%.

‡CONNIE CLAUSEN ASSOCIATES, WEST COAST FICTION BRANCH, 10966 Elderwood Rd., San Diego CA 92131. (619)578-1888. Agent contact: Susan Lipson. Agency estab. 1976. Novels. Special interests: mainstream, children's. Usually obtains new clients via recommendations from editors. Currently represents 20 authors. Not presently accepting new clients. Send query letter with outline plus 2 or 3 sample chapters. Responds to queries in 3-4 weeks; to mss in 8-10 weeks. New/unpublished writers.
Recent Sales: *Act of Passion*, by Harrison Arnston (HarperCollins); *Innismere*, by Suzannah O'Neill (Harper/Collins); and *The Snow Pony*, by Anne Eliot Crompton (Henry Holt).
Terms: Agent's commision: 15% on domestic sales; 25% on foreign sales ("when *I* make the sale, not the publisher.")Charges for office expenses, postage and photocopies. 99% of income derived from commission on mss sales. "Study the query letter format, don't ramble and don't apologize for your lack of credentials if you have none; present yourself as a professional writer and send only your most polished work in its most professional presentation."

‡**DIANE CLEAVER, INC.**, 55 Fifth Ave., New York NY 10003. (212)206-5600. Affiliated with Sanford Greenburger Assoc. Estab. 1979. Novels. Also reads nonfiction (40%-60% fiction to nonfiction). No science fiction or romances. "I do like mysteries, suspense mainstream." Usually obtains new clients via recommendations from others; listings in directories. Occasionally accepts new clients. Query. Responds to queries in 1 week. Member I.L.A.A.
Terms: Agent's commission: 15% on domestic sales; 10% on foreign sales and 10% sub agent's commission.

HY COHEN LITERARY AGENCY, 111 W. 57th St., New York NY 10019. (212)757-5237. Fiction and nonfiction. Send sample chapters with SASE "if ms is to be returned." Represents approximately 30 writers. Obtains writers via recommendation, conferences, unsolicited mss and queries. New/unpublished writers: 85%.
Terms: Agent's commission: 10%.

RUTH COHEN, INC., Box 7626, Menlo Park CA 94025. (415)854-2054. Reviews fiction and nonfiction (60%-40% fiction to nonfiction). Special interests: detective mysteries, juvenile, young adult, historical romance. Usually obtains new clients via recommendations from others; at conferences. Currently represents 70 authors. Presently accepting new clients. Query letter and 10 pages of manuscript plus SASE. Responds to queries in 2-3 weeks; *no unsolicited mss.* Member of I.L.A.A.
Sales: *No Way Out* (Harper and Row); *Dear Baby* (Macmillan); *Knaves and Hearts* (Avon).
Terms: Agent's commission: 15% on domestic sales; 20% on foreign sales. Charges for photocopying expenses. 100% of income derived from commissions on ms sales. Writers must include SASE.

COLLIER ASSOCIATES, 2000 Flat Run Rd., Seaman OH 45679. (513)764-1234. Agency estab. 1976. Fiction and nonfiction books. Member of S.A.R. and I.L.A.A.
Recent Sales: *Mourning Becomes the Hangman*, by Mark McShane (Doubleday); *The Da Vinci Deception*, by Thomas F. Swan (Bantam Books).
Terms: Agent's commission: usually 15% on domestic sales (fee negotiable for authors with strong credits); 20% on foreign sales. Charges for express mail and copies of books ordered from publisher if author approves. 100% of income derived from commissions on mss sales. "This is a small agency run by two people, and it handles authors and contracts dating back to the 1960s from predecessor agencies. So agency is extremely selective in accepting new authors—at most two or three new clients a year are tried out, including through referrals."

FRANCES COLLIN LITERARY AGENT, (formerly Marie Rodell-Frances Collin Literary Agency), 110 W. 40th St., New York NY 10018. (212)840-8664. Also reviews nonfiction (50%-50% fiction to nonfiction). Special interests: general adult trade books. Query with SASE only. No unsolicited manuscripts. Member of S.A.R.
Terms: Agent's commission: 15% on domestic sales; 20% on foreign sales.

COLUMBIA LITERARY ASSOCS., INC., 7902 Nottingham Way, Ellicott City MD 21043. (301)465-1595. Contact: Linda Hayes. Adult novels (mass market). Special interest: mainstream and category woman's fiction. Represents 40-50 writers. Query with publishing credits, synopsis, first chapter and submission history (pubs/agents). Cannot respond without SASE. Also reviews commercial nonfiction (70%-30% fiction to nonfiction). Writer is billed for specific project expenses (shipping, long distance calls, photocopy). Obtains new clients via referrals and queries. Presently accepting "very few" new clients. Member of I.L.A.A.
Terms: Agent's commission: 15%.
Advice: Does *not* handle short stories or collections, juvenile/young adult books, science fiction/fantasy, poetry, pornography, men's adventure, category historical/Regency novels.

MOLLY MALONE COOK LITERARY AGENCY, INC., Box 338, Provincetown MA 02657. (508)487-1931. Novels, short story collections. Query. "Queries and/or mss without return postage will not be acknowledged or returned." Also reviews nonfiction (50%-50% fiction to nonfiction).

BILL COOPER ASSOCIATES, INC., Suite 411, 224 West 49th St., New York NY 10019. (212)307-1100. Agency estab. 1964. Novels. Presently accepting new clients. Special interest: mainstream. Usually obtains new clients via recommendations. Send outline/proposal. Responds to queries in 2-3 weeks.
Terms: Agent's commission: 15% on domestic sales. *Charges reading fee to unpublished authors*, if material interesting and to be considered. Payment of fee does not ensure representation.

BONNIE R. CROWN INTERNATIONAL LITERATURE AND ARTS, 50 E. 10th St., New York NY 10003. (212)475-1999. Agency estab. 1976. Novels, novellas, story collections, including translations from Asian languages. Also reviews nonfiction (80%-20% fiction to nonfiction). Special interests: originality of style and tone, mainstream, and anything related to Asia. Usually obtains new clients via recommendation. Currently represents 12 authors. "I am a very small specialized agency." Presently accepting new clients. Send query with SASE for policy. Responds in 2 weeks. New/unpublished writers: 10%.
Recent Sales: *Wings of Stone*, by Linda Casper (Readers International); *The Haiku Handbook*, by William Hisginson (Kodansha International); *Haiku Around the World* (Simon and Schuster).
Terms: Agent's commission: 15% on domestic sales; 20% on foreign sales. "I am particularly interested in any work which has been influenced by some Asian experience, the Asian-American experience, anything cross-cultural."

‡LIZ DARHANSOFF LITERARY AGENCY, 1220 Park Ave., New York NY 10128. (212)534-2479. Agency estab. 1975. Reviews novels, novellas, short stories, story collections. Also reviews nonfiction (70%-30% fiction to nonfiction). Special interest: literary fiction. Usually obtains new clients through recommendations. Currently represents 95 writers. Presently accepting new clients. Send sample chapters. Responds "immediately" to queries; to mss in 3 weeks. New/unpublished writers: 10%. Member of I.L.A.A.
Recent Sales: *Very Old Boxes*, by William Kennedy (Penguin USA); an untitled novel by Harriet Doerr (HBJ); *A Cure for Dreaming*, by Kaye Gibbons (Algonquin Books); *A Relative Stranger*, stories by Charles Boxter (Norton).
Terms: Agent's commission: 10% on domestic sales; 20% on foreign sales. Charges for "major Xeroxing, foreign postage."

ELAINE DAVIE LITERARY AGENCY, Village Gate Square, 274 N. Goodman St., Rochester NY 14607. (716)442-0830. President: Elaine Davie. Agency estab. 1986. Novels and nonfiction (60%-40% fiction to nonfiction). Special interests: "all types of adult, popular fiction. Both mainstream and category manuscripts are reviewed." No juvenile fiction. "I write several articles each year on 'agenting' for various trade journals. We're always looking for new, talented writers." Currently represents 110 authors. Presently accepting new clients. Query or send outline plus sample chapters. Reports on queries in 2 weeks; on mss in 4 weeks. New/unpublished writers: 60.
Sales: *Perfect Morning*, by Marcia Evanick (Bantam); *City of Glass*, by Paul Bagdon (Dell); *Defiant Captive*, by Christina Skye (Dell).
Terms: Agent's commission: 15% on domestic sales; 20% on foreign sales. 100% of income derived from commission on ms sales. "Our agency specializes in adult fiction and nonfiction by and for women. We are particularly successful in placing genre fiction (romances, historicals, mysteries, suspense, westerns). We welcome queries from non-published writers as well as published authors, and we never charge a fee of any kind."

‡DOROTHY DEERING LITERARY AGENCY, 1507 Oakmont Dr., Acworth GA 30101. (404)591-2051. FAX: (404)591-0369. Contact: Dorothy Deering or V.L. Richardson. Editorial Director: M. Sewell Causey. Marketing Director: Charles Deering. Estab. 1989. Novels, novellas and story collections. Also reviews nonfiction (75%-25% fiction to nonfiction). Special interests: historical fiction and nonfiction, mainstream, mystery, romance, humor, juvenile, science-fiction, horror. Usually obtains new clients via conferences, active solicitation, recommendations, and through *Writer's Market*. Currently represents 47 authors. Presently accepting new clients. Send entire ms. Reports in 6-8 weeks on queries; 2 weeks on mss. New/unpublished writers: 65%.
Terms: Agent's commission: 12% on domestic sales; 15% on foreign sales. *Charges reading fee: $100 up to 100,000 words; $125 over 100,000 words; $25 short stories.* "We critique each book length manuscript free of charge. We offer a one to two page professional critique written by myself, Dorothy Deering, or a professional editor on staff. Author is responsible for postage, packaging, long distance calls, office expenses." 95% of income derived from commission on ms sales; 5% from reading fees or criticism services. Payment of criticism fee does not ensure agency will represent a writer.

‡ANITA DIAMANT: THE WRITERS' WORKSHOP, INC., 310 Madison Ave., New York NY 10017. (212)687-1122. Agency estab. 1917. Novels. Also reviews nonfiction (50%-50% fiction to nonfiction). Special interests: "any areas except children's and science fiction." Usually obtains new clients via recommendations and unsolicited queries. Currently represents 100 authors. Presently accepting new clients. Query. Responds to queries in 1 week; to mss in 4-6 weeks. New/unpublished writers: 25%.

Recent Sales: *Web of Dreams*, by V.C. Andrews (Pocket); *Crazy English*, by Richard Lederer (Pocket); *Houston in the Rear View Mirror*, by Susan Cooper (St. Martin's); and *Death of a Joyce Scholar*, by Bartholomew Gill (Morrow).
Terms: Agent's commission: 10-15% on domestic sales; 20% on foreign sales. 100% of income derived from commissions on ms sales. "Queries by mail preferred over telephone queries and unannounced visits."

SANDRA DIJKSTRA LITERARY AGENCY, Box 4500, Del Mar CA 92014. (619)755-3115. Agent contact: Sandra Dijkstra. Associate: Katherine Goodwin. Agency estab. 1978. Novels and story collections. Also reviews nonfiction (20%-80% fiction to nonfiction). Special interests: mainstream, literary. Usually obtains new clients via "recommendations from authors, editors, reviewers, booksellers, etc.; conferences; 'over the transom.'" Currently represents 90 authors. Presently accepting new clients selectively. Send query, synopsis and sample chapters plus SASE. Responds in 2-6. New/unpublished writers: 30%. Member of I.L.A.A.
Recent Sales: *The Joy Luck Club*, by Amy Tan (Putnam's); *The Horse Latitudes*, by Robert Ferrigno (William Morrow); *Catering to Nobody*, by Diane Davidson (St. Martin's); *A Woman's Glory*, by Franchesca Forrer (Harper Collins).
Terms: Agent's commission: 15% on domestic sales; 20% (British) and (translation) on foreign sales. Charges for postage, Xerox and phone expenses. "We ask an expense fee of $225/year (in which we are active) which seems to be average expended."

‡THE JONATHAN DOLGER AGENCY, Suite 9B, 49 East 96th St., New York NY 10128. (212)427-1853. Agent contact: Jonathan Dolger. Estab. 1980. Novels and short stories. Also reviews nonfiction (20%-80% fiction to nonfiction).Special interests: Mainstream. Usually obtains new clients via referrals. Currently represents 75 authors. Presently accepting new clients, but selectively. Sendy query with outline/proposal plus SASE. Responds to queries 3 weekss; to mss 5 weeks. New/unpublished writers: 10%-15%.
Sales: *A Real Man and Other Stories*, by Shylah Boyd (British American House); *A Bed by the Window*; by M. Scott Peck (Bantam Books); *The Exception*, by Susan Trott (Carroll & Graf).
Terms: Agent's commission: 15%on domestic sales; 25-35% on foreign sales. Charges for marketing fee, office expenses, postage, and photocopying expenses. 100% of income derived from commission on ms sales, domestic and foreign excluding dramatic rights, software etc.

THE DORESE AGENCY, 37-965 Palo Verde, Cathedral City CA 92234. (619)321-1115. Agent contact: Alyss Dorese. Estab. 1979. Novels, story collections. Also reviews nonfiction (50%-50% fiction to nonfiction). Special interest: mainstream. Usually obtains new clients via recommendations from others. Currently represents 35 authors. Presently accepting new clients. Query or send outline/proposal. Responds to queries in 3 weeks; to mss in 3 months. New/unpublished writers: 15%. Member of WGA.
Terms: Agent's commission: 15% on domestic sales; 20% on foreign sales. Charges $75 reading fee to unpublished authors. 95% of income derived from commissions on ms sales; 5% of income derived from criticism service.

DUPREE/MILLER AND ASSOC., INC., 5518 Dyer St., Ste. 3, Dallas TX 75206. (214)692-1388. Agent contact: Jan Miller. Agency estab. 1984. Accepts full-length projects only; no stories, children's projects, or poetry. Also reviews nonfiction (40%-60% fiction to nonfiction). "Prefer proposal format for nonfiction; fiction submissions should include a brief overall synopsis, sample chapters and chapter-by-chapter outline." Responds to queries in 10-12 weeks. New/unpublished writers: 60%. No reading fee; however there is a $10 processing fee and we require a properly posted SASE.
Recent Sales: *Storming Intrepid*, by Payne Harrison (Crown); *The Great Depression of 1990*, by Ravi Batra (Simon and Schuster); *The Seven Habits of Highly Effective People*, by Stephen Covey (Simon and Schuster).
Terms: "Minimal handling fee due when contract to represent project is signed." 100% of income derived from commission on ms sales.

ETHAN ELLENBERG LITERARY AGENT/CONSULTANT, 548 Broadway, #5-C, New York NY 10012. (212)431-4554. Agency estab. 1983. Quality fiction and nonfiction. (75% fiction to 25% nonfiction.) Special interests: first novels, thriller, horror, spy, science fiction. Usually obtains new clients via referrals (75%) or solicitations (25%). Currently represents 50 clients. Query. Responds to queries in 10 days; to mss in 21 days. New/unpublished writers: 50%.

Recent Sales: *Brack*, by Johnney Quarles (Berkley); *Danang Diary*, by Tom Yarborough (St. Martin's); and *Homicide*, by Charles Sasser (Pocket); *Rolling Thunder IV + V*, by Mark Berent (Putnam's/Berkley). **Terms:** Agent's commission: 15% on domestic sales. "75% of income derived from commission on ms sales; 25% of my business is derived from selling translations and performance rights. I only take clients I feel I can help, and I will not take a new client lightly. I usually give a quick response. I am actively seeking clients."

‡ANN ELMO AGENCY INC., 60 East 42nd St., New York NY 10165. (212)661-2880. Agent contact: Ann Elmo or Lettie Lee. Agency estab. 1940s. Novels. Also reviews nonfiction. Special interests: mainstream, children's. Usually obtains new clients via recommendations. Currently represents 50 authors. Not presently accepting new clients. Send query or entire ms. Responds to queries within a week; to mss "depending on length." Member of S.A.R.
Recent Sales: "Romances. 2 western series going at one a month and nonfiction." (Harlequin, NAL and Berkley; Wm. Morrow and Simon & Schuster for nonfiction.)"
Terms: Agent's commission: 15% on domestic sales; 20% on foreign sales.

‡THE FALLON LITERARY AGENCY, 1456 2nd Ave. #108, New York NY 10021. (212)744-6680. Agent Contact: Eileen Fallon. Agency estab. 1990. Novels. Also reviews nonfiction (70% -30% fiction to nonfiction.) Special interests: mainstream , mysteries and romance. Usually obtains new clients via recommendations from other others, solicitation, at conferences, etc. Currently represents 25 writers. Presently accepting new clients. Send query. Responds to queries in 1 week; to mss 4-6. New/unpublished writers: 10%.

JOHN FARQUHARSON LTD., 250 W. 57th St., New York NY 10107. (212)245-1993. Agent contact: Deborah Schneider. Agency estab. 1911. Novels. Also reviews nonfiction (50%-50% fiction to nonfiction). Special interests: mainstream, literary, mysteries. Usually obtains new clients via recommendations. Currently represents 125 authors. Presently accepting new clients, but very few. Query. Responds to queries in 1-2 weeks; to mss in 4-6 weeks. Member of S.A.R. and I.L.A.A.
Terms: Agent's commission: 10% on domestic sales; 20% on foreign sales. 100% of income derived from commissions on ms sales.

MARJE FIELDS — RITA SCOTT, Room 1205, 165 W. 46th St., New York NY 10036. (212)764-5740. Agent Contact: Ray Powers. Agency estab. 1961. Novels. Also nonfiction. Special interests: "All kinds, but we do not represent children's books." Currently represents 40 authors. Presently accepting new clients. Query. Responds to queries in 1 day.
Sales: *Live Free or Die*, by Ernest Hebert (Viking); *Exit Wounds*, by John Westermann (Soho); *Death of a Blue Movie Star*, by Jeff Deaver (Bantam).
Terms: Agent's commission: 15% on domestic sales; 20% on foreign sales.

FRIEDA FISHBEIN LTD., 2556 Hubbard St., Brooklyn NY 11235. (212)247-4398. Contact: Janice Fishbein. Agency estab. 1926. Novels. Also reviews nonfiction: (75%-25% fiction to nonfiction). Special interest: mainstream. Usually obtains new clients via recommendations and referral by staff readers. Currently represents 37 authors. Presently accepting new clients. "Responds to query letters in two weeks. Partial or complete manuscripts are not to be sent with query letter; sends criticism of manuscripts accepted for review in 4-6 weeks."
Sales: *Dr. Death* Series, by Herb Fisher (Berkley); *The Frenchwoman* and *The Queen's War* (two books), by Jeanne Mackin (St. Martin's Press).
Terms: Agent's commission: 10% on domestic sales; 15% on foreign sales. *Charges reading fee for new, unpublished authors* — $75 for first 50,000 words, pro-rated thereafter at $1 per thousand. Offers criticism service. "Analysis (criticism) and summary done by staff reader. If ms found marketable, it is referred to myself or an associate." 75% of income derived from commission on ms sales; 25% from criticism service.

FLANNERY, WHITE & STONE, Suite 110, 180 Cook, Denver CO 80206. Estab. 1987. Novels, screenplays, true crime. Also reviews nonfiction, business and children's literature. (50%-50% fiction to nonfiction). Special interests: literary, mainstream, gay, women's fiction, true crime. Usually obtains new clients via recommendations, some through advertisements in literary journals. Currently represents approximately 25 clients. Query, send outline proposal or outline plus 2 sample chapters. Responds to queries in 2 weeks; to mss in 6 weeks. New/unpublished writers 90%.

Sales: *I Get on the Bus*, by Reginald McKnight (Little Brown); *The Powwow Highway*, by David Seals (NAL); *Baby Lust* (Zebra Books); and *How to Run Your Business So You Can Leave It In Style*, by John Brown (Amacom).
Terms: Agents commission: 15% on domestic sales: 20% on foreign sales. *Sometimes will charge a reading fee for authors with no publishing credits.* Will critique manuscripts and edit for a fee. 75% of income derived from commission on ms sales. "Only submit work that is polished to the best of your ability."

THE FOLEY AGENCY, 34 E. 38th St., New York NY 10016. (212)686-6930. Contact: Joan or Joe Foley. Novels and nonfiction (50%-50% fiction to nonfiction). Query first by letter with SASE. No manuscripts. Accepts very few new clients.
Terms: Agent's commission: 10%.

JAY GARON-BROOKE ASSOCIATES, INC., 415 Central Park West, New York NY 10025. (212)866-3654. Contact: Jay Garon. "Mainstream, male and female action, adventure, mainstream romance (contemporary), frontier novels with authentic research, non-category horror novels, generational suspense sagas." Area of specialization: "whatever is selling at a given time; fiction and nonfiction." Query first; no phone calls. No magazine shorts or articles. Represents approximately 110 writers. Presently accepting new clients with credits via queries and recommendations only. New/unpublished writers: queries only.
Terms: Agent's commission: 15% domestic; 30% foreign sales.

GELLES-COLE LITERARY ENTERPRISES, 320 E. 42d St., New York NY 10017. (212)573-9857. Agency estab. 1983. Novels. Also reviews nonfiction (75%-25% fiction to nonfiction). Special interests: mainstream and "relationship" novels. Usually obtains new clients via recommendations from others or at conferences. Currently represents 25 authors. Presently accepting new clients. Query. Responds to queries in 2 weeks; to mss in 3½-4 weeks. New/unpublished writers: 5%.
Recent Sales: *Striving*, by Roberta Grimes (Berkley); *The Beyond*, by Barry Herington (Berkley).
Terms: Agent's commission: 15% on domestic sales; 20% on foreign sales. *Charges reading fee:* $75-proposal; $100-novel under 250 pages; $150-over 250 pages. Offers criticism service: "This is very varied from project to project. We've charged between $500 and $10,000. The book is completely analyzed and then edited by me." Charges for overseas phone calls, photocopying for multiple submissions, overnight mail expenses. "These two areas of the agency (ms sales and editorial service) are separate—many writers in editorial service come to me from other agents or publishers. I frequently place writers in editorial service with other agents. Usually the literary agency clients are *not* out of the editorial service. In fact there are only two."

THE GERSH AGENCY, 222 N. Canyon Dr., Beverly Hills CA 90210. (213)274-6611. Agent Contact: Nancy Nigrosh (formerly Blaylock). Estab. 1962. Novels, novellas, short stories. Also reviews nonfiction (90%-10% fiction to nonfiction). Special interests: "mainstream—convertible to film and television." Usually obtains new clients via professional referrals. Presently accepting new clients. Send entire ms. Responds to ms in 4 weeks. New/unpublished writers: less than 10%.
Sales: *Hot Flashes*, by Barbara Raskin (Weintraub Entertainment); *Donato & Daughter* (Universal); *Libra* by Don Dellio (A&M).
Terms: Agent's commission: 10% on domestic sales. "We strictly deal in *published* manuscripts in terms of potential film or television sales, on a strictly 10% commission—sometimes split with a New York literary agency—various top agencies."

‡GLADDEN UNLIMITED, Box 12001, Portland OR 97212. (503)287-9015. Agent Contact: Carolan Gladden. Estab. 1987. Novels. Also reviews nonfiction (80%-20% fiction to nonfiction). Special interests: mainstream, horror/thriller, action/adventure, sci-fi/fantasy. "No romance or children's." Usually obtains new clients via reference book listings, advertising, recommendations. Currently represents 10 authors. Presently accepting new clients. Query. Responds is 2 weeks on queries; 2 months on mss. New/unpublished writers: 95%.
Terms: Agent's commission: 15% on domestic sales; 20% on foreign sales. *Charges evaluation fee:* $100 (refundable on placement of project) is charged for diagnostic marketability evaluation. Offers 6-8 pages of specific recommendations to turn the project into a salable commodity. "We also include a copy of our handy guide 'The Writer's Simple, Straightforward, Common Sense Rules of Marketability,' with guidance and encouragement." 90% of income derived from commission on sales. Payment

of fee does not ensure agency representation. "This agency is dedicated to helping new authors achieve publication."

GOODMAN ASSOCIATES, 500 West End Ave., New York NY 10024. Contact: Elise Simon Goodman. Agency estab. 1976. General adult fiction and nonfiction. Usually obtains new clients via letters of inquiry, recommendations. Currently represents approximately 100 authors. Presently accepting new clients on a very selective basis. Query with SASE. Responds to queries in 10 days; to mss in 4 weeks. Member of I.L.A.A. (Arnold Goodman is currently president of I.L.A.A.)
Terms: Agent's commission: 15% on domestic sales; 20% on foreign sales. Also bills for certain expenses: faxes, telexes, toll calls, overseas postage, photocopying of mss and proposals, book purchases. 100% of income derived from commissions on ms sales. Does not handle "poetry, sci fi and fantasy, articles, individual stories, or children's or YA material."

CHARLOTTE GORDON LITERARY AGENCY, 235 E. 22nd St., New York NY 10010. (212)679-5363. Agent contact: Charlotte Gordon. Estab. 1986. Novels. Also nonfiction (60%-40% fiction to nonfiction). "Mainstream and literary fiction, mysteries, YA novels." Usually obtains new clients via recommendations. Currently represents 18 authors. Presently accepting new clients. Query. Responds to queries and mss in 3 weeks. New/unpublished writers: 20%.
Sales: *An Almost Perfect Summer*, (Bantam); *The Tarot*, (Paragon House); *What Your Dreams Mean*, (Berkley).
Terms: Agent's commission: 15% on domestic sales; 10% on foreign sales. Charges for photocopying expenses. 95% of income derived from commission on ms sales.

SANFORD J. GREENBURGER ASSOCIATES, 55 5th Ave., New York NY 10003. (212)206-5600. Adult novels only (no short fiction, poetry). Send query letter and detailed description or approximately 50-page sample with synopsis of balance. Also reviews nonfiction (50%-50% fiction to nonfiction). Presently accepting new clients. Interested in new/beginning novelists. Member of I.L.A.A.
Terms: Agent's commission: 15%.

‡MAIA GREGORY ASSOCIATES, 311 East 72nd St., New York NY 10021. Agent contact: Maia Gregory. Estab. 1976. Novels, novellas, story collections. Also reads nonfiction (25%-75% fiction to nonfiction). Special interests: literary fiction—no romance or popular fiction. Currently represents 10 clients. Presently accepting very few new clients. Query or send outline/proposal. Responds to query in 2 weeks; to ms in 1 month. New/unpublished writers: 50%.
Terms: Agent's commission: 10 or 12% on domestic sales; 20% on foreign sales. Charges for Xeroxing and foreign calls and mailings. 100% of business is derived from commissions on ms sales.

CHARLOTTE GUSAY LITERARY AGENCY, 10532 Blythe Ave., Los Angeles CA 90064. (213)559-0831. Agent contact: Charlotte Gusay. Estab. 1988. Novels, novellas, children's and story collections. Also reads nonfiction (50%-50% fiction to nonfiction). No science fiction, fantasy, mysteries *per se*. Usually obtains new clients via recommendations, query letters; sometimes by solicitation. Currently represents 10 authors. Presently accepting new clients. Query. Responds to queries in 6 weeks; to mss in 2-4 months. New/unpublished writers: 65%.
Recent Sales: *Wearing Dad's Head*, by Barry Yourgrau (Peregrine Smith); *Dressing Mary Slowly*, by Gail Wronsky (Peregrine Smith); *A Visit to the Art Galaxy*, by Annie Reiner (Green Tiger Press).
Terms: Agent's commission: 15% on domestic sales; 10% on foreign sales. Some basic costs for printing, photocopying and mailing may later be assessed, usually agreed upon between author and agent. 100% of income derived from commission on ms sales.

REECE HALSEY AGENCY, 8733 Sunset Blvd., Los Angeles CA (213)652-2409. Query only with SASE. Also reviews nonfiction ("no set ratio"). Interested in new/beginning novelists, but not presently accepting new clients.
Terms: Agent's commission: 10%.

‡ALEXANDRIA HATCHER AGENCY, 150 W. 55th St., New York NY 10019. (212)757-8596. Agency estab. 1976. Novels. Also reviews nonfiction (20%-80% fiction to nonfiction). Special interest: mainstream. Usually obtains new clients via recommendations. Currently represents 15-20 authors. No unsolicited mss. Not presently accepting new clients. Query by telephone. Responds to queries in 3 weeks; to mss in 8 weeks. New/unpublished writers: 75%. Member of I.L.A.A.

Terms: Agent's commission: 15% on domestic sales; 20% on foreign sales, including foreign agent's fee. *Charges $50 handling fee with all new material submitted for the first time.* Responds with comments on "why I think I can't sell it—what needs to be done to make it saleable, if possible." Charges for out-of-pocket expenses. 95% of income derived from commissions on ms sales; 5% from criticism services.

THE JEFF HERMAN AGENCY, INC., 500 Greenwich Street, Suite #501-C, New York NY 10013. (212)941-0540. Agent contact: Jeffrey H. Herman. Estab. 1985. Novels. Also reviews nonfiction (25%-75% fiction to nonfiction). Usually obtains new clients via referrals. Currently represents 75 clients. Presently accepting new clients. "First-timers welcome" Send query. Responds to queries in 10 days; to mss in 4 weeks. New/unpublished writers: 25%. Member of I.L.A.A.
Recent Sales: More than 100 titles sold.
Terms: Agent's commission: 15% on domestic sales; 10% on foreign sales. Charges for manuscript/proposal photocopying costs, overseas electronic communications. 100% of income derived from commission on ms sales.

FREDERICK HILL ASSOCIATES, 1842 Union St., San Francisco, CA 94123. (415)921-2910. Agency estab. 1979. Novels. Also reviews nonfiction. Special interests: literary and mainstream fiction. Usually obtains new clients via recommendations from others; solicitation; at conferences. Currently represents 100 authors. Presently accepting new clients. Query.
Terms: Agent's commission: 15% on domestic sales; 20% on foreign sales. 100% of income derived from commissions on ms sales.

ALICE HILTON LITERARY AGENCY, (formerly Warren/Hilton Agency), 13131 Welby Way, Suite B, North Hollywood CA 91606. (818)982-2546. Agent contact: Alice Hilton. Agency estab. 1985. Novels and story collections. "Preliminary query appreciated." Also reviews nonfiction (80%-20% fiction [and films] to nonfiction). Special interests: mainstream, science fiction, romance, quality humor and wit, children's. Usually obtains new clients via *Writer's Market, LMP,* other trade publications, referrals. Currently represents 22 clients. Presently accepting new clients. Query or send entire ms. Responds to queries in 2 weeks; to mss in 6 weeks. New/unpublished writers: 60%.
Terms: Agent's commission: 10% on domestic sales; 20% on foreign sales. *Charges reading fee: approx. $150 for 300-page ms.* "Where I am able, I do the evaluating myself, but I use outside readers who are highly qualified in various areas of expertise." 80% of income derived from commission on sales; 20% derived from reading fees. Payment of fees does not ensure agency representation.

HULL HOUSE LITERARY AGENCY, 240 East 82 St., New York NY 10028. (212)988-0725. Agent contact: David Stewart Hull, President. Lydia Mortimer, Associate. Estab. 1987. Novels. Does *not* handle short stories unless written by regular clients who concentrate on full-length books. Also reviews nonfiction (50%-50% fiction to nonfiction). Special interests: mainstream commercial fiction. Usually obtains new clients via recommendations. Currently represents 38 authors. Presently accepting new clients. Query. Responds to queries in 1 week; to mss in 1 month. New/unpublished writers: 15%.
Sales: *His Vision of Her,* by G.D. Dess (Harper & Row); *The Pact,* by Sharon Salvato (Berkley); and *The Haven,* by Sharon Salvato (Berkley).
Terms: Agent's commission: 15% on domestic sales; 20% on foreign sales. Charges for photocopying expenses. 100% of income derived from commission on ms sales.

SHARON JARVIS & CO., INC., 260 Willard Ave., Staten Island NY 10314. (718)273-1066. Agency estab. 1982. Novels. Also reviews nonfiction (60%-40% fiction to nonfiction). Special interests: "category/genre fiction, especially science fiction, fantasy, horror; mainstream nonfiction: true crime, nonfiction occult." Usually obtains new clients via conferences and references. Currently represents 80 authors. New/unpublished writers: 20%. Member of SFWA, WWA, MWA, RWA, I.L.A.A., INFO.
Sales: *Rainy North Woods,* by Vince Kohler (St. Martin's); *The Star Scroll,* (Dragon Prince series-Daw Books) by Melanie Rawn; *Encyclopedias Galacitica & Horrifica,* by Michael Kurland (Prentice Hall).
Terms: New policy: The agency will only take on new clients if (1) they come recommended by someone we know, who has read and can discuss the work; (2) they have met me at a conference and I have read the material and indicated interest. In the former, such a recommendation would have to come from a professional in the publishing field; an editor, writer or an editorial consultant. Send query letter only, with a brief description of project and length, and bio. A self-addressed, stamped envelope MUST be included.

ASHER D. JASON ENTERPRISES, INC., 111 Barrow St., New York NY 10014. (212)929-2179. Agency estab. 1983. Novels. Also reviews nonfiction (20%-80% fiction to nonfiction). Special interests: mainstream, suspense/espionage/mystery and romance. Usually obtains new clients via recommendations. Currently represents 30 authors. Presently accepting new clients. Query with outline plus sample chapters. Responds to queries immediately; to mss in 3 weeks. New/unpublished writers: 35%.
Terms: Agent's commission: 15% on domestic sales; 20% on foreign sales. Charges for photocopying expenses. 100% of income derived from commission on ms sales.

JCA LITERARY AGENCY, INC., 27 West 20th St., New York NY 10011. (212)807-0888. Agent Contacts: Jane Cushman, Jeff Gerecke, Tony Outhwaite. Agency estab. 1978. Novels. Also reviews nonfiction (60%-40% fiction to nonfiction. Special interests: "literary fiction, thrillers/adventure and mysteries, commercial fiction." Currently represents 100 authors. Presently accepting new clients. Send query. No unsolicited mss. Responds to queries in 2 weeks; to mss in 6 weeks. New/unpublished writers: 10%. Member of S.A.R.
Sales: *The Geography of Desire*, by Robert Boswell (Knopf); *Manifest Destiny*, by Brian Garfield (Otto Denzler Books/Mysterious Press); *Criss Cross*, by Tom Kakonis (St. Martin's Press).
Terms: Agent's commission: 10% on domestic sales; 20% on foreign sales. Charges for cost of bound galleys and copies of books to be submitted are deducted from author earnings. 100% of income derived from commission on ms sales.

JET LITERARY ASSOCIATES, INC., 124 E. 84th St., New York NY 10028. (212)879-2578. Agent contact: Jim Turpin. Agency estab. 1976. Novels. Also reviews nonfiction (40%-60% fiction to nonfiction). "Mainstream only. No children, sci fi or young adult." Usually obtains new clients via recommendation. Currently represents 80 authors. Not presently accepting new clients. Query. Responds to queries in 2 weeks; to mss in 1 month. New/unpublished writers: 5%.
Sales: *When Do Fish Sleep?*, by David Feldman (Harper & Row); *Juice*, by Robert Campbell (Poseidon/Pocket Books); *Age Wave*, by Dr. Ken Dychtwald (Tarcher/Bantam).
Terms: Agent's commission: 15% on domestic sales; 25% on foreign sales. Charges for photocopying long distance phone calls, postage expenses. 100% of income derived from commissions on ms sales.

‡LLOYD JONES LITERARY AGENCY, 4301 Hidden Creek, Arlington TX 76016. Agent Contact: Lloyd Jones. Estab. 1988. Novels. Also reviews nonfiction (30%-70% fiction to nonfiction). Special interests: mystery, childrens, romance, male adventure. Usually obtains new clients via recommendations. Currently represents 20+ authors. Presently accepting new clients. Send outline/proposal. Responds to queries in 2 weeks; to mss in 4-6 weeks. New/unpublished writers: 40%.
Recent Sales: *On My Honor, I Will*, by Randy Pennington and Mark Bockman (Warner); *The Blood Covenant*, by Rena Chynoweth and Dean Shapiro (Eakin Publishing); and *Abuse: A Handbook for Adult Survivors of Child Abuse*, by Dee Ann Parrish (Station Hill Press).
Terms: Agent's commission: 15% on domestic sales; 20% on foreign sales. 100% of income derived from commissions on sales. "I would like a brief bio on author plus a list of publishers shopped."

LARRY KALTMAN LITERARY AGENCY, 1301 S. Scott St., Arlington VA 22204. (703)920-3771. Agent contact: Larry Kaltman. Agency estab. 1984. Novels, novellas. Also reviews nonfiction (75%-25% fiction to nonfiction). Special interest: mainstream. Usually obtains new clients via recommendations from others and solicitation. Currently represents 12 authors. Presently accepting new clients. Responds to queries in 2 weeks; to mss in 2 weeks. New/unpublished writers: 75%.
Sales: *RASTUS on Capitol Hill*, by Samuel Edison (Hunter House); *Anything That's All*, by Shirley Cochrane (Signal Books); *Wheel of Fortune*, by Larry Kaltman (Washington Post).
Terms: Agent's commission: 15% on domestic and foreign sales. *Charges reading fee of $150 for 300 pages*; 50¢ for each additional page. "The author receives an approximately 1,200-word letter commenting on writing style, organization and marketability." 80% of income derived from commissions on ms sales; 20% from criticism service.

KEARNS & ORR ASSOCIATES, Suite 1166, 305 Madison Ave., New York NY 10165. Agent contact: Alice Harron Orr. Agency estab. 1987. Novels. Also reviews nonfiction (70%-30% fiction to nonfiction). Special interests: women's fiction (genre and mainstream), mystery/suspense, horror, and commercial nonfiction. Lectures nationally and obtains new clients through conferences and recommendations. Currently represents 65-75 writers. Presently accepting new clients, but "very selective." Send outline and first three chapters. "For an SASE we will send free guidelines on how to write a synopsis."

Responds to manuscript proposals in 6-8 weeks. New/unpublished writers: 50%. Ms. Orr represents all client work.

Terms: Agent's commission: 15% on domestic sales. "When I see work I think has potential for me to represent, I will offer suggestions on how to make it more saleable, no fees." 100% of income derived from commissions on ms sales.

Advice: "Don't send out a proposal until it is absolutely your best work. The market is cautious. Work must bc original and executed skillfully."

‡J. KELLOCK & ASSOCIATES LTD., 11017 80 Ave., Edmonton, Alberta T6G 0R2 Canada (403)433-0274. Agent contact: Joanne Kellock. Estab. 1981. Novels. Also review nonfiction (60%-40% fiction to nonfiction). Special interests: literary fiction, mainstream, children's, science fiction/fantasy, mysteries, thrillers—all genre writing. Currently represents 50 authors. Presently accepting new clients. Send query with sample chapters. Responds to queries in 1 week; to mss in 2 months. New/unpublished writers: 20%.

Recent Sales: *The Delany Bride* and *Pride of the De Vaux*, by Jo Beverley (Zebra); *The Gospel According to Mary Magdalen*, by Clive Doucet (Black Moss Press); and *The Great Science Fair Disaster*, by Martyn Godfrey (Scholastic, NY).

Terms: Agent's commission: 15% on domestic sales; 20% on foreign sales. *Charges "$75 for reading three chapters.* If style working with subject, my major concern, I read balance free of charge. Fee charged previously unpublished writers only." "If novel is good/borderline, and more work needed in order to sell. I charge by number of words, fee can reach for say a five hundred page novel: $300. Writers receive a detailed report basically on style: character development, action, dialogue either by myself or my qualified reader." Charges for all postage, necessary long distance, FAX, photocopying of ms. 75% of earnings derived from commission on ms sales; 25% from criticism service. Payment of fee does not ensure agency representation.

KIDDE, HOYT & PICARD, 335 E. 51st St., Apt. 1G, New York NY 10022. (212)755-9461. Novels and nonfiction (70%-30% fiction to nonfiction). Special interests: mainstream, literary and romantic fiction. Usually obtains new clients via recommendations from others, solicitations. Currently represents 50 authors. Presently accepting a few new clients. Query. Responds to queries in 1-2 weeks; to mss in 2-4 weeks. Associate member S.A.R. Dramatic Affiliate: Joel Gotler, L.A. Literary Associates. Foreign Rights: A.M. Heath & Co., Ltd., London

Recent Sales: *Nightlight*, by Michael Cadnum (St. Martin's); *The Last Frame*, by Jim Wright (Carroll and Graf); *Something to Hide*, by Patricia Robinson (St. Martin's and Readers' Digest Press).

Terms: Agent's commission: 10% on domestic sales. Charges postage and phone call expenses. 100% of income derived from commissions on ms sales.

DANIEL P. KING, LITERARY AGENT, 5125 N. Cumberland Blvd., Whitefish Bay WI 53217. (414)964-2903; FAX: (414)964-6860; Telex: 724389. Contact: Daniel P. King. Estab. 1974. Novels, novellas, short stories, story collections. Also reviews nonfiction (80%-20% fiction to nonfiction). Special interests: mystery, crime, science fiction, romance. Usually obtains new clients via conferences, recommendations from present clients. Currently represents 65 authors. Presently accepting new clients. Send query and outline plus 1 or 2 sample chapters. Responds to queries in 10 days; to mss in 2 months. New/unpublished writers: 75%. Member of Association for Authors, Crime Writers' Association.

Sales: *Twice a Victim*, by Cyril Joyce (Pageant); *Widows' Beads*, by Cyril Joyce (Pageant); *Cast a Shadow at Midnight*, by John D'Arcy (Romas Books).

Terms: *Charges reading fee.* Varies up to $175. Fee charged only to writers without major book or magazine credits. 99% of income derived from commission on ms sales; payment of fees does not ensure agency representation. "We are interested in newer authors and are most impressed by a concise query letter citing any previous credits and a synopsis plus the first and second chapters of the ms. We are very interested in fiction and nonfiction for the European, South American and Japanese markets. Genre fiction is the most salable (mystery, suspense, crime, romance) as well as general nonfiction."

HARVEY KLINGER, INC., 301 W. 53rd St., New York NY 10019. (212)581-7068. Agency estab. 1977. Novels. Also reviews nonfiction (40%-60% fiction to nonfiction). Special interest: mainstream. Usually obtains new clients via referrals from publishers and existing clients. Currently represents 75 authors. Presently accepting new clients. Query with outline/proposal. Responds to queries in 2 weeks; to mss in 6-8 weeks. New/unpublished writers: 15-20%.

Sales: *Green City in the Sun*, by Barbara Wood (Random House); *Butterfly*, by Kathryn Harvey (Villard); *The Final Opus of Leon Solomon*, by Jerome Badanes (Knopf).
Terms: Agent's commission: 15% on domestic sales; 25% on foreign sales.

BARBARA S. KOUTS, LITERARY AGENT, 788 Ninth Ave. 3A, New York NY 10019. (212)265-6003. Agency estab. 1980. Novels. Also reviews nonfiction (50%-50% fiction to nonfiction). Special interests: literary, mainstream, women's and children's novels. Usually obtains new clients via recommendations from others; at conferences; by queries. Currently represents 50 authors. Presently accepting new clients. Query with outline/proposal. Responds to queries in 3 weeks; to mss in 4-8 weeks. New/unpublished writers: 70%.
Sales: *The Talking Eggs*, by Robert San Souci (Dial Books for Young Readers); *Bed & Breakfast Across North America*, by Hal Gieseking (Simon & Schuster).
Terms: Agent's commission: 10% on domestic sales; 20% on foreign sales. 100% of income derived from commissions on ms sales.

LUCY KROLL AGENCY, 390 West End Ave., New York NY 10024. Send mss to 2211 Broadway, New York NY 10024. (212)877-0556. Contact: Lucy Kroll or Barbara Hogenson. Novels. Special interest: contemporary. Represents 35 writers (including playwrights and screenwriters). Query. Also reviews nonfiction (50%-50% fiction to nonfiction). Obtains new clients via recommendations from others; queries occasionally. "Not actively seeking new clients, but we take them on occasionally."

PETER LAMPACK AGENCY, INC., Suite 2015, 551 5th Ave., New York NY 10017. (212)687-9106. Agent Contact: Peter Lampack. Agency estab. 1977. Novels, novellas. Also represents nonfiction (60%-40% fiction to nonfiction). Special interests: commercial fiction, especially contemporary relationships, out-of-category male-oriented action adventure, distinguished issue-oriented nonfiction and literary fiction. Usually obtains new clients via recommendations from others. Currently represents 60 authors. Presently accepting new clients. Query—no unsolicited mss. Responds to queries in 2 weeks. New/unpublished writers: 15%.
Sales: *Rightfully Mine*, by Doris Mortman (Bantam); *Dragon*, by Clive Cussler (Simon & Schuster); *Mine*, by Robert McCammon (Pocket Books); *The Glitter and The Gold*, by Fred Mustard Stewart (NAL).
Terms: Agent's commission: 15% on domestic sales; 20% on foreign sales. Author is responsible for supplying all submission copies. 100% of income derived from commissions on ms sales.

THE ROBERT LANTZ/JOY HARRIS LITERARY AGENCY, 888 7th Ave., New York NY 10106. (212)586-0200. Contact: Joy Harris. Special interest: mainstream. Also reviews nonfiction (50%-50% fiction to nonfiction). Represents 60 writers. Usually obtains new writers via recommendations and writer's conferences. Presently accepting new clients on limited basis. New/unpublished writers: 10%. Member of S.A.R.

MICHAEL LARSEN/ELIZABETH POMADA LITERARY AGENTS, 1029 Jones St., San Francisco CA 94109. (415)673-0939. Agency estab. 1972. Novels. Also reviews nonfiction. Special interests: mainstream, historical, contemporary, literary, commercial, romance and mysteries. Usually obtains new clients via recommendations from others. Currently represents 75 authors. Presently accepting new clients. Send first 30 pages of completed manuscript and a synopsis with SASE. Responds to queries in 6-8 weeks. New/unpublished writers: 50%. Member of I.L.A.A.
Recent Sales: *Chantal*, by Yvone Lenard (Dell); *Candle in the Window*, by Christina Dodd (HarperCollins); and *Dragon Revenant*, by Katharine Kerr (Bantam).
Terms: Agent's commission: 15% on domestic sales; 20% on foreign sales. "As agents, we desperately seek good new novelists, who are the lifeblood of the publishing world."

THE LAZEAR AGENCY INCORPORATED, Suite 416, 430 First Avenue North, Minneapolis MN 55401. (612)332-8640. Agent contacts: Jonathan Lazear, Virginia See, Kathy Erickson, Mary Meehan, Peggy Kelly, Wendy Lazcar. Estab. 1984. Novels and story collections. Also reviews nonfiction (40%-60% fiction to nonfiction). Special interests: adult fiction and nonfiction, young adult, mainstream, science fiction, mysteries, romance, westerns. Usually obtains new clients via recommendations and solicitations. Currently represents 300+ authors. Presently accepting new clients. Query. Responds to queries in 2 weeks; to mss in 8-10 weeks. New/unpublished writers: 50%. Member of ABA.

Recent Sales: *Eagle-Eye Ernie* series, by Susan Pearson (Simon & Schuster); 2 untitled novels by James Lileks (Pocket Books); *The River*, by Gary Paulsen (Delacorte); *Next Thing to Strangers*, by Sheri Cooper Sinykin (Lothrop, Lee and Shepard).
Terms: Agent's commission: 15% on domestic sales; 20% on foreign sales. Charges for federal express and photocopying expenses. 75% of income derived from ms sales; 25% from motion picture and television sales.

THE L. HARRY LEE LITERARY AGENCY, Box 203, Rocky Point NY 11778. (516)744-1188. Agent contacts: Vito Brenna, Lisa Judd, Holli Rovitti, Dawn Dreyer, Ralph Schiano (Sci Fi), Charles Rothery (Humor), Katie Polk (Mainstream), Charis Biggis (Action/Adventure), Colin James (Horror/Mystery). Agency estab. 1979. Novels. Does not review nonfiction. Special interests: mainstream, SF, historical, war, horror, humor, occult, mystery, suspense, modern sexy romance, western, adventure, thrillers, spy and literary works. Usually obtains new clients via recommendations, solicitations, conferences, watering holes. Currently represents 175 authors, 100 of whom are screenwriters or playwrights. Presently accepting new clients. Query. Responds to queries in 3-4 weeks; to mss in 4-6 weeks. New/ unpublished writers: 20%. Member of S.A.R., I.L.A.A., WGA, East, Inc.
Recent Sales: *The Gizmo Delicious*, by Holli Rovitti (Dorchester); *Brianne*, by Patti Roenbeck (Leisure); *Neighbors*, by Maureen Pusti (Dorchester); *Curtains for Sure*, by Ken Copel; *Snake-Check*, by James E. Colaneri.
Terms: Agents commission: 15% on domestic sales; 20% on foreign sales. *Charges $85 reading fee* "for 1st 55 pages; $75 for the rest of the novel regardless of length. That's with a critique." Offers criticism service by "competent associates who have years of experience. Critiques range from 3-6 pages. Plus a marked-up manuscript." Charges fee for "postage, handling (includes phone calls, letters, packaging), file set-up, responses to rejections etc. Copyright forms available. Associates available at all times." 90% of income derived from commissions on mss; 10% from criticism service. "Good story telling essential. Good writing essential. The market is getting tougher and tougher, so you have to be good to sell today."

ELLEN LEVINE LITERARY AGENCY INC., 15 East 26th Street, 18th Floor, New York NY 10010. (212)889-0620. Agents: Ellen Levine, Diana Finch, Anne Dubuisson. Reviews novels and nonfiction (50%-50% fiction to nonfiction). Usually obtains new clients through recommendations from clients and editors. Presently accepting new clients. Query letter first, do not look at unsolicited mss. Responds to queries in 2 weeks; to mss in 4-6 weeks. Member of S.A.R. and I.L.A.A.
Terms: Agent's commision: 10% on domestic sales; 20% on foreign sales.

LIGHTHOUSE LITERARY AGENCY, P.O. Box 1000, Edgewater FL 32132-1000. Agent contact: Sandy Kangas. Agency estab. 1988. Novel, novellas, story collections. Also reviews nonfiction (71%-29% fiction to nonfiction). Special interests: genre fiction, contemporary, literary, adventure, young adult. Usually obtains new clients via recommendations and professional organizations. Currently represents 68 authors. Presently accepting new clients. Send entire ms if complete; otherwise, send query or proposal package. Responds in 1 month. New/unpublished writers: 35%. Member of the Authors Guild.
Recent Sales: *The Draper Solution*, by Galen C. Dukes (Ballantine); *Power P.R.*, by D.C. Hill (Fell); *The Goose Got Loose*, by Laura Happel (Little, Brown).
Terms: Agent's commission: 15% on domestic sales; 20% on foreign sales. *Charges $45 to review unsolicited mss for acceptance or rejection.* May be waived if previously published. *Offers criticism service:* will critique 300/page novel for $300. We promise prompt response to proposals, submissions and analysis requests, whether we offer to represent the author or not. We do not believe in holding up an author's work."

MAXWELL J. LILLIENSTEIN, 7 Rest Ave., Ardsley NY 10502. Agent Contact: Maxwell J. Lillienstein. Agency estab. 1979. Novels. Also reviews nonfiction (80%-20% fiction to nonfiction). Special interests: mainstream, historical romances, fantasy, science fiction. Usually obtains new clients via recommendations from others. Currently represents 6 authors. Presently accepting new clients "only published authors." Send 3 sample chapters. Responds to ms in 30 days.
Terms: Agent's commission: 10% on domestic sales; 10% on foreign sales.

RAY LINCOLN LITERARY AGENCY, 107 B Elkins Park House, 7900 Old York Rd., Elkinspark PA 19117. (215)635-0827. Agency estab. 1974. Novels. Also reviews nonfiction (50%-50% fiction to nonfiction). "I particularly like biographies and popular science." Special interests: "mainstream—contemporary, historical, science fiction, children's—only for ages 5 and upward; mostly young adult; no picture books; no plays; no poetry." Usually obtains new clients by recommendation. Presently accepting new clients. "I prefer a query letter first (with SASE); then if I'm interested I ask for two sample chapters with overview, then on to full ms if promising." Responds to queries in 1-2 weeks; to mss in 3-4 weeks.

Recent Sales: *Bronze Mirror*, by Jeanne Larsen (Henry Holt); *The Fourth Grade Rats*, by Jerry Spinelli (Scholastic); and *Will the Nurse Make Me Take My Underwear Off?*, by Joel L. Schwartz (Dell).

Terms: Agent's commission: 15% on domestic sales; 20% on foreign sales. "If I think a ms is very promising and agree to handle it, then I'll make suggestions for changes in order to make it even better. For this there is no fee."

‡THE LITERARY GROUP, 262 Central Park West, New York NY 10024. (212)873-0972. Agent Contact: Frank Weimann. Estab. 1985. Novels, story collections. Also reviews nonfiction (75%-25% fiction to nonfiction). Special interests: mystery and thrillers. Usually obtains new clients by referrals. Currently represents 40 authors. Presently accepting new clients. Query with sample chapters. Responds to queries in 1 week; to mss in 1 month. New/unpublished writers: 50.

Recent Sales: *Play Dead*, by Harian Coben (British American); *Doublecross*, by Sam Giancarna (Warner).

Terms: Agent's commission: 15% on domestic sales; 20% on foreign sales. 100% of income derived from commissions on sales.

LITERARY/BUSINESS ASSOCIATES, Box 2415, Hollywood CA 90078. (213)465-2630. Contact: Shelley Gross. Agency estab. 1979. Novels, novellas. Also reviews nonfiction (40%-60% fiction to nonfiction). Special interests: mystery, New Age, occult, holistic healing, humor and contemporary, business. Usually obtains new clients via recommendations; solicitations; at conferences. Currently represents 5 authors. Presently accepting new clients. Query with brief outline. Responds to queries in 2 weeks; to mss in 4-6 weeks. SASE. New/unpublished writers: 85-90%.

Terms: Agent's commission: 15% on domestic sales; 20% on foreign sales. *Charges $85 evaluation fee* for up to 300-page ms. "Critique includes detailed analysis plus free literary nonfiction or fiction 1-page guide sheet." Charges marketing fee of $60. 60% of income derived from commissions on ms sales; 40% from criticism service. "Marketing fee is refundable after sale has been made."

‡STERLING LORD LITERISTIC, INC., One Madison Ave., New York NY 10010. (212)696-2800. Estab. 1952. Novels, novellas, short stories, story collections. Also reviews nonfiction (50%-50% fiction to nonfiction). Special interests: mainstream. Usually obtains new clients via recommendations. Currently represents 500+ authors. Presently accepting new clients. Query. Member S.A.R. and W.G.A.

Terms: Agent's commission: 10% on domestic sales; 20% on foreign sales. Charges fees for photocopying; some foreign mailing. 100% of income derived from commission on sales.

LOS ANGELES LITERARY ASSOCIATES, 8955 Norma Place, Los Angeles CA 90069. (213)275-6330. Contact: Joel Gotler. Agency estab. 1987. Novels. Also reviews nonficiton (70%-30% fiction to nonfiction). Special interest: mainstream. Usually obtains new clients via recommendations from others. Query. Responds to queries in 2 weeks. "If send submissions, postage must be included if they are to be returned." New/unpublished writers: 10%.

Sales: *Brain Building*, by Marilyn Vos Savant (Bantam); *Rockets Red Glare*, by Greg Dinallo (St. Martin's Press).

Terms: Commission: 10% minimum on domestic sales but rate varies; 20% on foreign sales.

LOWENSTEIN ASSOCIATES, 121 W. 27th St., New York NY 10001. (212)206-1630. Agent contact: Norman Kurz. Agency estab. 1978. (50%-50% fiction to nonfiction). Usually obtains new clients via recommendations from clients and published authors, conferences. Currently represents 150 authors. Presently accepting new clients. Send query. Responds to queries in 4 weeks; to mss in 6-8 weeks. Member of I.L.A.A.

Terms: Agent's commission: 15% on domestic sales; 20% on foreign sales. 100% of income derived from commission on ms sales.

MARGARET McBRIDE LITERARY AGENCY, Box 8730, La Jolla CA 92038. (619)459-0559. Contact: Winifred Golden, associate; Sheri Douglas, assistant. Fiction and nonfiction for adult mainstream market. Prefers query letter. No unsolicited mss. Member of I.L.A.A.

Terms: Agent's commission: 15%.

DONALD MacCAMPBELL INC., 12 E. 41st St., New York NY 10017. (212)683-5580. Agent Contact: Donald MacCampbell. Agency estab. 1940. Book-length fiction only. Special interests: adult fiction, specializing in the women's market. Usually obtains new clients via recommendations from others. Presently accepting new clients; no unpublished writers. Query with entire ms. Responds to queries in 2 weeks.
Sales: *Kate*, by Joanna McGauran (Pocket Books); *Thunder*, by Lynne Scott-Drennan (Doubleday); *China Silk*, by Florence Hurd (Ballantine).
Terms: Agent's commission: 10% on domestic sales; 20% on foreign sales. 100% of income derived from commissions on ms sales. "This is a small, highly selective agency for professional writers who write full time in the commercial fiction markets."

RICHARD P. McDONOUGH, LITERARY AGENT, 812 Centre St., Box 1950, Boston MA 02130. (617)522-6388. Agent contact: R. McDonough. Novels and story collections. Also reads nonfiction (25%-75% fiction to nonfiction). Special interests: literary. Usually obtains new clients via recommendations. Currently represents 30 authors. Presently accepting new clients. Query letters only. New/unpublished writers: 50%.
Sales: *The Way That Water Enters Stone*, by John Dufresne (Norton).
Terms: Agent's commission: 15% on domestic sales; 15% on foreign. Charges for some extraordinary expenses on sale only. 100% of income derived from commission on ms sales.

JANET WILKENS MANUS LITERARY AGENCY INC., 370 Lexington Ave., New York NY 10017. (212)685-9558. Agency estab. 1981. 50%-50% fiction to nonfiction. Special interests: mainstream, thrillers, mystery, suspense, true crime, horror, children's, psychology, health. Usually obtains new clients via conferences, recommendations from others. Currently represents 35 authors. Presently accepting new clients. Query with 2-3 sample chapters. Responds to queries in 2-3 weeks; to mss in 5-6 weeks. New/unpublished writers: 25%. Member of I.L.A.A.
Recent Sales: *Innocence Lost*, by Carlton Stowers; *A Cold Killing* and *Fatal Recall*, by Stephen "Deforest" Day; *Personal Effects*, by Marissa Pasman.
Terms: Agent's commission: 15% on domestic sales; 20% on foreign sales. 100% of income derived from commissions on ms sales.

DENISE MARCIL LITERARY AGENCY, INC., 685 West End Ave., #9C, New York NY 10025. Agency estab. 1977. Novels. Also reviews nonfiction (65%-35% fiction to nonfiction). Special interests: women's fiction, commercial fiction, horror, psychological suspense. Usually obtains new clients via recommendations from others, conferences, and through query letters. Currently represents 100 authors. Presently accepting few new clients. Query with SASE. Responds to queries in 2 weeks; to mss in 3 months. New/unpublished writers: 80% "were unpublished at the time I began representing them." Member of I.L.A.A.
Sales: *Pearls of Sharah* series, by Fayrene Preston (Bantam); *Betrayals*, by Anne Harrell (Berkley).
Terms: Agent's commission: 15% on domestic sales; 20% on foreign sales. *Charges $45 for first three chapters and outlines only if we request material.* "If I sell the author's work, I charge for disbursements." 99.9% of income derived from commissions on ms sales; .1% from reading service.

‡BARBARA MARKOWITZ, 117 N. Mansfield Ave., Los Angeles CA 90036. (213)939-5927. Agent Contact: Barbara Markowitz, Judith Rosenthal, associate. Estab. 1981. Novels, story collections. Also reviews nonfiction (75%-25% fiction to nonfiction). "No sci-fi." Special interests: contemporary fiction and historical novels. Usually obtains new clients by recommendations, solicitation and the *LMP*. Currently represents 14 authors. Presently accepting new clients. Query with SASE and outline/proposal. Responds to queries in 1 week; to mss in 4-6 weeks. New/unpublished writers: 90%.
Recent Sales: *The Legend of Jimmy Spoon*, by K. Gregory (Harcourt Brace Jovanovich).
Terms: Agent's commission: 15% on domestic sales; 15% on foreign sales. Charges postage. 100% of income derived from commission on sales. "Succinct query; do not tell me all your friends and relatives love your ms."

ELAINE MARKSON LITERARY AGENCY, 44 Greenwich Ave., New York NY 10011. (212)243-8480. Contacts: Elaine Markson, Geri Thoma. Query letter first. *Do not* send unsolicited mss. "Authors should write to us (*don't call*) and we will respond." Also reviews nonfiction (about 50%-50% fiction to nonfiction). Presently accepting new clients. ("Very rarely, but we do accept clients if we are very impressed with their potential.") Interested in new/beginning novelists. Member of I.L.A.A. "We can't respond to queries unless you include SASE."

Terms: Agent's commission: 15%.

THE EVAN MARSHALL AGENCY, 228 Watchung Ave., Upper Montclair NJ 07043. (201)744-1661. Agent contact: Evan Marshall. Estab. 1987. Novels. Also reviews nonfiction (50%-50% fiction to nonfiction). Special interests: general adult fiction. Usually obtains new clients via recommendations from current clients and editors; solicitations; writers conferences. Presently accepting new clients. Query. Responds to queries in 2 weeks; to mss in 1 month. Member of I.L.A.A.
Terms: Agent's commission: 15% on domestic sales; 20% on foreign sales. *Fee for unpublished writers.*

MEWS BOOKS LTD., 20 Bluewater Hill, Westport CT 06880. (203)227-1837. Contact: Sidney B. Kramer/Fran Pollak, secretary. Novels. Also reviews nonfiction (20% fiction, 20% nonfiction, 50% juvenile, 10% miscellaneous). Special interests: "juvenile (pre-school thru young adult) and adult fiction." Currently represents 35 authors. Presently accepting new clients. Query with outline/proposal with character description and writing sample.
Terms: Agent's commission: 10% on domestic sales for published authors; 15% on domestic sales for unpublished; 20% on foreign sales; $500 minimum commission, if book is published. For new authors without professional recommendations, if the work is accepted by Mews, *charges $350 for circulation* to 4-5 publishers, applied against commission. Charges for direct expenses (photocopying, postage, etc.). Payment of fees does not ensure agency representation.

THE PETER MILLER AGENCY, INC., Box 760, Old Chelsea Sta., New York NY 10011. (212)929-1222. Agent contacts: Peter Miller and Jennifer Robinson. Agency estab. 1976. Novels of all kinds. Also reviews nonfiction (40%-60% fiction to nonfiction). "Interested in category fiction, particularly fiction (or nonfiction) which has television and motion picture potential." Usually obtains new clients via referral and reputation as established literary agent for over 15 years. Also writing conferences, and speaking engagements at colleges and universities. Currently represents 50 authors. Presently accepting new clients. Send query. Responds to query quickly; to mss in approximately 3-6 weeks. New/unpublished writers: 40%.
Recent Sales: *Lullaby and Good Night*, by Vincent Bugliosi (NAL); *Hollywood at Home: A Family Album 1950-1965*; photography by Sid Avery, written by Richard Schickel (Crown); *Infiltrators, Penetrators* and *Operators*, series by Mark Harrell (Berkley, a MCA Universal Co.).
Terms: *Charges reading fee for unpublished writers* (refundable out of first monies earned for author) for full-length novels. Will critique 300-page novel for $225 (nonrefundable out of first moneys earned for author). Critiques are 3-5 pages in length and written by the owner, Peter Miller, and a staff of highly qualified editorial consultants. Charges minimal marketing expenses, including photocopies, deliveries, Federal Express, long distance phone calls, and legal fees. 97% of income derived from commission on ms sales; 2-3% from criticism service. Payment of fees does not ensure agency representation. The agency specializes in representing "true-crime projects and all books that have significant television and motion picture potential and is particularly interested in developing agent/client relations. Agency has established relationships with co-agents throughout the world."

‡DAVID H. MORGAN LITERARY AGENCY, INC., P.O. Box 14810, Richmond VA 23221. Agent Contact: David H. Morgan. Estab. 1987. Novels. Also reviews nonfiction (50%-50% fiction to nonfiction). Special interests: "all except formula romance." Usually obtains new clients via recommendations, conferences, ads. Currently represents 25 authors. Presently accepting new clients. Query. Responds to queries in 1 week; to mss in 4-6 weeks. New/unpublished writers: 40%.
Terms: Agent's commission: 15% on domestic sales; 20% on foreign sales. *Charges a reading fee.* Offers criticism service. "Writer must pay for copies of ms to be submitted to publishers; writer pays for out of ordinary mail costs (overnight) where deemed necessary and mutually agreed upon." 70% of income derived from commission on sales. Payment of fee does not ensure representation.

HOWARD MORHAIM LITERARY AGENCY, 175 5th Ave., Room #709, New York NY 10010. (212)529-4433. Novels principally. Query. Also reviews nonfiction (70%-30% fiction to nonfiction). Member of I.L.A.A.
Terms: Agent's commission: 15%.

‡HENRY MORRISON, INC., P.O. Box 235, Bedford Hills NY 10507. (914)666-3500. Estab. 1965. Novels. Also reviews nonfiction (95%-5% fiction to nonfiction). Special interest: mainstream, international thrillers. Usually obtains new clients via recommendations. Currently represents 50 authors. Presently

accepting new clients. Query. Responds to queries in 2 weeks, to ms in 4-6 weeks. New/unpublished writers: 10%.
Recent Sales: *The Bourne Ultimatum*, by Robert Ludlum (Random House/Bantam); *The Moscow Club*, by Joseph Finder (Viking/NAL); and *Mollie Pride*, by Beverly S. Martin (Bantam Books).
Terms: Agent's commission: 15% on domestic sales; 20% on foreign sales. Charges fees for photocopies, bound galleys and books. 100% of income derived from commission from sales.

MULTIMEDIA PRODUCT DEVELOPMENT, INC., Suite 724, 410 S. Michigan Ave., Chicago IL 60605. (312)922-3063. Agent Contact: Jane Jordan Browne. Agency estab. 1971. Novels. Also reviews nonfiction (35%-65% fiction to nonfiction). Special interests: mainstream, mystery, and romance. Usually obtains new clients via recommendations, word-of-mouth, conferences. Currently represents 100 authors. Presently accepting new clients. Query. Responds to queries in 5 days; to mss in 1 month. New/unpublished writers: 2%. Member of I.L.A.A.
Recent Sales: *The Detective and Mr. Dickens*, by William J. Palmer (St. Martin's Press); *Swing Sisters*, by Jeane Westin (Scribner's); and *Silken Dreams*, by Lisa Bingham (Pocket).
Terms: Agent's commission: 15% on domestic sales; 20% on foreign sales. Charges for photocopying expenses and overseas phone calls. 100% of income derived from commissions on ms sales.

JEAN V. NAGGAR LITERARY AGENCY, INC., 216 E. 75th St., New York NY 10021. (212)794-1082. Agent contacts: Jean Naggar, Teresa Cavanaugh. Novels and nonfiction. Special interests: mainstream fiction (literary and commercial), suspense, science fiction and mystery; no category romances. Query with SASE. No unsolicited mss. Represents 80 writers. Obtains clients via recommendations, solicited mss, queries and writers' conferences. Presently accepting new clients only on a highly selective basis. Interested in some new/beginning novelists. Member of I.L.A.A. and S.A.R.
Terms: Agent's commission: 15% domestic; 20% foreign.

RUTH NATHAN, 648 Broadway, #402B, New York NY 10012. (212)529-1133. Agency estab. 1980. Novels. Also reviews nonfiction (20%-80% fiction to nonfiction). Special interests: mainstream, biography, illustrated books on art and decorative arts and show biz. Usually obtains new clients through recommendations, solicitation or at conferences. Currently represents 12 authors. Presently accepting new clients. Send sample chapters. Responds to queries in 4 weeks; to mss in 6-8 weeks. New/unpublished writers: 20%.
Terms: Agent's commission: 15% on domestic sales; 10% on foreign sales.

‡THE NATIONAL WRITERS LITERARY AGENCY, Suite 620, 1450 S. Havana, Aurora CO 80012. (303)751-7844. Agent Contact: Don Bower. Agency Estab. 1989. Novels, novellas. Also reviews nonfiction (60%-40% fiction to nonfiction.) All categories. Usually obtains new clients through the National Writers Club. Currently represents 12 authors. Presently accepting new clients, "if members of NWC." Send entire ms with outline plus 3 sample chapters. Responds to queries in 3 weeks; to mss in 6 weeks. New/unpublished writers: 80%.
Terms: Agent's commission: 15% on domestic sales; 20% on foreign sales. Charges $25 for making copies. 100% of income derived from commission on ms sales. "All clients must be active members of The National Writers Club."

‡CHARLES NEIGHBORS, INC., Suite 3607A, 7600 Blanco Rd., San Antonio TX 78216. (512)342-5324. Agent contact: Margaret Neighbors, vice president. Agency estab. 1966. Novels, story collections. Also reviews nonfiction (60%-40% fiction to nonfiction). Special interest: mainstream, male adventure, romance, mysteries, suspense, westerns and historical. No juveniles. Usually obtains new clients via 90% recommendations from clients and editors, 5% conferences, 5% inquiries. Currently represents 55 authors. Presently accepting new clients. Query with outline/proposal, ms samples and SASE. New/unpublished writers: 15%. Responds to queries in 1 week; to mss in 1 month.
Sales: *War Horse*, by Wayne Barton and Stan Smith (Pocket Books); *Manual of the Mercenary Soldier*, by Paul Balor (Dell).
Terms: Agent's commission: 15% on domestic sales; 20% on foreign and co-agent motion picture sales. 95% of income derived from commissions on ms sales. Also offers fee-paid editorial services.

B.K. NELSON LITERARY AGENCY, 409 North Broadway, Townhouse 23, Yonkers NY 10701. (914)376-2022. FAX: (914)476-7552. Agency estab. 1979. Novels. Also reviews nonfiction (10%-90% fiction to nonfiction). Special interest: mainstream. Usually obtains new clients via recommendations by others. Currently represents 12 authors. Presently accepting new clients. Query. Responds to que-

ries in "a few days"; to mss in 2 weeks. New/unpublished writers: 100%.
Sales: *Brecher's Odyssey*, by Gerhard Brecher (Pueblo Press); *Cafe Pierre*, by W. Ware Lynch and Charles Romine (Random House).
Terms: Agent's commission: 15% on domestic sales; 10% on foreign sales. *Charges a reading fee of $230 for a completed ms.* 99% of income derived from commissions on ms; 1% on criticism service.

THE BETSY NOLAN LITERARY AGENCY, 50 West 29th St., 9W, New York NY 10001. (212)779-0700. Contact: Betsy Nolan. Agency estab. 1982. Novels. Also reviews nonfiction (30%-70% fiction to nonfiction). Special interest: mainstream. Presently accepting new clients. Query with outline/proposal. Responds to queries in 2 weeks; to mss in 6-8 weeks. New/unpublished writers: 50%.
Terms: Agent's commission: 15% on domestic sales; 20% on foreign sales.

THE NORMA-LEWIS AGENCY, 521 Fifth Ave., New York NY 10175. (212)751-4955. Agent contact: Norma Liebert. Estab. 1980. Novels. Also reviews nonfiction (50%-50% fiction to nonfiction). Special interest: mainstream, mystery, suspense, children's, YA. Usually obtains new clients by listings in directories. Presently accepting new clients. Query. Responds to queries in 2 weeks; to ms in 4 weeks.
Terms: Agent's commission: 15% on domestic sales; 20% on foreign sales. 100% on income derived from commission on sales.

‡NORTHWEST LITERARY SERVICES, Box 165, Shawnigan Lake, British Columbia V0R 2W0 Canada. (604)743-9169. Agent Contact: Brent Laughren. Agency estab. 1986. Novels, novellas, short stories, story collections. Also reviews nonfiction (80%-20% fiction to nonfiction.) Special interests: "Literary primarily, all other genres considered." Usually obtains new clients via recommendations from others. Currently represents 20 writers. Presently accepting new clients. Send query with outline plus 2 sample chapters. Responds to queries in 2 weeks; to mss in 6 weeks. New/unpublished writers: 80%.
Terms: Agent's commission: 15% on domestic sales; 20% on foreign sales. Sometimes charges reading fee. Manuscript criticism (up to 20,000 words)-$100; reading fee, includes summary and recommendations, outline and sample chapters, $40; short story critique- $20." Written reports on literary merit and marketability with editorial suggestions." Charges for photocopying. 90% of income derived from commission on ms sales; 10% from reading fees or criticism service. Payment of fees does not ensure representation. "This agency is particularly interested in the development and marketing of new and unpublished authors."

NUGENT & ASSOCIATES, INC., 170 10th St. N., Naples FL 33940. (813)262-3683. Agent contact: Ray E. Nugent. Agency estab. 1983. Nonfiction. Also reviews novels (30%-70% fiction to nonfiction). Special interests: sports, health, true crime and celebrity biographies. "We do also handle a fairly large amount of fiction." Usually obtains new clients via publicity, other writers, writing conferences. Currently represents 44 authors. Presently accepting new clients. Send query and sample chapters and summary along with SASE. Responds to queries in 30 days; to mss in 90 days. New/unpublished writers: 40%. Book scouts located in other cities.
Recent Sales: *The 50+ Wellness Program*, (John Wiley & Sons); *P.O.W. Hanoi* (Ballantine); *The Jay Barbree Story* (New Horizon).
Terms: Agent's commission: 15% on domestic sales; 25% on foreign sales. "We charge for all clerical expenses directly associated with the preparation, mailing and materials required for the offering of a client's material. Long distance calls and wires are also billed to the clients." 100% of income derived from commission on ms sales. "We only charge our clients for expenses that they would normally incur if they were to attempt to bring their material to market without an agent."

‡HAROLD OBER ASSOCIATES, INC., 425 Madison Ave., New York NY 10017. (212)759-8600. Novels and general nonfiction. Reads all kinds, category and mainstream. Query first. About 75%-25% fiction to nonfiction. Currently representing 400 writers. Presently accepting new clients but very limited numbers. Represents British agencies also. Member of S.A.R.
Terms: Agent's commission: 10% US; 15% British; 20% other foreign.

FIFI OSCARD ASSOCIATES, 19 W. 44th St., New York NY 10036. (212)764-1100. Novels. Also reviews nonfiction (50%-50% fiction to nonfiction). Special interests: literary, mainstream. Usually obtains new clients via recommendations. Currently represents over 100 authors. Presently accepting new clients. Query. Responds to queries in 2 weeks; to mss in 2-3 weeks. New/unpublished writers: 10%. Member of S.A.R.

Recent Sales: *TekWar*, by William Shatner (G.P. Putnam's); *Cardinal Numbers*, by Hob Broun (Knopf); *Tower to Heaven*, by Ruby Dee (Henry Holt); *The New Edgar Winners*, the 1990 Anthology from Mystery Writers of America (Wynwood Press).
Terms: Agent's commission: 15% on domestic sales; 20% on foreign sales. 100% of income derived from commissions.

‡**THE RICHARD PARKS AGENCY**, 138 E. 16th St., #5B, New York NY 10003. (212)254-9067. Agent Contact: Richard Parks. Estab. 1988. (50%-50% fiction to nonfiction). Special interest: mainstream nonfiction; commercial and literary fiction." Usually obtains new clients by recommendations from others. Presently accepting "a few" clients. Query only with SASE. Responds in 2 weeks. Member of I.L.A.A.
Recent Sales: *The Little Brother*, by Bill Eidson (Henry Holt & Co.); *The Road to Bobby Joe*, by Louis Berney (Harcourt Brace Jovanovich); and *Following the Bloom*, by Douglas Whynott (Stackpole Books).
Terms: Agent's commission: 15% on domestic sales; 20% on foreign sales. Charges photocopying fee. 100% of income derived from commission on sales.

‡**KATHI J. PATON LITERARY AGENCY**, 19 W. 55th St., New York NY 10019-4914. (212)265-6586. Agent contact: Kathi J. Paton. Estab. 1987. Novels and story collections. Also reviews nonfiction (35%-65% fiction to nonfiction). Special interest: adult quality mainstream and literary novels and short stories. Usually obtains new clients via recommendations from others. Currently represents 30 + authors. Presently accepting new clients. Query. ("Please send first 40 pages and plot summary, or 3 short stories."). Responds to queries in 1-14 days; to ms in 1-30 days. New/unpublished writers: 15%. Member of I.L.A.A. (pending).
Recent Sales: *Wives and Husbands*, edited by Michael Nagler & William Swanson (NAL); *The Rat Becomes Light*, by Donald Secreast (Harper & Row).
Terms: Agent's commission: 15% on domestic sales; 20% on foreign sales. Charges photocopying fee. 100% of income derived from commission on sales. "To ensure response, please enclose a SASE."

RODNEY PELTER, LITERARY AGENT, 129 E. 61st St., New York NY 10021. (212)838-3432. Contact: Rodney Pelter. Fiction and nonfiction. Query with SASE, résumé and first 50 pages. Represents 15-25 writers. Obtains clients via recommendations, unsolicited mss and queries. Presently accepting new clients. New/unpublished writers: "probably a majority."
Terms: Agent's commission: 15% on US book sales.

‡**PERKINS' LITERARY AGENCY**, P.O. Box 48, Childs MD 21916. (301)398-2647. Agent Contact: Esther R. Perkins. Estab. 1979. Novels. Special interest: mainstream, mysteries, men's adventure, intrigue, historical, regency. Usually obtains new clients via word of mouth and listing in *LMP*. Currently represents 40 authors. Query with outline/proposal. Responds to queries in 1 week; to mss in 3 weeks. New/unpublished writers: 50%.
Recent Sales: *Brazen Virginia Bride*, by Millie Criswell (Zebra); *Time-Spun Rapture*, by Thomasina Ring (Leisure); and *Lady Maryann's Dilemma*, by Karla Hocker (Zebra).
Terms: Agent's commission: 15% on domestic sales; 20% on foreign sales. Charges a reading fee for anyone not published in past 2 years. Criticism service comes with fee. Type of critique "depends on what and how much mss requires. I do all reading and critique." 95% of income derived from commission on sales. Payment of fee does not ensure representation.

‡**ALISON PICARD, LITERARY AGENT**, P.O. Box 2000, Cotuit MA 02635. (508)888-3741. Agent Contact: Alison Picard. Estab. 1985. Novels, short stories and story collections. Also reviews nonfiction (40%-60% fiction to nonfiction.) Special interests: suspense/mystery/thrillers, contemporary and historical romances, westerns, children's/Y.A.) Usually obtains new clients via recommendations from others and queries. Currently represents 40 authors. Presently accepting new clients. Query first. Responds to queries in 1 week; to mss in 1 month. New/unpublished writers: 20%.
Recent Sales: *Toby's Folly*, by Margot Arnold (Foul Play Press); *Over on the Lonesome Side*, by James Ritchie (Walker & Co); *Rainbow Wishes, Winter Dreams*, by Jacqueline Case (Meteor Publishing Co.).
Terms: Agent's Commission: 15% on domestic sales; 15% on foreign sales. Charges for photocopying expenses. 100% of income derived from commissions on ms sales.

SIDNEY PORCELAIN AGENCY, Box 1229, Milford PA 18337. (717)296-6420. Agent contact: Sidney Porcelain. Agency estab. 1952. Novels, novellas, short stories. Fiction and nonfiction (75%-25%, fiction to nonfiction). Special interests: novels, mysteries, children's. Usually obtains clients through recommendations; market lists. Currently represents 20 clients. Presently accepting new clients. Query. Responds to queries in a few days; to mss in 2 weeks. New/unpublished writers: 60%. SASE. **Terms:** Agent's commission: 10%. "If foreign agent, his fee is separate."

‡JULIAN PORTMAN & ASSOCIATES, 8033 Sunset Blvd., Suite 964, Los Angeles CA 90046. (213)871-8544. (CTV/motion picture scripts); Julian Portman and Associates, 7337 N. Lincoln Avenue, Suite 283, Chicago IL 60646. (312)509-6421. (book manuscripts). Agency estab. 1972. Novels. Also reviews nonfiction (45%-55% fiction to nonfiction). Special interests: mainstream, bios, adventure, historical. Usually obtains new clients via recommendations, conferences. Currently represents 23 authors. Presently accepting new clients. Query with outline/proposal. Include SASE. Responds to queries in a minimum of 4 weeks. New/unpublished writers: 73%.
Recent Sales: *Escape From Terror*, by Julian John Portman (Pocket Books); *Pray For Me*, by Mike Blake and Walt Ny Kaza (Contempory Books); *Baseball Players Idiosyncrasies*, by Mike Blake (Wynwood Press).
Terms: Agent's commission: 15% on domestic and foreign sales. *$150 reading fee for up to 275 pages; charges $200 reading fee for 300-page or more novel.* Offers criticism service: "It is part of our reader's fee. Readers used, but final approval by Julian John Portman." Payment of fees ensures agency representation if writers follow constructive critiques. "Our agency is heavily involved in turning out mss that would be suitable for television."

THE AARON M. PRIEST LITERARY AGENCY INC., 122 East 42nd St., New York NY 10168. (212)818-0344. Contact: Aaron Priest or Molly Friedrich. Fiction and nonfiction. Presently accepting new clients. Send SASE with query letter only. Not accepting ms at this time.
Terms: Agent's commission: 15% (foreign mailing and copying charged to author).

SUSAN ANN PROTTER, LITERARY AGENT, 110 West 40th St., New York NY 10018. (212)840-0480. Agent contact: Susan Ann Protter. Agency estab. 1971. Novels. Fiction and nonfiction (50%-50% fiction to nonfiction). Special interests: contemporary and medical novels, thrillers, mysteries, science fiction and fantasy. Currently represents 45 clients. Presently accepting some new clients. Query (letters only). Responds to queries in 2 weeks. New/unpublished writers: 20%. Member of I.L.A.A.
Recent Sales: *Woman of the Mists*, by Lynn McKee (Charter/Diamond); *The Hollow Earth*, by Rudy Rucker (Morrow/Avon); *A Cat in the Manger*, by Lydia Adamson (Signet/NAL); and *Carl's Lawn and Garden*, by Terry Bisson (Omni).
Terms: Agent's commission: 15% on domestic sales; 25% on foreign sales (includes sub-agent's commissions). 100% of income derived from commissions on ms sales.

QUICKSILVER BOOKS LITERARY AGENTS, 50 Wilson St., Hartsdale NY 10530. (914)946-8748. Agent contact: Bob Silverstein, president. Agency estab. 1973 (as packager); 1987 (as literary agency). Novels. Also reviews nonfiction (50%-50% fiction to nonfiction). Special interests: mainstream, New Age, literary, mystery/suspense. Usually obtains new clients via recommendations from others, listings in sourcebooks. Currently represents 40 authors. Presently accepting new clients. Send query with outline, plus SASE. Responds to queries in 1 week; to mss in 2-3 weeks. New/unpublished writers: 50%.
Sales: *James Baldwin: Artist on Fire*, by W.J. Weatherby (Donald I Fine); *When You Can Walk on Water, Take the Boat*, by John Harricharan (Berkley); and *The Paradoxical Power*, by Greg Johanson and Ron Kurtz (Bell Tower/Harmony).
Terms: Agent's commissions: 15% on domestic sales; 20% on foreign sales. 100% of income derived from commission on ms sales.

HELEN REES LITERARY AGENCY, 308 Commonwealth Ave., Boston MA 02116. (617)262-2401. Agent contact: Catherine Mahar. Agency estab. 1980. Novels, novellas, short stories, story collections. Also reviews nonfiction (15%-85% fiction to nonfiction). Special interests: mainstream, mystery, suspense, gay, literary and commercial. Usually obtains new clients via solicitations, referrals, some through submissions. Currently represents 60 authors. Presently accepting new clients. Query. Responds to queries in 5-10 days; to mss in 2 weeks. Member of I.L.A.A.
Sales: *In The Falcon's Claw*, by Chet Raymo (Viking); *Water From the Moon*, by Lawrence Kinsman (Knights Press); *Ghost Riders*, by Rick Boyer (Ballantine).
Terms: Agent's commission: 15% on domestic sales; 20% on foreign. Charges "reimbursement for expenses (mail, phone, copying)." 100% of income derived from commissions on ms sales.

‡**RHODES LITERARY AGENCY NY**, 140 West End Ave., New York NY 10023. (212)580-1300. Agent contacts: Joe Rhodes. Agency estab. 1974. Novels. Also reviews nonfiction 40%-60% fiction to nonfiction). Usually obtains new clients via recommendations and inquiries. Currently represents 30 authors. Presently accepting new clients. Query with SASE. Reponds to queries in 10 days. Member of I.L.A.A.
Terms: Agent's commission: 10% on domestic sales. 100% of income derived from commissions on ms sales.

‡**RIGHTS UNLIMITED**, 156 5th Ave., New York NY 10010. (212)741-0404. Agent contact: Bernard Kurman. Estab. 1984. Novels. Also reviews nonfiction (80%-20% fiction to nonfiction). Special interests: mainstream, childrens. Usually obtains new clients via recommendations from others, and at conferences. Currently represent 57 authors. Presently accepting new clients. Query with entire ms. Responds to queries in 2 weeks; to mss in 4 weeks. New/unpublished writers: 5%.
Sales: *Step-by-Step Language Books*, by Charles Berlitz (Wynwood Press); *Bird Song Experiment*, by Norman Lang (Harper and Row); and *James Dean: Behind the Scene*, by Leith Adams and Keith Burns (Carol Publishing/Birch Lane Press).
Terms: Agent's commission: 15% on domestic sales; 20% on foreign sales.

SHERRY ROBB LITERARY PROPERTIES, Suite 102, 7250 Beverly Blvd., Los Angeles CA 90069. (213)965-8780. Contact: Sherry Robb, Sasha Goodman. Agency estab. 1979. Novels. Also reviews nonfiction (50%-50% fiction to nonfiction). Special interests: commercial mainstream, offbeat and literary, mysteries, thrillers and women's genre. Usually obtains new clients via client referrals, introductions via conferences and directories. Presently accepting new clients. Send entire ms (for literary, mystery, thrillers and offbeat novels); outline or proposal plus 3 sample chapters for mainstream or genre. Responds to queries in 2 weeks; to whole ms in 3 months; 2 months for outline/proposal. New/unpublished writers: 60%.
Recent Sales: *No Easy Place To Be* (literary), by Steven Corbin (Simon & Schuster); *Mistresses* (mainstream), by Trevor Meldal-Johnsen (Pinnacle); *Magnificent Passage* (historical romance) by Kat Martin (Crown).
Terms: "We do require authors—especially since we work with so many 'first-timers'—to pay for their own Xeroxing and postage charge."

THE ROBBINS OFFICE, INC., 12th Floor, 866 2nd Ave., New York NY 10017. (212)223-0720. Agency estab. 1978. General fiction and nonfiction, TV and motion picture rights (no scripts) (35%-65% fiction to nonfiction). Special interests: mainstream hardcover, literary. *No unsolicited mss, by referral only;* submit outline and sample chapters (fiction). Currently represents 150 authors. Presently accepting new clients. Responds to queries in 2 weeks.
Recent Sales: *Biodegradable Soap*, by Amy Ephron (Houghton Mifflin); *Article 35*, by Michael G. Grant (Bantam); *Playing the Dozens*, by William D. Pease (Viking).
Terms: Agent's commission: 15%. "Specific expenses incurred in doing business for a client are billed back including express mail, messenger and copying." 100% of income derived from commissions on ms sales.

‡**IRENE ROGERS, LITERARY REPRESENTATIVE**, 9454 Wilshire Blvd. Suite 600, Beverly Hills CA 90212. (213)837-3511. Estab. 1977. Novels. Also reviews nonfiction (50%-50% fiction to nonfiction). Special interest: mainstream. Usually obtains new clients from referrals. Currently represents 10 authors. Not presently accepting new clients "but this changes from month to month." Query. Responds to queries in 6-8 weeks. New/unpublished writers: 10%. Member of S.A.R. and I.L.A.A.
Recent Sales: *Cross of Stone*, by V. Gregory (Random House); *King James*, by S. Stewart (Crown); *A Gathering*, by J. Kelley (MacMillan).
Terms: Agent's commission: 10% on domestic sales; 5% on foreign sales.

THE MITCHELL ROSE LITERARY AGENCY, Suite 410, 799 Broadway, New York NY 10003. (212)551-1528. Agent contact: Mitchell Rose. Agency estab. 1986. Novels, story collections. Also reviews nonfiction (40%-60% fiction to nonfiction). Special interests: commercial fiction, mystery and literary fiction. Usually obtains new clients via recommendations. Currently represents 45 authors. Presently accepting new clients. Query or send outline plus sample chapters. Responds to queries in 3 weeks; to mss in 6 weeks. New/unpublished writers: 20%. Member of Authors Guild.

Sales: *Victorian Tales*, by Michael Patrick Hearn (Pantheon/Random House); *To Laredo*, by Jim Shaffer (St. Martin's); *Chain Reaction*, by Josh Pachter (Alliance Entertainment).

Terms: Agent's commission: 15% on domestic sales; 20% on foreign sales involving a sub-agent. Charges fee for high-volume photocopying, telexes, overseas phone calls. 100% of income derived from commission on mss sales. "For talented writers with promising projects, we can offer extensive editorial guidance when required."

‡ROSENSTONE/WENDER, 3 E. 48th St., New York NY 10017. (212)832-8330. Novels, novelettes, short stories, short story collections, plays and screenplays. Query. Does not accept unsolicited mss. Also reviews nonfiction (50%-50% fiction to nonfiction).

Terms: Agent's commission: 10%. Member of S.A.R.

JANE ROTROSEN AGENCY, 318 E. 51st St., New York NY 10022. (212)593-4330. Agents: Andrea Cirillo, Margaret Ruley, Stephanie Laidman. Agency estab. 1973. Reviews novels, novellas, story collections. Also reviews nonfiction (60%-40% fiction to nonfiction). Special interest: commercial fiction. Usually obtains new clients through referrals. Represents 140+ writers. Presently accepting new clients. Query first. Responds to queries in 10 days if SASE included; to mss in 6-8 weeks. Member of I.L.A.A.

Terms: Agent's commission: 15% on domestic sales; 20% on foreign sales (10% to co-agent; 10% to JRA).

RUSSELL & VOLKENING, INC., 50 W. 29th St., Apt. 7E, New York NY 10001. (212)684-6050. Novels, nonfiction. Send query letter with SASE. Member of S.A.R. Agents in all countries.

RAPHAEL SAGALYN, INC., LITERARY AGENCY, 1520 New Hampshire Ave., Washington DC 20036. Member of I.L.A.A.

SBC ENTERPRISES, INC., 11 Mabro Dr., Denville NJ 07834-9607, (201)366-3622. Agent contact: Alec Bernard, Eugenia Cohen. Agency estab 1979. Novels and story collections (where bulk are previously published). Also reviews nonfiction (75%-25% fiction to nonfiction). Special interest: mainstream, science projection, espionage. Usually obtains new clients via recommendations, conferences, advertising. Currently represents 25 authors. Presently accepting new clients. Query with SASE. Responds immediately to queries. New/unpublished writers: 90%.

Sales: *Maximizing Cash Flow*, by Emery Toncré (Wiley); *Action-Step Plan to Owning & Operating Business*, by Toncré (Montclair Press reprint).

Terms: Agent's commission: 15% on domestic sales if advance under $10,000, 10% thereafter; 20% on foreign sales. *Will critique 300-page novel for $2/page reading fee.* 100% of income derived from commission on ms sales.

JACK SCAGNETTI, 5330 Lankershim Blvd. #210, N. Hollywood CA 91601. (818)762-3871. Agency estab. 1974. Novels and scripts. Also reviews nonfiction (40%-60% fiction to nonfiction). Special interest: mainstream. Usually obtains new clients by referrals from other clients or free listings. Currently represents 35 authors. Presently accepting new clients. Query with outline. Responds to queries in 2 weeks; to mss in 4-6 weeks. New/unpublished writers: 75%. Signatory to Writers Guild of America–West.

Recent Sales: *Superstition Gold*, by Melissa Bowesock (Dorchester Publishing); *Successful Car Buying*, by Steve Ross (nonfiction). Script sales: *Family Ties, Women's Penitentiary 3000, Highway to Heaven.*

Terms: Agent's commission: 10% on domestic sales; 15% on foreign sales. No reading fees for screenplays. No reading fees for books unless detailed critique is requested. Offers criticism service: $100 for 400 pages; $125 for 500 pages. Will detail critique 300-page novel for $75. "Experienced readers/analysts write critiques." Charges for one-way postage for multiple submissions. 100% of income derived from commission on ms sales. Payment of fees does not ensure agency representation. "Also handle screenwriters; spend more time reading/selling screenplays than books; represent more screenwriters than authors."

SCHAFFNER AGENCY, INC., 6625 N. Casas, Adobes Rd., Tucson AZ 85705. (602)797-8000. Agency Contact: Timothy Schaffner or Patrick Delahunt. Agency estab: 1948. Novels and story collections. Also reviews nonfiction. Special interest: mainstream, science fiction, fantasy, literary fiction and serious nonfiction. Usually obtains new clients via referrals, conventions and by reading magazine fiction. Currently represents 35 authors. Presently accepting new clients. Query with outline. "No

unsolicited manuscripts, please." Responds to queries in 2 weeks; to mss in 4-6 weeks. Member of S.A.R. and I.L.A.A.
Recent Sales: *The Watch*, by Rick Bass (novel); *Remember Who You Are*, by Ester Mautzig (Crown); *Confessions of an Eco-Warrior*, by Dave Forman (Crown).
Terms: Agent's commission: 15% on domestic sales; 20% on foreign sales. Charges for return postage or $15 if SASE not included. 100% of income derived from commission on ms sales.

SCHLESSINGER-VAN DYCK AGENCY, 2814 PSFS Bldg., 12 S. 12th St., Philadelphia PA 19107. (215)627-4665. Agent contact: Blanche Schlessinger or Barrie Van Dyck. Agency estab. 1987. Novels. Also represents nonfiction (25%-75% fiction to nonfiction). Usually obtains new clients via recommendations from others. Currently represents 50 clients. Presently accepting new clients. Send query or outline plus sample chapters. Responds to queries or mss in 4-6 weeks. New/unpublished writers: 15%. Must include SASE for a response.
Sales: *Indecent Proposal*, by Jack Engelhard (Donald I. Fine); *Maggie Among the Seneca* and *The Bread Sister of Sinking Creek*, by Robin Moore (Harper & Row).
Terms: Agent's commission: 15% on domestic sales; 20% on foreign sales. 100% of income derived from commission on sales.

SUSAN SCHULMAN LITERARY AGENCY, INC., 454 West 44th St., New York NY 10036. (212)713-1633. FAX: (212)581-8830. Agent contact: Susan Schulman. Estab. 1978. Fiction and nonfiction (50%-50% fiction to nonfiction). Special interests: all types of nonfiction, parenting, psychology, sciences; mainstream novels, literary fiction and women's stories (genre fiction). Usually obtains new clients via recommendations from current clients. Presently accepting new clients. Send outline plus 3 sample chapters. Responds to queries in 6 days; to ms in 6 weeks. New/unpublished writers: 20%. Member of S.A.R., I.L.A.A.
Recent Titles: *Prayer Devil*, by Christopher Fawles (Ballantine, horror); and *The Dark Vision of Lorraine Hansberry*, by Margaret Wilkerson (Little, Brown); *Hard Tack*, by Barbara D'Amato (Scribner's, mystery); *Dreamland*, by Margaret Keilstrup (Bantam, mystery)..
Terms: Agent's commission: 15% on domestic sales; 20% foreign sales. Charges $50 reading fee for any length ms. "I do the reading, evaluating and writing myself." Charges for postage and photocopying expenses. 99% of income derived from commission on ms sales; less 1% from criticism service.

LYNN SELIGMAN LITERARY AGENCY, 400 Highland Ave., Upper Montclair NJ 07043. (201)783-3631. Agent contact: Lynn Seligman. Estab. 1985. Novels, short stories and story collections. Also reviews nonfiction (20%-80% fiction to nonfiction). Special interests: women's novel, literary mainstream, fantasy. Usually obtains new clients via recommendations. Currently represents 35 authors. Presently accepting new clients. Query with letter or outline/proposal (for nonfiction) with SASE. Responds to queries in 1-2 weeks; to mss in 2 months. New/unpublished writers: 50%.
Recent Sales: *Everything You've Heard is True*, by Frances Sherwood (Johns Hopkins University Press); *Fly by Night*, by Carol McD. Wallace (St. Martin's Press); and *Tourists*, by Lisa Goldstein (Simon and Schuster).
Terms: Agent's commission: 15% on domestic sales; 25% on foreign sales. Charges for photocopying and unusual mail or transatlantic calls. 100% of income derived from commission on ms sales.

‡THE SHEPARD AGENCY, 73 Kingswood Dr, Bethel CT 06801. (203)790-4230; 743-1879. Novels, novellas and story collections. Also reviews nonfiction (65% nonfiction). Special interests: mainstream, children's. Usually obtains new clients via recommendations from others. Currently represents 32 authors. Presently accepting new clients. Query or send entire ms (fiction—1st novel) or outline. Responds to queries in 4 weeks; to ms in 8 weeks. New/unpublished writers: 70%.

BOBBE SIEGEL AGENCY, 41 West 83rd St., New York NY 10024. (212)877-4985. Bobbe Siegel and Associate: Richard Siegel. Agency estab. 1975. Novels. Also reviews nonfiction (45%-55% fiction to nonfiction). Special interests: mainstream, literary, science fiction, mystery, historical, any fiction. "But I do not handle children's books or cookbooks." Usually obtains new clients via "referral from editors and authors I know or whom I represent." Currently represents 60 authors. Presently accepting new clients. Query with letter. Responds to queries in 2-3 weeks; to mss in 6-8 weeks. New/unpublished writers: 30%.

Recent Sales: *The 6th Day & Other Tales*, by Primo Levi (Summit); *North of the Sun*, by Fred Hatfield (Birch Lane Press); and *Rebel Without a Clue*, by Holly Uyemoto (Crown).
Terms: Agent's commission: 15% on domestic sales; 10% on foreign sales. Charges for airmail FAX, overseas phone, photocopy etc. 100% of income derived from commission on ms sales. "I will not read any manuscript or proposal that is not preceded by a letter. Do not send unless I ask to see—and always send with return postage, otherwise material will not be returned."

EVELYN SINGER LITERARY AGENCY INC., Box 594, White Plains NY 10602. Contact: Evelyn Singer. Agency estab. 1951. Novels. Also reviews nonfiction (25%-75% fiction to nonfiction). Special interests: fiction and particularly nonfiction adult and juvenile books. Interested in fiction for general trade departments and suspense or mystery. Usually obtains new clients via recommendations. Currently represents 50-75 writers. "Accepting writers who have earned $20,000 from freelance material." Query or send outline plus 2-3 sample chapters. New/unpublished writers: 15%. Responds to queries in 2-4 weeks; to mss in 2-6 weeks.
Recent Sales: *Pursuit of Fear*, by William Beechcroft (Carroll & Graf); *Run Baby Run*, by Cruz with Buckingham (Bridge); *Snakes & Other Reptiles*, by Mary Elting (Simon & Schuster).
Terms: Agent's commission: 15% on domestic sales; 20% on foreign sales. Charges for: "Long distance calls; copyright; charges other than local postage, phone and overhead, that are special for a particular property." 100% of income derived from commission on ms sales. "Include bio pertinent to literary background; type double-space (or use letter-quality printer; I cannot read dot matrix) on 8½x11 paper. Do not bind ms. Paginate consecutively. Do not send sample material from a section of the ms; send first part and outline. Include SASE for reply and/or return of material. Write; do not phone."

SINGER MEDIA CORPORATION, 3164 Tyler Ave., Anaheim CA 92801. (714)527-5650. FAX: (714)527-0268. Agent contact: John J. Kearns. Agency estab. 1945. Novels. Also reviews nonfiction (95%-5% fiction to nonfiction). Special interests: contemporary romance, adventure, suspense, mysteries. Usually obtains new clients via conferences, word of mouth. Presently accepting new clients. Query or send entire ms. Responds to queries by return mail; to mss in 6 weeks. New/unpublished writers: 80%.
Terms: Agent's commission: 15% on domestic sales; 20% on foreign sales. Charges reading fee for unpublished authors; $200 for 300-page novel. "Compilation of readers' reports." Payment of fees ensures agency representation if marketable.

MICHAEL SNELL LITERARY AGENCY, Box 655, Truro MA 02666. (508)349-3718. Patricia Smith. Estab. 1980. Reviews novels. Also reads nonfiction (20%-80% fiction to nonfiction). Special interests: mystery, suspense, thrillers. Usually obtains news clients through *LMP*, word of mouth, publishers. Currently represents 200 clients. Presently accepting new clients. Send outline/proposal and query. Reports on queries in 1 week; on mss in 2 weeks.
Sales: *Blood Dawn, Blood Moon, Blood Tide*, by Kalish (3-book series) (Harvest/Avon); *The Brothers K*, by Duncan (Doubleday).
Terms: Agent's commission: 15% on domestic and foreign sales. 100% of business is derived from commission on mss sales.

SOUTHERN WRITERS, INC., Suite 1020, 635 Gravier St., New Orleans LA 70130. (504)525-6390. Agent contact: Pamela Ahearn. Agency estab: 1979. Novels and novellas. Also reviews nonfiction (65%-35% fiction to nonfiction). Special interest: fiction with a Southern flavor or background and romances—both contemporary and historical. Usually obtains new clients via recommendations from others, at conferences, and from listings. Currently represents 25-30 authors. Presently accepting new clients. Query. Responds to queries in 2 weeks; to mss in 4 weeks. New/unpublished writers: 35%.
Recent Sales: *Where the Towers Pierce the Sky*, by Marie Goodwin (Macmillan); *When Angels Fall*, by Meagan McKinney (Dell); *The Heart's Haven*, by Jill Barnett (Pocket).
Terms: Agent's commission: 15% on domestic sales; 20% on foreign sales. Foreign Representatives: Abner Stein (UK); Uwe Luserke (Europe). *Charges $175 reading fee to new writer* on 300-page ms. "We charge a reading fee to unpublished authors and to those writing in areas other than that of previous publication." Offers criticism service for $275. Descripton of criticism service: "A letter (3-4 pp. single-spaced) evaluating work on the basis of style, content and marketability, offering constructive advice on this work and pointers for future writing." Charges for office expenses, which are deducted from royalties if book is sold. 65% of income derived from commission on ms sales; 35% from criticism service and reading fees.

DAVID M. SPATT, ESQ., P.O. Box 19, Saunderstown RI 02874. (401)789-5686. Estab. 1987. Novels, novellas, short stories. "All fiction, but especially sci-fi, fantasy, horror, mystery and stories with a New England flavor." Usually obtains new clients via recommendations. Currently represents under 10 authors. Presently accepting new clients. Query. Responds to queries in 2 months; to mss in 2 months. New/unpublished writers: 50%.
Terms: Agent's commission: 15% on domestic sales; 15% on foreign sales. "Costs which are directly attributed to marketing of the writers work. No general office expenses. This is an arts/entertainment law firm which has recently begun acting as a literary agent for the benefit of its clients, but now is looking to expand with new writers and previously published" writers, especially in the New England area.

PHILIP G. SPITZER LITERARY AGENCY, 788 9th Ave., New York NY 10019. (212)265-6003. Agency estab. 1969. Novels and nonfiction (50%-50% fiction to nonfiction). Special interest: quality fiction, suspense fiction. Obtains new clients primarily via recommendation. Currently represents 50 authors. Query. Also reviews nonfiction (50%-50% fiction to nonfiction). Accepting few new clients. Send outline/proposal. Responds to queries in 1 week; to mss in 6 weeks. New/unpublished writers: 25%.
Sales: *Black Cherry Blues*, by James Lee Burke (Little, Brown); *Selected Stories*, by Andre Dubus (Vintage); *Fall From Grace: The Failed Crusade of the Christian Right*, by Michael D'Antonio (Farrar, Straus & Giroux).
Terms: Agent's commission: 10% on domestic sales; 20% on foreign sales. 100% of income derived from commission on ms sales.

LYLE STEELE & CO., LTD., LITERARY AGENTS, 511 E. 73d St., Suite 7, New York NY 10021. (212)288-2981. Agent contact: Lyle Steele. Agency estab. 1984. Novels and nonfiction (75%-25% fiction to nonfiction). Special interests: mysteries, horror, particularly continuing series, true crime, current events, and general nonfiction. Currently represents 50 clients. Presently accepting new clients. Query. Responds to queries in 1 week; to mss in 3 weeks. New/unpublished writers: .05%.
Recent Sales: *Cracking the 50 plus Job Market*, by J. Robert Connor (New American Library).
Terms: Agent's commission: 10% on domestic sales; 10% on foreign sales (foreign agent also takes 10%). 100% of income derived from commission on mss sales.

STEPPING STONE, 59 West 71st St., New York NY 10023. (212)362-9277. Agent contact: Sarah Jane Freymann. Agency estab. 1974. Novels. Also reviews nonfiction (50%-50% fiction to nonfiction). Special interests: mainstream, self help, women's fiction, women's issues, spiritual themes, psychology, mystery and current events. Currently represents 75 clients. Presently accepting new clients. Query with outline/proposal. Responds to queries in 2 weeks; to mss in 1 month. New/unpublished writers: 10%. Member of I.L.A.A.
Terms: Agent's commission: 15%. 100% of income derived from commission on ms sales.

GLORIA STERN AGENCY, 1230 Park Ave., New York NY 10128. (212)289-7698. Agent contact: Gloria Stern. Agency estab. 1976. Also reviews nonfiction (20%-80% fiction to nonfiction). Represents 35 writers. Not presently accepting new clients unless referred by established writer or editor or previously published. Query with one-page outline plus 1 sample chapter. No unsolicited manuscripts. SASE. Member of I.L.A.A.
Terms: Agent's commission: 15% on domestic sales; 20% on foreign sales. "I am sorry that I cannot take any short stories at the present time."

JO STEWART AGENCY, 201 E. 66th St., New York NY 10021. (212)879-1301. Agent contact: Jo Stewart. Agency estab. 1976. Novels. Also reviews nonfiction. Special interest: "all kinds of fiction and nonfiction—young adult fiction." Usually obtains new clients via recommendations of other writers and editors. Presently accepting new clients. Query first or send synopsis plus 2-3 sample chapters.
Terms: Agent's commission: 15% on unpublished writers on domestic sales; 10% on published authors on domestic sales; 20% on foreign sales.

GUNTHER STUHLMANN AUTHOR'S REPRESENTATIVE, Box 276, Becket MA 01223. (413)623-5170. Agent Contact: Barbara Ward. Agency estab. 1954. Fiction and nonfiction books; no sci-fi. Special interest: quality literary fiction. Usually obtains new clients via recommendations. Query with outline and SASE. Responds to queries in 2 weeks.

Recent Sales: *Goldbug Variations*, by Richard Powers (Morrow); *Hunting Hemingway's Trout*, by Lauri Anderson (Atheneum).
Terms: Agent's commission: 10% on domestic sales; 20% on foreign sales; 15% British Commonwealth. 100% of income derived from commission on ms sales.

H.N. SWANSON, INC., 8523 Sunset Blvd., Los Angeles CA 90069. (213)652-5385. FAX: (213)652-3690. President and Founder: H.N. Swanson. Vice President: N.V. Swanson. Head of Operations: Tom Shanks. Agents: Michael Siegel and Sanford Weinberg. Agency estab. 1934. Novels, novellas and story collections. Also reviews nonfiction (90%-10% fiction to nonfiction). Special interests: mainstream, adventure and thrillers. Usually obtains new clients via recommendations from others. Currently represents 125 authors. Presently accepting new clients. Query with outline plus sample chapters. Responds to queries in 1 week; to mss in 4 weeks.
Recent Sales: *Killshot*, by Elmore Leonard; *Get Shorty*, by Elmore Leonard; *Among Schoolchildren*, by Tracy Kidder (film); and *The Music Room*, by Dennis McFarland (film).
Terms: Agent's commission: 10% on domestic sales; 15% on foreign sales. 100% of income derived from commission on ms sales.

‡TARC LITERARY AGENCY, P.O. Box 64785, Tucson AZ 85740-1785. Agent contact: Martha R. Gore. Estab. 1987. Novels. Also reviews nonfiction (20%-80% fiction to nonfiction). Special interests: mainstream. Usually obtains new clients via recommendations from others. Currently represents 100 authors. Presently accepting new clients. Send query with 4 sample chapters. "Must include SASE if writer wants material returned. No collect calls." Responds to queries in 1 week; to mss in 2 months. New/unpublished writers: 90%.
Recent Sales: *Yearling*, by Williamson (Avon); *Untitled II*, by Williamson (Avon); and *Grey Pilgrim*, by Hayes (Walker).
Terms: Agent's commission 15% on domestic sales; 20% on foreign sales; "15% movie and TV sales." Will critique if requested by writer. "Critiques written by agent, includes some actual editing on manuscript." Charges for postage, telephone calls, faxing, photocopying. 99% of income derived from commission on sales; 1% critiques and editing fees. "Query letter should describe the book and information about the author, especially if knowledge in depth is required to make the book believeable. Very important if book includes factual descriptions, etc."

ROSLYN TARG LITERARY AGENCY, INC., 105 W. 13th St., New York NY 10011. (212)206-9390. Agent contact: Roslyn Targ. Estab. 1969. Novels. Also reads nonfiction. Special interest: mainstream. Usually obtains new clients via recommendations from others. Query with SASE, and where sending manuscripts. Responds to mss in 2-3 weeks. Member of S.A.R. and I.L.A.A.
Terms: Agent's commission: 15% on unpublished authors; 10% on published authors; 20% on foreign sales. 100% of income derived from commission on ms sales.

PATRICIA TEAL LITERARY AGENCY, 2036 Vista Del Rosa, Fullerton CA 92631. (714)738-8333. Contact: Patricia Teal. Agency estab. 1978. Novels. Also reviews nonfiction (75%-25% fiction to nonfiction). Special interest: category novels. Usually obtains new clients via recommendations from others, solicitation, at conferences. Currently represents 60 authors. Presently accepting "a few" new clients. Query. Responds to queries in 2 weeks; to requested mss in 1 month. New/unpublished writers: 50%. Member of I.L.A.A.
Recent Sales: *Bloody Waters*, by B.L. Wilson (Pocket Books); *Face of a Stranger*, by Patricia Warren (Zebra); *Jade*, by Jill Marie Landis (Berkley Publishing Group); *Dakota* and *Dream*, by Sharon MacIver (Damond/Charter), Berkley Publishing Group.
Terms: Agent's commission: 10-15% on domestic sales; 20% on foreign sales. "We do not read entire manuscripts, only queries or partials. Would not charge a fee for a book we asked to see." Charges for postage and telephone calls. 100% of income derived from commission on mss sales. "We do not welcome mainstream fiction by unpublished writers except through professional writer referral or through contact at conferences."

THOMPSON TALENT AGENCY, Box 4272, Modesto CA 95352. Agent contact: Sharon Harris, director of literary talent. Agency estab. 1982. Novels, novellas, short stories, story collections of a religious nature only. Also reviews nonfiction (60%-40% fiction to nonfiction). Special interests: novels. Presently accepting new clients. Query first. Responds to queries in 5-7 weeks; to mss in 3 months. New/unpublished writers: 25%. Member of S.A.R., I.L.A.A.

Terms: Agents commission: 10% on domestic sales. Offers criticism service. "Writer must provide all postage expenses for query and manuscript returns. Do not send money, check or money orders."

‡**PHYLLIS R. TORNETTA LITERARY AGENCY,** Box 423, Croton-on-Hudson NY 10521. (914)737-3464. Agent contact: Phyllis Tornetta. Agency estab. 1978. Novels. Special interests: romance, mainstream. Usually obtains new clients via recommendations from others, conferences. Currently represents 15 authors. Presently accepting new clients. Send outline/proposal. Responds to mss in 1 month. New/unpublished writers: 50%.
Sales: *Cats and Kings*, by Beverly Simmons (Harlequin); *Intimate Strangers*, by Sally Hoover (Harlequin).
Terms: 15% on domestic sales. Charges $75 reading fee. "I will answer all inquiries at no charge."

SUSAN P. URSTADT INC., P.O. Box 1676, New Canaan CT 06840. Agent contact: Susan P. Urstadt. Agency estab. 1975. Novels. Also reviews nonfiction (30%-70% fiction to nonfiction). Special interest: "thoughtful, quality fiction—commercial, literary and accessible with psychological insight." Usually obtains new clients via recommendations from others. Currently represents 50 authors. Presently accepting new clients. Send outline plus 1 sample chapter and SASE with short author biography. Responds to queries in 3-4 weeks. New/unpublished writers: 10%. Member of I.L.A.A. "Please do not phone."
Terms: Agent's commission: 15% on domestic sales; 20% on foreign sales. Charges for photocopying, airmail and foreign postage.

RALPH M. VICINANZA, LTD., 432 Park Ave., New York NY 10016. (212)725-5133. Contact: Chris Lotts. Estab. 1978. Novels. Also reviews nonfiction. Special interests: science fiction, fantasy, thrillers. New clients via recommendations only. Currently represents 50 clients. New/unpublished writer: 10%.
Terms: Agent's commission: 10% on domestic sales; 20% on foreign sales.

MARY JACK WALD ASSOCIATES, INC., 111 E. 14th Street, New York NY 10003. (212)254-7842. Contact: Mary Jack Wald. Agency estab. 1985 (1983-1985 was Wald-Hardy Associates, Inc.). Novels, "novellas if in or with a short story collection." Also reviews nonfiction (50%-50% fiction to nonfiction). Special interests: mainstream and literary fiction and nonfiction for the adult and juvenile audience. Usually obtains clients via recommendations from others. Currently represents 50 writers. Presently accepting new clients. Responds to queries in 3-4 weeks; to mss in 1-2 months. Member of The Authors Guild, The Society of Children's Book Writers and Authors League of America.
Recent Sales: *Multi-book Contract*, by Richie Tankersley Cusick (Pocket Books); *The Time of Trimming*, by Haim Be'er (Random House); *The Sleepytime Book*, by Jan Wahl (Wm. Morrow).
Terms: Agent's commission: 15% on domestic sales; 15% on foreign sales.

THE GERRY B. WALLERSTEIN AGENCY, 2315 Powell Ave., Suite 12, Erie PA 16506. (814)833-5511. Contact: Ms. Gerry B. Wallerstein. Agency estab. 1984. Novels, novellas, short stories, story collections for adult market only. Also reads adult nonfiction (25%-75% fiction to nonfiction). Usually obtains new clients through (1) ongoing ad in *Writer's Digest*; (2) recommendations; (3) referrals from existing clients; (4) writers' groups. Currently represents 40 clients. Presently accepting new clients. Query. "Brochure is sent right away; responds to ms in approximately 6-8 weeks; no ms until writer sees brochure." New/unpublished writers: 25%. Member of Author's Guild and Society of Professional Journalists.
Terms: Agent's commission: 15% on domestic sales; 15% on dramatic sales; 20% on foreign sales. *"I charge a reading/critique fee* (waived for some published writers), which must accompany your material, on the following basis: $50 for each manuscript under 5,000 words; $100 for each manuscript of 5,000 to 20,000 words; $200 for each manuscript 20,000 to 65,000 words; $250 for each manuscript 65,000 to 85,000 words; $300 for each manuscript 85,000 to 105,000 words; $350 for each manuscript 105,000 to 125,000 words. Query for manuscript over 125,000 words. A critique will be provided, including my assessment of the work's marketability. If the work requires revision or editing to make it salable, it will be up to you to do it, if you so decide, based on the advice I give you; I will re-read the revised manuscript without additional charge. Clients accepted for representation are charged for copyright applications, photocopying manuscripts, typing manuscripts, legal fees (if required and approved by author), my travel (if required and approved by author), $20 monthly mail/telephone fee." 50% of income derived from commissions on ms sales; 50% derived from reading fees and criticism services. "Quality must be high for today's fiction marketplace."

JOHN A. WARE LITERARY AGENCY, 392 Central Park West, New York NY 10025. (212)866-4733. Agency estab. 1978. Novels and story collections "if individual stories have been placed." Also reviews nonfiction (40%-60% fiction to nonfiction). Special interests: literary, thrillers, mysteries, mainstream. "No romances, men's adventure or science fiction, please." Usually obtains new clients via referrals or at conferences. Currently represents 50 authors. Presently accepting new clients. Please query first. Responds to queries in 2 weeks; to mss in 1 month. New/unpublished writers: 25%.
Recent Sales: *Fires in the Sky,* by Phillip Parotti (Ticknor & Fields); *The Old Way,* by Lucy Taylor (New American Library); *Heathern,* by Jack Womack (Tor).
Terms: Agent's commission: 10% on domestic sales; 20% on foreign sales.

JAMES WARREN LITERARY AGENCY, (formerly Warren/Hilton Agency), 13131 Welby Way, Suite B, North Hollywood CA 91606. (818)982-5423. Agent contacts: James Warren, Romilde-Ann Dicke, Bob Carlson. Agency estab. 1969. Novels, novellas, stories and story collections, "but query first." Also reviews nonfiction (70%-30% fiction to nonfiction). Special interests: mainstream, adventure, gothic, history, historical romance, science fiction, mystery, horror, humor. Usually obtains new clients via *Writer's Market, LMP,* other trade publications, referrals. Currently represents 48 clients. Presently accepting new clients. Query or send entire ms. Responds to queries in 1 week; to mss in 1 month. New/unpublished writers: 60%.
Terms: Agent's commission: 10% on domestic sales; 20% on foreign sales. *Charges reading fee:* $150 for 300-page ms typed with pica typeface; $225 or more for ms typed with elite typeface. "On rare occasions we may charge a submission fee if we think the material is excellent but has little chance of publication." 80% of income derived from commission on sales; 20% derived from reading fees. Payment of fees does not ensure agency representation.

WATERSIDE PRODUCTIONS, INC, 832 Camino Del Mar, Del Mar CA 92014. (619)481-8335. Contact: Julie Castiglia, agent, fiction. Novels. Also reviews nonfiction (50%-50% fiction/nonfiction). Special interest: mainstream novels. Usually obtains new clients through recommendations from others. Currently represents 50 authors. Presently accepting new clients. Query, then send synopsis & two chapters. Responds to queries in 2 weeks. New/unpublished writers: 25%.
Recent Sales: *Red & Tight,* by Mike Dunn (Avon) *Month of Sundays* by Melody Martin (Knightsbridge); *A Vision of Nature,* by Michael Tobias. (Shambala/Random House).
Terms: Agent's commission: 15% on domestic sales; 25% on foreign sales. No initial reading fee. Editorial services for pre-determined fee. 99% of income derived from commission on ms sales; 1% from criticism service.

SANDRA WATT AND ASSOCIATES, Suite 4053, 8033 Sunset Blvd., Los Angeles CA 90046. (213)653-2339. Agent contact: Sandra Watt or Robert Drake. Agency estab. 1977. Novels. Special interests: women's fiction, men's action/adventure, mystery, thrillers, New Age, literary fiction, humor, cookbooks. Usually obtains new clients via client referrals and conferences. Currently represents 100+ clients. Presently accepting new clients. Query first. Responds to queries in 1 week; to mss in 8 weeks. Always SASE. New/unpublished writers: 15%. Member I.L.A.A. and Writer's Guild West.
Sales: *Hungry Women,* by Laramie Dunaway (Warner); *Walk on the Wild Side,* by Holly Woodlawn (New American Library); and *Half a Mind,* by Wendy Hornsby (New American Library).
Terms: Agent's commission: 15% on domestic sales and 25% on foreign sales. "We charge an unpublished writer of fiction a $100 marketing fee." 100% of income derived from commission of ms sales.

CHERRY WEINER LITERARY AGENCY, 28 Kipling Way, Manalapan NJ 07726. (201)446-2096. Agency estab. 1977. Novels. Also reviews nonfiction (80%-20% fiction to nonfiction). Special interests: mainstream, science fiction, romance. Usually obtains new clients via recommendations from others. Currently represents 40 authors. Query or send outline plus sample chapters. Responds "immediately" to queries; to mss in 4-6 weeks. New/unpublished writers: 15% — not taking without recommendation.
Terms: Agent's commission: 15%. 100% of income derived from commission on ms sales. Sub agents: Germany, Scandinavia, Japan, England, France.

 The double dagger before a listing indicates that the listing is new in this edition. New markets are often the most receptive to freelance contributions.

RHODA WEYR AGENCY, 151 Bergen St., Brooklyn NY 11217. Book length fiction and nonfiction. Query or send outline plus sample chapters. "The query letter should give any relevant information about the author and her/his work, publishing history, etc." Also represents nonfiction (about equal fiction to nonfiction). Presently accepting new clients. Interested in both fiction and nonfiction writers. Member of S.A.R and I.L.A.A. "Send letter/material, etc., with SASE to fit mss."
Terms: Agent's commission: 15% for domestic; 20% foreign.

WIESER & WIESER, 118 East 25th St., New York NY 10010. (212)260-0860. Agent contact: Olga Wieser. Agency estab. 1976. Novels. Also reviews nonfiction (40%-60% fiction to nonfiction). Special interests: mainstream, literary, historical and regency. Usually obtains new clients via recommendations from clients and other professionals. Currently represents 60 authors. Presently accepting new clients. Send outline plus sample chapters. Responds to queries in 1-2 weeks; to mss in 4 weeks.
Recent Sales: *Hammerheads*, by Dale Brown (Donald I. Fine, Inc.); *Final Approach*, by John Nance (Crown Books); and *Partners in Recovery*, by Carol Cox (Bantam Books).
Terms: Agent's commission: 15% on domestic sales; 20% on foreign sales; 15% motion picture rights sale. Offers criticism service. "No fees; if we decide to critique a work, we feel our input will improve the chances for publication." Charges for overseas cables and duplicating manuscript. 100% of income derived from commission on ms sales.

RUTH WRESCHNER, AUTHORS' REPRESENTATIVE, 10 W. 74th St., New York NY 10023. (212)877-2605. Contact: Ruth Wreschner. Agency estab. 1981. Novels. Also reviews nonfiction (15%-85% fiction to nonfiction). Special interests: mainstream, some romantic fiction, mysteries and science fiction. "Does not handle short stories." Usually obtains new clients via recommendations from others, solicitation, at conferences and listings. Represents about 50 writers. Send query and outline/proposal. Responds to queries in 2 days; to mss in 2-3 weeks. "Must enclose SASE."
Terms: Agent's commission: 15% on domestic sales; 20% on foreign sales. Charges for photocopy expenses "and when a book has been sold, I withhold certain funds for foreign mailings from the second advance." 100% of income derived from commission on ms sales. "While I avidly review fiction, I sell much more nonfiction. A first novel is very difficult to place, unless it really is superb."

ANN WRIGHT REPRESENTATIVES INC., Suite 2C 136 East 56th St., New York NY 10022. (212)832-0110. Agent contact: Dan Wright, head—literary department. Agency estab. 1962. Novels, novellas, short stories. Special needs: fiction that applies both to publishing and motion pictures/TV. Usually obtains clients via word of mouth, references from film industry. Currently represents 31 clients. Not presently accepting new clients. Query first. Responds to queries in 2 months; to mss in 3+ months. New/unpublished writers: 25%. Member of WGA.
Terms: Agent's commission: 10% on domestic sales; 20% on foreign sales.

‡STEPHEN WRIGHT, AUTHORS' REPRESENTATIVE, P.O. Box 1341, F.D.R. Station, New York NY 10150. Agent contact: Stephen Wright. Estab. 1984. Novels, novellas, short stories and story collections. Special interests: mystery and mainstream. Presently accepting new clients. Query or send outline plus 3 sample chapters (first 3). Responds to queries in 3 weeks; to mss in 30-60 days.
Terms: Agent's commission: 10-15% on domestic sales; 15-20% on foreign sales. *Charges a reading fee "only for new/unpublished writers.* No charge for professionals." Offers criticism service. Type of critique: "detailed critique of plot, character, etc., suggestions for improvement. Also, marketability of manuscript." Charges other fees if necessary. "Have a genuine talent and be a craftsman/woman. Try to do what your agent asks; be understanding of your agent's problems; and be courteous."

‡WRITER'S CONSULTING GROUP, P.O. Box 492, Burbank CA 91503. (818)841-9294. Agent contact: Jim Barmeier. Estab. 1983. Novels. Also reviews nonfiction (50%-50% fiction to nonfiction). Special interests: genre fiction—mystery, thriller, science fiction; also mainstream. Usually obtains new clients via recommendations and solicitation. Currently represents 12 authors. Presently accepting new clients. Send query with outline/proposal. Responds to queries in 2 weeks; to mss in 1-3 months. New/unpublished writers: 60%.
Terms: Agent's commission: 15% on domestic sales. *Charges reading fee:* "50 cents a page, up to a maximum of $200." 80% of income derived from commission on ms sales; 20% from criticism service.

WRITERS HOUSE, INC., 21 W. 26th St., New York NY 10010. President: Albert Zuckerman. Executive Vice President: Amy Beckower. Novels. Also reviews nonfiction (50%-50% fiction to nonfiction). Usually obtains clients via recommendations. Represents around 120 writers. Presently accepting new

clients. Query. Responds to queries in 2 weeks; to mss in 8 weeks. New/unpublished writers. "About 75% when they started with us."
Recent Sales: *Public Secrets*, by Nora Roberts; *Baby Sitters*, by Ann Martin; and *Good Omens*, by Terry Pletchett and Neil Gaman.
Terms: Agent's commission: 15% on domestic sales; 20% on foreign sales. 100% of income derived from commission on ms sales. "We are always on the lookout for skilled and talented writers."

WRITERS' PRODUCTIONS, Box 630, Westport CT 06881. Agent contact: David L. Meth. Agency estab. 1981. "Literary quality fiction; dramatic photo-essay books of exceptional quality on unique subjects; and works of nonfiction that are well researched, carefully planned and thought out, with a high degree of originality. We welcome health and fitness, and family-oriented books. We have a special interest in work by Asian Americans; work about Southeast Asia and the Far East." Usually obtains new clients by "word of mouth, though we read and respond to all work." Presently accepting new clients. Send one-page cover letter plus 30 pages and a SASE for return of ms. Responds to queries in 1 week; to mss in 1 month. New/unpublished writers: 50%.
Recent Sales: *Inspector Imanismi Investigates*, by Matsumoto Seicho (Japan), (Soho Press); *Trial by Fire*, by Kathleen Barnes (Thunder's Mouth Press); *The Day Care Kit*, by Debbie Spaide (Birch Lane Press).
Terms: Agent's commission: 15% on domestic sales; 20% on foreign sales; 20% dramatic sales. SASE must accompany ms for its return and any correspondence. No phone calls please.

MARY YOST ASSOCIATES, 59 E. 54th St., New York NY 10022. (212)980-4988. Contact: Mary Yost. Novels. Special interests: mainstream, women's. Query or send outline plus 50 pages. Also reviews nonfiction (40%-60% fiction to nonfiction). Obtains new clients via recommendations from other clients, editors, a few unsolicited mss. Presently accepting new clients. Member of S.A.R.
Terms: Agent's commission: 10%.

SUSAN ZECKENDORF ASSOCIATES, 171 W. 57th St., New York NY 10019. (212)245-2928. Contact: Susan Zeckendorf. Agency estab. 1979. Novels. Also reviews nonfiction (60%-40% fiction to nonfiction). Special interests: mainstream, thrillers, mysteries, and literary, historical, and commercial women's fiction. Usually obtains new clients via recommendations and solicitation. Represents 45 writers. Presently accepting new clients. Query. Responds to queries in 2 weeks; to solicited mss in 3 weeks. New/unpublished writers: 25%. Member of I.L.A.A.
Recent Sales: *Enticements*, by Una Mary Parker (NAL); *Came a Dead Cat*, by James N. Frey (St. Martin's Press); *Life Itself*, by Boyce Rensberger (Bantam).
Terms: Agent's commission: 15% on domestic sales; 20% on foreign sales. Charges for photocopying expenses. 100% of income derived from commission on ms sales.

Other literary agents

The following agents appeared in the 1990 edition of *Novel & Short Story Writer's Market* but not in the 1991 edition. Those who did not respond to our request for an update appear without further explanation below. Agents do not respond for a variety of reasons—they may be out of business, for example, or they may have received too many inappropriate submissions.

Bill Berger Associates
Book Peddlers of Deephaven (not accepting new clients)
Ned Brown Inc.
Robert Cornfield Literary Agency (asked to be deleted)
Richard Curtis Associates, Inc.
Nicholas Ellison, Inc. (not accepting new clients)
Estrada Literary Agency (asked

to be left out this year)
Farwestern Consultants Literary Agency
Max Gartenberg Literary Agent (moved; no forwarding address)
Lucianne S. Goldberg Literary Agents, Inc. Susan Herner Rights Agency (moved; no forwarding address)
Yvonne Hubbs Literary Agency

(out of business)
Arthur P. Schwartz
F. Joseph Spieler Literary Agency (asked to be left out this year)
Charles M. Stern Associates (asked to be deleted)
Larry Sternig Literary Agency (not accepting new clients)
The Wendy Weil Agency, Inc. (not accepting new clients)

Glossary

The following words are used differently when applied to writing and publishing than they are when spoken or written in other situations. For more general definitions and terms, check a standard dictionary.

Advance. Payment by a publisher to an author prior to the publication of a book, to be deducted from the author's future royalties.

All rights. The rights contracted to a publisher permitting a manuscript's use anywhere and in any form, including movie and book-club sales, without additional payment to the writer.

Anthology. A collection of selected writings by various authors or a gathering of works by one author.

Auction. Publishers sometimes bid for the acquisition of a manuscript that has excellent sales prospects. The bids are for the amount of the author's advance, guaranteed dollar amounts, advertising and promotional expenses, royalty percentage, etc.

Backlist. A publisher's list of its books that were not published during the current season but which are still in print.

Belles lettres. A term used to describe fine or literary writing more to entertain than to inform or instruct.

Book producer/packager. An organization that plans all elements of a book, from its initial concept to writing and marketing strategies, and then sells the package to a book publisher and/or movie producer.

Category fiction. See Genre.

Chapbook. A booklet of 15-30 pages of fiction or poetry.

Cliffhanger. Fictional event in which the reader is left in suspense at the end of a chapter or episode, so that interest in the story's outcome will be sustained.

Clip. Sample, usually from newspaper or magazine, of a writer's published work.

Cloak-and-dagger. A melodramatic, romantic type of fiction dealing with espionage and intrigue.

Commercial. Publishers whose chief concern is with salability, profit and success with a large readership.

Contemporary. Material dealing with popular current trends, themes or topics.

Contributor's copy. Copy of an issue of a magazine or published book sent to an author whose work is included; often the only form of payment from little/literary magazines and small presses.

Co-publishing. An arrangement in which the author and publisher share costs and profits.

Copyediting. Editing a manuscript for writing style, grammar, punctuation and factual accuracy.

Copyright. The legal right to exclusive publication, sale or distribution of a literary work.

Cover letter. A brief descriptive letter sent along with a complete manuscript submitted to an editor.

"Cozy" (or "teacup") mystery. Mystery usually set in a small British town, in a bygone era, featuring a somewhat genteel, intellectual protagonist.

Cyberpunk. Type of science fiction, usually concerned with computer networks and human-computer combinations, involving young, sophisticated protagonists.

Division. An unincorporated branch of a company (e.g. Penguin Books, a division of Viking, Penguin, Inc.).

Experimental fiction. Fiction that is innovative in subject matter and style; avant-garde, nonformulaic, usually literary material.

Exposition. The portion of the storyline, usually the beginning, where background information about character and setting is related.

Fair use. A provision in the copyright law that says short passages from copyrighted material may be used without infringing on the owner's rights.

Fanzine. A noncommercial, small-circulation magazine usually dealing with fantasy, horror or science-fiction literature and art.

First North American serial rights. The right to publish material in a periodical before it appears in book form, for the first time, in the United States or Canada.

Formula. A fixed and conventional method of plot development, which varies little from one book to another in a particular genre.

Frontier novel. Novel based upon the frontier history of "unwestern" places like Florida that has all the basic elements of traditional westerns.

Galleys. The first typeset version of a manuscript that has not yet been divided into pages.

Genre. A formulaic type of fiction such as romance, western or horror.

Gothic. A genre in which the central character is usually a beautiful young woman and the setting an old mansion or castle, involving a handsome hero and real danger, either natural or supernatural.

Hard-boiled detective novel. Mystery novel featuring a private eye or police detective as the protagonist; usually involves a murder. The emphasis is on the details of the crime.

Honorarium. A small, token payment for published work.

Horror. A genre stressing fear, death and other aspects of the macabre.

Imprint. Name applied to a publisher's specific line of books (e.g. Aerie Books, an imprint of Tor Books).

Interactive fiction. Fiction in book or computer-software format where the reader determines the path the story will take by choosing from several alternatives at the end of each chapter or episode.

International Reply Coupon (IRC). A form purchased at a post office and enclosed with a letter or manuscript to a foreign publisher, to cover return postage costs.

Juvenile. Fiction intended for children 2-12.

Libel. Written or printed words that defame, malign or damagingly misrepresent a living person.

Literary. The general category of serious, non-formulaic, intelligent fiction, sometimes experimental, that most frequently appears in little magazines.

Literary agent. A person who acts for an author in finding a publisher or arranging contract terms on a literary project.

Mainstream. Traditionally written fiction on subjects or trends that transcend experimental or genre fiction categories.

Malice domestic novel. A traditional mystery novel that is not hard-boiled; emphasis is on the solution. Suspects and victims know one another.

Manuscript. The author's unpublished copy of a work, usually typewritten, used as the basis for typesetting.

Mass market paperback. Softcover book on a popular subject, usually around 4×7, directed to a general audience and sold in drugstores and groceries as well as in bookstores.

Ms(s). Abbreviation for manuscript(s).

Multiple submission (also simultaneous submission). The practice of sending copies of the same manuscript to several editors or publishers at the same time.

MWA, Mystery Writers of America. Room 600, 236 W. 27th St., New York NY 10001. (212)255-7005. Organization open to professional writers in mystery and other fields, also to students and fans of mystery. The purpose is to enhance the prestige of mystery story and fact crime writing. Also sponsors workshops.

Narration. The account of events in a story's plot as related by the speaker or the voice of the author.

Narrator. The person who tells the story, either someone involved in the action or the voice of the writer.

New Age. A term including categories such as astrology, psychic phenomena, spiritual healing, UFOs, mysticism and other aspects of the occult.

Nom de plume. French for "pen name"; a pseudonym.

Novella (also novelette). A short novel or long story, approximately 7,000-15,000 words.

#10 envelope. 4×9½ envelope, used for queries and other business letters.

Offprint. Copy of a story taken from a magazine before it is bound.

One-time rights. Permission to publish a story in periodical or book form one time only.

Over the transom. Slang for the path of an unsolicited manuscript into the slush pile.

Page rate. A fixed rate paid to an author per published page of fiction.

Payment on acceptance. Payment from the magazine or publishing house as soon as the decision to print a manuscript is made.

Payment on publication. Payment from the publisher after a manuscript is printed.

Pen name. A pseudonym used to conceal a writer's real name.

Periodical. A magazine or journal published at regular intervals—not ordinarily referring to newspapers.

Plot. The carefully devised series of events through which the characters progress in a work of fiction.

Proofreading. Close reading and correction of a manuscript's typographical errors.

Proofs. A typeset version of a manuscript used for correcting errors and making changes, often a photocopy of the galleys.

Proposal. An offer to an editor to write a specific work, usually consisting of an outline of the work and one or two completed chapters.

Prose poem. Short piece of prose with the language and expression of poetry.

Protagonist. The principal or leading character in a literary work.

Public domain. Material that either was never copyrighted or whose copyright term has expired.

Pulp magazine. A periodical printed on inexpensive paper, usually containing lurid, sensational stories or articles.

Purple prose. Ornate writing using exaggerated and excessive literary devices.

Query. A letter written to an editor to elicit interest in a story the writer wants to submit.

Reader. A person hired by a publisher to read unsolicited manuscripts.

Reading fee. An arbitrary amount of money charged by some agents and publishers to read a submitted manuscript.

Regency romance. A genre romance, usually set in England between 1811-1820.

Remainders. Leftover copies of an out-of-print book, sold by the publisher at a reduced price.

Reporting time. The number of weeks or months it takes an editor to report back on an author's query or manuscript.

Reprint rights. Permission to print an already published work whose rights have been sold to another magazine or book publisher.

Roman à clef. French "novel with a key." A novel that represents actual living or historical characters and events in fictionalized form.

Romance. The genre relating accounts of passionate love and fictional heroic achievements.

Royalties. A percentage of the retail price paid to he author for each copy of the book that is sold.

RWA, Romance Writers of America. Suite 315, 13700 Veterans Memorial Dr., Houston TX 77014. An organization of professional writers, agents, editors, booksellers and others interested in the romance field.

SASE. Self-addressed stamped envelope.

Science fiction. Genre in which scientific facts and hypotheses form the basis of actions and events.

Second serial rights. Permission for the reprinting of a work in another periodical after its first publication in book or magazine form.

Self publishing. An independent publishing effort where full financial and editorial responsibility for the printing and marketing of a work is taken by its author.

Sequel. A literary work that continues the narrative of a previous, related story or novel.

Serial rights. The rights given by an author to a publisher to print a piece in one or more periodicals.

Serialized novel. A book-length work of fiction published in sequential issues of a periodical.

Setting. The environment and time period during which the action of a story takes place.

SFWA, Science Fiction Writers of America. Box 4236, West Columbia SC 29171. An organization of professional writers, editors, agents, artists and others in the science fiction and fantasy field.

Short short story. A condensed piece of fiction, usually under 1,000 words.

Simultaneous submission. See Multiple submission.

Slant. A story's particular approach or style, designed to appeal to the readers of a specific magazine.

Slice of life. A presentation of characters in a seemingly mundane situation which offers the reader a flash of illumination about the characters or their situation.

Slush pile. A stack of unsolicited manuscripts in the editorial offices of a publisher.

Speculation (or Spec). An editor's agreement to look at an author's manuscript with no promise to purchase.

Subsidiary. An incorporated branch of a company or conglomerate (e.g. Alfred Knopf, Inc., a subsidiary of Random House, Inc.).

Subsidiary rights. All rights other than book publishing rights included in a book contract, such as paperback, book club and movie rights.

Subsidy publisher. A book publisher who charges the author for the cost of typesetting, printing and promoting a book. Also Vanity publisher.

Suspense. A genre of fiction where the plot's primary function is to build a feeling of anticipation and fear in the reader over its possible outcome.

Tabloid. Publication printed on paper about half the size of a regular newspaper page (e.g. *The National Enquirer*).

Tearsheet. Page from a magazine containing a published story.

Theme. The dominant or central idea in a literary work; its message, moral or main thread.

Trade paperback. A softbound volume, usually around 5×8, published and designed for the general public, available mainly in bookstores.

Unsolicited manuscript. A story or novel manuscript that an editor did not specifically ask to see.

Vanity publisher. See Subsidy publisher.

Viewpoint. The position or attitude of the first- or third-person narrator or multiple narrators, which determines how a story's action is seen and evaluated.

Western. Genre with a setting in the West, usually between 1860-1890, with a formula plot about cowboys or other aspects of frontier life.

Whodunit. Genre dealing with murder, suspense and the detection of criminals.

Young adult. The general classification of books written for readers 12-18.

Category Index

The category index is a good place to begin searching for a market for your fiction.

Below is an alphabetized list of subjects of particular interest to the editors and agents listed in *Novel and Short Story Writer's Market*. The category index is divided into five sections: literary and small circulation magazines, commercial periodicals, small presses, commercial publishers and literary agents.

If you have prepared a manuscript for a science fiction novel, for example, check small press, commercial publisher or agents sections under Science Fiction. Then look up that publisher or agent you have selected in the Markets Index to find the correct page number. Read the listing *very* carefully.

Literary and Small Circulation Magazines

Adventure. Carolina Literary Companion, A; Amaranth; Amelia; Amherst Review; Animal Tales; Arnazella; Atalantik; Being; Black Jack; Blue Water Review; Blueline; Bradley's Fantasy Magazine, Marion Zimmer; Breakthrough!; Caffe, Il; Carousel Literary Arts Magazine; Chapter One; Chrysalis; Cicada; City Scriptum; Cochran's Corner; Cross Timbers Review; Dagger of the Mind; Dan River Anthology; Dangerous Times; Dream International/Quarterly; Ecphorizer; Eldritch Science; 11th Street Ruse; Emerald City Comix & Stories; Escapist; Event; Exit 13 Magazine; F.O.C. Review; Felicity; Garm Lu; Gas; Gestalt; Gotta Write Network Litmag; Grasslands Review; Green Mountains Review; Green's Magazine; Hawaii Pacific Review; Hemispheres; Hibiscus Magazine; Hippo; Hobo Jungle; Imagination; Indian Youth of America Newsletter; Innisfree; Jeopardy; Journal of Regional Criticism; Kana; Lactuca; Late Knocking; Leading Edge; Left-Footed Wombat; Legend; Lighthouse; Literary Creations; Living Among Nature Daringly Magazine; Llamas Magazine; Long Shot; Lost Creek Letters; MacGuffin; Merlyn's Pen; Minnesota Ink; Monocacy Valley Review; Negative Capability; New Methods; New Press; Nimrod; No Idea Magazine; Northwest Writers, Photographers and Design Artists; Ouroboros; P.I. Magazine; Paper Bag; Perceptions; Plowman; Portable Wall; Post; Prisoners of the Night; Pub; Queen's Quarterly; Rag Mag; Rambunctious Review; Re Arts & Letters; Renegade; Renovated Lighthouse Publications; Review La Booche; Riverwind; Salome: A Journal of the Performing Arts; Samisdat; Scream Magazine; Sensations; Shawnee Silhouette; Shoe Tree; Short Stuff Magazine for Grown-ups; Slate and Style; South Hill Gazette; Space and Time; SPSM&H; Storyzine; Sword of Shahrazad; Terse Tales; Thema; Thumbprints; Tickled By Thunder; Tucumcari Literary Review; Tyro Magazine; Ultimate Writer; Villager; Vincent Brothers Review; Vintage Northwest; Virginia Quarterly Review; West Texas Sun; Wide Open Magazine; Wisconsin Restaurateur; Words of Wisdom; Writers' Bar-B-Q; Writers Newsletter

Canada. ACTA Victoriana; Alchemist; Alpha Beat Soup; Antigonish Review; Atlantis (Nova Scotia); Breakthrough!; Canadian Author & Bookman; Canadian Fiction Magazine; Chalk Talk; Champagne Horror; Dalhousie Review; Dance Connection; Descant (Ontario); Dreams & Visions; Event; Fiddlehead; Fireweed; Garm Lu; Grain; Green's Magazine; Indigo; K; Kola; Legend; Lost; Malahat Review; New Quarterly; NeWest Review; Out Magazine; PARA*phrase; Plowman; Poetry Halifax Dartmouth; Pottersfield Portfolio; Prairie Fire; Prairie Journal of Canadian Literature; President Journal; Prism International; Quarry; Queen's Quarterly; Scrivener; Sidetrekked; Tabula Rasa; This Magazine; Tickled By Thunder; Tyro Magazine; Wascana Review; Whetstone; White Wall Review; Writ Magazine; Zymergy

Comics. Apaeros; Fat Tuesday; Processed World; Rag Mag; Sign of the Times; Working Classics

Confession. Amherst Review; Apaeros; Cacanadadada Review; Caffe, Il; Can(N)on Magazine; City Scriptum; Columbus Single Scene; D.C.; Dream International/Quarterly; Felicity; Fireweed; Garm Lu; Gas; Haight Ashbury Literary Journal; Hippo; Housewife-Writer's Forum; Imagination; K; Kana; Lactuca; Late Knocking; Ledge Poetry and Prose Magazine; Libido; Long Shot; MidCoaster; New Press; PARA*phrase; Perceptions; Plowman; Poetry Forum Short Stories; Processed World; Shattered Wig Review; SPSM&H; Storyzine; Tyro Magazine; Ultimate Writer; Village Idiot; Zero Hour

Condensed Novel. After Hours; Alabama Literary Review; Ararat Quarterly; Atalantik; Bahlasti Paper; Caffe, Il; Can(N)on Magazine; Chakra; Chaminade Literary Review; Chapter One; City Scriptum; Dangerous Times; Deviance; F.O.C. Review; Fireweed; G.W. Review; Garm Lu; Gestalt; Gulf Coast; Indian Youth of America Newsletter; Jazziminds Magazine; K; Kenyon Review; Lactuca; Language Bridges Quarterly; Libido; Limestone: A Literary Journal; Lost Creek Letters; Manoa; MidCoaster; NCASA News; New Methods; Northland Quarterly; Northwest Writers, Photographers and Design Artists; Perceptions; Poetry Motel; Pub; Renegade; River Styx; Satori; Snake Nation Review; Stone Drum;

Story; Storyzine; Sword of Shahrazad; Tandava; Toad Hiway; Tucumcari Literary Review; Two-Ton Santa; Tyro Magazine; Vincent Brothers Review; Vintage Northwest; West Texas Sun; Witness (Michigan); Word & Image; Zymergy

Contemporary. ACM, (Another Chicago Magazine); ACTA Victoriana; Adrift; Alabama Literary Review; Alaska Quarterly Review; Amaranth; Amaranth Review; Ambergris; Amelia; Amherst Review; Antaeus; Antietam Review; Antigonish Review; Antioch Review; Ararat Quarterly; Archae; Arnazella; Art Brigade; Artemis; Asylum; Atalantik; Aura Literary/Arts Review; Azorean Express; Bellowing Ark; Beloit Fiction Journal; Black Jack; Black Scholar; Black Warrior Review; Blatant Artifice; Blue Water Review; Blueline; Blur; Boulevard; Bradley's Fantasy Magazine, Marion Zimmer; Cacanadadada Review; Caesura; Caffe, Il; California Quarterly; Callaloo; Calliope; Calypso; Canadian Author & Bookman; Can(N)on Magazine; Caribbean Writer; Carolina Literary Companion, A; Carousel Literary Arts Magazine; Cathedral of Insanity; Central Park; Chapter One; Chariton Review; Chattahoochee Review; Chicago Review; Chiron Review; Kindred Spirit, The (see Chiron Review); Chrysalis; Cicada; Cimarron Review; Cipher; City Scriptum; Clockwatch Review; Coe Review; Cold-Drill Magazine; Colorado Review; Colorado-North Review; Columbus Single Scene; Concho River Review; Confrontation; Corona; Crab Creek Review; Crazyquilt; Crescent Review; Dan River Anthology; Dangerous Times; Delirium; Descant (Ontario); Descant (Texas); Deviance; Dream International/Quarterly; Ecphorizer; Elephant-ear; 11th Street Ruse; Emrys Journal; Epoch Magazine; Event; Exit 13 Magazine; F.O.C. Review; Farmer's Market; Fiction; Fine Madness; Fireweed; Fish Drum Magazine; Florida Review; Folio: A Literary Journal; Footwork; Four Quarters; G.W. Review; Gamut; Garm Lu; Gas; Gestalt; Gettysburg Review; Gotta Write Network Litmag; Grain; Grasslands Review; Great Stream Review; Green Mountains Review; Greensboro Review; Groundswell; Gulf Coast; Gulf Stream Magazine; Haight Ashbury Literary Journal; Hawaii Pacific Review; Hawaii Review; Hayden's Ferry Review; Hemispheres; Hibiscus Magazine; High Plains Literary Review; Hill and Holler; Hippo; Hobo Jungle; Hobo Stew Review; Housewife-Writer's Forum; Howling Dog; Imagination; Indian Youth of America Newsletter; Indiana Review; Indigo; Inlet; Innisfree; Interim; Jacaranda Review; Jazziminds Magazine; Jeopardy; Journal of Regional Criticism; Journal; K; Kana; Karamu; Kenyon Review; Key West Review; Kingfisher; Lactuca; Lake Effect; Late Knocking; Laurel Review; Ledge Poetry and Prose Magazine; Left Curve; Left-Footed Wombat; Lighthouse; Limestone: A Literary Journal; Long Shot; Long Story; Loonfeather; Lost and Found Times; Lost Creek Letters; Louisville Review; MacGuffin; Manoa; Mark; Maryland Review; Mati; MidCoaster; Minnesota Ink; Mississippi Review; Mississippi Valley Review; Missouri Review; Monocacy Valley Review; Mud Creek; NCASA News; Nebraska Review; Negative Capability; New Delta Review; New Laurel Review; New Letters Magazine; New Methods; New Orleans Review; New Virginia Review; Nexus; Nimrod; No Idea Magazine; North Dakota Quarterly; Northland Quarterly; Northwest Review; Northwest Writers, Photographers and Design Artists; NRG; Ohio Review; Old Hickory Review; Onionhead; Other Voices; Ouroboros; Oyez Review; Painted Bride Quarterly; Panhandler; Paper Bag; PARA*-phrase; Partisan Review; Pearl; Pennsylvania English; Perceptions; Pikestaff Forum; Pikeville Review; Pinehurst Journal; Plowman; Poetic Space; Poetry Forum Short Stories; Poetry Magic Publications; Poetry Motel; Pointed Circle; Poor Robert's Almanac; Portable Wall; Poskisnolt Press; Potato Eyes; Pottersfield Portfolio; Prairie Fire; Prairie Journal of Canadian Literature; Primavera; Prism International; Prisoners of the Night; Processed World; Puerto Del Sol; Quarterly West; Queen's Quarterly; Rag Mag; Rambunctious Review; Re Arts & Letters; Redneck Review of Literature; Renegade; Response; Review La Booche; River Styx; Riverwind; Rohwedder; Salome: A Journal of the Performing Arts; Salt Lick Press; Samisdat; San Gabriel Valley Magazine; Sanskrit; Santa Monica Review; Satori; Scream Magazine; Seattle Review; Sensations; Sewanee Review; Shattered Wig Review; Shawnee Silhouette; Shoe Tree; Shooting Star Review; Short Stuff Magazine for Grown-ups; Sing Heavenly Muse!; Skylark; Slate and Style; Slipstream; Snake Nation Review; Soundings East; South Carolina Review; South Dakota Review; Southern California Anthology; Southern Exposure; Southern Review; Spectrum (Massachusetts); Spindrift; Spirit That Moves Us; SPSM&H; Stone Drum; Story; Storyzine; Stroker Magazine; Struggle; Studio One; Sword of Shahrazad; Sycamore Review; Syzygy; Tabula Rasa; Tampa Review; Tandava; Terse Tales; Texas Review; Thema; Third World; This Magazine; Tickled By Thunder; Toad Hiway; Tramp; Triquarterly; Tucumcari Literary Review; Turnstile; Two-Ton Santa; Tyro Magazine; Underpass; University of Portland Review; Unmuzzled Ox; Valley Grapevine; Verve; Village Idiot; Vincent Brothers Review; Virginia Quarterly Review; Washington Jewish Singles Newsletter; Webster Review; Welter; West Branch; West Texas Sun; Wide Open Magazine; Widener Review; Wisconsin Restaurateur; Witness (Michigan); Word & Image; Words of Wisdom; Working Classics; Writers' Bar-B-Q; Writers' Forum; Writers Newsletter; Xavier Review; Zyzzyva

Erotica. Adrift; Alabama Literary Review; Alpha Beat Soup; Amaranth; Amelia; Apaeros; Arnazella; Art Brigade; Asylum; Baby Sue; Bahlasti Paper; Blatant Artifice; Brain Dead; Bvi-Pacifica Newsletter; Cacanadadada Review; Can(N)on Magazine; Central Park; Chattahoochee Review; Cicada; Coe Review; Cold-Drill Magazine; Crescent Review; Dangerous Times; Desert Sun; Dream International/Quarterly; Ecphorizer; Eidos; Emerald City Comix & Stories; Erotic Fiction Quarterly; Fat Tuesday; Fireweed; Fish Drum Magazine; Garm Lu; Gas; Gauntlet; Gay Chicago Magazine; Haight Ashbury Literary Journal;

HEATHENzine; Hippo; Hobo Jungle; It's a Mad Mad. . . World; Journal; K; Kiosk; Lactuca; Ledge Poetry and Prose Magazine; Left-Footed Wombat; Libido; Long Shot; Magic Changes; MidCoaster; New Blood Magazine; New Delta Review; Paper Bag; Paper Radio; PARA*phrase; Pinehurst Journal; Poetic Space; Poetry Motel; Poskisnolt Press; Prisoners of the Night; Rag Mag; Rambunctious Review; Riverwind; Salt Lick Press; Samisdat; Sanskrit; Scream Magazine; Shattered Wig Review; Sign of the Times; Slipstream; Snake Nation Review; SPSM&H; Star Route Journal; Starry Nights; Storyzine; Sub-Terrain; Sword of Shahrazad; Syzygy; Toad Hiway; Tramp; Two-Ton Santa; Village Idiot; Words of Wisdom; Writers' Bar-B-Q; Zero Hour

Ethnic. ACM, (Another Chicago Magazine); Acorn; ACTA Victoriana; Adrift; Alabama Literary Review; Amaranth; Amelia; American Dane; Amherst Review; Antietam Review; Ararat Quarterly; Arnazella; Atalantik; Aura Literary/Arts Review; Azorean Express; Bahlasti Paper; Being; Bella Figura, La; Bilingual Review; Black Jack; Black Scholar; Black Warrior Review; Black Writer Magazine; Blatant Artifice; Blue Light Red Light; Blue Water Review; Bridge; Caffe, Il; Callaloo; Caribbean Writer; Carolina Literary Companion, A; Carousel Literary Arts Magazine; Central Park; Chakra; Chaminade Literary Review; Chapter One; Cicada; City Scriptum; Coe Review; Cold-Drill Magazine; Colorado Review; Concho River Review; Crazyquilt; Cream City Review; Crescent Review; Cross Timbers Review; D.C.; Dan River Anthology; Dangerous Times; Deviance; Dream International/Quarterly; Elephant-ear; Epoch Magazine; Escapist; Felicity; Fireweed; Fish Drum Magazine; Five Fingers Review; Footwork; Garm Lu; Gauntlet; Gestalt; Grasslands Review; Groundswell; Gulf Coast; Gulf Stream Magazine; Haight Ashbury Literary Journal; Hawaii Pacific Review; Hawaii Review; Hayden's Ferry Review; HEATHENzine; Hemispheres; Hill and Holler; Hobo Jungle; Innisfree; It's a Mad Mad. . . World; Japanophile; Jeopardy; Journal of Regional Criticism; Journal; Kana; Kennesaw Review; Kenyon Review; Kola; Late Knocking; Left Curve; Left-Footed Wombat; Little Magazine; Long Shot; Long Story; Lost Creek Letters; MacGuffin; Mark; MidCoaster; Middle Eastern Dancer; Miorita, a Journal of Romanian Studies; NCASA News; Negative Capability; New Letters Magazine; New Press; Nimrod; North Dakota Quarterly; Northwest Writers, Photographers and Design Artists; Notebook/Cnaderno: A Literary Journal; Now & Then; Obsidian II: Black Literature in Review; Onionhead; Oxford Magazine; Painted Bride Quarterly; Panhandler; Paper Bag; Pennsylvania Review; Plowman; Poetic Space; Poetry Forum Short Stories; Poetry Motel; Pointed Circle; Poor Robert's Almanac; Portable Wall; Poskisnolt Press; Pottersfield Portfolio; President Journal; Puerto Del Sol; Rag Mag; Rambunctious Review; Reconstructionist; Response; River Styx; Riverwind; Rockford Review; Rohwedder; Salt Lick Press; Samisdat; San Jose Studies; Sanskrit; Seattle Review; Shattered Wig Review; Sing Heavenly Muse!; Skylark; Slipstream; Snake Nation Review; South Carolina Review; South Dakota Review; South Hill Gazette; Southern California Anthology; Southern Exposure; Spindrift; Spirit That Moves Us; Spoofing!; SPSM&H; Star Route Journal; Storyzine; Struggle; Studio One; Sword of Shahrazad; Syzygy; Tampa Review; Third Woman; Third World; This Magazine; Tramp; Tucumcari Literary Review; Tyro Magazine; Ultimate Writer; Valley Grapevine; Valley Women's Voice; Village Idiot; Vincent Brothers Review; Whispering Wind Magazine; Wicazo SA Review; Wide Open Magazine; Words of Wisdom; Working Classics; Writers' Bar-B-Q; Writers' Forum; Xavier Review; Zero Hour

Experimental. ACM, (Another Chicago Magazine); ACTA Victoriana; Adrift; Aerial; Alabama Literary Review; Alaska Quarterly Review; Alpha Beat Soup; Amaranth; Amelia; Amherst Review; Antietam Review; Antioch Review; Archae; Arnazella; Art Brigade; Artful Dodge; Asylum; Asymptotical World; Atalantik; Azorean Express; Baby Sue; Bad Haircut; Bahlasti Paper; Being; Black Ice; Blue Light Red Light; Blue Water Review; Blur; Bogg; Bottomfish Magazine; Boulevard; Bvi-Pacifica Newsletter; Cacanadadada Review; Cache Review; California Quarterly; Calliope; Calypso; Can(N)on Magazine; Carousel Literary Arts Magazine; Cathedral of Insanity; Ceilidh; Central Park; Chakra; Chaminade Literary Review; Chapter One; Chattahoochee Review; Chicago Review; Chiron Review; Kindred Spirit, The (see Chiron Review); Chrysalis; Cicada; Cipher; City Scriptum; Clockwatch Review; Cold-Drill Magazine; Collages and Bricolages; Colorado Review; Columbus Single Scene; Compost Newsletter; Conjunctions; Corona; Cream City Review; Crescent Review; D.C.; Dagger of the Mind; Dan River Anthology; Dangerous Times; Deathrealm; Delirium; Denver Quarterly; Deviance; Dream International/Quarterly; Dreams & Nightmares; Ecphorizer; Elephant-ear; 11th Street Ruse; Emerald City Comix & Stories; Eotu; Escapist; Experiment in Words; Explorations '91; F.O.C. Review; Fiction; Fine Madness; Fireweed; Fish Drum Magazine; Five Fingers Review; Florida Review; Footwork; G.W. Review; Gamut; Gas; Gaslight Review; Georgia Review; Gestalt; Gettysburg Review; Grain; Grasslands Review; Green Mountains Review; Greensboro Review; Groundswell; Gulf Coast; Gypsy; Haight Ashbury Literary Journal; Hawaii Pacific Review; Hawaii Review; Hayden's Ferry Review; HEATHENzine; Heaven Bone; Hippo; Hobo Jungle; Housewife-Writer's Forum; Howling Dog; Imagination; Indiana Review; Indigo; It's a Mad Mad. . .; Jacaranda Review; Jazziminds Magazine; Jeopardy; Journal of Regional Criticism; Journal; K; Kana; Kennesaw Review; Kenyon Review; Key West Review; Kingfisher; Kings Review; Kiosk; Late Knocking; Leading Edge; Left Curve; Left-Footed Wombat; Limestone: A Literary Journal; Little Magazine; Long Shot; Lost; Lost and Found Times; Lost Creek Letters; Louisville Review; MacGuffin; Madison Review; Mage; Merlyn's Pen; Mid-American Review; MidCoaster; Mind in Motion; Minnesota Ink; Minnesota

Review; Mississippi Review; Monocacy Valley Review; NCASA News; Negative Capability; New Blood Magazine; New Delta Review; New Letters Magazine; New Methods; New Moon; New Press; new renaissance, the; New Virginia Review; Next Phase; Nexus; Night Owl's Newsletter; Night Slivers; Nimrod; No Idea Magazine; Nocturnal Lyric; North Dakota Quarterly; Northwest Review; Northwest Writers, Photographers and Design Artists; NRG; Ohio Review; Old Hickory Review; Onionhead; Other Voices; Ouroboros; Oxford Magazine; Oyez Review; Painted Bride Quarterly; Panhandler; Paper Bag; Paper Radio; PARA*phrase; Partisan Review; Pavor Nocturnus; Pennsylvania Review; Perceptions; Phoebe; Pikeville Review; Pinehurst Journal; Poetic Space; Poetry Forum Short Stories; Poetry Halifax Dartmouth; Poor Robert's Almanac; Portable Wall; Poskisnolt Press; Pottersfield Portfolio; Prairie Fire; President Journal; Prisoners of the Night; Puckerbrush Review; Puerto Del Sol; Pulsar; Quarry; Queen's Quarterly; Rag Mag; Rambunctious Review; Re Arts & Letters; Red Cedar Review; Renegade; Renovated Lighthouse Publications; Response; Review La Booche; River Styx; Rockford Review; Rohwedder; Salt Lick Press; Samisdat; Sanskrit; Satori; Scream Magazine; Seattle Review; Shattered Wig Review; Shooting Star Review; Sign of the Times; Skylark; Slipstream; Snake Nation Review; (something); South Dakota Review; Southern California Anthology; Spectrum (Massachusetts); Spindrift; SPSM&H; Star Route Journal; Sterling Web; Story; Storyzine; Strange Plasma; Struggle; SubTerrain; Sword of Shahrazad; Sycamore Review; Syzygy; Tabula Rasa; Tampa Review; Tandava; Temm Poetry Magazine; Thema; Thin Ice; This Magazine; Toad Hiway; Tramp; Turnstile; 2 AM Magazine; Two-Ton Santa; Tyro Magazine; Ultimate Writer; Underpass; Verve; Videomania; Village Idiot; Vincent Brothers Review; Washington Jewish Singles Newsletter; Westview; Whetstone; Wide Open Magazine; Widener Review; Wisconsin Academy Review; Wisconsin Review; Witness (Michigan); Working Classics; Writers' Bar-B-Q; Writers Newsletter; Xavier Review; Zero Hour; Zoiks!; Zyzzyva

Fantasy. After Hours; Alabama Literary Review; Amelia; Amherst Review; Argonaut; Arnazella; Art Brigade; Asymptotical World; Bahlasti Paper; Bardic Runes; Being; Beyond; Blue Light Red Light; Bradley's Fantasy Magazine, Marion Zimmer; Brain Dead; Bvi-Pacifica Newsletter; Cacanadadada Review; Cache Review; Can(N)on Magazine; Carousel Literary Arts Magazine; Chapter One; City Scriptum; Coe Review; Cold-Drill Magazine; Columbus Single Scene; Companion in Zeor, A; Compost Newsletter; Corona; Crazyquilt; Crescent Review; Dagger of the Mind; Dan River Anthology; Dangerous Times; Deathrealm; Desert Sun; Deviance; Dream International/Quarterly; Dreams & Nightmares; Ecphorizer; Eldritch Science; Emerald City Comix & Stories; Escapist; F.O.C. Review; Felicity; Figment Magazine; Fireweed; Fish Drum Magazine; Gas; Gauntlet; Golden Isis Magazine; Gotta Write Network Litmag; Grasslands Review; Green's Magazine; Groundswell; Haunts; Hawaii Pacific Review; Hayden's Ferry Review; HEATHENzine; Heaven Bone; Hibiscus Magazine; Hippo; Hobo Jungle; Hobson's Choice; Hor-Tasy; Imagination; Inlet; Innisfree; It's a Mad Mad. . . World; Jeopardy; Journal of Regional Criticism; Kana; Kennesaw Review; Kenyon Review; Lake Effect; Language Bridges Quarterly; Late Knocking; Leading Edge; Legend; Long Shot; Lost Creek Letters; MacGuffin; Mage; Magic Changes; Merlyn's Pen; Minas Tirith Evening-Star; Mind in Motion; Minnesota Ink; Minnesota Review; Mississippi Review; Mythic Circle; Negative Capability; New Blood Magazine; New Laurel Review; New Moon; New Press; Next Phase; Night Owl's Newsletter; No Idea Magazine; Nocturnal Lyric; Northwest Writers, Photographers and Design Artists; Nuclear Fiction; Old Hickory Review; Once Upon A World; Ouroboros; Owlflight; Pablo Lennis; Paper Bag; Paper Radio; PARA*phrase; Pavor Nocturnus; Perceptions; Pléiades Magazine/Philae Magazine; Poetic Space; Poetry Forum Short Stories; Poetry Motel; Poskisnolt Press; Pottersfield Portfolio; Primavera; Prisoners of the Night; Processed World; Pub; Pulphouse; Pulsar; Quarry; Queen's Quarterly; Quintessential Space Debris; Rag Mag; Rampant Guinea Pig; Realms; Renaissance Fan; Renegade; Renovated Lighthouse Publications; Riverside Quarterly; Rockford Review; Salome: A Journal of the Performing Arts; Samisdat; Scream Magazine; Seattle Review; Sensations; Shoe Tree; Short Stuff Magazine for Grown-ups; Sidetrekked; Sing Heavenly Muse!; Skylark; Slate and Style; Slipstream; Snake Nation Review; Southern Humanities Review; Space and Time; SPSM&H; SPSM&H; Square One; Starsong; Sterling Web; Stone Drum; Storyzine; Strange Plasma; Sword of Shahrazad; Syzygy; Tabula Rasa; Tampa Review; Tandava; Terse Tales; Thin Ice; This Magazine; Tickled By Thunder; Trajectories; Tramp; Twisted; 2 AM Magazine; Tyro Magazine; Ultimate Writer; Verve; Videomania; Village Idiot; Vintage Northwest; Weirdbook; Wide Open Magazine; Witness (Michigan); Word & Image; Writers' Bar-B-Q, The

Feminist. ACM, (Another Chicago Magazine); Adrift; Alabama Literary Review; Alchemist; Amaranth; Amelia; Amelia; Amherst Review; Antietam Review; Apaeros; Arnazella; Art Brigade; Atlantis (Nova Scotia); Aura Literary/Arts Review; Bella Figura, La; Blatant Artifice; Bridge; Broomstick; Cacanadadada Review; Callaloo; Carousel Literary Arts Magazine; Central Park; Chapter One; Chattahoochee Review; Cicada; City Scriptum; Coe Review; Cold-Drill Magazine; Collages and Bricolages; Compost Newsletter; Corona; Creative Woman; Dangerous Times; Daughters of Sarah; Deviance; Earth's Daughters; Elephant-ear; Emrys Journal; Event; F.O.C. Review; Farmer's Market; Fiction; Five Fingers Review; Gamut; Garm Lu; Gauntlet; Gestalt; Groundswell; Gulf Coast; Gulf Stream Magazine; Gypsy; Haight Ashbury Literary Journal; Hayden's Ferry Review; HEATHENzine; Heresies; Hobo Jungle; Hobo Stew Review; Hurricane Alice; Iowa Woman; It's a Mad Mad. . . World; Jeopardy; Journal; K; Kana; Kennesaw

Review; Kenyon Review; Key West Review; Kiosk; Late Knocking; Left-Footed Wombat; Limestone: A Literary Journal; Little Magazine; Long Shot; Long Story; Mati; MidCoaster; Minnesota Review; Moving Out; NCASA News; Negative Capability; New Moon; North Dakota Quarterly; Northland Quarterly; Northwest Review; Obsidian II: Black Literature in Review; Onionhead; Oxford Magazine; Oyez Review; Painted Bride Quarterly; Paper Bag; Pennsylvania Review; Perceptions; Pinehurst Journal; Poetic Space; Poetry Forum Short Stories; Poetry Motel; Poor Robert's Almanac; Portable Wall; Poskisnolt Press; Pottersfield Portfolio; Primavera; Prisoners of the Night; Rag Mag; Rainbow City Express; Rambunctious Review; Re Arts & Letters; Red Cedar Review; Renegade; Renovated Lighthouse Publications; Response; River Styx; Riverwind; Rockford Review; Rohwedder; Room of One's Own; Salome: A Journal of the Performing Arts; Salt Lick Press; Samisdat; Sanskrit; Scream Magazine; Seattle Review; Shattered Wig Review; Sing Heavenly Muse!; Sinister Wisdom; Skylark; Slipstream; Snake Nation Review; Southern California Anthology; Southern Exposure; Southern Humanities Review; Spirit That Moves Us; SPSM&H; Star Route Journal; Struggle; Studio One; Syzygy; Third Woman; Third World; Two-Ton Santa; Valley Women's Voice; Videomania; Village Idiot; Vincent Brothers Review; Virginia Quarterly Review; Wide Open Magazine; Wisconsin Restaurateur; Witness (Michigan); Woman of Power; Words of Wisdom; Working Classics; Writers' Bar-B-Q; Zero Hour; Zymergy

Gay. ACM, (Another Chicago Magazine); Adrift; Alchemist; Amaranth; Amelia; Amherst Review; Apaeros; Arnazella; Art Brigade; Bahlasti Paper; Blatant Artifice; Can(N)on Magazine; Carousel Literary Arts Magazine; Central Park; Chattahoochee Review; City Scriptum; Coe Review; Cold-Drill Magazine; Compost Newsletter; Corona; Crazyquilt; Dangerous Times; Deviance; Fag Rag; Fish Drum Magazine; Five Fingers Review; Garm Lu; Gaslight Review; Gauntlet; Gay Chicago Magazine; Groundswell; Gulf Coast; Gulf Stream Magazine; Haight Ashbury Literary Journal; Hayden's Ferry Review; HEATHENzine; It's a Mad Mad. . . World; Journal; Kana; Kennesaw Review; Kenyon Review; Key West Review; Kiosk; Left-Footed Wombat; Libido; Little Magazine; Long Shot; MidCoaster; Minnesota Review; NCASA News; Northwest Gay & Lesbian Reader; Onionhead; Out Magazine; Oxford Magazine; Painted Bride Quarterly; Pennsylvania Review; Pinehurst Journal; Poetic Space; Poetry Motel; Poskisnolt Press; Pottersfield Portfolio; Primavera; Prisoners of the Night; Puckerbrush Review; Renovated Lighthouse Publications; River Styx; Salt Lick Press; Samisdat; Sanskrit; Scream Magazine; Seattle Review; Sensations; Shattered Wig Review; Sign of the Times; Slipstream; Snake Nation Review; Southern Exposure; Spirit That Moves Us; SPSM&H; Star Route Journal; Storyzine; Syzygy; This Magazine; Tramp; Two-Ton Santa; Village Idiot; White Review, The James; Wide Open Magazine; Working Classics; Writers' Bar-B-Q; Yellow Silk; Zero Hour

Historical. Agora; Alabama Literary Review; Amaranth; Amelia; Amherst Review; Appalachian Heritage; Archae; Arnazella; Atalantik; Black Writer Magazine; Breakthrough!; Cache Review; Callaloo; Caribbean Writer; Carolina Literary Companion, A; Central Park; Chapter One; Chrysalis; Cicada; City Scriptum; Cochran's Corner; Concho River Review; Crazyquilt; Cross Timbers Review; Dan River Anthology; Dangerous Times; Daughters of Sarah; Deviance; Dream International/Quarterly; Ecphorizer; 11th Street Ruse; Felicity; Fireweed; Garm Lu; Gaslight Review; Gestalt; Gettysburg Review; Gotta Write Network Litmag; Hayden's Ferry Review; Hobo Jungle; Housewife-Writer's Forum; Indian Youth of America Newsletter; Journal of Regional Criticism; Kana; Kenyon Review; Lake Effect; Language Bridges Quarterly; Late Knocking; Left Curve; Legend; Lighthouse; Linington Lineup; Literary Creations; Living Among Nature Daringly Magazine; Llamas Magazine; MacGuffin; Merlyn's Pen; Minnesota Review; Miorita, a Journal of Romanian Studies; Monocacy Valley Review; Mountain Laurel; Negative Capability; New Methods; Nomos; North Atlantic Review; North Dakota Quarterly; Notebook/Cnaderno: A Literary Journal; Ouroboros; Pinehurst Journal; Pipe Smoker's Ephemeris; Pléiades Magazine/Philae Magazine; Plowman; Poetry Forum Short Stories; Portable Wall; Queen's Quarterly; Rambunctious Review; Re Arts & Letters; Renegade; Renovated Lighthouse Publications; Response; Resurgens; Review La Booche; Riverwind; Rockford Review; Samisdat; Scream Magazine; Seattle Review; Sensations; Shawnee Silhouette; Shoe Tree; Short Stuff Magazine for Grown-ups; Six Lakes Arts; South Hill Gazette; Southern California Anthology; Spectrum (Massachusetts); Spindrift; SPSM&H; Storyzine; Struggle; Sword of Shahrazad; Sycamore Review; Syzygy; Tampa Review; Thumbprints; Tucumcari Literary Review; Tyro Magazine; Ultimate Writer; Village Idiot; Villager; Vincent Brothers Review; Vintage Northwest; Washington Jewish Singles Newsletter; West Texas Sun; Westview; Wide Open Magazine; Wisconsin Academy Review; Word & Image; Words of Wisdom; Working Classics; Writers' Bar-B-Q; Writers Newsletter; Xavier Review; Yesterday's Magazette

Horror. After Hours; Amaranth; Amherst Review; Argonaut; Art Brigade; Asymptotical World; Bahlasti Paper; Being; Brain Dead; Bvi-Pacifica Newsletter; Cache Review; Carousel Literary Arts Magazine; Champagne Horror; Chapter One; Cicada; City Scriptum; Cochran's Corner; Cold-Drill Magazine; D.C.; Dagger of the Mind; Dan River Anthology; Dangerous Times; Dark Side; Dark Tome; Deathrealm; Delirium; Desert Sun; Deviance; Dream International/Quarterly; Dreams & Nightmares; Eldritch Tales; Event; Figment Magazine; Gas; Gauntlet; Gestalt; Grasslands Review; Grue Magazine; Haunts; Hemispheres; Hor-Tasy; Indigo; It's a Mad Mad. . . World; Journal of Regional Criticism; Kennesaw Review;

Late Knocking; Left-Footed Wombat; Long Shot; Lost; Mage; Merlyn's Pen; MidCoaster; Miss Lucy Westenra Society of the Undead; New Blood Magazine; Next Phase; Night Slivers; No Idea Magazine; Nocturnal Lyric; Northwest Writers, Photographers and Design Artists; Nuclear Fiction; Ouroboros; Paper Bag; Pavor Nocturnus; Pinehurst Journal; Pléiades Magazine/Philae Magazine; President Journal; Pub; Pulphouse; Renegade; Riverwind; Scream Magazine; Seattle Review; Sensations; Shoe Tree; Snake Nation Review; South Carolina Review; Space and Time; SPSM&H; Square One; Starsong; Sterling Web; Storyzine; Sword of Shahrazad; Syzygy; Tabula Rasa; Terror Time Again; Thin Ice; Tickled By Thunder; Twisted; 2 AM Magazine; Two-Ton Santa; Tyro Magazine; Ultimate Writer; Videomania; Weirdbook; Wide Open Magazine; Writers' Bar-B-Q, The

Humor/Satire. ACM, (Another Chicago Magazine); ACTA Victoriana; After Hours; Agora; Alabama Literary Review; Amelia; Amherst Review; Animal Tales; Ararat Quarterly; Archae; Arnazella; Art Brigade; Atalantik; Atrocity; Azorean Express; Baby Sue; Bad Haircut; Bahlasti Paper; Big Two-Hearted; Black Jack; Blatant Artifice; Blue Water Review; Blueline; Bradley's Fantasy Magazine, Marion Zimmer; Breakthrough!; Bvi-Pacifica Newsletter; Cacanadadada Review; Cache Review; Caffe, Il; Callaloo; Canadian Author & Bookman; Can(N)on Magazine; Caribbean Writer; Carolina Literary Companion, A; Carousel Literary Arts Magazine; Cathedral of Insanity; Chakra; Chaminade Literary Review; Chapter One; Chattahoochee Review; Chiron Review; Kindred Spirit, The (see Chiron Review); Cicada; City Scriptum; Clockwatch Review; Cochrans Corner; Cold-Drill Magazine; Collages and Bricolages; Columbus Single Scene; Companion in Zeor, A; Compost Newsletter; Concho River Review; Corona; Crab Creek Review; Crazyquilt; Cream City Review; Crescent Review; Cross Timbers Review; D.C.; Dan River Anthology; Dangerous Times; Delirium; Desert Sun; Deviance; Dream International/Quarterly; Dreams & Nightmares; Eidos; Elephant-ear; 11th Street Ruse; Emerald City Comix & Stories; Escapist; Explorations '91; F.O.C. Review; Farmer's Market; Fat Tuesday; Fiction; Fireweed; Five Fingers Review; G.W. Review; Gamut; Garm Lu; Gas; Gaslight Review; Gauntlet; Gestalt; Gettysburg Review; Gotta Write Network Litmag; Grasslands Review; Green Mountains Review; Green's Magazine; Groundswell; Gulf Coast; Gulf Stream Magazine; Haight Ashbury Literary Journal; Hawaii Pacific Review; Hawaii Review; Hayden's Ferry Review; HEATHENzine; Hemispheres; Hibiscus Magazine; High Plains Literary Review; Hill and Holler; Hippo; Hobo Jungle; Hobo Stew Review; Hobson's Choice; Housewife-Writer's Forum; Howling Dog; Imagination; Indigo; Inlet; Iowa Woman; It's a Mad Mad. . . World; Jeopardy; Journal of Polymorphous Perversity; Journal of Regional Criticism; K; Kaleidoscope; Kana; Kennesaw Review; Kenyon Review; Key West Review; Kiosk; Lake Effect; Language Bridges Quarterly; Late Knocking; Leading Edge; Ledge Poetry and Prose Magazine; Left Curve; Left-Footed Wombat; Lighthouse; Limestone: A Literary Journal; Literary Creations; Little Magazine; Llamas Magazine; Long Shot; Lost Creek Letters; MacGuffin; Mark; Maryland Review; Merlyn's Pen; MidCoaster; Mind in Motion; Minnesota Ink; Mississippi Review; Monocacy Valley Review; Mountain Laurel; NCASA News; Nebraska Review; New Delta Review; New Letters Magazine; New Press; new renaissance, the; Night Owl's Newsletter; No Idea Magazine; Nocturnal Lyric; Nomos; North Dakota Quarterly; Northwest Writers, Photographers and Design Artists; Notebook/Cnaderno: A Literary Journal; Onionhead; Oregon East; Other Voices; Ouroboros; Oxford Magazine; P.I. Magazine; P.U.N. (Play on Words); Panhandler; PARA*phrase; Pearl; Pegasus Review; Pinehurst Journal; Pipe Smoker's Ephemeris; Poetic Space; Poetry Halifax Dartmouth; Poetry Magic Publications; Poetry Motel; Portable Wall; Poskisnolt Press; Potato Eyes; Pottersfield Portfolio; President Journal; Primavera; Processed World; Prophetic Voices; Queen's Quarterly; Quintessential Space Debris; Rambunctious Review; Red Cedar Review; Renegade; Response; River Styx; Riverwind; Rockford Review; Salome: A Journal of the Performing Arts; Samisdat; San Gabriel Valley Magazine; San Jose Studies; Sanskrit; Satori; Scream Magazine; Seattle Review; Sensations; Shattered Wig Review; Shawnee Silhouette; Shoe Tree; Short Stuff Magazine for Grown-ups; Sing Heavenly Muse!; Six Lakes Arts; Skylark; Slate and Style; Slipstream; Snake Nation Review; Snake River Reflections; Sneak Preview; (something); South Hill Gazette; Southern California Anthology; Southern Exposure; Southern Humanities Review; Space and Time; Spirit That Moves Us; Spoofing!; SPSM&H; Star Route Journal; Starsong; Sterling Web; Stone Drum; Storyzine; Struggle; Studio One; Sub-Terrain; Sword of Shahrazad; Sycamore Review; Syzygy; Tabula Rasa; Tampa Review; Terse Tales; Thema; Thin Ice; Thumbprints; Tickled By Thunder; Toad Hiway; Trajectories; Tramp; Tucumcari Literary Review; Turnstile; 2 AM Magazine; Two-Ton Santa; Tyro Magazine; Ultimate Writer; Verve; Videomania; Village Idiot; Villager; Vincent Brothers Review; Vintage Northwest; Virginia Quarterly Review; Wascana Review; Washington Jewish Singles Newsletter; West Texas Sun; Wide Open Magazine; Wisconsin Academy Review; Wisconsin Restaurateur; Word & Image; Words of Wisdom; Working Classics; Writers' Bar-B-Q; Writers Newsletter; Yesterday's Magazette; Zero Hour; Zoiks!

Juvenile. Acorn; Atalantik; Black Scholar; Chalk Talk; Chapter One; Cochran's Corner; Creative Kids; Dangerous Times; Dream International/Quarterly; Felicity; Lighthouse; Plowman; Shattered Wig Review; Six Lakes Arts; Spoofing!; Two-Ton Santa; Tyro Magazine; Ultimate Writer; Young Voices Magazine

Lesbian. ACM, (Another Chicago Magazine); Adrift; Alchemist; Amaranth; Amelia; Amherst Review;

Apaeros; Arnazella; Art Brigade; Bahlasti Paper; Bella Figura, La; Blatant Artifice; Can(N)on Magazine; Carousel Literary Arts Magazine; Central Park; Cicada; City Scriptum; Coe Review; Cold-Drill Magazine; Common Lives/Lesbian Lives; Compost Newsletter; Corona; Dangerous Times; Deviance; Fireweed; Fish Drum Magazine; Five Fingers Review; Garm Lu; Gaslight Review; Gay Chicago Magazine; Groundswell; Gulf Coast; Haight Ashbury Literary Journal; HEATHENzine; Heresies; Hurricane Alice; It's a Mad Mad. . . World; Kana; Kenyon Review; Key West Review; Kiosk; Left-Footed Wombat; Libido; Little Magazine; Long Shot; MidCoaster; Minnesota Review; Moving Out; Northwest Gay & Lesbian Reader; Onionhead; Oxford Magazine; Painted Bride Quarterly; Pennsylvania Review; Pinehurst Journal; Poetic Space; Poetry Motel; Poskisnolt Press; Pottersfield Portfolio; Primavera; Prisoners of the Night; Renovated Lighthouse Publications; River Styx; Room of One's Own; Salt Lick Press; Samisdat; Sanskrit; Scream Magazine; Seattle Review; Sensations; Shattered Wig Review; Sign of the Times; Sinister Wisdom; Slipstream; Snake Nation Review; Southern Exposure; Spirit That Moves Us; SPSM&H; Star Route Journal; Syzygy; This Magazine; Tramp; Two-Ton Santa; Valley Women's Voice; Videomania; Village Idiot; Visibilities; Wide Open Magazine; Working Classics; Writers' Bar-B-Q, The

Preschool/Picture Book. Acorn; Can(N)on Magazine; Chapter One; Cochran's Corner; Corona; Plowman; Two-Ton Santa

Prose Poem. ACM (Another Chicago Magazine); ACTA Victoriana; Adara; Agni; Alabama Literary Review; Alaska Quarterly Review; Alpha Beat Soup; Amaranth; Amelia; Amherst Review; Antaeus; Antietam Review; Antigonish Review; Apaeros; Appalachian Heritage; Archae; Argonaut; Arnazella; Art:Mag; Artful Dodge; Asylum; Bad Haircut; Being; Bella Figura, La; Beloit Fiction Journal; Big Two-Hearted; Black Warrior Review; Black Writer Magazine; Blue Light Red Light; Blueline; Bogg; Bottomfish Magazine; Boulevard; Brain Dead; Cacanadadada Review; Cache Review; Callaloo; Calypso; Can(N)on Magazine; Caribbean Writer; Carousel Literary Arts Magazine; Ceilidh; Central Park; Chapter One; Cipher; City Scriptum; Clockwatch Review; Cochran's Corner; Collages and Bricolages; Colorado-North Review; Columbia: A Magazine of Poetry & Prose; Companion in Zeor, A; Confrontation; Corona; Cream City Review; D.C.; Dan River Anthology; Deviance; Dream International/Quarterly; Ecphorizer; Emerald City Comix & Stories; Eotu; Escapist; Explorer Magazine; F.O.C. Review; Fat Tuesday; Felicity; Fine Madness; Fireweed; Fish Drum Magazine; Five Fingers Review; Folio: A Literary Journal; G.W. Review; Gamut; Gas; Gestalt; Gotta Write Network Litmag; Grain; Grasslands Review; Haight Ashbury Literary Journal; Hawaii Review; Hayden's Ferry Review; HEATHENzine; Hemispheres; Hippo; Hobo Jungle; Imagination; It's a Mad Mad. . . World; Jacaranda Review; Jazziminds Magazine; Jeopardy; Journal; Kaleidoscope; Kenyon Review; Kings Review; Kiosk; Lactuca; Language Bridges Quarterly; Leading Edge; Ledge Poetry and Prose Magazine; Left Curve; Left-Footed Wombat; Lighthouse; Limestone: A Literary Journal; Literary Creations; Little Magazine; Long Shot; Loonfeather; Lost; Lost and Found Times; Louisville Review; MacGuffin; Madison Review; Magic Changes; Mid-American Review; Mind in Motion; Monocacy Valley Review; Mythic Circle; NCASA News; Negative Capability; New Delta Review; New Moon; New Press; new renaissance, the; Nimrod; Northwest Writers, Photographers and Design Artists; Now & Then; NRG; Oregon East; Painted Bride Quarterly; Paper Bag; Paper Radio; PARA*phrase; Partisan Review; Pearl; Pegasus Review; Pennsylvania Review; Perceptions; Phoebe; Pikeville Review; Pinehurst Journal; Plowman; Poetic Space; Poetry Forum Short Stories; Poetry Halifax Dartmouth; Poetry Magic Publications; Poetry Motel; Pointed Circle; Portable Wall; Poskisnolt Press; Pottersfield Portfolio; Prairie Fire; Prairie Journal of Canadian Literature; Prism International; Prisoners of the Night; Prophetic Voices; Puerto Del Sol; Rag Mag; Rainbow City Express; Rambunctious Review; Renegade; Renovated Lighthouse Publications; Response; River Styx; Riverwind; Salome: A Journal of the Performing Arts; Samisdat; Sanskrit; Seattle Review; Sensations; Shattered Wig Review; Sing Heavenly Muse!; Six Lakes Arts; Skylark; Slipstream; Snake Nation Review; Sneak Preview; (something); Soundings East; South Hill Gazette; Spindrift; Spirit That Moves Us; Star Route Journal; Starsong; Storyzine; Struggle; Studio One; Sword of Shahrazad; Syzygy; Tabula Rasa; Tampa Review; Tandava; Thema; This Magazine; Thumbprints; Tickled By Thunder; Toad Hiway; Trajectories; Tramp; Twisted; 2 AM Magazine; Two-Ton Santa; Tyro Magazine; Underpass; Unmuzzled Ox; Valley Women's Voice; Verve; Village Idiot; Villager; Vincent Brothers Review; West Branch; Willow Springs; Wisconsin Academy Review; Worcester Review; Word & Image; Words of Wisdom; Working Classics; Wormwood Review; Writers Newsletter; Xavier Review; Zymergy; Zyzzyva

Psychic/Supernatural/Occult. After Hours; Alchemist; Amaranth; Amherst Review; Asymptotical World; Atalantik; Bahlasti Paper; Being; Bradley's Fantasy Magazine, Marion Zimmer; Bvi-Pacifica Newsletter; Can(N)on Magazine; Cathedral of Insanity; Chapter One; Cicada; City Scriptum; Coe Review; Compost Newsletter; Converging Paths; Corona; Crescent Review; D.C.; Dan River Anthology; Dangerous Times; Dark Tome; Deathrealm; Deviance; Dream International/Quarterly; Ecphorizer; Eldritch Tales; Fat Tuesday; Felicity; Figment Magazine; Fish Drum Magazine; Gas; Gestalt; Golden Isis Magazine; Grue Magazine; Haunts; Hayden's Ferry Review; Heaven Bone; Hippo; Imagination; Indigo; It's a Mad Mad. . . World; Journal of Regional Criticism; Kennesaw Review; Left-Footed Wombat; Long Shot; Lost; MacGuffin; Negative Capability; Night Slivers; Nocturnal Lyric; Northwest Writers,

Photographers and Design Artists; Ouroboros; Pablo Lennis; PARA*phrase; Pavor Nocturnus; Perceptions; Poskisnolt Press; President Journal; Prisoners of the Night; Pub; Rainbow City Express; Renegade; Renovated Lighthouse Publications; San Gabriel Valley Magazine; Scream Magazine; Seattle Review; Shattered Wig Review; Snake Nation Review; Space and Time; Starsong; Sterling Web; Stone Drum; Sword of Shahrazad; Syzygy; Thema; Thin Ice; Tickled By Thunder; Twisted; 2 AM Magazine; Tyro Magazine; Washington Jewish Singles Newsletter; Weirdbook; Wide Open Magazine; Writers' Bar-B-Q; Zero Hour; Zoiks!

Regional. Agora; Alabama Literary Review; Amherst Review; Appalachian Heritage; Arnazella; Aura Literary/Arts Review; Azorean Express; Big Two-Hearted; Blue Water Review; Blueline; Breakthrough!; Bridge; Cache Review; Callaloo; Carolina Literary Companion, A; Chapter One; Chattahoochee Review; Cicada; Clockwatch Review; Coe Review; Cold-Drill Magazine; Concho River Review; Confrontation; Corona; Cream City Review; Crescent Review; Cross Timbers Review; Dan River Anthology; Descant (Texas); Door County Almanak; Ecphorizer; Elephant-ear; Emrys Journal; Event; Exit 13 Magazine; Farmer's Market; Fish Drum Magazine; Five Fingers Review; Gamut; Garm Lu; Gestalt; Gettysburg Review; Grasslands Review; Great Stream Review; Green Mountains Review; Groundswell; Gulf Coast; Gulf Stream Magazine; Hawaii Pacific Review; Hawaii Review; Hayden's Ferry Review; Heaven Bone; High Plains Literary Review; Hill and Holler; Hippo; Hobo Jungle; Innisfree; Japanophile; Jeopardy; Journal of Regional Criticism; Journal; Kana; Kennebec; Kennesaw Review; Key West Review; Lactuca; Lake Effect; Left Curve; Left-Footed Wombat; Lighthouse; Limestone: A Literary Journal; Loonfeather; Lost Creek Letters; Louisiana Literature; Mark; Merlyn's Pen; MidCoaster; Middle Eastern Dancer; Minnesota Ink; Miorita, a Journal of Romanian Studies; Monocacy Valley Review; Mountain Laurel; NCASA News; Negative Capability; New Methods; New Mexico Humanities Review; NeWest Review; Nexus; Northern Review; Northland Quarterly; Notebook/Cnaderno: A Literary Journal; Now & Then; Onionhead; Oregon East; Oyez Review; Partisan Review; Pennsylvania Review; Phoebe; Plowman; Poetic Space; Pointed Circle; Portable Wall; Potato Eyes; Pottersfield Portfolio; Prairie Journal of Canadian Literature; Rag Mag; Re Arts & Letters; Red Cedar Review; Renovated Lighthouse Publications; Response; Riverwind; Rockford Review; Rohwedder; Samisdat; San Jose Studies; Sanskrit; Satori; Scream Magazine; Seattle Review; Sensations; Shattered Wig Review; Shawnee Silhouette; Shooting Star Review; Short Stuff Magazine for Grown-ups; Six Lakes Arts; Skylark; Snake Nation Review; Snake River Reflections; Sneak Preview; South Dakota Review; South Hill Gazette; Southern California Anthology; Southern Exposure; Southern Humanities Review; Spindrift; Spoofing!; SPSM&H; Struggle; Studio One; Sword of Shahrazad; Sycamore Review; Thema; This Magazine; Thumbprints; Tucumcari Literary Review; Turnstile; Tyro Magazine; Vincent Brothers Review; Washington Review; West Texas Sun; Widener Review; Wind Magazine; Wisconsin Academy Review; Word & Image; Words of Wisdom; Working Classics; Writers' Bar-B-Q; Writers' Forum; Writers Newsletter; Xavier Review; Zyzzyva

Religious/Inspirational. Agora; Apaeros; Ararat Quarterly; Arnazella; Being; Beloit Fiction Journal; Black Writer Magazine; Breakthrough!; Carousel Literary Arts Magazine; Chakra; Chaminade Literary Review; Chapter One; Christian Outlook; Cochran's Corner; Converging Paths; Daughters of Sarah; Dreams & Visions; Escapist; Explorer Magazine; Felicity; Fish Drum Magazine; Garm Lu; Heaven Bone; Journal of Regional Criticism; Language Bridges Quarterly; Left-Footed Wombat; Living Streams; Modern Liturgy; New Press; North American Voice of Fatima; Now & Then; Pablo Lennis; Pegasus Review; Perceptions; Plowman; Poetry Forum Short Stories; Queen of All Hearts; Rainbow City Express; Renegade; Response; Riverwind; Skylark; Spirit That Moves Us; Starlight; Storyzine; Tickled By Thunder; Two-Ton Santa; Tyro Magazine; Ultimate Writer; Valley Women's Voice; Vintage Northwest; West Texas Sun; Word & Image; Writers Newsletter; Xavier Review; Yesterday's Magazette

Romance. Amaranth; Amherst Review; Apaeros; Atalantik; Aura Literary/Arts Review; Breakthrough!; Carousel Literary Arts Magazine; Chapter One; Cicada; Cochran's Corner; Corona; Dan River Anthology; Delirium; Dream International/Quarterly; Eagle's Flight; Explorer Magazine; Felicity; Gay Chicago Magazine; Gotta Write Network Litmag; Hayden's Ferry Review; Hemispheres; Housewife-Writer's Forum; Imagination; Jeopardy; Journal of Regional Criticism; Ledge Poetry and Prose Magazine; Lighthouse; Merlyn's Pen; Minnesota Ink; Negative Capability; Northland Quarterly; Northwest Writers, Photographers and Design Artists; Peoplenet; Plowman; Poetry Forum Short Stories; Poskisnolt Press; PSI; Rambunctious Review; Renegade; Salome: A Journal of the Performing Arts; Sensations; Shawnee Silhouette; Short Stuff Magazine for Grown-ups; South Hill Gazette; SPSM&H; Sword of Shahrazad; Terse Tales; Thumbprints; Tyro Magazine; Ultimate Writer; Village Idiot; Villager; Virginia Quarterly Review; Washington Jewish Singles Newsletter; Word & Image; Writers Newsletter

Science Fiction. Acorn; Agora; Alabama Literary Review; Amaranth; Amelia; Amherst Review; Apaeros; Argonaut; Arnazella; Art Brigade; Atalantik; Aura Literary/Arts Review; Bahlasti Paper; Being; Beyond; Brain Dead; Bvi-Pacifica Newsletter; Cacanadadada Review; Cache Review; Callaloo; Can(N)on Magazine; Carousel Literary Arts Magazine; Ceilidh; Chapter One; Chrysalis; Cicada; City Scriptum; Cochran's Corner; Coe Review; Cold-Drill Magazine; Collages and Bricolages; Companion in Zeor, A; Compost Newsletter; Cosmic Landscapes; Crazyquilt; Crescent Review; Dagger of the Mind;

Dan River Anthology; Dangerous Times; Deathrealm; Desert Sun; Deviance; Dream International/Quarterly; Dreams & Nightmares; Ecphorizer; Eldritch Science; Emerald City Comix & Stories; Escapist; Explorer Magazine; F.O.C. Review; Fat Tuesday; Felicity; Figment Magazine; Gas; Gaslight Review; Gestalt; Gotta Write Network Litmag; Grasslands Review; Green's Magazine; Hawaii Pacific Review; Hayden's Ferry Review; Hibiscus Magazine; Hippo; Hobo Jungle; Hobson's Choice; Imagination; Indigo; Innisfree; It's a Mad Mad. . . World; Jeopardy; Journal of Regional Criticism; K; Late Knocking; Leading Edge; Left Curve; Long Shot; Lost Creek Letters; MacGuffin; Mad Engineer; Mage; Magic Changes; Mark; Mati; Merlyn's Pen; Mind in Motion; Minnesota Ink; Minnesota Review; Negative Capability; New Methods; New Moon; Next Phase; Nimrod; No Idea Magazine; Nocturnal Lyric; Nomos; Northwest Writers, Photographers and Design Artists; Nuclear Fiction; Once Upon A World; Other Worlds; Ouroboros; Owlflight; Pablo Lennis; Paper Radio; PARA*phrase; Pavor Nocturnus; Perceptions; Poetry Forum Short Stories; Poetry Motel; Portable Wall; Pottersfield Portfolio; Primavera; Prisoners of the Night; Processed World; Pulphouse; Pulsar; Quarry; Queen's Quarterly; Quintessential Space Debris; Re Arts & Letters; Renaissance Fan; Renegade; Renovated Lighthouse Publications; Riverside Quarterly; Salome: A Journal of the Performing Arts; Samisdat; Sanskrit; Scream Magazine; Seattle Review; Sensations; Shawnee Silhouette; Shoe Tree; Short Stuff Magazine for Grown-ups; Sidetrekked; Skylark; Slipstream; Snake Nation Review; South Hill Gazette; Space and Time; Spindrift; SPSM&H; Square One; Star Route Journal; Starsong; Sterling Web; Storyzine; Strange Plasma; Struggle; Syzygy; Tabula Rasa; Tandava; Terse Tales; Thema; Tickled By Thunder; Toad Hiway; Trajectories; Twisted; 2 AM Magazine; Tyro Magazine; Ultimate Writer; Village Idiot; Vincent Brothers Review; Wide Open Magazine; Writers' Bar-B-Q, The

Senior Citizen/Retirement. Amelia; Carolina Literary Companion, A; Chapter One; Cicada; Corona; Dan River Anthology; Dream International/Quarterly; Felicity; Hayden's Ferry Review; Heartland Journal; Imagination; Kana; Kenyon Review; Left-Footed Wombat; Lighthouse; Living Among Nature Daringly Magazine; Minnesota Ink; Moving Out; Negative Capability; Pléiades Magazine/Philae Magazine; Plowman; Poetry Forum Short Stories; Portable Wall; Poskisnolt Press; Shattered Wig Review; Short Stuff Magazine for Grown-ups; Snake Nation Review; SPSM&H; Struggle; Terse Tales; Thumbprints; Tucumcari Literary Review; Two-Ton Santa; Tyro Magazine; Village Idiot; Vincent Brothers Review; Vintage Northwest; Washington Jewish Singles Newsletter; Wide Open Magazine; Word & Image; Yesterday's Magazette

Serialized/Excerpted Novel. Agni; Alabama Literary Review; Antaeus; Apaeros; Art Brigade; Bellowing Ark; Black Jack; Blatant Artifice; Bvi-Pacifica Newsletter; Cache Review; Caffe, Il; Callaloo; Cathedral of Insanity; Ceilidh; Central Park; Coe Review; Cold-Drill Magazine; Compost Newsletter; Crazyquilt; Dangerous Times; Deviance; Dream International/Quarterly; Ecphorizer; F.O.C. Review; Farmer's Market; Garm Lu; Gestalt; Gettysburg Review; Green Mountains Review; Groundswell; Gulf Stream Magazine; Gypsy; Hobo Jungle; Hobo Stew Review; It's a Mad Mad. . . World; K; Kingfisher; Madison Review; Mid-American Review; Mud Creek; Mystery Notebook; NCASA News; New Press; New Virginia Review; Northland Quarterly; Northwest Writers, Photographers and Design Artists; Now & Then; Other Voices; Phoebe; Pléiades Magazine/Philae Magazine; Poor Robert's Almanac; Prairie Journal of Canadian Literature; Pub; Puerto Del Sol; Quarry; Realms; Red Bass; Resurgens; Salome: A Journal of the Performing Arts; Samisdat; Scream Magazine; Seattle Review; Shattered Wig Review; Six Lakes Arts; Skylark; South Dakota Review; Southern California Anthology; Spindrift; Trajectories; Tyro Magazine; Virginia Quarterly Review; Washington Jewish Singles Newsletter; Widener Review; Willow Springs; Writ Magazine; Writers' Bar-B-Q; Xavier Review

Sports. Amelia; Beloit Fiction Journal; Blue Water Review; Cache Review; Carousel Literary Arts Magazine; Chapter One; Chrysalis; F.O.C. Review; Folio: A Literary Journal; Magic Changes; MidCoaster; New Press; Now & Then; Portable Wall; Riverwind; Samisdat; Skylark; Spirit That Moves Us; Spitball; Sycamore Review; Thema; Thumbprints; Tyro Magazine; Valley Women's Voice; West Texas Sun; Witness (Michigan)

Suspense/Mystery. Acorn; After Hours; Alabama Literary Review; Amaranth; Amelia; Amherst Review; Arnazella; Atalantik; Bahlasti Paper; Blue Water Review; Bradley's Fantasy Magazine, Marion Zimmer; Breakthrough!; Bvi-Pacifica Newsletter; Byline; Cache Review; Can(N)on Magazine; Carolina Literary Companion, A; Carousel Literary Arts Magazine; Chapter One; Chrysalis; Cicada; City Scriptum; Cochran's Corner; Cold-Drill Magazine; Columbus Single Scene; Crazyquilt; Crescent Review; Dagger of the Mind; Dan River Anthology; Deviance; Dream International/Quarterly; Eagle's Flight; Ecphorizer; 11th Street Ruse; Emerald City Comix & Stories; Escapist; F.O.C. Review; Felicity; Folio: A Literary Journal; Gas; Gauntlet; Gestalt; Grasslands Review; Green's Magazine; Groundswell; Gulf Stream Magazine; Hardboiled; Hawaii Pacific Review; Hemispheres; Hibiscus Magazine; Hobo Jungle; Housewife-Writer's Forum; Imagination; Innisfree; It's a Mad Mad. . . World; Late Knocking; Left-Footed Wombat; Lighthouse; Linington Lineup; Living Among Nature Daringly Magazine; Long Shot; Merlyn's Pen; MidCoaster; Minnesota Ink; Mystery Notebook; Mystery Time; Negative Capability; New Blood Magazine; No Idea Magazine; Nocturnal Lyric; Nomos; Northwest Writers, Photographers and

Design Artists; Ouroboros; P.I. Magazine; Paper Bag; Perceptions; Pinehurst Journal; Pléiades Magazine/Philae Magazine; Poetry Forum Short Stories; Post; President Journal; Prisoners of the Night; PSI; Pub; Renegade; Salome: A Journal of the Performing Arts; Samisdat; Scream Magazine; Seattle Review; Sensations; Shawnee Silhouette; Shoe Tree; Short Stuff Magazine for Grown-ups; Sing Heavenly Muse!; Six Lakes Arts; Skylark; Snake Nation Review; Snake River Reflections; South Hill Gazette; SPSM&H; Square One; Storyzine; Struggle; Tabula Rasa; Terse Tales; Thema; Tickled By Thunder; Tucumcari Literary Review; 2 AM Magazine; Tyro Magazine; Ultimate Writer; Village Idiot; Villager; Vincent Brothers Review; Vintage Northwest; Washington Jewish Singles Newsletter; Wide Open Magazine; Writers' Bar-B-Q; Writers Newsletter

Translations. ACM, (Another Chicago Magazine); Adrift; Aerial; Agni; Alabama Literary Review; Alaska Quarterly Review; Amelia; Amherst Review; Antaeus; Antigonish Review; Antioch Review; Ararat Quarterly; Archae; Arnazella; Art Brigade; Artful Dodge; Asylum; Atalantik; Bad Haircut; Bella Figura, La; Black Ice; Blatant Artifice; Cacanadadada Review; Cache Review; Caffe, Il; Callaloo; Can(N)on Magazine; Ceilidh; Central Park; Chakra; Chaminade Literary Review; Chariton Review; Chattahoochee Review; Cicada; Cipher; Coe Review; Cold-Drill Magazine; Colorado Review; Columbia: A Magazine of Poetry & Prose; Confrontation; Conjunctions; Crab Creek Review; Cream City Review; Dangerous Times; Descant (Ontario); Deviance; Dream International/Quarterly; Ecphorizer; Escapist; Fiction; Fine Madness; Fireweed; Folio: A Literary Journal; Footwork; G.W. Review; Gamut; Garm Lu; Gestalt; Green Mountains Review; Groundswell; Gulf Coast; Gypsy; Hawaii Pacific Review; Hawaii Review; Hobo Jungle; Hobo Stew Review; It's a Mad Mad... World; Jacaranda Review; Jazziminds Magazine; Jeopardy; Kana; Kenyon Review; Kingfisher; Kiosk; Language Bridges Quarterly; Late Knocking; Left Curve; Left-Footed Wombat; MacGuffin; Manoa; Mati; Mid-American Review; MidCoaster; Miorita, a Journal of Romanian Studies; Mississippi Review; Mud Creek; NCASA News; Negative Capability; New Delta Review; New Laurel Review; New Letters Magazine; New Moon; New Orleans Review; New Press; new renaissance, the; Nexus; Nimrod; Northwest Review; Oregon East; Oxford Magazine; Painted Bride Quarterly; Partisan Review; Pennsylvania Review; Phoebe; Pikeville Review; Pinehurst Journal; Plowman; Poetic Space; Poor Robert's Almanac; Portable Wall; President Journal; Prism International; Puerto Del Sol; Quarry; Quarterly West; Red Bass; Renegade; Response; River Styx; Riverwind; Rohwedder; Salome: A Journal of the Performing Arts; Samisdat; Sanskrit; Satori; Seattle Review; Shattered Wig Review; Shooting Star Review; Signal; South Dakota Review; Spindrift; Spirit That Moves Us; SPSM&H; Star Route Journal; Story; Storyzine; Struggle; Sycamore Review; Tampa Review; Third Woman; Third World; Toad Hiway; Translation; Triquarterly; Unmuzzled Ox; Village Idiot; Vincent Brothers Review; Virginia Quarterly Review; Webster Review; West Branch; Willow Springs; Writ Magazine; Writers' Bar-B-Q; Xavier Review; Zero Hour; Zoiks!

Western. Amelia; Amherst Review; Azorean Express; Black Jack; Carousel Literary Arts Magazine; Chapter One; City Scriptum; Cold-Drill Magazine; Concho River Review; Cross Timbers Review; Dan River Anthology; Delirium; Dream International/Quarterly; Felicity; Gestalt; Hemispheres; Hibiscus Magazine; Hippo; Indian Youth of America Newsletter; Lighthouse; Living Among Nature Daringly Magazine; Long Shot; Merlyn's Pen; Minnesota Ink; New Methods; Paper Bag; Pléiades Magazine/Philae Magazine; Plowman; Poskisnolt Press; Riverwind; Samisdat; San Gabriel Valley Magazine; Seattle Review; Short Stuff Magazine for Grown-ups; Skylark; Snake River Reflections; South Hill Gazette; SPSM&H; Sword of Shahrazad; Thema; Tickled By Thunder; Tucumcari Literary Review; Ultimate Writer; Valley Grapevine; Village Idiot; West Texas Sun; Westview; Wide Open Magazine

Young Adult/Teen. Acorn; Black Scholar; Bradley's Fantasy Magazine, Marion Zimmer; Chapter One; Cochran's Corner; Creative Kids; Dream International/Quarterly; Felicity; Gotta Write Network Litmag; Hobo Stew Review; Language Bridges Quarterly; Merlyn's Pen; Minnesota Ink; Plowman; Poetry Forum Short Stories; Poskisnolt Press; Reflections; Review La Booche; Shattered Wig Review; Shooting Star Review; Spoofing!; Struggle; Tyro Magazine

Commercial Periodicals

Adventure. American Accent Short Story Magazine; Art Times; Bostonia Magazine; Bowbender; Bowhunter Magazine; Boys' Life; Buffalo Spree Magazine; Career Focus; College Preview; Journey; Visions; Catholic Forester; Cavalier Magazine; Cosmopolitan Magazine; Crusader Magazine; Dialogue; Florida Wildlife; Flyfishing News, Views and Reviews; Georgia Sportsman; Horse Illustrated; International Bowhunter; Mainstreet USA; Modern Gold Miner and Treasure Hunter; Modern Short Stories; Modern Woodmen; New Hampshire Life; Northcoast View; Plain Dealer Magazine; Pockets; Prime Times; Radiance; Ranger Rick Magazine; Road King Magazine; Senior Life Magazine; Sporting Times; Sports Afield; Sun and Sonlight Christian Newspapers; Trailer Boats Magazine

Canada. Atlantic Advocate; Atlantic Salmon Journal; Bowbender; Canadian Messenger; Chickadee; Indian Life Magazine; Messenger of the Sacred Heart; Vancouver Child; Western People

Comics. Freeway

Condensed Novel. Arizona Coast; Bostonia Magazine; Buzzworm; Northcoast View; Senior Life Magazine; Tikkun; Virtue; Women's American ORT Reporter

Confession. Jive; Modern Short Stories

Contemporary. American Accent Short Story Magazine; American Atheist; Art Times; Atlanta Singles Magazine; Atlantic Monthly; Baby Connection News Journal; B'nai B'rith International Jewish Monthly; Bomb Magazine; Boston Review; Bostonia Magazine; Buffalo Spree Magazine; Career Focus; Catholic Forester; Cosmopolitan Magazine; Dialogue; Family Magazine; First; Good Housekeeping; Harper's Magazine; Lady's Circle; Mademoiselle Magazine; Military Lifestyle; Modern Short Stories; Modern Woodmen; Moment Magazine; Náamat Woman; New Hampshire Life; Northcoast View; Northeast; Northwest Magazine; Orange Coast Magazine; Organica Quarterly; Other Side; Oui Magazine; Plain Dealer Magazine; Playboy Magazine; Pockets; Portland Magazine; Prime Times; Radiance; Redbook; St. Anthony Messenger; St. Joseph's Messenger; Sassy Magazine; Tikkun; Trailer Boats Magazine; Virtue; Woman's Day

Erotica. Cavalier Magazine; Contact Advertising; Drummer; First Hand; Genesis Magazine; Gent; Gentleman's Companion; Guys; Harvey for Loving People; Hustler; Hustler Busty Beauties; Manscape; Northcoast View; Nugget; Options; Private Letters; Radiance; Swank Magazine; Turn-on Letters

Ethnic. American Citizen Italian Press; American Dane; Art Times; Baltimore Jewish Times; B'nai B'rith International Jewish Monthly; Bomb Magazine; Boston Review; Bostonia Magazine; Buffalo Spree Magazine; Career Focus; Catholic Forester; Christmas; Detroit Jewish News; Emerge Magazine; Hadassah Magazine; India Currents; Indian Life Magazine; Inside; Jive; Midstream; Moment Magazine; Northcoast View; Organica Quarterly; Other Side; Plain Dealer Magazine; Pockets; Prime Times; Radiance; Sassy Magazine; Women's American ORT Reporter

Experimental. Bomb Magazine; Boston Review; Bostonia Magazine; Career Focus; Modern Gold Miner and Treasure Hunter; Modern Short Stories; Northcoast View; Organica Quarterly; Other Side; Sassy Magazine

Fantasy. American Accent Short Story Magazine; Art Times; Asimov's Science Fiction Magazine, Isaac; Buzzworm; Contact Advertising; Dragon Magazine; Emerge Magazine; Magazine of Fantasy and Science Fiction; Modern Short Stories; New Hampshire Life; Northcoast View; Northwest Magazine; Omni; Oui Magazine; Playboy Magazine; Pockets; Radiance; Ranger Rick Magazine; Trailer Boats Magazine; Weird Tales; Woman's Day; Young American

Feminist. American Atheist; Art Times; Buffalo Spree Magazine; Catholic Forester; Contact Advertising; Mother Jones Magazine; Náamat Woman; Other Side; Radiance; Redbook; Sassy Magazine; Tikkun; Vancouver Child; Women's American ORT Reporter

Gay. Art Times; Bear; Contact Advertising; Drummer; First Hand; Guide Magazine; Guide; Guys; Hot Shots; In Touch for Men; Manscape; Mother Jones Magazine; Options; Sassy Magazine; Tikkun; Xtra Magazine

Historical. American Accent Short Story Magazine; American Atheist; American Citizen Italian Press; Arizona Coast; Art Times; Atlantic Advocate; Atlantic Salmon Journal; Beckett Baseball Card Monthly; B'nai B'rith International Jewish Monthly; Career Focus; Christmas; Lady's Circle; Midstream; Modern Gold Miner and Treasure Hunter; Modern Short Stories; Modern Woodmen; Moment Magazine; Montana Senior Citizens News; Northcoast View; Plain Dealer Magazine; Pockets; Portland Magazine; Purpose; Radiance; Senior Life Magazine; Sun and Sonlight Christian Newspapers; Tikkun

Horror. Bostonia Magazine; Cavalier Magazine; Horror; Modern Short Stories; New Mystery; Northcoast View; Omni; Playboy Magazine; Weird Tales

Humor/Satire. American Accent Short Story Magazine; American Atheist; American Citizen Italian Press; Art Times; Atlanta Singles Magazine; Atlantic Advocate; Atlantic Salmon Journal; Baby Connection News Journal; Balloon Life; Beckett Baseball Card Monthly; B'nai B'rith International Jewish Monthly; Boston Review; Bostonia Magazine; Boys' Life; Buffalo Spree Magazine; Career Focus; Catholic Forester; Dialogue; Emerge Magazine; First; Freeway; Georgia Sportsman; Golf Journal; Harper's Magazine; Horse Illustrated; Ideals Magazine; Lady's Circle; Mainstreet USA; Metro Singles Lifestyles; Midstream; Modern Gold Miner and Treasure Hunter; Modern Short Stories; National Lampoon; New Hampshire Life; Northcoast View; Northwest Magazine; Oh! Idaho; Orange Coast Magazine; Other Side; Oui Magazine; Outlaw Biker; Plain Dealer Magazine; Playboy Magazine; Prime Times; Radiance; Ranger Rick Magazine; Reform Judaism; Road King Magazine; St. Joseph's Messenger; Sassy Magazine; Senior Life Magazine; Singlelife Magazine; Sports Afield; Sun and Sonlight Christian Newspapers; Tikkun; Trailer Boats Magazine; Virtue; Vista; Women's American ORT Reporter; Young American

Juvenile. Associate Reformed Presbyterian; Beckett Baseball Card Monthly; Chickadee; Child Life; Children's Digest; Children's Playmate; Clubhouse; Cricket Magazine; Crusader Magazine; Discoveries; Friend Magazine; Highlights for Children; Home Altar; Humpty Dumpty's Magazine; Jack and Jill;

Junior Trails; Kid City; Kindergarten Listen; Ladybug; Lollipops Magazine; Modern Woodmen; My Friend; Noah's Ark; On the Line; Pennywhistle Press; R-A-D-A-R; Ranger Rick Magazine; Single Parent; Sporting Times; Story Friends; Touch; Turtle Magazine for Preschool Kids; Vancouver Child; Wee Wisdom Magazine; Wonder Time; Young Crusader, The

Lesbian. Art Times; Contact Advertising; Guide; Mother Jones Magazine; On Our Backs; Options; Oui Magazine; Tikkun; Xtra Magazine

Preschool/Picture Book. Baby Connection News Journal; Vancouver Child; Wee Wisdom Magazine

Prose Poem. Baby Connection News Journal; Boston Review; Career Focus; Church Herald; Ideals Magazine; Mature Years; Metro Singles Lifestyles; My Friend; Northwest Magazine; Pennywhistle Press; Radiance; Sassy Magazine; Student Leadership Journal; Young American

Psychic/Supernatural/Occult. Emerge Magazine; Horror; Modern Short Stories; Northcoast View; Plain Dealer Magazine; Weird Tales

Regional. Aloha; Atlantic Advocate; Atlantic Salmon Journal; Boston Review; Bostonia Magazine; Catholic Forester; Chesapeake Bay Magazine; Country America; Dialogue; First; Flyfishing News, Views and Reviews; Georgia Sportsman; Modern Short Stories; New Hampshire Life; Northcoast View; Northeast; Oh! Idaho; Orange Coast Magazine; Palouse Journal; Plain Dealer Magazine; Portland Magazine; Sassy Magazine; Sunday Journal Magazine; Vancouver Child; Washingtonian; Western People; Yankee Magazine

Religious/Inspirational. Alive Now!; Associate Reformed Presbyterian; Baltimore Jewish Times; B'nai B'rith International Jewish Monthly; Bread; Campus Life Magazine; Canadian Messenger; Christian Living For Senior Highs; Christmas; Church Herald; Clubhouse; Crusader Magazine; Detroit Jewish News; Discoveries; Evangel; Family; Freeway; Friend Magazine; Gem; HiCall; High Adventure; Home Altar; Home Life; Ideals Magazine; In Touch; Inside; Junior Trails; Kindergarten Listen; Lady's Circle; Liguorian; Live; Living with Teenagers; Lookout; Lutheran Journal; Magazine for Christian Youth!; Mature Living; Mature Years; Messenger of the Sacred Heart; Metro Singles Lifestyles; Midstream; Modern Short Stories; Moment Magazine; My Friend; New Era Magazine; Noah's Ark; Other Side; Pockets; R-A-D-A-R; Reform Judaism; St. Anthony Messenger; St. Joseph's Messenger; Seek; Senior Life Magazine; Standard; Story Friends; Straight; Student Leadership Journal; Student; Sun and Sonlight Christian Newspapers; Teen Power; Teens Today; Touch; TQ; Virtue; Vision; Vista; With Magazine; Wonder Time; Young Salvationist/Young Soldier

Romance. American Accent Short Story Magazine; Baby Connection News Journal; Career Focus; Cosmopolitan Magazine; Good Housekeeping; Jive; Lady's Circle; Metro Singles Lifestyles; Modern Short Stories; Prime Times; St. Anthony Messenger; St. Joseph's Messenger; Sun and Sonlight Christian Newspapers; Virtue; Woman's World Magazine

Science Fiction. Aboriginal Science Fiction; American Accent Short Story Magazine; Analog Science Fiction/Science Fact; Art Times; Asimov's Science Fiction Magazine, Isaac; Boys' Life; Career Focus; Emerge Magazine; Magazine of Fantasy and Science Fiction; Modern Short Stories; New Hampshire Life; Northcoast View; Northwest Magazine; Omni; Plain Dealer Magazine; Playboy Magazine; Radiance; Ranger Rick Magazine; Trailer Boats Magazine

Senior Citizen/Retirement. Arizona Coast; Catholic Forester; Dialogue; Lady's Circle; Mature Living; Mature Years; Modern Gold Miner and Treasure Hunter; Modern Woodmen; Montana Senior Citizens News; New Hampshire Life; St. Anthony Messenger; St. Joseph's Messenger; Senior Life Magazine; Vista

Serialized/Excerpted Novel. Analog Science Fiction/Science Fact; Arizona Coast; Bomb Magazine; Boston Review; Bostonia Magazine; Capper's; Moment Magazine; New Hampshire Life

Sports. Balloon Life; Beckett Baseball Card Monthly; Bike Report; Black Belt; Boston Review; Bowbender; Bowhunter Magazine; Boys' Life; Career Focus; College Preview; Journey; Visions; Catholic Forester; Emerge Magazine; Florida Wildlife; Flyfisher; Flyfishing News, Views and Reviews; Georgia Sportsman; Golf Journal; Horse Illustrated; Inside Texas Running; Insights; International Bowhunter; Mainstreet USA; Modern Short Stories; New York Running News; Outlaw Biker; Plain Dealer Magazine; Playboy Magazine; Prime Time Sports and Fitness; Radiance; Senior Life Magazine; Sporting Times; Sports Afield; Sun and Sonlight Christian Newspapers; Surfing Magazine; Young American

Suspense/Mystery. American Accent Short Story Magazine; bePuzzled; Bostonia Magazine; Boys' Life; Buffalo Spree Magazine; Career Focus; Catholic Forester; Cosmopolitan Magazine; Dialogue; Emerge Magazine; Hitchcock's Mystery Magazine, Alfred; Horse Illustrated; Modern Gold Miner and Treasure Hunter; Modern Short Stories; New Hampshire Life; New Mystery; Northcoast View; Orange Coast Magazine; Other Side; Oui Magazine; Plain Dealer Magazine; Playboy Magazine; Pockets; Portland Magazine; Queen's Mystery Magazine, Ellery; Radiance; Ranger Rick Magazine; Road King Magazine; Senior Life Magazine; Trailer Boats Magazine; Woman's World Magazine; Young American

Translations. American Citizen Italian Press; Boston Review; India Currents; Midstream; Moment Magazine; New Hampshire Life; Northcoast View; Tikkun

Western. Arizona Coast; Country America; Modern Short Stories; Montana Senior Citizens News; Playboy Magazine; Road King Magazine; Senior Life Magazine

Young Adult/Teen. American Newspaper Carrier; Associate Reformed Presbyterian; Beckett Baseball Card Monthly; Boys' Life; Bread; Campus Life Magazine; Career Focus; Christian Living For Senior Highs; HiCall; High Adventure; In Touch; Insights; Magazine for Christian Youth!; Modern Woodmen; New Era Magazine; Noah's Ark; Northwest Magazine; On the Line; Pennywhistle Press; Radiance; Sassy Magazine; Scholastic Scope; Seventeen; Sporting Times; Straight; Student; 'Teen Magazine; Teen Power; Teens Today; TQ; Vision; Vista; Wee Wisdom Magazine; With Magazine; Young Salvationist/Young Soldier

Small Press

Adventure. Aegina Press, Inc.; Ariadne Press; Barlow Press; Black Heron Press; Borealis Press; Bryans & Bryans; Cave Books; Council for Indian Education; Dan River Press; Fasa Corporation; Jesperson Press Ltd.; Lighthouse Publications; Marron Publishers, Inc.; Mey-House Books; Our Child Press; Pando Publications; Paper Bag Press; Read 'n Run Books; Satchell's Publishing; Scojtia Publishing Company; Soho Press; Starburst Publishers; University Editions; Willowisp Press, Inc.; Woodsong Graphics Inc.; Wyrick & Company

Canada. Annick Press Ltd.; Black Moss Press; Borealis Press; Cacanadadada; Cuff Publications Ltd., Harry; Dundurn Press; Goose Lane Editions; Hyperion Press Limited; Newest Publishers Ltd.; Orca Book Publishers Ltd.; Porcupines Quill, Inc.; Prairie Journal Press; Prairie Publishing Company; Press Gang Publishers; Quarry Press; Red Deer College Press; Reference Press; Thistledown Press; Turnstone Press; Women's Press; York Press

Comics. Mosaic Press

Contemporary. Aegina Press, Inc.; Applezaba Press; Ariadne Press; Barlow Press; Black Heron Press; Black Tie Press; Books for All Times, Inc.; Borealis Press; Breitenbush Books, Inc.; Bryans & Bryans; Carolina Wren Press; Carpenter Press; Catbird Press; Coffee House Press; Confluence Press Inc.; Creative Arts Book Co.; Cross-cultural Communications; Dan River Press; Dawnwood Press; Dayspring Press, Inc.; Dragonsbreath Press; Dundurn Press; Esoterica Press; Feminist Press at the City University of New York; Four Walls Eight Windows; Fromm International Publishing Corporation; Goose Lane Editions; Griffon House Publications; Guernica Editions; Haypenny Press; Hermes House Press; Independence Publishers Inc.; Lighthouse Publications; Lincoln Springs Press; Marron Publishers, Inc.; Mey-House Books; Milkweed Editions; New Rivers Press; Ommation Press; Orca Book Publishers Ltd.; Our Child Press; Paper Bag Press; Papier-Mache Press; Paycock Press; Peachtree Publishers, Ltd.; Pikestaff Publications, Inc.; Pineapple Press; Pocahontas Press, Inc.; Porcupine's Quill, Inc.; Press Gang Publishers; Primal Publishing; Puckerbrush Press; Ramalo Publications; Read 'n Run Books; Red Deer College Press; Scojtia Publishing Company; Second Chance Press and the Permanent Press; Seven Buffaloes Press; Simon & Pierre Publishing Company Limited; Starburst Publishers; Station Hill Press; Teal Press; Times Eagle Books; Tudor Publishers, Inc.; University Editions; University of Illinois Press; Willowisp Press, Inc.; Woman in the Moon Publications; Women's Press; Woodsong Graphics Inc.; York Press; Zephyr Press; Zoland Books, Inc.

Erotica. Carlton Books; Creative Arts Book Co.; Dragonsbreath Press; Paper Bag Press; Press Gang Publishers; Primal Publishing; Red Alder Books

Ethnic. Acadia Publishing Co.; Alaska Native Language Center; Arte Publico Press; Bilingual Press/Editorial Bilingüe; Breitenbush Books, Inc.; Carolina Wren Press; China Books; Clarity Press; Coffee House Press; Council for Indian Education; Cross-cultural Communications; Eighth Mt. Press; Esoterica Press; Feminist Press at the City University of New York; Griffon House Publications; Guernica Editions; Haypenny Press; Heritage Press; Island House; Kitchen Table: Women of Color Press; Lincoln Springs Press; Marron Publishers, Inc.; Mey-House Books; New Seed Press; Open Hand Publishing, Inc.; Paper Bag Press; Path Press, Inc.; Pocahontas Press, Inc.; Press Gang Publishers; Read 'n Run Books; Sandpiper Press; Satchell's Publishing; Scojtia Publishing Company; Seal Press; Seven Buffaloes Press; Soho Press; Soleil Press; Third Woman Press; University Editions; Waterfront Press; Woman in the Moon Publications; Wyrick & Company; Zephyr Press

Experimental. Aegina Press, Inc.; Applezaba Press; Black Heron Press; Black Tie Press; Breitenbush Books, Inc.; Cacanadadada; Carolina Wren Press; Carpenter Press; Clothespin Fever Press; Coffee House Press; Cross-cultural Communications; Dan River Press; Dragonsbreath Press; Feminist Press at the City University of New York; Fiction Collective Two; Four Walls Eight Windows; Griffon House

Publications; Haypenny Press; Hermes Hosue Press; Independence Publishers Inc.; Island House; Lincoln Springs Press; Milkweed Editions; New Directions; New Rivers Press; Ommation Press; Paper Bag Press; Paycock Press; Pikestaff Publications, Inc.; Pineapple Press; Primal Publishing; Puckerbrush Press; Quarry Press; Read 'n Run Books; Red Deer College Press; Re/Search Publishing; Scojtia Publishing Company; Station Hill Press; Textile Bridge Press; Thistledown Press; Turnstone Press; Ultramarine Publishing Co., Inc.; University Editions; University of Illinois Press; Women's Press; Wyrick & Company; York Press; Zephyr Press; Zoland Books, Inc.

Faction. Aegina Press, Inc.; Island House

Fantasy. Aegina Press, Inc.; Ansuda Publications; Applezaba Press; Ariadne Press; Carpenter Press; Dan River Press; Dragon's Den Publishing; Dragonsbreath Press; Haypenny Press; Jesperson Press Ltd.; Kubicek and Associates; Marron Publishers, Inc.; Our Child Press; Paper Bag Press; Porcupine's Quill, Inc.; Press of Macdonald and Reinecke; Read 'n Run Books; Satchell's Publishing; Scojtia Publishing Company; Space and Time; Starburst Publishers; Ultramarine Publishing Co., Inc.; University Editions; W.W. Publications; Woman in the Moon Publications; Yith Press

Feminist. Applezaba Press; Ariadne Press; Calyx Books; Carolina Wren Press; Clothespin Fever Press; Creative Arts Book Co.; Eighth Mt. Press; Feminist Press at the City University of New York; Firebrand Books; Frog in the Well; Hermes House Press; Kitchen Table: Women of Color Press; Lincoln Springs Press; Mother Courage Press; New Seed Press; New Victoria Publishers; Ommation Press; Papier-Mache Press; Post-Apollo Press; Press Gang Publishers; Quarry Press; Read 'n Run Books; Samisdat; Seal Press; Silverleaf Press, Inc.; Third Woman Press; University Editions; Véhicule Press; Woman Sleuth Mystery Series; Women's Press; Zephyr Press; Zoland Books, Inc.

Gay. Alyson Publications, Inc.; Applezaba Press; Banned Books; Carolina Wren Press; Eighth Mt. Press; Feminist Press at the City University of New York; Gay Sunshine Press and Leyland Publications; Knights Press; Los Hombres Press; Primal Publishing; Samisdat; Woman in the Moon Publications; Zephyr Press; Zoland Books, Inc.

Historical. Aegina Press, Inc.; Ariadne Press; Barlow Press; Borealis Press; Breitenbush Books, Inc.; Bryans & Bryans; Council for Indian Education; Creative Arts Book Co.; Dan River Press; Dragon's Den Publishing; Esoterica Press; Feminist Press at the City University of New York; 1st Amendment Publishers Inc.; Goose Lane Editions; Independence Publishers Inc.; Jayell Enterprises; Kruza Kaleidoscopix, Inc.; Library Research Associates, Inc.; Lighthouse Publications; Lincoln Springs Press; Long Publishing Co., Hendrick; Marron Publishers, Inc.; Mosaic Press; Open Hand Publishing, Inc.; Pando Publications; Paper Bag Press; Path Press, Inc.; Pineapple Press; Pocahontas Press, Inc.; Porcupine's Quill, Inc.; Press of Macdonald and Reinecke; Quarry Press; Read 'n Run Books; Scojtia Publishing Company; Simon & Pierre Publishing Company Limited; Soho Press; Starburst Publishers; Tudor Publishers, Inc.; University Editions; Women's Press; Woodsong Graphics Inc.; Zephyr Press

Horror. Aegina Press, Inc.; Ansuda Publications; Bryans & Bryans; Dan River Press; Dragon's Den Publishing; Kubicek and Associates; Paper Bag Press; Read 'n Run Books; Scare Ware; Space and Time; Starburst Publishers; University Editions; Willowisp Press, Inc.

Humor/Satire. Acadia Publishing Co.; Applezaba Press; Ariadne Press; Barlow Press; Beil, Publisher, Inc., Frederic C.; Black Heron Press; Black Moss Press; Bryans & Bryans; Catbird Press; Coffee House Press; Confluence Press Inc.; Creative with Words Publications; Cross-cultural Communications; Dan River Press; Dragonsbreath Press; Fromm International Publishing Corporation; Haypenny Press; Homestead Publishing; Independence Publishers Inc.; Jesperson Press Ltd.; Lighthouse Publications; Mosaic Press; Overlook Press; Pando Publications; Paper Bag Press; Paycock Press; Press Gang Publishers; Press of Macdonald and Reinecke; Ramalo Publications; Read 'n Run Books; Simon & Pierre Publishing Company Limited; University Editions; Woodsong Graphics Inc.; Wyrick & Company; Zephyr Press; Zoland Books, Inc.

Juvenile. Acadia Publishing Co.; Advocacy Press; Annick Press Ltd.; Black Moss Press; Borealis Press; Carolina Wren Press; Council for Indian Education; Creative with Words Publications; Cross-cultural Communications; Double M Press; Esoterica Press; Green Tiger Press; Homestead Publishing; Jesperson Press Ltd.; Kar-Ben Copies, Inc.; Kruza Kaleidoscopix, Inc.; Lollipop Power Books; Long Publishing Co., Hendrick; Misty Hill Press; New Seed Press; Open Hand Publishing, Inc.; Orca Book Publishers Ltd.; Our Child Press; Overlook Press; Pando Publications; Pippin Press; Prairie Publishing Company; Read 'n Run Books; Satchell's Publishing; Scojtia Publishing Company; Shoe Tree Press; Simon & Pierre Publishing Company Limited; University Editions; Women's Press; Woodsong Graphics Inc.; Lighthouse Publications; Willowisp Press, Inc.

Lesbian. Alyson Publications, Inc.; Applezaba Press; Banned Books; Calyx Books; Carolina Wren Press; Clothespin Fever Press; Eighth Mt. Press; Feminist Press at the City University of New York; Firebrand Books; Frog in the Well; Kitchen Table: Women of Color Press; Los Hombres Press; Mother Courage Press; Naiad Press, Inc.; New Victoria Publishers; Pocahontas Press, Inc.; Post-Apollo Press; Press Gang Publishers; Primal Publishing; Rising Tide Press; Samisdat; Seal Press; Silverleaf Press, Inc.; Woman in the Moon Publications; Woman Sleuth Mystery Series; Zephyr Press; Zoland Books, Inc.

Military/War. Dan River Press; 1st Amendment Publishers Inc.; Haypenny Press; Lighthouse Publications; Nautical & Aviation Publishing Co. of America Inc.; Pando Publications; Paper Bag Press; Read 'n Run Books; Starburst Publishers

Novella. Hermes House Press; Teal Press

Preschool/Picture Book. Black Moss Press; Council for Indian Education; Double M Press; Homestead Publishing; Our Child Press; Read 'n Run Books; Scojtia Publishing Company; Willowisp Press, Inc.

Prose Poem. Ommation Press

Psychic/Supernatural/Occult. Ansuda Publications; Carolina Wren Press; Dan River Press; Dragon's Den Publishing; Kubicek and Associates; Overlook Press; Read 'n Run Books; Scare Ware; Space and Time; Starburst Publishers; Woman in the Moon Publications; Woodsong Graphics Inc.

Regional. Aegina Press, Inc.; Barlow Press; Beil, Publisher, Inc., Frederic C.; Breitenbush Books, Inc.; Carolina Wren Press; Confluence Press Inc.; Council for Indian Education; Creative Arts Book Co.; Cuff Publications Ltd., Harry; Dan River Press; Feminist Press at the City University of New York; Frog in the Well; Haypenny Press; Independence Publishers Inc.; Kubicek and Associates; Library Research Associates, Inc.; Lighthouse Publications; Long Publishing Co., Hendrick; Mosaic Press; New Seed Press; Pando Publications; Peachtree Publishers, Ltd.; Pineapple Press; Pocahontas Press, Inc.; Press Gang Publishers; Ramalo Publications; Read 'n Run Books; Samisdat; Seven Buffaloes Press; Three Continents Press; Times Eagle Books; Tudor Publishers, Inc.; University Editions; University of Idaho Press; University of Utah Press; Véhicule Press; Watermark Press, Inc.; Woodley Memorial Press; Wyrick & Company; Zephyr Press

Religious/Inspirational. Bethel Publishing; Double M Press; Dragon's Den Publishing; Lighthouse Publications; Mosaic Press; Post-Apollo Press; Read 'n Run Books; Satchell's Publishing; Shaw Publishers, Harold; Star Books, Inc.; Starburst Publishers

Romance. Bryans & Bryans; Lighthouse Publications; Marron Publishers, Inc.; Mosaic Press; Read 'n Run Books; Satchell's Publishing; Scojtia Publishing Company; Starburst Publishers; University Editions; Woodsong Graphics Inc.

Science Fiction. Aegina Press, Inc.; Black Heron Press; Carpenter Press; Dan River Press; Dayspring Press, Inc.; Dragon's Den Publishing; Dragonsbreath Press; Fasa Corporation; Feminist Press at the City University of New York; Haypenny Press; Kubicek and Associates; Lighthouse Publications; Mey-House Books; Overlook Press; Pando Publications; Press Gang Publishers; Read 'n Run Books; Re/Search Publishing; Scojtia Publishing Company; Space and Time; Ultramarine Publishing Co., Inc.; University Editions; W.W. Publications; Woodsong Graphics Inc.

Short Story Collections. Aegina Press, Inc.; Ansuda Publications; Applezaba Press; Barlow Press; Beil, Publisher, Inc., Frederic C.; Bilingual Press/Editorial Bilingüe; Black Moss Press; Books for All Times, Inc.; Breitenbush Books, Inc.; Calyx Books; Carolina Wren Press; Clothespin Fever Press; Coffee House Press; Confluence Press Inc.; Creative Arts Book Co.; Dan River Press; Daniel and Company, Publishers, John; Dragon's Den Publishing; Dragonsbreath Press; Ecco Press; Eighth Mt. Press; Esoterica Press; Feminist Press at the City University of New York; Four Walls Eight Windows; Frog in the Well; Fromm International Publishing Corporation; Goose Lane Editions; Graywolf Press; Haypenny Press; Hermes House Press; Homestead Publishing; Independence Publishers Inc.; Intertext; Island House; Kitchen Table: Women of Color Press; Lincoln Springs Press; Longstreet Press; New Rivers Press; Papier-Mache Press; Path Press, Inc.; Peachtree Publishers, Ltd.; Post-Apollo Press; Press Gang Publishers; Press of Macdonald and Reinecke; Quarry Press; Ramalo Publications; Read 'n Run Books; Red Deer College Press; Seal Press; Seven Buffaloes Press; Silverleaf Press, Inc.; Teal Press; Textile Bridge Press; Thistledown Press; Three Continents Press; Ultramarine Publishing Co., Inc.; University Editions; University of Arkansas; University of Idaho Press; University of Illinois Press; University of Utah Press; Véhicule Press; Watermark Press, Inc.; Woman in the Moon Publications; Women's Press; Zephyr Press; Zoland Books, Inc.

Sports. Path Press, Inc.; Pocahontas Press, Inc.; Reference Press; Starburst Publishers

Suspense/Mystery. Aegina Press, Inc.; Ansuda Publications; Ariadne Press; Carlton Books; Cliffhanger Press; Creative Arts Book Co.; Dragon's Den Publishing; Lighthouse Publications; Marron Publishers, Inc.; Pando Publications; Papyrus Publishers; Press Gang Publishers; Read 'n Run Books; Second Chance Press and the Permanent Press; Simon & Pierre Publishing Company Limited; Soho Press; Starburst Publishers; Tudor Publishers, Inc.; Woman Sleuth Mystery Series; Woodsong Graphics Inc.

Translations. Applezaba Press; Beil, Publisher, Inc., Frederic C.; Bilingual Press/Editorial Bilingüe; Calyx Books; Carolina Wren Press; Catbird Press; Creative Arts Book Co.; Cross-cultural Communications; Esoterica Press; Feminist Press at the City University of New York; Four Walls Eight Windows; Fromm International Publishing Corporation; Griffon House Publications; Hermes House Press; Independence Publishers Inc.; Intertext; Italica Press; New Rivers Press; Overlook Press; Paycock Press; Pocahontas Press, Inc.; Post-Apollo Press; Read 'n Run Books; Simon & Pierre Publishing Company Limited; Station Hill Press; Three Continents Press; Translation Center; University Editions; University of Arkansas Press; Véhicule Press; Waterfront Press; Women's Press; York Press; Zoland Books, Inc.

Western. Council for Indian Education; Creative Arts Book Co.; Dan River Press; Homestead Publishing; Lighthouse Publications; Ramalo Publications; Read 'n Run Books; Starburst Publishers; Sunstone Press; University of Utah Press; Woodsong Graphics Inc.

Young Adult/Teen. Acadia Publishing Co.; Bethel Publishing; Borealis Press; Council for Indian Education; Cross-cultural Communications; Davenport Publishers, May; Double M Press; Esoterica Press; Haypenny Press; Homestead Publishing; Hyperion Press Limited; Lighthouse Publications; Long Publishing Co., Hendrick; Marron Publishers, Inc.; Mosaic Press; New Seed Press; Open Hand Publishing, Inc.; Orca Book Publishers Ltd.; Our Child Press; Pando Publications; Pocahontas Press, Inc.; Porcupine's Quill, Inc.; Read 'n Run Books; Satchell's Publishing; Scojtia Publishing Company; Shaw Publishers, Harold; Shoe Tree Press; Simon & Pierre Publishing Company Limited; Star Books, Inc.; Tudor Publishers, Inc.; W.W. Publications; Willowisp Press, Inc.; Women's Press; Woodsong Graphics Inc.

Commercial Publishers

Adventure. Bethany House Publishers; Bouregy & Company, Inc., Thomas; Branden Publishing Co.; Broadman Press; Cloverdale Press Inc.; Crossway Books; Crown Publishing Group; Dell Publishing; Fearon/Janus/Quercus; Harlequin Enterprises, Ltd.; Herald Press; Holiday House, Inc.; Holloway House Publishing Company; Holt & Company, Henry; Horizon Publishers & Dist., Inc.; Morrow and Company, Inc., William; Naval Institute Press; Pocket Books; Random House, Inc.; St. Martin's Press; Scribner's Sons, Charles; Stoddart; Vesta Publications, Ltd; Villard Books; Walker and Company; Warner Books; Worldwide Library; Zebra Books; Zondervan

Canada. Doubleday Canada Limited; Harlequin Enterprises, Ltd.; Macmillan of Canada; Stoddart; Vesta Publications, Ltd; Western Producer Prairie Books; Worldwide Library

Comics. Eclipse Books/Eclipse Comics; Fantagraphics Books

Confession. St. Martin's Press

Contemporary. Ace Charter Books; Ballantine Books; Blair, Publisher, John F.; Bookcraft, Inc.; Branden Publishing Co.; Carroll & Graf Publishers, Inc.; Crossway Books; Crown Publishing Group; Dell Publishing; Fearon/Janus/Quercus; Harvest House Publishers; Holiday House, Inc.; Holloway House Publishing Company; Holt & Company, Henry; Knopf Alfred A.; Louisiana State University Press; Morrow and Company, Inc., William; Pocket Books; Random House, Inc.; St. Martin's Press; Scribner's Sons, Charles; Sierra Club Books; Smith, Publisher, Gibbs; University of Minnesota Press; Vesta Publications, Ltd; Villard Books; Warner Books; Zebra Books

Erotica. Carroll & Graf Publishers, Inc.; Pocket Books; St. Martin's Press

Ethnic. Branden Publishing Co.; Fearon/Janus/Quercus; Holloway House Publishing Company; Pocket Books; St. Martin's Press; University of Minnesota Press; Vesta Publications, Ltd

Experimental. Holloway House Publishing Company; Morrow and Company, Inc., William; St. Martin's Press; Smith, Publisher, Gibbs; University of Minnesota Press; Vesta Publications, Ltd

Faction. Vesta Publications, Ltd

Fantasy. Avon Books; Baen Books; Bantam Spectra Books/Foundation Books; Berkley/Ace Science Fiction; Carroll & Graf Publishers, Inc.; Cloverdale Press Inc.; Crossway Books; Daw Books, Inc.; Del Rey Books; Delacorte/Dell Books for Young Readers; Doubleday-Foundation Books; Holloway House Publishing Company; Iron Crown Enterprises, Inc.; New American Library; Pocket Books; St. Martin's Press; Tor Books; TSR, Inc.; University of Minnesota Press; Vesta Publications, Ltd; Warner Books; Zondervan

Feminist. Academy Chicago Publishers; Ballantine Books; Braziller, Inc., George; Holt & Company, Henry; Morrow and Company, Inc., William; St. Martin's Press; Scribner's Sons, Charles; University of Minnesota Press; Vesta Publications, Ltd

Gay. Morrow and Company, Inc., William; New American Library; St. Martin's Press; University of Minnesota Press

Historical. Academy Chicago Publishers; Avon Books; Ballantine Books; Bookcraft, Inc.; Branden Publishing Co.; Broadman Press; Cloverdale Press Inc.; Crown Publishing Group; Dell Publishing; Fearon/Janus/Quercus; Godine, Publisher, Inc., David R.; Harvest House Publishers; Herald Press; Holloway House Publishing Company; Holt & Company, Henry; Horizon Publishers & Dist., Inc.; Leisure Books; Morrow and Company, Inc., William; Naval Institute Press; New American Library; Pocket Books; Presidio Press; Random House, Inc.; University of Minnesota Press; Vesta Publications, Ltd; Villard Books; Winston-Derek Publishers; Zebra Books; Zondervan

Horror. Avon Books; Cloverdale Press Inc.; Crown Publishing Group; Daw Books, Inc.; Dell Publishing; Dorchester Publishing Co., Inc.; Doubleday-Foundation Books; Holloway House Publishing Company; Leisure Books; Morrow and Company, Inc., William; New American Library; Pocket Books; Scribner's Sons, Charles; TSR, Inc.; Villard Books; Walker and Company; Warner Books; Wildstar Books/Empire Books; Zebra Books

Humor/Satire. Broadman Press; Crown Publishing Group; Doubleday Canada Limited; Harvest House Publishers; Holt & Company, Henry; Horizon Publishers & Dist., Inc.; Larksdale; Morrow and Company, Inc., William; Pocket Books; Potter, Inc., Clarkson N.; Price Stern Sloan, Inc.; St. Martin's Press; Scribner's Sons, Charles; Smith, Publisher, Gibbs; Vesta Publications, Ltd; Villard Books

Juvenile. Holt and Company, Henry; Ace Charter Books; Atheneum Books for Children; Bethany House Publishers; Boyds Mills Press; Bradbury Press, Inc.; Broadman Press; Camelot Books; Childrens Press; Clarion Books; Crossway Books; Delacorte/Dell Books for Young Readers; Dell Publishing; Dial Books for Young Readers; Doubleday Canada Limited; Eakin Press; Farrar, Straus & Giroux/Children's Books; Gareth Stevens, Inc.; Gemstone Books; Gessler Publishing Company; Godine, Publisher, Inc., David R.; Grosset & Dunlap, Inc.; Harcourt Brace Jovanovich; HarperCollins Children's Books; Herald Press; Holiday House, Inc.; Horizon Publishers & Dist., Inc.; Interlink Publishing Group, Inc.; Joy Street Books; Knopf Books for Young Readers; Larksdale; Little, Brown And Company Children's Books; Lodestar Books; Lucas/Evans Books; McElderry Books, Margaret K.; Macmillan Children's Books; Modern Publishing; Morrow Junior Books; Multnomah; Pantheon Books; Pelican Publishing Company; Potter, Inc., Clarkson N.; Prentice-Hall Books for Young Readers; Price Stern Sloan, Inc.; St. Paul Books and Media; Scribner's Sons Books for Young Readers, Charles; Trillium Press; Troll Associates; Vesta Publications, Ltd; Western Producer Prairie Books; Western Publishing Company, Inc.; Whitman & Company, Albert; Winston-Derek Publishers; Yearling; Zolotow Books, Charlotte (see Harper & Row Junior Books)

Lesbian. Morrow and Company, Inc., William; St. Martin's Press; University of Minnesota Press

Military/War. Avon Books; Branden Publishing Co.; Cloverdale Press Inc.; Crown Publishing Group; Dell Publishing; Holloway House Publishing Company; Horizon Publishers & Dist., Inc.; Larksdale; Naval Institute Press; Pocket Books; Presidio Press; Vesta Publications, Ltd; Warner Books; Zebra Books

Preschool/Picture Book. Atheneum Books for Children; Boyds Mills Press; Farrar, Straus & Giroux/Children's Books; Four Winds Press; Gareth Stevens, Inc.; Gessler Publishing Company; Grosset & Dunlap, Inc.; Harcourt Brace Jovanovich; HarperCollins Children's Books; Harvest House Publishers; Joy Street Books; Knopf Books for Young Readers; McElderry Books, Margaret K.; Modern Publishing; Morrow Junior Books; Multnomah; Prentice-Hall Books for Young Readers; St. Paul Books and Media; Scribner's Sons Books for Young Readers, Charles; Troll Associates; Vesta Publications, Ltd; Warner Books; Western Publishing Company, Inc.

Psychic/Supernatural/Occult. Avon Books; Cloverdale Press Inc.; Dell Publishing; Pocket Books; St. Martin's Press; Vesta Publications, Ltd; Wildstar Books/Empire Books; Winston-Derek Publishers

Regional. Bethany House Publishers; Blair, Publisher, John F.; Fearon/Janus/Quercus; Interlink Publishing Group, Inc.; Vesta Publications, Ltd

Religious/Inspirational. Abingdon Press; Accent Books; Ballantine/Epiphany Books; Bethany House Publishers; Bookcraft, Inc.; Broadman Press; Crossway Books; Harvest House Publishers; Herald Press; Horizon Publishers & Dist., Inc.; Larksdale; Multnomah; St. Martin's Press; Tyndale House Publishers; Vesta Publications, Ltd; WindSong Books; Winston-Derek Publishers; Zondervan

Romance. Bethany House Publishers; Bookcraft, Inc.; Bouregy & Company, Inc., Thomas; Branden Publishing Co.; Crown Publishing Group; Dorchester Publishing Co., Inc.; Fearon/Janus/Quercus; Harlequin Enterprises, Ltd.; Harvest House Publishers; Heartfire Romance; Holloway House Publishing Company; Horizon Publishers & Dist., Inc.; Leisure Books; Loveswept; Morrow and Company, Inc., William; New American Library; Pocket Books; St. Martin's Press; Silhouette Books; Vesta Publications, Ltd; Villard Books; Walker and Company; Warner Books; Wildstar Books/Empire Books; Zebra Books; Herald Press

Science Fiction. Avon Books; Baen Books; Bantam Spectra Books/Foundation Books; Berkley/Ace Science Fiction; Carroll & Graf Publishers, Inc.; Cloverdale Press Inc.; Crossway Books; Crown Publishing Group; Daw Books, Inc.; Del Rey Books; Dorchester Publishing Co., Inc.; Doubleday Canada Limited; Doubleday-Foundation Books; Fearon/Janus/Quercus; Holloway House Publishing Company; Horizon Publishers & Dist., Inc.; Iron Crown Enterprises, Inc.; Morrow and Company, Inc., William; New American Library; St. Martin's Press; Tor Books; TSR, Inc.; University of Minnesota Press; Vesta Publications, Ltd; Warner Books; Zondervan

Short Story Collections. Branden Publishing Co.; Braziller, Inc., George; Doubleday-Foundation Books; Fearon/Janus/Quercus; Gessler Publishing Company; Louisiana State University Press; Macmillan of Canada; Random House, Inc.; Resource Publications, Inc.; Smith, Publisher, Gibbs; University of Georgia Press; University of Minnesota Press; Vesta Publications, Ltd

Suspense/Mystery. Academy Chicago Publishers; Bethany House Publishers; Branden Publishing Co.; Carroll & Graf Publishers, Inc.; Cloverdale Press Inc.; Dell Publishing; Dembner Books; Doubleday Canada Limited; Fearon/Janus/Quercus; Godine, Publisher, Inc., David R.; Holloway House Publishing Company; Holt & Company, Henry; Knopf Alfred A.; Macmillan of Canada; Morrow and Company, Inc., William; Mysterious Press; New American Library; Pocket Books; Random House, Inc.; St. Martin's Press; Scribner's Sons, Charles; Stoddart; Tor Books; Vesta Publications, Ltd; Villard Books; Walker and Company; Warner Books; Wildstar Books/Empire Books; Zebra Books; Zondervan

Translations. Academy Chicago Publishers; Branden Publishing Co.; Braziller, Inc., George; Gessler Publishing Company; Holt & Company, Henry; Interlink Publishing Group, Inc.; Morrow and Company, Inc., William; Smith, Publisher, Gibbs; University of Minnesota Press; Vesta Publications, Ltd

Western. Avon Books; Bookcraft, Inc.; Bouregy & Company, Inc., Thomas; Cloverdale Press Inc.; Evans & Co., Inc., M.; Fearon/Janus/Quercus; Holloway House Publishing Company; Jameson Books; Leisure Books; New American Library; Tor Books; Walker and Company; Warner Books; Wildstar Books/Empire Books

Young Adult/Teen. Archway Paperbacks; Atheneum Books for Children; Avon Books; Boyds Mills Press; Bradbury Press, Inc.; Broadman Press; Clarion Books; Cloverdale Press Inc.; Crossway Books; Delacorte/Dell Books for Young Readers; Dell Publishing; Evans & Co., Inc., M.; Fearon/Janus/Quercus; Harcourt Brace Jovanovich; HarperCollins Children's Books; Herald Press; Holt & Company, Henry; Horizon Publishers & Dist., Inc.; Knopf Books for Young Readers; Larksdale; Little, Brown And Company Children's Books; Lodestar Books; Lucas/Evans Books; McElderry Books, Margaret K.; Morrow Junior Books; Multnomah; Pantheon Books; Pelican Publishing Company; Point Books; Prentice-Hall Books for Young Readers; St. Paul Books and Media; Scribner's Sons Books for Young Readers, Charles; Stoddart; Tab Book Club; Trillium Press; Troll Associates; Vesta Publications, Ltd; Walker and Company; Weiss Associates, Inc., Daniel; Western Producer Prairie Books; WindSong Books; Winston-Derek Publishers

Literary Agents

Adventure. Amsterdam Agency, Marcia; Authors' Marketing Services Ltd.; Becker, Maximilian; Garon-Brooke Associates, Inc., Jay; Gladden Unlimited; JCA Literary Agency, Inc.; Jones Literary Agency, Lloyd; Kearns & Orr; Lampack Agency, Inc., Peter; Lee Literary Agency, The L. Harry; Lighthouse Literary Agency; Neighbors, Inc., Charles; Perkins' Literary Agency; Singer Media Corporation; Swanson, Inc., H.N.; Warren Literary Agency, James; Watt and Associates, Sandra

Canada. Kellock & Associates Ltd., J.

Contemporary. Authors' Marketing Services Ltd.; Kroll Agency, Lucy; Larsen/Elizabeth Pomada Literary Agents, Michael; Lighthouse Literary Agency; Lincoln Literary Agency, Ray; Literary/Business Associates; Markowitz, Barbara; Protter, Literary Agent, Susan Ann; Southern Writers, Inc.

Ethnic. Crown International Literature and Arts, Bonnie R.; Writers' Productions

Fantasy. Allen Literary Agency, James; Butler, Art & Literary Agent, Jane; Collier Associates; Jarvis & Co., Inc., Sharon; Kellock & Associates Ltd., J.; Lillienstein, Maxwell J.; Protter, Literary Agent, Susan Ann; Schaffner Agency, Inc.; Seligman Literary Agency, Lynn; Spatt, Esq., David M.; Vicinanza, Ltd., Ralph M.

Feminist. Flannery, White & Stone

Gay. Flannery, White & Stone; Rees Literary Agency, Helen

Historical. Allen Literary Agency, James; Butler, Art & Literary Agent, Jane; Carvainis Agency, Inc., Maria; Cohen, Inc., Ruth; Collier Associates; Deering Literary Agency, Dorothy; Larsen/Elizabeth Pomada Literary Agents, Michael; Lee Literary Agency, The L. Harry; Lillienstein, Maxwell J.; Markowitz, Barbara; Multimedia Product Development, Inc.; Neighbors, Inc., Charles; Nugent & Associates, Inc.; Perkins' Literary Agency; Siegel Agency, Bobbe; Southern Writers, Inc.; Warren Literary Agency, James; Wieser & Wieser; Zeckendorf Associates, Susan

Horror. Allan Agency, Lee; Allen Literary Agency, James; Amsterdam Agency, Marcia; Authors' Marketing Services Ltd.; Browne Ltd., Pema; Butler, Art & Literary Agent, Jane; Deering Literary Agency, Dorothy; Ellenberg Literary Agent/Consultant, Ethan; Garon-Brooke Associates, Inc., Jay; Gladden Unlimited; Jarvis & Co., Inc., Sharon; JCA Literary Agency, Inc.; Kearns & Orr; Lee Literary Agency, The L. Harry; Lowenstein Associates; Manus Literary Agency Inc., Janet Wilkens; Marcil Literary Agency, Inc., Denise; Protter, Literary Agent, Susan Ann; Snell Literary Agency, Michael; Spatt, Esq., David M.; Steele & Co., Ltd., Literary Agents, Lyle; Swanson, Inc., H.N.; Vicinanza, Ltd., Ralph M.;

Ware Literary Agency, John A.; Warren Literary Agency, James; Zeckendorf Associates, Susan

Humor/Satire. Amsterdam Agency, Marcia; Deering Literary Agency, Dorothy; Hilton Literary Agency, Alice; Lee Literary Agency, The L. Harry; Lincoln Literary Agency, Ray; Portman & Associates, Julian; Warren Literary Agency, James; Watt and Associates, Sandra

Juvenile. Casselman Literary Agency, Martha; Clark Literary Agency, SJ; Cohen, Inc., Ruth; Deering Literary Agency, Dorothy; Elmo Agency Inc., Ann; Flannery, White & Stone; Gusay Literary Agency, Charlotte; Hilton Literary Agency, Alice; Jones Literary Agency, Lloyd; Kellock & Associates Ltd., J.; Kouts, Literary Agent, Barbara S.; Lincoln Literary Agency, Ray; Manus Literary Agency Inc., Janet Wilkens; Mews Books Ltd.; Norma-Lewis Agency; Porcelain Agency, Sidney; Rights Unlimited; Shepard Agency; Singer Literary Agency Inc., Evelyn; Wald Associates, Inc., Mary Jack

Military/War. Collier Associates; Lee Literary Agency, L. Harry

Novella. Baldi Literary Agency Inc., Malaga; Blake Group Literary Agency; Borchardt Inc., Georges; Brandt & Brandt Literary Agents, Inc.; Chester Literary Agency, The Linda; Crown International Literature and Arts, Bonnie R.; Gersh Agency; Gusay Literary Agency, Charlotte; Kaltman Literary Agency, Larry; King, Literary, Daniel P.; Lampack Agency, Inc., Peter; Lighthouse Literary Agency; Lord Literistic, Inc., Sterling; Porcelain Agency, Sidney; Rhodes Literary Agency NY; Rosenstone/Wender; Swanson, Inc., H.N.; Thompson Talent Agency; Wald Associates, Inc., Mary Jack; Warren Literary Agency, James; Wright Representatives Inc., Ann

Preschool/Picture Book. Browne Ltd., Pema; Mews Books Ltd.

Psychic/Supernatural/Occult. Clark Literary Agency, SJ; Jarvis & Co., Inc., Sharon; Lee Literary Agency, The L. Harry; Literary/Business Associates; Marcil Literary Agency, Inc., Denise

Regional. Crown International Literature and Arts, Bonnie R.; Southern Writers, Inc.; Spatt, Esq., David M.; Writers' Productions

Religious/Inspirational. Stepping Stone; Thompson Talent Agency

Romance. Browne Ltd., Pema; Carvainis Agency, Inc., Maria; Cohen, Inc., Ruth; Collier Associates; Columbia Literary Assocs., Inc.; Davie Literary Agency, Elaine; Deering Literary Agency, Dorothy; Elmo Agency Inc., Ann; Garon-Brooke Associates, Inc., Jay; Hilton Literary Agency, Alice; Jason Enterprises, Inc., Asher D.; Jones Literary Agency, Lloyd; Kearns & Orr; Kidde, Hoyt & Picard; King, Literary, Daniel P.; Larsen/Elizabeth Pomada Literary Agents, Michael; Lazear Agency Incorporated; Lee Literary Agency, The L. Harry; Lillienstein, Maxwell J.; Lowenstein Associates; Multimedia Product Development, Inc.; Neighbors, Inc., Charles; Robb Literary Properties, Sherry; Singer Media Corporation; Southern Writers, Inc.; Teal Literary Agency, Patricia; Tornetta Literary Agency, Phyllis R.; Weiner Literary Agency, Cherry; Wreschner, Authors' Representative, Ruth

Science Fiction. Allan Agency, Lee; Allen Literary Agency, James; Amsterdam Agency, Marcia; Becker, Maximilian; Bova Literary Agency, The Barbara; Butler, Art & Literary Agent, Jane; Deering Literary Agency, Dorothy; Ellenberg Literary Agent/Consultant, Ethan; Gladden Unlimited; Hilton Literary Agency, Alice; Jarvis & Co., Inc., Sharon; Kearns & Orr; Kellock & Associates Ltd., J.; King, Literary, Daniel P.; Lazear Agency Incorporated; Lillienstein, Maxwell J.; Lincoln Literary Agency, Ray; Naggar Literary Agency, Inc., Jean V.; Protter, Literary Agent, Susan Ann; Quicksilver Books Literary Agents; Schaffner Agency, Inc.; Siegel Agency, Bobbe; Spatt, Esq., David M.; Teal Literary Agency, Patricia; Vicinanza, Ltd., Ralph M.; Warren Literary Agency, James; Weiner Literary Agency, Cherry; Wreschner, Authors' Representative, Ruth; Writer's Consulting Group

Short Story Collections. Blake Group Literary Agency; Borchardt Inc., Georges; Brandt & Brandt Literary Agents, Inc.; Chester Literary Agency, The Linda; Crown International Literature and Arts, Bonnie R.; Darhansoff Literary Agency, Liz; Dolger Agency, The Jonathan; Dorese Agency; Gersh Agency; Gusay Literary Agency, Charlotte; Hilton Literary Agency, Alice; King, Literary, Daniel P.; Lazear Agency Incorporated; Lord Literistic, Inc., Sterling; Macdonough, Richard P., Literary Agent; Paton Literary Agency, Kathi J.; Porcelain Agency, Sidney; Rhodes Literary Agency NY; Rosenstone/Wender; Swanson, Inc., H.N.; Thompson Talent Agency; Wald Associates, Inc., Mary Jack; Warren Literary Agency, James; Wright Representatives Inc., Ann

Suspense/Mystery. Abel Literary Agency, Inc., Dominick; Allan Agency, Lee; Allen Literary Agency, James; American Play Co. Inc.; Amsterdam Agency, Marcia; Axelrod Agency, Inc.; Baldi Literary Agency Inc., Malaga; Becker, Maximilian; Bova Literary Agency, The Barbara; Brod Literary Agency, Ruth Hagy; Butler, Art & Literary Agent, Jane; Carvainis Agency, Inc., Maria; Clark Literary Agency, SJ; Cleaver, Inc., Diane; Cohen, Inc., Ruth; Collier Associates; Davie Literary Agency, Elaine; Deering Literary Agency, Dorothy; Ellenberg Literary Agent/Consultant, Ethan; Farquharson Ltd., John; Garon-Brooke Associates, Inc., Jay; Gordon Literary Agency, Charlotte; Jason Enterprises, Inc., Asher D.; JCA Literary Agency, Inc.; Jones Literary Agency, Lloyd; Kearns & Orr; Kellock & Associates Ltd., J.; King, Literary, Daniel P.; Larsen/Elizabeth Pomada Literary Agents, Michael; Lazear Agency Incorporated; Lee Literary Agency, The L. Harry; Literary Group; Literary/Business Associates; Manus Literary Agency

Inc., Janet Wilkens; Marcil Literary Agency, Inc., Denise; Morrison, Inc., Henry; Multimedia Product Development, Inc.; Naggar Literary Agency, Inc., Jean V.; Neighbors, Inc., Charles; Norma-Lewis Agency; Nugent & Associates, Inc.; Porcelain Agency, Sidney; Protter, Literary Agent, Susan Ann; Quicksilver Books Literary Agents; Rees Literary Agency, Helen; Robb Literary Properties, Sherry; Rose Literary Agency, The Mitchell; Siegel Agency, Bobbe; Singer Media Corporation; Snell Literary Agency, Michael; Spatt, Esq., David M.; Spitzer Literary Agency, Philip G.; Stepping Stone; Tornetta Literary Agency, Phyllis R.; Ware Literary Agency, John A.; Warren Literary Agency, James; Watt and Associates, Sandra; Wreschner, Authors' Representative, Ruth; Wright, Authors' Representative, Stephen; Writer's Consulting Group; Zeckendorf Associates, Susan

Western. Allan Agency, Lee; Carvainis Agency, Inc., Maria; Davie Literary Agency, Elaine; Elmo Agency Inc., Ann; Lazear Agency Incorporated; Lee Literary Agency, The L. Harry; Teal Literary Agency, Patricia

Young Adult/Teen. Amsterdam Agency, Marcia; Browne Ltd., Pema; Carvainis Agency, Inc., Maria; Cohen, Inc., Ruth; Gordon Literary Agency, Charlotte; Lazear Agency Incorporated; Lighthouse Literary Agency; Lincoln Literary Agency, Ray; Mews Books Ltd.; Norma-Lewis Agency; Stewart Agency, Jo

Markets Index

Your Guide to Getting Published

Learn to write publishable material and discover the best-paying markets for your work. Subscribe to *Writer's Digest*, the magazine that has instructed, informed and inspired writers since 1920. Every month you'll get:

- Fresh markets for your writing, including the names and addresses of editors, what type of writing they're currently buying, how much they pay, and how to get in touch with them.
- Insights, advice, and how-to information from professional writers and editors.
- In-depth profiles of today's foremost authors and the secrets of their success.
- Monthly expert columns about the writing and selling of fiction, nonfiction, poetry and scripts.

Plus, a $12.00 discount. Subscribe today through this special introductory offer, and receive a full year (12 issues) of *Writer's Digest* for only $18.00—that's a $12.00 savings off the $30 newsstand rate. Enclose payment with your order, and we will add an extra issue to your subscription, absolutely **free**.

Detach postage-free coupon and mail today!

Writer's ®
DIGEST

Guarantee: If you are not satisfied with your subscription at any time, you may cancel it and receive a full refund for all unmailed issues due you.

Subscription Savings Certificate
Save $12.00

Yes, I want professional advice on how to write publishable material and sell it to the best-paying markets. Send me 12 issues of *Writer's Digest* for just $18...a $12 discount off the newsstand price. (Outside U.S. add $4 and remit in U.S. funds.)

☐ Payment enclosed (Send me an extra issue free—13 in all)
☐ Please bill me

Name (please print)

Address _____ Apt.

City

State _____ Zip

Basic rate, $24.

VMSS1

Writer's®
DIGEST

How would you like to get:

- up-to-the-minute reports on new markets for your writing
- professional advice from editors and writers about what to write and how to write it to maximize your opportunities for getting published
- in-depth interviews with leading authors who reveal their secrets of success
- expert opinion about writing and selling fiction, nonfiction, poetry and scripts
- ...all at a $12.00 discount?